Principles of Criminal Law

Simon Bronitt and Bernadette McSherry

HEAD OFFICE: 100 Harris Street PYRMONT NSW 2009
Tel: (02) 8587 7000 Fax: (02) 8587 7100
For all sales inquiries please ring 1800 650 522
(for calls within Australia only)

INTERNATIONAL AGENTS & DISTRIBUTORS

CANADA
Carswell Co
Ontario, Montreal,
Vancouver, Calgary

HONG KONG
Sweet & Maxwell Asia
Hennessy Road, Wanchai

Bloomsbury Books Ltd
Chater Road, Central

MALAYSIA
Sweet & Maxwell Asia
Petaling Jaya, Selangor

NEW ZEALAND
Brooker's Ltd
Wellington

SINGAPORE
Sweet & Maxwell Asia
Albert Street

UNITED KINGDOM & EUROPE
Sweet & Maxwell Ltd
London

UNITED STATES
Wm W Gaunt & Sons, Inc
Holmes Beach, Florida

William S Hein Co Inc
Buffalo, New York

JAPAN
Maruzen Company Ltd
Tokyo

Principles of Criminal Law

Simon Bronitt

LLB (Bristol), LLM (Cantab)
Senior Lecturer, Faculty of Law, The Australian National University

and

Bernadette McSherry

BA (Hons), LLB (Hons), LLM (Melb), D Jur (York, Can)
Senior Lecturer, Faculty of Law, Monash University

LBC Information Services 2001

Published in Sydney by

LBC Information Services
    100 Harris Street, Pyrmont, NSW

First edition 2001

National Library of Australia
    Cataloguing-in-Publication entry

Bronitt, Simon.
    Principles of Criminal Law.

    Bibliography.
    Includes index.
    ISBN 0 455 21740 8.
    1. Criminal law — Australia. I. McSherry, Bernadette. II. Title.

345.94

Internal Design by Vivien Valk Design
Product Developer: Catherine Dunk
Senior Editor: Jessica Perini

Typeset in Meta Plus, 9 on 14 point, by RE Typesetting, Woy Woy, NSW
Printed by Ligare Pty Ltd, Riverwood, NSW

Preface

In 1995, we fortuitously met at a workshop on health, law and ethics in Canberra and quickly discovered a mutual interest in interdisciplinary and comparative legal studies. We also shared a desire to teach our students to question conventional ahistorical, timeless and self-evident accounts of the criminal law. This book is a result of our commitment to showing how the principles of criminal law reflect the changing social, political and moral concerns about wrongful conduct and particular groups.

We set ourselves the daunting task of describing criminal laws across every Australian jurisdiction and, wherever possible, challenging these accounts from interdisciplinary vantage points. Reflecting our broad variety of interests, we have drawn upon a range of disciplines including criminology, criminal justice studies, feminism, legal history, human rights, legal theory, medicine, psychology and sociology, to illuminate the substance and operation of the criminal law. We have also focused on procedural issues such as jurisdiction, and substantive crimes such as public order and drug offences that have traditionally received little, if any, attention in standard texts.

Reflecting both the limits of our expertise and publishing constraints, our account of criminal law is necessarily selective and incomplete. There will be many issues that we have simply omitted or glossed over in a cursory manner. What we do hope to impart is a critical orientation to the criminal law, rather than simply a description of the rules, principles and substantive definitions applicable in every jurisdiction. In terms of presentation, we deliberately set out to differentiate this book from other textbooks by including case studies, perspectives sections and shorter aside boxes, tables and diagrams. We hope that this translates into a user-friendly book that provides starting points for critical reflection, class discussion and further research into specific areas.

Beyond providing critiques of the law, we are keen to point the way toward reform. In this regard, we have discussed (where relevant) the proposals and recommendations of the Model Criminal Code Officers Committee, which has been given the unenviable task of formulating an Australian Model Criminal Code. We have also attempted to provide an overview of relevant academic debate in particular areas.

Our ambition to write a "critical text" in criminal law is not novel. There is a strong commitment to both critical and contextual perspectives in criminal law scholarship: see, for example, A Bates, T Buddin and D Meure, *The System of Criminal Law — Cases and Materials* (Sydney: Butt, 1979), D Brown, D Farrier and D Weisbrot, *Criminal Laws* (2nd ed, Sydney: Federation Press, 1996) and N Lacey and C Wells, *Reconstructing Criminal Law* (2nd ed, London: Butt, 1998). Our book is distinctive in one respect — conceived as a commentary on the law rather than as a casebook, it has a much stronger narrative focus. Rather than representing the criminal law through a mass of textual fragments, we have provided readers with *our story* about the criminal law. We encourage readers, especially law students, to step beyond the boundaries of our text and to engage independently with the original material. Reading cases and/or articles in their original unedited form is essential, we believe, for the development of effective legal research and writing skills.

Writing about law from an interdisciplinary perspective is not without its own hazards and pitfalls. As Harry Arthurs, a distinguished Canadian law professor, noted in "The Political Economy of Canadian Legal Education" (1998) 25 (1) *Journal of Law and Society* 14 at 26:

> Law professors who prefer to continue to teach and write in the classic black-letter tradition sometimes resent and disparage their more adventurous colleagues; deans who feel pressure to staff "core" courses or to respond to professional expectations of conventional scholarship, sometimes fail to support interdisciplinary initiatives; scholars in other disciplines do not always appreciate encroachments by their neighbours; and interdisciplinary scholars alienated by unsympathetic students, colleagues or administrators — and by the intrinsic difficulty of their task — sometimes become disillusioned and resentful (footnotes omitted).

In the Australian context, interdisciplinary perspectives are further challenged by the mandatory "core" legal topics to be studied within the law degree.

On 1 April 1992 the Consultative Committee of State and Territorial Law Admitting Authorities, chaired by Mr Justice Priestley, prescribed eleven "areas of knowledge" that must be covered by students during their law degrees in order to satisfy the academic requirements for admission. The mandated syllabus, aptly known as the "Priestley Eleven", is now embodied in rules and regulations in each jurisdiction, and each educational institution is required to certify that students have complied with these requirements. The prescribed course of Criminal Law and Procedure is as follows:

1. The definition of crime.
2. Elements of crime.
3. Aims of the criminal law.
4. Homicide and defences.
5. Non-fatal offences against the person and defences.
6. Offences against property.
7. General doctrines.
8. Selected topics chosen from attempts, participation in crime, drunkenness, mistake, strict responsibility.
9. Elements of criminal procedure. Selected topics chosen from classification of offences, process to compel appearance, bail, preliminary examination, trial of indictable offences.

OR

topics of such breadth and depth as to satisfy the following guidelines:

> The topics should provide knowledge of the general doctrines of the criminal law and particular examination of both offences against the person and against property. Selective treatment should also be given to various defences and to elements of criminal procedure.

Clearly there is considerable flexibility in how a criminal law course may be structured within this framework. Needless to say, we believe that our book complies with these requirements.

Although not expressly precluded from the syllabus, a criminal law course may comply with "Priestley" requirements without addressing any theoretical, contextual and interdisciplinary perspectives. The above list of topics embody a traditional conception of the criminal law comprised of a "general part" that will be revealed through an examination of a narrow range of doctrines and selected offences. Not only is this concept of criminal law contestable, from a practical perspective it ignores significant substantive areas such as public order and drug offences. The prescribed syllabus also maintains the dualism between the core and context of law, with the danger that the latter is viewed as an "optional extra" to be pursued in advanced elective courses, or worse still, viewed as completely redundant from both academic and practical perspectives. The distinction drawn in legal education between the core and context, like the division between academic and vocational legal education, is highly problematic. Our holistic vision of criminal law and legal education requires the integration of interdisciplinary perspectives, an approach that we believe will pay practical as well as academic dividends. While we endorse Harry Arthurs' observation about the intrinsic difficulty of applying interdisciplinary perspectives to law, we have greater optimism that the Australian legal community will be receptive to such endeavours.

While one author wrote the initial draft of each chapter, we contributed text and other sources for each other's chapters wherever possible. Bernadette wrote the first drafts of Chapters 3, 4, 5, 6, 7, 9, 10 and 11, whilst Simon wrote the first drafts of Chapters 1, 2, 12, 13, 14 and 15. Chapter 8, which aptly deals with complicity, was a shared responsibility.

As convention demands, the law is current as at 1 November 2000 and we alone are responsible for any errors.

ACKNOWLEDGMENTS

We thank all of those at LBC for their enthusiasm and encouragement throughout this project. Judith Fox, the Commissioning Editor, was an early and formative influence. Her vision for a critical book on criminal law was present in the original book proposal in 1995, which set the task for the authors to produce a "fresh approach to the subject, designed to reflect the distinctive Australian jurisprudence which has come into being in the last decade". It also acknowledged that "the reconstruction of criminal law around gender issues, race issues and minority issues has further changed the terrain". At its inception, it was envisaged that the book would include interdisciplinary sections dealing with history, empirical research and academic debates. Judith has since departed LBC, moving onto a successful literary career as a novelist: see J Fox, *Bracelet Honeymyrtle* (St Leonards, NSW: Allen and Unwin, 1995). In more recent times, Catherine Dunk (Product Developer) and Jessica Perini (Senior Editor) have both played significant roles in making the original vision a reality. We were fortunate that LBC was persuaded, largely as a result of Judith Fox's skills of advocacy, to provide financial support for the project in the form of a small grant, as well as advances on royalties. Research assistants have worked tirelessly behind the scenes, chasing down errant references, re-checking sources and saving the authors from embarrassment. Simon would like to thank Henry Mares for his diligent research assistance throughout this and other projects, and Syvi Boon for lending assistance over the past six months. Bernadette would like to thank her research assistants, Owen Griffiths and Robyn Sweet for their excellent work. There has also been a significant contribution from law students who have challenged the law through class discussion, essays and theses.

Bernadette would particularly like to acknowledge the following:

The Monash University Law Faculty has long been renowned for its depth and breadth of scholarship in the criminal law field. The scholarly trinity of Professors Louis Waller, Bob Williams and Richard Fox has provided invaluable support and guidance. Thanks also to my former tutors Megan Bowman, Melissa Castan, Maria Hyland and Amanda Williams for keeping me on my toes and to my colleagues in crime, Kumar Amarasekara, Sandy Caspi Sable, Jonathan Clough, Gail Hubble, Pat Kilbride and Bronwyn Naylor for the helpful discussions over the past few years. Nick Pengelley and Lisa Smith provided expert assistance with tracking down material. My thanks also to Professors Stephen Parker and Marcia Neave for their enthusiasm and encouragement of contextual approaches to the study of law. Many people have supported me in my pursuit of interdisciplinary studies. However, I must single out Associate Professor Ellen Berah, Dr Tom Faunce and Professors Tom Campbell, John Devereux, Ian Freckelton, Shelley Gavigan, Paul Mullen and Margot Somerville for leading the way in breaking down the boundaries between the law and other disciplines and encouraging me to do the same.

Thanks to Van for the inspiration, to my brothers, Tony, Paul and Mark and to my late father, Michael, for their love and support. Most of all thanks to my mother, Doris, for her unfailing love and understanding and for putting up with me working on the computer at Inverloch!

Simon would particularly like to acknowledge the following:

My colleagues, David Hambly, John Seymour and Peter Waight, have made an immeasurable contribution to broadening my knowledge of criminal law and the criminal justice system over the past decade. Since their recent retirement, Kumar Amirthalingam, Miriam Gani and Declan Roche, have provided new sources of collegiality and support. Aside from my colleagues in criminal law, Peter Bailey, Juliet Behrens, Tom Campbell, Hilary Charlesworth, Jim Davis, Patricia Easteal, Gerry Simpson and Phillipa Weeks have generously taken time to discuss, make comments and answer queries on various topics. I am also indebted to Dr Stephen Mugford, formerly of the Department of Sociology at ANU, who shared a vision for creating an elective criminology course as part of the LLB. My involvement in that course had a profound influence on my approach to law. Stephen's ideas about the law and the sociology of crime and justice, particularly in relation to drug reform, can be seen in Chapters 1 and 15. My interest in criminology has been further stimulated by my close association over the past five years with the Australian Institute of Criminology. I am grateful to Drs Adam Graycar and Peter Grabosky, for involving me in interesting projects and providing a research haven during non-teaching periods. I am also grateful to Dr Toni Makkai, for her friendship and formidable expertise in illicit drugs, which once again helped immeasurably with Chapter 15. Finally, I would like to thank my colleagues at the University of Hong Kong, for welcoming me as a Visiting Associate Professor in 1999. I am grateful to those colleagues who shared their courses with me, Johannes Chan, Michael Jackson, Janice Brabyn and Michael Sandor, and who tolerated my heretical ideas about criminal law and legal education.

To my parents, Basil and Sheena, who have been an unfailing source of love and inspiration.

And finally to my loving wife, Jane, whose care and positive support lifted my spirit on dark days, bringing some measure of balance between "the book" and the "other project", our son Aaron. Thank you.

The publisher would also like to give particular thanks to the following lecturers for their detailed feedback on chapters of the draft manuscript: John Anderson (University of Newcastle), Michael Grant (University of Adelaide), Geraldine Mackenzie (Queensland University of Technology) and Associate Professor John Willis (La Trobe University).

We hope that this book will foster a desire to learn more about the social context in which the principles of criminal law evolve. We also hope it will whet your appetite for research into disciplines other than law. If you have any suggestions or comments, Simon can be contacted at simon.bronitt@anu.edu.au and Bernadette at Bernadette.McSherry@law.monash.edu.au.

Simon Bronitt

Bernadette McSherry

Canberra and Melbourne

November 2000

Acknowledgments

The following extracts listed herein, which made this textbook possible, have been reprinted with the kind permission of

Allen & Unwin: "Feminism and Criminology" (1997), p 110, by N Naffine; "Law's Truth/Women's Experience" in R Graycar (ed), *Dissenting Opinions — Feminist Explorations in Law and Society* (1990), p 14.

Almqvist & Wiksell, Stockholm: Lundstedt, *Legal Thinking Revisited* (1956), p 140.

American Psychiatric Association, Washington DC: *Diagnostic and Statistical Manual of Mental Disorders* (4th ed, 1994).

Ashgate Publishing, London: L Farmer, "The Law of the Land; Criminal Jurisdiction 1747-1908" in P Rush, S McVeigh and A Young (eds), *Criminal Legal Doctrine* (1997) Ch 3; P Alldridge, *Relocating Criminal Law* (2000) pp 5, 140.

Auckland University, Law School, NZ: A Turner, "Criminal Liability and AIDS" (1995) 7 *Auckland University Law Review* 857 at 887.

AusInfo: Hansard House of Representatives, *Criminal Code Amendment Bill 1999*, Second Reading Speech by the Hon. Daryl Williams, Attorney-General, 24 November 1999; *Aboriginal Customary Law — Recognition*, Discussion Paper No 17 (1980), p 52; Review Committee of Commonwealth Criminal Law, *Principles of Criminal Responsibility and other Matters*, July 1990 (Interim Report), p 398; Legislation Working Group, *Model Domestic Violence Laws*, Report (April 1999); Australian Law Reform Commission, *Multiculturalism and the Law*, Report No 57 (1992), p 179; Family Law Council, *Female Genital Mutilation*, Report (June 1994), p 31; Law Commission, *Criminal Law: Attempt and Impossibility in Relation to Attempt, Conspiracy and Incitement*, Report No 102 (1980), para 2.97; *Model Criminal Codes*.

Australian Feminist Law Foundation: A Orford, "Liberty, Equality, Pornography: The Bodies of Women and Human Rights Discourse" (1994) 3 *Australian Feminist Law Journal* 72 at 79, 97-99.

Australian Institute of Criminology: Data from T Makkai, "Drug Use Monitoring in Australia" (1999) Annual Report on Drug Use Among Adult Detainees, AIC Research and Public Policy Series, No. 26 (Chart); *"Australian Crime" — Facts and Figures*, p 10-11; A Cossins, "A Reply to the NSW Royal Commission Inquiry into Paedophilia: Victim Report Studies and Child Sex Offender Profiles — A Bad Match?" (1999) 32(1) *ANZ Journal of Criminology* 42 at 46-54; I Leader-Elliot, "Prohibition Against Heroin Use: Can They be Justified" (1986) 19 *ANZ Journal of Criminology* 225, p 244-245; Australian Illicit Drug Report 1997-1998 (1999), p 1, 3, 41, 42, 90, 95 Australian Bureau of Criminal Intelligence.

Basic Books: JQ Wilson, *Thinking About Crime* (1983), p 50.

Blackwell Publishers, UK: N Lacey, "A Clear Concept of Intention: Elusive or Illusory?" (1998) 56 *Modern Law Review* 621; R Cotterrell, "Why Must Legal Ideas Be Interpreted Sociologically" (1998) 25 *Journal of Law and Society* 171 at 183, 192; A Goldsmith and C Parker, "Failed Sociologists in the Marketplace: Law Schools in Australia" (1998) 25(1) *Journal of Law and Society* 33 at 47; S Edwards, *Female Sexuality and the Law* (1981), p 87.

Bloomsbury Publishing, London: T Jefferson, "Declaration of Independence" (original draft) in J Daintith (ed), *Bloombury's Thematic Dictionary of Quotations* (1991), p 198.

Butterworths Australia: D O'Connor and PA Fairall, *Criminal Defences* (3rd ed, 1996), pp 232-233; P Rush, *Criminal Law* (1997), p 353; S Yeo, "Coercing Wives into Crime" (1992) 6 *Australian Journal of Family Law* 214-228 at 224; M Otlowski, "The Legal Fallout from the APPM Dispute" (1992) 5 *Australian Journal Labour Law* 287 at 292; *Australian Capital Territory Reports* (ACTR); *Australian Law Reports* (ALR); *Supreme Court Reports* (SCR); *New South Wales Reports* (NSWR).

Butterworths, London: NLacey and C Wells, *Reconstructing Criminal Law* (2nd ed, 1998), p 23; S Edwards, "No Defence for Sadomasochistic Libido" (1994) *New Law Journal* 406; "No Shield for a Sadomasochistic Libido" (1993) *New Law Journal* 406 at 407; S Yeo, "Battered Woman Syndrome in Australia" (1993) 143 *New Law Journal* 13; P Alldridge, "Manslaughter and Causing Death by Driving Recklessly" (1980) 144 *Justice of the Peace* 569 at 571; *All England Law Reports* (All ER).

Cambridge University Press: L Farmer, *Criminal Law, Tradition and Legal Order* (1997), Ch 1, p 12; B Fisse and J Braithwaite, *Corporations, Crime and Accountability* (1993), p 47.

Canada Law Book: "Fraud and Consent in Rape: Comprehension of the Nature and Character of the Act and its Moral Implications" (1976) 18 Crim LQ 312 at 319; *Canada Criminal Cases* (CCC); *Dominion Law Reports* (DLR).

Carswell, Canada: EA Tollefson and B Starkman, *Mental Disorder in Criminal Proceedings* (1993), p 31; E Mee, "The Law of Criminal Attempt — a Treatise" (1984) *Western Weekly Reports* (WWR).

Chatto & Windus, London: H Kennedy, *Eve was Framed: Women and British Justice* (1993), pp 4, 5, 12.

Clarendon Press: David Garland, *Punishment and Modern Society* (1990), p 252, 271; N Lacey, *Criminology, Criminal Law and Criminalization* (2nd ed, 1997), Ch 11, p 448 in Maguire, R Morgan and R Reiner (eds), *The Oxford Handbook of Criminology* (1997); HLA Hart, *Punishment and Responsibility* (1968), pp 4-5; J Braithwaite and P Pettit, *Not Just Deserts — A Republican Theory of Criminal Justice* (1990), pp 57, 68, 76; KJM Smith, *A Modern Treatise on the Law of Criminal Complicity* (1991), p 22, 64, 204, 209, 211.

Council of Law Reporting for New South Wales: *New South Wales Law Reports* (NSWLR); *Weekly Notes NSW* (WN NSW).

Council of Law Reporting for Victoria: *Victorian Law Reports* (VLR), *Victorian Reports* (VR).

Council of Law Reporting for Queensland: *Queensland Reports* (Qd R).

Council of Law Reporting for New Zealand: *New Zealand Law Reports* (NZLR).

Dartmouth Publishing, UK: S McVeigh and P Rush, "Cutting Our Losses: Criminal Legal Doctrine" in P Rush, S McVeigh and A Young (eds), *Criminal Legal Doctrine* (1997), pp 188-193:

Donadio & Ashworth, Inc., New York: M Puzo, *The Godfather*.

Faber & Faber, UK: WH Auden from "Law Like Love", in AW Allison et al, *The Norton Anthology of Poetry* (1975), p 177.

Federation Press: N Seddon, *Domestic Violence in Australia — The Legal Response* (2nd ed, 1993), Ch 5; C Reynolds, *Public Health Law in Australia* (1995), p 204; D Brown, D Farrier and D Weisbrot, *Criminal Laws* (2nd ed, 1996), p 370.

Harcourt, Inc, USA: RL Atkinson, RC Atkinson, EE Smith and DJ Bern, *Introduction to Psychology* (10th ed, 1990), p 412.

Hart Publishing: N Lacey, *Unspeakable Subjects* (1998), p 88.

Harvard University Press: C MacKinnon, *Toward a Feminist Theory of the State* (1989), p 175.

Harvard University, School of Law: IP Robbins, "Double Inchoate Crimes" (1989) 26(1) *Harvard Journal on Legislation* 1 at 115.

Hawkins Publications: D Dixon, "Issues in the Legal Regulation of Policing" (1999) in D Dixon (ed), *A Culture of Corruption*.

HMSO (Her Majesty's Stationary Office), UK: *Laskey, Jaggard & Brown v United Kingdom*, 19 Feb 1997, Reports of Judgments and Decisions; Clause 27(6) of the *Draft Criminal Code*: The Law Commission, *Criminal Law: A Criminal Code for England and Wales*, No 177 (1989); Law Commission of England, *Assisting and Encouraging Crime*, Consultation Paper No 131 (1993), p 48; *Report of the Committee on Homosexual Offences and Prostitution* (Cmnd 247, 1957), p 25.

Human Rights Equal Opportunity Commission: H Charlesworth, "The Australian Reluctance About Rights" in P Alston (ed), *Towards an Australian Bill of Rights* (1994), p 49.

Hutchinson & Co Ltd, UK: F Forsyth, *The Day of the Jackal* (1971), pp 354-355; , K Popper, *The Logic of Scientific Discovery* (1939), p 59.

Indiana University, Law School: J Hall, "Mental Disease and Criminal Responsibility" (1958) 33 *Indiana Law Journal* 212, 223.

Journal of Drug Issues Inc, USA: E Drucker, "Drug Prohibition and Public Health: It's Model of Drug Addiction" P Dance and S Mugford, 'The St Oswald's Day Celebrations: 'Carnival' v 'Sobriety' in an Australian Drug Enthusiast Group" (1992) 22(3) *Journal of Drug Issues* 591 at 603.

Kluwer Netherlands: L Pineau, "Date Rape: A Feminist Analysis" (1989) 9 *Law and Philosophy* 217 at 234, 240.

LBC Information Services (formerly The Law Book Co), a part of Thomson Legal & Regulatory Group Asia Pacific Limited: S Yeo, "Private Defences, Duress and Necessity" (1991) 15 Crim LJ 139 at 143; M Goves, "Commentary" (1998) 22 Crim LJ 357 at 359; D Lanham, "Hale, Misogyny and Rape" (1983) 7 Crim LJ 148 at 156; M Kirby, "The Future of Criminal Law" (1999) 23 Crim LJ 263 at 272-273; *Defina* (1994) 18 Crim LJ 293 at 317; M Ashby, "Hard Cases, Causation and Care of the Dying" (1995) 3(2) *Journal of Law and Medicine* 152 at 152; I Freckelton, "Masochism, Self-mutilation and the Limits of Consent" (1994) (1) *Journal of Law and Medicine* 48 at 50; J Crawford, "International Law and the Recognition of Aboriginal Customary Law" in B Hocking (ed), *International Law and Aboriginal Human Rights* (1988) p 53; B Fisse, *Howard's Criminal Law* (5th ed, 1990), p 179; *Commonwealth Law Reports* (CLR); *Federal Law Reports* (FLR); *South Australia State Reports* (SASR); *Tasmanian Reports* (TasR); *Australian Criminal Reports* (A Crim R).

Law Institute Victoria: J Lipton, "Property Offices in the Electronic Age" (1998) 72 *Law Institute Journal* 54 at 54.

Law Reform Commission of Canada: *Criminal Law, the General Part: Liability and Defences*, Working Paper 28 (1982), p 48.

D Mackay Co, New York: J Dulles, "US Politician and Diplomat, on being asked whether he had ever been wrong" in H Temianka, *Facing the Musician, Irreverent Close-up of the Real Concert World* (1973).

Macmillan Press, UK: D McBarnet, *Conviction: Law, the State and the Construction of Justice* (1981), pp 8, 156.

Maxwell Macmillan, Sydney: S Mugford, "Controlled Drug Use Among Recreational Users: Sociological Perspectives" in N Heather, W Miller and J Greely (eds), *Self Control and the Addictive Behaviours* (1991), Ch 8.

Methuen & Co Ltd, UK: A Pope, "To Lord Bathurst" (1733) in FW Bateson, (ed), *The Poems of Alexander Pope*, Vol 111, Epistles to Several People 1.155-156 (1951), p 106.

New South Wales Bureau of Crime Statistics & Research: R Jochelson, "Aborigines and Public Order Legislation in NSW" (1997) 34 *Crime and Justice Bulletin*, p 15.

New South Wales Law Reform Commission: *Partial Defences to Murder: Diminished Responsibility* Report No 82 (May 1997), pp 49, 56.

Northwestern University, School of Law, Chicago: SJ Morse, "Immaturity and Irresponsibility" (1998) 88(1) *The Journal of Criminal Law and Criminology* 16-67.

Ohio University Press: R Browning, "By the Fireside" (1855) Stanza 46 in RJ King (ed), *The Complete Works of Robert Browning* (1981), Vol 5, p 200.

Oxford University Press, Melbourne: D Manderson, *From Mr Sin to Mr Big — A History of Australian Drug Laws* (1993), pp 105, 110; R Ford, " 'Lady-friends' and 'Sexual Deviationists', Lesbians and Law in Australia" 1920-1950 in D Kirkby (ed), *Sex, Power and Justice* (1995), Ch 3, pp 47-48.

Oxford University Press, New York: F Allen, *The Habits of Legality — Criminal Justice and the Rule of Law* (1996), p 39; J Braithwaite and I Ayres, *Responsive Regulation* (1983).

Oxford University Press, UK: G Simpson, "On Magic Mountain: Teaching Public International Law" (1999) 10 *European Journal of International Law* 70 at 80; K Hawkins, "Law as Law Resort" in R Baldwin, C Scott and C Hood (ed), *A Reader on Regulation* (1998), p 288; A Duff and D Garland, *A Reader on Punishment* (1994), p 239; J Young, "Incessant Chatter: Recent Paradigms in Criminology" in M Maguire, R Morgan and R Reiner (eds), *The Oxford Handbook of Criminology* (2nd ed, 1997), p 486; HLA Hart, *Law, Liberty and Morality* (1963), p 50; A Ashworth, *Principles of Criminal Law* (3rd ed, 1999), pp 30,31, 59; M Moore, *Act and Crime* (1993), p 4; A Ashworth, "Taking the Consequences" in S Shute (ed), *Action and Value in Criminal Law* (1993); M Gelder, D Gath, R Mayou and P Cowen, *The Oxford Textbook of Psychiatry* (3rd ed, 1996), p 57; K Daley, "Criminal Justice Ideologies and Practices in Different Voices: Some Feminist Questions about Justice" in N Lacey (ed), *Criminal Justice* (1994), p 240; L Lustgarten, "The Police and the Substantive Criminal Law" (1987) *British Journal of Criminology* 24 at 29.

Pantheon Books: CG Jung, *Erinnerungen, Traume, Gedanker*, recorded and edited by A Jaffe, translated from German by R and C Winston, (1973), p 361.

Pearson, UK: T Moore, "Morality" in *The Poetical Works of Thomas Moore* (1860), p 2931.15-18, (Green, Longman & Roberts).

Penguin, UK: JS Mill, *On Liberty* (1974), p 11; J Webster (1580-1625) *The Duchess of Malfi*, IV:2 Line 260 (1972), p 260; E Burke, *Reflections on the Revolution in France* (1970), p 372.

Routledge, UK: D Galligan, "Preserving Public Protest: the Legal Approach" in L Gostin (ed), *Civil Liberties in Conflict* (1988), p 54-55.

Sage Publications: RD Hare and SD Hart, "Psychopathy, Mental Disorder and Crime" in S Hodgins (ed), *Mental Disorder and Crime*, Newbury Park, CA; C Smart, *Law, Crime and Sexuality* (1995), p 104; D Manderson, "Substances as Symbols: Race Rhetoric and the Tropes of Australian Drug History" (1997) 63(3) *Social and Legal Studies* 383 at 384.

Simon & Schuster, New York: J Wilson and R Herrnstein, *Crime and Human Nature* (1985).

South Australian Attorney-General: South Australian Attorney-General's Office, *Intoxication and Criminal Responsibility*, Discussion Paper (July 1998); South Australian Penal Methods and Law Reform Commission's Report on "The Substantial Criminal Law" (1977), p 309.

Stanford University Press, California USA: J Braithwaite "Inequality and Republican Criminology" in J Hagan and RD Peterson (eds), *Crime and Inequality* (1995), p 279.

Sweet & Maxwell, UK: H Biggs, "Euthanasia and Death with Dignity: Still Poised on the Fulcrum of Homicide" (1996) Crim LR 878 at 883; *R v Simcox* (1964) Crim LR 402 at 403; A Ashworth and M Blake, "Resumption of Innocence in English Criminal Law" (1996) Crim LR 306 at 314; A Ashworth, "Crime, Community and Creeping Consequentialism" (1996) Crim LR 229; P English, "Homicide Other than Murder" (1977) Crim LR 79 at 89; DW Elliott, "Law and Fact in Theft Act Cases" (1976) Crim LR 707 at 711; D Ormerod, "Cheating the Revenue" (1998) Crim LR 627; G Williams, "Complicity, Purpose and the Draft Code-1" (1990) Crim LR 4 at 4; P Glazebrook, "Should We Have a Law of Attempted Crime?" (1969) 85 *Law Quarterly Review* 28 at 35; TH Jones, "Insanity, Automatism and the Burden of Proof on the Accused" (1995) 111 *Law Quarterly Review* 475-516 at 477, 492; G Williams, *Textbook of Criminal Law* (2nd ed, 1983), pp 27, 125; G Williams, *Criminal Law: The General Part* (1961), pp 287, 288; *R v Boyea* (1992) Crim LR, p 575; *Criminal Appeal Reports* (Cr App R); *English Reports* (ER).

Taylor & Francis, Inc (http://www.routledge-ny.com): W Blackstone, *Commentaries on the Laws of England* (9th ed, 1978), Book IV, p 251.

The Incorporated Council of Law Reporting for England & Wales: *Reports on Appeal Cases* (AC), *Kings Bench* (KB), *Queens Bench* (QB), *Law Reports* (LR), *Weekly Law Reports* (WLR).

The Scholars' Press Limited: R Burns (1759-1796) "Man was Made to Mourn" in R Burns, *Poems 1786 & 1787* (1971), p 160.

University of Adelaide: S Bronitt and G Williams, "Political Freedom as an Outlaw: Republican Theory and Political Protest" (1996) 18(2) *Adelaide Law Review* 289 at 294.

University of Melbourne: J Morgan, "Rape in Medical Treatment: The Patient as Victim" (1991) 18 MULR 403 at 413; S Chandra-Shekeran, "Theorising the Limits of the 'Sadomasochistic Homosexual' Identity" in *R v Brown* (1977) 21 MULR 584 at 592; W Morgan, "Identifying Evil for What It Is: Tasmania, Sexual Perversity and the United Nations" (1994) (19)3 MULR 740 at 756.

University of New South Wales: DGT Williams, "Freedom of Assembly and Free Speech: Changes and Reforms in England" (1975) 1(2) UNSW LJ 97 at 100-101.

University of Sydney: S Yeo, "Sex, Ethnicity, Power of Self-Control and Provocation" (1996) 18 *Sydney Law Review* 304-322 at 316.

University of Western Australia: J Scutt in "Consent versus Submission: Threats and the Element of Fear in Rape" (1977) 13 Uni of WA Law Review 52 at 63-64, 66.

Victorian Law Reform Committee: "Criminal Liability for Self-induced Intoxication Report" (May 1999).

Victorian Law Reform Commission: *Criminal Liability of Married Persons*, Report No. 3 (1975), para 16; *Death Caused by Dangerous Driving*, Discussion Paper 21 (July 1991), p 15.

Viking Press, New York: Lord Byron, "Fare Thee Well" (1973) Stanza 12, p 259, in WH Auden and NH Pearson (eds), *Romantic Poets*.

Weidenfield & Nicholson Ltd: A Norrie, *Crime, Reason and History* (1993), p 9.

Western Australian Attorney-General: *Western Australian Law Reports* (WALR).

LBC Information Services (formerly The Law Book Co), a part of Thomson Legal and Regulatory Group Asia Pacific Limited (TLRG), is grateful to all the publishers and authors above who have allowed us to reproduce extracts of their work in this book. While every care has been taken to establish and acknowledge copyright, TLRG, tenders its apology for any accidental infringement. The publisher would be pleased to come to a suitable agreement with the rightful owners in each case.

Thank you.

Summary of Contents

Table of Contents

PART II   JUSTIFICATIONS AND EXCUSES

PART III EXTENDING CRIMINAL RESPONSIBILITY

PART IV   SPECIFIC CRIMES

Table of Cases

Table of Statutes

NEW SOUTH WALES

QUEENSLAND

SOUTH AUSTRALIA

UNITED STATES

Bibliography

Books and Reports

Alcorn, P, Zahra P and Arden R, *Drug Law in the Code States* (Sydney: Federation Press, 1993)

Alldridge, P, *Relocating Criminal Law* (Aldershot: Ashgate, 2000)

Allen, CK, *Legal Duties and Other Essays in Jurisprudence* (Oxford: Oxford University Press, 1931)

Allen, FA, *The Habits of Legality — Criminal Justice and the Rule of Law* (New York: Oxford University Press, 1996)

American Psychiatric Association, *Diagnostic and Statistical Manual of Mental Disorders* (4th ed, Washington, DC: APA, 1994)

Archbold, JF, *Archbold's Pleading, Evidence and Practice in Criminal Cases* (London: Sweet & Maxwell, 1822)

Ashworth, A, *The Criminal Process* (2nd ed, Oxford: Oxford University Press, 1998)

Ashworth, A, *Principles of Criminal Law* (3rd ed, Oxford: Oxford University Press, 1999)

Attorney-General's Office (SA), *Intoxication and Criminal Responsibility*, Discussion Paper (July, 1998)

Australian Bureau of Criminal Intelligence, *Australian Illicit Drug Report 1997-1998* (Canberra: ABCI, 1999)

Australian Bureau of Statistics, *Women's Safety Survey* (Canberra: Office of the Status of Women, 1996)

Australian Institute of Criminology, *Australian Crime, Facts and Figures* (Canberra: AIC, 1999)

Australian Law Reform Commission, *Aboriginal Customary Law — Recognition*, Discussion Paper No 17 (Canberra: AGPS, 1980)

Australian Law Reform Commission, *The Recognition of Aboriginal Customary Laws*, Final Report (1988)

Australian Law Reform Commission, *Multiculturalism and the Law*, Report No 57 (1992)

Australian Law Reform Commission, *Multiculturalism: Criminal Law*, Discussion Paper No 48 (1991)

Australian Law Reform Commission, *Evidence*, Report No 26 (Interim) (1985)

Australian Law Reform Commission, *Domestic Violence*, Report No 30 (1986)

Australian Law Reform Commission, *Evidence*, Report No 38 (1987)

Australian Medical Association, *Female Genital Mutilation*, Position Statement (1994)

Australian Medical Association, *Position Statement on Care of Severely and Terminally Ill Patients* (1996)

Bartholomew, A, *Psychiatry, the Criminal Law and Corrections* (Bundalong: Wiseman Publications, 1987)

Bates, A, Buddin T and Meure D, *The System of Criminal Law* (Sydney: Butterworths, 1979)

Battin, M, *The Least Worst Death* (New York: Oxford University Press, 1994)

Beauchamp, TL and Childress JF, *Principles of Biomedical Ethics* (4th ed, Oxford: Oxford University Press, 1994)

Becarria, C, *An Essay on Crimes and Punishment* (1764) (Birmingham, Alabama: Legal Classics Library, 1991)

Becker, H, *Outsiders: Studies in the Sociology of Deviance* (London: Collier McMillan, 1963)

Bennett, B, *Law and Medicine* (Sydney: LBC Information Services, 1997)

Blackstone, W, *Commentaries on the Laws of England* (Oxford: Clarendon Press, 1769)

Bottomley, S and Parker S, *Law in Context* (2nd ed, Sydney: Federation Press, 1997)

Braithwaite, J and Ayres I, *Responsive Regulation* (New York: Oxford University Press, 1992)

Braithwaite, J and Pettit P, *Not Just Deserts — A Republican Theory of Criminal Justice* (Oxford: Clarendon Press, 1990)

Braithwaite, J, *To Punish or Persuade: Enforcement of Coal Mine Safety* (Albany: State University of New York Press, 1985)

Braithwaite, J, *Crime, Shame and Reintegration* (Cambridge: Cambridge University Press, 1989)

Brakel, SJ, Parry J and Weiner BA, *The Mentally Disabled and the Law* (3rd ed, Chicago: American Bar Foundation, 1985)

Brennan, F, *Too Much Order With Too Little Law* (St Lucia, Qld: University of Queensland Press, 1983)

Bronitt, S, *Criminal Liability Issues Associated with a Heroin Trial, Working Paper No 13, Feasibility Research into the Controlled Availability of Opioids Stage 2* (Canberra: NCEPH and AIC, 1995)

Brown, D and Ellis T, *Policing low-level disorder: Police Use of Section 5 of the Public Order Act 1986* (London: HMSO, 1994)

Brown, D and Hogg R, *Rethinking Law and Order* (Annandale: Pluto Press, 1998)

Brown, D, Farrier D and Weisbrot D, *Criminal Laws* (2nd ed, Sydney: Federation Press, 1996)

Brownmiller, S, *Against Our Will: Men, Women and Rape* (Harmondsworth: Penguin Books, 1975)

Bryan, JW, *The Development of the English Law of Conspiracy* (New York: Da Capo Press, 1970)

Burns, JH and Hart HLA, *Jeremy Bentham: Introduction to the Principles of Morals and Legislation* (London: Methuen, 1982)

Campbell, E and Whitmore H, *Freedom in Australia* (revised ed, Sydney: Sydney University Press, 1973)

Campbell, TD, *The Legal Theory of Ethical Positivism* (Brookfield, Vt: Dartmouth Publishing Co, 1996)

Cannold, L, *The Abortion Myth* (Sydney: Allen and Unwin, 1998)

Carmody, M, *Sexual Assault of People With an Intellectual Disability* (Sydney: NSW Women's Coordination Unit, 1990)

Carter, J, *Rape in Medieval England: An Historical and Sociological Study*, (Lanham: University Press of America, 1985)

Cashmore, J, *Legal and Social Aspects of the Physical Punishment of Children* (ACT: Commonwealth of Australia, May 1995)

Cato, C, *The Law and Practice of Criminal Litigation* (Sydney: LBC, 1998)

Chan, J, *Annotated Bills of Rights Ordinance* (Hong Kong: Butterworths, 1999)

Chappell, D and Wilson P, *The Australian Criminal Justice System: The Mid 1990s* (Sydney: Butterworths, 1994)

Charlesworth, M, *Bioethics in a Liberal Society* (Cambridge: Cambridge University Press, 1993)

Clarke, A, *Women's Silence, Men's Violence: Sexual Assault in England 1770-1845* (London: Pandora, 1987)

Clough, J and Mulhern C, *Butterworths Tutorial Series: Criminal Law* (Sydney: Butterworths, 1999)

Cohen, S, *Folkdevils and Moral Panics* (London: Paladin, 1973)

Colvin, E, Linden S and Bunney L, *Criminal law in Queensland and Western Australia* (Sydney: Butterworths, 1998)

Commonwealth Partnerships Against Domestic Violence, *Report: Model Domestic Violence Laws* (1999)

Community Law Reform Committee of the Australian Capital Territory, *Public Assemblies and Street Offences: Issues Paper No 10* (Canberra: ACT Government, 1994)

Cook, S and Bessant J (eds), *Women's Encounters with Violence — Australian Experiences* (Thousand Oaks, CA: Sage Publications Inc, 1997)

Cornish, WR and Clarke G, *Law and Society in England 1750-1950* (London: Sweet & Maxwell, 1989)

Criminal Code Officers Committee, *Chapter 2: General Principles of Criminal Responsibility*, Final Report (Canberra: AGPS, December 1992)

Criminal Law and Penal Methods Reform Committee of South Australia, *The Substantive Criminal Law*, 4th Report (Adelaide: Government Printer SA, 1978)

Criminal Law Revision Committee, *Offences Against the Person*, Fourteenth Report (London: HMSO, Cmnd 7844, 1980)

Criminal Law Revision Committee, *Sexual Offences*, Fifteenth Report (London: HMSO, 1984)

Criminal Law Revision Committee, *Theft and Related Offences,* Eighth Report (London: HMSO, Cmnd 2977, 1966)

Cunneen, C, Fraser D and Tomsen S (eds), *Faces of Hate — Hate Crime in Australia* (Sydney: Hawkins Press, 1997)

Davenport-Hines, R, *Sex, Death and Punishment* (London: Collins, 1990)

de Smith, SA, *Constitutional and Administrative Law* (7th ed, Harmondsworth: Penguin, 1996)

Dept of Foreign Affairs and Trade, *Human Rights Manual* (1998)

Dept of Justice (Vic*)*, *Rape Law Reform Evaluation Project — The Crimes (Rape) Act 1991* (1997)

Devlin, P, *The Enforcement of Morals* (London: Oxford University Press, 1965)

Dixon, D, *Law in Policing: Legal Regulation and Police Practices* (Oxford: Clarendon Press, 1997)

Dixon, D, Lynskey M and Hall W, *Running the Risks: Heroin, Health and Harm in South West Sydney*, NDARC Monograph No 38 (Sydney: National Drug and Alcohol Centre, UNSW, 1998)

Domestic Violence Legislation Working Group, *Model Domestic Violence Laws*, Discussion Paper (Canberra: AGPS, November 1997)

Domestic Violence Legislation Working Group, *Model Domestic Violence Laws,* Report (Canberra: AGPS, April 1999)

Douglas, M, *Purity and Danger*, (London: Routledge & Kegan Paul, 1992)

Duff, RA, *Intention, Agency and Criminal Liability* (Oxford: Oxford University Press, 1990)

Duff, RA, *Criminal Attempts* (Oxford: Oxford University Press, 1996)

Dworkin, R, *Taking Rights Seriously* (London: Duckworth, 1977)

Dworkin, R, *Law's Empire* (London: Fontana, 1986)

Dworkin, R, *Life's Dominion. An Argument about Abortion and Euthanasia* (London: Harper Collins, 1993)

Easteal, P, *Voices of the Survivors* (Melbourne: Spinifex Press, 1994)

Easteal, P, *Shattered Dreams: Marital Violence Among Overseas-born in Australia* (Canberra: AGPS, 1996)

Easteal, P (ed), *Balancing the Scales: Rape, Law Reform and Australian Culture* (Sydney: Federation Press, 1998)

Edwards, S, *Female Sexuality and the Law* (Oxford: Martin Robertson, 1981)

Edwards, S, *Sex and Gender in the Legal Process* (London: Blackstone Press, 1996)

English Law Commission, *Defences of General Application*, Working Paper No 55 (1974)

English Royal Commissions, *Royal Commission on Capital Punishment* (1949-1953)

Evans, EP, *The Criminal Prosecution and Capital Punishment of Animals* (London: Faber and Faber, 1987)

Family Law Council, *Female Genital Mutilation*, Discussion Paper (January 1994)

Family Law Council, *Female Genital Mutilation,* Report (June 1994)

Family Law Council, *Parental Child Abduction,* A Report to the Attorney-General (January 1998)

Farmer, L, *Criminal Law, Tradition, and Legal Order* (Cambridge: Cambridge University Press, 1997)

Favazza, AR, *Bodies Under Siege* (Baltimore: John Hopkins University Press, 1992)

Federal Human Rights Commission, *Civil Disobedience and the Use of Arrest as Punishment: Some Human Rights Issues* (1986)

Feeley, M, *The Process is the Punishment* (New York: Russell Sage Foundation, 1979)

Feinberg, J, *The Moral Limits of the Criminal Law — Volume 1 — Harm to Others* (New York: Oxford University Press, 1984); *Volume 2 — Harm to Self* (New York: Oxford University Press, 1986); *Volume 3 — Offence to Others* (New York: Oxford University Press, 1988)

Feldman, D, *Civil Liberties and Human Rights in England and Wales* (Oxford: Clarendon Press, 1993)

Fijnaut, C and Marx G (eds), *Undercover — Police Surveillance in Comparative Perspective* (The Hague: Kluwer, 1995)

Findlay, M and Duff P (eds), *The Jury Under Attack* (Sydney: LBC, 1988)

Findlay, M and Hogg R, *Understanding Crime and Criminal Justice* (Sydney: Law Book Company Ltd, 1988)

Findlay, M, Odgers S and Yeo S, *Australian Criminal Justice* (2nd ed, Melbourne: Oxford University Press, 1999)

Findlay, M, *Globalisation of Crime* (Cambridge: Cambridge University Press, 1999)

Fine, B and Millar R (eds), *Policing the Miners' Strike* (London: Lawrence and Wishart, 1985)

Fingarette, H, *The Meaning of Criminal Insanity* (Berkeley: University of California Press, 1972)

Finnane, M, *Police and Government* (Melbourne: Oxford University Press, 1994)

Finnane, M, *Punishment in Australian Society* (Melbourne: Oxford University Press, 1997)

Fisse, B and Braithwaite J, *Corporations, Crime and Accountability* (Cambridge: Cambridge University Press, 1993)

Fisse, B, Fraser D and Coss G, *The Money Trail: Confiscation of Proceeds of Crime, Money Laundering and Cash Transaction Reporting* (Sydney: Law Book Company Ltd, 1992)

Fisse, B, *The Impact of Publicity on Corporate Offenders* (Albany: State University of New York Press, 1983)

Fisse, B, *Howard's Criminal Law* (5th ed, Sydney: Law Book Company Limited, 1990)

Fletcher, G, *Rethinking Criminal Law* (Boston: Little Brown, 1978)

Flick, G, *Civil Liberties in Australia* (Sydney: Law Book Company Ltd, 1981)

Foucault, M, *The Birth of the Clinic* (New York: Vintage Press, 1975)

Foucault, M, *Discipline and Punish — The Birth of the Prison* (New York: Pantheon Books, 1977)

Garland, D, *Punishment in Modern Society* (Chicago: University of Chicago Press, 1990)

Gaze, B and Jones M, *Law, Liberty and Australian Democracy* (Sydney: Law Book Company Ltd, 1990)

Gearty, C and Ewing K, *Freedom Under Thatcher: Civil Liberties in Modern Britain* (Oxford: Clarendon Press, 1990)

Gelder, M, Gath D, Mayou R and Cowen P, *Oxford Textbook of Psychiatry* (3rd ed, Oxford: Oxford University Press, 1996)

Gelles, RS and Straus MA, *Intimate Violence* (New York: Simon and Schuster, 1988)

Gibbs Committee, *Review of Commonwealth Criminal Law: Interim Report on Computer Crime* (1988)

Gibbs Committee, *Review of Commonwealth Criminal Law, Interim Report: Principles of Criminal Responsibility and Other Matters,* Chapter 10, Intoxication (1990)

Gibbs Committee, *Review of Commonwealth Criminal Law,* Interim Report (1991)

Gillies, P, *The Law of Criminal Conspiracy* (Sydney: Law Book Company Ltd, 1981)

Gillies, P, *Criminal Law* (4th ed, Sydney: LBC, 1997)

Gilligan, C, *In A Different Voice* (Cambridge, MA: Harvard University Press, 1982)

Gilmore, WC, *Dirty Money: The Evolution of Money Laundering Counter-Measures* (The Netherlands: Council of Europe Press, 1995)

Glissan, J and Tilmouth S, *Australian Criminal Trial Directions* (Sydney: Butterworths, 1996)

Godwin, J, Hamblin J, Patterson D and Buchanan D, *Australian HIV/AIDS Legal Guide* (2nd ed, Sydney: Federation Press, 1993)

Goldstein, A, *The Insanity Defense* (New Haven: Yale University Press, 1967)

Goode, M, *Criminal Conspiracy in Canada* (Toronto: Carswell, 1975)

Gordon, G, *The Criminal Law of Scotland* (2nd ed, Edinburgh: Green, 1978)

Grabosky, P and Smith R, *Crime in the Digital Age* (Sydney: Transaction Publishers/Federation Press, 1998)

Grabosky, P, *Sydney in Ferment* (Canberra: ANU Press, 1977)

Graycar, R and Morgan J, *The Hidden Gender of Law* (Sydney: Federation Press, 1990)

Gunn, J and Taylor P (eds), *Forensic Psychiatry: Clinical, Legal and Ethical Issues:* (Oxford: Butterworth-Heinemann, 1993)

Hale, M, *The History of the Pleas of the Crown* (London: Professional Books Limited, 1971) (original publication 1736)

Hall, J, *Theft, Law and Society* (2nd ed, Bloomington, IN: Bobbs-Merrill Company Inc, 1952)

Hall, J, *General Principles of Criminal Law* (2nd ed, Indianapolis: The Bobbs-Merrill Company Inc, 1960)

Hart, HLA and Honoré A, *Causation in the Law* (Oxford: Clarendon Press, 1959) (2nd ed, 1985)

Hart, HLA, *The Concept of Law* (Oxford: Clarendon Press, 1961)

Hart, HLA, *Law, Liberty and Morality* (London: Oxford University Press, 1963)

Hart, HLA, *Punishment and Responsibility: Essays in the Philosophy of Law* (Oxford: Oxford University Press, 1968)

Hawkins, K, *Environment and Enforcement* (Oxford: Clarendon Press, 1983)

Hawkins, W, *A Treatise of the Pleas of the Crown*, Vol 1 (London: J Curwood, 1824)

Hayes, SC and Craddock G, *Simply Criminal* (2nd ed, Sydney: Federation Press, 1992)

Hazell, R, *Conspiracy and Civil Liberties* (London: Bell, 1974)

Healey, K (ed), *Euthanasia* (Sydney: The Spinney Press, 1997)

Heenan, M and McKelvie H, *Rape Law Reform Evaluation Project, Report No 2; The Crimes (Rape) Act 1991: An Evaluation Project* (Melbourne: Dept of Justice, 1997)

Heilbron Committee, *Report of the Advisory Group on the Law of Rape* (1975)

Hermann, D, *The Insanity Defense* (Springfield: CC Thomas, 1983)

Hiller, A, *Public Order and the Law* (Sydney: Law Book Company Ltd, 1983)

Hogg, R and Brown D, *Rethinking Law and Order* (Annandale: Pluto Press, 1998)

Holdsworth, W, *A History of English Law* (London: Sweet and Maxwell, 1966)

Holmes, OW, *The Common Law* (Boston: Little, Brown, 1881)

Home Office, *Violence: Reforming the Offences Against the Person Act* 1861 (1998)

Hopkins, A, *Making Safety Work: Getting Management Commitment to Occupational Health and Safety* (St Leonard's: Allen & Unwin, 1995)

House of Lords Select Committee, *Report of the Select Committee on Murder and Life Imprisonment* (London: HMSO, 1989)

Howe, A (ed), *Sexed Crime in the News* (Sydney: Federation Press, 1998)

Hughes, G, *Data Protection in Australia* (Sydney: Law Book Company Ltd, 1991)

Human Rights and Equal Opportunity Commission, *Racist Violence* (Canberra: AGPS, 1991)

Human Rights and Equal Opportunity Commission, *Toomelah Report* (Sydney: HREOC, 1988)

Hunt, A and Wickham G, *Foucault and the Law — Towards a Sociology of Law as Governance* (London: Pluto, 1994)

Hunter, J and Cronin K, *Evidence, Advocacy and Ethical Practice* (Sydney: Butterworths, 1995)

Husak, D, *Drugs and Rights* (Cambridge: Cambridge University Press, 1992)

Indian Law Commission, *A Penal Code Prepared by the Indian Law Commissioners* (Birmingham, Alabama: Legal Classics Library, 1987)

Joint Select Committee into Safe Injection Rooms, Parliament of New South Wales, *Report on the Establishment or Trial of Safe Injection Rooms* (Sydney: 1998)

Kennedy, H, *Eve Was Framed — Women and British Justice* (London: Vintage Books for Chatto & Windus, 1993)

Kenny, RG, *An Introduction to Criminal Law in Queensland and Western Australia* (5th ed, Sydney: Butterworths, 2000)

Kercher, B, *An Unruly Child: A History of Law in Australia* (Sydney: Allen & Unwin, 1995)

Kerruish, V, *Jurisprudence as Ideology* (London and New York: Routledge, 1991)

King, M, *Framework of Criminal Justice* (London: Croom Helm, 1981)

Kirkby, D (ed), *Sex, Power and Justice* (Melbourne: Oxford University Press, 1995)

Krivanek, J, *Heroin — Myths and Reality* (Sydney: Allen and Unwin, 1988)

Lacey, N and Wells C, *Reconstructing the Criminal Law* (2nd ed, London: Butterworths, 1998)

Lacey, N, *State Punishment: Political Principles and Community Values* (London: Routledge, 1988)

Lacey, N, *Unspeakable Subjects — Feminist Essays in Legal and Social Theory* (Oxford: Hart Publishing, 1998)

Lanham, D, *Cross-Border Criminal Law* (Melbourne: FT Law & Tax Asia Pacific, 1997)

Laster, K, *Law as Culture* (Sydney: Federation Press, 1997)

Law Commission, *Assisting and Encouraging Crime*, Consultation Paper No 131 (London: HMSO, 1993)

Law Commission, *Attempt and Impossibility in Relation to Attempt, Conspiracy and Incitement*, Report No 102 (London: HMSO,1980)

Law Commission, *Binding Over*, Report No 222 (London: HMSO, 1994)

Law Commission, *Consent in the Criminal Law*, Consultation Paper 139 (London: HMSO, 1995)

Law Commission, *Criminal Law: A Criminal Code for England and Wales*, Report No 177 (London: HMSO, 1989)

Law Commission, *Criminal Law: Consent and Offences against the Person*, Consultation Paper No 134 (London: HMSO, 1994)

Law Commission, *Criminal Law: Corroboration of Evidence in Criminal Trials*, Report No 202 (London: HMSO, 1991)

Law Commission, *Criminal law: Report on Conspiracy and Criminal Law Reform*, Report No 76 (London: HMSO, 1976)

Law Commission, *General Principles, Parties, Complicity and Liability for the Acts of Another*, Working Paper No 43 (London: HMSO, 1972)

Law Commission, *Legislating the Criminal Code: Intoxication and Criminal Liability*, Report No 229 (London: HMSO, 1995)

Law Commission, *Parties, Complicity and Liability for the Act of Another*, Working Paper No 43 (London: HMSO, 1972)

Law Commission of England and Wales, *Legislating the Criminal Code: Fraud and Deception*, Consultation Paper No 155 (London: HMSO, 1999)

Law Reform Commission of Canada, *Aboriginal Peoples and Criminal Justice,* Report No 34 (1991)

Law Reform Commission of Canada, *Criminal Law, The General Part: Liability and Defences*, Working Paper 29 (1982)

Law Reform Commission of Canada, *Homicide*, Working Paper No 33 (1984)

Law Reform Commission of Canada, *Secondary Liability: Participation in Crime and Inchoate Offences*, Working Paper No 45 (1985)

Law Reform Commission of Victoria, *Criminal Responsibility: Intention and Gross Intoxication,* Report No 6 (1986)

Law Reform Commission of Victoria, *Death Caused by Dangerous Driving*, Discussion Paper 21 (1991)

Law Reform Commission of Victoria, *Homicide*, Report No 40 (1991)

Law Reform Commission of Victoria, *Mental Malfunction and Criminal Responsibility*, Report No 34 (1990)

Law Reform Commission of Victoria, *Mental Malfunction and Criminal Responsibility*, Discussion Paper No 14 (1988)

Law Reform Commission of Victoria, *Rape: Reform of Law and Procedure*, Report No 43 (1991)

Law Reform Commissioner of Victoria, *Criminal Procedure: Miscellaneous Reforms* (1974)

Law Reform Commissioner of Victoria, *Criminal Liability of Married Persons*, Report No 3 (1975)

Law Reform Commissioner of Victoria, *Duress Necessity and Coercion*, Report No 9 (1980)

Law Reform Commissioner of Victoria, *Provocation and Diminished Responsibility as Defences to Murder*, Report No 12 (1982)

Law Reform Committee of Victoria, *Criminal Liability for Self-Induced Intoxication,* Report (1999)

Leader-Elliott, D and White JM, *Legal Approaches to Alcohol-Related Violence: A Summary*, Report 6A for the National Symposium on Alcohol Misuse and Violence (Canberra: AGPS, July 1994)

Leaver, A, *Investigating Crime* (Sydney: LBC, 1997)

Lees, S, *Ruling Passions: Sexual Violence, Reputation and the Law* (Buckingham: Open University Press, 1997)

Legal Working Party of the Intergovernmental Committee on AIDS, *Legislative Approaches to Public Health Control of HIV Infection* (1992)

Luker, K, *Abortion and the Politics of Motherhood* (Berkeley: University of California Press, 1984)

Lundstedt, AV, *Legal Thinking Revisited* (Stockholm: Almqvist & Wiksell, 1956)

MacKinnon, C, *Toward A Feminist Theory of the State* (Cambridge MA: Harvard University Press, 1989)

Makkai, T, *Drug Use Monitoring in Australia — 1999 Annual Report on Drug Use Among Adult Detainees*, Australian Institute of Criminology, Research and Public Policy Series, No 26 (Canberra: AIC, 2000)

Manderson, D, *From Mr Sin to Mr Big — A History of Australian Drug Laws* (Melbourne: Oxford University Press, 1993)

Marx, G, *Undercover — Police Surveillance in America* (Berkeley: University of California Press, 1988)

McAuley, F, *Insanity, Psychiatry and Criminal Responsibility* (Dublin: The Round Hall Press, 1993)

McBarnet, D, *Conviction: Law, The State and the Construction of Justice* (London: MacMillan Press, 1981)

McCabe, S and Wallington P, *The Police, Public Order and Civil Liberties: Legacies of the Miners' Strike* (London: Routledge, 1988)

Model Criminal Code Officers Committee, *Chapter 3: Theft, Fraud, Bribery and Related Offences*, Final Report (1995)

Model Criminal Code Officers Committee, *Model Criminal Code, Chapter 5: Sexual Offences Against the Person*, Discussion Paper (1996)

Model Criminal Code Officers Committee, *Chapter 3: Conspiracy to Defraud*, Report (1997)

Model Criminal Code Officers Committee, *Chapter 5: Non Fatal Offences Against the Person*, Discussion Paper (1996)

Model Criminal Code Officers Committee, *Chapter 5: Non Fatal Offences Against the Person*, Report (1998)

Model Criminal Code Officers Committee, *Chapter 5: Fatal Offences Against the Person*, Discussion Paper, (1998)

Model Criminal Code Officers Committee, *Chapter 6: Serious Drug Offences*, Report (1998)

Model Criminal Code Officers Committee, *Chapter 8: Public Order Offences — Contamination of Goods*, Report (1998)

Model Criminal Code Officers Committee, *Chapter 9: Offences Against Humanity — Slavery* (1998)

Model Criminal Code Officers Committee, *Discussion Paper on Model Forensic Procedures Bill; DNA Database Provisions*, Report (1999)

Model Criminal Code Officers Committee, *Chapter 5: Sexual Offences Against the Person*, Report (1999)

Model Criminal Code Officers Committee, *Chapter 4: Damage and Computer Offences*, Discussion Paper (2000)

McConville, M, Sanders A and Leng R, *The Case for the Prosecution* (London: Routledge, 1991)

McDonald, D, Moore R, Norberry J, Wardlaw G and Ballenden N, *Legislative Options for Cannabis in Australia* (1994) *National Drug Strategy Monograph*, No 26

Meehan, E, *The Law of Criminal Attempt — A Treatise* (Calgary: Carswell Legal Publications, 1984)

Mezey, G and King M, *Male Victims of Sexual Assault* (Oxford: Oxford University Press, 1991)

Mill, JS, *On Liberty* (London: JM Dent & Sons,1960, first published 1859)

Miller, R, *The Case for Legalizing Drugs* (New York: Prager, 1991)

Mitchell Committee, *Criminal Law and Penal Methods Reform Committee of South Australia* (Adelaide: Government Printer, 1977)

Mommsen, T, Krueger P and Watson A, (edited and translated), *The Digest of Justinian* (Pennsylvania: University of Pennsylvania Press, 1985)

Moore, MS, *Law and Psychiatry: Rethinking the Relationship* (New York: Cambridge University Press, 1984)

Moore, M, *Act and Crime* (Oxford: Oxford University Press, 1993)

Moore, M, *Placing Blame: A General Theory of the Criminal Law* (Oxford: Oxford University Press, 1997)

Moran, L, *The Homosexual(ity) of Law* (London: Routledge, 1996)

Morgan, J and Graycar R, *The Hidden Gender of Law* (Sydney: Federation Press, 1990)

Mukherjee, S, Carcach C and Higgins K, *A Statistical Profile of Crime in Australia* (Canberra: AIC, 1997)

Mullen, P, Pathé M and Purcell R, *Stalkers and Their Victims* (Cambridge: Cambridge University Press, 2000)

Murugason, R and McNamara L, *Outline of Criminal Law* (Sydney: Butterworths, 1997)

Naffine, N and Owens R, *Sexing the Subject of Law* (Sydney: LBC, 1997)

National Committee on Violence, *Violence: Directions for Australia* (Canberra: Australian Institute of Criminology, 1990)

National Crime Authority, *Taken to the Cleaners: Money Laundering in Australia*: *Vol 1* (Canberra: AGPS, 1992)

National Drug Strategy, *Report of the Task Force on Cannabis* (Canberra: AGPS, 1994)

National HIV/AIDS Strategy (Canberra: AGPS, 1989)

Neal, D, *The Rule of Law in A Penal Colony* (Cambridge: Cambridge University Press, 1991)

New South Wales Bureau of Crime Statistics and Research, *Statistical Report* (1978), Series 2, No 9

New South Wales Sexual Assault Committee, *Sexual Assault Phone-In Report* (Sydney: Ministry for the Status and Advancement of Women, 1993)

New South Wales Department for Women, *Heroines of Fortitude: The Experience of Women in Court as Victims of Sexual Assault* (Woolloomooloo: Dept for Women, 1996)

New South Wales Law Reform Commission, *Partial Defences to Murder: Diminished Responsibility*, Report No 82 (1997)

New South Wales Law Reform Commission, *Partial Defences to Murder: Provocation and Infanticide*, Report No 83 (1998)

New Zealand Criminal Law Reform Committee, *Report on Intoxication as a Defence to a Criminal Charge* (1984)

Norrie, A, *Crime, Reason and History* (London: Weidenfeld & Nicolson, 1993)

O'Connor, D and Fairall PA, *Criminal Defences* (3rd ed, Sydney: Butterworths, 1996)

O'Donovan, K, *Sexual Divisions in Law* (London: Weidenfeld and Nicolson, 1985)

O'Neill, N and Handley R, *Retreat From Injustice* (Sydney: Federation Press, 1995)

Orth, JV, *Combination and Conspiracy: A Legal History of Trade Unionism, 1721-1906* (Oxford: Clarendon Press, 1991)

Packer, H, *The Limits of the Criminal Sanction* (Stanford: Stanford University Press, 1968)

Royal Commission into the New South Wales Police Service, *Paedophile Inquiry Report* (1997)

Parliament of the Commonwealth of Australia, *A Right To Protest* (Canberra: AGPS, 1997)

Pettit, P, *Republicanism — A Theory of Freedom and Government* (Sydney: Oxford University Press, 1997)

Pinchbeck, I and Hewitt M, *Children in English Society*, Vol 1 (London: Routledge and Kegan Paul, 1973)

Pratt, J, *Governing the Dangerous: Dangerousness, Law and Social Change* (Sydney: Federation Press, 1997)

Queensland Criminal Justice Commission, *Residential Burglary in Queensland,* Research Paper Series, Vol 3(1), (1996)

Queensland Law Reform Commission, *Female Genital Mutilation*, Report No 47(1994)

Rachels, J, *The End of Life* (Oxford: Oxford University Press, 1986)

Radzinowicz, L, *A History of English Criminal Law and its Administration from 1750* (London: Stevens & Sons Ltd, 1956)

Rawls, J, *A Theory of Justice* (Cambridge, Mass: Harvard University Press, 1980)

Reicher, H (ed), *Australian International Law* (Sydney: Law Book Company Ltd, 1995)

Report by the Senate Legal and Constitutional Legislation Committee, Human Rights (Sexual Conduct) Bill 1994 (December 1994)

Report of the Committee on Homosexual Offences and Prostitution (London: HMSO, Cmnd 247, 1957)

Report of the Committee on Mentally Abnormal Offenders (London: HMSO, Cmnd 6244, 1975)

Review [Committee] of Commonwealth Criminal Law, *Interim Report: Principles of Criminal Responsibility and Other Matters*, July 1990 (Canberra: AGPS, 1990)

Reynolds, C, *Public Health Law in Australia* (Sydney: Federation Press, 1995)

Rinaldi, F and Gillies P, *Narcotic Offences* (Sydney: Law Book Company Ltd, 1991)

Robertson, G, *The Justice Game* (London: Chatto and Windus, 1988)

Robinson, P and Darley J, *Justice, Liability and Blame* (Boulder, Co: Westview, 1995)

Robinson, P, *Structure and Function in Criminal Law* (Oxford: Oxford University Press, 1997)

Roskill Committee, *Fraud Trials Committee Report* (London: HMSO, 1986)

Royal Commission into Aboriginal Deaths in Custody, *National Report — Overview and Recommendations* (Canberra: AGPS, 1991)

Royal Commission into the New South Wales Police Service, *Final Report* (1997)

Rush, P, *Criminal Law* (Sydney: Butterworths, 1997)

Rush, P, McVeigh S and Young A (eds), *Criminal Legal Doctrine* (Aldershot: Ashgate, 1997)

Sandler, M, *Mental Illness in Pregnancy and the Puerperium* (Oxford: Oxford University Press, 1978)

Scutt, J, *Women and The Law* (Sydney: Law Book Company Ltd, 1990)

Seddon, N, *Domestic Violence in Australia — The Legal Response* (2nd ed, Sydney: Federation Press, 1993)

Senate Legal and Constitutional Legislation Committee, *Consideration of Legislation Referred to the Committee: Euthanasia Laws Bill 1996* (1997)

Senate Standing Committee on Legal and Constitutional Affairs, *Gender Bias and the Judiciary* (1994)

Seymour, J, *Foetal Welfare and the Law: A Report of an Inquiry Commissioned by the Australian Medical Association* (1995)

Seymour, J, *Childbirth and the Law* (Oxford: Oxford University Press, 2000)

Shorter, E, *A History of Psychiatry* (New York: Wiley, 1997)

Shute, S, Gardner J and Horder J, *Action and Value in Criminal Law* (Oxford: Clarendon Press, 1993)

Skene, L, *Law and Medical Practice: Rights, Duties, Claims and Defences* (Sydney: Butterworths, 1998)

Smart, C, *Law, Crime and Sexuality* (London: Sage, 1995)

Smith, JC and Hogan B, *Criminal Law* (7th ed, London: Butterworths, 1992)

Smith, KJM, *A Modern Treatise on the Law of Criminal Complicity* (Oxford: Clarendon Press, 1991)

South Australian Criminal Law and Penal Methods Reform Committee, *The Substantive Criminal Law, Fourth Report* (1977)

Steiner, H and Alston P, *International Human Rights in Context* (Oxford: Clarendon Press, 1996)

Stephen, J, *Digest of the Criminal Law* (3rd ed, London: Richard Clay & Sons, 1883)

Stone, J and Wells WAN, *Evidence: Its History and Policies* (Sydney: Butterworths, 1992)

Stubbs, J (ed), *Women, Male Violence and the Law* (Sydney: The Institute of Criminology, 1994)

Stychin, C, *Law's Desire: Sexuality and the Limits of Justice* (London: Routledge, 1995)

Supperstone, M, *Brownlie's Law of Public Order and National Security* (2nd ed, London: Butterworths, 1981)

Sweeney, D and Williams N, *Commonwealth Criminal Law* (Sydney: Federation Press, 1990)

Taylor, I, Walton P and Young J, *The New Criminology* (London: Routledge and Kegan Paul, 1973)

Temkin, J, *Rape and the Legal Process* (London: Sweet & Maxwell, 1987)

Teubner, G, *Law as an Autopoietic System* (Oxford: Basil Blackwell, 1993)

Thompson, EP, *Whigs and Hunters* (London: Penguin, 1975)

Thornton, M, *The Liberal Promise* (Melbourne: Oxford University Press, 1990)

Thornton, M (ed), *Public and Private: Feminist Legal Debates* (Melbourne: Oxford University Press, 1995)

Tollefson, EA and Starkman B, *Mental Disorder in Criminal Proceedings* (Toronto: Carswell, 1993)

Tooley, M, *Abortion and Infanticide* (Oxford: Clarendon Press, 1983)

Tyler, T, *Why People Obey the Law* (New Haven: Yale University Press, 1990)

Victorian Sentencing Committee, *The Report of the Victorian Sentencing Committee,* Vol 1 (Melbourne: Attorney-General's Department, 1988)

Waller, L and Williams CR, *Brett Waller and Williams, Criminal Law — Text and Cases* (8th ed, Sydney: Butterworths, 1997)

Watson, S and Ayers M, *Australian Criminal Law — Federal Offences* (Sydney: LBC, 2000)

Weeks, J, *Coming Out: Homosexual Politics in Britain from the 19ÆMDSUØth Century to the Present* (London: Quartet Books, 1977)

Wells, C, *Corporations and Criminal Responsibility* (Oxford: Oxford University Press, 1993)

White, R and Alder C (eds), *The Police and Young People in Australia* (Cambridge: Cambridge University Press, 1994)

White, R and Haines F, *Crime and Criminology* (Melbourne: Oxford University Press, 1996)

White, R (ed), *Youth Subcultures: Theory, History and the Australian Experience* (Hobart: National Clearinghouse for Youth Studies, 1993)

Williams, CR, *Property Offences* (3rd ed, Sydney: LBC, 1999)

Williams, D, *Keeping the Peace* (London: Hutchinson, 1967)

Williams, G, *The Sanctity of Life and the Criminal Law* (London: Faber, 1958)

Williams, G, *Criminal Law — The General Part* (2nd ed, London: Stevens & Sons, 1961)

Williams, G, *Textbook of Criminal Law* (2nd ed, London: Stevens & Sons, 1983)

Wilson, J and Herrnstein R, *Crime and Human Nature* (New York: Simon and Schuster, 1985)

Wilson, JQ, *Thinking About Crime* (Revised ed, New York: Basic Books, 1983)

Winfield, PH, *The History of Conspiracy and Abuse of Legal Procedure* (Cambridge: Cambridge University Press, 1921)

Wodak, A and Owens R, *Drug Prohibition: A Call for Change* (Sydney: UNSW Press, 1996)

Wootton, B, *Social Science and Social Pathology* (London: Allen & Unwin, 1959)

Yeo, S, *Compulsion in the Criminal Law* (Sydney: Law Book Company Ltd, 1990)

Zahra, P, Arden R, Lerace M and Schurr B, *Drug Law in New South Wales* (Sydney: Federation Press, 1998)

Zinberg, N, *Drug, Set and Setting: The Basis for Controlled Intoxicant Use* (New Haven, CT: Yale University Press, 1984)

Articles and Chapters in Books

Alldridge, P, "Manslaughter and Causing Death by Driving Recklessly" (1980) 144 *Justice of the Peace* 569

Amirthalingam, K, "Mistake of Law: A Criminal Offence or a Reasonable Defence?" (1994) 18 *Criminal Law Journal* 271

Armistead, C, "Piercing Thoughts", *Guardian Weekly*, 17 July 1994

Andrews, K, Murphy L, Munday R and Littlewood C, "Misdiagnosis of the Vegetative State: Retrospective Study in a Rehabilitation Unit" (1996) 313 *British Medical Journal* 13

Asai, A, "Should a Patient in a Persistent Vegetative State Live?" (1999) 18(2) *Monash Bioethics Review* 25

Ashby, M, "Hard Cases, Causation and Care of the Dying" (1995) 3(2) *Journal of Law and Medicine* 152

Ashworth, A and Blake M, "Presumption of Innocence in English Criminal Law" [1996] *Criminal Law Review* 306

Ashworth, A, "Excusable Mistake of Law" [1974] *Criminal Law Review* 652

Ashworth, A, "Concepts of Criminal Justice" [1979] *Criminal Law Review* 412

Ashworth, A, "Criminal Attempts and the Role of Resulting Harm under the Code, and in the Common Law" (1988) 19 *Rutgers Law Journal* 725

Ashworth, A, "Taking the Consequences" in S Shute (ed), *Action and Value in Criminal Law* (1993)

Ashworth, A, "Crime, Community and Creeping Consequentialism" [1996] *Criminal Law Review* 220

Ashworth, A, "Editorial — The Value of Empirical Research in Criminal Justice" [1997] *Criminal Law Review* 533

Ashworth, A, "Should the Police Be Allowed to Use Deceptive Practices" (1998) 114 *Law Quarterly Review* 108

Ashworth, A, "What is Wrong with Entrapment" [1999] *Singapore Journal of Legal Studies* 293

Atkinson, L and McDonald D, "Cannabis, the Law and Social Impacts in Australia" *Trends and Issues in Crime and Criminal Justice*, Paper No 48 (Canberra: AIC, 1995)

Bagaric, M, "The Disunity of Sentencing and Confiscation" (1997) 21 *Criminal Law Journal* 191

Bagaric, M, "Active and Passive Euthanasia: Is There a Moral Distinction and Should There Be a Legal Difference?" (1997) 5(2) *Journal of Law and Medicine* 143

Bagaric, M, "Incapacitation, Deterrence and Rehabilitation: Flawed Ideals or Appropriate Sentencing Goals" (2000) 24(1) *Criminal Law Journal* 21

Bailey, P, "Fair Trial" in *Halsbury's Laws of Australia* (Sydney: Butterworths, 1991)

Baines, P, "Attempting the Impossible" (1990) 154 *Justice of the Peace* 67

Bamforth, N, "Sado-masochism and Consent" [1994] *Criminal Law Review* 661

Bandalli, S, "Abolition of the Presumption of Doli Incapax and the Criminalisation of Children" (1998) 37(2) *Howard Journal of Criminal Justice* 114

Barry, J, "Suicide and the Law" (1965) 5 *Melbourne University Law Review* 1

Bartholomew, T, "Legal and Clinical Enactment of the *Doli Incapax* Defence in the Supreme Court of Victoria, Australia" (1998) 5(1) *Psychiatry, Psychology and Law* 95

Barton, J, "The Story of Marital Rape" (1992) 108 *Law Quarterly Review* 260

Baume, P and O'Malley E, "Euthanasia: Attitudes and Practices of Medical Practitioners" (1994) 161(2) *Medicial Journal of Australia* 137

Bavin-Mizzi, J, "Understandings of Justice: Australian Rape and Carnal Knowledge Cases 1876-1924" in D Kirkby (ed), *Sex, Power and Justice: Historical Perspectives on Law in Australia* (Melbourne: Oxford University Press, 1995)

Bayes, H, "Punishment is Blind: Mandatory Sentencing of Children in Western Australia and the Northern Territory" (1999) 22 *University of New South Wales Law Journal* 286

Benyon, H, "Causation, Omissions and Complicity" [1987] *Criminal Law Review* 539

Bibbings, L and Alldridge P, "Sexual Expression, Body Alteration and the Defence of Consent" (1993) 20(3) *Journal of Law and Society* 356

Biggs, H, "Euthanasia and Death with Dignity: Still Poised on the Fulcrum of Homicide" [1996] *Criminal Law Review* 878

Blay, S, "The International Covenant on Civil and Political Rights and the Recognition of Customary Law Practices of Indigenous Tribes: the Case of Australian Aborigines" (1986) *19 Comparative and International Law Journal of Southern Africa* 199

Blazey-Ayoub, P, "Doli Incapax" (1996) 20 *Criminal Law Journal* 34

Boyle, GJ, Svoboda, JS, Price CP and Turner JN, "Circumcision of Healthy Boys: Criminal Assault?" (2000) 7(3) *Journal of Law and Medicine* 301

Bradfield, "Is Near Enough Good Enough? Why Isn't Self-Defence Appropriate for the Battered Woman?" (1998) 5(1) *Psychiatry, Psychology and Law* 71

Bradfield, R, "Case and Comment: *Attorney-General's Reference No 1 of 1996 Re Weiderman*" (1999) 23 *Criminal Law Journal* 41

Bradley, D, "Policing" in K Hazlehurst (ed), *Crime and Justice* (Sydney: LBC, 1996)

Braithwaite, J, "Inequality and Republican Criminology" in J Hagan and RD Peterson (eds), *Crime and Inequality* (Stanford, California: Stanford University Press, 1995)

Braithwaite, J, "Introduction" in K Hazlehurst (ed), *Crime and Justice: An Australian Textbook in Criminology* (Sydney: LBC, 1996)

Brereton, D, "Real Rape, Law Reform and the Role of Research: The Evolution of the Victorian *Crimes (Rape) Act* 1991" (1994) 27 *Australian New Zealand Journal of Criminology* 74

Brett, P, "Mistake of Law as a Criminal Defence" (1966) 5 *Melbourne University Law Review* 179

Brett, P, "The Physiology of Provocation" [1970] *Criminal Law Review* 634

Bronitt, S and Amitrthalingam K, "Cultural Blindness — Criminal Law in Multicultural Australia" (1996) 21 *Alternative Law Journal* 38

Bronitt, S and Ayers M, "Criminal Law and Human Rights" in D Kinley (ed), *Human Rights in Australian Law* (Sydney: Federation Press, 1998)

Bronitt, S and McSherry B, "The Use and Abuse of Counselling Record in Sexual Assault Trials: Reconstructing the 'Rape Shield'" (1997) 8(2) *Criminal Law Forum* 289

Bronitt, S and Roche D, "Between Rhetoric and Reality: Sociolegal and Republican Perspectives on Entrapment" (2000) 4(2) *International Journal of Evidence And Proof* 77

Bronitt, S and Williams G, "Political Freedom as an Outlaw: Republican Theory and Political Protest" 18(2) *Adelaide Law Review* 289

Bronitt, S, "Criminal Liability for the Transmission of HIV/AIDS" (1992) 16 *Criminal Law Journal* 85

Bronitt, S, "Defending Giorgianni — Part One: The Fault Required for Complicity" (1993) 17 *Criminal Law Journal* 242

Bronitt, S, "Defending Giorgianni — Part Two: New Solutions for Old Problems in Complicity" (1993) 17 *Criminal Law Journal* 305

Bronitt, S, "Donating HIV-infected Blood: A Public Nuisance?" (1994) 1 *Journal of Law and Medicine* 245

Bronitt, S, "Electronic Surveillance, Human Rights and Criminal Justice" (1997) 3(2) *Australian Journal of Human Rights* 183

Bronitt, S, "Fracturing the Criminal Law: Disease Control and the Limits of Law-making" (1996) 4(1) *Health Care Analysis* 59

Bronitt, S, "Rape and Lack of Consent" (1992) 16 *Criminal Law Journal* 289

Bronitt, S, "Spreading Disease and the Criminal Law" [1994] *Criminal Law Review* 21

Bronitt, S, "The Direction of Rape Law in Australia: Toward a Positive Consent Standard" (1994) 18 *Criminal Law Journal* 249

Bronitt, S, "The Right to Sexual Privacy, Sadomasochism and the *Human Rights (Sexual Conduct) Act* 1994 (Cth)" (1995) 21(2) *Australian Journal of Human Rights* 59

Bronitt, S, "The Rules of Recent Complaint: Rape Myths and the Legal Construction of the 'Reasonable' Rape Victim" in P Easteal (ed), *Balancing the Scales: Rape, Law Reform and Australian Culture* (Sydney: Federation Press, 1998)

Bronitt, S, "The Transmission of Life-Threatening Infections: A New Regulatory Strategy" in R Smith (ed), *Health Care Crime and Regulatory Control* (Sydney: Hawkins Press, 1998)

Brookbanks, W "Recent Developments in the Doctrine of Mistake of Law" (1987) 11 *Criminal Law Journal* 195

Brookbanks, W, "Colour of Right and Offences of Dishonesty" (1987) 11 *Criminal Law Journal* 153

Brookbanks, W, "Officially Induced Error as a Defence to a Crime" (1993) 17 *Criminal Law Journal* 380

Brown, D, "Lionel Murphy and the Criminal Law" in M Coper and G Williams, *Justice Lionel Murphy: Influential or Merely Prescient?* (Sydney: Federation Press, 1997)

Brown, RA, "Military Justice in Australia: W(h)ither Way?" (1989) 13 *Criminal Law Journal* 263

Brown, R, "Federal Drug-Control Laws: Present and Future" (1977) 8 *Federal Law Review* 435

Brownlie, I, "The Renovation of Affray" [1965] *Criminal Law Review* 479

Buxton, R, "Complicity in the Criminal Code" (1969) 85 *Law Quarterly Review* 252

Campbell, IG, "Recklessness in Intentional Murder Under the Australian Codes" (1986) 10 *Criminal Law Journal* 3

Campbell, S, "Gypsies: The Criminalisation of a Way of Life?" [1995] *Criminal Law Review* 28

Chaikin, DA, "International Extradition and Parental Child Abduction" (1993) 5 *Bond Law Review* 129

Chamallas, M, "Consent, Equality and the Legal Control of Sexual Conduct" (1988) 61 *Southern California Law Review* 777

Chan, J, "Policing Youth in 'Ethnic' Communities", in R White and C Alder (eds), *The Police and Young People in Australia* (Cambridge: Cambridge University Press, 1994)

Chandra-Shekeran, S, "Theorising the Limits of the 'Sado-masochistic homosexual' identity in *R v Brown*" (1997) 21 MULR 584

Charlesworth, H and Chinkin C, "Violence against Women" in J Stubbs (ed), *Women, Male Violence and the Law* (Sydney: Institute of Criminology, 1994)

Charlesworth, H, "The Australian Reluctance About Rights" in P Alston (ed), *Towards an Australian Bill of Rights* (Canberra: CIPL and HREOC, 1994)

Charlesworth, H, "Taking the Gender of Rights Seriously" in B Galligan and C Sampford (eds), *Rethinking Human Rights* (Sydney: Federation Press, 1997)

Cica, N, "The Inadequacies of Australian Abortion Law" (1991) 5 *Australian Journal of Family Law* 37

Clarkson, C, "Complicity, Powell and Manslaughter" [1998] *Criminal Law Review* 556

Clarkson, C, Cretney A, Davies G and Shepherd J, "Assaults: The Relationship between Seriousness, Criminalisation and Punishment" [1994] *Criminal Law Review* 4

Clarkson, CMV, "Complicity. Powell and Manslaughter" [1998] *Criminal Law Review* 556

Clemens, JH and Bennett JM, "Historical Notes on the Law of Mental Illness in New South Wales" (1962-1964) 4 *Sydney Law Review* 49

Cohen, M, "Inciting the Impossible" [1979] *Criminal Law Review* 239

Coles, EM and Jang D, "A Psychological Perspective on the Legal Concepts of 'Volition' and 'Intent'" (1996) 4 *Journal of Law and Medicine* 60

Coles, EM and Armstrong SM, "Hughlings Jackson on Automatism as Disinhibition" (1998) 6 *Journal of Law and Medicine* 73

Colvin, E, "Recent Developments in Canadian Criminal Law" (1995) 19 *Criminal Law Journal* 139

Connelly, AM, "Problems of Interpretation of Article 8 of the European Convention on Human Rights" (1986) 35 *International and Comparative Law Quarterly* 567

Cook, R, "Legal Abortion: Limits and Contributions to Human Life" in R Porter and M O'Connor (eds) *Ciba Foundation Symposium 115 — Abortion: Medical Progress and Social Implications* (London: Pitman Publishing, 1985)

Coss, G, "'God is a righteous judge, strong and patient: and God is provoked every day': A Brief History of the Doctrine of Provocation in England" (1991) 13 *Sydney Law Review* 570

Cossins, A, "Tipping The Scales in Her Favour: The Need to Protect Counselling Records in Sexual Assault Trials" in P Easteal (ed), *Balancing the Scales: Rape, Law Reform and Australian Culture* (Sydney: Federation Press, 1998)

Cossins, A, "A Reply to the NSW Royal Commission Inquiry into Paedophilia: Victim Report Studies and Child Sex Offender Profiles — A Bad Match?" (1999) 32(1) *Australian New Zealand Journal of Criminology* 42

Coughlin, A, "Excusing Women" (1994) 82 *California Law Review* 1

Crawford, J, "International Law and the Recognition of Aboriginal Customary Law" in B Hocking (ed), *International Law and Aboriginal Human Rights* (Sydney: Law Book Co, 1988)

Cretney, A and Davis G, "Prosecuting 'Domestic' Assault" [1996] *Criminal Law Review* 162

Crofts, T, "Rebutting the Presumption of Doli Incapax" (1998) 62(2) *Journal of Criminal Law* 185

Cross, R, "The Reports of the Criminal Law Commissioners (1833 —1849) and the Abortive Bills of 1853" in PR Glazebrook (ed), *Reshaping the Criminal Law* (London: Stevens & Sons, 1978)

Cunneen, C, "The Policing of Public Order: Some Thoughts on Culture, Space and Political Economy" in M Findlay and R Hogg (eds), *Understanding Crime and Criminal Justice* (Sydney: LBC, 1988)

Cunneen, C, "Enforcing Genocide? Aboriginal Young People and the Police", in R White and C Alder (eds), *The Police and Young People in Australia* (Cambridge: Cambridge University Press, 1994)

Daintith, T, "Disobeying a Policeman. A Fresh Look at *Duncan v Jones*" [1966] *Public Law* 248

Daly, K, "Criminal Justice Ideologies and Practices in Different Voices: Some Feminist Questions about Justice" in N Lacey (ed), *Criminal Justice* (Oxford: Oxford University Press, 1994)

Dance, P and Mugford S, "The St Oswald's Day Celebrations: 'Carnival' versus 'Sobriety' in an Australian Drug Enthusiast Group" (1992) 22(3) *Journal of Drug Issues* 591

Danto, A, "Basic Action" (1965) 2 *American Philosophical Quarterly* 141

Darbyshire, P, "An Essay on the Importance and Neglect of the Magistracy" [1997] *Criminal Law Review* 627

Darbyshire, P, "The Lamp that Shows that Freedom Lies — Is it Worth the Candle?" [1991] *Criminal Law Review* 740

Davies, S, "Child Killing in English Law" [1937] *Modern Law Review* 203

Dell, S, "Diminished Responsibility Reconsidered" (1982) *Criminal Law Review* 809

Dennis, I, "The Rationale of Criminal Conspiracy" (1977) 93 *The Law Quarterly Review* 39

Dennis, IH, "The Mental Element for Accessories" in P Smith (ed), *Criminal Law: Essays in Honour of JC Smith* (London: Butt, 1987)

"Developments in the Law — Criminal Conspiracy" (1959) 72 *Harvard Law Review* 920

Devlin, P, "The Conscience of the Jury" (1991) 107 *Law Quarterly Review* 398

Dresser, R, "Culpability and Other Minds" (1993) 2(1) *Southern California Interdisciplinary Law Journal* 41

Drucker, E, "Drug Prohibition and Public Health: It's A Crime" (1995) 28 *Australian and New Zealand Journal of Criminology* 67

Duff RA, "Acting, Trying and Criminal Liability", in S Shute (ed), *Action and Value in Criminal Law* (1993)

Duff, A, "Principle and Contradiction in the Criminal Law: Motives and Criminal Liability" in A Duff (ed), *Philosophy and the Criminal Law: Principle and Critique* (Cambridge: Cambridge University Press, 1998)

Duggan, KP, "Reform of the Criminal Law with Fair Trial as the Guiding Star" (1995) 19 *Criminal Law Journal* 258

Dunford, L and Pickford V, "Is There a Qualitative Difference Between Physical and Psychiatric Harm in English Law?" (1999) 7 *Journal of Law and Medicine* 36

Easteal P, "Beyond Balancing" in P Easteal (ed), *Balancing the Scales: Rape, Law Reform and Australian Culture* (Sydney: Federation Press, 1998)

Easteal, P, "Rape in Marriage: Has the Licence Lapsed" in P Easteal (ed), *Balancing the Scales: Rape, Law Reform and Australian Culture* (Sydney: Federation Press, 1998)

Easteal, P, "Suppressing the Voices of Survivors: Sexual Exploitation by Health Practitioners" (1998) 33 (1) *Australian Journal of Social Issues* 211

Eastman, K and Ronalds C, "Using Human Rights Laws in Litigation" in D Kinley (ed), *Human Rights in Australian Law* (Sydney: Federation Press, 1998)

Eburn, M, "The Legal Status of a Living Abortus" (1997) 4(4) *Journal of Law and Medicine* 373

Edwards, S, "No Defence for a Sado-Masochistic Libido" (1993) 143 *New Law Journal* 406

Egger, S and Findlay M, "The Politics of Police Discretion" in M Findlay and R Hogg (eds), *Understanding Crime and Criminal Justice* (Sydney: Law Books Co, 1988)

Eisenberg, A, "The Politics of Individual and Group Difference in Canadian Jurisprudence" (1994) 27 *Canadian Journal of Political Science* 1

Elliot, DW, "Law and Fact in Theft Act Cases" [1976] *Criminal Law Review* 707

Elliot, DW, "Dishonesty in Theft: A Dispensible Concept" [1982] *Criminal Law Review* 395

Elliott, I, "Australian Letter" [1969] *Criminal Law Review* 511

Elliott, I, "Recklessness in Murder" (1981) 5 *Criminal Law Journal* 84

English, P, "Homicide other than Murder" [1977] *Criminal Law Review* 79

Ericson, R, "The Royal Commission on Criminal Justice Surveillance" in M McConville and L Bridges, *Criminal Justice in Crisis* (Aldershot: Edward Elgar Publishing, 1995)

Evans, R, "*Peters*" (1998) 22 *Criminal Law Journal* 230

Evatt, E, "Cultural Diversity and Human Rights" in P Alston (ed), *Towards an Australian Bill of Rights*, (Canberra: Centre of International and Public Law, Australian National University & Human Rights and Equal Opportunity Commission, 1994)

Faigman, D, "The Battered Woman and Self Defence: A Legal and Empirical Dissent" (1986) 72 *Virginia Law Review* 619

Fairall, PA and Johnston PW, "Antisocial personality disorder (APD) and the insanity defence" (1987) 11 *Criminal Law Journal* 78

Fairall, PA, "The Exculpatory Force of Delusions — A Note on the Insanity Defence" (1994) 6 *Bond Law Review* 57

Fairall, PA, "Before the High Court: Imprisonment without Conviction in New South Wales: *Kable v Director Public Prosecutions*" (1995) 17(4) *Sydney Law Review* 573

Farmer, L, "The Obsession with Definition" (1996) *Social and Legal Studies* 57

Farmer, L, "The Law of the Land: Criminal Jurisdiction 1747-1908" in P Rush, S McVeigh and A Young (eds), *Criminal Legal Doctrine* (Aldershot: Ashgate, 1997)

Farrugia, PJ, "The Consent Defence: Sports Violence, Sadomasochism and the Criminal Law" (1997) 8(2) *Auckland University Law Review* 472

Faulkner, J, "*Mens Rea* in Rape: *Morgan* and the Inadequacy of Subjectivism" (1991) 18 *Melbourne University Law Review* 60

Favour, CD, "Puzzling Cases about Killing and Letting Die" (1996) 1 *Res Publica* 18

Fedele, NM, Golding ER, Grossman FK and Pollack WS, "Psychological Issues in Adjustment to First parenthood" in GY Michaels and WA Goldberg, *The Transition to Parenthood* (New York: Cambridge University Press, 1988)

Feldman, D, "The King's Peace, The Royal Prerogative and Public Order: The Roots and Early Development of Binding Over Powers" (1988) 47(1) *Cambridge Law Journal* 101

Fenwick, P, "Somnambulism and the Law: A Review" (1987) 5 *Behavioural Sciences and the Law* 343

Finn, J, "Case and Comment: *Machirus*" (1997) 21 *Criminal Law Journal* 51

Finnis, JM, "Bland: Crossing the Rubicon?" (1993) 109 *Law Quarterly Review* 329

Fisse, B, "Complicity in Regulatory Offences" (1968) 6 *Melbourne University Law Review* 278

Fisse, B, "Corporate Criminal Responsibility" (1991) 15 *Criminal Law Journal* 166

Fisse, B, "Criminal Law: The Attribution of Criminal Liability to Corporations: A Statutory Model" (1991) 13 *Sydney Law Review* 277

Flew, A, "The Principle of Euthanasia" in AB Downing and B Smoker (eds), *Voluntary Euthanasia: Experts Debate the Right to Die* (London: Peter Owen, 1986)

Flynn, M, "Fixing a Sentence: Are there any Constitutional Limits?" (1999) 22 *UNSW Law Journal* 280

Ford, R, "'Lady-friends' and 'sexual deviationists': Lesbians and law in Australia, 1920-1950s" in D Kirkby (ed), *Sex, Power and Justice* (Melbourne: Oxford University Press, 1995)

Fraser, D, "Father Knows Best: Transgressive Sexualities and the Rule of Law" (1995) 7(1) *Current Issues in Criminal Justice* 82

Freckelton, I, "Withdrawal of Life Support: The 'Persistent Vegetative State Conundrum'" (1993) 1(1) *Journal of Law and Medicine* 35

Freckelton, I, "Masochism, Self-mutilation and the Limits of Consent" (1994) 2(1) *Journal of Law and Medicine* 48

Freckelton, I, "When Plight Makes Right: The Forensic Abuse Syndrome" (1994) 18 *Criminal Law Journal* 29

Frieberg, A, "Criminal Confiscation, Profit and Liberty" (1992) 25 *Australian and New Zealand Journal of Criminology* 44

Freiberg, A, "The Disposition of Mentally Disordered Offenders in Australia: 'Out of Mind, Out of Sight' Revisited" (1994) 1(2) *Psychiatry, Psychology and Law* 97

Freiberg, A, "Australian Drug Courts" (2000) 24 *Criminal Law Journal* 213

Galligan, D, "Preserving Public Protest: the Legal Approach" in L Gostin (ed), *Civil Liberties in Conflict* (London and New York: Routledge, 1988)

Galligan, D, "Regulating Pre-Trial Decisions" in N Lacey (ed), *A Reader on Criminal Justice* (Oxford: Oxford University Press, 1994)

Gans, J, "Rape Trial Studies: Handle with Care" (1997) 30 *Australian and New Zealand Journal of Criminology* 27

Gardiner, S, "Recklessness Refined" (1993) 109 *Law Quarterly Review* 21

Gardiner, S, "Appreciating Olugboja" (1996) 16(3) *Legal Studies* 275

Garkawe, S, "Human Rights in the Administration of Justice" (1994) 1 *Australian Journal of Human Rights* 371

Garnsey, D, "Rugby League Player Jailed for On-Field Assault" (1995) 5(2) *ANZSLA Newsletter* 7

Gaylin, W, Kass LR, Pellegrino ED and Siegler M, "Doctors Must Not Kill" in RM Baird and SE Rosenbaum, *Euthanasia: The Moral Issues* (New York: Prometheus Books, 1989)

Giles, M, "Judicial Law Making in the Criminal Courts: The Case of Marital Rape" (1991) *Criminal Law Review* 407

Giles, M, "*R v Brown*: Consensual Harm and the Public Interest" (1994) 57 *Modern Law Review* 101

Gillett, G, "Euthanasia, Letting Die and the Pause" (1988) 14 *Journal of Medical Ethics* 61

Goode, M, "Stalking: Crime of the Nineties?" (1995) 19 *Criminal Law Journal* 21

Goode, M, "Two New Decisions on Criminal 'Jurisdiction': The Appalling Durability of Common Law" (1996) 20 *Criminal Law Journal* 267

Goode, M, "Case and Comment: Keane v Police" (1998) 22 *Criminal Law Journal* 237

Goodhart, A, "Public Meetings and Processions" (1936) 6 *Cambridge Law Journal* 161

Gordon, P, "Racist Harassment and Violence", in E Stanko (ed), *Perspectives on Violence* (London: Quartet Books, 1994)

Grabosky, P, "Counterproductive Regulation" (1995) 23 *International Journal of the Sociology of Law* 347

Grant, I, "The Impact of *Vaillancourt v The Queen* on Canadian Criminal Law" (1990) XXVIII (2) *Alberta Law Review* 443

Greenberg, N, "The Rhetoric of Risk" 22 (1) *Alternative Law Journal* 11

Greene, J, "A Provocation Defence for Battered Women Who Kill" (1989) 12 *Adelaide Law Review* 145

Griew, E, "Dishonesty: The Objections to *Feely* and *Ghosh*" [1985] *Criminal Law Review* 341

Grisso, T, "Society's Retributive Response to Juvenile Violence: A Developmental Perspective" (1996) 20 *Law and Human Behavior* 229

Groves, M, "Are You Old Enough? In Defence of Doli Incapax" (1996) April *Law Institute Journal* 38

Groves, M, "Commentary" (1998) 22 *Criminal Law Journal* 357

Gunn, M and Ormerod D, "The Legality of Boxing" (1995) 15(2) *Legal Studies* 181

Haberfield, L, "The Transplantation of Human Foetal Tissue is Australia: Abortion, Consent and Other Legal Issues" (1996) 4 *Journal of Law and Medicine* 144

Hale, R, "Peaceful Picketing in Australia: The Failure to Guarantee a Basic Human Right" in *The Right Of Peaceful Protest Seminar, Human Rights Commission Occasional Paper No 14*

Hall, J, "Mental Disease and Criminal Responsibility" (1958) 33 *Indiana Law Journal* 212

Halpin, A, "The Test for Dishonesty" [1996] *Criminal Law Review* 283

Hammond, G, "Theft of Information" (1984) 100 *Law Quarterly Review* 252

Handley, R, "'Serious Affront' and the NSW Public Assemblies Legislation" (1986) 10(5) *Criminal Law Journal* 287

Handley, R, "Preventive Powers and NUM Pickets" (1986) 10 *Criminal Law Journal* 93

Harris, W, "Entrapment" (1994) 18 *Criminal Law Journal* 197

Hart, HLA, "The House of Lords on Attempting the Impossible" (1981) 1 *Oxford Journal of Legal Studies* 149

Hay, D, "Property, Authority and the Criminal Law" in D Hay et al, *Albion's Fatal Tree* (New York: Pantheon, 1975)

Heilpern, D and Rayner G, "Drug Law and Necessity" (1997) 22(4) *Alternative Law Journal* 188

Henderson, E, "Of Signifiers and Sodomy: Privacy, Public Morality and Sex in the Decriminalisation Debates" (1996) 20 *Melbourne University Law Review* 1023

Henning, T and Bronitt S, "Rape Victims on Trial: Regulating the Use and Abuse of Sexual History Evidence" in P Easteal (ed), *Balancing the Scales: Rape, Law Reform and Australian Culture* (Sydney: Federation Press, 1998)

Hocking, B, "Commentary" on *Dellapatrona* and *Duffield* (1995) 19 *Criminal Law Journal* 169

Hogg, R, "Mandatory Sentencing Laws and the Symbolic Politics of Law and Order" (1999) 22 *UNSW Law Journal* 262

Homel, R and Bull M, "Under the Influence: Alcohol, Drugs and Crime" in K Hazlehurst (ed), *Crime and Justice — An Australian Textbook in Criminology* (Sydney: LBC, 1996)

Honoré, T, "Responsibility and Luck" (1988) 104 *Law Quarterly Review* 530

Hope, J, "A Constitutional Right to A Fair Trial? Implications for the Reform of the Australian Criminal Justice System" (1996) 24 *Federal Law Review* 173

Horder, J, "Intention in the Criminal Law — A Rejoinder" (1995) 58 *Modern Law Review* 678

Horder, J, "Two Histories and Four Hidden Principles of Mens Rea" (1997) 113 *Law Quarterly Review* 95

Horder, J, "Reconsidering Psychic Assault" [1998] *Criminal Law Review* 392

Horwitz, M , "The Historical Contingency of the Role of History" (1981) 90 *Yale Law Journal* 1057

Hubble, G, "Feminism and the Battered Woman: The Limits of Self-Defence in the Context of Domestic Violence" (1997) 9(2) *Current Issues in Criminal Justice* 113

Hubble, G, "Rape by Innocent Agent" (1997) 21(4) *Criminal Law Journal* 104

Hughes, B, "Female Genital Mutilation: The Complementary Roles of Education and Legislation in Combating the Practice in Australia" (1995) 3 *Journal of Law and Medicine* 202

Hughes, G, "Computers, Crime and the Concept of 'Property" (1990) 1 *Intellectual Property Journal* 154

Hunter, R and Mack K, "Exclusion and Silence: Procedure and Evidence" in N Naffine and R Owens, *Sexing the Subject of Law* (Sydney: LBC, 1997)

Hunter, R and Stubbs J, "Model Laws or Missed Opportunity" (1999) 24(1) *Alternative Law Journal* 12

Husak, D, "Ignorance of Law and Duties of Citizenship" (1994) 14 *Legal Studies* 105

Ierodiaconou, M, "'Listen to Us!' Female Genital Mutilation, Feminism and the Law in Australia" (1995) 20 *Melbourne University Law Review* 562

Ivamy, E, "The Right of Public Meeting" (1949) 2 *Current Legal Problems* 183

Jack, A, "A Judicial Step Too Far" [1995] *New Law Journal* 315

Jackson, J and Doran S, "Judge and Jury: Towards a New Division of Labour in Criminal Trials" (1997) 60(6) *Modern Law Review* 759

James, S and Sutton A, "Joining the War Against Drugs? Assessing Law Enforcement Approaches to Illicit Drug Control" in D Chappell and P Wilson (eds), *Australian Policing — Contemporary Issues* (2nd ed, Sydney: Butt, 1996)

James, S and Warren I, "Police Culture", in J Bessant, K Carrington and S Cook (eds), *Cultures of Crime and Violence* (Bundoora: La Trobe University Press, 1995)

Jeffreys, S, "Consent and the Politics of Sexuality" (1993) 5(2) *Current Issues in Criminal Justice* 173

Jochelson, R, "Aborigines and Public Order Legislation in New South Wales" (1997) 34 *Crime and Justice Bulletin* 1

Jochelson, R, "Household Break-ins and the Market for Stolen Goods" in *Crime and Justice Bulletin*, No 24, (Sydney: NSW Bureau of Crime Statistics and Research, 1995)

Johnson, PE, "The Unnecessary Crime of Conspiracy" (1973) 61(5) *California Law Review* 1137

Jones, TH, "Insanity, Automatism and the Burden of Proof on the Accused" (1995) 111 *Law Quarterly Review* 475

Kadish, SH, "Complicity, Cause and Blame: A Study in the Interpretation of Doctrine", (1985) 73 *California Law Review* 324

Keith (Lord) of Avonholm, "Some Observations on Diminished Responsibility" (1959) *Juridical Review* 109

Kell, D, "Bodily Harm in the Court of Appeal" (1993) 109 *Law Quarterly Review* 199

Kell, D, "Consent to Harmful Assaults Under the Queensland *Criminal Code*: Time for a Reappraisal?" (1994) 68 *Australian Law Journal* 363

Kell, D, "Social Disutility and the Law of Consent" (1994) 14 *Oxford Journal of Legal Studies* 121

Kelman, M, "Interpretive Construction in the Substantive Criminal Law" (1981) 33 *Stanford Law Review* 591

Keown, IJ, "The Scope of the Offence of Child Destruction" (1988) 104 *Law Quarterly Review* 120

Kerridge, I, McPhee J, Lowe M and Flynn B, "Advance Directives" (1997) Issues Paper No 5, *Australian Institute of Health, Law and Ethics: Topics for Attention*

Kerridge, I, Lowe M and McPhee J, "The Persistent Vegetative State and Brainstem Death" in *Ethics and Law for the Health Professions* (Katoomba, NSW: Social Science Press, 1998)

Kirby, J, "The Future of Criminal Law" (1999) 23 *Criminal Law Journal* 263

Klinck, DR, "'Specific Delusions' in the Insanity Defence" (1982-83) 25 *Criminal Law Quarterly* 458

Koffman, L, "Conditional Intention to Steal" [1980] *Criminal Law Review* 463

Koh, H, "Two Cheers for Feminist Procedure" (1993) 61 *University of Cincinnati Law Review* 1201

Konic, N, "Say Goodbye Doli? Age and Criminal Responsibility?" (1994) 19(3) *Alternative Law Journal* 140
Kuhse, H and Singer P, "Voluntary Euthanasia and the Nurse: An Australian Study" (1993) 4 *International Journal of Nursing Studies* 311

Kuhse, H and Singer P, "Active Voluntary Euthanasia, Morality and the Law" (1995) 3(2) *Journal of Law and Medicine* 129

Kuhse, H, Singer P, Baume P, Clark M and Maurice R, "End-of-Life Decisions in Australian Medical Practice" (1997) 166(4) *Medical Journal of Australia* 191

Kyriagis, M, "Marijuana — Just What the Doctor Ordered?" (1997) 20(3) *UNSW Law Journal* 594

Lacey, N, "A Clear Concept of Intention: Elusive or Illusory?" (1993) 56(5) *Modern Law Review* 621

Lacey, N, "Criminology, Criminal law and Criminalization" in M Maguire, R Morgan and R Reiner (eds), *The Oxford Handbook of Criminology* (2nd ed, Oxford: Oxford University Press, 1997)

Lacey, N, "In(de)terminable Intentions" (1995) 58 *Modern Law Review* 692

Lacey, N, "Introduction — Making Sense of Criminal Justice" in N Lacey, *A Reader on Criminal Justice* (Oxford: Oxford University Press, 1994)

Lanham, D, "Accomplices and Withdrawal" (1981) 97 *Law Quarterly Review* 575

Lanham, D, "Felony Murder — Ancient and Modern" (1983) 7 *Criminal Law Journal* 90

Lanham, D, "Hale, Misogyny and Rape" (1983) 7 *Criminal Law Journal* 148

Lanham, D, "Wilful Blindness and the Criminal Law" (1985) 9 *Criminal Law Journal* 261

Lanham, D, "Danger Down Under" [1999] *Criminal Law Review* 960

Lansdowne, R, "Infanticide: Psychiatrists in the Plea Bargaining Process" (1990) 16(1) *Monash University Law Review* 41

Leader-Elliot, I, "Prohibitions Against Heroin Use: Can They Be Justified" (1986) 19 *Australian and New Zealand Journal of Criminology* 225

Leader-Elliott, I, "Battered But Not Beaten: Women Who Kill in Self Defence" (1993) 15 *Sydney Law Review* 403

Leader-Elliott, I, "Case note: Insanity, Involuntariness and the Mental Element in Crime" (1994) 18 *Criminal Law Journal* 347

Leader-Elliott, I, "Sex, Race and Provocation: In Defence of *Stingel*" (1996) 20 *Criminal Law Journal* 72

Levine, H, "The Discovery of Addiction: Changing Conceptions of Habitual Drunkenness in America" (1978) 39(1) *Journal of Studies on Alcohol* 143

Lipton, J, "Property Offences in the Electronic Age" (1998) 72 *Law Institute Journal* 54

Lipton, J, "Property Offences into the 21st century" (1999) (1) *The Journal of Information Law and Technology* (

Lofgren, N, "Aboriginal Community Participation in Sentencing" (1997) 21(3) *Criminal Law Journal* 127

LSE Jury Project, "Juries and the Rules of Evidence" [1973] *Criminal Law Review* 208

Lucashenko, M, "Violence Against Indigenous Women: Public and Private Dimensions" in S Cook and J Bessant (eds), *Women's Encounters with Violence — Australian Experiences* (Thousand Oaks, CA: Sage Publications Inc, 1997)

Lustgarten, L, "The Police and the Substantive Criminal Law" [1987] *British Journal of Criminology* 24

Mack, K, "'You Should Scrutinise Her Evidence With Great Care': Corroboration of Women's Testimony About Sexual Assault" in P Easteal (ed), *Balancing the Scales: Rape, Law Reform and Australian Culture* (Sydney: Federation Press, 1998)

Magnusson, RS, "The Recognition of Proprietary Rights in Human Tissue in Common Law Jurisdictions" (1992) 18 *Melbourne University Law Review* 601

Maher, L, Dixon D, Lynskey M and Hall W, *Running the Risks: Heroin, Health and Harm in South West Sydney* (Sydney: National Drug and Alcohol Centre, UNSW, 1998) NDARC Monograph No 38

Makkai, T, "Drug Courts: Issues and Prospects" in *Trends and Issues* No 95 (Canberra: AIC, 1998)

Makkai, T, "Drugs and Property Crime" in *Australian Illicit Drug Report 1997-1998* (Canberra: Australian Bureau of Criminal Intelligence, 1999)

Manderson, D, "Metamorphoses: Clashing Symbols in the Social Construction of Drugs" (1995) 25 *Journal of Drug Issues* 799

Manderson, D "Substances as Symbols: Race Rhetoric and the Tropes of Australian Drug History" (1997) 6(3) *Social and Legal Studies* 383

Marks, R, "Prohibition or Regulation: An Economist's View of Australian Heroin Policy" (1990) 23 *Australian and New Zealand Journal of Criminology* 65

Martyn, K, "Technological Advances and *Roe v Wade*: The Need to Rethink Abortion Law (1982) 29 *UCLA Law Review* 1194

Mason, A, "The Influence of International and Transnational Law on Australian Municipal Law" (1996) 7 *Public Law Review* 20

Mason, A, "The Role of the Judiciary in the Development of Human Rights in Australian Law" in D Kinley (ed), *Human Rights in Australian Law* (Sydney: Federation Press, 1998)

Mason, A, "The Courts as Community Institutions" (1998) 9 *Public Law Review* 83

Mason, B, "From Shamans to Shaming: A History of Criminological Thought" in K Hazlehurst (ed), *Crime and Justice: An Australian Textbook in Criminology* (Melbourne: LBC, 1996)

Mason, G, "Reforming the Law of Rape: Incursion into the Masculinist Sanctum" in D Kirkby (ed), *Sex, Power and Justice: Historical Perspectives on Law in Australia* (Melbourne: Oxford University Press, 1995)

McAuley, F, "The Intoxication Defence in Criminal Law" (1997) XXXII *The Irish Jurist* 243

McBarnet, DJ, "False Dichotomies in Criminal Justice Research" in J Baldwin and AK Bottomley, *Criminal Justice: Selected Readings* (London: Martin Robertson and Company, 1978)

McCutcheon, JP, "Omissions and Criminal Liability" (1993-1995) 28-30 *Irish Jurist* 56

McDonald, PL, "Helping with the Termination of an Assaultive Relationship" in B Pressman, G Cameron and M Rothery (eds), *Intervening with Assaulted Women* (Hillsdale: Eribaum, 1989)

McHugh, G, "Power of Self-Control in Provocation and Automatism" (1992) 14 *Sydney Law Review* 3

McNamara, L and Solomon T, "The Commonwealth Racial Hatred Act 1995: Achievement or Disappointment?" (1996) 18(2) *Adelaide Law Review* 259

McSherry, B, "The Return of the Raging Hormones Theory: Premenstrual Syndrome, Postpartum Disorders and Criminal Responsibility" (1993) 15 *Sydney Law Review* 292

McSherry, B, "Defining What is a 'Disease of the Mind': The Untenability of Current Legal Interpretations" (1993) 1(2) *Journal of Law and Medicine* 76

McSherry, B, "Automatism in Australia Since *Falconer's* Case" (1996) 6 *International Bulletin of Law and Mental Health* 3

McSherry, B, *Access to Medical Records*, AIHLE, Topics for Attention, Issues Paper No 1, 1996

McSherry, B, "Getting Away with Murder? Dissociative States and Crminal Responsibility" (1998) 21(2) *International Journal of Law and Psychiatry* 163

McSherry, B, "'Dangerousness' and Public Health" (1998) 23(6) *Alternative law Journal* 276

McSherry, B, "Sexual Assault Against Individuals with Mental Impairment: Are Criminal Laws Adequate?" (1998) 5(1) *Psychiatry, Psychology and Law* 107

McSherry, B, "Constructing Lack of Consent" in P Easteal (ed), *Balancing the Scales* (Sydney: Federation Press, 1998)

McSherry, B, "A Review of the New South Wales Law Reform Commission's Report, *People with an Intellectual Disability and the Criminal Justice System*" (1999) 25(1) *Monash University Law Review* 166

McSherry, B, "Criminal Detention of Those with Mental Impairment" (1999) 6 *Journal of Law and Medicine* 216

McSherry, B, "Mental Impairment and Criminal Responsibility: Recent Australian Legislative Reforms" (1999) 23(3) *Criminal Law Journal* 135

McVeigh, S and Rush P, "Cutting Our Losses: Criminal Legal Doctrine" in P Rush, S McVeigh and A Young (eds), *Criminal Legal Doctrine* (Aldershot: Dartmouth, 1997)

Mickell, WE, "Is Suicide Murder?" (1903) 3 *Columbia Law Review* 379

Möller, C, "Legislation Comment: Serious Money, Funny Legislation: Tasmania and the Politics of Criminal Forfeiture" (1998) 22 *Criminal Law Journal* 99

Moloney, GJ, "Attempts" (1991) 15 *Criminal Law Journal* 175

Morgan, J, "Rape in Medical Treatment: the Patient as Victim" (1991) 18 *Melbourne University Law Review* 403

Morgan, J, "Equality Rights in the Australian Context: A Feminist Assessment" in P Alston (ed), *Towards an Australian Bill of Rights* (Canberra: Centre for International and Public Law, Canberra, 1994)

Morgan, P, "The Legislation of Drug Law: Economic Crisis and Social Control" (1978) 8(1) *Journal of Drug Issues* 53

Morgan, W, "Identifying Evil for What it is: Tasmania, Sexual Perversity and the United Nations" (1994) 19(3) *Melbourne University Law Review* 740

Morrison, W, "Modernity, Knowledge and the Criminalisation of Drug Usage" in I Loveland (ed), *Frontiers of Criminality* (London: Sweet and Maxwell, 1995)

Morse, SL, "Immaturity and Irresponsibility" (1998) 88(1) *The Journal of Criminal Law and Criminology* 15

Mugford, S, "Controlled Drug Use Among Recreational Users: Sociological Perspectives" in N Heather, W Miller and J Greeley (eds), *Self Control and the Addictive Behaviours* (Sydney: Macmillan, 1991)

Mugford, S, "Least Bad Solutions to the 'Drugs Problem'" (1991) 10 *Drug and Alcohol Review* 401

Mugford, S, "Policing of Euphoria: The Politics and Pragmatics of Drug Control" in P Moir and H Eijkman (eds), *Policing Australia: Old Issues, New Perspectives* (South Melbourne: MacMillan, 1992)

Mugford, S, "Harm Reduction: Does it Lead Where its Proponents Imagine?" in N Heather, A Wodax, E Nadelmann and P O'Hare, *Psychoactive Drugs and Harm Reduction: From Faith to Science* (London: Whurr Publishers, 1993)

Mugford, S, "Recreational Cocaine Use in Three Australian Cities" (1994) 2 *Addiction Research* 95

Mugford, S, "Studies in the Natural History of Cocaine Use — Theoretical Afterword" (1994) 2(1) *Addiction Research* 127

Mullen, P and Pathé M, "Stalking and the Pathologies of Love" (1994) 28 *Australian and New Zealand Journal of Psychiatry* 469

Mullen, P and Pathé M, "The Pathological Extensions of Love" (1994) 165 *British Journal of Psychiatry* 614

Mullen, P, Pathé M and Purcell R, *Stalkers and Their Victims* (Cambridge: Cambridge University Press, 2000)

Mullen, P, Pathé M, Purcell R and Stuart G, "A Study of Stalkers" (1999) 156 *American Journal of Psychiatry* 1244

Mullen, P, "Euthanasia: An Impoverished Construction of Life and Death" (1995) 3 *Journal of Law and Medicine* 121

Mullen, P, "The Dangerousness of the Mentally Ill and the Clinical Assessment of Risk" in W Brookbanks (ed), *Psychiatry and the Law: Clinical and Legal Issues* (Wellington: Brooker's, 1996)

Multi-Society Task Force on PVS, "Medical Aspects of the Persistent Vegetative State" Part One (1994) 330(21) *New England Journal of Medicine* 1499 and Part Two (1994) 330(22) *New England Journal of Medicine* 1572

Naffine, N, "Windows on the Legal Mind: The Evocation of Rape in Legal Writings" (1992) 18 *Melbourne University Law Review* 741

Naffine, N, "Possession: Erotic Love in the Law of Rape" (1994) 57 *Modern Law Review* 10

Neal, D, "Corporate Manslaughter" [1996] *Law Institute Journal* 39

Nelken, D, "Criminal Law and Criminal Justice: Some Notes on their Interrrelation" in IH Dennis (ed), *Criminal Law and Justice* (London: Sweet & Maxwell, 1987)

Nicolson, D, "The Citizen's Duty to Assist the Police" [1992] *Criminal Law Review* 661

Nielsen, J and Martin G, "Indigenous Australian Peoples and Human Rights" in D Kinley, *Human Rights in Australian Law* (Sydney: Federation Press, 1998)

Niemann, G, "Attempts" (1991) 2(3) *Criminal Law Forum* 549

Norrie, A, "Oblique Intention and Legal Politics" [1989] *Criminal Law Review* 793

Norrie, A, "Legal and Moral Judgment in the 'General' Part" in P Rush, S McVeigh and A Young (eds), *Criminal Legal Doctrine* (Aldershot: Ashgate/Dartmouth Publishing Company Limited, 1997)

Norrie, S, "Abortions in Great Britain: One Act, Two Laws" [1985] *Criminal Law Review* 475

O'Donovan, K, "Book Review: Public and Private Feminist Legal Debates" (1996) 18(1) *Adelaide Law Review* 113

O'Malley, P and Mugford S "Heroin Policy and Deficit Models — The Limits of Left Realism" (1991) 15 *Crime, Law and Social Change* 19

O'Malley, P and Mugford S, "The Demand for Intoxicating Commodities: Implications for the 'War on Drugs'" (1991) 18(4) *Social Justice* 49

O'Malley, P and Mugford S, "Moral Technology: The Political Agenda of Random Drug Testing" (1991) 18 *Social Justice* 122

O'Malley, P and Mugford S, "Crime, Excitement and Modernity" in G Barak (ed), *Varieties of Criminology* (Praeger, Westport, 1994)

O'Regan, RS, "Intoxication and Criminal Responsibility Under the Queensland Code" (1977-1978) 10 *University of Queensland Law Journal* 70

Odgers, SJ, "Criminal Cases in the High Court of Australia" (1996) 20 *Criminal Law Journal* 43

Opie, H, "Aussie Rules Player Jailed for Behind-Play Assault" (1996) 6(2) *ANZSLA Newsletter* 3

Orchard, GF, "Criminal Responsibility for the Acts of Innocent Agents" (1990) 2 *Criminal Law Forum* 45

Orchard, GF, "Impossibility and Inchoate Crimes — Another Hook in a Red Herring" [1993] *New Zealand Law Journal* 426

Ormerod, D, "Cheating the Revenue" [1998] *Criminal Law Review* 627

Otlowski, M, "The Legal Fallout from the APPM Dispute" (1992) 5 *Australian Journal of Labour Law* 287

Padfield, N, "Consent and the Public Interest" [1992] *New Law Journal* 430

Palmer, H, "Dr Adams' Trial for Murder" [1957] *Criminal Law Review* 365

Parssinen, T and Kerner K, "Development of the Disease Model of Drug Addiction in Britain, 1870-1926" (1980) 24 *Medical History* 275

Pathé, M and Mullen P, "The Impact of Stalkers on their Victims" (1997) 170 *British Journal of Psychiatry* 12

Pearce, A and Easteal P, "The 'Domestic' in Stalking" (1999) 24(4) *Alternative Law Journal* 165

Perrone, S, "Workplace Fatalities and the Adequacy of Prosecution" (1995) 13(1) *Law in Context* 81

Pickard, T, "Culpable Mistakes and Rape: Relating Mens Rea to the Crime" [1980] *University of Toronto Law Journal* 75

Pineau, L, "Date Rape: A Feminist Analysis" (1989) 9 *Law and Philosophy* 217

Pollard, C, "Victims and the Criminal Justice System: A New Vision" [2000] *Criminal Law Review* 5

Power, P, " 'An Honour and Almost a Singular One' A Review of the Justices' Preventive Jurisdiction" (1982) 8 *Monash University Law Review* 69

Price, DPT, "How Viable is the Present Scope of the Offence of Child Destruction?" (1987) 16 Anglo-*American Law Review* 220

Price, DPT, "Selective Reduction and Feticide: The Parameters of Abortion" [1988] *Criminal Law Review* 199

Price, D, "The Criminal Liability of Children" (1995) 69 (8) *Australian Law Journal* 593

Pritchard, S, "The Jurisprudence of Human Rights: Some Critical Thought and Developments in Practice" (1995) 2(1) *Australian Journal of Human Rights*

Rachels, J, "Active and Passive Euthanasia" (1975) *New England Journal of Medicine* 78

Reaugh, DM, "Presumptions and the Burden of Proof" (1942) 36 *Illinois Law Review of Northwestern University* 703

Reed, A, "The Need for a New Anglo-American Approach to Duress" (1997) 61(2) *The Journal of Criminal Law* 209

Reilly, A, "Loss of Self-Control in Provocation" (1997) 21 *Criminal Law Journal* 320

Reiner, R, "Policing and the Police", in M Maguire, R Morgan and R Reiner (eds), *The Oxford Handbook of Criminology* (Oxford: Oxford University Press, 1994)

Remick, L, "Read Her Lips: An Argument For a Verbal Consent Standard in Rape" (1993) 141 *University of Pennsylvania Law Review* 1103

Review of Commonwealth Criminal Law, *Drug Offences — Discussion Paper No 13* (April 1988)

Reynolds, C, "Can We Make Sense of Drug Laws in Australia? A Case Study of the South Australian Legislation" (1995) 1 *Flinders Journal of Law Reform* 73

Rhoden, N, "Trimesters and Technology: Revamping *Roe v Wade*" (1986) 95 *Yale Law Journal* 639

Ribiero, RA, "Criminal Liability for Attempting the Impossible — Lady Luck and the Villains" (1974) 4 *Hong Kong Law Review* 109

Richards, D, "Male Circumcision: Medical or Ritual" (1996) 3(4) *Journal of Law and Medicine* 371

Robbins, IP, "Double Inchoate Crimes" (1989) 26(1) *Harvard Journal on Legislation* 1

Roberts, G, "Dr Bolduc's Speculum and the Victorian Rape Provisions" (1984) 8 *Criminal Law Journal* 296

Roberts, P, "Consent to Injury: How Far Can You Go?" (1997) 113 *Law Quarterly Review* 27

Roche, D, "Mandatory Sentencing", *Australian Institute of Criminology — Trends and Issues*, No 138 (1999)

Ronalds, C, "Anzac Day and the Aftermath" (1983) 8 *Law Society Bulletin* 133

Rubenfeld, J, "On the Legal Status of the Proposition that "Life Begins at Conception" " (1991) 43 *Stanford Law Review* 599

Rubin, G, "Thinking Sex: Notes for a Radical Theory of the Politics of Sexuality" in C Vance (ed), *Pleasure and Danger* (London: Pandora, 1989)

Sadurski, W, "Racial Vilification, Psychic Harm and Affirmative Action", in T Campbell and W Sadurski (eds), *Freedom of Communication* (Aldershot: Dartmouth, 1994)

Sallmann P and Willis J, "Editorial: Criminal Conspiracy: Takes One to Tango?" (1982) 15 *Australian and New Zealand Journal of Criminology* 129

Saunders, K, "Controlling (hetero)sexuality: The implementation and operation of contagious diseases legislation in Australia, 1868-1945" in D Kirkby (ed), *Sex, Power and Justice: Historical Perspectives on Law in Australia* (Melbourne: Oxford University Press, 1995)

Sayre, FB, "Criminal Conspiracy" (1923) 35 *Harvard Law Review* 393

Sayre, FB, "Criminal Attempts" (1928) 41 *Harvard Law Review* 821

Schuller, RA and Vidmar N, "Battered Woman Syndrome Evidence in the Courtroom" (1992) 16(3) *Law and Human Behavior* 273

Scott, ES, Dickon Reppucci N and Woolard J L, "Evaluating Adolescent Decision Making in Legal Contexts" (1995) 19 *Law and Human Behavior* 221

Scrimshaw, S, "Infanticide in Human Populations: Societal and Individual Concerns" in G Hausfater and S Hardy (eds), *Infanticide: Comparative and Evolutionary Perspectives* (New York: Aldue Publishing Co, 1984)

Scutt, J, "Consent Versus Submission: Threats and the Element of Fear in Rape" (1977) 13 *University of Western Australia Law Review* 52

Scutt, J, "Fraud and Consent in Rape: Comprehension of the Nature and Character of the Act and its Moral Implications" (1976) 18 *Criminal Law Quarterly* 312

Sharpe, A, "The precarious position of the transsexual rape victim" (1994) 6(2) *Current Issues in Criminal Justice* 303

Sheehey, E, Stubbs J and Tolmie, "Defending Battered Women on Trial: The Battered Woman Syndrome and its Limitations" (1992) 16 *Criminal Law Journal* 369

Sheehy, E, "Personal Autonomy and the Criminal Law: Emerging Issues" *Background Paper, Canadian Advisory Council on the Status of Women* (1987)

Sherman, L and Barnes G, *Restorative Justice and Offenders Respect for the Law*, Paper 3, Reintegrative Shaming Experiment, Working Paper, Law Program (Canberra: ANU, 1997)

Simester, AP, "Mistakes in Defence" (1992) 12(2) *Oxford Journal of Legal Studies* 295

Singh, RU, "History of the Defence of Drunkenness in English Criminal Law" (1933) 49 *Law Quarterly Review* 528

Skegg, P, "A Justification for Medical Procedures Performed Without Consent" (1974) 90 *Law Quarterly Review* 512

Smart, C, "Law's Truth/Women's Experience" in R Graycar (ed), *Dissenting Opinions — Feminist Explorations in Law and Society* (Sydney: Allen and Unwin, 1990)

Smith, ATH, "Constructive Trusts in the Law of Theft" [1977] *Criminal Law Review* 395

Smith, ATH, "The Idea of Criminal Deception" [1982] *Criminal Law Review* 721

Smith, ATH, "Judicial Lawmaking in the Criminal Law" (1984) 100 *Law Quarterly Review* 46

Smith, JC, "Commentary on *R v Feely*" [1973] *Criminal Law Review* 192

Smith, JC, "Criminal Damage" [1981] *Criminal Law Review* 393

Smith, JC, *Commentary* [1995] *Criminal Law Review* 571

Smith, JC, "Criminal Liability of Accessories" [1997] 113 *Law Quarterly Review* 453

Smith, JC, "Criminal Liability of Accessories: Law and Law Reform" (1997) 113 *Law Quarterly Review* 453

Smith, JC, "Obtaining Cheques by Deception or Theft" [1997] *Criminal Law Review* 396

Smith, KJM, "Withdrawal from Criminal Liability for Complicity and Inchoate Offences" (1983) 12 *Anglo-American Law Review* 200

Smith, KJM, "Complicity and Causation" [1986] *Criminal Law Review* 663

Spencer, JR, "Trying to Help Another Person Commit a Crime" in PF Smith (ed), *Criminal Law: Essays in Honour of J C Smith* (London: Butterworths, 1987)

Steel, A, "The Appropriate Test for Dishonesty" (2000) 24 *Criminal Law Journal* 46

Stuart, D, "Sexual Assault: Substantive Issues Before and After Bill C-49" (1993) 35 *Criminal Law Quarterly* 241

Stubbs, J and Tolmie J, "Feminisms, Self-Defence, and Battered Women: A Response to Hubble's 'Straw Feminist'" (1998) 10(1) *Current Issues in Criminal Justice* 75

Stuhmcke, A, "The Legal Regulation of Foetal Tissue Transplantation" (1996) 4(2) *Journal of Law and Medicine* 131

Stychin, C, "Unmanly Diversions: The Construction of the Homosexual Body (Politic) in English Law" (1994) 32 *Osgoode Hall Law Journal* 503

Sullivan, C, "The Response of the Criminal Law in Australia to Electronic Funds Transfer Abuse" in G Hughes (ed), *Essays on Computer Law* (Melbourne: Longman Professional, 1990)

Sundby, SE, "The Reasonable Doubt Rule and the Meaning of Innocence" (1988) 40 *Hastings Law Journal* 457

Syrota, G, "A Radical Change in the Law of Recklessness" [1982] *Criminal Law Review* 97

Syrota, G, "Criminal Fraud in Western Australia: A Vague, Sweeping and Arbitrary Offence" (1994) 24 *Western Australian Law Review* 261

Syrota, G, "Rape: When does Fraud Vitiate Consent?" (1995) 25 *West Australian Law Review* 334

Temkin, J, "Impossible Attempts: Another View" (1976) 39 *Modern Law Review* 55

Temkin, J, "The Limits of Reckless Rape" [1983] *Criminal Law Review* 5

Thornton, M, "The Public/Private Dichotomy: Gendered and Discriminatory" (1991) 18 *Journal of Law and Society* 448

Triggs, G, "Australia's War Crimes Trials" in TLH McCormack and GJ Simpson, *The Law of War Crimes: National and International Approaches* (The Hague: Kluwer Law International, 1997)

Tunkel, V, "Modern Anti-Pregnancy Techniques and the Criminal Law [1974] *Criminal Law Review* 461

Tunkel, V, "Late Abortions and the Crime of Child Destruction: (1) A Reply" [1985] *Criminal Law Review* 133

Turner, A, "Criminal Liability and AIDS" [1995] *Auckland University Review* 875

Turner, JN, "The James Bulger Case: A Challenge to Juvenile Justice Theories" (1994) 68(8) *Law Institute Journal* 734

Tyler, L, "Towards a Redefinition of Rape" (1994) *New Law Journal* 860

Urlich, R, "Physical Discipline in the Home" [1994] *Auckland University Law Review* 851

Van der Maas, PJ, et al, "Euthanasia and Other Medical Decisions Concerning the End of Life" (1991) 338 *The Lancet* 669

Van der Maas, P , et al, "Euthanasia, Physician-Assisted Suicide and Other Medical Practices Involving the End of Life in the Netherlands, 1990-1995" (1996) 335 *New England Journal of Medicine* 1699

Van Groningen, J, "Detained at the Governor's Pleasure: The Consequence of the Insanity Verdict and Unfitness to Stand Trial" in D Greig and I Freckelton (eds), *Emerging Issues for the 1990s in Psychiatry, Psychology and Law*, Proceedings of the 10th Annual Congress of the Australian and New Zealand Association of Psychiatry, Psychology and Law (Melbourne: ANZAPPL, 1989)

Verdun-Jones, S, "The Insanity Defense in Canada" (1994) 17 *International Journal of Law and Psychiatry* 175

Wade, H, "The Law of Public Meeting" (1938) 2 *Modern Law Review* 177

Walker, LE, "Understanding Battered Woman's Syndrome" (1995) 31(2) *Trial* 30

Walker, N, "Unscientific, Unwise, Unprofitable or Unjust?" (1982) 22 *British Journal of Criminology* 276

Waller, L, "Tracy Maund Memorial Lecture: Any Reasonable Creature in Being" (1987) 13 *Monash Law Review* 37

Walsh, B, "Offensive Language" in D Eades (ed), *Language in Evidence* (Sydney: University of New South Wales Press, 1995)

Wardlaw, G, "Drug Control Policies and Organised Crime" in M Findlay and R Hogg (eds), *Understanding Crime and Criminal Justice* (Sydney: Law Book Company Ltd, 1988)

Warner, K, "Sentencing for Rape" in P Easteal (ed), *Balancing the Scales* (Sydney: Federation Press, 1998)

Warren, MA, "Abortion" in P Singer (ed), *A Companion to Ethics* (Oxford: Blackwell, 1991)

Warren, SD and Brandeis LD, "The Right to Privacy" (1890) 4 *Harvard Law Review* 193

Warren, I, "Violence, Sport and the Law: A Critical Discussion" in D Hemphill, *All Part of the Game: Violence and Australian Sport* (Melbourne: Walla Walla Press, 1998)

Wasik, M, "Mens Rea, Motive and the Problem of 'Dishonesty' in the Law of Theft" [1979] *Criminal Law Review* 543

Waye, V, "Rape and the Unconscionable Bargain" (1991) 16 *Criminal Law Journal* 94

Weinert, HR, "Social Hosts and Drunken Drivers: A Duty to Intervene?" (1985) 133 *University of Pennsylvania Law Review* 867

Wells, C, "Stalking: The Criminal Law Response" [1997] *Criminal Law Review* 463

Wells, C, "Swatting the Subjectivist Bug" [1982] *Criminal Law Review* 209

Wheeler F, "The Doctrine of Separation of Powers and Constitutionally Entrenched Due Process in Australia" (1997) 23(2) *Monash University Law Review* 248

White, DV, "Sports Violence as Criminal Assault: Development of the Doctrine by Canadian Courts" (1986) 6 *Duke Law Journal* 1030

Widiger, TA and Corbett EM, "Antisocial Personality Disorder" in WJ Livesey (ed), *The DSM-IV Personality Disorders* (New York: Guildford Press, 1995)

Wilkinson, T, "Doli Incapax — RIP?" (1994) 138 *Solicitor's Journal* 662

Wilkinson, T, "Doli Incapax Resurrected" (1995) 139 *Solicitor's Journal* 338

Williams, CR, "Psychopathy, Mental Illness and Preventive Detention: Issues Arising from the *David* Case" (1990) 16(2) *Monash University Law Review* 161

Williams, CR, "The Shifting Meaning of Dishonesty" (1999) 5 *Criminal Law Journal* 275

Williams, DGT, "Freedom of Assembly and Free Speech: Changes and Reforms in England" (1975) 1(2) *UNSW Law Journal* 97

Williams, DGT, "The Principle of *Beatty v Gillbanks*: A Reappraisal" in A Doob and E Greenspan (eds), *Perspectives* in DGT Williams, *Criminal Law: Essays in Honour of John Edwards* (Ontario: Canada Law Book Inc, 1985)

Williams, DGT, "Criminal Law and Administrative Law: Problems of Procedure and Reasonableness" in P Smith (ed), *Criminal Law: Essays in Honour of JC Smith* (London: Butterworths, 1987)

Williams, G, "Arrest for Breach of the Peace" [1954] *Criminal Law Review* 578

Williams, G, "Venue and Ambit of Criminal Law" (1965) 81 *Law Quarterly Review* 518

Williams, G, "The Mathematics of Proof" [1979] *Criminal Law Review* 297

Williams, G, "Three Rogues' Charters" [1980] *Criminal Law Review* 263

Williams, G, "Recklessness Redefined" (1981) 40(2) *Cambridge Law Journal* 252

Williams, G, "Temporary Appropriation Should be Theft" [1981] *Criminal Law Review* 129

Williams, G, "Offences and Defences" (1982) 2 *Legal Studies* 233

Williams, G, "The Standard of Honesty" (1983) 133 *New Law Journal* 636

Williams, G, "Oblique Intention" (1987) 46 *Cambridge Law Journal* 417

Williams, G, "The Draft Code and Reliance on Official Statements" (1989) 9 *Legal Studies* 177

Williams, G, "Victims and Other Exempt Parties in Crime" (1990) 10 *Legal Studies* 245

Williams, G, "Obedience to Law as a Crime" (1990) 53 *Modern Law Review* 445

Williams, G, "Complicity, Purpose and the Draft Code — 1" [1990] *Criminal Law Review* 4

Williams, G, "Criminal Omissions — the Conventional View" (1991) 107 *Law Quarterly Review* 86

Williams, G, "The Problem of Domestic Rape" (1991) 141 *New Law Journal* 205

Williams, G, "Innocent Agency and Causation" (1992) 3 *Criminal Law Forum* 289

Williams, G, "Rape is Rape" (1992) 142 *New Law Journal* 11

Williamson, L, "Infanticide: An Anthropological Analysis" in M Kohl (ed), *Infanticide and the Value of Life* (New York: Prometheus Books, 1978)

Willis, J, "Felony Murder at Common Law in Australia" (1977) 1 *Criminal Law Journal* 231

Woolard, JL, Dickon Repucci N and Redding RN, "Theoretical and Methodological Issues in Studying Children's Capacities in Legal Contexts" (1996) 20 *Law and Human Behaviour* 219

Wright, G, "Capable of Being Born Alive?" (1981) 131 *New Law Journal* 188

Wright, G, "The Legality of Abortion by Prostaglandin" [1984] *Criminal Law Review* 347

Wright, G, "Late Abortions and the Crime of Child Destruction: (2) A Rejoinder" [1985] *Criminal Law Review* 140

Yeo, S, "Proportionality in Criminal Cases" (1988) 12 *Criminal Law Journal* 211

Yeo, S, "Private Defences, Duress and Necessity" (1991) 15 *Criminal Law Journal* 139

Yeo, S, "Coercing Wives into Crime" (1992) 6 *Australian Journal of Family Law* 214

Yeo, S, "Battered Woman Syndrome in Australia" (1993) 143 *New Law Journal* 13

Yeo, S, "Editorial — Recognition of Aboriginal Criminal Jurisdiction" (1994) 18 *Criminal Law Journal* 193

Yeo, S, "Native Criminal Jurisdiction After Mabo" (1994) 6 *Current Issues in Criminal Justice* 9

Yeo, S, "Sex, Ethnicity, Power of Self-Control and Provocation Revisited" (1996) 18 *Sydney Law Review* 304

Young, J, "Incessant Chatter: Recent Paradigms in Criminology", in M Maguire, R Morgan and R Reiner (eds), *The Oxford Handbook of Criminology* (2nd ed, Oxford: Oxford University Press, 1997)

Zdenkowski, G, "Defending the Indigent Accused in Serious Cases: A Legal Right to Counsel?" (1994) 18 *Criminal Law Journal* 135

Zdenkowski, G, "Mandatory Imprisonment of Property Offenders in the Northern Territory" (1999) 22 *UNSW Law Journal* 302

PART I

Theory and Principles

1

Theory and the Criminal Law

> Theories are nets to catch the world,
> to rationalise, to explain and to master it

K Popper, *The Logic of Scientific Discovery*
(London: Hutchinson, 1939), p 59

> Theory is here and law/doctrine is there.
> Students all too often fall into the gap
> between the two

G Simpson, "On the Magic Mountain:
Teaching Public International Law" (1999) 10
*European Journal of International
Law* 70 at 80

1. WHAT IS THEORY? AND WHO REALLY CARES?

Michael King in *Framework of Criminal Justice* (London: Croom Helm, 1981) defines theory as the "many general principles or set of principles formulated to explain the events in the world or relation between such events": p 8. The test of the validity of such general principles is not whether they are accepted by police or lawyers "but the extent to which they offer useful insights into the operation of the criminal justice system": p 9. This positive view that theory expands the boundaries of legal knowledge is countered by cynicism that theory adds little value to our understanding of the criminal law as teachers, students and practitioners. Theoretical debate often seems divorced from the real world, raising legitimate questions about its relevance (if any) to the study and practice of criminal law. Beyond the introductory lecture, theory is usually left to be pursued furtively in further reading and footnotes.

This chapter sets out to explore the role and value of theory in understanding the function, structure and processes of the criminal law. It may be viewed as an essay on the role and value of theory in constructing and reconstructing the criminal law.

1.1 MAPPING THE THEORETICAL TERRAIN

Legal analysis is often represented as a process of "mapping" the divisions and boundaries of law. As Lindsay Farmer in *Criminal Law, Tradition and Legal Order* (Cambridge: Cambridge University Press, 1997) has noted, the criminal law is concerned not only with geographical space or territory, but also with the metaphysical space in which the law is imagined and represented: Ch 1. In Farmer's view, legal scholarship may be regarded as a form of legal cartography (pp 2-3):

> Just as maps recreate space by the use of imaginary or scientific devices, the law, in the form of doctrine or academic treatises, must be capable of representing itself. Legal doctrine is a guide, not to the geographical territory, but to the territory of the law, to the imaginary space that the law occupies. From their earliest days law students are taught that to venture into this territory without a map is foolhardy. It is vast and ancient, full of unseen dangers. It is possessed of a strange and wonderful beauty that cannot be perceived by the untrained eye. The law as it is taught and written is always an attempt to impose an order on this unruly country by marking out the "greater divisions and principal cities". It is always the result of a process of selection, and the symbolic order that is constructed mirrors, or more precisely refracts, the legal ordering of space.

This process of mapping can be productive, exposing the underlying contradictions within the substantive law and providing a guide for reform. It may also be repressive, concealing and suppressing the range of issues considered appropriate for "legitimate" legal consideration. As we shall see below, the theory of legal positivism, the concept of law as an autonomous body of legal rules distinct from morality, sociology or politics, has been criticised for excluding other perspectives, such as ethnicity, gender and power, from legal analysis.[1]

Mapping Jurisprudence: A Theory of Aesthetics and Critical Pluralism

Desmond Manderson in "Beyond the Provincial: Space, Aesthetics, and Modernist Legal Theory" (1996) 20(4) *Melbourne University Law Review* 1048 suggests that legal theory more generally may be viewed as a form of legal cartography. Legal philosophers map boundaries and divisions, determining "provinces" and constructing "empires". Manderson argues against such geographic reification proposing instead that law should be understood not in spatial terms, but as an aesthetic enterprise —

---

1   The repressive aspects of analytical jurisprudence are explored in V Kerruish, *Jurisprudence as Ideology* (London and New York: Routledge, 1991).

as a process of signification. Rather than suppress complexity and diversity, the aesthetic approach values pluralism. He characterises this approach as "critical pluralism" (at 1069):

> The aesthetic of critical pluralism, in keeping with this aesthetic spirit, celebrates multiplicity in stark contradiction to the legal trinity of coherence/order/control. Uncertainty, indeterminacy, unpredictability, particularity: these are not *failures* of analysis if we abandon the equation of order with beauty and chaos with ugliness. Pluralism *is* local knowledge and local action, a recognition of the cultural, communal and individual construction of legality. No reification or systemisation of "space" or "time" can capture the complexity of legal meaning as each of us experience it, because each of us experience it differently.

Theorists claim that their ideas about the law provide the legal community with guides or blueprints for constructing and reconstructing the law. Yet is this really so? The criminal law has certainly provided the doctrinal grist for much thinking and re-thinking about the nature and purpose of law. Until recently, the bulk of this theorising has been concerned with determining the legitimate conditions, in both moral and political terms, of criminal liability and punishment. A leading American legal scholar George Fletcher has gone so far as to claim that the criminal law *itself* is a "species of moral and political philosophy": *Rethinking Criminal Law* (Boston: Little Brown, 1978), p xix. As a consequence, much theoretical debate has been concerned with exploring the conditions under which individuals should be held morally and legally responsible for their conduct. In most textbooks, theoretical engagement is focused on the "principles of responsibility" in *general* terms, at the expense of critical examination of the aims and limits of the criminalisation in *specific* contexts. As Peter Alldridge in *Relocating Criminal Law* (Aldershot: Ashgate, 2000) has observed (p 5):

> There are other problems in the criminal law than those to do with attribution of responsibility ... They too can generate important problems requiring contributions from philosophical and other extradoctrinal sources. So long as the crimes under consideration are homicide and assaults there is little controversy as to what the law should require people to do (not kill or hit one another) but there are many areas where it is precisely that question which requires attention.
>
> Whatever the standpoint, it is important to realise that "general principles" are not the full extent of theorising about criminal law.

From the perspective of criminal law *as* moral philosophy, criminal law doctrine appears to be a spectacular failure. Textbooks often seem to be a litany of complaint about the failure of the courts and legislatures to uphold "fundamental" principles, such as the presumption of subjective fault. These traditional accounts proceed with little or no appreciation of the social, political, historical or practical context within which the criminal law has developed and currently operates. Legal scholarship seems preoccupied with the search for universal principles of responsibility applicable to *all* crimes, and has been characterised fundamentally as a "rationalising enterprise".[2]

---

2   A Norrie, *Crime, Reason and History* (London: Weidenfeld & Nicolson, 1993), p 8, citing M Horwitz, "The Historical Contingency of the Role of History" (1981) 90 *Yale Law Journal* 1057.

At the same time, there is an emerging "critical" consciousness that an alternative basis for the study of the criminal law is necessary, one which seriously engages with the external disciplinary perspectives offered by sociology, psychology, feminism, human rights, legal history and so on.[3] Most significantly, criminal law scholars are increasingly disputing the traditional disciplinary segregation of criminal law from criminal justice studies and criminology. By exploring the nature and purpose of the criminal process, critical scholars have exposed the ideology and contradictions within the concept of "criminal justice". Drawing on such broader insights, an holistic approach may be developed that conceives the criminal law as merely one component of a larger legal apparatus involved in the detection, prosecution and punishment of offenders.

In this chapter, we describe, evaluate and critique various theories of the criminal law and criminal justice, as well as laying the foundation for a critical pluralistic theory of the criminal law, which Nicola Lacey has called "criminalization".[4]

Types of Theory

When thinking about the function and significance of different theories of the criminal law, a distinction is sometimes drawn between explanatory and normative models. The former explains how the criminal law works, while the latter is concerned with how it *ought* to work. As John Braithwaite has generally observed "sound policy analysis involves a combination of explanatory and normative theory": K Hazlehurst (ed), *Crime and Justice: An Australian Textbook in Criminology* (Sydney: LBC, 1996), p 5. This simple binary classification can be misleading since explanatory analysis is invariably founded upon an implicit normative model. Reflecting this integrated approach, this chapter organises the material around the ideas of "constructing" and "reconstructing" the criminal law, a distinction that traverses both explanatory and normative terrain.

---

3   While foreign to Anglo-American criminal law, this non-exclusive approach to the discipline is the norm in the civil law systems of Continental Europe: P Alldridge, *Relocating Criminal Law* (Aldershot: Ashgate, 2000), pp 18-19.

4   This theory is developed in N Lacey, "Criminology, Criminal Law, and Criminalization" in M Maguire, R Morgan and R Reiner (eds), *The Oxford Handbook of Criminology* (2nd ed, Oxford: Clarendon Press, 1997), Ch 11.

2. CONSTRUCTING THE CRIMINAL LAW

WH Auden, "Law Like Love",
in AW Allison et al, *The Norton Anthology of Poetry* (New York: WH Norton & Company Inc, 1975), p 117

> Yet law-abiding scholars write;
> Law is neither wrong nor right;
> Law is only crimes
> Punished by places and by times

2.1 DEFINING CRIME AND THE RULE OF LAW

The criminal law is conventionally defined as a set of legal norms for determining the conditions under which individuals may be held liable to punishment. Glanville Williams in his *Textbook of Criminal Law* (2nd ed, London: Stevens and Sons, 1983) viewed the criminal law as comprised of "crimes" which he defined (p 27) as follows:

> A crime (or offence) is a legal wrong that can be followed by criminal proceedings which
> may result in punishment.

In this account, the criminal law is defined by reference to the legal norms (rules and principles) for identifying and punishing proscribed conduct rather than by reference to the inherent wrongful *quality* of that conduct. Crime is simply whatever the law-makers (legislatures or courts) at a particular time have decided is punishable as a crime.

> As the criminal law reflects the social, political and cultural values of the period in which it developed, it has been described as a "sociopolitical artifact": H Packer, *The Limits of the Criminal Sanction* (Stanford: Stanford University Press, 1968), p 364.

While some sociologists and criminologists define crime in qualitative terms that transcend formal legal categories, such as "deviance",[5] for the purpose of legal analysis and, more importantly, adjudication, crime is simply any conduct which is proscribed by law as being criminal and punishable accordingly. As Lord Atkin concluded in *Proprietary Articles Trade Association v Attorney-General (Canada)* [1931] AC 310 at 324:

> the domain of criminal jurisprudence can only be ascertained by examining what acts at
> any particular period are declared by the State to be crimes, and the only common nature
> they will be found to possess is that they are prohibited by the State and that those who
> commit them are punished.

---

5   D Downes and P Rock, *Understanding Deviance* (Oxford: Oxford University Press, 1988). For a review of the different definitions of crime see R White and F Haines, *Crime and Criminology* (2nd ed, Melbourne: Oxford University Press, 2000), pp 3-5.

Under these definitions, the power of the State to label and punish conduct as criminal is the defining or unifying characteristic of "crime". Many legal norms prohibit conduct, but only the criminal law has the power to impose punishment in the name of the State following a verdict of guilt. Laws can proscribe conduct as "unlawful", but without the imposition (or at least threat) of punishment, they cannot be described as "criminal". For example, provisions in the *Workplace Relations Act* 1996 (Cth) prohibit employers from paying workers engaged in industrial action, though breach of these provisions does not constitute an offence.[6] Though deemed unlawful, this conduct only gives rise to a right under civil law to compensation for damage caused or an injunction to restrain unlawful conduct in the future. Although civil remedies such as injunctions or exemplary damages have coercive qualities, from the viewpoint of legal classification they do not constitute criminal punishment since they do not flow from a determination of guilt following criminal proceedings. In Chapter 15, pp 866ff, we explore, in the context of drug offences, the coercive and punitive effect of the civil powers of confiscation under proceeds of crime legislation.

The concept of the criminal law as a system of legal norms for guiding action backed by the threat of state punishment confronts, in the words of Lacey, "a serious challenge of legitimation".[7] This challenge is tackled at two levels. At the level of substantive legal doctrine, legitimation is addressed by appealing to the objective and timeless status of the legal standards being applied, and then basing these standards in common understandings or shared commitments. At the level of criminal process, legitimacy is addressed by respecting the values of justice, legality, fairness, equality and privacy, and so on. This is reflected in the growing importance attached to respecting human rights in the administration of criminal justice: Ch 2, pp 111-114. Embodied in general principles, these normative standards play a significant role in legitimating the criminal law.

In liberal democratic societies, the legitimacy of punishment is addressed through the principle of legality or, as it is more traditionally known, the rule of law.[8] The rule of law secures legitimation by purporting to constrain arbitrary power in a number of ways. A key idea is that no person may be punished except for a breach of law established in the ordinary manner before the courts. Another important component is that no person is above the law — that every person is subject to these laws without exception, thus ensuring equality before the law. Judges are required to do justice *according to the law*, rather than by reference to arbitrary and discretionary notions of fairness or morality. Associated with these ideals of legality is the principle against retrospectivity, which is embodied in maxims such as:

> *Nulla crimen sine lege* (no crime without law); and
>
> *Nulla poena sine lege* (no punishment without law).

---

6 The question of whether a prohibition creates a criminal offence is a matter of statutory interpretation, though in this context, the *Workplace Relations Act* 1996 (Cth) expressly states that contravention of the section is not an offence: s 187AA(3).

7 N Lacey, "Criminology, Criminal Law, and Criminalization" in M Maguire, R Morgan and R Reiner (eds), *The Oxford Handbook of Criminology* (2nd ed, Oxford: Clarendon Press, 1997), p 444.

8 The phrase "rule of law" is commonly associated with the 19th century English constitutional writing of AV Dicey, *Introduction to the Study of the Law of the Constitution* (10th ed, London: Macmillan, 1959), pp 202-203. The idea of rule by law rather than by men has an older lineage traceable to the *Magna Carta* (1215), the Glorious Revolution (1668) and the United States Declaration of Independence (1776) and Constitution (1787). For an excellent essay examining the rule of law, see D Clark, "The Many Meanings of the Rule of Law" in K Jayasuriya (ed), *Law, Capitalism and Power in Asia* (London and New York: Routledge, 1999).

Fidelity to these ideals and principles leads to the rejection of retrospective criminal laws and punishment without trial, as well as imposing constraints on judicial creativity in expanding the scope of criminal laws.

The ideals behind the rule of law are largely the product of the Enlightenment. As Farmer has noted, these ideals emerged in the 18th century "as part of a movement that sought to restrict arbitrary royal power, and defend the absolute value of law" and, as such, are "inextricably bound up with views of the modernity of law": *Criminal Law, Tradition and Legal Order* (Cambridge: Cambridge University Press, 1997), p 23. In the context of early colonial Australia, the rule of law played important roles in constraining the absolute powers of the Governor and facilitating the transformation of a penal settlement into a free and civil society. In the modern context, where disempowered subjects are denied civil and political rights, the concept of legality and the rule of law continue to provide one of the few means (though not always effective) of rendering the State accountable for its actions.[9]

Colonial Visions of the Rule of Law and Criminal Justice

The extent to which the rule of law operated to constrain the exercise of arbitrary State power, or conversely legitimate the power of the ruling elite, is a matter of continuing debate in the Australian context: see D Neal, *The Rule of Law in A Penal Colony* (Cambridge: Cambridge University Press, 1991), Ch 3; B Kercher, *An Unruly Child: A History of Law in Australia* (Sydney: Allen & Unwin, 1995). For earlier discussions of the significance of the rule of law in the administration of criminal justice in 18th century England, see EP Thompson, *Whigs and Hunters: The Origins of the Black Act* (London: Allen Lane, 1975); D Hay, "Property, Authority and the Criminal Law" in D Hay, P Linebaugh, J Rule, EP Thompson and C Winslow (eds), *Albion's Fatal Tree: Crime and Society in 18th Century England* (NY: Pantheon, 1975); J Langbein, *Albion's Fatal Flaws* (1983) 98 *Past and Present* 96. These sources are extracted and discussed in D Brown, D Farrier and D Weisbrot, *Criminal Laws* (2nd ed, Sydney: Federation Press, 1996), pp 43-60.

These ideals and principles encompassed within the rule of law play an influential role in constructing the legal subject — the offender. An important premise behind the rule of law is that the State punishes criminal conduct, not criminal types. As Francis Allen points out in *The Habits of Legality — Criminal Justice and the Rule of Law* (New York: Oxford University Press, 1996), p 15:

> Although the point seems not often made, the *nulla poena* principle has important implications not only for the procedures of justice but also for the substantive criminal law. It speaks to the questions, What is a crime? and Who is the criminal? The *nulla poena* concept assumes that persons become criminals because of their acts, not simply because of who or what they are.

---

9   Within developing Asian economies, the rule of law is primarily used as a means of legitimating strong government rather than protecting democratic, liberal values: K Jayasuriya (ed), *Law, Capitalism and Power in Asia* (London and New York: Routledge, 1999). British colonial powers have not been averse to supplying legal rights in lieu of democracy: C Jones, "Politics Postponed: Law as a Substitute for Politics in Hong Kong and China", K Jayasuriya (ed), *Law, Capitalism and Power in Asia* (London and New York: Routledge, 1999), p 45.

According to Allen, drafting criminal laws to punish individuals because they possess characteristics perceived to be dangerous or anti-social is incompatible with the principles of legality. As we shall explore below, criminological theories based on biological determinism supported such approaches to criminalisation, and were influential in Nazi and Soviet legal systems: see p 30. It would be incorrect, however, to assume that legal systems based on the rule of law did not enact offences targeting the defective character of offenders rather than their conduct. Throughout the 19th century, "status" offences were widely enacted to deal with vagrants, prostitutes, drunks and habitual criminals. As we shall explore below, the modern criminal law continues to identify types of offenders through the range of special laws and powers enacted to deal with "dangerous offenders".

Such derogations from the rule of law are significant. They reveal that the ideals of legality, upon closer scrutiny, are often hedged with qualifications. The value of legality is not so much instrumental, but rather symbolic and ideological. Its importance resides in its capacity to confer legitimacy on the criminal law. By abstracting the offence from the political and social context of its enactment and enforcement, the law may be applied (or so it is claimed) in a neutral and impartial manner. This has the effect of excluding the *subject* of the criminal law — the offender — from legal view, suppressing the relevance and significance of personal characteristics such as class, ethnicity, sexuality and gender.

> **The abstraction of offenders from their social and political context may be viewed as part of an historical project of reconstructing notions of criminal responsibility in the late 19th century.[10] Until this period, the idea of responsibility in the criminal law was determined largely by reference to the offender's character, rather than conduct: M Wiener, *Reconstructing the Criminal* (Cambridge: Cambridge University Press, 1991). This idea was reflected in the moral conception of subjective fault based on malice and wickedness. Only gradually were these normative notions of fault displaced with descriptive neutral concepts such as intention and knowledge: see Ch 3, 3.4 'Fault Elements' p 173.**

Legal discourse struggles to suppress the political dimensions of the criminal law. It is never completely successful. While political questions about criminalisation and enforcement policies are deemed non-justiciable at trial, they are often relevant at the pre-trial stage (influencing police or prosecutorial discretion) or post-conviction (influencing sentencing). The political dimensions of particular conduct are sometimes exposed in the application of substantive legal rules. For example, feminists have revealed that the legal definitions of homicide, self-defence and provocation (while formally gender-neutral) are constructed around and condone masculine understandings of legitimate excusable violence. As we shall see in Chapters 4 and 5, the socio-political construction of homicide has severely limited the range and scope of defences available to battered women who kill abusive partners. Critical scholarship recognises as important a wide range of questions about the nature of the crime, the type of offender, and the impact of law enforcement — matters that *should* have crucial implications for legal responses to crime.

---

10   A Norrie, *Crime, Reason and History* (London: Weidenfeld & Nicolson, 1993); L Farmer, *Criminal Law, Tradition and Legal Order* (Cambridge: Cambridge University Press, 1997), Ch 1.

To constrain and legitimate the power of the State to punish, the rule of law places a premium on the clarity, rationality and coherence of the criminal law.[11] Debates in the criminal law are often represented as a dialogic tension between the interests of legality and the countervailing needs of securing individualised justice: F Allen, *The Habits of Legality — Criminal Justice and the Rule of Law* (New York: Oxford University Press, 1996), p 21. This tension is stamped across many compartments of the criminal law. However, it is not only justice that tempers legality. Broader community values and interests are often viewed as imposing limitations on legality. For example, the rules governing intoxication reveal how strict legal logic has been qualified by policy considerations based on "common-sense" and "community interests". The tensions between the principle of legality and other legal values such as fairness are further explored in Chapter 2: pp 95-97.

2.2 LEGAL POSITIVISM AND A CONCEPT OF CRIMINAL LAW

Notwithstanding the emergence of alternative theoretical perspectives in the form of Critical Legal Scholarship, socio-legal studies and law in context, most legal scholarship (and thus legal education) remains "broadly positivist".[12] From both explanatory and normative perspectives, legal positivism fixes clear boundaries around the criminal law. Criminal law is viewed as a discrete and autonomous field which may be understood and applied without reference to politics, economics, morality, history, psychology and sociology. To the extent that analysis does extend beyond cases and legislation, it is limited to contextualising law within a set of legal values (informed broadly by liberalism) relating to autonomy, equality, fairness, privacy, and so on.

Conceiving the criminal law as a discrete system of rules and principles has the effect of quarantining questions about the nature of crime, punishment and the criminal process from legal analysis. By viewing crimes as "given" acts of law-creation, relevant political and criminological issues are quietly removed from the legal agenda.[13] The ideological exclusion of criminology, as well as other non-legal perspectives, conceals important insights into the role of offenders, victims, the public and the State in understanding crime and the legal responses to it.

Criminology, as well as providing theoretical perspectives on the criminal law and criminal justice system, offers empirical insights on the practical operation of specific laws. It opens a disciplinary space for critical scholarship to explore the gap between "law in action" and "law in the books". We explore this crucial distinction below at p 36. Empirical research undoubtedly produces

---

11   The centrality of these values to legal culture is reinforced by legal theory itself. Lon Fuller in *The Morality of Law* (Rev. ed., New Haven: Yale University Press, 1969) has suggested that the "inner morality of law" rests on 8 precepts: there must be rules; these rules must be prospective, not retrospective; they must be published; intelligible; not contradictory; capable of being complied with; not constantly changing; and that there must be congruence between the declared rules and those applied by officials.

12   N Lacey, "Feminist Perspectives on Ethical Positivism" in T Campbell and J Goldsworthy (eds), *Judicial Power, Democracy and Legal Positivism* (Aldershot: Ashgate, 2000), p 92. This essay reviews how feminism has challenged positivism's claims of objectivity, neutrality, centrality, unity and rationality for law.

13   N Lacey, "Criminology, Criminal Law, and Criminalization" in M Maguire, R Morgan and R Reiner (eds), *The Oxford Handbook of Criminology* (2nd ed, Oxford: Clarendon Press, 1997), p 440.

better policy-making and law reform — it serves to counteract the belief of lawyers, judges as well as legislators pursuing "law and order" agendas, that social and cultural change by criminal prohibition is inevitable and achievable: A Ashworth, "Editorial — The Value of Empirical Research in Criminal Justice" [1997] *Criminal Law Review* 533. As we shall explore in Chapter 12, recent empirical studies in Australia have shown that, notwithstanding the abolition of many discriminatory rules and practices in rape trials, the treatment of complainants has not significantly improved. Indeed, in many areas the reforms have been counterproductive. Criminologists and sociologists have exposed the limits of legality in regulatory terms. Peter Grabosky has highlighted the risk of new laws being neutralised through "creative adaptation" and "unintended consequences": "Counterproductive Regulation" (1995) 23 *International Journal of the Sociology of Law* 347.

Liberal accounts view the criminal law as the ultimate prohibitory norm that should only be used as a measure of "last resort": A Ashworth, *Principles of Criminal Law* (3rd ed, Oxford: Oxford University Press, 1999), pp 32-37. This concern about overcriminalisation is shared by critical scholars, who accuse lawmakers of squandering the criminal law through an "uncivil politics of law and order": R Hogg and D Brown, *Rethinking Law and Order* (Sydney: Pluto Press, 1998), Ch 1. This trend is apparent in many areas, such as public order and drug offences, where new police powers and offences have been enacted to combat perceived threats to the community's social, political, economic and even international interests.

Notwithstanding this image of an omnipotent criminal law in need of restraint, it must be acknowledged that the regulatory power of criminalisation can be surprisingly weak. To criminalise conduct places the subject and conduct practically and symbolically beyond the boundaries of legality and civil society. The criminal is literally and legally rendered *out*law. This is the paradox of criminalisation. The process of criminalisation, while potently symbolic, weakens the instrumental capacity of law to regulate the prohibited conduct. For example, where there exists a continuing market for goods or services that have been prohibited, such as illicit drugs or prostitution, the regulatory impact of the criminal law may be marginal or even counterproductive. Criminalisation may simply serve to stimulate the illegal market by increasing the profit to be gained from the delivery of illicit goods and services. It may also undermine law enforcement more generally by increasing the likelihood of police corruption and weakening public confidence in the administration of justice.

While criminal prohibition may have undesirable and unintended effects, it does not necessarily mean that legal regulation must be abandoned. As David Dixon recently observed in relation to illicit drugs:

> Indeed, the prohibition/legalisation dichotomy is unhelpfully stark: the significant issue is not whether we choose prohibition or legalisation, but rather how we regulate markets in ways which minimise the harms caused by the activities and by their prohibition.[14]

Similar concerns about counterproductive effects of criminalisation have been raised in relation to recent offences prohibiting HIV transmission and female genital mutilation discussed in Chapters 11 and 12. The counterproductive effects of prohibition of illicit drugs are explored in Chapter 15.

---

14 D Dixon, "Issues in the Legal Regulation of Policing" in D Dixon (ed), *A Culture of Corruption* (Sydney: Hawkins Press, 1999).

Another weakness of the positivist conception of law is that the sources of its rules and principles are restricted to *formal* authorities, namely legislation and case law. The role of criminal justice institutions, such as the police and the prosecution, in the interpretation and enforcement of the criminal law is ignored. This focus is maintained notwithstanding the empirical research demonstrating that policies of selective law enforcement, charge and plea-bargaining play a significant role in defining and determining the boundaries of the criminal law. Keith Hawkins in *Environment and Enforcement* (Oxford: Clarendon Press, 1983) found that prosecution of environmental offences only proceeded in cases where there was evidence of an *intentional* violation of the law by the accused. This restriction applied notwithstanding the legal reality that these offences, being crimes of strict liability, did not *technically* require proof of intention. In a recent essay "Law as Last Resort" in R Baldwin, C Scott and C Hood (eds), *A Reader on Regulation* (Oxford: Oxford University Press, 1998), Hawkins concluded (p 288) that the values and policies of the prosecutors, not the substantive legal definitions, were determinative of prosecution:

> Practical criminal law — the enforcement of the norms embodied in that branch of the law — is ... founded not so much in the substantive acts it deems unlawful, but rather on the principles that define its proper realm and procedure.

Combined with the reality that most suspects plead guilty, the legal rules (encapsulated in procedural, evidential and substantive definitions) operate primarily as "bargaining chips" for the police, prosecution and defence lawyers in negotiating charges and pleas.

Selective law enforcement may also sustain a cloak of invisibility around certain forms of wrongdoing. Santina Perrone's empirical study of work-related fatalities in Victoria revealed how these events were typically constructed as "accidents" even in the face of credible evidence that could support charges of corporate manslaughter by criminal negligence. Corporations were more likely to be prosecuted, if at all, for breaches of provisions of the *Occupational Health and Safety Act* 1985 (Vic) resulting in modest fines on companies and directors.[15] Prosecutorial discretion can be exercised in a discriminatory manner. As we shall explore in Chapter 3 at p 154, the enforcement of the criminal law against "corporate killers" is also hampered by the restrictive scope of corporate criminal responsibility.

Positivist accounts of the criminal law ignore how legal rules and principles are mediated through the criminal process — the rules of the criminal law simply define and prohibit particular conduct and states of mind. Such accounts rarely consider how legal rules articulated in the higher courts are "translated" in the lower courts. Little attention is paid to the influential role of jury directions and legal summation in shaping the meaning of key legal concepts, such as intention, consent or dishonesty. These issues are further explored below in Chapter 2: pp 123-126 'The Law/Fact Distinction: The Boundaries of Judicial Impartiality'. It has recently been suggested that the number and extent of these directions pose a threat to the independence of the jury: G Flatman and M Bagaric, "Juries Peers or Puppets — The Need to Curtail Jury Instructions" (1998) 22 Crim LJ 207.

---

15   S Perrone, "Workplace Fatalities and the Adequacy of Prosecutions" (1995) 13(1) *Law in Context* 81; see also R White and S Perrone, *Crime and Social Control* (Melbourne: Oxford University Press, 1997), pp 102-105.

Formal accounts of the criminal law also ignore the role of judicial texts, such as "bench books", which provide both specimen directions and constitute an authoritative source of criminal law for trial judges. It is often the paraphrase of the relevant legal rule contained in the bench book, rather than the primary source itself, that guides the trial judge, jury or magistrate. To achieve a deeper understanding of the criminal law, both practically and theoretically, a wider range of legal sources, both formal and informal, must be studied: N Lacey, "Criminology, Criminal Law, and Criminalization" in M Maguire, R Morgan and R Reiner (eds), *The Oxford Handbook of Criminology* (2nd ed, Oxford: Clarendon Press, 1997), pp 443-444.

Postivist accounts of the criminal law focus exclusively on the instrumental, as opposed to the expressive or symbolic, aspects of law and legal power.[16] Literary perspectives on law expose more broadly the role of narrative and story-telling in the construction of legal discourse. Feminist and critical scholars in the field of criminal law have explored how female sexuality is constructed through legal discourse including the content of jury directions, case law, legislation and even academic scholarship.

Criminal Law as Narrative

As feminist scholars have pointed out, legal scholarship is deeply implicated in the construction of the legal narrative and imagery surrounding sexuality, both male and female. This narrative has been influential in constructing the law governing consent and credibility in rape cases: N Naffine, "Windows on the Legal Mind: The Evocation of Rape in Legal Writings" (1992) 18 *Melbourne University Law Review* 741; N Naffine, "Possession: Erotic Love in the Law of Rape" (1994) 57 *Modern Law Review* 10; A Young, "The Waste Land of the Law, the Wordless Song of the Rape Victim" (1998) 22 *Melbourne University Law Review* 435. Feminists have argued that it is possible to reconstruct such narratives to empower rather than disempower women. For an imaginative example, drawing on crime fiction, see N Naffine, *Feminism and Criminology* (Sydney: Allen and Unwin, 1997), Chapter 5.

2.3 REINSTATING HISTORY AND PROCEDURE

The positivist "concept of law" may also be criticised for conceiving its rules and principles in *ahistorical* terms. Legal history, if considered at all, is only used to trace the pedigree of legal rules or principles along lines of authority. This is a form of legal antiquarianism — an exploration of the past for the purpose of demonstrating how far we have progressed. As Alan Norrie observed in *Crime, Reason and History* (London: Weidenfeld & Nicolson, 1993), p 9:

> To the extent that lawyers think historically about the law, they tend to think in terms of the slow evolution of legal forms from the crude to the sophisticated, and not in terms of the particular connections between different legal forms and different kinds of society.

---

16 N Lacey, "Feminist Perspectives on Ethical Positivism" in T Campbell and J Goldsworthy (eds), *Judicial Power, Democracy and Legal Positivism* (Aldershot: Ashgate, 2000), p 108.

This suppression of history, especially the impact of procedural changes, reinforces the conception of the criminal law as a rational *system* of rules. Crimes are dissected into components, such as "ingredients" or "elements" of offences or defences, rather than viewed as a historical *process* of criminalisation which is responsive to changing social, cultural and political forces.

Historical analysis produces a more complex and comprehensive understanding of the criminal law. It has exposed the contingency and contradictions of "general principles" of the criminal law, as well the social, political and economic forces shaping the development of specific crimes. Norrie's *Crime, Reason and History* (London: Weidenfeld & Nicolson, 1993) uses historical sources to develop a powerful critique of the dominant subjectivist theory of fault in the criminal law. In relation to specific crimes, we explore the significance of historical research in reshaping our approach to the criminalisation of illicit drugs in Chapter 15: pp 834ff.

Farmer has sought to meld the historical and procedural perspectives into a theory of criminal law called "critical positivism": *Criminal Law, Tradition and Legal Order* (Cambridge: Cambridge University Press, 1997), Ch 1. Farmer argues that a better understanding of rules and principles may be gained from historical study of the relationship between criminal law and its procedures. He suggests that historical approaches to criminal law must not confine themselves to tracing the influence of liberal philosophy on the development of the "principles of criminal responsibility" from the 18th century onwards. He is dismissive of the current "fetish" for contextualising the criminal law through inter-disciplinary critique, which leads in his view to a growing confusion about how the criminal law fits together (particularly of what constitutes the "core" and the "context") and "increasingly diffuse accounts of social control": p 12. By contrast, his theory of "critical positivism" offers the prospect of a deeper appreciation of the criminal law through its relationship with criminal justice (p 12):

> The study of the doctrine of the criminal law must therefore begin by shifting attention on the relationship between legal practices and moral philosophy itself. It should look at its origins, the way that this has been invested with significance, and its actual significance to the operation of the criminal justice system. This entails looking at it as one practice within a complex of practices — the philosophising of the criminal law in the field of the administration of criminal law and criminal justice — where the relationship is not given, once and for all, but must always be in the process of re-establishing itself. The true significance of each of these practices in a specific period must be traced and weighed against the others. The organising concepts of the criminal law do not have an *a priori* existence, springing fully formed from the head of some god-like philosopher. They emerge from institutional practices and their study must begin by looking at their uses in this system of practices.

2.4 BEYOND LEGAL POSITIVISM

The principal weakness of the positivist definition of "crime" is its tendency to conceal or suppress its deeply-contested normative character. Farmer suggests in "The Obsession with Definition: The Nature of Crime and Critical Legal Theory" (1996) 5 *Social and Legal Studies* 57 at 66, that the tendency of modern lawyers and judges to define crime in neutral procedural terms, rather than by reference to its normative qualities, simply "reflects the diversity of functions of law in the interventionist state. There is no single, simple moral or other purpose that is capable of holding the whole together". He traces this diversity in the criminal law to the administrative transformations in the 19th century criminal justice system, in particular the growth of regulatory offences triable by summary procedures. While these new forms of crime promoted public welfare, social order and efficiency, they could no longer be justified in terms of protecting the moral or political order. As a consequence, explanations of the criminal law became increasingly neutral.

Normative suppression performs an important legitimating function related to the separation of powers. According to the ideals of legal positivism, the function of the courts should be confined to the interpretation and application of existing rules or principles.[17] Within the constraints of adjudication, the courts have the power to refine and clarify definitions and concepts and to apply existing rules to new situations. Higher courts have the additional power to correct doctrinal mistakes and to develop the law in accordance with its fundamental principles. Positivism contends that if there are no clear rules or principles, then it is for parliament, not the courts, to fill the gaps. Questions of what the criminal law *is* are primarily technical legal matters for the courts. Questions of what the law *should* be are political matters for the legislature.[18]

> **In the context of technology outpacing copyright law, McHugh and Kirby JJ observed in**
> **_Phonographic Performance Company of Australia Limited v Federation of Australian_**
> **_Commercial Television Stations_ (1998) 195 CLR 158 at 181:**
>
> > **Courts have sometimes been slow to adapt to new circumstances.**
> > **Sometimes there will be no other way of dealing with the problem than**
> > **by legislative amendment.[53]**
>
> > **[53] Courts cannot always, in the manner of Star Trek's Captain Jean-Luc Picard,**
> > **say "Make it so!"**

The positivist's "concept of law" is clearly contestable as a sociological depiction of adjudicative practices within systems based on the common law tradition. The interpretative process permits judges at every level considerable discretion, or "leeways" to use Julius Stone's phrase, to refashion and create legal doctrine.[19] Judicial creativity is admittedly constrained by legal conventions

---

17   HLA Hart, *The Concept of Law* (Oxford: Clarendon Press, 1961); R Dworkin, *Law's Empire* (London: Fontana, 1986).

18   This ideal is strongly promoted in Tom Campbell's *The Legal Theory of Ethical Positivism* (Brookfield, Vt: Dartmouth Publishing Co, 1996). This explicitly normative theory of law emphasises the importance of democratic institutions and separation of powers with the effect of imposing strict limits on judicial law-making. Ethical positivism however is open to the same criticisms that have been levelled at its ancestors: it adopts a narrow conception of legal and political power and denies the relevance of external disciplinary perspectives on law: N Lacey, "Feminist Perspectives on Ethical Positivism" in T Campbell and J Goldsworthy (eds), *Judicial Power, Democracy and Legal Positivism* (Aldershot: Ashgate, 2000).

19   See J Stone, *Legal System and Lawyer's Reasonings* (London: Stevens and Sons, 1964); J Stone, *Precedent and Law: Dynamics of Common Law Growth* (Sydney: Butt, 1985). Responding to accusations of inappropriate levels of judicial activism, some judges have addressed the issue of the legitimacy and limits of judicial law-making in extra-curial speeches: M McHugh, "The Law-Making Function of the Judicial Process — Part I" (1988) 62 ALJ 15 and "The Law-Making Function of the Judicial Process — Part II" (1988) 62 ALJ 116; A Mason, "The Role of the Courts at the Turn of the Century" (1993) 3 *Journal of Judicial Administration* 156; A Mason, "The Courts as Community Institutions" (1998) 9(2) *Public Law Review* 83.

governing the proper use of precedent, interpretation of statutes and beliefs about the appropriate constitutional limits of judicial law-making. Indeed, most common law systems would deny any inherent judicial power to create "new" crimes in the public interest, Scotland being an exception.[20]

Judicial law-making in the criminal law field does however occur indirectly — the High Court has exercised its power to abolish outmoded common law offences (such as battery manslaughter) or restrict the scope of particular defences. In some cases, this process of incremental doctrinal development raises concern about the legitimate limits of criminalisation by judicial pronouncement rather than legislative enactment. For example, judicial decisions in England and Australia have held that the marital rape immunity is no longer part of the common law. This refusal to recognise the historical immunity may be viewed as a judicial act of law-creation, criminalising spousal rape where no such crime previously existed. Although potentially conflicting with the principle against retrospectivity, the courts clearly have some latitude in moulding the law in accordance with changing social and political attitudes. The demise of the marital rape immunity is further explored in Chapter 12: pp 599ff.

This process of judicial law-making is also facilitated by the breadth of offence definitions that allow the courts to apply existing laws to emerging and unforeseen social threats. For example, "catch-all" offences of public nuisance and endangerment, recognised by common law and statute, have been used to criminalise individuals organising "raves" (*R v Shorrock* [1993] WLR 698), and individuals who engage in sexual intercourse that exposes others to the risk of HIV transmission (*Mutemeri v Cheeseman* [1998] 4 VR 484).

Legal rhetoric, in keeping with positivist ideals, is compelled to deny the true extent of judicial creativity. The inherent flexibility and discretion within interpretation and adjudication provides the space for theory to inform and guide legal development. These normative resources may be framed in terms of common-sense, experience or conventional moral or political philosophy. Whether the legal community is conscious of the value of theory, legal rules are shaped and outcomes determined by reference to ideas about how the criminal law does and should operate.

2.5 THE RELATIONSHIP BETWEEN CRIME AND PUNISHMENT

According to conventional definitions above, the criminal law is tied to punishment. Punishment, it is said, has several competing aims and effects. These aims and effects are typically represented as retribution, deterrence, incapacitation and rehabilitation. The question, often overlooked by criminal law scholars, is whether it is *appropriate* to consider the criminal law as an "adjunct to punishment". Nor is the practical question addressed as to whether the aims of punishment are empirically achievable through the criminal law. Are these aims offered as an explanatory or normative account of the criminal law, or both? The justifying aims of the criminal law are represented simply as "practical common-sense", with little appreciation of the historical origins of these ideas. Although

---

20 L Farmer, *Criminal Law, Tradition and Legal Order* (Cambridge: Cambridge University Press, 1997), p 23, citing *Rachel Wright* (1809): "The genius of our law rests on a principle diametrically opposite to that of England; the Courts of criminal jurisdiction being authorised to punish crimes with any positive enactment", per Clerk Hope LJ.

typically examined in the first few pages of the standard criminal law text, these ideas rarely intrude into subsequent discussion about the nature, scope and limits of the criminal law. This type of approach has profound political implications for the criminal law as a discipline:

> Conventional criminal law scholars generally provide a brief resumé of the moral/retributive, incapacitative, and deterrent aspects of criminal justice. They go on to give a terse statement of the competing concerns of fairness and social protection, due process, and crime control which are taken to inform the development of the criminal law in liberal societies. From this point on, they take the idea of "crimes" as given by acts of law-creation. In this way both political and criminological issues are quietly removed from the legal agenda.[21]

In the next section, we search more deeply for answers to questions about the proper relationship of punishment to the criminal law.

Since punishment flows from a verdict of guilt, theoretical discussion of the criminal law is customarily prefaced with an exploration of the legitimacy of state punishment. As HLA Hart in *Punishment and Responsibility* (Oxford: Clarendon Press, 1968) said, punishment in legal terms must (pp 4-5):

== **involve pain or other consequences normally considered unpleasant;**

== **be for an offence against legal rules;**

== **be of an actual or supposed offender for an offence;**

== **be intentionally administered by human beings other than the offender; and**

== **be imposed and administered by an authority constituted by a legal system against which the offence is committed.**

To view the criminal law as an adjunct to punishment draws us inevitably into a philosophical discussion of the purposes and justification of punishment. This is represented as an ideologically polarised debate between retributivists seeking "just deserts" and utilitarians seeking to prevent crime by deterrence, rehabilitation or incapacitation: "such crude extremism readily spills over to create rival caricatures of the criminal law as a whole": S Shute, J Gardner and J Horder, *Action and Value in Criminal Law* (Oxford: Clarendon Press, 1993), p 3.

There is tendency in debating the nature of criminal punishment to muddle the purposes, consequences and justifications. As Hart conceded, theories of punishment do not necessarily explain what punishment is or achieves, but rather constitute "moral claims as to what justifies the practice of punishment — claims as to why, morally, it should or may be used": *Punishment and Responsibility* (Oxford: Clarendon Press, 1968), p 72. Discussion of punishment is highly normative. These various theories of punishment have influenced a wide range of issues including criminalisation, the basis and scope of criminal responsibility; the availability of defences or excuses;

---

21   N Lacey, "Criminology, Criminal Law, and Criminalization" in M Maguire, R Morgan and R Reiner (eds), *The Oxford Handbook of Criminology* (2nd ed, Oxford: Clarendon Press, 1997), p 440.

and sentencing. In the following section, we examine the background and philosophical ideas behind these rival theories of punishment and evaluate their impact on and significance to the modern criminal law.

RETRIBUTION

For many people, retribution is the primary purpose of punishment.[22] Retribution is a communal and institutionalised expression, with appropriate safeguards, of the human instinct to retaliate or seek revenge when harmed.

> The *lex talonis* is usually traced to the Old Testament injunction "an eye for an eye, a tooth for a tooth": *Exodus*, 21:24. Paradoxically, this provision of Jewish law relates not to a measure of punishment, but rather a principle of just compensation in the civil law: M Lew, *The Humanity of Jewish Law* (London: The Soncino Press, 1985), Ch 1.

To distinguish itself from vengeance, retribution holds that an offender should receive punishment proportionate to the harm caused and blameworthiness or guilt: R Fox, "The Meaning of Proportionality in Sentencing" (1994) 19 *Melbourne University Law Review* 489. There is no further purpose behind punishment, such as prevention of crime by deterrence or rehabilitation. As a consequence, retribution is "backward-looking" because it focuses on the criminal act and the offender's criminal responsibility. The revival of retributive ideals "has coincided with widespread dissatisfaction with both the deterrent and rehabilitative goals" of punishment: R Murugason and L McNamara, *Outline of Criminal Law* (Sydney: Butt, 1997), p 10.

In its incantation as "A Theory of Just Deserts", retribution occupies a dominant place in modern sentencing principles and practices.[23] This theory stipulates that there must not only be proportionality between punishment and blameworthiness, but that there must also be a proportionate relationship between the harm done and the nature and degree of punishment. In colloquial terms, the "punishment must fit the crime". Retribution is increasingly being disputed by ideas of "Restorative Justice": P Pettit and J Braithwaite, *Not Just Deserts — A Republican Theory of Criminal Justice* (Oxford: Clarendon Press, 1990). The key ideas of republican theory, and the central importance of reintegrative shaming to criminal justice, are explored below: 3.5 'Republican Theories of Criminal Justice', pp 59-63.

The theory of retribution also has implications for the substantive law. The principle of proportionality suggests lesser penalties for inchoate offences, such as attempts, since the punishment must be proportioned according to whether or not harm has been caused: see, for example, *Crimes Act* 1958 (Vic), s 321P; Ch 9, p 436. Although a person who attempts to commit a crime may possess the equivalent level of culpability as a person who is successful, the importance

---

22 Retribution is sometimes considered to be a synonym for punishment: G Davies and K Raymond, "Do Current Sentencing Practices Work" (2000) 24 Crim LJ 236 at 238. Such definitions erroneously imply that interventions promoting rehabilitation, deterrence or incapacitation are not punishment.

23 This revival has been promoted by Andrew Von Hirsch in *Doing Justice: The Choice of Punishments* (New York: Hill and Wang, 1976); *Past or Future Crimes: Deservedness and Dangerousness in the Sentencing of Criminals* (New Brunswick: Rutgers University Press, 1985); *Censure and Sanctions* (Oxford: Oxford University Press, 1993).

of proportionality in relation to *harm* justifies their different treatment. Similarly, if an accused attacks another, intending to cause grievous bodily harm, he or she will be punished less severely if the victim survives than if the victim dies. The level of blameworthiness may be the same, but the punishment will differ according to the consequences of the accused's actions.

Sentencing Aims: Retribution and Punitive Practices

In the context of modern sentencing, retribution is an important, but not overriding, consideration. At common law, the aims of sentencing may be found scattered in judicial dicta, many of which are contradictory. To promote consistency, the purpose and principles guiding sentencing discretion have been cast in legislative form in most jurisdictions. However, legislation tends to adopt a "smorgasbord" approach, allowing judges to consider a range of factors including whether the sentence is "just" and would serve the goals of rehabilitation, deterrence, denunciation and community protection: *Crimes Act* 1900 (ACT), s 429; *Penalties and Sentences Act* 1992 (Qld), s 3; *Criminal Law (Sentencing) Act* 1988 (SA), s 10; *Sentencing Act* 1997 (Tas), s 3; *Sentencing Act* 1991 (Vic), s 5(1).

Concern about lenient sentences and early release on parole has led to a law and order campaign to reinstate "truth in sentencing". To achieve greater certainty, legislation in many jurisdictions provides that offenders must serve the minimum or fixed term of imprisonment set by the court: for example, *Sentencing Act* 1989 (NSW), s 3. These political forces, combined with the victims' rights movement, have produced the controversial "mandatory sentencing" laws in Western Australia and the Northern Territory. These sentencing laws deny judges any discretion in relation to specified property and juvenile offences. It is difficult in these cases to identify any coherent philosophical justification for punishment beyond giving force to the punitive rhetoric of "law and order" politics. The discriminatory effect of these laws is explored below in Chapter 2: 3.4.3, pp 139-141.

DETERRENCE

Deterrence, unlike retribution, is concerned with preventing crime. In this sense, it is "forward-looking", viewing punishment in terms of its capacity to prevent individuals (either the accused or the general public) from breaking the criminal law. Punishment is not legitimate unless it serves as an effective deterrent: see generally JH Burns and HLA Hart, *Jeremy Bentham: Introduction to the Principles of Morals and Legislation* (London: Methuen, 1982). Deterrence is modelled on particular assumptions about human nature, namely, that since individuals are rationally motivated to maximise pleasure and avoid pain, they will freely choose not to commit crimes. It is the threat of punishment, rather than moral "goodness", that ensures compliance with the law. To motivate rational people, the punishment must also be proportionate to both harm and culpability. Punishment is measured to have maximum individual and general deterrent effect. Not only may it prevent recidivism (recurrence of crime) by punishing the offender, it also has the general effect of deterring other members of society from engaging in criminal conduct. As Burns and Hart point out these two aspects of deterrence are often confused: p 17.

Punishment can only have a deterrent effect, both general and specific, where the person has freely chosen to break the law. According to Bentham, punishment should not be applied to conduct which, morally speaking, is involuntary. As Norrie noted, this exemption of involuntary conduct would excuse "individuals who could not know the law, who have acted without intention, who have done the evil innocently, under an erroneous supposition, or by irresistible constraint": *Crime, Reason and History* (London: Weidenfeld & Nicolson, 1993), p 21. Also, to be effective as a deterrent, the criminal law must be formulated in advance in clear and accessible terms, and there must be certainty and consistency of enforcement.

Deterrence theory is a product of 18th and 19th century theorising about the nature of crime, human conduct and reason. As a general theory, it assumes that individuals are similarly situated socially, politically and economically, each rationally capable of weighing and attaching similar values to the opportunities and costs of particular courses of conduct. The difficulty with this model of human behaviour is that it generalises about human behaviour and abstracts individuals from the context of their offending.

The deterrent effect of laws is dependent on a wide range of factors including the publicity of the offence, the nature of the offence, the risk of detection and certainty of prosecution, and the social stigma attached to the offence and punishment. Empirical research on the deterrent effects of environmental crimes has suggested that a deterrent effect is correlated to two factors: the certainty of punishment, that is, the likelihood of prosecution, trial and conviction; and, to a lesser extent, the severity of punishment.[24] Clearly for these "white collar" crimes, the deterrent effect may be reasonably high since potential offenders, being successful corporate players, are more likely to be economically rational and self-interested, knowledgeable about the law and occupy a high social standing where the stigma of conviction involves significant social and professional costs. For the wider population, it is unrealistic to presume knowledge of every crime and, most significantly relevant sentencing tariffs given the range and diversity of regulatory offences contained in the modern criminal law.[25] Although it is often claimed that the prospect of being caught and going to gaol does have some deterrent effect in a general way,[26] the likelihood of detection, conviction, let alone imprisonment for many offences is very remote. This is strikingly represented in this summary of data on the "size of crime" published in Hogg and Brown, *Rethinking Law and Order* (Annandale: Pluto Press, 1998), p 10, based on data gathered by the Australian Institute of Criminology:

> **FOR EACH 1000 "CRIMES" COMMITTED**
> **400 ARE REPORTED TO THE POLICE**
> **320 ARE RECORDED BY THE POLICE AS CRIMES**
> **64 ARE DETECTED**
> **43 RESULT IN CONVICTIONS**
> **1 PERSON IS JAILED**

---

24 J Norberry, "Environmental Offences: Australian Responses" in D Chappell and P Wilson (eds), *The Australian Criminal Justice System: the Mid 90s* (Sydney: Butt, 1994), p 167, discussing research undertaken by Duncan Chappell in Canada.

25 M Moore, *Act and Crime* (Oxford: Clarendon Press, 1993) estimates that the criminal law in modern industrialised societies comprises 7000 offences: p 1. A Ashworth, *Principles of Criminal Law* (3rd ed, Oxford: Oxford University Press, 1999) estimates that there are 8000 crimes in English criminal law: p 21.

26 G Davies and K Raymond, "Do Current Sentencing Practices Work" (2000) 24 Crim LJ 236 at 239.

Clearly a complex array of factors explain legal conformity beyond the deterrent effect of punishment. Nevertheless there remains a widespread belief within the legal and wider community that punishment (specifically imprisonment) does deter crime. It is an ideology that is sustained and nourished by political "law and order" campaigns.

Although the assumptions behind deterrence (that individuals are calculating and rational agents) may be true for some people, some of the time, they do not generalise easily into a "theory of punishment". Even Jeremy Bentham, the founding father of "Deterrence Theory", had to concede the limitations of his rationalist assumptions about human nature. As Norrie observed in *Crime, Reason and History* (London: Weidenfeld & Nicolson, 1993), p 24: "The sad truth, Bentham acknowledges, for his own deterrent theory is that people know what they ought to do, but nonetheless do what they ought not to do".

Notwithstanding its shaky empirical foundations, the idea of deterrence remains politically and morally significant in criminal justice debates. With increasing scepticism in the 1970s that crime was rooted in "social factors" and that imprisonment failed to reform or rehabilitate, there was a revival of deterrence as the primary focus for crime control. Embracing deterrence was justified on pragmatic rather than philosophical grounds. As leading American criminal justice scholar, James Q Wilson, conceded in his manifesto for criminal justice reform, *Thinking About Crime* (Revised ed, New York: Basic Books, 1983), the deterrence model was favoured (p 50):

> not necessarily because of a belief that the "causes of crime" are thereby eradicated but
> because behavior is easier to change than attitudes, and because the only instruments
> society has by which to alter behavior in the short run require it to assume that people act
> in response to the costs and benefits of alternative courses of action.

Whatever the political and pragmatic appeal of this "new" approach to crime control, it suffers from the same weakness as earlier theories of deterrence. It rests on crude generalisations about human nature and the motivations to commit crime, and it removes offenders from the social and political context of their offending.

REHABILITATION

Another important aim of punishment is the rehabilitation of offenders. Rehabilitation, like deterrence, is concerned with the prevention of crime. However, it differs from deterrence by seeking to modify behaviour by changing the moral outlook of the offender rather than simply threatening or imposing a measure of pain sufficient to induce conformity. Rehabilitation views criminal behaviour as a "social disease" that, through proper treatment, is curable and preventable. The history of rehabilitation is tied to the rise of prisons and the emergence of pathological models for explaining crime in the 19th century. Until the middle of the 20th century, rehabilitation remained a plausible account of the purpose of punishment supported by sociological theories of deviance. According to these theories, criminal behaviour was "learned", the product of attitudes to offending shaped and influenced by social groups, friends and family. Faulty learning could be rectified through, among other things, psychological therapy and treatment. Due to the focus of treatment on the *individual* needs of the offender, rehabilitation is criticised from a retributivist perspective because it leads to inconsistent sentences for the same offence. Whilst rehabilitation remained popular until the 1960s and 1970s, particularly in relation to the treatment of juveniles, it has been somewhat overtaken by the revival of retributive and deterrent theories. As we shall see in Chapter 15, pp 826-827, rehabilitation is making a partial comeback with the establishment of specialised drug courts in Australia, which have been specifically constituted to provide judicial supervision of drug treatment and rehabilitation: A Freiberg, "Australian Drug Courts" (2000) 24(4) Crim LJ 213.

Rehabilitation and the Rise of the Model Prison

In terms of the history of punishment, the penitentiary model emerged as an instrument of "carceral" discipline directed to training the mind or soul of the offender. It displaced an earlier form of "corporeal" discipline directed to the physical body: M Foucault, *Discipline and Punish: The Birth of the Prison* (New York: Pantheon Books, 1977). Using Michel Foucault's theoretical approach, Mark Finnane in *Punishment in Australian Society* (Melbourne: Oxford University Press, 1997) traces these shifts through the demise of transportation and the emergence of "model prisons" in Australia: see Ch 2. The penitentiary incorporated the pervasive surveillance technology of Bentham's Panoptican and social isolation of prisoners as means of achieving "reform through suffering": see below, p 44. This new architecture of penality was supported by the emerging discipline of criminology and penology, which offered scientific explanations for offending that progressed from crude pathological or biological accounts, to more complex psychological explanations: see generally J Hirst, "The Australian Experience: The Convict Colony" in N Morris and D Rotham (eds), *The Oxford History of the Prison* (New York: Oxford University Press, 1998).

Rehabilitation uses a medical or pathological model for determining the motivations and proper treatment of offenders. This approach searches for the latent abnormalities of offenders and then deems these correlated "characteristics" as the underlying causes of crime. Deviance (whether moral, social or legal) may be constructed in terms of a "sickness" that requires diagnosis and treatment. However, these pathological conditions are not objective categories existing independently from medico-legal discourse. As the construction and subsequent de-construction of "homosexuality" as a type of sexual disorder in the 20th century demonstrates, there is a complex relationship between law and medical science in defining and punishing deviance.[27]

An emphasis on rehabilitation necessarily suppresses these wider historical, political and social forces shaping the process of criminalisation. In Chapter 15, we explore how the discovery of drug addiction as a disease in the late 19th century generated the "deficit model" of drug use that has continued to shape legal policy on illicit drugs through to the present day. By conceptualising drug use as a disease of addiction, the range of criminal justice interventions are limited to treatment options such as counselling, detoxification or maintenance programs. While the medical model undoubtedly has the capacity to blunt the criminal law, it has also diverted our attention away from controlled drug-use and alternative market-based regulatory strategies, that are now used to control other historical "vices" such as gambling and prostitution.

---

27 On the changing medico-legal status of homosexuality, and the political movement within psychology and psychiatry to remove it as a sexual disorder see E Shorter, *A History of Psychiatry* (New York: Wiley, 1997); see also L Moran, *The Homosexual(ity) of Law* (London: Routledge, 1996).

While not excluding other punishment aims, Art 10(3) of the International Covenant on Civil and Political Rights prioritises rehabilitation as the principal purpose of imprisonment:

> The penitentiary system shall comprise treatment of prisoners the essential aim of which shall be their reformation and social rehabilitation.

INCAPACITATION

Nigel Walker suggests that the "incapacitation" of those known to be dangerous should be regarded as a justification that is as sound as retributive notions of just deserts and proportionality, or notions of deterrence or the need for treatment: "Unscientific, Unwise, Unprofitable or Unjust?" (1982) 22 *British Journal of Criminology* 276. Punitive considerations of desert and proportionality, rehabilitation and deterrence cannot be applied to an accused who is not criminally responsible for his or her actions or who is incapable of rational free choice. Nevertheless the person who is dangerous and mentally impaired needs to be prevented from committing further harm.

Since the 19th century, the criminal law achieved this balance through the recognition of the verdict of "not guilty by reason of insanity". This qualified acquittal justified detention for indefinite duration in a secure psychiatric institution: see Ch 4, p 220. This sort of preventive detention is based on the presumption that an accused who caused harm once because of mental impairment, will be driven to do so again. In *Veen v The Queen (No 2)* (1988) 164 CLR 465 Deane J stated (at 495):

> The protection of the community obviously warrants the introduction of some acceptable statutory system of preventive restraint to deal with the case of a person who has been convicted of violent crime and who, while not legally insane, might represent a grave threat to the safety of other people by reason of mental abnormality if he [or she] were to be released as a matter of course at the end of what represents a proper punitive sentence. Such a statutory system could, one would hope, avoid the disadvantages of indeterminate prison sentences by being based on periodic orders for continuing detention in an institution other than a gaol and provide a guarantee of regular and thorough review by psychiatric and other experts.

The idea of "dangerousness" which underscores incapacitation is a highly malleable concept, shaped by historical, cultural and political forces: J Pratt, *Governing the Dangerous: Dangerousness, Law and Social Change* (Sydney: Federation Press, 1997). The concept was initially applied to justify the detention and treatment of individuals suffering from a mental disorder who posed a danger to themselves or others, though in recent years the concept has been used to justify preventive legislation that extends (extra-judicially) the incarceration of prisoners deemed to be "dangerous" beyond the term of their original sentence.[28]

---

28 The introduction of such extraordinary measures in Victoria is discussed in P Fairall, "Violent Offenders and Community Protection in Victoria — The Gary David Experience" (1993) 17(1) Crim LJ 40. The doctrine of separation of powers implied into State and Federal Constitutions prevents the executive or legislature usurping judicial functions. The High Court has held that an order of involuntary detention of a penal or punitive character that was not imposed pursuant to a judicial determination of guilt violated the separation of powers doctrine: *Kable v DPP (NSW)* (1996) 189 CLR 51; P Fairall, "Before the High Court: Imprisonment without Conviction in New South Wales: *Kable v Director of Public Prosecutions*" (1995) 17(4) *Sydney Law Review* 573.

The protection of society as a justification for removing an individual from it has been criticised as conflicting with the backward-looking notion of punishment for what one has done, rather than for what one might do.[29] As Anthony Duff and David Garland have observed in *A Reader on Punishment* (Oxford: Oxford University Press, 1994) (p 239):

> it is wrong, in principle, to punish offenders for their predicted future conduct: they should
> be punished for what they have done, not in respect of what they will or might do. We
> should treat individuals (unless they are insane) as moral agents who can choose whether
> or not to desist from future crimes.

There has been, however, growing acceptance that preventive detention on the basis of the protection of society is an unavoidable issue: CR Williams, "Psychopathy, Mental Illness and Preventive Detention" (1990) 16(2) *Monash University Law Review* 161 at 178.

Empirical Claims of Punishment: Fact and Fiction

In a recent article, Mirko Bagaric critically examines the utilitarian justifications of punishment: "Incapacitation, Deterrence and Rehabilitation: Flawed Ideals or Appropriate Sentencing Goals?" (2000) 24(1) Crim LJ 21. Bagaric searches for empirical evidence to support the claims that punishment does promote incapacitation, deterrence and rehabilitation. He concludes there is little empirical evidence to support any of these claims except for general deterrence. Since general deterrence is the only effective basis for punishment, specific deterrence and rehabilitation should be abolished as sentencing objectives. Bagaric's empirical claims rely on an historical analysis of outbreaks of lawlessness during police strikes, including the strike in Melbourne in 1923. With the removal of the police and therefore the threat of punishment, the bonds of civil society dissolved and anarchy inevitably followed. This finding supports his conclusion (at 45) that:

> experience shows that absent the threat of punishment for criminal
> conduct, the social fabric of society would readily dissipate. Crime
> would escalate and overwhelmingly frustrate the capacity of people to
> lead happy and fulfilled lives. Thus while there is only one objective of
> punishment which the utilitarian can invoke [general deterrence], this
> is more than sufficient to justify the practice of State imposed
> unpleasantness on those who violate the criminal law.

While we may share Bagaric's uncertainty about the empirical foundation for existing theories of punishment, his analysis of the instrumental effect of punishment, like much of the discourse he critiques, is over-determined. He ignores the other forces that operate to encourage the conditions of lawlessness during police strikes, most

---

29 See, for example, CR Williams, "Psychopathy, Mental Illness and Preventive Detention" (1990) 16(2) *Monash University Law Review* 161 at 168 and 178; Victorian Sentencing Committee, *The Report of the Victorian Sentencing Committee*, Vol 1 (Melbourne: Attorney-General's Department, 1988), pp 120-121.

obviously in the context of the Melbourne police strike in 1923, the social and economic conditions caused by the mass demobilisation of soldiers at the end of the First World War and the onset of the Great Depression. Rather than search for an explanation and justification of punishment in instrumental terms, it may be more fruitful to explore the symbolic dimensions of punishment.

SOCIOLOGICAL PERSPECTIVES

Punishment

David Garland in *Punishment and Modern Society* (Oxford: Clarendon Press, 1990) conceives punishment as a social and cultural institution, rather than merely as an instrument of state coercion. This approach provides a more complex and useful understanding of the multiple roles and meanings of punishment in modern society. Garland set out to develop a comprehensive theory drawing on insights from earlier theorists including Durkheim, Foucault, "the Marxists" and others. In reviewing the various theories of punishment over the 20th century, he highlights a number of weaknesses in earlier accounts. In Garland's view, penality "communicates meaning not just about crime and punishment, but also about power, authority, legitimacy, morality, personhood, social relations, and a host of other tangential matters": p 252. It has a powerful moralising effect: "punishment expresses and projects a definite conception of social relations, holding out an imagery of the ways in which individuals relate — or ought to relate — to one another in society": p 271.

Earlier approaches to punishment suffered from "over-determination", that is, the tendency of theorists to subscribe to a "single causal principle or functional purpose for punishment be it 'morals' or 'economics', 'state control' or 'crime control'": p 280. The complexity of punishment and its multiple layers of meaning — its *polysemic* quality — are inconsistent with mono-causal explanations. Instead of searching for a single explanatory principle, we need to grasp the facts of multiple causality, multiple effects and multiple meanings: p 281. Garland suggests that punishment should be viewed as a "social institution" with expressive and symbolic aspects (p 287):

> Punishment is, on the face of things, an apparatus for dealing with criminals — a circumscribed, discrete, legal-administrative entity. But it is also, as we have seen, an expression of state power, a statement of collective morality, a vehicle for emotional expression, an economically conditioned social policy, an embodiment of current sensibilities, and a set of symbols which display a cultural ethos and help create a social identity.

Within modern legal systems, the symbolic value of punishment may be more important than its instrumental functions. When viewed in instrumental terms, punishment is a signal failure. This is because the most effective means of inducing social conformity — those processes of socialisation that are based on an internalised sense of morality, duty, trust, loyalty, shame and so on, lie outside the jurisdiction of existing penal institutions. Approached in this broader sociological way, punishment is no longer glorified as a functionally important social institution.

Rather its limitations and alternatives to punishment are exposed, "and to the extent that punishment is deemed unavoidable, it should be viewed as a morally expressive undertaking rather than a purely instrumental one": p 292.

This sociological approach to punishment has profound implications for the criminal law. Recognition of the polysemic quality of punishment affects (or rather infects) the criminal law in many ways. Rather than be viewed as an instrument of retribution, deterrence, rehabilitation or incapacitation, the criminal law may be viewed as a part of a wider practice of cultural signification that contains and expresses multiple and contradictory meanings. A sociological approach suggests that greater attention needs to be paid to the range and diversity of the criminal law's expressive functions. These functions include both the positive capacity to produce "normality" and conformity, as well as the negative capacity to suppress and stigmatise deviance. From this perspective the criminal trial, including the law as propounded in the higher courts, far from being unimportant as early legal realists contended, assumes considerable significance as a site where fundamental "meanings" of the criminal law are expressed and contested.

While theories of punishment have influenced the shape of the modern law, it is important to recognise that the criminal law need not *necessarily* be tied to the search for the legitimacy of state punishment. Although presented as a distinctive feature of criminal law, punishment does not *always* follow a finding of guilt. A conviction may be imposed without any painful or unpleasant consequences beyond the finding of guilt. Admittedly condemnation as a "criminal" is an unpleasant consequence for most people. Even in relation to condemnation, however, a sentencing court may exercise its discretion not to record a conviction, an acknowledgment that the punitive effect of condemnation is not always needed or desirable. As we shall explore below, there is a growing international social movement in favour of reconstructing criminal justice as "Restorative Justice". Under this increasingly influential model, the search for legitimacy is redirected away from the State and its power to punish towards community-based initiatives that offer the prospect of reintegration and restoration for offenders, victims and communities affected by crime. Rather than punishment, the justifying aim of the criminal law could be viewed as the realisation of justice for offenders, victims and the community more generally.

2.6 CRIMINOLOGY AND THE CRIMINAL LAW

As a discipline, criminal law is occupied with the study and rationalisation of legal doctrine, its rules and general principles. By contrast, criminology as an applied discipline, employs a wide-range of external perspectives — drawing from sociology, history, economics, psychology, anthropology, and so on — to identify the causes of crime and to develop effective responses to "crime problems".[30]

---

30 Some criminologist tie the discipline firmly to the boundaries of the criminal law. Edwin Sutherland in *Criminology* (New York: Lippincott Co, 1974) viewed the discipline as concerned with the making, breaking and enforcement of the criminal law. Others adopt a wider focus that embraces social deviance generally: D Downes and P Rock, *Understanding Deviance* (Oxford: Oxford University Press, 1988). For an overview of the various schools of criminological thought see R White and F Haines, *Crime and Criminology* (2nd ed, Melbourne: Oxford University Press, 1996).

Theories about crime are historically contingent, shaped and re-modelled by a kaleidoscope of changing social, economic and political forces.[31] For criminal justice scholars writing in the Age of Enlightenment during the 18th century, knowledge about crime and the operation of the criminal law was pursued through scientific rationality and classification. The model of a rational and ordered criminal law emerged as a reaction to the punitive and arbitrary nature of the criminal justice system of the previous century where the criminal law served primarily to instil legal terror in the lower orders through its draconian laws and extensive use of capital punishment. Against the backdrop of this "Bloody Code", justice was not found in the fabric of substantive or procedural law, but rather was promoted post-conviction through sentence mitigation or executive clemency in the form of pardons or transportation.[32] At this time, the legitimacy of criminal law and punishment became the central focus of attention. In England, Jeremy Bentham, both a legal academic and campaigner for law reform, argued that deterrence was the only legitimate purpose for imposing criminal punishment. According to Bentham, the system of criminal law in England was both ineffective and unjust. Primarily sourced from the common law, the criminal law itself was difficult to discover and subject to gross judicial manipulation in the courts. As Norrie noted, "Bentham called it 'dog law' for it condemned individuals after the event, in the way that a person punishes his [or her] dog. The dog only learns after the punishment that what it has done is wrong."[33]

Bentham's utilitarianism challenged this approach to punishment, proposing in its stead a rational and humane system of laws and penalties. To maximise rationality and deterrence there must be proportionality between the crime and the punishment — the level of punishment must be equal or proportionate to the level of harm inflicted by the accused. Under this approach, the self-interested person would conclude that the costs of punishment outweighed the benefits of crime and therefore make the rational decision to desist from its commission. Punishment was justified on the utilitarian theory of deterrence based upon an individual rational calculation of self-interest. Norrie in *Crime, Reason and History* (London: Weidenfeld & Nicolson, 1993) summarised this theory as follows (p 21):

> In England, the utilitarian reformer Bentham wrote that mankind was placed under two sovereign masters, pain and pleasure, and possessed an innate tendency to avoid one and seek the other. The ability to calculate rationally the consequences of actions combined with the pain/pleasure principle to enable the individual to maximise his [or her] self interest.

Bentham took the view that a criminal code based on legislation rather than common law would be a more effective deterrent. Law must be certain and knowable to operate as an effective deterrent.

---

31 The historical material in this section is based on B Mason, "From Shamans to Shaming: A History of Criminological Thought" in K Hazlehurst (ed), *Crime and Justice* (Sydney: LBC, 1996), Ch 2.

32 A Norrie, *Crime, Reason and History* (London: Weidenfeld & Nicolson, 1993), pp 18-19. See further EP Thompson, *Whigs and Hunters: The Origins of the Black Act* (London: Allen Lane, 1975). In the Australian context, the extent to which transportation constituted a form of punishment or an opportunity for rehabilitation is discussed in M Finnane, *Punishment in Australian Society* (Melbourne: Oxford University Press, 1997), Ch 1.

33 A Norrie, *Crime, Reason and History* (London: Weidenfeld & Nicolson, 1993), p 21. Bentham's preference for legislation over common law stood in stark contrast to the earlier views of Blackstone who eulogised the common law in *Commentaries on the Laws of England* (9th ed, London: Garland, 1978) (first published, 1765).

To achieve this, rational and systematic codes of offences, along the lines of those adopted in civil law systems, were required. Bentham predicted that adopting a comprehensive criminal code would reduce crime to virtually nil. Although Bentham's ambitions for the codification of criminal law were unsuccessful in England, they did take root in several Australian jurisdictions. We explore the differences between Code and common law jurisdictions in Chapter 2: pp 70-74.

The impact of these liberal utilitarian values on law has been significant and enduring. The modern criminal law is stamped throughout with liberal assumptions about "freewill" and "rationality" as measures of culpability. The emergence of the "reasonable man" in both the civil and criminal law may be viewed as the fictive embodiment of the rational, self-interested person against whom the conduct of ordinary people will be judged: A Norrie, *Crime, Reason and History* (London: Weidenfeld & Nicolson, 1993), pp 22-26. The influence of this conception of human action has been profound, constituting "the major model of human behaviour held to by agencies of social control in all advanced industrial societies": I Taylor, P Walton and J Young, *The New Criminology* (London: Routledge and Kegan Paul, 1973), pp 9-10.

CRIMINOLOGICAL PERSPECTIVES

Freewill versus Determinism

Bentham's theories concerning the criminal law coalesced with the new science of crime — criminology — emerging in Continental Europe. The emergence of this new discipline concerned with the nature and cause of crime is tied to the history of the bickering Italian "schools" of the 18th and 19th centuries. The father of the "Classical School of Criminology", Cesare Beccaria, published *Essay on Crimes and Punishments* (London: F Newberry, 1770, first published 1764) which set out a manifesto for criminal justice reform. Beccaria, like Bentham, wrote against the backdrop of an arbitrary and severe criminal justice system. His conception of crime was rooted in the liberal values of the Enlightenment; crime was explained as a matter of free choice exercised by rational individuals, rather than being caused by evilness or the supernatural forces. Both Beccaria and Bentham shared the view that the criminal law must incorporate the principle of hedonism — that is, since humans are possessed of free will and rational choice, they will choose to obey the law because the pain of punishment will outweigh the pleasure. To minimise interference with individual freedom, the punishment meted out must be no more than is necessary to prevent or deter crime.

Arguments about the perceived value of deterrence from explanatory and moral perspectives have waxed and waned with criminological theories about the nature of crime and criminals. The liberal values and optimism of the "Classical School" was dented by the emergence of the rival "Positivist School". The father of Positivism, Cesare Lombroso (1835-1909), explained criminal behaviour in biological terms. By measuring the skulls of cadavers, Lombroso observed that features of convicted criminals had "atavistic anomalies" — they appeared primitive and inferior. He therefore hypothesised that individuals were born "criminal" and that this was part of their nature (pathology and biology). From modern eyes, Lombroso's "science", based on observations from decomposing corpses hardly seems credible, but at the time, it seemed a natural implication drawn from Charles Darwin's theory of human evolution. As a form of "social Darwinism", Positivism had implications for the criminal law as B Mason,

"From Shamans to Shaming: A History of Criminological Thought" in K Hazlehurst (ed), *Crime and Justice* (Sydney: LBC, 1996) states (p 20):

> As the criminal's behaviour was largely determined by factors such as biology, the needs of society could best be served by adopting measures to prevent the criminal from committing further offences. For "born criminals" elimination or incapacitation (and, later medical correction of defects) was the only answer. Rehabilitation was useless where defects could not be altered.

In the Australian context, these competing conceptions of crime and criminals served to polarise and sustain a division in early colonial society between the free-born settlers (The Exclusives) and those who bore the "convict stain", the transported convicts and their descendants (The Emancipists): D Neal, *The Rule of Law in A Penal Colony* (Cambridge: Cambridge University Press, 1991), Ch 2.

By the middle of the 20th century, Positivism had been thoroughly discredited as a result of its flirtation with fascism in the 1930s, which lent scientific credence to eugenic programs and genocide for "inferior" human races. In the post-war period, biological explanations of criminal behaviour gave way to social or sociological explanations. These "modern schools" viewed crime as a social phenomenon that was, to some degree, determined beyond the capacity of the individual to freely resist. It was in a social, rather than biological sense, that crime was determined. A broader range of theories emerged, united in the hypothesis that the roots of crime lie in social structures and institutions. Theories, like Edwin Sutherland's "theory of differential association", suggested that criminal behaviour was "learned", that through interaction with others who advocate crime, deviance is normalised and encouraged.[34] Other theories stressed the causative role of social alienation and social, economic and political powerlessness. Drawing on Durkheim's theory of "anomie", Robert Merton viewed crime as a product of the discrepancy (or strain) between the aspirations of an individual and the means and opportunities available for achieving them. The weakness of the "strain theory" was that it predicted "too little bourgeois criminality and too much proletarian criminality": I Taylor, P Walton and J Young, *The New Criminology* (London: Routledge and Kegan Paul, 1973), p 107.

The post-war period was confronted by a "crisis of aetiology and penality" — notwithstanding the emergence of the welfare state, improving standards of education and prosperity, crime levels continued to rise.[35] At this time, the State, and its role in defining crime, also became a focus of study. Rather than search for "causes" of crime, researchers explored the State's role in construction of deviance and the "labelling" of crime. Crime did not exist, in an objective or natural sense, separate from the laws defining and enforcing crime: "deviance is not a quality of the act the person commits, but rather a consequence of the application by others of

---

34 Discussed in B Mason, "From Shamans to Shaming: A History of Criminological Thought" in K Hazlehurst (ed), *Crime and Justice* (Sydney: LBC, 1996), pp 22-24. This theory had the advantage of explaining working class crime and "white collar" crime committed by persons of high social class.

35 J Young, "Incessant Chatter: Recent Paradigms in Criminology", in M Maguire, R Morgan and R Reiner (eds), *The Oxford Handbook of Criminology* (2nd ed, Oxford: Oxford University Press, 1997), pp 480-482.

rules and 'sanctions' to the offender".[36] Accordingly, the role of the State in responding to moral panics, spawning new categories of crime and criminals, such as "hooliganism", became the subject of study: S Cohen, *Folk Devils and Moral Panics* (London: Paladin, 1973).

The idealism of "New Criminology" in the 1970s went even further, viewing criminality and criminalisation as essentially political acts of resistance and control respectively: I Taylor, P Walton and J Young, *The New Criminology* (London: Routledge and Kegan Paul, 1973). Criminal behaviour, it was argued, is normal and natural, merely an assertion of human diversity in a society of inequality of wealth, power and property. Criminality, on the other hand, is merely a social construct invented by the powerful to protect the interests of capital. As crime is a function of the existing social, economic and political arrangements, it would disappear when these inequalities were eradicated. Needless to say, this revolutionary Marxist idealism was short-lived.

Realist left criminology emerged as a reaction to this leftist extremism, regaining political credibility by "taking crime seriously". It aimed to be faithful to the reality of crime, recognising that victims, as well as offenders, were also drawn from the powerless sections of society. Left realism is critical of the partial approach of left idealism and its tendency to separate the causes of crime from reactions by the criminal justice system. This involves a synthesis of approaches, recognising that "all crimes must, of necessity, involve rules and rule breakers (that is, criminal behaviour and reaction against it) and offenders and rule breakers": J Young, "Left Realist Criminology" in M Maguire, R Morgan and R Reiner (eds), *The Oxford Handbook of Criminology* (2nd ed, Oxford: Oxford University Press, 1997), p 485. Jock Young conceives the nature and form of crime in terms of a "square of crime", a model of opposing dyads of victim-offender and actions-reactions: of crime and its control.

DIAGRAM 1:   The Square of Crime

The Oxford Handbook of Criminology (2nd ed, Oxford: Oxford University Press, 1997), p 486.

In relation to any crime, its nature and form are the consequence of social relationships and interactions between individuals (offender, victims and members of the public) and formal and informal agencies of social control (police, schools and family). These relationships vary for different crimes. In relation to burglary, for example, the relationship between the police and

---

36   Howard Becker, cited in B Mason, "From Shamans to Shaming: A History of Criminological Thought" in K Hazlehurst (ed), *Crime and Justice* (Sydney: LBC, 1996), p 29.

public determines the efficiency of policing; the relationship between the offender and victim determines the impact of the crime; the relationship between the state and the offender determines levels of recidivism. Left realism is concerned to restore the offender into the picture — while avoiding the biological reductionism of the past, left realists do not reject the correlations between biology and crime, whether that involves body size, hormones, size and age. Put simply, there are "facts" about crime that any theory ought to fit — such as the fact that crime is committed disproportionately by individuals who are male and young, aged between 15-25 years: J Braithwaite, *Crime, Shame and Reintegration* (Cambridge: Cambridge University Press, 1989), Ch 3.

With an increasing sense that "nothing works", many academics have abandoned criminology as a flawed discipline.[37] Others criminologists, rejecting "social" accounts of crime, have returned to the classical ideas, such as James Q Wilson's revival of deterrence and free-will theories of crime in the United States, discussed above: p 22. Others have sought to identify the causes of crime in the deficits and characteristics of individuals, denying any relationship between crime and broader social structures. Avoiding the over-determined approach to crime of biological positivism, these theorists established a multiplicity of "causal relations" between crime and other factors including genetics; low intelligence; inadequate child-rearing; inadequate single mothers; inadequate socialisation in the first five years of life.[38]

There have also been attempts to synthesise freewill and determinist theories of criminal behaviour. According to these accounts, while people do exercise choice over whether or not to commit crime, social and biological conditions may impose constraints on the choices available. This search for synthesis and comprehensive theory is evident in J Wilson and R Herrnstein's *Crime and Human Nature* (New York: Simon and Schuster, 1985). In this book, which became criminology's first "best-seller", the authors highlight the importance of "constitutional factors", such as low IQ, in explaining patterns of crime (p 103):

> social forces cannot deter criminal behavior in 100 percent of a population, and that the distributions of crime within and across societies may, to some extent, reflect underlying distributions of constitutional factors ... crime cannot be understood without taking into account individual predispositions and their biological roots.[39]

These forms of determinism are less crude than their positivist forebears. Crime is a matter of free choice, albeit exercised within a biologically and socially determined framework. However as a *general* theory, it has significant limitations. As Braithwaite observes in *Crime, Shame and Reintegration* (Sydney: Cambridge University Press, 1989), it cannot account for the massive reality of white collar crime: p 36.

---

37 Carol Smart has argued that criminology is a problematic enterprise, which marginalises the significance of gender and thus has little to offer feminism: *Law, Crime and Sexuality* (London: Sage Publications, 1995), Chs 2-3.

38 These theorists are discussed in J Young, "Incessant Chatter: Recent Paradigms in Criminology" in M Maguire, R Morgan and R Reiner (eds), *The Oxford Handbook of Criminology* (2nd ed, Oxford: Oxford University Press, 1997), pp 479-480.

39 See discussion in B Mason, "From Shamans to Shaming: A History of Criminological Thought" in K Hazlehurst (ed), *Crime and Justice* (Sydney: LBC, 1996), pp 34-35.

The search for synthesis has occupied criminologists on both the right and left of politics. In striving for this complex synthesis for Left Realism, Jock Young in "Incessant Chatter: Recent Paradigms in Criminology", in M Maguire, R Morgan and R Reiner (eds), *The Oxford Handbook of Criminology* (2nd ed, Oxford: Oxford University Press, 1997) offers the following definition of crime (p 106):

> As an activity, crime involves a moral choice at a certain point in time in changing determinant circumstances. It has neither the totally determined quality beloved of positivism, nor the wilful display of rationality enshrined in classicist legal doctrine. It is a moral act, but one which must be constantly assessed within a determined social context. It is neither an act of determined pathology, nor an obvious response to desperate situations. It involves both social organization and disorganization.

Such broad statements demonstrate the futility of criminology as an enterprise that searches for universal truths about "crime". Critical scholars who have come to reject criminology, such as Carol Smart, have doubted the value of Young's "synthesis": *Law, Crime and Sexuality* (London: Sage Publications, 1995), pp 38-39. As Young's definition itself concedes, the reasons for deviance and conformity are more complex and varied than any single "school" of criminology, theory or model of human behaviour can explain.

Notwithstanding criminology's increasingly pluralistic (and postmodern) explanations of crime, the criminal law clings firmly to traditional assumptions about the rationality and freewill of offenders. As subsequent chapters will reveal, the presumption of rationality and freewill underscore many of the key principles of criminal responsibility. The idea that these behavioural attributes are "typical" or "normal" is not supported by empirical research. Recent studies suggest that many (if not most) offenders processed before the courts have committed their crime while under the influence of alcohol and/or illicit drugs, casting doubt on the presumption that criminal conduct is the product of a rational mind possessed of free will: see Chs 4 and 15, p 199 and p 828 respectively. Legal academics, law reformers, politicians and judges nevertheless place great weight on the liberal values of clarity and predictability in deterring crime, and promoting a more effective and just criminal law. We may reasonably conclude that the assumptions about human behaviour that inform legal doctrine are truly normative ideals derived from liberalism, rather than explanatory truths supported by empirical study. There is nothing wrong with striving for a criminal law that promotes liberal values. Indeed, we shall explore below how republican theorists have set out to rehabilitate liberalism as a normative guide for the criminal law and criminal justice reform: 3.5 'Republican Theories of Criminal Justice', pp 59-63. The problem with existing approaches to the criminal law is that liberal and individualistic assumptions about agency and responsibility are represented as universal truths, rather than as normative ideals that are politically and morally contestable.

The failure to consider criminology and other external perspectives can blind lawyers, judges, legislatures and reformers to the complexities of crime and effects of criminalisation. Law reform is weakest when conceived solely as an exercise in improving the internal rationality and coherence of the law. As we shall explore in Chapter 15, in relation to serious drug offences, the Model Criminal Code Officers Committee engaged in a lengthy analysis of existing drug offences and confiscation powers without examining their historical development; the rationale for criminalisation; the validity of the distinctions drawn between different drugs and types of users; the relevance of culture and setting to drug use; and the effectiveness of alternative approaches to drug control based on regulation rather than criminalisation: pp 830ff. Such issues were deemed "political questions" beyond the scope of the Committee's terms of reference.

Criminological and sociological perspectives on crime and the criminal process are essential not merely for providing an *external* critique, but also as the foundation for *internal* critiques of the criminal law. The attempt to develop a critical theoretical synthesis of these external and internal perspectives, which Lacey calls "criminalization", is explored below, pp 45-47.

2.7 THEORIES OF CRIMINAL JUSTICE

Concerns about the legitimacy of the criminal law, as already noted, are linked to its processes as well as its substantive content. As we shall explore in Chapter 2, the general principles relating to fairness, equality and privacy play an increasingly important role in ensuring legitimacy within the criminal justice system. As Herbert Packer recognised in *The Limits of the Criminal Sanction* (Stanford, CA: Stanford University Press, 1968), theoretical discussion about the criminal law must address questions about the nature of criminal punishment, culpability (criminal responsibility) *and* the criminal process.

The purpose of the criminal process is typically represented in terms of "crime control", namely, that the guilty should be detected, convicted and duly sentenced: A Ashworth, "Concepts of Criminal Justice" [1979] *Criminal Law Review* 412. Legitimacy in this mission is ensured by proper observance of "due process of law". Packer constructed these objectives as two competing models of criminal process — "the normative antinomy at the heart of the criminal law": p 153.

MODELS OF CRIMINAL JUSTICE: CRIME CONTROL AND DUE PROCESS

Models have been a popular way of analysing the criminal justice system. Packer's theory of criminal justice draws two models of criminal process into dialogic tension — "Crime Control" *versus* "Due Process". As the Crime Control Model is concerned with the repression of criminal conduct, its emphasis is on social control and maintaining public order. In this sense, "the criminal process is a positive guarantor of social freedom": p 158. Considerable attention is paid to promoting efficiency, with stress on effectiveness and the avoidance of legal rules that are obstacles to this objective. However, the efficient apprehension and disposition of offenders does not take place in a political vacuum: the quantity and quality of resources available for crime control are not infinite. Thus, efficiency is an important consideration that demands both "speed and finality". Speed depends on informality, while finality is achieved by minimising opportunities for challenge. The process must not be cluttered by steps that impede the closure of a case. This consideration favours reliance on administrative rather than judicial procedures. Hence Packer coins the metaphor of an "assembly-line" for the Crime Control Model: p 159. Informal but efficient procedures are given priority, leading to widespread reliance on confessions as a means of inducing guilty pleas and the efficient disposal of cases. The efficient handling of cases demands a system that screens out cases unlikely to result in convictions whilst securing convictions in the remainder as expeditiously as possible with the minimum opportunity for challenge. This depends on the earliest possible determination of guilt or innocence.

According to Packer, the key factor determining whether a case proceeds further is the presumption of guilt: "The presumption of guilt is what makes it possible for the system to deal efficiently with large numbers, as the Crime Control Model demands": p 160. Packer goes on to deal with the relationship between this presumption of guilt and its "polestar" — the presumption of innocence. The development of the presumption of innocence and its role in ensuring fairness is explored in Chapter 2: pp 114-123. Since these two concepts are directed to different ends, they should not be viewed as opposites. The presumption of innocence is a direction as to how officials are to proceed: that even in the face of overwhelming evidence the suspect is to be treated as innocent. In contrast, the presumption of guilt that operates as part of the Crime Control Model is purely and simply a prediction of outcome: "the presumption of guilt is descriptive and factual; the presumption of innocence is normative and legal": pp 161-162. The presumption of guilt is central to the Crime Control Model: the dominant goal of repressing crime can be achieved through summary processes, without loss of efficiency, because of the probability that the preliminary screening processes used by the police and the prosecution contain adequate guarantees of reliable fact-finding. It follows that the criminal process must place as few restrictions as possible on administrative fact-finding and, in particular, on police powers. Minimal control over the police is a central feature of the Crime Control Model. Another way that Packer puts this is that the "center of gravity" of the process lies at the early stages of fact-finding *before* trial: p 162. Subsequent stages are relatively unimportant. The Crime Control Model has very little use for many conspicuous features of the adjudicative process, and in real life works out a number of ingenious compromises with them, such as plea-bargaining.

Crime Control is counter-balanced by the Due Process Model. Packer uses the metaphor of an "obstacle course": a series of procedures designed to impede the suspect's further progress through the system: p 163. Packer rejects the idea that Due Process is the obverse of the Crime Control Model. The Due Process Model is not founded on the idea that repression of crime is socially undesirable, although some critics often assert this. Its starting point is different. The focus in this Model is not on the prevention of crime but on the control of State power in a liberal democracy. Within liberal democracies, the primacy of the individual is stressed: "The aim of the process is at least as much to protect the factually innocent as it is to convict the factually guilty": p 165. The Due Process Model stresses the possibility of error in fact finding. For example, witnesses may be mistaken or confessions may be unreliable. Hence, there is a suspicion of informal fact-finding and a premium placed on the use of legal procedures of formal, adjudicative, and adversarial processes for discovering and evaluating evidence. These concerns about fallibility predominate, supporting the wide availability of reviews and appeals: "The demand for finality is thus very low in the Due Process Model": p 164.

In reconciling the competing demands of efficiency and reliability, the Crime Control Model will tolerate some degree of error. By contrast, Due Process insists on the prevention and elimination of such mistakes. Rules are developed, such as the presumption of innocence and the burden of proof, that have nothing to do with the factual question of guilt, but are designed to ensure the observance of standards that limit the exercise of official power. As Packer concedes, it is unconvincing to say that a person who, after police investigation, is charged with a crime is probably innocent. What Due Process requires is that the State must be forced to prove its case and this brings into operation a whole series of rules designed to limit the use of the criminal sanction against the individual, and increase the accused's opportunity of securing a favourable outcome: p 167. Even when a person's guilt is clear, the legitimacy of the process is what matters: it is more important to constrain errant police and prosecutors than to secure a conviction.

CRIME CONTROL AND DUE PROCESS: A FALSE DICHOTOMY?

Packer's use of models to explain the criminal justice system, in particular the dichotomy drawn between Crime Control and Due Process, has attracted significant criticism. His construction of the criminal justice system draws a distinction between the role of the police (who promote Crime Control) and the courts (who uphold Due Process). Presented in these binary terms, the models are antagonistic: when the system promotes one set of values, it necessarily undermines the other.

Doreen McBarnet in *Conviction: Law, the State and the Construction of Justice* (London: MacMillan, 1981) is highly critical of the validity and assumptions of this distinction from a sociological and theoretical perspective. McBarnet argues that empirical analysis of the criminal process reveals Packer's models as drawing a "false distinction": p 156. The dichotomy underlying Packer's theories reflects the earlier distinction drawn by American Legal Realists between "law in action" and "law in the books". Crime Control is what happens, Due Process is what *should* happen: pp 4-5.[40] This binary conception of criminal justice leads lawyers to believe that reforms require merely greater fidelity to the values of due process and legality in the criminal process, rather than subjecting the values themselves to further independent or critical scrutiny.[41]

McBarnet argued that this approach was unsatisfactory. Her research suggested (p 156) that "law in action", rather than being a deviation from the "law in books", was condoned by the law.

> If the practice of criminal justice does not live up to its rhetoric, one should not only look to the interactions and negotiations of those who put the law into practice but to the law itself ... Deviation from the rhetoric of legality and justice is institutionalised within the law itself.

Due Process did not set a standard of legality from which the police deviated, but rather provided police, lawyers and judges with a licence to ignore the rhetoric of legality and justice in many cases. McBarnet concludes (p 156):

> If we bring due process down from the dizzy heights of abstraction and subject it to empirical scrutiny, the conclusion must be that due process is *for* crime control.

---

40 Packer would reject this criticism since he argued that his models "are not labelled Is and Ought, nor are they to be taken in that sense": *The Limits of the Criminal Sanction* (Stanford, CA: Stanford University Press, 1968), p 153.

41 See for example FA Allen, *The Habits of Legality — Criminal Justice and the Rule of Law* (NY: Oxford University Press, 1996). Other legal scholars have argued that the principles of due process and legality should be subject to critical evaluation and reconstruction using external normative sources, such as ethics and human rights: see A Ashworth, *The Criminal Process* (2nd ed, Oxford: Oxford University Press, 1998), Ch 3; S Bronitt and M Ayers, "Criminal Law and Human Rights" in D Kinley (ed), *Human Rights in Australian Law* (Sydney: Federation Press, 1998), Ch 6.

McBarnet's inversion of the conventional rhetoric of justice has been criticised as an "over-generalisation".[42] While it must be conceded that due process does impose some constraints on crime control, McBarnet's thesis usefully highlights the importance of empirical research in exposing the realities and contradictions behind the rhetoric of criminal justice.

The "gap" between the rhetoric and realities of criminal justice are managed in a number of ways. Both in its substance and structure, the law provides considerable room for judicial manoeuvre. Fundamental principles are subject to numerous judicial and legislative qualifications. For example, a core idea at the heart of due process is the "fair trial". However, a closer examination of legal doctrine reveals that this so called fundamental common law right is only an entitlement to a trial as *fair as the courts can make it*. In Chapter 2, we further explore the contradictions between one rhetoric and realities of the fair trial principle in Australian law: pp 95-97. General principles may be venerated in judicial rhetoric, while simultaneously distinguished and confined by the "particular facts" of the case. McBarnet notes that this flexibility in adjudication allows lawyers and judges to balance the contradictory demands of crime control and due process, and to manage the gap between the rhetoric and practice "out of existence": p 161.

McBarnet's research also drew attention to "two tiers of justice" within the criminal justice system, contrasting the "ideology of triviality" that pervaded the lower courts with the "ideology of justice" available for public consumption in the higher courts.[43] This finding is significant bearing in mind that the bulk of criminal matters are initiated and determined in the magistrates' court.

Australian Crime — Facts and Figures 1999 (Australian Institute of Criminology)

- Over 1.7 million cases were initiated in magistrates' courts in 1997-1998. These cases accounted for 98.2% of matters initiated in the criminal courts.

- Only 1.5% of cases were initiated in the intermediate courts and 0.3% of cases in the supreme courts.

- 66% of the criminal matters initiated in magistrates' courts were of a minor nature.

- There has been a 21% increase in the number of matters initiated throughout Australia since 1994-1995.

- Nationally, there were approximately 543,000 court hearings in 1997-1998, 390,783 of a criminal nature.

- The majority of criminal hearings (93%) took place in the magistrates' court: p 39.

---

42 Russell Hogg has criticised McBarnet's conclusion on the ground that it simply replaces one abstraction with another, namely, suggesting that "the law is essentially about one thing (crime control) rather than another (due process):" "Policing and Penality" in K Carrington and B Morris (eds), *Politics, Prisons and Punishment* (1991), cited in D Brown, D Farrier and D Weisbrot, *Criminal Laws* (2nd ed, Sydney: Federation Press, 1996), pp 240-241.

43 D McBarnet, *Conviction: Law, the State and the Construction of Justice* (London: MacMillan Press, 1981), Ch 7; D McBarnet, "Two Tiers of Justice" in N Lacey (ed), *Criminal Justice* (Oxford: Oxford University Press, 1994).

As these statistics reveal, the proceedings of magistrates courts are not confined to trivial matters. Nearly half of the criminal matters heard by magistrates (44%) could be characterised as "serious". Magistrates are not confined to regulatory or minor crimes. They deal with a wide range of offences, many carrying the risk of several years of imprisonment or substantial fines. What is truly striking is that so little legal and academic attention is paid to this part of the criminal process. As McBarnet concludes: "what happens in the lower courts is not only trivial, it is not really law": p 153. This process of inversion means that 93% of criminal proceedings, many of which have serious consequences for the parties involved, are constructed as "exceptions" to the rule of due process. As we shall explore in Chapter 2, this is certainly a valid criticism of the right to a fair trial, which has been restricted by the High Court to trials of "serious offences" and excludes pre-trial proceedings such as committals conducted before a magistrate. In Chapter 13, we shall also explore the implications of these two modes of fact-finding (jury versus magistrate) for the test of dishonesty in theft. Although most legal discussion proceeds on the assumption that a jury will determine the meaning of dishonesty by reference to the standards of "ordinary decent people", in the majority of cases this issue is determined by a magistrate sitting without a jury. Judicial involvement in the construction of "community standards" using moral rather than strictly legal values gives rise to concern that the attribution of legal blame is less objective, neutral and apolitical than is commonly claimed.

McBarnet's theory has many implications for our understanding of the criminal process and the direction of criminal justice research. It encourages deeper reflection on the structure and functions of law in the criminal process and the apparent tensions and contradictions within legal doctrine and its fundamental principles. These perspectives are further explored in our critical review of general principles in Chapter 2. The acceptance of Packer's model by researchers has tended to conceal or minimise the role of law in constituting criminal justice practices. McBarnet criticises sociologists and criminologists who study the behaviour of police, prosecutors and judges, but who ignore the role that law plays in shaping and constituting such behaviour.[44]

An excellent example of research that does recognise the significance of law to understanding criminal justice practices is David Dixon's *Law in Policing: Legal Regulation and Police Practices* (Oxford: Oxford University Press, 1997). This empirical study of English and Australian policing reveals that the law for the police is not conceived as a "rule book" to be either followed or ignored, but rather serves as a "tool" or normative resource that is used by police officers in performing their diverse roles of maintaining social order, and preventing and apprehending crime. His study exposes the complexity and contingency of law in policing and concludes "law's relationship with policing depends upon the nature of the law, the type of policing, and the social and political contexts": p 318.

The value of studying criminal process lies not merely in gaining knowledge about the legal rules and practices governing criminal investigation and conduct of a trial. Rather, it provides the resources for developing an appreciation of how changes to substantive law have had an impact on methods of

---

44   D McBarnet, "False Dichotomies in Criminal Justice Research" in J Baldwin and K Bottomley (eds), *Criminal Justice* (London: Martin Robertson, 1978).

investigation and procedure, and vice versa. The focus on confession evidence in modern policing is undoubtedly related to the increasing emphasis placed on subjective mental states from the late 19th century onwards, and the gradual displacement of constructive or imputed forms of criminal fault. Lindsay Farmer has traced similar synergies between the massive expansion of the summary jurisdiction during in the 19th century and legislative efforts to impose stricter forms of liability for a wider range of "regulatory" offences — measures which were designed to improve the administrative efficiency and reach of the criminal law: L Farmer, *Criminal Law, Tradition and Legal Order* (Cambridge: Cambridge University Press, 1997), pp 122-126.

Another weakness of Packer's models of criminal process is the unproblematic view of "crime". The difficulty with the Crime Control Model is that the notions of "guilt" and "offenders" are conceived as existing, in some phenomenological sense, distinct from the institutions and practices involved in investigation and the production of evidence. As we explore below, this approach fails to recognise that guilt is not simply the product of legal rules applied at trial, but is "constructed" at an earlier stage by the key players within the system such as police, prosecutors and informers. Also, the Crime Control Model does not conceive repression of *police* illegality as part of its mission. Pro-active policing techniques involving illegality by the police, such as unlawfully inciting others to commit crimes, cuts across Packer's distinction which was drawn between "the criminal" and "the crime-controller". In Chapter 15 we explore the pervasive practice of police entrapment in drug law enforcement: pp 870ff.

BEYOND BALANCING CRIME CONTROL AND DUE PROCESS: PROMOTING HUMAN RIGHTS

At the core of Packer's binary conception of criminal justice implicitly lies the importance of ensuring "balance" between the normative antinomies of Crime Control and Due Process. Andrew Ashworth rejects Packer's conception of criminal justice as a "balance" between two poles. In an article called "Concepts of Criminal Justice" [1979] *Criminal Law Review* 412, Ashworth recognised that the general justifying aim of the criminal process was crime control, though this was subject to three main qualifiers (at 413):

▰ **considerations of system (that is, resources);**

▰ **principles of fairness; and**

▰ **control of abuse.**

Unlike Packer's model, where Due Process is the only constraint on Crime Control, Ashworth's concept of criminal justice accommodates both economic and public policy interests as legitimate constraints. Considerations of "system" impose economic limitations on the criminal process — since full enforcement of the criminal law would impose an unreasonable cost on society, decisions to arrest and prosecute must be discretionary. This approach supports practices that encourage cooperation such as sentencing discounts, plea-bargaining and infringement notice systems for minor offences. Controlling abuse by law enforcement officials is a further qualifier. It is not an end in itself, but rather a means of maintaining the balance between the State and the citizen. Not only does it have instrumental value, subjecting police to the rule of law, it also serves to maintain public confidence in the administration of criminal justice. In the Australian context, the importance of maintaining public confidence underlies the judicial discretion to exclude evidence that was illegally or improperly obtained (*Bunning v Cross* (1978) 141 CLR 54) and the inherent power to grant a stay of proceedings on the ground of "abuse of process" in order to prevent an unfair trial (*Dietrich v The Queen* (1992) 177 CLR 292).

Debates about criminal justice reform tend to pivot on the need to "balance" the rights of suspects against the public interest in detecting, preventing and prosecuting crime. The weakness of this approach is that it suggests that Due Process and Crime Control exist in some sort of hydraulic relationship to one another.[45] Far from maintaining the perfect equilibrium, the criminal justice system, as McBarnet contends, consistently favours the interests of the State and the community over the individual.

Ashworth in "Crime, Community and Consequentialism" [1996] *Criminal Law Review* 220 has similarly pointed to the distorting effect of balancing metaphors in debates about criminal justice reform. Rather than balancing interests or rights, Ashworth proposes that reformers must first determine the aim of a given part of the criminal process and then ascertain what rights *ought* to be ascribed to the affected parties (the law enforcement agency, prosecution and defence counsel, suspects, accused and the community): at 229. In a powerful critique of balancing, he proposes that criminal justice reform, rather than adopting a utilitarian approach, should ensure maximum protection for fundamental human rights. Balancing metaphors are banished and instead careful consideration is given to the justification of rights and their relative strength: "Conflicts cannot always be avoided, and choices have to be made, but the principle should be maximum respect for rights": at 230. The flawed approach of balancing rights is further explored in Chapter 2: pp 104-109.

This approach of promoting rights is not unproblematic. As we shall explore in the next chapter, some feminist and critical scholars have rejected "rights discourse": pp 128ff. Rights have traditionally favoured liberal political agendas, promoting individual over collective or social interests. There has been a lively debate about the value of rights, with critical legal scholars exposing the failure of rights to remedy disadvantage within marginalised communities. Other theorists have not abandoned rights discourse, viewing the challenge as involving the reconstruction of key concepts (such as fairness, equality and privacy) around a different set of priorities and goals. Rather than simply promote rights as unqualified liberal goods or as ends in themselves, we shall explore below how these legal tools may be employed strategically to realise alternative social or "republican" conceptions of justice.

RISK MANAGEMENT: BUREAUCRATIC AND TECHNOCRATIC MODELS OF CRIMINAL JUSTICE

The increasing emphasis on promoting "efficiency" in the criminal process has led some theorists to represent the concept of criminal justice in bureaucratic or managerial terms. Michael King in *The Framework of Criminal Justice* (London: Croom Helm, 1981), sketches a bureaucratic model of criminal

---

45   D Dixon, *Law in Policing: Legal Regulation and Police Practices* (Oxford: Clarendon Press, 1997), p 284 citing
     J Braithwaite, *Crime, Shame and Reintegration* (Cambridge: Cambridge University Press, 1989), pp 158-159.

justice: pp 21-23. Within this model, the aim of the system is the efficient processing and disposal of cases, a model that is most prevalent in the lower courts: p 22. Efficiency is the key objective though it is not restricted to the narrow interests of "crime control" in the sense of maximising the detection and conviction of the guilty. The emphasis is on gathering and managing information about suspects and offenders, as well as minimising the costs associated with the administration of criminal justice.

Such a model prioritises administrative processes over formal legal procedures. The ubiquitous use of the police caution is justified in terms of efficiency in disposing of a case without trial. The system of "cautioning" assists in the management of suspects. It provides "formal" notice to suspects that they are "known to the police" and may therefore act as a deterrent. From an internal bureaucratic perspective cautions (though not resulting in a conviction) are counted as "clearances" for the purpose of measuring police performance. With only limited opportunities for suspects to challenge the legality of cautions,[46] the working informal definitions of illegality and permissible excuses used by the police stand mostly unchallenged.

Other practices within the criminal justice system have similar qualities, such as infringement notices used to deal with minor offences, such as speeding. However, the presumed efficiency gains of promoting infringement schemes in lieu of prosecution must be subject to critical scrutiny. As we shall explore below, the power to issue infringement notices in relation to possession of small quantities of cannabis has resulted in significant increases in court appearances and convictions for drug offences. Mandatory sentencing laws may also be understood in terms of promoting efficiency. Removing sentencing discretion not only promotes (formal) equality, it also dramatically streamlines the sentencing process. It dispenses with the need for lengthy hearings where evidence is tendered and contested on the nature of the offence, the background of offenders' and the prospects for rehabilitation.

As the next section reveals, there is a danger that "efficient" disposal mechanisms privilege bureaucratic concerns over other values, such as due process and protection of human rights.

Actuarial Justice: The New Criminal Law

The term "Actuarial Justice" was first coined by Malcolm Feeley and Jonathon Simon to denote the "New Penology" based on management of risk: "Actuarial Justice: The Emerging New Criminal Law" in D Nelken (ed), *The Futures of Criminology* (London: Sage Publications). Many initiatives in criminal justice (including new criminal laws) have been directed to identifying and managing "dangerousness" in the community. This trend has justified the use of incapacitation and preventive detention and the profiling of offenders posing a risk of danger to the community. For a collection of articles exploring these developments see P O'Malley (ed), *Crime and the Risk Society* (Aldershot: Ashgate, 1998).

---

46 Cautions are warnings given by the police that they believe an offence has been committed, but have exercised their discretion not to proceed. Cautions, while practically significant, have no formal legal status, and there is limited scope for challenging the grounds of a caution: R May, "The Legal Effect of a Police Caution" [1997] *Criminal Law Review* 491.

PERSPECTIVES

Technocratic Justice: "Decriminalising" Cannabis

Pat O'Malley has explored the rise of managerialism in the criminal justice system, which he calls "technocratic justice": "Technocratic Justice in Australia" (1984) 2 *Law in Context* 31. The use of infringement notices and expiation schemes, commonly known as "on-the-spot-fines", may be viewed as measures of technocratic justice. Infringement or expiation schemes are now widely used by the police and other law enforcement officials, such as health and safety inspectors, to manage an increasing range of offences. These offences are no longer confined to minor traffic infringements, but extend to serious offences such as the possession of narcotics. These diversionary schemes offer, at first glance, significant savings in terms of system costs since there is no hearing and the "penalty" paid covers enforcement costs. The failure to pay the penalty is made a distinct offence, though only in cases where the person has not elected to contest the notice of infringement. From the offender's perspective, irrespective of guilt or innocence, compliance with the scheme is encouraged because the negative cost of prosecution and conviction outweighs the relatively minor pecuniary burden of the penalty. O'Malley's conclusion is that the displacement of due process from the system in effect "de-moralises crime and renders it merely a breach of administrative regulation": at 46.

There is an increasing range of "civil offences" of a morally ambiguous character: p 45. These include the possession of small quantities of cannabis which has been "decriminalised" through the introduction of infringement notice schemes in the Australian Capital Territory and South Australia. These reforms were initially welcomed by law enforcement officials and reformers as sensible alternatives to prohibition that would promote "harm minimisation". However, these schemes have neither increased diversion from the criminal justice system or blunted the coercive edge of the criminal law. Indeed, there have been significant increases in the number of prosecutions and convictions for minor drug offences in both jurisdictions: L Atkinson and D McDonald, "Cannabis, the Law and Social Impacts in Australia" *Trends and Issues in Crime and Criminal Justice,* No 48 (Canberra: AIC, 1995). As a result, many lower courts have become clogged with prosecutions of defaulters for non-payment of fines as well as possession of drugs. These "unintended consequences" are related to the wide use of infringement notices in preference to cautions for minor offences, and the high levels of fine-default. Unlike individuals who receive "on-the-spot" fines for minor motoring offences, drug users who typically come to the attention of the police are, from a socio-economic perspective, poorly placed to pay the fine and thus avoid prosecution.

> The trend toward de-moralisation of the modern criminal law, though strong, is not pervasive. Kathy Laster and Pat O'Malley have identified a counter-narrative of emotionality in some areas of the criminal law, such as rape and domestic violence: "Sensitive New-Age Laws: The Reassertion of Emotionality in Law" (1996) 24(1) *International Journal of the Sociology of Law* 21. The authors compare the emergent emotional paradigm with technocratic and positive/rationalist paradigms, concluding that the law must strive to integrate all three legal paradigms.

To manage and control suspect populations efficiently, bureaucratic models rely heavily on knowledge of suspect populations. Attention is focused on how knowledge about crime and criminals is generated, managed and deployed by the institutions and processes of criminal justice. As Russell Hogg has pointed out, it is important to recognise that the objects under scrutiny, namely "crime" and "criminals", are not external to the practices of criminal justice: "Perspectives on the Criminal Justice System" in M Findlay, S Egger and J Sutton (eds), *Issues in Criminal Justice Administration* (Sydney: Allen & Unwin, 1983). Hogg is critical of the prevailing models, including McBarnet's, for its failure to examine the process by which knowledge is created within the institutions and process of criminal justice: p 9. Hogg's approach is overtly influenced by Foucault's ideas about power and the production of knowledge: "Power operates in and alongside the processes of knowledge formation, designating certain objects of knowledge, while blocking others, constraining the analyses that might be constructed": p 10.

Knowledge about crime and criminal justice is produced at a number of different levels and locations. There are internal informal sources of knowledge generated into day-to-day policing through stereotyping and informers: R Settle, *Police Informers* (Sydney: Federation Press, 1995). There are also other popular sources that generate knowledge about criminal justice (such as the media, both news and fiction) that then feed back into research and policy: A Howe (ed), *Sexed Crime in the News* (Sydney: Federation Press, 1998). As we shall explore in later chapters, there is a complex interrelationship between community fear, the politics of law and order and criminalisation. Fears about "stalking", "drug raves", "consumer terrorism", "homosexual pedophiles" and even "hooning" have justified the creation of new police powers and offences. The responsiveness of public order law to community fear and the politics of law and order is explored below in Chapter 14: pp 744ff.

The significant role played by the police in the construction of knowledge about "suspects" is borne out by the research of Mike McConville, Andrew Saunders and Roger Leng in *The Case for the Prosecution* (London: Routledge, 1991). This empirical study supported a theory of "case construction", namely, that police accounts of any event may be represented in numerous ways: "official accounts are problematic, selective renderings of complex realities": p 7. The process of case construction is continuous. At each stage the question of "what happened?" is the subject of "interpretation, addition, subtraction, selection and reformulation": p 12. In short, evidence is "constructed" rather than merely discovered. As a result of case construction, pre-trial processes are often determinative of outcome. Although theoretically the outcome of an investigation might depend on the application of the correct legal definition of fault required for an offence, in practice, the police simply direct their efforts to obtaining a confession for the purpose of inducing a guilty plea so that technical definitional questions are rendered redundant.

This process is apparent in other areas of the law. In Chapter 14, for example, we shall explore how the police play a determinative role in constructing "disorder" in one realm of public order law. Police definitions of "good order" are practically and legally unassailable. As Lawrence Lustgarten concluded in "The Police and the Substantive Criminal Law" (1987) 27(1) *British Journal of Criminology* 23 at 29: "a key characteristic of all preventive public order offences, is that the police are a complainant, judge, and, in all but a few cases, jury as well". The extent to which public order law imposes restrictions on political protest, or conversely upholds fundamental human rights of peaceful assembly, association or expression, has less to do with formal legal definitions and more to do with police culture and training. The police, as gatekeepers of the system, make crucial decisions in the management of cases that do not rest exclusively on formal legal judgments.

Surveillance is integral to the process of creating and managing knowledge of suspect populations. Indeed, its prevalence within modern societies leads some scholars to suggest that the dominant objective of the criminal process is no longer crime control, but rather surveillance. Surveillance is not limited to suspect populations, but also extends to law enforcement officials and institutions. This trend toward "system surveillance" explains the increasing use of Royal Commissions to generate knowledge about the criminal justice system and notorious miscarriages of justice: R Ericson, "The Royal Commission on Criminal Justice Surveillance" in M McConville and L Bridges (eds), *Criminal Justice in Crisis* (Edward Elgar Publishing, Aldershot, 1995), Ch 11. In Australia, this trend has not been limited to general structural concerns, but has focused on specific crime threats and even particular suspects. The ad hoc Royal Commission is now supplemented by specialised investigative bodies, such as the Independent Commission Against Corruption and the National Crime Authority. In New South Wales, the *Royal Commission into the New South Wales Police Service* established to investigate claims of corruption and paedophilia led to the establishment of a permanent specialised investigative agency, called the Police Integrity Commission, to investigate, prevent and detect serious corruption: *Police Integrity Commission Act 1996* (NSW). As Richard Ericson concludes, these trends pose considerable dangers to fundamental human rights since "[s]uspects' rights are displaced by system rights. Justice becomes a matter of just knowledge production for the efficient management of suspect populations": pp 139-140.

Foucault on Crime and Punishment

Surveillance in the modern context not only produces knowledge about crime and criminals, it also has disciplinary dimensions. In *Discipline and Punish — The Birth of the Prison* (New York: Pantheon Books, 1977), Michel Foucault traces the transformation of disciplinary technologies from their initial focus on the "corporeal" (capital punishment), to the "carceral" (the rise of the penitentiary) and finally, to the emergence of "risk management". He examined the new surveillance technologies developed in the 19th century that aimed to produce "docile bodies", such as Bentham's model prison that incorporated the Panoptican. The Panoptican's circular design subjected prisoners to the constant but invisible threat of surveillance from a central observation point. In his famous essay "The Panoptican versus New South Wales" (1802) Bentham trumpeted the model of prison reform as a preferable solution to transportation: M Finnane, *Punishment in Australian Society* (Melbourne: Oxford University Press, 1997), Ch 2.

Another implication of Foucault's theorising for law is that since governance is always incomplete and partial, it leads inevitably to further attempts at governance, which themselves are incomplete and partial, and thus the cycle of governance perpetuates itself: A Hunt and G Wickham, *Foucault and Law — Towards a Sociology of Law as Governance* (London: Pluto Press, 1994).

2.8 TOWARDS CRITICAL SYNTHESIS: A THEORY OF "CRIMINALISATION"

Legal scholarship plays a significant role in constituting the conceptual boundaries and vocabulary of the criminal law. As this chapter has demonstrated, there is no single *concept* of criminal law. Rather there are multiple and contradictory accounts of its nature and function. Yet many textbooks (to the extent they acknowledge theory at all) restrict themselves to the province of analytical jurisprudence and liberal theory. As we shall further explore in Chapters 2 and 3, the theoretical foundations of general principles in the criminal law are firmly based in the moral and political concerns of liberalism, particularly the need to provide a legitimate basis for State interference with individual liberty, especially the right to freedom of person and property.

Liberal accounts of the criminal law have not gone unchallenged. In the 1980s, Critical Legal Scholarship (CLS) emerged in the United States.[47] In the field of criminal law, Mark Kelman exposed through close textual analysis the internal "politics" of legal discourse. This internal or immanent critique unmasked the indeterminacy and contradictions of "general principles" in the criminal law. Kelman demonstrated that, notwithstanding a subjectivist rhetoric underlying doctrines such as subjective fault elements, the law wavered between "freewill" and "determinist" accounts of human action. The principal weakness of the early CLS movement was its failure to develop an "external critique", or to engage in normative reconstruction within the structure of law. As Lacey concludes, developing an internal critique requires engagement with a broader set of "historical, political, and social questions about the conditions and existence and efficacy of particular doctrinal arrangements".[48]

In recent years, this deficiency in critical scholarship has been largely rectified. Norrie's *Crime, Reason and History* (London: Weidenfeld and Nicolson, 1993) is an outstanding example of the meshing of internal and external perspectives on the evolution and role of subjective fault elements in the criminal law. In this book, Norrie uses legal history to critique the modern principles of criminal responsibility. His study reveals that the criminal law's commitment to subjectivism, rather than being a timeless and universal principle, was formed in the crucible of social and political forces in the 19th century and remains, in the 20th century, the site of struggle and contradiction.

> Roger Cotterrell in "Why Must Legal Ideas Be Interpreted Sociologically" (1998) 25 *Journal of Law and Society* 171 suggests that a socio-legal approach requires an appreciation of the political, social and cultural contexts of legal development, as well as a commitment to theorising law as a social phenomenon: at 183. Such sociological perspectives are not merely a "desirable supplement but an essential means of legal understanding": at 192.

---

47 The emergence of "CLS" is reviewed in N Lacey, "Criminology, Criminal Law, and Criminalization" in M Maguire, R Morgan and R Reiner (eds), *The Oxford Handbook of Criminology* (2nd ed, Oxford: Clarendon Press, 1997), pp 440-441; and D Nelken, "Criminal Law and Criminal Justice: Some Notes on their Irrelation" in I Dennis (ed), *Criminal Law and Criminal Justice* (London: Sweet and Maxwell, 1986), pp 152-155.

48 N Lacey, "Criminology, Criminal Law, and Criminalization" in M Maguire, R Morgan and R Reiner (eds), *The Oxford Handbook of Criminology* (2nd ed, Oxford: Clarendon Press, 1997), p 443.

Socio-legal perspectives reject the notion that "crime" is a given act of law creation. The study of the crimes must be placed within a wider disciplinary terrain that encompasses the criminal law, criminology and criminal justice studies. Lacey uses the term "criminalization" to describe this broader conceptual framework:

> the idea of criminalization captures the dynamic nature of the field as a set of interlocking practices in which the moments of "defining" and "responding to" crime can rarely be completely distinguished. It accommodates the full range of relevant institutions within which those practices take shape and the disciplines which might be brought to bear upon their analysis; it allows the instrumental and symbolic aspects of the field to be addressed, as well as encompassing empirical, interpretive and normative projects.[49]

An important aspect of this project, beyond attention to formal legal analysis, is a close examination of the rhetorical and aesthetic structure of legal doctrine. The unrelenting quest for integrity in law — order, rationality and coherence — has an important symbolic and ideological function. As explored above, the prospect that the criminal law can be stated in rational and principled terms is essential to the notion of legality and the rule of law. This concept of criminal law directs our disciplinary efforts to "tidying up" the criminal law. However, resolving incoherence through conceptual analysis often masks the internal contradictions within the law and limits the normative choices available for reform. Legal scholarship is deeply implicated in this process of constructing the criminal law. An approach that draws only on a narrow brand of (liberal) moral and political philosophy severely inhibits the potential to imagine the criminal law and its organising principles differently.

The challenge offered to scholars and students who embrace "criminalization" is awesome. Since the conception of the criminal law is less bounded than traditional accounts, the potential disciplinary terrain is vast. Peter Alldridge in *Relocating Criminal Law* (Aldershot: Ashgate, 2000) similarly proposes that the discipline must be broadened to encompass crime, criminal law and criminal justice. Adopting this broadened perspective brings into focus questions related to human rights, victims and globalisation of crime: pp 18-23. This "no-exclusions" approach to criminal law is certainly daunting. The only strategy for coping with this approach is to become conscious and comfortable with the "gaps" in our knowledge. In many areas, the process of critically (re)thinking and (re)reading the criminal law from internal and external perspectives is at an embryonic stage of development. Forays beyond doctrinal analysis or analytical (liberal) jurisprudence are undoubtedly hampered by the conservative nature of legal culture. New sources of knowledge and ideas may engender hostility from within the profession and the academy on the grounds that they fragment and disorder the discipline of law. Critical scholarship is necessarily "messy", producing more complex, fractured and pluralistic accounts of the criminal law. As Manderson has pointed out, rather than viewing this quality as a form of legal anarchy in need of order, an aesthetic theory of law, building on traditions of legal pluralism and critical scholarship, would value and celebrate legal diversity: "Beyond the Provincial: Space, Aethestics, and Modernist Legal Theory" (1996)

---

49 N Lacey, "Criminology, Criminal Law, and Criminalization" in M Maguire, R Morgan and R Reiner (eds), *The Oxford Handbook of Criminology* (2nd ed, Oxford: Clarendon Press, 1997), p 448.

20(4) *Melbourne University Law Review* 1048 at 1069. Celebration of diversity stands in stark contrast to the uncritical "principled approach" to criminal law that understands "inconsistency" as "incoherence" requiring remediation. Through its many editions, *Howard's Criminal Law* (5th ed, Sydney: Law Book Company Ltd, 1990) searched for its principles through the conceptual rationalisation of the law governing a narrow range of substantive offences and defences. While highly influential, such texts have failed to provide an explicit explanatory or normative platform (beyond the promotion of clarity, coherence and rationality) upon which to evaluate the criminal law.

An understanding of legal principle must step beyond an inquiry into clarity, coherence and rationality. The study of criminal law must seek to expose rather than conceal doctrinal contingency and contradiction. It can no longer focus exclusively on "serious crimes" for which imprisonment is the usual penalty. More importantly, it must place these principles of law in a broader context using a variety of external disciplinary perspectives. As Lacey observed in *Unspeakable Subjects* (Oxford: Hart Publishing, 1998), a critical approach towards the criminal law need not necessarily descend into "disempowering relativism" where one interpretation is as good as another: p 228. The process of exposing contradictions in legal doctrine need not be an exercise in mindless "trashing" — it opens up spaces for normative reconstruction which are often concealed by traditional accounts of legal doctrine.

We believe that adopting a socio-legal and socio-theoretical approach to the criminal law pays both academic and practical dividends. Broader perspectives not only encourage more realistic accounts of the criminal law, they also encourage more imaginative debate about the scope, possibilities and limits of law reform. These perspectives may be used to challenge and subvert the law's epistemological claims of objectivity, universality and neutrality. As we shall explore in Chapters 5 and 6, the tests for self-defence and provocation are based on "objective" gender-neutral standards. Liberal concerns about equality are addressed simply by replacing the overtly discriminatory standard of the "reasonable man" with the genderless "reasonable or ordinary person". However, as feminists have observed, law reform that only tackles formal discrimination does little to address the myths and stereotypes about women as potential victims and perpetrators of violence that may influence the assessment of "reasonableness" of a woman's conduct by the judge, jury or magistrate. Notwithstanding its purported neutrality, the "reasonableness" of the defensive actions and beliefs of a woman who kills her abusive partner, or who carries an irritant spray because she lives in constant fear of male violence, continues to be defined in masculine terms: *R v Taikato* (1996) 186 CLR 454. Feminist scholarship has been directed to confronting this gendered reality and reconstructing the "reasonable" and "ordinary" standards in the law in more inclusive terms. Such a project, in both academic and practical terms, is aided by external disciplinary perspectives. Insights from psychology on the "battered women syndrome" (mediated through expert evidence) have been used to bolster claims of provocation and self-defence. As we shall review in Chapter 6, the benefits and pitfalls of such forensic strategies continue to be hotly debated both inside and outside the courtroom. There remains considerable scepticism whether such "external" perspectives on violence against women are credible in terms of psychology or law: Ch 6, 2.8 'Battered Women and Self-Defence', pp 306-310.

3. RECONSTRUCTING THE CRIMINAL LAW

In the process of rational construction and reconstruction of the criminal law, the legal community (that is, the broader interpretive community comprised of lawyers, judges and legal academics) is influenced by a wide range of normative theories.[50] Normative discussion may not be explicit, but rather remains latent within legal discourse. The concealment of the "ethical" in legal discussion may be viewed as a symptom of modernity. It forms part of positivism's efforts to separate law and morality and denial of the existence of normative choices within the criminal law. As a consequence, the dichotomy between constructing and reconstructing the criminal law, between explanatory and normative perspectives, is often conflated. Indeed, the unconscious slippage from the "is" to the "ought" is a powerful rhetorical strategy of legal persuasion used by lawyers, judges and academics alike. Even in relation to contextual and critical scholarship, there is a tendency to merge "the question of explaining legal doctrine with the rationale reconstruction of arguments and justifications for particular legal provisions": D Nelken, "Criminal Law and Criminal Justice: Some Notes on their Irrelation" in I Dennis (ed), *Criminal Law and Criminal Justice* (London: Sweet and Maxwell, 1986), p 154.

To provide resources for normative reconstruction, this section provides an overview of some significant theories. The purpose of this section is to review the origins, aims and key tenets of these theories, as well as highlight their implications for the reform of the criminal law. While some theories relate to protecting liberal values, such as preventing harm to individuals and limiting the power of the state, others are concerned with communitarian or social interests, such as welfare or the republican hybrid of "social freedom".

The normative ideas addressed in this chapter are not exhaustive. The contribution of feminism to reconstructing the criminal law is not separately addressed in this chapter. This deficiency is rectified in the next chapter, which reviews the feminist critique and reconstruction of the fundamental notions of justice, fairness, equality and privacy in the context of the criminal law. Later chapters address feminist critiques of defences such as provocation and self-defence, and specific crimes such as rape and domestic violence.

This section pays limited attention to another increasingly influential external perspective — Law and Economics. This external perspective on law, which is highly influential in the United States, has only limited explanatory and normative power for the criminal law. Its fundamental weakness, like deterrence theory, is that it presumes that individuals are always self-interested and rational actors. Economic analysis suffers from an overdetermined view of human behaviour. As Alldridge notes in *Relocating Criminal Law* (Aldershot: Ashgate, 2000), "[w]hen applied at all, it seems to have had greatest influence in punishments, procedural rather than substantive law and in relation to acquisitive crime rather than other offences": p 13.

---

50   For an exploration of the concepts of "community" in legal discourse, its power to create and legitimate communities by defining and excluding others, is explored in N Lacey, *Unspeakable Subjects* (Oxford: Hart Publishing, 1998), Ch 5.

The Chicago School of Criminal Law

Law and Economics offer useful insights in relation to the criminalisation of commodities such as drugs, but viewed as a grand theory for regulating of types of behaviour, it necessarily involves crude forms of reductionism. For example, rape has been conceived as an appropriation of sexual intercourse — viewed as a commodity — on "unjust terms": D Dripps, "Beyond Rape: An Essay on the Difference Between the Presence of Force and the Absence of Consent" (1992) 92 *Columbia Law Review* 1780. On this view, the law of rape simply operates, or should operate, to protect the proprietary interests in one's own body. Posner's analysis of rape is discussed in P Alldridge, *Relocating Criminal Law* (Aldershot: Ashgate, 2000), p 14. As feminists point out a significant drawback to the objectification or commodification of sex is that it can attach no value to other non-material interests connected with sexuality requiring legal protection, such as pleasure, communication, trust, respect and sexual health. For a useful review of Law and Economics see S Parker and S Bottomley, *Law In Context* (2nd ed, Sydney: Federation Press, 1998), Chapters 11-15. For essays specifically addressing criminal law issues, see R Posner and F Parisi (eds), *Law and Economics Volume II: Contracts, Torts and Criminal Law* (Cheltenhan UK: Edward Elgar Publishing Limited, 1997) and J Coleman and J Lange (eds), *Law and Economics Volume I* (Aldershot: Dartmouth Publishing Company Limited, 1992), Part V.

3.1 THE PREVENTION OF HARM

Liberalism has exerted a significant influence on both the shape and substance of the criminal law. Liberal political theory in the 19th century had a profound impact on criminal law since it required those creating laws, and thus interfering with individual freedom, to *justify* state intervention in the lives of citizens. Liberalism conceives personal liberty and autonomy as matters of prime importance. Individual freedom should not be curtailed simply to promote public morals or the interests of the State.

As a principle of political philosophy, this idea was championed in the mid 19th century by John Stuart Mill in *On Liberty* (London: Harmondsworth, Penguin, 1974) (first published, 1859). Restrictions on individual liberty must be curtailed and are justifiable only in order to prevent harm to others (p 68):

> [T]he only purpose for which power can be rightfully exercised over any member of a civilised community, against his [or her] will, is to prevent harm to others. His [or her] own good, either physical or moral, is not a sufficient warrant. He [or she] cannot rightfully be compelled to do or forbear because it will be better for him [or her] to do so, because it will make him [or her] happier, because, in the opinion of others, to do so would be wise, or even right.

The criminal law should not be used to prohibit non-harmful behaviour, or to prevent individuals from harming themselves, or simply to enforce a particular conception of morals or public interest. As Norrie notes in *Crime, Reason and History* (London: Weidenfeld and Nicolson, 1993), the harm principle is a product of 19th century liberalism, reflecting a view that the social world is founded upon individual self-interest and rights: p 19. It aims to accommodate the principal concerns of the State whilst respecting individual freedom and autonomy. The harm principle has played an influential role in the criminal law, informing debates over whether homosexuality and prostitution pose a sufficient threat of "harm to others" to warrant criminal sanction. It has also provided the philosophical framework for debating the scope of consent in the context of sadomasochistic assaults: see Ch 11, pp 562ff.

Law Reform and Liberal Agendas

Law reform projects have been largely preoccupied with promoting liberal process values of certainty, coherence and rationality. A recent review of the law of consent by the Law Commission in the United Kingdom marked a significantly different approach to the role of theory in providing a framework for reform. The Commission engaged in (albeit in an Appendix) an extended philosophical discussion divided into two stages. Stage One examined the criminalisation of harmful activity from the approaches of liberalism, paternalism; and legal moralism. Stage Two examined the impact of criminalisation on the process values, such as the importance of "the Rule of Law" and efficiency in the administration of justice: Law Com (CP No 39), *Consent in the Criminal Law* (London: HMSO, 1995), pp 245-283. This theoretical discussion is largely disconnected from the substantive discussion. The paper also fails to discuss competing theories, such as the principle of welfare. Adopting Joel Feinberg's rejection of "legal paternalism and moralism" (see below), communitarian concerns are crudely depicted in negative terms. Notwithstanding these limitations, the relative theoretical sophistication of the paper is striking compared to the previous paper on this topic that avoided any engagement in abstract philosophical questions: cf Law Com (CP No 122), *Offences against the Person and General Principles* (London: HMSO, 1992).

The primary difficulty with the harm principle is the central notion of "harm to others". The definition of what constitutes "harm to others" is notoriously unstable and difficult to apply.

There is considerable disagreement over whether offensive or insulting behaviour is conduct that causes "harm to others". Joel Feinberg in *The Moral Limits of the Criminal Law: Harm to Others* (New York: Oxford University Press, 1984) explored this aspect of the harm principle, proposing a broader conception of harm that encompasses a "setback to a person's interest": p 215; see also J Schonsheck, *On Criminalisation: An Essay in the Philosophy of the Criminal Law* (Dordecht: Kluwer, 1994). In his later work, *Offense to Others* (New York: Oxford University Press, 1985) Feinberg refines these ideas through the development of the "offense principle", which would permit the use of criminal prohibitions in order to prevent serious offense or hurt to other persons. As we shall further explore in Chapter 14, while superficially attractive, the history of criminalising "offensive conduct" reveals that the concept of offensiveness is legally constructed and enforced in ways that can discriminate against minority groups: pp 792ff. Another difficulty with Feinberg's theory, as noted by Ashworth, is that it fails to address the moral, political and cultural nature of the interests "set back": *Principles of Criminal Law* (3rd ed, Oxford: Clarendon Press, 1999), p 32.

Further questions and uncertainties concerning the scope of the harm principle have also arisen:

=== **Must harm be direct, or can it be indirect?**

=== **Is it based on the notion of physical harm or can it include psychological or economic harm?**

=== **To what extent, if at all, does the principle accommodate conduct involving potential harm?**[51]

There are often sound moral, social and political reasons for broadening the harm principle to include conduct which causes *indirect* harm to others. As we shall explore in Chapter 12, this argument is often used by feminists to justify tighter criminal regulation of pornography — obscene publications are claimed to cause harm indirectly by increasing the likelihood of sexual assault and perpetuating discrimination against women: pp 653ff. In Chapter 14, we will examine how some theorists have argued for the criminalisation of racial vilification on the ground that it is necessary to prevent harm in the form of "psychic injury": pp 769ff.

From a traditional liberal perspective, such expanded notions of harm significantly weaken the harm principle as a means of maximising freedom and curbing State power. In addition to the problems of indeterminacy and elasticity, another limitation is that the harm principle is anthropocentric in its focus. This means that it is difficult to justify criminal prohibitions where conduct causes harm to the environment but has no harmful effects on human beings.[52] It also has an individualistic focus which would confine the criminal law to measures preventing harm to individuals rather than preventing harm to communities or groups.

As a normative resource for the criminal law, the harm principle operates as an *exclusory* guide. It explains why some activities should *not* be criminalised, but it does not explain why activities *should* be criminalised. Not only do we have problems in defining harm, but the harm principle is hardly descriptive of the modern criminal law. Many regulatory offences prohibit conduct that does not cause *direct* harm to others, while other crimes restrict conduct that only indirectly causes harm. Nevertheless, the harm principle holds an enormous sway over debates in the criminal law. As Nicola Lacey and Celia Wells in *Reconstructing the Criminal Law* (2nd ed, London: Butt, 1998) conclude, the harm principle is best viewed "neither as an ideal nor as an explanation but rather as an ideological framework in terms of which policy debate about criminal law is expressed": pp 7-8.

3.2 MORALITY

The normative quality of labelling and punishing wrongdoing underscores the idea that the criminal law serves, and ought to serve, the function of enforcing morality. Morality may be conceived either in religious or secular terms. In legal systems where religious and secular law is aligned, for example, in jurisdictions applying Islamic law, religious morality has legal force. In common law systems, the

---

51 The harm principle certainly supports the existence of crimes such as murder, assault and rape, but falters in explaining the criminalisation of many regulatory offences and inchoate crimes such as attempts or conspiracy unless an extremely elastic notion of harm is adopted: R Murgason and L McNamara, *Outline of Criminal Law* (Sydney: Butt, 1997), p 6.

52 In debates about the legality of abortion, the further question arises whether the rubric "harm to others" extends to embryos and foetuses. See further, J Seymour, *Childbirth and the Law* (Oxford: Oxford University Press, 2000), Ch 8.

Christian religion (more specifically the canons of the Church of England) has exerted an influence on secular law through the ecclesiastical jurisdiction. The ecclesiastical jurisdiction has left its vestigial mark on the criminal law through offences of perjury and blasphemy, and defences (now abolished) such as the "benefit of clergy" and marital rape immunity.

> **Most of ecclesiastical crimes have been abolished — the principal exception being the crime of perjury (lying under oath). However, the rationale of perjury has changed over time. From its original religious rationale of protecting individuals from damnation for bearing false witness, perjury has been remodelled into a secular offence protecting the integrity of the administration of justice. For a review of the transition of criminal process from a religious to a secular system of justice, see J Hunter and K Cronin, *Evidence, Advocacy and Ethical Practice* (Sydney: Butt, 1995), pp 9-24.**

Religious morality has exerted some influence on the shape of the criminal law, but the normative principle that the criminal law *ought* to be used only to enforce morals was revived this century by Lord Devlin, a distinguished English judge. Devlin sought to defend morality as the organising principle for criminalisation against encroachment from the harm principle in a series of lectures in the 1950s, published later as *The Enforcement of Morals* (London: Oxford University Press, 1965). This book has been described as a "classic example of a populist morality justification" for the criminal law: N Bamford, *Sexuality, Morals and Justice* (London: Cassel, 1997), p 179. Devlin contended that there existed a common positive morality that binds members of a society together and that "society may use the law to preserve morality in the same way as it uses it to safeguard anything else that is essential to its existence": p 11. According to Devlin, the "suppression of vice is as much the law's business as the suppression of subversive activities"; legislating against immorality was just as necessary as legislating against treason: pp 13-14. Rather than being gifted divinely from God, morality was "populist", derived from the shared moral beliefs of the majority of the community. Accordingly, morality could vary across cultures and history. A common morality could be determined by inquiring into what "every right-minded person" presumes to consider immoral: p 15. Whether specific conduct ought to be criminalised depended upon whether it attracted a widespread feeling of reprobation, a mixture of "intolerance, indignation, and disgust": p 17. Morality for this purpose was concerned simply with the "distinction between virtue and vice, between good and evil so far as it affects our actions": pp 18-19.

There were limitations however in this approach. Devlin acknowledged that a prima facie entitlement to use the criminal law to enforce morality could be rebutted by other considerations. These "loose principles" acknowledged the practical difficulties removing criminal laws once moral attitudes had changed; the importance of respecting personal privacy as far as possible and, most importantly in his view, that the criminal law should be concerned with established minimum rather than maximum standards of conduct.[53]

Lord Devlin's theory concerning morality and the criminal law must be understood in its political-historical context. His lectures were delivered as a conservative counter-offensive against the gathering political momentum in the 1950s to "liberalise" offences against homosexuality and prostitution. He suggested that the Wolfenden Committee was wrong to adopt the harm principle as

---

53   These principles are critically reviewed in N Bamford, *Sexuality, Morals and Justice* (London: Cassel, 1997), p 181.

the basis for decriminalising homosexual acts performed in private between consenting adults: *Report of the Committee on Homosexual Offences and Prostitution* (London: HMSO, Cmnd 247, 1957). Devlin argued that since there is a general abhorrence of homosexuality, society would be entitled to use the law to prohibit or impose some regulation on these objectionable practices. The moral standards of a community are based on those of the "reasonable man": p 24. Since no society can teach morality exclusively by religion, the law must base itself on Christian morals and, to its ability, enforce them (p 25):

> not simply because they are the morals of most of us, nor simply because they are the morals which are taught by the established Church ... but for the compelling reason that without the help of Christian teaching the law will fail.

While the religious basis of Devlin's normative claims is problematic, his proposal to use law to enforce common moral values is supported by empirical research that suggests people are much more likely to follow laws that they believe are morally correct, and much more likely to break laws that counter their views of morality: T Tyler, *Why People Obey the Law* (New Haven: Yale University Press, 1990).

Devlin's theory, however effective it might be in terms of enforcement, runs into problems. This first difficulty is the claim that a common shared morality can be identified. Although modern society is comprised of many different cultures and religions, Devlin maintained that it was possible to identify shared moral values. In his view, morality in England in the 1950s was derived "broadly speaking" from Christian teachings. At the start of the 21st century, such claims are difficult to sustain in secular societies where religion does not buttress the law, and where separation of Church and State is vigilantly defended and constitutionally entrenched.

There have been attempts by "new natural law" theorists to conceive morality as an objective set of secular values rather than as divinely-derived or populist morals. By separating morality from religion "new" natural law philosophers, such as John Finnis, have attempted to widen its legitimacy and acceptability: *Natural Law and Natural Rights* (Oxford: Oxford University Press, 1980). Finnis has developed an argument, in the context of defending laws prohibiting homosexuality, that the criminal law should be used to reinforce moral conceptions of right and wrong conduct. He argues that notions of right and wrong in this context are determined objectively by reference to "basic human goods" necessary for human flourishing — such as life, knowledge, play and the like. The problem of subjectivity is addressed by reference to "practical reasonableness". Goods such as "family" are conceived in exclusively heterosexual terms tied to procreative capacity, with the inevitable effect of relegating all sex acts outside this framework to the category of moral worthlessness and an appropriate area for legal repression. As Nicholas Bamforth cogently points out in *Sexuality, Morals and Justice* (London: Cassel, 1997), such secular theories of morality rest on barely concealed theological foundations: "in reality his arguments make little or no sense unless one supports a conservative interpretation of Catholic sexual morality": p 174.

Both populist and new natural law theories of morality have the potential to discriminate against minority groups. The image of a reasonably harmonious society bound by shared moral values sits uncomfortably with the realities of modern secular, pluralistic and multicultural communities within which moral disagreement rages over issues such as abortion, euthanasia, pornography, prostitution, drug use and the like. The stability of a common morality is questionable even in relation to apparently uncontroversial crimes, such as murder, which purport to uphold the most fundamental of moral principles, namely the "sanctity of human life". Consider, for example, the scope of admissible defences for women who kill abusive partners. Early approaches to the problem of "battered wives" admitted no excuse or defence (provocation or self defence). Indeed, the justification for denying such claims was cast in terms of the importance of maintaining the sanctity of human life and fending off moral and social disintegration. In recent years, however, the courts have made significant changes to the law to recognise the realities confronting victims who, subject to repeated psychological and physical violence, resort to deadly force in order to defend themselves: Chs 5 and 6.

Devlin's contention that the enforcement of communal morality is necessary for "social preservation" — the disintegration thesis — is also contestable. The moral foundations of society do not, as an empirical fact, disintegrate as a result of the increasing secular nature of modern society. As legal positivist, HLA Hart, pointed out, Devlin produced no evidence to support his contention that deviation from accepted morality, such as homosexuality, threatens the existence of society. No reputable historian has maintained this thesis, and there is indeed much evidence against it. As a proposition of fact, Hart suggested that it was entitled to no more respect than the Roman Emperor Justinian's statement that homosexuality was the cause of earthquakes: HLA Hart, *Law, Liberty and Morality* (London: Oxford University Press, 1963), p 50. Hart then went on to criticise Devlin for moving from the acceptable proposition that some shared morality binds a society together to the "unacceptable proposition that a society is identical with its morality ... so that a change in its morality is tantamount to the destruction of a society": p 51. The fact that morality may change in a permissive direction does not mean that society is going to be destroyed. Hart also criticised Devlin's notion of the populist model of common morality on the ground of its capacity to trample on minority rights (p 79):

> The central mistake is a failure to distinguish the acceptable principle that political power
> is best entrusted to the majority from the unacceptable claim that what the majority do
> with that power is beyond criticism and must never be resisted.

It is questionable as to whether Devlin actually made the latter claim, but there may be a problem with distinguishing between common morality and popular prejudice. From a normative perspective, Hart proposed that using the criminal law to enforce common morality would significantly curb individual freedom since it may be used to protect individuals from causing harm (both physical and moral harm) to themselves or where no harm is caused at all.

Devlin's concept of the criminal law fits better with certain areas of the criminal law. The moralising force of the criminal law is most powerfully felt in relation to the laws governing sexual conduct. In Chapter 12 we shall explore the wide range of *crimes against morality* that proscribe as unlawful "unnatural acts" or "acts against nature". These legal euphemisms deal with a catalogue of sexual acts ranging from incest to bestiality to sexual acts between males. In relation to the latter, "homosexual offences", unlike other sexual offences, apply irrespective of the age or consent of the parties involved. Indecency and obscenity laws have also similarly evolved to protect moral interests, though as we shall see, the objectives of the law have shifted from protecting (religious) morality to protecting (secular) community standards of decency. A similar trend is also evidence in relation to property offences (Chapter 13) and public order offences (Chapter 14), where the jury is invited to apply "community standards" to determine whether conduct is dishonest or offensive respectively.

In developing the law governing sexual conduct, judges often appeal to the moral foundations of the criminal law. For example, in *Shaw v DPP* [1962] AC 220, the House of Lords revived a common law offence of "conspiracy to corrupt public morals" in order to criminalise the publishers of the "Ladies Directory" which listed contact details of prostitutes. The justification for taking action against conduct promoting prostitution and promiscuity was cast in moral terms. Viscount Simonds held (at 267) that:

> In the sphere of criminal law I entertain no doubt that there remains in the courts of law a residual power to enforce the supreme and fundamental purpose of the law, to conserve not only the safety and order but also the moral welfare of the State, and that it is their duty to guard it against attacks which may be more insidious because they are novel and unprepared for.

See further Chapter 9, pp 459-460. While it may be conceded that many serious offences (such as offences against the person and property crimes) have a moral dimension, the modern criminal law does not universally promote or enforce any particular conception of morals. The bulk of offences lack any explicit moral foundation being essentially regulatory in nature, such as motor traffic regulations. Even in relation to the question of criminal responsibility, the commitment to moral blame is weakened by the rise of strict and absolute liability offences that dispense with fault. As explored above, this trend toward technocratic and actuarial models of criminal justice has largely "de-moralised" our notions of crime and criminal responsibility.

The most important insight in relation to the role of morals in the criminal law is its symbolic and ideological effect — that is, the widespread *belief* in the community that the criminal law serves a moral function by creating and reinforcing moral consensus and conformity. Once again, consistent with Garland's approach to punishment explored above, it is the symbolic and expressive functions of criminal laws in upholding core moral values that are more important than their instrumental effects.

3.3 THE PUBLIC INTEREST

Rather than appeal to divinely inspired abstract moral principles, modern judges and lawyers justify the criminal law in secular terms of the interests and values of "the public". While appearing to be neutral and objective, the public interest is a highly political concept. As we shall explore in Chapter 2, the "public" is shaped by the "private", and vice versa. Feminist scholarship has revealed that public/private dichotomy is a malleable legal construct, with the power to render legally invisible the discrimination of women, children, gays/lesbians and other minority groups.

At the substantive level, concepts of public interest and public policy are built into the structure of many criminal offences and defences. For example, in relation to the law of assault, the courts have placed "public interest" limitations on the scope of consent as a defence. As we explore in Chapter 11, public interest has played a controversial and variable role in legal discussion of the legitimacy of sadomasochism. This case study reveals the malleability and contingency of the "public interest" in the criminal law.

Judicial fall-back on the "public interest" can lead to uncertainty. Its overt and discriminatory manipulation in some cases leads to the conclusion that the "public interest" is a legal device for cloaking the individual political and moral views of judges in neutral and legitimate terms. Less cynically, it may be argued that the increasing judicial resort to the language of public interest and community values reflects a changing conception within the judiciary of the courts as "community institutions".[54] The adjudication process serves an important discursive function, communicating ideas about law to the wider community not merely to parties to the litigation. As part of this educative mission, the courts are increasingly sourcing "contemporary community values" from international legal sources, rather than from judicial "common sense", "experience" or conceptions of morality and justice. In this context, those human rights contained in international treaties are increasingly used by domestic courts to assist and justify legal decisions. As the High Court has repeatedly recognised, such sources are a legitimate influence on the development of the common law, as an expression of contemporary values or fundamental rights: *Mabo v Queensland (No 2)* (1992) 175 CLR 1 at 42, per Brennan J; *Dietrich v The Queen* (1992) 177 CLR 292 at 321, per Brennan J. In Chapter 2, we further explore the role of human rights law in shaping the general principles of the criminal law: pp 111-114.

Both the courts and the legislature are concerned that the criminal justice system must maintain public confidence in the administration of criminal justice. However, "public opinion" on specific issues, particularly of a technical doctrinal nature, is difficult for either judges or legislatures to gauge. In the United States, Paul Robinson and John Darley in *Justice, Liability and Blame* (Boulder, Co: Westview, 1995) undertook an empirical study on this question that revealed significant discrepancies between public opinion on the assignment of criminal responsibility and legal doctrine. In the field of self-defence, their research revealed a gap between public opinion and legal doctrine: public opinion was extremely supportive of "self-help remedies" far in excess of those permissible under the law. Since legal observance is influenced by the extent to which laws are believed to be morally correct, the authors conclude that the efficacy of the criminal law would be significantly improved by "closing this gap".

The difficulty with this approach is that concepts like public interest or public opinion are neither neutral nor autonomous. They are highly contingent upon historical, political and social contexts. Responses to particular conduct are often shaped by moral panics and the politics of law and order. As we shall examine in Chapter 15, the enactment of Australian drug laws have been influenced by successive international moral crusades. These began with a campaign against the Chinese vice of opium-smoking in the 19th century, and continue today in the form of an international "War Against Drugs". A fundamental difficulty with Robinson and Darley's approach is that it overlooks the role of criminalisation in forming and reinforcing public attitudes to certain types of conduct — moral views held within the community do not exist in a legal vacuum. The increasing public awareness of "domestic violence" and "drink-driving" as crimes has dramatically changed the community's moral outlook on previously acceptable conduct. In this way, the law, through education and enforcement, plays a role in creating and (re)forming public opinion towards particular wrongdoing.

---

54 A Mason, "The Courts as Community Institutions" (1998) 9 *Public Law Review* 83. For a collection of essays debating the roles and limits of judicial versus parliamentary law-making, see T Campbell and J Goldsworthy (eds), *Judicial Power, Democracy and Legal Positivism* (Aldershot: Ashgate, 2000), Chs 10-18.

While public interest or public opinion are malleable concepts, and thus dubious guides for criminalisation, they have considerable symbolic and rhetorical force. As Lacey and Wells conclude in *Reconstructing Criminal Law* (2nd ed, London: Butt, 1998) (p 63):

> Both in terms of the developing definition of crime and it terms of its enforcement, the intangible phenomenon of *"public opinion"* and, perhaps more importantly, perceptions of that phenomenon, are enormously influential.

3.4 THE PRESERVATION OF WELFARE

The principle of welfare arises from a dissatisfaction with asocial individualism (liberalism and the harm principle) or paternalism (legal moralism) as the guides for the criminal law. Societal welfare is a broad, but tangible concept that is capable of promotion by the criminal law.[55] What is, or should be considered, a crime depends upon an evaluation of what is "best" for society as a whole. Thus, legislation that prohibits conduct that may lead to environmental damage can be supported on the basis that it promotes the well-being of the community. A similar justification may be made for offences relating to regulating traffic flow and workplace practices. One of the subsidiary benefits of the preservation of social welfare is the avoidance of unnecessary hardship and financial cost to the community. Welfare may justify the criminalisation of consensual conduct, such as failure to wear seat belts or drug use, on the ground that resulting injuries may impose burdens on the community through provision of health care and social services. Such costs could have been avoided by the regulation of these activities. Welfare is often viewed in terms of imposing a balance or check on the principle of autonomy. For example, the voluntary taking of drugs may be considered an expression of personal autonomy under the harm principle, but the preservation of social welfare may call for the criminalisation of such conduct because of the costs, financial and social, to the community. We explore the tension between the principles of autonomy and welfare in our discussion of drug prohibition in Chapter 15.

Modern criminal law doctrine substantially reflects liberal values and conceptions of rights in its understandings of fundamental concepts. As we shall explore in Chapter 2, liberalism has a profound and enduring influence on our legal understanding of the fundamental principles of fairness, equality and privacy. Rival normative theories on how the criminal law should operate, such as Lacey's principle of welfare, provide resources for reconstructing the criminal law around a different set of collective goals. Her principle of welfare includes "the fulfilment of certain basic interests such as maintaining one's personal safety, health and capacity to pursue one's chosen life plan": *State Punishment* (London: Routledge, 1986), p 104. To address the potentially unlimited scope for criminalisation, Lacey grounds welfare in those values, needs and interests which a society has decided through its democratic processes are fundamental to its collective social functioning, and therefore require protection by the criminal law. These community values are democratically rather than theologically derived, and so can be distinguished from Devlin's approach.

---

55 AV Lundstedt, *Legal Thinking Revisited* (Stockholm: Almqvist & Wiksell, 1956), p 137. See also, N Lacey, *State Punishment: Political Principles and Community Values* (London/New York: Routledge, 1988), Chs 2 and 7; N Lacey, *Unspeakable Subjects* (Oxford: Hart Publishing, 1998), Ch 2.

The dichotomy between liberalism and welfare is often overstated since much "liberalism orthodoxy *is* welfarist": N Lacey, *Unspeakable Subjects* (Oxford: Hart Publishing, 1998), p 54. Ashworth concedes that "criminalisation on the basis of welfare as well as on the basis of autonomy cannot be put in doubt": *Principles of Criminal Law* (3rd ed, Oxford: Oxford University Press, 1999), p 31. The difficulty with an unqualified acceptance of welfare as the basis for criminalisation is defining with any precision its goals. Anders Vilhelm Lundstedt has written in *Legal Thinking Revisited* (Stockholm: Almqvist & Wiksell, 1956), p 140 that the goals of social welfare include:

> such things as suitable and well-tasting food, appropriate and becoming clothes ... dwellings furnished in the best and most comfortable way, security of life, limb and "property", the greatest possible freedom of action and movement ... in brief, all conceivable material comfort as well as the protection of spiritual interests.

These are obviously very general aspirations and there are dangers, even when the identification of these goals are entrusted to the democratic process, that the principle of welfare may lead to overcriminalisation and to harsh and intrusive policies of law enforcement.

In most instances, the principle of welfare is not conceived as an overriding principle but rather as a rival to the harm principle that mediates and limits arguments based on the importance of autonomy. Ashworth in *Principles of Criminal Law* (3rd ed, Oxford: Oxford University Press, 1999) concludes (p 31) that: "the principles of autonomy and welfare have a degree of mutual interdependence, which should be recognised and structured": p 31. Though in his liberal-welfare framework, the danger is that the promotion of communal interests is legitimate only to the extent that they do not significantly encroach upon individual autonomy and freedom.

Across many compartments of the criminal law, there is a conflict or tension between individual and collective interests. It is possible to reconcile this tension, as Ashworth observes (p 30):

> Clearly there are conflicts between the two principles [of welfare and autonomy], but that may not always be the case. If the principle of autonomy is taken to require a positive form of liberty rather than merely negative liberty, then the principle of welfare may work towards the same end by ensuring the citizens benefit from the existence of facilities and structures, which are protected, albeit in the last resort, by the criminal law.

As we shall explore below, republicanism is a normative theory concerned with the promotion of positive social freedom (rather than negative individual freedom) that has profound implications for criminal justice reform. Along these lines, in Chapter 2, we explore how fundamental principles in the criminal law relating to fairness, equality and privacy, may be reconstructed in ways that transcend the individual/communal divide, accommodating a wider range of interests and values.

The considerations of welfare intrude into the substantive law in a number of areas. As we shall explore in Chapters 11 and 12, the defence of consent purports to uphold the liberal principle of autonomy (individual interest), but is subject to limits deemed necessary in the public interest (community interests). Legal debate is trapped within an *either/or* dialogue between liberalism and welfare, either the law should prioritise the interests of individuals over community, or vice versa. As we shall explore in our discussion of sexual assault in Chapter 12, it is possible to transcend this dichotomy. Rather than being viewed as rival models, autonomy and welfare may be drawn into a more constructive dialogue, one that offers the prospect of remodelling consent through the adoption of standards based on positive communication and disclosure of risks.

3.5 REPUBLICAN THEORIES OF CRIMINAL JUSTICE

In *Not Just Deserts — A Republican Theory of Criminal Justice* (Oxford: Clarendon Press, 1990), John Braithwaite and Phillip Pettit propose a comprehensive normative theory of criminal justice. The criminal justice system is conceived in terms of interrelated sub-systems of investigation, prosecution, guilt-determination and punishment. This comprehensive aspect of republican theory is consistent with Lacey's approach to criminalization. *Not Just Deserts* provides new theoretical resources, not merely for reconstructing the aims of punishment around non-retributive goals (as the title of their book suggests), but also for redefining the aims and scope of the criminal law and criminal process.

What follows is necessarily a brief description of a complex theory that combines insights from criminological and sociological research on crime (particularly theories of reintegrative shaming), and the political philosophy of republicanism: J Braithwaite, *Crime, Shame and Reintegration* (Sydney: Cambridge University Press, 1989) and P Pettit, *Republicanism — A Theory of Freedom and Government* (Sydney: Oxford University Press, 1997), respectively. Using insights from both criminology and philosophy, *Not Just Deserts* builds a case against the retributive and utilitarian models for the criminal justice system. Retributive justice is rejected by the authors because it has no purposes. It conceives criminal justice as the *means* of ensuring offenders receive their just deserts (that is, punishment proportionate to their wrongdoing) rather than in terms of *ends or consequences*. While deterrence is not susceptible to this criticism, the utilitarian model is also rejected because maximising happiness or the welfare of the majority is a potent threat to individual freedom. Utilitarianism renders rights unstable: "it fails to provide the criminal justice authorities with reason to take the rights seriously, attaching moral as well as legal force to them": p 44. Furthermore, where necessary to maximise overall happiness, utilitarian models would subscribe to penalisation of the innocent, "preventionism" and overcriminalisation: p 52.

Republican Inequality Perspectives on Crime and Criminal Justice

Republicanism integrates explanatory and normative accounts of crime. Braithwaite's research has identified that inequality was an important factor in understanding criminal behaviour, discovering striking correlations between levels of homicide and inequality with society. Low crime societies were characterised by active community engagement in defending the institutions of freedom. As crime is conceived as the domination by one person over another, legal responses to crime must promote freedom as non-domination. Freedom, equality and community are "key explanatory variables and central normative ideals": J Braithwaite, *Regulation, Crime, Freedom*

> (Aldershot: Ashgate: 2000), p xii. This collection of previously published essays and articles provides an excellent overview of the key elements of republican theory and the empirical research that underscored its development and refinement.

Not Just Deserts offers a comprehensive and consequentialist theory of criminal justice geared to achieving republican goals. According to this theory, the purpose of the criminal justice system should be directed to the promotion of a republican conception of liberty called "dominion" or "freedom as non-domination": p 51. Republicanism is concerned with freedom, though it is not the conception of liberty offered by classical liberalism. Both in its negative and positive forms, liberalism envisages an *asocial* concept of individual freedom that must not be interfered with by others: p 57. Republican theory reconceives freedom in *social* and *relational* terms (p 58):

> Republicans differ from classical liberals ... in arguing for a different interpretation of what the ideal of negative liberty is more or less bound to involve. According to the classical liberal interpretation, the sort of condition required is that of being left alone, a condition exemplified *par excellence* in the solitary individual. According to the republican interpretation, it is the condition of citizenship or equality before the law.

Braithwaite has summarised "dominion" as follows:

> Dominion is a republican conception of liberty. Whereas the liberal conception of freedom is the freedom of an isolated atomistic individual, the republican conception of liberty is the freedom of a social world. Liberal freedom is objective and individualistic. Negative freedom for the liberal means the objective fact of individuals' being left alone by others. For the republican, however, freedom is defined socially and relationally. You only enjoy republican freedom — dominion — when you live in a social world that provides you with an intersubjective set of assurances of liberty. You must subjectively believe that you enjoy these assurances, and so must others believe. As a social, relational conception of liberty, by definition it also has a comparative dimension. To fully enjoy liberty, you must have equality-of-liberty with other persons. If this is difficult to grasp, think of dominion as a conception of freedom that, by definition, incorporates the notions of *liberté, égalité,* and *fraternité*; then you have the basic idea.[56]

THE PRINCIPLES AND PRESUMPTIONS OF REPUBLICANISM

Dominion has three components. A person enjoys full dominion if and only if (pp 64-65):

▬ the person enjoys no less a prospect of liberty than that which is available to other citizens;

▬ this condition is common knowledge among citizens, so that the person and nearly everyone else knows that the person enjoys the prospect mentioned, they and nearly everyone else knows that the others generally know this too, and so on; and

---

56 J Braithwaite, "Inequality and Republican Criminology" in J Hagan and R Peterson (eds), *Crime and Inequality* (Stanford, CA: Stanford University Press, 1995), p 279.

⸻ the same person enjoys no less a prospect of liberty than the best that is compatible with the same prospects for all citizens.

It is the subjective aspect of dominion which sets Braithwaite and Pettit's theory apart from other consequentialist theories such as utilitarianism. By defining their goal in such a way, republican theory aims to protect individuals in a way that other consequentialist theories do not: A von Hirsch, *Censure and Sanctions* (Oxford: Oxford University Press, 1993), p 22. Braithwaite and Pettit argue that securing this state of "subjective dominion" is critical to the protection of individual rights (p 68):

> one of the most common ways in which dominion can be reduced in a society is through subjective erosion: through people, even perhaps those people who have reasonable liberty prospects, coming to lose faith in the prospects provided ... Montesquieu writes in suitable vein "The political liberty of the subject is a tranquility of mind, arising from the opinion each has of his safety. In order to have this liberty, it is requisite the government be so constituted as one man need not be afraid of another" (footnotes omitted).

Braithwaite and Pettit offer the example of convicting an innocent person to placate an angry mob. A republican will not countenance this, even where a utilitarian might, because to do so would threaten the right not to be convicted of an offence unless guilty (p 76):

> it is part of the very concept of having dominion — that a person cannot enjoy dominion fully if she perceives or suspects that the agents of the state, or indeed any other powers in the land, will not be scrupulous in respecting her rights.

To assist in interpreting the abstract goal of dominion, Republican theory identifies four general presumptions, which serve as middle range principles:

(1) **Parsimony** — the presumption in favour of parsimony, or in other words, the "presumption ... in favour of less rather than more criminal justice activity": p 87. This presumption arises because any criminal justice intervention does immediate and unquestionable damage to someone's dominion (whether the intervention be investigation, arrest, detention, prosecution or punishment) whereas the benefits of the initiative are always of "a distant and probabilistic character". Thus, the onus of proof should be on those justifying any intervention.

(2) **Checking of Power** — this is the presumption that the power enjoyed by criminal justice authorities will always be subject to checks. This presumption arises because in its absence people's subjective dominion is threatened. This presumption supports the recognition of rights (such as the right to a fair trial) as well as checking mechanisms such as accountability mechanisms.

(3) **Reprobation** — this is the presumption in favour of reprobation, or disapproval of crime, based in the recognition that such reprobation promotes dominion by reducing crime, and also by improving people's understanding of what the criminal justice system does (which promotes subjective dominion).

(4) **Reintegration** — this is the presumption that the criminal justice system "should pursue reintegration in the community, in particular the restoration of dominion, for those citizens who have had their dominion invaded by crime or punishment": p 91.

As a consequentialist theory, the purpose of the criminal justice system and its integrated sub-systems is conceived in terms of the maximisation of dominion. Unlike the harm principle, republicanism has a positive target — the promotion of dominion — rather than a negative one — the prevention of harm to others.

Responsive Regulation

Liberal as well as republican theories counsel restraint in the use of the criminal law through "presumption of parsimony". The concept promotes the use of non-legal forms of regulation (informal social norms and practices), reserving criminalisation and coercion as a method of last resort. For republican theorists, parsimony is placed within a framework of regulation characterised as an "enforcement pyramid".

DIAGRAM 2: Enforcement Pyramid

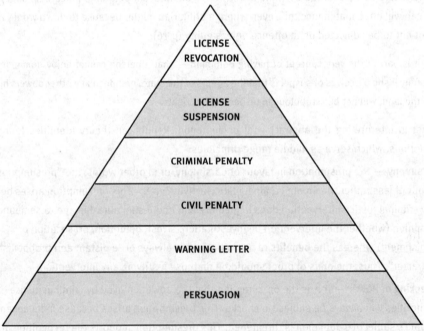

The pyramid first appeared in J Braithwaite and I Ayres, *Responsive Regulation* (New York: Oxford University Press, 1993). This version appears in J Braithwaite, "Inequality and Republican Criminology" in J Hagan and R Peterson (eds), *Crime and Inequality* (Stanford, CA: Stanford University Press, 1995), p 299. The pyramid may be adapted across a range of areas. See, for example, the pyramid dealing with intervention in cases of domestic violence in Chapter 14: p 761.

The republican regulatory approach has implications for a wide range of debates in the criminal law including: the objectives and priorities of policing; the acceptable limits of surveillance, investigation and prosecution; the scope and type of criminal laws; and sentencing: pp 92-132.

Reflections on Republican Criminal Laws

The authors of *Not Just Deserts* discussed reform of substantive areas of the criminal law in general terms. Legal academics have recently begun the process of exploring the implications of republican theory for laws dealing with public order, public health and police illegality: S Bronitt and G Williams, "Political Freedom as an Outlaw: Republican Theory and Political Protest" (1996) 18 *Adelaide Law Review* 289; S Bronitt, "The Transmission of Life-Threatening Infections: A New Regulatory Strategy" in R Smith (ed), *Health Care, Crime and Regulatory Control* (Sydney: Hawkins Press, 1998), Ch 13; S Bronitt and D Roche, "Between Rhetoric And Reality: Socio-legal and Republican Perspectives on Entrapment" (2000) 4 *International Journal of Evidence and Proof* 77. For a review of the implications of republican theory for reshaping constitutional law, see G Williams, *Human Rights under the Australian Constitution* (Melbourne: Oxford University Press, 1998), Ch 1.

Republicanism, like all of the theories discussed above, has strengths and weaknesses. Dominion is conceived in terms of "citizenship" or "equality before the law", and a central principle is "equality-of-liberty-opportunity". By using these concepts, the authors hope to avoid the limitations of formal or strict equality, and therefore offer remedies for individuals and groups who have typically been denied liberty by virtue of their status as non-citizens, such as women, children and Aboriginal persons. However, the right to equality, including the right to equality of opportunity, has been subject to extensive criticism. As we shall explore in Chapter 2, critical scholars and feminist theorists have expressed scepticism as to whether equality jurisprudence, conceived as the right to same treatment rather than respect for difference, can address entrenched structural disadvantage: pp 127-132. The failure of anti-discrimination laws based on promoting "equality of opportunity" to remedy gender and race-based disadvantage is a challenge that republican theorists must confront and resolve.

The centrality of "rights" to the promotion of republican goals may also attract criticism. As we shall explore in Chapter 2, there is a large body of literature examining the value and dangers of casting interests in these terms — the so-called "critique of rights debate": pp 128ff. There is a strong tendency in liberal discourse to fetishise rights. Legal rights are considered as "self-executing" taking no account of the social and cultural disadvantage of individuals who theoretically possess particular rights. While the structural and historical limitations of rights must be acknowledged, republicanism attaches considerable value to the instrumental and symbolic functions of rights. From a symbolic perspective, rights as a juridical form, particularly those designated as fundamental or human rights, have a powerful moralising and normative effect. Rights need not be abandoned, but redefined and harnessed to promote the republican goal of dominion. Groups that have been traditionally disenfranchised are rightfully sceptical of the empancipatory potential of social liberalism based on liberté, égalité, and fraternité (or sorority). In re-fashioning concepts and rights in a manner that most effectively promotes a social concept of liberty, "freedom as non-domination", republicanism must be sensitive to these issues of structural disadvantage.

4. CONCLUSION: INTEGRATING CRIMINAL LAW AND THEORY

As the pair of introductory quotations suggest, theory offers the tantalising prospect of a deeper, more authentic, understanding of the criminal law. Yet, in relation to the criminal law, theory very often fails to live up to its promise. Students, teachers and practitioners may legitimately question the value of theoretical perspectives on the criminal law. After all, competent legal analysis and a lifetime of criminal practice may be undertaken without any conscious intrusion of theory. However, ideas about the criminal law — how it works and ought to work — do inform our understanding of the process and substance of the criminal law. Whether packaged as "common-sense" or "fundamental principles", theories about how the law is or should be constructed are influential both in instrumental and symbolic terms. As we shall see in Chapters 2 and 3, liberalism has played a powerful role in the modern constitution of the criminal law, especially in the development of general principles and principles of criminal responsibility. Engagement with critical perspectives reveals the contingent and contradictory nature of these principles, providing scope for their normative reconstruction using alternate social, political and moral ideas.

Criminal law as a discipline defines its own jurisdiction. Its "territory" is presently narrowly defined in terms of the principles of criminal responsibility, a focus that fosters an atheoretical, ahistorical obsession with definition: L Farmer, "The Obsession with Definition" (1996) *Social and Legal Studies* 57. This preoccupation with criminal responsibility has other disciplinary consequences. Deeper engagement in theoretical questions raised by feminist, critical, historical, medico-legal and socio-legal scholarship is considered unnecessary or even disruptive to the traditional analytical enterprise. Indeed, the exclusion of these "eclectic" perspectives is sometimes justified by the demands of practical legal education. Much debate within legal education circulates around an unproductive polarity between its "academic" versus "practical" objectives. In a recent essay titled "Failed Sociologists in the Marketplace: Law Schools in Australia" (1998) 25(1) *Journal of Law and Society* 33, Andrew Goldsmith and Christine Parker explore this tension and sketch a "transformative vision of legal education". In their view, the tension between academic and practical objectives, which daily confronts law students, teachers, practitioners and judges, should be embraced positively rather than negatively. They suggest that Australian law schools should reconstitute themselves by embracing and entrenching (p 47):

═══ A broad conception of the legal knowledge which we are responsible for passing on, a knowledge based on a variety of disciplines from the humanities, social sciences and elsewhere, that allow law students to study the diverse meanings and consequences of law as a social and human variable in everyday life;

and:

═══ An expanded conception of the field of legal practice for which we prepare our students so as to integrate a critically and ethically oriented understanding of how lawyers and others carry law and legal institutions into the communities in which they live and work.

Understanding the criminal law, or any other legal subject, as a complex social phenomenon rather than simply a set of legal rules requires engagement with a wide array of perspectives. In promoting this multi-perspective approach, we have paid particular attention to neglected historical and comparative perspectives on the criminal law: P Alldridge, *Relocating Criminal Law* (Aldershot: Ashgate, 2000), pp 23-24. We envisage that this chapter, which functions both as an introduction and conclusion, will provide the explanatory and normative foundations for a deeper understanding of the meanings and limits of the criminal law in modern Australian society.

2

General Principles

> The truth is, that the law is always approaching, and never reaching, consistency. It is forever adopting new principles from life at one end, and it always retains old ones from history at the other, which have not yet been absorbed or sloughed off. It will become entirely consistent only when it ceases to grow

Oliver Wendell Holmes,
The Common Law (Boston: Little, Brown and Co, 1881), p 36

1. INTRODUCTION

This chapter explores the place of "general principles" in the criminal law. The concept of general principles embodies fundamental ideas about how the criminal process and substantive law operate, or rather *should* operate. General principles encompass both procedural and substantive matters. They also perform explanatory and normative functions. This distinction has been explained in Chapter 1, p 6. This chapter offers critical perspectives on the structure and function of general principles through an examination of the principles of territoriality, fairness, equality and privacy. It focuses primarily on principles governing the criminal process and punishment, rather than criminal responsibility. The latter principles, which are separately considered in Chapter 3, determine the conditions under which conduct or individuals should be held criminally liable. As we shall explore in the next section, the idea of general principles universally applying across all offences, while normatively significant, is a highly contestable representation of the existing law. Although claimed to be the "General Part" of the criminal law, many of these principles are routinely subject to derogation and qualification in the context of *specific* offences — for example, the presumption of a fault element is displaced for many crimes including serious drug and public order offences.

This chapter examines the process and reasoning behind the criminal law's designation of certain principles as "fundamental" and "universal". By exploring their historical, moral and political foundations, the chapter provides resources for a critical re-examination of their claims of centrality in the criminal law. The chapter is necessarily selective in its coverage. It claims neither to be an authoritative nor exhaustive account of those principles that have shaped the criminal law over time. Returning to our introductory quotation by Oliver Wendell Holmes, it is important to recognise that the law is perpetually engaged in the process of identifying new principles, reforming existing ones and abolishing obsolete ones. The chapter offers some observations on that process of doctrinal representation, laying the foundation for developing critical perspectives on the roles — symbolic as well as instrumental — of general principles within the criminal law.

2. THE STRUCTURE AND FUNCTION OF GENERAL PRINCIPLES

2.1 THE CONCEPT OF GENERAL PRINCIPLES

General principles have been a major focus of modern criminal law scholarship. The conceptual task of developing a framework for understanding the criminal law is regarded as fundamental, with practical as well as theoretical implications for the structure or form of criminal liability: P Robinson, *Structure and Function in Criminal Law* (Oxford: Oxford University Press, 1997). A "principled approach" promises a high degree of conceptual unity for criminal law. Rather than focus on the doctrinal particularities of specific crimes, attention is redirected towards "the fundamentals", that is, the *core* concepts and doctrines of the criminal law. Traditionally textbook discussion is structured around the "General Part", focusing attention on those doctrines applicable to physical and fault elements, as well as general defences. In some cases, this discussion may be prefaced by a cursory survey of selected principles governing criminal procedure and punishment.

General principles are fundamental to the promotion of the "liberal" values of certainty, consistency and predictability in the criminal law, as explored previously in Chapter 1 in 2.1 'Defining Crime and the Rule of Law': pp 7ff. As such they are an essential precondition for the modernisation and codification of the criminal law. As philosopher Michael Moore has argued in *Act and Crime* (Oxford: Oxford University Press, 1993), p 4:

> The criminal law thus needs some structure if its codification is to be possible and if adjudication under such codes is to be non-arbitrary. More specifically, it needs some general doctrines — doctrines applying to all types of action prohibited by a criminal code — in order to avoid an ungodly repugnancy and a woeful incompleteness.[1]

In jurisdictions that codify the criminal law, general principles are elevated to the status of positive law. However, reconciling these abstract general principles with the specific elements of individual

---

1   See also P Robinson, *Structure and Function in Criminal Law* (Oxford: Oxford University Press, 1997).

crimes has caused interpretational difficulties, as we explore in the next section 'Codification: Reconciling the General and Specific Part'.

General principles not only assist our understanding of the law, they also perform an important normative function. By establishing normative parameters for legal development, these principles provide lawyers, judges and academics with the tools for determining the "proper" direction for the criminal law. Operating at a higher level of abstraction than rules, principles are highly flexible. By resorting to principles, judges and lawyers free themselves from the constraints of existing doctrine. Contradictory precedent can be rationalised and reconciled, while simultaneously preserving flexibility for the development of the criminal law in future cases.

Principles generate legal rules, but they do not dictate their development. As Andrew Ashworth in *Principles of Criminal Law* (3rd ed, Oxford: Oxford University Press, 1999) has observed (p 59):

> principles may or should operate both as reasons for creating certain rules and as reasons
> for interpreting and applying the law in particular ways. They are termed "principles"
> because they amount to strong arguments based on moral or political foundations rather
> than absolute precepts: a principle can be still treated as such even if on occasion it is
> outweighed by another principle or countervailing consideration.

On this view, tension is inevitable because principles reflect a wide range of competing political and moral ideas about the legitimate scope and function of the criminal law. Sometimes principles are trumped for policy reasons. For example, the practical difficulties of proving subjective mental states in relation to drug dealing, combined with a strong political and legislative commitment to the "War Against Drugs", has displaced the presumption of a fault element in relation to drug possession and trafficking offences. The widespread derogation from the normal principles of fault attribution and cherished procedural values such as the burden of proof is further discussed in Chapter 14: pp 846-847.

As Ashworth acknowledges, there is a strong relationship between theoretical ideas and general principles. Principles, like theories, can provide "blueprints" for the development of the criminal law. This process is facilitated by theorists casting their ideas (or rather ideals) as "principles", see for example, John Stuart Mill's "harm principle"; Nicola Lacey's "principle of welfare" and the "republican principles" of John Braithwaite and Philip Pettit reviewed in Chapter 1, 3 'Reconstructing the Criminal Law'. Theoretical and general principles may share normative concerns about the proper nature and scope of the criminal law, but they perform distinct functions. Theoretical principles address "macro-level questions", such as the general nature and functions of the criminal law and criminal justice. As explained in the previous chapter, the harm principle has provided the conceptual framework for the liberalisation of homosexual offences and prostitution in the late 20th century: see pp 49-51. General principles, by contrast, address "micro-level questions", such as the forms and structure of the criminal process (how a trial should be conducted) and criminal responsibility (when a person should be found guilty). This macro-micro dichotomy should not be overstated. Theoretical contributions are not restricted to providing "guiding principles" for legislative reform. As we shall reveal in Chapter 3, the principles governing criminal responsibility dealing with agency, fault and causation have been influenced (overtly and covertly) by a range of different philosophical perspectives. Indeed, philosophical disagreement over the attribution of fault has fuelled fierce doctrinal disagreement over whether a subjective or objective mental state is the true principle of fault in the criminal law.

PERSPECTIVES

Codification: Reconciling the General and Specific Part

The identification of a set of general principles for the criminal law formed part of a modernisation project that commenced in the 19th century. Codification into a single Act of Parliament logically demands a "General Part" that deals with principles applicable to every offence. The General Part of a Code operates, in effect, as a constitution for the criminal law — setting the parameters for judging all criminal conduct. General principles, based on reason and logic, promise to curb the irrational and illogical tendencies of the common law. Since codification places the responsibility for development of the criminal law with the legislature rather than the judiciary, it represents an important instantiation of liberal values. It removes from judges their quasi-legislative power to extend the criminal law by remodelling offences and defences and minimises the risk of violation to the principle of non-retrospectivity discussed in the previous chapter. As the embodiment of Enlightenment thinking, codification sought to impose the elegance of form, structure and rationality of European Penal Codes (such as the French *Code Napoleon*) upon the substance of the common law: A Norrie, *Crime, Reason and History* (London: Weidenfeld and Nicolson, 1993), Ch 2. It became the life-long work of liberal reformers such as Jeremy Bentham and James Fitzjames Stephen in England, and Samuel Griffiths (the first Chief Justice of the High Court) in Australia.

In England, codification has proved elusive. Even today the criminal law is a hotch-potch of common law and statutory consolidations.[2] By contrast, many British colonies in the 19th century embraced the idea of codification. Codification was attractive to these transplanted British societies; it offered a comprehensive legislative Code of the English criminal law devised by the most distinguished jurists of the time. Rather than rely on the vagaries of the inherited common law, the Code provided colonial societies with a "ready-made" criminal law. In Australia, the process of codification was relatively late in its development. Codes based on a draft produced by Samuel Griffiths in 1897 were enacted in Queensland (1899), Western Australia (1902, re-enacted 1913), Tasmania (1924) and the Northern Territory (1983).[3] Griffiths envisaged that the Code should be a collected and explicit statement of the criminal law in a form that could be ascertained by an intelligent person.[4]

---

2   There has been no progress in implementing the Draft Criminal Code produced by the Law Commission in 1989: Law Comm No 177.

3   See *Criminal Code Act* 1899 (Qld); *Criminal Code Act* 1913 (WA); *Criminal Code Act* 1924 (Tas); *Criminal Code Act* 1983 (NT) respectively. The Griffith Code was also adopted in a number of British colonies and dependencies such as Papua (1902) and New Guinea (1921). On the migration of the Code see R O'Regan, *New Essays on the Australian Criminal Codes* (Sydney: Law Book Company Ltd, 1988), pp 103-120

4   Sir Samuel Griffith, "Explanatory Letter to the Attorney-General Queensland with Draft Code" in E Edwards, R Harding and I Campbell, *The Criminal Codes* (4th ed, Sydney: Law Book Company Ltd, 1992), p 5.

The liberal promise of codification can be overstated. The differences between codified and uncodified jurisdictions are not as structurally significant as often claimed. The legal assertion of the Code's primacy over the common law may be viewed simply as an application of the doctrine of parliamentary sovereignty — the fundamental status of precedent has neither been altered nor diminished in Code jurisdictions.[5] In terms of clarity, a Code, like any legislation, is not free of ambiguity. The provisions of the General Part have posed considerable challenges for the courts, either being too abstract or condensed to be construed according to their "ordinary" meaning. Since Code provisions are not self-executing, precedent develops to guide interpretation. Conversely, in those jurisdictions that have resisted codification, namely the Australian Capital Territory, New South Wales, South Australia and Victoria, it would be wrong to assume that criminal law is sourced *exclusively* from the common law. Even in these so-called "common law jurisdictions", the bulk of offences and defences have been enacted in consolidating legislation. What remains significant by comparison with the Code jurisdictions is that the common law survives as a reservoir of residual offences and doctrines available for revival by prosecutors and judges as needed.[6]

In both common law and Code jurisdictions, the High Court has played a significant role in promoting uniformity. In a number of recent decisions, the High Court has held that common law should be viewed as a "unitary" system — that there is a "common law of Australia", as distinct from nine separate systems of Federal, State and Territory common law. As McHugh J observed in *Kable v DPP (NSW)* (1996) 189 CLR 51 (at 112):

> Unlike the United States of America where there is a common law of each State, Australia has a unified common law which applies in each State but is not itself the creation of any State.

The importance of developing a consistent and unitary concept of Australian common law in relation to the test of criminal jurisdiction has been recently stressed by the High Court in *Lipohar v The Queen* (1999) 168 ALR 8 at 12-17, per Gaudron, Gummow and Hayne JJ. This decision is explored below at pp 86-88.

Codification has produced two distinct but related cultures of criminal jurisprudence in Australia. The primary difference between adjudication under a Code and other criminal legislation relates to the approach taken to statutory interpretation. As a special type of legislation, Codes are governed by their own distinct principles of interpretation. In *Charlie v The Queen* (1999) 162 ALR 463, Kirby J summarised these principles as follows (at 466):

---

5   The centrality of precedent in Code jurisdictions is apparent from the retention of "casebooks" for explaining the criminal law: see E Colvin, S Linden and L Bunney, *Criminal Law in Queensland and Western Australia* (2nd ed, Sydney: Butt, 1998).

6   For example, the concept of assault and "bodily harm" has been expanded beyond the application or threats of physical force. Recent cases prosecuted in England and Canada have held that the infliction of psychological harm and infection with a serious disease may constitute an assault: see *R v Ireland* [1997] 4 All ER 225 (HL); *R v Cuerrier* [1998] 2 SCR 371 (SC Can). As a result of this judicial innovation, special offences of stalking or transmission of HIV could be considered unnecessary: see C Wells, "Stalking: The Criminal Law Response" [1997] Crim LR 463. See further Ch 11, pp 568-570.

The first loyalty, as it has been often put, is to the code. Where there is ambiguity, and especially in matters of basic principle, the construction which achieves consistency in the interpretation of like language in similar codes of other Australian jurisdictions will ordinarily be favoured. But before deciding that there is ambiguity, the code in question must be read as a whole. The operation of a contested provision of a code, or any other legislation, cannot be elucidated by confining attention to that provision. It must be presumed that the objective of the legislature was to give an integrated operation to all of the provisions of the code taken as a whole, and an effective operation to provisions of apparently general application, except to the extent that they are expressly confined or necessarily excluded (footnotes omitted).[7]

To give effect to the liberal promise of coherence, an "integrated" approach to Code interpretation is needed. There are, however, significant difficulties reconciling the Code's "General Part" with specific offences that follow. Doubts have arisen as to whether or not general provisions dealing with criminal responsibility in fact displace or qualify the terms of specific offences. There has been a tendency toward viewing the general part of Codes as primarily educative in function, consisting of:

wide abstract statements of principle about criminal responsibility framed rather to satisfy the analytical conscience of an Austinian jurist than to tell a judge at a criminal trial what he [or she] ought to do.[8]

On this view, the meaning of general provisions cannot be determined in the abstract. Rather, "it is only by specific solutions of particular difficulties raised by the precise facts of given cases that the operation of [general provisions] can be worked out judicially".[9] General principles are subordinated to the definitional constraints of specific Code provisions rather than vice versa. Even when expressed in a Code, the idea of "fundamental" and "universal" principles guiding the interpretation and application of all offences is rhetorical and illusory.

The criminal law in the Code jurisdictions generates its own distinct jurisprudence,[10] though it would be incorrect to characterise the differences as a form of legal apartheid. In many areas, especially those relating to fundamental principles, the High Court has promoted convergence between the Codes and the common law. This is particularly apparent in cases reviewing the scope and meaning of concepts originating in the common law, such as provocation and self-defence. For example, the High Court in *Stingel v The Queen* (1990) 171 CLR 312 has

---

7   These principles are derived from dicta in *R v Barlow* (1997) 188 CLR 31-33; *Boughey v The Queen* (1986) 161 CLR 10 at 30; and *R v Jervis* [1993] 1 Qd R 643 at 647 and 670-671.

8   *Vallance v The Queen* (1961) 108 CLR 56 at 61, per Dixon CJ.

9   *Vallance v The Queen* (1961) 108 CLR 56 at 61, per Dixon CJ. In *Kenny Charlie v The Queen* [1999] HCA 23, the majority of the High Court (Kirby and Hayne JJ dissenting) held that General Part provisions in the *Criminal Code* (NT) dealing with mental states were excluded by the definition of intent specifically included in the offence of murder. Kirby J concluded (at para 20) that the general part of the Code was an "overarching provision ... a core principle of general application, a core tenet of our criminal law. It is not one which would ordinarily be confined or narrowed".

10   See R Kenny, *An Introduction to Criminal Law in Queensland and Western Australia* (Sydney: Butt, 1997); E Colvin, S Linden and L Bunney, *Criminal Law in Queensland and Western Australia* (2nd ed, Sydney: Butt, 1998).

observed (at 320) that there is a large degree of conformity in the law of provocation whether it be common law or statutory:

> in this particular field of criminal law, the common law, the Codes and other statutory provisions, and judicial decisions about them, have tended to interact and to reflect a degree of unity of underlying notions.

Although the ordinary person test developed in that case was confined to the Tasmanian Code, the subsequent decision of the High Court in *Masciantonio v The Queen* (1995) 183 CLR 58 at 66 affirmed that the test equally applied to the common law defence in Victoria. Such judicial efforts to promote uniformity in the criminal law are constrained by the language of the statute under consideration, thus restricting judicially imposed uniformity to cases involving ambiguity. As Kirby J observed in *Charlie v The Queen* (1999) 162 ALR 463 at 466, judicial loyalties should remain, first and foremost, to the provisions of the Code.

Recent proposals for codification have been part of a broader project promoting harmonisation or uniformity of criminal laws in Australia. However, consensus on the scope and content of general principles and specific offences has proven difficult to achieve. From a political perspective, the adoption of a uniform *Criminal Code* requires cooperation between the Commonwealth, States and Territories. Until recently, the Commonwealth has played only a limited role in the field of criminal law as its power to legislate is circumscribed by the heads of power in the Commonwealth Constitution. Since the enactment of a national *Criminal Code* would lack a solid legal basis under the Constitution, harmonisation of Federal, State and Territory criminal laws has been viewed as the next best alternative.

Harmonisation involves each jurisdiction enacting the same (or substantially similar) criminal laws. In 1990, the Standing Committee of Attorneys-General (SCAG) placed on its agenda the question of the development of a uniform *Criminal Code* for Australian jurisdictions. Before 1990, the pattern of harmonisation in the criminal law was ad hoc. For example, as we shall explore in Chapter 13, partial uniformity in relation to property offences was achieved in the Australian Capital Territory, Northern Territory and Victoria by the adoption of statutory provisions modelled on the *Theft Act* 1968 (UK).

SCAG established the Model Criminal Code Officers Committee (MCCOC) to draft a Criminal Code for the Commonwealth, which would provide the model for codes adopted in the States and Territories. As one of the drafters, Mathew Goode has pointed out, the aims of the *Model Criminal Code* are codification and uniformity: "Codification of the Australian Criminal Law" (1992) 16 Crim LJ 5 at 7. Codification, the principal aim, should be systematic and comprehensive, offering the prospect of a criminal law that is "easy to discover, easy to understand, cheap to buy and democratically made and amended": p 8. Significantly, the MCCOC gave priority to the codification of principles of criminal responsibility over preliminary procedural issues "as these were the very foundation of any system of criminal justice": CLOC/SCAG, *Model Criminal Code: Chapter 2 — General Principles of Criminal Responsibility* (1992), ii. The recommendations contained in this report have been enacted by the *Criminal Code Act* 1995 (Cth). Chapter 1 of the Code abolishes common law crimes, stating that the only offences against laws of the Commonwealth are those offences created by, or under the authority of, the Code or any other Act. Chapter 2 deals with "General Principles of Criminal Responsibility". Section 2.1 states:

> The purpose of this Chapter is to codify the general principles of criminal responsibility under laws of the Commonwealth. It contains all the general principles of criminal responsibility that apply to any offence, irrespective of how the offence is created.
>
> The principles of criminal responsibility are examined below and other proposals relating to specific offences will be explored in subsequent chapters.

2.2 THE ABSTRACTION OF PRINCIPLES: AN ELUSIVE OR ILLUSORY SEARCH?

Principles are claimed to provide a means for promoting coherence and rationality in the criminal law. Even scholars who structure their accounts in terms of principles are prepared to concede the existence of widespread disagreement and incoherence in the criminal law. As Ashworth has explained, the power of principles to promote coherence in the criminal law is limited in a number of ways — principles possess rivals that inevitably clash, and even those principles deemed to be "fundamental" may be outweighed for countervailing policy considerations: *Principles of Criminal Law* (3rd ed, Oxford: Oxford University Press, 1999). Though significant limitations on the explanatory and normative power of principles, such "qualifications" rarely justify the re-evaluation of claims that some principles have attained a fundamental and universal status in the criminal law.

Some degree of disjunction between principles and the *actual* law would seem inevitable. Since general principles embody normative ideals — a state of legal perfection — it is hardly surprising that imperfect human judges and lawmakers fall into error. When structured in terms of principles, academic discussion of the criminal law "flits between the descriptive and the normative": A Ashworth, *Principles of Criminal Law* (3rd ed, Oxford: Oxford University Press, 1999), p 60. This slippage between the language of descriptive and normative analysis has a significant ideological function, smoothing over doctrinal rifts and contradictions in the criminal law.

Critical scholars have expressed profound scepticism with the quest for general principles in the criminal law. Lacey has described the rationalising enterprise of orthodox criminal scholarship as involving:

> eliciting, articulating, and, where necessary, prescribing the proper principles informing criminal law, ironing out and rationalising apparent contradictions and exceptions, and paving the way for a clear, consistent and coherent theory and practice of criminal law on the basis of a loosely speaking liberal set of principles.[11]

---

11 N Lacey, "A Clear Concept of Intention: Elusive or Illusory?" (1993) 56 *Modern Law Review* 621. See generally N Lacey and C Wells, *Reconstructing Criminal Law* (2nd ed, London: Butt, 1998), Ch 1; D Brown, D Farrier and D Weisbrot, *Criminal Laws* (2nd ed, Sydney: Federation Press, 1996), p 4.

She concludes that in many areas of the criminal law, such as the meaning of intention, the search for transcendent, universal principles is not only elusive, it is illusory.[12] The conflicts and contradictions that exist within doctrine, the apparent multiple meanings of fundamental concepts, is "symptomatic of deeper substantive political questions that cannot be submerged by doctrinal rationalisation or by formal conceptual analysis".[13]

Critical scholarship has also rendered transparent the fact that many of the organising principles of the criminal law are sourced directly or indirectly from liberal philosophy. With the rise of legal positivism in the 19th century, law was conceptualised as a system of positive legal rules — in John Austin's terms, as commands of the sovereign backed by coercive threats: see generally P Parkinson, *Tradition and Change in Australian Law* (2nd ed, Sydney: LBC, 2001), Ch 2. This liberal project demanded the separation of legality from morality — the authority of modern law no longer required moral underwriting from God or natural law ideas. Legitimacy within this framework is primarily addressed by constraining arbitrary power through the strict observance of legal rules and procedures: see Ch 1, 2.1 'Defining Crime and the Rule of Law'. Principles and rules could be justified largely in terms of their own logic and rationality; in this sense, the authority of the modern criminal law is self-referential.[14] In the latter half of the 20th century, legal logic and rationality has been bolstered by arguments from moral and political philosophy, with the tenets of liberalism providing the principal "external" perspective for explaining, justifying and reconstructing the criminal law.

There is now a significant body of "analytical criminal jurisprudence", that strives to synthesise from existing legal doctrine the fundamental and universal principles of criminal law.[15] The primary philosophical focus of this body of scholarship is "the principles of criminal responsibility" which govern the identification of the legitimate conditions for attributing blame for wrongful conduct. Monograph after monograph examines fundamental concepts such as intention, free-will, agency, causation, attempt, complicity and so on.[16] Moral blameworthiness provides the template for legal guilt at the expense of other external explanatory and normative perspectives, such as criminology, psychology, ethics or human rights.

---

12   Lacey's critique of intention was explored by Jeremy Horder, "Intention in the Criminal Law — A Rejoinder" (1995) 58 *Modern Law Review* 678. Jeremy Horder proposed that the multiple meanings of intention reflects the multiple roles performed by the concept, such as the liberal values of protecting autonomy and representative labelling. From this perspective, the present guidance on intention in murder constituted a legitimate compromise permitting juries, within defined legal parameters, to engage in moral evaluation in the labelling process of distinguishing murder from manslaughter. See further N Lacey, "In(de)terminable Intentions" (1995) 58 *Modern Law Review* 692.

13   N Lacey, "A Clear Concept of Intention: Elusive or Illusory?" (1993) 56 *Modern Law Review* 621 at 637.

14   The authority for principles and rules is drawn from "ordinary" or "common-sense" understanding of concepts, an approach that Lacey calls "stipulative analysis": "A Clear Concept of Intention: Elusive or Illusory?" (1993) 56 *Modern Law Review* 621 at 624.

15   G Williams, *Criminal Law — The General Part* (London: Stevens and Sons, 1961, 2nd ed); G Fletcher, *Rethinking the Criminal Law* (Boston, MA: Little, Brown, 1978); J Feinberg, *The Moral Limits of the Criminal Law — Volume 1 — Harm to Others* (New York: Oxford University Press, 1984); *Volume 2 — Harm to Self* (New York: Oxford University Press, 1986); *Volume 3 — Offense to Others* (New York: Oxford University Press, 1988).

16   See, for example, HLA Hart, *Punishment and Responsibility* (Oxford: Oxford University Press, 1968); RA Duff, *Intention, Agency and Criminal Liability* (Oxford: Blackwell, 1990); RA Duff, *Criminal Attempts* (Oxford: Oxford University Press, 1996); RA Duff (ed), *Philosophy and the Criminal law: Principle and Critique* (Cambridge: Cambridge University Press, 1998); M Moore, *Placing Blame: A General Theory of the Criminal Law* (Oxford: Oxford University Press 1997); S Shute, J Gardner and J Horder (eds), *Action and Value in Criminal Law* (Oxford: Oxford University Press, 1993); KJM Smith, *A Modern Treatise on the Law of Criminal Complicity* (Oxford: Oxford University Press, 1991); AP Simester and ATH Smith (eds), *Harm and Culpability* (Oxford: Oxford University Press, 1996).

This concept of criminal law is exclusive rather than inclusive. Questions about the purpose and limits of punishment — for example, whether the criminal law and punishment should be legitimately used — are distinguished from questions about the conditions of individual responsibility. Questions of individual justice are divorced from broader questions of criminal justice, thereby suppressing the sociological and normative significance of the key institutions involved in the administration of the criminal law such as police, prosecutors and juries: N Lacey, "Introduction — Making Sense of Criminal Justice" in N Lacey, *A Reader on Criminal Justice* (Oxford: Oxford University Press, 1994), p 3.

The narrow focus of this "philosophy of the criminal law" sustains a strict division between criminal law, criminal justice and criminology. As outlined in Chapter 1, the criminal law may be more meaningfully understood as part of a broader framework bridging these divisions, an approach Lacey calls "criminalization": "Criminology, Criminal law and Criminalization" in M Maguire, R Morgan and R Reiner (eds), *The Oxford Handbook of Criminology* (2nd ed, Oxford: Oxford University Press, 1997), Ch 11.

The increasing scepticism over treating moral and political philosophy as *the* conceptual framework for the criminal law has encouraged scholars to search more widely for explanatory and normative insights. Modern criminal scholarship draws increasingly from feminism, psychology, history, sociology, literary theory, human rights, economics, and so on. The range of perspectives on the criminal law should have "no exclusions": P Alldridge, *Relocating Criminal Law* (Aldershot: Ashgate, 2000), pp 18-19. Clearly the grip of liberal philosophy on the criminal law is not inevitable. Indeed, Nicola Lacey has recently called for an alternate "social theory" for the criminal law, one that is grounded in sociology and criminology rather than analytical jurisprudence: "'Philosophical Foundations of the Common Law': Social Not Metaphysical" in J Horder (ed), *Oxford Essays in Jurisprudence* (Oxford: Oxford University Press, 2000), p 17.

Theoretical pluralism need not be a descent into eclecticism. While rejecting the idea of grand theory or theoretical monopoly, it is important to realise that some perspectives have greater explanatory power than others in certain contexts. While feminism has the potential to reconceptualise our notions of sexual harm, psychology offers explanatory and normative resources for reshaping fundamental concepts of criminal responsibility. As we shall explore in Chapter 15, economic, sociological and medical perspectives may shed light on the nature of drug markets and the potential counterproductive impact of criminalisation of "pleasurable commodities".

Viewing criminal law as a "species of moral and political philosophy" as suggested by George Fletcher in *Rethinking Criminal Law* (Boston: Little, Brown, 1978), p xix, sustains an acute form of historical myopia. As noted in Chapter 1 conventional accounts of the criminal law tend to be ahistorical, concealing the contingency and conflict surrounding the development of principles and doctrines.[17] Through processes of abstraction, general principles are represented as self-evident, eternal moral and political truths about the criminal law. By contrast, historical perspectives on the development of legal concepts and specific forms of crime can expose the fragility of principles that claim universal and fundamental status. Rather than possessing transcendent qualities, the criminal

---

17   "Analytic scholarship is anti-historical: it regards history as subversive because it exposes the rationalising enterprise": MJ Horwitz, "The Historical Contingency of the Role of History" (1981) 90 *Yale Law Journal* 1057.

law is contingent, reflecting the social, political and moral concerns about wrongful conduct and particular groups at certain times. Adopting this perspective on the general principles of responsibility, Alan Norrie in *Crime, Reason and History* (London: Weidenfeld and Nicolson, 1993), Ch 11, concludes that concepts of agency and responsibility emerged in the criminal law in the 19th century were modelled on a psychological and political concept of individualism that abstracted the "legal subject" (in this context the accused) from his or her social and political context.

Conventional accounts of the criminal law often conceal or suppress the fact that the obsession with "general principles" has been an academic rather than a judicial or legislative project. Paradoxically, modern legal scholarship tends to minimise or deny its own role in synthesising and creating general principles. The concept of a "criminal law" as a unified corpus of general principles and doctrines, as distinct from the "law of crimes", emerges only in the 19th century.[18] Shaun McVeigh and Peter Rush suggest that this reconceptualisation of criminal discourse may be traced to the first self-styled textbook on "criminal law", published in 1863 by James Fitzjames Stephen, one of the most distinguished English judges and jurists of his time.[19] This text represented a significant transition in the order of representation of the criminal doctrine. As McVeigh and Rush point out:

> Stephen collapses the disparate traditions of the law of public wrongs and pleas of the Crown, that is the Institutists and the common lawyers. This sets in train the transition from the laws of crime to criminal law.[20]

Unlike previous criminal texts, Stephen distinguished "criminal law doctrine" from the rules of procedure and evidence, and subordinated specific crimes to general principles. This approach continues to represent the dominant model for thinking, rethinking and reforming the criminal law.[21]

The search for general principles may be viewed as an academic enterprise, only recently attracting the attention of law reformers and the appellate courts. From a judicial perspective, general principles are ill-suited to the common law method. The judicial ability to articulate fundamental principles of universal application is hampered by the constraints of legal adjudication. Since adjudication is based on precedent, which naturally inclines to inductive reasoning, incrementalism and pragmatism, judges rarely identify the principles underlying their

---

18 While some principles claim an ancient pedigree, such as the tautological maxim *Actus non facit reum nisi mens sit rea* (an act does not make a person guilty of a crime unless that person's mind be also guilty), their meaning and scope change significantly over time. During the 19th century, the principle has moved from a normative moral understanding of fault (malice or evil) to a descriptive psychological understanding (intention, knowledge or recklessness): A Norrie, *Crime, Reason and History* (London: Weidenfeld and Nicolson,1993), especially Chs 3 and 4.

19 S McVeigh and P Rush, "Cutting Our Losses: Criminal Legal Doctrine" in P Rush, S McVeigh and A Young (eds), *Criminal Legal Doctrine* (Aldershot: Dartmouth, 1997), pp 188-193.

20 S McVeigh and P Rush, "Cutting Our Losses: Criminal Legal Doctrine" in P Rush, S McVeigh and A Young (eds), *Criminal Legal Doctrine* (Aldershot: Dartmouth, 1997), p 189. Liberal reformer Jeremy Bentham also played a significant role in creating a new conceptual framework for understanding criminal punishment and legislation: see A Norrie, *Crime, Reason and History* (London: Weidenfeld and Nicolson,1993), Ch 2.

21 G Williams, *Criminal Law — The General Part* (2nd ed, London: Stevens and Sons, 1961). Discussion of legal doctrine is commonly organised around principles. This convention is not limited to academic texts, but is employed in leading practice texts, such as *The Laws of Australia*, which represent and reduce the law to neat propositional forms.

decisions.[22] As a consequence, a significant part of legal scholarship is devoted to the extrapolation and synthesis of the "hidden principles" of the criminal law: see for example, J Horder, "Two Histories and Four Hidden Principles of *Mens Rea*" (1997) 113 *Law Quarterly Review* 95.

Adopting a "principled" approach to the study of criminal law also dramatically narrows the scope of intellectual engagement. Crimes that derogate from general principles are "exceptional", governed by their own special rules and doctrines. Though numerically significant, minor crimes of strict or absolute liability that do not require proof of a subjective fault element are viewed as unworthy of consideration. As Doreen McBarnet points out in *Conviction: Law, The State and the Construction of Justice* (London: MacMillan Press, 1981), this conception of the criminal law sustains an "ideology of triviality" around summary crimes and processes: Ch 7. This ideology sustains academic invisibility around offences that deviate from general principles such as minor crimes of a regulatory nature, as well as more serious crimes such as drug dealing. The latter, far from being an exception, "is the single crime that most clearly drives the contemporary criminal justice system": P Alldridge, *Relocating Criminal Law* (Aldershot: Ashgate, 2000), p 23. As Lacey has concluded, critical perspectives provide a powerful antidote to the constraints of current legal constructions, requiring law students, teachers and practitioners to search "beyond the boundaries of criminal law and its doctrines to its social meanings, its enforcement practices, its ideological functions and so on": "A Clear Concept of Intention: Elusive or Illusory?" (1993) 56 *Modern Law Review* 621 at 639.

Adopting critical perspectives on general principles do not deny their normative significance or standing within legal culture. General principles represent an ideal (or idealised) image of how the process and substance of the criminal law *should* operate. As well as offering guidance to scholars, lawyers, judges and lawmakers, these principles also strive to confer legitimacy — both moral and political — on the criminal law. Modern legal scholarship has been primarily concerned with demonstrating how the criminal law fails to live up to its principles. Critical scholars do not regard this "gap" between rhetoric and reality as a remediable derogation, but rather as something which is constitutive of the law itself. By resorting to a higher level of abstraction, general principles minimise and conceal disagreement (which often reflects wider moral and political conflict in society) within legal doctrine. Moreover, analysis and reconstruction of law in terms of general principles tends to inscribe liberal values *as* legal values. This performs a disciplinary function, defining the intellectual boundaries beyond which the criminal law (as well as its students, scholars, practitioners and judges) must not venture. Feminist and critical legal scholars have exposed the "common-sense" liberal assumptions behind many of these principles. While liberalism may dominate our legal understanding of what is "fundamental", the range and scope of general principles are not immutable. As we shall explore below, in the context of the criminal law there is plenty of scope for reconstructing the principles of fundamental justice, fairness, equality and privacy in a more radical and socially-inclusive way.

---

22 An exception is the discussion of "general principles" in the context of drug offences in *He Kaw Teh v The Queen* (1985) 157 CLR 523. Brennan J divided his judgment into a statement of "The General Principles", at 564ff, and then "Application of the General Principles to s 233B(b) and (c)" at 582ff.

3. PRINCIPLES OF CRIMINAL PROCESS

3.1 THE RELATIONSHIP BETWEEN CRIMINAL LAW AND PROCEDURE

Many criminal law courses and textbooks examine process issues in a cursory and descriptive fashion.[23] There is little attempt to examine how legal rules and principles impinge, if at all, on law enforcement practices and trial procedures. Criminal procedure is typically marginal to criminal law, represented as having practical rather than academic significance.[24] Neither has criminal procedure been a priority for law reformers. Nearly a decade after the Model Criminal Code Officers Committee began its work, the section of the Code that deals with principles of criminal procedure (Chapter 1) has not yet been released. The MCCOC took the view that the "general principles of criminal responsibility" were fundamental and therefore a more important priority.

By contrast, critical scholarship has highlighted the significance of the criminal process. David Nelken has highlighted the *irrelation* between criminal process and the substantive law; namely, how legal rules are translated, sometimes distorted, by the criminal process: "Criminal Law and Criminal Justice: Some Notes on their Irrelation" in I Dennis (ed), *Criminal Law and Criminal Justice* (London: Sweet and Maxwell, 1986). Building on these critical perspectives, Lindsay Farmer proposes that the criminal law is best understood not in terms of "general principles of responsibility", but rather through an examination of the impact of historical and procedural changes in specific areas. Farmer began his review of the criminal law of Scotland by exploring the growth of the "summary jurisdiction" in the 19th century and its role in transforming key concepts of criminal responsibility in the common law: L Farmer, *Criminal Law, Tradition, and Legal Order* (Cambridge: Cambridge University Press, 1997). The relationship between process and substantive law in specific contexts is explored in subsequent chapters. In this chapter, we focus on four principles that have general application to the criminal law: territoriality, fairness, equality before the law and privacy.

---

23 The segregation of criminal law from criminal justice is further entrenched by the emergence of "criminal justice" as a distinct field of legal study, supported by its own texts: eg M Findlay, S Odgers and S Yeo, *Australian Criminal Justice* (2nd ed, Sydney: Oxford University Press, 1999); A Ashworth, *The Criminal Process* (2nd ed, Oxford: Oxford University Press, 1998).

24 Textbooks on criminal procedure tend to adopt a practical rather than academic perspective: C Cato, *The Law and Practice of Criminal Litigation* (Sydney: LBC, 1998); J Bishop, *Criminal Procedure* (Sydney: Butt, 1998).

3.2 THE PRINCIPLE OF TERRITORIALITY

> All crime is local. The jurisdiction over the crime belongs to the country where the crime is committed, and, except over her own subjects, Her Majesty and the Imperial Legislature have no power whatever

MacLeod v Attorney-General (NSW)
[1891] AC 455 at 458-459,
per Halsbury LC

The idea that the criminal law is "territorial" in the sense of being bound to a defined geographic territory is considered to be a "general thesis of the common law": *Thompson v The Queen* (1989) 169 CLR 1 at 33, per Deane J. This image of territoriality as the jurisdictional norm for the criminal law is reinforced by the presumption (albeit rebuttable) that offences do not have extra-territorial effect.[25]

The principle of territoriality appears to be unproblematic — it is rarely addressed in standard criminal textbooks, regarded as having greater practical rather than academic significance.[26] Far from being of marginal significance, jurisdiction is a fundamental concept that creates and defines the boundaries of the criminal law. As Farmer notes:

> The power of law is always a territorial question. The law draws physical boundaries in geographic space. The law orders the interior of this space into political and administrative units. Legal sovereignty means nothing without these physical aspects of space and organisation. The law is also always the law of the land.[27]

The idea of territoriality reinforces ideas of national sovereignty by promoting centralisation and uniformity, rather than localisation in the administration of criminal justice: P Alldridge, *Relocating Criminal Law* (Aldershot: Ashgate, 2000), p 138. By aligning criminal jurisdiction with geographical and political space, territoriality displaces alternate grounds for claiming jurisdiction, such as the status of the parties or nature of the conduct:

---

25 The presumption that criminal offences do not have extraterritorial effect may be rebutted expressly or impliedly: *Pearce v Florenca* (1976) 135 CLR 507; *Treacy v DPP* [1971] AC 537 at 561 per Lord Diplock. See C Dellitt, B Fisse and P Keyzer, Chapter 5, 'Territorial and Extraterritorial Jurisdiction' in 9 Criminal Law Principles, 9.1 'The Criminal Laws', *The Laws of Australia* (Sydney: Law Book Company Ltd, 1993–).

26 See C Dellitt, B Fisse and P Keyzer, Chapter 5, 'Territorial and Extraterritorial Jurisdiction' in 9 Criminal Law Principles, 9.1 'The Criminal Laws', *The Laws of Australia* (Sydney: Law Book Company Ltd, 1993–), paras 109-149; A Leaver, *Investigating Crime* (Sydney: LBC, 1997), pp 33-50. By contrast the principle of territoriality is rarely addressed by standard criminal texts: see B Fisse, *Howard's Criminal Law* (Sydney: LBC, 1990). Falling between criminal law and conflicts of law, criminal jurisdiction has become an area of discrete specialisation: see D Lanham, *Cross-Border Criminal Law* (Melbourne: FT Law & Tax Asia Pacific, 1997), Ch 1.

27 L Farmer, "The Law of the Land: Criminal Jurisdiction 1747-1908" in P Rush, S McVeigh and A Young (eds), *Criminal Legal Doctrine* (Aldershot: Ashgate, 1997), Ch 3. See also *Criminal Law, Tradition, and Legal Order* (Cambridge: Cambridge University Press, 1997), Ch 3.

> With the privileging of the *forum deliciti* [the jurisdiction where the offence occurred] the law is moving away from the face to face control of individuals towards the control of actions with particular legal space. The legal subject is abstracted from particularities of place, time and biography.[28]

These views reflect the modern conception of criminal jurisdiction that emerged in the late 18th and 19th century. A closer historical review reveals that criminal jurisdiction has never been *perfectly* aligned with territorial borders. In many respects, the common law evolved a highly localised view of jurisdiction that limited trials to the locality in which the crime occurred.[29] These derogations from territoriality reveal the concealed significance of the nature of the crime and the status of the parties in determining the reach of the criminal law. Criminal jurisdiction could be "universal" extending "beyond the seas" as in the case of piracy.[30] In relation to status, Crown immunity was the most significant deviation from territoriality as the basis for jurisdiction — neither the Courts nor Parliament had power over crimes committed by the Sovereign.[31] Until the 18th century, status could be regularly invoked as a basis for denying criminal jurisdiction — many accused escaped trial by claiming the "benefit of clergy". By invariably disingenuous claims of clerical ordination (thereby invoking ecclesiastical jurisdiction over the crime) educated accused were furnished with a means of defeating jurisdiction on a technicality![32] Although such fictions were not open to those accused of crimes in colonial Australia — because of the failure to legislate for an Established Church in Australia — status nevertheless played a significant role in determining the scope and application of the criminal law. Members of the military and convicted prisoners were subject to their own distinct codes of disciplinary offences. Moreover, during the first 40 years of colonisation, some judges refused to apply English criminal law to Indigenous crimes, invoking the "Aboriginal" status of an offender and the "tribal" nature of the offence as grounds for denying criminal jurisdiction.[33] In due course, such claims based on native law and jurisdiction were suppressed by the fiction of "terra nullius" — that is, the continent of Australia was uninhabited territory, barren of Indigenous

---

28 In Scots law, the power to punish under feudal customary law survived until its gradual displacement by the introduction of a centralised "summary" procedure in the 19th century. The army and church also reserved its own jurisdiction: L Farmer, "The Law of the Land: Criminal Jurisdiction 1747-1908" in P Rush, S McVeigh and A Young (eds), *Criminal Legal Doctrine* (Aldershot: Ashgate, 1997), pp 66-69.

29 The importance of venue related to the need to ensure that the jury empanelled to hear the matter had "local knowledge" of the offender and offence: see discussion, A Leaver, *Investigating Crime* (Sydney: LBC, 1997), p 37.

30 Crimes committed on the high seas (such as piracy) eventually became a matter for Admiralty jurisdiction: D Lanham, *Cross-Border Criminal Law* (Melbourne: FT Law & Tax Asia Pacific, 1997), pp 2-3.

31 *MacLeod v Attorney-General (NSW)* [1891] AC 455 at 458-459, per Halsbury LC.

32 By the 18th century, the benefit was no longer confined to religious orders and any person who could read received the benefit subject to being branded on the thumb to prevent a second claim. The range of "clergyable crimes" was reduced and from 1718 onwards, a condition of the claim was that the offender submit to transportation for seven years: WR Cornish and G Clarke, *Law and Society in England 1750-1950* (London: Sweet & Maxwell), p 558. Although diminishing in its authority, the ecclesiastical courts retained jurisdiction to try members of their parish for crimes, such as drunkeness, adultery, incest, brawling and failure to attend church, until the late 18th century: p 546.

33 As Jennifer Clarke points out "In 1841, a Port Phillip judge, Willis J, expressed the view that Aboriginal crimes inter se were a matter for the 'tribes' under their own law on the United States model. This view was inconsistent with an earlier New South Wales Supreme Court decision (*R v Jack Congo Murrell* (1836) Legge 73) and was overruled by the Colonial Office with the support of the New South Wales Chief Justice": "Indigenous People and Constitutional Law" in P Hanks and D Cass, *Australian Constitutional Law* (Sydney: Butt, 1999), p 57.

peoples and systems of law.[34] Such claims have only recently been revived in the wake of the recognition of native title in *Mabo v Queensland (No 2)* (1992) 175 CLR 1. The implications of claims of Aboriginal criminal jurisdiction for the "Principle of Equality Before the Law" are further explored below, pp 132-135.

As this brief historical digression suggests, the idea of a unitary domestic criminal law bound tightly to the geographical and political borders of the State has always competed with alternate non-territorial bases for jurisdiction. It would seem that the territorial idea of criminal jurisdiction, the idea of criminal law as the "law of the land", has always been under threat from countervailing forces of fragmentation and legal pluralism.

At its core, the question of jurisdiction — the power of judging and punishing crimes[35] — is a political matter involving "important questions of policy, justice and international law and practice": G Williams, "Venue and Ambit of Criminal Law — Part III" (1965) 81 *Law Quarterly Review* 276 at 276. As Alldridge in *Relocating Criminal Law* (Aldershot: Ashgate, 2000) observes (p 140):

> At the intersection of criminal law and international relations is the question of jurisdiction. Bad relations between states will lead to refusal to extradite, generous provision as to asylum and strict geographical limits upon jurisdiction. Good relations, or interdependence between states will lead to shared police information, shared policing, mutual cooperation and either reciprocal jurisdiction, or to granting "full faith and credit" to the laws of the other, with mechanistic extradition arrangements, including extradition without double criminality, or both.

For domestic lawyers, the question of which polity — state, federal, supra national or international — should exercise legal authority over criminal conduct or individuals is translated into legal tests of criminal jurisdiction. Judicial attempts to suppress the political dimensions of this issue behind technical formulations are rarely successful. Indeed, there is increasing judicial recognition that "policy considerations" are relevant, and that there is "no mechanical answer" to jurisdictional questions: *DPP v Doot* [1973] AC 807 at 817, per Lord Wilberforce. Determining whether a person should be brought to justice in one system rather than another is influenced by a range of political and practical questions. For example, the prosecutor's decision over venue is only partially influenced by the application of the principle of territoriality. As one survey of the law concludes: "the more recent trend in the law has been to focus less on territoriality and more on exercising jurisdiction with a view to bolstering international or federal law enforcement".[36]

While there is a large and growing body of law governing jurisdiction, in practice, most jurisdictional uncertainties are resolved through informal negotiation between law enforcement agencies and prosecutors rather than through litigation. In rare cases where defence counsel

---

34 On the doctrine of terra nullius and its consequences for Aboriginal law see S Bottomley and S Parker, *Law in Context* (2nd ed, Sydney: Federation Press, 1997), pp 245-251.

35 "Criminal jurisdiction, termed the Power of the Sword, is a Power of judging and punishing crimes" (Forbes, 1730, 215), quoted in L Farmer, "The Law of the Land: Criminal Jurisdiction 1747-1908" in P Rush, S McVeigh and A Young (eds), *Criminal Legal Doctrine* (Aldershot: Ashgate, 1997), p 65.

36 C Dellitt, B Fisse and P Keyzer, Chapter 5, 'Territorial and Extraterritorial Jurisdiction' in 9 Criminal Law Principles, 9.1 'The Criminal Laws' *The Laws of Australia* (Sydney: Law Book Company Ltd, 1993–), para 110, p 86.

challenge jurisdiction, the matter is determined by the jury: "when an issue is raised as to locality of the offence the jury may have to decide the issue in order to determine whether the conduct charged falls within the territorial ambit of the law of the forum".[37]

TESTS OF CRIMINAL JURISDICTION: FROM TERRITORIALITY TO TERRITORIAL NEXUS

The tests of territoriality developed by courts and legislatures, while not always determinative, provide the legal framework within which jurisdiction is negotiated, and where necessary, determined by the jury or tribunal of fact. The principle of territoriality is rarely visible, revealing itself only in cases where criminal conduct and individuals traverse domestic or international frontiers.

CASE STUDIES

The Principle of Territoriality Under Common Law

The leading case of *Ward v The Queen* (1980) 142 CLR 308, provided the High Court with the opportunity for a sustained examination of the common law principles governing criminal jurisdiction. The accused, standing on the Victorian bank of the Murray River, shot and killed his victim who was standing on the opposite bank in New South Wales. The accused was tried and convicted of murder in Victoria. On appeal, the accused challenged the jurisdiction and the High Court considered that the question of jurisdiction fell to be determined either by:

(1) the place where the *conduct* causing death initiated (the *initiatory theory*); or

(2) the place where the *consequences* of that conduct occurred (the *terminatory theory*).[38]

Under international law either of these tests, which are termed subjective and objective territoriality respectively, will suffice for claiming domestic criminal jurisdiction: Ivan Shearer, "Jurisdiction" in S Blay, R Piotrowicz and M Tsamenyi (eds), *Public International Law: An Australian Perspective* (Melbourne: Oxford University Press, 1998), p 167.

The High Court in *Ward* first had to resolve the territorial limits of New South Wales.[39] The Court then considered and confirmed that the second approach — the terminatory theory — applied to these facts. Accordingly, New South Wales rather than Victoria had jurisdiction to try the accused for murder. This question was not merely an academic exercise, as Murphy J observed (at 340), since the defence of diminished responsibility was available in New South Wales, but not in Victoria. Clearly, decisions to submit to or challenge jurisdiction involve a range of tactical as well as substantive legal considerations.

---

37 *Thompson v The Queen* (1989) 169 CLR 1 at 22, per Brennan J. Where raised, the jury should be directed to return a special verdict on the issue of jurisdiction before considering guilt. Where territoriality is not established on the balance of probabilities, the accused should be discharged rather than acquitted — using this special verdict prevents the accused relying on his acquittal to defeat proceedings in another jurisdiction on the grounds of double jeopardy: at 30, per Mason CJ and Deane J. See further A Leaver, *Investigating Crime* (Sydney: LBC, 1997), pp 38-39.

38 These theories, and the authorities cited supporting them, are discussed in D Lanham, *Cross-Border Criminal Law* (Melbourne: FT Law & Tax Asia Pacific, 1997), Ch 1. The High Court relied extensively on an article reviewing these competing theories: see G Williams, "Venue and Ambit of Criminal Law — Part III" (1965) 81 *Law Quarterly Review* 518. As Lanham notes (p 6), the High Court omitted to mention that Glanville Williams favoured the initiatory rather than the terminatory theory!

As David Lanham points out, the "cross border rules" laid down in *Ward* are modelled on crimes that have "one core element which dictates where it may be tried": *Cross-Border Criminal Law* (Melbourne: FT Law & Tax Asia Pacific, 1997), p 3. These rules do not easily apply to crimes that have multiple elements that may be committed at different times and from different locations. As Gleeson CJ recently remarked in *Lipohar v The Queen* (1999) 168 ALR 8 at 13: "Discussion of the rule [governing jurisdiction in cases of conspiracy to defraud] usually proceeds upon the assumption that the offence is committed in only one place. That assumption is not a logical necessity, and whether it should be revised is a question that may be addressed in some future case." The tests may also be criticised as anthropocentric being modelled around human individuals rather than corporations. As Alldridge has observed, the process of jurisdiction becomes an even more "metaphysical activity" where the criminal conduct and responsibility is diffused across the organisational structure of multi-national corporations: *Relocating Criminal Law* (Aldershot: Ashgate, 2000), p 142.

The terminatory test in *Ward v The Queen* has been widely regarded as being the basis for criminal jurisdiction under the common law, applicable in the Australian Capital Territory, New South Wales, South Australia and Victoria.[40] However, it is not clear whether the principle of territoriality (based on the terminatory theory) endorsed in *Ward* was intended to apply beyond the offence of homicide. As Lanham points out, the common law rules for determining the jurisdiction for murder in many respects were "exceptional": *Cross-Border Criminal Law* (Melbourne: FT Law & Tax Asia Pacific, 1997), Ch 1. They were framed against the historical background of murder as a felony punishable by death. Extending the jurisdiction for homicide was a politically sensitive matter with the potential to unhinge relations between States: pp 8-9. In these circumstances, it was not surprising that the courts adopted a test of jurisdiction that rested on territorial borders, rather than some other base such as nationality or domicile of the victim or the accused.

While *Ward* is often represented as the general principle for determining jurisdiction, as we shall explore below, others courts have acknowledged the limitations of the terminatory theory and have adopted more flexible tests or conceptions of territoriality. A broader, inclusive test is particularly evident in cases where the criminal conduct appears genuinely to have a multi-jurisdictional dimension.[41] To widen the basis of territoriality in

---

39 The High Court held that the border between the two States ran along the top of the southern bank of the Murray River. Stephen J (with whom the rest of the High Court agreed) discussed a wide range of legal and historical sources, including the Constitution of New South Wales: *Ward v The Queen* (1980) 142 CLR 308 at 337. As the Constitution defined the State as extending across the "whole Watercourse", Stephen J reviewed the legal effect of floods and tides on jurisdiction.

40 C Dellitt, B Fisse and P Keyzer, Chapter 5, 'Territorial and Extraterritorial Jurisdiction' in 9 Criminal Law Principles, 9.1 'The Criminal Laws', *The Laws of Australia* (Sydney: Law Book Company Ltd, 1993–), para 116, p 90. The terminatory test has been incorporated into the tests of territorial jurisdiction in the Codes adopted in Queensland, Tasmania and Western Australia.

41 Dishonest and false representations made in one jurisdiction may result in obtaining of property or services in another: see *R v Hansford* (1974) 8 SASR 164, discussed in D Lanham, *Cross-Border Criminal Law* (Melbourne: FT Law & Tax Asia Pacific, 1997), p 11.

cases of conspiracy, the courts have categorised the physical elements of the offence as being "continuing" in nature, conveniently placing the agreement and its objective in the same jurisdiction.[42]

Legislative reforms have modified or substantially qualified the traditional territorial test of jurisdiction. In Queensland and Western Australia, the legislature has adopted a composite test, fusing the initiatory and terminatory theories: *Criminal Code* (Qld), s 12; *Criminal Code* (WA), s 12. Other jurisdictions, such as the Australian Capital Territory, New South Wales and South Australia, have supplemented the common law with a statutory test of jurisdiction based on "territorial nexus": see also *Crimes Act* 1900 (ACT), s 3A; *Crimes Act* 1900 (NSW), s 3A; *Criminal Law Consolidation Act* 1935 (SA), s 5C. The New South Wales provision provides as follows:

3A: Territorial application of the criminal law of the State

(1) An offence against the law of the State is committed if:

(a) all elements necessary to constitute the offence (disregarding territorial considerations) exist; and

(b) a territorial nexus exists between the State and at least one element of the offence.

(2) A territorial nexus exists between the State and an element of an offence if:

(a) the element is or includes an event occurring in the State; or

(b) the element is or includes an event that occurs outside the State but while the person alleged to have committed the offence is in the State.

Significantly, these statutory provisions do not abrogate the common law. While territorial nexus seems to constitute a significant departure from the terminatory theory, it is unclear whether the legislative test will provide greater flexibility than the common law, particularly in light of recent developments in the High Court, which are discussed below.[43] These legislative provisions and relevant case law are reviewed in M Hinton and C Lind, "The Territorial Application of the Criminal Law — When Crime is Not Local" (1999) 23 Crim LJ 285.

---

42 *DPP v Doot* [1973] AC 807. "The concept of a continuing offence is invoked to expand the scope of territorial jurisdiction. That concept is used to circumvent the difficulties of pinpointing when and where a crime takes effect": C Dellitt, B Fisse and P Keyzer, "Chapter 5 — Territorial and Extraterritorial Jurisdiction" in 9 Criminal Law Principles, 9.1 'The Criminal Laws', *The Laws of Australia* (Sydney: Law Book Company, 1993–), para 120, p 97. The complex body of authority on conspiracy to commit crime abroad or in another Australian jurisdiction is discussed in M Goode, "Two New Decisions on Criminal 'Jurisdiction': The Appalling Durability of Common Law" (1996) 20 Crim LJ 267 at 273-281.

43 It has been suggested that territorial nexus has "similar effect" to the real and substantial link test: C Dellitt, B Fisse and P Keyzer, Chapter 5, 'Territorial and Extraterritorial Jurisdiction' in 9 Criminal Law Principles, 9.1 'The Criminal Laws', *The Laws of Australia* (Sydney: Law Book Company Ltd, 1993–), para 118, p 92. Some early decisions adopted a restrictive approach to the provision, leading one commentator to conclude that "It appears at this stage that the courts will so interpret [the provision] to achieve nothing that was not already achieved by common law": M Goode, "Two New Decisions on Criminal 'Jurisdiction': The Appalling Durability of Common Law" (1996) 20 Crim LJ 267 at 282.

As jurisdictional challenges are resolved "case-by-case", there is some uncertainty whether the principle, theory or test of territoriality endorsed applies to all offences or is crime-specific. As a recent review of the concept of territoriality concluded: "Any reader seeking a common thread of reason, rationale or plain legal reasoning in these and other decisions will be bitterly disappointed": M Goode, "Two New Decisions on Criminal 'Jurisdiction': The Appalling Durability of Common Law" (1996) 20 Crim LJ 267 at 269.

Resolving jurisdiction exclusively by reference to the terminatory test can be overly restrictive. In addition to legislative modifications discussed above, the test of jurisdiction has also been broadened by judicial development of the common law. In cases where the criminal activity has trans-jurisdictional dimensions, some judges have resorted to more flexible tests of jurisdiction, that fall broadly into one of two categories:

(1) whether the conduct of the accused affects "the peace, welfare and good government of the State"[44] — this is also known as the "Queen's Peace" test[45] or the protective theory of jurisdiction;[46] or

(2) whether there is a "real and substantial link" between the offence and the jurisdiction seeking to try it.[47]

The first test, which dispenses with the need to establish any physical connection to a territory, is particularly broad. Notwithstanding the inherent vagueness and legal malleability of this test, it has been "applied enthusiastically to drug and terrorism offences": *Chapter 4 — Damage and Computer Offences*, Discussion Paper (2000), p 164.

The second test, which offers similar flexibility though at the cost of some certainty, has recently been examined by the High Court in *Lipohar v The Queen* (1999) 168 ALR 8. The case involved determining jurisdiction in relation to conspiracy to defraud. The accused had devised a fraudulent scheme involving activity in Indonesia, Thailand, Queensland, Victoria and South Australia. The intended victim was a company based in Adelaide, and it was in South Australia that

---

44 *R v Hansford* (1974) 8 SASR 164 at 195, per Wells J. The origins of this formulation lie in *Board of Trade v Owen* [1957] AC 602 at 624, per Tucker LJ. The House of Lords held that it could be conspiracy to enter into an agreement in England to commit a crime abroad provided that the contemplated crime abroad would be indictable had it occurred in England: "it is necessary to recognise the offence to aid in the preservation of the Queen's peace and the maintenance of law and order within the realm": at 624-625. The Australian courts have recast this formulation into "peace, welfare and good government" a phrase from the plenary power to legislate contained in State Constitutions: *Union Steamship of Australia Pty Ltd v King* (1988) 166 CLR 1 at 6, see T Blackshield and G Williams, *Australian Constitutional Law and Theory: Commentary and Materials* (2nd ed, Sydney: Federation Press, 1998), pp 380-381. As a principle of jurisdiction, the phrase is vague and imposes few real restrictions: *R v Fan* (1991) 24 NSWLR 60.

45 A Leaver, *Investigating Crime* (Sydney: LBC, 1997), pp 43-47.

46 It has been suggested that this principle comes from the period of radical nationalism which produced the French and American revolutions, and was originally limited to national security crimes: Model Criminal Code Officers Committee/Standing Committee of Attorneys-General, *Ch 4: Damage and Computer Offences*, Discussion Paper (2000), p 162.

47 The Supreme Court of Canada discarded the old territoriality tests in favour of recognising jurisdiction where there is "a real and substantial link between the offence and the country: *Libman v The Queen* (1985) 21 CCC (3d) 206 at 232. This test was endorsed by the Privy Council in *Liangsiriprasert v Government of the USA* [1991] 1 AC 225.

proceedings were instituted against the accused. In this case, the parties conceded that the territorial nexus test in s 5C of the *Criminal Law Consolidation Act* 1953 (SA) did not confer jurisdiction (see p 85 above), and so the High Court examined the common law tests.

The majority of the High Court, affirming jurisdiction on these facts, applied various approaches to jurisdiction including whether there was: (a) a "sufficient connection" (at 17, per Gleeson CJ; at 42, per Gaudron, Gummow and Hayne JJ); or (b) a "real link" (at 84, per Callinan J) between the offence and the jurisdiction. Kirby J, dissenting, adhered to the existing test of jurisdiction based on territoriality. He had been initially attracted to the Supreme Court of Canada's "real and substantial link" test, noting (at 62) the desirability of adopting simple rules of jurisdiction within a federal system. Although not pressed by counsel, he noted that the Commonwealth Constitution could provide a basis for uniform rules. In this case, the matter fell to be determined by the rules enacted by the legislature or judges applying the common law. In South Australia the legislature had enacted remedial provisions in the form of a territorial nexus test. In Kirby J's view, the courts must restrain their enthusiasm to repair omissions appearing in such legislation. In his view, abandoning the principle of territoriality in the common law would require resort to legal fictions to bring conduct within the jurisdiction — such an approach would have the effect of creating new offences and applying them retrospectively. It would also require the courts to subvert the territorial division of Australia, reflected in the Constitution, into separate geographical areas of States and Territories.

Since these new tests of jurisdiction extend the criminal law beyond conventional boundaries, there is an increased possibility of concurrent claims of jurisdiction between the Commonwealth, States and Territories, as well as overseas jurisdictions. An obvious consequence of greater inclusivity is that the issue of jurisdiction requires greater judicial attention to policy matters such as maintaining good relations between States (also known as the requirements of international comity), as well as practical law enforcement considerations such as the necessary resources and evidence for a successful prosecution. As La Forest J acknowledged in *Libman v The Queen* [1985] 2 SCR 178 at 213-214: "Just what may constitute a real and substantial link in a particular case, I need not explore ... The outer limits of the test may, however, well be coterminous with the requirements of international comity". Jurisdiction is determined not simply by the application of formal legal rules, but rather involves the exercise of judicial discretion and the weighing of competing policy considerations, both national and international.[48] This issue of comity has recently been addressed by the High Court in *Lipohar v The Queen*, where Gaudron, Gummow, and Hayne JJ held (at 35) that considerations of comity would have no bearing on relations between jurisdictions within a federal system: "Within Australia, any rationale for the common law rule respecting comity between what became the States disappeared with federation". Similar comments were made by Gleeson CJ (at 17) and Kirby J (at 55).

---

48 D Lanham reviews authorities in which non-legal factors were considered relevant to jurisdiction, representing them as a check-list of "policy considerations": *Cross-Border Criminal Law* (Melbourne: FT Law & Tax Asia Pacific, 1997), pp 16-20. The breadth of a principle informed by policy or comity would not violate international law since a State may claim criminal jurisdiction unless there is proved to be a rule of international law to the contrary: *Lotus Case* (1927) PCIJ Series A No 10, discussed in I Shearer, *Starke's International Law* (11th ed, Sydney: Butt, 1994), pp 183-184. The decision has been the subject of criticism: I Brownlie, *Principles of International Law*, (5th ed, Oxford: Clarendon Press, 1998), p 305.

As reflected in these statutory and common law developments, the modern trend is against the view that all crime is local. Broader tests of territoriality based on territorial nexus, or real sufficient link or connection further cast doubt on the hitherto fundamental assumption that there is only one core element of an offence that situates the crime in a particular jurisdiction. Until *Lipohar v The Queen*, the Australian courts remained faithful to territoriality as the appropriate test of jurisdiction.[49] Indeed, the Model Criminal Code Officers Committee expressed concern that the real and substantial link test, which mirrored that applied to determine jurisdiction in torts cases, would lead to uncertainty in the application of the criminal law: *Chapter 4 — Damage and Computer Offences*, Discussion Paper (2000), p 170. The MCCOC concluded (p 170) that such uncertainty explained the reluctance of the Australian courts "to abandon the cloak of territorialism". The Canadian approach has, however, support from legal commentators: see for example, M Goode, "Two New Decisions on Criminal 'Jurisdiction': The Appalling Durability of Common Law" (1996) 20 Crim LJ 267 at 279-280. *Lipohar v The Queen* represents yet another "nail in the coffin" for territorality.

Notwithstanding the diversity of tests and theories underlying the principle of territoriality, jurisdiction rarely forms the basis for an objection by the defence. This is probably because the tests of jurisdiction under the common law and statute are inclusive rather than exclusive:

> The disparities in formulation rarely affect the outcome in practice. In any given juris-
> diction, it is rare to find a case where a sufficient territorial connection cannot be found
> under one or other of the tests which apply.[50]

The uncertainties in the present law do not significantly impair the functioning of the administration of criminal justice. Indeed, the current patchwork of competing common law "theories" merely provides a flexible framework within which police, prosecutors and defence negotiate jurisdiction. Only where such negotiation fails will a judge be required to direct the jury on the topic of territoriality, which the prosecution must establish on the balance of probabilities.[51]

BEYOND TERRITORIALITY: ENLARGING THE SCOPE OF CRIMINAL JURISDICTION

Criminal jurisdiction under the common law has never been confined strictly to conduct within its physical borders. Some offences are non-territorial. For the purpose of military criminal law, for example, the *status* of the accused as a member of the Australian Defence Forces, rather than

---

49 The Canadian test of real and substantial link had been criticised in *Re Hamilton-Byrne* [1995] 1 VR 129 at 139-140, 142; *Isaac, Tajeddine & Elachi* (1996) 87 A Crim R 513 at 522.

50 C Dellitt, B Fisse and P Keyzer, Chapter 5, 'Territorial and Extraterritorial Jurisdiction' in 9 Criminal Law Principles, 9.1 'The Criminal Laws', *The Laws of Australia* (Sydney: Law Book Company Ltd, 1993–), para 119, p 96.

51 *Thompson v The Queen* (1989) 169 CLR 1, per Mason CJ, Dawson and Gaudron JJ. Since venue will often affect the range of defences and level of punishment, the minority (Brennan and Deane JJ)) took the view that in cases where liability in the "other" jurisdiction is materially different, then the prosecution must establish jurisdiction "beyond reasonable doubt". Under the common law, the burden of proof lies with the prosecution. In some jurisdictions, this has been displaced by a presumption that territorial nexus exists unless the contrary is proved: *Crimes Act* 1900 (NSW), s 3A(4).

territorial location of the alleged conduct, confers jurisdiction on the Advocate General and members of the Courts-Martial.[52]

The adoption of flexible tests of jurisdiction that transcend territoriality is related to an increased awareness of the "globalisation of crime"[53] and that law enforcement must be coordinated at the federal, regional and international level. This expanded approach blurs the conventional representation of domestic criminal jurisdiction in terms of a polarity between territoriality and extra-territoriality. The extra-territorial extension of the criminal law can no longer be regarded as exceptional, confined to "international" crimes with universal jurisdiction such as war crimes.

Reflecting the perception that crime is increasingly globalised, the legal trend is firmly against territoriality as the *exclusive* basis for criminal jurisdiction. This expansion of jurisdiction is reflected in the principles proposed for inclusion in the *Model Criminal Code*.[54] Rather than adopt the flexible test of "territorial nexus", the Code has retained the common law as the "standard geographical jurisdiction", supplemented by four bases of "extended geographical jurisdiction". The Code proposals claim to "provide more certainty about the geographical reach of various offences, and, will turn the mind of the legislature to this very important issue in all contexts".[55]

Summary of the Rules Governing Jurisdiction under the Model Criminal Code

Criminal Code Act *1995* (Cth) — Part 2.7 — *Geographical Jurisdiction*
Standard Geographic Jurisdiction (Division 14, Section 14.1)

The "default" test applies where the offence provision does not address jurisdiction: similar to the principle of territoriality, applying where the "conduct" or a "result" required by the offence occur wholly or partly in Australia.

Extended Geographic Jurisdiction (Division 15, Sections 15.1-15.4)

- **CATEGORY A — covers Australian citizens or body corporates anywhere in the world, subject to a foreign law defence.[56]**

- **CATEGORY B — covers Australian citizens, body corporates and residents anywhere in the world, subject to a foreign law defence.[57]**

---

52 Military and civil jurisdiction is concurrent and potentially overlapping. The scope of military criminal law is limited by the Constitution which imposes restraints on the nature of offences which may be validly enacted by the Commonwealth: see *Re Tracey; Ex parte Ryan* (1989) 166 CLR 518, upholding the constitutional validity of service offences provided they are sufficiently connected with the regulation of the forces and the good order and discipline of defence members: see RA Brown, "Military Justice in Australia: W(h)ither Way?" (1989) 13 Crim LJ 263; W Walsh-Buckley, "Military Courts-Martial in Australia" (1999) 23(6) Crim LJ 335.

53 For a theoretical review of this concept, see M Findlay, *Globalisation of Crime* (Cambridge: Cambridge University Press, 1999).

54 The proposals are contained in the Criminal Code Amendment (Theft, Fraud, Bribery and Related Offences) Bill 1999. These far-reaching proposals were reviewed in a Discussion Paper dealing with computer crimes issued *after* the release of the Bill, effectively by-passing the opportunity for public consultation on the proposals: Model Criminal Code Officers Committee/Standing Committee of Attorneys-General, *Damage and Computer Offences*, Discussion Paper (2000).

55 Criminal Code Amendment (Theft, Fraud, Bribery and Related Offences) Bill 1999, Explanatory Memorandum, p 5.

56 It is a defence if there is no crime in the foreign jurisdiction which corresponds to the Commonwealth offence.

57 It is a defence if the accused is not an Australian citizen or body corporate, and there is no crime in the foreign jurisdiction that corresponds to the Commonwealth offence.

- **CATEGORY C** — covers anyone anywhere regardless of citizenship or residence, subject to a foreign law defence.[58]
- **CATEGORY D** — covers anyone anywhere regardless of citizenship or residence, no foreign law defence.

The *Model Criminal Code* establishes that territoriality (based on the terminatory theory) is defined as the default, supplemented by four non-territorial bases for jurisdiction (Categories A-D) of varying breadth. Categories A-D do not require the crime to be geographically connected to the territory. Jurisdiction extends overseas because of the citizenship or resident status of the accused and/or nature of the offence, not because of any geographic or territorial connection with Australia. Since these categories are truly non-geographic, the phrase "Extended Geographic Jurisdiction" is somewhat misleading.

The *Model Criminal Code* provisions aim to rectify the uncertainty in the present law by removing some of the discretion in the present tests of jurisdiction: the question of whether an offence should be extended beyond Australia's territorial shores is presented as a matter exclusively for Parliament, rather than the courts. The law requires Parliament to address jurisdictional policy considerations prior to enactment, rather than compel judges to address these matters in the context of litigation. Discretion however cannot be entirely removed from the courts. For example, in relation to the foreign law defence (that applies if there is no crime in the foreign jurisdiction which corresponds to the Commonwealth offence) there will doubtless be uncertainties over the characterisation of foreign laws as either criminal or civil.

The obvious danger with the new "global" approach to jurisdiction is over-inclusiveness. The option of "extending" (in effect, abrogating) territorial or geographic jurisdiction will be hard for legislators to resist. Attempting to allay such fears, the Federal Attorney-General offered the following reassurance in the Second Reading Speech:

> Naturally, it is intended that extended forms of jurisdiction will only be applied where there
> is justification for this, having regard to considerations of international law, comity and
> practice.[59]

Even where Parliament has extended jurisdiction, the permission of the Attorney General is required to institute proceedings against a non-citizen/resident of Australia in relation to conduct that occurs wholly in a foreign country. Notwithstanding these safeguards, the domestic pressures to be seen to fight crime at the international level may be difficult to resist. The process of normalisation of extra-territoriality in the criminal law will be fostered and legitimated by the large (and increasing) number

---

58 It is a defence if the accused is not an Australian citizen or body corporate, and there is no crime in the foreign jurisdiction that corresponds to the Commonwealth offence.

59 The Parliament of the Commonwealth of Australia, House of Representatives, Criminal Code Amendment (Theft, Fraud, Bribery and Related Offences) Bill 1999, Second Reading Speech by The Hon Daryl Williams, Attorney-General.

of international treaties dealing with transnational and global crime.[60] Drug law, more than any other area of domestic law, has been shaped by international law. As we shall see in Chapter 15, the extensive proliferation of drug offences (supply, possession, import/export, cultivation, manufacture, drug-dealing, trafficking) and provisions against money-laundering has been mandated by international treaties.

Prior to the *Model Criminal Code* provisions on jurisdiction, the principles of international law have exercised only marginal influence on the concepts of territoriality and extra-territoriality in domestic law. The concept of jurisdiction under international and domestic law is traditionally viewed as having differing and potentially conflicting meanings.[61] The new Federal law, which is proposed as a model for Australia, would represent a radical departure from this approach. This model might be considered acceptable for Federal criminal law since "Commonwealth legislation does not deal with the general law (except where it needs to be applied for specific situations) but with particular interests and concerns that, being of a national character, fall within the Commonwealth sphere".[62] There are, however, dangers of over-extension of State and Territory jurisdiction; the pressures of "law and order" politics to fight crime nationally and globally will be equally hard to resist.

Categories A-D shadow the principles of international law governing jurisdiction. To avoid disputes between sovereign nations, five "principles" have emerged for evaluating the legitimacy of national claims of criminal jurisdiction under international law:

(1) the *territoriality principle*, either on subjective or objective accounts, which applies where the offence occurred within the territory of the prosecuting state;

(2) the *nationality principle*, which applies where the offender is a national of the prosecuting state;

(3) the *protective principle*, which applies where an extra-territorial act threatens the integrity of the prosecuting state;

(4) the *passive personality principle*, which applies where the victim of the offence is a national of the prosecuting state; and

(5) the *universality principle*.[63]

International law provides a mandate for the overseas extension of domestic criminal laws. There are many offences where Federal, State and Territory legislatures have exercised their sovereign power

---

60 As the Model Criminal Code Officers Committee noted: "Sometimes extended jurisdiction needs to be asserted in the interests of effectively dealing with serious transnational crimes. Many international treaties recognise this, and in relation to particular offences call for countries to exercise jurisdiction even though the conduct in question has occurred beyond their boundaries": Model Criminal Code Officers Committee/Standing Committee of Attorneys-General, *Chapter 4: Damage and Computer Offences*, Discussion Paper (2000), p 177. See generally, M Findlay, *The Globalisation of Crime* (Cambridge: Cambridge University Press, 1999).

61 As was noted in *Polyukovich v Commonwealth* (1991) 172 CLR 501 at 658, per Toohey J: "The term 'jurisdiction' has different meanings in international and municipal law".

62 Model Criminal Code Officers Committee/Standing Committee of Attorneys-General, *Ch 4: Damage and Computer Offences*, Discussion Paper (2000), p 177.

63 "There is no exhaustive list of bases upon which a state may exert authority over an individual in international law nor is there precise agreement between commentators as to categorisation": *Polyukovich v Commonwealth* (1991) 172 CLR 501 at 659, per Toohey J. See further, H Reicher (ed), *Australian International Law* (Sydney: Law Book Company Ltd, 1995), pp 243-246.

to apply the criminal law beyond their territorial borders (often expressly stating that the provision "applies outside Australia"). The extra-territorial reach of such offences can raise complex questions of international law, but they are not, by virtue of extra-territoriality, domestically unconstitutional. In *Polyukovich v Commonwealth* (1991) 172 CLR 501, the High Court upheld the validity of the *War Crimes Act* 1945 (Cth) as a proper exercise of the Commonwealth's external affairs power in the Constitution pursuant to s 51(vi), (xxiv). The majority concluded that the legislation was a valid exercise of these powers, notwithstanding the fact that it had extra-territorial effect, and applied to past conduct of persons who at the relevant time had no connection with Australia.[64]

Extra-territorial offences are not limited to international crimes recognised as having "universal jurisdiction".[65] There is a global trend to enact "crimes against human rights", such as torture, terrorism, slavery, sexual trafficking in women and children, and so on. A recent example is the legislation enacted criminalising acts of child sex tourism committed overseas by Australian citizens and residents: see, for example, *Crimes (Child Sex Tourism) Amendment Act* 1994 (Cth), inserting Pt IIIA into the *Crimes Act* 1914 (Cth). Also, responding to international concerns, the *Criminal Code Act* 1995 (Cth) has enacted extra-territorial offences against slavery and sexual servitude: Pt 9.1 of the *Criminal Code Act* 1995 (Cth), inserted by *Criminal Code Amendment Act (Offences Against Humanity)* 1999 (Cth). The latter offences were enacted as part of a new Chapter of the *Model Criminal Code* to align with "Offences Against Humanity": *Model Criminal Code: Chapter 9, Offences Against Humanity — Slavery* (1998).

The increasingly international character of criminal law, and its focus on human rights violations, is reflected in the prosecution of the former President of Chile, Augusto Pinochet, for alleged acts of torture committed on Spanish citizens in Chile. Extradition proceedings were instituted against Pinochet in the United Kingdom: *R v Bow Street Metropolitan Stipendiary Magistrate; Ex parte Pinochet Ugarte (No 3)* [1999] 2 All ER 97. Christine Chinkin has described the litigation as representing "the globalization of human rights law through the affirmation that the consequences of, and jurisdiction over, gross violations are not limited to the state in which they (mostly) occur": "International Decisions: *Regina v Bow Street Metropolitan Stipendiary Magistrate; Ex parte Pinochet Ugarte (No 3)* [1999] 2 WLR 827" (1999) 93 *American Journal of International Law* 703 at 711. See also the discussion at (1999) 93 *American Journal of International Law* 690-703. As Alldridge has observed, this process of internationalisation, both in terms of the impact on jurisdiction and content of the substantive rules, constitutes a significant challenge to the traditional national sovereign character of the criminal law: *Relocating Criminal Law* (Aldershot: Ashgate, 2000), p 160.

---

64   The *War Crimes Act* 1945 (Cth), as amended by the *War Crimes Amendment Act* 1988 (Cth). "War crime" is defined in ss 6, 7 and 8. Section 11 provides that only Australian nationals or residents may be prosecuted for war crimes. See further, G Triggs, "Australia's War Crimes Trials" in TLH McCormack and GJ Simpson (eds), *The Law of War Crimes: National and International Approaches* (The Hague: Kluwer Law International, 1997).

65   Crimes of universal jurisdiction are those that international law regards as so "grave and heinous" that every nation is entitled to try them irrespective of where the conduct occurred. There is disagreement over what crimes fall within this category. It is commonly agreed that war crimes, piracy and slavery fall within it. Other crimes recognised under international law (by treaty or customary law) do not necessarily confer universal jurisdiction, for example, drug trafficking offences.

AUSTRALIAN CRIMINAL LAW: THE GROWTH OF THE FEDERAL JURISDICTION

Federalism undoubtedly complicates conceptions of territoriality in Australia. In the field of criminal law, Federal, State and Territory substantive laws and procedures for enforcement overlap. This overlap between laws has grown significantly in recent years because of the expansion of Federal criminal jurisdiction.[66]

The Commonwealth's legislative power to enact criminal law is restricted by the Constitution. Since the Constitution does not include an express power to legislate in the field of criminal law, to be constitutionally valid, Federal offences must be "incidental" to an existing head of power. The High Court has construed these heads of power broadly, providing a wide mandate for the "federalisation" of criminal law and procedure. For example, in relation to drugs, Federal jurisdiction derives from the Commonwealth's legislative power under the Constitution to regulate "trade and commerce", as well as "external affairs": Commonwealth Constitution, s 51(i), (xxiv). In relation to the latter, the power to legislate is triggered by Australia's ratification of many international treaties and conventions dealing with drugs: see Ch 15, pp 859ff.

International treaties do not merely supply the legal basis for enacting Federal laws to fight international and transnational crime. As we shall see, international human rights law has the potential to limit the scope of national criminal law and procedure. As explored below, the right to privacy contained in the International Covenant on Civil and Political Rights[67] (ICCPR) has provided the legal basis for Commonwealth legislation that protects sexual conduct between consenting adults from arbitrary interference by Federal, State or Territory laws: pp 141ff.

At the level of enforcement, there are national cooperative arrangements for prosecution in specific areas, such as the arrangements governing the prosecution of offences enacted under the uniform *Corporations Law*. Under coordinating legislation, the Commonwealth Director of Public Prosecutions (DPP) has been assigned the role of prosecuting offences under uniform State and Territory laws, in effect "federalising" crimes in areas where the Commonwealth otherwise lacks constitutional authority to legislate. In the recent case of *R v Hughes* (2000) 171 ALR 155, the High Court highlighted that these national enforcement arrangements must satisfy the test of Constitutional validity. As Kirby J noted (at 189):

> Under our Constitution, criminal liability and punishment, when provided in a federal law, must be supported by demonstrable constitutional authority. Convenience and desirability are not enough if the constitutional foundation is missing.

In this case, the authority of the Commonwealth DPP to prosecute corporate offences passed the constitutional test since the activity by the accused impinged on trade and commerce with other

---

66 The expansion of Federal criminal law is reflected in the recent publication of a three volume loose-leaf service, RS Watson and M Ayers, *Australian Criminal Law — Federal Offences* (Sydney: LBC, 2000–); D Sweeney and N Williams, *Commonwealth Criminal Law* (Sydney: Federation Press, 1990).

67 Aus TS 1980 No 23; 999 UNTS 171; New York, adopted 16 December 1966, entered into force 23 March 1976. For a discussion of Australia's human rights obligations and texts of relevant treaties see Department of Foreign Affairs and Trade, *Human Rights Manual* (1998).

countries and affairs external to Australia. Consequently, the federal laws authorising the DPP to exercise enforcement powers under the *Corporations Act* in Western Australia were valid in so far as they affected the accused. However, the constitutional basis for prosecuting these offences is constrained by the heads of power, creating uncertainty in individual cases over whether the facts confer upon the Commonwealth DPP the authority to enforce State and Territory laws. As Kirby J concluded (at para 120), this provides "a fragile foundation for a highly important national law. The present accused fails in his challenge. But the next case may not present circumstances sufficient to attract the essential constitutional support".

●　　●　　●　　●　　●　　●

The principle of territoriality, traditionally conceived, minimises and conceals the transnational dimensions of the criminal law. As territoriality is expanded or transcended, a fragmented and pluralistic picture of criminal law emerges. The kaleidoscopic quality of criminal jurisdiction has implications for other general principles, such as fairness and equality before the law. For example, in negotiating and determining venue, law enforcement officials, prosecutors and judges must be mindful of the danger that the accused may be unfairly subject to prosecution and punishment in another State or Territory for the same conduct, thereby violating the principle against "double jeopardy": D Lanham, *Cross-Border Criminal Law* (Melbourne: FT Law & Tax Asia Pacific, 1997), Ch 3. These concerns are specifically addressed in the *Model Criminal Code* rules governing jurisdiction, discussed above, that permit the accused to raise as a defence the fact that the conduct overseas does not constitute an offence that corresponds to the domestic offence charged. The increasingly pluralistic and fragmented nature of jurisdiction in Australian law also provides scope for the recognition of Indigenous or native criminal jurisdiction.[68] As we explore below at pp 132-135, the emergence of a status-based principle of criminal jurisdiction may lead to conflict with the fundamental principle of equality, particularly the ideal that individuals should be subject to the same treatment before the law.

3.3 THE PRINCIPLE OF FAIRNESS

Geoffery Robertson QC,
The Justice Game (London:
Vintage, 1999), p 386

> For all the grandiose descriptions that have been offered of the adversary system of trial, and for all the pomp and self-esteem that tends to affect its professional participants, it is the best method we have yet devised for giving the suckers an even break

---

68　Cf *Walker v NSW* (1994) 182 CLR 45. J Nielsen and G Martin, "Indigenous Australian Peoples and Human Rights" in D Kinley (ed), *Human Rights in Australian Law* (Sydney: Federation Press, 1998), pp 110-114.

THE RHETORIC OF FAIRNESS AND CRIMINAL JUSTICE

Alongside legality and the rule of law, the principle of fairness plays an important legitimating function in the criminal law. It holds out to the accused, victims and the wider community the promise of obtaining justice from the substantive law and criminal process. From a philosophical perspective, justice has been conceived in a number of different ways. Liberal theorists have conceived justice in terms of "fairness", equality of treatment and respect for individual rights.[69] The centrality accorded to individuals and their rights within this conception of justice has attracted substantial criticism. Feminist legal theorists have exposed how liberal conceptions of justice have only a limited ability to address structural and group-based discrimination that lies beyond the public sphere.[70] Republican theorists have similarly rejected ideas of criminal justice as "just deserts" or retribution, arguing instead for a theory based on the promotion of social freedom or dominion: see Ch 1, pp 59-63. Such theoretical debates about the meaning of justice have practical as well a philosophical implications for the criminal law, especially when translated into concrete legal rights and claims based on fairness, equality and privacy.

Fairness in the administration of law is regarded as "fundamental". It promises legitimacy for the criminal process through maintaining a balance between the State and the citizen. This state of equilibrium is reflected in the concept of "equality of arms" that underscores the right to a fair trial in international human rights law.[71] As McBarnet has observed in *Conviction: Law, The State and the Construction of Justice* (London: MacMillan Press, 1981), p 8:

> The criminal justice process is the most explicit coercive apparatus of the state and the idea that the police and the courts can interfere with liberties of citizens only under known law and by means of *due process of law* is thus a crucial element in the ideology of the democratic state (emphasis in original).

This relationship between legality and fairness in upholding justice is complex. Fairness functions as a curative for the strict unbending quality of legality. The inherent opposition between these two concepts is captured within the phrase "fair trial according to law" or the American version "due process of law" entrenched by the Fourteenth Amendment to the United States Constitution. Gaudron J noted in *Dietrich v The Queen* (1992) 177 CLR 292 at 362:

> It is fundamental to our system of criminal justice that a person should not be convicted of an offence save after a fair trial according to law. The expression "fair trial according to law" is not a tautology. In most cases a trial is fair if conducted according to law, and unfair

---

69　See J Rawls, *A Theory of Justice* (Cambridge, Mass: Harvard University Press, 1980); R Dworkin, *Taking Rights Seriously* (London: Duckworth, 1977) respectively. For a review of the competing conceptions of justice see T Campbell, *Justice* (2nd ed, Houndmills, Hamps: Macmillan, 2001).

70　While the theories of Rawls and Dworkin presume the existence of the welfare state and may be described as broadly welfarist, they nevertheless take individuals and their rights as the starting point. Being addressed to political action in the public sphere, the theories have only restricted scope for achieving social justice: see N Lacey, *Unspeakable Subjects: Feminist Essays in Legal and Social Theory* (Oxford: Hart Publishing, 1998), Ch 2.

71　This principle has been drawn from the fair trial guarantees in Art 6 of the *European Convention on Human Rights*: A Ashworth, *The Criminal Process* (2nd ed, Oxford: Oxford University Press, 1998), p 60.

> if not. If our legal processes were perfect that would be so in every case. But the law recognizes that sometimes, despite the best efforts of all concerned, a trial may be unfair even though conducted strictly in accordance with law. Thus, the overriding qualification and universal criterion of fairness! (citations omitted)

See also Deane J at 326. The centrality accorded to the "trial" by the common law reflects the limited judicial control over criminal investigation and prosecution within adversarial systems. With the exception of judicial supervision of pre-trial warrants, the trial is the forum where judges can demonstrate their fidelity to the principles of legality and fairness. Thus, the courts have recognised a right to a fair trial "in the interests of seeking to ensure that innocent people are not convicted of criminal offences": *Jago v District Court (NSW)* (1989) 168 CLR 23, at 42, per Mason CJ. As we will examine below, the judicial commitment to avoiding unfairness is embodied in a wide-range of procedural rules, such as the presumption of innocence and burden of proof as well as rules governing the admissibility and exclusion of evidence. The denial of a fair trial to an accused is a ground for setting aside a conviction on the grounds of miscarriage of justice.[72]

The fairness principle is directed towards the process, not the substance, of the criminal law. It does not require the criminalisation or decriminalisation of any type of conduct. Rather, it merely insists that criminal proceedings operate in a way that avoids an unfair trial by minimising the risk of innocent people being convicted. So while there may be evidence that law enforcement policies and definitions of substantive crimes discriminate against certain groups within society, judges can be relied upon to apply the rules governing fact and guilt determination during the trial in an objectively fair manner. The importance of fair treatment plays a vital role in preserving public confidence in the administration of justice. As Ashworth has noted "there is ample evidence that people place great emphasis on the fairness of procedures, even when they disagree with the outcome".[73]

This representation of criminal justice as a "balance" between crime control and due process is problematic: see Ch 1, pp 36-40. Critical and socio-legal research has suggested that due process values such as fairness, while performing important ideological functions, are largely illusory. In lower courts, where most suspects are processed, an "ideology of triviality" pervades summary proceedings.[74] Rather than venerate fairness values, empirical research has revealed that trial procedures, especially those in lower courts, operate as ritualised degradation ceremonies.[75] Though the jury trial occupies a central place in our image of criminal justice, the majority of legal proceedings are summary in nature presided over by a magistrate sitting without a jury. Indeed, the cherished right to jury trial has been extensively abrogated by legislation — summary proceedings

---

72 In *McKinney v The Queen* (1990) 171 CLR 468, the High Court observed, in the context of jury warnings relating to uncorroborated confession evidence, that "the central thesis of the administration of criminal justice is the entitlement of an accused person to a fair trial according to law" and wherever this is not met there will be a miscarriage of justice: at 478.

73 A Ashworth, "Crime, Community and Creeping Consequentialism" [1996] *Criminal Law Review* 220 at 228, citing T Tyler, *Why People Obey the Law* (New Haven: Yale University Press, 1990).

74 D McBarnet, *Conviction: Law, The State and the Construction of Justice* (London: MacMillan Press, 1981), especially Chs 7 and 8.

75 K Laster, *Law as Culture* (Sydney: Federation Press, 1997), pp 294-302; M Feeley, *The Process is the Punishment* (New York: Sage, 1979). On the positive use of shame to reintegrate rather than stigmatise offenders, see J Braithwaite, *Crime, Shame and Reintegration* (Cambridge: Cambridge University Press, 1989).

are so pervasive that the symbolic function of the jury now far outweighs its practical significance. As we shall explore in Chapter 13 at p 677, although most theft cases will be determined by a magistrate, the test of dishonesty presumes that relevant community standards will be applied by a jury. The role and impact of judicial instructions on the independence of jury deliberations is further explored below at pp 123-126.

A Constitutional Right to Trial by Jury

No doubt conscious of the trend toward the increasing dominance of summary justice in the late 19th century, the drafters of the Commonwealth Constitution included the following guarantee in s 80: "The trial on an indictment of any offence against any law of the Commonwealth shall be by jury". Notwithstanding a powerful dissenting judgment by Deane J, the High Court has affirmed that s 80 has procedural rather than substantive effect, leaving the legislature completely free to determine whether crimes should be "deemed" summary and thus tried without a jury: *Kingswell v The Queen* (1985) 159 CLR 264. For a review of the "dissenting jurisprudence" on s 80, and Murphy J's contribution, see D Brown, "Lionel Murphy and the Criminal Law" in M Coper and G Williams (eds), *Justice Lionel Murphy: Influential or Merely Prescient?* (Sydney: Federation Press, 1997), pp 85-89. See also G Williams, *Human Rights Under the Constitution* (Melbourne: Oxford University Press, 1999), pp 36-37, 103-110.

Even in superior courts, where the rhetorical assurances of fair treatment are strongest, McBarnet concludes that the rhetoric of legality and fairness rarely stands in the way of conviction: "if we bring due process down from the dizzy heights of abstraction and subject it to empirical scrutiny, the conclusion must be that due process is for crime control".[76] Her point is *not* that the police, prosecutors and judges collude in deviating from legality and fairness, but rather that the law itself licences this deviation. Judicial rhetoric venerates fairness and legality in the administration of criminal justice while systematically denying them in the specific application of rules, discretions and remedies: see Ch 1, pp 36-40. The challenge for critical scholars has not only been to expose the dichotomy between rhetoric and reality, but also to engage in the radical reconstruction and expansion of the principle of fairness.

CLASSIFICATION OF OFFENCES AND CRIMINAL PROCEEDINGS

Felony v Misdemeanour

Historically, the distinction between felonies and misdemeanours developed in the English common law to distinguish between the type of punishment to be applied. Felonies were capital crimes. The effect of passing a sentence of death (whether or not commuted to transportation or imprisonment) was "attainder". Attainder (which means "to blacken" in Latin and is probably the source of the "convict taint") resulted in convicted felons losing all civil rights, including the right to hold property

---

76   D McBarnet, *Conviction: Law, the State and the Construction of Justice* (London: MacMillan Press, 1981), pp 155-156.

and institute legal proceedings. The property of felons was therefore forfeited to the Crown. The felon suffered a form of "legal death". Misdemeanours were less serious offences that did not result in civil incapacitation, but were punishable by imprisonment or fine. Following the statutory relaxation of attainder in relation to forfeiture of property in the late 19th century and demise of capital punishment generally, the distinction lost much of its practical significance. These reforms did not address the continuing incapacity of persons convicted of a capital felony to bring civil actions. Although attainder was rarely invoked, the High Court in *Dugan v Mirror Newspapers Ltd* (1979) 142 CLR 583, confirmed that the English doctrine, though archaic, had been received into New South Wales in 1828. Gibbs J noted (at 589) that in the early colonial period, the doctrine had been largely evaded in practice by judges requiring proof of conviction and sentence from England. However, since the doctrine had not been abolished by statute, a person convicted of a capital felony could not bring proceedings in defamation. This anomaly was quickly remedied by legislation in jurisdictions retaining the distinction: for example, *Felons (Civil Proceedings) Act* 1981 (NSW). It should be noted that the forfeiture of property, pre-trial as well as post-conviction, has been revived by special legislative provisions relating to the confiscation of proceeds of crimes. For further discussion of these measures in the context of drug trafficking, see Chapter 15, pp 866ff.

Historical Perspectives on the Convict Taint

In early colonial New South Wales, the full force of the doctrine of attainder was not applied. To establish order and respect for legality, the courts ignored the doctrine allowing civil proceedings to be instituted by and on behalf of convicted felons. The first civil case in 1788 was instituted by Henry and Susannah Kable (both convicted felons) to recover compensation for goods "lost" during their transportation. For a discussion of the relative civil freedom of convicts in Australia, see D Neal, *The Rule of Law in a Penal Colony* (Cambridge: Cambridge University Press, 1991), Ch 1; B Kercher, *The Unruly Child: A History of Law in Australia* (Sydney: Allen & Unwin, 1995), Ch 2 and *Debt, Seduction and other Disasters: The Birth of Civil Law in Convict New South Wales* (Sydney: Federation Press, 1996), Ch 3.

Although having lost most of its original significance, the term "felony" is still employed in New South Wales, though it is defined by legislation simply as an offence punishable by imprisonment: *Crimes Act* 1900 (NSW), s 9. It has been specifically abolished in the Australian Capital Territory, South Australia, and Victoria: *Crimes Act* 1900 (ACT), s 9; *Criminal Law Consolidation Act* 1935 (SA), s 5D; *Crimes Act* 1958 (Vic), s 322B(1). The Commonwealth never introduced the felony/misdemeanour distinction, simply dividing crimes into indictable or summary offences: *Crimes Act* 1914 (Cth), ss 4G-4H. In the Commonwealth, Australian Capital Territory, Tasmania and Victoria, crimes are referred to simply as indictable offences and summary offences. The Code States abolished the common law classifications and with them the doctrine of attainder. The Codes simply divide offences into categories: crimes, misdemeanours and simple offences (and regulatory offences in Western Australia): *Criminal Code* (NT), s 3; *Criminal Code* (Qld), s 3; *Criminal Code* (Tas), s 5; *Criminal Code* (WA), s 3. The distinctions are relevant to determining the mode of trial (indictable/summary).

The persistence of the distinction in New South Wales, and the division of indictable offences into "crimes" and "misdemeanours" in the Northern Territory, Queensland and Western Australia, make for complexities in terminology when reviewing Australian criminal law. Since this book will be concerned predominantly with the law relating to indictable offences, we will refrain from further dividing them into felonies or crimes as opposed to misdemeanours and will simply use the generic term "offences".

In the modern criminal law, the classification of offences is most significant for determining the mode of trial used to adjudicate guilt. Crimes are conventionally divided into the following classes:

━━ offences triable on indictment before a jury, known as "indictable offences";

━━ offences triable summarily before a magistrate, known as "summary offences";

━━ offences triable either way, known as "hybrid offences".

T A B L E 1 : Types of Offences and Terminology

JURISDICTION	OFFENCES TRIABLE BY JUDGE AND JURY (most serious)	OFFENCES TRIABLE BY JUDGE AND JURY (less serious)	OFFENCES TRIABLE BY MAGISTRATE
CTH	indictable	indictable	summary
ACT	indictable	indictable	summary
NSW	felony	misdemeanour	summary
NT	crime	crime	simple or regulatory[77]
QLD	crime	misdemeanour	simple or regulatory[78]
SA	indictable	indictable	summary
TAS	indictable	indictable	summary
VIC	indictable	indictable	summary
WA	crime	misdemeanour	simple[79]

Typically, indictable offences are determined before a judge and jury, and so are usually reserved for more serious offences. Summary offences require trial before a magistrate, who sits as both the tribunal of law and fact. There are also "hybrid offences", where the accused in an indictable matter may elect to be tried before a single judge sitting without a jury. For example, in New South Wales,

---

77 *Criminal Code* (NT), s 3.

78 *Criminal Code* (Qld), s 3.

79 *Criminal Code* (WA), s 3.

a person prosecuted on indictment has a general right to elect for trial by judge alone: *Criminal Procedure Act* 1986 (NSW), ss 30-33. There are also indictable offences, scheduled under this Act, that must be dealt with summarily unless the prosecution elects to proceed by way of indictment. There is also another type of hybrid offence: the summary offence that may be heard by a Supreme Court judge sitting without a jury. In New South Wales, this procedure has been introduced to deal with complex "white collar" crimes: *Crimes Act* 1900 (NSW), s 475B. Commercial fraud trials can be extremely complex (arguably too complex for a jury) and may take many months. This section provides a quicker procedure for dealing with such cases. However, s 475B clearly indicates that it is only the accused who can elect for this type of trial.

Indictable v Summary Offences

Indictable offences take their name from the indictment, which is a written document prepared on the behalf of the *Crown* (commonly the Director of Public Prosecutions). Hence cases are listed as *R v Smith* ("R" representing either "Regina" during the reign of a Queen or "Rex" during the reign of a King). Originally the bill of indictment was laid before a "grand jury" of 23 men who had to decide whether the bill was "true", that is, whether there was a case for the accused to answer. If it was true, the case would then proceed to trial by a "petty jury" consisting of 12 men. In early colonial Australia, the summary trial without jury was established as the norm. Trial by jury was considered impractical within a society comprised largely of felons, and was only gradually introduced in the mid-19th century as a result of a concerted political campaign by Emancipists: D Neal, *The Rule of Law in a Penal Colony* (Cambridge: Cambridge University Press, 1991), Ch 7. In the 20th century the bifurcated grand jury system was replaced by the committal or preliminary hearing conducted by a magistrate. (The grand jury system still survives in some common law jurisdictions such as the United States). The committal or preliminary hearing considers whether there is sufficient evidence to justify the trial.

The overwhelming majority of criminal matters (98.2%) are initiated by way of summons (hence "summary offences"): Ch 1, p 37. As a result, most proceedings are conducted before a magistrate sitting without a jury. Rather than the norm, indictable matters heard before a jury may be viewed as exceptional. As a creation of statute, the summary procedure only applies where stipulated by legislation. The Act creating the offence must expressly state that the crime is a summary offence or that the offence must be tried by a magistrate. Whilst indictable offences are prosecuted on behalf of the Crown, in summary matters the proceedings are initiated in the name of the informant, that is, the person who lays the information before the magistrate. The informant can be anyone, but is usually the arresting officer or the officer responsible for conducting prosecutions in that police station.

Criminal proceedings may be commenced by way of summons, as an alternative to arrest. A summons is a notice served on the defendant by a court official instructing the defendant to appear before the court on a particular date. The courts have construed the power to arrest or proceed by way of summons in a manner that provides maximum protection to individual liberty: see, for example, *Williams v The Queen* (1986) 161 CLR 278.

The function of the committal is to operate as a procedural filter with the objectives of:

(1) eliminating weak cases;

(2) disclosing the prosecution case;

(3) identifying guilty pleas early in the prosecution process; and

(4) rehearsing the case and clarifying the issues.[80]

Empirical research suggests that very few committals result in discharge. In Salmelainen's study, only 7.6% of cases were discharged at the committal: "Understanding Committal Hearings" (1992) 18 *Crime and Justice Bulletin* 2. This finding would be consistent with McBarnet's thesis of an ideology of triviality and that magistrates are operating merely as "rubber stamps" for the prosecution: Ch 1, pp 37ff. Indeed, the power of the magistrate to throw out a matter for lack of evidence may be circumvented by the power of the Director of Public Prosecutions (DPP) to lay an indictment against a person who was discharged by the magistrate during the committal. The filtering and safeguard function of the committal is even further undermined by the power of the DPP to lay an "ex officio" indictment in cases where there has been no committal: for example, *Criminal Procedure Act* 1986 (NSW), s 4(2). It has been held that the power to lay an ex officio indictment is not amenable to judicial review: *Barton v The Queen* (1980) 147 CLR 75. For fuller discussion of the rules governing the institution of criminal proceedings see C Cato, *The Law and Practice of Criminal Litigation* (Sydney: LBC, 1998), Ch 2. A less sceptical explanation of the low rate of discharge is that the committal stage has a disciplinary effect on prosecutors, leading to the careful selection and preparation of cases.

The second function of the committal is that it allows the accused to be informed of the prosecution's case and the evidence that will be called at trial. Pre-trial disclosure helps the defence prepare its case, though the extent of this obligation under the fair trial principle is murky: *Lawless v The Queen* (1979) 142 CLR 659. Although pleading and discovery have not been features of criminal trials, there are increasing moves in the name of efficiency to impose formal pre-trial disclosure obligations on both the prosecution and the defence. These obligations are typically imposed by prosecution guidelines or practice statements issued by the courts, though in Victoria these duties of disclosure have been formalised in legislation: *Crimes (Criminal Trials) Act* 1999 (Vic). To promote litigation efficiency, the Act casts obligations on the accused to disclose the nature of the defence before trial. Similar non-legislative schemes, based on voluntary defence disclosure, have been adopted under the rubric of "case management" in many jurisdictions: R Refshauge, "Frankenstein's Monster — Creating a Criminal Justice System for the 21st Century" (2000) 9(4) *Journal of Judicial Administration* 185. This has raised concerns about the negative impact of these efficiency reforms on the right to a fair trial, in particular, the extent to which they threaten the presumption of innocence by requiring the accused to furnish evidence of his or her own guilt: S Bronitt and M Ayers, "Criminal Law and Human Rights" in D Kinley (ed), *Human Rights in Australian Law* (Sydney: Federation Press, 1998), pp 130-132. Others have argued that the recent reforms enacted in Victoria are measured and justifiable responses for promoting efficiency, and do not abrogate fundamental principles of criminal justice: G Flatman and M Bagaric, "Accused Disclosure — Measured Response or Abrogation of the Presumption of Innocence" (1999) 23 Crim LJ 327. For further discussion of law and ethical consideration governing pre-trial procedures see J Hunter and K Cronin, *Evidence, Advocacy and Ethical Practice* (Sydney: Butt, 1995), Ch 4.

---

80   P Salmelainen, "Understanding Committal Hearings" (1992) 18 *Crime and Justice Bulletin* 2.

McBarnet's research suggests that the quality of justice in summary proceedings is inferior compared to the guarantees offered by trial by jury. Nevertheless, for minor matters, the summary procedure is justified for its efficiency. Although the accused loses the right to a trial by jury, the benefits of a summary trial are two-fold. First. it provides for a speedier trial, as Blackstone noted in his *Commentaries on the Laws of England* (1765), Book IV, p 280:

> There is no intervention of a jury, but the party accused is acquitted or condemned by the suffrage of such person as the statute has appointed for his judge. An institution designed professedly for the greater ease of the subject, by doing him speedy justice.

Secondly, summary offences limit the range of penalties available to the judge. For example, in the Australian Capital Territory, the Magistrates' Court is limited to a maximum imprisonment term of two years and maximum fine of $10,000: *Crimes Act* 1900 (ACT), s 477(10). Notwithstanding the ideology of triviality that pervades summary justice, the modern trend is firmly in favour of expanding summary jurisdiction and the range of sentencing powers of magistrates: P Darbyshire, "An Essay on the Importance and Neglect of the Magistracy" [1997] Crim LR 627. For a discussion of "technocratic justice" and the increasing emphasis placed on promoting efficiency within the criminal justice system, see Chapter 1, 2.8 'Theories of Criminal Justice' at pp 40-42.

Plea-Bargaining in the Shadow of the Criminal Law

The rarity of the trial is a reflection of the ubiquity of the guilty plea, which often follows discussion between the prosecution and the defence. For an excellent survey of plea-bargaining which combines empirical research and discussion of reform see K Mack and S Anleu, "Reform of Pre-Trial Criminal Procedure: Guilty Pleas" (1998) 22 Crim LJ 263. See also J Bishop, *Prosecution Without Trial* (Sydney: Butt, 1989).

THE RIGHT TO A FAIR TRIAL: *DIETRICH v THE QUEEN*

Although the fair trial principle is claimed to be fundamental and universal — indeed, a basic human right protected by international law — its scope and effect are *legally* circumscribed in a number of ways. The judicial duty is not to ensure fairness in the criminal process, but rather to prevent the accused being subjected to an unfair trial and the risk of wrongful conviction. Limiting this duty in this way means that judges do not have the responsibility for ensuing fairness during investigation. That said, what happens before a trial may hamper the ability of the court to conduct a fair trial. For example, serious pre-trial delay may have a negative impact on the ability of accused persons to conduct their defence: *Jago v District Court (NSW)* (1989) 168 CLR 23. In this "indirect" way, procedural and evidential rules for ensuring fairness during the trial impinge on pre-trial methods of investigation and prosecution decision-making.[81] As Lord Scarman has observed, "The judge's control of the criminal process begins and ends with the trial, though his influence may extend beyond its beginning and conclusion": *R v Sang* [1980] AC 402 at 455.

---

81 The impact of law on investigative practices is often overstated, as recent Australian research reveals, many leading High Court decisions that had an impact on investigative powers were not communicated to the police or were misconstrued: D Dixon, *Law in Policing: Legal Regulation and Police Practices* (Oxford: Oxford University Press, 1997), p 205.

Further practical limitations to the fair trial principle emerge when it is applied to *specific* contexts. The judicial rhetoric of fairness shifts from one of "universal absolutes" to a "fundamental principle subject to reasonable qualifications". As we shall explore below, the fair trial principle is dependent on the gravity of the offence. For example, in *Dietrich v The Queen* (1992) 177 CLR 292 the majority of the High Court held that the lack of legal representation for an accused charged with a "serious crime" may result in an unfair trial. While the High Court did not hold that the right to a fair trial was inapplicable to proceedings for minor crimes (this was not the question being litigated), there is some indication that the standards of fairness are not truly universal or absolute. Indeed, the right to a fair trial may be viewed as right to a trial that is *reasonably* fair in the circumstances. Like the notion of "perfect justice", the fair trial is a normative ideal for which judges should strive to achieve. As Brennan J pointed out in *Jago v District Court (NSW)* (1989) 168 CLR 23 at 49 (emphasis added):

> If it be said that judicial measures cannot always secure perfect justice to an accused, we should ask whether the ideal of perfect justice has not sounded in rhetoric rather than in law and whether the legal right of an accused, truly stated, is a *right to a trial as fair as the courts can make it*. Were it otherwise, trials would be prevented and convictions would be set aside when circumstances outside judicial control impair absolute fairness.[82]

There are clearly constitutional limits on the judicial obligation to ensure a fair trial. The courts cannot address the resource implications of the fair trial principle, such as the availability and allocation of resources for legal aid. The separation of the spheres of governmental responsibility — judicial, executive and legislative — reinforces judicial independence and authority. The doctrine of separation of powers places the law above and beyond politics. However, the constitutional confinement of judicial responsibility for the fair trial effectively sequesters the courts from the wider political contexts of the administration of criminal justice. Yet, fairness within the criminal process is not *solely* a judicial or even legal responsibility. It is a responsibility that should be shared between judicial, political and social institutions. Indeed, this is consistent with the position under the *International Covenant on Civil and Political Rights*, which imposes enforceable obligations in relation to the fair trial on *all* organs of State, including the legislature, executive and judiciary.[83]

There is considerable indeterminacy surrounding many aspects of the principle of fairness. Many fundamental questions remain unresolved including:

What is a "fair" trial?

How far does the fair trial principle extend?

Does the principle apply pre-trial to preliminary hearings or committals?

Does the principle apply to the methods of gathering evidence?

If the fair trial principle confers legal rights and duties, what remedies are available for breach?

---

82 This dicta was approved in *Dietrich v The Queen* (1992) 177 CLR 292 at 345, per Dawson J. Gaudron J similarly noted: "A trial is not necessarily unfair because it is less than perfect": at 365.

83 See Art 2(2) of the International Covenant on Civil and Political Rights, as clarified by the United Nations Human Rights Committee General Comment, Nos 2 and 3, 36 UN GAOR, Supp No 40 (a/36/40), Annex VII.

▬ Does the inherent judicial power to halt or stay legal proceedings apply where the unfairness to the accused is caused or sanctioned by statute?

▬ Does the Commonwealth Constitution contain an implied right to a fair trial, and does this extend to State as well as Federal proceedings?[84]

At its core, the definition of "fairness" in the fair trial principle proves to be elusive. In *Dietrich v The Queen* (1992) 177 CLR 292 (at 300 and 353), members of the High Court acknowledged that the right to a fair trial under the common law, by its nature, is an evolving concept incapable of exhaustive definition. Acknowledging its contingency, Gaudron J observed (at 364) that,

> what is fair very often depends on the circumstances of the particular case. Moreover, notions of fairness are inevitably bound up with prevailing social values ... And, just as what might be fair in one case might be unfair in another, so too what is considered fair at one time may, quite properly, be adjudged unfair at another.

While the fair trial concept in domestic law remains narrowly circumscribed, there are signs that the principle under international law is evolving into a fundamental value that extends throughout the criminal process. This is evident in a recent decision of the European Court of Human Rights, which held that evidence obtained by deliberate police entrapment violated the right to a fair trial under Art 6. The Court affirmed that the guarantee of fairness is not limited to legal proceedings, but underpins the whole course of the criminal process including the way in which evidence was taken.[85] The judicial discretion to exclude evidence gathered by entrapment in Australia, which is based on public policy considerations rather than fairness, is further discussed in Chapter 15. There are signs that the concept of the fair trial under the common law is capable of expansion into the pre-trial phase. As Mason CJ observed in *Jago v District Court (NSW)* (1989) 168 CLR 23 at 29: "there is no reason why the right should not extend to the whole course of the criminal process". The role of international human rights law on the development of the right to fair trial and its remedies is further explored below.

FEMINIST PERSPECTIVES

The Fair Trial Principle: A Flawed Balance?

Normative disagreement over the fair trial principle is related not only to structural issues, such as its scope and possible remedies. More fundamentally, feminists have raised concern that the concept of fairness that underlies the adversarial system is constrained by its traditional "binary" or "bipolar" construction.[86] That is, the State's interests are pitted against the individual accused

---

84 Discussion of these issues is beyond the scope of this chapter. For further discussion, see P Bailey, "Civil and Political Rights: (8) The Right to a Fair Trial" in D Heydon (ed), *Halsbury's Laws of Australia*, (Sydney: Butt, 1997), Vol 4, para 80-1575ff; S Bronitt and M Ayers, "Criminal Law and Human Rights" in D Kinley (ed), *Human Rights in Australian Law* (Sydney: Federation Press, 1998), pp 120-124. On the constitutional developments, see J Hope, "A Constitutional Right to A Fair Trial? Implications for the Reform of the Australian Criminal Justice System" (1996) 24 *Federal Law Review* 173 at 181-189 and F Wheeler, "The Doctrine of Separation of Powers and Constitutionally Entrenched Due Process in Australia" (1997) 23(2) *Monash University Law Review* 248.

85 *Teixeira de Castro v Portugal* (9 June 1998), *Reports of Judgments and Decisions* 1998-IV, para 34, citing *Van Mechelen v the Netherlands* (23 April 1997), *Reports of Judgments and Decisions* 1997-III, p 711, § 50.

86 P Easteal, "Beyond Balancing" in P Easteal (ed), *Balancing the Scales: Rape, Law Reform and Australian Culture* (Sydney: Federation Press, 1998), Ch 14. These attributes also apply to civil procedure: see R Hunter and K Mack, "Exclusion and Silence: Procedure and Evidence" in N Naffine and R Owens (eds), *Sexing the Subject of Law* (Sydney: LBC, 1997), Ch 9.

and the judge's obligation is to maintain a fair balance between these two parties. To ensure that the power and superior resources of the State do not upset this balance, the law develops safeguards against wrongful conviction of the innocent such as the presumption of innocence and the standard of proof.

This image of balancing the interests of the State and the accused is reinforced in popular culture and legal iconography. As Patricia Easteal notes in *Balancing the Scales: Rape, Law Reform and Australian Culture* (Sydney: Federation Press, 1998), p 205:

> another striking flaw in the portrayal of justice is that the scales [of justice] are held by a woman, the goddess Astraea; an ironic use of female imagery since women have and continue to play such a marginal and silent role in the legal system.

The imagery is deficient not only because there are so few female judges, but also because it excludes victims, their families and the wider community from the scales of justice. In the modern criminal process, victims have no special status beyond their position as a potential witness for the prosecution: C Pollard, "Victims and the Criminal Justice System: A New Vision" (2000) Crim LR 5. While there is an increasing commitment at the international level to improving the treatment of victims of crime,[87] prosecutors are not representatives or advocates for victims, or the communities affected by crime. The wider interests of the State and victims do not necessarily coincide. This has been evident, for example, in recent cases where those accused of rape have sought access to the complainant's confidential medical and/or counselling records.[88]

While the principle of equality has provided the basis for the reform of sexual assault laws, the fair trial principle has provided a foundation for challenging such initiatives. In recent years, defence counsel have argued that rape trials should be permanently stayed on the ground that "rape shield laws", which aim to limit humiliating and degrading cross-examination on the complainant's sexual history, violate the accused's right to a fair trial.[89] The principle has also been invoked to stay proceedings where the complaint is substantially delayed because the complaint relates to sexual abuse perpetrated on the victim as a child.[90]

---

87 See United Nations, *Declaration of Basic Principles of Justice for Victims of Crime and Abuse of Power*, GA Res 40/34, UN GAOR, 40th Session, Supp No 53, at 213, UN Doc A/40/53 (1985). This has resulted in the widespread adoption of "Victims' Charters", leading to compensation schemes and the introduction of "victim impact statements" at the sentencing stage.

88 A Cossin, "Tipping The Scales in Her Favour: The Need to Protect Counselling Records in Sexual Assault Trials" in P Easteal (ed), *Balancing the Scales: Rape, Law Reform and Australian Culture* (Sydney: Federation Press, 1998), Ch 7. For a survey comparing approaches in Canada, Australia and the United States, see S Bronitt and B McSherry, "The Use and Abuse of Counselling Records in Sexual Assault Trials: Reconstructing the 'Rape Shield'" (1997) *Criminal Law Forum* 259.

89 See T Henning and S Bronitt, "Rape Victims on Trial: Regulating the Use and Abuse of Sexual History Evidence" in P Easteal (ed), *Balancing the Scales: Rape, Law Reform and Australian Culture* (Sydney: Federation Press, 1998), Ch 6.

90 A prosecution of a doctor for alleged sexual abuse of children patients was stayed on the grounds of the victims "inexcusable delay": *Geoffrey Davis v DPP* (SC No 782 of 1994) discussed in P Easteal, "Suppressing the Voices of Survivors: Sexual Exploitation by Health Practitioners" (1998) 33(1) *Australian Journal of Social Issues* 211 at 222-227.

The traditional adversarial conception of the criminal process in terms of a "battle model" — the State versus the individual — is clearly open to challenge. Feminists have argued for wider use of alternate dispute resolution, such as mediation, claiming that these processes are more "culturally feminine" and better able to accommodate the female subject: R Graycar and J Morgan, *The Hidden Gender of Law* (Sydney: Federation Press, 1990), pp 410-412. This feminine approach to dispute resolution is contrasted with the masculine construction of "justice" in terms of rights, autonomy and impartiality.[91] While mediation offers advantages in terms of contextualising disputes and enabling parties to produce a consensual outcome, it poses the danger (especially vivid in the criminal justice context) of concealing legal wrongs against women from public scrutiny. As Rosemary Hunter and Kathy Mack point out: "The emphasis on privacy and confidentiality [in mediation] can reinforce the law's construction of sexed harms to women as not suitable for consideration or remedy by formal legal processes": "Exclusion and Silence: Procedure and Evidence" in N Naffine and R Owens (eds), *Sexing the Subject of Law* (Sydney: LBC, 1997), p 188. Thus far, mediation in the criminal context has been selectively employed for a narrow range of offences, as a diversionary option where guilt is not contested.[92] The dichotomy has also been challenged at a more fundamental level. Kathy Daly has pointed out that the common feminist accusation of "justice" as being masculine and therefore incapable of feminine "care" is an oversimplified representation of existing criminal processes: "Criminal Justice Ideologies and Practices in Different Voices: Some Feminist Questions about Justice" in N Lacey (ed), *Criminal Justice* (Oxford: Oxford University Press, 1994). In many areas, such as the discretion to prosecute and the sentencing stage, considerations of "care" do intrude, taking into account the potential negative impact of prosecution or imprisonment on dependent family members: p 238.

Rather than abandon the adversarial system, there is scope for re-conceptualising the fair trial principle in holistic and inclusive terms. As Gaudron J pointed out in *Dietrich v The Queen* (1992) 177 CLR 292 (at 364), the concept of fairness is not immutable and may properly take account of changing social values. The adversarial system is neither undermined nor its "balance" upset by valuing the legitimate interests of victims. Indeed, adjustment to the traditional balance may be essential for achieving "justice". As Helena Kennedy observed in *Eve Was Framed — Women and British Justice* (London: Vintage Books for Chatto & Windus, 1993) (at p 12):

> Civilised men and women adhere to a social contract requiring them to settle disputes
> in courtrooms rather than with pistols at dawn. That involves the provision by courts of
> symbolic retribution, an assuagement for the victims and their families as well as
> society. But the contract ceases to operate effectively if victims are not dealt with fairly

---

91 Carol Gilligan argues that the legal voice, which is implicitly male, is based on logic of justice, whereas the female voice attaches greater value to the "ethic of care": *In A Different Voice* (Cambridge, MA: Harvard University Press, 1982), discussed in K Daly, "Criminal Justice Ideologies and Practices in Different Voices: Some Feminist Questions about Justice" in N Lacey (ed), *Criminal Justice* (Oxford: Oxford University Press, 1994).

92 Early research on restorative conferences suggests that compared to ordinary criminal proceedings, conferences are perceived by offenders as being more procedurally fair: L Sherman and G Barnes, *Restorative Justice and Offenders Respect for the Law*. Paper 3, Reintegrative Shaming Experiment, Working Paper, Law Program (Canberra: ANU, 1997).

in the courts or defendants cannot be guaranteed a fair trial. There is a constant
tension between the needs of those who suffer crime and those who are accused of it,
and it is within that tension that justice is defined. There has to be a constant fine
tuning to a changing world and a willingness to shed preconceptions.

Under international human rights law, there are signs that the concept of fair trial is evolving to
accommodate the rights of victims and other participants in the criminal process such as
witnesses. The European Court of Human Rights has recently held that, in relation to the needs of
preserving the anonymity of witnesses and victims, the fair trial principle in Art 6 is broad enough
to encompass the interests of victims and their families.[93] Reconceiving justice in terms of
victims' interests addresses the traditional exclusion of women from the scales of justice, yet
victims' interests cannot be paramount. Kathy Daly has pointed to the dangers of reconstructing
criminal law and justice practices exclusively from the standpoint of victims:

> A victim-centred strategy can easily lead to a feminist law and order stance, and we
> should be wary of this for several reasons. It can spill over to a more punitive treatment
> of women defendants, and it can have especially harsh consequences for ethnic
> minority men.[94]

Feminists understandably express some scepticism toward "rights-based" reformist agendas
that draw exclusively from the traditional catalogue of human rights in which political and civil
rights are privileged over social and economic ones.[95] The classical liberal freedoms protected by
Bills of Rights and to a lesser extent, by the common law, maintain and inscribe boundaries
between public and private spheres. This approach offers only limited opportunities for
remedying entrenched gender discrimination occurring outside the public sphere. Feminist
scholarship has produced both a "critique of rights", as well as engaging in the reconstruction of
concepts, such as equality and privacy, in ways that better protect the interests of women. The
public/private dichotomy is explored further in 'The Public/Private Dichotomy: Malleable and
Discriminatory': below at pp 143-145.

Gender discrimination is structurally embedded within the substance and procedure of
the criminal law. The media has highlighted "unfair" sexist and insensitive judicial comments
made during rape trials. Closer scrutiny of these remarks reveal that judicial "gender bias" is
often based on established evidential and procedural rules, such as the requirement to give a

---

93 *Doorson v The Netherlands* (1996) 22 EHRR 330; *Van Mechlen v Netherlands* [1997] HRCD 431; *Jasper v the United
    Kingdom* (unrep, 16/2/2000, Eur Ct HR, 27052/95). In relation to these cases Ashworth concludes: "Although the
    issues are complex, it is important to build upon this small beginning": *The Criminal Process* (2nd ed, Oxford:
    Oxford University Press, 1998), p 60. A report by JUSTICE, a leading non-governmental human rights and law reform
    organisation, has similarly proposed: "A fundamental principle of criminal justice is that it must show integrity
    towards both victims and offenders": *Victims in Criminal Justice* (London: JUSTICE, 1998), Recommendation 1.2, p 5.

94 K Daly, "Criminal Justice Ideologies and Practices in Different Voices: Some Feminist Questions about Justice" in
    N Lacey (ed), *Criminal Justice* (Oxford: Oxford University Press, 1994), p 240.

95 H Charlesworth, "Taking the Gender of Rights Seriously" in B Galligan and C Sampford (eds), *Rethinking Human
    Rights* (Sydney: Federation Press, 1997), Ch 3.

corroboration warning in sexual cases.[96] An inclusive notion of fairness, that both avoids the pitfalls of "balancing" and accommodates a wider range of interests, could provide a more effective basis for tackling structural discrimination within the criminal process: P Easteal, "Beyond Balancing" in P Easteal (ed), *Balancing the Scales: Rape, Law Reform and Australian Culture* (Sydney: Federation Press, 1998), Ch 14. It could provide the normative principle for challenging and reconstructing discriminatory rules of evidence that unfairly discredit the testimony of women and children in sexual offences cases. One such rule is the requirement to give mandatory jury warnings in trials involving sexual offences that it was dangerous to rely on the uncorroborated testimony of the complainant or that a failure to make a prompt complaint may render the testimony less credible and worthy of belief.[97] The discriminatory basis of these special evidential rules, and recent reforms, are critically evaluated in Chapter 12 at pp 630ff. A more expansive notion of fairness may also support the widening of "legal standing", facilitating and providing resources for independent legal representation for victims. These developments would provide the first step toward "the generation of 'feminist procedure' in these cases — a procedure that would incorporate women's experiences and knowledges".[98]

Historical Perspectives: The Victim as Prosecutrix/Prosecutor

The idea of "public prosecution" is a relatively recent innovation. Before the 19th century, few criminal prosecutions were instituted or resourced by the State. In England, most crime was prosecuted by victims (or prosecution associations or societies established to assist them) rather than police or lawyers acting on behalf of the Attorney-General: see D Hay, "Controlling the English Prosecutor" in A Sanders (ed), *Prosecution in Common Law Jurisdictions* (Brookfield, Vermont: Dartmouth, 1996). In Australia, colonial police forces established in early 19th century Australia were not confined to preventing crime and protecting property. Unlike their English counterparts, colonial police assumed a wide-range of governmental responsibilities including prosecution and administering punishment: see M Finnane, *Police and Government: Histories of Policing in Australia* (Melbourne: Oxford University Press, 1994), Ch 1.

Images of balance pervade debates about criminal justice. In Chapter 1, we explored Herbert Packer's theory of criminal justice as a balance between the competing models of "Crime Control" and "Due Process": pp 39ff. Balancing represents the state of perfect equilibrium between competing

---

96 See Senate Standing Committee on Legal and Constitutional Affairs, *Gender Bias and the Judiciary* (1994). This Federal inquiry was prompted by publicity given to judicial remarks by Justice Bollen during a rape trial: see Ch 12, p 585. The Committee concluded that the directions were largely sanctioned by law, and that the problem of gender bias was systemic rather than individual: para 18.

97 Notwithstanding the statutory abolition or modification of these warnings in most jurisdictions, the judicial practice of offering informal warnings on these dangers of false accusation persist: K Mack, "'You Should Scrutinise Her Evidence With Great Care': Corroboration of Women's Testimony About Sexual Assault" in P Easteal (ed), *Balancing the Scales: Rape, Law Reform and Australian Culture* (Sydney: Federation Press, 1998), Ch 5.

98 R Hunter and K Mack, "Exclusion and Silence: Procedure and Evidence" in N Naffine and R Owens (eds), *Sexing the Subject of Law* (Sydney: LBC, 1997), p 192, citing H Koh, "Two Cheers for Feminist Procedure" (1993) 61 *University of Cincinnati Law Review* 1201 at 1202-1203.

interests. Judges, lawyers and law reformers seem constantly to be engaged in "balancing acts". For example, the Australian Law Reform Commission in reforming the rules of criminal evidence concluded, a "critical issue is the way the balance is struck between the prosecution and the defence".[99] Yet there is increasing scepticism, even within liberal circles, as to whether "balancing" is a useful concept. Ashworth has warned of the dangers of "creeping consequentialism" associated with balancing rhetoric that reduces criminal justice reform to the utilitarian calculus of weighing, trading and trumping competing interests. The rhetoric of balancing obscures and suppresses the rights and interests in conflict, such as the rights of victims and the community. Instead of "balancing", Ashworth proposes in "Crime, Community and Creeping Consequentialism" [1996] *Criminal Law Review* 220 a "principled approach" to reform which accords maximum respect for rights (at 229):

> The first step should be to ascertain what the aim of a given part of the criminal process is, and then to ascertain what rights ought to be accorded to suspects, defendants and victims. If there are conflicts, as there often are, then the justifications for the rights and their relative strength must be examined with care. To short circuit this process with bland assertions of "balance" leads to sloppy reasoning.

In later work, he suggests that resolving avoidable conflicts in a "principled" rather than a "balanced" fashion requires maximum respect for fundamental human rights and the right to consistent (or equal) treatment in the enjoyment of these rights.[100] The significance of the principle of equality before the law for the criminal process is examined in the next section. While sympathetic to the concern that utilitarian balancing invariably means Crime Control trumps Due Process, the limitations of Ashworth's "principled approach" have been identified above: first, it tends to conceal the contested nature of fundamental legal concepts, and secondly, it tends to inscribe a narrow set of liberal values *as* legal values.

INTERNATIONAL PERSPECTIVES ON THE FAIR TRIAL PRINCIPLE[101]

While fairness may be said to be a fundamental value of criminal justice guiding legal development, its formulation as a distinct "right" that confers remedies under the common law is a recent innovation. In Australia, international human rights law has been influential in the domestic recognition of the common law right to a fair trial. Article 14 of the *International Covenant on Civil and Political Rights* (ICCPR) guarantees the general right, in both criminal and civil proceedings, to a "fair and public hearing by a competent, independent and impartial tribunal established by law".[102]

---

99 Australian Law Reform Commission, *Evidence*, Report No 38 (Canberra: AGPS, 1987), pp 19-10, following the "balancing" approach adopted by the *Royal Commission into Criminal Procedure* (1981) in the United Kingdom.

100 A Ashworth, *The Criminal Process*, (2nd ed, Oxford: Oxford University Press, 1998), p 51. These rights and principles are drawn directly from the liberal jurisprudence of Ronald Dworkin, *Taking Rights Seriously* (London: Duckworth, 1977).

101 This section is drawn from S Bronitt and M Ayers, "Criminal Law and Human Rights" in D Kinley (ed), *Human Rights in Australian Law* (Sydney: Federation Press, 1998), pp 120-124.

102 Aust TS 1980 No 23; 999 UNTS 171; New York, adopted 16 December 1966, entered into force 23 March 1976.

It then specifies a number of due process safeguards: Art 14(2) contains the "presumption of innocence" (considered below). Article 14(3) states:

> In the determination of any criminal charge against him [or her], everyone shall be entitled to the following minimum guarantees, in full equality:
>
> **(a)** To be informed promptly and in detail in a language which he [or she] understands of the nature and cause of the charge against him [or her];
>
> **(b)** To have adequate time and facilities for the preparation of his [or her] defence and to communicate with counsel of his [or her] own choosing;
>
> **(c)** To be tried without undue delay;
>
> **(d)** To be tried in his [or her] presence, and to defend himself [or herself] in person or through legal assistance of his [or her] own choosing; to be informed, if he [or she] does not have legal assistance, of this right; and to have legal assistance assigned to him [or her], in any case where the interests of justice so require, and without payment by him [or her] in any such case if he [or she] does not have sufficient means to pay for it;
>
> **(e)** To examine, or have examined, the witnesses against him [or her] and to obtain the attendance and examination of witnesses on his [or her] behalf under the same conditions as witnesses against him [or her];
>
> **(f)** To have the free assistance of an interpreter if he [or she] cannot understand or speak the language used in court;
>
> **(g)** Not to be compelled to testify against himself [or herself] or to confess guilt.

As noted above, the idea of the fair trial as a distinct right under the common law was first recognised by the High Court in *Jago v District Court (NSW)* (1989) 168 CLR 23. This case considered whether undue pre-trial delay had violated the accused's right to a fair trial resulting in a miscarriage of justice. Although the High Court made no reference to the ICCPR in support of this common law right, Kirby P in the New South Wales Court of Criminal Appeal expressly referred to Australia's obligation under Art 14(3)(c) to guarantee trial "without undue delay": *Jago v District Court (NSW)* (1988) 12 NSWLR 558 at 569.

Three years later, in *Dietrich v The Queen* (1992) 177 CLR 292, the High Court reconsidered the right to fair trial in the context of an indigent accused who had been tried and convicted of a serious drug offence without legal representation. By contrast with *Jago*, the judgments in *Dietrich* took judicial notice of the fair trial guarantees in the ICCPR and the equivalent provisions contained in the *European Convention on Human Rights* (ECHR) and the Canadian Charter of Fundamental Rights and Freedoms.[103] The majority held that, although there is no right to legal representation at public

---

103 See discussion of Art 14 of the *International Covenant of Civil and Political Rights* (ICCPR) in the following judgments in *Dietrich v The Queen* (1992) 177 CLR 292, Mason CJ and McHugh J at 300, 305-307, Deane J at 337, Toohey J at 351, 359-361, and Gaudron J at 373. Although dissenting, Brennan J viewed the ICCPR as an expression of "contemporary values" and therefore was relevant in general terms to the development of the common law: at 321. His refusal to extend the right to a fair trial however was motivated by concern about the appropriate limits of judicial intervention in the law-making process. Dawson J, dissenting, also accepted that the common law was inconsistent with Art 14(3)(d), but concluded that the ICCPR had no bearing on the development of the common law since the relevant case law was clear and unambiguous: at 347-349.

expense under the common law, compelling an indigent accused to face serious criminal charges without legal representation could result in an unfair trial. Although the terms of Art 14(3)(d) of the ICCPR provided limited assistance in shaping the common law right, the majority of the High Court noted that their "qualified approach" to legal representation followed the interpretation adopted by the European Court of Human Rights and the Supreme Court of Canada: at 307-309, per Mason CJ and McHugh J.

In *Jago* and *Dietrich* the High Court significantly expanded the notion of the fair trial under the common law. Procedural fairness is no longer simply an aspirational value of the criminal justice system, rather it is a *legally enforceable right* that imposes upon the courts an obligation to stay legal proceedings that are unfair.[104] The decision has a significant impact on governmental priorities and policies of Legal Aid Commissions around Australia.[105] As we shall explore below, the decision in *Dietrich* signified a new "transnational approach" to legal adjudication. Binding obligations under international law, including those contained in the ICCPR, could be considered a legitimate influence on the judicial development of the common law.[106] Undoubtedly, in further elaborating the content of this right, legal practitioners and judges may draw upon the "minimum guarantees" laid down in Art 14(3) and the jurisprudence and commentary that has developed around the ICCPR and its European and Canadian counterparts: KP Duggan, "Reform of the Criminal Law with Fair Trial as the Guiding Star" (1995) 19 Crim LJ 258 at 271.

PERSPECTIVES

International Human Rights and the Criminal Law

International human rights law has exerted an influence on domestic criminal process principally in the fields of procedure and evidence. However, this impact should not be overstated: A Mason, "The Influence of International and Transnational Law on Australian Municipal Law" (1996) 7 *Public Law Review* 20. While the High Court has held that international human rights law may be relevant to the development of the common law as "an expression of contemporary values" or "fundamental rights", it does *not* constitute an overriding source of law.[107] Under the Australian legal system, international law has no *direct* legal effect until incorporated into domestic legislation.[108] While judges may strenuously assert the right or even their duty to consider international human rights law in developing the common law or interpreting statutes, this

---

104 The duty of the trial judge to grant a stay of proceedings to prevent an unfair trial was first recognised in *Barton v The Queen* (1980) 147 CLR 75 at 95-96; see also *Williams v Spautz* (1992) 107 ALR 635.

105 G Zdenkowski, "Defending the Indigent Accused in Serious Cases: A Legal Right to Counsel?" (1994) 18 Crim LJ 135 and S Garkawe, "Human Rights in the Administration of Justice" (1994) 1 *Australian Journal of Human Rights* 371. In Victoria, the effect of *Dietrich v The Queen* (1992) 177 CLR 292 has been abrogated by statute, although the courts have been given the power to order Legal Aid to provide legal representation in cases where the accused is unable to receive a fair trial: see *Crimes Act* 1958 (Vic), s 360A.

106 See also *Mabo v Queensland (No 2)* (1992) 175 CLR 1. See further, A Mason, "The Influence of International and Transnational Law on Australian Municipal Law" (1996) 7 *Public Law Review* 20.

107 *Dietrich v The Queen* (1992) 177 CLR 292 at 321, per Brennan J. Dawson J dissenting, found that the present law clearly conflicted with the *International Covenant on Civil and Political Rights* (ICCPR), but concluded that ICCPR had no relevance since the authorities were clear and unambiguous: at 347-349.

108 See A Mason, "The Role of the Judiciary in the Development of Human Rights in Australian Law" in D Kinley (ed), *Human Rights in Australian Law* (Sydney: Federation Press, 1998).

freedom to incorporate indirectly human rights into Australia law is constrained by precedent and parliamentary sovereignty. As Kirby J recently observed in *R v Swaffield; Pavic v The Queen* (1998) 192 CLR 159 at 214 (emphasis added, footnotes omitted):

> To the fullest extent possible, *save where statute or established common law authority is clearly inconsistent with such rights*, the common law in Australia, when it is being developed or re-expressed, should be formulated in a way that is compatible with such international and universal jurisprudence.

Any such judicial development that widens the basis of criminal liability must be cognisant of the dangers of retrospective application. The principle that a person should not be held liable or punished for conduct that was not clearly criminal at the time of its commission (*nullum crimen/nulla poena sine lege*) is itself a fundamental human right protected by Art 15 of the ICCPR: Ch 1, p 8. While the principle of non-retrospectivity operates as a brake on arbitrary exercises of judicial power, it does not preclude common law development in the criminal law. International human rights law accepts that absolute certainty and predicability is impossible within common law jurisdictions. The European Court of Human Rights held that the House of Lords' development of the common law (in this case abolishing the marital rape immunity) would not offend the principle against non-retrospectivity "provided that the resultant development is consistent with the essence of the offence and could reasonably be foreseen": *CR v the United Kingdom* and *SW v the United Kingdom* (1996) 21 EHRR 363. Nevertheless, such cases raise legitimate concerns about the limits of judicial law-making within a liberal democracy: M Giles, "Judicial Law-making in the Criminal Courts: The Case of Marital Rape" [1992] Crim LR 407. Where domestic law is either undeveloped or ambiguous, the judiciary is clearly faced with a dilemma — should it wait for Parliament to legislate (which may never happen because of political inertia or stalemate), or should it develop common law doctrine in a manner that is consistent with international human rights standards? See further Chapter 12, pp 600ff.

International law also influences the interpretation of domestic statutes. In accordance with ordinary principles of statutory interpretation, where Australian legislation incorporates or refers to a provision of an international human rights instrument, wholly or in part, the "prima facie legislative intention is that the transposed text should bear the same meaning in the domestic statute as it bears in the treaty".[109] Moreover, courts should interpret such provisions in light of the decisions of relevant international tribunals: *Dietrich v The Queen* (1992) 177 CLR 292 at 304-305. In relation to general legislation that does not specifically incorporate or refer to international human rights provisions, there is a rebuttable presumption that Parliament intended to conform to its fundamental human rights obligations.[110] Thus, legislation must be construed, as far as its language permits, consistently with these human rights.[111]

---

109 *Applicant A v Minister of Immigration and Ethnic Affairs* (1997) 71 ALJR 381 at 383 per Brennan CJ. This principle of interpretation is reflected in statute in some jurisdictions: see *Acts Interpretation Act* 1901 (Cth), s 15AB(2).

110 *Dietrich v The Queen* (1992) 177 CLR 292 at 306 per Mason CJ and McHugh J, at 348-349 per Dawson J. The English courts have restricted the presumption that Parliament intended to legislate in conformity with the European Convention on Human Rights to cases of "ambiguity": *R v Secretary of State of Home Office Department; Ex parte Brind* [1991] 1 All ER 720. The *Human Rights Act* 1998 (UK) requires the courts to adopt an interpretation which is compatible with the Convention or, if this is impossible, to make a declaration of incompatibility: s 4.

111 The uses of international human rights law in domestic litigation is explored in K Eastman and C Ronalds, "Using Human Rights Laws in Litigation" in D Kinley (ed), *Human Rights in Australian Law* (Sydney: Federation Press, 1998), Ch 14.

Within "dualist" legal systems, such as Australia, which maintain a strict divide between domestic and international law, the principal route for vindicating human rights protected by international law is litigation before the appropriate international court or tribunal. Following Australia's ratification of the Optional Protocol of the ICCPR in 1991, individuals may challenge before the United Nations Human Rights Committee, Commonwealth, State or Territory laws that violate rights protected by the ICCPR. The Committee may issue a ruling that requires Contracting States to take steps to remedy any violation, including repeal or modification of existing laws. The optional Protocol's impact on the criminal law is potentially far-reaching. Immediately after its ratification, offences under the *Criminal Code* 1924 (Tas) prohibiting sodomy and gross indecency between consenting adult males were challenged before the Committee. The Committee held that the existence of these offences violated the rights of privacy protected under the ICCPR: *Toonen v Australia* (1994) 1 PLPR 50, Communication No 488/1992, UN Doc CCPR/C/50/D/488/1992, 4 April 1994. The subsequent failure to repeal these laws in Tasmania led the Federal Parliament, relying upon its external affairs power under the Constitution, to enact a right to privacy in relation to sexual conduct for adults that has the effect of rendering these laws inoperative. As we shall explore in Chapter 12 at p 636, the Federal privacy shield has the potential to limit the scope of many national laws governing sexual activity, such as the rules concerning the age of consent.

The failure of the courts, as well as the legislature or executive, to protect the fundamental rights under the ICCPR may give rise to litigation before the United Nations Human Rights Committee. The impact of the ICCPR on the substantive law in Australia thus far has been limited to challenging draconian homosexual offences. There is considerable scope of contesting criminal laws, especially those derived from the common law, on the grounds of uncertainty and retrospectivity. As we shall explore in Chapter 11 at p 557, the common law defence of "reasonable chastisement" has been successfully challenged before the European Court of Human Rights as a violation of the right not to be subjected to "torture or inhuman or degrading treatment or punishment". While such challenges are a cause for optimism, there are many cases where international human rights law has failed to curb judicial enthusiasm for common law development at the expense of the principles of certainty and non-retrospectivity. In addition to upholding the judicial abolition of marital rape immunity, the European Court of Human Rights recently held that the notoriously elusive common law definition of "breach of the peace", which lies at the heart of public order offences and powers, complied with the *European Convention on Human Rights*: see Ch 14, pp 751ff. For a negative assessment of the potential contribution of international human rights law to the substantive criminal law in the United Kingdom, see R Buxton, "The Human Rights Act and the Substantive Criminal Law" [2000] Crim LR 331.

Notwithstanding such reservations, there is a strong case (subject to the constraints of adjudication identified by Kirby J in *R v Swaffield and Pavic* above) for developing domestic criminal law in conformity with international human rights law. In the criminal field, the impact of the international human rights law has been much stronger in relation to the law of evidence and procedure. The fair trial guarantees in the ICCPR have been used by Australian courts to develop the common law governing the right to silence, hearsay, prosecution disclosure and sentencing discretion. Compliance with the ICCPR is also a factor relevant to the exercise of discretion under many rules of evidence and procedure. Indeed, the Uniform Evidence Act specifically provides that the failure to comply with the ICCPR is a factor that *must* be considered in the exercise of the judicial discretion to exclude improperly obtained evidence: *Evidence Act* 1995 (Cth), s 138(3); *Evidence Act* 1995 (NSW), s 138(3). See generally S Bronitt and M Ayers, "Criminal Law and Human Rights" in D Kinley (ed), *Human Rights in Australian Law* (Sydney: Federation Press, 1998).

Human rights law is exerting an increasingly powerful normative force on the process and substance of the criminal law. Nearly 30 years ago, Murphy J foreshadowed the melding of domestic and international human rights law, coining the phrase "the common law of human rights" to denote the broader role for the common law in the protection of individual rights.[112] In the face of widespread political apathy toward the protection of human rights, judges must be specially vigilant. As Murphy J observed: "Often courts cannot remedy denial of human rights which occurs outside of the judicial system, but there is no excuse for tolerating it within the system": *McInnis v The Queen* (1979) 143 CLR 575 at 593. As this brief survey has demonstrated, international human rights law can no longer be viewed as a discrete area of specialisation for international lawyers, but rather forms an integral part of domestic criminal law and practice.

THE PRESUMPTION OF INNOCENCE: FUNDAMENTAL PRINCIPLE OR LEGAL FICTION?

In this section we focus on two of the most famous attributes of the fair trial — the right to be presumed innocent and the criminal standard of proof "beyond reasonable doubt".

The "presumption of innocence" is the cornerstone of the fair trial principle, celebrated in both legal and popular culture.[113]

> **A useful filmography, providing sources of fictional material with significant courtroom scenes illustrating the dramatic and tactical aspects of adversarial practice, has recently been produced by Kathy Laster with Krista Breckweg and John King, *The Drama of the Courtroom* (Sydney: Federation Press, 2000).**

The presumption of innocence is a fundamental human right embodied in Art 14(2) of the ICCPR: "Everyone charged with a criminal offence shall be presumed innocent until proven guilty".[114] This familiar concept, which rarely requires further judicial elaboration for juries, simply means that the prosecution must prove that the accused is guilty of an offence.[115] The use of the term "presumption" is somewhat perplexing. It is not a "presumption" in the sense commonly understood by lawyers.

---

112 *Controlled Consultants Pty Ltd v Commissioner for Corporate Affairs* (1985) 156 CLR 385 at 394-395 and *Pyneboard v TPC* (1983) 45 ALR 609 at 621-622, where Murphy J described the privilege against self-incrimination as part of the "common law of human rights".

113 In TV fiction the presumption of innocence — the golden thread of the criminal law — is cherished as the key protection against State tyranny, an image most famously and regularly invoked by Rumpole of the Bailey: J Mortimer, *Rumpole* (London: The Folio Society Ltd, 1994).

114 The presumption has been codified in some jurisdictions: see *Criminal Code* (NT), s 5.

115 For the effect of acquittal, see the discussion by Gibbs CJ, Aickin, Wilson and Brennan JJ in *R v Darby* (1982) 148 CLR 668 at 675 of Lord Salmon's judgment in *DPP v Shannon* [1975] AC 717.

Presumptions are evidential devices for deeming the normal expected conditions or state of affairs to exist unless proven otherwise: "The presumption, in short, is nothing more than a rule of thumb worked out by courts on its experience of the probabilities in that kind of situation".[116] Thus, when executing a will or contract, a party is presumed to have legal capacity unless there is evidence to the contrary. By contrast, the presumption of innocence does not reflect the normal or expected state of affairs that a person charged with an offence is or will be proven innocent of the offence. Rather, the function of the presumption is to serve as a formal caution to those parties concerned with guilt determination — judges, lawyers and jurors — that the prosecution (usually the State) has to prove guilt, rather than the defence having to prove innocence. It reflects the adversarial nature of the legal process, that the party who "avers" must prove the case, and that a fair "balance" is maintained between the State and the individuals who are accused of a criminal offence.

The presumption of innocence performs an important constitutional function related to the fair trial principle. The burden of proof directs the fact-finder as to which party must prove or disprove a particular element of an offence or establish a defence. It is regarded as a matter of substantive law rather than a rule of evidence because

> [r]ules for determining the incidence of the legal burden of proof are not something over
> and above the substantive rules to which the burden relates. Rather we speak of the
> 'burden of proof' because of the nature of the adversarial process. It is placed on one party
> or the other according to the terms of substantive rules.[117]

To determine the burden of proof careful attention must be paid to the terms of the legislation and/or available authorities. The rules governing standard of proof, by contrast, tell the jury what to do when faced with uncertainty over the facts. Strangely, the ICCPR makes no provision about the standard of proof that should be applied in criminal proceedings.

The meaning of the burden and standard of proof is governed by the common law. Since the Codes of the Northern Territory, Queensland, Tasmania and Western Australia are silent on the question of burden of proof, it has been held that the common law applies.[118] Even the comprehensive codification of these rules by s 13 of the *Criminal Code Act* 1995 (Cth) restate the common law, without elaboration of fundamental concepts such as "beyond reasonable doubt".

The common law rules governing proof claim an ancient and distinguished pedigree in the criminal law. As Viscount Sankey LC observed in *Woolmington v DPP* [1935] AC 462 at 481-482:

> Throughout the web of the English Criminal Law one golden thread is always to be seen,
> that it is the duty of the prosecution to prove the prisoner's guilt subject to what I have
> already said as to the defence of insanity and subject also to any statutory exception. If, at
> the end of the whole of the case, there is a reasonable doubt, created by the evidence,
> given by either the prosecution or the prisoner ... the prosecution has not made out its case

---

116 J Stone and WAN Wells, *Evidence: Its History and Policies* (Sydney: Butt, 1992), p 62.

117 Australian Law Reform Commission, *Evidence* (1985), Report No 28 (Interim), p 15. By contrast, the rules of evidence assist the judge to determine whether material should be heard (admissibility) and the tribunal of fact to determine the weight to be attached to evidence (credibility).

118 *R v Packett* (1937) 58 CLR 190 at 212 per Dixon J; *R v Mullen* (1938) 59 CLR 124 at 136 per Dixon J, at 132 per Rich J, at 138 per McTiernan J.

and the prisoner is entitled to an acquittal. No matter what the charge or where the trial, the principle that the prosecution must prove the guilt of the prisoner is part of the common law and no attempt to whittle it down can be entertained.

This famous "Golden Thread" speech was made in the context of the rules governing murder at common law. *Woolmington* cast doubt on the well-established practice of directing juries that once the prosecution had proved that the accused caused the death of the victim, the killing was presumed to be murder unless the accused could prove that the killing was "involuntary" manslaughter.[119]

The Platitudes of Innocence: A Golden Thread or Recent Invention

A famous essay by CK Allen on the presumption of innocence, published four years before *Woolmington*, traced how English law from early times contained many "platitudes of innocence". However, as Allen observed, the presumption of innocence did not emerge distinctly until the early 19th century:

> we may conclude that four hundred years ago in all criminal trials of which we have any record, the dice were loaded heavily against the accused. The presumption of innocence was not only absent from, but antagonistic to, the whole system of penal procedure.[120]

Allen traced the growing judicial commitment to the presumption of innocence over the intervening period to two sources: the changed social conditions and decreasing lawlessness in England after 1688, and the "building up" of the law of evidence, particularly the principle that a person who makes a claim under either civil or criminal law must positively prove it: *Legal Duties and Other Essays in Jurisprudence* (Oxford: Oxford University Press, 1931), pp 273-276.

The fragility of the historical claims surrounding the presumption of innocence also hints at its marginal place in the modern criminal law. While the presumption is much vaunted in legal rhetoric, this fundamental principle has been significantly eroded by legislation. Although Viscount Sankey held that no attempt to "whittle" the golden thread should be entertained, he recognised two instances where the legal burden was lifted from the prosecution: the insanity defence at common law and exceptions provided by legislation. If the defence raises evidence of mental impairment, it bears both the legal and evidential burden of proof to establish the defence of mental impairment on

---

119 Viscount Sankey LC in *Woolmington v DPP* [1935] AC 462 at 473-474, refers to the discussion of this rule in *Foster's Crown Law* (1762). However he dismisses its authority on the basis that this statement, though made by a distinguished judge, appeared in a textbook unsupported by precedent! Paradoxically, Viscount Sankey LC offered scant legal authority for his "golden thread" in English criminal law.

120 CK Allen, *Legal Duties and Other Essays in Jurisprudence* (Oxford: Oxford University Press, 1931), pp 257-258, extracted in N Lacey and C Wells, *Reconstructing the Criminal Law* (2nd ed, London: Butt, 1998), pp 18-19. One such platitude of innocence was the idea that it is better that 10 guilty men should escape punishment than one innocent person be wrongfully convicted. It emerged as a maxim in the 16th century but the ratio was initially 20:1. The 10:1 ratio was fixed as the preferred ratio in *R v Hobson* (1823) 1 Lew CC 261.

the standard of the balance of probabilities. The nature and role of the burdens of proof in relation to mental state defences is further explored in Chapter 4, pp 219-220. The role of the evidential burden is explained below.

The second exception in *Woolmington* relates to statutory offences that place the legal burden on the accused to prove or disprove certain facts. Such statutory provisions do not expressly state that the burden is "reversed", but rather have the effect (or rather are construed) as placing a legal duty on the accused to prove or disprove certain facts. They are a common feature of strict or absolute liability offences such as trafficking in drugs, which provide that where a person possesses a prescribed quantity of a proscribed drug, it is presumed that the drug is possessed for the purpose of trafficking unless the accused proves otherwise. A similar provision applies to the possession of stolen goods. Where the legal burden is placed on the accused, the standard of proof is the civil standard, the balance of probabilities: *Colle* (1991) 95 Cr App R 67.

Recent empirical research conducted in England by Ashworth and Meredith Blake suggests offences that derogate from the presumption of innocence are not exceptional: "Presumption of Innocence in English Criminal Law" [1996] Crim LR 306.[121] Indeed, no fewer than 40% of indictable offences studied violated the presumption in the sense that the burden of proof did not lie with the prosecution in all respects. The findings are more striking since the research was confined to indictable rather than summary proceedings. Deviation from the fundamental principle seemed ubiquitous and unprincipled; it was neither the preserve of "trivial" summary offences nor "serious" crimes involving drugs or terrorism. The study concluded (p 314) that the deviation was the result of the wide scope given to Parliament by the common law to dispense or modify the requirement that the prosecution must prove a subjective fault element on the part of the accused:

> Perhaps the limited terms of Viscount Sankey's speech in *Woolmington* holds the key: what he said, in effect, is that courts should invariably place the burden of proof on the prosecution, but that Parliament may do what it pleases.

The statutory in-roads to the common law's "presumption of innocence" has implications for the conception of "general principles". After reviewing this area of law, Lacey and Wells in *Reconstructing Criminal Law* (2nd ed, London: Butt, 1998) pose the following rhetorical questions (p 23):

> At what stage do exceptions become so extensive as to undermine the status of "general principle"? Are the symbolic and ideological functions of the presumption of innocence and other features of due process in legitimising criminal law more significant than their material effects in safeguarding defendants' interests?

While Art 14(2) of the ICCPR proclaims that everyone charged with an offence should be presumed innocent, the concept has not yet been interpreted as limiting Parliament's sovereign power to impose "reasonable" qualifications. In jurisdictions where the fair trial principle is constitutionally entrenched, the presumption has the power — at least potentially — to invalidate offences that alter

---

121 The offences departed from *Woolmington* in a number of ways including reverse onus provisions, rebuttable presumptions and irrebuttable presumptions (or deeming provisions): pp 310-313. No comparable research has been undertaken in Australia, though it is unlikely that the findings would be significantly different.

the burden of proof. This issue has been considered by the Privy Council in *Attorney-General for Hong Kong v Lee Kwong-kut* [1993] AC 951.[122] In Hong Kong, the presumption of innocence in the ICCPR has been entrenched by the Bill of Rights Ordinance. The appeal to the Privy Council alleged that reverse burden provisions in several Ordinances violated the presumption of innocence. The Privy Council held that the offence of possession of stolen goods was invalid because it placed a burden on the accused in relation to the most important element of the offence, namely, whether the goods were known to be stolen. By contrast, the reverse-burden provision in an offence penalising involvement in drug trafficking was upheld. Since the burden of proving the substance of the offence (that is, involvement with known or suspected traffickers) remained with the prosecution it was reasonable for the legislature to place the burden of proof in relation to elements of the statutory defence on the accused. In determining whether a reverse burden provision went too far, the Privy Council observed at 969:

> Some exceptions will be justifiable, others will not. Whether they are justifiable will in the end depend upon whether it remains primarily the responsibility of the prosecution to prove the guilt of an accused to the required standard and whether the exception is reasonably imposed, notwithstanding the importance of maintaining the principle which Art 11(1) [presumption of innocence] enshrines. The less significant the departure from the normal principle, the simpler it will be to justify an exception. If the prosecution retains the responsibility for proving the essential ingredients of the offence, the less likely it is that an exception will be regarded as unacceptable.

In Canada, the courts have adopted a less discretionary approach to stricter forms of liability. The principle of "fundamental justice" contained in s 7 of the *Charter of Rights and Freedoms* confers substantive not merely procedural rights, and thus has invalidated offences that dispense with fault while carrying imprisonment as a possible penalty.[123] The principle of fundamental justice in Canada has been used to initiate a wide-ranging review of the law of criminal responsibility: E Colvin, "Recent Developments in Canadian Criminal Law" (1995) 19 Crim LJ 139. It provides the clearest example in a common law jurisdiction of how constitutionalising abstract principles (in this case "fundamental justice" rather than "fairness") can produce significant rethinking of traditional doctrinal concepts and strengthen judicial commitment to basic values.

DISTINGUISHING BURDENS: LEGAL OR EVIDENTIAL?

As noted above, the burden of proof, which is sometimes referred to as the onus of proof, relates to the duty placed on a party to prove certain facts. The term "burden of proof" is used in two different senses:

▬ the legal burden of proof; and

▬ the evidential burden of proof.

---

122 For further discussion of the Hong Kong case law on the entrenched nature of the presumption of innocence, see J Chan, *Annotated Bills of Rights Ordinance* (Hong Kong: Butt, 1999).

123 Section 7 provides: "Everyone has the right to life, liberty and security of the person and the right not to be deprived thereof except in accordance with the principles of fundamental justice": *Constitutional Act* 1982 (Can).

DIAGRAM 1: Burden of Proof

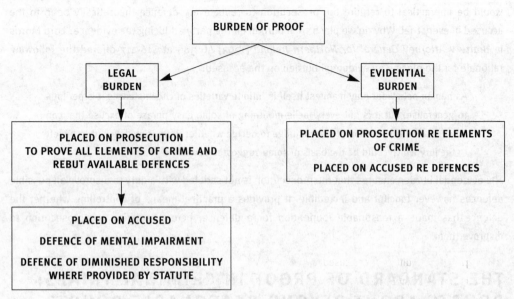

The most significant burden of proof is the *legal* or *persuasive burden*. In criminal cases, the general rule is that the prosecution bears the legal burden of proving all the elements of the crime and rebutting any defences.[124] It is a persuasive burden in the sense that the prosecution bears the risk of losing the case if there is a failure to persuade the trier of fact that a proposition has been made out: *Woolmington v DPP* [1935] AC 462 at 482 per Viscount Sankey LC. The legal burden remains on the prosecution for the whole trial. In exceptional cases, where the legal burden is placed on the accused (for example, the defence of mental impairment), the lower civil standard, the balance of probabilities, applies.

The other burden of proof, the *evidential* or *tactical burden*, relates to the duty to produce some evidence to support a claim. The evidential burden, unlike the legal burden can rest on either party. The duty is placed on one of the parties to produce sufficient evidence to permit the matter to be left to the jury for consideration. This burden does not require the party to prove the issue. It is for the judge to decide whether the issue has the support of evidence so that it can be considered by the jury. A distinction is generally drawn between the evidential burden in relation to offences and defences. Except where otherwise provided by statute, the prosecution bears the evidential burden in relation to proving elements of the crime.[125] However, in relation to defences, the evidential burden is placed upon the accused.[126]

---

124 *Woolmington v DPP* [1935] AC 462; *R v Mullen* (1938) 59 CLR 124; *Chan Kau v The Queen* [1955] AC 206; *Thomas v The Queen* (1960) 102 CLR 584; *La Fontaine v The Queen* (1976) 135 CLR 62; *Van Leeuwen v The Queen* (1981) 36 ALR 591; *Chamberlain v The Queen (No 2)* 153 CLR 521; *Hoch v The Queen* (1988) 165 CLR 292; *R v Falconer* (1990) 171 CLR 30.

125 *DPP v Morgan* [1976] AC 182; *Tsang Ping-Nam v The Queen* [1981] 1 WLR 1462; *May v O' Sullivan* (1955) 92 CLR 654.

126 *Mancini v DPP* [1942] AC 1; *Chan Kau v The Queen* [1955] AC 206; *Ryan v The Queen* (1967) 121 CLR 205 at 215-216 per Barwick CJ; *Marwey v The Queen* (1977) 138 CLR 630 at 641 per Stephen J; *R v O' Connor* (1980) 146 CLR 64 at 88 per Barwick CJ; *Moffa v The Queen* (1977) 138 CLR 601 at 607per Barwick CJ; *Viro v The Queen* (1978) 141 CLR 88 at 95 per Barwick CJ, at 117 per Gibbs J, at 146 per Mason J, at 147-148 per Jacobs J; *R v Lawrence* [1980] 1 NSWLR 122; *Spautz v Williams* [1983] 2 NSWLR 506 at 534 per Hunt J; *He Kaw Teh v The Queen* (1985) 157 CLR 523 at 534-535 per Gibbs CJ, at 593 per Dawson J; *R v Youssef* (1990) 50 A Crim R 1 (CCA NSW).

The rationale for placing an evidential burden on the accused in relation to defences is that it would be impractical to require the prosecution to rebut every defence theoretically open to the accused in every trial. Why do we place such burden on the party adducing the evidence? Lord Morris in *Bratty v Attorney General for Northern Ireland* [1963] AC 386 at 416-417 offered the following rationale for the placing an evidential burden on the accused:

> As human behaviour may manifest itself in infinite varieties of circumstances it is perilous to generalise, but it is not every facile mouthing of some easy phrase of excuse that can amount to an explanation. It is for a judge to decide whether there is evidence fit to be left to the jury which could be the basis of some suggested verdict.

The evidential burden ensures that the prosecution is not saddled with a duty to disprove all possible defences however fanciful and incredible. It provides a practical means of controlling whether the defence has made a reasonable foundation for a defence, before requiring the prosecution to disprove them.

THE STANDARD OF PROOF IN CRIMINAL TRIALS: DOUBTS ABOUT BEYOND REASONABLE DOUBT?

While the burden of proof deals with which party bears the duty of proving a particular issue, the standard of proof relates to the quantum or level of proof: how much evidence is required to convict the accused? The criminal standard of proof — "beyond reasonable doubt" — again occupies a central place in legal and popular culture.[127]

DIAGRAM 2: Standard of Proof

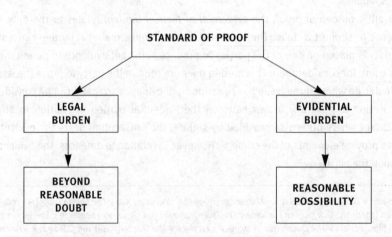

---

127 Since *Woolmington v DPP* [1935] AC 462, the criminal standard has been repeatedly affirmed: *R v Mullen* (1938) 59 CLR 124; *Chan Kau v The Queen* [1955] AC 206; *Thomas v The Queen* (1960) 102 CLR 584; *La Fontaine v The Queen* (1976) 135 CLR 62; *Van Leeuwen v The Queen* (1981) 36 ALR 591; *Chamberlain v The Queen (No 2)* 153 CLR 521; *Hoch v The Queen* (1988) 165 CLR 292; *R v Falconer* (1990) 171 CLR 30.

Although regularly affirmed by the courts today, historical research reveals that prior to *Woolmington* there was little legal authority supporting the criminal standard of proof as beyond reasonable doubt. Since he doubted whether there was any "true difference" between a balance of probabilities and a reasonable certainty (the converse of reasonable doubt), CK Allen concluded that "the principle of 'reasonable doubt' therefore seems to be little more than a counsel of prudence; and there is considerable judicial authority for this view".[128] Julius Stone similarly viewed beyond reasonable doubt as a "neutralising weapon" that addressed the frailties of human tribunals, particularly the normal tendency for the mere fact of criminal accusation to interfere with the degree of impartiality necessary for a fair trial: J Stone and WAN Wells, *Evidence* (Sydney: Butt, 1991), p 69.

"Beyond reasonable doubt" is commonly defined and contrasted by its antinomy, the civil standard of proof — the "balance of probabilities". Any further attempt to elaborate on the time-honoured formula of beyond reasonable doubt by resort to mathematical analogies or percentages can provide grounds for an appeal.[129]

> **Where the evidence proffered by the prosecution is only circumstantial, the judge may elaborate upon the traditional standard by directing the jury to acquit unless the facts are not only consistent with the accused's guilt but also inconsistent with any other rational explanation.[130] A body of case law has developed in relation to role of the criminal standard in relation to prosecutions that rely substantially upon "circumstantial evidence". The High Court in *Shepherd v The Queen* (1990) 170 CLR 573 held that where:**
>
> ━━ **a prosecution case relies upon circumstantial evidence; and**
>
> ━━ **an intermediate conclusion of fact in the inferential process constitutes an indispensable link in a chain of reasoning towards an inference of guilt,**
>
> **such fact must itself be proved beyond reasonable doubt: at 579, 581 per Dawson J. See further S Odgers, *Uniform Evidence Law* (4th ed, Sydney: LBC, 2000), p 382.**

Judges are strongly discouraged from elaborating more generally on the meaning of "beyond reasonable doubt" except to reiterate that the standard does not require absolute certainty and is stricter than the civil standard of "balance of probabilities", another allegedly familiar concept which requires no further elaboration. As the Privy Council has observed in *Ferguson v The Queen* [1979] 1 All ER 877 at 882:

> The time-honoured formula is that the jury must be satisfied beyond reasonable doubt ... attempts to substitute other expressions have never prospered. It is generally sufficient and safe to direct a jury that they must be satisfied beyond reasonable doubt so that they feel sure of the defendant's guilt. Nevertheless, other words will suffice, so long as the message is clear.

---

128 CK Allen, *Legal Duties and Other Essays in Jurisprudence* (Oxford: Oxford University Press, 1931), discussed in N Lacey and C Wells, *Reconstructing the Criminal Law* (2nd ed, London: Butt, 1998), p 20.

129 *Dawson v The Queen* (1961) 106 CLR 1 at 18, per Dixon CJ; *Thomas v The Queen* (1960) 102 CLR 584; *Green v The Queen* (1971) 126 CLR 28; *La Fontaine v The Queen* (1976) 135 CLR 62.

130 *Re Hodge* (1838) 2 Lew CC 227; 168 ER 1136; *Plomp v The Queen* (1963) 110 CLR 234; *Grant v The Queen* (1975) 11 ALR 503; *Barca v The Queen* (1975) 133 CLR 82; *R v Trimboli* (1979) 21 SASR 577; *R v Lawrence* [1980] 1 NSWLR 122 at 124 per Nagel CJ and Yeldham J; *Stanton v The Queen* [1981] WAR 185; *R v Sorby* [1986] VR 753.

The likelihood and severity of punishment affect the degree of certainty required to "feel sure". As Helena Kennedy observed in *Eve Was Framed — Women and British Justice* (London: Vintage Books for Chatto & Windus, 1993), p 4:

> The wording invariably used by judges today is that jurors must be "satisfied so that they are sure", an expression more likely to conjure up advertisements for Cadbury's chocolate. Does the concept of satisfaction or "being sure" drive one to the level of certainty which should be required before we surrender a citizen to sentencing and the likely loss of liberty? For the most part the only people who mention proof "beyond reasonable doubt" are defence lawyers.

The formula impresses upon the jury the importance of prudence in criminal matters because of risks to liberty and reputation posed by conviction. Yet in this regard, the jury is not well placed to gauge the weight of these matters since they are invariably ignorant of the gravity of the consequences of a guilty verdict, such as whether the offence carries imprisonment. By contrast, the civil standard, discussed below, impresses on the fact-finder (a judge rather than a jury) the importance of such consequential factors.

The position in relation to the standard of the evidential burden of proof is similarly shrouded with uncertainty. In *Bratty v Attorney-General for Northern Ireland* [1963] AC 386 Lord Denning spoke of the requirement that the evidential burden on the defence in relation to sane automatism would be fulfilled if the evidence amounted to a "proper foundation": at 413. Moreover, in *Hill v Baxter* [1958] 1 QB 277 Lord Devlin referred to the requirement of "prima facie evidence": at 285. More recently, the New South Wales Court of Criminal Appeal stated in *Youssef* (1990) 50 A Crim R 1 (at 3) that:

> [T]he accused bears an *evidentiary* onus to point to or to produce evidence (or material in an unsworn statement) from which it could be inferred that ... there is at least a reasonable possibility that, for example, the act of the accused was accidental, or that it was provoked or done in self-defence.

Just what amounts to a "proper foundation" or "prima facie evidence" or a "reasonable possibility" will be a matter for a judge to determine.

The distinction between the criminal and civil standard of proof is further blurred when the meaning of "balance of probabilities" is subject to close critical scrutiny. Although the phrase is suggestive of "51 out of 100 per cent",[131] the civil standard of proof has been held to be case or context-dependent. What constitutes the amount of proof necessary for "reasonable satisfaction" in a civil matter varies, as Sir Owen Dixon in *Briginshaw v Briginshaw* (1938) 60 CLR 336 at 361-362 observed:

> But reasonable satisfaction is not a state of mind that is attained or established independently of the nature and consequence of the fact or facts to be proved. The seriousness of an allegation made, the inherent unlikelihood of an occurrence of a given

---

131 See generally G Williams, "The Mathematics of Proof" [1979] Crim LR 297.

description, or the gravity of the consequences flowing from a particular finding are considerations which must affect the answer to the question whether the issue has been proved to the reasonable satisfaction of the tribunal.[132]

Since jury trials are rare in civil matters, the metaphysical dimensions of a case or context-dependent standard of proof have not been subject to further judicial elaboration. It demonstrates the degree of uncertainty that may shroud fundamental principles that are seemingly applied everyday in the criminal courts.

> The Supreme Court of Canada has taken a different approach to the criminal standard of proof. Unlike Australian and English courts, the Supreme Court in *R v Lifchus* [1997] 3 SCR 320, held that a trial judge must offer proper guidance to the jury on the meaning of "beyond reasonable doubt" — it was insufficient for juries to be told that this standard was a familiar concept determined by its ordinary meaning. In directing the jury, the Court emphasised (at 333) that judges should draw a link between the standard of proof and the presumption of innocence — reasonable doubt was described as "a doubt based on reason and common sense which must be based upon the evidence or lack of evidence". See further, G Ferguson, "Recent Developments in Canadian Criminal Law" (2000) 24 Crim LJ 248 at 262-263.

THE LAW/FACT DISTINCTION: THE BOUNDARIES OF JUDICIAL IMPARTIALITY

In terms of the division of labour, the judge decides matters of law, whereas the jury decides matters of fact. In matters of fact, the jury may be said to be sovereign. The judge's duty is to direct the jury as to the relevant law and it is the duty of the jurors to apply the law to the facts. The judge directs the jury as to the law during the summing up at the end of the trial just before the jury retires. In the summing up, the judge may also express an opinion as to the evidence, but must be careful not to usurp the function of the jury.[133]

The complexity of the judicial role in commenting on evidence has recently been examined by the High Court in *RPS v The Queen* (1999) 168 ALR 729. The appeal examined whether inferences of guilt could be drawn from the accused's failure to testify. The majority (Gaudron ACJ, Gummow, Kirby and Hayne JJ) held that where the prosecution adduced direct evidence of guilt, the accused's silence could not be used to infer guilt. This general inhibition on the evidential use of silence was related to the fundamental feature of criminal trials, namely, that the accused was not bound to give evidence and that the prosecution must prove its case beyond reasonable doubt. At the end of their judgment (paras 41-42), the majority took the unusual step of offering general guidance on the function of jury instructions (at 741):

---

132 The case involved an appeal against a divorce on the grounds of adultery. There remains uncertainty over this formulation: "as the seriousness of the allegation increases does the standard of satisfaction vary or does the standard remain the same but more cogent proof is needed?": Australian Law Reform Commission, *Evidence*, Report No 26 (Interim) (Canberra: AGPS, 1985), p 45, fn 25.

133 For a description of the duties involving in "summing up" see C Cato, *The Law and Practice of Criminal Litigation* (Sydney: LBC, 1998), pp 304-306.

Judicial instructions in criminal trials

41. Before parting with the case, it is as well to say something more general about the difficult task trial judges have in giving juries proper instructions. The fundamental task of a trial judge is, of course, to ensure a fair trial of the accused. That will require the judge to instruct the jury about so much of the law as they need to know in order to dispose of the issues in the case. No doubt that will require instructions about the elements of the offence, the burden and standard of proof and the respective functions of judge and jury. Subject to any applicable statutory provisions it will require the judge to identify the issues in the case and to relate the law to those issues. It will require the judge to put fairly before the jury the case which the accused makes. In some cases it will require the judge to warn the jury about how they should *not* reason or about particular care that must be shown before accepting certain kinds of evidence.

42. But none of this must be permitted to obscure the division of functions between judge and jury. It is for the jury, and the jury alone, to decide the facts. As we have said, in some cases a judge must give the jury warnings about how they go about that task. And, of course, it has long been held that a trial judge may comment (and comment strongly) on factual issues. But although a trial judge *may* comment on the facts, the judge is not bound to do so except to the extent that the judge's other functions require it. Often, perhaps much more often than not, the safer course for a trial judge will be to make no comment on the facts beyond reminding the jury, in the course of identifying the issues before them, of the arguments of counsel (footnotes omitted).

Although the division of judicial and jury responsibilities is firmly drawn, in many respects the law/fact dichotomy is misleading. Judges are called upon to make judgments on many factual questions in the course of the trial. Preliminary hearings may be held to determine the admissibility of evidence; for example, a voir dire (a hearing in the absence of a jury) may be held to determine the admissibility of a confession alleged to be involuntary. At the end of the prosecution case, the judge may be called upon to rule whether there is a prima facie case for the accused to answer, that is whether there is insufficient evidence to allow the case to proceed.[134] Conversely, the jury is not confined exclusively to the facts. Since the jury renders the general verdict, and is not required to provide reasons, it has considerable power to nullify laws and prosecutions considered to be abusive or unjust.[135] The capacity of the jury to temper the strictness of legality — its power to be "above the law" — is often represented as bulwark of liberty against unfair and unjust offences enacted by the legislature over which the courts, due to the doctrine of parliamentary supremacy, are powerless: P Devlin, "The Conscience of the Jury" (1991) 107 *Law Quarterly Review* 398 at 404. While jury

---

134 *Doney v The Queen* (1990) 171 CLR 207; see C Cato, *The Law and Practice of Criminal Litigation* (Sydney: LBC, 1998), pp 301-302. J Jackson and S Doran, "Judge and Jury: Towards a New Division of Labour in Criminal Trials" (1997) 60(6) *Modern Law Review* 759 at 767.

135 See further P Devlin, *Trial By Jury* (London: Stevens and Sons, 1966); J Hunter and K Cronin, *Evidence, Advocacy and Ethical Practice* (Sydney: Butt, 1995), pp 120-122.

nullification can always occur, its practical significance is tempered by the rarity of contested criminal matters and the dominance of summary trials conducted without a jury.[136]

The formal segregation of the functions of judge from jury also ignores the wide-range of "mixed" issues of law and fact. This may be illustrated by the standard directions concerning the meaning of grievous bodily harm or serious injury. In determining whether the harm or injury caused is grievous or serious, the jury does not have a completely free hand with the facts. The judge will direct the jury as to the type and quantum of injuries that satisfy the particular legal definition. As we shall explore in Chapter 11, the judge may (depending on the facts) direct the jury that:

▬ **the injury must be serious, not trivial;**

▬ **the accused must take the victim as he or she finds them; and**

▬ **harm is not limited to physical injury, but includes psychological harm provided that it amounts to a "recognisable psychiatric disorder".**

In both direct and indirect ways, judges impose limits on the freedom of the jury to determine the facts as it sees fit.

The judge also exerts significant influence over fact-determination through the "summing up" delivered before the jury retires. The summation may legitimately traverse both matters of law and fact. As foreshadowed above, the rules of evidence may impose a judicial duty to direct or warn the jury on matters relating to issues of credibility, such as the failure of the victim to make a prompt complaint in a sexual offences trial, or the requirement to give a warning that it is dangerous to rely on the complainant's evidence in the absence of corroboration. Moreover, Australia has inherited the English tradition (which has not been followed in the United States) of giving judges considerable latitude in commenting on the strengths and weaknesses of the defence and prosecution case. The extent to which a trial judge may express personal views on the credibility of witnesses threatens to undermine the independence of the jury. As Helena Kennedy observed in *Eve Was Framed — Women and British Justice* (London: Vintage Books for Chatto & Windus, 1993) (at p 5):

> When jurists from other countries see the extent to which our judiciary give rein to their own views and try to influence juries in the summing-up at the end of the trial, they are appalled; it appears a usurping of the jury's function, contrary to the principle of jury trial.

Indeed, the guidance offered by the High Court in *RPS v The Queen* (1999) 168 ALR 729 may be viewed as an attempt to minimise undue judicial interference with jury deliberations. See further G Flatman and M Bagaric, "Juries Peers or Puppets — The Need to Curtail Jury Instructions" (1998) 22 Crim LJ 207.

Available research on jury decision-making reveals the strong influence of judicial directions on the minds of the jury. In a famous study by John Baldwin and Mike McConville, *Jury Trials* (Oxford:

---

136 J Hunter and K Cronin note that trial by jury occurs in less than 1% of the total charges laid, a figure which is likely to continue to diminish: *Evidence, Advocacy and Ethical Practice* (Sydney: Butt, 1995), p 97. See also P Darbyshire, "The Lamp that Shows that Freedom Lies — Is it Worth the Candle?" [1991] Crim LR 740; M Findlay and P Duff (eds), *The Jury Under Attack* (Sydney: Law Book Company Ltd, 1988).

Clarendon Press, 1979) the researchers identified cases where much of the jury's deliberation was actually taken up with seeking to discover what was in the judge's mind and with trying to produce a verdict with which the judge would agree!: p 78. For a review of recent research on the jury, see J Hunter and K Cronin, *Evidence, Advocacy and Ethical Practice* (Sydney: Butt, 1995), pp 124-135. A recent empirical study in New Zealand suggests that juries, while confronting difficulties, did perform their tasks competently and with integrity: W Young, Y Tinsley and N Cameron, "The Effectiveness and Efficiency of Jury Decision-Making" (2000) 24 Crim LJ 89.

Empirical research has revealed that judges often hamper rather than assist jury decision-making. Research using mock juries in England suggests that judicial warnings about evidence that is considered potentially unreliable, such as the mandatory corroboration warning in sexual offences trials, can be counterproductive, having the opposite effect than that which was intended by the judge.[137] While perhaps ineffective, such warnings embody discriminatory myths and stereotypes about female sexuality. The "special" evidential and procedural rules governing sexual offences are explored in Chapter 12, 'Perspectives: Special Procedural and Evidential Rules for Sexual Offences': pp 630-631.

To avoid the danger of unduly prejudicing the jury and rendering the trial unfair, the summing-up must be "balanced" between the prosecution and defence:

> a judge is obliged to give a fair and balanced account of the prosecution and the defence case ... He or she must exhibit a judicial balance so that the jury is not deprived of understanding and giving effect to the evidence and matters relied upon in support of the defence.[138]

Even where the direction is balanced, the language and tone can play a significant role: "The judge's usual linguistic device is to express an opinion and then add the rider that 'of course, members of the jury, it is a matter for you'. But juror's perceive this as the judge tipping them the wink as to how they should be thinking": H Kennedy, *Eve Was Framed — Women and British Justice* (London: Vintage Books, 1993), p 5. Indeed, these judicial cues and qualifications may explain why evidence of intoxication or an unreasonable mistake, though technically capable of negating the required mental state for the offence, rarely result in an acquittal.

As this section has revealed, for academic as well practical reasons, greater attention must be paid to procedural context within which so-called fundamental principles operate.

---

137 LSE Jury Project, "Juries and the Rules of Evidence" [1973] Crim LR 208, discussed in J Hunter and K Cronin, *Evidence, Advocacy and Ethical Practice* (Sydney: Butt, 1995), pp 80-81. In cases where the warning was given, juries were more likely to convict. One possible explanation is that the warning that it is dangerous to convict without corroboration requires the judge to identify what evidence is corroborative. This serves to highlight implicating material against the accused and so underscores (rather than undermines) the prosecution case.

138 C Cato, *The Law and Practice of Criminal Litigation* (Sydney: LBC, 1998), pp 305-306, citing *B v R* (1992) 63 A Crim R 225 at 229, per Brennan J.

3.4 THE PRINCIPLE OF EQUALITY BEFORE THE LAW

> **[The poor] have to labour in the face of the majestic equality of the law, which forbids the rich as well as the poor to sleep under bridges, to beg in the streets, and to steal bread**
>
> Anatole France,
> *Le Lys Rouge* (1894), Ch 7

Equality before the law is a fundamental principle ensuring that individuals are not subject to discrimination in the enjoyment of their legal rights or entitlements. The *Universal Declaration of Human Rights* (adopted and proclaimed by the General Assembly resolution 217A (III) of 10 December 1948) provides that: "All are equal before the law and are entitled without discrimination to equal protection of the law": Art 7. The *International Covenant on Civil and Political Rights* contains a similar provision in Art 26, which states that "the law shall prohibit any discrimination and guarantee to all persons equal and effective protection against discrimination on any ground such as race, colour, sex, language, religion, political or other opinion, national or social origin, property, birth or other status". The equal right of men and women to enjoy these rights is further recognised in Art 3. The right to equality before the law was the subject of a major law reform project by the Australian Law Reform Commission, *Equality Before the Law*, Report No 69 (1994). The Report recommended Federal legislation (not yet implemented) that would "guarantee that everyone is entitled to equality in law" and would render inoperative "any law, policy, programme, practice or decision which is inconsistent with equality in law on the ground of gender": p 65.

The principle of equal *treatment* before the law is directed to procedural rather than substantive ends. As formal or strict equality promotes sameness of treatment, it may conceal the substantive political, social and economic inequality of disadvantaged groups or individuals. Acknowledgment of these limitations has generated remedial versions of equality, such as equality of opportunity. Yet, both formal and remedial conceptions of equality have been criticised from a feminist perspective. Lacey has summarised the feminist critique as follows:

> In the case of equality, it has been argued that liberal notions of equality are fundamentally premised on the idea of sameness: equal treatment is due to all who are similarly situated to the full liberal subject. Hence, if the subject is implicitly marked as masculine — is understood in terms of bodily and psychic characteristics which have been culturally understood to be associated with men — then the strategy of equality amounts to the assimilation of women to a norm set by and for men.[139]

---

139 N Lacey, *Unspeakable Subjects — Feminist Essays in Legal and Social Theory* (Oxford: Hart Publishing, 1998), p 240, and Ch 1 generally.

Inequality is approached from the liberal (and invariably legal) standpoint of individualism. By conceiving discrimination as the different treatment of individuals on specified grounds such as gender or race, there is only limited scope for addressing and remedying group-based disadvantage.[140] Rejecting the concept of "equality as sameness", feminists have focused instead on subordination.[141] There is considerable scope for the "normative reconstruction" of equality in broader pluralistic terms such as "equality as acceptance" or "equality as respect for difference".[142] It has been suggested that the implicit maleness of the norm of comparison underlying anti-discrimination legislation can only be addressed by targeting the provisions specifically at the groups that have been significantly disadvantaged.[143]

There is also concern about the packaging of equality, or indeed any normative claim, in terms of "rights". Dissatisfied with the privileging of liberalism within conventional rights discourse, some critical and feminist scholars have rejected the concept of rights entirely.[144] Valerie Kerruish in *Jurisprudence as Ideology* (London and New York: Routledge, 1991) rejects (p 145) the prevailing politico-morals ideas for using rights, claiming it is wrong to support rights as "claims of liberal ideals of liberty, equality and democratic community, or of justice or human rights or whatever". Rather, she argues that rights should be construed as "claims by people bearing the heaviest burdens of our way of life, which express resistance to the established order of things". This approach recognises the empowering effect of the language of rights within legal and political discourse. As Hilary Charlesworth concludes:

> The assertion of rights can have great symbolic force for oppressed groups within a society
> offering a significant vocabulary to formulate political and social grievances which is
> recognised by the powerful.[145]

---

140 N Lacey, *Unspeakable Subjects — Feminist Essays in Legal and Social Theory* (Oxford: Hart Publishing, 1998), p 25.

141 C MacKinnon, *Toward a Feminist Theory of the State* (Cambridge, Mass: Harvard University Press, 1989), Ch 12; J Morgan and R Graycar, *The Hidden Gender of Law* (Sydney: Federation Press, 1990), pp 41-43, discussing the adoption of the subordination principle as the theoretical perspective for reviewing criminal law in Canada: E Sheehy, "Personal Autonomy and the Criminal Law: Emerging Issues", *Background Paper, Canadian Advisory Council on the Status of Women* (1987). See also proposals for a gendered equality right for a Bill of Rights which specifically addresses women's subordination: J Morgan, "Equality Rights in the Australian Context: A Feminist Perspective" in P Alston (ed), *Towards an Australian Bill of Rights* (Canberra: CIPL and HREOC, 1994), p 144.

142 N Lacey, *Unspeakable Subjects — Feminist Essays in Legal and Social Theory* (Oxford: Hart Publishing, 1998), pp 239-241, discussing the work of feminist theorists, Drucilla Cornell and Luce Irigaray.

143 See, for example, the Australian Law Reform Commission minority report which proposed the adoption of a Status of Women Act for the purpose of establishing a specific right to equality in law *for women*: H Charlesworth, "Taking the Gender of Rights Seriously" in B Galligan and C Sampford (eds), *Rethinking Human Rights* (Sydney: Federation Press, 1997), p 48.

144 For a review of this debate see H Charlesworth, "Taking the Gender of Rights Seriously" in B Galligan and C Sampford (eds), *Rethinking Human Rights* (Sydney: Federation Press, 1997), pp 32-35 and J Morgan, "Equality Rights in the Australian Context: A Feminist Perspective" in P Alston (ed), *Towards an Australian Bill of Rights* (Canberra: CIPL and HREOC, 1994), pp 123-131.

145 H Charlesworth, "The Australian Reluctance About Rights" in P Alston (ed), *Towards an Australian Bill of Rights* (Canberra: CIPL and HREOC, 1994), p 49. See also H Charlesworth, "Taking the Gender of Rights Seriously" in B Galligan and C Sampford (eds), *Rethinking Human Rights* (Sydney: Federation Press, 1997), Ch 3.

Equality is clearly a contested notion with multiple meanings. While being flawed and limited in fundamental respects, the principle of equality before the law continues to influence many debates about the reform of the criminal law. It holds out the promise of liberation for the disadvantaged within society. In the following sections, we review the struggles over the different and contested meanings of equality in debates concerning the treatment of women and Indigenous peoples by the criminal law.

FEMINIST PERSPECTIVES ON GENDER DISCRIMINATION AND THE CRIMINAL LAW

There have been some significant reforms aimed at improving the treatment of women by the criminal justice system. As we shall explore in Chapter 12, feminist concerns about the rules of evidence and procedure that discriminate against women who allege sexual abuse have led to wide ranging reforms in Australia: pp 630-631. However, recent empirical studies suggest that rape law reform has not significantly improved the treatment of victims by the legal process.[146] Arguments based on equality have also supported the abolition of substantive rules that discriminate against women such as the marital rape immunity. Yet, the case of marital rape reveals the limits of legal strategies for achieving gender equality. While formal legal and evidential hurdles to the prosecution of men who rape their wives have been removed, discriminatory attitudes of prosecutors and judges during sentencing continue to downgrade the seriousness of marital and acquaintance rape: P Easteal, *Balancing the Scales: Rape, Law Reform and Australian Culture* (Sydney: Federation Press, 1998), Ch 8. As Lacey concludes in *Unspeakable Subjects* (Oxford: Hart Publishing, 1998), the criminal law has only limited potential to achieve sexual equality in marriage "because of all sorts of other flows of power — economic power being significant among them — which cannot be affected except by very radical social change which cannot be engendered directly by legal means": p 241.

International human rights law can provide a *legal* basis, as distinct from a purely philosophical basis, for using equality to evaluate and reform the criminal law. In the context of discrimination against women, this process has been bolstered by international treaties such as the *Convention on the Elimination of All Forms of Discrimination Against Women* (CEDAW), adopted by the United Nations in 1979, that contains specific obligations on Contracting States to take steps to eliminate discrimination against women.[147] The Convention does not address the general topic of violence against women, though the subsequent *Declaration on the Elimination of Violence Against Women* (DEVAW) stated that "gender based violence" as a form of discrimination is prohibited under CEDAW. As noted above at p 92, these international human rights treaties have supported the recent enactment of extraterritorial offences against sexual trafficking and child sex tourism.

There is considerable potential for international law, particularly relating to human rights, to operate as a legitimate influence on the development of the common law in Australia. The

---

146 Department of Women (NSW), *Heroines of Fortitude* (1996); Department of Justice (Vic), *Rape Law Reform Evaluation Project — The Crimes (Rape) Act 1991* (1997). See generally P Easteal (ed), *Balancing the Scales: Rape, Law Reform and Australian Culture* (Sydney: Federation Press, 1998); G Mason, "Reforming the Law of Rape" in D Kirkby (ed), *Sex, Power and Justice* (Melbourne: Oxford University Press, 1995), Ch 4.

147 See generally, H Charlesworth and C Chinkin, "Violence against Women" in J Stubbs (ed), *Women, Male Violence and the Law* (Sydney: Institute of Criminology, 1994), Ch 2.

permissible interpretive strategies for incorporating international human rights into domestic criminal law have been considered above at pp 111-114. A recent Canadian decision provides an example of how these international treaties may used productively to remove discriminatory concepts embedded in the substantive law. In *R v Ewanchuk* [1999] 1 SCR 330 the Supreme Court of Canada remoulded the common law definition of consent for the purpose of sexual assault. The Supreme Court unanimously rejected a submission that the common law recognised a defence of "implied consent" to sexual assault. Not only did a defence of implied consent give inadequate weight to the importance of sexual autonomy, it also perpetuated the "no means yes" discriminatory stereotype of females' sexual passivity. Feminist criticism of the law governing consent is reviewed in Chapter 12, p 607.

The strategy of reshaping the common law adopted by the Supreme Court of Canada was preferred to a direct constitutional challenge that these laws violated the guarantee of equality under the Canadian Charter of Rights. In developing the common law, L'Heureux-Dubé J drew extensively on provisions in CEDAW and DEVAW, pointing to the obligation on Contracting States to "ensure that laws against family violence and abuse, rape, *sexual assault and other gender-biased violence give adequate protection to all women, and respect their integrity and dignity*": *R v Ewanchuk* [1999] 1 SCR 330 at 364 (emphasis in original). The obligation included protecting sexual activity that occurs because of force, threats or fear. L'Heureux-Dubé J highlighted (at 365) the importance of tackling discrimination in the form of gender bias in the judiciary, pointing to the obligation in Art 4(j) of DEVAW that required States to adopt:

> all appropriate measures, especially in the field of education, to modify the social and
> cultural patterns of conduct of men and women *and to eliminate prejudices*, customary
> practices and all other practices based on the idea of the inferiority or superiority of either
> of the sexes and *on stereotyped roles for men and women*.

In light of these international obligations, L'Heureux-Dubé J viewed the judicial task as involving the correction of "myths and stereotypes" evident both in the substantive legal rules and the gender-biased language employed in the judgments of the lower courts: at 369-376. She concluded (at 376):

> It is part of the role of this Court to denounce this kind of language, unfortunately still used
> today, which not only perpetuates archaic myths and stereotypes about the nature of
> sexual assaults but also ignores the law.

The experience in Canada suggests that these provisions of CEDAW and DEVAW may be used to develop the Australian common law in a similar manner.[148] A similar sensitivity to issues of discrimination is evident in recent judicial efforts to re-define self-defence in a way that may take into account the experiences of battered women: see Ch 6, 2.8 'Battered Women and Self Defence' at pp 306-310.

---

148 The notion of "actual bodily harm" under the common law of assault has traditionally excluded the infliction of psychological and psychiatric distress: cf, the wider definition emerging in English law in *R v Ireland* [1997] 4 All ER 225. By contrast, gender-based violence under the *Convention on the Elimination of all Forms of Discrimination against Women* (CEDAW) covers "acts that inflict physical, mental or sexual harm or suffering, threats of such acts, coercion and other deprivations of liberty": *General Recommendation* No 19 (11th Session 1992). CEDAW provides the mandate for widening the common law definition of assault and developing new statutory crimes of stalking: see Ch 11.

Feminist and cultural claims to equality can often collide. Articles 18 and 27 of the International Covenant on Civil and Political Rights specifically protect ethnic and cultural rights under the guarantee of freedom of religion and the right of ethnic, religious or linguistic minorities to enjoy their own culture, religion or language. "Rights conflicts" are most problematic in cases where individual rights collide with group rights. Human rights lawyers often reject the contention that rights are hierarchial and that specific individual rights trump general collective rights. Competing tensions between rights must be resolved through "balancing". Rights are rarely absolute. Concepts like proportionality are liberally employed to accommodate competing interests while maximising respect for human rights.[149] However, there are problems in this "balanced" image of human rights. The structural constraints of "balancing" have been previously explored in the context of the fair trial principle: see above, pp 104-109. In this context, the process of balancing conceives individual and group rights as mutually exclusive: to promote individual rights is necessarily to subvert collective rights, and vice versa. The reduction of conflict to these simple binary terms conceals the composition and complexity of the values in opposition.[150] Concern has also been expressed that individual rights have tended to trump collective interests.[151]

Dissatisfied with the privileging of liberalism, some feminists have argued for a pluralistic conception of equality that promotes rather than suppresses difference. Difference is not confined to gender but includes anything that plays a role in constituting identity including culture, religion, language, sexuality and so on.[152] The "difference perspective" cuts across the binary distinction of individuals and groups since it is concerned both with *individual* differences such as personal expression and characteristics and *group* differences such as language, culture and religion. Adopting this approach, the values underlying respective claims are transparent and may be negotiated more constructively.

In the criminal law, tensions within the concept of equality have manifested themselves in debates over the extent to which defences should incorporate discriminatory cultural beliefs about female sexuality. In the context of provocation, examined in Chapter 5 at pp 270-273, there is controversy over whether the cultural attitudes and ethnic background of the accused should be considered relevant, not only to determining the gravity of the provocation, but whether the provocation was such as could cause an "ordinary person" to act in the way in which the accused did. The difficulty arises in cases where the accused's response to the provocation is founded on cultural belief or customs that are discriminatory and condone or legitimate violence against

---

149 The difficulties of upholding this image of universality across many and varied cultures is evident in many controversies in human rights: see H Steiner and P Alston, *International Human Rights in Context* (Oxford: Clarendon Press, 1996), Ch 4.

150 For an analysis of Canadian rights jurisprudence that support this conclusion see A Eisenberg, "The Politics of Individual and Group Difference in Canadian Jurisprudence" (1994) 27 *Canadian Journal of Political Science* 1.

151 Avigail Eisenberg proposes that the sterility of the individual versus group rights approaches in Canadian jurisprudence should be abandoned in favour of the "difference perspective". By focusing on identity-related difference, the courts can frame its reasoning in terms of the values actually at stake: "The Politics of Individual and Group Difference in Canadian Jurisprudence" (1994) 27 *Canadian Journal of Political Science* 1.

152 There is a danger that feminism replaces one (masculine) universalism with two. As Lacey concludes "We need, in other words, to ... locate the ethical impulse to attend to otherness not just within the vector of sexual difference but within those of racial, ethnic, national, class and other differences too": *Unspeakable Subjects — Feminist Essays in Legal and Social Theory* (Oxford: Hart Publishing, 1998), p 245.

women and children. From a practical perspective, it is important that cultural claims that incorporate and perpetuate gender discrimination are evaluated carefully — culture is neither monolithic or immutable. Without careful interrogation of the centrality of these cultural beliefs to identity, there is a real danger that the courts may stereotype the values and beliefs of "other" races and cultures, paradoxically perpetuating discriminatory myths.

Respecting gender and cultural differences involve complex political and moral questions. In cases of irreconcilable conflict between these imperatives it has been suggested that the legislature rather than the courts should choose which values should prevail in a specific context: K Amirthalingam and S Bronitt, "Cultural Blindness and the Criminal Law" (1996) 20(2) *Alternative Law Journal* 58 at 60. Anticipating the potential clash between cultural and feminist claims to equality, the DEVAW sets out that "States should condemn violence against women and should not invoke any custom, tradition or religious consideration to avoid their obligations with respect to its elimination": Art 4. The DEVAW draws on the rights contained in the *Universal Declaration of Human Rights* 1948 (UDHR) and the *International Covenant on Civil and Political Rights* (ICCPR). The UDHR and ICCPR contain the right not to be subject to torture, or to cruel, inhuman or degrading treatment or punishment and the right to liberty and security of person. In Chapter 11 at pp 550ff, we consider the conflict between feminist and cultural claims to equal treatment in relation to "female genital mutilation". Should this practice be outlawed as a form of torture? To what extent should the law accommodate harmful cultural differences? Is it possible to achieve a balance between feminist and cultural claims?

EQUALITY BEFORE THE LAW: DENYING INDIGENOUS CRIMINAL LAW AND JURISDICTION

The paradox of equality before the law — its capacity to perpetuate and thereby condone disadvantage — is apparent in debates over the recognition of Indigenous "customary law". As noted in our discussion of jurisdiction above, in the colonial period there were legal challenges (ultimately unsuccessful) suggesting that Indigenous people were not amenable to criminal jurisdiction in all situations.[153] In recent years, this issue of native criminal jurisdiction has been re-agitated by the High Court's recognition of native title in *Mabo v Queensland (No 2)* (1992) 175 CLR 1. The decision left open a basis for argument, by analogy to native title, that Indigenous criminal laws (including customary defences) may have survived British occupation. As Deane and Gaudron JJ observed in *Mabo* (at 79):

> The common law so introduced was adjusted in accordance with the principle that, in
> settled colonies, only so much of it was introduced as was "reasonably applicable to the
> circumstances of the colony". This left room for the continued operation of some local laws
> or customs among the native people and even the incorporation of some of those laws and
> customs as part of the common law.

---

153 See *R v Murrell* (1836) 1 Legge 72; *R v Peter* 29/6/1860 Argus; *R v Jemmy* 7/9/1860 Argus; *R v Wedge* [1976] 1 NSWLR 581; *R v Walker* [1989] 2 Qd R 79, discussed in N O'Neill and R Handley, *Retreat From Injustice* (Sydney: Federation Press, 1994), p 409.

Not long after *Mabo*, Stanley Yeo drawing the analogy with native title, argued that Aboriginal criminal jurisdiction survived unless clearly abrogated by Parliament or Executive action.[154] Yeo suggested that even if Aboriginal criminal jurisdiction was held to have been abrogated, *Mabo* provided a moral basis for its reinstatement as a gesture of reconciliation consistent with the trend toward recognition of Indigenous rights to self-determination or self-management: at 196.

The extent of the extinguishment of native criminal jurisdiction is yet to be resolved authoritatively by the High Court. However, the prospects of success seem remote in light of the reasoning in *Walker v New South Wales* (1994) 182 CLR 45. This case concerned an attempt to claim, through the civil courts, that the Commonwealth and State Parliaments lacked the power to legislate over Aboriginal people without their consent. During the course of oral argument, the plaintiff introduced a further argument that Aboriginal criminal customary law had not been extinguished by British settlement. Refusing leave to appeal, Mason CJ noted that an argument framed in terms of Indigenous sovereignty and rights of self-determination was doomed to failure, as they were in *Mabo (No 2)*. The second argument also failed on the ground that the recognition of two concurrent, potentially overlapping, systems of criminal law would be confusing to citizens and more fundamentally, contradicted the principle of equality before the law (at 50):

> It is a basic principle that all people should stand equal before the law. A construction which results in different criminal sanctions applying to different persons for the same conduct offends that basic principle. The general rule is that an enactment applies to all persons and matters within the territory to which it extends, but not to any other persons and matters. ... The presumption applies with added force in the case of the criminal law, which is inherently universal in its operation, and whose aims would otherwise be frustrated.

Mason CJ continued (at 50) that even if it was assumed that the customary criminal law of Aboriginal peoples had survived settlement, it had been extinguished by the passage of criminal statutes of general application. No analogy could be drawn with native title:

> English criminal law did not, and Australian criminal law does not, accommodate an alternative body of law operating alongside it. There is nothing in *Mabo (No 2)* to provide any support at all for the proposition that criminal laws of general application do not apply to Aboriginal people.

This approach, based on the principle of equality before the law, is not beyond challenge. As our discussion of jurisdiction above has revealed, the simple ideal of territoriality in the criminal law has been subject to significant qualifications and exceptions. As Jennifer Neilsen and Gary Martin point out, the rejection of Indigenous criminal law in *Walker* ignores "the pluralism already inherent within the Australian federation, which is comprised of three tiers of law-making authority, each of which is supposed to complement the others".[155] As noted above, criminal jurisdiction within Australia is

---

154 S Yeo, "Native Criminal Jurisdiction After Mabo" (1994) 6 *Current Issues in Criminal Justice* 9; S Yeo, "Editorial — Recognition of Aboriginal Criminal Jurisdiction" (1994) 18 Crim LJ 193.

155 J Nielsen and G Martin, "Indigenous Australian Peoples and Human Rights" in D Kinley (ed), *Human Rights in Australian Law* (Sydney: Federation Press, 1998), p 111.

already fragmented, divided between the nine jurisdictions of the Commonwealth, States and Territories. It is also overlaid by the military criminal jurisdiction for defence services personnel. Legal and administrative mechanisms have been developed to "share" criminal jurisdiction and to resolve potential conflicts. For example, federal offences may be tried in State or Territory courts, though in accordance with State or Territory rather than Federal rules of evidence and procedure. In some spheres, Federal law has an overriding effect: State and Territory offences may be subject to claims that they are inoperative to the extent of inconsistency with Commonwealth legislation.[156] The problem of potential conflict between Indigenous and non-Indigenous criminal jurisdiction is not insurmountable, and could be resolved, as in the case of native title, by legislation which clarified the scope and limits of Indigenous law.

The formalistic conception of equality offered by Mason CJ in *Walker* severely limits the scope of claims for recognition of Aboriginal criminal laws and jurisdiction. As Neilsen and Martin point out: "[T]his formal reading of the notion of equality is out of kilter with international jurisprudence, and so the continued denial of the Indigenous criminal justice system contravenes the cultural rights of Indigenous Australians".[157] A similarly contested concept of equality informs the discussion in Report 31 of the Australian Law Reform Commission (ALRC) on *The Recognition of Aboriginal Customary Laws* (1988). The ALRC considered that special laws or defences for Aboriginal people had to comply with the principle of equality before law. This did not rule out different treatment for indigenous people where it was a necessary and reasonable response to the special needs of Aboriginal persons: paras 404-412. Consequently, the ALRC rejected special offences and defences in favour of addressing the issue of Aboriginality and Aboriginal law, where appropriate, within existing substantive and procedural laws. Rather than conceptualise equality as "equal versus special treatment", the Law Reform Commission of Canada has recognised the limits of equality discourse, proposing instead the higher goal of "ensuring equal access to justice, equitable treatment and respect" for Aboriginal peoples within the criminal justice system: *Aboriginal Peoples and Criminal Justice,* Report No 34 (1991), Ch 3. On this view, the principle of equality before the law would be consistent, rather than antagonistic, with the creation of parallel systems of Indigenous criminal justice.

The principle of equality before the law is limited in another way. The right to equality is usually conceived in procedural rather than substantive terms. Equality before the law ensures that all persons accused of crime receive the same minimum level of treatment from the criminal justice system. Thus, discretion relating to law enforcement, prosecution and sentencing *should* be structured and exercised in a consistent and non-discriminatory manner. In relation to pre-trial decision-making, Denis Galligan has pointed out that values such as fairness, consistency and equality before the law, do not ordinarily attach to substantive purposes or policies. Ensuring even-handedness in the administration of justice does not address the substantive discrimination that may be embedded in the purpose and policies of criminalising certain conduct. Substantive offences based on loose definitions such as "offensiveness" and "indecency" have a disproportionate impact

---

156 See, for example, the impact of the *Human Rights (Sexual Conduct) Act* 1994 (Cth) on homosexual offences and age of consent laws in States and Territories, discussed in Chapter 12, p 636.

157 J Nielsen and G Martin, "Indigenous Australian Peoples and Human Rights" in D Kinley (ed), *Human Rights in Australian Law* (Sydney: Federation Press, 1998), p 111.

on ethnic and minority groups. As we shall explore in Chapter 14: pp 792ff, empirical research has revealed that offensive conduct crimes are used primarily to deal with individuals who are intoxicated, swear at the police or otherwise demonstrate disrespect to authority. Such offences provide the police with flexible legal tools for defining and responding to social disorder, with adverse consequences for young persons particularly those from Indigenous and ethnic communities.

SENTENCING AND EQUALITY BEFORE THE LAW

The principle of equality before the law also influences sentencing. The racial and ethnic background of an offender tests the principle of equality in a number of ways. Race is not in itself a ground for differential treatment in sentencing. To do so would violate the *Race Discrimination Act* 1975 (Cth). Nevertheless, as Brennan J concluded in *Neal v The Queen* (1982) 149 CLR 305 (at 326), the principle of equality may require the sentencing court to consider rather than ignore *the effects* that flow from the offender's ethnic and racial background:

> The same sentencing principles are to be applied, of course, in every case, irrespective of the identity of a particular offender or his membership of an ethnic or other group. But in imposing sentences courts are bound to take into account, in accordance with those principles, all material facts including those facts which exist only by reason of the offender's membership of an ethnic or other group. So much is essential to the even administration of criminal justice.

The political and social context of the offending conduct in *Neal* is further explored in Chapter 15, pp 796-797.

It is often said that the socio-economic conditions within Indigenous communities (including alcohol abuse) may be taken into account in mitigation where relevant: *Rogers and Murray* (1989) 44 A Crim R 301 at 307; *Fernando* (1992) 76 A Crim R 58. However, there is a concern that the "check list" approach to Aboriginal disadvantage in mitigation of sentence do not give sufficient weight to the negative effect of the dispossession of land, culture and law as a contributing cause of offending: J Nicholson, "The Sentencing of Aboriginal Offenders" (1999) 23 Crim LJ 85.

A review of the recent authorities reveal considerable judicial ambivalence about the extent to which the accused's Aboriginal background may be taken into account particularly in cases where the violence occurs *within* Indigenous communities. In *R v Daniel* [1997] QCA 139 (30 May 1997), Fitzgerald P observed that it is not possible to reconcile all the judicial statements taken from these cases:

> Although the public, politicians and the media generally seem unaware of the complexity of sentencing, it involves principles and considerations which are potentially contradictory, as is not only recognised by the courts but established by legislative statements of Parliamentary intention. The public has competing interests, which are visible in the conflicting interests of victim and offender. Shortly put, some factors favour severity and some favour leniency of punishment; thus, for example, deterrence of crime, both general and personal to a particular offender, which is necessary for the protection of the community, punishment for the wrong done to the victim of an offence and society, and

vindication of the rights of the victim indicate the need for a sufficient penalty, while leniency can be attracted by favourable considerations which are personal to the offender and the prospect of his or her rehabilitation. Nonetheless, these factors which are inherent in the sentencing process cannot fully explain the divergent views expressed in the authorities concerning the sentencing of members of Aboriginal communities. (footnotes omitted)

Similar judicial ambivalence is evident in cases where the offender has been or will be punished in accordance with Indigenous law or practices. Judicial notice is taken of customs and practices within Indigenous communities that shed light on the seriousness of the individual offender's wrongdoing. This may operate to either mitigate or aggravate the penalty, though sentencing courts are warned not to consider such matters without credible independent evidence on Indigenous law and customs: *Minor* (1992) 59 A Crim R 227 at 237 per Mildren J. As we shall explore below, judges and law reformers alike have struggled to understand and recognise, within limits, the relevance of "payback" within Indigenous communities to sentencing.

CULTURAL PERSPECTIVES

"Payback": The Recognition of Indigenous Justice

Although Australian courts have persistently denied Indigenous criminal jurisdiction, they been prepared to recognise practices sanctioned by Indigenous law *indirectly* as a factor relevant to sentencing. "Payback" is an Aboriginal—English term used to describe the wide range of methods used to punish wrongdoers and to appease victims within some Indigenous communities. It is not a form of revenge, but constitutes an admission of responsibility, typically involving some form of restitution or gift to the victim, or acceptance of punishment by the wrongdoer.[158] Forms of payback vary widely, ranging from death, spearing and duelling, through to shaming, education, compensation or exclusion: Australian Law Reform Commission (ALRC), *Recognition of Aboriginal Customary Laws*, Report No 31 (1986), para 500. In some communities, payback may be purely symbolic involving no more than merely touching the accused on the thigh with a spear: *Minor* (1992) 59 A Crim R 227 at 229 per Asche CJ. The type of payback varies according to the severity of the breach of Indigenous law, the factors surrounding the offence, the parties involved and any other relevant matters. Once the type of payback is determined and carried out, that is regarded as the end of the matter and the potential for further violence between the clans is averted. Judges in the Northern Territory and Western Australia have a long history of recognising such Indigenous "customary law" in sentencing decisions.[159]

The ALRC has recognised the relevance of Aboriginal customary law to sentencing and recommended that lawful forms of traditional punishment could be incorporated into sentencing

---

158 *Jadurin v The Queen* (1982) 44 ALR 424 at 427-428 contains a vivid description of a payback ceremony and its consequences for those involved.

159 *Minor* (1992) 59 A Crim R 227 at 237 per Mildren J. This was aided by legislation that permitted the court in murder cases to receive any evidence on native law or custom in mitigation of penalty: *Criminal Law Amendment Ordinance* 1939 (NT).

orders. However, the ALRC refused to sanction the incorporation of traditional punishment into sentencing orders that would involve a breach of the general law. Partial recognition of Aboriginal law was justified as being consistent with Art 27 of the *International Covenant on Civil and Political Rights* (ICCPR), which provides:

> In those states in which ethnic, religious or linguistic minorities exist, persons belonging to such minorities shall not be denied the right, in community with others of the group to enjoy their own culture, to profess and practice their own religion or to use their own language.

Debate over recognition of "customary law" in sentencing decisions has tended to fixate negatively upon "payback by spearing" rather than positively on the restorative nature of Indigenous community-based punishment.[160] While accepting the inevitability of payback involving the infliction of serious injury within some Indigenous communities, the courts point out that payback is not retribution or vengeance and that the deliberate infliction of serious harm cannot be judicially condoned.[161] This position of judicial "neutrality" allows the courts to factor payback into sentencing, while deftly avoiding judicial consideration of the question of its legality under either domestic and international law.[162] Yet, this position is difficult to maintain in cases of prospective payback where the courts impose punishment *conditional* upon payback. In *R v Walker*,[163] the sentencing court adopted a "hands on" approach, requiring in the sentencing order that the Director of Correctional Services report back to the court as to whether payback occurred within a reasonable time. The judicial incorporation of payback into the sentencing order in *Walker* raises the question whether Australian law is sanctioning, perhaps even facilitating, "cruel, inhuman or degrading treatment or punishment" prohibited by Art 7 of the ICCPR. This argument has not been raised before either domestic or international courts, but James Crawford has suggested that nothing in the ICCPR prevents Australian courts from taking traditional spearing into account in sentencing decisions:

---

160 For a typical media depiction of payback see *The Independent* (May 1994) where the front-page banner "Bloody Justice" is pierced by a blood-splattered spear. On the importance of Indigenous involvement in sentencing see N Löfgren, "Aboriginal Community Participation in Sentencing" (1997) 21 Crim LJ 127.

161 *Jadurin* (1982) 7 A Crim R 182 at 187, per St John, Toohey and Fisher JJ; *Minor* (1992) 59 A Crim R 227 at 240, per Mildren J.

162 It has been suggested, obiter, that payback may not constitute an assault: *Minor* (1992) 59 A Crim R 227. The Northern Territory Code provided that an assault is not illegal where it is authorised by the victim, and the person who commits the assault does not intend to kill or cause grievous bodily harm. According to Mildren J, a person who administered payback on behalf of the Aboriginal community does not intend to kill or cause grievous bodily harm. Neither does the person who administers the payback inflict grievous bodily harm. Mildren J pointed to recent authority which supported the view that mere spearing into the thigh muscle may not in fact cause any permanent injury to health so as to fall within the definition of grievous bodily harm. This aspect of the judgment in *Minor* represents a novel approach to offences against the person. Previously, severe forms of payback by spearing had been assumed to be unlawful even where the victim consents. The approach is not consistent. In a Western Australian case, the judge refused to grant bail to an accused to allow him to undergo payback on the grounds that the spearing would be "unlawful": "Judge Rejects Spear Justice" in *The Western Australian*, 4 October 1997, p 3.

163 *R v Walker* (unrep, 10/2/1994, SC NT Martin CJ, SCC No 46 of 1993), discussed in (1994) 68(3) *Aboriginal Law Bulletin* 26.

The question, then, is whether the Covenant requires States Parties actively to suppress all treatment considered "cruel" or "degrading", even where the treatment occurs with the consent of the parties concerned, and as an aspect of the traditions and customs of the ethnic group within which it occurs, and no matter what other consequences such suppression, with its associated policing, would involve for the group in question. Quite apart from the question whether such punishment is "cruel" or "degrading", the answer must be that it does not. Nothing in the Covenant prevents the law enforcement authorities from adopting a policy of intervening in indigenous communities only upon complaint, in cases not involving threats of life or suppression of complaints.[164]

This approach again side-steps the issue of legality, hiding behind the prosecutorial discretion not to proceed in the absence of a complaint. From an international perspective, the toleration of payback by domestic law poses a significant challenge to the universality of human rights. As we have explored above, international law, while accepting some "margin of appreciation" in the application of human rights, is reluctant to dilute the universal quality of fundamental rights. This claim of universality is strongest in relation to rights that are not qualified such as Art 7 of the ICCPR that prohibits torture, cruel, inhuman or degrading treatment or punishment. The ALRC has acknowledged in its Discussion Paper No 17, *Aboriginal Customary Law — Recognition* (1980), that it is impossible to escape the culturally determined nature of fundamental concepts (p 52):

> But by what standard are the notions of human rights to be measured? Obviously there is a wide gap in some areas between Western notions of human rights and those which apply in Aboriginal society. These issues pose questions of justice which have never been answered satisfactorily anywhere and which are probably unanswerable. There is a direct clash between the imperative of imposed law and indigenous custom, a clash between irreconcilable moral imperatives.

As considered above, the clash requires the legal system — domestic and international — to choose between competing rights. After reviewing these issues, the ALRC concluded that the right to culture under Art 27 was "qualified" by Art 7: "Article 27 protects the right of a minority 'to profess and practice' its religion. It does not in terms protect cruel or inhumane punishments connected with it": at 53. On balance, the ALRC was satisfied that prohibiting cruel punishment would not have a significant detrimental effect on Aboriginal culture since there were other means of preserving Aboriginal culture such as land rights and language.

Payback involving spearing exposes the limits of equality and rights discourse, presenting challenges which the criminal justice system has only just begun to address. The ALRC's solution is an example of the tendency of individual rights to trump collective rights. It also reveals the

---

164 See J Crawford, "International Law and the Recognition of Aboriginal Customary Law" in B Hocking (ed), *International Law and Aboriginal Human Rights* (Sydney: Law Book Company Ltd, 1988), p 43 at p 63; S Blay, "The International Covenant on Civil and Political Rights and the Recognition of Customary Law Practices of Indigenous Tribes: the Case of Australian Aborigines" (1986) 19 *Comparative and International Law Journal of Southern Africa* 199 at 203-207; Australian Law Reform Commission, *Aboriginal Customary Law — Recognition,* Discussion Paper No 17 (1980), p 53.

process by which laws and cultural practices of "others" can be constructed as "inhuman and degrading punishment", denying legal recognition to practices that play a vital role in sustaining individual and group identities. As we shall explore in Chapter 11, what is striking by comparison is the "unseen" legitimation of a wide array of lawful "homosocial violence" within Australian society in the form of religious or cultural practices (such as male circumcision), violent sports (such as boxing and rugby), and general larrikinism or "rough horseplay".

MANDATORY SENTENCING: (IN)EQUALITY BEFORE THE LAW

Political debates about crime and punishment in Australia have degenerated into "uncivil politics of law and order": R Hogg and D Brown, *Rethinking Law and Order* (Annandale: Pluto Press, 1998), Ch 1. Within these debates, the rhetoric of equality and victims' rights, crudely and formalistically understood, can have a negative, often counterproductive, impact on the most disadvantaged within our community. This is clearly evident in relation to the controversial mandatory sentencing laws introduced in Western Australia and the Northern Territory: *Criminal Code* (WA), s 401 (adults and juveniles); *Sentencing Act* 1995 (NT), s 78A (adults); *Juvenile Justice Act* 1996 (NT), s 53(1) (juveniles). These laws were a response to a moral panic that the criminal justice system was not taking victims rights seriously, and that sentencing courts, by considering factors such as race and socio-economic deprivation, were passing inconsistent and excessively lenient sentences. These laws were also influenced by Bill Clinton's penal policy of "Three Strikes and You're Out" introduced in the United States.

Under these laws, the sentencing court is required to impose a minimum sentence of imprisonment in relation to designated offences, with escalating severity for repeat offending. For example, the Northern Territory law requires imprisonment for 14 days for the first offence, 90 days for the second offence and one year for the third offence.[165] As Declan Roche has pointed out, notwithstanding political claims to the contrary, there is scant empirical evidence that these laws have had any significant deterrent effect: "Mandatory Sentencing", *Australian Institute of Criminology — Trends and Issues*, No 138 (1999). While incapacitation limits the capacity of an individual to commit crime, it violates the principle that a person should be punished for what they have done, not for what they may do in the future: see Ch 1, p 25.

The costs of mandatory imprisonment are high in social as well as financial terms. The social cost for the Indigenous community was vividly demonstrated by the recent suicide of a young Aboriginal male while serving a prison sentence for minor theft. Rather than tackle discrimination within the sentencing process, these laws perpetuate disadvantage within the least powerful communities in society. As Roche concludes (p 6), mandatory sentencing is morally questionable, particularly as it routinely disadvantages the poor and marginalised. The laws do not apply to "white collar crimes" but rather are restricted to a narrow range of property crimes that are most likely to be committed by individuals from disadvantaged communities.

---

165 See H Bayes, "Punishment is Blind: Mandatory Sentencing of Children in Western Australia and the Northern Territory" (1999) 22 *University of New South Wales Law Journal* 286; G Zdenkowski, "Mandatory Imprisonment of Property Offenders in the Northern Territory" (1999) 22 *University of New South Wales Law Journal* 302.

Mandatory sentencing aims at consistency of treatment between offenders by removing or fettering judicial discretion during sentencing. Judges have expressed concern that these laws simply require heavier sentences where not justified on the facts. As Mildren J has observed:

> Prescribed minimum mandatory sentencing provisions are the very antithesis of just sentences. If a court thinks that a proper just sentence is the prescribed minimum or more, the minimum prescribed penalty is unnecessary. It therefore follows that the sole purpose of a prescribed minimum mandatory sentencing regime is to require sentencers to impose heavier sentences than would be proper according to the justice of the case.[166]

Mandatory sentencing flatly contradicts the recommendation of the Royal Commission into Aboriginal Deaths in Custody that every jurisdiction should enact legislation "to enforce the principle that imprisonment should be utilised only as a sanction of last resort": see *National Report — Overview and Recommendations* (Canberra: AGPS, 1991), Recommendation 92. The United Nations Human Rights Committee has also observed that the mandatory sentencing laws in Australia, which were viewed as imposing disproportionate punishment and being inconsistent with strategies to reduce the over-representation of Indigenous people in the criminal justice system, raised serious issues of compliance with various Articles of ICCPR: *Concluding Remarks of the Human Rights Committee — Australia*, CCPR/CO/69 AUS, para 17 (28 July 2000).

> **Although a decade has passed since the Royal Commission into Aboriginal Deaths in Custody, the levels of Aboriginal deaths in custody have continued to rise, comprising nearly one quarter of all deaths in 1999: V Dalton, "Australian Deaths in Custody & Custody-Related Police Operations 1999" (2000) *Trends & Issues in Crime and Criminal Justice*, No 153.**

These laws can be challenged and resisted in a range of informal and formal ways. Concern about the punitiveness of these policies may influence decisions made by the police and prosecutors to caution or divert the offender from the criminal justice process: D Roche, "Mandatory Sentencing", *Australian Institute of Criminology — Trends and Issues in Crime and Criminal Justice*, No 138 (1999), pp 4-5. Mandatory sentencing may also have an impact on the jury, encouraging "not guilty" verdicts as a protest against these harsh laws. Judges may also interpret the terms of the legislation, contrary to its obvious intent, in a manner most favourable to the accused. The power of Parliament to abrogate sentencing raises questions of constitutional significance relating to the doctrine of separation of powers: M Flynn, "Fixing a Sentence: Are there any Constitutional Limits?" (1999) 22 *University of New South Wales Law Journal* 280. Moreover, there have been calls for the Commonwealth Parliament to intervene and exercise its power to disallow the Northern Territory laws as in the case of the legislation enacted to legalise voluntary euthanasia.

The case of mandatory sentencing reveals the importance of ensuring that the principle of equality before the law is not politically and morally corrupted by the "uncivil politics of law and order": R Hogg, "Mandatory Sentencing Laws and the Symbolic Politics of Law and Order" (1999) 22 *University of New South Wales Law Journal* 262. Criminal justice reform requires a complex and

---

166 *Terry Ernest Curnow v Leonard David Pryce* [1999] NTSC 116 at para 12, per Mildren J.

contextual understanding of equality — a discourse of feminist and Indigenous rights — that both acknowledges and addresses the disadvantage faced by offenders and victims within marginalised communities.

3.5 THE PRINCIPLE OF PRIVACY

Privacy is a concept that influences and constrains the scope of the criminal law in many ways. Since the right to privacy protects citizens from arbitrary intrusion into their homes or private lives, it imposes limits on both procedural and substantive laws. While the common law has always attached considered value to the inviolability of property, it has never recognised invasion of privacy as a distinct tort: *Victoria Park Racing v Taylor* (1937) 58 CLR 479 at 496, per Latham CJ. The importance of property is reflected in the common law's historical antipathy toward general warrants,[167] and the strict construction of warrants authorising the search, seizure or surveillance of property.[168]

The legal conception of a "right to privacy" is a relatively recent innovation, emerging first in American legal scholarship during the late 19th century.[169] This period of legal development witnessed a significant shift in focus from the protection of physical interests (such as property) to less tangible, psychological interests (such as privacy): P Alldridge, *Relocating Criminal Law* (Aldershot: Ashgate, 2000), pp 107-108.

PRIVACY: A SHIELD AGAINST ARBITRARY STATE INTRUSION

In the modern era, privacy is a fundamental human right protected by Art 17 of the International Covenant on Civil and Political Rights (ICCPR):

(1) No one shall be subjected to arbitrary or unlawful interference with his privacy, family, home or correspondence, nor to unlawful attacks on his honour and reputation.

(2) Everyone has the right to the protection of the law against such interference or attacks.

In the field of criminal process, this provision has operated as a shield against intrusive methods of investigation. Since privacy is not absolute, interference through the use of electronic surveillance may be legitimate where it is reasonably necessary for the prevention of disorder or crime.[170] Provided that the domestic law imposes appropriate legal and/or administrative safeguards against

---

167 *Entick v Carrington* (1765) 95 ER 807 is the classic authority for this proposition. While affirming the inviolability of an Englishman's property with legal authority, the court acknowledged that the power to issue search warrants for stolen goods had crept into the common law by stealth!

168 In relation to listening devices warrants, the High Court has held interference with the rights of ownership are justified only where it has been authorised or excused by law: *Coco* (1994) 68 ALJR 410 at 403.

169 The legal conception of privacy is traced to a famous article in the *Harvard Law Review* in 1890 by Warren and Brandeis (both subsequently United States Supreme Court Justices). Drawing analogies from a range of civil law remedies, the authors rationalised the right to privacy as "the right to be let alone": S Warren and L Brandeis, "The Right to Privacy" (1890) 4 *Harvard Law Review* 193 at 193.

170 *Klass v Federal Republic of Germany* (1978) 2 EHRR 214 (ECHR Series A, No 28, 1978); *Kruslin v France* (1990) 12 EHRR 547 (ECHR, Series A, No 176B, 1990).

abuses, intrusive investigative activity will not constitute an arbitrary interference with privacy. With increasingly sophisticated and inexpensive surveillance technologies, the right to privacy provides a normative principle for imposing limits and ensuring accountability for intrusive investigative methods in the public and private sector.[171] With advances in forensic sciences, such as DNA testing, the threats to privacy emerge at the molecular level — not surprisingly, the law has considerable difficulty in keeping pace with these technological advances.[172]

Privacy plays an important role in limiting the exercise of State power. As the High Court observed when considering the judicial discretion to exclude evidence obtained by improper or illegal means, "it is not fair play that is called into question but rather society's right to insist that those who enforce the law themselves respect it, so that a citizen's precious right to immunity from arbitrary and unlawful intrusion into the daily affairs of private life may remain unimpaired": *Bunning v Cross* (1978) 141 CLR 54 at 75, per Stephen and Aickin JJ. In this context, respect for legality (the rule of law) is not merely an end in itself, but also a means of protecting privacy: see further, Ch 1, 2.1 'Defining Crime and the Rule of Law'.

Privacy also has an impact on the substantive law. As we shall explore in subsequent chapters, privacy has influenced debates about the criminalisation of a wide-range of conduct previously falling outside the scope of the criminal law, such as computer hacking, stalking and domestic violence. In terms of decriminalisation, the principle has exerted the most influence in the "liberalisation" of homosexual and prostitution offences. The principle of privacy however operates spasmodically. In the sexual field, it is more likely to confer protection to conventional rather than transgressive forms of sexuality. This issue is further explored in Chapter 12, 1.1 'Constructing Sexual Crimes: Sexual Violence or Violent Sex': pp 581ff. In other areas, privacy has had negligible impact. As Alldridge notes in *Relocating Criminal Law* (Aldershot: Ashgate, 2000) "privacy does not seem to have any substantial contemporary relevance to the drug debate": p 116.

Australia's accession to the Optional Protocol to the ICCPR, which created the right of individual petition, provided a new legal avenue for challenging domestic laws which violate the right to privacy: see above at p 113. In *Toonen v Australia* (1994) 1 PLPR 50, the United Nations Human Rights Committee ruled that criminalisation of sexual conduct between consenting adult males under the *Criminal Code* (Tas) violated the right to privacy under the ICCPR: para 8.2. With no immediate prospect of State legislation repealing the offending sections, the Federal Government, as a party to the ICCPR, was obliged to provide the applicant with the "effective remedy" required by the Human Rights Committee. The resulting legislation, the *Human Rights (Sexual Conduct) Act* 1994 (Cth), created a right to sexual privacy under Federal law:

---

171 The extent to which the present statutory framework for electronic surveillance in Australia satisfies these international obligations is considered in S Bronitt, "Electronic Surveillance, Human Rights and Criminal Justice" (1997) 3(2) *Australian Journal of Human Rights* 183. Threats to privacy also derive from "private policing" and its extensive use of surveillance cameras (CCTV) in workplaces and shopping malls.

172 On the legal issues surrounding the use of forensic evidence and the proposal to establish a National DNA Database, see Model Criminal Code Officers Committee of the Standing Committee of Attorneys-General, *Model Forensic Procedures Bill; DNA Database Provisions Report*, Discussion Paper (1999). The Model Bill has been enacted in the Commonwealth, South Australia and Victoria: *Crimes Act* 1914 (Cth), Pt 1D; *Criminal Law (Forensic Procedures) Act* 1998 (SA); *Crimes Act* 1958 (Vic), Pt 4.

Arbitrary interferences with privacy

4(1) Sexual conduct involving only consenting adults acting in private is not to be subject, by or under any law of the Commonwealth, a State or a Territory, to any arbitrary interference with privacy within the meaning of Article 17 of the International Covenant on Civil and Political Rights.

(2) For the purposes of this section, an adult is a person who is 18 years old or more.

Although protecting only one aspect of the right to privacy under Art 17 of the ICCPR — the right to sexual privacy — it is generally accepted that the Act is a valid exercise of the Commonwealth's legislative power under the external affairs provision in the Constitution: Report by the Senate Legal and Constitutional Legislation Committee, *Human Rights (Sexual Conduct) Bill 1994* (December 1994), para 1.72. The impact of this provision on domestic criminal laws is further considered in Chapter 12.

THE PUBLIC/PRIVATE DICHOTOMY: MALLEABLE AND DISCRIMINATORY

The scope of the protection accorded by Art 17 of the ICCPR, reflected in *Toonen* and the resulting Federal Act, rests upon the public/private dichotomy. The idea that there exist spheres of "private" activity that cannot legitimately be subject to State intervention — which underlies the "harm principle"[173] — has been influential in the liberalisation of laws governing homosexuality and prostitution: see Ch 1, 3.1 'The Prevention of Harm', pp 49-51.

Like equality, privacy has been the subject of extensive feminist critique. Feminists have noted that the legal division between the public and the private has played, and continues to play, a significant role in concealing and legitimating the subordination of certain groups in society. The private sphere of the "family" remains the site for female subordination.[174] By placing "domestic" violence and "marital" rape firmly within the private sphere, these crimes are not viewed as proper matters for state regulation. Although the spousal immunity for rape has been removed from the substantive law, in practice, the authorities are reluctant to interfere with violence which occurs within the family. The public sphere is claimed to be constructed around male interests.

Theorists exploring gay and lesbian rights also share similar concerns. Wayne Morgan argues that juridical discourses of privacy, including those employed in *Toonen*, conceal and contribute to the subordination of homosexuality by constructing this type of sexuality as powerless, dangerous and deviant.[175] By contrast, Morgan advances equality as the preferable basis for protecting and extending gay and lesbian rights. While it is true that privacy has traditionally done little to validate

---

173 JS Mill, *On Liberty* (London: Harmondsworth, Penguin, 1974, first published 1859). Mill provided the philosophical basis for the Wolfenden Committee's proposals for reform of the criminal law governing homosexuality and prostitution: *Report of the Committee on Homosexual Offences and Prostitution* (London: HMSO, 1957).

174 See generally K O'Donovan, *Sexual Divisions in Law* (London: Weidenfeld and Nicolson, 1985); and R Graycar and J Morgan, *The Hidden Gender of Law* (Sydney: Federation Press, 1990), Ch 1.

175 See W Morgan, "Identifying Evil for What it is: Tasmania, Sexual Perversity and the United Nations" (1994) 19 *Melbourne University Law Review* 740.

or celebrate different sexualities, our discussion of equality in the preceding section reads as a catalogue of failure on the part of the courts and legislatures to provide effective remedies for addressing the structural causes of disadvantage affecting marginalised groups in society. It is not a question of abandoning privacy in favour of equality, but rather engaging in the normative reconstruction of both concepts.[176]

In relation to privacy, it has been suggested that the right to respect for private life could be reconceptualised. The boundaries between the spheres of public and private are neither immutable nor universal. As Margaret Thornton observes, "the public/private dichotomy of liberal thought, far from constituting two analytically discrete realms, is a malleable creation of the public realm".[177] Working within this traditional framework, it is possible to reconstruct privacy in ways that provide individuals with greater freedom to express and fulfil their emotional needs. Privacy may be viewed not merely as a shield, but as a positive basis for the recognition of personal needs and aspirations. The European Commission has observed that the right to privacy protected under the *European Convention on Human Rights* includes "to a certain extent, the right to establish and to develop relationships with other human beings, especially in the emotional field for the development and fulfilment of one's own personality".[178] This approach expands the *negative* conception of privacy as freedom from unwarranted state intrusion into one's private life, to include the *positive* right to establish, develop and fulfil one's own emotional needs.[179] This glimmer of "privacy as autonomy"[180] underlies legal moves for recognising rights of access to personal information, such as medical and counselling records.[181]

By reconstructing privacy in this way, the scope of private sexual conduct can be redefined to include some types of public behaviour. A redefined concept of privacy could offer protection against laws that unreasonably interfere with sexual activity in public spaces such as public displays of homosexuality. Under the present law, a wide range of homosexual conduct is indirectly criminalised through public indecency and offensive conduct laws. This reconstruction of privacy would have considerable practical significance since empirical research in Australia indicates that, even before the decriminalisation of homosexual activity "in private", the bulk of prosecutions for homosexual

---

176 For an excellent review of the "critique of rights" debate in this context see J Morgan, "Equality Rights in the Australian Context: A Feminist Assessment" in P Alston (ed), *Towards an Australian Bill of Rights* (Canberra: CIPL/HREOC, 1994), p 123.

177 M Thornton, "The Public/Private Dichotomy: Gendered and Discriminatory" (1991) 18 *Journal of Law and Society* 448 at 459. See generally, M Thornton (ed), *Public and Private: Feminist Legal Debates* (Melbourne: Oxford University Press, 1995).

178 App No 6825/74, 5 Eur Com HR Dec & Rep 86 at 87. This broader conception of privacy is reflected in *Dudgeon v United Kingdom*, 45 Eur Ct HR (ser A) (1981); 4 Eur HR Rep 149 (1982).

179 It has been suggested that the state should assume a greater role in *promoting*, rather than simply protecting, the right to respect for private life under Art 8: AM Connelly, "Problems of Interpretation of Article 8 of the *European Convention on Human Rights*" (1986) 35 *International and Comparative Law Quarterly* 567 at 574-575.

180 P Alldridge, *Relocating Criminal Law* (Aldershot: Ashgate, 2000), pp 114.

181 *Gaskin v United Kingdom* (1990) 12 Eur HR Rep 36 held that refusal to allow a patient access to her medical records breached the right to privacy protected by the *European Convention on Human Rights*. See further, B McSherry, "Access to Medical Records" AIHLE, Topics for Attention, Issues Paper No 1, 1996. Rights to privacy may conflict with competing rights such as the right to a fair trial. The legal arguments surrounding defence access to the counselling records of rape victims are explored in S Bronitt and B McSherry, "The Use and Abuse of Counseling Records in Sexual Assault Trials: Reconstructing the 'Rape Shield'" (1997) 8(2) *Criminal Law Forum* 289.

activity concerned public acts of some kind: New South Wales Bureau of Crime Statistics and Research, *Statistical Report* (1978), Series 2, No 9, p 38. Although privacy has the potential to protect many facets of personhood, the present sphere of protection continues to be drawn along traditional liberal and therefore negative lines. As we shall explore in Chapter 12 at pp 644ff, rather than respect and celebrate sexual difference, privacy jurisprudence simply maintains an oppressive legal closet around conduct that is considered to be sexually deviant or transgressive.

4. CONCLUSION: THE FUTURE OF GENERAL PRINCIPLES?

General principles embody a set of political, moral and ethical values that are considered fundamental to the operation of the criminal law and criminal process. In this chapter, we have examined the contested meaning and scope of a selection of principles relating to territoriality, fairness, equality before the law and privacy. Rather than exhibiting universal and immutable qualities, these principles are historically contingent, evolving to accommodate changing social, political and moral expectations about the proper function and limits of the criminal law. The legitimacy of the principles discussed in this chapter increasingly derives from the moral and political authority of international law, in particular those treaties protecting fundamental human rights.[182] Many basic concepts of the criminal law are being challenged and reformed by reference to the principles of international law. The growing internationalisation of criminal jurisdiction is one example of this trend. We predict that international jurisprudence will exert an increasing influence on the future development of the substantive criminal law.

This chapter has also explored the contribution of critical scholarship to the understanding and reconstruction of general principles. While conventional legal scholars, practitioners, judges and liberal reformers view their task as forcing the law to live up to its rhetoric, critical scholars have suggested that the dichotomy between the rhetoric and reality of criminal justice reveals something fundamental, indeed constitutive, about the law and legal ideology. The "gap" between rhetoric and reality reflects the profound normative disagreement within legal doctrine, a conflict that is often concealed or minimised within principled accounts of criminal law. Critical and feminist scholars have also exposed the limits of general principles as a means of remedying the entrenched political, social and economic disadvantage of marginalised groups. In this chapter, we hope to have demonstrated that the adoption of critical perspectives need not lead to mindless "trashing" or "deconstruction" of the criminal law. While some critical scholars remain deeply sceptical of general principles,[183] we believe that normative perspectives (whether packaged as theories or principles) are essential for the future vitality of the criminal law. By revealing the contingent and contradictory nature of the principles relating to territoriality, fairness, equality and privacy, we have opened spaces for re-imagining these fundamental concepts in radically different ways. This process, which Lacey calls

---

182 A framework of criminal justice based on promotion of principles, particularly those derived from international human rights law, is sketched in A Ashworth, *The Criminal Process* (2nd ed, Oxford: Oxford University Press, 1998).

183 D Brown, D Farrier and D Weisbrot, *Criminal Laws* (2nd ed, Sydney: Federation Press, 1996), p 4.

"normative reconstruction", is not confined to general principles. In the next chapter, we review the principles governing criminal responsibility adopting a similar perspective. By drawing insights from psychology and other disciplines, we will critically examine the fundamental principles governing the fault and physical elements of offences, and will provide alternative normative frameworks for understanding and reconstructing notions of responsibility within the criminal law.

3

Principles of Criminal Responsibility

Thomas Moore, "Morality" in
The Poetical Works of Thomas Moore
(London: Longman, Green, Longman
and Roberts, 1860), p 293, l. 15-18

I find the doctors and the sages
Have differ'd in all climes and ages,
And two in fifty scarce agree
On what is pure morality

1. INTRODUCTION

The principles that underlie the criminal law are dependent upon the idea of a person as a rational being, capable of making choices between right and wrong and able to control conscious actions.[1] The idea that children and those with mental impairment lack the ability to reason and therefore should be excused from responsibility for criminal acts has been pervasive throughout the history of the criminal law. For example, in the 18th century, Sir Matthew Hale considered that infants under the age of 14 were incapable of discerning between good and evil and that the lack of understanding in the insane precluded them from criminal sanctions: *The History of the Pleas of the Crown* (London: Professional Books Ltd, 1971) (original publication 1736), Chs III and IV, pp 16-37. The criminal law continues to excuse children and those with mental impairment from criminal responsibility and this is briefly explained below.

---

[1]   For an analysis of the concept of "personhood" in the criminal law see P Alldridge, *Relocating Criminal Law* (Aldershot: Ashgate, 2000), Ch 3.

The attribution of criminal responsibility has not, however, been confined to human persons. For example, at times, the law has attributed criminal responsibility to animals: EP Evans, *The Criminal Prosecution and Capital Punishment of Animals* (London: Faber and Faber, 1987). One of the developing areas of criminal law is the attribution of criminal responsibility to corporations and the question of whether or not corporations can commit crimes is now subject to a growing field of literature. It was once claimed that "the punishment of corporations is of small relevance to the purposes of the criminal law": G Williams, *Criminal Law: The General Part* (2nd ed, London: Stevens & Sons, 1961), p 865. This no longer holds true as the inquiry into corporations and criminal responsibility has increased in tandem with the growth in sociological analyses of corporate crime and increasing social concern with the serious forms of harms resulting from corporate activities.

As well as developing general principles relating to who may commit a crime, the principles governing criminal responsibility has been concerned to ensure that only a person who is considered "blameworthy" should be convicted of a crime. There has thus been a division made between the physical and fault elements of serious offences. This is expressed in the Latin maxim, *actus non facit reum, nisi mens sit rea*, which may be loosely translated as "an act does not make a person guilty of a crime unless that person's mind be also guilty".[2] A variety of terms have been used to describe these physical and fault elements, the most common being those stemming from the Latin maxim, namely *actus reus* and *mens rea*.

The use of these Latin terms persists in common law states despite constant criticism. In *R v Miller* [1983] 2 AC 161, Lord Diplock stated (at 174):

> [I]t would ... be conducive to clarity of analysis of the ingredients of a crime that is created by statute ... if we were to avoid bad Latin and instead to think and speak ... about the conduct of the accused and his [or her] state of mind at the time of the conduct, instead of speaking of *actus reus* and *mens rea*.

The Code jurisdictions do not refer to *mens rea* or *actus reus* and do not use any synonyms for these terms. Physical and fault elements are determined by the nature and definition of the crime under consideration. For example, in *Widgee Shire Council v Bonney* (1907) 116 CLR 353 (at 356) Griffith CJ stated in relation to the *Criminal Code* (Qld):

> [I]t is never necessary to have recourse to the old doctrine of *mens rea,* the exact meaning of which has been the subject of much discussion.

The Model Criminal Code Officers Committee (MCCOC) avoids using the terms *mens rea* and *actus reus* and simply uses the generic terms "physical" and "fault elements": *Criminal Code Act* 1995 (Cth), Pt 2.2. Because of the criticism of the Latin terms and their lack of use in the Code jurisdictions, we will follow the MCCOC's lead and simply refer to physical and fault elements throughout this book.

It should, however, be noted that the distinction itself between physical and fault elements has also been criticised on the basis that it lacks clarity and there is often an overlap between the

---

2   *Haughton v Smith* [1975] AC 476 at 491-492; per Lord Hailsham (translation of maxim adopted). The maxim appears to have originated with Sir Edward Coke: *Institutes of the Laws of England*, Part 3 (London: Lee & Pakeman, 1644), 3 Inst 6.

two elements.[3] This becomes particularly apparent in the analysis of automatism which is explored in Chapter 4. In addition, a large range of statutory crimes can be classified as ones of strict or absolute liability: see below p 191. These offences enable a person (or corporation) to be convicted despite having acted without intention, recklessness or negligence. At the other end of the scale, individuals can be punished for certain conduct that is preliminary to a substantive offence being carried out. The intention to commit a crime becomes the principal ingredient of the offences of attempts, conspiracy and incitement. These are considered further in Chapter 9.

In this chapter, we will first consider criminal responsibility in terms of who may commit a crime before turning toward an exploration of the traditional division between physical and fault elements and the rise of strict and absolute liability offences.

2. WHO MAY COMMIT CRIMES?

2.1 INDIVIDUALS WITH MENTAL IMPAIRMENT

There is a presumption in criminal law that individuals do not suffer from mental impairment.[4] In general, this presumption may be displaced by the defence proving on the balance of probabilities that the accused was suffering from mental impairment at the time of the commission of the crime. Such mental impairment must have affected the accused's ability to know the nature and quality of the conduct or that the conduct was wrong or, in some jurisdictions, affected the accused's capacity to control his or her conduct. If a person is found not guilty because of mental impairment, he or she is generally detained in a psychiatric institution. The defence of mental impairment will be dealt with in more detail in Chapter 4.

2.2 CHILDREN

Like those with some form of mental impairment, children have traditionally been viewed as lacking the ability to reason. For example, Aristotle associated children with animals because of their lack of reason and rational desire: *The Nichomachean Ethics,* translated by T Irwin (Indianapolis: Hackett Publishing Co, 1985), i 9 1100a1. In the criminal law, children under a certain age have been exempted from criminal responsibility because of their incapacity to understand the consequences of their acts and because they have not fully developed an appreciation of the difference between right and wrong.

---

3   See for example, B Fisse, *Howard's Criminal Law* (5th ed, Sydney: Law Book Company Ltd, 1990), p 11; R Murgason and L McNamara, *Outline of Criminal Law* (Sydney: Butt, 1997), p 19.

4   *Criminal Code Act* (Cth), s 7.2(3); *Crimes Act* 1900 (ACT), s 428N (this is inferred on the basis that "mental dysfunction" must be established on the balance of probabilities); *Criminal Code* (NT), s 6; *Criminal Code* (Qld), s 26; *Criminal Law Consolidation Act* 1935 (SA), s 269D; *Criminal Code* (Tas), s 15; *Crimes (Mental Impairment and Unfitness to be Tried) Act* 1997 (Vic), s 21(1); *Criminal Code* (WA), s 26.

Having a minimum age of criminal responsibility is occasionally questioned, particularly when a serious crime is committed by a child. The murder of two-year-old James Bulger in Liverpool, England, by Robert Thompson and Jon Venables, both of whom were aged 10 at the time gave rise to much public concern and outrage.[5] In *R v Secretary of State for the Home Department; Ex parte Venables; R v Secretary of State for the Home Department; Ex parte Thompson* [1997] 3 WLR 23 Lord Hope of Craighead pointed out (at 76) that had the two boys been born a few months later, they could not have been held responsible for the crime. The accused subsequently complained to the European Court of Human Rights that they had been denied a fair trial.[6] There was evidence that the accused had found the trial distressing and frightening and had not been able to concentrate during it. The Court held by 16 votes to one that there had been a violation of the right to a fair trial under Art 6 of the *European Convention on Human Rights*. This was on the basis that given their immaturity and emotional state and the tense court room and public scrutiny, they would not have been capable of consulting with their lawyers and giving them information for the purposes of their defence.

The main rationale behind treating children as not criminally responsible is that they are viewed as somehow morally different to adults. This has been questioned by social science researchers who argue that children and adolescents' moral reasoning in the sense of knowing the difference between right and wrong, may be very similar to that of adults.[7] The main difference between children and adolescents as compared to adults is that children differ in relation to judgment and self-control. Morse writes in "Immaturity and Irresponsibility" (1998) 88(1) *The Journal of Criminal Law and Criminology* 15 that in relation to adolescents, they:

> (1) have a stronger preference for risk and novelty; (2) subjectively assess the potentially
> negative consequences of risky conduct less unfavorably; (3) tend to be impulsive and
> more concerned with short-term than long-term consequences; (4) subjectively experience
> and assess the passage of time and time periods as longer; and (5) are more susceptible to
> peer pressure.

Morse argues that differential treatment of children because of these findings is a normative judgment that only society can make.

The way in which children have been treated by the criminal law has differed markedly according to societal concepts of childhood. In the 17th and 18th centuries, children were treated as miniature adults and were subject to fierce punishments such as whipping, branding and even hanging: see in general, I Pinchbeck and M Hewitt, *Children in English Society* (London: Routledge

---

5   The trial was held in the Preston Crown Court before Morland J in November 1993. Alan Norrie has analysed the responses in the context of law's hegemony over such events: "Legal and Moral Judgment in the 'General' Part" in P Rush, S McVeigh and A Young (eds), *Criminal Legal Doctrine* (Aldershot: Ashgate, 1997), pp 4-8. For an outline of the facts of the case and references to newspaper reports at the time, see JN Turner, "The James Bulger Case: A Challenge to Juvenile Justice Theories"(1994) 68(8) *Law Institute Journal* 734.

6   *T v United Kingdom; V v United Kingdom* (unrep, 16/12/1999, Strasbourg, Application No 00024724/94).

7   See for example, T Grisso, "Society's Retributive Response to Juvenile Violence: A Developmental Perspective" (1996) 20 *Law and Human Behavior* 229; JL Woolard, N Dickon Repucci and RE Redding, "Theoretical and Methodological Issues in Studying Children's Capacities in Legal Contexts" (1996) 20 *Law and Human Behavior* 219; L Steinberg and E Cauffman, "Maturity of Judgement in Adolescence: Psychosocial Factors in Adolescent Decision Making" (1996) 20 *Law and Human Behavior* 249; ES Scott, N Dickon Reppucci and JL Woolard, "Evaluating Adolescent Decision Making in Legal Contexts" (1995) 19 *Law and Human Behavior* 221.

and Kegan Paul, 1973), Vol 1. It was only in the 19th century that children began to be treated differently and only at the turn of the 20th century that separate courts for children's crime were established in common law countries: J Turner, "The James Bulger Case: A Challenge to Juvenile Justice Theories" (1994) 68(8) *Law Institute Journal* 734 at 735. The special procedures and rules governing the investigation, adjudication and sentencing of juveniles in Australia are reviewed in K Warner, "The Legal Framework of Juvenile Justice" in R White and C Alder (eds), *The Police and Young People in Australia* (Melbourne: Cambridge University Press, 1994), Ch 2.

The minimum age for criminal responsibility is 10 years of age in Australia except in Tasmania. At common law, there is an irrebuttable presumption that a child aged seven or under cannot be guilty of a crime.[8] In Tasmania, the phrase used is "under 7 years of age": *Criminal Code* (Tas), s 18(1). In the Australian Capital Territory, New South Wales, the Northern Territory, Queensland, South Australia, Victoria and Western Australia, the minimum age of criminal responsibility has been raised to 10,[9] so that a person under that age cannot be found guilty of a crime. This mirrors the position taken in the *Model Criminal Code*, reflected in s 7.1 of the *Criminal Code Act* 1995 (Cth).

THE REBUTTABLE PRESUMPTION

Under both common law and statute, when a child reaches the age of 14 he or she is regarded as an adult in terms of criminal responsibility.[10] The problem arises as to how to treat those children of and over the minimum age of criminal responsibility but below the age of 14.

There is a common law presumption that once a child reaches the age of seven but is under the age of 14, he or she does not "know the difference between right and wrong and [is] therefore incapable of committing a crime because of lack of *mens rea*".[11] This is sometimes referred to by the Latin term *doli incapax* (incapable of wrongdoing). A rationale for the presumption is that it protects children from the "full rigour of criminal law enforcement": B Fisse, *Howard's Criminal Law* (5th ed, Sydney: Law Book Company Ltd, 1990), pp 479-480. The *doli incapax* presumption has been codified by legislation in the Australian Capital Territory, Commonwealth, Northern Territory, Queensland, Tasmania and Western Australia, and survives as part of the common law in New South Wales, South Australia and Victoria.[12]

---

8   Sir William Holdsworth, *A History of English Law* (London: Sweet and Maxwell, 1966), Vol 3, p 372; Sir James Stephen, *A History of the Criminal Law of England* (London: 1883), Vol 2, p 98.

9   *Children and Young People Act* 1999 (ACT), s 71; *Children (Criminal Proceedings) Act* 1985 (NSW), s 5; *Criminal Code* (NT), s 38(1); *Criminal Code* (Qld), s 29(1); *Young Offenders Act* 1993 (SA), s 10; *Children and Young Persons Act* 1989 (Vic), s 127; *Criminal Code* (WA), s 29.

10 The standard of behaviour expected by the law may be lower than that of an adult. In the context of provocation the High Court, however, has stated that "[t]here is, we think, adequate justification in policy, reason and authority for taking age, in the sense of immaturity, into account in setting the standard of self-control required by reference to the ordinary [person] ...": *Stingel v The Queen* (1990) 171 CLR 312 at 330.

11 *Archbold's Criminal Pleading Evidence and Practice* (1993) Vol 1, para 1.96. For a discussion of sentencing issues in relation to the two 10-year-old boys convicted of the murder of James Bulger, see *R v Secretary of State for the Home Department; Ex parte Venables; R v Secretary of State for the Home Department; Ex parte Thompson* [1997] 3 WLR 23; [1997] 3 All ER 97; [1977] 2 FLR 471; [1997] Fam Law 786.

12 *Criminal Code Act* 1995 (Cth), s 7.2; *Children and Young People Act* 1999 (ACT), s 71; *Children (Criminal Proceedings) Act* 1985 (NSW), s 5; *Criminal Code* (NT), s 38(2); *Criminal Code* (Qld), s 29(2); *Young Offenders Act* 1993 (SA), s 10; *Criminal Code* (Tas), s 18(2); *Children and Young Persons Act* 1989 (Vic), s 127; *Criminal Code* (WA), s 29.

The presumption that a child between the minimum age of criminal responsibility and 14 is incapable of committing a crime was severely criticised by Laws J sitting in the Divisional Court of Queen's Bench Division in *C (a minor) v DPP* [1994] 3 WLR 888. In that case, two 12-year-old boys were caught tampering with a motorcycle. One boy held the handlebars while the other used a crowbar in an attempt to force open the padlock and chain around the motorcycle. The police approached on foot and one chased C who climbed a wall, but who was then caught by another officer. C was convicted of interfering with a motor vehicle with the intention to commit theft. The magistrate considered a submission that C was *doli incapax*, but held that the presumption had been rebutted on the basis that it could be inferred from C's running away and the criminal damage, that C knew that what he was doing was wrong. The Divisional Court dismissed C's appeal on the basis that the presumption of *doli incapax* was outdated and should be treated as being no longer good law.

In the course of his judgment, Laws J criticised the presumption on a number of grounds. One criticism (at 895-896) was that the presumption operated in favour of children with impoverished backgrounds and antisocial tendencies:

> It must surely nowadays be regarded as obvious that, where a morally impoverished upbringing may have led a teenager into crime, the facts of his [or her] background should not go to his [or her] guilt, but to his [or her] mitigation; the very emphasis placed in modern penal policy upon the desirability of non-custodial disposal designed to be remedial rather than retributive ... offers powerful support for the view that delinquents ... who may know no better than to commit anti-social and sometimes dangerous crimes, should not be held immune from the criminal justice system, but sensibly managed within it.

The judgment of the Divisional Court was overturned by the House of Lords which held that abolition of the presumption was a matter for Parliament.[13] Lord Lowry addressed the above criticism of Laws J as well as a number of others set out by the latter and stated that the main purpose of the presumption is to protect children of this age group from the full force of the criminal law: at 396-399. He stated (at 403):

> [t]he distinction between the treatment and the punishment of child "offenders" has popular and political overtones, a fact which shows that we have been discussing not so much a legal as a social problem, with a dash of politics thrown in.

The pros and cons of retaining the presumption that a child aged above the minimum age of criminal responsibility and under 14 is incapable of wrongdoing have been explored in recent academic material.[14] Thus far, the presumption remains firmly in place in Australia, but s 34 of the *Crime and*

---

13 *C (a minor) v DPP* [1995] 2 WLR 383. For a brief discussion of this case see DC Price, "The Criminal Liability of Children" (1995) 69 ALJ 593-594.

14 T Bartholomew, "Legal and Clinical Enactment of the *Doli Incapax* Defence in the Supreme Court of Victoria, Australia" (1998) 5(1) *Psychiatry, Psychology and Law* 95; M Grove, "Are You Old Enough? In Defence of *Doli Incapax*" (1996) *Law Institute Journal* 38; P Blazey-Ayoub, "*Doli Incapax*" (1996) 20 Crim LJ 34; D Price, "The Criminal Liability of Children" (1995) 69 (8) ALJ 593; N Konic, "Say Goodbye Doli? Age and Criminal Responsibility?" (1994) 19(3) *Alternative Law Journal* 140; T Wilkinson, "*Doli Incapax* — RIP?" (1994) 138 SJ 662; T Wilkinson, "*Doli Incapax* Resurrected" (1995) 139 SJ 338; S Bandalli, "Abolition of the Presumption of *Doli Incapax* and the Criminalisation of Children" (1998) 37(2) *Howard Journal of Criminal Justice* 114; A Jack, "A Judicial Step Too Far" [1995] *New Law Journal* 315; G Hubble, "Juvenile Defendants: Taking the Human Rights of Children Seriously" (2000) 25(3) *Alternative Law Journal* 116.

Disorder Act 1998 (UK) has abolished the presumption. A joint report of the Australian Law Reform Commission and the Human Rights and Equal Opportunity Commission recommended that the principle of *doli incapax*, implementing the recommendations of the *Model Criminal Code*, should be applied consistently throughout Australia and be legislatively based: ALRC, *Seen and Heard: Priority For Children in the Legal Process*, Report No 84 (1997), para 18.20.

It is important to note that the presumption is just that, and is capable of being rebutted. The prosecution bears the legal burden of rebutting the presumption. It must prove that the child committed the criminal act with the requisite fault element and that he or she had a sufficient understanding to know that what he or she did was wrong. That is, the prosecution must prove that the child knew the offence was wrong rather than simply naughty or mischievous.[15]

Just what is meant by the term "wrong" is unclear. One standard that has been used is that of "seriously wrong": *IPH v Chief Constable of South Wales* [1987] Crim LR 42; *R v Gorrie* (1918) 83 JP 136. Proof that the child knew that the act was morally wrong may not be sufficient to establish the requisite understanding,[16] but proof that he or she knew that the act would result in criminal punishment may be enough.[17] Another standard is that akin to the definition of "wrong" for the purposes of the common law of insanity. In *R v M* (1977) 16 SASR 589 and *R (a child) v Whitty* (1993) 66 A Crim R 462 the standard referred to was that of wrong according to the ordinary principles of reasonable people, a standard laid down by the High Court in *Stapleton v The Queen* (1952) 86 CLR 356 in relation to the defence of insanity.

There is also some degree of uncertainty as to what will amount to sufficient evidence to rebut the presumption and allow a conviction.[18] Lord Lowry stated in *C (a minor) v DPP* [1995] 2 WLR 383 (at 401-402) that evidence of the offence itself was not enough on its own to show that a child knew that the act was wrong. However, in *A v DPP* [1997] Crim LR 125 the Divisional Court of Queen's Bench held that consideration of conduct closely associated with the criminal act and the nature of the offence charged (in this case, indecent assault) may be relevant factors in deciding whether guilty knowledge was in all the circumstances proved.

In *T v DPP; L v DPP; H v DPP* [1977] Crim LR 127 the Divisional Court of Queen's Bench held that the prosecution was not required to lead direct evidence such as psychiatric evidence specifically relating to the child's knowledge of wrongfulness. It is sufficient that the circumstances of the case lead to an inference about the child's knowledge.

Evidence that a child knew that the act was wrong may include:

▬▬ evidence of the child's upbringing;[19]

▬▬ admissions to the police that the child knew that the conduct was wrong;[20]

---

15   *R v M* [1977] 16 SASR 589; *C (a minor) v DPP* [1994] 3 WLR 888 at 894; *IPH v Chief Constable of South Wales* [1987] Crim LR 42.

16   *JM (a minor) v Runeckles* (1984) 79 Cr App R 255.

17   *R (a child) v Whitty* (1993) 66 A Crim R 462.

18   See in general on this point T Crofts, "Rebutting the Presumption of *Doli Incapax*" (1998) 62(2) *Journal of Criminal Law* 185.

19   *X v X* [1958] Crim LR 805; *B v The Queen* (1960) 44 Cr App R 1; *F v Padwick* [1959] Crim LR 439.

20   *Ex parte N* [1959] Crim LR 523; *F v Padwick* [1959] Crim LR 439; *R v M* (1977) 16 SASR 589 at 593 per Bray CJ; *R (a child) v Whitty* (1993) A Crim R 462.

▰▰ conduct after the criminal act including attempts at concealment[21] or running away when disturbed;[22]

▰▰ conduct and demeanour in court;[23]

▰▰ mental capacity;[24] and

▰▰ any relevant prior convictions.[25]

2.3 CORPORATIONS

Celia Wells writes that the "history of the development of corporate criminal liability has a number of intervening strands and the resulting cloth is uneven": *Corporations and Criminal Responsibility* (Oxford: Oxford University Press, 1993), p 94. The criminal responsibility of corporations was virtually unknown until the latter half of the 19th century and then, it was on the basis of vicarious liability. The immediate response to the question as to who can be convicted of a crime is to envisage a human being. That may partly explain the slow development in attributing criminal responsibility to corporations as does the tendency to associate regulatory rather than criminal law with corporate actions: pp 3ff. The need for rules as to corporate criminal responsibility has developed in tandem with the growth of corporations and the occurrence of recent major disasters such as the Air New Zealand Mount Erebus crash, the Bhopal disaster in India, the Chernobyl nuclear explosion and the Exxon Valdez oil spill. For an excellent collection of essays on this topic, see P Grabosky and A Sutton (eds), *Stains on A White Collar: Fourteen Studies in Corporate Crime or Corporate Harm* (Sydney: Federation Press, 1989). In Australia, there are a significant number of work related deaths occurring every year.

> In a study of occupational health and safety offences, Santina Perrone found that between January 1987 and December 1990, 353 work related deaths had occurred in Victoria alone: "Workplace Fatalities and the Adequacy of Prosecutions" (1995) 13(1) *Law in Context* 81 at 87. Of those deaths, 203 occurred in a corporate context and 25 of those were related to an "extreme level of company negligence" sufficient to establish criminal culpability to sustain a conviction of manslaughter: p 87. The legal construction of these events as minor breaches of Occupational Health and Safety regulations rather than criminal acts of manslaughter is discussed further in Chapter 13.

The law now has moved beyond vicarious liability to direct liability, but the Model Criminal Code Officers Committee (MCCOC) has suggested that the present state of the law does not go far enough. An alternative framework for corporate criminal liability which has been suggested by the MCCOC will be discussed after the current state of the law is outlined.

---

21   *JM (a minor) v Runeckles* (1984) 79 Cr App R 255.
22   *A v DPP* [1977] Crim LR 125.
23   *JM (a minor) v Runeckles* (1984) 79 Cr App R 255; *Ex parte N* [1959] Crim LR 523.
24   *JBH and JH (minors) v O' Connell* [1981] Crim LR 632.
25   *R v B; R v A* [1979] 3 All ER 460.

A corporation is considered a legal person[26] and may therefore be criminally liable to the same extent as a natural person. The main restriction to this principle is that a corporation cannot be tried for an offence which can only be punished by imprisonment[27] and therefore it is arguable that a corporation cannot be held criminally responsible for the crime of murder.[28] There is no reason, however, for a corporation to be exempted from prosecution for manslaughter: *R v P & O European Ferries (Dover) Ltd* (1991) 93 Cr App R 73.

> In *R v Denbo Pty Ltd & Timothy Ian Nadenbousch* (unrep, 14/6/1994, SC Vic) the accused corporation pleaded guilty to manslaughter resulting from a workplace death. This was the first case of "corporate manslaughter" in Australia. One of the corporation's truck drivers died in a truck accident after attempting to drive down a steep incline of which he had not been warned. The truck itself had faulty brakes and the manslaughter charge was based on the argument that the corporation had failed to set up an adequate maintenance system for its plant and vehicles, had failed to train its employees properly and had allowed the truck to be used without proper maintenance. Teague J fined the corporation $120,000. Nadenbousch, one of the corporation's two shareholders pleaded guilty to two charges of wilful neglect under the *Occupational Health and Safety Act* 1985 (Vic) and was fined $10,000. The company however was wound up before sentencing and never paid the fine. See S Chesterman, "The Corporate Veil, Crime and Punishment: *The Queen v Denbo Pty Ltd and Timothy Ian Nadenbousch*" (1994) 19(4) *Melbourne University Law Review* 1066.

A corporation cannot be held criminally responsible for certain crimes which only an individual can commit such as perjury or bigamy. It may, however, be held criminally liable for the offences of complicity,[29] conspiracy,[30] attempt[31] and incitement.[32]

---

26 *Acts Interpretation Act* 1901 (Cth), s 22; *Interpretation Act* 1967 (ACT), s 14(1); *Interpretation Act* 1987 (NSW), ss 8(d), 21(1); *Interpretation Act* (NT), ss 19, 38B; *Acts Interpretation Act* 1954 (Qld), s 36; *Acts Interpretation Act* 1915 (SA), s 4; *Acts Interpretation Act* 1931 (Tas), s 35; *Acts Interpretation Act* 1984 (Vic), s 38; *Interpretation Act* 1984 (WA), s 5. Section 1 of the *Criminal Code* (Qld) and s 1 of the *Criminal Code* (WA) also provide that the definition of "person" in relation to property, include corporations of all kinds. Section 1 of the *Criminal Code* (NT) provides a similar definition of the word "owner". Section 46(1) of the *Acts Interpretation Act* 1954 (Qld) and s 69(1) of the *Acts Interpretation Act* 1984 (WA) also make it clear that every enactment relating to any offence applies to corporations as well as individuals.

27 *R v ICR Haulage Ltd* [1944] KB 551 at 556; [1944] 1 All ER 691; *R v Murray Wright Ltd* [1970] NZLR 476 at 484 per McCarthy J. For example, s 3 of the *Crimes Act* 1958 (Vic) imposes a mandatory prison sentence for the crime of murder.

28 Brent Fisse argues, however, that even if no suitable sentencing option is available for a crime such as murder, the stigmatic effect of a conviction would still support a corporation being found liable: *Howard's Criminal Law* (5th ed, Sydney: Law Book Company Ltd, 1990), p 611.

29 *Lewis v Crafter* [1942] SASR 30; *Smith v Trocadero Dansant Ltd* [1927] St R Qd 39 (FC); *R v Robert Millar (Contractors) Ltd* [1970] 2 QB 54; [1970] 2 WLR 541; [1969] 3 All ER 257; 54 Cr App R 158 (CA); *John Henshall (Quarries) Ltd v Harvey* [1965] 2 QB 233; [1965] 2 WLR 758; [1965] All ER 725; *National Coal Board v Gamble* [1959] 1 QB 11; [1958] 3 WLR 434; [1958] 3 All ER 205.

30 *Canadian Dredge & Dock Co Ltd v The Queen* (1985) 19 DLR (4th) 314; 19 CCC (3d) 1 (SC Canada).

31 *Trade Practices Commission v Tubemakers of Australia Ltd* (1983) 76 FLR 455 (Fed Ct).

32 *Invicta Plastics Ltd v Clare* [1976] Crim LR 131 (QB).

Because a corporation does not have a physical existence, it can only act or form an intention through its directors or employees. There are two ways in which corporate criminal liability may be established:

▬ **by holding a corporation vicariously liable for the conduct of its employees where those employees were acting within the scope of their employment (the agency model); or**

▬ **by holding a corporation directly liable for the acts of certain persons such as the corporation's board of directors, its managing director or person to whom the functions of the board have been delegated, who are considered to be the embodiment of the company (the identification model).**

VICARIOUS LIABILITY

Borrowing from civil law principles, it is now well established that a corporation may be held vicariously liable for the acts of its employees providing that they acted within the scope of their employment.[33] The status of the employee is irrelevant for this purpose. However, a corporation will not be vicariously responsible for the conduct of an independent contractor except where so provided by statute.[34] It is usually in respect of strict liability offences that corporations will be found vicariously liable for the acts of their employees: see below at p 191.

In general, the prosecution needs to prove three elements for vicarious criminal liability to be established:

1. The relevant legislation must intend that legal liability be applied vicariously. In *Mousell Bros Ltd v London and Northwestern Railway Co* [1917] 2 KB 836 Lord Atkin stated (at 845):

   > [R]egard must be had to the object of the statute, the words used, the nature of the duty laid down, the person upon whom it is imposed, the person by whom it would in ordinary circumstances be performed, and the person upon whom the penalty is imposed.

2. The employee must have committed the relevant act within the course of employment or within the scope of his or her authority. In this regard, there is no requirement that the corporation authorise the employee to commit the offence.[35] Nor does it appear that there is a requirement that the employee act with the intention of benefiting the corporation.[36]

---

33 *Christie v Foster Brewing Co Ltd* (1982) 18 VLR 292; *R and Minister for Customs and Australasian Films Ltd* (1921) 29 CLR 195; *Morgan v Babcock and Wilcox Ltd* (1929) 43 CLR 163; *Alford v Riley Newman Ltd* (1934) 34 SR(NSW) 261; *Fraser v Dryden's Carrying & Agency Co Pty Ltd* [1941] VLR 103; *Australian Stevedoring Industry Authority v Overseas and General Stevedoring Co Pty Ltd* (1959) 1 FLR 298.

34 *Allen v United Carpet Mills Pty Ltd* [1989] VR 323; *Goodes v General Motors Holden's Pty Ltd* [1972] VR 386.

35 *Fraser v Dryden's Carrying & Agency Co Pty Ltd* [1941] VLR 103; *Australian Stevedoring Industry Authority v Overseas & General Stevedoring Co Pty Ltd* (1959) 1 FLR 298 (Fed Ct); *Canadian Dredge & Dock Co Ltd v The Queen* (1985) 19 DLR (4th) 314 (SC Can).

36 An intent to benefit is not required under s 84 of the *Trade Practices Act* 1974 (Cth); *Walplan Pty Ltd v Wallace* (1985) 8 FCR 27; (Fed Ct); *Trade Practices Commission v Tubemakers of Australia Ltd* (1983) 76 FLR 455.

3. The employee must have possessed the state of mind required for the offence in question, unless the offence is one of strict or absolute liability: *Moussell Bros Ltd v London and Northwestern Railway Co* [1917] 2 KB 836.

DIRECT LIABILITY

Corporate criminal liability for serious offences such as manslaughter is based on direct liability. Rather than holding the corporation criminally responsible *for* the acts of its employees, direct liability views the employee's acts as those *of* the corporation.[37] The mere fact that an employee performed an act will not be sufficient to establish liability for a serious offence. It must be shown that an act or omission was performed by someone with authority to act *as the corporation*. That person must be said to embody the corporation and this is sometimes referred to as "the identity rule" or "the attribution rule" or "alter-ego rule". The leading authority in this area is that of *Tesco Supermarkets Ltd v Nattrass* [1972] AC 153.

In *Tesco*, the company operated over 800 supermarkets throughout the United Kingdom. It was charged under the *Trade Descriptions Act* with offering goods to consumers at a price for which they could not be bought. An assistant had placed normally priced soap powder on the shelf despite it having been advertised at a reduced price. The assistant had failed to notify the manager of the store and he had failed to check that the soap powder was displayed at the advertised price. It was held at first instance and by the Court of Appeal that the company was vicariously liable for the manager's lack of care. The House of Lords held, however, that the company was not liable as the manager was not of sufficient station within the company's organisation for his lack of care to be attributable to the company. He did not, as it were, "embody" the company. The company's conviction was therefore quashed.

The *Tesco* principle limits the criminal liability of a company to the conduct and fault of those who may be said to embody the company such as the company's board of directors, its managing director or person to whom the function of the board has been fully delegated.[38] Brent Fisse and John Braithwaite write that this principle amounts to "vicarious liability for the fault of a restricted range of representatives exercising corporate functions": *Corporations, Crime and Accountability* (Cambridge: Cambridge University Press, 1993), p 47. These authors go on to criticise the *Tesco* principle in the following way (p 47):

> This compromised form of vicarious liability is doubly unsatisfactory because the compromise is struck in a way that makes it difficult to establish corporate criminal liability against large companies. Offences committed on behalf of large concerns are often visible only at the level of middle management whereas the *Tesco* principle requires proof of fault of a top-level manager. By contrast, fault on the part of a top-level manager is much easier to prove in the context of small companies.

---

37 See in general, R Tomasic and S Bottomley, *Corporations Law in Australia* (Sydney: Federation Press, 1995), Ch 11.

38 See also *Collins v State Rail Authority (NSW)* (1986) 5 NSWLR 209; *R v Roffel* [1985] VR 511 (FC); *Cook's Hotel Pty Ltd v Pope* (1983) 34 SASR 292 (FC); *Brambles Holdngs Ltd v Carey* (1976) 15 SASR 270; *Lamb v Toledo-Berkel Pty Ltd* [1969] VR 343; *Ex parte Falstein; Re Maher* (1948) 49 SR(NSW) 133; *Freeman v CT Warne Pty Ltd* [1947] VLR 279; *Ex parte Colonial Petroleum Oil Pty Ltd; Re Byrne* (1944) 44 SR (NSW) 306; *Fraser v Dryden's Carrying & Agency Co Pty Ltd* [1941] VLR 103; *Stephens v Robert Reid & Co Ltd* (1902) 28 VLR 82.

There appears to be some truth in this criticism. In *R v AC Hatrick Chemicals Pty Ltd* (unrep, 29/11/1995, SC Vic) the corporation, a plant engineer and a plant manager were charged with manslaughter in relation to a tank which had exploded during a welding operation, causing the death of one worker and serious injury to another. The manslaughter charges against the individuals were withdrawn prior to committal and Hampel J directed a verdict of acquittal against the corporation on the basis of legal argument prior to the trial. One of the main arguments forming the basis of the direction was that the plant engineer and the plant manager were not "the guiding mind" of the company: see further, D Neal, "Corporate Manslaughter" (1996) 70(10) *Law Institute Journal* 39.

Despite criticisms of the *Tesco* principle, it has been widely followed in Australia.[39] Subsequent English cases, however, have been prepared to modify the *Tesco* principle somewhat.

In *Director General of Fair Trading v Pioneer Concrete (UK) Ltd* [1995] 1 AC 456 the House of Lords was prepared to attribute the actions of the executives of the company to the company itself, despite the Board not knowing what the executives had done and in fact giving instructions that the employees should not do what the executives had in fact done. Lord Templeman stated (at 465) that an uncritical transposition of the *Tesco* principle:

> would allow a company to enjoy the benefit of restrictions outlawed by Parliament and the benefit of arrangements prohibited by the courts provided that the restrictions were accepted and implemented and the arrangements were negotiated by one or more employees who had been forbidden to do so by some superior employee identified in argument as a member of the "higher management" of the company or by one or more directors of the company identified in argument as "the guiding will" of the company.

Similarly, in *Meridian Global Funds Management Asia Ltd v Securities Commission* [1995] 3 WLR 413 the Privy Council held the company liable for the actions of its chief investment officer and its senior portfolio manager despite the actions being unknown to the board of directors and its managing director. The Privy Council found that knowledge of the employee's actions could be attributed to the company, but were careful to point out (at 423) that it will be a "matter of construction in each case as to whether the particular rule requires that the knowledge that an act has been done, or the state of mind with which it was done, should be attributed to the company".

It should be noted that corporate liability particularly in relation to manslaughter is in a period of development given the preparedness of the authorities to prosecute corporations in this regard[40] and the readiness of the courts, at least in England, to modify the *Tesco* principle in certain circumstances.

In relation to defences, where an employee whose conduct is attributable to a corporation has a personal defence such as mental impairment or self-defence, this defence may be available to

---

39   *AC Hatrick Chemicals Pty Ltd* (unrep, 29/11/1995, SC Vic Hampel J); *Hamilton v Whitehead* (1988) 63 ALJR 80; *Collins v State Rail Authority of New South Wales* (1986) 3 NSWLR 209; *S&Y Investments (No 2) Pty Ltd v Commercial Union Assurance Co of Australia Ltd* (1986) 85 FLR 285; *GJ Coles & Co Ltd v Goldsworthy* [1985] WAR 183; *R v Roffel* [1985] VR 510; *Cook's Hotel Pty Ltd v Pope* (1983) 34 SASR 292; *Linehan v Australian Public Service Association* (1983) 67 FLR 412; *Trade Practices Commission v Tubemakers of Australia Ltd* (1983) 47 ALR 719; *Universal Telecasters (Qld) Ltd v Guthrie* (1978) 18 ALR 531; *Brambles Holdings Ltd v Carey* (1976) 15 SASR 270; *Kehoe v Dacol Motors Pty Ltd; Ex parte Dacol Motors Pty Ltd* [1972] Qd R 59.

40   See D Neal, "Corporate Manslaughter" (1996) 70(10) *Law Institute Journal* 39.

the corporation.[41] That is, a corporation will not be held criminally liable if the employee's conduct was excusable or justifiable.

In relation to offences of strict liability, the defence of honest and reasonable mistake of fact may also be available: see below at p 191, Ch 7.

PERSPECTIVES

Reforming Corporate Criminal Responsibility

Sections 12.1-12.6 of the *Criminal Code Act* 1995 (Cth) deal with corporate criminal responsibility. Section 12.1 confirms that the Code applies to bodies corporate in the same way as for individuals and that a body corporate may be found guilty of any offence, including one punishable by imprisonment.

Section 12.2 states that the physical element of an offence may be attributed to a corporation where an employee, agent or officer committed the physical element whilst acting within the actual or apparent scope of his or her employment. This is similar to the principle of vicarious liability. But if the relevant offence contains a fault element, s 12.3 requires that intention, knowledge or recklessness must also be attributed to the corporation.

It is in relation to fault elements that the Code departs from the *Tesco* principle. Section 12.3(1) states that a fault element will be attributed where the corporation "expressly, tacitly or impliedly authorised or permitted the commission of the offence". Section 12.3(2) then lists four situations whereby such permission or authorisation may be established:

(a) proving that the body corporate's board of directors intentionally, knowingly or recklessly carried out the relevant conduct, or expressly, tacitly or impliedly authorised or permitted the commission of the offence; or

(b) proving that a high managerial agent of the body corporate intentionally, knowingly or recklessly engaged in the relevant conduct, or expressly, tacitly or impliedly authorised or permitted the commission of the offence; or

(c) proving that a corporate culture existed within the body corporate that directed, encouraged, tolerated or led to non-compliance with the relevant provision; or

(d) proving that the body corporate failed to create and maintain a corporate culture that required compliance with the relevant provision.

The idea of "corporate culture" as a way of proving the authorisation of an offence is an interesting one and draws on the work of Brent Fisse and John Braithwaite on corporate liability.[42] "Corporate culture" is defined as "an attitude, policy, rule, course of conduct or practice existing within the body corporate generally or in the part of the body corporate in which the relevant activities take place": *Criminal Code Act* 1995 (Cth), s 12.3(6). In its Final Report on *Chapter 2:*

---

41   *Tesco Supermarkets Ltd v Nattrass* [1972] AC 153; *Brambles Holdings Ltd v Carey* (1976) 15 SASR 270; *GJ Coles & Co Ltd v Goldsworthy* [1985] WAR 183; (1985) 57 LGRA 122; *McKenzie v GJ Coles & Co Ltd* [1986] WAR 224; *Adams v Eta Foods Ltd* (1987) 19 FCR 93; *Woolworths Ltd v Luff* (1988) A Crim R 144.

42   See for example, B Fisse, "Corporate Criminal Responsibility" (1991) 15 Crim LJ 166 at 173; B Fisse, "Criminal Law: The Attribution of Criminal Liability to Corporations: A Statutory Model" (1991) 13 *Sydney Law Review* 277 at 281ff; B Fisse and J Braithwaite, *Corporations, Crime and Accountability* (Cambridge: Cambridge University Press, 1993).

General Principles of Criminal Responsibility (1992), the Model Criminal Code Officers Committee explained that this idea would allow (pp 111-113):

> the prosecution to lead evidence that the company's unwritten rules tacitly authorised non-compliance or failed to create a culture of compliance. It would catch situations where, despite formal documents appearing to require compliance, the reality was that non-compliance was expected. For example, employees who know that if they do not break the law to meet production schedules (eg by removing safety guards on equipment) they will be dismissed. The company would be guilty of intentionally breaching safety legislation.

The *Criminal Code Act* 1995 (Cth) also contains provisions dealing with negligent actions by a corporation: ss 12.4, 5.5. Negligence may be evidenced by inadequate corporate management, control or supervision of the conduct of one or more of the corporation's employees, agents or officers or by the failure to provide adequate systems for conveying relevant information to relevant persons in the body corporate: s 12.4(3).

The proposed provisions may go some way toward securing a greater measure of corporate accountability, but more may be necessary to ensure the accountability of *individuals* whose combined actions have led to the death of an employee. One of the elements of environmental protection legislation in some jurisdictions is the nomination of senior company officials as those personally liable for breaches of legislation by the company.[43] Andrew Hopkins suggests that nominated accountability has caused directors of large companies to take their organisation's environmental responsibilities very seriously: *Making Safety Work: Getting Management Commitment to Occupational Health and Safety* (St Leonard's: Allen & Unwin, 1995), pp 105-107. This model could be adapted to corporate homicide in order to avoid the

> perennial problem in dealing with corporate crime that a complex corporate activity gives a picture of confused accountability for any wrong doing. Everyone can blame someone else.[44]

One other problem associated with corporate criminal responsibility lies in the sanctions that may be enforced against a corporation. There is some reason to believe that fines have a limited deterrent effect when imposed on corporations: S Perrone, "Workplace Fatalities and the Adequacy of Prosecutions" (1995) 13(1) *Law in Context* 94 at 100. Fisse has suggested that other forms of sanctions should be used such as adverse publicity orders, punitive injunctions and liquidation orders against the company.[45]

Certainly, these suggestions for reform should be seriously considered in order to find a way around the current theoretical and practical problems associated with corporate criminal responsibility.

---

43 See for example, *Environmental Offences and Penalties Act* 1989 (NSW), s 10; *Environment Protection Act* 1993 (SA), s 129.

44 J Braithwaite, *To Punish or Persuade: Enforcement of Coal Mine Safety* (Albany: State University of New York Press, 1985), p 159.

45 B Fisse, "Sentencing Options Against Corporations" (1990) 1(2) *Criminal Law Forum* 211. See also J Braithwaite and B Fisse, *The Impact of Publicity on Corporate Offenders* (Albany: State University of New York Press, 1983).

3. THE ELEMENTS OF A CRIME

The traditional common law explanation of the elements of a crime is that the latter is divided into two parts, both of which must be proven before a conviction can be made out. The first part encompasses the external or physical elements of the crime; the second refers to the fault element or requisite state of mind of the accused.

In this section we will outline the components of both physical and fault elements before turning to the rise of strict and absolute liability offences.

3.1 PHYSICAL ELEMENTS

The physical elements of an offence may refer to:

▬ **A specified form of conduct such as:**
  — **an act**
  — **an omission**
  — **a state of affairs**

▬ **Conduct which occurs in specified circumstances; or**

▬ **Results or consequences of conduct.**

DIAGRAM 1: **Physical Elements**

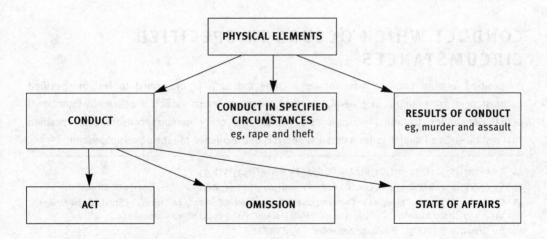

A SPECIFIED FORM OF CONDUCT

An Act

The physical element of most offences will consist of the commission of an act or series of acts by the accused. The main issue here relates to identifying the relevant act, and voluntariness and causation are relevant in this regard. The latter principles will be explained at pp 163, 164 respectively.

An Omission

The early common law imposed a duty on individuals to "Keep the King's Peace". On the duties and powers of individuals to prevent a breach of the peace, see Chapter 14, at p 763. Also, failure to report a felony amounted to the offence of misprision of felony. In the modern law, there is no legal obligation for persons to act so as to prevent harm or wrongdoing. There is no general duty to prevent a crime[46] nor does an individual commit a crime or become a party to it simply because he or she could reasonably have prevented it:[47] see further Ch 8, p 382. An omission to act may give rise to criminal liability in situations where a duty arises at common law or is imposed by statute.[48] At common law, a duty to act may arise as a result of a family relationship between the parties[49] or as a result of a person undertaking to care for another who is unable to care for him or herself.[50] In *R v Miller* [1983] 2 AC 1 (at 176) Lord Diplock also referred to there being "no rational ground for excluding from conduct capable of giving rise to criminal liability, conduct which consists of failing to take measures that lie within one's power to counteract a danger that one has oneself created". Statutory examples of the imposition of a duty to act include a duty to provide necessities[51] in certain jurisdictions and, in the Northern Territory, a duty to rescue or provide help to a person urgently in need of it and whose life may be endangered if it is not provided.[52] Omission is further discussed in Chapter 10, pp 512ff.

A State of Affairs

There are certain offences which criminalise a state of affairs, or perhaps more precisely, a state of "being" rather than conduct. An example is that of being drunk and disorderly in a public place[53] or offences relating to vagrancy.[54] While these are usually summary offences, other status offences, such as being "knowingly concerned" in the importation of illicit drugs, carry the maximum penalty of life imprisonment: see further Ch 15, pp 842ff.

CONDUCT WHICH OCCURS IN SPECIFIED CIRCUMSTANCES

A specified form of conduct may not be a crime *unless* it is performed in certain specified circumstances. For example, in general, the crime of rape or sexual assault is defined by intentional sexual penetration (conduct) which occurs without the other person's consent (the specified circumstance). See Chapter 12 for a detailed analysis of the offence of rape or sexual assault.

---

46   *R v Instan* [1893] 1 QB 450; (1893) 17 Cox CC 602; *R v Russell* [1933] VLR 59.

47   *R v Coney* (1882) 8 QBD 534; 15 Cox CC 46; *R v Russell* [1933] VLR 59; *Wilcox v Jeffrey* [1951] 1 All ER 464.

48   See further, M Kelman, "Interpretive Construction in the Substantive Criminal Law" (1981) 33 *Stanford Law Review* 591 at 637; JP McCutcheon, "Omissions and Criminal Liability" (1993-1995) 28-30 *Irish Jurist* 56.

49   *R v Russell* [1933] VLR 59; *R v Clarke and Wilton* [1959] VR 645.

50   *R v Instan* [1893] 1 QB 450; (1893) 17 Cox CC 602; *Lee v The Queen* (1917) 13 Cr App R 39 at 41 per Darling J; *Gibbins v The Queen* (1918) 13 Cr App R 134; *R v Stone and Dobinson* [1977] QB 354; *Taktak* (1988) 34 A Crim R 334.

51   *Crimes Act* 1900 (NSW), s 44; *Criminal Code* (NT), s 183; *Criminal Code* (Qld), s 285; *Criminal Law Consolidation Act* 1935 (SA), s 30; *Criminal Code* (Tas), s 144; *Criminal Code* (WA), s 262.

52   *Criminal Code* (NT), s 155; considered in *Salmon v Chute* (1994) 94 NTR 1.

53   See for example, *Summary Offences Act* 1966 (Vic), ss 13-16. The public order offences and powers dealing with public intoxication are reviewed in Ch 14, pp 779ff.

54   For example, up until 1979 it was an offence in New South Wales to have no visible lawful means of support: *Police Offences Act* 1901 (NSW), s 22.

RESULTS OR CONSEQUENCES OF CONDUCT

The physical element of an offence may sometimes refer to the results or consequences of conduct rather than the conduct itself. For example, what is prohibited in the crime of murder is the death of the victim rather than the conduct which caused the death. It is irrelevant what conduct was undertaken which caused the death; providing the conduct of the accused *results* in the death of the victim, the physical element of murder will be established. Where the physical element of a crime refers to the results or consequences of conduct, it will be necessary for the prosecution to prove that the conduct *caused* the requisite consequences: see 3.3 'Causation'.

3.2 VOLUNTARINESS

The requisite physical element of a crime must be performed voluntarily in the sense that it must be willed.[55] There are three ways in which an act may be considered at law to be involuntary:

- when the criminal act was accidental;

- when the criminal act was caused by a reflex action; or

- when the conduct was performed whilst the accused was in a state of impaired consciousness.

In the first two examples of involuntary conduct, the act is not "willed" in that it is not an intended action. To say that an act was caused by accident means that it was caused without intention, recklessness or criminal negligence of the accused's part. An act caused by a reflex action is an act founded on an external cause rather than intention: *Ryan v The Queen* (1967) 121 CLR 205 at 215 per Barwick CJ, at 245 per Windeyer J. The latter expressed misgivings about the use of the phrase "reflex action" to denote involuntary conduct. Humphreys J in *Kay v Butterworth* (1945) 61 TLR 452 (at 453)[56] suggested that a driver would not be responsible if his or her car went out of control and caused the death of a passerby where the driver had been attacked by a swarm of bees or wasps. Because of the connection between willing an action and intending it, the traditional division between external or physical elements and mental or fault elements becomes blurred.

The third example of involuntary conduct is the one that has been the most discussed in case law. Automatism is the term generally used to refer to conduct performed in a state of impaired consciousness. Automatism is discussed in detail in Chapter 4, where the divergent legal and psychological conceptions of voluntary conduct are explored.

---

55 *Criminal Code* (NT), s 31; *Criminal Code* (Qld), s 23; *Criminal Code* (Tas), s 13(1); *Criminal Code* (WA), s 23; *R v Vickers* [1957] 2 QB 664 at 672; [1957] 3 WLR 326; [1957] 2 All ER 741 per Lord Goddard CJ (CCA); *R v Scott* [1967] VR 276 at 288-289 per Gillard J (FC SC Vic); *R v Haywood* [1971] VR 755; *R v Tait* [1973] VR 151; *R v Dodd* (1974) 7 SASR 151; *Woolmington v DPP* [1935] AC 462 at 482; [1935] All ER 1; (1935) 25 Cr App R 72 per Viscount Sankey LC; *Ryan v The Queen* (1967) 121 CLR 205.

56 See also *Hill v Baxter* [1958] 1 QB 277 at 286 per Pearson J.

3.3 CAUSATION

When the physical element of a crime requires the occurrence of specified results or consequences, the prosecution must prove that the conduct *caused* those results or consequences. Alan Norrie points out that legal causation "involves an unstable interface between individualistic and political considerations": *Crime, Reason and History* (London: Weidenfeld and Nicolson, 1993), p 152. Causation is of particular relevance to the crimes of murder and manslaughter in which it must be proved that the accused's conduct caused the death of the victim. It is in the context of these crimes that the tests of causation have been developed.

Causation is a question of fact for the jury[57] and whilst the members of the jury must be instructed as to the legal requirements for causation, they are expected to apply their "common sense" in determining whether an accused's conduct caused the death of a victim.[58]

In ordinary speech and common usage, the notion of causation is used loosely. In the criminal law, causation has a distinctive legal meaning and the courts have developed a number of tests in order to assess whether an accused's conduct caused the requisite result or consequence. These may be broadly defined as:

- the reasonable foreseeability test;

- the substantial cause test; and

- the natural consequence test.

Each test has found favour with different courts at different times. The more modern cases appear, however, to favour the substantial cause test, but it is not unusual for the courts to refer to these tests interchangeably. The tests, and any potential differences between them, became apparent only in cases where it is alleged that there is a *novus actus interveniens*, that is, an external event that severs the causal link between the accused's conduct and the prohibited harmful consequence: see generally, K Arenson, "Causation in the Criminal Law: A Search for Doctrinal Consistency" (1996) 20 Crim LJ 189; S Yeo, "Blamable Causation" (2000) 24 Crim LJ 144. A word of warning in relation to this area was sounded by McHugh J in *Royall v The Queen* (1991) 172 CLR 378 when he stated (at 448):

> Judicial and academic efforts to achieve a coherent theory of common law causation have not met with significant success. Perhaps the nature of the subject matter when combined with the lawyer's need to couple issues of factual causation with culpability make achievement of a coherent theory virtually impossible.

Royall v The Queen is the most recent High Court case on causation and it shows that there is no consensus as to which test *should* be used. In that case, a majority (Mason CJ, Deane and Dawson JJ) favoured applying the natural consequences test. Toohey and Gaudron JJ showed the greatest fidelity to the substantial cause test and Brennan and McHugh JJ in separate judgments, favoured a reasonable foreseeability test.

---

57 *R v Evans & Gardiner (No 2)* [1976] VR 523 at 527; *R v Pagett* (1983) 76 Cr App R 279 at 290-291.

58 *Campbell v The Queen* [1981] WAR 286 at 290 per Burt CJ.

All of the tests used by the courts are objective in the sense that they are not based on what the accused subjectively intended or foresaw. This objective requirement may be difficult to apply, particularly in relation to the reasonable foreseeability test. In obiter statements in *Royall v The Queen*, Mason CJ, Brennan and McHugh JJ blurred the distinction between causation and the fault element of a crime. Mason CJ stated (at 390):

> [I]n some situations, the accused's state of mind will be relevant to that issue [causation] as, for example, where there is evidence that the accused intended that injury should result in the same way in which it did and where, in the absence of evidence of intention, the facts would raise a doubt about causation.

How can intention be relevant to causation? Suppose a person has an unreasonable phobia concerning spiders. The accused knows of this person's phobia and intends to cause injury by showing the person a spider. Suppose the victim is so frightened that she or he jumps out of a window and is seriously hurt. This reaction may not be a natural consequence of exposure to spiders, but causation may be established because of the accused's intention. Brennan and McHugh JJ in their separate judgments agreed that in some unusual cases, intention may be relevant to causation.[59] Causation as an issue rarely arises in practice and, it would seem that cases that blur intention and causation are likely to remain in the realm of the hypothetical. The role of subjective fault in proving causation is further explored in S Yeo, "Blamable Causation" (2000) 24 Crim LJ 144 at 152-156.

> **For crimes of strict or absolute liability, such as pollution offences, where proof of fault is no longer in issue, the concept of causation performs an important role in allocating blame: see N Padfield, "Clean Water and Muddy Causation: Is Causation A Question of Law or Fact, or Just a Way of Allocating Blame?" [1995] Crim LR 683. In these cases, the judicial attention to the accused's blameworthiness in assessing causation would ensure that strict and absolute liability does not operate in an unfair or unjust manner.**

THE REASONABLE FORESEEABILITY TEST

The reasonable foreseeability test involves examining whether the consequences of the accused's conduct were reasonably foreseeable. It is generally cast as an objective test in the sense of considering what a reasonable person would have foreseen rather than an inquiry into the accused's appreciation of the consequences of his or her conduct: *R v Hallett* [1969] SASR 141 at 149. In *Royall v The Queen* (1991) 172 CLR 378, the High Court considered that legal causation and foreseeability were closely connected, but the majority stated that juries should not be directed in terms of

---

59 "[A]s causation requires proof that the taking of a final fatal step by a victim was objectively reasonable (or proportionate) and was foreseen by an accused or was reasonably foreseeable, the facts tendered to prove a specific mental element may be relevant in some cases to the existence of facts tending to prove causation": *Royall v The Queen* (1991) 172 CLR 378 at 400 per Brennan J. McHugh J, in favouring a reasonable foreseeability test also blurred the distinction between causation and intention: "[A]n accused should not be held to be guilty unless his or her conduct induced the victim to take action which resulted in harm to him or her and that harm was either intended by the accused or was of a type which a reasonable person could have foreseen as a consequence of the accused's conduct": at 451.

foreseeability because of the risks of confusion in foreseeability as an objective standard as a subjective state of mind.[60] For example, Deane and Dawson JJ stated (at 412):

> On occasions forseeability may play some part in a jury's inquiry into the cause of death,
> but in directing a jury, it is, for practical purposes, desirable to keep causation and intent
> separate as far as possible and to avoid the introduction of forseeability in relation to
> causation.

The minority in *Royall* did, however, favour the use of a reasonable foreseeability test[61] which suggests that it may not have been completely laid to rest.

THE SUBSTANTIAL CAUSE TEST

The substantial cause test was developed in the earlier cases on causation and, in particular, by the Supreme Court of South Australia in *R v Hallett* [1969] SASR 141. In that case, the accused had attacked the victim on a beach, rendering the latter unconscious. The forensic evidence suggested that the victim died from drowning in shallow water. The accused claimed that he had not drowned the victim, but had simply left him in what he thought was a position of apparent safety with the victim's ankles in a few inches of water. The accused was convicted of murder and appealed to the Supreme Court of South Australia which (at 149) posed the test as follows:

> The question to be asked is whether an act or series of acts (in exceptional cases an
> omission or series of omissions) consciously performed by the accused is or are so
> connected with the event that it or they must be regarded as having a sufficiently
> substantial causal effect which subsisted *up* to the happening of the event, without being
> spent or without being in the eyes of the law sufficiently interrupted by some other act or
> event.

Sometimes, this test is referred to as the significant cause test[62] or the operating and substantial cause test.[63]

The Supreme Court held in *Hallett* that the accused's original blow which rendered the victim unconscious started the events which led to the victim drowning. It could not be said that the tide coming in broke the chain of causation.

The accused's conduct need not be the sole cause of death in relation to the crimes of murder and manslaughter: *R v Pagett* (1983) 76 Cr App R 279. Death may result from several causes, but all that must be proved is that the accused's conduct was a substantial cause.

---

60   *Royall v The Queen* (1991) 172 CLR 378 per Mason CJ at 390, per Deane and Dawson JJ at 412 and per Toohey and
     Gaudron JJ at 425.

61   *Royall v The Queen* (1991) 172 CLR 378 per Brennan J at 399, and per McHugh J at 449.

62   *Royall v The Queen* (1991) 172 CLR 378 at 398 per Brennan J, 411 per Deane and Dawson JJ; *R v Cheshire* [1991] 3 All
     ER 670 at 677; *R v Pagett* (1983) 76 Cr App R 279.

63   *R v Evans (No 2)* [1976] VR 523 at 529.

THE NATURAL CONSEQUENCE TEST

The natural consequence test may apply to situations where the victim has contributed to his or her death by seeking to escape or attempting to avoid being attacked by the accused. The main case that sets out this test is that of *Royall v The Queen* (1991) 172 CLR 378. The victim died after falling from the bathroom window of a sixth floor flat. The victim had previously been assaulted by the accused and the prosecution argued that the victim had either been forced from the window or had fallen from the window in retreating from an attack or had jumped in order to escape from an attack. Mason CJ stated (at 389) the test as follows:

> where the conduct of the accused induces in the victim a well-founded apprehension of physical harm such as to make it a natural consequence (or reasonable) that the victim would seek to escape and the victim is injured in the course of escaping, the injury is caused by the accused's conduct.

Mason CJ, Deane and Dawson JJ in *Royall* applied this "commonsense" natural consequences test of causation. However, as stated above, the other members of the court differed in the test of causation to be applied. This is explored further in the next section.

EXAMPLES OF NOVUS ACTUS INTERVENIENS

If a subsequent event renders the prohibited consequence no longer a reasonably foreseeable, substantial cause or natural consequence of the accused's conduct, the courts have held that this amounts to a *novus actus interveniens* which breaks the chain of causation. Some courts have stressed that the intervening act must be of an unexpected or extraordinary nature. In *R v Hallett* [1969] SASR 141 the Supreme Court of South Australia held that the incoming tide was not unexpected or an event which would break the chain of causation as opposed to, for example, an extraordinary tidal wave.

While *Hallett's* case was concerned with acts of nature as possible intervening events, in general, the courts have been asked to consider human acts as breaking the chain of causation. There are two kinds of *novus actus interveniens* that have been considered by the courts:

═══ **the acts of the victim; and**

═══ **the acts of a third party.**

The Acts of the Victim

The case law deals with three different types of acts of the victim that may break the chain of causation:

═══ **seeking to escape violence;**

═══ **failing to take medical advice; and**

═══ **suicide.**

Seeking to Escape Violence

Where a victim is killed seeking to escape the violence of the accused, the victim's actions may break the chain of causation. In *Royall v The Queen* (1991) 172 CLR 378 the High Court unanimously held that the victim's actions of falling or jumping from the bathroom window of her sixth floor flat to avoid an attack was not to be regarded as a *novus actus interveniens*.

The members of the High Court, however, divided over the test of causation to be applied in such circumstances. As stated above, Mason CJ, Deane and Dawson JJ in the majority applied a natural consequence test to the victim's reaction in preference to a reasonable foreseeability test.

There is a question as to whether or not the victim's act of self-preservation must be reasonable. The majority of judges believed that it should be, but came to this conclusion via different reasoning. Brennan J (at 398) stated that the victim's act of self-preservation must be reasonable having regard to the nature of the accused's conduct and the fear that it was likely to have induced. That is, the victim's attempt at self-preservation must be proportionate to that conduct. According to Deane and Dawson JJ (at 412-413), the victim's attempt at self-preservation does not break the causal link if (a) the victim's fear or apprehension is well-founded or reasonable in all the circumstances and (b) the victim's act of escape or self-preservation was the natural consequence of the accused's behaviour. Toohey and Gaudron JJ (at 425) followed the substantial cause test that originated in *Hallett*. They stated that a "jury may be told that if the victim's reaction to the act of the defendant ... was quite disproportionate to the act or was unreasonable, the chain of causation was broken". Mason CJ and McHugh J, however, concluded that the victim's act of self-preservation need not be reasonable. Mason CJ considered the authorities and held (at 390) that there was no requirement that the steps taken to escape be reasonable.

McHugh J (at 449) took the most radical approach to causation. He recognised the need to clarify and rationalise the relevant principles and was concerned to achieve a coherent theory of causation in both the criminal and civil law. He applied the test of reasonable foreseeability and criticised the substantial cause test that he viewed as nothing more than a disguised "but for" test which is used in tort law. He stated that persons subjected to violence or the threat of violence do not always think rationally or act reasonably. The instinct of self-preservation often causes them to flee or to take action which, while avoiding the immediate danger, places them in greater peril. According to McHugh J (at 450), if unreasonable refusal to take medical treatment does not operate as a *novus actus interveniens* (explored in the next section), then neither should the unreasonable conduct of a victim in escaping an attack.

Failing to Take Medical Advice

There have been some cases where injuries sustained by a victim might not have resulted in death except for the fact that he or she failed to take medical advice. In these cases, the courts have been reluctant to find that the victim's actions break the chain of causation. For example in *R v Bingapore* (1975) 11 SASR 469 the accused had assaulted the victim, causing injuries to the head. The victim left hospital after treatment against medical advice. About six hours later he returned to the hospital by ambulance needing urgent attention and he died the next day. The Supreme Court of South Australia held that there had been no *novus actus interveniens*, there had only been the loss of a possible opportunity of avoiding death. Similarly, in *R v Holland* (1841) 2 M & Rob 351; 174 ER 313 the accused assaulted the victim and injured one of the latter's fingers. The victim rejected the advice of a surgeon to have the finger amputated. Two weeks later, the victim died of lockjaw. Maule J rejected the accused's submission that the cause of death was not the wound inflicted, but the victim's refusal to have the finger amputated.

The tort law principle that people must take their victims as they find them may also be relevant here. In *R v Blaue* [1975] 1 WLR 1411 the victim who had been stabbed by the accused was a Jehovah's Witness and refused to have a blood transfusion which would probably have saved her life. The English Court of Appeal held (at 1415) that the victim's refusal to have a transfusion did not break the chain of causation:

> It has long been the policy of the law that those who use violence on other people must take their victims as they find them. This in our judgment means the whole man [or woman], not just the physical man [or woman]. It does not lie in the mouth of the assailant to say that his victim's religious beliefs which inhibited him from accepting certain kinds of treatment were unreasonable. The question for decision is what caused her death. The answer is the stab wound. The fact that the victim refused to stop this end coming about did not break the causal connection between the act and death.

Suicide

There have been some rare cases where the victim has committed suicide after being assaulted. Two American cases again show a reluctance by the courts to see the victims' acts as breaking the chain of causation. In *People v Lewis,* 124 Cal 551 (1899) the victim cut his own throat to hasten his death after sustaining fatal injuries from an assault by the accused. The court held that the victim's actions did not amount to a *novus actus interveniens*. In *Stephenson v State*, 179 NE 633 (1933), the accused brutally raped the victim, biting her all over the body. While being held captive, she took a large dose of mercury bichloride tablets. The accused refused to get medical help for her, kept her in a hotel for some hours before dumping her on the doorstep of her home. She died a month later partly from bichloride poisoning and perhaps partly because of an abscess caused by the bites. The jury issued a special verdict which found that the victim had taken the poison as a result of pain and shame and convicted the accused of murder. The Supreme Court of Indiana upheld the conviction on the basis that the consumption of poison was not a *novus actus interveniens*.

Acts of a Third Party — Medical Treatment

The act of a third party may, in rare instances, break the chain of causation. The main circumstance in which this will arise is where a victim receives medical treatment which may be an independent cause of death. However, the case of *R v Pagett* (1983) 76 Cr App R 279 refers to acts of a third party in a wider sense and stands for the principle that the act of a third party will only be considered a *novus actus interveniens* when it is a voluntary act in the sense that it is "free, deliberate and informed": at 289.

In *Pagett*, the accused shot at armed police, whilst using his ex-girlfriend as a shield. The police returned his fire and, in the course of doing so, a police officer shot and killed the ex-girlfriend. The accused was convicted of manslaughter. On appeal, he argued that the victim's death was caused by her being shot by the police officer and this was an act of a third party which was a *novus actus interveniens*. The English Court of Appeal rejected this argument.

The Court held that in determining whether or not a homicide may be attributed to those cases where the immediate cause of death was the act of another, the ordinary principles of causation apply. The Court pointed out that the trial judge had erred in directing the jury that it was a matter or law (and therefore a matter for the judge) to determine whether the accused's conduct caused the death. The trial judge should have merely directed the jury as to the relevant principles relating to causation, leaving it to the jury to determine whether the causal connection between the accused's conduct and the death had been established.

The Court reviewed the relevant principles of causation and in particular those external factors that may operate to break the chain of causation. The Court unusually made reference to the treatise on causation by Herbert Hart and Tony Honoré, *Causation in the Law* (Oxford: Clarendon Press, 1959) (now see 2nd ed, 1985). After a comprehensive review of the authorities, Hart and Honoré concluded that the intervention of a third party will have the effect of breaking the chain of causation only where the intervention was "free, deliberate and informed": (2nd ed, Oxford: Clarendon Press, 1985), pp 326ff. The Court concluded (at 289) that the police officer's actions were not free and deliberate. The shooting was an act performed for the purpose of self-preservation and in performance of a legal duty:

> [A] reasonable act of self-preservation, being of course itself an act caused by the accused's own act, does not operate as a *novus actus interveniens*.

The Court held that the chain of causation was not broken between the victim's death and the accused's unlawful and dangerous acts of firing at the police and holding the victim as a shield in front of him when the police might fire shots at him in self-defence. Arguably, this case may stretch the bounds of causation too far, since here the accused is said to be causing the death of the victim by the unintended actions of another. Clearly the Court's generous approach to causation in this case was influenced by the underlying criminal recklessness of the accused, which had placed the victim in a position of acute danger.

The case law in this area is mostly concerned with whether or not medical treatment given by a third party may break the chain of causation. It appears that it will only be in the most exceptional circumstances that medical treatment, even if given negligently, will be held to be a *novus actus interveniens*.

R v Jordan (1956) 40 Cr App R 152 is one of the rare cases where negligent medical treatment has been found to break the chain of causation. In that case, the victim was admitted to hospital after being stabbed by the accused and the wound was stitched up. The victim died a week later and there was evidence called on appeal that death had not been caused by the stab wound but by the administration of terramycin after the victim had shown an intolerance to it and by the intravenous introduction of abnormal quantities of liquid which led to broncho-pneumonia.

There is some controversy as to what was decided by the English Court of Criminal Appeal in this case. The headnote (at 152) reads that "death resulting from any normal treatment employed to deal with a felonious injury may be regarded as caused by the felonious injury, but the same principle does not apply where the treatment employed is abnormal". This summary in the headnote is not supported by the judgment itself. The Court of Criminal Appeal quashed the accused's conviction and held that whether or not medical treatment was sufficient to break the chain of causation was a question of fact for the jury. The Court (at 158) was convinced that if the jury had heard this evidence, they "would have felt precluded from saying that they were satisfied that death was caused by the stab wound". The Court thought that treatment which was "palpably wrong" could be regarded as a *novus actus interveniens* which could break the chain of causation.

Subsequent cases, however, have stated that *Jordan* should be regarded as a case decided on its own special facts.[64] In *R v Smith* [1959] 2 QB 35 the victim, a soldier in the Gloucestershire Regiment received two bayonet wounds in the course of a fight with a private in the King's Regiment. Unknown to anyone, one blow pierced the victim's lung and caused a haemorrhage. The victim was dropped twice by accident when he was being carried to a medical station. An unsuccessful attempt was made at the station to give him a saline transfusion. He was then given oxygen and artificial respiration. The victim died about two hours after the stabbing. There was evidence that the treatment given to the victim was "thoroughly bad" and that if the victim had received a blood transfusion, there was a 75% chance he might not have died: at 42. The accused was convicted of murder and appealed on the basis that the "abnormal" medical treatment broke the chain of causation. The English Court Martial Appeals Court dismissed the appeal. Lord Parker CJ stated (at 42-43):

> It seems to the court that if at the time of death the original wound is still an operating cause and a substantial cause, then the death can properly be said to be the result of the wound, albeit that some other cause of death is also operating ... [O]nly if the second cause is so overwhelming as to make the original wound merely part of the history can it be said that the death does not flow from the wound.

Smith's case was referred to with approval in *R v Hallett* [1969] SASR 141 (at 150) and followed in *R v Evans & Gardiner (No 2)* [1976] VR 523. In the latter case, the victim was stabbed in the stomach by two fellow prisoners at Pentridge prison. A successful bowel resection operation was performed. The victim resumed an apparently healthy life, but died 11 months later. The immediate cause of death was a fibrous ring that caused a stricture in the small bowel at the site of the resection operation. There was medical evidence that the stricture was not an uncommon occurrence after a resection operation. There was also evidence that the victim's condition should have been diagnosed and an operation performed to rectify it. Despite this evidence as to the immediate cause of death, the Full Court of the Supreme Court of Victoria upheld the two accuseds' convictions for murder.

The decision in *Evans & Gardiner* is difficult to reconcile with the earlier English decision in *Jordan*. The Supreme Court in *Evans & Gardiner* took a broad view of causation, approaching the issue in the following way (at 534):

> The failure of the medical practitioners to diagnose correctly the victim's condition, *however inept and unskilful*, was not the cause of death and the real question for the jury was whether the blockage was due to the stabbing (emphasis added).

---

64   The Full Court of the Supreme Court of Victoria in *R v Evans & Gardiner (No 2)* [1976] VR 523 at 531 agreed with Lord Parker's opinion in *R v Smith* [1959] 2 QB 36 that *Jordan* should be confined to its facts and nor regarded as an authority relaxing the common law approach to causation. In *R v Malcharek; R v Steel* [1981] 1 WLR 690 at 696, Lord Lane CJ stated "In the view of this court, if a choice has to be made between the decision in *R v Jordan* and that in *R v Smith,* which we do not believe it does (*R v Jordan* being a very exceptional case), then the decision in *R v Smith* is to be preferred".

In *R v Cheshire* [1991] 1 WLR 844 the English Court of Appeal reiterated that only in the most extraordinary circumstances will medical treatment, however negligent, break the chain of causation. In *Cheshire*, the accused was shot by the accused in the leg and stomach. He was admitted to an intensive care unit where he developed respiratory problems and a tracheotomy tube was placed in his windpipe for four weeks to assist breathing. The victim suffered further chest infections and other complications and more than two months after the shooting, he died in hospital of cardio-respiratory failure because his windpipe had been obstructed due to a narrowing where the tracheotomy had been performed. At the accused's trial for murder, evidence was given by a surgeon that the victim's wounds no longer threatened his life at the time of death and that the death was caused by the negligent failure of the medical staff to diagnose and treat his respiratory condition. The accused was convicted of murder and an appeal against conviction was dismissed. The Court of Appeal held that the victim's respiratory problems were a direct consequence of the accused's act which remained a significant cause of death, despite the evidence of medical negligence. Beldam LJ in delivering the judgment of the Court stated (at 852):

> Even though negligence in the treatment of the victim was the immediate cause of his death, the jury should not regard it as excluding the responsibility of the accused unless the negligent treatment was so independent of his acts, and in itself so potent in causing death that they regard the contribution made by his acts as insignificant.

The cases since *Jordan* show a marked reluctance on the part of the courts to break the chain of causation even where medical negligence is an immediate cause of death. It will only be in the most extraordinary cases where there is gross negligence that medical treatment may be considered a *novus actus interveniens*. As a matter of legal policy, it seems that accused must take both their victims and their healthcare systems as they find them!

Another aspect of medical treatment which needs consideration in this area is the withdrawal of life support machines. In *R v Malcharek; R v Steel* [1981] 2 All ER 422 the English Court of Appeal considered this issue in relation to two similar fact situations. In the first case, the accused stabbed his wife in the stomach. She received treatment in hospital and appeared to be recovering, but several days later whilst still in hospital, she collapsed and shortly afterwards, her heart stopped beating. After surgery was performed to remove a blood clot from the pulmonary artery and after some 30 minutes, her heart started beating again. The victim was put on a life-support system because of the danger that brain damage had occurred during the time her heart had stopped beating. Tests confirmed that she had suffered irreversible brain damage and the life-support system was disconnected. The victim died shortly afterwards. In the second case, the victim suffered head injuries after being attacked by the accused. She was taken to hospital and put on a life-support system. Tests showed that her brain had ceased to function and two days later, the life-support system was disconnected. The victim died shortly afterwards.

At each trial for murder, the judge withdrew the issue of causation from the jury on the basis that the infliction of the original injuries was the substantial cause of death. Both accused were convicted and both appealed on the basis that the jury in each case should have been allowed to consider the issue of causation. The appeals were dismissed. The Court of Appeal held that where competent medical treatment involved placing a victim on a life-support system, the decision to disconnect that system could not break the chain of causation between the infliction of the original injury and the victim's death. Since there was no evidence in either case that the original injury had ceased to be a substantial cause of death, the issue of causation had been correctly withdrawn from the jury.

3.4 FAULT ELEMENTS

Traditionally, the fault elements of crimes have been divided into subjective and, occasionally, objective elements.

DIAGRAM 2: Fault Elements

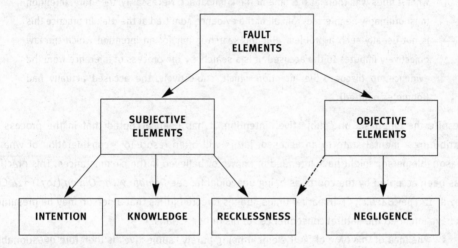

PERSPECTIVES

Subjective versus Objective Fault

The subjective components of fault are interconnected. For example, in *Giorgianni v The Queen* (1985) 156 CLR 473 (at 505) Wilson, Deane and Dawson JJ referred to intention as being *based on* knowledge. Where the fault element for a particular crime is subjective, the prosecution must prove beyond reasonable doubt that at the time of the commission of the crime, the accused possessed the requisite state of mind. This may often be a difficult task.

In the absence of an admission or confession, it is impossible to know beyond reasonable doubt what the accused was thinking at the time of the commission of the crime. The law in this area is based upon a "deeply entrenched"[65] approach to mental state attribution known as "folk psychology". This "involves interpreting someone as a perceiver with beliefs and desires which lead him [or her] to act in the world": P Smith and O Jones, *The Philosophy of Mind* (New York: Cambridge University Press, 1986), p 172. What the trier of fact is being asked to do in assessing

65   PM Churchland, *Matter and Consciousness* (Cambridge, Mass: MIT Press, 1988), p 59.

a person's intention, knowledge or recklessness is to see whether one of these mental states can be attributed to the person, taking into account his or her behaviour and experiences. This model of mental state attribution relates to our everyday interpretation of others' behaviour in attributing to them mental states they "ought to have, in light of [their] environment, perceptual capacities, interests, and past experiences. Moreover, we expect that [they] will act as ... rational agent[s]": R Dresser, "Culpability and Other Minds" (1992) 2(1) *Southern California Interdisciplinary Law Journal* 41 at 78.

The difficulty of determining intention or knowledge was recognised by Kirby J in *Peters v The Queen* (1998) 192 CLR 493 (at 551):

> Absent a comprehensive and reliable confession, it is usually impossible for the prosecution actually to get into the mind of the accused and to demonstrate exactly what it finds was there at the time of the criminal act. Necessarily, therefore, intention must ordinarily be inferred from all of the evidence admitted at the trial. In practice this is not usually such a problem. But the search is not for an intention which the law objectively imputes to the accused. It is a search, by the process of inference from the evidence, to discover the intention which, subjectively, the accused actually had (footnotes omitted).

Despite the emphasis on "subjective" intention, it has been accepted that in the process of attributing a mental state to an accused, jurors will often resort to a consideration of what a reasonable person might have intended or known or believed in the circumstances. This practice has been accepted by the courts as being unavoidable: see *Pemble v The Queen* (1971) 124 CLR 107 at 120 per Barwick CJ. In earlier times, judges directed juries that a person may be presumed to have intended the natural consequences of his or her actions.

The idea of this type of fault element being purely "subjective" is therefore questionable. What the notion of subjectivity in this context really means is that the trier of fact must make an assessment of fault in relation to the particular accused, taking into account his or her behaviour, experiences and characteristics such as age, social and cultural background.

The difficulty in proving intention, knowledge or recklessness beyond reasonable doubt is one factor in the rise of offences where the fault element is expressed as an objective one. Some crimes incorporate an element of negligence as the basis upon which criminal responsibility is assigned. Negligent behaviour is usually assessed by reference to an external standard such as the behaviour of the reasonable person. In the common law jurisdictions, there are also a growing number of offences of strict and absolute liability where the prosecution need not prove any fault element; the establishment of the requisite physical element of the crime will be sufficient for a conviction: see below at p 191.

The courts have generally shown a preference for subjective fault elements in relation to serious crimes: see, for example, *DPP v Morgan* [1976] AC 182, discussed in Chapters 9 and 12. This preference may be related to the liberal philosophical justification for criminal punishment in terms of "free will": see Ch 1, p 29. In *Punishment and Responsibility* (Oxford: Oxford University Press, 1968) Herbert Hart posited that the principle of criminal punishment should be restricted to those who have voluntarily broken the law. This principle suggests that a person should be punished when he or she had recognised the harmful aspect of his or her conduct or its consequences. In other words, the accused must intend, know or at least be aware of the risk (that is, be reckless) as to the particular harm occurring. Significantly, Hart's theorising about the conditions of punishment and responsibility did not exclude the possibility of imposing criminal blame on the basis of negligence, though he expressed some reservation in cases where the accused, due to physical or mental infirmity, could not attain the standard of the reasonable person: see Chs 2 and 5. The principle that a person should not be punished without proof of fault is at the heart of the criminal law and it helps explain the modern judicial reluctance to countenance "no-fault" liability in the criminal law.

INTENTION

The fault element of most serious crimes is generally expressed as an intention to bring about the requisite physical element of the offence. Intention, a word used daily in legal practice, has evaded precise legal definition.

In relation to the physical element as a specified form of conduct or conduct that occurs in specified circumstances, intention refers to the accused meaning to perform the conduct. In this sense of intentional conduct, it is closely connected with the requirement that conduct be voluntary in the sense of it being willed or consciously performed.

In relation to the physical element as the results or consequences of conduct, the prosecution must prove that the accused's *purpose* was to bring about the results or consequences of the conduct.[66] Where an accused has this purpose, he or she acts intentionally even where, to that person's knowledge, the chance of him or her causing the result are small: *Leonard v Morris* (1975) 10 SASR 528 at 531-532. If an accused does not have this purpose, he or she does not act intentionally, even though to his or her knowledge, the chances of causing the result are high. In this circumstance, however, recklessness may be made out.[67]

The difference in intention as it relates to conduct and as it relates to consequences is sometimes referred to as a distinction between basic and specific intent.[68] In *He Kaw Teh v The Queen* (1985) 157 CLR 523 Brennan J drew a number of distinctions in the use of the term "intention" in criminal offences. He stated (at 569-570):

> General intent and specific intent are ... distinct mental states. General intent or basic intent relates to the doing of the act involved in an offence; special or specific intent relates to the results caused by the act done. In statutory offences, general or basic intent is an intent to do an act of the character prescribed by the statute creating the offence; special or specific intent is an intent to cause the results to which the intent is expressed to relate.

---

66 *La Fontaine v The Queen* (1976) 136 CLR 62; *R v Crabbe* (1985) 156 CLR 464; *Boughey v The Queen* (1986) 161 CLR 10; *R v Demirian* [1989] VR 97.

67 See also the discussion on oblique intention below at p 176.

68 For further discussion of this distinction, see 4 'Intoxication' in Chapter 4: pp 244ff.

Where a person intends to commit the requisite physical element, he or she may still be convicted even where the victim is not the intended victim[69] or where the crime takes effect in a manner which is unforeseen or unintended.[70]

Intention is not the same as motive which is generally referred to as an emotion prompting an act. In *Hyam v DPP* [1975] AC 55 Lord Hailsham stated (at 73):

> The motive for murder ... may be jealousy, fear, hatred, desire for money, perverted lust, or
> even, as in so-called "mercy killings", compassion or love. In this sense, motive is entirely
> distinct from intention or purpose. It is the emotion which gives rise to the intention and it
> is the latter and not the former which converts an *actus reus* into a criminal act.

Motive, however, may be relevant in attributing intention to an accused. It may form part of the circumstantial evidence that may establish that the accused did have the requisite state of mind. In some areas, such as the meaning of dishonesty for property offences, motive does become legally relevant: see further Ch 13, p 688. While the legal suppression of motive keeps the political, social and cultural explanations of offending out of the courtroom at the trial stage, motive is highly relevant at sentencing.

Direct and Oblique Intention

Brennan J stated (at 569) in *He Kaw Teh v The Queen* (1985) 157 CLR 523 that intention "connotes a decision to bring about a situation so far as it is possible to do so — to bring about an act of a particular kind or a particular result". This is a narrow interpretation of intention, sometimes referred to as direct intention. The most popular legal synonym for this form of intention is "purpose".

However, the courts have also developed a broader form of intention, which is commonly referred to as oblique intention.[71] This term relates to the situation where the outcome of the accused's conduct was not directly linked to his or her intention, but emerges obliquely as the consequence of that conduct. The following hypothetical is often used to illustrate the point. Imagine that a person intends to collect the insurance on a plane by placing a bomb on the plane timed to explode in mid-air. The person does not have the direct intention to cause the death of the crew, but is aware that these deaths are virtually certain to follow from his or her action. Should that person's awareness or belief that particular consequences are virtually certain be regarded as intention for the purposes of the criminal law?

The English courts have grappled with this issue for more than 20 years in the context of the law relating to murder.[72] The facts of *Hyam v DPP* [1975] AC 55 provide a good example of the problems associated with implying a broader approach to intention. The accused, Hyam, poured petrol through a neighbour's letter box and lit it in order, she claimed, to frighten a woman in the house. In the ensuing fire, two of the woman's daughters died. Hyam claimed that she did not intend to kill them. The House of Lords defined intention broadly to include not only direct intention but also

---

69 *R v Saunders* (1575) Fost 371; 75 ER 706; *R v Latimer* (1886) 17 QBD 359; [1886-90] All ER 386.

70 *R v Michael* (1840) 2 Mood 121; 169 ER 48; *R v Evans (No 2)* [1976] VR 523.

71 See G Williams, "Oblique Intention" (1987) 46 *Cambridge Law Journal* 417; A Norrie, "Oblique Intention and Legal Politics" [1989] Crim LR 793.

72 For an excellent review of the legal development of oblique intention see N Lacey, "A Clear Concept of Intention: Elusive or Illusory?" (1993) 56(5) *Modern Law Review* 621 and A Norrie, "After *Woollin*" [1999] Crim LR 532.

foresight of a probable consequence. Lord Hailsham (at 78) took the view that intentionally and deliberately doing an act which exposes a victim to the risk of probable grievous bodily harm or death are "morally indistinguishable". That is, if the accused foresaw that death was a probable consequence of her actions, then she had the relevant intent to kill.

The effect of *Hyam*'s case was to introduce into the criminal law a broad definition of "intention" which overlaps with recklessness. As we shall explore in Chapter 10, in Australia, recklessness in relation to murder is defined as foresight of a probable consequence,[73] and in relation to other offences, as foresight of a possible consequence: *R v Crabbe* (1985) 156 CLR 464.

Subsequent decisions have attempted to restrict the level of foresight required for oblique intention. The House of Lords reconsidered the *Hyam* decision in *R v Moloney* [1985] AC 905. The accused shot his stepfather with a shotgun at close range, but claimed that he had not possessed any intention to kill or hurt his victim. The accused (and the victim) had been drinking alcohol, but this was not raised in defence. The accused gave evidence that he had argued with his stepfather about the former wanting to leave the army. They then started talking about guns and his stepfather claimed that he was faster than the accused at loading, drawing and shooting a gun. The accused went upstairs and brought down two shotguns, presumably so that they could compete with one another. The accused loaded his shotgun faster than the stepfather who said "I didn't think you got the guts, but if you have, pull the trigger".

Without expressly departing from the decision in *Hyam*, the House of Lords held that the degree of foresight has to be "little short of overwhelming before it will suffice to establish the necessary intent": at 925 per Lord Bridge. According to Lord Bridge (at 926), the meaning of intention is best left to the jury to decide:

> The golden rule should be that, when directing the jury on the mental element necessary in a crime of specific intent, the judge should avoid any elaboration or paraphrase of what is meant by intent, and leave it to the jury's good sense to decide whether the accused acted with the necessary intent, unless the judge is convinced that, on the facts and having regard to the way that the case has been presented to the jury in evidence and argument, some further explanation or elaboration is strictly necessary to avoid misunderstanding.

It would seem that as a result of this case the scope for giving a direction on oblique intention has been restricted quite substantially.[73] In practice, facts situations giving rise to an analysis of oblique intention in Australia can usually fall within the concept of recklessness, at least for the purpose of the law of homicide: see Ch 10.

Transferred Intention

The doctrine of transferred intention generally applies where an accused intends a particular crime and commits the requisite physical element of that crime, but with a different victim in mind. In these circumstances, the accused is still held criminally responsible for his or her conduct:

---

73   See also *R v Hancock; R v Shankland* [1986] AC 455; *R v Nedrick* [1986] 3 All ER 1; *R v Woollin* [1998] 4 All ER 103. In the latter case, the House of Lords clarified that foresight of the consequence (death or GBH) as a "virtual certainty" was required to establish intent for murder.

[I]f an accused strike at one and missing him [or her] kills another, whom he [or she] did not intend, this is felony and homicide, and not casualty or *per infortunium*.[74]

Usually, transferred intention is considered in the context of murder, but it may apply to other crimes such as malicious wounding: see *R v Latimer* (1886) 17 QBD 359.

In recent years, there has been an exploration of whether or not the doctrine of transferred intention can apply to the situation where a child dies following antenatal injuries caused when the accused assaulted the then pregnant mother. Up until 1997, it was generally accepted that an accused who inflicts the injuries to the foetus may be guilty of murder or manslaughter depending on what fault element existed at the time of the action.[75] However, in *Attorney-General's Reference (No 3 of 1994)* [1997] 3 WLR 421 the House of Lords unanimously held that only manslaughter and not murder may be committed in these circumstances.

In *Kwok Chak Ming v The Queen* [1963] HKLR 349 the Hong Kong Court of Appeal held that the doctrine may be used in assessing an accused's liability for the death of a child from an antenatal injury. In that case, the accused stabbed a nine months pregnant woman in the abdomen and chest. Her child died three days after its birth as a result of the injuries sustained. The accused was convicted of the manslaughter of the child. On appeal, he argued that homicide could not be committed where there was no malice aforethought against the child. This argument was rejected by the Court of Appeal (at 354) on the basis that it was immaterial that the malice aforethought may have been directed against the mother rather than the child:

> The principle that where A, intending to kill or seriously injure B, unintentionally but, in pursuit of that purpose, kills C may be indicted for the murder of C, applies we think with equal force even where C was only an embryo or foetus at the time when the malice was manifested and the injury inflicted but is subsequently born alive and dies of the injury.

This same argument was accepted by the Court of Appeal in *Attorney-General's Reference (No 3 of 1994)* [1996] QB 581. That case arose out of the following facts. "B" stabbed his pregnant girlfriend, "M", several times. B knew that M was almost six months pregnant and that he was the father of the child. There were several stab wounds, one of which punctured M's uterus and entered the abdomen of the foetus. M made a good recovery from her wounds, but about two weeks after the stabbing she went into labour and gave birth to the child, "S". The medical evidence was that the period of gestation was around six and a half months and S had only a 50% chance of survival. S survived for four months, spending her entire life in intensive care. The injuries to her abdomen had been repaired and the evidence was that she died from the failure of her lungs to perform adequately due to her premature birth.

While S was still alive, B pleaded guilty to wounding with intent to cause M grievous bodily harm and was sentenced to four years' imprisonment. Although he knew M was pregnant, there was no evidence that he intended to destroy or cause injury to the foetus. B was then charged with the

---

74   M Hale, *The History of the Pleas of the Crown* (London: Professional Books Ltd, 1971) (original publication, 1736), Ch 1 p 38. *Per infortunium* means "through misfortune".

75   *R v West* (1848) 2 Cox CC 500; *Kwok Ming v The Queen (No 1)* [1963] HKLR 349; *Martin* (1995) 85 A Crim R 587 (SC WA).

murder of S. The trial judge accepted that there was evidence that B had caused the child's death, but acquitted him on the basis that he could not be found guilty of murder or manslaughter because when the stab wound was inflicted, there was an absence of a human being who could be killed.

The Attorney-General then made a reference on this point of law to the Court of Appeal under s 36(1) of the *Criminal Justice Act* 1972 (UK). The question before the Court of Appeal was whether B could be guilty of the murder or manslaughter of the child. The Court of Appeal answered this question in the affirmative. In delivering the judgment of the court, Lord Taylor of Gosforth CJ stated (at 594) that "we can see no reason to hold that malice can only be transferred where the person to whom it is transferred was in existence at the time of the act causing death".

This argument was rejected on further appeal to the House of Lords. Lord Mustill analysed the origins of the doctrine of transferred intention and found that while it could be retained "notwithstanding its lack of any sound intellectual basis" (*Attorney-General's Reference (No 3 of 1994)* [1997] 3 WLR 421 at 434) it was not broad enough to encompass the facts before the court. To find otherwise, would require a double "transfer" of intent, "first from the mother to the foetus and then from the foetus to the child as yet unborn. Then one would have to deploy the fiction (or at least the doctrine) which converts an intention to commit serious harm into the *mens rea* of murder. For me, this is too much": at 435.

It is unclear whether Australian courts will follow the approach of the House of Lords in holding that transferred intention cannot be used to hold an accused guilty of the death of a child who had suffered antenatal injuries. In *Martin* (1995) 85 A Crim R 587 Owen J held that a conviction for "unlawful killing" under the *Criminal Code* (WA) could arise out of similar circumstances to those in *Attorney-General's Reference (No 3 of 1994)*. An appeal against this finding was dismissed by the Full Court of the Supreme Court of Western Australia in *Martin (No 2)* (1996) 86 A Crim R 133. Interestingly, the doctrine of transferred intention was not considered in *Martin's* case and it may be that because the law of homicide in Australia has developed in a different way to that of England, the doctrine will have limited relevance in this area.

KNOWLEDGE

An accused may be held criminally responsible if he or she acts with knowledge that a particular circumstance exists or awareness that a particular consequence will result from the performance of the conduct. The requirement for the existence of knowledge or awareness relates to the physical element of the crime as conduct that occurs in specified circumstances and the physical element as the results or consequences of conduct.

An accused may claim a mistaken belief in order to show that he or she did not possess the requisite knowledge. For example, the crime of rape occurs where a person intentionally penetrates another without that person's consent while being aware that the person is not consenting or might not be consenting: see Ch 12. An accused may claim that although the victim was not in fact consenting, he honestly *believed* she was. This mistaken belief in certain jurisdictions has the effect of negating the requirement that the accused be aware that the victim was not consenting: see further Ch 7, 2 'Mistake of Fact and Subjective Fault Elements'; Ch 12, 2.2 'Fault Elements for Rape and Sexual Assault'.

KNOWLEDGE AND THE ROLE OF WILFUL BLINDNESS

In some cases, an accused has been deemed to possess the requisite knowledge for an offence where he or she deliberately refrained from making inquiries or wilfully shut his or her eyes for fear that he or she may learn the truth.[76] This is sometimes referred to as "wilful blindness".

In recent cases the High Court has shown a reluctance to equate wilful blindness with actual knowledge. In *Kural v The Queen* (1987) 162 CLR 502 the High Court had to determine the meaning of "intention to import a prohibited import" in s 233B(1)(b) of the *Customs Act* 1901 (Cth). The majority held that this intention did not require actual knowledge of what was being imported. A belief, falling short of actual knowledge, could sustain an inference of intention. However, the majority pointed out that wilful blindness was not an alternative fault element for this offence, it was simply evidence that a jury could use to infer intention.[77]

In *Pereira v DPP* (1988) 82 ALR 217 the High Court considered the offence of possession of a prohibited import in contravention of the *Customs Act* 1901 (Cth). The accused was delivered a package from Bombay containing cricket balls and a jewellery case that had inside them a quantity of cannabis resin. The accused had taken delivery of the package but had not opened it when the police raided her premises. The trial judge directed the jury as to the importance of proving knowledge and that wilful blindness is the equivalent of knowledge. The jury was directed that the accused could be considered wilfully blind if her suspicions about receiving a parcel from overseas were aroused and she refrained from making any inquiries for fear that she would learn the truth.

The majority of the High Court made some observations about the role of knowledge and wilful blindness. They referred to the previous High Court decision in *Kural* and held that in contrast to the offence of importing a prohibited import, the offence of the possession of a prohibited import *did* require actual knowledge. The majority then went on to state that knowledge means *actual knowledge* and not *imputed knowledge*. A state of mind *less than* actual knowledge is not sufficient. However, the accused's suspicion coupled with a failure to inquire, may be evidence from which a jury can infer knowledge. This reflects Kirby J's comments in *Peters v The Queen* (1998) 151 ALR 51 (at 93) that intention must be inferred from the evidence, the focus being on discovering the intention which subjectively the accused had rather than searching for an intention which the law objectively imputes to the accused.

The majority decisions in *Kural* and *Pereira* relegate wilful blindness to an evidential role. This seems to echo the restriction of the concept of oblique intention. For both intention and knowledge, there appears to be a tension between the technical rules governing the meaning of intention and knowledge and the broad practical application of those rules by the jury.

---

76   D Lanham, "Wilful Blindness and the Criminal Law" (1985) 9 Crim LJ 261.

77   *Giorgianni v The Queen* (1985) 156 CLR 473; *Kural v The Queen* (1987) 162 CLR 502; *Saad v The Queen* (1987) 70 ALR 667; 61 ALJR 243; 29 A Crim R 20; *R v Crabbe* (1985) 156 CLR 464; *Pereira v DPP* (1988) 82 ALR 217; 63 ALJR 1; 35 A Crim R 382; *Zakaria* (1992) 62 A Crim R 259 at 266 per Crockett and Marks JJ; *R v Dykyj* (1993) 29 NSWLR 672; *McConnell* (1993) 69 A Crim R 39.

RECKLESSNESS

The term "recklessness" describes the state of mind of a person who, whilst performing an act, is aware of a risk that a particular consequence is *likely* to result. Awareness of a risk is thus the essence of recklessness. However, this fault element is also formulated as one of knowledge, foresight or realisation that a consequence is likely to result. The usual shorthand for recklessness is foresight, in the sense of foresight of the likelihood of a consequence or of a circumstance occurring.

An accused is said to be reckless where he or she acts in the knowledge that a consequence is a probable or possible result of his or her conduct.[78] For example, under the common law a person who foresees death or grievous bodily harm as a probable consequence of his or her conduct is said to be reckless as to those consequences and may be convicted of murder if death results.[79] An accused may also be said to be reckless where he or she is aware of the possible existence of certain circumstances but acts regardless of their existence. For example, an accused who intentionally sexually penetrates another without that person's consent whilst being aware that the other person might not be consenting is said to be reckless as to the absence of consent and may be guilty of rape: see Ch 12 at pp 623ff.

Recklessness is treated on the same scale as intention because of the notion of blameworthiness. This was explained in *R v Crabbe* (1985) 156 CLR 464 as follows (at 469):

> The conduct of a person who does an act, knowing that death or grievous bodily harm is a probable consequence, can naturally be regarded for the purposes of the criminal law as just as blameworthy as the conduct of one who does an act intended to kill or do grievous bodily harm.

Whether couched in terms of probability or possibility, what is important is that recklessness relates to a subjective attribution of awareness of risks that are substantial and the "real and not remote" chance that the consequences will occur: *Boughey v The Queen* (1986) 161 CLR 10 at 21 per Mason, Wilson and Deane JJ.

As stated previously, there is a similarity or overlap between recklessness and oblique intention, the latter referring to foresight of a particular consequence as a virtual certainty. Wilful blindness may also overlap with recklessness in that individuals may close their eyes to a fact after becoming aware of the risk of that fact existing. However, Glanville Williams in *Textbook of Criminal Law* (2nd ed, London: Stevens & Sons, 1983), p 125 states that courts must be careful, and that judges should not equate wilful blindness with recklessness because there is a danger of inferring knowledge if a person has been reckless:

> If knowledge is judicially made to include wilful blindness, and if wilful blindness is judicially deemed to equal recklessness, the result is that a person who has no knowledge is judicially deemed to have knowledge if he [or she] is found to have been reckless.

---

78 *Pemble v The Queen* (1971) 124 CLR 107; *La Fontaine v The Queen* (1976) 136 CLR 62; *Nydam v The Queen* [1977] VR 430; *R v Crabbe* (1985) 156 CLR 464; *R v Demirian* [1989] VR 97; *Filmer v Barclay* [1994] 2 VR 269.

79 *La Fontaine v The Queen* (1976) 136 CLR 62; *R v Crabbe* (1985) 156 CLR 464.

RECKLESSNESS AND INDIFFERENCE

In some statutes, recklessness is formulated as "reckless indifference". For example, s 18(1)(a) of the *Crimes Act* 1900 (NSW) states that:

> Murder shall be taken to have been committed where the act of the accused, or thing by him [or her] omitted to be done, causing the death charged, was done or omitted with reckless indifference to human life.

The High Court in *R v Crabbe* (1985) 156 CLR 464 (at 470) stressed that under the common law definition of recklessness, it was not necessary that an accused's knowledge of the probable consequences of his or her actions be accompanied by indifference:

> It is not the offender's indifference to the consequences of his [or her] act but his [or her] knowledge that those consequences will probably occur that is the relevant element.

The members of the High Court in *Crabbe* expressly stated that their interpretation of recklessness only applied to the common law. Notwithstanding this rider, the Federal Court has held that murder under the equivalent s 18 of the *Crimes Act* 1900 (ACT) should follow the common law position: *R v Brown* (1987) 78 ALR 368. The Federal Court held that although s 18 refers to "reckless *indifference* to human life", it is immaterial whether or not the accused was indifferent to the risk. The sole question is whether or not the accused at the relevant time foresaw the probability of causing death.[80]

This approach to indifference in recklessness reflects the criminal law's stance on the irrelevance of motive. Requiring indifference on the part of the accused would be tantamount to regarding motive as relevant to liability. If indifference is not required, as the High Court suggests, then how do we protect conduct that involves the high risk of harm to others, but is done for a legitimate reason?

In *Crabbe*, the High Court referred (at 470) to the example of a doctor who performs a surgical operation that involves the high risk of death to the patient. Every day, doctors are aware that death or serious injury is a likely consequence of medical procedures. How does the law protect doctors from liability under the criminal law when their procedures fail? There are two ways to protect individuals who take risks for legitimate reasons. The first way is to allow them to raise the defence of necessity. Necessity or justification is a complete defence and would render the doctor's conduct lawful. But the onus is on the accused to raise some evidence that the conduct was justified. The scope of the defence of necessity is further explored in Chapter 6.

Alternatively, the second way to protect individuals who take risks for legitimate reasons is to adopt a narrower definition of recklessness by requiring an accused's risk-taking to be unjustifiable. In deciding whether an act is justifiable its social purpose or social utility is important: C Howard, *Howard's Criminal Law* (4th ed, Sydney: Law Book Company Ltd, 1982), pp 54-55, 357-359. Recklessness in this sense could be defined as substantial and unjustifiable risk-taking. Doctors regularly foresee the risk of harm occurring, but as the risk is one that is socially justifiable, doctors are not considered to be reckless.

---

80 *R v Crabbe* (1985) 156 CLR 464 is not followed in New South Wales with respect to reckless indifference to human life: "Section 18 [of the *Crimes Act* 1900 (NSW)] departs from the common law in that it requires foresight of the probability of death; foresight of the probability of grievous bodily harm is not enough": *Royall v The Queen* (1990) 172 CLR 378 at 395 per Mason CJ. See further, Chapter 10.

This notion of requiring an accused's risk-taking to be unjustifiable was set out in the American Law Institute's *Model Penal Code*[81] and found favour with Fisse in *Howard's Criminal Law* (5th ed, Sydney: Law Book Company Ltd, 1990), pp 486ff. It has now been adopted by the Model Criminal Code Officers Committee in the *Criminal Code Act* 1995 (Cth). Section 5.4(1) of that Act defines "recklessness" as substantial and unjustifiable risk-taking.

RECKLESSNESS AND WILFUL BLINDNESS

We have already noted that the High Court has relegated the concept of wilful blindness to an evidential role and is wary of equating knowledge with wilful blindness. The High Court in *R v Crabbe* (1985) 156 CLR 464 (at 470-471) was similarly critical of the direction used by the trial judge with regard to wilful blindness and foresight of a particular consequence being likely to result.

The High Court in *Crabbe's* case made it clear that the test of recklessness for murder at common law is knowledge that death or grievous bodily harm will probably result from one's actions. This demonstrates the concern of the courts to ensure that the law of murder reflects distinctions of moral culpability. The High Court believed that punishing an accused for murder when death or grievous bodily harm was foreseen as a mere possibility would spread the scope of murder too far. However, this strict definition of recklessness does not apply for less serious offences.

For offences other than murder, the courts have not applied the high level of recklessness based on foresight of probable consequence. In *R v Coleman* (1990) 19 NSWLR 467 the New South Wales Court of Criminal Appeal considered the definition of recklessness with regard to the offence of maliciously inflicting actual bodily harm with intent to have sexual intercourse: *Crimes Act* 1900 (NSW), s 61. The term "maliciously" has been interpreted as meaning that intention or recklessness is required for this offence. The accused had appealed against conviction on the ground that the trial judge had misdirected the jury on recklessness by not applying the *Crabbe* formulation. The New South Wales Court of Criminal Appeal held that for all statutory offences other than murder, recklessness is defined as foresight of possibility not probability.

As a result of these cases, it is most important that the trial judge direct the jury as to the appropriate meaning of recklessness. In *La Fontaine v The Queen* (1976) 136 CLR 62 the High Court made two suggestions regarding recklessness. First, that in murder trials the issue of recklessness should not be left to the jury unless it arises as a real possibility on the facts. Secondly, the High Court suggested that the term "reckless" should not be used in the trial judge's direction to the jury, as it is liable to confuse. Rather, the jury should be directed that the accused must foresee that the death or grievous bodily harm is a probable consequence of his or her action.

There is a great deal of merit in this second recommendation. In *R v Williams* (1990) 50 A Crim R 213 the New South Wales Court of Criminal Appeal considered the meaning of recklessness for the purpose of assault. Badgery-Parker J stated (at 222):

> The word reckless is a word well-known in ordinary speech and a person is said to be reckless who acts without regard to the possible consequences of the act in question. In most contexts the law gives to the word the same meaning that it has in ordinary speech.

---

81 *Proposed Official Draft*, s 2.02(2)(c): "A person acts recklessly with respect to a material element of an offence when he [or she] consciously disregards a substantial and unjustifiable risk that the material element exists or will result from his [or her] conduct. The risk must be of such a nature and degree that, considering the circumstances known to him [or her], its disregard involves a gross deviation from the standard of conduct that a law-abiding person would observe in the actor's situation."

However, the ordinary "common sense" use of the term recklessness is much broader than its legal use. The definition of recklessness in the *Macquarie Dictionary* (Second Revision, North Ryde: Macquarie University, 1988) is "utterly careless of the consequences of action; without caution": p 1419. Carelessness generally uses an objective rather than a subjective standard. Without proper guidance on the meaning of recklessness, a jury would be likely to depart from a subjective standard and apply an objective standard of carelessness instead. This would mean that the division between recklessness and negligence would break down.

CASE STUDIES

Caldwell Recklessness

It is necessary to emphasise that the concept of recklessness in Australia differs from that under English law. In the early 1980s, the English courts developed a dual meaning for recklessness. In *Commissioner of Police of the Metropolis v Caldwell* [1982] AC 341 the House of Lords broadened the interpretation of recklessness in statutory offences to include an objective standard. This second meaning of recklessness is often described in shorthand as *Caldwell* recklessness. The case concerned the meaning of "recklessly" under the statutory offence of criminal damage. The objective definition was also applied to reckless driving: *R v Lawrence* [1982] AC 510.

The House of Lords held that in interpreting the word "recklessly", the courts must apply the ordinary meaning and usage of the word. The House of Lords held that recklessness has two meanings. It embraces a *subjective* awareness of a risk: the person who is aware of a risk but goes ahead in any case. But it also embraces an *objective* aspect: the person who fails to appreciate the risk when the risk would be obvious to the reasonable person. The House of Lords concluded that inadvertence to an obvious risk was as morally culpable as subjective risk-taking.

The decision in *Caldwell* caused uproar in the legal community. However, the *Caldwell* definition of recklessness still applies in England (*R v Reid* [1992] 1 WLR 793) and has been extended to other statutory offences. Many academics were extremely critical of this departure from subjectivism in the fault element of a crime.[82] It certainly appears to blur the distinction between recklessness and criminal negligence. *Caldwell* recklessness has not generally been applied in Australia. However, there appears to be some movement toward a modified standard relating to recklessness in the field of sexual offences in New South Wales.[83]

For a general discusssion of *Caldwell* recklessness, see R Card, *Criminal Law* (14th ed, London: Butt, 1998), pp 58-68.

---

82 JC Smith, "Criminal Damage" [1981] Crim LR 393 and 410; G Syrota "A Radical Change in the Law of Recklessness" [1982] Crim LR 97; L Leigh and J Temkin, "Note on *Caldwell* and *Lawrence* (1982) 45 *Modern Law Review* 198; RA Duff "*Caldwell* and *Lawrence*: The Retreat from Subjectivism" (1983) 3 *Oxford Journal of Legal Studies* 77; G Williams, "Recklessness Redefined" (1981) 40(2) *Cambridge Law Journal* 252; S Gardiner, "Recklessness Refined" (1993) 109 *Law Quarterly Review* 21.

83 *R v Tolmie* (1995) 37 NSWLR 660 at 672 per Kirby J; *R v Kitchener* (1993) 29 NSWLR 696 at 703 per Carruthers J. See Chapter 12, p 624. Paradoxically, *Caldwell* recklessness has been rejected for the statutory offence of rape in the United Kingdom: *R v Satnam*; *R v Kewal* (1983) 78 Cr App R 149.

NEGLIGENCE

Negligence is measured on an objective standard and therefore does not sit well with the concept of the fault element of a crime as a guilty mind. It is therefore sometimes placed in a separate category to that of intention, knowledge or recklessness. However, negligence shares with these other forms of fault elements the fact that it is an element that determines criminal responsibility.

Negligence may apply to any form of the physical element. The objective standard in negligence is generally that of *reasonableness*, often expressed by the term reasonable person. Generally, the accused's behaviour is assessed by reference to what a hypothetical reasonable person would have known, foreseen or done in the circumstances. Often it will be difficult to distinguish reckless from negligent conduct, purely on an external basis. The distinction lies in the accused's subjective awareness of the danger that he or she is creating.[84]

Because of the general reluctance to use objective standards in the criminal context, the courts have developed a narrow meaning for negligence and have been concerned to draw a distinction between criminal and civil concepts of negligence. Simple lack of care that may constitute civil liability is normally not enough for a crime to be committed negligently.[85]

The leading case on criminal negligence is that of *Nydam v The Queen* [1977] VR 430. In that case, the accused threw petrol over two women and ignited it. He claimed that he only intended to take his own life. The trial judge directed the jury as to murder and also manslaughter by criminal negligence. The accused was convicted of murder. On appeal, the Supreme Court of Victoria considered the trial judge's direction on the meaning of criminal negligence for manslaughter. The Court found that the weight of authority favoured an objective rather than a subjective test. It stated (at 445) that for manslaughter by negligence to be made out, it must be proved that the accused's behaviour involved "such a great falling short of the standard of care which a reasonable [person] would have exercised and which involved such a high degree of risk that death or grievous bodily harm would follow that the doing of the act merit[s] criminal punishment". Sometimes the term "gross negligence" is used in this regard.

For manslaughter by criminal negligence, there are thus three components:

▬ The accused's conduct must involve a great falling short of the standard of care required of a reasonable person;

▬ The reasonable person, in the position of the accused, would have foreseen the risk of the particular consequence occurring; and

▬ The doing of the act must merit criminal punishment.

This last component is inherently circular. It is like defining a crime by saying "X is criminal when X is sufficient to justify punishment". This aspect of manslaughter by criminal negligence should be treated with some scepticism. It is perhaps best explained by the court's concern to distinguish criminal negligence from the standard of negligence applied in tort law.

---

84   *Andrews v DPP* [1937] AC 576 at 583; *Mamote-Kulang of Tamagot v The Queen* (1964) 111 CLR 62 at 79.

85   *Andrews v DPP* [1937] AC 576; *R v Adomako* [1995] 1 AC 171; *Callaghan v The Queen* (1952) 87 CLR 115; *Nydam v The Queen* [1977] VR 430; *R v Buttsworth* [1983] 1 NSWLR 658.

The standard of criminal negligence may differ according to the nature of the offence. If the offence is a serious one, it would seem that the departure from the standard of reasonableness must be greater than if the offence is minor: *New South Wales Sugar Milling Co-op Ltd v EPA* (1992) 59 A Crim R 6.

There is one major problem related to using an objective standard in assessing criminal negligence. This problem bedevils objective standards in law generally. Who precisely *is* the "reasonable person"? The reasonable person standard assumes a community consensus about what constitutes reasonable and unreasonable conduct. By using this hypothetical person to judge the accused's conduct, the law is ignoring important personal characteristics of the accused such as race and gender. The standard is in fact highly discretionary because judges or juries will be constructing the standard of judgment according to their own values. Because the standard is expressed as "objective" and "neutral" it is given the veneer of legitimacy: see S Bronitt and K Amirthalingam, "Cultural Blindness and the Criminal Law" (1996) 20(2) *Alternative Law Journal* 58.

Even if the "reasonable person" can be identified, the objective standard poses severe problems for those people who are unable to reach the standards of the reasonable person because of some inherent physical or intellectual disability. For example, in *R v Stone and Dobinson* [1977] 1 QB 354 the two accused, a 67-year-old man and a 43-year-old woman, both of whom suffered from physical and intellectual disabilities were convicted of manslaughter by negligent omission. The deceased, the male accused's sister, had been living with the two accused who had assumed responsibility for her care. There was evidence that the sister suffered from anorexia nervosa and when she died, she weighed only five stone and five pounds. She died from toxaemia and prolonged immobilisation. The victim was found dead in bed in "a scene of dreadful degradation": at 359. She was soaked in urine and excreta and had ulcers on her legs that contained maggots. Both accused had made some ineffectual attempts to obtain medical attention for the sister and the female accused had given her food. On appeal, the English Court of Appeal held that both accused had undertaken a duty of care for the woman and that they had been negligent in failing to give her proper care.

The facts of this case show that the objective standard can operate harshly against those who have a physical or intellectual disability. The Victorian Law Reform Commission was critical of the decision in *Stone and Dobinson* and recommended that special circumstances may exist where an accused is incapable of meeting a reasonableness standard: *Homicide*, Report No 40, (1990), p 116. The Commission proposed that any person charged with manslaughter by criminal negligence should be afforded a defence if by reason of some physical or intellectual disability he or she could not reach the standard expected from non-disabled persons.

The Model Criminal Code Officers Committee, whilst not dealing specifically with the situation of an accused with a physical or intellectual disability, has suggested that the objective standard for negligence "require the reasonable person to step into the shoes of the [accused] at the relevant time": *Chapter 5 — Fatal Offences Against the Person*, Discussion Paper (1998), p 153.

The problems associated with the "reasonable" or "ordinary person" will be taken up when we consider provocation in Chapter 5 and self-defence in Chapter 6. The controversy surrounding the adoption of objective fault standards based on the "reasonable man/person" in the law of rape is explored in Chapter 12, pp 618ff.

PHILOSOPHICAL PERSPECTIVES

Moral Blameworthiness

Legal philosophers have debated the role of consequences and outcome-luck in relation to moral blameworthiness and the criminal law. To illustrate the topic, consider the following examples provided by Andrew Ashworth:

"A and B each shoot at their victims, A hits and kills his victim but B misses. In both cases, A and B share the identical intention."

"D and E each throw a punch at someone, both punches are identical but in D's case the victim sustains a bruised cheek, while in E's case, the victim falls and sustains brain damage and dies."[86]

Whether A, B, D and E are considered guilty depends on two competing philosophical models for attributing blame — the subjectivist and objectivist models.

According to the "subjectivist" view, harmful consequences of actions are strictly matters outside the control of the individual. Thus, blame should be ascribed on the basis of an individual's intention, not consequences, accompanying such action. Blame should depend on individual choices made and not merely on luck or chance. Applied to the criminal law, consequences are relevant to culpability *only* where they are intended or foreseen.[87] Subjectivism has implications for the following debates in the criminal law such as:

— *Inchoate Liability*: Since subjective intention is the touchstone of liability it does not matter if the offence is incomplete. A person should be held liable for criminal acts through the law of attempt, conspiracy or incitement even where the acts are physically (or even legally) impossible to complete. This is taken up in Chapter 7, p 355.
— *Participation in an offence*: A subjectivist model would not hold that a person who assists or encourages another person to commit crime should be liable *irrespective* of whether the commission of the perpetrator's crime actually occurred. This is explored in Chapter 8, pp 404ff.
— *Constructive Liability*: Imposing criminal liability for consequences that are unforeseen or beyond the control of the accused would be incompatible with subjectivism. Thus, constructive crimes, such as felony murder or battery manslaughter, should be abolished. Such constructive crimes are considered in Chapter 10, p 497.

Objectivists, on the other hand, argue that "outcome-luck" ought to play a role in ascribing moral and criminal responsibility: RA Duff, *Intention, Agency and Criminal Liability* (Oxford: Oxford University Press, 1990), pp 184-192. In their view, consequences have a role to play in

---

86 These examples are borrowed from A Ashworth, "Taking the Consequences" in S Shute, J Gardner and J Horder (eds), *Action and Value in Criminal Law* (Oxford: Clarendon Press, 1993).

87 As Ashworth points out in relation to risk taking "if the harm did occur, this may provide evidence which assists in assessing magnitude and probability, but resulting harm does not alter the intrinsic seriousness of the risk-taking": "Taking the Consequences" in S Shute, J Gardner and J Horder (eds), *Action and Value in Criminal Law* (Oxford: Clarendon Press, 1993), p 123.

determining questions of moral and legal blame even where the actor has no control over them. Theorists like Duff have explored this question in the context of criminal attempts. Analytically, Duff doubts whether consequences are truly severable from the action giving rising to them.[88] He also points to empirical evidence that people commonly tend to judge conduct by reference to consequences.

From a moral perspective, the different sentiments expressed here are significant. Consider, for example, an act of careless driving resulting in a "near miss" and an identical act of driving that results in the death of a child. The capacity to express moral relief at the "near miss", which is not available to the driver causing the death of a child, suggests that these situations ought to be morally differentiated. Moreover, imposing strict equivalence of blame would not mark the effect of consequences on the driver. The driver who caused a "near miss" is provided with an opportunity to avoid occurrence of death in the future, an opportunity that is not available to the person who caused death. Most importantly, not taking account of consequences undermines the censuring function of the criminal law. It would convey the message that, morally speaking, causing actual harm is unimportant and there is no distinction between completed and attempted offences: RA Duff, *Intention, Agency and Criminal Liability* (3rd ed, Oxford: Oxford University Press, 1990), pp 184-192.

As explored in Chapter 2, moral philosophy plays a significant role in shaping the criminal law. The tendency is to view these different approaches as competing models or paradigms, as explanatory and normative blueprints for the criminal law. As Ashworth concludes (p 124):

> If a subjectivist were drafting a new criminal code, all these cases would be made to depend on the defendant's culpability rather than the outcome in a particular case. The effect of this on the form of the criminal law would be quite radical, since many offences are currently defined by reference to the result.

Subjectivists must concede that the criminal law does not perfectly correspond to their ideal. Nevertheless the fundamental importance of subjectivist ideals can be preserved by viewing the plethora of strict and absolute liability offences as both "exceptional" and "trivial": see A Ashworth, *Principles of Criminal Law* (3rd ed, Oxford: Oxford University Press, 1999), pp 167-176. This disjunction may be viewed, to borrow Doreen McBarnet's phrase, as yet another "false dichotomy" in our system of criminal law: "False Dichotomies in Criminal Justice Research" in J Baldwin and AK Bottomley, *Criminal Justice: Selected Readings* (London: Martin Robertson and Company, 1978). Rather than view objective forms of liability as a deviation from the "true" principle of fault, the better view is that there is a perpetual tension between subjective and objective accounts of culpability in the criminal law. Fault in the criminal law lies on a spectrum between these subjective and objective models. The apparent instability of fault in the criminal law may simply be a reflection of the diversity of functions performed by the modern criminal law.

---

88 RA Duff, "Acting, Trying and Criminal Liability" in S Shute, J Gardner and J Horder (eds), *Action and Value in Criminal Law* (Oxford: Clarendon Press, 1993). "If actions and outcomes were not ascribed to us on the basis of our bodily movements and their mutual accompaniments, we could have no continuing history or character": T Honoré, "Responsibility and Luck" (1988) 104 *Law Quarterly Review* 530 at 543, quoted in A Ashworth, "Taking the Consequences" in S Shute, J Gardner and J Horder (eds), *Action and Value in Criminal Law*, p 112.

At certain historical moments, for some crimes, intentions not consequences, are all-important, and vice versa. Our conclusion may simply be that the meaning of fault in the criminal law is historically contingent, and that any quest for the "grand universal theory" to account for all forms of culpability may prove to be illusive, if not illusory.

4. STRICT LIABILITY AND ABSOLUTE LIABILITY OFFENCES

The courts have recognised a tripartite classification of statutory offences. An offence may:

▬ involve a subjective fault element;

▬ be a strict liability offence where no fault element need be proved, but evidence of honest and reasonable mistake of fact is open to the accused; or

▬ be an absolute liability offence where no fault element needs to be proved.[89]

At common law and in the Code jurisdictions, it will be a matter of statutory interpretation as to the category in which the offence falls. In the common law jurisdictions, there is a range of matters that may be considered in construing the classification of an offence. However, in the Code jurisdictions, the type of offence is constructed solely by the provisions of the section creating the offence and the relevant *Criminal Code*.[90] If the section creating the offence does not contain a fault element, the provisions of the relevant Code relating to criminal responsibility apply.[91]

Crimes of strict and absolute liability share two distinctive features. First, strict and absolute liability offences are creatures of statute. Secondly, these offences, like those satisfied by criminal negligence, depart from the paradigm offences that require a subjective fault element. The prosecution need only prove that the accused committed the physical element of the crime. In many textbooks, these types of offences are marginalised to the periphery of the criminal law and described as exceptional and regulatory in nature. In reality, in terms of numbers of offences, the bulk of crimes do not require proof of a subjective fault element. See, for example, the extensive derogation from the subjective fault element in drug offences, some of which carry the penalty of life imprisonment: Ch 15, pp 849ff.

---

89   *Chiou Yaou Fa v Morris* (1987) 46 NTR 1 at 19 per Asche J; *He Kaw Teh v The Queen* (1985) 157 CLR 523.

90   *Pregelj v Mansion* (1987) 31 A Crim R 383 at 393 per Nader J; *Bennett v The Queen* (1991) Tas R 11.

91   *Thomas v McEather* [1920] St R Qd 166; (1920) 14 QJPR 160; *Bennett v The Queen* (1991) Tas R 11; *Vallance v The Queen* (1961) 108 CLR 56; *McPherson v Cairn* [1977] WAR 28; *Defiance Enterprises Pty Ltd v Collector of Customs (Queensland)* (1990) 96 ALR 697; *GJ Coles & Co Ltd v Goldsworthy* [1985] WAR 183; (1985) 57 LGRA 122; *Brimblecombe v Duncan; Ex parte Duncan* [1958] Qd R 8; (1958) 52 QJPR 83; *Smith v Le Mura* [1983] Qd R 535.

4.1 THE PRESUMPTION OF SUBJECTIVE FAULT AT COMMON LAW

The preference for a subjective fault element manifests itself in a judicial reluctance to dispose of this requirement too readily for statutory offences. In the 19th century, in the face of a growing number of statutory crimes that did not require proof of a subjective fault element, the courts developed a common law presumption that all crimes (common law and statutory) involve some form of subjective fault element.[92] This presumption does not apply to the Code jurisdictions.[93]

This presumption of subjective fault may, however, be rebutted. Gibbs CJ pointed out in *He Kaw Teh v The Queen* (1985) 157 CLR 523 (at 528-530) that there are four factors that need to be assessed in determining whether or not the presumption of subjective fault has been displaced:

▬ the language of the section creating the offence;

▬ the subject matter of the statute;

▬ the consequences for the community of an offence; and

▬ the potential consequences for an accused, if convicted.

THE LANGUAGE OF THE SECTION

If the section creating the offence uses words such as "knowingly" or "dishonestly" or "wilfully",[94] it will be difficult to show that the presumption of subjective fault has been displaced.[95] The absence of such words, however, does not immediately imply that an offence will be one of strict or absolute liability.[96] Other factors must also be taken into account.

THE SUBJECT MATTER OF THE STATUTE

Brennan J states (at 576) in *He Kaw Teh v The Queen* (1985) 157 CLR 523 that the "purpose of the statute is the surest guide of the legislature's intention as to the mental state to be implied". If the subject matter of the statute is to regulate behaviour in some way and the prohibited acts "are not criminal in any real sense, but are acts which in the public interest are prohibited under a penalty"[97] then it is likely that the presumption of subjective fault will be displaced. One of the factors behind the rise of strict liability offences is that of administrative efficiency. The presumption of subjective

---

92 *Sherras v De Rutzen* [1895] 1 QB 918.

93 *Thomas v McEather* [1920] St R Qd 166; (1920) 14 QJPR 160; *Vallance v The Queen* (1961) 108 CLR 56; *Martin v The Queen* [1963] Tas SR 103; *Pregelj v Manison* (1987) 51 NTR 1; *TTS Pty Ltd v Griffiths* (1991) 105 FLR 255; *Hogan v Sawyer; Ex parte Sawyer* [1992] 1 Qd R 32; (1990) 51 A Crim R 46; *Bennett v The Queen* (1991) Tas R 11; *McMaster v The Queen* (1994) 4 NTLR 92.

94 *Environment Protection Agency v N* (1992) 26 NSWLR 352; (1992) 59 A Crim R 408 provides an example of interpretation of a provision containing the word "wilfully".

95 *He Kaw Teh v The Queen* (1985) 157 CLR 523 at 594 per Dawson J.

96 *He Kaw Teh v The Queen* (1985) 157 CLR 523 at 594 per Dawson J; *Lim Chin Aik v The Queen* [1963] AC 160 at 176 per Viscount Radcliffe, Lord Evershed and Lord Devlin; *Von Lieven v Stewart* (1990) 21 NSWLR 52; *Davis v Bates* (1986) 43 SASR 149 at 150 per King CJ.

97 *Sherras v De Rutzen* [1895] 1 QB 918 at 922.

fault has been held to have been displaced in offences dealing with adulterated food[98] and serving liquor to certain people,[99] perhaps partly because it would lead to delays in the court system if subjective fault had to be proved for such offences on each occasion.

THE CONSEQUENCES FOR THE COMMUNITY

This requirement is generally weighed directly against the potential consequences for the accused if convicted. Consequences to the community have outweighed the latter in the case of environmental damage[100] and speeding offences[101] and the presumption of subjective fault has been displaced.

POTENTIAL CONSEQUENCES FOR THE ACCUSED

In general, the more serious the potential consequences for the accused on conviction, the less likely it is that the presumption of subjective fault will be displaced. In *He Kaw Teh v The Queen* (1985) 157 CLR 523 a majority of the High Court held that the severe penal provisions relating to the importation and possession of heroin enforced the presumption that subjective fault was required and should not be displaced. If, on the other hand, the potential consequences to the accused involve a financial penalty, it is likely that the presumption of subjective fault will be displaced.

The implications of *He Kaw Teh* for the fault elements of drug offences, and its impact on drug law enforcement, are explored further in Chapter 15, p 850.

4.2 STRICT LIABILITY VERSUS ABSOLUTE LIABILITY

The courts have been reluctant to categorise offences as those of absolute liability in the absence of a clear legislative intention that this be the case. Street CJ stated in *R v Wampfler* (1987) 11 NSWLR 541 (at 547) that "[t]here is a discernible trend in modern authorities away from construing statutes as creating absolute liability and towards recognising statutes as falling within the middle or second category [strict liability]". This appears to be because the courts are uneasy about punishing an accused on the basis of the physical element alone.

With strict liability offences, the accused's state of mind and lack of culpability may be raised by way of the defence of honest and reasonable mistake of fact. This defence is explored in Chapter 7. The prosecution need not prove a fault element in relation to strict liability offences. However, an accused may raise an honest and reasonable belief in a state of facts which, if they existed, would render the act innocent: *Proudman v Dayman* (1941) 67 CLR 536; see Ch 7. Provided the accused satisfies the evidential burden in this regard, the prosecution must prove beyond reasonable doubt that the accused did not have an honest or reasonable belief as to the facts asserted: *He Kaw Teh v The Queen* (1985) 157 CLR 523.

---

98 *Parker v Alder* [1899] 1 QB 20 (adulterated milk); *R v Woodrow* (1846) 15 M & W 404; 153 ER 907 (adulterated tobacco).

99 *Cundy v Le Cocq* (1884) 13 QBD 207 (serving liquor to a drunken person).

100 *Allen v United Carpet Mills Pty Ltd* [1989] VR 323.

101 *Kearon v Grant* [1991] 1 VR 321.

The courts have interpreted certain offences dealing with the regulation of social or industrial conditions or protecting revenue as imposing absolute liability. For example, the offence of exceeding 60 kilometres per hour in a 60 kilometre zone contrary to cl 1001(1)(c) of the *Road Safety (Traffic) Regulations* 1988 (Vic) has been held to be an absolute liability offence[102] as has causing pollution to waters under s 39(1) of the *Environment Protection Act* 1970 (Vic).[103] In these two cases, the courts were persuaded that the beneficial consequences for the community overrode any potential negative consequences to the accused. Other "regulatory" offences that have been interpreted as absolute liability offences include selling alcohol to underage persons in breach of s 114 of the *Liquor Act* 1982 (NSW),[104] refusing or failing to submit to breath testing pursuant to s 4E(7) of the *Motor Traffic Act* 1909 (NSW)[105] and publishing a name in breach of a suppression order under ss 69 and 71 of the *Evidence Act* 1929 (SA).[106] The effect of absolute liability is to place on individuals engaged in potentially hazardous or harmful activity a legal obligation of extreme (not merely reassonable) care. Empirical research into the enforcement of environmental offences, explored in Chapter 1 at p 13 suggests that regulatory agencies only prosecute where there is evidence that polluters knew (after repeated warnings) that they were breaching the law. Prosecution discretion and policies, operating in the shadow of the law, ameliorate the coercive and potentially unjust nature of "no-fault" liability.

Because of the harshness of holding a person criminally responsible in the absence of any fault on his or her part, the courts may take into account whether any purpose will be served by characterising the offence as one of absolute liability which could just as effectively be served by characterising the offence as one of strict liability.[107] Absolute liability will not be inferred "merely in order to find a luckless victim".[108]

5. CONCURRENCE OF PHYSICAL AND FAULT ELEMENTS

In order for an accused to be convicted of an offence, it must be proved that the fault element coincided with, or existed at the same time as, the physical element.[109] This model of criminal responsibility separates an accused's thoughts from his or her actions. This dualist approach to responsibility has been criticised, most notably by the philosopher RA Duff who points out that in practice, ordinary people do not adopt such a refined notion of human behaviour which separates act from will: *Intention, Agency and Criminal Liability* (Oxford: Oxford University Press, 1990). Neither do

---

102 *Kearon v Grant* [1991] 1 VR 321.

103 *Allen v United Carpet Mills Pty Ltd* [1989] VR 323.

104 *Hickling v Laneyrie* (1991) 21 NSWLR 730.

105 *R v Walker* (1994) 35 NSWLR 384; 77 A Crim R 236.

106 *Nationwide News Pty Ltd v Bitter* (1985) 38 SASR 390.

107 *Hawthorn (Department of Health) v Morcam Pty Ltd* (1992) 29 NSWLR 120 at 129-130 per Hunt CJ.

108 *Lim Chin Aik v The Queen* [1963] AC 160 at 174 per Judicial Committee of the Privy Council.

109 *Ryan v The Queen* (1967) 121 CLR 205; *R v Miller* [1983] 2 AC 161; *R v Demirian* [1989] VR 97; *Royall v The Queen* (1990) 172 CLR 378 at 458 per McHugh J.

philosophers. Ludwig Wittgenstein maintained that intending to do something is not a mental state dissociated from the act but rather part and parcel of the act: see G Fletcher, *Rethinking Criminal Law* (Boston: Little, Brown & Co, 1978), p 437. People thus make a global judgment of behaviour that encompasses both act and attitude. This dualist approach to criminal behaviour also causes problems with separating voluntariness from the fault element of a crime.

Occasionally, the dualist approach to criminal behaviour causes a problem with the concurrence of the fault and physical elements and this has tested the ingenuity of the courts. The courts have occasionally stretched this requirement such that fault element has been imposed upon a series of acts or a "continuing act". The main cases in which this has occurred are *Thabo Meli v The Queen* [1954] 1 WLR 228; *Fagan v Metropolitan Commissioner* [1969] 1 QB 439; *R v Miller* [1983] 2 AC 161 and *Jiminez v The Queen* (1992) 173 CLR 572.

5.1 FAULT ELEMENT IMPOSED UPON A SERIES OF ACTS

In *Thabo Meli*, in accordance with a preconceived plan, the accused men took the victim to a hut, gave him beer so that he was partially intoxicated, then hit him on the back of the head. They then took the victim out of the hut and, believing him to be dead, rolled him over a cliff to create the appearance of an accident. The victim was in fact still alive at that stage and later died of exposure.

At the trial the defence took a "frame-by-frame" approach to concurrence and argued that there were two acts: the first act was the attack in the hut and whilst the fault element coincided with this act, it was not the cause of death. The second act was the rolling of the victim off the cliff and while this could be said to be the cause of death, it was not accompanied by the fault element. On appeal against conviction, the Privy Council held that it was impossible to divide up what was really a series of acts in this way. Their Lordships preferred to regard the whole of the conduct as one indivisible transaction causing death or as one continuing act. On this reading, the fault element and physical element coincided because the accused possessed the requisite fault element at the time they started the series of acts. Lord Reid stated (at 374):

> There is no doubt that the accused set out to do all these acts in order to achieve their plan, and as parts of their plan: and it is much too refined a ground of judgment to say that, because they were under a misapprehension at one stage and thought that their guilty purpose had been achieved before, in fact, it was achieved, therefore they are to escape the penalties of the law.

This "series of acts" approach to the coincidence of the fault element and *actus reus* has been followed in *R v Le Brun* [1991] 4 All ER 673.[110]

Thabo Meli does not contain a clear statement as to *how* the law overcomes the problem of concurrence, except that the criminal law will not be frustrated by an overly refined application of its general principles. Two later decisions do, however, attempt to provide a firmer conceptual basis for dealing with concurrence problems.

---

110 See also *R v Church* [1966] 1 QB 59; *R v McConnell, McFarland & Holland* [1977] 1 NSWLR 714.

5.2 FAULT ELEMENT IMPOSED UPON A CONTINUING ACT

Another way of approaching concurrence, is to view the physical element as a continuing act. In *Fagan v Metropolitan Commissioner* [1969] 1 QB 439 the accused drove his car (the accused maintained accidentally) onto the foot of a police constable after being told to park his car in a particular space. When the victim told the accused to move the car which was on his foot, the accused said "Fuck you, you can wait" and stopped the engine. The accused eventually moved the car off the victim's foot.

On appeal against a conviction for assault, the accused argued that the act of the wheel moving onto the police constable's foot occurred without the fault element. A majority of the Court of Queen's Bench rejected this argument. James J, with whom Lord Parker LJ agreed, held (at 445) that the relevant act was a continuing one which started when the wheel was driven onto the victim's foot and ended when it was removed. Viewed this way, the fault element could be super-imposed upon the physical element:

> It is not necessary that [the fault element] should be present at the inception of the [physical element]; it can be superimposed upon an existing act. On the other hand the subsequent inception of [the fault element] cannot convert an act which has been completed without [the fault element] into an assault.

The issue of concurrence also arose in *R v Miller* (1983) 2 AC 161. In that case, the accused (a homeless person) fell asleep in a derelict house while smoking and whilst asleep, his bed caught fire. He awoke to find the mattress smouldering, but instead of extinguishing the fire, he arose and moved into another room of the house and went back to sleep. The house then caught fire and damage was caused.

The accused was charged with and convicted of arson, an offence that requires a fault element of intention or recklessness as to damage to property. The problem of concurrence arose because at the time that the initial act of damage occurred, the accused lacked intention or recklessness as to damage. The prosecution relied on the accused's recklessness *after* he had become aware that the bed was on fire.

The English Court of Appeal took a "continuing act" approach to the problem of concurrence, but justified it on the basis of a duty arising from the creation of a dangerous situation. Lord Diplock stated (at 176):

> I see no rational ground for excluding from conduct capable of giving rise to criminal liability, conduct which consists of failing to take measures that lie within one's power to counteract a danger that one has oneself created, if at the time of such conduct one's state of mind is such as constitutes a necessary ingredient of the offence.

The Court of Appeal therefore held that once the accused became aware of the danger he created, a duty arose to take reasonable steps to counteract that danger.

The High Court also took a relaxed approach to concurrence in *Jiminez v The Queen* (1992) 173 CLR 572. This is an important decision because it demonstrates that concurrence problems are not restricted to crimes that contain fault elements. *Jiminez* also raises concerns about voluntariness. The facts were that the accused was driving from the Gold Coast to Sydney with three companions. He took over the driving at 3.30 am and two and a half hours later, he fell asleep at the wheel of the car. The car went off the road and crashed into some trees, killing the front seat passenger. The accused claimed that he had not felt tired before the accident and that he had no warning of the onset of sleep.

The accused was charged and convicted of causing death by culpable driving contrary to s 52A of the *Crimes Act* 1900 (NSW). The physical element of the offence is driving and causing death. There is no fault element required, although the prosecution must prove that the accused was driving the car in a manner dangerous to the public "at the time of the impact".

The principle of concurrence here requires the accused's driving to be both dangerous and cause death. The facts of *Jiminez* posed a problem because *at the time of the impact* that caused death the accused had momentarily fallen asleep and he therefore argued that he was not driving. The High Court affirmed that a person who is asleep is not acting voluntarily and therefore such a person cannot be regarded as driving whilst asleep. However, the majority (at 575-585) solved this problem of concurrence by focusing on the earlier conduct of the accused. The Court examined whether the accused was driving in a manner dangerous to the public *before* he fell asleep. This occasioned examining whether he was so tired that his driving was dangerous.

This approach is an inversion of the *continuing* act approach: the court is looking at *earlier* conduct which is sufficiently culpable to ground criminal responsibility rather than conduct occurring *after* a dangerous event which was the situation in *Miller's* case. In *Jiminez*, the High Court was prepared to relax the strict requirement of concurrence, to bridge the gap where the accused's lapse of consciousness was momentary.

In all, the courts have shown a willingness to construct concurrence by either imposing the fault element over a series of acts, or upon a continuing act. In *Miller* the failure to act after awareness of a dangerous situation was enough to make out criminal responsibility. In *Jiminez*, the High Court was prepared to look at antecedent conduct in order to impose criminal responsibility. All these cases show that the courts are prepared to take a very flexible approach to the problem of concurrence.

For further critical examination of *Jiminez* see JP McCutcheon, "Involuntary Conduct and the Case of the Unconscious 'Driver': Reflections on *Jiminez*" (1997) 21 Crim LJ 71.

6. CONCLUSION

In this chapter, we have considered criminal responsibility in two main ways. The first part of the chapter outlined the principles dealing with *who* may be considered criminally responsible and the difficulties associated with corporate criminal responsibility. The second part dealt with the conditions that need to be fulfilled before an accused can be convicted of a crime. We outlined the traditional view of offences having a physical element and a fault element, before examining those offences that require no fault element.

In Chapter 1, we pointed out that in order to promote certainty and coherence, the criminal law, both as a system of law and as a scholarly discipline, is a "rationalising enterprise": A Norrie, *Crime, Reason and History* (London: Weidenfeld & Nicolson, 1993), p 8. In terms of criminal responsibility, the law is "rationalised" or "legitimised" by relying on the idea of the criminal subject as a rational being and stressing the importance of both fault and physical elements as components of a crime. Examined more closely, however, these notions of individual agency and the importance of moral blameworthiness break down in relation to corporate responsibility and the rise of strict and absolute liability offences. The broadening of criminal offences to encompass corporate liability and offences displacing the fault element cannot be explained by reliance on traditional notions alone. This broadening of criminal offences can be seen as a dynamic process. It can partially be explained as a response to the rise in work-related deaths, the occurrence of major disasters caused by corporate negligence and the growth of statutory offences in areas such as public health and safety.

Even if a person can be considered criminally responsible, it may be that circumstances existed in which the person's conduct can be considered justified or excusable. In the next three chapters, we turn to an examination of criminal defences.

PART II

Justifications and Excuses

4

Mental State Defences

> All my faults perchance
> thou knowest,
> All my madness none can know

Lord Byron, "Fare Thee Well",
Stanza 12 in WH Auden and NH Pearson (eds),
Romantic Poets
(New York: The Viking Press, 1973), p 259

1. INTRODUCTION

The concept of criminal responsibility is based on the notion that individuals possess the capacity to make rational choices in performing or refraining from performing acts. A person will be considered to be criminally responsible for a criminal act which was made voluntarily and intentionally and where the individual understood the significance of the act. However, some forms of mental impairment may exculpate an individual from criminal responsibility. For example, a person suffering from a severe form of mental illness may be found not guilty because of mental impairment and be liable to a supervision order on the basis that he or she could not understand the significance of the act. Further, if an individual commits a crime whilst in a state of automatism, he or she may be acquitted on the basis that the act was unwilled or involuntary. It has also been accepted that severe intoxication may divorce the will from the movements of the body so that they are truly involuntary or, perhaps more frequently, prevent the formation of the requisite intention for the crime charged.

The rules in relation to the burden of proof and who may raise evidence of mental impairment differ in relation to automatism, the defence of mental impairment and intoxication. There is some overlap between these three categories of mental impairment and this should be kept in mind when reading the following sections.

2. MENTAL IMPAIRMENT

In the criminal law, the notion that children and the insane lack the ability to reason has long been found in laws excusing them from responsibility for criminal acts. This notion may be found in Roman law through Justinian's codification in the 6th century that an "infant or a madman who kills a man is not liable under the *lex cornelia*, the one being protected by the innocence of his intent, the other excused by the misfortune of his condition".[1] The same conclusion was reached in Henrici de Bracton's first systematic treatise on the laws and customs of England when he stated that the "lack of reason in committing the act" excused the madman and "the innocence of design" protected the infant from the boundaries of the criminal law.[2]

The modern conception of the defence of mental impairment follows this tradition in that it serves to exculpate an accused from criminal responsibility because of the accused's inability to know the nature and quality of the conduct or that the conduct was wrong. In some jurisdictions, there is an added component of the mental impairment causing an inability to control one's conduct. Most jurisdictions follow the rules established in *M' Naghten* (1843) 8 ER 718 at 722. Whilst the name of the defence differs across jurisdictions, we will use the term "defence of mental impairment" as this is the term used by the Model Criminal Code Officers Committee.

The *M' Naghten Rules* arose out of the controversy surrounding the 19th century case of Daniel M'Naghten. M'Naghten was tried for the murder of Edward Drummond, the private secretary of the Prime Minister of England, Sir Robert Peel. Evidence was led to show that M'Naghten suffered from the delusion that he was being persecuted by "the Tories" and that in order to end this persecution, he shot and killed Drummond whom he supposedly mistook for Peel. Lord Tindal CJ instructed the jury that it could return a verdict of not guilty on the ground of insanity if it was of the opinion that the accused did not have the use of his understanding so as not to know that he was doing a wrong or wicked act.

M'Naghten was accordingly found not guilty on the ground of insanity by the jury. This led to a detailed debate that took place in the House of Lords concerning the question of whether or not the rules of law governing the defence of insanity were satisfactory. In June 1843, certain questions were placed before the common law judges on the existing law of insanity, with particular reference to the subject of delusions.

The Spelling of M'Naghten

Daniel M'Naghten gave his name to the case that resulted in the traditional rules concerning the defence of mental impairment. But what is the correct spelling of his name? *M'Naghten* is the customary spelling in the English and American law reports, but other versions have emerged such as M'Naughten, McNaughton, Macnaghten and even the original Gaelic Mhicneachdain. For a discussion of the correct spelling and to examine a sample signature from the man himself, see BL Diamond "On the Spelling of Daniel M'Naghten's Name" in D West and A Walk (eds), *Daniel McNaughton* [sic]: *His Trial and the Aftermath* (Kent: Gaskell Books, 1977), pp 86-90.

---

1 T Mommsen, P Krueger and A Watson (eds and translators), *The Digest of Justinian* (Pennsylvania: University of Pennsylvania Press, 1985) Book Forty-Eight, 8.12.

2 Henrici de Bracton, *De Legibus et Consuetudinibus Angliae* 135b quoted in FB Sayre, "*Mens Rea*" (1932) *Harvard Law Review* 974 at 985-986.

With one dissent, the judges agreed on the answers and these have become known as the *M' Naghten Rules*. The most well-known rule states:

> [T]o establish a defence on the ground of insanity, it must be clearly proved that, at the time of the committing of the act, the party accused was labouring under such defect of reason, from disease of the mind, as not to know the nature and quality of the act he [or she] was doing; or, if he [or she] did know it, that he [or she] did not know he [or she] was doing what was wrong.[3]

Many authors have criticised the emphasis in the *M' Naghten Rules* on cognitive factors (the effect on knowledge), rather than emotional and volitional factors (the effect on the ability to control conduct) which leads to the traditional insanity defence being very limited in its scope.[4] The Australian jurisdictions base the current defence of mental impairment on the *M' Naghten Rules*, but some broaden the scope of the defence by including a volitional component. The following table summarises the elements of the defence across Australian jurisdictions.

TABLE 1:

Elements of the Defence of Mental Impairment

JURISDICTION AND RELEVANT LAW	NAME OF DEFENCE	COMPONENTS OF MENTAL STATE	NATURE AND QUALITY OF CONDUCT	KNOWLEDGE THAT CONDUCT IS WRONG	INABILITY TO CONTROL CONDUCT
CTH *Criminal Code Act* 1995 (*M' Naghten Rules* apply until this Act is brought into force)	mental impairment	senility, intellectual disability, mental illness, brain damage, severe personality disorder	did not know the nature and quality of the conduct	did not know that the conduct was wrong	unable to control the conduct
	s 7.3(1)	s 7.3(8)	s 7.3(1)(a)	s 7.3(1)(b)	s 7.3(1)(c)
ACT *Crimes Act* 1900	mental impairment	mental dysfunction defined as a disturbance or defect, to a substantially disabling degree, of perceptual interpretation, comprehension, reasoning, learning, judgment, memory, motivation or emotion	incapable of knowing what he or she was doing	incapable of understanding that what he or she was doing was wrong	—
	s 428N(1)	s 428B	s 428N(1)(a)	s 428N(1)(b)	

---

3   *M' Naghten's case* (1843) 10 Cl and Fin 200 at 210; 8 ER 718 at 722.

4   See, for example, SJ Brakel, J Parry and BA Weiner, *The Mentally Disabled and the Law* (3rd ed, Chicago: American Bar Foundation, 1985), p 710; H Fingarette, *The Meaning of Criminal Insanity* (Berkeley: University of California Press, 1972), p 144; A Goldstein, *The Insanity Defense* (New Haven: Yale University Press, 1967), pp 47-49; D Hermann, *The Insanity Defense* (Springfield: CC Thomas, 1983), pp 37, 138; F McAuley, *Insanity, Psychiatry and Criminal Responsibility* (Dublin: The Round Hall Press, 1993), p 23.

Table 1 continued

JURISDICTION AND RELEVANT LAW	NAME OF DEFENCE	COMPONENTS OF MENTAL STATE	NATURE AND QUALITY OF CONDUCT	KNOWLEDGE THAT CONDUCT IS WRONG	INABILITY TO CONTROL CONDUCT
NSW Common law M' Naghten Rules Mental Health (Criminal Procedure) Act 1990	mental illness s 25	defect of reason caused by a disease of the mind	did not know the nature and quality of the act he or she was doing	did not know that what he or she was doing was wrong	–
NT Criminal Code	insanity s 35	abnormality of mind arising from a condition of arrested or retarded development of mind or inherent causes or induced by disease, illness or injury ss 35(1) and 1	capacity to understand what he or she was doing s 35(1)	capacity to know that he or she ought not do the act, make the omission or cause the event s 35(1)	capacity to control his or her actions s 35(1)
QLD Criminal Code	insanity s 27	mental disease or natural mental infirmity s 27(1)	capacity to understand what the person is doing s 27(1)	capacity to know that the person ought not to do the act or make the omission s 27(1)	capacity to control the person's actions s 27(1)
SA Criminal Law Consolidation Act 1935	mental incompetence ss 269C and 269E	mental impairment: includes: mental illness, intellectual disability or a disability or impairment of the mind resulting from senility s 269A(1)	does not know the nature and quality of the conduct s 269C(a)	does not know that the conduct is wrong s 269C(b)	is unable to control the conduct s 269C(c)
TAS Criminal Code	insanity s 16	mental disease s 16(1)	incapable of understanding the physical character of the act or omission s 16(1)(a)(i)	incapable of knowing that the act or omission was one that he or she ought not to do or make s 16(1)(a)(ii)	the act or omission was done or made under an impulse which he or she was in substance deprived of any power to resist s 16(1)(b)

Table 1 continued

JURISDICTION AND RELEVANT LAW	NAME OF DEFENCE	COMPONENTS OF MENTAL STATE	NATURE AND QUALITY OF CONDUCT	KNOWLEDGE THAT CONDUCT IS WRONG	INABILITY TO CONTROL CONDUCT
VIC *Crimes (Mental Impairment and Fitness to be Tried) Act 1997*	mental impairment	no definition	did not know the nature and quality of the conduct	did not know that the conduct was wrong	—
	s 20	s 20(1)(a)	s 20(1)(b)		
WA *Criminal Code*	insanity	unsoundness of mind; state of mental impairment meaning intellectual disability, mental illness, brain damage or senility	capacity to understand what he or she is doing	capacity to know that he or she ought not to do the act or make the omission	capacity to control his or her actions
	s 27	ss 27, 1	s 27	s 27	

2.1 DEFINING MENTAL IMPAIRMENT

Just what conditions will constitute mental impairment for the purposes of this defence varies from jurisdiction to jurisdiction. The following section outlines some of the terms used and the conditions that have been held to fall within them. It should be noted that the Victorian legislation uses the term "mental impairment" without any definition, which may leave the door open to a wide interpretation of the term. See further B McSherry, "Mental Impairment and Criminal Responsibility: Recent Australian Legislative Reforms" (1999) 23 Crim LJ 135.

DISEASE OF THE MIND

The traditional *M' Naghten Rules* referred to a "defect of reason" arising from a "disease of the mind". This is still followed in New South Wales. In Queensland and Tasmania, the term "mental disease" is used. This is a problematic term in that it has no medical relevance and is purely a legal construct. Under the old common law, conditions that have been held to fall within the insanity defence include psychotic disorders,[5] cerebral arteriosclerosis,[6] epilepsy,[7] and hyperglycaemia.[8]

---

5   "[T]he major mental diseases, which the doctors call psychoses, such as schizophrenia, are clearly diseases of the mind": *Bratty v Attorney-General for Northern Ireland* [1963] AC 386 at 412 per Lord Denning.

6   *R v Kemp* [1957] 1 QB 399.

7   *R v Cottle* [1958] NZLR 999; *R v Sullivan* [1984] AC 156; *R v Foy* [1960] Qd R 225 (CA Qld); *R v Mursic* [1980] Qd R 482 (CA Qld); *R v Meddings* [1966] VR 306; *Youssef* (1990) 50 A Crim R 1 (CCA NSW).

8   *R v Hennessy* [1989] 1 WLR 287.

The common thread amongst these conditions is that they are seen as arising from an *internal* rather than an external cause. Martin JA explained this internal/external distinction in the Canadian case of *R v Rabey* (1977) 37 CCC (2d) 461 as follows (at 477):

> In general, the distinction to be drawn is between a malfunctioning of the mind arising from some cause that is primarily internal to the accused, having its source in his [or her] psychological or emotional make-up, or in some organic pathology, as opposed to a malfunctioning of the mind which is the transient effect produced by some specific external factor such as, for example, concussion.

The problems in distinguishing between an internal malfunctioning of the mind and a condition caused by external factors will be discussed in the section dealing with automatism: see 3.4 'Sane and Insane Automatism', p 229.

There have been some statements that a disease of the mind simply means mental illness. In *R v Radford* (1985) 42 SASR 266, King CJ of the Supreme Court of South Australia stated (at 274):

> The expression "disease of the mind" is synonymous, in my view, with "mental illness" ... The essential notion appears to be that in order to constitute insanity in the eyes of the law, the malfunction of the mental faculties called "defect of reason" in the *M' Naghten rules*, must result from an underlying pathological infirmity of the mind, be it of long or short duration and be it permanent or temporary, which can be properly termed mental illness, as distinct from the reaction of a healthy mind to extraordinary external stimuli.

This statement was accepted by the members of the High Court in *R v Falconer* (1990) 171 CLR 30: at 53 per Mason CJ, Brennan and McHugh JJ, at 60 per Deane and Dawson JJ, at 85 per Gaudron J.

What, however, is mental illness? The next section explores this further.

MENTAL ILLNESS

According to *The Oxford Textbook of Psychiatry* "most psychiatrists begin by separating mental handicap and personality disorder from mental illness ... they diagnose mental illness if there are delusions, hallucinations, severe alterations of mood, or other major disturbances of psychological functions. In practice, most psychiatrists allocate psychiatric disorders to diagnostic categories such as schizophrenia, affective disorders, organic mental states, and others; by convention, they agree to group these diagnostic categories together under the rubric mental illness": M Gelder, D Gath, R Mayou and P Cowen, *The Oxford Textbook of Psychiatry* (3rd ed, Oxford: Oxford University Press, 1996), p 57.

The modern psychiatric conception of mental illness views it as "a pervasive inability to engage reality: as a failure of 'reality testing' to use the term of art favoured by psychiatrists": F McAuley, *Insanity, Psychiatry and Criminal Responsibility* (Dublin: The Round Hall Press, 1993), p 35. This is why psychotic disorders which involve the inability to engage reality are generally distinguished from neurotic and personality disorders.

The term "mental illness" is specifically included in s 269A(1) of the *Criminal Law Consolidation Act* 1935 (SA) and in the Model Criminal Code Officers Committee's conception of mental impairment: *Criminal Code Act* 1995 (Cth), s 7.3(1). The *Criminal Code* (WA) uses the term "a state of mental impairment" which is defined in s 1 as meaning "intellectual disability, mental illness, brain damage or senility". The definitions of "mental illness" in these provisions, however, follow along the traditional legal rather than psychiatric conception of the term. Section 7.3(9) of the *Criminal Code Act* 1995 (Cth) relies on King CJ's words in *Radford's* case in defining mental illness as "an underlying pathological infirmity of the mind, whether of long or short duration and whether permanent or temporary, but does not include a condition that results from the reaction of a healthy mind to extraordinary external stimuli". Section 7.3(9) also goes on to state that "such a condition may be evidence of a mental illness if it involves some abnormality and is prone to recur".[9]

The vagueness of the legal concept of "underlying pathological infirmity of mind" has perhaps been necessary because the courts have traditionally been influenced by policy rather than medical reasons in determining which mental conditions fall within the defence of mental impairment: B McSherry, "Defining What is a 'Disease of the Mind': The Untenability of Current Legal Interpretations" (1993) 1 *Journal of Law and Medicine* 76. However, it is possible to have a more meaningful conception of what should fall within the scope of mental impairment.

Section 428N(1) of the *Crimes Act* 1900 (ACT) perhaps comes closest to the psychiatric conception of mental illness. This section uses the term "mental dysfunction" which is further defined in s 428B as "a disturbance or defect, to a substantially disabling degree, of perceptual interpretation, comprehension, reasoning, learning, judgment, memory, motivation or emotion". This appears to be a broad definition, but it is flexible enough to accord with changing medical conceptions of mental disorders. It is also perhaps of more guidance to medical experts than the concept of "an underlying pathological infirmity of mind".

ABNORMALITY OF MIND

Section 35 of the *Criminal Code* (NT) refers to the term "abnormality of mind". That term is defined in s 1 as an "abnormality of mind arising from a condition of arrested or retarded development of mind or inherent causes or induced by disease, illness or injury". This is the same definition as for the defence of diminished responsibility (see Chapter 5, p 276) and may potentially go further than traditional conceptions of "a disease of the mind" under the common law. For example, concussion arising from an injury such as a blow to the head may fall within an abnormality of mind under this definition, whereas this has been excluded from the traditional insanity defence: see the discussion of sane automatism, below at 3.4 'Sane and Insane Automatism', p 229.

Conditions that have fallen within the scope of an abnormality of mind for the purpose of the defence of diminished responsibility have traditionally been much broader than those accepted for the defence of mental impairment: see Ch 5, pp 276ff. The latter should only be available to those who experience a failure in "reality testing" and the term "abnormality of mind" should be read down accordingly.

---

9   The definition of "mental illness" in South Australia is similar: *Criminal Law Consolidation Act* 1935 (SA), s 269A(1). It does not, however, mention recurrence. The Western Australian definition of mental illness in s 1 of the *Criminal Code* simply repeats King CJ's definition without mentioning an abnormality of mind and recurrence.

INTELLECTUAL DISABILITY AND DEMENTIA

The *Diagnostic and Statistical Manual of Mental Disorders*[10] defines "mental retardation" the onset of which must occur before the age of 18, as "significantly subaverage general intellectual functioning that is accompanied by significant limitations in adaptive functioning in at least two of the following skill areas: communication, self-care, home living, social/interpersonal skills, use of community resources, self-direction, functional academic skills, work, leisure, health, and safety".[11]

A number of disorders are classed within the general term "dementia" in the *Diagnostic and Statistical Manual of Mental Disorders*. They are generally "characterized by the development of multiple cognitive deficits (including memory impairment) that are due to the direct physiological effects of a general medical condition, to the persisting effects of a substance, or to multiple etiologies (eg, the combined effects of cerebrovascular disease and Alzheimer's disease)".[12]

When the *M' Naghten Rules* were formulated, there is some reason to believe that intellectual disabilities and dementia were regarded as a form of insanity and therefore the defence was intended to encompass them.[13] Certain jurisdictions refer to terms that appear to encompass these conditions.

Section 269A(1) of the *Criminal Law Consolidation Act* 1935 (SA) and s 1 of the *Criminal Code* (WA) include intellectual disability within their definition of "mental impairment". The South Australian definition also includes a "disability or impairment of the mind resulting from senility and the Western Australian definition refers to "brain damage or senility". Section 27(1) of the *Criminal Code* (Qld) refers to "natural mental infirmity" and Sch 1 s 1 of the *Criminal Code* (NT) refers to an abnormality of mind "arising from a condition of arrested or retarded development of mind" both of which appear to cover the same conditions. Section 7.3(1) of the *Criminal Code Act* 1995 (Cth) also refers to senility, intellectual disability and brain damage as falling within the definition of mental impairment.

Although intellectual disability and dementia must be distinguished from mental illness in that they concern restrictions in physical and cognitive abilities, rather than a failure in reality testing, they may affect a person's ability to know what he or she is doing is wrong and therefore it is important that these conditions are included within the concept of mental impairment. For the purpose of law reform "dementia" is probably a better term than "senility" because the latter is not a medical term and the former covers dementia due to head trauma, so that "brain damage" is encompassed.

---

10 American Psychiatric Association, *Diagnostic and Statistical Manual of Mental Disorders* (4th ed, Washington, DC: APA, 1994).

11 American Psychiatric Association, *Diagnostic and Statistical Manual of Mental Disorders* (4th ed, Washington, DC: APA, 1994), p 39.

12 American Psychiatric Association, *Diagnostic and Statistical Manual of Mental Disorders* (4th ed, Washington, DC: APA, 1994), p 133.

13 S Hayes and G Craddock, *Simply Criminal* (2nd ed, Sydney: Federation Press, 1992), pp 140-141; G Williams, *Criminal Law: The General Part* (2nd ed, London: Stevens & Sons, 1961), p 447; J Clemens and J Bennett, "Historical Notes on the Law of Mental Illness in New South Wales" (1962) 4 *Sydney Law Review* 49 at 53.

PERSONALITY DISORDERS

Section 7.3(1) of the *Criminal Code Act* 1995 (Cth) includes "severe personality disorder" within its definition of mental impairment. This inclusion is problematic and it is interesting to note that the South Australian legislature omitted this term from its proposed defence after intensive lobbying. The term "personality disorder" is very loose and what can be considered a "severe" personality disorder is unclear. The *Diagnostic and Statistical Manual of Mental Disorders*[14] refers to a number of personality disorders including "avoidant", "dependent" and "histrionic" personality disorders. Should severe manifestations of such disorders serve to excuse individuals from criminal responsibility? The term "antisocial personality disorder" and "psychopath" are often used as loose labels in order to diagnose an extremely broad range of people who have exhibited behaviour that may be classified as antisocial.[15] The category of antisocial personality disorder as set out in various editions of the *Diagnostic and Statistical Manual of Mental Disorders* has been criticised as contributing to an overdiagnosis of the disorder in criminal and forensic settings because it over-emphasises overt criminal acts to the neglect of personality traits.[16] It has been stated that the diagnosis of psychopathic disorder has is "a 'pseudo-diagnosis' used just to get patients through the customs-barrier of the courts": J Gunn and P Taylor (eds), *Forensic Psychiatry: Clinical, Legal and Ethical Issues* (Oxford: Butterworth-Heinemann, 1993), p 402; see also M Cavadino, "Death to the Psychopath" (1998) 9(1) *Journal of Forensic Psychiatry* 5.

Perhaps more importantly, the weight of psychiatric opinion appears to be that antisocial personality disorder, the disorder most "linked" to criminal conduct, should not be equated with mental illness or mental impairment. As stated earlier, modern psychiatrists see mental illness as leading to a failure in "reality testing". Those with antisocial personality disorders have no problem dealing with reality. Robert Hart and Stephen Hare state that antisocial personality disorder is either unassociated with, or negatively associated with, most Axis 1 Clinical Disorders in the *Diagnostic and Statistical Manual of Mental Disorders*.[17] Personality disorders are generally viewed in a separate category to neurotic or psychotic disorders because the former are manifested by a lifelong pattern of deviant behaviour as regards cultural norms rather than mental or emotional symptoms. It is because those with antisocial personality disorders are able to "reason", that a series of Australian cases suggest that antisocial personality disorder cannot be put forward as an independent basis for the defence of mental impairment.[18]

---

14 American Psychiatric Association, *Diagnostic and Statistical Manual of Mental Disorders* (4th ed, Washington: APA, 1994).

15 There have, however, been attempts to delineate what is meant by these terms: RD Hare, *The Hare Psychopathy Checklist — Revised* (Toronto: Multi-Health Systems, 1991); B Dolan and J Coid, *Psychopathic and Antisocial Personality Disorders: Treatment and Research Issues* (London: Gaskell/Royal College of Psychiatrists, 1993).

16 For an overview of such criticisms, see TA Widiger and EM Corbett, "Antisocial Personality Disorder" in WJ Livesey (ed), *The DSM-IV Personality Disorders* (New York: Guildford Press, 1995), p 103; RD Hare, "Comparison of Procedures for the Assessment of Psychopathy" (1985) 53 *Journal of Consulting and Clinical Psychology* 7; RD Hare, SD Hart and TJ Harpur, "Psychopathy and the DSM-IV Criteria for Antisocial Personality Disorder" (1991) 100(3) *Journal of Abnormal Psychology* 391.

17 RD Hare and SD Hart, "Psychopathy, Mental Disorder and Crime" in S Hodgins (ed), *Mental Disorder and Crime* (Newbury Park, CA: Sage Publications, 1993), p 104.

18 *Willgoss v The Queen* (1960) 105 CLR 295; *Jeffrey v The Queen* [1982] Tas R 199; *Hodges* (1985) 19 A Crim R 129.

It is also paradoxical to allow the antisocial record of an accused to be used as an argument in his or her favour: B Wootton, *Social Science and Social Pathology* (London: Allen & Unwin, 1959), pp 249ff, 333-334. The concept of excusing an accused of an offence by virtue of his or her background is one that has not generally been accepted at law. This is because of the dominance of "free-will" as a basis for explaining crime rather than "determinism": see Ch 1, pp 29ff.

For these reasons, it is of grave concern that the Model Criminal Code Officers Committee's conception of mental impairment has been so broadened as to excuse those suffering from severe personality disorders from criminal responsibility.

2.2 KNOWLEDGE AND UNDERSTANDING

To establish the defence of mental impairment, it must be proved that the mental impairment had the effect that the accused did not *know* or, in the Code jurisdictions, *understand* the nature and quality of the conduct or that the conduct was wrong. There are two ways in which the word "know" may be interpreted. It may mean to know in a "verbalistic" sense: that is, in a sense akin to learning a mathematical formula by rote. The second interpretation of "know" connotes some deeper form of understanding as in the appreciation of the effect of conduct upon other people. The actual use of the term "understanding" rather than "know" in the Code jurisdictions reflects this idea of a deeper form of appreciation.

In *Willgoss v The Queen* (1960) 105 CLR 295 however, the High Court held that a mere intellectual apprehension of the wrongness of the act amounts to knowledge under the *M' Naghten Rules*. The Court rejected an argument to the effect that "knowledge" requires a moral appreciation of the effect of conduct. The High Court's decision in *Willgoss* therefore follows the narrow interpretation of the verb "to know". Part of the rationale behind this decision may lie in the fact that the Court did not wish to excuse a person with an antisocial personality disorder from criminal responsibility. If knowledge is said to require a moral appreciation of the effect of an act on others, a person with an antisocial personality disorder could be viewed as not having this requisite degree of knowledge, resulting in him or her being found not guilty because of mental impairment.

There therefore appears to be some discrepancy between the Code and other jurisdictions in relation to the scope of the effect of the mental impairment on the accused's cognitive capacities.

2.3 NATURE AND QUALITY OF CONDUCT

The first alternative for the establishment of the defence of mental impairment in New South Wales, South Australia, Victoria and at a Federal level is to show that the accused's mental impairment had the effect that he or she did not know the nature and quality of the conduct. This is based on the first limb of the *M' Naghten Rules* which has rarely been used.

There is some ambiguity in the case law as to the meaning of the words "nature and quality". The English Court of Criminal Appeal in *R v Codere* (1916) 12 Cr App R 21 and a line of Canadian cases have held that "nature and quality" refers only to the physical character of the conduct.[19] However,

---

19   *R v Barnier* (1980) 51 CCC (2d) 193; [1980] 1 SCR 1124; 13 CR (3d) 129; *R v Kjeldsen* (1981) 24 CR (3d) 289; 64 CCC (2d) 161; *R v Abbey* (1982) 68 CCC (2d) 394; *R v Kirkby* (1985) 21 CCC (3d) 31; *R v Landry* (1991) 2 CR (4th) 268; 62 CCC (3d) 117.

other cases suggest that "nature and quality" not only refers to the physical character of the conduct, but also to the *significance* of the conduct itself. For example, the High Court in *Willgoss v The Queen* (1960) 105 CLR 295 (at 300) states that the nature and quality of the conduct "refers to the physical character of the act, in this case, a capacity to know or understand the significance of the act of killing". Similarly, in the Canadian case of *Cooper v The Queen* (1979) 51 CCC (2d) 129 Dickson J stated (at 145) that the test for appreciating the nature and quality of the conduct involved the "estimation and understanding of the consequences of the act".

It would seem that if the first, narrower interpretation of the words "nature and quality" hold sway, a smaller group of people will be afforded the defence of mental impairment. This proposition is exemplified by the English case of *R v Dickie* [1984] 3 All ER 173 in which the accused was charged with arson. The accused had set fire to a wastepaper basket and sat watching a blank television screen while the fire burned the carpet and smoke filled the room. There was evidence that he was in the manic phase of manic-depressive psychosis and that he was not aware of the dangerousness of his conduct. The court found that the accused did know the nature and quality of his actions because he knew he was setting fire to a wastepaper basket; the fact that his psychosis prevented him from appreciating the dangerousness of his conduct was deemed irrelevant.

The Code jurisdictions and the Australian Capital Territory avoid using the words "nature and quality" and instead refer to the capacity to understand what the accused is doing. This appears to follow the broader approach to the question set out in *Willgoss*. Section 16(1)(a)(i) of the *Criminal Code* (Tas) refers to the capacity to understand the "physical character of the act or omission". This may reflect the narrower approach set out in *Codere*.

In practice, this branch of the defence is rarely used, so that this discussion is largely semantic. Most cases of mental impairment fall within the following branch.

2.4 WRONG

The second alternative for the establishment of the defence of mental impairment is to show that the accused did not know that the conduct was wrong or, in the Code jurisdictions, that he or she ought not do the act or omission. Again, this is based upon the *M'Naghten Rules* and, in particular, Dixon J's interpretation of the term "wrong" in *R v Porter* (1933) 55 CLR 182 (at 190):[20]

> What is meant by wrong is wrong having regard to the everyday standards of reasonable people ...
>
> [T]he main question ... is whether ... [the accused] was disabled from knowing that it was a wrong act to commit in the sense that ordinary reasonable [people] understand right and wrong and that he [or she] was disabled from considering with some degree of composure and reason what he [or she] was doing and its wrongness.

In s 7.3(1)(b) of the *Criminal Code Act* 1995 (Cth) and s 20(1)(b) of the *Crimes (Mental Impairment and Unfitness to be Tried) Act* 1997 (Vic), these words have now been summarised to read "he or she could not reason with a moderate degree of sense and composure about whether the conduct, as perceived by reasonable people, was wrong".

---

20 This view was expressly approved in *Stapleton v the Queen* (1952) 86 CLR 358.

This interpretation of "wrong" makes it clear that there is more than just a legal component to the term. It is significant in fact situations like that of *R v Hadfield* (1800) 27 St Tr 1281. In that case, the accused attempted to kill King George III. The accused was motivated by the belief that he (Hadfield) was destined, by dying, to save the world. He knew that killing was contrary to law and he therefore shot at the king in order to be hanged. Knowledge of the illegality of the act was his very reason for doing it. Under Dixon J's interpretation of the word "wrong", a person in Hadfield's position would be found not criminally responsible, whereas if it only means contrary to law, a person in Hadfield's position would not be afforded a defence of mental impairment.

There will be little difficulty in most instances as what is legally wrong will be perceived as morally wrong. However, there may be problems in attempting to measure popular morality in relation to offences such as abortion (see Ch 10, p 518) or euthanasia: see Ch 10, pp 465ff; see generally, Ch 1, pp 51ff. The Canadian authors, Tollefson and Starkman in their book *Mental Disorder in Criminal Proceedings* (Toronto: Carswell, 1993), p 31, have been particularly critical of this notion of the perception of reasonable people:

> How is the appropriate moral standard to be proved in a socially diverse country ...? Will it
> be necessary for the Crown and the defence to conduct polls to determine what people
> think is morally wrong? Is the court going to determine wrong in accordance with the view
> of the majority ... or may the view of a significant minority also be used as the basis for
> determining what is "morally wrong"?

There is also no guidance in the legislation or case law as to what is meant by the accused's inability to "reason with a moderate degree of sense and composure". This seems to echo the "defect of reason" requirement in the *M' Naghten Rules* and it would seem that this is a matter which would be left to the jury to decide as a matter of fact after hearing expert evidence.

2.5 CAPACITY TO CONTROL CONDUCT

The Code jurisdictions and now, South Australia, include a third alternative to the establishment of the defence of mental impairment. Legislation in these jurisdictions refers to the capacity to control the accused's conduct or actions. Section 16(1)(b) of the *Criminal Code* (Tas) is a little different in referring to whether or not the act or omission was done or made "under an impulse which he or she was in substance deprived of any power to resist". The Model Criminal Code Officers Committee has also included a "volitional" component to its model defence: *Criminal Code Act* 1995 (Cth), s 7.3(1)(c).

There have been two ways in which the lack of capacity to control one's conduct can be interpreted. One way is to see it as broadening the defence considerably so that it covers those who know that they ought not do the act but are unable to resist an impulse to act. This was referred to by McMillan J in *R v Moore* (1908) 10 WALR 64 (at 66) as follows:

> This section [*Criminal Code* (WA), s 27] deals with the defence of insanity, and it shows in
> what cases persons who would otherwise be responsible for their acts are free from
> responsibility because they are insane. It treats as insane certain persons who under the old

law would not have been treated as insane. It accepts the medical theory of uncontrollable impulse, and treats people who are insane to the extent that they have not the capacity to control their actions, whether from mental disease or natural mental infirmity, as being persons who are irresponsible.

This notion of "uncontrollable impulse" is reflected in the wording of the Tasmanian provision (*Criminal Code* (Tas), s 16) and is also reflected in *Wray v The King* (1930) 33 WALR 67 (at 68-69).

In the other jurisdictions that do not include a separate volitional component, the lack of capacity to control conduct can be taken into account in assessing whether or not the accused knew that the conduct was wrong. As Dixon J explained in *Sodeman v The Queen* (1952) 86 CLR 358 (at 215):

[I]t is important to bear steadily in mind that if through disorder of the faculties a prisoner is incapable of controlling his [or her] relevant acts, this may afford the strongest reason for supposing that he [or she] is incapable of forming a judgment that they are wrong, and in some cases even of understanding their nature.

Mason CJ, Brennan and McHugh JJ in *R v Falconer* (1990) 171 CLR 30 appear to have interpreted the volitional component quite differently to the approach in *Moore* and the common law approach. They took the question of the capacity to control conduct as concerning the capacity to perform a voluntary act. They stated (at 40-41):

Because we assume that a person who is apparently conscious has the capacity to control his [or her] actions, we draw an inference that the act is done by choice ... The presumption that the acts of a person, apparently conscious, are willed or voluntary is an inference of fact and, as a matter of fact, there must be good grounds for refusing to draw the inference. Generally speaking, grounds for refusing to draw the inference appear only when there are grounds for believing that the actor is unable to control his [or her] actions.

If this is the case, the third limb of the defence of mental impairment is redundant, as the question of voluntariness falls within the separate area of automatism. It would seem that if the third limb is to have any relevance at all, the approach in *Moore* and *Wray* should hold sway.

In practice, the volitional arm of the defence of mental impairment has been used very rarely in the Australian jurisdictions in which it exists. In fact, of the few reported cases in which the accused applied for leave to appeal against conviction on the basis that he was unable to control his conduct, the appeal court concerned has invariably dismissed the appeal.[21] Only in one reported case was an appeal against conviction upheld and that was on the basis of uncontradicted medical evidence that the accused was suffering from dementia praecox, which deprived him of the capacity to control his actions: *Wray v The King* (1930) 33 WALR 67.

The rarity of the use of the volitional component may be explained in part because the accused's lack of capacity to control his or her actions must be a result of a "mental disease" or the like, which has not in the past been interpreted to include personality or impulse-control disorders.

---

21   *R v Moore* (1908) 10 WAR 64; *Hitchens v The Queen* [1962] Tas SR 35; *O' Neill v The Queen* [1976] Tas SR 66; *Jeffrey v The Queen* [1982] Tas R 199.

Where the issue has been raised, its lack of success may be due to the fact that "it might be perceived as an 'easy out' for persons who are seeking an excuse for yielding to temptation": EA Tollefson and B Starkman, *Mental Disorder in Criminal Proceedings* (Toronto: Carswell, 1993), p 41.

There are a number of specific criticisms that may be aimed at excusing persons from criminal responsibility on the basis of loss of control.

First, the problem with loss of control tests in general is that it is impossible to devise an objectively verifiable test to determine when an accused could not control his or her conduct and when he or she would not: AS Goldstein, *The Insanity Defense* (New Haven, CT: Yale University Press, 1967), pp 67-68. Certainly it can be argued that the question raised is really not so different from the questions of degree that arise throughout the law. It is impossible to draw absolute lines when considering other legal concepts such as "intention" or "knowledge" or "negligence", or determining "loss of control" for provocation.

However, there remains a further problem with loss of control tests and that is that such tests are based on an abandoned system of faculty psychology which divided the mind into separate and unrelated compartments. According to James Chaplin's *Dictionary of Psychology* (2nd ed, New York: Dell, 1982) "faculty psychology" refers to "the discredited doctrine that the mind is constituted of a number of powers or agencies, such as intellect, will, judgment and attentiveness, which produce mental activities": p 174. While introductory psychology texts may still separate "cognition" from "emotion",[22] much contemporary research is based on an holistic model that explores the interaction between feelings and thought processes. For example, one textbook speaks of the "three components of emotion — cognitive, physiological, and behavioral"[23] and another refers to the interconnections between emotion and cognition.[24] According to the holistic model, there can be no serious impairment of one mental function without some form of impairment of the others. For example, modern psychological research implies that in "complex emotional experiences, such as pride, disappointment, jealousy, or contempt, cognitive appraisal must play a role": RL Atkinson, RC Atkinson, EE Smith and DJ Bern, *Introduction to Psychology* (10th ed, Fort Worth: Harcourt Brace Jovanovich, 1990), p 412.

The law relating to mental impairment stems from the notion that an individual must possess the ability to reason about the significance of conduct in order for the criminal law to apply. Loss of control tests assume that a person can know what he or she is doing is wrong, yet be unable to control his or her actions. In reality, such tests assume that cognition remains completely unaffected, and this contradicts not only the holistic standpoint of modern psychology but also the view that the ability to reason plays an essential part in controlling conduct. Jerome Hall writes in his article "Mental Disease and Criminal Responsibility" (1958) 33 *Indiana Law Journal* 212 at 223:

---

22 For example, C Wade and C Tarris, *Psychology* (4th ed, New York: Harper Collins, 1996); H Gleitman, *Psychology* (4th ed, New York: W W Norton & Company, 1995); P Gray, *Psychology* (2nd ed, New York: Worth Publishers, 1994); M Matlin, *Psychology* (Fort Worth: Harcourt Brace College Publishers, 1992); R Atkinson, R Atkinson, E Smith and D Bern, *Introduction to Psychology* (10th ed, Fort Worth: Harcourt Brace Jovanovich, 1990).

23 M Matlin, *Psychology* (Fort Worth: Harcourt Brace College Publishers, 1992), p 402.

24 C Wade and C Tarris, *Psychology* (4th ed, New York: HarperCollins, 1996), pp 389-390.

What the proponents of "irresistible impulse" are in effect telling us is that the most distinctive and potent function on earth — human understanding in its full amplitude — can be normal but nonetheless impotent even as regards killing or raping or robbing. That is the thesis they are advancing and do not forget that. It can only mean that intelligence is unrelated to the control of human conduct.

It appears to be more logical from a psychological viewpoint to take the approach of Dixon J in *Sodeman v The King* (1936) 55 CLR 192 and simply take into account an incapacity to control conduct as evidence that the accused did not know that what he or she was doing was wrong. If knowledge of wrongfulness is defined as the ability of a person to reason "with a moderate degree of sense and composure", it is not necessary to prove the *complete* absence of a person's ability to reason before that person can be excused from criminal responsibility. This liberalises the strict cognitive approach of the traditional *M'Naghten Rules*, while preventing those who are able to reason about their conduct from being so excused. Such a test sits far more readily with traditional concepts of criminal responsibility than does a strict test of volition.

Having a separate volitional arm to the defence of mental impairment is therefore fraught with difficulties from a conceptual viewpoint. It is unfortunate that the Model Criminal Code Officers Committee has recommended broadening the defence in such a way as to enable those whose ability to reason is not impaired to be found not guilty because of mental impairment on the ground that they could not control their actions.

PSYCHIATRIC PERSPECTIVES

Delusions and Criminal Responsibility

The *M'Naghten Rules* drew a distinction between insanity and a "partial delusion". Their Lordships stated in *M'Naghten's* case [1843] Cl & F 200 at 201; 8 ER 718 at 723 that if an accused

> labours under [a] partial delusion only, and is not in other respects insane, we think he must be considered in the same situation as to responsibility as if the facts with respect to which the delusion exists were real. For example, if under the influence of his delusion he supposes another man to be in the act of attempting to take away his life, and he kills that man, as he supposes in self-defence, he would be exempt from punishment. If his delusion was that the deceased had inflicted a serious injury to his character and fortune, and he killed him in revenge for such supposed injury, he would be liable to punishment.

This part of the rules has been enacted in the Code jurisdictions.[25] For example, s 35(2) of the *Criminal Code* (NT) states:

> A person whose mind, at the time of his [or her] doing, making or causing an act, omission or event, was affected by delusions on some specific matter or matters, but who is not otherwise entitled to the benefit of the foregoing provisions of this section,

---

25 *Criminal Code* (NT), s 35(2); *Criminal Code* (Qld), s 27(2); *Criminal Code* (Tas), s 16(3); *Criminal Code* (WA), s 27.

is criminally responsible for the act, omission or event to the same extent as if the real state of things has been such as he [or she] was induced by the delusions to believe to exist.

How can one suffer from a delusion and not be considered mentally impaired? From the psychiatric standpoint, delusions form one of the characteristic symptoms of schizophrenia that has traditionally been viewed as a disease of the mind for the purposes of the insanity defence.[26] The *Diagnostic and Statistical Manual of Mental Disorders* does, however, refer to the category of "delusional disorder" which can be differentiated from schizophrenia.[27] This usually involves "nonbizarre" delusions "such as being followed, poisoned, infected, loved at a distance, or deceived by spouse or lover, or having a disease"[28] and there is generally little impairment in social functioning and behaviour. According to Gelder, Gath, Mayou and Cowen in *The Oxford Textbook of Psychiatry* (3rd ed, Oxford: Oxford University Press, 1996), p 300:

> The essence of the modern concept of delusional disorder is that of a permanent and unshakeable delusional system developing insidiously in a person in middle or late life. This delusional system is encapsulated, and there is no impairment of other mental functions. The patient can often go on working, and his [or her] social life may sometimes be maintained fairly well. In clinical practice, cases conforming strictly to the definitions are rare.

It may be that this is the sort of disorder that is meant to fall within the concept of a "partial delusion". Yet from a psychiatric perspective, delusional disorders are a form of psychosis and it is difficult to accept that the defence of mental impairment would not come into play in the rare instance of an accused suffering from such a disorder. In *Grosser* (1999) 106 A Crim R 125 the South Australian Court of Criminal Appeal held that the trial judge had correctly directed the jury that psychiatric evidence that the accused had "a predominance or persecutory ideation or persecutory ideas" could be taken into account in assessing his belief that he was acting in self-defence. The accused had shot at and wounded a police officer in the course of a raid on his farmhouse. However, the psychiatric evidence was that he was not suffering from delusions or a mental illness, but that he had a severe paranoid personality disorder. As discussed above, personality disorders are separated by psychiatrists from mental illnesses because the former do not involve a failure of "reality testing".

The main case dealing with delusions is that of *Walsh* (1991) 60 A Crim R 419; see also Ch 7, p 342. The accused had been a soldier in Korea where he had been severely wounded by a mortar explosion. He had spent some months convalescing in Japan and then in a military hospital in Australia. He suffered continuing health problems that led to five admissions to the Repatriation Hospital and to receiving "shock treatment" (electroconvulsive therapy). He had also

---

26 "[T]he major mental diseases, which the doctors call psychoses, such as schizophrenia, are clearly diseases of the mind": *Bratty v Attorney-General (Northern Ireland)* [1963] AC 386 at 412 per Lord Denning.

27 American Psychiatric Association, *Diagnostic and Statistical Manual of Mental Disorders* (4th ed, Washington: APA, 1994), p 296.

28 American Psychiatric Association, *Diagnostic and Statistical Manual of Mental Disorders* (4th ed, Washington: APA, 1994), p 301.

been attacked and badly beaten by five men in Sydney in 1988. The accused was charged with the murder of an acquaintance whom he killed by firing a shotgun from a distance of approximately three metres. The accused had alighted from a car with the victim and the third man. The victim's dogs were barking nearby. The accused's account of the killing in an unsworn statement to the court was as follows (at 421):

> I sang out to Peter [the victim] "For God's sake Peter take control of those dogs" … I had
> been nursing the gun in the car and I just carried it with me … I stopped a little way
> from the wheels and axle and turned towards the car. Peter was walking from the rear
> of the vehicle to the driver's side door. He just turned and headed straight towards me.
> His eyes were squinting. I sensed danger. I can't say why I just knew it. I knew he
> was going to bash me. I said, "Stop Pete". He kept coming. I said, "Stop Peter". He still
> kept coming. I can't explain why it happened. It just clicked. I had to stop him. He
> was only two or three yards away. I fired. I have no idea where I hit him. I just had to
> stop him … I don't know when I flicked the safety catch off on the gun.

The defence sought to lead expert evidence from a psychiatrist to show that the accused was suffering from a delusion that he was under attack and that this formed the basis for the defence of self-defence. Section 46 of the *Criminal Code* (Tas) states that a person is justified in using in defence of him or herself "such force as, in the circumstances as he [or she] believes them to be, it is reasonable to use". The defence argument was therefore that the accused believed that the victim was going to bash him and that he had to use force to stop him.

The defence did not wish to raise the defence of insanity under s 16(1) of the *Criminal Code* (Tas). The trial judge, Slicer J, conducted a voir dire and considered medical files dealing with the accused's "Post Traumatic Stress Disorder" (PTSD) resulting from his war experience and evidence from the psychiatrist that the killing could have occurred during a "dissociative flash back episode in which [the accused] acted as he might have done if he'd been on active service in Korea": at 422.

Slicer J ruled that if such evidence of PTSD was led, it was evidence of a disorder for the purpose of s 16 as a whole and not just for the purpose of s 16(3) which deals with a delusion divorced from insanity. He stated that a jury would have to consider whether the delusion gave rise to the insanity defence first before considering s 16(3). It might then be the case that the jury did not accept that the disorder amounted to a "mental disease" for the purpose of the insanity defence, or that, if the jury accepted that it was a mental disease it did not have the requisite effect on the accused's understanding the act, knowledge that he or she ought not do the act or power to resist an impulse.

Slicer J stated that if the jury found that the delusion was not a disorder falling within the insanity defence, it could then consider s 16(3) and its relation to the defence of self-defence. On the facts of the case, the jury could "consider whether, if the accused had a deluded belief, such belief could be a circumstance which the accused believed, so as to justify him in using force in the defence of himself, and that such belief, although deluded, made it reasonable to use such force": at 428.

The evidence led at the voir dire was then put in more detail to the jury. The judge directed the jury to consider first whether there was a homicide, secondly, if so, whether the homicide was caused by an act intended to or likely to cause death or bodily harm and whether or not it was justified as an act of self-defence. Slicer J directed the jury that at this stage they could only consider the "sane beliefs" of the accused, rather than those arising from a disordered mind.

Thirdly, the members of the jury were directed that if they were satisfied that the homicide was not justified, they had to consider whether it was murder or manslaughter. Fourthly, they were directed to consider the accused's criminal responsibility for the act, paying regard to the defence of insanity. Finally, if they were satisfied that insanity was not made out, they could then consider s 16(3) and whether the deluded belief that the accused was under attack made it reasonable to use the force he used.

The jury convicted the accused of murder. An appeal was made to the Full Court of the Supreme Court of Tasmania which quashed the conviction for murder and substituted a finding of not guilty on the ground of insanity: *Walsh* (unrep, 19/8/1993, FC SC Tas, CCA 47/1992, A68/1993). The first ground of appeal was that the trial judge had erred at the second point of his direction in directing the jury that it could only take into account the "sane beliefs" of the accused in regard to self-defence. This ground was rejected on the basis that on the evidence heard on the voir dire, for the purposes of self-defence, the jury was only entitled to pay regard to the sane beliefs of the accused. Crawford J went on to say that the trial judge had been incorrect in directing the jury to reconsider self-defence after considering the defence of insanity. Crawford J stated that on the evidence, deluded beliefs were necessarily excluded by the jury because it had rejected the defence of insanity. He went on to say (at para 26):

> I do not say that evidence concerning a mental disease and its effects may never be regarded by a jury when considering s 46 in circumstances where the defence of insanity has been rejected. But when that defence has been rejected the presumption of sanity remains. With respect the learned judge was in error by failing to instruct the jury accordingly and by returning to s 46 and leaving them with deluded beliefs for further consideration. The result was that the appellant had a more favourable summing-up than that to which he was entitled.

The second ground of appeal was that the verdict of the jury was unsafe and satisfactory. This was upheld on the basis that there were only two verdicts available on the evidence, that of murder and that of not guilty on the ground of insanity and that the psychiatric evidence supported the latter verdict.

The decision of the Supreme Court with regard to the evidence of a delusion is correct in that the delusion could be seen as a form of mental impairment which had the effect that the accused did not know that what he was doing was wrong. It therefore fell squarely within the insanity defence. This approach is supported by the decision of the majority in the Canadian Supreme Court case of *R v Chaulk* (1990) 62 CCC(3d) 193. In that case, the two accused were aged 15 and 16 and there was evidence that they suffered from a paranoid psychosis which made them believe they had the power to rule the world and that killing was a necessary means to this end. They entered a house, took property from it and bludgeoned the occupant to death. They raised the defence of insanity at trial, but were convicted of murder. An appeal to the Manitoba Court of Appeal was dismissed. A majority of the Supreme Court of Canada upheld the further appeal and sent the matter back for retrial. Five of the nine judges held that the existing provision dealing with partial delusions in s 16(3) of the *Criminal Code* (Can)[29] was obsolete because those suffering from delusions would fall within the general insanity defence. This provision was later omitted from the reformulated defence.[30]

In *Conlon* (1993) 69 A Crim R 92 it was pointed out by Hunt CJ (at 101) that the emphasis in self-defence is placed on the accused's belief which has to be reasonable, rather than the hypothetical reasonable person in the position of the accused. It is necessary to take into account all the relevant characteristics of the accused and surrounding circumstances in assessing whether or not the accused believed on reasonable grounds that he or she was being threatened or attacked and whether the force applied was necessary in self-defence. In *Conlon*, Hunt CJ presided without a jury at the trial of the accused on two counts of murder. He acquitted the accused on the first count on the basis that the accused's voluntarily induced intoxication affected his belief that he was being threatened and the reasonableness of his response to that danger.

The effect of drugs on perception seems, however, different from the situation where a person is suffering from a delusional disorder. The only other case dealing with the effect of a partial delusion relates to the defence of provocation: see also Ch 7, p 343. In *R v Voukelatos* [1990] VR 1 the Supreme Court of Victoria considered the situation of insane delusions as they pertain to provocation. The accused was found guilty of the murder of his wife by shooting her twice with a shotgun after she attempted to leave him. There was psychiatric evidence led at the trial that the accused was suffering from a delusional disorder and that he falsely believed his wife to be having an affair with their neighbour. Both insanity and provocation were raised by the defence. The trial judge directed the jury that provocation could be considered if it rejected the defence of insanity and stated that there had to be some conduct on the part of the deceased which amounted to provocation. The accused appealed against conviction on the basis that provocation could be based solely on the accused's delusional beliefs. Hampel J (at 26) was of the view that provocation does not extend to "self-generated or entirely imaginary circumstances which cause a loss of self-control", and dismissed the appeal.

Young CJ and Murphy J, however, said that in theory, evidence of provocation should be left to the jury even where the accused's belief in provocation was wholly the product of a delusion. Young CJ (at 5) went on to say that even if one accepted that the accused was suffering from the delusion that his wife was unfaithful, there was no evidence to suggest that he was *provoked* by that belief to kill her:

> There was simply nothing in the evidence to suggest that the applicant killed his wife because he was provoked by his deluded belief.

Similarly, Murphy J agreed (at 19) that the concession to human frailty made by the defence of provocation should not be lessened whether "the facts said to constitute the provocation are real or imagined, or whether they are volunteered by the victim or 'self-induced' by the accused". On the facts, however, he found that there was no evidence to show that the accused had lost

29 An analysis of this section can be found in D Klinck, "'Specific Delusions' in the Insanity Defence" (1982-83) 25 *Criminal Law Quarterly* 458.

30 Section 16 of the *Criminal Code* (Can), inserted by c 43 in 1991: R.S. c. C-34, s 16; 1991, c. 43, s 2.

self-control and shot the deceased in the "heat of passion". Both Murphy (at 20) and Hampel JJ (at 26) were critical of the provocation defence, Murphy J calling for its abolition.

Hampel J's approach to the evidence of a delusion is preferable to that of the majority. It would seem that such a delusional disorder, if in existence, should give rise to the defence of mental impairment rather than provocation. However, even if the majority's approach were accepted, it would seem difficult for a jury or magistrate to accept that the ordinary person could or might have lost control in the way the accused did because, in assessing this question, no personal characteristic apart from age may be taken into account. See the defence of provocation discussed in Chapter 5. It would be very difficult for provocation to be accepted on this basis.

The Model Criminal Code Officers Committee (MCCOC) appears to have wanted to exclude or curtail the use of delusions to bolster defences other than that of mental impairment. Section 7.3(7) of the *Criminal Code Act* 1995 (Cth) states:

> If the tribunal of fact is satisfied that a person carried out conduct as a result of a delusion caused by a mental impairment, the delusion cannot otherwise be relied on as a defence.

Paul Fairall refers to the meaning of this section as "obscure": "The Exculpatory Force of Delusions — A Note on the Insanity Defence" (1994) 6 *Bond Law Review* 57 at 62. It could perhaps be interpreted as meaning that a delusion that is not caused by a mental impairment *can* be relied on as a defence. However, this was clearly not the intention of the MCCOC. In its final report on *General Principles of Criminal Responsibility*, the Committee stated that it took the view "that delusions are symptoms of an underlying pathology and that such defendants should be confined to the mental impairment defence": Criminal Law Officers Committee of the Standing Committee of Attorneys-General, *General Principles of Criminal Responsibility*, Final Report, (December 1992), p 47. Whether or not s 7.3(7) expresses this intention well enough is debatable.

While the MCCOC's proposals seek to draw firmer lines between general defences and mental impairment, the main problem with the idea of "partial delusions" is that it is does not coincide with current medical opinion. The Law Reform Commission of Canada summarises this point:

> Medical opinion rejects the idea of partial insanity and legal scholarship stresses the injustice and illogicality of applying to the mentally abnormal a rule requiring normal reactions within their abnormality; a paranoiac killing his [or her] persecutor will be acquitted only if the imagined persecution would have justified the killing by way of self-defence — the law requires him [or her] to be sane in his [or her] insanity. For this reason it is suggested that the rule on insane delusion be abandoned.[31]

---

31 Law Reform Commission of Canada, *Criminal Law, The General Part: Liability and Defences*, Working Paper 29 (Ottawa: Minister of Supply and Services Canada, 1982), p 48. See also Criminal Law and Penal Methods Reform Committee of South Australia, 4th Report, *The Substantive Criminal Law* (Government Printer South Australia, 1978), p 43, para 13.2.

2.6 BURDEN AND MODE OF PROOF OF MENTAL IMPAIRMENT

The traditional defence of insanity has provided an exception to the general rule that was recognised by the House of Lords in *Woolmington v DPP* [1935] AC 462 that the legal burden of proof in criminal trials rests on the prosecution. There is a presumption in the Code jurisdictions and at common law that every person is presumed to be sane or "of sound mind".[32] The party raising the defence of mental impairment bears the burden of rebutting this presumption on the balance of probabilities.[33]

It is difficult to justify why the burden and standard of proof differ in relation to the defence of mental impairment as opposed to other offences. The traditional explanation as to why the burden and standard of proof differs is that it developed simply as an historical anomaly. Glanville Williams writes in his article, "Offences and Defences" (1982) 2 *Legal Studies* 233 (at 235):

> The defence ... is an anomalous exception, explicable only as a survival from a time before the present rules of burden of proof were established.

The defence of insanity set out in the *M' Naghten Rules* was produced at a time when the distinction between the legal and evidentiary burdens of proof "was not so fully marked by the courts"[34] and it is highly unlikely that the words "it must be clearly proved" were intended to lay down a special rule for the insanity defence.[35] Indeed, historical research reveals that the placing of the burden of proof on the prosecution was a relatively recent innovation, and that before *Woolmington* the law regularly required the accused to establish general defences: see Ch 2, pp 114ff.

The modern rationale for the standard of proof lies in the fear that if an accused only has to bear an evidentiary burden in relation to mental impairment, more individuals would be found not criminally responsible than should be the case. One author has described this as the fear of "swinging the jail door open to any individual who can stand up in court and claim insanity": S Sundby, "The Reasonable Doubt Rule and the Meaning of Innocence" (1988) 40 *Hastings Law Journal* 457 at 500. It seems difficult to support this standard in relation to mental impairment and not in relation to other defences. There appears little support for the proposition that it may be easier to fake a claim of mental impairment than say duress or automatism and Jones writes in his article, "Insanity, Automatism and the Burden of Proof on the Accused" (1995) 111 *The Law Quarterly Review* 475 at 477:

---

32 *Criminal Code Act* 1995 (Cth), s 7.2(3); *Crimes Act* 1900 (ACT), s 428N (this is inferred on the basis that "mental dysfunction" must be established on the balance of probabilities); *Criminal Code* (Qld), s 26; *Criminal Code* (NT), s 6; *Criminal Law Consolidation Act* 1935 (SA), s 269D; *Criminal Code* (Tas), s 15; *Crimes (Mental Impairment and Unfitness to be Tried) Act* 1997 (Vic), s 21(1); *Criminal Code* (WA), s 26.

33 *Criminal Code Act* 1995 (Cth), s 7.3(3); *Crimes Act* 1900 (ACT), s 428N(2); *Criminal Law Consolidation Act* 1935 (SA), s 269F; *Criminal Code* (Tas), s 381; *Crimes (Mental Impairment and Unfitness to be Tried) Act* 1997 (Vic), s 21(2)(b); *R v Porter* (1933) 55 CLR 182 at 183-184; *Sodeman v The Queen* (1936) 55 CLR 192; *R v Ayoub* [1984] 2 NSWLR 511; *R v Falconer* (1990) 171 CLR 30; 50 A Crim R 244.

34 *R v Bonnor* [1957] VR 227 at 260 per Sholl J. See also D Reaugh, "Presumptions and the Burden of Proof" (1942) 36 *Illinois Law Review of Northwestern University* 703 at 706-713.

35 TH Jones, "Insanity, Automatism and the Burden of Proof on the Accused" (1995) 111 *The Law Quarterly Review* 475 at 477.

> One would also have thought that the special disposal arrangements for those found not guilty by reason of insanity ... made false claims of insanity rather less likely than those of more conventional defences.

At common law, if the accused has put his or her state of mind at issue, such as in relation to the defence of diminished responsibility or automatism, the prosecution can then raise the issue of mental impairment against the wishes of the defence.[36] It cannot, however, give evidence of mental impairment as part of its initial case. If the prosecution raises mental impairment in such circumstances, the standard is still that of the balance of probabilities.[37] This position is codified in s 381 of the *Criminal Code* (Tas), but the other Code jurisdictions are silent on the matter.

Section 7.3(3) of the *Criminal Code Act* 1995 (Cth) retains the main common law principles in relation to the presumption of sanity and burden and standard of proof. It states:

> A person is presumed not to have been suffering from ... a mental impairment. The presumption is only displaced if it is proved on the balance of probabilities (by the prosecution or the defence) that the person was suffering from such a mental impairment.

The Model Criminal Code Officers Committee, however, concluded that there should be a midway position in relation to who may raise the issue of mental impairment. Section 7.3(4) states that the prosecution can only rely on mental impairment if the court gives leave. This has also been incorporated into the Australian Capital Territory, South Australian and Victorian provisions.[38] In these jurisdictions, therefore, the prosecution may raise the defence of mental impairment without having the defence first put the accused's state of mind at issue. While there is the rider that the court must give leave for this to be done, there is the possibility that an accused may be acquitted on the ground of mental impairment contrary to his or her wishes and "could be kept in some form of psychiatric detention for a longer period than [he or she] would serve if convicted and sentenced to prison": S Verdun-Jones, "The Insanity Defense in Canada" (1994) 17 *International Journal of Law and Psychiatry* 175 at 183.

Before 1991 in Canada, the prosecution was able to raise the issue of mental impairment even against the wishes of the defence. However, in *R v Swain* (1991) 63 CCC (3d) 481 the Supreme Court of Canada held that such a rule infringed the accused's right to liberty and security of the person. It is to be hoped that in the relevant Australian jurisdictions, the requirement that the prosecution be given leave of the court to raise the issue of mental impairment will limit the prosecution's power in this regard.

2.7 DISPOSITION

Traditionally, those found guilty on the basis of insanity were locked away in secure mental health faculties or kept in prison "at the Governor's Pleasure". The prospect of indeterminate detention for

---

36 *R v Joyce* [1970] SASR 184; *R v Ayoub* [1984] 2 NSWLR 511; *Walsh* (1991) 60 A Crim R 419.

37 *R v Ayoub* [1984] 2 NSWLR 511 at 516 per Street CJ, Slattery J concurring.

38 *Crimes Act* 1900 (ACT), s 428N(3); *Criminal Law Consolidation Act* 1935 (SA), s 269E(b); *Crimes (Mental Impairment and Unfitness to be Tried) Act* 1997 (Vic), s 22(1).

their clients has led to defence counsel shying away from the use of the insanity defence. The traditional justification for detaining those found not criminally responsible centres upon the notion or incapacitation to prevent further harm to the public. Occasionally, there is reference made to justifying such detention in order to provide "treatment". See, for example, C Williams, "Psychopathy, Mental Illness and Preventive Detention: Issues Arising from the *David* Case" (1990) 16(2) *Monash University Law Review* 161 at 169. This notion is difficult to support, given that many detained under traditional Governor's Pleasure orders have been detained in prisons rather than hospitals, and many did not receive any treatment at all.

Governor's Pleasure Detainees and Treatment

In 1988, 66% of Governor's Pleasure detainees in Victoria were kept in G Division at Pentridge Prison[39] and in that same year the Victorian Law Reform Commission found that a quarter of Governor's Pleasure detainees had received no treatment since being detained.[40]

The system of detention following the special verdict is best described as a system of preventive detention. On the rationales behind incapacitation for the dangerous, see Chapter 1, pp 24ff. There is a presumption that a person who has committed a crime once because of his or her mental impairment will be driven to do so again. In this sense, those found not criminally responsible have generally been detained on the basis of "dangerousness". That is, they are perceived as dangerous individuals who may do harm again.

Recent cases have accepted the justification of "protecting society" as a legitimate factor to be taken into account in fixing an appropriate sentence[41] and have also accepted it in upholding systems of preventive detention for those with mental impairment or considered dangerous who have been found guilty of serious crimes.[42] In a perfect world, individuals would not be detained on the basis that they might do harm in the future. However, it is also true that, in some instances, there may be a connection between previous mental impairment and the risk of future harm. Some studies suggest there is an association, though not necessarily a causal link, between having mental illness, particularly schizophrenia, and an increased risk of behaving in a violent manner.[43] The problem really lies in drawing up appropriate criteria which will lead to the detention of those who really may do harm in the future, whilst allowing for the absolute discharge of those who do not pose a risk to the public.

---

39 A Freiberg, "The Disposition of Mentally Disordered Offenders in Australia: 'Out of Mind, Out of Sight' Revisited" (1994) 1(2) *Psychiatry, Psychology and Law* 97 at 103.

40 Victorian Law Reform Commission, *Mental Malfunction and Criminal Responsibility*, Discussion Paper No 14 (Melbourne: Victorian Government Printing Service, 1988) discussed in J Van Groningen, "Detained at the Governor's Pleasure: The Consequence of the Insanity Verdict and Unfitness to Stand Trial" in D Greig and I Freckelton (eds), *Emerging Issues for the 1990s in Psychiatry, Psychology and Law* Proceedings of the 10th Annual Congress of the Australian and New Zealand Association of Psychiatry, Psychology and Law (Melbourne: ANZAPPL, 1989), p 149.

41 *Veen v The Queen (No 2)* (1988) 164 CLR 465 at 472.

42 *R v Carr* [1996] 1 VR 585; *R v Moffatt* [1998] 2 VR 229; cf *Kable v DPP (NSW)* (1996) 138 ALR 577.

43 For an excellent overview of the literature in this regard, see P Mullen, "The Dangerousness of the Mentally Ill and the Clinical Assessment of Risk" in W Brookbanks (ed), *Psychiatry and the Law: Clinical and Legal Issues* (Wellington: Brooker's, 1996), p 93.

Recent changes to the legislation in most Australian jurisdictions have enabled a wider range of dispositional options other than indefinite detention.[44] For example, s 23 of the *Crimes (Mental Impairment and Unfitness to Be Tried) Act* 1997 (Vic) states that on a finding of not guilty because of mental impairment, the court must make a supervision order or order that the accused be released unconditionally. A supervision order may commit the person to custody in an approved mental health service or residential service in a prison or release the person on conditions decided by the court and specified in the order.

There is some reason to believe that the courts will take a cautious approach to the disposition of those found not guilty on the ground of mental impairment: B McSherry "Criminal Detention of Those with Mental Impairment" (1999) 6 *Journal of Law and Medicine* 216. Nevertheless, it is important that flexible dispositional options are available to ensure that the defence is in fact used where relevant: RD Mackay and G Kearns, "More Fact(s) About the Insanity Defence" [1999] Crim LR 714.

3. AUTOMATISM

One of the fundamental principles of the criminal law is that an accused can only be considered criminally responsible where he or she performed the criminal act voluntarily in the sense that it must be willed or conscious.[45] There is no practical difference between the Australian jurisdictions as to the law relating to voluntariness. Section 13(1) of the *Criminal Code* (Tas) states that "no person shall be criminally responsible for an act, unless it is voluntary". Similarly, s 23 of the *Criminal Code* (Qld) and *Criminal Code* (WA) state that "a person is not criminally responsible for an act or omission which occurs independently of the exercise of his [or her] will". There is no such express provision in the *Criminal Code* (NT), but the common law principle would appear to operate in that jurisdiction.

There are three ways in which an act may be considered at law to be involuntary:

- when the criminal act was accidental;

- when the criminal act was caused by a reflex action; or

- when the conduct was performed whilst the accused was in a state of impaired consciousness.

Automatism is the term most often used to refer to involuntary conduct in the third sense of it being conduct performed in a state of impaired consciousness. Automatism when it relates to

---

44 *Crimes Act* 1914 (Cth), s 20BJ (the Model Criminal Code Officers Committee has also circulated the *Mental Impairment Bill* 1994 (Cth)); *Crimes Act* 1900 (ACT), ss 428Q, 428R (accused comes within the jurisdiction of the Mental Health Tribunal); *Mental Health (Criminal Procedure) Act* 1990 (NSW), s 39; *Criminal Law Consolidation Act* 1935 (SA), s 269O; *Crimes (Mental Impairment and Unfitness to Plead Act* 1997 (Vic), s 23; *Criminal Law (Mentally Impaired Defendants) Act* 1996 (WA), s 22. In other jurisdictions, indefinite detention still applies: *Criminal Code* (NT), s 382; *Criminal Code* 1899 (Qld), s 647; *Criminal Code* (Tas), s 382.

45 *R v Vickers* [1957] 2 QB 664 at 672 per Lord Goddard CJ (CCA); *R v Scott* [1967] VR 276 at 288-289 per Gillard J (FC SC Vic); *R v Haywood* [1971] VR 755; *R v Tait* [1973] VR 151; *R v Dodd* (1974) 7 SASR 151; *Woolmington v DPP* [1935] AC 462 at 482 per Viscount Sankey LC; *Ryan v The Queen* (1967) 121 CLR 205.

involuntariness is not a "defence" in the same sense as the defence of mental impairment because the burden of proof is always upon the prosecution to prove beyond reasonable doubt that an accused's conduct was voluntary.

There has been a great deal of confusion in the development of the law of automatism as it not only relates to involuntary conduct, but may also be subsumed within the defence of mental impairment. The concept of voluntariness itself is often difficult to separate from the fault element of intention. The notion of an act being willed often overlaps with the notion of intentional action. That is, voluntary conduct has generally been understood as under the mental direction of the accused who has the opportunity to choose not to perform the act.

The main decision dealing with automatism is that of the High Court in *R v Falconer* (1990) 171 CLR 30. The distinction between automatism as it relates to involuntariness and automatism as it relates to the defence of mental impairment can only be understood by reference to this case.

CASE STUDIES

Evidence of Dissociation

Falconer's case concerns the law relating to voluntary action and the defence of insanity in Western Australia, but has relevance to the law in other jurisdictions. The facts showed a long history of violence by Gordon Falconer towards his wife, Mary Falconer. The latter had obtained a non-molestation order against her husband and criminal proceedings had been preferred against him in relation to allegations that he had sexually abused two of their daughters over a period of years. Mary Falconer shot Gordon Falconer dead after he unexpectedly came to where she was staying and assaulted her. She claimed that she remembered nothing after he had reached out to grab her hair until she found herself slumped against an archway with a shotgun nearby. The latter had been kept in a wardrobe and Mary Falconer said she had no recollection of picking it up or loading it.

At the trial, after the Crown case had closed and the accused and other witnesses had given evidence, counsel for the defence sought to call evidence from two psychiatrists to show that the accused's conduct was consistent with a state of automatism which rendered her conduct involuntary. The Commissioner presiding at the trial conducted a voir dire to test the admissibility of the evidence. Both psychiatrists gave evidence to the effect that the circumstances leading up to and surrounding the shooting could have produced a dissociative state where, according to one of the psychiatrists, "part of her personality would be sort of segmented and not functioning as a whole and she became disrupted in her behaviour, without awareness of what she was doing": *Falconer* (1989) 46 A Crim R 83 at 109.

The Commissioner ruled the evidence inadmissible and the accused was convicted. On appeal, the Western Australian Court of Criminal Appeal held that the evidence was admissible on the issue of voluntariness, allowed the appeal against conviction and ordered a retrial: *Falconer* (1989) 46 A Crim R 83. The Crown then sought special leave to appeal against that order, seeking restoration of the conviction and of the sentence of life imprisonment which accompanied it.

All seven judges of the High Court agreed that leave to appeal should be granted because the case raised exceptionally important questions of law, but that the appeal should be dismissed because the Commissioner erred in rejecting the evidence of dissociation. All agreed that the evidence led raised no issue of insanity, but it did raise the question of whether or not the accused's act of discharging the gun was involuntary.

Section 23 of the *Criminal Code* (WA) provides that "a person is not criminally responsible for an act or omission which occurs independently of the exercise of his [or her] will". The insanity defence is set out in s 27 of the Code:

> A person is not criminally responsible for an act or omission if at the time of doing the act he [or she] is in such a state of mental disease or natural mental infirmity as to deprive him [or her] of capacity to understand what he [or she] is doing, or of capacity to control his [or her] actions, or of capacity to know that he [or she] ought not to do the act or make the omission.

All seven members of the High Court were of the opinion that s 27 of the Code encompasses involuntary action where the automatism resulted from a mental disease, natural mental infirmity or disorder of the mind. If, however, it is shown that the automatism arose from a mental condition which could *not* be classified as a result of a mental disease, natural mental infirmity or disorder of the mind and the act occurred involuntarily because of this mental condition, the accused would be entitled to a complete acquittal.

This distinction between automatism as relating to involuntariness and automatism as subsumed within the defence of mental impairment is well ingrained in the common law.[46] The *Criminal Code Act* 1995 (Cth) also makes the traditional distinction between involuntary conduct arising from impaired consciousness[47] and conduct which is willed but committed whilst mentally impaired.

After the High Court decision, the matter was set down for a retrial so that the issue of automatism could be put to the jury. However, Mary Falconer decided at that stage to plead guilty to manslaughter. The plea was heard on 19 March 1991 before Nicholson J. On 27 March 1991, Nicholson J passed a sentence of six years imprisonment, but after allowing for the time already served, he stated that a suspended sentence was the appropriate disposition: B McSherry, "Automatism and Criminal Responsibility: The Position in Australia Since *Falconer's* Case" in I Freckelton, D Greig and M McMahon (eds), *Forensic Issues in Mental Health* (Melbourne: ANZAPPL, 1991), pp 209-217 at pp 216-217.

---

46   *Rabey v The Queen* [1980] 2 SCR 513 at 524 per Dickson J; *R v Cottle* [1958] NZLR 999 at 1007 per Gresson P; *R v Falconer* (1990) 171 CLR 30.

47   Section 4.2(3) of the *Criminal Code Act* 1995 (Cth) gives as an example of conduct that is not voluntary: "an act performed during impaired consciousness depriving the person of the will to act".

3.1 CONDITIONS GIVING RISE TO AUTOMATISM

A state of automatism may be caused by concussion from a blow to the head,[48] sleep disorders,[49] the consumption of alcohol or other drugs,[50] neurological disorders,[51] hypoglycaemia,[52] epilepsy[53] or dissociation arising from extraordinary external stress.[54] Evidence of some degree of control over bodily movements does not preclude automatism.[55] It does not matter what the cause of automatism is, providing that the accused's actions are rendered involuntary.[56]

3.2 CONSCIOUSNESS AND AUTOMATISM

There are conflicting decisions relating to whether or not some degree of consciousness on the part of the accused will defeat a claim of automatism. Some cases have equated automatism with a *complete* lack of consciousness.[57] This appears to be on the grounds that a lack of consciousness is more readily tested than a lack of volition and the "familiarity of consciousness as a test of liability": D O'Connor and PA Fairall, *Criminal Defences* (3rd ed, Sydney: Butt, 1996), p 282. However other cases have suggested that because automatism is related to the concept of involuntariness

---

48 *R v Minor* (1955) 112 CCC 29 (CA Saskatchewan); *R v Stripp* (1978) 69 Cr App R 318 at 323 per Ormrod LJ; *Ziems v Prothonotary of the Supreme Court of New South Wales* (1957) 97 CLR 279; *Re Wakefield* (1958) 75 WN (NSW) 66; *Cooper v McKenna; Ex parte Cooper* [1960] Qd R 406; *Re Budd* [1962] Crim LR 49; *R v Scott* [1967] VR 276 (SC Vic); *Hall* (1988) 36 A Crim R 368; *Wogandt* (1988) 33 A Crim R 31.

49 *R v Boshears*, The Times, 18 February 1961; *R v Cogdon* [1951] Res Jud 29; *R v Holmes* [1960] WAR 122 at 125; *R v Scarth* [1945] St R Qd 38; *R v Smith* [1979] 1 WLR 1445; *Cordwell v Carley* (1985) 31 A Crim R 291; *Kroon v The Queen* (1990) 55 SASR 476; *Jiminez v The Queen* (1992) 173 CLR 572 (HC); *R v Parks* [1992] 2 SCR 871 (SC Can) (sane automatism); *R v Burgess* [1991] 2 QB 92 (CA) (insane automatism).

50 *R v O'Connor* (1980) 146 CLR 64 (HC); *Martin* (1984) 16 A Crim R 87 (HC); *Jeffs v Graham* (1987) 8 NSWLR 292; *R v Keogh* [1964] VR 400; *R v Meddings* [1966] VR 306; *R v Dodd* (1974) 7 SASR 151; *R v Daviault* [1994] 3 SCR 63 (SC Can).

51 *Police v Bannin* [1991] 2 NZLR 237; (Klein-Levin syndrome); *Hughes* (1989) 42 A Crim R 270 (myotonia).

52 *Watmore v Jenkins* [1962] 2 QB 572; *August v Fingleton* [1964] SASR 22; *R v Quick and Paddison* [1973] QB 910 (CA); *R v Bailey* [1983] 1 WLR 760; *Broome v Perkins* (1986) 85 Cr App R 321; *R v Hennessy* [1989] 1 WLR 287 (hyperglycaemia viewed as insane automatism).

53 Generally, epilepsy is viewed as insane automatism: *R v Cottle* [1958] NZLR 999; *Bratty v Attorney-General (Northern Ireland)* [1963] AC 386; *R v Sullivan* [1984] 1 AC 156; *R v Foy* [1960] Qd R 225; *R v Meddings* [1966] VR 306; *Youssef* (1990) A Crim R 1; *Battle v The Queen* (unrep, 26/2/1993, CCA WA, 149 of 1992).

54 *R v Tsigos* [1964-65] NSWR 1607; *R v K* (1970) 3 CCC (2d) 84 (Ont HC of Justice); *Re Wiseman* (1972) 46 ALJ 412; *R v Sproule* (1975) 26 CCC (2d) 92; *R v Rabey* (1977) 37 CCC (2d) 461 (CA Ont); approved in *R v Rabey* (1981) 54 CCC 1 (SC Can); *R v Isitt* (1978) 67 Cr App R 44; *Williams v The Queen* [1978] Tas SR 98; *R v Radford* (1985) 42 SASR 266 (SC SA); *Radford v The Queen (No 2)* (1986) 11 Crim LJ 231; *R v Falconer* (1990) 171 CLR 30; *Milloy v The Queen* [1993] 1 Qd R 298; *R v M* (unrep, 18/3/1994, SC Vic Hampel J); *R v Mansfield* (unrep, 5/5/1994, SC Vic Hampel J); *R v Joudrie* (unrep, 9/5/1996, Court of Queen's Bench, Alberta, No 9501-1280-C6).

55 *R v Radford* (1985) 42 SASR 266 at 275-276; per King CJ; *R v Burr* [1969] NZLR 736 at 745 per Turner J.

56 *Jiminez v The Queen* (1992) 173 CLR 572 at 581.

57 *R v Joyce* [1970] SASR 184; *R v Burr* [1969] NZLR 734; *Broome v Perkins* (1987) 85 Cr App R 321; *R v Isitt* (1977) 67 Cr App R 44; [1977] RTR 211; *Haynes v MOT* (1988) 3 CRNZ 587.

rather than consciousness,[58] a degree of awareness or cognitive function is not necessarily fatal to automatism being accepted by the trier of fact.[59] In *Ryan v The Queen* (1967) 121 CLR 205 Barwick CJ stated (at 217):

> [I]t is important ... not to regard [automatism] as of the essence of the discussion, however convenient an expression automatism may be to comprehend involuntary deeds where the lack of concomitant or controlling will to act is due to diverse causes. It is that lack of will which is the relevant determinant ... It is of course the absence of the will to act or, perhaps, more precisely, of its exercise rather than lack of knowledge or consciousness which ... decides criminal liability.

The acceptance that some degree of consciousness is not fatal to a claim of automatism is of great importance in relation to dissociative states. An accused may claim that he or she was in a state of dissociation such that he or she could not control his or her conduct, but he or she was aware of events occurring as if they were in a dream.[60]

It is probably misleading to think of consciousness in terms simply of it being present or not. North P has stated that "one cannot move a muscle without a direction given by the mind": *R v Burr* [1969] NZLR 736 at 742. The main question is whether or not there was an absence of the exercise of the will such that the accused acted automatically.[61] While amnesia is often linked to a state of automatism, amnesia of itself is not a defence to a crime.[62]

PSYCHOLOGICAL PERSPECTIVES

Conceptions of Voluntary Conduct

In law, conduct is viewed as either voluntary or involuntary. Psychological conceptions of conduct, however, start from the premise that there is a continuum between involuntary and voluntary conduct and that conduct performed in states of impaired consciousness may be goal-directed. The broadening of the legal concept of involuntary conduct to include automatism has led to acquittals in circumstances where the accused has performed goal-directed behaviour.[63] This is particularly concerning given that from the psychological viewpoint, it is questionable that acts performed in states of impaired consciousness can truly be termed "involuntary".

---

58   *Ryan v The Queen* (1967) 121 CLR 205 at 214 per Barwick CJ; *R v Pantelic* (1973) 21 FLR 253 per Fox J; *R v Dodd* (1974) 7 SASR 151; *Jeffs v Graham* (1987) 8 NSWLR 292; *Barker v Burke* [1970] VR 884 at 891.

59   *R v Radford* (1985) 42 SASR 266 at 275-276 per King CJ; *R v Burr* [1969] NZLR 736 at 745 per Turner J. Compare Kilmuir LC's statement in *Bratty v Attorney-General (Northern Ireland)* [1963] AC 386 at 401: "[Automatism] means unconscious voluntary action and it is a defence because the mind does not go with what is being done".

60   In *R v Mansfield* (unrep, SC Vic Hampel J, acquittal 5/5/1994), the accused stated that the events leading up to his stabbing his wife were "like watching an Arnold Schwarzenegger movie or something". See B McSherry, "Automatism in Australia Since *Falconer's* Case" (1996) 6 *International Bulletin of Law and Mental Health* 3 at 6.

61   *R v Burr* [1969] NZLR 736 at 745 per North P; *Ryan v The Queen* (1967) 121 CLR 205 at 214 per Barwick CJ.

62   *R v Hartridge* (1966) 57 DLR (2d) 332; *R v Matchett* [1980] 2 WWR 122 at 134 per Walker DCJ (Saskatchewan Dist Ct).

63   B McSherry, "Automatism in Australia Since *Falconer's* Case" (1996) *International Bulletin of Law and Mental Health* 3; B McSherry, "Getting Away with Murder? Dissociative States and Criminal Responsibility" (1998) 21(2) *International Journal of Law and Psychiatry* 163.

There are numerous ways of explaining human action. At the simplest level, there are bodily movements that result from the contraction or relaxation of muscles. Arthur Danto has referred to the "basic actions" such as waving, walking, picking up objects and so on: "Basic Action" (1965) 2 *American Philosophical Quarterly* 141. In relation to criminal conduct, the explanation for behaviour becomes much more complex. Michael Moore writes that "[s]ince in law and morals it is *persons* performing actions with which we are concerned, we may put aside the behaviourist sense of action, which reduces it without remainder to bodily motions": MS Moore, *Law and Psychiatry: Rethinking the Relationship* (New York: Cambridge University Press, 1984), p 70.

Certainly, behaviourism — as a psychological theory that emphasises the scientific study of observable behavioural responses — is limited in the assistance it can give to the complexities of criminal responsibility. The functional approach to the theory of behaviour is perhaps of more relevance given that it looks at sensory input, neural mechanisms and resulting behaviour as a complex set of interactions: P Churchland, *Matter and Consciousness: A Contemporary Introduction to the Philosophy of the Mind* (Cambridge, Mass: MIT Press, 1988), p 36. It also appears to have the most current support amongst cognitive psychologists and philosophers: R Dresser, "Culpability and Other Minds" (1993) 2(1) *Southern California Interdisciplinary Law Journal* 41.

In the psychological literature, automatism is the term used to explain compulsive repetitive simple behaviours usually associated with a psychomotor epileptic attack: J Pinel, *Biopsychology* (3rd ed, Needham Heights, MA: Allyn & Bacon, 1997), p 138. There is thus an immediate difference in the language used in this area by lawyers and psychologists.

Further, a clear-cut distinction between involuntary and voluntary behaviour is foreign to most philosophical and psychological thinking. Joel Feinberg, for example, refers to voluntariness as "a variable concept, determined by higher and lower cut-off points depending on the nature of the circumstances, the interests at stake, and the moral or legal purposes to be served": *Harm to Self* (Oxford: Oxford University Press, 1986), p 117.

In his classic work on epilepsy last century, Hughlings Jackson posited that volitional and automatistic behaviours are not polar opposites, but part of a continuum: "Evolution and Dissolution of the Nervous System: Croonian Lectures Delivered at the Royal College of Physicians, March 1884" (1884) 1 *British Medical Journal* 591. From a clinical perspective it is therefore common to talk of the "most and least volitional, or least and most automatic": E Coles and S Armstrong, "Hughlings Jackson on Automatism as Disinhibition" (1998) 6 *Journal of Law and Medicine* 73. The functional approach to the study of mind and behaviour thus views behaviour as much more complex than the legal concept of acts as either voluntary or involuntary, a notion which has its basis in Cartesian dualism: R Dresser, "Culpability and Other Minds" (1993) 2(1) *Southern California Interdisciplinary Law Journal* 41.

In recent years, "dissociative states" have clinically come to the fore, particularly in the context of individuals recovering from traumatic events such as physical and sexual abuse. Dissociation is defined in the *Diagnostic and Statistical Manual of Mental Disorders* as "a disruption in the usually integrated functions of consciousness, memory, identity, or perception of the environment": American Psychiatric Association, *Diagnostic and Statistical Manual of Mental Disorders* (4th ed, Washington, DC: APA, 1994), p 477. Steinberg has categorised five core symptoms of dissociation: amnesia, depersonalization, derealization, identity confusion and identity alteration: *Handbook for the Assessment of Dissociation: A Clinical Guide* (Washington: American Psychiatric Press, 1995), pp 8-13. She argues that all of these symptoms must be present before a diagnosis of dissociation can be made. She has also invented the *Structured Clinical Interview for DSM-IV Dissociative Disorders* which may be useful in diagnosing and assessing the presence and severity of these dissociative symptoms: *Structured Clinical Interview for DSM-IV Dissociative Disorders* (Revised ed, Washington: American Psychiatric Press, 1994).

Steinberg writes that "[d]uring a dissociative episode, the mental contents that are dissociated from full consciousness remain on some peripheral level of awareness; from this perspective dissociation can also be defined as a fragmentation of consciousness": *Handbook for the Assessment of Dissociation: A Clinical Guide* (Washington: American Psychiatric Press, 1995), p 23. Michael Coles and S Armstrong agree that goal-directed behaviour can occur in states of impaired consciousness where some partial awareness exists. In their view only reflex movements or well learned "habits" such as those explored in experimental psychology under the term "automaticity" can truly be considered involuntary in the sense that they are not goal-directed behaviours: "Hughlings Jackson on Automatism as Disinhibition" (1998) 6 *Journal of Law and Medicine* 73.

It is at this point that the psychological and legal concepts of involuntary conduct may be able to converge. Imagine that involuntary behaviour in the legal context is confined to accidental acts and reflex actions. This can be justified in the sense that such behaviour is at the "least volitional" end of the act continuum. What then of those acts which are committed in a state of impaired consciousness? From a psychological perspective, it is difficult to view such acts as "involuntary" in the same sense as accidental or reflex actions. One alternative that is worth exploring is to move away from viewing these acts as "involuntary" and instead bring them within the realm of the defence of mental impairment. The Canadian Psychiatric Association has suggested that automatism be subsumed within the existing defence of not criminally responsible on account of mental disorder.[64] This suggestion was based on the view that automatism always involves some form of mental impairment.

There certainly appears to be a difference between accidental and reflex actions and goal-directed behaviour performed in a state of impaired consciousness. In particular, a diagnosis of dissociation as a reaction to extreme stress does not fit well with legal requirements for holding an accused criminally responsible. If a major crime such as homicide has been committed, it may often be difficult to determine whether the accused was in a state of dissociation at the time of the killing or suffered a dissociative state as a *reaction* to the trauma of killing another person. Further, because one of the symptoms of dissociation is amnesia, which can be easily simulated,[65] it can be very problematic for clinicians to diagnose this condition accurately and even more difficult for the prosecution to prove beyond reasonable doubt that the accused was *not* in a state of dissociation.

---

64 Canadian Psychiatric Association, *Brief to the House of Commons Standing Committee on Justice and the Solicitor General, Subcommittee on the Reform of the General Part of the Criminal Code*, 9 November 1992.

65 TA Kiersch, "Amnesia: A Clinical Study of Ninety-Eight Cases" (1962) 119 *American Journal of Psychiatry* 57.

The main benefit of subsuming automatism within a general defence of mental disorder is that once a person has been found not criminally responsible, a range of dispositional options can then become available. More flexible dispositional options apart from indefinite detention are gradually being enacted in common law jurisdictions along with the introduction of a reformulated defence of mental disorder or impairment: B McSherry, "Mental Impairment and Criminal Responsibility: Recent Australian Legislative Reforms" (1999) 23 Crim LJ 135. An assessment of an accused's mental disorder could take place at the dispositional stage in determining whether or not an individual should be discharged absolutely or be subject to some form of medical treatment.

At present, the outcome of criminal proceedings where evidence of dissociation is raised will largely depend upon the credibility of medical evidence called at the trial. Having a defence of mental disorder that encompasses automatism will help avoid the problems associated with the issue of legal versus psychological concepts of voluntariness.

3.3 AUTOMATISM AND THE DEFENCE OF MENTAL IMPAIRMENT

If automatism arises from a condition that is not considered to be a form of mental impairment, the focus will be on whether or not the conduct was involuntary as a result of that condition. Impaired consciousness arising in this sense will be seen as depriving the accused of the will to act. If, however, automatism arises from a condition which may be viewed as a form of mental impairment then the defence of mental impairment may be relevant.

Whether or not mental impairment exists is a question of fact for the jury to decide,[66] but expert evidence in this regard will be of crucial importance. Traditionally, the term "disease of the mind" has been central to judicial considerations concerning whether or not to classify a condition as a form of mental impairment. The next section sets out the common law in relation to the division between what has been termed "sane" and "insane" automatism.

3.4 SANE AND INSANE AUTOMATISM

Under the common law, the traditional distinction between sane and insane automatism was based on the concept of a "disease of the mind". This distinction has repercussions for both the substantive law and procedural matters. If an accused is acquitted on the basis of "sane" automatism, he or she is entitled to a complete acquittal because he or she had been deprived of the will to act. However, if the automatism arose from what has been termed a disease of the mind, it is considered "insane" automatism. Under the common law, the accused was then detained at the Governor's Pleasure under a special verdict: see above, at 2.7 'Disposition', p 220.

---

66   See, for example, *Crimes (Mental Impairment and Unfitness to be Tried) Act* 1997 (Vic), s 21(2).

What conditions were legally determined to be a "disease of the mind" has been largely based upon policy considerations.[67] Three criteria or tests have been developed by the courts in order to define what should be considered to be a disease of the mind:

▬ The *recurrence/continuing danger test*, which holds that if a mental condition is prone to recur, it should be considered to be a disease of the mind;[68]

▬ The *internal/external test*, which provides that if the mental state is "internal" to the accused, as opposed to arising from an external cause, it should be defined as a disease of the mind;[69] and

▬ The *sound/unsound mind test*, which is a more sophisticated version of the second test and which has been used to categorise certain "dissociative" states. A disease of the mind is considered on this test to be evidenced by the reaction of an unsound mind to its own delusions or external stimuli.[70]

In *R v Parks* [1992] 2 SCR 871 (SC Can) La Forest J stated (at 902) that the internal/external test is "really meant to be used only as an analytical tool and not as an all encompassing methodology": see also *R v Falconer* (1990) 171 CLR 30 at 50-51 per Mason CJ, Brennan and McHugh JJ, at 77 per Toohey J, at 84 per Gaudron J. The same may be said in relation to all these tests as they are really artificial means of deciding who should be set free and who should be subject to some form of detention: see B McSherry, "Defining What is a 'Disease of the Mind': The Untenability of Current Legal Interpretations" (1993) 1 *Journal of Law and Medicine* 76 at 89. In the recent Canadian case of *R v Stone* [1999] 2 SCR 290, Bastarache J in delivering the judgment of the majority, stated (at 396) that the "continuing danger" test and the "internal/external" test are both relevant in determining whether the condition of automatism was a relevant factor. He also pointed out (at 398) that other policy factors may also be taken into account to provide a "holistic" approach.

Since most Australian jurisdictions now have a range of dispositional options available for those found not guilty by reason of mental impairment, the necessity of trying to pigeonhole mental conditions as "diseases of the mind" may not be as imperative as before. However, the tests do give some indication of what conditions could fall within the defence of mental impairment and it is therefore of some value to consider them in more detail.

---

67 *R v Rabey* (1977) 37 CCC (2d) 461 at 473 per Martin JA (CA Ontario); *R v Parks* [1992] 2 SCR 871.

68 *Bratty v Attorney-General (Northern Ireland)* [1963] AC 386 at 412 per Lord Denning (HL); *R v Carter* [1959] VR 105 at 110 per Sholl J; *R v Meddings* [1966] VR 306 at 309 per Sholl J.

69 *R v Falconer* (1990) 171 CLR 30; *R v Quick and Paddison* [1973] QB 910 (CA); *R v Sullivan* [1984] AC 156; *R v Rabey* (1977) 37 CCC (2d) 1; *R v Radford* (1985) 42 SASR 266 at 276 per King CJ; *R v Hennessy* [1989] 1 WLR 297 at 292 per Lord Lane CJ.

70 In *R v Radford* (1985) 42 SASR 266 at 276 King CJ stated: "the significant distinction is between the reaction of an unsound mind to its own delusions or to external stimuli on the one hand and the reaction of a sound mind to external stimuli, including stress producing factors, on the other hand". This statement was approved by the High Court in *R v Falconer* (1990) 171 CLR 30.

THE RECURRENCE OR CONTINUING DANGER TEST

In *R v Kemp* [1957] 1 QB 399 (at 407) it was stated that a mental disorder for the purposes of the common law defence of insanity may be permanent or temporary, curable or incurable. In *Bratty v Attorney General (Northern Ireland)* [1963] AC 386 (at 412) Lord Denning attempted to put a rider on this by stating that:

> [A]ny mental disorder which has manifested itself in violence and is prone to recur is a disease of the mind. At any rate it is the sort of disease for which a person should be detained in hospital rather than be given an unqualified acquittal.

This recurrence element found favour with Sholl J in *R v Carter* [1959] VR 105 and *R v Meddings* [1966] VR 306. In the latter case, Sholl J stated (at 309) that the:

> potentiality of repetition ... might be regarded as a discrimen between cases of irrational behaviour due to some transient cause affecting the mind, other than disease of the mind, and cases of irrational behaviour due to defective reason from disease of the mind.

This test has been criticised on the basis that it may unfairly hold that conditions such as epilepsy, sleepwalking, hypoglycaemia and hyperglycaemia must of necessity be diseases of the mind because they are likely to recur, despite such conditions lending themselves to control through medication and good health practices.[71] It does appear that this test is not used as often as the internal/external test. However, in *R v Stone* [1999] 2 SCR 290, the Supreme Court of Canada referred to the possibility of continuing danger as one of the factors to be taken into account in categorising a condition as sane or insane automatism.

THE INTERNAL/EXTERNAL TEST

The internal/external test was developed by Martin JA in the Canadian case of *R v Rabey* (1977) 37 CCC (2d) 461[72] in which he stated (at 477):

> In general, the distinction to be drawn is between a malfunctioning of the mind arising from some cause that is primarily internal to the accused, having its source in his [or her] psychological or emotional make-up, or in some organic pathology, as opposed to a malfunctioning of mind which is the transient effect produced by some specific external factor such as, for example, concussion.

This distinction is aimed at placing mental states such as those caused by physical blows, hypnotic influences or drugs firmly in the camp of automatism as it relates to voluntary conduct. The rationale appears to be that an internal weakness may be more likely to lead to recurrent violence than automatism brought about by some intervening and usually external cause. Therefore automatism caused by some internal factor should be subsumed within a defence of mental impairment in order that the accused may be detained rather than completely acquitted.

---

71 See B McSherry, "Defining What is a 'Disease of the Mind': The Untenability of Current Legal Interpretations" (1993) 1 *Journal of Law and Medicine* 76 at 83; D O'Connor and PA Fairall, *Criminal Defences* (3rd ed, Sydney: Butt, 1996), p 284.

72 Affirmed on appeal by the Supreme Court of Canada in *Rabey v The Queen* (1981) 54 CCC 1.

The internal/external test can be criticised because it may lead to arbitrary results. For example, in *R v Quick* [1989] 1 WLR 287 the English Court of Appeal held that hypoglycaemia which was brought on by the accused's use of insulin amounted to sane automatism because it was brought on by an external factor. However, in *R v Hennessy* [1973] 1 QB 910 Lord Lane CJ suggested at 293 that hyperglycaemia caused by a failure to take insulin is an "inherent defect" which could be subsumed within the defence of insanity. In addition, some conditions may not lend themselves to being easily classified as arising from internal or external causes. For example, Fenwick writes that because sleepwalking is known to run in families and has a marked genetic component, it can be viewed as arising from internal factors: "Somnambulism and the Law: A Review" (1987) 5 *Behavioural Sciences and the Law* 343 at 350. At the same time, however, he points out (at 350) that "external trigger factors such as tiredness, drugs, alcohol, stress, also often play a part".

The internal/external test may therefore be of assistance in relation to distinguishing between clear-cut cases as, for instance, a blow to the head producing concussion from severe mental disorders such as schizophrenia. However, it is of limited use in relation to complex medical conditions such as hyperglycaemia, hypoglycaemia and sleepwalking.

THE SOUND/UNSOUND MIND TEST

The sound/unsound mind test is a more sophisticated version of the internal/external distinction aimed specifically at "dissociative states". The latter may arise from external stress factors or as a result of some forms of neurological or other general medical conditions. Dissociative states are explained loosely in the *Diagnostic and Statistical Manual of Mental Disorders* (4th ed, Washington: APA, 1994) (at 477) as follows:

> The essential feature of the Dissociative Disorders is a disruption in the usually integrated functions of consciousness, memory, identity, or perception of the environment. The disturbance may be sudden or gradual, transient or chronic.

In *R v Radford* (1985) 42 SASR 266 King CJ set out the test for determining whether dissociative states should fall within automatism as it relates to voluntary conduct or automatism subsumed within the defence of mental impairment as a "disease of the mind". In that case, Radford shot and killed a woman whom he believed to have been the lover of his ex-wife. Radford had served in Vietnam and at the time of the shooting he claimed that he thought he was shooting a soldier dressed in army gear. He stated that he had become very detached from the situation as though he "had gone into a sort of cocoon": at 268. Psychiatric evidence was called by the defence to the effect that the accused had been in a "state of derealization" which was closely akin to dissociation and this had been brought about by the emotional stress of the accused's marriage break-up. The psychiatrist was also of the opinion that this state was not caused by any disease, chronic disorder or disturbance of the mind.

The trial judge ruled that this evidence did not raise the issue of involuntary action apart from insanity. Counsel for the defence did not wish to raise insanity and therefore confined the issue to whether or not intention had been proved. Radford was convicted of murder. On appeal, the Supreme Court of South Australia set aside the conviction and ordered a retrial[73] on the basis that the

---

73 On a retrial, Radford was convicted of murder and this was upheld by the Court of Criminal Appeal of South Australia: *R v Radford (No 2)* (1987) 11 Crim LJ 231.

question of automatism as it relates to voluntary conduct should have been left to the jury. In the course of his judgment, King CJ stated (at 276):

> The significant distinction is between the reaction of an unsound mind to its own delusions or to external stimuli on the one hand and the reaction of a sound mind to external stimuli, including stress producing factors, on the other hand.

In *R v Falconer* (1990) 171 CLR 30 Toohey J, Mason CJ, Brennan and McHugh JJ all approved of this test for distinguishing between dissociative states which relate to voluntary conduct and those which are subsumed within the defence of mental impairment. Gaudron J (at 85) adopted a similar test, but introduced the concept of states of mind experienced by a "normal" person:

> [T]he fundamental distinction is necessarily between those mental states which, although resulting in abnormal behaviour, are or may be experienced by normal persons (as, for example and relevant to the issue of involuntariness, a state of mind resulting from a blow to the head) and those which are never experienced by or encountered in normal persons.

Mason CJ, Brennan and McHugh JJ also proposed an objective standard gloss to the sound/unsound mind distinction. They stated (at 55):

> [T]he law must postulate a standard of mental strength which, in the face of a given level of psychological trauma, is capable of protecting the mind from malfunction to the extent prescribed in the respective definitions of insanity. That standard must be the standard of the ordinary person: if the mind's strength is below that standard, the mind is infirm; if it is of or above that standard, the mind is sound or sane. This is an objective standard which corresponds with the objective standard imported for the purpose of provocation.

The result of these statements appears to be that where a state of dissociation is in issue, King CJ's test will be applied and the standard will be an objective one, that of the "ordinary" or "normal" person.

The main difficulty with this test lies in distinguishing between the reaction of an unsound mind and that of a sound mind, given the vagaries of determining who is an "ordinary" or "normal" person. The distinction between the two may largely depend upon the susceptibility of the accused to emotional shock and stress. For example, if there is evidence that the accused was not normally affected by stress, then he or she may have a good defence if the psychological blow is severe. On the standard of the ordinary normal person, he or she would be displaying abnormal behaviour which an ordinary person might very well experience in the same circumstances. On the other hand, if the accused's dissociative state is triggered by an "everyday" form of stress, then he or she is to be regarded as having an unsound mind on the basis that the reaction of a normal person would not be so severe. What is the real difference? In the latter case, the accused is simply more susceptible to stress.

There is an added difficulty in determining what amounts to "stress producing factors" for the purposes of assessing the external stimuli which may cause a sound mind to react. In *R v Mansfield* (unrep, SC Vic Hampel J, acquittal 5/5/1994) the accused was acquitted on the basis that he was in a dissociative state as a result of the external stress of a marital breakdown when he stabbed his estranged wife to death. It is debatable whether or not a relationship breakdown is sufficient external stimuli to cause an ordinary, normal person to cause another to act in an involuntary way. King CJ sounded this warning in *R v Radford (No 2)* (1987) 11 Crim LJ 231 (at 232):

Feelings of jealousy and resentment over the breakdown of matrimonial and other sexual relationships and hatred of a rival lover are commonplace human emotions. The law must firmly repress any tendency for people harbouring such dark emotions to give in to them by way of murderous violence.

The ordinary/reasonable person standard is confronted by similar challenges in the context of provocation and self-defence: see Chs 5, 6, pp 270, 305.

As stated earlier, the three tests used to distinguish between automatism as it relates to voluntary conduct and automatism which may be subsumed within the defence of mental impairment are artificial and should only be used as guides rather than rigidly followed: *R v Falconer* (1990) 171 CLR 30 at 50-51 per Mason CJ, Brennan and McHugh JJ, at 77 per Toohey J, at 84 per Gaudron J.

3.5 PRESUMPTION OF MENTAL CAPACITY

There is a presumption of mental capacity in the common law that the accused acted pursuant to an exercise of will.[74] This presumption may be displaced by evidence that leaves the jury in doubt as to whether or not the actions were voluntary.[75] The defence therefore has the evidential burden in relation to the issue of automatism.[76] The standard of the evidential burden of proof in relation to automatism appears to be sufficient evidence from which it may be inferred that the conduct was involuntary: *Youseff* (1990) 50 A Crim R 1 at 3 per Hunt J. In *Bratty v Attorney-General (Northern Ireland)* [1963] AC 386 (at 413) Lord Denning spoke of the requirement that the evidential burden would be fulfilled if the evidence amounted to a "proper foundation". Similarly, in *Hill v Baxter* [1958] 1 QB 277 (at 285) Lord Devlin referred to the requirement of "*prima facie* evidence". Just what amounts to a "proper foundation" or "*prima facie* evidence" will be a matter for the trial judge to determine.

3.6 BURDEN OF PROOF

If automatism is raised by the defence as a subset of the defence of mental impairment, the burden will be on the accused to prove mental impairment on the balance of probabilities: *R v Falconer* (1990) 171 CLR 30. If the defence raises automatism to show that the act was involuntary, the defence bears the evidential burden and the onus is on the prosecution to negate automatism beyond reasonable doubt.[77]

---

74 *R v Falconer* (1990) 171 CLR 30 at 41-42 per Mason CJ, Brennan and McHugh JJ (approving *R v Radford* (1985) 42 SASR 266).

75 *R v Falconer* (1990) 171 CLR 30 at 41-42 per Mason CJ, Brennan and McHugh JJ (approving *R v Radford* (1985) 42 SASR 266).

76 See Chapter 2, p 118 as to the meaning of the evidential burden. See also *Wogandt* (1988) 3 A Crim R 31; *Ryan v The Queen* (1967) 121 CLR 205 at 215-216 per Barwick CJ: *Bratty v Attorney General for Northern Ireland* [1963] AC 386 at 406 per Viscount Kilmuir LC (HL); *Hill v Baxter* [1958] 1 QB 277 at 285 per Devlin J.

77 *R v Falconer* (1990) 171 CLR 30 at 61-62 per Deane and Dawson JJ, at 86 per Gaudron J. Compare the decision of the minority on this point, Mason CJ, Brennan and McHugh JJ at 56 who favoured placing both the evidentiary and legal burden of proof on the defence where automatism is raised. This latter approach has been taken up by a majority of the Supreme Court of Canada in *R v Stone* [1999] 2 SCR 290.

The defence may wish to raise automatism as relating to involuntary conduct in order to gain a complete acquittal. The prosecution may then want to raise the issue of automatism as a form of mental impairment in order to have the option of detention or a supervision order available rather than a complete acquittal. This complicates the procedure relating to the burden and standard of proof.

In *R v Falconer* (1990) 171 CLR 30 the majority was of the opinion that there was no need to modify the ordinary rules as to the burden and standard of proof. The jury therefore needs to be instructed according to a five-step procedure.

DIAGRAM 1: Five-Step Procedure

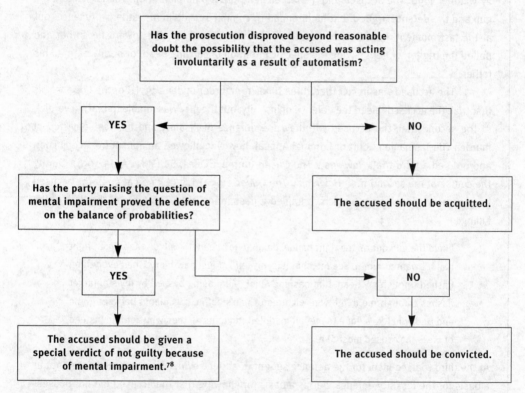

Deane and Dawson JJ added (at 63) further comments about the defence of mental impairment in general, concluding that if there is evidence that would support a verdict of not guilty because of mental impairment, the prosecution could rely upon it in asking for a special verdict of supervision as an alternative to conviction. They take the realistic approach that it is more often in the interests of the prosecution to raise the issue of mental impairment rather than in the interests of the accused because of the attendant consequences of supervision orders.

---

78 This Diagram is based on the procedure set out in *R v Falconer* (1990) 171 CLR 30 at 62-63 per Deane and Dawson JJ, at 77-78 per Toohey J and at 80 per Gaudron J. According to s 21 of the *Crimes (Mental Impairment and Unfitness to be Tried) Act* 1997 (Vic) the legal burden is on the party raising the defence of mental impairment and the standard of proof is on the balance of probabilities. The prosecution can only raise this defence with the leave of the trial judge: *Crimes (Mental Impairment and Unfitness to be Tried) Act* 1997 (Vic), s 22(1).

CASE STUDIES

Mental Impairment and Intention

Evidence of mental impairment may be raised not only for the purpose of the defence of mental impairment, but also to show that there was not the requisite intention for the crime charged. The leading decision in this area is that of *Hawkins v The Queen* (1994) 179 CLR 500.

In *Hawkins*, the High Court considered a number of sections of the *Criminal Code* 1924 (Tas) which deal with concepts of voluntariness, soundness of mind and intention. The facts giving rise to the Court's decision concerned the shooting of a father by his 16 year-old son on 27 October 1990. The accused and his father went into a pine plantation. The accused had a gun and the defence argued that he intended to commit suicide in his father's presence, but at the last moment, in a disturbed state of mind, he turned the rifle toward his father and pulled the trigger without having the specific intention of causing death or bodily harm to his father.

The accused was in fact tried three times for murder under s 157(1) of the Code. At his first trial, the accused raised the defence of insanity, but the jury was unable to reach a verdict. At the second trial, the accused withdrew the defence of insanity and he was convicted of murder. The Tasmanian Court of Criminal Appeal, however, allowed an appeal from conviction and ordered a third trial: *Hawkins v The Queen* (unrep, SC Tas, Serial No A105/1991). During the course of the second trial (*Hawkins v The Queen* (1994) 179 CLR 500 at 505), the accused gave an unsworn statement which contained a description of his thoughts at the time of the killing:

> I held the gun out on the right hand side up to my head, thumb on the trigger, right hand. I wanted him to see me shot [sic] myself ... I just saw him ... then everything flashed through my head. Him bashing Mum, Mum being bashed by my stepfather flashes through me mind were pictures of nan's coffin, arguments between Mum and Dad, what he's done to me, all muddled thoughts — then why not him instead of me — he caused most of it.

At the third trial, counsel for the defence sought to adduce evidence of mental disease not as a basis for the insanity defence, but as a basis for showing that the accused did not possess the requisite intention for the crime of murder. Underwood J conducted a voir dire to determine the relevance and admissibility of this evidence. Two expert witnesses were called by the defence. One gave evidence that the accused was suffering from a diagnosable mental disease at the time of the shooting which he labelled an "adolescent identity disorder". The other expert stated that the accused had been suffering from an "adolescent adjustment disorder" which could be regarded in law as a mental disease.

Underwood J ruled that this medical evidence was inadmissible for any purpose other than the insanity defence. The Court of Criminal Appeal of Tasmania dismissed an appeal by the accused on the ground that the ruling that the evidence was inadmissible did not cause any miscarriage of justice: *Hawkins (No 2)* (1993) 68 A Crim R 1. The accused then appealed to the High Court.

In a joint judgment, the High Court agreed that evidence of mental disease should be excluded in determining the issue of the voluntariness of the criminal act. This followed its earlier decision in *R v Falconer* (1990) 171 CLR 30. A distinction was drawn between mental states caused by factors other than "diseases of the mind" which could be considered in relation to voluntary conduct and mental states caused by "diseases of the mind" which lead to a consideration of the insanity defence.

However, the High Court went on to hold that there was no reason "for excluding evidence of mental disease in determining whether an act done by a person who is criminally responsible for the act was done with a specific intent": *Hawkins v The Queen* (1994) 179 CLR 500 at 513. It held that since evidence of intoxication may be led to negate intention, "it would be anomalous to exclude evidence of other forms of mental abnormality in determining the same issue": at 514. The High Court remitted the matter to the Court of Criminal Appeal of Tasmania to either make an order dismissing the appeal if it considered that no substantial miscarriage of justice had actually occurred or alternatively, to consider substituting a conviction of manslaughter instead of ordering a new trial. The Court of Criminal Appeal by a majority of two to one subsequently ordered that there be a fourth trial of the matter: *Hawkins v The Queen (No 3)* (1994) 4 Tas R 376. The accused then pleaded guilty to manslaughter and was sentenced on 11 July 1995 by Cox J to six years imprisonment to date from the 29th October 1990 when he had first been taken into custody.

In its judgment, the High Court cautioned that the use of evidence of mental disease to negate intention can arise "only on the hypothesis that the accused's mental condition at the time when the incriminated act was done fell short of insanity": *Hawkins v The Queen* (1994) 179 CLR 500 at 517. In reaching this conclusion, the High Court relied upon a series of Canadian cases in which mental disorder falling short of "insanity" has been held to negate the fault element.[79] Ian Leader-Elliott summarises the procedural effect of *Hawkins* as follows:

> If the evidence of mental disease is supplemented by evidence of one or other of the elements necessary to the defence of insanity, the jury will be instructed to return an insanity verdict if satisfied, on the balance of probabilities, that the defence is made out.
>
> The issue of intention falls to be considered:
>
> **(a)** if the evidence of mental disease is not capable of supporting an insanity defence; or
>
> **(b)** if the jury is not persuaded on the balance of probabilities that the defence is made out.

---

79 *More v The Queen* [1963] 3 CCC 289 at 291-292 (SC Can); *R v Lacjance* [1963] 2 CCC 14 at 17 (CA Ont); *R v Kirkby* (1985) 21 CCC (3d) 31 at 61; *R v Baltzer* (1974) 27 CCC (2d) 118 at 141 (CA NS); *R v Meloche* (1975) 34 CCC (2d) 184; *R v Browning* (1976) 34 CCC (2d) 200 at 202-203; *R v Hilton* (1977) 34 CCC (2d) 206 at 208; *R v Lechasseur* (1977) 38 CCC (2d) 319; *R v Allard* (1990) 57 CCC (3d) 397 at 401; *R v Stevenson* (1990) 58 CCC (3d) 464 at 488.

> Evidence of mental disease is admissible on the issue of intention and the prosecution must establish intention beyond reasonable doubt: I Leader-Elliott, "Case note: Insanity, Involuntariness and the Mental Element in Crime" (1994) 18 Crim LJ 347 at 351-352.

Hawkin's case only deals with mental impairment as it relates to intention. If intention is not made out for the crime of murder, for example, the decision in *Hawkins* allows a fall-back position for the accused to be convicted of manslaughter rather than be given a complete acquittal. It is unclear, however, whether or not evidence of mental impairment may be admissible in relation to recklessness or negligence. Leader-Elliott argues (at 355) that mental impairment may be relevant to these fault elements as well as intention. It could be argued that mental impairment prevented the accused from realising the probability of harm to the victim or that the accused was incapable of meeting ordinary standards of care. In this sense, *Hawkins* may open the way for a complete acquittal if the requisite fault elements are not made out. This point is yet to be decided by the courts.

4. INTOXICATION

A research report prepared by Ian Leader-Elliott and Jason White for the National Symposium on Alcohol Misuse and Violence found clear evidence that "police frequently deal with intoxicated suspects": *Legal Approaches to Alcohol-Related Violence: A Summary*, Report 6A for the National Symposium on Alcohol Misuse and Violence (Canberra: AGPS, July 1994), p 29. Recent empirical studies on adult detainees have confirmed high levels of illicit drug use across a wide range of offences: see Ch 15, p 827. Using evidence of such intoxication (whatever the drug) in court, however, is a double-edged sword. Intoxication is not in itself a defence to a criminal charge,[80] but may negate the elements of a crime if it causes a condition inconsistent with criminal responsibility. However, evidence of intoxication may be damaging for the defence as it may invite an inference of intention[81] or motive[82] from the very fact that the accused was intoxicated.

The prosecution may claim that evidence of self-induced intoxication showed that the accused became intoxicated in order to commit the crime, alcohol being known as a disinhibitor.[83] Evidence of intoxication may therefore be used by the prosecution to explain the accused's behaviour.[84] Murphy J in *R v O'Connor* (1980) 146 CLR 64 described the use of evidence of intoxication as follows (at 114):

---

80 *Viro v The Queen* (1978) 141 CLR 88 at 109 per Gibbs J; *R v O'Connor* (1980) 146 CLR 64; *R v Murray* [1980] 2 NSWLR 526; *Sullivan* (1981) 6 A Crim R 259; *R v Kamipeli* [1975] 2 NZLR 610.

81 *Owens* (1987) 30 A Crim R 59; *R v Kingston* [1994] 3 WLR 519.

82 *O'Leary v Daire* (1984) 13 A Crim R 404 at 411 per White J (SC SA).

83 *Attorney-General (Northern Ireland) v Gallagher* [1963] AC 349 at 382 per Denning LJ (HL) (the expression "Dutch courage" is sometimes used in this context). *O'Leary v Daire* (1984) 13 A Crim R 404 at 411 per White J (SC SA).

84 *R v Stokes* (1990) 51 A Crim R 25 at 33 per Hunt J (CCA NSW); *R v Hamilton* (1985) 31 A Crim R 167 (CCA NSW); *R v Perks* (1986) 41 SASR 335 at 340-341 per White J; *R v Leaf-Milham* (1987) 47 SASR 499; *O'Leary v Daire* (1984) 13 A Crim R 404 at 411 per White J (SC SA).

The inferences to be drawn from intoxication are not all one way: evidence of intoxication may result in absence of proof beyond reasonable doubt of the requisite fault element, or in a more ready acceptance that the fault element exists on the supposition that intoxication reduces inhibitions.

Evidence of intoxication may also be used by the prosecution to show negligence or recklessness in relation to charges such as culpable or dangerous driving.[85]

The history of intoxication and criminal responsibility is an interesting one. In early Anglo-Saxon law, no concession was made in practice to an intoxicated accused: RU Singh, "History of the Defence of Drunkenness in English Criminal Law" (1933) 49 *Law Quarterly Review* 528 at 529: see also D McCord, "The English and American History of Voluntary Intoxication to Negate *Mens Rea*" (1992) 11 *Journal of Legal History* 372. It was only in the 19th century, that a line of cases began to emerge allowing evidence of intoxication in relation to the material question as to whether the accused's act was premeditated or done impulsively: F McAuley, "The Intoxication Defence in Criminal Law" (1997) 32 *Irish Jurist* 243. In 1849 Coleridge J mentioned the relationship between intoxication and specific intention. In *R v Monkhouse* (1849) 4 Cox CC 55 (at 56) he stated:

> [W]here [intoxication] is available as a partial answer to a charge ... it is not enough that
> [the accused] was excited or rendered more irritable, unless the intoxication was such as ...
> to take away the power of forming any specific intention.

It was in *DPP v Beard* [1920] AC 479 that the House of Lords fully established the common law relating to intoxication. In general, that decision set out the rule that an accused can use evidence of self-induced intoxication to show that he or she did not have the intent for "specific intent" crimes, but is not allowed to use evidence of self-induced intoxication to show that he or she did not have the intent required for "basic intent" offences. This approach was further set out in the case of *DPP v Majewski* [1977] AC 443, and the distinction is explained below: p 246.

The Australian common law has diverged from that of England. However, the *Beard/Majewski* approach is still reflected in the Code jurisdictions' approach to intoxication. The Code jurisdictions of Queensland, Tasmania and Western Australia as well as New South Wales have followed the English approach of dividing crimes into those where intoxication may be taken into account and those where evidence of intoxication is irrelevant. In Queensland and Western Australia, intoxication may be considered in relation to crimes that have "an intention to cause a specific result" as an element of the offence: *Criminal Code* (Qld), s 28; *Criminal Code* (WA), s 28. The Tasmanian provision simply refers to the element of "specific intent essential to constitute the offence": *Criminal Code* (Tas), s 17(2). Similarly, in New South Wales, self-induced intoxication may only be taken into account in relation to whether the accused "had the intention to cause the specific result necessary for an offence of specific intent": *Crimes Act* 1900 (NSW), s 428C.

This amendment in New South Wales was introduced following the controversy in
R v Paxman **(NSW District Court 21/6/95) where the accused, convicted of man-slaughter, received a sentence of only 3 years imprisonment. The perceived leniency was (wrongly) blamed by the media on the availability of intoxication as an excuse, pressuring the New South Wales Government to introduce these reforms.**

---

85 *R v Guthrie* (1981) 52 FLR 171; *R v McBride* [1962] 2 QB 167.

The *Criminal Code* (NT) is somewhat different to the other jurisdictions in that it does not expressly state that intoxication may negate the fault element of a crime. Section 7(1)(b) sets out a presumption that the accused foresaw the natural and probable consequences of his or her conduct unless the intoxication was involuntary. This seems to suggest that self-induced intoxication will be irrelevant to the question of intention.

Interestingly enough, the Model Criminal Code Officers Committee rejected the division of crimes into those where intoxication is relevant and those where it is irrelevant. It recommended that the approach in *O' Connor's* case be followed: *Model Criminal Code, Chapter 2: General Principles of Criminal Responsibility,* Final Report (December 1992), p 51. However, s 8.2(1) of the *Criminal Code Act* 1995 (Cth) was nevertheless enacted stating that self-induced intoxication can only be considered in relation to offences involving specific intent.

The leading common law decision in Australia dealing with intoxication is *R v O' Connor* (1980) 146 CLR 64. In that case, the accused was caught rifling through a car owned by a police officer. When the officer found the accused, the latter had removed a map and a knife from the car. The accused went to run away, but the officer caught him and arrested him. During the arrest, the accused opened the blade of the knife and stabbed the officer. There was evidence led that the accused had been taking an hallucinogenic drug and that he had been drinking a substantial amount of alcohol during the day of the occurrence.

The accused was charged with theft and with wounding with intent to resist arrest. The trial judge directed the jury that these were crimes of specific intent and intoxication could be taken into account when considering these charges but that it was irrelevant to an alternative charge of unlawful wounding. The jury accordingly found the accused not guilty of theft and wounding with intent to resist arrest, but guilty of unlawful wounding.

The accused appealed to the Supreme Court of Victoria. It allowed the appeal and entered a verdict of acquittal on the alternative charge of unlawful wounding. The Solicitor-General of Victoria applied for special leave to appeal to the High Court. Special leave was granted and a majority of the Court consisting of Barwick CJ, Stephen, Murphy and Aickin JJ all delivered separate judgments dismissing the Solicitor-General's appeal. The majority was of the opinion that evidence of intoxication may be tendered to assist in raising a doubt as to the voluntary character of the criminal conduct and that such evidence may be tendered even where the offence is one of strict liability. They also held that evidence of intoxication could be relevant to cast doubt as to whether or not the accused possessed the requisite fault element in relation to the unlawful act.

The minority, consisting of Wilson, Gibbs and Mason JJ preferred to follow the English approach to evidence of intoxication set out in *DPP v Majewski* [1977] AC 443. In that case, the House of Lords drew a distinction between crimes of basic and specific intent and held that evidence of intoxication was only relevant to the latter.[86] The minority was concerned with public policy in reaching their decisions. Mason J stated (at 110):

---

86   The House of Lords has since expressed some doubt concerning the application of the distinction between crimes of basic and specific intent in relation to the admissibility of evidence of intoxication: *R v Kingston* [1994] 3 All ER 353 at 364 per Lord Mustill.

[T]here are two strands of thought whose thrust is to deny that drunkenness is an excuse for the commission of crime. One is essentially a moral judgment — that it is wrong that a person should escape responsibility for his [or her] actions merely because he [or she] is so intoxicated by drink or drugs that his [or her] act is not willed when by his [or her] own voluntary choice he [or she] embarked on the course which led to his [or her] intoxication. The other is a social judgment — that society legitimately expects for its protection that the law will not allow to go unpunished an act which would be adjudged to be a serious criminal offence but for the fact that the perpetrator is grossly intoxicated.

The majority of the High Court refused to follow *Majewski* because:

▬ first, the distinction between crimes of specific and basic intent lacks logic;[87] and

▬ secondly, the social policy arguments in favour of holding an accused liable for depriving him or herself of the capacity to act voluntarily or intentionally would provide an unjustifiable exception to fundamental common law principles.

Stephen J stated (at 101) that the *Majewski* approach "operates by means of uncertain criteria, in a manner not always rational and which serves an end which I regard as doubtful of attainment". Barwick CJ stated (at 87) that the blameworthiness which may be attached to the accused's behaviour in becoming intoxicated in the first place should not be superimposed over the criminal conduct so as to presume that the accused acted voluntarily or with the requisite state of mind.

While the majority's approach to evidence of intoxication in *O'Connor's* case caused political and media controversy, there is no evidence that it has given rise to an increase in acquittals on the ground of intoxication: see, for example, Victorian Law Reform Commission, *Criminal Responsibility: Intention and Gross Intoxication,* Report No 6 (Melbourne: VLRC, 1986), p 19; G Smith, "A Footnote to *O'Connor's* case" (1981) 5 Crim LJ 270 at 276-277.

In 1997, the common law relating to intoxication in *O'Connor* came under fire after a well known member of a professional rugby club, Noa Nadruku Kurimalawi was acquitted by a magistrate of assaulting two women on the basis that he was so intoxicated that he did not know what he did and did not form any intent as to what he was doing: *SC Small v Noa Kurimalawi* (ACT Magistrates' Court No CC97/01904, 22 October 1997). The resulting uproar concerning the acquittal gave rise to the drafting of legislation which is intended to implement the relevant provisions of the *Criminal Code Act* 1995 (Cth).[88] The South Australian and Victorian Parliaments also subsequently conducted inquiries into the law relating to intoxication.[89]

---

87 Stephen J pointed out that murder is generally characterised as a crime of specific intent, yet other serious crimes such as rape and manslaughter are characterised as crimes of basic intent. He stated that such a distinction is "neither clearly defined not easily recognisable [and] ... does not reflect or give effect to any coherent attitude either as the relative wrongfulness of particular conduct or the degree of social mischief which that conduct is thought to involve": *R v O'Connor* (1980) 146 CLR 64 at 104; 4 A Crim R 348.

88 Clause 4 will if passed, insert a new s 428XC into the *Crimes Act* 1900 (ACT). This amendment was referred to the Justice and Community Safety Committee (ACT) in May 1998.

89 Attorney-General's Office (SA), *Intoxication and Criminal Responsibility*, Discussion Paper (July 1998); Victorian Law Reform Committee, *Inquiry Into Criminal Liability for Self-Induced Intoxication*, Report (May 1999).

This is one area of the law where there are no easy answers as to how evidence of intoxication should be taken into account. In summary, evidence of intoxication may be used by the defence, depending upon the jurisdiction, to support a claim that:

- the criminal conduct was performed involuntarily;

- the conduct was not intended or the accused did not have the requisite fault element for the offence;

- it caused mental impairment for the purposes of the defence of mental impairment;

- it helps substantiate a claim of self-defence or provocation; or

- in some jurisdictions, it negated criminal responsibility because it was unintentional.

We will outline the present law relating to intoxication, then look briefly at the difference between principle and policy in guiding what the law should be.

4.1 INTOXICATION AND VOLUNTARINESS

An accused can only be considered criminally responsible where he or she performed the criminal act voluntarily in the sense that it was willed.[90] At common law, the High Court majority decision in *R v O'Connor* (1980) 146 CLR 64 affirms that evidence of intoxication in extreme cases may support the claim that the accused's actions were involuntary. This was the position in Victoria prior to *O'Connor's* case.[91]

The situation in the Code jurisdictions, however, appears to differ. None of the *Criminal Codes* refer to the relevance of self-induced intoxication in relation to the question of voluntary conduct. The case law appears to hold that where an offence charged does not require proof of an intention to cause a specific result, evidence of self-induced intoxication cannot provide a foundation for a plea of involuntariness.[92]

In *R v Kusu* [1981] Qd R 136 the majority read s 28, the intoxication provision of the *Criminal Code* (Qld), as qualifying s 23(1) which states that a person is not criminally responsible for an act that occurs independently of the exercise of the person's will. In that case, Macrossan J in dissent stated that an accused whose intoxication leads to conduct occurring independently of the will can rely on s 23, even where the elements of the offence do not include an intention to cause a specific result. Malcolm CJ in *Cameron* (1990) 47 A Crim R 397 had sympathy for this view, stating that it was

---

90 *Criminal Code* (NT), s 31; *Criminal Code* (Qld), s 23; *Criminal Code* (Tas), s 13; *Criminal Code* (WA), s 23; *R v Vickers* [1957] 2 QB 664 at 672 per Lord Goddard CJ (CCA); *R v Scott* [1967] VR 276 at 288-289 per Gillard J (FC SC Vic); *R v Haywood* [1971] VR 755; *R v Tait* [1973] VR 151; *R v Dodd* (1974) 7 SASR 151; *Woolmington v DPP* [1935] AC 462 at 482 per Viscount Sankey LC; *Ryan v The Queen* (1967) 121 CLR 205. See Chapter 3 at 3.2 'Voluntariness'.

91 *R v Keogh* [1964] VR 400; *R v Haywood* [1971] VR 755.

92 *R v Martin* [1979] Tas R 211 at 213; (1979) 1 A Crim R 85; *Arnol* (1981) 7 A Crim R 291; *Palmer v The Queen* [1985] Tas R 138; *Bennett* (1989) 45 A Crim R 45; *R v Kusu* [1981] Qd R 136; *R v Miers* [1985] 2 Qd R 138; *Cameron* (1990) 47 A Crim R 397 at 410; *R v Battle* (1993) 8 WAR 449; *Haggie v Meredith* (1993) 9 WAR 206.

consistent with the approach taken to automatism by the High Court in *R v Falconer* (1990) 171 CLR 30. However, he accepted that the weight of authority supported the majority view in *Kusu* and there was no room for the question of s 23 in an intoxication case.

Section 13(1) of the *Criminal Code* (Tas) requires an act to be voluntary and intentional in order for criminal responsibility to be made out. In *Snow v The Queen* [1962] Tas SR 271 the majority held that intoxication was irrelevant to this section unless it had caused a disease of the mind and brought into play the defence of insanity. In dissent, Crawford J stated that intoxication could, on rare occasions, be relevant to whether the act of an accused was voluntary and intentional or as to whether the act occurred by chance. The decision of the majority in *Snow's* case was affirmed by the Supreme Court of Tasmania in *Attorney-General's Reference No 1 of 1996: Re David John Weiderman* (unrep, 26/2/1998, SC Tas, CCA, No 12/98).[93]

Section 428G of the *Crimes Act* 1900 (NSW) now makes it clear that self-induced intoxication cannot be taken into account in determining whether the relevant conduct was voluntary.

Evidence of intoxication is used most commonly in order to negate the fault element of a crime rather than as grounds for involuntary conduct: *R v Tucker* (1984) 36 SASR 135. This is perhaps partly because of the difficulty in getting a jury to accept that the accused could carry out often complicated conduct, yet claim that this conduct was unwilled due to intoxication. Indeed, the idea that the movements of the body can be divorced from the will has been the subject of debate in philosophical literature.[94]

Because evidence of intoxication is used most often to negate the requisite fault element, a jury direction in relation to voluntariness will usually be unnecessary. King CJ has explained this in *R v Tucker* (1984) 36 SASR 135 at 139 as follows:

> If intent is proved, voluntariness is proved ipso facto. In all such cases a direction as to the
> effect of alcohol on the existence of volition is unnecessary and could well confuse the jury.

On the other hand, if intent is not proved, a verdict of not guilty results irrespective of whether or not the conduct was involuntary.

At common law, partial intoxication as well as total intoxication may be relevant to the issue of whether or not the criminal conduct was involuntary: *Martin* (1983) 9 A Crim R 376 at 404. Desmond O'Connor and Paul Fairall write:

> The effect of partial intoxication may be one of several discrete factors (for example,
> epilepsy, concussion, nervous shock) put forward by way of explanation for D's involuntary
> conduct. Such factors should be viewed collectively, and not in isolation. The jury should
> be directed to take into account any evidence of intoxication (whether partial or total) in
> deciding whether the act was a product of the will.[95]

---

93 See R Bradfield, "Case and Comment: *Attorney-General's Reference No 1 of 1996 Re Weiderman*" (1999) 23 Crim LJ 41.

94 See, for example, HLA Hart, *Punishment and Responsibility* (Oxford: Clarendon Press, 1968), pp 90-112; E Coles and D Jang, "A Psychological Perspective on the Legal Concepts of 'Volition' and 'Intent'" (1996) 4 *Journal of Law and Medicine* 60.

95 D O'Connor and P Fairall, *Criminal Defences* (3rd ed, Sydney: Butt, 1996), pp 232-233.

It should be pointed out that in *O'Connor's* case, the majority of the High Court did not itself conclude that O'Connor's actions were involuntary, but held that this matter should have been left to the jury to decide.[96]

4.2 INTOXICATION AND FAULT ELEMENTS

Subjective fault elements have traditionally been divided into intention, knowledge and recklessness: see Ch 3, 3.4 'Fault Elements'. A further fault element is expressed in the objective element of negligence. Evidence of intoxication may be raised to negate some of these subjective fault elements depending upon the jurisdiction, but will not afford any assistance to the defence in relation to casting a doubt as to negligent conduct. In the latter case, it may be used by the prosecution to show negligence in relation to charges such as culpable or dangerous driving.[97] This is discussed below at p 247.

INTOXICATION AND INTENTION, KNOWLEDGE AND RECKLESSNESS

At common law, evidence of intoxication may be relevant to show that the accused did not possess the requisite intention or knowledge for the offence or to negate recklessness.[98] This ruling as set out in *R v O'Connor* (1980) 146 CLR 64 can be viewed as the logical consequence of fidelity to the principle of subjective fault. However, while the majority of the High Court held that intoxication was relevant in assessing subjective fault, jury directions usually stress that evidence of intoxication will not preclude intent, but may serve to loosen inhibitions such that "a drunken intent is an intent nevertheless".[99] Such a "mixed-message" jury direction as to intention has been described by Alan Norrie as "having one's subjectivist cake and eating it": A Norrie, *Crime, Reason and History* (London: Weidenfeld & Nicolson, 1993), p 52.

As outlined in Chapter 3, the fault element of most serious crimes is generally expressed as an intention to bring about the requisite physical element of the offence. In relation to the physical element as a specified form of conduct or conduct that occurs in specified circumstances, intention refers to the accused *meaning* to perform the conduct. In relation to the physical element as the results or consequences of conduct, the prosecution must prove that the accused's *purpose* was to bring about the results or consequences of the conduct.[100] Evidence of intoxication may therefore be raised to show that the accused did not mean to perform the conduct or did not act with the purpose of bringing about the results or consequences of the conduct.

---

96 Barwick CJ spent some time discussing the issue of voluntariness. The other judges did not discuss the issue in as much detail and it is therefore unclear as to what level of importance they placed upon the issue.

97 *R v Guthrie* (1981) 52 FLR 171; *R v McBride* [1962] 2 QB 167.

98 *R v O'Connor* (1980) 146 CLR 64 at 87-88 per Barwick CJ, at 105 per Stephen J, at 113-114 per Murphy J, at 125-126 per Aickin J; *Martin* (1984) 16 A Crim R 87.

99 For model jury directions on intoxication in these terms, see J Glissan and S Tilmoth, *Australian Criminal Trial Directions* (Sydney: Butt, 1996), para 5-1400-1, p 7601.

100 *La Fontaine v The Queen* (1976) 136 CLR 62; *R v Crabbe* (1985) 156 CLR 464; *Boughey v The Queen* (1986) 161 CLR 10; *R v Demirian* [1989] VR 97.

An accused may be held criminally responsible if he or she acts with knowledge that a particular circumstance exists or awareness that a particular consequence will result from the performance of the conduct. Evidence of intoxication may therefore be relevant here to show that the accused did not act with the requisite knowledge or awareness.

An accused is said to be reckless where he or she acts in the knowledge that a consequence is a probable or possible result of his or her conduct.[101] Evidence of intoxication may be relevant here to show that the accused did not foresee the likelihood of a consequence or circumstance occurring. For example, in relation to a charge of murder, intoxication may be relevant where the mental element the prosecution must prove is reckless indifference to human life.[102] The test for recklessness which may satisfy the fault element of a crime involves an assessment of whether the accused was aware of the possible consequences of committing the criminal act and whether he or she decided to disregard them and act without caring for the consequences.[103]

The Code jurisdictions take a different approach to the question of intention. In Queensland and Western Australia, intoxication may be considered in relation to crimes that have "an intention to cause a specific result" as an element of the offence: *Criminal Code* (Qld), s 28; *Criminal Code* (WA), s 28. Similarly, in New South Wales, self-induced intoxication may only be taken into account in relation to whether the accused "had the intention to cause the specific result necessary for an offence of specific intent": *Crimes Act* 1900 (NSW), s 428C. Section 17(2) of the *Criminal Code* (Tas) sets out the requirement that evidence of intoxication go to whether or not the accused was "incapable of forming the specific intent essential to constitute the offence". In *Attorney-General's Reference No 1 of 1996; Re Weiderman* (unrep, 26/2/1998, CCA SC Tas, 12/98) the Supreme Court of Tasmania seems to imply that intoxication may be relevant to negate other fault elements such as knowledge: see R Bradfield, "Case and Comment: *Attorney-General's Reference No 1 of 1996 Re Weiderman*" (1999) 23 Crim LJ 41.

The *Criminal Code* (NT) is somewhat different to the other jurisdictions in that it does not expressly state that intoxication may negate the fault element of a crime. Section 7(1)(b) sets out a presumption that the accused foresaw the natural and probable consequences of his or her conduct unless the intoxication was involuntary. This seems to suggest that self-induced intoxication will be irrelevant to the question of intention.

The obvious question that arises here is what are crimes of basic as opposed to specific intent? The following table shows the practical division between the two, but we shall see that theoretically, the division is difficult to explain or justify: for a detailed criticism of the basic/specific intent distinction see T Quigley, "Specific and General Nonsense?" (1987) 11 *Dalhousie Law Journal* 75.

---

101 *Pemble v The Queen* (1971) 124 CLR 107; *La Fontaine v The Queen* (1976) 136 CLR 62; *Nydam v The Queen* [1977] VR 430; *R v Crabbe* (1985) 156 CLR 464; *R v Demirian* [1989] VR 97; *Filmer v Barclay* [1994] 2 VR 269.

102 *R v Stones* (1955) 56 SR (NSW) 25 at 34; *R v Gordon* [1964] NSWR 1024; *Peterkin* (1982) A Crim R 351; *Commissioner of Police of the Metropolis v Caldwell* [1982] AC 341.

103 *R v O'Connor* (1980) 146 CLR 64 at 85 per Barwick CJ; *R v Crabbe* (1985) 156 CLR 464; *R v Brown* (1987) 78 ALR 368; *R v Solomon* [1980] 1 NSWLR 321; *Stokes* (1990) 51 A Crim R 25.

TABLE 2:

The Division Between Crimes of Basic and Specific Intent

CRIMES OF BASIC INTENT (intoxication not relevant)	CRIMES OF SPECIFIC INTENT (intoxication may be relevant)
manslaughter[104]	murder[105]
assault and unlawful wounding[106]	wounding with intent to resist arrest[107]
unlawfully causing grievous bodily harm[108]	rape[109]
unlawful use of a motor vehicle[110]	stealing and larceny[111]
—	unlawfully entering premises[112]
—	robbery[113]
—	inchoate offences such as attempts and conspiracy[114]
—	incest[115]

Lord Simon in *DPP v Morgan* [1976] AC 182 stated (at 216):

> By "crimes of basic intent", I mean those crimes whose definition expresses (or, more often, implies) a *mens rea* which does not go beyond the *actus reus*. The *actus reus* generally consists of an act and some consequence. The consequence may be very closely connected with the act, or more remotely connected with it: but with a crime of basic intent the *mens rea* does not extend beyond the act and its consequence, however remote, defined in the *actus reus*.

This quotation appears to refer to the division between conduct as an element of an offence and the physical element as the results or consequences of conduct. It is relatively simple on that division to

---

104 *R v Howell* [1974] 2 All ER 806; *R v Martin* [1979] Tas R 211; *Martin* (1984) 16 A Crim R 87.

105 *DPP v Majewski* [1977] AC 443; *R v O'Connor* (1980) 146 CLR 64; *R v Lovet* [1986] 1 Qd R 305 at 57 per Kelly SPJ.

106 *R v O'Connor* (1980) 146 CLR 64; *DPP v Majewski* [1977] AC 443; *Duffy v The Queen* [1981] WAR 72.

107 *R v O'Connor* (1980) 146 CLR 64.

108 *Bennett* (1989) 45 A Crim R 45 (CCA Tas).

109 *R v Hornbuckle* [1945] VLR 281. Compare *Holman v The Queen* [1970] WAR 2; *R v Thompson* [1961] 1 Qd R 503 at 516 per Stable J.

110 *R v Kaeser* [1961] QWN 11.

111 *R v O'Connor* (1980) 146 CLR 64; *R v Mathieson* (1906) 25 NZLR 879.

112 *Police v Bannin* [1991] 2 NZLR 237.

113 *Kaminski v The Queen* [1975] WAR 143.

114 *R v Mohan* [1976] QB 1.

115 *R v O'Regan* [1961] Qd R 78.

see that murder is a crime of specific intent. What is prohibited in the crime of murder is the death of the victim rather than the conduct that caused the death. It is irrelevant what conduct was undertaken which caused the death; providing the conduct of the accused *results* in the death of the victim, the physical element of murder will be established.

The other rationale for the distinction in *Majewski* is that crimes of basic intent are those satisfied by recklessness: G Orchard, "Drunkeness as a 'Defence' to 'Crime'" (1977) Crim LJ 59 at 132. On this view, the reckless act of voluntary intoxication supplies the requisite blameworthiness to hold the accused responsible. The equation of fault is imperfect and, as a result, Lord Simon's explanation – the "ulterior intent" test – has been preferred.

But why should rape be a crime of specific intent? Rape is generally defined by intentional sexual penetration (conduct) which occurs without the other person's consent (the specified circumstance). It is a crime that has as its physical element conduct that occurs in specified circumstances rather than a result or consequence of conduct.

It is also very difficult to find any rationale for holding that intoxication is relevant to certain offences and not to others. For example, why should intoxication be taken into account in relation to an attempt to commit an offence of basic intent and yet not in relation to the latter? The division is often arbitrary and inconsistent without any guiding principles or rationale.

Section 17(2) of the *Criminal Code* (Tas) sets out the requirement that evidence of intoxication is relevant to whether or not the accused was "incapable of forming the specific intent essential to constitute the offence". Such evidence therefore goes to the question of capacity rather than the fact of intention.[116] In Queensland and Western Australia and at common law, it is clear that capacity is not in issue and it is a misdirection to suggest otherwise.[117]

Where evidence of intoxication is raised by the defence to negate the requisite fault element, the prosecution may attempt to counteract this by claiming that the evidence showed that the accused became intoxicated in order to commit the crime, alcohol being known as a disinhibitor.[118] Evidence of intoxication may be used by the prosecution to explain the accused's behaviour.[119]

INTOXICATION AND NEGLIGENCE

Evidence of intoxication may be raised by the prosecution to show that the accused acted negligently: *R v Guthrie* (1981) 52 FLR 171 (SC ACT). In the case of serious offences based on negligence where death or serious injury has resulted, the prosecution must prove that the accused's behaviour fell grossly short of the standard expected of a reasonable, sober person: *Nydam v The Queen* [1977]

---

116 *Bennett* (1989) 45 A Crim R 45; *Palmer v The Queen* [1985] Tas R 138; *McCullough v The Queen* [1982] Tas R 43 at 50-51; *Snow v The Queen* [1962] Tas SR 271.

117 *R v Gordon* (1963) 63 SR(NSW) 631; *R v Kampeli* [1975] 2 NZLR 610 at 616; *R v Hart* [1986] 2 NZLR 408; *Viro v The Queen* (1978) 141 CLR 88; *Helmhout v The Queen* (1980) 49 FLR 1 at 5-6; *Herbert v The Queen* (1982) 62 FLR 302 at 313 per Toohey and Sheppard JJ; *R v Tucker* (1984) 36 SASR 135; *Summers* (1986) 22 A Crim R 47 at 48 per King CJ; *R v Coleman* (1990) 19 NSWLR 467; *Cameron* (1990) 47 A Crim R 397 at 407 per Malcolm CJ; *R v Ball* (1991) 56 SASR 126.

118 *Attorney-General (Northern Ireland) v Gallagher* [1963] AC 349 at 382 per Denning LJ (HL) (the expression "Dutch courage" is sometimes used in this context). *O' Leary v Daire* (1984) 13 A Crim R 404 at 411 per White J (SC SA).

119 *Stokes* (1990) 51 A Crim R 25 at 33 per Hunt J (CCA NSW); *Hamilton* (1985) 31 A Crim R 167 (CCA NSW); *R v Perks* (1986) 41 SASR 335 at 340-341 per White J; *R v Leaf-Milham* (1987) 47 SASR 499; *O' Leary v Daire* (1984) 13 A Crim R 404 at 411 per White J (SC SA).

VR 430. The only way in which evidence of intoxication may perhaps aid the defence in negligence-based crimes is where there is evidence that the accused became intoxicated accidentally.[120] This may occur by the stratagem or fraud of another person[121] or the error of a physician or chemist.[122]

The *Criminal Code Act* 1995 (Cth) has codified this requirement by applying the standard of a reasonable person who is not intoxicated: s 8.3(1). It also makes a concession for an accused whose intoxication is not self-induced. Section 8.3(2) states that in this situation, "regard must be had to the standard of a reasonable person who is not intoxicated".

Section 154(1) of the *Criminal Code* (NT) makes it an offence for a person to do a dangerous act where an ordinary person would have clearly foreseen such danger. If the act is performed while the accused is intoxicated, s 154(4) enables up to four years imprisonment to be added to the sentence.

INTOXICATION AND MENTAL IMPAIRMENT

In all jurisdictions, if intoxication induces a condition such as *delirium tremens* or permanent brain damage, then the defence of mental impairment may be raised.[123] It is unlikely that a temporary state of intoxication will be considered to be a form of mental impairment for the purpose of the defence.[124] Rather, there must be some continuing underlying condition caused by intoxication or exacerbated by it for the defence to apply.[125] For example, a pre-existing condition such as epilepsy may be exacerbated by intoxication: *R v Meddings* [1966] VR 306 at 310 per Sholl J.

In the Northern Territory, Queensland and Western Australia, the defence of mental impairment cannot be raised where the accused intentionally caused him or herself to become intoxicated.[126] This means that the effect of self-induced intoxication on a pre-existing condition is not recognised.

Evidence of intoxication may be considered in relation to an abnormality of mind for the purpose of the defence of diminished responsibility (see Chapter 5, p 276) providing it is protracted and has caused some injury to the accused's brain.[127] A temporary state of self-induced intoxication has not been considered enough to constitute an abnormality of mind for the purpose of the defence.[128]

---

120 *Flyger v Auckland City Council* [1979] 1 NZLR 161; *Rooke v Auckland City Council* [1980] 1 NZLR 680; *O' Neill v Ministry of Transport* [1985] 2 NZLR 513; *Ministry of Transport v Crawford* [1988] 1 NZLR 762.

121 *Barker v Burke* [1970] VR 884.

122 *Pearson's Case* (1835) 2 Lew CC 144; 168 ER 1108.

123 *Criminal Code* (NT), s 36; *Criminal Code* (Qld), s 28(1); *Criminal Code* (Tas), s 17(1); *Re Attorney-General's Reference No 1 of 1996* (unrep, 26/2/1998, CCA SC Tas, Cox CJ, Underwood, Wright, Crawford and Zeeman JJ, No 12/98); *Criminal Code* (WA), s 28; *DPP (UK) v Beard* [1920] AC 479 at 500-501 per Birkenhead LJ; *R v Stones* (1955) 56 SR (NSW) 25; 72 WN (NSW) 465 at 468 per the Court; *R v Connolly* (1958) 76 WN (NSW) 184; *R v Meddings* [1966] VR 306 at 310 per Sholl J.

124 *R v Davis* (1881) 14 Cox CC 563; *Dearnley v The Queen* [1947] St R Qd 51 at 61 per Philp J.

125 *R v Falconer* (1990) 171 CLR 30 at 49-56 per Mason CJ, Brennan and McHugh JJ.

126 *Criminal Code* (NT), s 36 (s 35 only applies where person is in a state of abnormality of mind caused by involuntary intoxication); *Criminal Code* (Qld), s 28; *Criminal Code* (WA), s 28. See 4.3 'Unintentional Intoxication'.

127 *R v Chester* [1982] Qd R 252; *R v Whitworth* [1989] 1 Qd R 437 at 457 per Derrington J.

128 *R v Nielsen* [1990] 2 Qd R 578 at 582; *R v Whitworth* [1989] 1 Qd R 437; *R v Tandy* (1988) 87 Cr App R 45; (1987) 31 A Crim R 453 at 462; *R v Morgan; Ex parte Attorney-General* [1987] 2 Qd R 627; *R v Miers* [1985] 2 Qd R 138; *Jones* (1986) 22 A Crim R 42 at 44 per Street CJ; *R v Gittens* [1984] QB 698; *R v Fenton* (1975) 61 Cr App R 261; *R v Kuzmenko* [1968] QWN 49; *R v Di Duca* (1959) 43 Cr App R 167; R O'Regan, "Intoxication and Criminal Responsibility Under the Queensland Code" (1977) 10 *University of Queensland Law Journal* 70 at 81.

4.3 INTOXICATION AND OTHER DEFENCES

A mistake of fact resulting from intoxication may negate the fault element of an offence. For example, in *Gow v Davies* (1992) A Crim R 282 on a charge of trespass, the accused claimed that due to his intoxicated state, he had mistakenly entered the house of another believing it to be his own. Evidence of intoxication was held to be relevant to support the accused's mistaken belief that he was not trespassing. Mistake is considered further in Chapter 7.

In relation to self-defence, at common law, the accused must have honestly believed on reasonable grounds that he or she was being threatened or attacked[129] and that the force applied by him or her was necessary in self defence.[130] Similarly, in relation to the use of lethal force in Queensland, Western Australia and the Northern Territory, the accused must believe on reasonable grounds that he or she cannot otherwise preserve him or herself or another from death or grievous bodily harm.[131]

This entails an analysis of first, what the accused believed, and secondly, whether or not this belief was based on reasonable grounds. Section 46 of the *Criminal Code* (Tas) states that a "person is justified in using, in the defence of himself [or herself] or another person, such force as, in the circumstances as he [or she] believes them to be, it is reasonable to use". Similarly, the South Australian provision allows an accused to use force if that person believes that the force is necessary and reasonable for self-defence.[132] Here the focus is on the accused's belief about necessity and reasonableness, rather than on whether or not the accused's belief was honest *and* based on reasonable grounds. This is taken up further in Chapter 6.

Evidence of intoxication may be relevant to the assessment of the accused's belief that he or she was being threatened or attacked and that the force applied was necessary: *Conlon* (1993) 69 A Crim R 92 (SC NSW). However, in those jurisdictions where the belief must be based on reasonable grounds, it may be difficult for intoxication to be taken into account at this stage. In *McCullough v The Queen* [1982] Tas R 43 the Tasmanian Supreme Court noted (at 53):

> The criterion of reasonableness is in its nature an objective one, and in our view it would be incongruous and wrong to contemplate the proposition that a person's exercise of judgment might be unreasonable if he [or she] was sober, but reasonable because he [or she] was drunk.

These words, however, relate to the Tasmanian provision that has now been replaced and there appears to be no firm authority on the matter.

---

129 *Zecevic v DPP* (1987) 162 CLR 645 at 651-652 per Mason CJ, at 656-657 per Wilson, Dawson and Toohey JJ, at 672-673 per Deane J, at 683 per Gaudron J; *Viro v The Queen* (1978) 141 CLR 88 at 146 per Mason J.

130 *Zecevic v DPP* (1987) 162 CLR 645 at 656 per Mason CJ, 661 per Wilson, Dawson and Toohey JJ, at 666 per Brennan J; at 681 per Deane J, at 683 per Gaudron J; *Dziduch* (1990) 47 A Crim R 378 (CCA NSW).

131 *Criminal Code* (NT), s 28; *Criminal Code* (Qld), s 271 (reasonable apprehension); *Criminal Code* (WA), s 248.

132 *Criminal Law Consolidation Act* 1935 (SA), s 15(1) as amended by the *Criminal Law Consolidation (Self-Defence) Amendment Act* 1997.

The elements of the defence of provocation are set out by the common law which is followed in South Australia and Victoria and reflected in the statutory provisions of the Australian Capital Territory, New South Wales, the Northern Territory and Tasmania.[133] It appears that the common law rules apply to the interpretation of provocation under s 304 of the *Criminal Code* (Qld), but it remains open as to whether or not the common law applies to s 281 of the *Criminal Code* (WA). Provocation is explored in Chapter 5.

In general, the test for provocation consists of both subjective and objective elements. There must be some evidence that the accused was in fact acting under provocation. The content and extent of the provocative conduct is assessed from the viewpoint of the particular accused. This is the subjective element of the defence. In addition, however, there is an objective requirement that the provocation be of such a nature that could or might have moved an ordinary person to act as the accused did. Evidence of intoxication may be relevant to the subjective component of the defence of provocation, but it will be irrelevant to the consideration of the ordinary person test.[134]

4.4 UNINTENTIONAL INTOXICATION

In the Code jurisdictions and New South Wales, which restrict intoxication as an excuse, special rules as to accidental or unintentional intoxication that are not present in the common law have been enacted. The *Criminal Code* (Tas) draws no distinction between self-induced and unintentional intoxication. In *Snow v The Queen* [1962] Tas R 271 Burbury CJ, Cox and Crawford JJ suggested (at 295) that a common law defence of unintentional intoxication may operate in Tasmania by virtue of s 8 of the *Criminal Code* which preserves common law defences. However, as such a separate defence does not operate in the Australian common law, this seems to be no longer the case.

In Queensland and Western Australia, an accused is not criminally responsible for an act if his or her mind is disordered by unintentional intoxication so as to deprive him or her of the capacity to understand what he or she is doing, to control his or her actions, or to know that he or she ought not to do the act or make the omission.[135]

Section 1 of the *Criminal Code* (NT) defines "involuntary intoxication" as meaning:

> The person concerned is under the influence of an intoxicating substance caused by the involuntary ingestion of it, his [or her] honest and reasonable mistake as to the nature of it, some physical idiosyncrasy of which he [or she] was unaware or the coercion, mistake or deception of another.

Section 36 then allows involuntary intoxication to be considered for the purpose of establishing whether the accused had an abnormality of mind so as to deprive him or her of the capacity to understand what he or she was doing or of capacity to control his or her actions or of the capacity to

---

133 *Crimes Act* 1900 (ACT), s 13(2); *Criminal Code* (NT), s 34; *Crimes Act* 1900 (NSW), s 23(2); *Criminal Code* (Tas), s 160(2).

134 *R v Perks* (1986) 41 SASR 335; *R v Cooke* (1985) 39 SASR 225; *Censori v The Queen* [1983] WAR 89; *R v O' Neill* [1982] VR 150; *R v Webb* (1977) 16 SASR 309; *R v Croft* [1981] 1 NSWLR 126; *Taylor v The King* [1948] 1 DLR 545.

135 *Criminal Code* (Qld), s 28; *Criminal Code* (WA), s 28; *R v Smith* [1949] St R Qd 126 at 130 per Macrossan CJ (approved in *Re Bromage* [1991] 1 Qd R 1; *R v Corbett* [1903] St R Q 246 at 249 per Griffith CJ; *R v Kusu* [1981] Qd R 136 at 141 per WB Campbell J; *Nosworthy v The Queen* (1983) 8 A Crim R 270.

know he or she ought not do the act. However, if a person is excused from criminal responsibility on this basis, he or she is found not guilty by reason of intoxication and may be subject to an order for the payment of compensation and restitution: *Criminal Code* (NT), s 383.

In the *Crimes Act* 1900 (NSW) it is stated that intoxication that is not self-induced may be taken into account in relation to offences other than an offence of specific intent (s 428D(b)) and in assessing whether the conduct was voluntary (s 428G). Intoxication that is not self-induced is defined as intoxication which is involuntary or which results from fraud, sudden or extraordinary emergency, accident, reasonable mistake, duress or force, or results from the administration of a prescription drug in accordance with the recommended dosage: s 428A. The New South Wales provisions echo those set out in the *Criminal Code Act* 1995 (Cth), although the interpretation of intoxication that is not self-induced is slightly broader in New South Wales.

These provisions that distinguish between unintentional and self-induced intoxication do so presumably on the basis that a person who becomes unintentionally intoxicated is less blameworthy than one who makes a choice to become intoxicated.

4.5 BURDEN OF PROOF

The prosecution bears the legal burden of proving all the elements of the crime are made out despite evidence of intoxication.[136] The standard of proof remains that of beyond reasonable doubt. The defence carries the evidential burden.

PERSPECTIVES

Principle and Policy and Reform of the Law of Intoxication

There have been numerous law reform proposals that have looked at how intoxication should be taken into account in assessing criminal responsibility. The Law Reform Commission and the Law Reform Committee of Victoria,[137] the South Australian Mitchell Committee,[138] the New Zealand Criminal Law Reform Committee,[139] the Law Commission of England and Wales[140] and the Model Criminal Code Officers Committee[141] have all recommended that the *O'Connor* approach to evidence of intoxication conforms best to general principles of criminal law. Ashworth refers to this approach as the "simplest" one: *Principles of Criminal Law* (3rd ed, Oxford: Oxford University

---

136 *Stokes* (1990) 51 A Crim R 25; *Dearnley v The King* [1947] St R Q 51; (1947) 41 QJPR 71. As to legal and evidentiary burdens see Chapter 2, p 118.

137 Law Reform Commission of Victoria, *Mental Malfunction and Criminal Responsibility*, Report No 34 (1990), paras 218-219; Law Reform Committee of Victoria, *Criminal Liability for Self-Induced Intoxication*, Report (May 1999).

138 South Australian Criminal Law and Penal Methods Reform Committee, *The Substantive Criminal Law*, Fourth Report (1977), p 48.

139 New Zealand Criminal Law Reform Committee, *Report on Intoxication as a Defence to a Criminal Charge* (1984), para 45.

140 Law Commission, *Legislating the Criminal Code: Intoxication and Criminal Liability* (London: HMSO, 1995).

141 Criminal Law Officers Committee of the Standing Committee of Attorneys-General, *Chapter 2: General Principles of Criminal Responsibility*, Final Report (1992), p 51.

Press, 1999), p 225. See also G Orchard, "Surviving Without *Majewski* — A View From Down Under" [1993] Crim LR 426. The Supreme Court of Canada in *R v Daviault* [1994] 3 SCR 63 has departed from *Majewski*, though the majority opted for the middle-ground that permitted intoxication to be raised in relation to crimes of basic intent only where the intoxication was "extreme" and involved an absence of awareness akin to mental impairment or automatism. The decision caused a storm of controversy in the press, and has since been partially reversed by statute: now see *Criminal Code* (Can), s 33.1.

We have already outlined the problems with dividing offences into strict and basic offences for the purpose of evidence of intoxication. The main argument against the *O' Connor* approach is that it may lead to what are seen as undeserved acquittals. In 1995, the Law Commission noted in *Legislating the Criminal Code: Intoxication and Criminal Liability* (London: HMSO, 1995) (LAW COM No 229, 1995), paras 5.20, 5.22 pp 45-46:

> We think it significant that on consultation many respondents concerned with the
> practical operation of the *Majewski* rule — namely the Bar and a significant minority of
> the Queen's Bench Division judges — expressed support for ... the abolition of the
> *Majewski* principle without replacement ... We were, however, impressed by the
> practical considerations urged upon us by, in particular, the majority of judges of the
> Queen's Bench Division. They expressed concern about the effect of
>
>> even one high profile case where there was an acquittal because the
>> alleged offender was too drunk to form the required intent. The
>> majority believe that such an acquittal would be viewed by the public
>> as another example of the law, and inevitably the judges who apply
>> that law, being out of touch with public opinion and public perception
>> of fault.

There is a natural urge to want to punish a person for getting so intoxicated in the first place that he or she causes harm in circumstances where an ordinary person would have foreseen it as a likelihood. But if that is the case, why not simply create an offence of committing a dangerous act whilst under the influence of intoxication? Section 154 of the *Criminal Code* (NT) provides an example of such an offence.

Whilst law reform bodies tend to concentrate on principles of criminal responsibility in assessing the law relating to intoxication, parliaments tend to look toward special rules to govern those who commit crimes whilst intoxicated. In a Discussion Paper prepared for the South Australian Attorney-General,[142] Matthew Goode writes:

> Parliaments tend to the opinion that letting defendants such as Mr Nadruku escape the
> criminal sanction is scandalous and should not be allowed to happen. In this they may
> well be representing the views of the public as a general proposition — certainly a
> vocal section of the general public. The courts and law reform bodies tend to say that
> letting the occasional defendant such as Mr Nadruku escape the criminal net is a small

---

142 Attorney-General's Office, *Intoxication and Criminal Responsibility*, Discussion Paper (July 1998).

price to pay for keeping away any alternative which will be complex, confusing and unjust to others. If both views may be conceded to have some justice, taken from their particular perspective, what then?

This tension between "principle" and "policy" explains why there is so much confusion about the effects of intoxication on criminal responsibility. Even some law reform bodies, whilst agreeing with the logic of *O'Connor's* case, have used policy grounds to justify departures from the *O'Connor* approach.[143]

Law and order politics have dictated that governments ignore legal principle in favour of policy. For example, in New South Wales, the *Majewski* approach was reintroduced into the law by the *Crimes Legislation Amendment Act* 1996 (NSW), which inserted ss 428A-428I into the *Crimes Act* 1900 (NSW). In the Second Reading speech, the Minister for Police noted:

> The preference for the *Majewski* approach is based on important public policy considerations. The Standing Committee of Attorneys-General, in particular, took the view that to excuse otherwise criminal conduct in relation to simple offences of basic intent — such as assault — because the accused is intoxicated to such an extent, is totally unacceptable at a time when alcohol and drug abuse are such significant social problems. The standing committee considered that if a person voluntarily takes the risk of getting intoxicated then he or she should be responsible for his or her actions. This Government agrees with and strongly supports this approach.[144]

This contrasts starkly with the views of law reform agencies, which have consistently favoured *O'Connor*. For example, the Victorian Law Reform Committee recently recommended that *O'Connor's* case continue to govern the law in Victoria (p 114) in its report on *Criminal Liability for Self-Induced Intoxication* (May 1999):

> The Committee believes that it is crucial that legal principles be applied consistently and simply on the basis of evidence available. The Committee concludes that the proposition arising from *O'Connor's* case, that a person should not be held criminally responsible for an unintended or involuntary act is logical, easy to apply and makes good sense.

While there is no consensus as to how intoxication should be taken into account, the Committee noted that it will be rare for an accused to be acquitted of a crime because of evidence of intoxication and cases like that of *Nadruku* are exceptions to general practice: p 107.

---

143 The Gibbs Committee, *Review of Commonwealth Criminal Law, Interim Report: Principles of Criminal Responsibility and Other Matters*, Chapter 10, Intoxication (Canberra: AGPS, 1990), paras 10.21 and 10.24; Law Com No 229, *Legislating the Criminal Code: Intoxication and Criminal Liability* (London: HMS, 1995), paras 5.19-5.28.

144 Mr Whelan, New South Wales Minister for Police, *New South Wales Parliamentary Debates*, Legislative Assembly, 6 December 1995.

5. CONCLUSION

In Chapter 3 we pointed out that the principles that underlie the criminal law are dependent upon the idea of a person as a rational being. In this chapter we have outlined how those who are considered to lack the ability to reason through mental impairment, automatism or intoxication may be excused from responsibility for criminal acts.

In relation to mental impairment, there is always a balance to be made between how broad or limited the defence should be. A comprehensive definition of the term "mental impairment" would give expert witnesses and juries some guidance as to what will serve to excuse an accused from criminal responsibility. The definition set out in s 428B of the *Crimes Act* 1900 (ACT) serves as a model in this regard. This section defines mental "dysfunction" as "a disturbance or defect, to a substantially disabling degree, of perceptual interpretation, comprehension, reasoning, learning, judgment, memory, motivation or emotion". This legal definition accords with modern medical conceptions of mental disorder.

We have pointed out the problems with broadening the defence to include personality disorders and the volitional component. The defence should be available only to those who experience a failure of "reality testing" and whose reasoning capacities are affected. In the past, because of the fear of being detained indefinitely at the "Governor's Pleasure", the defence was rarely used. With more dispositional options now available, it may be that this defence will be raised more often in the future.

We have also explored how the "all or nothing" legal conception of conduct being either voluntary or involuntary does not sit well with the psychological view of a continuum between volitional and automatistic behaviours. Further, the attempts to distinguish between sane and insane automatism has led to the law becoming very complex in this area and it may be time to subsume automatism within the broadened defence of mental impairment.

The question of how intoxication should be taken into account in determining criminal responsibility is inherently problematic because of the tension generated between an approach based on principle and an approach based on policy. In assessing this debate, it should be kept in mind that in practice, acquittals on the basis of intoxication are rare and there is some reason to believe that those accused who raise intoxication will show some elements of awareness of intention sufficient to warrant conviction.[145]

Finally, an important theme underlying this chapter is the importance of those working toward law reform in the area of mental state defences taking into account recent developments in other disciplines, such as psychiatry and psychology. This also holds true of the partial defence of diminished responsibility that is discussed in the next chapter.

---

145 R Shiner, "Intoxication and Responsibility" (1990) 13 *International Journal of Law and Psychiatry* 9; C Mitchell, "The Intoxicated Offender — Refuting the Legal and Medical Myths" (1988) 11 *International Journal of Law and Psychiatry* 77.

5

Partial Defences

Alexander Pope, "To Lord Bathurst" (1733)
in FW Bateson (ed),
*The Poems of Alexander Pope, Vol 111,
Epistles to Several People* l. 155-156 (London:
Methuen & Co Ltd, 1951), p 106

> The ruling Passion,
> be it what it will,
> The ruling Passion conquers
> Reason still

1. INTRODUCTION

There are three defences that can be considered as partial defences in the sense that they reduce a charge of murder to manslaughter. These are:

=== the defence of provocation which exists in all States and Territories;

=== the defence of diminished responsibility which exists in the Australian Capital Territory, New South Wales, the Northern Territory and Queensland; and

=== infanticide which is both an offence and operates as an alternative verdict to murder (and therefore in effect reduces murder to manslaughter) in New South Wales, Tasmania, Victoria and Western Australia.

These partial defences do not operate to negate the fault element of the crime of murder. The accused will be potentially guilty of murder because both the physical and fault elements of the offence will exist. What these defences do, instead, is recognise and provide a concession to "human frailty". Andrew Ashworth points out in *Principles of Criminal Law* (3rd ed, Oxford: Oxford University Press, 1999) that there is a symbolic function of the labels "murder" and "manslaughter" applied by the law and courts to criminal conduct: p 274. The availability of the lesser offence of manslaughter in certain circumstances is therefore available to mark significant differences in culpability.

The nature and role of provocation is best understood in its historical context. The early criminal law distinguished between the most serious types of killing which required proof of malice aforethought and killings that were unpremeditated and occurred on the spur of the moment in response to an act of provocation. The early law mitigated the punishment of the latter type of killing and the evolution of provocation as a defence, rather than merely as a mitigating factor, emerged in the 17th and 18th centuries. This was an epoch where insults or attacks upon honour were expected to be avenged with resort to lethal weapons. Sir William Holdsworth writes in *A History of English Law* (London: Sweet and Maxwell, 1966), Vol 8, p 302:

> [T]he readiness with which all classes resorted to lethal weapons to assert their rights, or to avenge any insult real or fancied, gave abundant opportunity for elaborating the distinctions between various kinds of homicide.

The need to draw such distinctions followed from the fact that murder at this time was a capital felony. The accused could escape capital punishment only if he or she lacked malice aforethought. Manslaughter was only available where the killing had occurred "suddenly" and in "hot blood" in response to an act of provocation by the deceased.

The defence of diminished responsibility is similar to that of provocation in that it takes into account the accused's frailty in the sense of an "abnormality of mind". This defence originated in the Scottish courts in the mid-18th century as a way of dealing with "mental weakness" falling short of insanity, by convicting the accused but with a recommendation to mercy: G Gordon, *The Criminal Law of Scotland* (2nd ed, Edinburgh: Green, 1978), p 386. At first, it began as a plea in mitigation, but became a fully fledged defence in the mid-19th century case of *HM Advocate v Dingwall* (1867) 5 Irvine 446.

Infanticide can be seen as closely allied to the defence of diminished responsibility in that it centres on the concept of a "mental imbalance" caused by the effects of childbirth. It only became a crime and a partial defence in England in 1922 (*Infanticide Act* 1922 (UK)) but attempts had been made in previous centuries to curb the incidence of infanticide whilst showing some mercy to the accused because of the circumstances of the killing: S Davies, "Child Killing in English Law" [1937] *Modern Law Review* 203 at 219.

These three defences have been criticised on a number of grounds and the Model Criminal Code Officers Committee in its Discussion Paper on *Fatal Offences Against the Person* (June 1998) has called for the abolition of all these partial defences: pp 87-139. We shall consider the abolition of partial defences at the end of this chapter.

2. PROVOCATION

Provocation operates as a partial defence to murder in that successful reliance on the defence reduces the charge of murder to manslaughter. It is derived from the common law and it now finds statutory expression in all jurisdictions apart from South Australia and Victoria.[1]

---

1   *Crimes Act* 1900 (ACT), s 13; *Crimes Act* 1900 (NSW), s 23; *Criminal Code* (NT), s 34; *Criminal Code* (Qld), s 304; *Criminal Code* (Tas), s 160; *Criminal Code* (WA), s 281.

The defence may be raised in relation to all forms of murder, including reckless murder[2] and constructive felony murder.[3] It may not, however be available to a charge of attempted murder: *R v Farrar* [1992] 1 VR 207 at 208-209 per Hampel J. Before provocation becomes a relevant defence in a murder trial, the prosecution must have satisfied the jury beyond reasonable doubt that the accused has committed murder: *Lee Chun-Chuen v The Queen* [1963] AC 220 at 231 per Lord Devlin.

As stated previously, provocation emerged as a partial defence to murder during the 17th century as a way of avoiding mandatory capital punishment[4] and it was developed as a concession to human frailty. This defence recognises that an individual may suffer a temporary loss of self-control in certain circumstances and attempts to distinguish between intentional killings which are committed in "cold blood" and those which occur in an extreme emotional state and which are unpremeditated: see A Reilly, "Loss of Self-Control in Provocation" (1997) 21 Crim LJ 320 at 320.

The early decisions relating to provocation sought to identify the fact situations where the defence could operate.[5] A physical assault could amount to provocation. However, the gravest insult at this time would be the discovery of a wife with a lover; adultery being considered at this time to be an offence and an attack both upon a gentleman's honour and property. The common law defence was thus constructed around male conceptions of sexual jealousy, anger and revenge. The courts required a sudden violent retaliation. Where there was an opportunity for the "blood to cool", the defence was not available.

Aspects of this early law have survived through to the current law. Suddenness and the absence of delay or premeditation are no longer substantive rules, but they may provide evidence that an ordinary person faced by that degree of provocation could have acted in the way in which the accused did.

The common law underwent significant changes, particularly in response to the philosophical currents of liberal theory in the 19th century. As explored in Chapter 3, that century witnessed many developments in the criminal law. The courts began to use the morally neutral terms, "intention" and "recklessness" rather than "malice" or a "wicked" or "evil mind" and the accused's motive or reason for acting was no longer considered relevant to responsibility. This changed understanding of criminal responsibility made an impact on the defence of provocation in several ways. First, the focus of the defence became, and remains, the accused's "loss of self control" rather than morally excusable retribution. Secondly, as a means of controlling the scope of the defence, the courts developed and applied an objective test that manifested itself in the following ways.

First, the "reasonable man" test emerged in *R v Welsh* (1869) 11 Cox 336. In that case, Keating J stated (at 338):

> The law contemplates the case of the reasonable man, and requires that the provocation
> shall be such as that such a man might naturally be induced, in the anger of the moment,
> to commit the act.

---

2 *Johnson v The Queen* (1976) 136 CLR 619 at 634 per Barwick CJ; *Cufley v The Queen* (1983) 78 FLR 359.

3 *Edwards v The Queen* [1973] AC 648; *R v Fry* (1992) 58 SASR 424; cf *R v Scriva (No 2)* [1951] VLR 298 at 304 per Smith J.

4 *Royley's* case (1612) Cro Jac 296; 79 ER 254; *Nugget* (1666) 18 Car 2; 84 ER 1082; *R v Mawgridge* (1707) 84 ER 1107. See also G Coss, "God is a Righteous Judge, Strong and Patient: and God is Provoked Every Day: A Brief History of the Doctrine of Provocation in England" (1991) 13 *Sydney Law Review* 570.

5 For example, *R v Mawgridge* (1707) 84 ER 1107. See discussion in J Greene, "A Provocation Defence for Battered Women Who Kill" (1989) 12 *Adelaide Law Review* 145 at 147.

In recent times, the reasonable man has transmogrified into the ordinary person. Barwick CJ in *Moffa v The Queen* (1977) 138 CLR 601 noted (at 606) that it is preferable to characterise the objective standard in terms of an ordinary rather than a reasonable person because the use of the term "reasonable" might be taken as excluding severe emotional reactions from consideration.

Secondly, the courts began to apply a test of proportionality that required a correlation or measured correspondence between the act of provocation and the accused's retaliation. This is no longer a separate requirement under the common law, but it may be relevant to the question as to whether or not the provocation was sufficient to have induced an ordinary person to have lost self control and acted in the way in which the accused did.

Provocation is often raised in cases of homicide between adult sexual intimates. In 2.5 'Provocation and Battered Women' we will explore the difficulties battered women who kill their partners after years in an abusive relationship face in raising the defence.

> In a study of all prosecutions for murder and manslaughter in Victoria between 1981 and 1987, the Law Reform Commission of Victoria found that provocation was an issue in 75 cases (23.5%). Men raised provocation in 65 of these cases, two-thirds of which involved a male victim (43 cases) and one-third a female victim (22 cases). Women raised provocation in the remaining 10 cases, nine of these involving a male victim. Interestingly, none of the women who raised provocation was convicted of murder. Only 11.6% of men who argued provocation were convicted of murder where the victim was male, compared with 36.4% where the victim was female. This suggested that more men used provocation as a defence than women both in absolute terms and as a proportion of all accused charged with murder. Where women raised the defence, they were more likely to be successful. However, the Commission points out that it is difficult to draw conclusions because of the small number of prosecutions and the probable operation of other defences: Law Reform Commission of Victoria, *Homicide Prosecutions Study*, Report No 40 (Melbourne: VGPS, October 1991), Appendix 6, pp 75-80.

In Chapter 6, we discuss the traditional distinction in the common law between killings that were justified and those that were excused. Defences "excusing" an accused from criminal responsibility are generally viewed as concentrating on the personal characteristics of the accused whereas defences "justifying" a crime focus on the act of the accused rather than on any personal characteristics: P Alldridge, "The Coherence of Defences" [1983] Crim LR 665; S Yeo, "Proportionality in Criminal Defences" (1988) 12 Crim LJ 209 at 212-213. Provocation, however, can be viewed as containing elements of both excuse and justification. It is excusatory in its focus on the accused's lack of self-control and justificatory in its focus on the provocative conduct of the victim and the acceptability of the accused's actions. Because of this combination of elements of excuse and justification, the conceptual basis for the defence of provocation is often confused. This in turn helps explain why there have been calls for its abolition. This will be discussed later in this chapter.

The elements of the defence of provocation are set out by the common law which is followed in South Australia and Victoria and reflected in the statutory provisions of the Australian Capital Territory, New South Wales, the Northern Territory and Tasmania.[6] The common law also has been

---

6   *Crimes Act* 1900 (ACT), s 13(2); *Crimes Act* 1900 (NSW), s 23(2); *Criminal Code* (NT), s 34; *Criminal Code* (Tas), s 160(2).

held to apply to the interpretation of provocation under s 304 of the *Criminal Code* (Qld) which sets out provocation as a partial defence to murder.[7] It seems, however, that the definition of provocation that applies as a defence to assault also applies to the partial defence to murder set out in s 281 of the *Criminal Code* (WA).[8] Section 245 of the *Criminal Code* (WA) defines "provocation" as any wrongful act or insult as to be likely, when done to an ordinary person, to deprive him or her of the power of self-control.

The leading High Court case dealing with the defence of provocation is that of *Stingel v The Queen* (1990) 171 CLR 312. Stingel had made an unsworn statement that he had found his ex-girlfriend with whom he was obsessed engaging in sexual activities with a man, Taylor, in a car. According to Stingel, when he opened the car door, Taylor had said "Piss off you cunt, piss off". Stingel fetched a butcher's knife from his car and stabbed Taylor to death. Stingel stated that seeing his ex-girlfriend with Taylor and the latter's words had caused him to lose self-control. The trial judge ruled that the evidence was not sufficient for a defence of provocation and this was therefore not left for the jury. An appeal to the Tasmanian Court of Criminal Appeal was dismissed and the High Court dismissed a subsequent appeal. In the course of their unanimous judgment, the members of the High Court clarified the law relating to provocation.

Although the case concerned provisions of the *Criminal Code* (Tas), the High Court observed (at 320) that there is a large degree of conformity in the law of provocation whether it be common law or statutory. The High Court subsequently affirmed that the test in *Stingel* equally applied to the common law: see *Masciantonio v The Queen* (1995) 183 CLR 58 at 66. The role of the High Court in harmonising the criminal law across Code and common law jurisdictions was explored earlier in Chapter 2, pp 70ff.

In general, the test for provocation consists of both subjective and objective elements. There must be some evidence that the accused was in fact acting under provocation. The content and extent of the provocative conduct is assessed from the viewpoint of the particular accused. This is the subjective element of the defence. In addition, however, there is an objective requirement that the provocation be of such a nature that could or might have moved an ordinary person to act as the accused did.

The defence can thus be divided into three fundamental requirements:

- **there must be provocative conduct;**
- **the accused must have lost self-control as a result of the provocation; and**
- **the provocation must be such that it was capable of causing an ordinary person to lose self-control and to act in the way the accused did.**

We will examine each of these three elements in turn.

---

7 *Van Den Hoek v The Queen* (1986) 161 CLR 158 at 168 per Mason J; *R v Johnson* [1964] Qd R 1; *Kaporonovski v The Queen* (1973) 133 CLR 209.

8 *Censori v The Queen* [1983] WAR 89; *Mehemet Ali v The Queen* (1957) 59 WALR 28; *Sreckovic v The Queen* [1973] WAR 85; *Roche v The Queen* [1988] WAR 278.

2.1 PROVOCATIVE CONDUCT

Before an accused can rely on the defence of provocation, there must be evidence of some form of conduct that caused the accused to lose self-control. In the past, the case law referred to the existence of a clearly identifiable triggering incident or series of incidents: *R v Croft* [1981] 1 NSWLR 126 at 140 per O'Brien J. That requirement has been lessened to some degree in recent years. In *Chhay* (1994) 72 A Crim R 1 Gleeson CJ stated (at 13):

> [T]imes are changing, and people are becoming more aware that a loss of self-control can develop even after a lengthy period of abuse, and without the necessity for a specific triggering incident.

What is important is the cumulative effect of all the circumstances including the background and history leading up to the accused's loss of control.[9] For example, in *Parker v The Queen* (1964) 111 CLR 665 the Privy Council found that the victim's provocative conduct included "hanging about" the accused's wife, speaking of her in disparaging terms to the accused and ultimately persuading the accused's wife to leave the accused and their six children. These circumstances were enough to form the basis for the defence of provocation. Lord Morris stated (at 679):

> The jury might well have taken the view that the [accused] was tormented beyond endurance. His wife whom he loved was being lured away from him and from their children despite protests, appeals and remonstrances. In open defiance of his grief and his anguish his wife was being taken by one who had jeered at [the accused's] lesser strength and who had spoken with unashamed relish of his lascivious intents. Though there was an interval of time between the moment when the [accused's] wife and the deceased went away and the moment when the [accused] overtook them and then caused the death of the deceased a jury might well consider and would be entitled to consider that the deceased's whole conduct was such as might "heat the blood to a proportionable degree of resentment and keep it boiling to the moment of the fact" [*East's Pleas of the Crown* (1803), p 238].

Similarly, an incident or words which of themselves may seem inoffensive may amount to provocation when placed in the context of an abusive relationship. In *R v R* (1981) 28 SASR 321 the accused killed her husband with an axe after he had stroked her arm and cuddled up to her in bed telling her that they would be one happy family and two of their daughters would not be leaving. The accused had recently been informed that her husband had sexually abused each of their five daughters. She gave evidence that while he slept, she sat smoking one cigarette after another thinking about her daughters before going to the shed and getting the axe. The court held that the victim's conduct had to be placed against a background of brutality, sexual assault, intimidation and manipulation.

Examples of incidents that have been held to constitute provocation include the sight of a wife committing adultery[10] and persistent homosexual advances.[11]

---

9   *Parker v The Queen* (1963) 111 CLR 610 at 665; *Moffa v The Queen* (1977) 138 CLR 601; *R v Jeffrey* [1967] VR 467; *R v R* (1981) 28 SASR 321; *Chhay* (1994) 72 A Crim R 1.

10 *R v Maddy* (1672) 1 Ventris 158; 86 ER 108; (1707) Kel J 119; 84 ER 1107; *Roche v The Queen* [1988] WAR 278; (1987) 29 A Crim R 168; *Holmes v DPP* [1946] AC 588; *R v Arden* [1975] VR 449; *R v Lyden* [1962] Tas SR 1.

11 *Green v The Queen* (1997) 191 CLR 334 at 347 per Brennan CJ.

INSULTING WORDS

Insulting words may amount to provocation when accompanied by gestures or other conduct. The provisions in the Australian Capital Territory and New South Wales require the words to be "grossly insulting": *Crimes Act* 1900 (ACT), s 13(2)(a); *Crimes Act* 1900 (NSW), s 23(2)(a). There is a reservation on the part of the courts towards accepting insulting words on their own as provocation because it appears to be generally accepted that violent acts rather than insulting words are more likely to induce an ordinary person to lose self-control.

CASE STUDIES

Words Designed to Enrage

The main case on this point is that of *Moffa v The Queen* (1977) 138 CLR 601. The accused, an Italian man, killed his wife by striking her on the head and neck with a piece of iron piping. He claimed that she had rejected his sexual advances, told him that she was "screwing with everybody in the street" and that she was leaving him, called him a "black bastard" and threw a telephone and photographs of herself naked (most of which the accused himself admitted having taken) at him. There was no evidence that the telephone hit the accused or that the victim had been violent towards him in any other way.

The accused successfully appealed to the High Court against conviction for murder. Gibbs J, in his dissenting judgment held that the words of the victim may have been calculated to disturb or enrage but were not of a "violently provocative" character to amount to provocation.

The conclusions of the majority that there was sufficient evidence of provocation were reached on different grounds and it is therefore difficult to find support for the proposition that insulting words alone can amount to provocation from this case.

Barwick CJ held that the insulting words of themselves were not enough to amount to provocation. However, he stated (at 606) "the threat of physical violence to reinforce [the victim's] rejection of [the accused], the throwing of the telephone as an expression of contempt and the use of the nude photographs, form part of the whole situation". The words in all these circumstances were enough to amount to provocation in Barwick CJ's opinion. Stephen J agreed with this analysis, but placed emphasis (at 619) on the victim having not simply admitted to adultery, but "boasted of wholesale promiscuity with the men in the suburban street where she and her husband lived and had brought up their family".

Mason J seems to have gone further than Barwick CJ and Stephen J in stating (at 620):

> There is no absolute rule against words founding a case of provocation. The existence of such an absolute rule would draw an arbitrary distinction between words and conduct which is insupportable in logic.

Murphy J was of the opinion that the question of whether or not certain words amounted to provocation reflected the attitudes of society, "or even of particular judges". He saw this (at 624) as "by-product of the reasonable man test" which, according to Murphy J was no longer part of the law of homicide. Murphy J's critique of the objective test is further explored below at p 270.

Perhaps all that can be gleaned from the majority judgments in *Moffa* is that insulting words may amount to provocation when viewed against all the circumstances. This seems to have been followed in *R v R* (1981) 28 SASR 321 where the victim telling the accused that they would be one happy family and two of their daughters would not be leaving amounted to provocation when the history of their relationship was taken into account. King CJ stated (at 326):

> Words or conduct cannot amount to provocation unless they are spoken or done to or in the presence of the killer ... although, of course, such words or conduct may be important as part of the background against which what is said or done by the deceased to the killer is to be assessed.

One case that does lend some, albeit slight, support to the proposition that insulting words in themselves may amount to provocation is that of *R v Dutton* (1979) 21 SASR 356. In that case, the 36-year-old accused injured his back in a work accident. This affected his general health and made sexual intercourse difficult with his 20-year-old wife. In the ensuing 10 months after the accident, the accused's wife left him more than once. On the last occasion she went to stay with friends and a week and a half later, after spending the night drinking, the accused went to where his wife was staying. In an unsworn statement, he stated that his wife taunted him with his inability to satisfy her sexually and that her last words were "I can get paid for what you can't give me". The accused then said he lost self-control and shot the victim several times.

The Supreme Court of South Australia ordered a retrial on the basis that the trial judge had failed to adequately direct the jury on the law relating to the ordinary person test. However, all three judges did not question whether or not the victim's alleged taunts were enough to amount to provocation. Cox J (at 376) referred to *Moffa's* case, regarding it as abolishing any distinction between conduct and words as the allowable cause for provocation.

It could be argued that the words in *Dutton's* case were interpreted against a background of arguments in a relationship gone sour. In *R v Romano* (1984) 36 SASR 283 the accused shot his wife after she had called him a "useless man". The Supreme Court of South Australia ordered a retrial on the ground that the trial judge should have left provocation for the jury to consider. King CJ (at 287) referred to the victim's words in the context of a background of alleged taunts concerning the accused's mental health as well as her interest in "a new boyfriend".

In *R v Webb* (1977) 16 SASR 309 a threat to "scream rape" unless paid money was also held to amount to provocation. However, as Desmond O'Connor and Paul Fairall point out in *Criminal Defences* (3rd ed, Sydney: Butt, 1996), p 214, the words in *Webb's* case are not insulting as such, but may seem more similar to threats to cause serious bodily harm which have been recognised as possible provocation.

It is therefore still unclear as to whether insulting words alone will amount to provocation. Obviously the more evidence there is of a background of taunts or violence, the more likely a jury will be to accept such evidence. It is also worthwhile heeding the words of Mason J in *Moffa's* case (at 620-621):

[A] case of provocation by words may be more easily invented than a case of provocation by conduct, particularly when the victim was the wife of the accused. There is, therefore, an element of public policy as well as common sense requiring the close scrutiny of claims of provocation founded in words, rather than conduct.

PROVOCATIVE CONDUCT AND LAWFULNESS

There is no requirement at common law that the provocative conduct or insult be unlawful.[12] The *Criminal Codes* of the Northern Territory, Tasmania and Western Australia do, however, require that there be a "wrongful act or insult".[13] A wrongful act need not mean contrary to law, but includes an act that is wrong by the ordinary standards of the community.[14]

A lawful arrest or a lawful restraint may not be classified as provocation. In *R v Scriva (No 2)* [1951] VLR 298 the accused stabbed a person to death who had intervened to restrain him from attacking a motorist who had run down the accused's daughter. The Full Court of the Supreme Court of Victoria held that where death was caused by the intentional use of force in resisting a lawful restraint, the fact that there was provocation from the other person cannot reduce murder to manslaughter. The court held that in any case, there was insufficient evidence of provocation on the facts.

An unlawful arrest, on the other hand, may amount to provocation if the illegality was known to the accused,[15] or, in Tasmania, if the accused believed on reasonable grounds that the arrest was illegal: *Criminal Code* (Tas), s 160(5).

PROVOCATION IN THE PRESENCE OF THE ACCUSED

Some cases have referred to a requirement that the provocation take place in the sight or hearing of the accused.[16] For example, in *R v Arden* [1975] VR 449 the accused's de facto wife who was two months pregnant told him that she had been raped by a man who was asleep in another room of the house. She showed the accused her torn pantyhose and pants. The accused confronted the man who denied the allegation. The accused attacked and killed him with an iron pipe. Menhennit J excluded the defence of provocation on the basis that being told by a third person of an incident is an insufficient basis for the defence. He stated (at 452):

> The rationale of this rule appears to me to be as follows. If a person actually sees conduct taking place in respect to a third person and he [or she] is provoked thereby, it is understandable that he [or she] may be provoked to the extent of taking the other person's life and in circumstances which would reduce murder to manslaughter. Where, however, all that happened is that the accused is told something by a third person there enters immediately the element of belief, and there is nothing tangible upon which the accused can be said to have acted.

---

12   *R v R* (1981) 28 SASR 321 at 327 per King CJ, at 342 per Jacobs J, cf at 339 per Zelling J; *Stingel v The Queen* (1990) 171 CLR 312 at 322-324 per the Court; *Roche v The Queen* [1988] WAR 278.

13   *Criminal Code* (NT), s 1 (definition of provocation); *Criminal Code* (Tas), s 160(2); *Criminal Code* (WA), s 245.

14   *Roche v The Queen* [1988] WAR 278 at 280 per Burt CJ; *Jabarula v Poore* (1989) 68 NTR 26 at 31.

15   *Hugget's Case* (1666) Kel 59; 84 ER 1082; *Criminal Code* (Tas), s 160(5); *Criminal Code* (WA), s 245.

16   *R v R* (1981) 28 SASR 321 at 326 per King CJ; *R v Terry* [1964] VR 248; *R v Arden* [1975] VR 449; *R v Quartly* (1986) 11 NSWLR 332; *R v Earley* (unrep, 6/4/1990, CCA SA King CJ, Milhouse, Olsson JJ, 6/1990).

However, this requirement may have been softened somewhat by the move towards accepting a history of provocative incidents, many of which may not have occurred in the presence of the accused.[17]

It is unclear in the situation where provocation occurs in the presence of the accused, whether or not the victim must have been aware of the accused's presence.[18] It is clear, however, that the provocation must have emanated from the victim.[19] However, the provocation need not be aimed at the accused, but may be indirect in the sense that it is aimed at a person with whom the accused has a familiar or close relationship.[20] In *R v Terry* [1964] VR 248 Pape J stated (at 250-251) that:

> the mere fact that provocation was not offered by the deceased to the accused, but was offered to the deceased's wife and the accused's sister, does not prevent the operation of the principle that provocation will reduce murder to manslaughter provided that the provocation was offered in the presence of the accused, and provided all the other elements of provocation are present.

Pape J was of the opinion that provocation could be aimed at not only a relative of the accused but also at other persons in some form of relationship to the accused, but he did not go on to define the required relationship.

The defence of provocation does not apply where the provocation was self-induced by the accused.[21] A distinction has been drawn at common law in this regard between inducing provocation as an excuse to kill and risking a provocative reaction from the victim.[22] In the latter case, provocation may still be applicable if the victim's reaction was unexpected or unpredictable: *Edwards v The Queen* [1973] AC 648.

2.2 THE ACCUSED'S LOSS OF SELF-CONTROL

For the defence of provocation to be successful, the accused must have lost the power of self-control as a result of the provocative conduct. In *R v McGregor* [1962] NZLR 1069 North J stated (at 1078):

> [I]t is of the essence of the defence of provocation that the acts or words of the dead man [or woman] have caused the accused a sudden and temporary loss of self-control, rendering him [or her] so subject to passion as to make him [or her] for the moment not master of his [or her] mind.

---

17 *Parker v The Queen* (1964) 111 CLR 665; *Moffa v The Queen* (1977) 138 CLR 601; *R v R* (1981) 28 SASR 321; *Gardner* (1989) 42 A Crim R 279; *Chhay* (1994) 72 A Crim R 1.

18 *Gardner* (1989) 42 A Crim R 279. Cf *R v Fricker* (1986) 42 SASR 436 at 449 per Zelling J.

19 *Gardner* (1989) 42 A Crim R 279; *R v Davies* [1975] 1 QB 691; *Simpson* (1915) 11 Cr App R 218; *Roche v The Queen* [1988] WAR 278 at 280 per Burt CJ.

20 *R v Terry* [1964] VR 248; *R v Earley* (unrep, 6/4/1990, CCA SA King CJ, Milhouse, Olsson JJ, 6/1990).

21 *R v Voukelatos* [1990] VR 1 at 19; *Allwood* (1975) 18 A Crim R 120 at 132-133 per Crockett J; *R v Newman* [1984] VLR 61 at 66. See A Ashworth, "Self-induced Provocation and the Homicide Act" [1973] Crim LR 483.

22 *Edwards v The Queen* [1973] AC 648; *R v Voukelatos* [1990] VR 1 at 19; *R v Newman* [1948] VLR 61 at 66; *Allwood* (1975) 18 A Crim R 120.

The loss of self-control must have been caused by the provocation rather than another factor such as intoxication.[23]

When considering whether or not an accused actually lost self-control, the jury must consider all the relevant characteristics of the accused[24] and "the totality of the deceased's conduct".[25] While anger is the usual response to provocation, the courts have taken into account other emotions such as fear or panic in causing a loss of self-control.[26] In *Van Den Hoek v The Queen* (1986) 161 CLR 158 Mason CJ stated (at 168):

> [T]here can now be no convincing reason for confining the doctrine [of provocation] to loss of self-control arising from anger or resentment. The doctrine naturally extends to a sudden and temporary loss of self-control due to an emotion such as fear or panic ... This extension ... conforms ... to the conceptual relationship between the doctrine and the mental elements in the offences of murder and manslaughter.

The loss of self-control may vary in intensity from "icy detachment" to "going berserk": *Phillips v The Queen* [1969] 2 AC 130 at 137 per the Court. Wood J stated in *Peisley* (1990) 54 A Crim R 42 at 48:

> More is required than anger or loss of temper or building resentment. There must, in my view, be a loss of self-control which I understand to include a state in which the blood is boiling or a state of fear or terror, in either case, to the point where reason has been temporarily suspended.

The jury may consider the significance of any time-delay in assessing whether or not the accused lost self-control.[27] There is no separate requirement that the accused lose self-control suddenly or immediately following the provocative conduct.[28] Any evidence of a "cooling-off period" will merely be a factor that the jury can consider: *Parker v The Queen* (1963) 111 CLR 610 at 630 per Dixon CJ.

2.3 THE ORDINARY PERSON TEST

The defence of provocation will only be successful where the provocation was of such a nature as to be "capable of causing an ordinary person to lose self-control and to act in the way the accused did".[29] The ordinary person test involves two questions:

---

23 *R v Perks* (1986) 41 SASR 335 per White J; *R v Cooke* (1985) 39 SASR 225 at 235 per King CJ; *Censori v The Queen* [1983] WAR 89.

24 *Stingel v The Queen* (1990) 171 CLR 312 at 326.

25 *Moffa v The Queen* (1977) 138 CLR 601 at 606; *Stingel v The Queen* (1990) 171 CLR 312 at 326.

26 *R v Hunter* [1988] 1 Qd R 663 at 667 per Connolly J; *Jeffrey v The Queen* [1982] Tas R 199 at 229 per Cosgrove J; *R v Newman* [1948] VLR 61 at 66-67; *Chhay* (1994) 72 A Crim R 1 at 14 per Gleeson CJ (CCA NSW).

27 *R v Fisher* (1837) 8 Car and P 182; 173 ER 452; *Albis* (1913) 9 Cr App R 158.

28 *Parker v The Queen* (1963) 111 CLR 610 at 655; *Moffa v The Queen* (1977) 138 CLR 601; *R v Jeffrey* [1967] VR 467; *R v R* (1981) 28 SASR 321.

29 *Masciantonio v The Queen* (1995) 183 CLR 58 at 66 per Brennan, Deane, Dawson and Gaudron JJ; *Stingel v The Queen* (1990) 171 CLR 312 at 325-327.

▬▬ given that the accused actually lost self-control, was the provocation of such a nature as to be capable of causing an ordinary person to lose self-control? This is usually referred to as assessing the gravity of the provocation; and

▬▬ given that the ordinary person would have lost self-control, was the provocation such as could cause an ordinary person to act in the way in which the accused did? [30]

The first part of the ordinary person test involves an assessment of the content and the extent or the provocation; the second involves an assessment of whether the provocation would have caused an ordinary person to kill another or whether an ordinary person would have maintained self-control. Peter Rush explains this in *Criminal Law* (Sydney: Butt, 1997), p 353 as follows:

> The possibility being envisaged here by the judiciary is that, although the ordinary person
> would have lost their self-control to the same extent the [accused] did, the ordinary person
> would have laughed it off or told the victim to go jump in the lake whereas the actual
> accused killed the victim.

The second part of the ordinary person test has been formulated in various ways. In the Northern Territory, Queensland, South Australia, Tasmania, Victoria and Western Australia, the question is whether or not an ordinary person *would* have lost self-control to the point of acting in the way in which the accused did. [31] Under s 23(2)(b) of the *Crimes Act* 1900 (NSW) there is a requirement that an ordinary person *could* be induced to form an intent to kill or to cause grievous bodily harm. Under s 13(2)(b) of the *Crimes Act* 1900 (ACT) there is the requirement that an ordinary person *could* be induced to form an intent to kill or could have been recklessly indifferent to the probability of causing the accused's death. The slight differences in wording between the jurisdictions is of little consequence. Brennan, Dean, Dawson and Gaudron JJ pointed out in *Masciantonio v The Queen* (1995) 183 CLR 58 at 66:

> Since the provocation must be such as could cause an ordinary person to lose self-control
> and act in a manner which would encompass the accused's actions, it must be such as could
> cause an ordinary person to form an intention to inflict grievous bodily harm or even death.

Different personal characteristics may be taken into account in applying the ordinary person test in these two ways. These are explored below.

The rationale for having an objective standard was expressed by Wilson J in *R v Hill* [1986] 1 SCR 313 (at 324) as follows:

> The objective standard ... may be said to exist in order to ensure that in the evaluation of
> the provocation defence there is no fluctuating standard of self-control against which
> accuseds are measured. The governing principles are those of equality and individual
> responsibility, so that all persons are held to the same standard notwithstanding their
> distinctive personality traits and varying capacities to achieve the standard.

---

30 *Masciantonio v The Queen* (1995) 183 CLR 58 at 66 per Brennan, Deane, Dawson and Gaudron JJ; *Stingel v The Queen* (1990) 171 CLR 312 at 325-327.

31 *Criminal Code* (NT), s 34(2)(d) (refers to whether "an ordinary person similarly circumstanced would have acted in the same or a similar way"); *Criminal Code* (Tas), s 160(2); *Hutton v The Queen* [1986] Tas R 24 at 38; *Criminal Code* (WA), s 245; *Censori v The Queen* [1983] WAR 89.

An ordinary person is not equivalent to the reasonable person in tort law[32] nor is the ordinary person to be construed as a juror in the position of the accused: *Stingel v The Queen* (1990) 171 CLR 312 at 327-328 per the Court. Just what *does* constitute the ordinary person is the subject of much debate and this will be considered further in the section dealing with criticisms of the objective test.

THE GRAVITY OF THE PROVOCATION

In assessing the gravity of the provocation, any relevant characteristic of the accused may be attributed to the ordinary person: *Stingel v The Queen* (1990) 171 CLR 312 at 325-327. Brennan, Deane, Dawson and Gaudron JJ provided a rationale for this requirement in *Masciantonio v The Queen* (1995) 183 CLR 58 (at 67):

> Conduct which might not be insulting or hurtful to one person might be extremely so to another because of that person's age, sex, race, ethnicity, physical features, personal attributes, personal relationships or past history. The provocation must be put into context and it is only by having regard to the attributes or characteristics of the accused that this can be done.

There is some debate concerning just what characteristics of the accused are relevant to the gravity issue. In the past, the courts have taken into account factors such as the accused's physical disability,[33] mental instability or weakness,[34] delusions,[35] intoxication,[36] religious[37] and ethnic[38] background in assessing whether or not the conduct was of such a nature to be sufficient to deprive an ordinary person of the power of self-control. In *R v Morhall* [1995] 3 All ER 659 the House of Lords held that the accused's history of "glue-sniffing" could be relevant in determining the gravity of the provocation.

Ian Leader-Elliott has argued in "Sex, Race and Provocation: In Defence of Stingel" (1996) 20 Crim LJ 72 that there are limitations on the types of characteristics that may be attributed to the ordinary person for the purpose of assessing the gravity of the deceased's conduct. He states (at 77) that "[w]hen gravity is in issue, the ordinary person is often a near double of the accused", but that there are "limits to the process of attributing the peculiarities of the accused to this imagined being". He argues (at 79) that provocation "is grave only if ordinary people would consider it grave".

Leader-Elliott bases this view on the following passage in *Stingel v The Queen* (1990) 171 CLR 312 (at 325):

> The central question posed by the objective test — ie of such a *nature* as to be *sufficient* — obviously cannot be answered without the identification of the content and relevant

---

32 *R v Enright* [1961] VR 663 at 669 per the Court; *Johnson v The Queen* (1976) 136 CLR 619 at 635 per Barwick CJ; *Stingel v The Queen* (1990) 171 CLR 312 at 327 per the Court.

33 *DPP v Camplin* [1978] AC 705 at 724 per Lord Simon.

34 *Stingel v The Queen* (1990) 171 CLR 312 at 326.

35 *R v Lukins* (1902) 19 WN (NSW) 90.

36 *R v Cooke* (1985) 39 SASR 225 at 235 per King CJ; *R v Webb* (1977) 16 SASR 309 at 314.

37 *R v Dincer* [1983] VR 460; *R v Saliba* (1986) 10 Crim LJ 420.

38 *Baraghith* (1991) 54 A Crim R 240; *R v Dincer* [1983] VR 460; *R v Saliba* (1986) 10 Crim LJ 420.

implications of the wrongful act or insult and an objective assessment of its gravity in the circumstance of the particular case.

Imbuing the ordinary person with *all* the characteristics of the accused would certainly seem to be moving away from an "objective assessment" of the gravity of the provocation. It has previously been stated that the ordinary person will not be invested with "exceptional excitability or pugnacity or ill-temper"[39] and in the New Zealand case of *R v McGregor* [1962] NZLR 1069 North J stated (at 1081):

> The characteristic must be something definite and of sufficient significance to make the offender a different person from the ordinary run of mankind, and have also a sufficient degree of permanence to warrant its being regarded as something constituting part of the individual's character and personality.

On the other hand, a little later in *Stingel's* case (at 326), the High Court appears to be getting close to making the ordinary person a mirror image of the accused:

> [T]he content and extent of the provocative conduct must be assessed from the viewpoint of the particular accused. Were it otherwise, it would be quite impossible to identify the gravity of the particular provocation. In that regard, none of the attributes or characteristics of a particular accused will be necessarily irrelevant to an assessment of the content and extent of the provocation involved in the relevant conduct. For example, any one or more of the accused's age, sex, race, physical features, personal attributes, personal relationships and past history may be relevant to an objective assessment of the gravity of a particular wrongful act or insult. Indeed, even mental instability or weakness of an accused could, in some circumstances, itself be a relevant consideration to be taken into account in the determination of the content and implications of particular conduct.

Perhaps the real limitation that occurs in relation to imbuing the ordinary person with the characteristics of the accused lies in the link that must occur between the provocative conduct and the accused's characteristics. That is, the conduct and/or words must be gravely provocative to the individual because they relate to a personal characteristic. If a person is "exceptionally pugnacious" and the provocative conduct consists or words relating to that fact, then there appears to be no reason why the ordinary person cannot be imbued with that characteristic.

THE ORDINARY PERSON AND THE EXTENT OF LOSS OF CONTROL

With regard to the question as to whether or not the ordinary person could or might have lost control in the way the accused did, the High Court has ruled that no personal characteristic may be taken into account apart from age: *Stingel v The Queen* (1990) 171 CLR 312 at 326-327, at 330-331 per the Court. In *Masciantonio v The Queen* (1994-95) 183 CLR 58 Brennan, Deane, Dawson and Gaudron JJ (at 67) spoke of the ordinary person test as follows:

---

39   *DPP v Camplin* [1978] AC 705 at 726 per Lord Simon. See also *Mancini v DPP* [1942] AC 1 at 9 per Viscount Simon; *R v Croft* [1981] 1 NSWLR 126; *R v O'Neill* [1982] VR 150.

The test involving the hypothetical ordinary person is an objective test which lays down the minimum standard of self-control required by the law. Since it is an objective test, the characteristics of the ordinary person are merely those of a person with ordinary powers of self-control. They are not the characteristics of the accused, although when it is appropriate to do so because of the accused's immaturity, the ordinary person may be taken to be of the accused's age.

There is no separate requirement that the retaliation be reasonably proportionate to the provocation offered.[40] Brennan, Deane, Dawson and Gaudron JJ referred (at 67) with approval to Barwick CJ's comments in *Johnson v The Queen* (1976) 136 CLR 619 at 636 that "it is the formation of an intent to kill or do grievous bodily harm which is the important consideration rather than the precise form of physical reaction".

Prior to *Stingel's* case, there existed a line of cases in the Northern Territory that imbued the ordinary person with the accused's Aboriginal background.[41] After *Stingel's* case was decided, the Supreme Court of the Northern Territory stated that the ordinary person test was not "intended to be applied in a vacuum and without regard to such of the accused's personal characteristics, attributes or history as served to identify the implications and to affect the gravity of the particular wrongful act or insult": *Mungatopi v The Queen* (1992) 2 NTR 1. The Court then went on to speak of the ordinary 29-year-old Aborigine, but it is unclear whether it was applying this to both parts of the ordinary person test. The Court did point out (at 6) that the provisions of the *Criminal Code* (NT) were different to that of the *Criminal Code* (Tas) and seemed to suggest that ethnicity could be taken into account in assessing whether or not the requisite conduct was such as to provoke an ordinary Aboriginal person living in the environment and culture of a fairly remote Aboriginal settlement to retaliate "to the degree and method and continuance of violence which produces the death": affirming *Holmes v DPP* [1946] AC 588 at 597.

Stanley Yeo in "Sex, Ethnicity, Power of Self-Control and Provocation" (1996) 18 *Sydney Law Review* 304 (at 316) criticises this line of cases on the basis that they regard Aboriginal people as possessing lesser capacity for self-control than other ethnic groups:

Doubtless, the judges who delivered these decisions had fairness and justice as their paramount aims. However, their decisions had the effect of promoting a great evil, namely, a negative stereotype of Aborigines being at a lower order of the evolutionary scale that other ethnic groups.

This aspect of the ordinary person test has been the subject of debate and is examined in the following section.

---

40 *Johnson v The Queen* (1976) 136 CLR 619 at 636 per Barwick CJ; *R v Webb* (1977) 16 SASR 309 at 314 per Bray CJ; *Masciantonio v The Queen* (1995) 183 CLR 58 at 67 per Brennan, Deane, Dawson and Gaudron JJ.

41 *R v Patipatu* (1951-1976) NTJ 18; *R v MacDonald* (1951-1976) NTJ 186; *R v Muddarubba* (1951-1976) NTJ 317; *R v Jimmy BalirBalir* (1951-1976) NTJ 633; *R v Nelson* (1951-1976) NTJ 327; *Jabarula v Poore* (1989) 42 A Crim R 479.

PERSPECTIVES

Critique of the Ordinary Person Test

The ordinary person test in provocation has drawn much criticism from both judges and academic commentators. In *Moffa v The Queen* (1977) 138 CLR 601 Murphy J (at 625-626) called for its abolition:

> The objective test is not suitable even for a superficially homogeneous society, and the more heterogeneous our society becomes, the more inappropriate the test is. Behaviour is influenced by age, sex, ethnic origin, climatic and other living conditions, biorhythms, education, occupation and, above all, individual differences. It is impossible to construct a model of a reasonable or ordinary South Australian for the purpose of assessing emotional flashpoint, loss of self-control and capacity to kill under particular circumstances ... The same considerations apply to cultural sub-groups such as migrants. The objective test should not be modified by establishing different standards for different groups in society. This would result in unequal treatment ... The objective test should be discarded. It has no place in rational criminal jurisprudence.[42]

Peter Brett in his article "The Physiology of Provocation" [1970] Crim LR 634 reviewed the sociological and physiological studies that demonstrate that the old common law was grounded on a number of fallacies about human nature. He examined the judicial view of "controllable anger", that is, the idea that individuals who have lost self-control are in a position to control the degree of retaliation. This conception was embodied in the requirement of proportionality between the insult and the retaliation. Brett noted that the human body under stress prepares for strenuous action, a phenomenon known as the "fight or flight" reaction. The changes that occur have something of an all or nothing quality; the reaction is not nicely proportioned to the threat which is expected of the ordinary person. Brett concluded (at 638) that "the all or none quality of the reaction make it pointless to draw a distinction of nicety between different types of provocative act". He also argued that how individuals cope with stress varies much from one individual to another in that some individuals "are highly vulnerable to stress, others are strikingly resistant to it": at 637. This provides another reason why it is difficult to identify the response of an ordinary person.

Another criticism of the defence of provocation concerns what characteristics should be taken into account in relation to the ordinary person. Alex Reilly refers to this as "[o]ne of the most intractable debates surrounding the defence": "Loss of Self-Control in Provocation" (1997) 21 Crim LJ 320 at 326.

Some authors and judges have called for a modification of the ordinary person test so that further characteristics of the accused in addition to that of age be taken into account in assessing whether or not the ordinary person could or might have lost self-control in the same way as the accused did. In *Masciantonio v The Queen* (1995) 183 CLR 58 McHugh J recanted that with which he had concurred in *Stingel's* case and stated (at 74) that:

---

42 This reasoning was adopted by the Irish Court of Appeal which abandoned the objective test in *The People v MacEoin* (1978) 112 ILTR 43.

> [U]nless the ethnic or cultural background of the accused is attributed to the ordinary person, the objective test of self-control results in inequality before the law. Real equality before the law cannot exist when ethnic or cultural minorities are convicted or acquitted or murder according to a standard that reflects the values of the dominant class but does not reflect the values of those minorities.

In reaching this conclusion, McHugh J stated that he was influenced by Stanley Yeo's criticisms of the objective test in his article "Power of Self-Control in Provocation and Automatism" (1992) 14 *Sydney Law Review* 3 at 12-13.

Interestingly enough, Yeo subsequently altered his position after reading the work of Leader-Elliott: see for example I Leader-Elliott, "Sex, Race and Provocation: In Defence of Stingel" (1996) 20 *Criminal Law Journal* 72. In 1996, Yeo wrote that imbuing the ordinary person with the accused's ethnic or cultural background may give rise to essentialist views of various cultures and thereupon give rise to racism: "Sex, Ethnicity, Power of Self-Control and Provocation Revisited" (1996) 18 *Sydney Law Review* 304-322.

There are dangers associated with the present test in that by excluding cultural and ethnic background as a relevant consideration, discrimination against minority groups may be concealed and perpetuated. When a tribunal of fact is called on to decide whether the accused's conduct complies with the standards of reasonableness or ordinariness imposed by the law, whose standard is being applied? Objective standards are predicated on the existence of a "community consensus" about what constitutes reasonable and ordinary behaviour, but where minority groups are not adequately represented either on juries or on the bench, objective standards will be determined by the values of the dominant Anglo-Saxon-Celtic culture exclusively: Australian Law Reform Commission, *Multiculturalism and the Law*, Report No 57 (1992), pp 183-184. In reality each tribunal is constructing the standard of judgment according to its own values, and though represented as an "objective" and "neutral" standard it produces a highly discretionary system of regulation: N Lacey, C Wells, and D Meure, *Reconstructing Criminal Law* (London: Weidenfeld and Nicolson, 1990), p 33.

On the other hand, the adoption of an ordinary person standard that is sensitive to cultural variation may also be problematic. Such a modified standard could accommodate cultural claims about the use of domestic violence to discipline women and children, providing a partial defence to murder in communities where violence is recognised as a culturally appropriate response to provocative acts of "domestic disobedience". This conflict of moral imperatives, between multicultural and feminist claims to equality, is irreconcilable. There is a tendency to obscure this conflict by means of a judicial "sleight of hand"; namely the law merely recognises but does not condone such cultural practices.[43] Certainly a multicultural model of provocation could legitimately refuse to recognise cultural claims which are discriminatory on the grounds of gender, sexuality or age. This limitation would be consistent with the protection offered under the law of assault, where violence inflicted for the purpose of "domestic discipline" is unlawful

---

43 Indeed a similar argument is used to justify sentencing decisions where payback by spearing within Aboriginal communities, while not condoned, is recognised as a factor relevant to the mitigation of sentence: see *R v Minor* (1992) 70 NTR 1 at 11, per Mildren J; *R v Wilson Jagamara Walker* (unrep, 10/2/1994, SC NT Martin CJ, SCC 46 of 1993). Payback is discussed in Chapter 2, p 136.

irrespective of the cultural practices or consent of the parties involved.[44] Moreover, it would conform to the position in international human rights law, where in cases of irreconcilable conflict, the right of minorities to enjoy their own culture, religion or language is qualified by individual rights to equality and non-discrimination.[45]

Another danger with accommodating different cultural perspectives relates to proof. In determining the reactions of an ordinary person of a particular ethnicity there is a risk (as Yeo acknowledges) that judges and juries may draw on discriminatory generalisations about the cultures of minority groups of which they have little or no understanding. These dangers can, however, be overcome by both "out of court" measures such as cross-cultural training for judges and lawyers, and better representation of minorities on juries and "in court" assistance from independent witnesses who have expertise in cultural issues: K Amirthalingam and S Bronitt, "Cultural Blindness — Criminal Law in Multicultural Australia" (1996) 21(2) *Alternative Law Journal* 58 at 60.

The most recent High Court case to consider the ordinary person test is that of *Green v The Queen* (1997) 191 CLR 334. The 22-year-old accused killed the 36-year-old male victim, one of his "best friends" after the latter had gently touched the accused's side, bottom and groin area. The accused punched the deceased about 35 times, banged his face against the wall and stabbed him with a pair of scissors about 10 times. In attempting to establish provocation at his trial, the accused sought to admit evidence that he was particularly sensitive to matters of sexual abuse as a result of being told by his sisters and mother that the father had sexually abused four of his sisters and after witnessing violent assaults by his father upon his mother. The trial judge directed the jury that this evidence was not relevant to the issue of provocation and the accused was convicted of murder.

On appeal to the New South Wales Court of Criminal Appeal, the Crown conceded that the trial judge had erred in law in determining that this evidence was not admissible in relation to the question as to whether or not the accused had in fact been provoked, but a majority of the Court (Priestley JA, Ireland J concurring, Smart J dissenting) dismissed the appeal on the basis that there was no miscarriage of justice. On a further appeal to the High Court all five judges agreed that there had been a misdirection but a majority of three judges, Brennan CJ, Toohey and McHugh JJ with Gummow and Kirby JJ dissenting held that there had been a miscarriage of justice and ordered a retrial.[46]

---

44   See *R v Watson* [1987] 1 Qd R 440. By contrast, the law still permits adults to use some force for the "reasonable chastisement" of children, though this has been challenged as a violation of international human rights law: Ch 11, p 556.

45   See E Evatt, "Cultural Diversity and Human Rights" in P Alston (ed), *Towards an Australian Bill of Rights,* Centre of International and Public Law (Canberra: Australian National University & Human Rights and Equal Opportunity Commission, 1994).

46   At his retrial, Green was convicted of manslaughter and sentenced to imprisonment for 10½ years. An appeal against sentence was dismissed: *Green v The Queen* (unrep, 18/5/1999, [1999] CCA NSW, 97). For further analysis of *Green's* case and the "homosexual advance defence" see G Coss, "Editorial — Revisiting Lethal Violence by Men" (1998) 22 Crim LJ 5; T Molomby, "Revisiting Lethal Violence by Men — A Reply" (1998) 22 Crim LJ 116; G Coss, "A Reply to Tom Molomby" (1998) 22 Crim LJ 119; New South Wales Attorney-General's Department, *Homosexual Advance Defence, Final Report of the Working Party* (September, 1998); R Bradfield, *"Green v The Queen"* (1998) 22 Crim LJ 296; S Tomsen, "Hatred, Murder and Male Honour: Gay Homicides and the 'Homosexual Panic Defence'" (1994) 6 *Criminology Australia* 2; S Tomsen and A George, "The Criminal Justice Response to Gay Killings: Research Findings" (1997) 9 *Current Issues in Criminal Justice* 56; R Mison, "Homophobia in Manslaughter: The Homosexual Advance as Insufficient Provocation" (1992) 80 *California Law Review* 133.

In the course of their judgments, the judges considered the application of the ordinary person test. Brennan CJ confirmed (at 339-340) that the ordinary person test set out in *Stingel* and *Masciantonio* also applies to the defence of provocation set out in s 23 of the *Crimes Act 1900* (NSW). Section 23(2)(b) of the *Crimes Act* 1900 (NSW) states that the provocation must be such "as could have induced an ordinary person in the position of the accused to have so far lost self-control as to have formed an intent to kill, or to inflict grievous bodily harm upon, the deceased". The appellant argued that the words "in the position of the accused" requires the ordinary person to be imbued with all the attributes or characteristics of the accused. Toohey J stated (at 673) that these words simply mean that in determining the *gravity* of the provocation to the accused, it is relevant to take into account the accused's own circumstances. Both Toohey and Gummow JJ referred (at 693) with approval to a statement made by Samuels JA in *Baragith* (1991) 54 A Crim R 240 (at 244) that "the words "in the position of the accused" so far as they make relevant attributes or characteristics of a particular accused do so only in assessing the gravity of the alleged provocation and are to be ignored in deciding whether the accused's response was or was not that of an ordinary person".

Similarly, McHugh J stated (at 682) that the words "in the position of the accused" "require that the hypothetical person be an ordinary person who has been provoked to the same degree of severity and for the same reasons as the accused". McHugh J (at 682) took the opportunity to repeat his position in *Masciantonio v The Queen* (1995) 183 CLR 58 at 74 in stating that there should be added "considerations of 'ethnic or cultural background of the accused' to age and maturity as relevant to any inquiry into the objective standard by which the self-control of an accused is measured".

Kirby J appears (at 716) to have taken a slightly different view of the meaning of the words "in the position of the accused", holding not that they deal with the gravity of the provocation, but rather, the "consideration to be given to the age and maturity of the accused person".

The end result of these judgments is that, in relation to the ordinary person test, the approach taken by the High Court in *Stingel* and *Masciantonio* still holds sway.

It may be that the difficulties associated with the ordinary person test are so intractable that it might be worthwhile considering other more radical solutions than attempting to modify it. The Model Criminal Code Officers Committee has recommended the abolition of the defence of provocation and this recommendation is discussed below: 5.1 'The Abolition of Provocation', p 285.

2.4 THE BURDEN OF PROOF

The prosecution bears the legal burden of negating provocation beyond reasonable doubt.[47] The legal burden may be discharged by proving that:

- **provocative conduct did not exist; or**

---

47   *Moffa v The Queen* (1977) 138 CLR 601 at 608 per Barwick CJ at 613, per Gibbs J at 628, per Murphy J; *Woolmington v DPP* [1935] AC 462; *McPherson* (1957) 41 Cr App R 213; *Holmes v DPP* [1946] AC 588 at 597; *R v Lilley* (1983) 12 A Crim R 335 at 339; *Stingel v The Queen* (1990) 171 CLR 312 at 333-334.

━━ the intention to kill or cause grievous bodily harm arose independently of the provocative conduct;[48] or

━━ the provocation was not such as to deprive the ordinary person of self-control in the way in which the accused did.[49]

The defence bears the evidential burden in relation to provocation. The trial judge should instruct the jury on provocation if there is material which suggests that the killing occurred when the accused lost self control.[50] This is the case even where the defence has not raised the defence or where the defence has conceded that provocation was not an issue.[51] The trial judge should direct the members of the jury to return a verdict of manslaughter if they are not satisfied beyond reasonable doubt that one or more of the elements of the defence was not present.[52] The trial judge may withdraw provocation from the jury if there is no credible narrative supporting the defence obtainable from the evidence.[53] This power to withdraw the defence should be exercised with caution.[54] In *Parker v The Queen* (1963) 111 CLR 610 Dixon CJ stated (at 616):

> [T]he issue before the Court of Criminal Appeal was whether by any possibility the jury might not unreasonably discover in the material before them enough to enable them to find a case of provocation. The selection and evaluation of the facts and factors upon which that conclusion would be based would be for the jury and it would not matter what qualifying or opposing considerations the Court might see: they would not matter because the question was, *ex hypothesi,* one for the jury and not for the Court.

Thus, the trial judge should be careful not to replace his or her views for that of the jury in assessing whether or not to withdraw the defence of provocation: *Moffa v The Queen* (1977) 138 CLR 601 at 613-614 per Gibbs J.

2.5 PROVOCATION AND BATTERED WOMEN

In the past, the use of the defence of provocation proved difficult for women who had killed their abusive partners. The common law traditionally required suddenness and a proportionate relationship between the provocation and the conduct undertaken. Since these two requirements are no longer separate rules, but matters to be taken into account overall, there has been a freeing up of the availability of the defence.

---

48 *Parker v The Queen* (1964) 111 CLR 665.

49 *Johnson v The Queen* (1976) 136 CLR 619 at 641 per Barwick CJ; *Moffa v The Queen* (1977) 138 CLR 601 at 612-613 per Gibbs J; *Caine* (1990) 48 A Crim R 464 at 471; *Shea (No 2)* (1990) 48 A Crim R 455 at 462 per McGarvie J; *R v Cooke* (1985) 39 SASR 225 at 233 per King CJ.

50 *Lee Chun-Chuen v The Queen* [1963] AC 220 at 231; *R v Anderson* [1965] NZLR 29.

51 *Van den Hoek v The Queen* (1986) 161 CLR 158 at 162 per Gibbs CJ, Wilson, Brennan and Deane JJ. *Pemble v The Queen* (1971) 124 CLR 107 at 117-118 per Barwick CJ; *Wardrope* (1987) 29 A Crim R 198 at 204 per Gray J; *Hutton v The Queen* [1986] Tas R 24 at 29 at 318 per Green CJ.

52 *Da Costa v The Queen* (1968) 118 CLR 186 at 213 per Owen J; *Parker v The Queen* (1964) 111 CLR 665 at 681.

53 *Da Costa v The Queen* (1968) 118 CLR 186; *Sreckovic v The Queen* [1973] WAR 85; *R v Callope* [1965] Qd R 456; *R v Vassiliev* [1968] 3 NSWLR 155; *Pepler* (1984) 13 A Crim R 476.

54 *Stingel v The Queen* (1990) 171 CLR 312 at 334; *Packett v The Queen* (1937) 58 CLR 190 at 220 per Evatt J.

For example, in *R v R* (1981) 28 SASR 321 the accused killed her abusive husband with an axe whilst he was sleeping: see above, p 260. The lack of suddeness in the provocative conduct was not a bar to provocation. The Supreme Court of South Australia accepted that the words and conduct of the deceased had to be seen in the context of the history of the relationship between the two.

Similarly, in *Hill* (1981) 3 A Crim R 397 the New South Wales Court of Criminal Appeal took a contextual approach to the traditional suddenness requirement and held that the accused's loss of self-control had to be seen in the context of a history of domestic violence. In that case, there was evidence that the husband had a propensity for violent conduct when he was drunk. On the day of the killing, he returned home from the pub drunk, swearing and "screaming his head off". The accused who had a rifle warned him not to come near her. She claimed she fired three shots, trying to frighten him away. One of the shots hit and killed her husband. The Court substituted a verdict of manslaughter and sentenced the accused to four and a half years in prison.

The real stumbling block in relation to battered women using the defence of provocation lies in the context of the ordinary person test. How can the experiences of a battered woman be taken into account if provocation depends upon whether or not an ordinary person would have lost self-control? Some have argued that the sexless ordinary person is really a male[55] and the challenge for the defence is to demonstrate that the male response to provocation is not necessarily the only reasonable response or ordinary reaction.

Evidence of "battered women syndrome" which will be considered more fully in Chapter 6 (at pp 306ff) in relation to the defence of self-defence, may be relevant to the questions as to whether or not the accused lost self-control and the gravity of the provocation. However, such evidence has no bearings on the powers of self-control expected of the ordinary person. Yeo points out in "Battered Woman Syndrome in Australia" (1993) 143 *New Law Journal* 13 at 13:

> [F]or the purposes of provocation, battered women are regarded as possessing normal levels of self-control and are not to be distinguished in this respect from the ordinary woman of the community. What the syndrome does do is to present the latest provocative incident in the light of a history of provocation, and contribute to the jurors' comprehension of how a person with such a history could have viewed the latest provocation.

Because of the difficulties of "fitting" the circumstances of battered women within the provocation defence, an accused who kills her partner after years of abuse may still be liable for murder. However, a man who kills his partner after discovering her in an act of adultery may be liable for manslaughter.

3. DIMINISHED RESPONSIBILITY

Like the defence of provocation, diminished responsibility serves to reduce a charge of murder to manslaughter. Unlike provocation which is available in all States and Territories, the defence of

---

55   See, for example, E Sheehy, J Stubbs and J Tolmie, "Defending Battered Women on Trial: The Battered Woman Syndrome and Its Limitations" (1992) 16 Crim LJ 369.

diminished responsibility is only available in the Australian Capital Territory, New South Wales, the Northern Territory and Queensland.[56]

Diminished responsibility began as a plea in mitigation in the Scottish courts in the mid-18th century as a way of dealing with "mental weakness" falling short of insanity and as a way of avoiding the death penalty.[57] It became a partial defence to murder in the mid-19th century case of *HM Advocate v Dingwall* (1967) 5 Irvine 446 and was later enacted in the United Kingdom under s 2 of the *Homicide Act* 1957 (UK).

Despite differences in the wording of the defence in the four Australian jurisdictions, diminished responsibility consists of three elements:

▬ the accused must have been suffering from an abnormality of mind;

▬ the abnormality of mind must have arisen from a specified cause; and

▬ the abnormality must have substantially impaired the accused's capacity to understand his or her actions or to know that he or she ought not to do the act or to control his or her actions.

The defence has been criticised both on conceptual grounds and on the basis of difficulties with each of these components. The criticisms dealing with the elements of the defence will be considered as each element is examined. That will be followed by consideration of whether or not the defence should be abolished.

3.1 ABNORMALITY OF MIND

The four Australian jurisdictions that have enacted the defence of diminished responsibility require that the accused was suffering from an "abnormality of mind".[58] Lord Parker CJ in *R v Byrne* [1960] 2 QB 396 (at 403) defined this term as follows:

> [A] state of mind so different from that of ordinary human beings that the reasonable [person] would term it abnormal. It appears ... to be wide enough to cover the mind's activities in all its aspects, not only the perception of physical acts and matters, and the ability to form a rational judgment as to whether an act is right or wrong, but also the ability to exercise will power to control physical acts in accordance with that rational judgment.

The abnormality of mind need not be a permanent feature,[59] but it does not include emotions such as anger, jealousy, bad temper or attitudes or prejudices arising from upbringing.[60]

---

56 *Crimes Act* 1900 (ACT), s 14; *Crimes Act* 1900 (NSW), s 23A; *Criminal Code* (NT), s 37; *Criminal Code* (Qld), s 304A. There is also a defence of diminished responsibility available under s 13 of the *Defence Force Discipline Act* 1982 (Cth).

57 G Gordon, *The Criminal Law of Scotland* (2nd ed, Edinburgh: Green, 1978), p 386; Lord Keith of Avonholm, "Some Observations on Diminished Responsibility" (1959) *Juridical Review* 109 at 110.

58 *Crimes Act* 1900 (ACT), s 14; *Crimes Act* 1900 (NSW), s 23A; *Criminal Code* (NT), s 37; *Criminal Code* (Qld), s 304A.

59 *Tumanako* (1992) 64 A Crim R 149; *R v Whitworth* [1989] 1 Qd R 437.

60 *R v Whitworth* [1989] 1 Qd R 437; *Hinz* (1986) 24 A Crim R 185 at 187-188 per Vasta J; *R v Purdy* [1982] 2 NSWLR 964 at 966; (1982) 7 A Crim R 122 per Glass JA.

In Queensland, there has been a suggestion that a narrow approach to what is an abnormality of mind should be followed. In *R v Rolph* [1962] Qd R 262 Hanger J referred to the broad approach set out in *Byrne's* case and stated (at 288):

> I do not believe that such a description would be an adequate direction to a Queensland jury. I would think it necessary to remind juries that normal people in the community vary greatly in intelligence, and disposition; in their capacity to reason, in the depth and intensity of their emotions; in their excitability, and their capacity to exercise self-restraint, etc, etc, the matters calling for mention varying with the facts of the particular case; and that until the particular quality said to amount to abnormality of mind, goes definitely beyond the limits marked out by the varied types of people met day by day, no abnormality exists.

The term "abnormality of mind" has been criticised on the grounds that it is an ambiguous term that does not conform to medical concepts. In consultations with the New South Wales Law Reform Commission, several psychiatrists pointed out that almost everyone who kills could be said to be suffering from an "abnormality of mind": *Partial Defences to Murder: Diminished Responsibility*, Report No 82 (1997), p 45. There has certainly been a wide range of conditions that have been held to fall within the term. For example, it has been held to encompass severe depression,[61] post-traumatic stress disorder[62] and personality disorders.[63]

It is interesting to note that, on the advice of psychiatrists and psychologists, the New South Wales Law Reform Commission recommended changing the term to "abnormality of mental functioning", but this term did not find its way into the amended defence: *Partial Defences to Murder: Diminished Responsibility,* Report No 82 (1997), p 55.

Ultimately what constitutes an abnormality of mind is a matter for the jury to decide. Thomas J in *R v Whitworth* [1989] 1 Qd R 437 explained this as follows (at 447):

> There is no doubt that juries and judges alike look for a test that gives the defence to the harassed and the incapable, and denies it to the wicked and the callous. In the end it must be for the jury to draw the line from case to case.

3.2 CAUSES OF THE ABNORMALITY OF MIND

For diminished responsibility to be made out, the abnormality of mind must arise from a prescribed factor.[64] The following Table summarises the different factors set out in the legislation.

---

61 *Chayna* (1993) 66 A Crim R 178; *R v Nielsen* [1990] 2 Qd R 578; *Seers* (1984) 79 Cr App R 261; *R v Morris* [1961] 2 QB 237.

62 *R v Neilsen* [1990] 2 Qd R 578.

63 *R v Whitworth* [1989] 1 Qd R 437; *R v McGarvie* (1986) 5 NSWLR 270; *Turnbull* (1977) 65 Cr App R 242; *Fenton* (1975) 61 Cr App R 261.

64 *Fenton* (1975) 61 Cr App R 261; *R v Gittens* [1984] QB 698; *Jones* (1986) 22 Cr App R 42; *R v Miers* [195] 2 Qd R 138.

TABLE 1:
Prescribed Factors

ACT *Crimes Act* 1900 s 14(1)	NSW *Crimes Act* 1900 s 23A(8)	NT *Criminal Code* s 1	QLD *Criminal Code* s 304A
a condition of arrested or retarded development of mind	"underlying condition" means a pre-existing mental or physiological condition, other than a condition of a transitory kind	a condition of arrested or retarded development of mind	a condition of arrested or retarded development of mind
any inherent cause		inherent causes	inherent causes
induced by disease or injury		induced by diseases, illness or injury	induced by disease or injury

This Table shows that the provisions in the Australian Capital Territory, the Northern Territory and Queensland are substantially the same, but the requirements in New South Wales have been recently amended by the *Crimes Amendment (Diminished Responsibility) Act* 1997 (NSW).

In the first three jurisdictions, the abnormality of mind must arise from one of three general factors, each of which will be explored in turn.

A CONDITION OF ARRESTED OR RETARDED DEVELOPMENT OF MIND

This provision is designed to take into account intellectual disabilities or organic brain damage. In Queensland, a condition of arrested or retarded development of mind has been interpreted as encompassing "natural mental infirmity" which is referred to in s 27 of the *Criminal Code* (Qld), the section which sets out the defence of insanity: *R v Rolph* [1962] Qd R 262. This in turn has been interpreted as going beyond organic disorders, but how far this extends is unclear.[65]

ANY INHERENT CAUSE

Any inherent cause has been held to be something that is a natural feature of the mind that has existed from birth or has developed by reason of an innate disposition or natural deterioration: *R v Whitworth* [1989] 1 Qd R 437 at 454 per Derrington J. An inherent cause must have some degree of permanency,[66] although an ephemeral manifestation of a permanent underlying condition may constitute an inherent cause: *R v McGarvie* (198) 5 NSWLR 270 at 272 per Street CJ. External factors

---

65 *Hodges* (1985) 19 A Crim R 129 (CCA WA). It is unclear whether or not natural mental infirmity extends to antisocial personality disorder: PA Fairall and PW Johnston, "Antisocial Personality Disorder (APD) and the Insanity Defence" (1987) 11 Crim LJ 78.

66 *Tumanako* (1992) 64 A Crim R 149 at 162 per Badgery-Parker J; *R v McGarvie* (1986) 5 NSWLR 270 at 272 per Street CJ.

such as environmental influences or stress cannot in themselves be considered inherent causes, but they may be taken into account if they have contributed to producing a pre-existing inherent cause: *R v Whitworth* [1989] 1 Qd R 437 at 453 per Derrington J, qualifying *R v McGarvie* (1986) 5 NSWLR 270.

The inclusion of abnormalities of mind stemming from inherent causes has attracted criticism. This is because of the anomaly of requiring the inherent cause to be permanent, yet the abnormality of mind need only be temporary: *R v McGarvie* (1986) 5 NSWLR 270. In addition, there may be some overlap between an "abnormality of mind" and an "inherent cause". Personality disorders are cited as common examples of where the abnormality and the inherent cause are considered indistinguishable. The courts appear to have accepted evidence of an "inherent abnormality" rather than an abnormality stemming from an inherent cause. For example, in *Tumanako* (1992) 64 A Crim R 149, Badgery-Parker J stated (at 162) that "[i]t will be sufficient that the abnormality of mind is itself shown to be inherent".

INDUCED BY DISEASE OR INJURY

A disease has been held to include all forms of physical deterioration caused by, for example, epilepsy[67] and delirium from fever: *R v Whitworth* [1989] 1 Qd R 437 at 450 per Derrington J. The provision in the Northern Territory also includes the term "illness",[68] but it is difficult to understand how this term would add anything further than that already covered by the broad scope of the term "disease".

"Injury" has been held to include injury caused either physically or psychologically, such as post-traumatic stress disorder: *R v Nielsen* [1990] 2 Qd R 578 at 585 per De Jersey J. It may also cover the situation of injury caused by protracted intoxication[69] and chronic alcoholism, but not a temporary self-induced state.[70]

UNDERLYING CONDITION

The New South Wales Law Reform Commission considered the traditional causes were "quite arbitrary and may generate a high level of complexity and confusion in relation to the expert evidence which is led in diminished responsibility cases": New South Wales Law Reform Commission, *Partial Defences to Murder: Diminished Responsibility*, Report No 82 (1997), p 49. Its proposal, which has now been enacted in s 23A of the *Crimes Act* (NSW) is that an abnormality of mind must arise from an "underlying condition" which is defined in s 23A(8) as a pre-existing mental or physiological condition, other than a condition of a transitory kind.

---

67 *R v Dick* [1966] Qd R 301; *Campbell* (1986) 84 Cr App R 255.

68 See the definition of "abnormality of mind" in s 1 of the *Criminal Code* (NT).

69 *R v Chester* [1982] Qd R 252; *R v Whitworth* [1989] 1 Qd R 437 at 457 per Derrington J; *R v Tandy* [1989] 1 WLR 350 (CA).

70 *R v de Souza* (unrep, 20/10/1995, SC NSW Dunford J) (abnormality of mind stemming from the use of anabolic steroids did not arise from any of the prescribed factors); *R v Nielsen* [1990] 2 Qd R 578 at 581 per Macrossan CJ, at 585-586 per de Jersey J; *R v Whitworth* [1989] 1 Qd R 437 at 453; *R v Morgan; Ex parte Attorney-General* [1987] 2 Qd R 637; *R v Miers* [1985] 2 Qd R 138; *Jones* (1986) 22 A Crim R 42; *R v Gittens* [1984] QB 698; *Fenton* (1975) 61 Cr App R 261; RS O'Regan, "Intoxication and Criminal Responsibility Under the Queensland Code" (1977) 10 *University of Queensland Law Journal* 70 at 81.

The New South Wales Law Reform Commission explained the rationale for this terminology as follows (at 56):

> The term "arising from an underlying condition" is intended to link the defence to a notion of a pre-existing impairment requiring proof by way of expert evidence, which impairment is of a more permanent nature than a simply temporary state of heightened emotions. This does not mean that the condition must be shown to be permanent. It simply requires that the condition be more than of an ephemeral or transitory nature. So, for example, a severe depressive illness which is curable would still be considered to come within the definition of "underlying condition", notwithstanding that it is not permanent. On the other hand, a transitory disturbance of mind brought about by heightened emotions, such as extreme anger in typical cases of "road rage", would be excluded from the definition of "underlying condition" and therefore could not form the basis of a plea of diminished responsibility.

3.3 SUBSTANTIAL IMPAIRMENT OF CAPACITY

The abnormality of mind must have substantially impaired the accused's capacity to understand events, the wrongness of the act or the ability to control his or her actions. In the old parlance, the term used was "mental responsibility", a term still used in the Australian Capital Territory.

TABLE 2:

Terms Describing Impairment of Capacity

ACT *Crimes Act* 1900 s 14(1)	NSW *Crimes Act* 1900 s 23A(8)	NT *Criminal Code* s 37	QLD *Criminal Code* s 304A
mental responsibility	capacity to understand events	capacity to understand what he or she was doing	capacity to understand what the person is doing
—	capacity to judge whether the person's actions were right or wrong	capacity to know that he or she ought not do the act, make the omission or cause that event	capacity to know that the person ought not do the act or make the omission
—	capacity to control himself or herself	capacity to control his or her actions	capacity to control the person's actions

There has been some case law in relation to what is meant by "substantially impaired". In *R v Byrne* [1960] 2 QB 396 Lord Parker CJ (at 404) in delivering the judgment of the court stated that substantial impairment was a matter of degree and that it signified more than "some impairment". In *R v Simcox* [1964] Crim LR 402 the English Court of Criminal Appeal stated (at 403):

It is a matter for the jury approaching the matter in a broad commonsense way and taking into consideration all the circumstances, not only the medical evidence but the [accused's] history, conduct, and the whole circumstances of the case.

In *R v Lloyd* [1967] 1 QB 175 the English Court of Criminal Appeal stated (at 176) that the jury should be directed that substantial "does not mean total ... [but at] the other end of the scale substantial does not mean trivial or minimal".[71]

The concept of substantial impairment is probably incapable of precise definition, yet its quantitative connotation appears sufficiently precise for the purposes of jury decision-making. In New South Wales, there is an added provision requiring that a person who would otherwise be guilty of murder is not to be convicted if the impairment was so substantial as to warrant liability for murder being reduced to manslaughter: *Crimes Act* 1900 (NSW), s 23A(1)(b). This provision was inserted to clarify that it is the jury that must determine the ultimate issue of whether or not the accused should be convicted of manslaughter rather than murder: New South Wales Law Reform Commission, *Partial Defences to Murder: Diminished Responsibility*, Report No 82 (May 1997), p 59.

The traditional diminished responsibility provisions and currently, the Australian Capital Territory provision, use the much criticised term "mental responsibility". In *R v Byrne* [1960] 2 QB 396 Lord Parker CJ stated (at 403):

The expression "mental responsibility for his acts" points to a consideration of the extent to which the accused's mind is answerable for his physical acts which include a consideration of the extent of his ability to exercise will power to control his physical acts.

This "definition" was accepted by the Judicial Committee of the Privy Council as authoritative and correct in *Rose v The Queen* [1961] AC 496 at 507. But what exactly does it mean? Is the question of mental responsibility akin to asking whether the accused's physical acts were voluntary as the traditional approach to automatism has it, or is it something different?

The Butler Committee in England pointed out that the term "mental responsibility" has no medical validity and, if it is a moral or legal concept, how can medical witnesses testify in relation to it?[72]

As noted above, the New South Wales and Northern Territory provisions avoid the problems associated with the term "mental responsibility" by replacing it with three capacities:

- **the capacity of the accused to understand what he or she is doing;**

- **the capacity to know that it was wrong; and**

- **the capacity to control his or her actions.**

In the Northern Territory and Queensland, these categories of capacity are the same as those prescribed for the defence of mental impairment: *R v Rolph* [1962] Qd R 262 at 271 per Mansfield CJ. See Chapter 4, p 210.

---

71 This direction was referred to by Hart J in *R v Biess* [1967] Qd R 470 at 475 as "the most satisfactory I have seen, on the meaning of substantially".

72 Report of the Committee on Mentally Abnormal Offenders, (London: HMSO Cmnd 6244, 1975), para 19.5: "It seems odd that psychiatrists should be asked to testify as to legal or moral responsibility. It is even more surprising that courts are prepared to hear that testimony".

As discussed in relation to the defence of mental impairment, the inclusion of the capacity to control one's actions is problematic. It is very difficult to assess whether or not an accused was incapable of controlling his or her actions as opposed to being capable, but choosing not to. There is also the risk that this component may afford a defence to those with an antisocial personality disorder who may argue that they were unable to control themselves because of their disorder.

3.4 BURDEN OF PROOF

Unlike provocation and infanticide, but like the defence of mental impairment, the accused bears the burden of proof in relation to the defence of diminished responsibility.[73] The standard of proof is on the balance of probabilities.[74]

There has been concern that this is inconsistent with the principle that the prosecution prove its case against the accused beyond reasonable doubt. It has been pointed out that where diminished responsibility and provocation are raised together, the jury may be confused by the distinctions in the burden and standard of proof of the two defences.[75]

As discussed previously in Chapter 4 in relation to the defence of mental impairment, it may be preferable for the evidential burden to be placed on the accused, but have the prosecution bear the burden of disproving the defence beyond reasonable doubt. For further discussion of the burden and standard of proof in criminal trials, see Chapter 2, pp 114ff.

4. INFANTICIDE

The practice of infanticide has had a long and controversial history. In the time of Plato and Aristotle, the exposure of weak and deformed infants was generally accepted and occasionally encouraged and the exposure of healthy infants was not regarded as a serious offence.[76] The general acceptance of infanticide in many different cultures appears to be related to the unavailability or ineffectiveness of contraception and some anthropologists have viewed it as a widely used method of population control.[77]

It was not until the 17th century that an Act was passed in England making it an offence to conceal the death of an illegitimate child: *An Act to Prevent the Destroying and Murthering of Bastard Children* 21 James 1 c 27 (1624). This was repealed by *Lord Ellenborough's Act* 43, Geo 3 c 58 in 1803 and infanticide was put on the same footing as homicide in that the prosecution had to prove that the child had been born alive and that someone, usually the mother, had killed it.

---

73   *Crimes Act* 1900 (ACT), s 14(2); *Crimes Act* 1900 (NSW), s 23A(4); *Criminal Code* (NT), s 6; *Criminal Code* (Qld), s 304A(2).

74   *R v Dunbar* [1958] 1 QB 1; *R v Ayoub* [1984] 2 NSWLR 511.

75   Criminal Law Revision Committee, *Offences Against the Person*, Report No 14 (London: HMSO, Cmnd 7844, 1980), para 94; Law Reform Commission of Victoria, *Provocation and Diminished Responsibility as Defences to Murder*, Report No 12 (1982), para 2.67.

76   M Tooley, *Abortion and Infanticide* (Oxford: Clarendon Press, 1983), p 316; L Williamson, "Infanticide: An Anthropological Analysis" in M Kohl (ed), *Infanticide and the Value of Life* (New York: Prometheus Books, 1978), p 61.

77   S Scrimshaw, "Infanticide in Human Populations: Societal and Individual Concerns" in G Hausfater and S Hardy (eds), *Infanticide: Comparative and Evolutionary Perspectives* (New York: Aldue Publishing Co, 1984), p 440.

Concealment of birth was subsequently made a separate offence.[78] This paved the way for a compassionate approach to women who killed their infants. It was not until 1922 that the *Infanticide Act* (UK) was passed which reduced the offence of murder to manslaughter. Section 1(1) of that Act made infanticide a partial defence where a woman caused the death of her "newly born" child "but at the time of the act or omission she has not fully recovered from the effect of giving birth to such child, but by reason thereof the balance of her mind was then disturbed". The *Infanticide Act* 1938 (UK) later changed the words "newly born" to "under the age of 12 months" and adding the concept of a woman's balance of mind being disturbed "by reasons of the effect of lactation consequent upon the birth of the child".

The Australian provisions follow this English model quite closely. In New South Wales, Tasmania, Victoria and Western Australia,[79] a woman may be charged with the offence of infanticide or, it can be used as a partial defence in the sense that if a woman has been charged with the murder of her child, she may be convicted of the alternative offence of infanticide.[80]

4.1 PHYSICAL ELEMENTS

Infanticide only applies to mothers who have caused their own infant's death by an act or omission. Adoptive mothers, fathers and other carers are excluded.[81] The Model Criminal Code Officers Committee (MCCOC) has pointed out that this discriminates against carers other than natural mothers who kill their children in identical circumstances: *Fatal Offences Against the Person*, Discussion Paper (1998), p 137.

The victim must also be under the age of 12 months.[82] This particular requirement has been criticised as leading to anomalous results: A Bartholomew, *Psychiatry, the Criminal Law and Corrections* (Bundalong: Wiseman Publications, 1987), pp 150-153.

At the time of the killing, the accused's state of mind must also have been disturbed by reason of childbirth or, in the relevant jurisdictions apart from Tasmania, the effect of lactation.[83] The medicalisation of infanticide has been criticised on the basis that it relies on antiquated medical opinion concerning the effects of lactation and childbirth.[84] This is taken up in the following section.

---

78 *Offences Against the Person Act* 1828 (UK), s XIV. This was amended by the *Offences Against the Person Act* 1861 (UK), s 60.

79 *Crimes Act* 1900 (NSW), s 22A; *Criminal Code* (Tas), s 165A; *Crimes Act* 1958 (Vic), s 6(1); *Criminal Code* (WA), s 287A.

80 *Crimes Act* 1900 (NSW), s 22A(2); *Criminal Code* (Tas), s 333(d); *Crimes Act* 1958 (Vic), s 6(2); *Criminal Code* (WA), s 595.

81 *Crimes Act* 1900 (NSW), s 22A(1), (2); *Criminal Code* (Tas), s 165A; *Crimes Act* 1958 (Vic), s 6(1), (2); *Criminal Code* (WA), s 281A(1).

82 *Crimes Act* 1900 (NSW), s 22A(1), (2); *Criminal Code* (Tas), s 165A; *Crimes Act* 1958 (Vic), s 6(1), (2); *Criminal Code* (WA), s 281A(2).

83 *Crimes Act* 1900 (NSW), s 22A(1), (2); *Criminal Code* (Tas), s 165A; *Crimes Act* 1958 (Vic), s 6(1), (2); *Criminal Code* (WA), s 281A(1).

84 B McSherry, "The Return of the Raging Hormones Theory: Premenstrual Syndrome, Postpartum Disorders and Criminal Responsibility" (1993) 15 *Sydney Law Review* 292; Report of the Committee on Mentally Abnormal Offenders, Cmnd 6244 (1975), p 24; Law Reform Commission of Canada, *Homicide*, Working Paper 33 (Ottawa: Supply and Services Canada, 1984), pp 75-77.

The Effect of Childbirth on Mental Health

Some women experience some form of mood disorder after childbirth. The "maternal blues" is estimated to affect between 50–70% of women, and gives rise to frequent and prolonged crying episodes which last for one to two days and which appear within four days following the birth. Postpartum depression affects between 10–20% of women and symptoms resemble those of clinical depression: see further, B McSherry "The Return of the Raging Hormones Theory: Premenstrual Syndrome, Postpartum Disorders and Criminal Responsibility" (1993) 15 *Sydney Law Review* 292 at 293ff and references therein. It has been suggested that social and psychological causes rather than biological are the most plausible explanations for these states: M Sandler, *Mental Illness in Pregnancy and the Puerperium* (Oxford: Oxford University Press, 1978), pp 84-88.

Postpartum disorders with psychotic disorders are estimated to occur in from one in 500 to one in 1000 births and are more common in those with a prior history of mood disorders: American Psychiatric Association, *Diagnostic and Statistical Manual of Mental Disorders* (4th ed, Washington, DC: APA, 1994), p 386. In the 19th century, postpartum psychoses were thought to be specific entities distinct from other mental illnesses: M Gelder, D Gath, R Mayou and P Cowen, *Oxford Textbook of Psychiatry* (3rd ed, Oxford: Oxford University Press, 1996), p 396. However, mental health professionals in the 20th century have treated the clinical features and the prognosis of postpartum psychosis as no different from other psychoses.[85]

Those suffering from postpartum psychosis could clearly avail themselves of the defence of mental impairment. There is little evidence to show that any of these postpartum disorders stem primarily from hormonal or chemical imbalances. Most researchers would in fact agree that all three types of postpartum disorders are associated with multiple factors such as psychological variables including low motivation for pregnancy and low level of psychological health, demographic variables such as socio-economic status, stress and previous psychiatric and genetic predispositions.[86] It would appear that biological factors cannot be blamed, but rather, a combination of external and internal factors may give rise to such conditions.

Kathy Laster has explored the historical development of infanticide and the biological/social assumptions about women who kill their children and its value in light of current feminist criminological thinking: K Laster, "Infanticide and Feminist Criminology: 'Strong' or 'Weak' Women?" (1990) 2(1) *Criminology Australia* 14 and "Infanticide: A Litmus Test For Feminist Criminological Theory" (1989) 22 *Australian and New Zealand Journal Of Criminology* 151.

85　M Gelder, D Gath, R Mayou and P Cowen, *Oxford Textbook of Psychiatry* (3rd ed, Oxford: Oxford University Press, 1996), p 396. See also M Bleuler, *The Schizophrenic Disorders* (New Haven: Yale University Press, 1972).

86　For an overview of research into such variables see NM Fedele, ER Golding, FK Grossman and WS Pollack, "Psychological Issues in Adjustment to First parenthood" in GY Michaels and WA Goldberg, *The Transition to Parenthood* (New York: Cambridge University Press, 1988), p 88.

4.2 FAULT ELEMENTS

The infanticide provisions in New South Wales, Tasmania and Victoria all require the existence of a "wilful" act or omission.[87] The adjective "wilful" has been interpreted as meaning intentional or reckless.[88] Section 281A of the *Criminal Code* (WA) requires the same fault element as for murder or wilful murder, that is, an intention to kill or cause grievous bodily harm: ss 278, 279(1); see further, Ch 10 'Unlawful Killing'.

5. THE ABOLITION OF PARTIAL DEFENCES

Various law reform commissions have recommended the abolition of the three partial defences discussed in this chapter. The following provides a brief overview of the various rationales behind these recommendations.

5.1 THE ABOLITION OF PROVOCATION

Because the defence of provocation contains elements of both justification and excuse, its rationale is often confused. Perhaps because of this conceptual confusion, this defence in particular has attracted a great deal of criticism.

The Model Criminal Code Officers Committee in its Discussion Paper, *Fatal Offences Against the Person* (1998), has recommended that the defence of provocation be abolished: pp 87ff. It mentions the following reasons in support of this:

▬ It engenders conceptual difficulties concerning intention. Those who rely on provocation intend to kill. Why does the fact that the accused lost self-control make a difference?

▬ Following on from the first argument, the existence of provocation can be reflected in sentencing. There is no need for a separate defence.

▬ Hot-blooded killers may be just as culpable as other killers.

Why is a husband who kills his wife because he found her committing adultery morally less guilty than a murderer? Why is a conservative Turkish Muslim father partially excused when he stabs his daughter to death because she refuses to stop seeing her boyfriend? [*R v Dincer* [1983] VR 460] Why do we partially excuse a man who kills another man who has made a homosexual advance on him? [*Green v The Queen* (1997) 191 CLR 334].[89]

---

87   *Crimes Act* 1900 (NSW), s 22A(1), (2); *Criminal Code* (Tas), s 165A; *Crimes Act* 1958 (Vic), s 6(1), (2).

88   *Iannella v French* (1968) 119 CLR 84 at 94, 95 per Barwick CJ; *Bergin v Brown* [1990] VR 888; *Gardenal-Williams v The Queen* [1989] Tas R 62.

89   Model Criminal Code Officers Committee, *Fatal Offences Against the Person*, Discussion Paper (1998), p 89.

▬ Provocation is gender biased in the sense that "suddenness", although no longer forming a separate (substantive) rule, may still be taken into account evidentially in assessing whether or not the accused lost self-control. This reflects male rather than female patterns of aggressive behaviour.

▬ The abolition of the doctrine of excessive self-defence (see Chapter 6, pp 302ff) has weakened the case for retaining a defence of provocation.

▬ Provocation is subject to abuse in that it may be difficult to separate those who lose their temper without provocation and those who lose self-control after being provoked. Often the accused's version of events will be the sole source of evidence of provocation and the above criticism is particularly relevant to cases of an alleged homosexual advance being the provocation claimed.

▬ Provocation may be a legal anomaly in that it does not reduce attempted murder to attempted manslaughter in some jurisdictions.

There are two main problems with abolishing provocation. First, it removes the consideration of explanations for violent conduct to the sentencing stage. Judges would still have to ascertain the basis for the killing. This undermines the role of the jury in apportioning criminal responsibility and raises the potential for inconsistent dealings with those who kill after losing self-control.

Secondly, Ashworth in *Principles of Criminal Law* (3rd ed, Oxford: Oxford University Press, 1999) points out (p 284) that whether provocation should exist as a defence is closely related to issues of stigma and fair labelling. He writes (at 284):

> [T]he label "murder" should be reserved for the most heinous of killings, and most people would accept that provoked killings are not in this group.

The rationale for the defence lies in the recognition that there is a difference between intentional killings that are committed in "cold blood" and those that occur in an extreme emotional state and which are unpremeditated: see A Reilly, "Loss of Self-Control in Provocation" (1997) 21 Crim LJ 320 at 320. It is unsettling at the very least to label a person who kills in the latter fashion a "murderer" with all the stigma that label invokes. Perhaps the better approach is to concentrate on developing a workable test of provocation rather than wiping the slate clean.

5.2 THE ABOLITION OF DIMINISHED RESPONSIBILITY

In New South Wales, the Law Reform Commission considered some of the criticisms of the defence of diminished responsibility, but recommended its retention and set out recommended amendments: *Partial Defences to Murder: Diminished Responsibility,* Report No 82 (1997). These were largely echoed in the *Crimes Amendment (Diminished Responsibility) Act* 1997 (NSW). In comparison, the Law Reform Commission of Victoria considered and rejected the possibility of enacting the defence in Victoria in 1991[90] and more recently, the Model Criminal Code Officers Committee (MCCOC) has recommended its abolition.[91]

---

90 Law Reform Commission of Victoria, *Homicide,* Report No 40 (Melbourne: VGPS, 1991).

91 Model Criminal Code Officers Committee, *Fatal Offences Against the Person*, Discussion Paper (1998), p 131.

The MCCOC considered a number of reasons as to why the defence should be abolished. First, because of the vagueness of the concept of "abnormality of mind" there is a difficulty in clearly defining the scope and operation of diminished responsibility. This has led to "a dichotomy of approaches" in attempting to distinguish this defence from that of the defence of mental impairment: *Fatal Offences Against the Person*, Discussion Paper (1998), p 123.

Secondly, there are practical problems associated with expert testimony relating to diminished responsibility. These include the problems with conflicting evidence and the possibility of "experts for hire" as well as the tendency of experts to answer the ultimate issue as to the effect of the abnormality of mind which is really a matter for the jury to decide. It should be noted however that s 80 of the *Evidence Act* 1995 (Cth), (NSW) abolished the common law rule preventing the admissability of expert opinion evidence on the ultimate issue. A further point not mentioned by the MCCOC is that psychiatrists and psychologists must of necessity rely on what the accused says. If the term abnormality of mind is given a broad definition as has occurred in the past, there is a danger that conditions may be fabricated, much more so than in the case of the defence of mental impairment.

Thirdly, there is a difficulty in directing juries concerning an accused having to prove that he or she is not fully sane and yet not mentally impaired for the purpose of the defence of mental impairment.

Fourthly, the need for the defence is questionable where there is flexibility in sentencing options. Susanne Dell explains that if "judges had discretion in sentencing murderers, the issue of diminished responsibility could be taken into account, as it is in all other cases, as a mitigating factor in sentencing": "Diminished Responsibility Reconsidered" (1982) Crim LR 809 at 814.

Finally, there may be difficulties in sentencing on the basis of manslaughter due to a successful defence of diminished responsibility where the accused presents a risk to the public. The MCCOC referred to the case of *Veen v The Queen (No 1)* (1979) 143 CLR 458 in which the accused had successfully raised diminished responsibility based on the effects of alcohol combined with high stress levels. The High Court rejected the prosecution argument that evidence that the accused was likely to kill again if exposed to the same conditions should offset any reduction in sentencing because of diminished responsibility. Subsequently, the accused did kill again on his release from prison. Diminished responsibility only has logical value if it serves to mitigate the severity of punishment otherwise thought appropriate. However, if those with antisocial personality disorders are considered to be suffering from an abnormality of mind, as has occurred in the past,[92] it suggests that the more "dangerous" the offender, the shorter the sentence has to be.

If the MCCOC's recommendation that provocation be abolished is followed, then more weight would be put on the defence of diminished responsibility, leading to its potential abuse.

There are also conceptual difficulties with this defence. Diminished responsibility is in essence an artificial concept aimed at lessening the severity of punishment, without going so far as to completely acquit an accused. There are profound difficulties with the concept of being partially but not wholly criminally responsible, but apart from that, when the concept is explored more fully, it appears that the defence is not about responsibility at all.

---

92 *Matheson* (1958) 42 Cr App R 145; *R v Byrne* [1960] 2 QB 396; *R v Clarke and King* [1962] Crim LR 836; *R v Harvey and Ryan* [1971] Crim LR 664; *Fenton* (1975) 61 Cr App R 261; *Turnbull* (1977) 65 Cr App R 242.

There are two questions that arise in the course of a criminal trial. First, was the accused responsible for his or her actions? Secondly, if found responsible, what form should the sentencing or disposition order take? The defence of diminished responsibility blurs these two questions. In fact, the primary emphasis seems to be on the question of sentencing or disposition rather than on a finding of responsibility. In reality, the defence exists *only* where the essential elements of murder are present. In truth, it is the sentence that is being *diminished* rather than the accused's responsibility.

Because the defence is primarily concerned with issues of mitigating punishment rather than responsibility, the courts have interpreted "abnormality of mind" so broadly that a wide variety of extenuating circumstances have been taken into account. The better approach may be to concentrate on reformulating the defence of mental impairment and enacting more flexible dispositional options rather than continuing with such a flawed defence: see Ch 4, p 220.

5.3 THE ABOLITION OF INFANTICIDE

The infanticide provisions have been widely criticised. The Butler Report in England, the Law Reform Commission of Canada, the New South Wales Law Reform Commission and the MCCOC have all recommended its abolition.[93] The MCCOC has pointed out that infanticide is ambiguous in terms of the fault element required. It also has an uncertain medical foundation, it is discriminatory and erroneously links women's biology to criminal responsibility and is unnecessary in jurisdictions with a discretionary sentence for murder.

However, it has been argued that despite its conceptual flaws, having a gender specific offence of infanticide enables special and sympathetic treatment for women unable to cope with the "onerous and unalleviated nature" of the responsibility of caring for infants: R Lansdowne, "Infanticide: Psychiatrists in the Plea Bargaining Process" (1990) 16(1) *Monash University Law Review* 41 at 61.

The Criminal Law Revision Committee in England, for example, recommended that the link between lactation and mental imbalance be removed, but that the medical model remain, despite its inadequacies, in order to take into account the socio-economic factors involved in child killing.[94]

If there is going to be an infanticide defence, then it should be based fairly and squarely on the existence of socio-economic factors and not on antiquated beliefs in the link between women's biology and (lack of) criminal responsibility. Since socio-economic factors are not otherwise used to excuse people from criminal responsibility, there seems to be no rationale for retaining infanticide. As the MCCOC points out in its Discussion Paper, *Fatal Offences Against the Person* (1998), the "justification for infanticide lies in policy [and consequently], the defence is contrary to fundamental criminal law principles": p 139.

---

93 Report of the Committee on Mentally Abnormal Offenders (London: HMSO Cmnd 6244, 1975) (The Butler Report) 245, Law Reform Commission of Canada, *Homicide*, Working Paper 33 (Ottawa: Supply and Servies Canada, 1984), pp 75-77; New South Wales Law Reform Commission, *Partial Defences to Murder: Provocation and Infanticide*, Report 83 (1998), pp 107-113; Model Criminal Code Officers Committee, *Fatal Offences Against the Person*, Discussion Paper (1998), pp 135-139.

94 Criminal Law Revision Committee, *Offences Against the Person*, Fourteenth Report (London: HMSO Cmnd 7844, 1980), para 103. See also Law Reform Commission of Victoria, *Mental Malfunction and Criminal Responsibility*, Fourteenth Report (1990), pp 54-62.

Those who do kill whilst suffering from a clinical mental disorder should be able to avail themselves of a workable defence of mental impairment with flexible dispositional options. Infanticide, like the defence of diminished responsibility, is conceptually flawed.

6. CONCLUSION

The partial defences of provocation, diminished responsibility and infanticide currently exist in certain jurisdictions in order to recognise and provide a concession to "human frailty". We have outlined how diminished responsibility and infanticide can be seen as conceptually flawed. The existence of an adequate defence of mental impairment and a wider range of dispositional options on a finding of not guilty on the basis of mental impairment would render diminished responsibility and infanticide unnecessary. It would therefore seem more logical to concentrate on reformulating the defence of mental impairment than on reformulating the latter two defences. In this regard, the MCCOC's call for the abolition of diminished responsibility and infanticide should be heeded.

Provocation, unlike diminished responsibility and infanticide, is firmly entrenched in all Australian jurisdictions. That fact alone may frustrate the MCCOC's call for this defence's abolition. We have outlined the difficulties associated with formulating an objective test for provocation and the "intractable debate" concerning what characteristics the hypothetical "ordinary" person should have. However it may be better to concentrate on developing a workable test rather than abolishing the defence entirely. This is because of the notion that the label "murder" should only attach to intentional or premeditated killings and because of the danger that inconsistencies may result if explanations for killing are considered only at the charging or sentencing stages.

6

Self-Help Defences

> We hold these truths to be sacred and undeniable;
> That all men are created equal and independent,
> That from that equal creation they derive
> Rights inherent and inalienable, among which are
> The preservation of life

Thomas Jefferson, "Declaration of Independence" (original draft) in J Daintith (ed), *Bloomsbury's Thematic Dictionary of Quotations* (London: Bloomsbury Publishing, 1991), p 198

1. INTRODUCTION

There was a traditional distinction in the common law between killings that were justified and those that were excused. A plea of justification was said to focus on the circumstances surrounding the act itself and if accepted, led to a total acquittal, entailing no forfeiture of goods and requiring no pardon. Excuses, on the other hand, were said to focus on the actor's state of mind and the consequences of a successful plea involved a pardon and the forfeiture of goods.

In 1828, forfeiture was abolished and therefore the division between justifiable and excusable homicide became obsolete. Nevertheless, academic writers have been drawn to a philosophical exploration of the distinction between justification and excuse: for example, GP Fletcher, *Rethinking Criminal Law* (Boston: Little Brown, 1978), pp 759ff. Robert Schopp in his book *Justification Defenses and Just Convictions* (Cambridge: Cambridge University Press, 1998) views the defences of self-defence, duress and necessity as falling within the category of "justification" defences. This categorisation, however, has been questioned. For example, in *Zecevic v DPP (Vic)* (1987) 162 CLR 645 at 658, Wilson, Dawson and Toohey JJ stated about self-defence:

> [I]n scope and in practice nowadays the plea has a greater connection with excusable homicide being in most cases related to the preservation of life and limb rather than the execution of justice.

The emphasis on what the accused believed in relation to self-defence may indeed place it in the category of an excuse. Similarly, the concepts of justification and excuse have both been used as rationales for the defence of necessity. However they are categorised, what defences such as self-defence, duress, marital coercion and necessity have in common is the notion that the accused committed a crime in order to "help" him or herself or another avoid serious harm.

The four defences of self-defence, duress, marital coercion and necessity that will be outlined in this chapter go beyond the realms of defences to unlawful killing. Self-defence where successful leads to acquittals on a range of charges from assault to murder. The other three defences are also available for a range of crimes including manslaughter, but controversy concerns whether they should be available in relation to murder. In practice, these three defences are rarely raised.

> In a study of all prosecutions for murder and manslaughter in Victoria between 1981 and 1987, the Law Reform Commission of Victoria found that duress was raised in only four cases (1.3%) and necessity was not raised at all. In comparison, self-defence was an issue in 66 cases (20.7%) and provocation in 75 cases (23.5%): Law Reform Commission of Victoria, *Homicide Prosecutions Study*, Report No 40 (Melbourne: VGPS, October 1991), Appendix 6, pp 75ff.

All Australian jurisdictions allow for the use of force in self-defence, defence of another or defence of property. The definition of self-defence differs between jurisdictions, but some common themes have emerged. In general, the use of force in defence of property is much more limited than in relation to the defence of persons, though there have been legislative developments clarifying this defence in New South Wales in relation to "home invasions": see Ch 13, p 729. Defences such as duress, marital coercion and necessity are relevant where an accused admits that the criminal act was willed and intended but claims that it was only performed because he or she was compelled by threats or by "natural exigencies" (situations of emergency) to do so. We will outline how these three defences have been limited in their scope because of public policy concerns that allowing acquittals will cause an increase in the use of "innocent" agents to commit crimes or will devalue the underlying principles of the criminal law such as the sanctity of human life.

2. SELF-DEFENCE

The defence of self-defence is available to crimes involving the use of or threat of force to the person such as murder and assault and it results in a complete acquittal. The definition of self-defence varies across the Australian jurisdictions. In general, the accused may raise evidence that he or she committed the crime as a result of a personal attack upon him or herself or another. It may also be raised in relation to the protection of personal property, although this is more restricted. The use of force in self-defence is closely allied to the right to use force in order to prevent the commission of a crime, to execute a lawful arrest and to escape false imprisonment.

The defence of self-defence arose out of the regulation of duels and other forms of combat. It developed in the context of fights between two men, the traditional scenario being a bar-room brawl or a one-off duel: I Leader-Elliott, "Battered But Not Beaten: Women Who Kill in Self-Defence" (1993) 15 *Sydney Law Review* 403 at 405. This scenario has made it difficult for some women to use the defence where they have killed a partner after experiencing years of abuse from him. This point is taken up later in 2.8 'Battered Women and Self-Defence', p 306.

The defensive use of force against personal attack has been accepted as an expression of personal autonomy. In *Palmer v The Queen* [1971] AC 814 the Privy Council stated (at 831):

> It is both good law and good sense that a man [or woman] who is attacked may defend himself [or herself]. It is both good law and good sense that he [or she] may do, but may only do, what is reasonably necessary. But everything will depend upon the particular facts and circumstances.

Self-defence is open-ended in its formulation in the sense that there are not many substantive rules limiting its scope and it is very much a matter of fact for the jury to decide: *DPP Reference (No 1 of 1991)* (1992) 60 A Crim R 43 at 46.

CASE STUDIES

Zecevic v DPP (Vic): A Simplified Test for Self-Defence

The leading case on self-defence at common law is that of *Zecevic v DPP (Vic)* (1987) 162 CLR 645. In that case, the accused killed his neighbour after an argument about the latter leaving security gates open and parking his car outside the garage. The accused argued that he believed the victim had a knife and that he might have a shotgun in his car. The accused ran into his unit after the initial altercation, fetched his gun and went outside again where he shot the neighbour. At the accused's trial for murder, the judge withdrew the issue of self-defence from the jury and the accused was convicted.

On appeal to the High Court, all seven judges allowed the appeal and ordered a retrial. Wilson, Dawson and Toohey JJ (at 661) set out the requirements for the defence as follows:

> The question to be asked in the end is quite simple. It is whether the accused believed upon reasonable grounds that it was necessary in self-defence to do what he [or she] did. If he [or she] had that belief and there were reasonable grounds for it, or if the jury is left in reasonable doubt about the matter, then he [or she] is entitled to an acquittal. Stated in this form, the question is one of general application and is not limited to cases of homicide.

This statement was expressly approved by Mason CJ (at 654) and Brennan J (at 666) with the dissenting judges seemingly not objecting to it: Deane J (at 681) and Gaudron J (at 685).

The decision in *Zecevic* greatly simplified the test for self-defence. Previously, Mason J had developed a six-stage test[1] that the majority judges (including Mason CJ) found in *Zecevic* to be unworkable in practice. The present test is an amalgamation of subjective and objective elements. It is not wholly subjective because the accused's belief must be tested by reference to reasonable grounds. There is, however, no requirement that the accused's belief be tested against that of the ordinary person; the question is what the accused might reasonably have believed in all the circumstances.

---

1   *Viro v The Queen* (1978) 141 CLR 88 at 146-147, Stephen and Aickin JJ concurring.

> There are no longer any separate requirements (at 663-664):
>
> — that the accused's response be proportionate to the attack; or
>
> — that the victim's attack be unlawful; or
>
> — that the accused retreat as far as possible before using force.
>
> It is sufficient that the accused believed on reasonable grounds that it was necessary to do what he or she did.

This formulation of self-defence applies in the Australian Capital Territory, New South Wales and Victoria. In South Australia and Tasmania, the legislation gives the defence slightly more of a subjective emphasis. Section 46 of the *Criminal Code* (Tas) states that a "person is justified in using, in defence of himself [or herself] or another person, such force as, in the circumstances as he [or she] believes them to be, it is reasonable to use". Similarly, the South Australian provision allows an accused to use force if that person believes that the force is necessary and reasonable for self-defence and conduct was reasonably proportionate to the threat that the accused genuinely believed to exist: *Criminal Law Consolidation Act* 1935 (SA), s 15(1) as amended by the *Criminal Law Consolidation (Self-Defence) Amendment Act* 1997.

In *R v Walsh* (unrep, 19/8/1993, SC Tas, A68/1993) Crawford J explained that the Tasmanian test is both subjective and objective:

> The subjective test can be said to involve two questions, whether the accused was acting in defence of himself [or herself] when he [or she] used the force in question, and what were the circumstances as he [or she] believed them to be which might be taken into account for the purpose of the objective test. The objective test is whether the force used was, in the circumstances as he [or she] believed them to be, reasonable to use.

The objective test here therefore relates to the reasonableness of the force rather than the reasonableness of the accused's belief. This also appears to be the case in South Australia.

The Queensland, Northern Territory and Western Australian *Criminal Codes* are more complex and supplement the core element of "reasonable necessity" with additional rules that limit the use of permissible force. The Queensland and Western Australian provisions distinguish between self-defence as it relates to provoked and unprovoked attacks. In relation to an unprovoked attack:

> [I]t is lawful for [the accused] to use such force to the assailant as is reasonably necessary to make effectual defence against the assault, provided that the force used is not intended and is not such as is likely, to cause death or grievous bodily harm.[2]

Here, the test is objective in determining whether or not the force used by the accused was reasonably necessary.

---

2   *Criminal Code* (Qld), s 283; *Criminal Code* (WA), s 260.

In addition, the use of lethal force may be used in certain prescribed circumstances such as where the attack is of such a nature as to cause reasonable apprehension of death or grievous bodily harm. This is also reflected in s 28(f) of the *Criminal Code* (NT). As a defence to homicide then, the test of self-defence is both subjective and objective. The jury must consider whether the accused apprehended death or grievous bodily harm and then assess on an objective basis whether the apprehension was a reasonable one.

Under ss 27(g), 28(f) of the *Criminal Code* (NT) the use of force in self-defence is justified unless it is "unnecessary". An accused may use non-lethal force to defend him or herself or another: s 27. Lethal force may be used where the nature of the attack is such as to cause the person using the force reasonable apprehension of death or grievous bodily harm: s 28. Section 1 of the *Criminal Code* (NT) defines "unnecessary force" as "force that the user of such force knows is unnecessary and disproportionate to the occasion and that the ordinary person, similarly circumstanced ... would regard as unnecessary for and disproportionate to the occasion".

The components of self-defence will be explored in more detail after its use in relation to the defence of others and the defence of property is outlined.

2.1 SELF-DEFENCE AND THE DEFENCE OF OTHERS

The actual word self-defence appears to imply that this defence can only be raised when the accused him or herself is under attack. This is not the case. Force may be used to defend other persons from harm. At common law, the traditional view has been that force may only be used in defence of another who falls within the relationships of "master and servant", child and parent and wife and husband. There are some indications, however, that these restrictions may be loosened.

In *R v Duffy* [1967] 1 QB 63 the accused went to the defence of her sister. The court stated (at 67):

> It is established that [self-defence] is not restricted to the person attacked. It has been said to extend to "the principal civil and natural relations". Hale's *Pleas of the Crown*, Vol 1, p 484, gives as instances master and servant, parent and child and husband and wife who, if they even kill an assailant in the necessary defence of each other, are excused, the act of the relative assisting being considered the same as the act of the party himself [or herself].
> But no reported cases goes outside the relations indicated.

In *Duffy*, the English Court of Criminal Appeal quashed the accused's conviction on the basis that it should have been left for the jury to decide whether the accused was intervening with the sole object of restoring the peace by rescuing the person being attacked. The Court (at 67) side-stepped the "technical limitations of self-defence" by stating that "there is a general liberty even as between strangers to prevent a felony": see also *Saler v Klingbeil* [1945] SASR 171 at 173. Thus, in *R v Williams (Gladstone)* (1984) 78 Cr App R 276[3] self-defence was available where the accused intervened in

---

3 Approved by the Privy Council in *R v Beckford* [1987] 3 WLR 611.

defence of a youth who was being assaulted. The accused was unaware that the assault was part of an alleged arrest for stealing by a private citizen. It was pointed out in *Duffy* (at 67-68) that there are limits placed on intervening to defend another:

> That is not to say of course, that a newcomer may lawfully join in a fight just for the sake of fighting. Such conduct is wholly different in law from that of a person who in circumstances of necessity intervenes with the sole object of restoring the peace by rescuing a person being attacked.

Where the attack is directed at another person, the accused may defend that person in the same way as he or she would defend him or herself.[4]

Apart from the law of self-defence, a person may intervene on another's behalf to prevent a breach of the peace.[5]

In Queensland and Western Australia, there are separate provisions that allow the use of force to defend another where it would be lawful for that other person to use the same degree of force in self-defence.[6] These provisions also allow the use of force to protect another who is a victim of an unprovoked assault because the Codes provide that it is lawful for such a person to use force in self-defence.[7] The self-defence provisions in the Northern Territory, South Australia and Tasmania all specifically allow the use of force in defence of another.[8]

2.2 SELF-DEFENCE AND THE PROTECTION OF PROPERTY

The principles of self-defence also apply to situations where there is no attack as such, but the accused acts in defence of property.[9] Most cases of this nature may also fall within the principles relating to arrest or crime prevention: see D O'Connor and PA Fairall, *Criminal Defences* (3rd ed, Sydney: Butt, 1996), p 181.

In *R v McKay* [1957] VR 560 a poultry farmer shot and killed a man whom he believed to have been stealing fowls from his farm. The defence of property in this case was held to be an insufficient rationale for the use of lethal force. Indeed, it would seem that the use of lethal force to protect property cannot be justified under the test of self-defence set out in *Zecevic v DPP (Vic)* (1987) 162 CLR 645. The question is whether or not the accused honestly believed, on reasonable grounds that it was necessary to do what was done in defence of property. Wilson, Dawson and Toohey JJ in *Zecevic* were of the opinion that lethal force could be justified only where a threat or attack caused a reasonable apprehension of death or serious harm. It is difficult to imagine how an attack on property in the absence of an attack on a person could satisfy the *Zecevic* test and therefore the use of self-defence in this regard may be very limited.

---

4   *R v Chisam* (1963) 47 Cr App R 130; *R v Fennell* [1971] 1 QB 428.
5   *R v Duffy* [1966] 2 WLR 229; *Lavin v Albert* [1982] AC 546. These powers are further explored in Chapter 14, pp 763ff.
6   *Criminal Code* (Qld), s 273; *Criminal Code* (WA), s 250.
7   *Criminal Code* (Qld), s 271; *Criminal Code* (WA), s 248.
8   *Criminal Code* (NT), ss 27(g), 28(f); *Criminal Law Consolidation Act* 1935 (SA), s 15; *Criminal Code* (Tas), s 46.
9   See, for example, *R v McKay* [1957] VR 560; *Conlon* (1993) 69 A Crim R 92 (SC NSW).

The statutory versions of self-defence in the Northern Territory, Queensland, Tasmania and Western Australia refer to the use of force to defend possession of property.[10] In these jurisdictions, the use of force to defend property reflects the common law in that the use must be reasonable and necessary. The Code jurisdictions have separate rules for the use of force in relation to the defence of real property and moveable property and defence of property with and without a claim of right. There are also distinctions made between the degrees of defensive force which may be used.

Section 15A(1)(b)(i) of the *Criminal Law Consolidation Act* 1935 (SA) refers to conduct to protect property from "unlawful appropriation, destruction, damage or interference". In such a circumstance, the accused must have believed that the conduct was necessary and reasonable and the conduct must be reasonably proportionate to the threat as perceived by the accused.

Following a series of highly publicised cases which raised doubt about the scope of force that householders may use to defend themselves against "home invasion", the New South Wales legislature enacted the *Home Invasion (Occupants Protection) Act* 1998 (NSW) to clarify the scope of the defence in these cases. The Act, reflecting the common law in *Zecevic*, authorises occupiers to act in defence of the property of, or within, a dwelling house (s 8) and whether the use of force is based on reasonable grounds is determined by reference to the occupier's beliefs (s 9). These reforms are further discussed in Chapter 13 at p 729. For empirical research on home invasion, see P Salmelainen, "'Home Invasions' and Robberies" (1996) *Crime and Justice Bulletin*, No 31, New South Wales Bureau of Crime Statistics and Research.

2.3 NATURE OF THE ATTACK

IMMINENCE

Self-defence may be raised not only where there was a physical attack upon the accused, but also where the accused perceived that there was a danger that an attack would occur. In *R v McKay* [1957] VR 560 Lowe J stated (at 562-563):

> Reasonable self-defence is not limited to cases in which the life of the person committing homicide is endangered or grave injury to his [or her] person is threatened. It is also available where there is a reasonable apprehension of such danger or grave injury. There is such a reasonable apprehension if the person believes on reasonable grounds that such danger exists.

The South Australian and Tasmanian provisions do not have any requirement that the attack should have actually commenced[11] and while the Queensland and Western Australian provisions refer to defence as an "assault", that term refers to threats of violence as well as its infliction.[12] Under s 28(f) of the *Criminal Code* (NT) there is a reference to an assault in relation to the use of force likely to kill or cause grievous bodily harm but not in relation to the law relating to a lesser degree of force: s 27(g). In that jurisdiction, "assault" also encompasses the threat of violence: s 187(b).

---

10   *Criminal Code* (NT), s 27(h)-(n); *Criminal Code* (Qld), ss 267, 274-278; *Criminal Code* (Tas), ss 40-44; *Criminal Code* (WA), ss 244, 251-255.

11   *Criminal Law Consolidation Act* 1935 (SA), s 15; *Criminal Code* (Tas), s 46.

12   *Criminal Code* (Qld), ss 271, 272, 245; *Criminal Code* (WA), ss 248, 249, 222.

There is therefore no need for the attack to have actually begun,[13] but if an attack is imminent, the accused may make a pre-emptive strike.[14]

There is no separate requirement that the attack be imminent. Pre-emptive strikes have been held to satisfy the criteria for self-defence on the basis of the accused's belief on reasonable grounds that it was necessary to so act.[15]

There is no clear definition in the case law of the kinds of physical injury suffered or threatened that will form the basis for the defence of self-defence. It appears that self-defence may be raised where the threats fall short of an apprehension of death or grievous bodily harm.[16] However, if the accused has killed by way of self-defence, then the attack must have involved a serious assault including threats of death or[17] serious bodily harm,[18] rape or sexual assault[19] and continuous acute pain.[20]

UNLAWFULNESS

At common law, there is no legal requirement that the attack be an unlawful one.[21] According to Wilson, Dawson and Toohey JJ in *Zecevic v DPP (Vic)* (1987) 162 CLR 645 (at 653):

> Whilst in most cases in which self-defence is raised the attack said to give rise to the need
> for the accused to defend himself [or herself] will have been unlawful, as a matter of law
> there is no requirement that it should have been so.

There is also no requirement in the Northern Territory, South Australia and Tasmania that the attack be unlawful.[22] In Queensland and Western Australia, however, the self-defence provisions refer to an "unlawful" assault.[23] Section 15(4) of the *Criminal Law Consolidation Act* 1935 (SA) states that in the situation where an accused resists another who is purporting to exercise a power of arrest or who is acting in response to an unlawful act committed by the accused, self-defence will only be available if the accused believes on reasonable grounds that the other person is acting unlawfully.

The Model Criminal Code Officers Committee (MCCOC), has followed the Queensland and Western Australian approach and suggested that self-defence not be available if the attack is a lawful one. Section 10.4(4) of the *Criminal Code Act* 1995 (Cth) states that self-defence does not apply if the accused is responding to lawful conduct and he or she knew that the conduct was lawful.

---

13 *Viro v The Queen* (1978) 141 CLR 88 at 146 per Mason J; *R v Lane* [1983] 2 VR 449 at 456 per Murphy J; *Morgan v Colman* (1981) 27 SASR 334 at 337 per Wells J.

14 *Beckford v The Queen* [1987] 3 WLR 611 at 619; *R v Conlon* (1993) 69 A Crim R 92.

15 *R v Secretary* (1996) 107 NTR 1; *R v Hickey* (unrep, 14/4/1992, SC NSW); *R v Kontinnen* (unrep, 30/3/1992, SC SA); *R v Zhou* (unrep, 4/10/1993, HC NZ).

16 *R v Johnson* [1964] Qd R 1 at 12 per Stanley J; *Walden* (1986) 19 A Crim R 444 at 447 per Street CJ.

17 *Viro v The Queen* (1978) 141 CLR 88 at 146 per Mason J.

18 *Viro v The Queen* (1978) 141 CLR 88 at 146 per Mason J.

19 *R v Howe* (1958) 100 CLR 448 at 460 per Dixon CJ; *Zecevic v DPP (Vic)* (1987) 162 CLR 645 per Deane J; *R v Lane* [1983] 2 VR 449; *Walden* (1986) 19 A Crim R 444 at 446.

20 *R v Lane* [1983] 2 VR 449 at 451; *Zikovic* (1985) 17 A Crim R 396 at 401; *Walden* (1986) 19 A Crim R 444 at 447.

21 *Zecevic v DPP (Vic)* (1987) 162 CLR 645; *Thomas v The Queen* (1992) 65 A Crim R 269 (CCA NSW); *Walsh* (1992) 60 A Crim R 419.

22 *Criminal Code* (NT), ss 27(g), 28(f); *Criminal Law Consolidation Act* 1935 (SA), s 15; *Criminal Code* (Tas), s 46.

23 *Criminal Code* (Qld), s 271; *Criminal Code* (WA), s 248.

Examples of lawful attacks suggested by the courts include an attack by a mentally impaired assailant or by an assailant who reasonably but mistakenly believes that the accused was about to attack him or her: see for example *R v Lawson* [1986] VR 515 at 527-528 per McGarvie J.

It will probably only be in rare situations that a lawful attack would provide reasonable grounds for self-defence. In *Fry v The Queen* (1992) 58 SASR 424 the accused raised self-defence at his trial for stabbing a police officer who was in the course of effecting a lawful arrest. The Court of Criminal Appeal of South Australia dismissed an appeal against a conviction for murder. White ACJ stated (at 443) that some passages in *Zecevic* indicated that "lawful arrest, even accompanied by some violence, is one of those situations where self-defence could hardly be said to arise — except perhaps in extreme cases of violence".

PROVOKED ATTACKS

In Queensland and Western Australia, a distinction is drawn between provoked and unprovoked attacks. If the attack is unprovoked, an accused may use such force as is reasonably necessary to make effectual defence against the assault and this can include lethal force where the attack is such as to cause reasonable apprehension of death or grievous bodily harm. In relation to the situation where the accused has originally provoked the attack, he or she can use such force as is reasonably necessary to preserve him or herself from death or grievous bodily harm where the violence caused a reasonable apprehension of such injury and the accused believed on reasonable grounds that it was necessary to so act: *Criminal Code* (Qld), ss 271, 272; *Criminal Code* (WA), ss 248, 249.

This rule as to provoked attacks does not apply where the accused began the assault with an intent to kill or to do grievous bodily harm to some person, nor where he or she endeavoured to kill or to do bodily harm before the necessity for self-defence arose.

To decide whether an attack is provoked or not, reference has to be made to the doctrine of provocation: *R v Muratovic* [1967] Qd R 15 at 28. See Ch 5, pp 256ff. Unless the behaviour of the accused would be sufficient to enable the victim to rely on provocation if the latter were charged with an offence, then the assault is unprovoked.

At common law, self-defence may only be relied on in such a situation if the accused's original aggression had ceased at the time of the victim's counter attack.[24] Wilson, Dawson and Toohey J in *Zecevic v DPP (Vic)* (1987) 162 CLR 645 explained this as follows (at 663):

> Where an accused person raising a plea of self-defence was the original aggressor and induced or provoked the assault against which he [or she] claims the right to defend himself [or herself], it will be for the jury to consider whether the original aggression had ceased so as to have enabled the accused to form a belief upon reasonable grounds, that his [or her] actions were necessary in self-defence. For this purpose, it will be relevant to consider the extent to which the accused declined further conflict and quit the use of force or retreated from it, these being matters which may bear upon the nature of the occasion and the use which the accused made of it.

---

24   *Zecevic v DPP (Vic)* (1987) 162 CLR 645; *R v Lawson* [1986] VR 515 at 533 per McGarvie J.

It seems, however, that in practice a person who initiates an attack upon him or herself may have difficulty in raising self-defence. This was recognised by Wilson, Dawson and Toohey JJ in the following passage (at 663):

> [W]here an accused person has created the situation in which force might lawfully be applied to apprehend him [or her] or cause him [or her] to desist — where, for example, he [or she] is engaged in criminal behaviour of a violent kind — then the only reasonable view of his [or her] resistance to that force will be that he [or she] is acting, not in self-defence, but as an aggressor in pursuit of his [or her] original design. A person may not create a continuing situation of emergency and provoke a lawful attack upon himself [or herself] and yet claim upon reasonable grounds the right to defend himself [or herself] against that attack.

2.4 THE ACCUSED'S BELIEF

At common law, the accused must have honestly believed on reasonable grounds that he or she was being threatened or attacked[25] and that the force applied by him or her was necessary in self-defence.[26] Similarly, in relation to the use of lethal force in Queensland, the Northern Territory and Western Australia, the accused must believe on reasonable grounds that he or she cannot otherwise preserve him or herself or another from death or grievous bodily harm.[27]

This entails an analysis of first, what the accused believed, and secondly, whether or not this belief was based on reasonable grounds. It is important to note that the requirement that the accused's belief be made on reasonable grounds does not mean a consideration of what a reasonable or ordinary person would have believed, but rather, what the accused him or herself might reasonably have believed in all the circumstances.[28]

Accordingly, in determining the reasonableness of the accused's belief, the jury may take into account all the facts within the accused's knowledge,[29] the prior conduct of the victim,[30] the relationships between the parties involved[31] and any excitement, affront or distress experienced by the accused.[32] Expert evidence may be admissible to assist jurors in relation to matters outside the realm of common knowledge such as reactions after a prolonged period of physical abuse.[33]

---

25 *Zecevic v DPP (Vic)*(1987) 162 CLR 645 at 651-652 per Mason CJ, at 656-659 per Wilson, Dawson and Toohey JJ, at 672-674 per Deane J, at 683 per Gaudron J; *Viro v The Queen* (1978) 141 CLR 88 at 146 per Mason J.

26 *Zecevic v DPP (Vic)* (1987) 162 CLR 645, at 654 per Mason CJ, 661 per Wilson, Dawson and Toohey JJ, at 666 per Brennan J, at 681 per Deane J, at 683 per Gaudron J; *Dziduch* (1990) 47 A Crim R 378.

27 *Criminal Code* (NT), s 28; *Criminal Code* (Qld), s 271(2) (reasonable apprehension); *Criminal Code* (WA), s 248.

28 *Viro v The Queen* (1978) 141 CLR 88 at 146 per Mason J; *Helmhout v The Queen* (1980) 49 FLR 1; *Conlon* (1993) 69 A Crim R 92 (SC NSW).

29 *R v Wills* [1983] 2 VR 201 at 210 per Lush J.

30 *R v Keith* [1934] St R Qd 155 at 177 per Webb J (CCA Qld); adopted in *R v Muratovic* [1967] Qd R 15 at 30 per Hart J (CCA Qld).

31 *R v Hector* [1953] VLR 543.

32 *R v Wills* [1983] 2 VR 201 at 211 per Lush J; *Dziduch* (1990) 47 A Crim R 378 at 380 per Hunt J (CCA NSW); *R v Johnson* [1964] Qd R 1 at 13-14 per Stanley J (CCA Qld).

33 *R v Runjanjic* (1991) 56 SASR 114; *R v C* (1993) 60 SASR 467.

Section 46 of the *Criminal Code* (Tas) states that a "person is justified in using, in defence of himself or another person, such force as, in the circumstances as he [or she] believes them to be, it is reasonable to use". Similarly, the South Australian provision allows an accused to use force if that person believes that the force is necessary and reasonable for self-defence.[34] Here the focus is on the accused's belief about necessity and reasonableness, rather than on whether or not the accused's belief was honest *and* based on reasonable grounds. It is a fine point, but these provisions are slightly more subjective in their approach than the other jurisdictions. The objective factor goes to the necessity and the reasonableness of the force used rather than to the accused's belief.

2.5 REACTION TO THE ATTACK

At common law, the force used in relation to a threat or an attack must be reasonably necessary.[35] Whilst the High Court in *Zecevic's* case did not specify whether or not the requirement for necessity means a minimum necessary response or a reasonably necessary response, a reference to the Privy Council case of *Palmer v The Queen* [1971] AC 814[36] indicates that necessity is used in the latter sense. In *Palmer* (at 831-832) Lord Morris described the element of necessity as follows:

> It is both good law and good sense that [the accused] may do, but may only do, what is reasonably necessary ... If there has been an attack so that defence is reasonably necessary it will be recognised that a person defending himself [or herself] cannot weigh to a nicety the exact measure of his [or her] necessary defensive action.

Sections 27, 28, 29(4) of the *Criminal Code* (NT) withhold justification where "unnecessary force" is used. In Queensland and Western Australia, the provisions refer to force that is reasonably necessary[37] or necessary.[38] In *R v Marwey* (1977) 138 CLR 630 Barwick CJ stated (at 637) in relation to the use of fatal force in self-defence under the *Criminal Code* (Qld):

> [W]hat the second paragraph of s 271 calls for is the actual belief by the accused on reasonable grounds of the necessity of the fatal act for his [or her] own preservation. That paragraph, it seems to me, when the occasion is appropriate makes the belief of the accused the definitive circumstances. As this belief must be based on reasonable grounds, there is no point in repeating the word "reasonably" before the word "necessary". That word — necessary — in the context of s 271 bears the sense ascribed to it by the *Shorter Oxford Dictionary* of "requisite" or "needful".

---

34 *Criminal Law Consolidation Act* 1935 (SA), s 15(1) as amended by the *Criminal Law Consolidation (Self-Defence) Amendment Act* 1997.

35 *Zecevic v DPP (Vic)* (1987) 162 CLR 645 at 654 per Mason CJ, at 661 per Wilson, Dawson and Toohey JJ, at 666 per Brennan J, at 681 per Deane J, at 683 per Gaudron J.

36 This passage was discussed in *Zecevic v DPP (Vic)* (1987) 162 CLR 645 at 661 and 665 per Wilson, Dawson and Toohey JJ, at 654 per Mason CJ.

37 *Criminal Code* (Qld), s 271 (1st para); *Criminal Code* (WA), s 248 (1st para).

38 *Criminal Code* (Qld), s 271 (2nd para); *Criminal Code* (WA), s 248 (2nd para).

Section 15(1)(a) of the *Criminal Code Consolidation Act* 1935 (SA) also refers to necessary conduct. However, there is no mention of the term in s 46 of the *Criminal Code* (Tas). This only refers to the accused's belief that the force is reasonable to use. In relation to the Tasmanian provision before amendment in 1987, the Tasmanian Court of Appeal in *Patterson* (1982) 6 A Crim R 331 (at 341-342) was of the view that self-defence could be made out even if the force used was more than was necessary for the purpose of self-defence.

There is no separate legal requirement in the Australian jurisdictions that the accused must retreat before attempting to defend him or herself.[39] Whether or not the accused retreated is simply a factor that may be considered in assessing whether or not the accused's conduct was reasonably necessary.[40] That is, if an accused had the opportunity to retreat, the jury may find that the accused's belief in the necessity to use the force he or she used was not based on reasonable grounds. However, Stanley J in *R v Johnson* [1964] Qd R 1 posed the following warning on this point (at 13):

> [A] jury should be warned against being wise after the event and that they must consider the
> matter from the point of view operative on the accused's mind in the stress of the moment.
> By turning away from an aggressor one might obviously lead to one's own destruction.

There is also a rider in Queensland and Western Australia in relation to provoked assaults where the accused causes death or grievous bodily harm; self-defence is only available where the accused retreated as far as practicable before the necessity to use force arose: *Criminal Code* (Qld), s 272; *Criminal Code* (WA), s 249.

There is no separate legal requirement in all jurisdictions apart from South Australia that the force used be proportionate to the attack: *Zecevic v DPP (Vic)* (1987) 162 CLR 645 at 662. Proportionality will simply be a factor to take into account in assessing the accused's belief that it was necessary to do what he or she did. In England, proportionality remains a separate element of self-defence (*Oatridge* (1992) 94 Cr App R 367) and this requirement has been recently introduced in South Australia. Under s 15(1)(b) of the *Criminal Law Consolidation Act* 1935 (SA), the accused's conduct must be, in the circumstances the accused genuinely believed them to be, reasonably proportionate to the threat the accused genuinely believed to exist. If the conduct was not reasonably proportionate, the accused may still be afforded a partial defence to a charge of murder that reduces the offence to manslaughter under s 15(2). This issue is taken up in the next section.

2.6 EXCESSIVE SELF-DEFENCE

Excessive self-defence has had an interesting history in Australian common law. For a time, it was a partial defence akin to provocation in that it reduced murder to manslaughter. Excessive self-defence was introduced into Australian law by the High Court in *R v Howe* (1958) 100 CLR 448 which adopted the reasoning of the Victorian Supreme Court a year before in *R v McKay* [1957] VR 560. It was then abolished by the Privy Council in *Palmer v The Queen* [1971] AC 814.

---

39 *Zecevic v DPP (Vic)* (1987) 162 CLR 645 at 663 per Wilson, Dawson and Toohey JJ; *Viro v The Queen* (1978) 141 CLR 88 at 115-116 per Gibbs J; *R v Howe* (1958) 100 CLR 448 at 462-464 per Dixon CJ.

40 *Zecevic v DPP (Vic)* (1987) 162 CLR 645 at 663 per Wilson, Dawson and Toohey JJ; *Viro v The Queen* (1978) 141 CLR 88 at 115-116 per Gibbs J; *R v Howe* (1958) 100 CLR 448 at 462-464 per Dixon CJ.

The issue came before the High Court again in 1978 when the Court decided that there was a requirement that the jury consider whether the force used by the accused was proportionate to the danger that he or she faced: *Viro v The Queen* (1978) 141 CLR 88 at 147. If the force used was disproportionate or excessive, the proper verdict should be manslaughter rather than murder. However, this doctrine was subsequently rejected by a five to two majority of the High Court in *Zecevic v DPP (Vic)* (1987) 162 CLR 645. Wilson, Dawson and Toohey JJ stated (at 654):

> [T]he use of excessive force in the belief that it was necessary in self-defence will not automatically result in a verdict of manslaughter. If the jury concludes that there were no reasonable grounds for a belief that the degree of force used was necessary, the defence of self-defence will fail and the circumstances will fall to be considered by the jury without reference to that plea. There is some force in the view, adopted by Stephen, Mason and Aickin JJ in *Viro,* that this may result in a conviction for murder of a person lacking the moral culpability associated with that crime. Experience would suggest, however, that such a result is unlikely in practice.

As stated above, proportionality may now only be taken into account as a relevant circumstance of the case rather than as a separate rule of law or determinative element. Wilson, Dawson and Toohey JJ stated in this regard (at 653):

> [I]t will in many cases be appropriate for a jury to be told that, in determining whether the accused believed that his [or her] actions were necessary in order to defend himself [or herself] and whether he [or she] held that belief on reasonable grounds, it should consider whether the force used by the accused was proportionate to the threat offered.

Accordingly, in *R v Lean; R v Aland* (1993) 66 A Crim R 296 the New South Wales Court of Criminal Appeal held that the trial judge had erred in directing the jury to consider the question of proportionality as a separate requirement. It confirmed (at 298 per Hunt CJ) that there is "no rule of law that the use of excessive force necessarily establishes that the accused did not act in self-defence".

Under the *Criminal Codes*, excessive force is unlawful and the accused's belief as to the appropriateness of the degree of force used is irrelevant. The partial defence of excessive force was never part of the law in Queensland and Western Australia.[41] Under s 283 of the *Criminal Code* (Qld) and s 260 of the *Criminal Code* (WA), the use of more force than is justified by law under the circumstances is unlawful. Section 52 of the *Criminal Code* (Tas) provides that a person authorised by law to use force is criminally responsible for any excess, according to the nature and quality of the act that constitutes such excess: *Masnec v The Queen* [1962] Tas SR 354. In the Northern Territory, if the force used is unnecessary, but was reasonably believed to be necessary, the killing is excused under s 32 of the *Criminal Code* (NT) which deals with a reasonable mistake of fact. If the force is unnecessary and the accused did not reasonably believe it to be necessary, self-defence does not apply and there is no "half-way house" available.

---

41   *R v Johnson* [1964] Qd R 1 at 7 per Philp J, at 11 per Stanley J; *Aleksovski v The Queen* [1979] WAR 1; *McCullough* (1982) 6 A Crim R 274.

Only South Australia has re-introduced excessive self-defence. In that jurisdiction, self-defence is only made out where the force used was reasonably proportionate to the threat that the accused genuinely believed: *Criminal Law Consolidation Act* 1935 (SA), s 15(1)(b). However, a partial defence of excessive force manslaughter has been statutorily introduced for those situations where the force used is not proportionate to the threat.[42]

The abolition of the doctrine of excessive self-defence has been criticised by various authors.[43] The main argument in support of excessive self-defence is based on a moral distinction between intentional killing and a killing based on an error of judgment. Mason J stated in *Viro v The Queen* (1978) 141 CLR 88 at 139:

> The underlying rationale ... is to be found in a conviction that the moral culpability of a person who kills another in defending himself [or herself] but who fails in a plea of self-defence only because the force which he [or she] believed to be necessary exceeded that which was reasonably necessary falls short of the moral culpability ordinarily associated with murder. The notion that a person commits murder in the circumstances should be rejected on the ground that the result is unjust. It is more consistent with the distinction which the criminal law makes between murder and manslaughter that an error of judgment on the part of the accused which alone deprives him [or her] of the absolute shield of self-defence results in the offence of manslaughter.

The Model Criminal Code Officers Committee (MCCOC), however, has recommended that excessive self-defence should not be re-introduced: *Chapter 5 — Fatal Offences Against the Person*, Discussion Paper (1998), p 113. This is the context of its recommendation that provocation be abolished (see Chapter 5, p 285), but the Committee was also concerned that excessive self-defence is "inherently vague" and that a sufficient test has not been promulgated by the courts.

The MCCOC states that if excessive self-defence is re-introduced it should be a subjective test along the lines suggested by Deane J in *Zecevic*. This test found favour with Brent Fisse in *Howard's Criminal Law* (5th ed, Sydney: Law Book Company Ltd, 1990), p 103. The MCCOC in particular mentioned the test set out by Menzies J in *R v Howe* (1958) 100 CLR 448 (at 477) which is that it is manslaughter if the accused "used greater force than was reasonably necessary for his [or her] self-protection and in doing so killed his [or her] assailant": *Chapter 5 — Fatal Offences Against the Person*, Discussion Paper (1998), p 111.

The South Australian provision changed from a purely subjective test of excessive self-defence to that of a partly objective one in 1997.[44] It will be interesting to see how often the South Australian provision is raised and whether or not it provides sufficient guidance to juries.

---

42 *Criminal Law Consolidation Act* 1935 (SA), s 15 (as amended by the *Criminal Law Consolidation (Self-defence) Act* 1997 (SA)).

43 For example B Fisse, *Howard's Criminal Law* (5th ed, Sydney: Law Book Company Ltd, 1990), pp 102ff; L Waller and CR Williams, *Brett, Waller and Williams: Criminal Law* (8th ed, Sydney: Butt, 1997), p 181.

44 *Criminal Law Consolidation (Self-Defence) Amendment Act* 1997 (SA) amending *Criminal Law Consolidation Act* 1935 (SA), s 15.

2.7 BURDEN OF PROOF

As with other defences such as duress, necessity and provocation, the accused bears the evidential burden in relation to self-defence. The prosecution bears the legal burden in negating beyond reasonable doubt the accused's assertion that he or she acted in self-defence.[45] In *Dziduch v The Queen* (1990) 47 A Crim R 378 Hunt J described (at 379) what is required as follows:

> The fundamental question which a jury has to establish in relation to the issue of self-defence is whether the Crown has established that the accused did not believe on reasonable grounds that it was necessary in self-defence to do what he [or she] did. The Crown may establish either that the accused had no such belief or that there was no reasonable grounds for such a belief. If the Crown fails to establish one or the other of those two alternatives, the accused is entitled to be acquitted of the charge.

PHILOSOPHICAL PERSPECTIVES

An Objective or a Subjective Test?

In its report on homicide, the Law Reform Commission of Victoria recommended that self-defence be made a fully subjective defence: *Homicide*, Report No 40 (1990), p 96. The Commission stated that this was "consistent with the emphasis on moral culpability and on the subjective mental state of the defendant": p 96.

In *Zecevic v DPP (Vic)* (1987) 162 CLR 645 the High Court unanimously rejected the argument that the test for self-defence be purely subjective. Deane J (at 673) was of the opinion that there was "simply no warrant for such a wholesale reversal" of what he termed "settled law" relating to self-defence. Wilson, Dawson and Toohey JJ (at 658) referred to the traditional rationale for the defence to support a partly objective test. They perceive self-defence as fitting within the concept of excusable killing that was not concerned "with the execution of justice but with the necessary and reasonable response to the preservation of life and limb". Accordingly, they stated (at 658):

> the history of the matter serves to explain why the requirement of reasonableness, which was a requirement of excusable homicide, has remained part of the law of self-defence. Moreover, it establishes why that requirement ought not to be regarded as a definitional element of the offence in question but as going rather to exculpation.

A purely subjective test does appear problematic. From a theoretical perspective, a subjective test fails to distinguish between the elements of an offence and the elements of a defence. Generally, if an offence requires a particular mental state as part of its definition, then a subjective test can be applied. However, a mental state forming part of a defence requires an objective test. This distinction is based on societal values. That is, before a society decides to exercise compassion by exculpating an accused from criminal liability, it is entitled to demand

---

45   As to the meaning of evidential and legal burden see Chapter 2 at pp 118ff.

that the accused lacked any blameworthiness in relation to the plea relied on. As Stanley Yeo in *Compulsion in the Criminal Law* (Sydney: Law Book Company Ltd, 1990) has pointed out (p 200), "[a]n unreasonable or negligently held belief would constitute blameworthiness denying the accused the excuse".

On a practical level, without some form of objective limitation such as reasonableness, it would seem that an accused who is, say, excessively fearful or apprehensive would be able to react violently towards others with perfect impunity.

The MCCOC has suggested a "simplified" test which, like the approach in *Zecevic* contains subjective and objective elements. Section 10.4(2) of the *Criminal Code Act* 1995 (Cth) states:

> A person carries out conduct in self-defence if and only if he or she believes the conduct is necessary:
>
> — to defend himself or herself or another person; or
>
> — to prevent or terminate the unlawful imprisonment of himself or herself or another person; or
>
> — to protect property from unlawful appropriation, destruction, damage or interference; or
>
> — to prevent criminal trespass to any land or premises; or
>
> — to remove from any land or premises a person who is committing criminal trespass;
>
> and the conduct is a reasonable response in circumstances as he or she perceives them to be.

As with s 46 of the *Criminal Code* (Tas), the test focuses on the belief of the accused, but there is an objective component in relation to whether the conduct was a reasonable response. This appears to be an adequate test for self-defence. Its emphasis on the subjective belief of the accused allows for sufficient account to be taken of an accused's personal characteristics such as sex, ethnicity, age and religion. The objective element provides for limitations on behaviour deemed appropriate by society as represented by members of the jury.

2.8 BATTERED WOMEN AND SELF-DEFENCE

The removal of the traditional legal requirements of proportionality[46] and the duty to retreat has made it somewhat easier for battered women who kill their abusive partners to avail themselves of the defence of self-defence. However there are still some problems with the use of the defence in this regard.

As mentioned earlier, the defence is based on "the paradigmatic case of a one-time bar-room brawl between two men of equal strength and size": *R v Lavallee* [1990] 1 SCR 852 at 876 per Wilson J. It does not easily "fit" the scenario of violence between intimates within the family. Nor does it recognise that women may experience and react to fear differently from men.

---

46 Except in South Australia, where the conduct must be reasonably proportionate to the threat that the accused genuinely believed to exist: *Criminal Law Consolidation Act* 1935 (SA), s 15.

In general, the law still qualifies a woman's belief in the necessity of her actions with the requirement of reasonableness. The test is not whether a reasonable woman with all the characteristics of the accused would have acted in self-defence, but rather, whether the accused's belief was based on reasonable grounds.

This requirement of reasonableness has been criticised by many feminist legal scholars. Although clothed in the language of rationality and objectivity, the underlying standard is a male one: E Sheehey, J Stubbs and J Tolmie, "Defending Battered Women on Trial: The Battered Woman Syndrome and its Limitations" (1992) 16 Crim LJ 369 at 372, 374. The challenge has been to demonstrate that the male response to aggression is not necessarily the only reasonable response. The task therefore is to demonstrate to the jury that the fear and reactions of a battered woman may indeed be reasonable in the circumstances.

One avenue in which this has been achieved with some success is through the admission of battered woman syndrome evidence. Wilson J in the Canadian case of *R v Lavallee* [1990] 1 SCR 852 (at 871-872) explained why expert evidence may be needed to explain the situation faced by a battered woman:

> The average member of the public (or of the jury) can be forgiven for asking: Why would a woman put up with this kind of treatment? Why should she continue to live with such a man? How could she love a partner who beats her to the point of requiring hospitalization? We would expect the woman to pack her bags and go. Where is her self-respect? Why does she not cut loose and make a new life for herself? Such is the reaction of the average person confronted with the so-called "battered wife syndrome". We need help to understand it and help is available from trained professionals.

The role of this expert evidence is therefore to answer some of these common questions and help support the claim that the accused believed *on reasonable grounds* that it was necessary to do what she did.

"Battered woman syndrome" can be traced back to a book published in 1979 by psychologist, Dr Lenore Walker: *The Battered Woman* (New York: Harper & Row, 1979). In 1984, she published a follow-up book detailing a study she had done with 400 battered women. She stated that a "cycle of violence" was characterised by three stages: tension building, the acute battering incident and loving contrition. She defined a "battered woman" as one who had gone through the cycle at least twice: *The Battered Woman Syndrome* (New York: Springer Pub Co, 1984). Walker emphasised that a battered woman finds it difficult to break out of this cycle because of "learned helplessness". This theory was based on experiments concerning the effect of electric shocks on two groups of dogs.[47]

In Australia, the first case to recognise the role of this type of evidence in a case of self-defence to murder was *R v Kontinnen* (1992) 16 Crim LJ 360. The accused shot and killed her de facto husband while he slept. The victim lived with the accused and another woman and her child. The accused claimed that the victim had abused her over many years, and that on the night of the shooting, threatened to kill her, the other woman and the child. The accused had been hospitalised 10 times in two years as a result of the beatings she suffered at the hands of the accused.

---

47 M Seligman and S Maier, "Failure to Escape Shock" (1967) 74 *Journal of Experimental Psychology* 1-9; M Seligman, *Helplessness: On Depression, Development and Death* (San Francisco: Freeman, 1975). See also LE Walker, *The Battered Woman Syndrome* (2nd ed, New York: Springer Pub Co, 1999).

At her trial, the defence raised both self-defence and provocation. Evidence of battered woman syndrome was led to allay the possible doubt of jurors that the accused's shooting the victim while he was asleep was necessary by way of self-defence. The evidence was admitted without objection by the Crown or the trial judge. The latter treated this evidence as relevant to two issues: first, it was relevant to whether or not the accused believed that it was necessary to shoot the victim and secondly, it was relevant to the question as to whether the belief was based on reasonable grounds. The jury acquitted the accused.

The New South Wales Supreme Court considered similar evidence in *R v Hickey* (1992) 16 Crim LJ 271. This again concerned a de facto relationship which had been abusive for several years. Mervyn Priestley was violent not only toward the accused but also toward their children, usually when he was intoxicated. The accused had separated from Priestley and at the time of the killing, was living with family and friends in a close-knit Aboriginal community. She visited Priestley with the children at the home of a mutual friend, believing it to be a safe environment. After some time spent drinking and after the accused refused to allow the children to stay overnight, Priestley became violent. He threw the accused on the bed, headbutted her and tried to strangle her. When Priestley stopped the attack and sat up and turned his back on the accused, she grabbed a knife and fatally stabbed him. During the trial for murder, expert psychological evidence was admitted without objection either by the Crown or the trial judge to support self-defence. The jury acquitted Hickey.

In his commentary on the case, Yeo points out that it is conceivable that Hickey could have been acquitted without the use of expert psychological evidence because there had been escalating violence in the relationship and a violent assault which occurred immediately before the killing: *R v Hickey* (1992) 16 Crim LJ 272-273. Yeo also states that many women who remain in violent relationships do so not because they have battered woman syndrome. There are often other more mundane social factors at play in these relationships, such as financial dependence and lack of sympathy and help from family members, social services or the police. According to Yeo, battered woman's syndrome should not be unduly emphasised.

There are indeed many problems associated with the use of battered woman syndrome. The "syndrome" itself and Walker's research methodology have been the subject of much criticism.[48] Walker herself admitted in 1995 that there is a definitional vagueness in the syndrome: "Understanding Battered Woman's Syndrome" (1995) 31(2) *Trial* 30. One problem with it in relation to self-defence is that it may explain why the accused didn't leave the relationship, but it is difficult to link "learned helplessness" with finally breaking out and killing an abusive partner.

A further problem lies in medicalising women's behaviour by the use of a "syndrome". Ian Freckelton has pointed out that it is difficult to translate a field of endeavour that has therapy as its purpose into a forensic context: "When Plight Makes Right: The Forensic Abuse Syndrome" (1994) 18 Crim LJ 29. Freckelton explains that in the medical context, the term "syndrome" is used to denote a

---

48 See, for example, P McDonald, "Helping with the Termination of an Assaultive Relationship" in B Pressman, G Cameron and M Rothery (eds), *Intervening with Assaulted Women* (Hillsdale: Eribaum, 1989); R Gelles & M Straus, *Intimate Violence* (New York: Simon and Schuster, 1988); D Faigman, "The Battered Woman and Self Defence: A Legal and Empirical Dissent" (1986) 72 *Virginia Law Review* 619; R Schuller and N Vidmar, "Battered Woman Syndrome Evidence in the Courtroom" (1992) 16(3) *Law and Human Behavior* 273; A Coughlin, "Excusing Women" (1994) 82 *California Law Review* 1; M McMahon, "Battered Women and Bad Science: The Limited Validity and Utility of Battered Woman Syndrome" (1999) 6(1) *Psychiatry, Psychology and Law* 23.

collection of symptoms that occur together where the cause of the symptom is not known. There is therefore some confusion between the medical use of the term syndrome which means that the cause of the symptoms is not identifiable and the legal and evidential use of the term which assumes that a cause can be identified. The advantage for the defence of using the term "syndrome" is that it cloaks the social and psychological explanation of the accused's conduct in a veneer of medical respectability to make it more acceptable to the jury.

There are several dangers in this medicalisation of women's experiences and behaviour. First, women who do not exhibit these symptoms will find it difficult to convince a jury that their reactions were reasonable. Although the legal rules of self-defence have moved away from the bar-room brawl model, the use of battered women syndrome means that women must now conform to a medical model for their evidence to be credible. Secondly, in crude terms, syndrome evidence suggests that the woman is not bad, but mad. This may suggest that the more appropriate defences are those of mental impairment or diminished responsibility. Again this pathologises the experience of battered women and takes their situation out of a social context: E Sheehy, J Stubbs and J Tolmie "Defending Battered Women on Trial: The Battered Woman Syndrome and its Limitations" (1992) Crim LJ 369; P Easteal "Battered Women Syndrome: What is Reasonable?" (1992) 17 *Alternative Law Journal* 203. See also S Murphy, "Assisting the Jury in Understanding Victimisation: Expert Psychological Testimony on Battered Women Syndrome and Rape Trauma Syndrome" (1992) 25 *Columbia Journal of Law and Social Problems*: 277. A similar debate has occurred in relation to the value of "rape trauma syndrome", see S Bronitt, "The Rules of Recent Complaint: Rape Myths and the Legal Construction of the 'Reasonable' Rape Victim" in P Easteal (ed), *Balancing the Scales: Rape, Law Reform and Australian Culture* (Sydney: Federation Press, 1998), Ch 4.

The introduction of battered women syndrome has to some extent been a necessary development because it has served an important role in disabusing juries and judges of myths and stereotypes concerning battered women. Because of its dangers, however, it is perhaps more useful to turn the focus back on the law of self-defence and provocation. Ian Leader-Elliott writes that the *Zecevic* model of self-defence is more accommodating to defensive acts impelled by necessity than other models and therefore there is less of a need to "emulate North American attempts to extend the operation of the law of self-defence by pleading incapacity, helplessness and mental disorder": "Battered But Not Beaten: Women Who Kill in Self Defence" (1993) 15 *Sydney Law Review* 403 at 460. Gail Hubble, however, has warned that the expansion of the scope of self-defence may interfere with the traditional reluctance of the law to accept that the choices of individuals are determined by their personal histories. She argues that if there is too much of a focus on past experiences as an explanation for a woman's violence, this "determinism" could have repercussions for the way in which the conduct of male criminals is explained: "Feminism and the Battered Woman: The Limits of Self-Defence in the Context of Domestic Violence" (1997) 9(2) *Current Issues in Criminal Justice* 113. Julie Stubbs and Julia Tolmie argue against this view, that new constructions of self-defence which reflect women's experiences do not have to be based on determinism.[49]

---

49 J Stubbs and J Tolmie, "Feminisms, Self-Defence, and Battered Women: A Response to Hubble's 'Straw Feminist'", (1998) 10(1) *Current Issues in Criminal Justice* 75 at 81. See also R Bradfield, "Is Near Enough Good Enough? Why Isn't Self-Defence Appropriate for the Battered Woman?" (1998) 5(1) *Psychiatry, Psychology and Law* 71.

While the debate about the gendered nature of self-defence will doubtless continue, Elizabeth Sheehy, Julie Stubbs and Julia Tolmie in "Defending Battered Women on Trial: The Battered Woman Syndrome and its Limitations" (1992) 16 Crim LJ 369 at 394 are correct in stating that:

Essentially [there] is not so much a problem with the doctrinal shape of the law on self-defence as the way it is applied in individual cases. Such offenders [battered women who kill] have difficulties in getting the circumstances surrounding their killings realistically appraised by the agents of the criminal justice system.

3. DURESS

The defence of duress, or compulsion as it is sometimes termed, operates to excuse an accused from criminal responsibility where the accused has committed a certain offence under a threat of physical harm to him or herself or to some other person should he or she refuse to comply with the threatener's command.[50] Lord Simon described in *DPP (Northern Ireland) v Lynch* [1975] AC 653 at 686 the defence as denoting:

such (well-grounded) fear, produced by threats, of death or grievous bodily harm (or unjustified imprisonment) if a certain act is not done, as overbears the actor's wish not to perform the act, and is effective, at the time of the act, in constraining him [or her] to perform it.

There has been some confusion in the case law as to whether or not duress operates to negate the fault element[51] or voluntariness[52] or is in fact an independent exculpatory factor which provides an excuse for conduct which would otherwise be criminal but for the presence of duress. It appears that the third way of approaching duress, that is, viewing it as an independent excuse is gaining currency at common law. For example, Cox J stated in *R v Palazoff* (1986) 43 SASR 99 (at 105):

[I]n a case of duress, the *actus reus* is voluntary, or willed, and intended, but is, in a real and very relevant sense, undesired. The maxim is *coactus volui*, but the force is not compulsion, strictly so called, but persuasion created by a dilemma.

---

50 *R v Hurley* [1967] VR 526 at 543 per Smith J; *R v Lawrence* [1980] 1 NSWLR 122; *R v Pakazoff* (1986) 43 SASR 99; *R v Darrington and McGauley* [1980] VR 353; *R v Dawson* [1978] VR 536; *Emery* (1978) 18 A Crim R 49.

51 Evidence of duress has occasionally been used to negate a particular state of mind. For example, in *R v Steane* [1947] 1 KB 997, the accused had been charged under the Defence Regulations with broadcasting during the Second World War to the allies with intent to assist the enemy. He claimed that he had only done so out of fear that he or his family would be placed into a concentration camp. This evidence was used to negate the requirement that he intended to assist the enemy.

52 Sometimes duress is referred to as overpowering the will of an individual. For example, in *Attorney-General v Whelan* [1934] IR 518 at 526, Munaghan J stated that "where the excuse of duress is applicable it must ... be clearly shown that the overpowering of the will was operative at the time the crime was actually committed, and, if there were reasonable opportunity for the will to reassert itself, no justification can be found in antecedent threats". However, equating duress with a lack of will is misleading as the conduct is voluntary, the actor is making a choice between the greater of two evils.

The defence is recognised at common law in the Australian Capital Territory, New South Wales, South Australia and Victoria. The statutory provisions in the Code jurisdictions of the Northern Territory, Queensland, Tasmania and Western Australia reflect the common law with some variation.[53]

If duress is successful, the accused will be acquitted. Limitations are, however, applied to when duress can be raised. The following Table refers to those crimes where duress cannot be raised.

TABLE 1:
Crimes Where Duress is Unavailable as a Defence

ACT, NSW, SA and VIC	NT	QLD	TAS	WA
murder[54]	murder[55]	murder	murder	murder
attempted murder[56]	manslaughter	crimes of intent to cause grievous bodily harm	attempted murder	crimes having the element of grievous bodily harm
—	crimes having the element of grievous bodily harm	piracy and offences deemed to be piracy[57]	treason	crimes of intent to cause grievous bodily harm[58]
—	crimes having the element of the intention to cause grievous bodily harm[59]	—	piracy and offences deemed to be piracy	—
—	—	—	armed robbery, robbery with violence and robbery	—
—	—	—	arson	—
—	—	—	causing grievous bodily harm, rape and forcible abduction[60]	—

53 *Criminal Code* (NT), s 40; *Criminal Code* (Qld), s 31(4); *Criminal Code* (Tas), s 20(1); *Criminal Code* (WA), s 31(4).

54 *R v Brown* [1968] SASR 467; *R v Harding* [1976] VR 129; *R v McConnell* [1977] 1 NSWLR 714. See also *R v Howe* [1987] 1 AC 417; *Abbott v The Queen* [1977] AC 755.

55 Section 41 of the *Criminal Code* (NT) allows for murder to be reduced to manslaughter if there was coercion of such a nature as to have caused a reasonable person similarly circumstanced to have acted in the same or a similar way.

56 *R v Gotts* [1992] 2 AC 412.

57 *Criminal Code* (Qld), s 31(2).

58 *Criminal Code* (WA), s 31(4).

59 *Criminal Code* (NT), s 40(2).

60 *Criminal Code* (Tas), s 20(1).

This Table shows that at common law the defence of duress is not available for the offences of murder and attempted murder. Otherwise, the defence may be raised in relation to all offences including manslaughter (except in the Northern Territory)[61] and treason (except in Tasmania).[62]

The rationale for limiting the scope of the defence to crimes other than murder or attempted murder lies in the policy argument that human life must be preserved and the purpose of the criminal law is to set a standard of conduct with which ordinary people must comply. In *R v Howe* [1987] AC 417 (at 433) Lord Hailsham described the situation:

> where the choice is between the threat of death or a fortiori of serious injury and deliberately taking an innocent life. In such a case a reasonable [person] might reflect that one innocent human life is at least as valuable as his [or her] own or that of his [or her] loved one. In such a case a [person] cannot claim that he [or she] is choosing the lesser of two evils. Instead he [or she] is embracing the cognate but morally disreputable principle that the end justifies the means.

In *R v Gotts* [1992] 2 AC 412 the House of Lords suggested that the scope of the defence should be further limited because of a climate of violence and rising terrorism. This further limitation has been taken up in the Code jurisdictions, Tasmania being the state with the most exclusions.

In some jurisdictions, there is a further limitation in that duress is not available to accessories to the crimes listed in Table 1. In *DPP (Northern Ireland) v Lynch* [1975] AC 653 a majority of the House of Lords held that duress should be available to an accessory to murder because an accessory bears a lesser degree of guilt than the person who actually commits the murder. In *R v Darrington and McGauley* [1980] VR 353 the Full Court of the Supreme Court followed this decision and held that the defence of duress was only denied to the principal offender: see also *R v McConnell* [1977] 1 NSWLR 714.

The decision in *Lynch's* case was overturned by the House of Lords in *R v Howe* [1987] AC 417 on the basis that the law should "stand firm recognising that its highest duty to protect the freedom and lives of those under it. The sanctity of human life lies at the root of this ideal": at 443-444 per Lord Griffiths.[63] Prior to the decision in *R v Darrington and McGauley*, other Australian cases did not allow for the defence of duress to be used by a secondary party to murder[64] and while the situation remains to be decided in Australia, it may be that *Howe's* case will be followed.

It is unclear at common law as to whether the defence is open to an accessory in relation to a charge of attempted murder. The weight of opinion at present seems to be that it is unavailable.[65]

In the Northern Territory, Queensland and Western Australia, duress is not available as a defence to accessories to an offence that falls within the exceptions listed in Table 1.[66] In contrast to

61 *R v Evans (No 1)* [1976] VR 517.
62 *R v Brown* [1968] SASR 467 at 492-493; *R v Purdy* (1946) 10 *Journal of Criminal Law* 182. Compare *R v Steane* [1947] KB 997 at 1005 per Godard LJ.
63 For a critique of this decision see A Reed, "The Need for a New Anglo-American Approach to Duress" (1997) 61(2) *Journal of Criminal Law* 209.
64 *R v Brown* [1968] SASR 467 at 490; *R v Harding* [1976] VR 129.
65 *R v Gotts* [1992] 2 AC 412. See also *R v Howe* [1987] 1 AC 417 at 445.
66 *Criminal Code* (NT), s 12; *Criminal Code* (Qld), s 7; *Criminal Code* (WA), s 7.

this strict approach, duress is available to accessories to an offence that falls within the exceptions in the *Criminal Code* (Tas): *Smith v The Queen* (unrep, 6/3/1979, CCA Tas Cosgrove, Crawford and Nettleford JJ). Duress may be raised by an accessory after the fact, including to the offence of murder: *R v Williamson* [1972] 2 NSWLR 281. In the Code jurisdictions, the involvement of an accessory falls after the commission of the crimes which are listed as exceptions.

Three of the five Law Lords in *Howe*[67] and various writers[68] have suggested that murder be reduced to manslaughter as a consequence of a successful defence of duress. This is currently the situation in the Northern Territory where s 41 of the *Criminal Code* (NT) allows for murder to be reduced to manslaughter where there was "coercion of such a nature that it would have caused a reasonable person similarly circumstanced to have acted in the same or a similar way". The rationale for reducing murder to manslaughter lies in the similarity between duress and provocation: both involve a killing by the accused whilst deprived of self-control or power to withstand an overwhelming threat. Others have argued that it should serve to exculpate an accused completely in certain circumstances.[69]

The Model Criminal Code Officers Committee (MCCOC) is of the view that there should not be any restrictions placed on the scope of the defence of duress: Criminal Code Officers Committee of the Standing Committee of Attorneys-General, *Chapter 2: General Principles of Criminal Responsibility*, Final Report (1992). It suggests that the objective element of duress is enough of a limitation as to its scope and quotes with approval the following passage written by Yeo in "Private Defences, Duress and Necessity" (1991) 15 Crim LJ 139 at 143:

> Once a person is under the influence of a threat, whatever he or she does depends on what the threatener demands. The crime demanded might be trivial or serious but it has no necessary connection with the type of threat confronting the accused. Policy reasons would, however, insist on a requirement that the accused's response was reasonably appropriate to the threat.

The MCCOC's approach follows that of the Law Reform Commission of Victoria which recommended in 1990 that the defence of duress be available to a charge of murder: *Homicide*, Report No 40 (1990), p 106. The reasons listed in favour of this approach do seem convincing. As well as Yeo's point, the following argument (p 104) is significant:

> Although someone who chooses to die rather than to kill another deserves praise, the criminal law should not require heroism on pain of conviction for murder.

Disallowing the defence of duress to a charge of murder does not act as a deterrent as the threat of immediate death constitutes a greater threat than that of future punishment.

---

67   *R v Howe* [1987] 1 AC 417 at 436 per Lord Bridge, at 438 per Lord Brandon, at 445 per Lord Griffiths. The Law Lords rejected this proposal on the ground that it was too late to be entertained by the common law.

68   B Fisse, *Howard's Criminal Law* (5th ed, Sydney: Law Book Company Ltd, 1990), p 546; D O'Connor and P Fairall, *Criminal Defences* (3rd ed, Sydney: Butt, 1996), p 156; Law Reform Commission of Victoria, *Duress, Necessity and Coercion*, Report No 9 (Melbourne: VLRC, 1980), para 4.19; Criminal Law and Penal Methods Reform Committe, South Australia, *The Substantive Criminal Law*, Fourth Report (Adelaide: 1977), para 12.5.

69   D O'Connor and P Fairall, *Criminal Defences* (3rd ed, Sydney: Butt, 1996), p 157; Law Reform Commission of Victoria, *Duress, Necessity and Coercion*, Report No 9 (Melbourne: VLRC, 1980), para 4.19; Criminal Law and Penal Methods Reform Committee, South Australia, *The Substantive Criminal Law*, Fourth Report (Adelaide: 1977), para 12.5.

The credibility of the accused's claims should be assessed by a jury. The possibility of fabrication would not seem any greater than in other defences.

3.1 ELEMENTS OF DURESS

The Victorian Supreme Court analysed the requirements for the defence of duress to be made out at common law in *R v Hurley and Murray* [1967] VR 526. Smith J stated (at 537) that a defence of duress would be relevant if eight factors existed:

- there was a threat that death or grievous bodily harm would be inflicted unlawfully upon a human being if the accused failed to do the act;

- the circumstances were such that a person of ordinary firmness of mind would have been likely to yield to the threat in the way the accused did;

- the threat was present, continuing, imminent and impending;

- the accused reasonably apprehended that the threat would be carried out;

- the accused was induced to commit the crime because of the threat;

- the crime was not murder, "nor any other crime so heinous so as to be excepted from the doctrine";

- the accused did not expose him or herself to the threat; and

- the accused had no means of preventing the execution of the threat.

In *Emery* (1985) 18 A Crim R 49 the Victorian Court of Criminal Appeal approved of this comprehensive analysis, but warned (at 56) that the jury should not be directed in such terms as this formulation wrongly implied that the burden of proof rested on the accused to establish the defence: see below, p 319 as to the burden of proof. It is worthwhile, however, considering Smith J's analysis in relation to the requirements of the defence in order to view how the Australian jurisdictions differ in each regard. The sixth point listed concerning murder has already been outlined.

THREATS OF THE INFLICTION OF DEATH OR GRIEVOUS BODILY HARM

The defence of duress is usually based upon threats of death or grievous bodily harm.[70] The latter has been held at common law to mean really serious injury[71] or, in the Code jurisdictions, bodily injury that endangers life or causes permanent injury to health or which is likely to do so.[72]

---

70 *Subramaniam v Public Prosecutor* [1956] 1 WLR 965; *R v Steane* [1947] KB 997 at 1005 per Lord Goddard CJ; *R v Valderrama-Vega* [1985] Crim LR 220; *R v Williamson* [1972] 2 NSWLR 281; *R v Lawrence* [1980] 1 NSWLR 122; *R v Brown* (1986) 43 SASR 33; *Criminal Code* (NT), s 40 (reference to "threats"); *Criminal Code* (Qld), s 31(d); *Criminal Code* (Tas), s 20; *Criminal Code* (WA), s 31(4).

71 *R v Perks* (1986) 41 SASR 335 at 346-347 per White J; *R v Smith* [1961] AC 290; *Pemble v The Queen* (1971) 124 CLR 107.

72 *Criminal Code* (NT), s 1; *Criminal Code* (Qld), s 1. The definition also encompasses serious disfigurement or the loss of a distinct part or an organ of the body: *Criminal Code* (Tas), s 1; *Criminal Code* (WA), s 1.

Section 40 of the *Criminal Code* (NT) does not specify the type of threat, but contains the limitation that a reasonable person similarly circumstanced would have acted in the same or a similar way.

The position concerning threats of unlawful imprisonment is uncertain. Such threats have been held to amount to duress in a number of cases,[73] but in *R v Foster* (1990) 14 Crim LJ 289 Lee CJ, with whom Hunt and McInerney JJ concurred, held that they could not form the basis for the defence of duress. Threats of violence[74] and threats of a "belting" without any specified limits[75] may also form the basis for the defence. Threats to property, however, are probably not sufficient[76] nor are threats to expose sexual immorality.[77] The common thread for identifying which threats will be accepted as forming the basis for the defence of duress appears to be that they are capable of overbearing the mind of a person of ordinary firmness of character: *R v Abusafiah* (1991) 24 NSWLR 531 at 545.

The threat at common law need not be directed at the accused but can be indirect in the sense that it is aimed at a third person, whether a member of the accused's family,[78] or not.[79] In *R v Hurley and Murray* [1967] VR 526 Smith J stated (at 543):

> [O]nce one goes beyond threats to the accused himself [or herself] I can see no justification, either in logic or convenience, for the laying down of a list of relationships of attachments which will define the limits of the doctrine … I consider that the true view is that a threat made known to the accused to kill or do grievous bodily harm to any human being can be sufficient to found a defence of duress.

The Northern Territory and Tasmanian provisions are silent as to this point,[80] but the Queensland provision was amended in 1997 to include threats to another.[81] Section 31(4) of the *Criminal Code* (WA) is the only provision that expressly limits the threats to those directed at the accused.

THE OBJECTIVE ELEMENT

At common law, the circumstances must have been such that a person of ordinary firmness of mind would have been likely to yield to the threat in the way in which the accused did.[82] Under s 40(1)(c) of the *Criminal Code* (NT) there is the requirement that "a reasonable person similarly circumstanced would have acted in the same or a similar way". In Queensland, Tasmania and Western Australia, there is no such requirement. All that matters is that the accused believed that he or she was unable

---

73 *R v Lawrence* [1980] 1 NSWLR 122 at 133 per Moffitt P; *R v Harding* [1976] VR 129 at 169 per Murphy J; *R v Steane* [1947] KB 997 at 1005 per Lord Goddard CJ; *DPP (Northern Ireland) v Lynch* [1975] AC 653 at 686 per Lord Simon.

74 *R v Harding* [1976] VR 129 at 169 per Murphy J; *R v Steane* [1947] KB 997 at 1005 per the Court.

75 *Goddard v Osborne* (1978) 18 SASR 481 at 489 per the Court.

76 *DPP (Northern Ireland) v Lynch* [1975] AC 653 at 686.

77 *R v Singh* [1973] 1 All ER 122; *R v Valderrama-Vega* [1985] Crim LR 220.

78 *R v Hurley and Murray* [1967] VR 526 (de facto wife); *Emery* (1978) 18 A Crim R 49 (de facto wife); *R v Brown* [1968] SASR 467 at 498 (wife, children or parents); *R v Abusafiah* (1991) 24 NSWLR 531 at 537 per Hunt J (family members generally).

79 *R v Brown* (1986) 43 SASR 33 at 55-56; *DPP (Northern Ireland) v Lynch* [1975] AC 653.

80 *Criminal Code* (NT), s 40; *Criminal Code* (Tas), s 20(1).

81 *Criminal Code* (Qld), s 31(d).

82 *R v Hurley and Murray* [1967] VR 526 at 543 per Smith J; *R v Palazoff* (1986) 43 SASR 99 at 108 per Cox J; *R v Valderrama-Vega* [1985] Crim LR 220.

otherwise to escape the carrying of the threats into execution.[83] In *R v Palazoff* (1986) 43 SASR 99 at 109 Cox J described the person of ordinary firmness of mind as having "the same age and sex and background and other personal characteristics (except perhaps strength of mind) as the [accused]": see also *R v Abusafiah* (1991) 24 NSWLR 531.

It is unclear whether imbuing the ordinary person with the characteristics of the accused is still good law given that the High Court in *R v Stingel* (1990) 171 CLR 312 held that only age is relevant in determining the standard of mental courage to be expected of the ordinary person. It could be argued, however, that *Stingel* relates only to the defence of provocation and may be distinguished from the defence of duress.

It is also unclear as to whether or not the degree of chance of an ordinary person yielding to the threat is one of possibility[84] or probability.[85] In *Lanciana* (1996) 84 A Crim R 268 the Victorian Court of Appeal stated (at 268) that the standard charge in relation to duress should instruct the jury to consider whether a person of ordinary firmness of disposition "could or might have been compelled" by the threats to commit the criminal act.

In *R v Runjanjic and Kontinnen* (1991) 56 SASR 114 the Supreme Court of South Australia held that evidence of "battered woman syndrome" may be relevant first to the question of whether or not a woman of ordinary firmness of mind would have been likely to yield to the threat in the way the accused did and secondly, to the question as to why such a woman would not choose to escape the situation rather than participate in criminal activity. (For an explanation of "battered woman syndrome" see 2.8 'Battered Women and Self-Defence'.)

CONTINUING AND IMMINENT THREATS

The threats made to the accused must be continuing in the sense that they are effective in acting upon the accused's mind at the time the criminal conduct occurred.[86] At common law[87] and in Queensland[88] and the Northern Territory,[89] the threatener need not be physically present when the criminal conduct was carried out. However, in Western Australia[90] and Tasmania[91] the threatener must be actually present at the time the offence is committed.

---

83 *Criminal Code* (Qld), s 31(d); *Criminal Code* (Tas), s 20; *Criminal Code* (WA), s 31(4).

84 The expression "might have yielded" is used in: *R v Palazoff* (1986) 43 SASR 99 at 108 per Cox J; *R v Brown* (1986) 43 SASR 33 at 39 per King CJ; *R v Runjanjic* (1991) 56 SASR 114 at 123 at 371 per Legoe J.

85 The expression "would have yielded" is used in *R v Abusafiah* (1991) 24 NSWLR 531 at 545 per Hunt J; *R v Dawson* [1978] VR 536 at 537; *R v Hurley* [1967] VR 526 at 543.

86 *R v Hurley and Murray* [1967] VR 526 at 543 per Smith J; *R v Hudson* [1971] 2 QB 202 at 206 per the Court; *R v Brown* (1986) 43 SASR 33; *Emery* (1978) 18 A Crim R 49 at 57; *Goddard v Osborne* (1978) 18 SASR 481 at 490; *R v Williamson* [1972] 2 NSWLR 281; *R v Valderrama-Vega* [1985] Crim LR 220.

87 *R v Hurley and Murray* [1967] VR 526 at 543 per Smith J; *R v Hudson* [1971] 2 QB 202 at 206 per the Court; *R v Brown* (1986) 43 SASR 33; *Emery* (1978) 18 A Crim R 49 at 57; *Goddard v Osborne* (1978) 18 SASR 481 at 490; *R v Williamson* [1972] 2 NSWLR 281; *R v Valderrama-Vega* [1985] Crim LR 220.

88 *Criminal Code* (Qld), s 31(d).

89 *Criminal Code* (NT), s 40.

90 *Criminal Code* (WA), s 31(4).

91 *Criminal Code* (Tas), s 20; *R v Pickard* [1959] Qd R 475 at 477 per Stanley J; *Clark* [1980] 2 A Crim R 90.

At common law, the threat of grievous bodily harm or death must generally be of an imminent nature in the sense that it will be carried out there and then, or within a short time thereafter.[92] This also appears to be the situation by implication in the Northern Territory: *Criminal Code* (NT), s 40. The other Code jurisdictions use the term "immediate" rather than "imminent".[93] This requirement of immediacy was referred to by Stanley J in *R v Pickard* [1959] Qd R 475 (at 476):

> In my opinion the word "immediate" qualifies the words "death" or "grievous bodily harm". In my opinion the word "immediate" obviously cannot mean some wholly indefinite future time and place. It must be related to some very short time after the doing or the omission of the act.

The main question here in all jurisdictions is really whether or not the threatened harm is too remote from the commission of the criminal conduct. In *R v Hudson* [1971] 2 QB 202 the English Court of Appeal explained this as follows (at 206-207):

> It is essential to the defence ... that the threat shall be effective at the moment when the crime is committed. The threat must be a "present" threat in the sense that it is effective to neutralise the will of the accused at that time ... a threat of future violence may be so remote as to be insufficient to overpower the will at that moment when the offence was committed ...
>
> When, however, there is no opportunity for delaying tactics, and the person threatened must make up his [or her] mind whether he [or she] is to commit the criminal act or not, the existence at that moment of threats sufficient to destroy his [or her] will ought to provide him [or her] with a defence even though the threatened injury may not follow instantly, but after an interval.

REASONABLE APPREHENSION THAT THE THREAT WOULD BE CARRIED OUT

Threats may often be factually demonstrable, but occasionally the matter will depend upon a belief by the accused. In such a case, the common law requires that the accused believed on reasonable grounds that the threat would be carried out.[94] Lord Lane CJ in *R v Graham* [1982] 1 WLR 294 put the question to be asked as follows (at 300):

> Was the defendant, or may he have been, impelled to act as he did because as a result of what he reasonably believed [the threatener] had said or done, he had good cause to fear that if he did not so act [the threatener] would kill him?

---

92 *R v Hudson and Taylor* [1971] 2 QB 202; *R v Williamson* [1972] 2 NSWLR 281; *R v Dawson* [1978] VR 536; *R v Brown* (1986) 43 SASR 33.

93 *Criminal Code* (Qld), s 31(d); *Criminal Code* (Tas), s 20(1); *Criminal Code* (WA), s 31(4).

94 *R v Graham* [1982] 1 WLR 294 at 300; [1982] 1 All ER 801; (1981) 74 Cr App R 235 per Lord Lane CJ; *R v Hurley and Murray* [1967] VR 526 at 543 per Smith J. See also S Yeo, "The Threat Element in Duress" (1987) 11 Crim LJ 165 at 176.

In the Northern Territory and Tasmania, the accused's belief that the threat would be carried out is tested subjectively in that it need not be based on reasonable grounds: *Criminal Code* (NT), s 40(1)(b); *Criminal Code* (Tas), s 20. In Queensland and Western Australia, there is no reference to a belief that the threat would be carried out. Rather, the belief pertains to being unable otherwise to escape the carrying out of the threats: *Criminal Code* (Qld), s 31(d); *Criminal Code* (WA), s 31(4).

3.2 THE NEXUS BETWEEN THE THREAT AND THE COMMISSION OF THE CRIME

The threat must have compelled the accused to commit the criminal conduct.[95] The defence will not be made out in the situation where the accused independently decided to commit the offence.

In *R v Dawson* [1978] VR 536 the Victorian Supreme Court appears to have taken a restrictive approach in holding that the offence committed must have been ordered specifically by the threatener. This seems to be an unnecessary restriction. The focus is on whether or not the accused believed that unless he or she committed the crime, the threat would be carried out. The focus of the defence is not on whether or not the threatener happened to direct the accused to commit a specific offence.

3.3 PRIOR FAULT AND DURESS

At common law, the defence of duress is not available to an accused who voluntarily enters a situation where duress may be predicted: *R v Hurley and Murray* [1967] VR 526 at 543 per Smith J. The situation usually envisaged here is that in which the accused joins a criminal association, the members of which subsequently threaten him or her in order to make him or her commit a crime.[96] The question here will be whether or not the accused knew that at the time of joining the association, that there was a risk of duress arising. This will be a matter of fact for the jury to decide: *R v Shepherd* (1987) 86 Cr App R 47.

In the Code jurisdictions, the defence is not available to a person who voluntarily became a party to a criminal or unlawful association.[97]

95 *R v Hurley and Murray* [1967] VR 526 at 543 per Smith J; *R v Abusafiah* (1991) 24 NSWLR 531 at 535 per Hunt J; *R v Brown* (1986) 43 SASR 33 at 57; *Criminal Code* (NT), s 40; *Criminal Code* (Qld), s 31(d); *Criminal Code* (Tas), s 20; *Criminal Code* (WA), s 31(4).
96 *R v Sharp* [1987] QB 853; *R v Galderwood and Moore* [1986] 2 WLR 294; *R v Burke* [1986] Crim LR 331.
97 *Criminal Code* (NT), s 40(2); *Criminal Code* (Qld), s 31(2); *Criminal Code* (Tas), s 20(1); *Criminal Code* (WA), s 31(4).

3.4 PREVENTION OF THE EXECUTION OF THE THREAT

In all jurisdictions, there is a legal duty on the accused to escape from the person making threats should a reasonable opportunity to do so present itself.[98]

At common law and in the Northern Territory, there is also an expectation that the accused report the threat to a police officer. However, the defence may be made out where the accused could have sought police protection but failed to do so because he or she thought that it would not be effective.[99] Evidence of battered woman syndrome has been accepted to explain why an accused did not escape the situation by seeking police protection: *R v Runjanjic and Kontinnen* (1991) 56 SASR 114 at 120 per King CJ.

3.5 BURDEN OF PROOF

The accused bears the evidential burden in relation to raising duress and the prosecution, the legal burden of establishing that the accused did not act under duress.[100] In *R v Smyth* [1963] VR 737 (at 738) Sholl J explained this as follows:

> [O]nce evidence is given on which a jury may hold that duress in the necessary sense was exercised, or once evidence is given that raises a reasonable doubt whether duress in that sense was exercised against the accused, the onus is on the Crown to rebut that evidence because (subject to the special rule as to insanity) the onus is always on the Crown in the ultimate result to prove that the criminal act alleged against the accused person was the free and voluntary act of a responsible individual.

In *R v Abusafiah* (1991) 24 NSWLR 531 Hunt J set out a model direction for the use by New South Wales courts in relation to the burden of proof. According to Hunt J (at 544-545), the jury should be directed that the legal burden is on the prosecution to eliminate any reasonable possibility that the accused acted under duress. In order to do this, the prosecution must establish either:

▬▬ **when the accused performed the criminal conduct, there was no reasonable possibility that he or she did so by reason of a threat that death or grievous bodily harm would be inflicted; or**

---

98 *R v Abusafiah* (1991) 24 NSWLR 531; *R v Palazoff* (1986) 43 SASR 99 at 106; *R v Brown* (1986) 43 SASR 33; *R v Lawrence* [1980] 1 NSWLR 122; *R v Dawson* [1978] VR 536 at 537; *Goddard v Osborne* (1978) 18 SASR 481 at 491; *R v Williamson* [1972] 2 NSWLR 281 at 285-286; *R v Hudson* [1971] 2 QB 202; *Criminal Code* (NT), s 40(1)(b) (belief that there was no other way to ensure that the threat was not executed); *Criminal Code* (Qld), s 31(d) (belief that complying with the threatener's order was the only way of avoiding the threat); *Criminal Code* (Tas), s 20(1) (belief that the threat will be executed); *Criminal Code* (WA), s 31(4) (belief that complying with the threatener's order was the only way of avoiding the threat).

99 *R v Brown* (1986) 43 SASR 33 at 40 per King CJ; *R v Dawson* [1978] VR 536 at 539; *Goddard v Osborne* (1978) 18 SASR 481 at 491; *R v Hudson* [1971] 2 QB 202 at 207; *Criminal Code* (NT), s 40(1)(d) (duress available where the nature of the threat was such that a reasonable person similarly circumstanced would not have reported that threat).

100 See Chapter 2 at pp 118ff as to legal and evidential burdens.

=== there was no reasonable possibility that a person of ordinary firmness of mind would have yielded to the threat in the way in which the accused did.

In *Lanciana* (1996) 84 A Crim R 268 the Victorian Court of Criminal Appeal generally approved of this direction, but were of the opinion that the words "could" or "might" should be substituted for the word "would" in the latter direction: at 272 per Callaway JA with whom Phillips CJ and Southwell AJA concurred. In *Lanciana*, the Court held that duress could be referred to as a "defence" as long as the true incidence of the burden of proof was made clear: at 270 per Callaway JA.

3.6 THE MODEL CRIMINAL CODE OFFICERS COMMITTEE APPROACH

Section 10.2 of the *Criminal Code* (Cth) sets out the model defence of duress as follows:

(1) A person is not criminally responsible for an offence if he or she carries out the conduct constituting the offence under duress.

(2) A person carries out conduct under duress if and only if he or she reasonably believes that:

(a) a threat has been made that will be carried out unless an offence is committed; and

(b) there is no reasonable way that the threat can be rendered ineffective; and

(c) the conduct is a reasonable response to the threat.

(3) This section does not apply if the threat is made by or on behalf of a person with whom the person under duress is voluntarily associating for the purpose of carrying out conduct of the kind actually carried out.

This defence largely codifies the common law in requiring a reasonable belief that the threat will be carried out; an implied duty to retreat where reasonable and an objective element in relation to the conduct. The main differences are that the type of threat is not set out; there is no mention of the test for reasonableness (will it still be a person of ordinary firmness of mind?); and, there are no exceptions as to the type of offence for which duress may be raised.

4. MARITAL COERCION

There was at common law a presumption that certain offences committed by a married woman in the presence of her husband were committed under his coercion. This presumption has been abolished in most Australian jurisdictions.[101] In South Australia, Victoria and Western Australia it is nevertheless still open for a married woman to be acquitted of certain offences on the basis that she was coerced

---

101 *Criminal Law and Procedure Ordinance* 1933 (NT) (repealed), s 55(2); *Crimes Act* 1900 (NSW), s 407A; *Criminal Code* (Qld), s 32 (now repealed); *Criminal Law Consolidation Act* 1935 (SA), s 328A; *Criminal Code* (Tas), s 20(2); *Crimes Act* 1958 (Vic), s 336(1); *Criminal Code* (WA), s 32. There is no equivalent provision in the Australian Capital Territory.

by her husband to commit the offence.[102] In New South Wales, while the common law presumption was abolished, the *Crimes Act* 1900 is silent as to the abolition of the common law defence of marital coercion and therefore it may still survive.

The existence of a defence of marital coercion has been justified on the basis that wives may be particularly vulnerable to pressure from their husbands to commit crimes. The Victorian Law Reform Commission has stated in *Criminal Liability of Married Persons*, Report No 3 (Melbourne: VLRC, 1975) (para 16):

> Where a wife, as is still commonly the case, has to look to her husband for support and shelter, and especially when she has young children to care for, the pressure upon her of insistent demands, and of threats of abandonment, may in many cases be just as difficult for her to resist as threats of physical violence sufficient to found a defence of duress. Moreover, the duty and habit of loyalty and co-operation which arise from the special relationship of husband and wife will commonly make it more difficult for a wife to resist pressure from her husband than from a stranger.

The abolition of the defence of marital coercion is occasionally called for on the basis that it unduly favours women over men and its underlying premise subjugates women under the will of men.[103] Sometimes when there are calls for the defence's abolition, it is recommended that the defence of duress be broadened at the same time.[104] The rarity of the use of the defence of marital coercion has supported calls for its abolition.[105] These arguments were considered by the Victorian Law Reform Commission in *Criminal Liability of Married Persons*, Report No 3 (1975), but abolition was rejected in favour of legislative changes to the *Crimes Act* 1958 (Vic). The Victorian sections on marital coercion were duly introduced in 1977 by the *Crimes (Married Person's Liability) Act* 1977 (Vic) and are now the most detailed in Australia.

It is significant that the *Criminal Code Act* 1995 (Cth) does not include a defence of marital coercion and it would seem that if the defence of duress is broadened as the Model Criminal Code Officers Committee (MCCOC) has suggested, then there is no reason to retain the gender specific defence of marital coercion.

The defences of duress and marital coercion at present overlap in that a woman who commits a crime because of threats from her husband would be able to use either defence. Marital coercion is not a defence in substitution for the defence of duress: *DPP (Northern Ireland) v Lynch* [1975] AC 653 at 684 per Lord Wilberforce, at 713 per Lord Edmund-Davies. However, the defence of marital coercion is broader than that of duress because the latter in most jurisdictions is confined to threats of death or grievous bodily harm whereas coercion is defined more broadly.

---

102 *Criminal Law Consolidation Act* 1935 (SA), s 328A; *Crimes Act* 1958 (Vic), s 336; *Criminal Code* (WA), s 32.

103 Model Criminal Code Officers Committee, *Principles of Criminal Responsibility and Other Matters*, Interim Report (1990), para 12.12. The defence has been abolished in Tasmania: *Criminal Code Act* 1924 (Tas), s 20(2).

104 Victorian Law Reform Commission, *Duress, Necessity and Coercion*, Report No 9 (1980), para 5.03; Review of Commonwealth Criminal Law, *Principles of Criminal Responsibility and Other Matters*, Interim Report (1990), paras 12.21 and 12.38.

105 JC Smith and B Hogan, *Criminal Law* (6th ed, London: Butt, 1988), p 240; English Law Commission, *Defences of General Application*, Working Paper No 55 (London: HMSO, 1974), para 63.

4.1 SCOPE OF THE DEFENCE

Section 336(2) of the *Crimes Act* 1958 (Vic) states:

> Where a woman is charged with an offence other than treason, [or] murder…[106] that woman
> shall have a complete defence to such charge if her action or inaction (as the case may be)
> was due to coercion by a man to whom she was then married.

This section places three limitations on the scope of the defence. It is unavailable where:

- the charge is one of murder or treason;

- there was no coercion or the coercion was not linked to the criminal conduct; or

- the threatener was not the husband of the accused.

"Coercion" is defined as pressure, whether in the form of threats or any other form: *Crimes Act* 1958 (Vic), s 336(3).

The legislative provisions in the other jurisdictions are similar in context, although slight variations do occur and these will be explored in the following sections.

As with the general defence of duress, the defence of marital coercion is not available on a charge of treason[107] or murder.[108] The rationale for this is that public policy requires that human life must be preserved and the purpose of the criminal law is to set a standard of conduct with which ordinary people must comply: see above, p 312. In Western Australia, the scope of the defence is even more limited in that it is not available to those offences that have the element of grievous bodily harm or an intention to cause such harm: *Criminal Code* (WA), s 32. It is more difficult to find a rationale for so limiting the scope of the defence in this regard.

The defence is only available to a lawfully married woman.[109] It is unavailable to a woman in a de facto marriage,[110] a polygamous marriage[111] or where the woman mistakenly believed she was legally married.[112]

The Law Reform Commission of Victoria when considering the defence of marital coercion received a submission that the defence be available for women living in de facto relationships. This was rejected on the ground that "the State does not have the same concern to preserve the stability of 'de facto' relationships as it has to preserve the stability of marriages": Victorian Law Reform Commission, *Criminal Liability of Married Persons*, Report No 3 (1975), para 83. It could be argued that this reliance on the sanctity of marriage is outdated given the rise in de facto cohabitation and greater societal acceptance of the fact. Yeo in "Coercing Wives into Crime" (1992) 6 *Australian Journal of Family Law* 214 argues (at 224):

---

106 The section also refers to "an offence specified in ss 4, 11 or 14 of this Act". All these sections have been abolished.

107 *Criminal Law Consolidation Act* 1935 (SA), s 328A; *Crimes Act* 1958 (Vic), s 336(2). There is no offence of treason in the *Criminal Code* (WA).

108 *Criminal Law Consolidation Act* 1935 (SA), s 328A; *Crimes Act* 1958 (Vic), s 336(2); *Criminal Code* (WA), s 32.

109 *Brennan v Bass* (1984) 35 SASR 311; *R v Court* (1912) 7 Cr App R 127 at 129; *R v Ditta* [1988] Crim LR 42; *Criminal Law Consolidation Act* 1935 (SA), s 328A; *Crimes Act* 1958 (Vic), s 336; *Criminal Code* (WA), s 32.

110 *Brennan v Bass* (1984) 35 SASR 311; *R v Court* (1912) 7 Cr App R 127 at 129.

111 *R v Ditta* [1988] Crim LR 42 at 44.

112 *Brennan v Bass* (1984) 35 SASR 311; *R v Ditta* [1988] Crim LR 42.

> It is highly contentious to confine the defence to legal marriages. Surely, a female partner of a de facto relationship would suffer just as much coercion as a legally married wife. The factors which create the possibility of coercion, namely, intimacy and gendered power imbalance, are found as much in de facto relationships as amongst legally married couples.

In Victoria, there is no requirement in the legislation that the husband be present at the time in which the accused commits the offence. In Western Australia, the act must be done in the presence of the husband: *Criminal Code* (WA), s 32. In South Australia, the husband's presence is also required, but this has been interpreted as the husband being close enough to influence the accused into doing what he wanted done: *Goddard v Osborne* (1978) 18 SASR 481 at 493.

In *Goddard v Osborne* (1978) 19 SASR 481 the Supreme Court of South Australia held that a woman's failure to report her husband's threats to the police would not preclude reliance on the defence of marital coercion. There is no legislative requirement in any of the jurisdictions that police protection first be sought.

4.2 MEANING OF COERCION

Section 336(3) of the *Crimes Act* 1958 (Vic) defines "coercion" as follows:

> For the purposes of this section, **"coercion"** means pressure, whether in the form of threats or in any other form, sufficient to cause a woman of ordinary good character and normal firmness of mind, placed in the circumstances in which the woman was placed, to conduct herself in the manner charged.

This definition of "coercion" is broader than the requirements for threats in the defence of duress. The term "pressure" is used which is a broader term than "threats" alone. It may, for example, encompass economic or moral pressure: *R v Richman* [1982] Crim LR 507. This could, for example, include claims that the husband would leave the accused and force her to bring up her children on her own or that he will cut off her access to income. For the defence of duress to be made out, the threat has to be one of death or grievous bodily harm. There is no such limitation in s 336(3).

The South Australian and Western Australian provisions do not specify the types of coercion that will form the basis for the defence. At common law, marital coercion has been interpreted broadly to include the application of moral pressure and threats of desertion: *R v Pierce* (1941) 5 *Journal of Criminal Law* 124; *R v White*, The Times, 16 February 1974.

In Victoria, the definition of "coercion" contains an objective element in that the gravity of the pressure will be measured according to its effect on a "woman of ordinary good character". This requirement is not relevant in South Australia or Western Australia or at common law.

In the common law defence of duress, the objective component centres solely upon the concept of a person of ordinary firmness of mind. The addition of the requirement in Victoria that the woman be of good character appears to inject a moral component into the defence of marital coercion. This has been criticised on the basis that the assumption underlying it, that a woman of bad character would be less hesitant in committing crimes than one of good character, is fallacious: S Yeo, "Coercing Wives into Crime" (1992) 6 *Australian Journal of Family Law* 214 at 222.

The other aspect to this objective element in Victoria is that the "woman of ordinary good character" must be placed in the position in which the accused was placed.

Section 336(4) of the *Crimes Act* 1958 (Vic) is relevant here:

> Without limiting the generality of the expression "the circumstances in which the woman was placed" in sub-section (3), such circumstances shall include the degree of dependence, whether economic or otherwise, of the woman on her husband.

Taking into account the circumstances in which the accused was placed provides a balance between having a purely objective component and a purely subjective one.

In all relevant jurisdictions, there must be a link between the pressure and the accused's commission of the crime.[113] The defence will fail if the accused acted independently of the pressure placed upon her: *R v Cohen* (1868) 11 Cox CC 99; *R v Torpey* (1871) 12 Cox CC 45.

4.3 BURDEN OF PROOF

As with the majority of defences, in Western Australia, Victoria and at common law, the accused bears the evidential burden in relation to the defence of marital coercion. Section 336(4) of the *Crimes Act* 1958 (Vic) states:

> The accused shall bear the burden of adducing evidence that she conducted herself in the manner charged because she was coerced by her husband, but if such evidence has been adduced, the prosecution shall bear the burden of proving that the action or inaction charged was not due to coercion by the husband.

This means that, as in the defence of duress, the accused bears the evidential burden in relation to raising duress and the prosecution, the legal burden of establishing that the accused did not act under duress. The jury direction set out by Hunt J in *R v Abusafiah* (1991) 24 NSWLR 531 (at 544-545) may be helpful here. Taking into account what the Victorian Court of Criminal Appeal said about this direction in *Lanciana* (1996) 84 A Crim R 268 the prosecution will need to prove beyond reasonable doubt that:

▬ **when the accused performed the criminal conduct, there was no reasonable possibility that she did so by reason of some form of pressure; or**

▬ **there was no reasonable possibility that a woman of ordinary good character and normal firmness of mind would have yielded to the pressure in the way in which the accused did.**

However, s 328a of the *Criminal Law Consolidation Act* 1935 (SA) states that it is a defence "to prove that the offence was committed in the presence, and under the coercion, of the husband". This implies that the accused bears the legal burden rather than just the evidential burden. In *Goddard v Osborne* (1978) 18 SASR 481 the Supreme Court of South Australia stated (at 495) that the effect of to transfer it to those of the acccused". Why the legal burden should be on the accused in South Australia in relation to marital coercion appears to be an inexplicable anomaly, particularly since duress is not treated in the same way in that State.

---

113 *Criminal Law Consolidation Act* 1935 (SA), s 328A; *Crimes Act* 1958 (Vic), s 336(2); *Criminal Code* (WA), s 32.

5. NECESSITY

The defence of necessity involves a claim by the accused that he or she was compelled to do what he or she did by reason of some extraordinary emergency. The concepts of justification *and* excuse have been used as rationales for the defence.

The accused's behaviour in a situation of necessity is sometimes described as justified because it is recognised that the law can on occasion be broken to avoid a greater harm than would occur by obeying it. This is sometimes referred to as the "greater good" principle.[114] For example, *Mouse's* case (1608) 77 ER 1341 concerned an action for trespass for throwing the plaintiff's goods overboard from a barge. It was held that not only the crew but also other passengers could do this in order to lighten the barge and prevent it capsizing in a storm. The rationale for this decision was that throwing the goods overboard was a lesser harm than the potential loss of lives.

The accused's behaviour in a situation of necessity is also said to be excused because of the situation of emergency confronting him or her.[115] Obedience to the law would impose an intolerable burden on the accused in such a situation. The Supreme Court of Canada in *R v Perka* (1985) 14 CCC (3d) 395 has described (at 386) the latter principle as follows:

> Necessity rests on a realistic assessment of human weakness, recognising that a liberal and humane criminal law cannot hold people to the strict obedience of laws in emergency situations where normal human instincts, whether of self-preservation or of altruism, overwhelmingly impelled disobedience. The defence must, however, be strictly controlled and scrupulously limited to situations that correspond to its underlying rationale. That rationale is that it is inappropriate to punish acts that are normatively involuntary.

As with the defence of duress, the defence of necessity is available where all the elements of the crime have been made out and the accused's ability to choose is affected by the emergency situation. As with duress also, the accused's ability to will the act remains unaffected; it is the accused's ability to choose between the lesser of two evils which is affected.[116]

The common law governs the defence in the Australian Capital Territory, New South Wales, South Australia and Victoria. Interestingly, the common law also appears to apply in Tasmania. The *Criminal Code* (Tas) is silent as to the defence and pursuant to s 8, it appears that the common law is applicable. The *Criminal Codes* of the Northern Territory, Queensland and Western Australia contain the defence of sudden or extraordinary emergency[117] which substantially follows the common law defence.

The main two Australian cases on necessity are that of *R v Davidson* [1969] VR 667 and *R v Loughnan* [1981] VR 443. In the former case, the accused was charged with unlawfully using an instrument to procure a miscarriage. Menhennit J stated that the defence of necessity was applicable

---

114 *Mouses's Case* (1608) 12 Co Rep 63; 77 ER 1341; *Re F (mental patient: sterilisation)* [1990] 2 AC 1.

115 *R v Loughnan* [1981] VR 443; *Moore v Hussey* (1609) Hob 93; 80 ER 243.

116 *R v Loughnan* [1981] VR 443 at 448. In *R v Perka* (1985) 14 CCC (3d) 395, the Supreme Court of Canada referred to this as "normative involuntariness" but this terminology may be confusing as necessity does not render the accused's actions involuntary in the usual legal sense.

117 *Criminal Code* (NT), s 33; *Criminal Code* (Qld), s 25; *Criminal Code* (WA), s 25.

in determining whether or not a therapeutic abortion was lawful or unlawful within the meaning of the statutory offence. Menhennit J ruled that for the defence to be made out, the accused must have believed on reasonable grounds that his actions were necessary to preserve the woman from serious danger to her life or her physical or mental health and that they were not out of proportion to the danger to be averted.

In *Loughnan's* case, the accused was charged with escaping from prison. He raised the issue of necessity, claiming that he had committed the offence to avoid being killed by his fellow prisoners. The Victorian Full Court comprising Young CJ, King and Crockett JJ were prepared to recognise a defence of necessity, but held that it had not been made out on the facts.

5.1 SCOPE OF THE DEFENCE

At common law, the defence of necessity is available to all offences except murder.[118] The statutory defence of sudden or extraordinary emergency in the Northern Territory, Queensland and Western Australia, however, is not limited in this way.

The rationale for why necessity is not available at common law to a charge of murder can be found in the 19th century case of *R v Dudley and Stephens* (1884) 14 QBD 273. Dudley, Stephens, Brooks and a 17-year-old boy, Parker were cast adrift in an open boat 1600 miles from land. On the 20th day, after nine days without food and seven without water, Dudley and Stephens agreed to kill Parker who was the weakest of the four and eat his flesh. Brooks refused to take part in the killing. Dudley then killed Parker and the three men survived by eating Parker's flesh. When they were subsequently rescued, Dudley and Stephens admitted what had happened and were charged with murder. The jurors declined to give their view as to whether the facts amounted to murder and asked for the advice of the Court of Queen's Bench. Lord Coleridge CJ in delivering the judgment of the Court held that the accused were guilty of murder and sentenced them to death. This mandatory penalty was later commuted by the Executive to six months' imprisonment.

In holding that the defence of necessity was not available to a charge of murder, Lord Coleridge CJ stated (at 287-288):

> To preserve one's life is generally speaking a duty, but it may be the plainest and the highest duty to sacrifice it. War is full of instances in which it is a man's duty not to live, but to die ... It is not correct, therefore, to say that there is any absolute or unqualified necessity to preserve one's life ... It is not needful to point out the awful danger of the principle which has been contended for. Who is to be the judge of this sort of necessity? By what measure is the comparative value of lives to be measured? Is it to be strength, or intellect, or what? It is plain that the principle leaves to him who is to profit by it to determine the necessity which will justify him deliberately taking another's life to save his own ... it is quite plain that such a principle once admitted might be made the legal cloak for unbridled passion and atrocious crime.

---

118 Necessity is not available to a charge of murder: *R v Dudley and Stephens* (1884) 14 QBD 273; *R v Howe* [1987] 1 AC 417. There are no Australian cases on point, but in Victoria it has been suggested that necessity may be available to a charge of murder: *R v Loughnan* [1981] VR 443 at 449 per Young CJ and King J.

For an engaging legal historical analysis of this case see A Simpson, *Cannibalism and the Common Law* (Chicago: University of Chicago Press, 1984).

This rationale for rejecting necessity as a defence for murder also underlies the House of Lords decision in *R v Howe* [1987] AC 417 that rejected duress as a defence to murder either by a principal in the first or second degree.

The Model Criminal Code Officers Committee (MCCOC) has followed the approach of the Code jurisdictions rather than the common law in formulating a defence of sudden or extraordinary emergency that is available in relation to all offences.[119] As with duress, having an objective element to the defence would appear to assuage the fear that it might become a cloak for unbridled passion and atrocious crime.

The scope of the defence of necessity is also restricted at common law in that it may be denied to an accused who has created the situation of emergency him or herself.[120] The Supreme Court of Canada has held that necessity may also fail if the accused contemplated or ought to have contemplated that his or her conduct bore the risk of giving rise to the emergency: *Perka v The Queen* (1985) 14 CCC (3d) 385 at 403 per Dickson J. The Court also held that no other alternatives must be open to the accused: at 386. There are no such explicit restrictions placed on the defence in the Northern Territory, Queensland or Western Australia.

Specific legal rules have been devised to cover the defence of necessity in medical emergency cases.[121] This defence will be examined at p 332.

5.2 ELEMENTS OF THE DEFENCE

In *R v Loughnan* [1981] VR 443 (at 448) Young CJ and King J summarised the elements of the defence of necessity as follows:

> [T]here are three elements involved in the defence of necessity. First, the criminal act or acts must have been done only in order to avoid certain consequences which would have inflicted irreparable evil upon the accused or upon others whom he [or she] was bound to protect ...
>
> The [second] element [is] that the accused must honestly believe on reasonable grounds that he [or she] was placed in a situation of imminent peril ... Thus if there is an interval of time between the threat and its expected execution it will be very rarely if ever that a defence of necessity can succeed.
>
> The [third] element of proportion simply means that the acts done to avoid the imminent peril must not be out of proportion to the peril to be avoided. Put in another way, the test is: would a reasonable [person] in the position of the accused have considered that he [or she] had any alternative to doing what he [or she] did to avoid the peril?

---

119 Criminal Law Officers Committee of the Standing Committee of Attorneys-General, *Chapter 2: General Principles of Criminal Responsibility*, Final Report (1992), p 67; *Criminal Code Act* 1995 (Cth), s 10.3.

120 *Perka v The Queen* (1985) 14 CCC (3d) 385 at 403 per Dickson J. See also *R v Roberts* (1990) 99 NBR (2d) 80; *R v Hendricks* (1988) 44 CCC (3d) 52.

121 *R v Davidson* [1969] VR 667; *R v Wald* (1971) 3 DCR (NSW) 25; *K v Minister for Youth and Community Services* [1982] 1 NSWLR 311; *Re F (mental patient: sterilisation)* [1990] 2 AC 1; [1989] 2 WLR 1025; *R v Bourne* [1939] 1 KB 687; [1938] 3 All ER 615; *Criminal Code* (Qld), s 282; *Criminal Code* (Tas), ss 51, 149; *Criminal Code* (WA), s 259.

The defence of sudden or extraordinary emergency in the Northern Territory, Queensland and Western Australia is similar in that there must be an emergency, the accused must have good cause to fear that death or serious injury and the situation must be such that an ordinary person possessing ordinary power of self-control could not reasonably be expected to act otherwise.

The MCCOC's version of the defence also follows this tripartite approach. Following the MCCOC's recommendation in its Final Report, *General Principles of Criminal Responsibility* (1992), p 67, s 10.3 of the *Criminal Code Act* 1995 (Cth) states:

(1) A person is not criminally responsible for an offence if he or she carries out the conduct constituting the offence in response to circumstances of sudden or extraordinary emergency.

(2) This section applies if and only if the person carrying out the conduct reasonably believes that:

(a) circumstances of sudden or extraordinary emergency exist; and

(b) committing the offence is the only reasonable way to deal with the emergency; and

(c) the conduct is a reasonable response to the emergency.

The three elements of the defence of necessity will be explored under the following categories:

=== the nature of the emergency;

=== the accused's belief; and

=== the ordinary person test.

THE NATURE OF THE EMERGENCY

The origin of the emergency that exerts pressure upon the accused to commit a crime may arise from a natural event or from threats by another.[122] The early case law held that necessity could not arise from threats from another as this was encompassed by the defence of duress: see, for example, *DPP (Northern Ireland) v Lynch* [1975] AC 653 at 694; [1975] 2 WLR 641; [1975] 1 All ER 913 per Lord Simon HL. This distinction has since been abandoned.

The common law has recognised threats of death[123] or serious physical harm,[124] sexual assault[125] and suicide[126] as giving rise to the defence of necessity.

In the Northern Territory, Queensland and Western Australia, the provisions refer to a "sudden or extraordinary emergency" which is not further explained. This seems to encompass all sorts of threatened harm. However, in *Larner v Dorrington* (1993) MVR 75 (at 79) the Supreme Court of Western Australia referred specifically to the fear of "death or serious physical injury".

---

122 *R v Loughnan* [1981] VR 443 (SC Vic); *Martin* (1989) 88 Cr App R 343; *R v Conway* [1989] QB 290.

123 *R v Loughnan* [1981] VR 443 at 448 per Young CJ and King J; *Martin* (1989) 88 Cr App R 343 per Simon Brown J.

124 *Martin* (1989) 88 Cr App R 343 per Simon Brown J.

125 *People v Lovecamp*, 118 Cal Rptr 110 (1975) referred to in *R v Loughnan* [1981] VR 443 at 448 per Young CJ and King J.

126 *Martin* (1989) 88 Cr App R 343; *R v Potter* (unrep, 16/10/1993, Dist Ct NSW Judge Dent QC).

In *R v Loughnan* [1981] VR 443 Young CJ and King J stated (at 448) that the range of threats forming the defence of necessity was a "matter of debate". Crockett J focused (at 460) on the concept of the balancing of harms to discover what amounted to "irreparable evil". In his view, any type of threatened harm could be relevant provided that the threatened harm was greater than or at least comparable to the crime committed by the accused to avoid it: see also *R v White* (1987) 31 A Crim R 194 at 198.

The "irreparable evil" spoken of in *Loughnan's* case may be aimed at a person other than the accused. It appears that this other person must bear a special relationship to the accused,[127] although this will not be a requirement in situations of necessary medical treatment. For example, in *R v Davidson* [1969] VR 667 the accused successfully argued that he used an instrument to procure a miscarriage (which is an offence contrary to s 66 of the *Crimes Act* 1958 (Vic)) because it was necessary to preserve the woman from serious danger to her life or physical or mental health. Menhennit J summarised (at 670) the scope of necessity as a defence for abortion in the following terms:

> For the use of an instrument with intent to procure a miscarriage to be lawful the accused
> must have honestly believed on reasonable grounds that the act done by him [or her] was
> (a) necessary to preserve the woman from a serious danger to her life or her physical or
> mental health (not being the normal dangers of pregnancy and childbirth) which the
> continuance of pregnancy would entail; and (b) in the circumstances not out of proportion
> to the danger to be averted.

The legality of medical abortion in Australian jurisdictions rests on the common law defence of necessity, which is notoriously uncertain in its scope and application: L Crowley-Cyr, "A Century of Remodelling: The Law of Abortion In Review" (2000) 7(3) *Journal of Law and Medicine* 252; K Petersen, "Abortion: Medicalisation and Legal Gatekeeping" (2000) 7(3) *Journal of Law and Medicine* 267. For a feminist critique of law reform which uses abortion as a case study see R Graycar and J Morgan, "A Quarter Century of Feminism In Law: Back To The Future" (1999) 24(3) *Alternative Law Journal* 117. Reproduction offences are further explored in Chapter 10, 7 'Abortion, Child Destruction and Concealment of Birth', p 517.

In the Northern Territory, Queensland and Western Australia, there is no express requirement of a special relationship between the accused and the person endangered.

At common law, the emergency situation must be an imminent one. As Young CJ and King J pointed out in *R v Loughnan* [1981] VR 443 (at 448) "if there is an interval of time between the threat and its expected execution it will be very rarely if ever that a defence of necessity will succeed".[128]

In *Re F (Mental Patient: Sterilisation)* [1990] 2 AC 1 the House of Lords indicated, albeit in a civil matter, that there could be some relaxation of the imminence requirement. The defence of necessity was raised with regard to the non-consensual sterilisation of an intellectually disabled woman who was in a sexual relationship. There was medical evidence that she would not be able to

---

127 In *R v Loughnan* [1981] VR 443 at 448, Young CJ and King J refer to the threat being inflicted "upon the accused or upon others whom he [or she] was bound to protect".

128 *Dixon-Jenkins* (1985) 14 A Crim R 372 at 278 per Starke J; *Perka v The Queen* (1985) 14 CCC (3d) 385 at 400 per Dickson J.

cope with pregnancy and giving birth, but it is questionable that the "peril" of getting pregnant was in fact "imminent". Lord Goff stated (at 75):

> [T]he relevance of an emergency is that it may give rise to a necessity to act in the interests of the assisted person, without first obtaining his [or her] consent. Emergency is however, not the criterion or even a prerequisite; it is simply a frequent origin of necessity which impels intervention. The principle is one of necessity not emergency.

The Code provisions do not refer to imminence but a "sudden or extraordinary emergency". A sudden emergency is one which is unexpected and this has been held to include a loud noise at the back of a car whilst it is being driven,[129] being told that one's horses have escaped onto a public road thereby causing danger to passing cars[130] and being chased at high speed by a car.[131]

An extraordinary emergency, on the other hand, may not entail this notion of suddenness or unexpectedness. It may persist over a period of time such as living in a war zone[132] or being cast adrift on the high seas.[133]

THE ACCUSED'S BELIEF

At common law, the accused must honestly believe on reasonable grounds that a situation of imminent peril has arisen. If the accused is ignorant of circumstances of necessity then the defence cannot be relied upon. In *Limbo v Little* (1989) 45 A Crim R 61 (at 88) Martin J, with whom Kearney and Rice JJ concurred, stated:

> [I]t is [not] relevant or permissible [in seeking to establish the defence of necessity] to attempt to prove facts which were not evident to the offender at the time of the offence.

The situation of imminent peril may not in fact exist. It will be enough if the accused honestly and reasonably (but mistakenly) believed that the situation existed.[134]

The *Criminal Codes* of the Northern Territory, Queensland and Western Australia all have general provisions relating to a mistake of fact[135] and reading these provisions together with the defence of sudden or extraordinary emergency, it would seem that the latter may still be relied upon even where an emergency does not, objectively speaking, exist. For example, in *R v Pius Piane* [1975] PNGLR 52 the accused was charged with dangerous driving causing death. He claimed that a loud noise at the back of his car that he was driving caused a momentary lack of attention. The Supreme Court of Papua New Guinea (at 56 per Lalor J) allowed the defence of emergency on that basis that "whether there was in fact a state of emergency or not, the situation was such that the driver could quite honestly and reasonably believe that there was an emergency in the back of the truck".

---

129 *R v Pius Piane* [1975] PNGLR 53 (SC).

130 *McHenry v Stewart* (unrep, 14/12/1976, CA WA).

131 *R v Warner* [1980] Qd R 207.

132 *Pagawa v Mathew* [1986] PNGLR 154 (National Court of Justice).

133 *R v Dudley and Stephens* (1884) 14 QBD 273.

134 *R v Loughnan* [1981] VR 443 at 448 per Young CJ and King J; *R v Conway* [1989] QB 290.

135 *Criminal Code* (NT), s 32; *Criminal Code* (Qld), s 24; *Criminal Code* (WA), s 24. See Ch 7.

THE ORDINARY PERSON TEST

All of the jurisdictions impose an objective standard in relation to necessity. At common law, the accused's response to the situation of imminent peril is measured against the reaction of an ordinary person in the position of the accused. Section 33 of the *Criminal Code* (NT) expressly refers to "an ordinary person similarly circumstanced". In *R v Martin* [1989] 1 All ER 652 Simon Brown J (at 653-654), in delivering the judgment of the Court of Appeal expressed the test as "would a sober person of reasonable firmness, sharing the characteristics of the accused, have responded to that situation by acting as the accused acted?" The use of the word "would" in this test implies probability rather than possibility as the degree of chance.[136]

The Queensland and Western Australian provisions refer to whether an ordinary person possessing ordinary power of self-control could not reasonably be expected to act otherwise. In *Larner v Dorrington* (1993) MVR 75 the Supreme Court of Western Australia referred (at 79) to the ordinary person as possessing the "characteristics of the accused person". The use of the word "could" in this test seems to convey a possible rather than a probable response.

It is unclear just what characteristics of the accused will be taken into account in relation to the ordinary person test. The Supreme Court of Victoria left this open in *R v Loughnan* [1981] VR 443 and other cases have not clarified the issue. In relation to the defence of duress, in *R v Palazoff* (1986) 43 SASR 99 Cox J described (at 109) the person of ordinary firmness of mind as having "the same age and sex and background and other personal characteristics (except perhaps strength of mind) as the [accused]".

If the defence of necessity is to echo the defence of duress, then the ordinary person test may well be the same.[137]

In some of the cases, a test of proportionality has been used in applying the ordinary person test. In *R v Davidson* [1969] VR 667 Menhennit J stated (at 671) that an important element of the objective test was that the accused's act was "not out of proportion to the danger to be averted".[138] In this regard, Des O'Connor and Paul Fairall write that:

> By parallel reasoning with self-defence and provocation, it is submitted that proportionality is but an element to be considered in determining whether the accused acted out of necessity.[139]

---

136 See *R v Loughnan* [1981] VR 443 at 448 per Young CJ and King J; *R v Conway* [1989] QB 290; *R v Abusafiah* (1991) 24 NSWLR 531 at 540-541 per Hunt J.

137 But see discussion above at p 315 regarding duress.

138 See also *R v Loughnan* [1981] VR 443 at 448 per Young CJ and King J, at 460 per Crockett J; *Re F (mental patient: sterilisation)* [1990] 2 AC 1 at 55 per Lord Brandon; *White* (1987) 31 A Crim R 194 at 198.

139 D O'Connor and P Fairall, *Criminal Defences* (Sydney: Butt, 1996), p 113. See also S Yeo, "Proportionality in Criminal Cases" (1988) 12 Crim LJ 211 at 220ff.

Necessity and Medical Treatment

Health professionals may be justified in performing emergency medical treatment on the basis of either implied consent, or on the basis of the defence of necessity: *Malette v Shulman* (1990) 67 DLR (4th) 321 at 328-329 (Ontario CA). In relation to implied consent, it is presumed that the patient would have consented to the treatment because it was necessary to save his or her life, but was unable to.

In relation to necessity providing the legal justification for emergency medical treatment, Lord Goff stated in *Re F (Mental Patient: Sterilisation)* [1990] 2 AC 1 (at 75):

> [N]ot only (1) must there be a necessity to act when it is not practicable to communicate with the assisted person, but also (2) the action taken must be such as a reasonable person would in all the circumstances take, acting in the best interests of the assisted person.

Lord Goff distinguished between emergency cases and those in which the disability is permanent. In relation to the former, he stated (at 77) that the treatment should be confined to that which is necessary in the short term in the patient's interests. These restrictions, however, would not apply in the case of a patient with a permanent disability such as an intellectual disability as the patient is incompetent to consent. In that situation, the health professional must act in the patient's best interests.

It is uncertain whether this precise test applies in Australia given that McHugh J in *Department of Health and Community Services (NT) v JWB* (1992) 175 CLR 218 stated (at 322):

> [T]he approach of their Lordships [in *Re F*] transfers the issue [of what medical treatment is appropriate] to the medical profession for determination ... Whatever may be the position in England, the approach of their Lordships is not consistent with the common law of Australia.

It would seem that in practice, a surgeon exercising proper medical judgment is generally able to proceed without risk of prosecution: P Skegg, "A Justification for Medical Procedures Performed Without Consent" (1974) 90 *Law Quarterly Review* 512.

In the Canadian case of *Murray v McMurchy* [1949] 2 DLR 442 Macfarlane J states (at 445) that the question to be determined is "whether [it] was *necessary* that the operation be done, not whether it was then more *convenient* to perform it". If there is no evidence that there is a danger to the patient if medical treatment is not performed, then unauthorised treatment is an assault: P Skegg, "A Justification for Medical Procedures Performed Without Consent" (1974) 90 *Law Quarterly Review* 512. Generally the patient will bring a civil action in trespass, but assault in the criminal sense has also been committed.

It appears that the defence of necessity will be irrelevant where emergency medical treatment is performed contrary to the patient's prior instructions. In *Malette v Shulman* (1990) 67 DLR (4th) 321 Robins JA stated (at 330):

> [A] doctor is not free to disregard a patient's advance instructions any more than he [or she] would be free to disregard instructions given at the time of the emergency.[140]

There are separate provisions in the *Criminal Codes* of Queensland and Western Australia that provide for a defence of necessity to those carrying out surgical operations. Section 150 of the *Criminal Code* (NT) provides for a test of medical treatment in relation to some defences, but expressly excludes cases of necessity. It is therefore silent as to a separate defence of necessity for medical treatment.

Sections 282 and 259 of the *Criminal Codes* of Queensland and Western Australia provide:

> A person is not criminally responsible for performing in good faith and with reasonable care and skill a surgical operation upon any person for his [or her] benefit, or upon an unborn child for the preservation of the mother's life, if the performance of the operation is reasonable, having regard to the patient's state at the time and to all circumstances of the case.

These provisions pose a different objective test to the general defence of necessity in that whether the performance of an operation is reasonable will generally involve looking at a body of relevant professional opinion. However, this will not necessarily be determinative in relation to the objective standard used in the defence of necessity in this area. In *Re F (mental patient: sterilisation)* [1990] 2 AC 1 (at 78) Lord Goff spoke of the health professional's conduct being measured against a responsible and competent body of relevant professional opinion. *Rogers v Whitaker* (1992) 175 CLR 479 (at 489-490) although dealing with the objective standard in relation to the law of negligence, is also relevant here. In that case, Mason CJ, Brennan, Dawson, Toohey and McHugh JJ agreed that:

> Whether a medical practitioner carried out a particular form of treatment in accordance with the appropriate standard of care is a question in the resolution of which responsible professional opinion will have an influential, often a decisive role to play.

Information about professional practices will therefore be relevant, if not determinative, in relation to the objective standard against which the health professional's actions will be measured.

The role of necessity in providing a legal justification for the medicinal/therapeutic use, possession and supply of cannabis is discussed in Chapter 15, p 846.

5.3 BURDEN OF PROOF

As with the defences of duress and marital coercion, the accused bears the evidential burden in relation to necessity whilst the legal burden is placed on the prosecution to negate any evidence of necessity beyond reasonable doubt. This was described by the Supreme Court of Canada in *Perka v The Queen* (1985) 14 CCC (3d) 385 at 386 as follows:

---

140 See further on this point I Kerridge, J McPhee, M Lowe and B Flynn, "Advance Directives" (1997) Issues Paper No 5, *Australian Institute of Health, Law and Ethics: Topics for Attention* 1-8.

Where the accused places before the court evidence sufficient to raise an issue that the situation created by external forces was so emergent that failure to act could endanger life or health and that, upon any reasonable view of the facts, compliance with the law was impossible, then the Crown must be prepared to meet that issue and there is no onus of proof on the accused.

6. CONCLUSION

Self-defence, duress, marital coercion and necessity share the notion that the accused committed a crime in order to "help" him or herself or another avoid serious harm. They all have a subjective and objective component, but differ substantially in how these are expressed. With self-defence, there is a growing emphasis on what the accused believed. Most jurisdictions require the belief to be based "on reasonable grounds", but it is clear that the focus is on what the accused (rather than an ordinary person) might reasonably have believed in all the circumstances. With duress and necessity, however, the objective component has been phrased in certain jurisdictions according to a form of the ordinary person test. However, it is unclear whether the ordinary person should be imbued with the personal characteristics of the accused or whether only age will be relevant.

We have outlined the following areas that need further consideration in relation to self-help defences:

- **Are current tests of self-defence adequate? Could self-defence be workable as a purely subjective defence?**

- **Should the doctrine of excessive self-defence be revived, as it has been in South Australia?**

- **Should the defences of duress and necessity be available against a charge of murder?**

- **Should the defence of marital coercion be abolished in those jurisdictions where it still exists?**

The Model Criminal Code Officers Committee's suggestion of following the Code jurisdictions, that is, of having a general defence of sudden or extraordinary emergency that is available to all offences, may go some way toward avoiding the confusion surrounding the objective component for necessity. However, the MCCOC's reformulation of the defence of duress may not go far enough in clarifying the objective component of this defence.

7

Mistake

1. INTRODUCTION

A mistake of fact may be loosely defined as an erroneous belief in the existence of a certain fact or facts. It may be relevant to the question of criminal responsibility in four different ways. It may:

━━ **prevent proof of the requisite fault element;**

━━ **give rise to a belief that forms an element of a defence such as self-defence, provocation, duress or necessity;**

━━ **give rise to a defence to strict liability offences; and**

━━ **have an effect on inchoate forms of liability, such as attempts.**

In Chapter 12, we will consider how the mistake of a complainant may negate consent in the context of the crime of rape. Here, however, we are concerned with how an accused's mistake may be used to avoid criminal responsibility.

At the beginning of the 19th century, it was well established that a mistake of fact could be raised as a defence but only where the mistake was reasonable. Cave J stated in *R v Tolson* (1889) 23 QBD 168 at 181 that "an honest and reasonable belief in the existence of circumstances, which if true, would make the act of the prisoner an innocent act, has always been held to be a good defence". This position had been reflected in the Australian *Criminal Codes* enacted in the 19th century.

It was only in *DPP v Morgan* [1976] AC 182 that a majority of the House of Lords drew a distinction between mistake as a "defence" to strict liability offences and mistake as negating proof of the requisite fault element. The majority in *Morgan's* case found that in the crime of rape, a mistaken belief in consent provided an evidential foundation for raising doubt as to whether the accused possessed the requisite mental state. Since rape required the accused to either know or be reckless as to whether the victim was consenting, as a matter of "inexorable logic", the majority of the House of Lords held that a mistaken belief in consent however unreasonable must negate liability for rape: at 214.

Thus, at common law, an important distinction exists between the operation of mistake as it relates to strict liability offences and mistake as it relates to offences which require proof of a subjective fault element. In relation to strict liability offences, a mistaken belief must not only be honestly held, but *must also be reasonable*. This defence of honest and reasonable mistake is recognised in all Australian jurisdictions. In comparison, when assessing the mental state of an accused, an honest belief in itself may show that the requisite fault element was not present. It is not a "defence" as such.

The situation in the Code jurisdictions is similar to the common law position in that if the accused's mistake is a denial of the fault element, then it need only be an honest one. However, if the mistake concerns a physical element of a crime such as whether or not a substance is a proscribed drug, then the mistake must be both honest and reasonable.[1] We shall explore the vagaries of this distinction between an honest mistake and an honest and reasonable one in 'Perspectives: Mistake and Rape' (p 338) and examine the matter further in Chapter 12: pp 618ff.

Criminal defences such as self-defence, provocation, duress and necessity all involve an assessment of what the accused believed the facts to be when he or she committed the offence. A mistake may therefore support a claim that the accused believed that he or she was, for example, acting in self-defence. Often, however, the particular defence will require the mistaken belief to have been based on reasonable grounds and this may be a difficult hurdle for the accused. The case law on mistake as it relates to criminal defences is few and far between, perhaps, because of this obstacle.

Finally, in relation to the inchoate offences of attempt, conspiracy and incitement, criminal responsibility may be questioned in relation to situations where the accused makes a mistake about the commission of the substantive offence. The question here is whether or not an accused can be found criminally responsible in circumstances when he or she mistakenly believes that the substantive offence can be carried out when in fact it cannot be. The mistake in this case has an inculpatory, rather than exculpatory effect.

In this chapter, we will explore the four scenarios in which an accused's mistake of fact may be relevant in assessing criminal responsibility. We shall explore also the concept of a mistake of law as opposed to a mistake of fact. While as a general rule, ignorance of the law is no excuse to criminal responsibility, there have been a number of exceptions developed where a mistake *of law* may also be taken into account. We will explore these exceptions separately at the end of this chapter.

---

1   *Criminal Code* (NT), s 32; *Criminal Code* (Qld), s 24; *Criminal Code* (Tas), s 14; *Criminal Code* (WA), s 24.

2. MISTAKE OF FACT AND SUBJECTIVE FAULT ELEMENTS

Where a subjective fault element[2] is part of an offence, the prosecution must prove beyond reasonable doubt that the accused possessed intention, knowledge or recklessness.[3] If the accused has an honest but mistaken belief in particular facts, this may indicate an absence of the requisite fault element and the prosecution will fail to prove its case.[4] For example, a person who picks up a book that belongs to someone else, mistakenly believing it to be his or her own, cannot be said to have an intention to deprive the owner of it. This is sometimes referred to as a mistaken belief negating intent,[5] although technically it applies to all the subjective fault elements.

In relation to offences that have subjective fault elements, the honest and mistaken belief held by the accused does not have to be based upon reasonable grounds.[6] However, reasonableness of the belief may be relevant in assessing whether or not the accused actually held the mistaken belief.[7] An accused will be entitled to an acquittal if the prosecution fails to negate the existence of a mistaken belief in certain facts and thus fails to prove that he or she possessed the requisite fault element of the offence charged.

The situation becomes complicated in Australia where knowledge is related to a physical element. It is in this situation that the common law and Code jurisdictions part company. In the Code jurisdictions, if there is a mistaken belief concerning a physical element of a crime, then the mistake must be both honest *and reasonable*.[8] This is not so in the common law jurisdictions. This is best explained by looking at possession of drugs.

In *Clare* (1993) 72 A Crim R 357, the accused was charged with possessing heroin contrary to s 9 of the *Drugs Misuse Act* 1986 (Qld). He admitted that he had in his possession a quantity of white powder, but claimed that he was told and had believed that it was a perfume base. The Queensland Court of Appeal dismissed the accused's appeal against conviction. The Court held that the prosecution had to prove that the accused knowingly had possession of the powder[9] and that the accused could have raised s 24 of the *Criminal Code* to show that he honestly *and reasonably* believed that it was a perfume base. However, on the facts, the Court held that the accused had been properly convicted, Pincus JA (at 377) referring to the accused's "improbable story".

There is also a divergence between the common law and Code jurisdictions in relation to mistaken belief in consent in the crime of rape. This is explored briefly in the following section.

---

2   For an explanation of subjective fault elements see Chapter 3 at p 173.

3   *He Kaw Teh v The Queen* (1985) 157 CLR 523. See Chapter 3 (pp 173ff) for an analysis of these terms.

4   *DPP v Morgan* [1976] AC 182; *He Kaw Teh v The Queen* (1985) 157 CLR 523; *R v McEwan* [1979] 2 NSWLR 926.

5   *R v McEwan* [1979] 2 NSWLR 926.

6   *R v Martin* [1963] Tas SR 103; *DPP v Morgan* [1976] AC 182; *Re A-G (WA) Reference (No 1 of 1977)* [1979] WAR 45; *Arnol* (1981) 7 A Crim R 291; *He Kaw Teh v The Queen* (1985) 157 CLR 523; *R v McEwan* [1979] 2 NSWLR 926.

7   *DPP v Morgan* [1976] AC 182; *R v Saragozza* [1984] VR 187.

8   *Criminal Code* (NT), s 32; *Criminal Code* (Qld), s 24; *Criminal Code* (Tas), s 14; *Criminal Code* (WA), s 24.

9   See further Chapter 15 as to the meaning of knowledge in drug offences: p 850.

PUBLIC POLICY VERSUS LEGAL PRINCIPLE

Mistake and Rape

As we shall explore in Chapter 12, pp 618ff, the requirement that the honest and mistaken belief does not have to be reasonable has been the subject of much criticism particularly with regard to the crime of rape. We set out how in the common law jurisdictions, the fault elements for rape are an intention to have sexual intercourse and knowledge that the victim was not consenting or recklessness in the awareness that the victim might not be consenting.[10] Thus, at common law, if the accused honestly believed the victim was consenting, the fault element cannot be made out. In comparison, there is no specific fault element set out in the rape provisions of the *Criminal Code* jurisdictions.[11] The prosecution need only prove the physical elements of the offence. However, the general defence of honest *and* reasonable mistake of fact is available.[12]

In most rape trials, an accused will argue that the complainant consented to sexual intercourse.[13] In the studies of rape prosecutions in Victoria, an accused argued a mistaken belief in consent in 6% of cases conducted in 1989[14] and only 2.2% of cases conducted in 1992-1993.[15] These percentages are perhaps so low because the accused is conceding that there was no consent. This is therefore a risky defence to run. In a further 17% of cases conducted in 1989[16] and 3.6% of cases conducted in 1992-1993,[17] the defence swung between claiming that the complainant consented, to claiming that even if there was no consent, the accused honestly believed that the complainant was consenting. The implications of this research are further explored in Chapter 12, p 627 'Perspectives: Empirical Data on Consent'.

The main area of concern in mistaken belief cases is whether or not the defence should only raise evidence of an 'honest' but mistaken belief or should be required to raise evidence of an honest *and* reasonable, but mistaken belief. In the common law jurisdictions, the defence need only raise evidence of an honest belief that is tested on a purely subjective basis. The question is simply: Did the accused honestly believe that the other person was consenting? In the Code jurisdictions, on the other hand, the belief must not only be honestly held, but it must also be reasonable. This imposes an objective standard. The question in these jurisdictions is this: Would a reasonable person have believed the other person was consenting?

---

10 *Crimes Act* 1900 (ACT), s 92D(1); *Crimes Act* 1900 (NSW), s 61R(1); *Criminal Law Consolidation Act* 1935 (SA), s 48; *Crimes Act* 1958 (Vic), s 38.

11 *Criminal Code* (NT), s 192(3); *Criminal Code* (Qld), s 347(1); *Criminal Code* (Tas), s 185; *Criminal Code* (WA), s 325.

12 *Criminal Code* (NT), s 32; *Criminal Code* (Qld), s 24; *Criminal Code* (Tas), s 14; *Criminal Code* (WA), s 24.

13 New South Wales Department for Women, *Heroines of Fortitude: The Experience of Women in Court as Victims of Sexual Assault* (Woolloomooloo: 1996), p 52; Law Reform Commission of Victoria, *Rape: Reform of Law and Procedure*, Appendices to Interim Report No 42 (Melbourne: VGPS, 1991), p 86.

14 Law Reform Commission of Victoria, *Rape: Reform of Law and Procedure*, Appendices to Interim Report No 42 (Melbourne: VGPS, 1991), p 87.

15 M Heenan and H McKelvie, *Rape Law Reform Evaluation Project, Report No 2: The Crimes (Rape) Act 1991: An Evaluation Project* (Melbourne: 1997), p 46.

16 Law Reform Commission of Victoria, *Rape: Reform of Law and Procedure*, Appendices to Interim Report No 42 (Melbourne: VGPS, 1991), p 87.

17 M Heenan and H McKelvie, *Rape Law Reform Evaluation Project, Report No 2: The Crimes (Rape) Act 1991: An Evaluation Project* (Melbourne: 1997), p 46.

The main case that governs the law in the Australian Capital Territory, New South Wales, South Australia and Victoria is that of the House of Lords decision in *DPP v Morgan* [1976] AC 182. In that case, Morgan invited three men who were younger than him and junior to him in rank in the RAF, to have sex with his wife. According to the three men, Morgan had told them they must not be surprised if his wife struggled a bit because she was "kinky" and this was the only way in which she could become "turned on". They admitted that the victim had indeed struggled and screamed for help to her young sons when the accused men had held her down and each had intercourse with her. However, they claimed that they honestly believed she was consenting. The three men were convicted of rape and Morgan of aiding and abetting them. (Even though Morgan also had intercourse with his wife without her consent, he was not charged with rape as in 1976 a husband could not be charged with raping his wife.)

On appeal to the House of Lords on a point of law, a majority of three to two held that if an accused honestly believes that the other person is consenting, no rape has occurred. The belief need not be reasonable. Reasonableness, however, can always be taken into account in assessing whether or not the accused in reality honestly believed the other person was consenting.[18] The more unreasonable the accused's alleged mistake, the less likely a jury will accept it.

On the facts, the majority held that it would have been extremely unlikely that any jury would have accepted that the accused men honestly believed the victim was consenting, and upheld their convictions.

Both the Law Reform Commission of Victoria and the Model Criminal Code Officers Committee have examined the principle in *Morgan's* case and have stated that the law should not be changed for the following reasons:

— having a subjective fault element which may be negated by a mistaken belief accords with fundamental principles of criminal responsibility;[19]

— there are no adequate policy reasons for treating rape differently from other serious criminal offences;[20] and

— the meaning of reasonableness is difficult to interpret in the context of sexual assaults.[21]

The primary argument against the principle set out in *Morgan's* case that an accused's belief in consent need only be honest is that it allows men to adhere to outdated notions about sexual behaviour and female sexuality. Lord Cross, one of the two dissenting judges in *Morgan's* case, stated (at 203) that a requirement that a belief in consent be reasonably justifiable on public policy grounds:

---

18   *DPP v Morgan* [1976] AC 182 at 214 per Lord Hailsham; *Crimes Act* 1958 (Vic), s 37(c); *Criminal Code* (NT), s 194A.

19   Model Criminal Code Officers Committee, *Model Criminal Code, Chapter 5: Sexual Offences Against the Person*, Discussion Paper (November 1996), p 67; Law Reform Commission of Victoria, *Rape: Reform of Law and Procedure*, Report No 43 (Melbourne: VGPS, September 1991), pp 10-12.

20   Law Reform Commission of Victoria, *Rape: Reform of Law and Procedure*, Report No 43 (Melbourne: VGPS, September 1991), pp 12-17.

21   Model Criminal Code Officers Committee, *Model Criminal Code, Chapter 5: Sexual Offences Against the Person*, Discussion Paper (November 1996), pp 67-68; Law Reform Commission of Victoria, *Rape: Reform of Law and Procedure*, Report No 43 (Melbourne: VGPS, September 1991), pp 17-18.

> [I]t can be argued with force that it is only fair to the woman and not in the least unfair
> to the man that he should be under a duty to take reasonable care to ascertain that she
> is consenting to the intercourse and be at the risk of a prosecution if he fails to take
> such care.

As with many other areas of the law, the public policy perspective set out by Lord Cross conflicts with the principle that subjective fault is necessary for serious crimes. We examined in Chapter 3 how this principle has been eroded by the plethora of strict and absolute liability offences. In Chapter 12 we will explore further how feminist academics such as Jennifer Temkin and Celia Wells have argued that subjectivism should give way here on policy grounds: pp 620-621.

2.1 CODIFYING HONEST AND REASONABLE BELIEF

The Criminal Law Officers Committee in its Final Report on *General Principles of Criminal Responsibility* (1992) recommended (at 55) that the common law approach to mistaken belief as it relates to intention, knowledge and recklessness should be codified. The Committee took the view that reasonableness should only be relevant to assessing whether or not the accused actually held the belief. Accordingly, s 9.1 (2) of the *Criminal Code Act* 1995 (Cth) states:

> In determining whether a person was under a mistaken belief about, or was ignorant of,
> facts, the tribunal of fact may consider whether the mistaken belief or ignorance was
> reasonable in the circumstances.

Andrew Ashworth in *Principles of Criminal Law* (3rd ed, Oxford: Oxford University Press, 1999), has argued along the lines of the approach taken by the Code jurisdictions that a mistaken belief must be both honest and reasonable. He states (at 242):

> [A subjective enquiry] focuses on D's attitude of mind at the time, but includes no reference
> to the circumstances of the act, to D's responsibilities, or to social expectations of conduct
> in that situation.

It may be that a more contextualised approach to mistake, as demonstrated by the additional requirement of reasonableness in the Code jurisdictions, provides a better way of assessing criminal responsibility. This point is taken up further in Chapter 12, pp 622-623.

3. MISTAKE OF FACT AND CRIMINAL DEFENCES

The availability of a defence such as self-defence, provocation, duress or necessity may be affected by the belief of the accused even where that belief is a mistaken one as to the relevant facts: see in general, AP Simester, "Mistakes in Defence" (1992) 12(2) *Oxford Journal of Legal Studies* 295. There is very little case law on mistake and the criminal defences, presumably because it is an unattractive argument to run. That is, a jury may not be too sympathetic toward an accused who claims he or she made a mistake about being provoked or acting in self-defence. The operation of how mistake might work in relation to each of these defences will be explored in turn.

3.1 SELF-DEFENCE

In Chapter 6 we set out how the law of self-defence in the Australian Capital Territory, New South Wales and Victoria is governed by the High Court decision in *Zecevic v DPP (Vic)* (1987) 162 CLR 645. The test (at 661) is whether the accused believed upon reasonable grounds that it was necessary in self-defence to do what he or she did. This implies that the belief that the accused's conduct was necessary, whether mistaken or not, must be reasonable in the circumstances.

In South Australia and Tasmania, the legislation gives the defence slightly more of a subjective emphasis. Section 46 of the *Criminal Code* (Tas) states that a "person is justified in using, in defence of himself or another person, such force as, in the circumstances as he [or she] believes them to be, it is reasonable to use". Similarly, the South Australian provision allows an accused to use force if that person believes that the force was necessary and reasonable for self-defence and the conduct was reasonably proportionate to the threat that the accused genuinely believed to exist: *Criminal Law Consolidation Act* 1935 (SA), s 15(1) as amended by the *Criminal Law Consolidation (Self-Defence) Amendment Act* 1997. However, the accused's belief still combines with a requirement of reasonableness and again, it would seem that an honest *and reasonable* mistaken belief may form the basis for the defence.

While the Queensland, Northern Territory and Western Australian provisions relating to self-defence are not couched in terms of the accused's belief,[22] it would seem that the general statutory provisions in these jurisdictions relating to an honest and reasonable, but mistaken belief can still be brought into play: *Criminal Code* (NT), s 32; *Criminal Code* (Qld), s 24; *Criminal Code* (WA), s 24.

What is clear from *Zecevic's* case and the statutory provisions in South Australia and Tasmania is that it is the belief of the accused rather than the ordinary person that must be reasonable. This is equally true of the general statutory provisions relating to an honest and reasonable, but mistaken belief in the other jurisdictions. This may require consideration of the accused's personal characteristics that might affect his or her appreciation of the gravity of the threat. Two cases have suggested that intoxication and mistaken beliefs may be taken into account in this regard.

In *R v Conlon* (1993) 69 A Crim R 92 the accused killed two men after they had broken into his farmhouse to steal the former's marijuana plants. The two men had wrestled with the accused and hit him on the head with a heavy plate. The accused ran into the lounge-room where he kept a loaded semi-automatic rifle and then shot both men and subsequently hit one with an axe and slit his throat with a knife. The accused had drunk just under a bottle of whisky in a six hour period before the

---

22   See Chapter 6 for an overview of these provisions: p 294.

event and had been smoking marijuana all afternoon. Hunt CJ presided without a jury at the trial of the accused on two counts of murder. He acquitted the accused on the first count on the basis that the accused's voluntarily induced intoxication affected his belief that he was being threatened and the reasonableness of his response to that danger. Hunt CJ then found the accused guilty of the manslaughter of the victim who was shot, struck with an axe and stabbed on the basis of diminished responsibility.

Hunt CJ pointed out (at 101) that in self-defence the emphasis is placed on the accused's belief, which must be reasonable, rather than the hypothetical reasonable person in the position of the accused. It is necessary to take into account all the relevant characteristics of the accused and surrounding circumstances in assessing whether or not the accused believed on reasonable grounds that he or she was being threatened or attacked and whether the force applied was necessary in self-defence.

The case of *R v Walsh* (1991) 60 A Crim R 419 is also generally cited in relation to mistake in self-defence. This was explored in the section on insane delusions in Chapter 4: pp 214ff. In *Walsh*, the accused argued that he was acting in self-defence when he fired a shotgun at an acquaintance at close range, mistakenly believing that he was defending himself from a Korean soldier. The defence did not rely on the issue of insanity at trial but only self-defence. Slicer J ruled on a voir dire that if such evidence was admitted, the prosecution could raise the issue of mental disease for the purpose of the insanity defence. He also ruled that if the jury found that the delusion was not a disorder falling within the insanity defence, it could then consider its relation to the defence of self-defence. He stated (at 428) that the jury could:

> consider whether, if the accused had a deluded belief, such belief could be a circumstance
> which the accused believed, so as to justify him in using force in the defence of himself,
> and that such belief, although deluded, made it reasonable to use such force.

The jury convicted the accused of murder. An appeal was made to the Full Court of the Supreme Court of Tasmania (unrep, 19/8/1993, CCA47/1992, No A68/19). The Supreme Court quashed the conviction for murder and substituted a finding of not guilty on the ground of insanity. The Supreme Court held that the jury was only entitled to pay regard to the sane beliefs of the accused in relation to the issue of self-defence. They held that the trial judge had been incorrect in directing the jury to reconsider self-defence after considering the defence of insanity because that left the jury with deluded beliefs for further consideration.

Walsh's case therefore supports the proposition that a mistaken belief may be taken into account providing it is "sane" and based upon reasonable grounds.

3.2 PROVOCATION

As explored in Chapter 5, the elements of the defence of provocation are set out by the common law which is followed in South Australia and Victoria and reflected in the statutory provisions of the Australian Capital Territory, New South Wales, the Northern Territory and Tasmania: *Crimes Act* 1900 (ACT), s 13(2); *Crimes Act* 1900 (NSW), s 23(2); *Criminal Code* (NT), s 34; *Criminal Code* (Tas), s 160(2). The common law also has been held to apply to the interpretation of provocation under s 304 of the *Criminal Code* (Qld) which sets out provocation as a partial defence to murder.[23] It seems, however, that the definition of provocation that applies as a defence to assault also applies to the partial defence to murder set out in s 281 of the *Criminal Code* (WA).[24]

The High Court in *Stingel v The Queen* (1990) 171 CLR 312 set out three fundamental requirements for the defence:

▬▬ **there must be provocative conduct;**

▬▬ **the accused must have lost self-control as a result of the provocation; and**

▬▬ **the provocation must be such that it was capable of causing an ordinary person to lose self-control and to act in the way the accused did.[25]**

For the defence of provocation to be successful, the accused must have lost the power of self-control as a result of the provocative conduct. When considering whether or not an accused actually lost self-control, the High Court in *Stingel* stated (at 326) that the jury must consider all the relevant characteristics of the accused and "the totality of the deceased's conduct".

On rare occasions, an accused because of his or her personal characteristics may mistakenly believe that an act of provocation has occurred. It appears that a mistake of fact can still be allowed as a basis for pleading provocation in these circumstances.

In *R v Voukelatos* [1990] VR 1 the accused shot and killed his wife after she attempted to leave him. There was psychiatric evidence led at the trial that the accused was suffering from a delusional disorder and that he falsely believed his wife to be having an affair with their neighbour. The accused appealed against conviction on the basis that provocation could be based solely on the accused's delusional beliefs. The majority, Young CJ and Murphy J, held that in theory, evidence of provocation should be left to the jury even where the accused's belief in provocation was wholly the product of delusion. Young CJ went on to say (at 5) that even if one accepted that the accused was suffering from the delusion that his wife was unfaithful, there was no evidence to suggest that he was provoked by that belief to kill her:

> There was simply nothing in the evidence to suggest that the applicant killed his wife because he was provoked by his deluded belief.

Whilst a mistaken belief in provocation may form the basis for the defence, it may be difficult for a jury to accept that the ordinary person would have lost control in the same way as the accused did. This is because in assessing this question, no personal characteristics apart from age may be taken into account: *Stingel v The Queen* (1990) 171 CLR 312 at 326-327, at 330-331 per the Court. See further Ch 5, p 266.

---

23 *Van Den Hoek v The Queen* (1986) 161 CLR 158 at 168 per Mason J; *R v Johnson* [1964] Qd R 1; *Kaporonovski v The Queen* (1973) 133 CLR 209.

24 *Censori v The Queen* [1983] WAR 89; (1982) 13 A Crim R 263; *Mehemet Ali v The Queen* (1957) 59 WALR 28; *Sreckovic v The Queen* [1973] WAR 85; *Roche v The Queen* [1988] WAR 278; (1987) 2 A Crim R 168.

25 For a discussion of these elements see Chapter 6: pp 297ff.

3.3 DURESS

In Chapter 6, we set out how the defence of duress is recognised at common law in the Australian Capital Territory, New South Wales, South Australia and Victoria. The statutory provisions in the Code jurisdictions of the Northern Territory, Queensland, Tasmania and Western Australia reflect the common law with some variation: *Criminal Code* (NT), s 40; *Criminal Code* (Qld), s 31(4); *Criminal Code* (Tas), s 20(1); *Criminal Code* (WA), s 31(4).

In *R v Hurley and Murray* [1967] VR 536, Smith J stated (at 543) that a defence of duress would be relevant if the following factors existed:

- there was a threat that death or grievous bodily harm would be inflicted unlawfully upon a human being if the accused failed to do the act;

- the circumstances were such that a person of ordinary firmness of mind would have been likely to yield to the threat in the way the accused did;

- the threat was present, continuing, imminent and impending;

- the accused reasonably apprehended that the threat would be carried out;

- the accused was induced to commit the crime because of the threat;

- the crime was not murder, "nor any other crime so heinous so as to be excepted from the doctrine";

- the accused did not expose him or herself to the application; and

- the accused had no means of preventing the execution of the threat.

It would seem from the English cases that an honest and reasonable, but mistaken belief may form the basis for a defence of duress. In *R v Graham* [1982] 1 WLR 294, Lord Lane CJ stated (at 300) that the correct direction in relation to the accused's belief should be:

> Was [the accused], or may he [or she] have been impelled to act as he [or she] did because, as a result of what he [or she] reasonably believed [the threatener] to have said or done, he [or she] had good cause to fear that if he [or she] did not so act [the threatener] would kill him [or her] ... or cause him [or her] serious physical injury?

There are no Australian cases directly on point, but it may be that Australian courts will also opt for an honest and reasonable belief approach in the same way that they have in relation to self-defence: see S Yeo, *Compulsion in the Criminal Law* (Sydney: Law Book Company Ltd, 1990), p 229.

3.4 NECESSITY

In Chapter 6 we outlined how the common law governs the defence of necessity in the Australian Capital Territory, New South Wales, South Australia, Tasmania and Victoria. The *Criminal Codes* of the Northern Territory, Queensland and Western Australia contain the defence of sudden or extraordinary emergency[26] which substantially follows the common law defence.

---

26 *Criminal Code* (NT), s 33; *Criminal Code* (Qld), s 25; *Criminal Code* (WA), s 25.

In *R v Loughnan* [1981] VR 443 Young CJ and King J (at 448) summarised the elements of the defence of necessity as follows:

[T]here are three elements involved in the defence of necessity. First, the criminal act or acts must have been done only in order to avoid certain consequences which would have inflicted irreparable evil upon the accused or upon others whom he [or she] was bound to protect.

The [second] element [is] that the accused must honestly believe on reasonable grounds that he [or she] was placed in a situation of imminent peril ... Thus if there is an interval of time between the threat and its expected execution it will be very rarely if ever that a defence of necessity can succeed.

The [third] element of proportion simply means that the acts done to avoid the imminent peril must not be out of proportion to the peril to be avoided. Put in another way, the test is: would a reasonable [person] in the position of the accused have considered that he [or she] had any alternative to doing what he [or she] did to avoid the peril?

The second element concerns an honest belief on reasonable grounds that a situation of imminent peril has arisen. The situation of imminent peril may not in fact exist and it appears that it will be sufficient if the accused honestly and reasonably (but mistakenly) believed that the situation existed. However, this may be difficult for the tribunal of fact to accept. For example, in *Limbo v Little* (1989) 45 A Crim R 61 the applicant Lenin Limbo claimed the defence of necessity regarding his trespass of the Pine Gap nuclear facility. He claimed that the human race and the planet were in danger of imminent destruction from nuclear war or accident and this made it necessary for him to take action. On appeal against conviction for trespass, Martin J stated (at 78) the "test of necessity ... is whether [the accused] honestly believed on reasonable grounds that he was placed in a situation of imminent peril, as at the time he trespassed". Martin J went on to say (at 88) "the word 'certain' in the foundation of the defence by the majority in *Loughnan* bears the sense of inevitable, something bound to happen or which could not otherwise be avoided, as opposed to something not named or specified". Martin J concluded that the defence of necessity had not been made out in this case because the situation was not one of inevitable peril.

4. MISTAKE OF FACT AND STRICT LIABILITY OFFENCES

There are many statutory offences that allow for criminal responsibility to be established upon proof of the physical element alone: see Ch 3, pp 189ff. However, in most instances, an honest and reasonable mistake in facts which, if they existed, would render the accused's conduct innocent, may afford an excuse.

This "defence" may be excluded expressly or by implication. If it is excluded, then the offence is said to be one of "absolute liability": see Ch 3, p 191. If it still operates, the offence is said to be one of "strict liability". Absolute liability offences are still rare in Australia and the defence of honest and reasonable mistake of fact is usually available to qualify the literal reading of the statutory offence.[27]

The "defence" of honest and reasonable mistake of fact is sometimes referred to as the *Proudman v Dayman* defence after the name of the High Court case that first developed it: (1941) 67 CLR 536. In that case, the accused was charged with allowing an unlicensed person to drive a motor vehicle on the road contrary to s 30 of the *Road Traffic Act* 1934-39 (SA). She was convicted and appealed to the Supreme Court of South Australia on the basis that she believed that the person who drove her car held a current licence and that she had reasonable grounds for that belief. Cleland J set aside the conviction. On further appeal to the Full Court, her conviction was restored. Special leave to appeal to the High Court was refused. In the course of considering the application for special leave, the court accepted that an honest and reasonable mistake may exculpate an accused, but held that this had not been made out on the facts. Dixon J stated (at 540):

> It is one thing to deny that a necessary ingredient of the offence is positive knowledge of the fact that the driver holds no subsisting licence. It is another to say that an honest belief founded on reasonable grounds that he [or she] is licensed cannot exculpate a person who permits him [or her] to drive. As a general rule an honest and reasonable belief in a state of facts which, if they existed, could make the defendant's act innocent affords an excuse for doing what would otherwise be an offence.

The "defence" at common law therefore has a number of components:

=== **there must be a mistake and not mere ignorance;**

=== **the mistake must be one of fact and not law;**

=== **the mistake must be honest and reasonable; and**

=== **the mistake must render the accused's act innocent.**

Mistake of fact is expressly referred to in the *Criminal Code* jurisdictions.[28] In Tasmania, the defence is similar to that at common law in that it is available only where no offence would have been committed on the facts as they were believed to be. In the Northern Territory, Queensland and Western Australia, the defence operates somewhat differently to that at common law and in Tasmania. It is somewhat broader in enabling a mistaken belief to lead to a conviction for a lesser offence as well as to an acquittal. In these jurisdictions, if an accused honestly and reasonable believed in facts that would render him or her guilty of a lesser offence or to a lower penalty, then he or she can be convicted of that lesser offence or given a lower penalty. The fourth component set out

---

27 *Hawthorn (Department of Health) v Morcam Pty Ltd* (1992) 29 NSWLR 120 (CCA NSW); *Pollard v DPP (Cth)* (1992) 28 NSWLR 659 (CCA NSW); *R v Wampfler* (1987) 11 NSWLR 541 at 547; *Strathfield Municipal Council v Elvy* (1992) 25 NSWLR 745 (CCA NSW); *Given v CV Holland (Holdings) Pty Ltd* (1977) 15 ALR 439; *Von Lieven v Stewart* (1990) 21 NSWLR 52; *Binskin v Watson* (1990) 48 A Crim R 33 (CA NSW); *Darwin Bakery Pty Ltd v Sully* (1981) 36 ALR 371; *Universal Telecasters (Qld) Ltd v Guthrie* (1978) 18 ALR 531; *Schmid v Keith Quinn Motor Co Pty Ltd* (1987) 47 SASR 96 (SC SA); *Cooper v ICI Australia Operations Pty Ltd* (1987) 31 A Crim R 267 (Land and Environment Ct NSW); *Browning v Barrett* [1987] Tas R 122 (SC Tas); *Minogue v Briggs* (1987) 79 ALR 525 (SC Tas).

28 *Criminal Code* (NT), s 32; *Criminal Code* (Qld), s 24; *Criminal Code* (Tas), s 14; *Criminal Code* (WA), s 24.

at common law that the mistake must render the accused's act "innocent" thus does not apply in the Northern Territory, Queensland and Western Australia.

The other components of the defence, however, are very similar in both Code and common law jurisdictions and we will examine these in turn. The Criminal Law Officers Committee in its Final Report on *General Principles of Criminal Responsibility* (1992) supported (at 55) the adoption of the defence of honest and reasonable mistake of fact in relation to strict liability offences. Section 9.2 of the *Criminal Code Act* 1995 (Cth) accordingly states:

(1) A person is not criminally responsible for an offence that has a physical element for which there is no fault element if:

(a) at or before the time of the conduct constituting the physical element, the person considered whether or not facts existed, and is under a mistaken but reasonable belief about those facts; and

(b) had those facts existed, the conduct would not have constituted an offence.

(2) A person may be regarded as having considered whether or not facts existed if:

(a) he or she had considered, on a previous occasion, whether those facts existed in the circumstances surrounding that occasion; and

(b) he or she honestly and reasonably believed that the circumstances surrounding the present occasion were the same, or substantially the same, as those surrounding the previous occasion.

4.1 MISTAKE RATHER THAN IGNORANCE

In all jurisdictions, there is a distinction made between a positive act of making a mistake and simply not thinking about the matter at all.[29] In *Proudman v Dayman* (1941) 67 CLR 536, the High Court refused the accused leave to appeal on the basis that she had not made a mistake, she had simply not adverted to the question as to whether or not the driver was licensed. A mistake therefore can only be made where there is a positive or affirmative belief present.[30]

A positive belief is more than a mere absence of knowledge or ignorance. The accused must have turned his or her mind to the relevant facts.[31] For example, in *Green v Sergeant* [1951] VR 500, the accused was charged with killing native game on a proclaimed sanctuary. He claimed that he did not know that the area was a sanctuary. It was held by Martin J that there was no defence available because (at 504-505):

his ignorance of the nature of the area in which he was engaged does not necessarily mean that he had an honest belief in a state of facts which, if they existed, would make his action innocent ... He really had no belief on the subject, for it never entered his head what was the nature of the property where he was.

---

29 *State Rail Authority (NSW) v Hunter Water Board* (1992) 28 NSWLR 721 at 724-726 per Gleeson CJ: *Australian Iron and Steel Pty Ltd v Environment Protection Authority* (1992) 29 NSWLR 497 at 507-513 per Abadee J.

30 *State Rail Authority (NSW) v Hunter Water Board* (1992) 28 NSWLR 721; *Von Lieven v Stewart* (1990) 21 NSWLR 52 at 66-67; *Bergin v Stack* (1953) 88 CLR 248 at 261 per Fullagar J; *Maher v Musson* (1934) 52 CLR 100.

31 *Gherashe v Boase* [1959] VR 1; *Bergin v Stack* (1953) 88 CLR 248.

Inadvertence will therefore not amount to a mistake.[32] The belief must also relate to the elements of the particular offence.[33]

In practice, however, there is reason to believe that the courts will take a flexible approach to the distinction between not turning one's mind to the facts and making a mistake. In *Mayer v Marchant* (1973) 5 SASR 567, the accused was the owner of a tanker that carried a load of distillate. The tanker was loaded and driven by the accused's employee. The distillate was of an unusually high density and the accused and his employee were both unaware of this. The tanker was found to be overloaded by one ton and the accused was charged with being the owner of an overloaded vehicle contrary to ss 144 and 146 of the *Road Traffic Act* 1961 (SA). Eighteen months previously, the accused had made a number of weighbridge checks of different samples of distillate to work out that 6,400 gallons was an appropriate limit. This amount of distillate would produce weights at or near the statutory limit and not more than two or three hundredweight in excess. The magistrate acquitted the accused of the charge and the prosecution then appealed to the Supreme Court of South Australia.

A majority of the Supreme Court agreed that the accused should be acquitted, but on the basis that the appropriate defence was that of an act of a stranger. In relation to the defence of honest and reasonable mistake of fact, the Court considered that it was not necessary to show that the accused had thought about whether or not the particular load in question was overweight. The accused's ignorance of the unusually high density of the distillate was irrelevant. Rather, the question concerned whether or not the accused had a general belief that a certain number of gallons of distillate would produce a load of a certain weight and whether this was an honest and reasonable belief.

Thus, the Supreme Court was prepared to look at whether a general mistake had been made rather than assessing the accused's ignorance of the actual weight of the load. This suggests that courts may take a rather flexible approach to the distinction between ignorance and mistake.

4.2 MISTAKE OF FACT

The mistake at common law must be one of fact and not law.[34] Under s 14 of the *Criminal Code* (Tas) the mistake must relate to a "state of facts", whereas in the other Code jurisdictions, the words "state of things" is used.[35] These words have been interpreted as meaning a belief in relation to *present* facts, rather than future events or consequences.[36]

It is often difficult to make a distinction between fact and law as there are no clear tests for determining the difference between the two. Glanville Williams in *Criminal Law: The General Part* (2nd ed, London: Stevens & Sons, 1961) stated (p 287) that:

---

32   *Von Lieven v Stewart* (1990) 21 NSWLR 52 at 66 per Handley JA; *State Rail Authority (NSW) v Hunter District Water Board* (1992) 65 A Crim R 101.

33   *State Rail Authority (NSW) v Hunter Water Board* (1992) 28 NSWLR 721.

34   *He Kaw Teh v The Queen* (1985) 157 CLR 523; *Iannella v French* (1968) 119 CLR 84 at 114-115 per Windeyer J; *Strathfield Municipal Council v Elvy* (1992) 25 NSWLR 745; *Von Lieven v Stewart* (1990) 21 NSWLR 52; *Griffin v Marsh* (1994) 34 NSWLR 52; *State Rail Authority v Hunter Water Board* (1992) 28 NSWLR 721.

35   *Criminal Code* (NT), s 32; *Criminal Code* (Qld), s 24; *Criminal Code* (WA), s 24.

36   *R v Gould and Barnes* [1960] Qd R 283; *R v McCullough* [1982] Tas R 43.

> Generally speaking a fact is something perceptible by the senses, while law is an idea in the minds of [individuals] ... the definition of a fact as something perceptible by the senses needs qualification in one respect. A state of mind is also a fact, though not directly perceptible by the senses.

Thus, questions concerning, for example, the speed at which a car was travelling, or whether the accused stabbed the victim can be considered questions of fact because the answers can be perceived by the senses. On the other hand, questions concerning the effect of a statutory provision, the elements of an offence, or whether a person or thing falls within a statutory description[37] are said to be matters of law. If there is some mixture between the two, that is "a mistake as to the existence of a compound event consisting of law and fact", the mistake will generally be treated as one of fact.[38] Thus, if a mistaken belief as to the law is flawed by an earlier mistake as to a relevant and important fact, the mistake will be taken to be one of fact: *Griffin v Marsh* (1994) 34 NSWLR 104 at 118 per Smart J.

For example, in *Thomas v The Queen* (1937) 59 CLR 279, the accused was convicted of bigamy. The High Court allowed an appeal and quashed his conviction on the basis that there had been an honest and reasonable mistake of fact. The accused argued that he had believed that he was an unmarried man and therefore free to marry because of a mistaken belief that his former marriage was void. The accused thought that his first wife was not validly divorced from her first husband because of an erroneous belief that there had not been a "decree absolute" or final order made. This complex mixture of mistaken beliefs was treated as a compound event consisting of law and fact and therefore ultimately one of fact which could provide a defence.

A mistake of law has been held to occur where the accused made a mistake as to the legal effect or legal significance of facts known to him or her[39] and where the accused mistakenly believed that the act in question was lawful because it was unregulated or because the requirements of law had been satisfied.[40]

Once all the facts are known, incorrect legal advice in relation to them has been taken to be a mistake of law.[41] The status of a mistake of law is examined below at p 363.

4.3 HONEST AND REASONABLE MISTAKE

The mistake made by the accused must not only be honestly held, it must also be based upon reasonable grounds.[42] An honest belief is simply one that is held in fact: *GJ Coles & Co Ltd v Goldsworthy* [1985] WAR 183 at 187 per Burt CJ. Although the qualification "honest" or "genuine" is

---

37 *Ianella v French* (1968) 119 CLR 84 at 114 per Windeyer J.

38 *R v Thomas* (1937) 59 CLR 279 at 306 per Dixon J; *Iannella v French* (1968) 119 CLR 84 at 115 per Windeyer J; *Power v Huffa* (1976) 14 SASR 337 at 344-345 per Bray CJ, at 355 per Zelling J, at 356 per Jacobs J.

39 *Pollard v DPP (Cth)* (1992) 28 NSWLR 659 at 678 per Abadee J; *Strathfield Municipal Council v Elvy* (1992) 25 NSWLR 745; *Khammash v Rowbottom* (1989) 51 SASR 172; *Griffin v Marsh* (1994) 34 NSWLR 104.

40 *Von Lieven v Stewart* (1990) 21 NSWLR 52.

41 *Pollard v DPP (Cth)* (1992) 28 NSWLR 659; *Crichton v Victorian Dairies Ltd* [1965] VR 49.

42 *Proudman v Dayman* (1941) 67 CLR 536; *He Kaw Teh v The Queen* (1985) 157 CLR 523; *Gherashe v Boase* [1959] VR 1; *Handmer v Taylor* [1971] VR 308.

logically redundant, it draws the jury's attention to the need to scrutinise claims of mistaken belief carefully. This function is further explored in the context of rape cases in Chapter 12, 'Restricting the Mistaken Belief in Consent Defence': p 622.

A belief based on reasonable grounds is one that is based upon the accused's "appreciation of primary objective fact that is in reason capable of sustaining the belief".[43] A mistake made carelessly is not a reasonable one: *GJ Coles & Co Ltd v Goldsworthy* [1985] WAR 183 at 188 per Burt CJ.

4.4 MISTAKE MUST RENDER THE ACCUSED'S ACT INNOCENT

At common law and in Tasmania, an honest and reasonable but mistaken belief in a set of facts will only exculpate an accused if the truth of the belief would mean that no offence was being committed, making the accused's act innocent.[44]

This reference to "innocent" in this regard has been taken to mean "not a breach of the criminal law".[45] For example, in *Bergin v Stack* (1953) 88 CLR 248 the accused, who was employed by a club, was charged with selling liquor without a licence. The accused had not inquired whether the club had a liquor licence, but simply assumed that it did. In any case, the accused sold the alcohol after 6 pm when no club could be licensed to sell liquor. It was held that the accused's mistake, if it could be called that, would not have rendered the act innocent as selling liquor after 6 pm was still a breach of the criminal law.

4.5 BURDEN OF PROOF

The prosecution bears the legal burden of disproving a mistake of fact: *Proudman v Dayman* (1941) 67 CLR 536. The defence bears the evidential burden of providing evidence of an exculpatory mistake of fact or pointing to evidence in the prosecution's case from which such a mistake may be inferred: *He Kaw Teh v The Queen* (1985) 157 CLR 523. Earlier cases seemed to suggest a higher burden be placed on the defence, but this is no longer correct. Dawson J stated in *He Kaw Teh v The Queen* (1985) 157 CLR 523 at 592-593:

> There is ... no justification since *Woolmington v DPP* [[1935] AC 462] for regarding the
> defence of honest and reasonable mistake as placing any special onus upon an accused
> who relies upon it. No doubt the burden of providing the necessary foundation in evidence
> will in most cases fall upon the accused. But it is not inconceivable that during the case for

---

43 *GJ Coles & Co Ltd v Goldsworthy* [1985] WAR 183 at 187-188 per Burt CJ; *Gibbon v Fitzmaurice* [1986] Tas R 137 at 154
    per Nettlefold J.
44 *Proudman v Dayman* (1941) 67 CLR 536 at 540 per Dixon J; *Bergin v Stack* (1953) 88 CLR 248 at 262 per Fullagar J;
    Criminal Code (Tas), s 14.
45 *Bergin v Stack* (1953) 88 CLR 248; *R v Reynhoudt* (1962) 107 CLR 381 at 389 per Kitto J; *R v Iannazzone* [1983]
    1 VR 649 at 655 per Brooking J.

the prosecution sufficient evidence may be elicited by way of cross-examination or otherwise to establish honest and reasonable mistake or to cast sufficient doubt upon the prosecution case to entitle the accused to an acquittal. The governing principle must be that which applies generally in the criminal law. There is no onus upon the accused to prove honest and reasonable mistake upon the balance of probabilities.

4.6 CRIMINAL NEGLIGENCE AND DUE DILIGENCE

Occasionally there are statements to the effect that there may be scope for developing a defence of due diligence at common law, independent of a defence of honest and reasonable mistake: see for example, *Australian Iron and Steel Pty Ltd v Environment Protection Authority* (1992) 29 NSWLR 497 at 498-499 per Badgery-Parker J. However, such a defence does not currently exist at common law[46] although statutory provisions may recognise such a defence.

It appears that the defence of honest and reasonable mistake of fact is not equivalent to an absence of negligence or the presence of due diligence[47] because taking reasonable steps to avoid an event is not the same as making a reasonable mistake. One case that suggests otherwise is that of *Allen v United Carpet Mills Pty Ltd* [1989] VR 323, a decision of a single judge of the Supreme Court of Victoria. In that case, Nathan J (at 327) was prepared to accept that a defence of taking all reasonable care and diligence could be subsumed within the concept of honest and reasonable mistake and should be available to offences of strict liability. It should be noted, however, that this statement was *obiter* as the case concerned an offence that was classified as one of absolute liability.

Due Diligence in Canada

In *R v City of Sault Ste Marie* (1978) 40 CCC (2d) 353, the Supreme Court of Canada held that a defence of honest and reasonable mistake would be established if the accused reasonably believed in a mistaken set of facts which if true would render the act innocent. This is the same position as the common law in Australia. However, the Court went on to say that a defence would also be available if the accused took all reasonable steps to avoid the particular event. Dickson J, in delivering the judgment of the Court, clarified (at 373) that the burden is on the accused to prove on the balance of probabilities that he or she acted with reasonable care. Placing the burden of proof on the accused has subsequently been held to be a reasonable limit on the guarantee to the presumption of innocence.[48]

---

46 *Australian Iron and Steel Pty Ltd v Environment Protection Authority* (1992) 29 NSWLR 497 at 510 per Abadee J.

47 *Australian Iron and Steel Pty Ltd v Environment Protection Authority* (1992) 29 NSWLR 497 at 509-510 per Abadee J.

48 *R v Wholesale Travel Group Inc* [1991] 3 SCR 154; *R v Ellis Don* (1992) 71 CCC(3d) 63n. See in general A Tuck-Jackson, "The Defence of Due Diligence and the Presumption of Innocence" (1990) 33(1) *Criminal Law Quarterly* 11; NJ Stranz, "Beyond *R v Sault Ste Marie*: The Creation and Expansion of Strict Liability and the 'Due Diligence' Defence" (1992) 30(4) *Alberta Law Review* 1233; J Keefe, "The Due Diligence Defence: A Wholesale Review (1993) 35(4) *Criminal Law Quarterly* 480.

For regulatory offences imposing strict or absolute liability, the legislature often makes available the defence of "due diligence". Due diligence is in law the converse of negligence: *Tesco Supermarkets v Nattrass* [1972] AC 153 at 199 per Lord Diplock. The question of whether an accused has taken "reasonable care" is a question of fact for the jury or magistrate, and it seems that different standards of care have been applied for different types of offences: D Parry, "Judicial Approaches to Due Diligence" [1995] Crim LR 695. In Australia, due diligence is a statutory defence for many consumer, corporate and environmental offences: see for example, *Environment Protection Act* 1997 (ACT), s 153; *Protection of the Environment Operations Act* 1997 (NSW), s 118; *Environment Protection Act* 1970 (Vic), s 66B(4B)(c); *Trade Practices Act* 1974 (Cth), s 85; P Lowe, "A Comparative Analysis of Australian and Canadian Approaches to the Defence of Due Diligence" (1997) 14 (2) *Environmental and Planning Law Journal* 102; S Christensen, "Criminal Liability of Directors and the Role of Due Diligence in their Exculpation" (1993) 11(6) *Company And Securities Law Journal* 340. Reliance on legal advice, even if mistaken, may support a claim of due diligence: K Amirthalingam, "Mistake of Law: A Criminal Offence or a Reasonable Defence? (1994) 18 Crim LJ 271 at 279-280. See generally W Duncan and S Traves, *Due Diligence* (Sydney: Law Book Company Ltd, 1995).

5. MISTAKE AND INCHOATE OFFENCES

In relation to the inchoate offences of attempt, conspiracy and incitement, criminal responsibility may be questioned in relation to situations where the accused makes a mistake about the commission of the substantive offence. Often dealt with under the title "impossibility", there are many scenarios that may be envisaged here. Antony Duff and Eugene Meehan both give numerous examples in their respective books on criminal attempts: RA Duff, *Criminal Attempts* (Oxford: Oxford University Press, 1996), Ch 3; E Meehan, *The Law of Criminal Attempt — A Treatise* (Calgary: Carswell Legal Publications, 1984), Ch 6. We will outline four main scenarios. The accused may intend to commit an offence, but makes a mistake concerning:

(1) *The conduct itself which is not in fact a crime*. For example, the accused may mistakenly believe that importing foreign currency is an offence or committing adultery is a crime. There is thus a belief in an "imaginary crime" and this is generally referred to as *legal* impossibility.

(2) *The means of carrying out the offence*. For example, the poison used was too little to kill or the victim was out of range of the rifle.

(3) *The existence of the person or thing aimed at*. For example, the accused stabs a corpse believing it to be a living person or there is no money in the pocket or safe.

(4) *The circumstances or facts accompanying the conduct such that an element of the offence was absent*. For example, the goods received were not stolen or the sexual partner was not under 16.

The third and fourth categories are often referred to as *factual* or *physical* impossibility. In *R v Donnelly* [1970] NZLR 980, Turner J stated (at 990-991) concerning this category:

[The accused] may find what he [or she] is proposing to do is after all impossible — not because of insufficiency of means, but because it is for some reason physically not possible, whatever means be adopted. He [or she] who walks into a room intending to steal, say a specific diamond ring, and finds that the ring is no longer there, but has been removed by the owner to the bank, is thus prevented from committing the crime which he [or she] intended, and which, but for the supervening physical impossibility imposed by events he [or she] would have committed.

The first category of mistake has traditionally permitted the accused to escape criminal responsibility for inchoate crimes. Where the most debate has occurred is between the categories of insufficiency of means and physical impossibility. In England, there was a distinction drawn between these categories such that physical impossibility was a bar to conviction for attempts, conspiracy and incitement. This distinction no longer exists in Australian jurisdictions except in South Australia.

Whether physical impossibility should be taken into account in exculpating an accused from criminal responsibility depends to a large extent upon whether one takes a fault-centred or act-centred approach to inchoate crimes. On a fault centred approach, both a mistake about insufficiency of means and physical impossibility will be irrelevant to criminal responsibility. If the accused believed that the offence could be committed in circumstances when it could not be, his or her state of mind is just as blameworthy as if the offence were able to be carried out. Ashworth writes in *Principles of Criminal Law* (3rd ed, Oxford: Oxford University Press, 1999), p 469:

> [W]e are justified in convicting the person who smuggles dried lettuce leaves in the belief that they are cannabis, and the person who puts sugar in someone's drink in the belief that it is cyanide, and the person who handles goods in the belief that they are stolen. In all these cases there is no relevant moral difference between their culpability and the culpability in cases where the substances *really* are cannabis, cyanide, and stolen goods.

If one takes an act-centred approach, however, physical impossibility should act as a bar to conviction. This approach emphasises the lack of harm or danger in circumstances where an offence cannot be carried out. That is, the criminal law should not be used to criminalise conduct that does not have the potential to cause harm: see J Temkin, "Impossible Attempts: Another View" (1976) 39 *Modern Law Review* 55. Liberal notions of the prevention of harm are explored in Chapter 1, pp 49ff. The alternate "subjective" approach places great weight on the accused's beliefs, with the resulting danger that convictions might be based on confessions that have been extracted through police pressure. This approach is taken up in 'A Criminal Process Perspective: Attempts and Physical Impossibility': see p 359.

We will first outline why it is that "legal impossibility" acts as a bar to criminal responsibility before dealing with the traditional distinction between insufficiency of means and physical impossibility.

5.1 MISTAKE AND LEGAL IMPOSSIBILITY

Traditionally, the common law has drawn a distinction between "legal" and "physical" or "factual" impossibility. Legal impossibility in relation to inchoate crimes refers to evidence of an intention to commit an imaginary crime such as importing an object believing it to be illegal to do so when it is not in fact prohibited. Physical impossibility deals with evidence of an intention to commit a crime, but a circumstance unknown to the accused prevents it from being accomplished.

In *R v Taaffe* [1984] AC 539, the accused brought some packages into England, believing them to contain foreign currency and believing this was prohibited. The packages actually contained cannabis, the importation of which was illegal, but the importation of currency was not prohibited. He was convicted of being "knowingly concerned in [the] fraudulent evasion" of the prohibition of certain goods. The Court of Appeal in *Taaffe* (1983) 77 Crim App R 82 at 85 upheld his appeal on the basis that he should be judged "against the facts that he believed them to be". That is, the accused believed he was importing currency and he mistakenly believed this was illegal. Lord Lane CJ (at 85-86) said that the accused's mistake of law:

> no doubt made his actions morally reprehensible. It did not ... turn what he ... believed to be the importation of currency into the commission of a criminal offence.

Duff in his book *Criminal Attempts* (Oxford: Oxford University Press, 1996) (p 93) points out that:

> Cases of *purely* imaginary crimes are unlikely to come to court; a repentant adulterer who walked into a British police station to give herself up for this supposed crime would be told to go home (emphasis in original).

But *Taaffe's* case obviously goes further than believing in a purely imaginary crime. Taaffe intended to commit a crime and he would have in fact committed a crime had he believed he was carrying cannabis rather than currency. Why should a mistake of law excuse in this instance when a mistake of law or ignorance of law will generally not provide an accused with a defence to a crime? Taking a subjectivist approach to criminalisation, Taaffe intended to break the law and, if caught early enough, should at least be convicted of attempting to commit a crime. As we point out in Chapter 10, the law of attempt is concerned with a set fault element, that of intention, but an undefined physical element. One could argue that this could be made out in the circumstances of *Taaffe*.

Ashworth agrees that a subjective approach would convict someone like Taaffe, but the subjectivist approach is here "outweighed by the principle of legality": "Criminal Attempts and the Role of Resulting Harm under the Code, and in the Common Law" (1988) 19 *Rutgers Law Journal* 725 at 762. In addition, Nix CJ of the Supreme Court of Pennsylvania has pointed out in *Henley*, 474 A 2d 1115 (1984) at 1120 that an "abstract inclination to violate the law must be concretized into an intent to engage in specific conduct which ... would amount to a violation of the criminal law". Criminal responsibility should thus reflect a willingness to engage in conduct that the law actually prohibits, not crime in the abstract.

Sections 11.1(4), 11.4(3), 11.5(3)(a) of the *Criminal Code Act* 1995 (Cth) (which deal with inchoate offences) state that a person may be found guilty even if committing the substantive offence is impossible. Similarly, the provisions dealing with attempts and conspiracy in the *Crimes Act* 1914 (Cth) enable a conviction where the substantive offence is impossible: *Crimes Act* 1914 (Cth), ss 7(3)(a), 86(4)(a). No such provision appears in s 7A dealing with incitement. These provisions appear to go further than the usual statutory ones that refer to impossibility in relation to circumstances or facts. Legal impossibility would also seem to be encompassed by these provisions.

In fact, the Criminal Law Officers Committee (CLOC) stated in 1992 in relation to attempts that "impossibility arising by reason of matters of fact *or law* should no longer be a bar to conviction" (emphasis added): *Chapter 2: General Principles of Criminal Responsibility*, Final Report (1992), p 81. CLOC, however, did not explain why a conviction would be appropriate in cases where it is legally impossible for the accused to commit the offence. In our view charging individuals with imaginary crimes would extend the criminal law much too far. It would be oppressive and ultimately unworkable. For example, many people believe that trespassing is a crime rather than a tort and signs on property reinforce this. Would this conduct now be a criminal offence? How would the judge determine the sentence? Would it be on the basis of what the accused believed would have been the punishment for committing this imagined offence? Upon closer examination this model of reform is simply unworkable and unjust.

5.2 MISTAKE AND PHYSICAL IMPOSSIBILITY

ATTEMPTS

In relation to attempts, all Australian jurisdictions, apart from South Australia, criminalise all cases of mistaken beliefs apart from those relating to imaginary crimes, providing the accused's conduct is sufficiently proximate to the offence.[49] Up until 1981, the English position was that only situations of mistake about the adequacy of means attracted criminal responsibility. This is still the case in South Australia as the Full Court of the Supreme Court followed this approach in *R v Collingridge* (1976) 16 SASR 117.

The House of Lords decision that distinguished between mistake concerning the adequacy of means used and situations of "physical" impossibility was *Haughton v Smith* [1975] AC 476. In that case, the police intercepted a van full of stolen corned beef. They allowed the van to proceed after two police officers installed themselves inside. They then arrested the accused when he met the van in order to unload the goods. Because the goods ceased to be stolen when the police intercepted them, the accused was charged with and convicted of attempting to handle stolen goods. This was on the basis that s 24(3) of the *Theft Act* 1968 (UK) stated that goods were not considered stolen "after they have been restored to the person from whom they were stolen or to other lawful possession or custody". The offence of handling is reviewed in Chapter 13, pp 729ff.

The House of Lords quashed the accused's conviction on the basis that it was physically impossible for the accused to commit the completed offence as the goods were no longer stolen. Lord Morris, observing (at 501) that the "goods that [the accused] had, in fact, handled were not stolen", posed the question: "How then, can it be said that he attempted to handle stolen goods?" Eugene Meehan in *The Law of Criminal Attempt — A Treatise* (Calgary: Carswell Legal Publications, 1984) writes of this (p 191):

---

49 *Crimes Act* 1914 (Cth), s 7(3)(a); *Criminal Code* (NT), s 4(3); *Criminal Code* (Qld), ss 4, 4(3); *Criminal Code* (Tas), s 2(2); *Crimes Act* (Vic), s 321N(3); *Criminal Code* (WA), s 4; *Britten v Alpogut* [1987] VR 929 at 938 per Murphy J; *R v Mai* (1992) 26 NSWLR 371 at 381-384 per Hunt CJ; *R v Lee* (1990) 1 WAR 411 at 423 per Malcolm CJ; *R v Prior* (1992) 91 NTR 53.

The House answered this question ill-advisedly. The Lords confused liability for an attempt and liability for the completed crime, and in the process eliminated attempt. Smith *did* attempt to receive the stolen goods; he was not in London to see the sights, he was there to direct the distribution of the previously stolen corned beef, which he was actually doing.

The decision in *Haughton v Smith* attracted much academic criticism[50] due to the difficulty in dividing situations into physical and other sorts of impossibility and because of its lack of clarity between an attempt and the substantive offence. The Law Commission of England and Wales conducted a major review of impossibility and inchoate crimes and recommended that physical impossibility should be irrelevant to criminal responsibility: Law Commission, *Attempt and Impossibility in Relation to Attempt, Conspiracy and Incitement*, Report No 102 (London: HMSO, 1980). Subsequently, the *Criminal Attempts Act* 1981 (UK) was enacted. Section 1(2) of that Act provides that a person may be guilty of an attempt "even though the facts are such that the commission of the offence is impossible".

The House of Lords initially had some difficulty in accepting the intention of Parliament in *Anderton v Ryan* [1985] AC 560. The accused had purchased a VCR believing it to be stolen, whereas in fact it was not. She was charged and convicted with attempted handling of stolen goods. The House of Lords held that she could not be guilty of attempt in these circumstances because her conduct was "objectively innocent". This decision flatly contradicted the clear intention of Parliament.

One year later the House of Lords acknowledged its mistake in *R v Shivpuri* [1987] AC 1. The accused believed that he was importing into the United Kingdom heroin and cannabis. He was arrested, but a chemical analysis proved that the substance imported was dried cabbage leaves. The House of Lords reversed the decision in *Anderton v Ryan* on the basis that the notion of "objective innocence" was unworkable. This case was one of factual or physical impossibility and the accused had been rightly convicted of attempt. Lord Bridge stated (at 21-22):

> I am satisfied on further consideration that the concept of "objective innocence" is incapable of sensible application in relation to the law of criminal attempts. The reason for this is that any attempt to commit an offence which involves "an act which is more than merely preparatory to the commission of the offence" but for any reason fails, so that in the event no offence is committed, must ... be "objectively innocent". What turns what would otherwise, from the point of view of the criminal law, be an innocent act into a crime is the intent of the actor to commit an offence ... These considerations lead me to the conclusion that the distinction sought to be drawn in *Anderton v Ryan* between innocent and guilty acts considered "objectively" and independently of the state of mind of the actor cannot be sensibly maintained.

The Victorian Supreme Court in *Britten v Alpogut* [1987] VR 929, decided that the reasoning in *Shivpuri* should apply in relation to s 233B of the *Customs Act* 1901 (Cth). In this case, the accused

---

50 See, for example, G Williams, *Textbook of Criminal Law* (London: Stevens, 1978), pp 397-398; R Ribiero, "Criminal Liability for Attempting the Impossible — Lady Luck and the Villains" (1974) 4 *Hong Kong Law Review* 109 at 131; HLA Hart, "The House of Lords on Attempting the Impossible" (1981) 1 *Oxford Journal of Legal Studies* 149 at 164.

believed that he was importing cannabis which is a prohibited drug. Upon analysis the substance was discovered to be an anaesthetic, procaine, which is not prohibited. The magistrate dismissed the case, relying on *Haughton v Smith*. The prosecution claimed before the Full Court of the Supreme Court of Victoria that the magistrate had erred in law. The Supreme Court held that impossibility is no answer to a charge of attempt, unless it was the accused's intent to commit an "imaginary crime". The same reasoning was applied to a charge of attempting to possess a prohibited import under the *Customs Act* 1901 (Cth) by the Supreme Court of Western Australia in *R v Lee* (1990) 1 WAR 411. This reasoning in *Britten v Alpogut* was also approved by Murray J in the Court of Criminal Appeal of Western Australia in *English* (1993) 68 A Crim R 96. Murphy J in *Britten v Alpogut* described (at 935) the rationale for holding an attempt had been made as follows:

> The criminality comes from the conduct intended to be done. That conduct intended must amount to an actual and not an imagined crime, but if it does, then it matters not that the gun is in fact unloaded, or the police intervene, or the victim is too far away, or in fact that the girl is over 16, or the pocket is empty, or the safe is too strong, or the goods are not cannabis.

The Australian cases that followed the approach in *Haughton v Smith* have narrowed the category of physical impossibility considerably. For example, the decision in *R v Gulyas* (1985) 2 NSWLR 260 demonstrates the lack of clarity between a mistake as to insufficiency of means and physical impossibility. In that case, the accused, a husband and wife, attempted to perpetrate a fraud against a lottery. They filled in the original form but removed the carbon paper. This meant that the duplicate was blank so that it could be filled in at a later stage when the winning numbers were published. The accused asked for the original form to check something and retained it. In due course, the accused claimed they had won. The original form, of course, was never found. However, the blank carbon paper was discovered and it was evident that this was a fraudulent claim. The accused were charged with attempting to obtain money by false pretences. The question of impossibility arose because it was a condition of entry that without the original form no prize money would be paid.

The New South Wales Court of Appeal agreed with the trial judge that this was a case of inadequate means rather than physical impossibility. The Court held that in order for an attempt not to be criminal, there must be an element of unconditional impossibility. Lee J (at 267) referred to physical impossibility as requiring "absolute impossibility not impossibility dependent upon conduct anticipated or otherwise". Grove J (at 267) stated that it was impossibility "unconditional upon human intervention". This appears to narrow the scope of factual impossibility to such a degree that it has no practical significance; only covering impossibility where there is no scope for human intervention, errors or frailties.

A similar case arose in South Australia in *Kristos* (1989) 39 A Crim R 86. The accused had presented a winning Lotto coupon but the receipt showed that he had not filled in that coupon when he paid for the game. The accused was convicted of attempting to obtain property by false pretences. On appeal to the South Australian Court of Criminal Appeal, the defence argued that the accused's cheating was physically impossible because of the safeguards built into the Lotteries Commission's computer system and the requirements of the Lotteries rules. Cox J rejected this submission on the basis that this was not a case of impossibility. At most it was highly unlikely that the accused's fraudulent claim would have succeeded. Cox J noted (at 93):

[T]here is a world of difference between impossibility and improbability, even great improbability, and the case for the appellant never really rose above the latter. It would be strange if the law were otherwise. It is hardly to be supposed, for example, that a defendant could escape a charge of attempted false pretences on the ground that his [or her] intended victim was so mean that the possibility of his [or her] responding favourably to a fraudulent claim on his [or her] charity could be dismissed as fanciful.

The status of mistake and attempts in New South Wales had been uncertain until the decision of *R v Mai* (1992) 26 NSWLR 371. The accused intended to smuggle a large quantity of heroin into Australia. The police intercepted his suitcase and discovered 6.9 kilos of heroin inside it. The police substituted the blocks of heroin with blocks of plaster containing small quantities of heroin and listening devices. The accused was arrested in possession of a plaster block that in fact contained no heroin at all. He was charged with attempting to possess heroin. Hunt CJ conceded that it was physically impossible for the accused to complete the crime of possessing heroin. The main issue in the case was whether *Haughton v Smith* was good law in New South Wales. Several earlier New South Wales decisions, including *R v Gulyas* (1985) 2 NSWLR 260 had affirmed the *Haughton v Smith* approach. However as Hunt CJ pointed out, this dicta in *Gulyas* had been strictly obiter since the court had concluded that the failure to complete the crime was due to the inadequacy of means rather than factual impossibility. Hunt CJ was influenced by several factors in reaching the conclusion that factual or physical impossibility was no answer to an attempt. He referred (at 381) to the decision in *Haughton v Smith* being reversed by statute, the House of Lords decision in *Shivpuri*, and the relevance of the decisions of the Supreme Courts of Victoria and Western Australia.

South Australia is now the only Australian jurisdiction that still follows *Haughton v Smith* in making a distinction between physical impossibility and insufficiency of means or the non-existence of a person or thing. Cox J in *Kristo* (1989) 39 A Crim R 86 at 94 noted that physical impossibility as a "defence" to a charge of attempt may "one day" require reconsideration. In practice, as mentioned above, the scope of physical impossibility has been narrowed considerably. In *R v Collingridge* (1976) 16 SASR 117, the accused was charged with the attempted murder of his wife. He had thrown the bare end of a live wire into the bath while she was in it. There was evidence that the victim could have been killed if the wire had made contact with her body, but the accused claimed he did not intend to touch the victim's body with the wire. The Supreme Court found that this was a case of insufficient means rather than physical impossibility.

The Code jurisdictions make it clear that physical impossibility is no bar to a conviction for attempt. For example, s 4(3) of the *Criminal Code* (WA) states that it is immaterial that by reason of circumstances not known to the offender, it is impossible to commit the offence: see also *Criminal Code* (NT), s 4(3); *Criminal Code* (Qld), s 4(3). Section 2(2) of the *Criminal Code* (Tas) states that an attempt may be committed whether under the circumstances it was possible to commit the crime or not.[52] Section 321N(3) of the *Crimes Act* 1958 (Vic) enables a conviction despite the existence of facts

---

52 It was thought that there was a conflict between s 2(1) and 2(2) of the *Criminal Code* (Tas). This conflict has been resolved by reading s 2(1) as meaning an attempt will be committed if the accused's acts form part of a series of events which if the accused's purpose were achieved, constitute the actual commission of the offence: *Haas v The Queen* [1964] Tas SR 1 at 27-28 per Neasey J, approved in *McGhee v The Queen* (1995) 183 CLR 82 at 106 per Toohey and Gaudron JJ.

that of which the accused is unaware which make the commission of the substantive offence impossible.

In 1990, the Gibbs Committee, which undertook a review of Commonwealth criminal law, recommended that future law should contain a statutory provision to the effect that a person may be convicted of an attempt, even though the facts are such that the commission of the offence is impossible.[53] This recommendation was followed by the insertion of s 7(3)(a) into the *Crimes Act* 1914 (Cth). As discussed above, this provision appears broader than the others in not confining impossibility to that of physical impossibility. Under this section, legal impossibility would not seem a barrier to conviction either.

A CRIMINAL PROCESS PERSPECTIVE

Attempts and Physical Impossibility

From a fault-centred perspective, there is little moral distinction between the person who intends to commit a crime and succeeds, and the person who intends to commit a crime but is frustrated because of ineptitude or physical impossibility. The problem with criminalising impossible attempts relates not to culpability, but rather with the impact it has on police and prosecutorial practices. There is a real danger that the offence of attempt can be used to cure deficiencies in the prosecution case. In this sense, it can be a backdoor method of convicting on the evidence of intention alone. As Andrew Ashworth in *Principles of Criminal Law* (3rd ed, Oxford: Oxford University Press, 1999) points out (p 469):

> [I]t is argued that there is a risk of oppression if the law criminalizes people in objectively innocent situations. Part of the concern here is that convictions might be based on confessions which are the result of fear, confusion or even police fabrication. Without the need to establish any objectively incriminating facts, the police might construct a case simply on the basis of remarks attributed to the accused person.

There is some evidence in the United Kingdom supporting this concern that the law relating to physical impossibility condones or even facilitates proactive policing methods such as entrapment. The propriety of entrapment from an evidential and procedural perspective is further explored in Chapter 15, pp 870ff. In 1990, Paul Baines, Chief Inspector of the Merseyside Police wrote an article for *Justice of the Peace*, which is a professional journal aimed at the police and magistrates called "Attempting the Impossible" (1990) 154 *Justice of the Peace* 67. Baines wrote about a police operation carried out in the Merseyside area to deal with the problem of car radio thefts and their resale. In Baines' words, the aim of the operation was to tackle "an Arthur Daley mentality about stolen car radios in that they were looked upon as nothing more than a bargain which had 'fell off a lorry'": at 67.

The police were instructed to identify suspect radios by noting, for example, a "top of the line" radio in an old car. (This decision would have had a disproportionate impact on policing of

---

53 Gibbs Committee Review of Commonwealth Criminal Law, *Principles of Criminal Responsibility and Other Matters*, Interim Report (1990), p 349. For commentaries on this Report, see G Niemann, "Attempts" (1991) 2(3) *Criminal Law Forum* 549 and G Moloney, "Attempts" (1991) 15 Crim LJ 175.

certain groups such as youths from the West Indian community). The car owner would then be interviewed, and if the radio had been purchased in suspicious circumstances, for example from someone in the pub, the radio was removed for examination. Where the police could not prove that the radio had been stolen, the suspect was charged with attempted handling. The fact that the owner had bought an expensive radio dirt cheap in suspicious circumstances provided circumstantial evidence of the suspect's knowledge that the radio was stolen.

In jurisdictions where impossibility no longer bars a conviction for attempts or other inchoate crimes, prosecutorial discretion is assumed to play a significant role. The Law Commission of England and Wales, in its Report *Criminal Law: Attempt and Impossibility in Relation to Attempt, Conspiracy and Incitement* (London: HMSO, 1980) noted that physical impossibility could provide a fall back position for attempt to be charged. Paragraph 2.97 of the Report notes:

> If it is right that an attempt should be chargeable (even though it is impossible to commit the crime intended) we do not think that we should be deterred by the fact that such a charge would also cover such extreme and exceptional cases ... an example would be where a person is offered goods at such a low price that he [or she] believes they are stolen, when in fact they are not; if he [or she] actually purchases them ... he [or she] would be liable for an attempt to handle stolen goods.

Although in such cases the accused would be guilty in theory, the Commission concluded that it would be unlikely that a complaint would be made or that a prosecution would ensue. In relation to the Merseyside operation, Baines stated (at 68) that a person who bought a radio which turned out not to be stolen, in the false belief that it was stolen, would not be charged. But clearly under the present law in the United Kingdom and Australia, such a person is guilty of attempted handling. The Merseyside police regarded the operation as a success since it led to a 22% drop in reported thefts from cars.

Limiting criminal responsibility for a mistake relating to insufficiency of means prevents the reliance upon proof of criminal intent alone, which in turn leads to reliance on confession evidence or other circumstantial evidence.

The danger with the present law is that the police can use the offence of attempt to cure prosecutions that would otherwise fail for lack of evidence. Perhaps *Haughton v Smith*, though conceptually confused, did have some practical value after all as a means of controlling police behaviour during criminal investigation.

CONSPIRACY

It is clear that in Victoria and federally, there will still be liability for conspiracy in situations of insufficiency of means and physical impossibility. Section 321(3) of the *Crimes Act* 1958 (Vic) states that there will be liability where an accused enters an agreement to commit acts that, unknown to the person at the time of the agreement, make the commission of the offence impossible. Section 86(4)(a) of the *Crimes Act* 1914 (Cth) enables a conviction for conspiracy even if committing the offence is impossible. As discussed above, legal impossibility does not appear a barrier to a conviction for a federal offence.

The common law is relevant in the other jurisdictions, including the Code jurisdictions in determining what constitutes conspiracy. Just what the common law position is in relation to conspiracy and physical impossibility is unclear.

In *DPP v Nock* [1978] AC 979, the House of Lords affirmed *Haughton v Smith's* division between insufficiency of means and physical impossibility, holding that there is no liability for conspiracy in the latter circumstances. In that case, the accused agreed to produce cocaine from a substance in their possession. Cocaine could not in fact be produced from the substance. They were convicted of conspiracy to produce a controlled drug contrary to the *Misuse of Drugs Act* 1971 (Eng). The House of Lords quashed their convictions on the basis that physical impossibility in conspiracy should be treated in the same way as physical impossibility in attempt. The House of Lords viewed both conspiracy and attempt as being criminal because they allowed the police to intervene to prevent the substantive offence being committed.

In contrast, in *R v Sew Hoy* [1994] 1 NZLR 257, the Court of Appeal of New Zealand held that physical impossibility is not a bar to conviction for conspiracy.[54] In that case, the accused agreed to produce falsified documents in order to have Customs officers wrongly classify men's clothing as women's clothing, the latter carrying a lower duty. There was evidence that this was bound to fail as Customs officers did not rely on documents, but on inspections of the goods. In the District Court, the jury was directed to return a verdict of not guilty on the basis that there could be no liability in circumstances of physical impossibility. The Crown then appealed on a reserved point of law.

The Court of Appeal ordered a retrial. While the Court considered that the facts could be interpreted as insufficiency of means, its decision was justified on the broader basis that physical impossibility was not a "defence" to conspiracy. The Court of Appeal declined to follow *Nock's* case because it was based on *Haughton v Smith* which had been rejected in Australia (except in South Australia) and legislatively overturned in England. The Court of Appeal was also of the opinion that conspiracy should not be viewed in the same way as attempt, but should be seen as "inherently culpable". The Court stated (at 267):

> It is the making of the agreement itself that is seen as inimical to the public good, whether
> it proceeds further or not ... It should not therefore be irrelevant that it may not be possible
> in fact to carry out the agreement.

The position of the common law in Australia is still unclear. In *R v Barbouttis* (1995) 37 NSWLR 256, the accused was charged with conspiracy to receive stolen property. It was alleged that he and others agreed to buy 50 boxes of cigarettes, believing them to be stolen. In circumstances reminiscent of the facts in *Haughton v Smith*, the boxes were in fact in the lawful possession of the police for the purpose of an undercover operation designed to catch the accused. The person from whom the boxes were to be bought was in fact an undercover policeman. The indictment was quashed in the District Court on the basis that there could not be a conspiracy where it was physically impossible to commit the substantive crime. The prosecution appealed on a point of law. A majority of the Court of Criminal Appeal of New South Wales rejected the appeal.

---

54 For a commentary on this case, see GF Orchard, "Impossibility and Inchoate Crimes — Another Hook in a Red Herring" [1993] *New Zealand Law Journal* 426.

Dunford and Smart JJ in the majority based their decisions on the agreement being one to purchase cigarettes which in itself was not an unlawful act. The accused's belief that the cigarettes were stolen was therefore irrelevant. Dunford J stated (at 278):

> [T]he conspiracy alleged in this case was not an agreement to do an unlawful act because the act agreed to be done, that is, receive the cigarettes, was not an unlawful act; nor was it an agreement to do a lawful act by unlawful means; and so it was not, in my view, a criminal conspiracy.

The reasoning employed here that supports an aquittal does not rest on physical impossibility. Gleeson CJ and Dunford J were in fact in agreement that physical impossibility could no longer be a bar to criminal responsibility for conspiracy. In contrast, Smart J (at 277) appeared to suggest that there may still be room for a "defence" of physical impossibility.

It would seem that the approach in *Sew Hoy* and the opinions of Gleeson CJ and Dunford J in *Barbouttis* should hold sway in order to bring the law relating to impossibility in conspiracy into line with that of attempt. In South Australia, the decision in *Nock* will probably still be relevant given that *Haughton v Smith* still applies. However, this may be reconsidered in the future. The Review Committee of Commonwealth Criminal Law recommended "for practical reasons" that physical impossibility should not defeat a prosecution: *Interim Report: Principles of Criminal Responsibility and Other Matters* (July 1990) (Canberra: AGPS, 1990), p 398. It gave the following example (at 398-399):

> A conspiracy to defeat the taxation laws or otherwise defraud the revenue may in fact be impossible to succeed because the Commissioner happens to know all the relevant circumstances; again the criminality of the conspiracy would seem to be just as great as if it had been possible of success.

Since the weight of opinion in recent cases is that physical impossibility should not bar a conviction for attempt, it seems likely that the same opinion would be reached for conspiracy if such a case were to come before an appeal court.

INCITEMENT

As with conspiracy, in Victoria physical impossibility is no bar to a conviction for incitement: *Crimes Act* 1958 (Vic), s 321G(3). Interestingly, the *Crimes Act* 1914 (Cth) does not include a provision dealing with impossibility in relation to incitement.

The situation at common law is still unclear. The early incitement cases held that physical impossibility was irrelevant to criminal responsibility for incitement. For example, in *R v McDonough* (1962) 47 Cr App R 37, the accused was convicted of three counts of incitement in relation to inciting another to receive stolen lamb carcasses. On one of the counts, there was no evidence that at the time of the incitement the carcasses existed. On the other two counts there was clear evidence that there were no stolen lamb carcasses in existence.[55]

---

55 See also *R v Shephard* [1919] 2 KB 125. For a commentary on these cases, see M Cohen, "Inciting the Impossible" [1979] Crim LR 239.

However, in *R v Fitzmaurice* [1983] QB 1083, the English Court of Appeal held that physical impossibility may excuse an accused from criminal responsibility for incitement. In that case, the accused's father thought up an elaborate scheme whereby he would be given a reward for informing a security firm that there was a plan to rob a security van. He asked the accused to arrange a robbery on a woman who was meant to be carrying wages from her company to the bank. The accused organised for three men to carry out the robbery. The accused and the three men did not know that the woman was part of the charade and a security van was going to be in the vicinity at the time the three men were meant to be robbing the woman. On the accused father's tip off, the three men were arrested for conspiracy to rob and the father subsequently received payment from the security firm for his information. The accused was convicted at the Central Criminal Court of having incited the three men to commit a robbery. On appeal, he argued that he could not be convicted of inciting other men to commit a crime that in fact could not be committed.

The Court of Appeal endorsed Lord Scarman's opinion in *DPP v Nock* [1978] AC 979 at 995 that emphasis must be placed on evidence of the offence that was to be the outcome of the conspiracy or incitement in order to see whether the offence was in fact impossible to achieve.

On the facts, the Court of Appeal held that the offence of robbery could have been achieved. Neill J in delivering the judgment of the Court stated (at 1092):

> [T]he appellant believed that there was to be a wage snatch and he was encouraging Bonham [one of the three men] to take part in it ... It is to be remembered that the particulars of offence in the indictment included the words "by robbing a woman in Bow".
> By no stretch of the imagination was that an impossible offence to carry out and it was that offence which the appellant was inciting Bonham to commit.

While the Court of Appeal therefore agreed that physical impossibility could bar a conviction for incitement, they were nevertheless able to find on the facts that this was not a case of physical impossibility.

Given that in all jurisdictions apart from South Australia, physical impossibility is no bar to a conviction for attempt, one would expect the common law in relation to incitement to develop in a similar manner. Section 11.4(3) of the *Criminal Code Act* 1995 goes further in holding that no form of impossibility (including legal) is a bar to conviction for incitement. As discussed above, this seems to be extending criminal responsibility too far.

6. MISTAKE OF LAW

At common law, a mistake of law or ignorance of law will generally not provide an accused with a defence to a crime.[56] The origins of this doctrine can be found in the Latin maxim *ignorantia juris non excusat* which, it appears, was introduced into the English common law in the 18th century by Sir William Blackstone: *Commentaries on the Laws of England* (1769), Book IV, p 27. Policy reasons for the doctrine include:

---

56 *R v Coote* (1873) LR 4 PC 599; *Iannella v French* (1968) 119 CLR 84; *Pollard v DPP (Cth)* (1992) 28 NSWLR 659; *Khammash v Rowbottom* (1989) 51 SASR 172.

━━━ the impossibility of ascertaining whether the accused was actually ignorant of the law and the difficulty in distinguishing between exculpatory and non-exculpatory mistakes of law;

━━━ the admission of the defence would encourage ignorance of the law;[57] and

━━━ citizens have a legal duty to acquaint themselves with their legal obligations;[58]

━━━ it would allow the substitution of a mistaken view of the law for what the law actually is.[59]

There are, however, numerous exceptions to the doctrine that ignorance of the law is no excuse. The four main exceptions are:

━━━ knowledge of unlawfulness as a *fault element*;

━━━ the defence of claim of right;

━━━ the non-discoverability of laws; and

━━━ the statutory defence of "with lawful excuse".[60]

We will examine these exceptions in turn. But first, it is worthwhile considering the cultural implications of ignorance of the law being no excuse.

MULTICULTURAL PERSPECTIVES

Ignorance as No Excuse

The rule that "ignorance of the law is no excuse" purports to uphold the principles of equality before the law: see Ch 2, 3.4 'The Principle of Equality Before the Law', p 127. However, the Australian Law Reform Commission (ALRC), in its Report No 57, entitled *Multiculturalism and the Law* (1992) recognised that this rule has the potential to operate harshly in a multicultural society. It can unfairly penalise individuals who are unaware of the relevant prohibition and who are hindered by language and cultural barriers from finding out. The ALRC nevertheless concluded (p 179):

> The basic principle of imposing responsibility on all members of the community to
> know what is and is not allowed should not be disturbed merely because it is difficult
> for some people to know what the law is. Instead, governments and responsible
> agencies should improve their efforts to communicate the substance of legal
> restrictions to those likely to be affected by them.

---

57 O Holmes, *The Common Law* (Boston: Little, Brown, 1881), p 48.

58 A Ashworth, *Principles of Criminal Law* (3rd ed, Oxford: Clarendon Press, 1999), p 244. The duties of citizenship rationale have been criticised, see D Husack, "Ignorance of Law and Duties of Citizenship" (1994) 14 *Legal Studies* 105.

59 J Hall, *General Principles of Criminal Law* (2nd ed, Indianapolis: The Bobbs-Merrill Company Inc, 1960), pp 382ff. For further discussion of the policy rationales for excluding such a defence, see K Amirthalingam, "Mistake of Law: A Criminal Offence or a Reasonable Defence?" (1994) 18 Crim LJ 271; A Ashworth, "Excusable Mistake of Law" [1974] *Criminal Law Review* 652; P Brett, "Mistake of Law as a Criminal Defence" (1966) 5 *Melbourne University Law Review* 179; W Brookbanks, "Recent Developments in the Doctrine of Mistake of Law" (1987) 11 Crim LJ 195.

60 Other exceptions which are in the process of development can be found in K Amirthalingam, "Mistake of Law: A Criminal Offence or a Reasonable Defence" (1994) 18 Crim LJ 271 at 276-279.

This recommendation can be criticised on two grounds. First, a person who acts in ignorance of the law may technically commit a crime, yet not be viewed as morally blameworthy. The principle of individual justice requires that criminal liability should not be imposed unless individuals had a fair opportunity to conform their conduct to the law.

Secondly, the ALRC's recommendation that the responsibility to know the law should be applied equally to all members of the community is based on a flawed notion of equality. Culpability is measured against a standard determined exclusively by reference to the dominant culture, in this context the ability and opportunity of members of the dominant culture to know and understand the applicable criminal laws.

To ameliorate unfairness, the ALRC (pp 179-181) did recommend that ignorance of the law based on cultural factors should be taken into account in the exercise of the court's sentencing discretion (including the discretion not to record a conviction) and the prosecutor's discretion not to prosecute. However, this is also problematic as it is widely acknowledged that minority groups are subject to a greater amount of discretionary justice and that discretion is often exercised in a discriminatory manner.

The ALRC argued that the enactment of widespread cultural exemptions would mean that the obligations under the criminal law would be determined by reference to one's membership of a particular cultural or ethnic group. It stated (p 177) that drawing the parameters of such exemptions would be difficult and having such exemptions would violate the principle of equality.

However, as an alternative to the ALRC's approach, some academic writers have called for the introduction of a defence based on justifiable ignorance of law.[61] Such a defence would have the qualification that the ignorance of law must be "reasonable in the circumstances" in order to counter frivolous claims and to ameliorate concern about proliferation of specious defences.

A defence of reasonable ignorance of law could apply in the situation where the accused, due to language or cultural barriers, did not know and could not reasonably be expected to know of the existence of the offence. This would demonstrate the legal system's commitment to the fundamental principle of individual justice. There may be fears that the defence could be abused for serious offences like murder, but such fears are unfounded. Cross-cultural claims of ignorance of law are unlikely to be justifiable for many core offences such as murder, assault, rape and theft that are regarded as crimes by citizens everywhere: see further N Lacey, *State Punishment* (London: Routledge and Kegan Paul, 1988). Accordingly, an accused raising ignorance of law in these cases would find it extremely difficult to establish that his or her ignorance of law was "reasonable" in the circumstances. Indeed, in South Africa the courts have developed a defence of mistake of law, negating the fault element, in *S v de Blom* (1977) (3) SA 513. Although extending to "unreasonable" mistakes of law, this development has not opened the floodgates for unmeritorious defences: see K Amirthalingam, "Distinguishing Between Ignorance and Mistake in the Criminal Law in Defence of the *de Blom* Principle" (1995) 8 *South African Journal of Criminal Justice* 12.

---

61 D Husak, "Ignorance of Law and Duties of Citizenship" (1994) 14 *Legal Studies* 105 at 115; K Amirthalingam, "Mistake of Law: A Criminal Offence or A Reasonable Defence" (1994) 18 Crim LJ 271; S Bronitt and K Amirthalingam, "Cultural Blindness — Criminal Law in Multicultural Australia" (1996) 21 *Alternative Law Journal* 38.

6.1 KNOWLEDGE OF UNLAWFULNESS AS A FAULT ELEMENT

Some offences require knowledge of unlawfulness as an element of an offence. For example, perjury is an offence that requires not only that the accused swore to that which was not true, but that this was done "wilfully" and "corruptly": *R v Smith* (1681) 2 Show KB 165. In this offence, the term wilfully means dishonestly, or at least awareness that the behaviour is unlawful. A mistake of law may thus exculpate an accused in circumstances where knowledge of unlawfulness is an element of the offence: *Jackon v Butterworth* [1946] VLR 330.[62]

6.2 THE DEFENCE OF CLAIM OF RIGHT

A person who honestly believes him or herself to be entitled to do what he or she is doing may be afforded the defence of an honest claim of right.[63] The defence is generally relevant to the situation where an accused has stolen, damaged or destroyed property and the fault element of the offence is negated by the existence of an honest claim of right to do the prohibited act.[64]

The defence is embodied in the theft legislation in the Australian Capital Territory, Northern Territory and Victoria: see Ch 13, p 676.

The belief must be honest, but it need not be reasonable[65] and what is essential is that the accused believed that there was a claim of right, regardless of whether or not one exists at law. For example, in *R v Bernhard* [1938] 2 KB 264 the accused was convicted of demanding money with menaces with intent to steal. The accused who was Hungarian, had been the mistress of an Englishman who had agreed to pay her £20 a month for a year after their affair ended. He paid the accused £80 to cover a period of four months, but failed to pay her the balance of £160 on the due date. The accused threatened to tell the Englishman's wife and the press about their affair if he did not pay her. On appeal against conviction, the accused argued that she had consulted a Hungarian lawyer and believed when she had ventured to England and demanded the money she was entitled to the money owing.

Her conviction was quashed on appeal. Charles J, in delivering the judgment of the Court of Criminal Appeal stated (at 270):

> We are ... bound by a series of long decisions ... to hold that ... a person has a claim of right, within the meaning of the section, if he [or she] is honestly asserting what he [or she] believes to be a lawful claim, even though it may be unfounded in law or in fact.

---

62 See generally K Amirthalingam, "Mistake of Law: A Criminal Offence or A Reasonable Defence" (1994) 18 Crim LJ 271 at 276.

63 *R v Cooper* (1914) 14 SR (NSW) 426; *R v Nundah* (1916) 16 SR (NSW) 482; *R v Pollard* [1962] QWN 13 at 29 per Gibbs J. See W Brookbanks, "Colour of Right and Offences of Dishonesty" (1987) 11 Crim LJ 153.

64 *R v Feely* [1973] QB 530; *R v Ghosh* [1982] 1 QB 1053; *R v Salvo* [1980] VR 401; *R v Love* (1989) 17 NSWLR 608; *Walden v Hensler* (1987) 163 CLR 561; *R v Sanders* (1991) 57 SASR 102; *Lenard v The Queen* (1992) 57 SASR 164; *Heywood v Canty* (unrep, 21/1/1993, SC Vic, Harper J, 11109 of 1991).

65 *R v Bernhard* [1938] 2 KB 264; *R v Love* (1989) 17 NSWLR 608.

6.3 THE NON-DISCOVERABILITY OF LAWS

Ignorance or mistake of law may afford an excuse where an offence is committed before publication of the law has been brought to the notice of the accused or in circumstances in which acquisition of knowledge of the existence of law is impossible.

In *Bailey* (1800) 168 ER 651, the accused was charged under a statute within a few weeks of it having been passed, at which time he was on the high seas and it was therefore physically impossible for the accused to know the law. The accused was found guilty, but was given an absolute pardon. At that time, the only way to correct a trial judge's erroneous ruling was to grant a pardon and it is therefore arguable that the pardon was given on the basis that the accused's conviction was wrong in law.

In *Burns v Nowell* (1880) 5 QBD 444, a similar fact situation occurred. In that case, a ship-owner sued a naval captain for damages for the illegal seizure of his ship. The latter had been seized under the *Pacific Islanders Protection Act* 1872 (Imp) which had come into effect during the voyage made by the captain of the ship in question. The Act made it illegal to carry natives without a permit from the Solomon Islands. The natives were used as divers. The Captain found out about the Act after the divers' work was finished and he was taking them back to their island homes. The shipowner failed in his claim for damages and his appeal was dismissed on the basis that the seizure of the ship had been made honestly and in good faith. Whilst it was not necessary to decide the point, the Court of Appeal went on to state (at 455) that the Act did not apply to the voyage because it was a continuous one and compliance with the legislation would have created "an act of cruelty in all probability as great as any which it was the avowed object of the act to prevent".

In *Lim Chin Aik v The Queen* [1963] AC 160, the accused was convicted of the offence of remaining in Singapore as a prohibited person. The Minister of Labour and Welfare had made an order prohibiting the entry of person into Singapore from the Federation of Malaya. There was no requirement that the order be published. At the accused's trial, there was evidence that he had entered Singapore from the Federation of Malaya after the Minister's order had been made and that he lived in Singapore. There was no evidence that any step had been taken to bring the order to the attention of the accused nor of anyone else.

The Judicial Committee of the Privy Council heard an appeal from the High Court of Singapore's decision to dismiss the accused's appeal against conviction. The Judicial Committee upheld the accused's appeal, Lord Evershed stating (at 171):

> [E]ven if the making of the order by the Minister be regarded as an exercise of the legislative as distinct from the executive or administrative function (as they do not concede), the maxim [*ignorantia juris neminem excusat*] cannot apply to such a case as the present where it appears that there is in the State of Singapore no provision ... for the publication in any form of an order of the kind made in the present case or any other provision designed to enable a man [or woman] by appropriate inquiry to find out what "the law" is.

The Judicial Committee therefore rejected the maxim that ignorance of the law is no excuse on the ground that non-publication of the order excluded the operation of the maxim.

An argument based on the non-discoverability of law is difficult to establish in Australia given that statutes are published by the government printer, are now available through the internet and there is usually a period of time before they come into effect. Subordinate legislation is also usually published in the relevant *Government Gazette*. Further, if an ordinance satisfies the necessary notification and publication requirements, it appears that the non-availability of the ordinance from the government printer or other appointed source will not postpone the operation of the statutory rule: *R v Sheer Metalcraft Ltd* [1954] 1 QB 586. In the Northern Territory and Queensland, there is some recognition of a defence of mistake or ignorance of delegated or subordinate legislation[66] and it may be that there is increasing support for such a defence to be recognised in other jurisdictions.[67]

6.4 THE STATUTORY DEFENCE OF WITH LAWFUL EXCUSE

An accused may be afforded a defence if he or she mistakenly believes that there was a lawful excuse to do what he or she did. This defence only applies to statutory crimes that require that the criminal act be performed "without lawful excuse".

In *R v Smith* [1974] 1 All ER 632,[68] the accused was charged under the *Criminal Damage Act 1971* (UK) with destroying property belonging to another without lawful excuse. The accused claimed that he honestly believed the property belonged to him. The Court of Appeal held that the accused's mistaken belief that he had a lawful excuse to destroy the property was a good defence. This case shows the readiness of the courts to take into account a mistake in relation to the legality of an act where a statutory provision allows for this.

The meaning and scope of "lawful" or "reasonable excuse" in relation to drug offences are explored in Chapter 15, pp 846ff.

PERSPECTIVES

Reliance on Incorrect Legal Advice from Those in Authority

Reliance upon legal advice is generally not a defence to a criminal charge. For example, in *R v Wheat and Stocks* [1921] 2 KB 119 the accused was convicted of bigamy despite receiving advice from counsel that his previous marriage was void. Similarly, in *Crichton v Victorian Dairies Ltd* [1965] VR 49 a company was convicted under the *Companies Act 1961* (Vic) for failing to appoint an auditor in circumstances in which the company had been advised by counsel that there was no duty to appoint: see also *Cooper v Simmons* (1862) 158 ER 654; *Olsen v Grain Sorghum Marketing Board* [1962] Qd R 580. More recent cases have also upheld this general rule: *Pollard v DPP (Cth)* (1992) 28 NSWLR 383; *Griffin v Marsh* (1994) 34 NSWLR 104.

---

66 *Criminal Code 1983* (NT), s 30(3); *Criminal Code* (Qld), s 22(3)-(4).

67 *Criminal Code Act 1995* (Cth), s 9.4(2)(c). See L Waller and CR Williams, *Brett, Waller and Williams: Criminal Law* (8th ed, Sydney: Butt, 1997), p 614.

68 This case could also be analysed in terms of claim of right, standing for the proposition that a mistaken belief that property is one's own negates the fault element.

The main rationale for not allowing a defence of mistake of law due to incorrect legal advice appears to be that a legal practitioner does not warrant the correctness of his or her advice and a client is free to reject advice and seek a second opinion. Another, more cynical rationale, is that if a defence of mistake of law based on incorrect legal advice were available, large corporations could "shop around" for a legal practitioner and exercise undue influence in order to obtain favourable advice. Glanville Williams has cautioned in "The Draft Code and Reliance on Official Statements" that allowing reliance on legal advice as a "defence" would enable corporations to avoid criminal responsibility in this manner: (1989) 9 *Legal Studies* 177 at 187-187.

If, however, the crime charged requires proof of some particular state of mind, evidence of legal advice may be relevant to show that the accused did not possess that state of mind. For example, in *R v Dodsworth* (1837) 173 ER 467 the accused was charged with falsely stating electoral qualifications. He claimed that he had acted honestly because he had acted on the advice of the election committee. Lord Denman (at 469) held that a person should not be convicted if he or she had acted bona fide and had "been guided in his [or her] conduct in a matter of law by persons who are conversant with law".

Reliance on official advice, like reliance on legal advice, does not enable a defence of mistake of law. In *Surrey County Council v Battersby* [1965] 2 QB 194 the accused was advised by a representative from the local council that she did not have to register a particular child-care arrangement under the *Children Act* 1968 (UK). In fact she did have to register it and the accused was convicted under the Act. It was held that the advice she was given was no defence: see also *Cambridgeshire County Council v Rush* [1972] 2 QB 426; sub nom *Howell v Falmouth Boat Construction Co* [1951] AC 837 at 845 per Lord Simonds.

This case has been the subject of much criticism[69] and in Canada and New Zealand the law is developing such that there may be a limited defence if a person relies on the advice of an official which purports to be definitive of the relevant law: see W Brookbanks, "Recent Developments in the Doctrine of Mistake of Law" (1987) 11 Crim LJ 195 at 199-201.

Ashworth argues that reasonable mistake of law should operate as an excuse: "Excusable Mistakes of Law" [1974] Crim LR 652; A Ashworth, *Principles of Criminal Law* (3rd ed, Oxford: Oxford University Press, 1999), p 247. He argues that this involves a form of "estoppel reasoning" such that the State and the courts should not convict those who have received incorrect advice from the officers of these institutions.

In practice, it is likely that those relying on incorrect legal advice from those in authority are not prosecuted or if convicted, receive substantial mitigation in sentence. The dearth of appeal cases in this area points to this conclusion: A Ashworth, "Excusable Mistakes of Law" [1974] Crim LR 652; A Ashworth, *Principles of Criminal Law* (3rd ed, Oxford: Oxford University Press, 1999), p 247. In *Postermobile v Brent LBC* (unrep, *The Times*, 8 December 1997) (discussed at [1998] Crim LR 435), Schiemann LJ of the English Divisional Court ordered that a prosecution be stayed as an abuse of process. In that case, a company erected advertising boards after being advised by members of the local council that this did not require planning consent. The Council subsequently brought a prosecution.

---

69   P Brett, "Mistake of Law as a Criminal Defence" (1966) 5 *Melbourne University Law Review* 179; W Brookbanks, "Officially Induced Error as a Defence to a Crime" (1993) 17 Crim LJ 380; L Waller and CR Williams, *Brett, Waller and Williams: Criminal Law* (8th ed, Sydney: Butt, 1997), pp 617-619.

> This case demonstrates that procedural measures may be taken to ensure that a reasonable mistake of law will afford some comfort to an accused despite such a "defence" not being currently available.

6.5 THE FUTURE OF MISTAKE OF LAW

The Criminal Law Officers Committee in its Final Report on *General Principles of Criminal Responsibility* (1992) recommended (at 59) that ignorance or mistake of law should not be an excuse unless it is so provided in statute or negates a fault element of the offence. This is simply reiterating the traditional view. The Committee was, however, prepared to enact a defence based on mistake or ignorance of subordinate legislation. Thus, s 9.4 of the *Criminal Code Act* 1995 (Cth) states:

> **(2)** Subsection (1) does not apply, and the person is not criminally responsible for the offence in those circumstances, if:
> **(a)** the subordinate legislation is expressly or impliedly to the contrary effect; or
> **(b)** the ignorance or mistake negates a fault element that applies to a physical element of the offence; or
> **(c)** at the time of the conduct, copies of the subordinate legislation have not been made available to the public or to persons likely to be affected by it, and the person could not be aware of its content even if he or she exercised due diligence.

The notion that there *must* be a general rule that ignorance of the law is no excuse is unsatisfactory. To avoid unfairness, the law has developed a number of exceptions. Unfortunately, these qualifications to the rule have developed in an ad hoc and unprincipled manner. It may be more useful for law reformers to move away from the strict approach towards a defence of reasonable mistake of law. A person who acts in the belief that conduct is not a crime or without knowing that it is a crime has made "a choice which is so ill-informed as to lack a proper basis": A Ashworth, *Principles of Criminal Law* (3rd ed, Oxford: Oxford University Press, 1999), p 244. Such conduct does not sit well with principles of criminal responsibility and moral blameworthiness. Nor does the criminal conduct of a person who relies on mistaken advice.

7. CONCLUSION

This chapter's exploration of how mistake may operate in different areas of the criminal law has shown that any doctrine of mistake has developed in a rather haphazard manner across the different contexts. We have outlined how the common law has stressed subjectivity in looking at mistake in the context of fault elements, while the notion of reasonableness is central in the Code jurisdictions and in other contexts such as strict liability and as a basis for certain defences.

Perhaps it is time for an objective approach to mistake to undercut all the different areas in which mistake may operate. Thus, an honest *and reasonable* mistake of fact could be relied upon to negate the fault element as well as to answer a charge of strict liability. Similarly, an honest *and reasonable* mistake of law should be a general defence to enable fairness and equality in a multicultural society.

PART III

Extending Criminal Responsibility

8

Complicity

> If two lives join,
> there is oft a scar

R Browning,
"By the Fireside" (1855)
Stanza 46

1. INTRODUCTION

The general rationale for the doctrine of complicity is that a person who promotes or assists the commission of a crime is just as blameworthy as the person who actually commits the crime. There is a tension in this area of the law because of the need to discourage acts that assist the commission of crime without imposing excessive sanctions on a much broader class of persons than those who directly commit a crime. As a consequence, some of the areas encompassed by the doctrine of complicity have developed in a rather haphazard and inconsistent fashion. In 1993, the Law Commission of England and Wales called for a new structure of statutory offences to replace the common law of complicity in order to clarify this complex area: The Law Commission, *Assisting and Encouraging Crime*, Consultation Paper No 131 (London: HMSO, 1993). This recommendation has, unfortunately, neither been heeded in England or Australia.

To understand the modern doctrine of complicity, considerable attention must be paid to its historical evolution.[1]

---

1   For an excellent review of the law of complicity in its historical context, see KJM Smith, *A Modern Treatise on the Law of Criminal Complicity* (Oxford: Clarendon Press, 1991).

1.1 HISTORICAL OVERVIEW OF COMPLICITY

The development of the substantive law of complicity is bound up with its "tortured procedural history": KJM Smith, *A Modern Treatise on the Law of Criminal Complicity* (Oxford: Clarendon Press, 1991), p 22. The common law evolved distinctions between modes of complicity based on the *nature* of the offence assisted or encouraged. In relation to felonies, the law identified several "degrees" of participation: the perpetrator of the offence was designated "principal in the first degree", whereas parties who were assisting or encouraging *during* the commission of perpetrator's crime were described as "principals in the second degree". Parties who were not physically present during the commission of the offence were divided into "accessories before the fact" (assisting or encouraging *before* the commission of the perpetrator's crime) or "accessories after the fact" (assisting *after* the commission of the perpetrator's offence). It should be noted, however, that these refined distinctions did not plague complicity in misdemeanors or treason. Due to the respective trivial and serious nature of these offences, the law deemed all accessories, irrespective of their precise participation, to be principals.

Keith Smith has pointed out that the distinctions between different modes of participation emerged from early judicial manoeuvres to overcome the derivative effects of accessorial liability. From the 13th century onwards, the common law developed a strict rule that an accessory to a felony could not be convicted unless there was proof that the perpetrator had been convicted and suffered punishment by way of "attainder", that is, sentence of death: see Ch 2, pp 97-98.[2] To overcome its manifest impracticality, the English courts in the 16th century resorted to a legal fiction that deemed accessories, who were present at the scene aiding and abetting the commission of the offence, to be principals.[3] These accumulated rules governing accessorial liability were restated in statutory form in the 19th century. As well as confirming the distinctions above, the *Accessories and Abettors Act* 1861 (UK) affirmed the common law principle of equal eligibility for punishment for all parties, that is, a person who aided, abetted, counselled or procured an offence was liable to be tried, indicted, and punished as a principal offender. Similar statutory provisions have been enacted in all Australian jurisdictions.[4]

---

2   KJM Smith suggests that the derivative nature of accessorial liability was established at the time Bracton's *Laws and Customs of England* were published in 1250: *A Modern Treatise on the Law of Criminal Complicity* (Oxford: Clarendon Press, 1991), p 22. For a discussion of these historical developments see Callinan J in *Osland v The Queen* (1998) 158 ALR 170 at 236.

3   *R v Griffith* (1553) 75 ER 152, discussed in KJM Smith, *A Modern Treatise on the Law of Criminal Complicity* (Oxford: Clarendon Press, 1991), p 23. This fiction was not however applied to accessories before the fact, consequently the strict rule requiring proof of attainder persisted until abolished by the *Criminal Law Act* 1848 (UK).

4   *Crimes Act* 1914 (Cth), s 5; *Crimes Act* 1900 (ACT), s 345; *Crimes Act* 1900 (NSW); *Criminal Code* (NT), ss 12, 346; *Criminal Code* (Qld), s 7; *Criminal Law Consolidation Act* 1935 (SA); *Criminal Code* (Tas), ss 3, 267; *Crimes Act* 1958 (Vic), ss 323; *Criminal Code* (WA), s 7.

In the modern context, the distinctions and terminology outlined above are largely of historical interest. Nevertheless, these distinctions and terminology continue to infect the language of lawyers and judges, even in those jurisdictions that have abolished the felony-misdemeanor classification: see Ch 2, 'Classification of Offences and Criminal Proceedings', pp 97ff.

Distinguishing between the different modes of participation does offer procedural advantages. As William Blackstone observed, defining the mode of participation allows the defence to know precisely the nature of the charge against the accused: W Blackstone, *Commentaries on the Laws of England* (1st ed, 1769), Vol IV; (reprinted 1966), pp 39-40. However, charging practices in cases of complicity involve tactical choices and the prosecution may be reluctant to narrow the legal or factual basis upon which it constructs the case against the accused. The tactical issues are explored below, at pp 424-426.

While deeming accessories to be principals for procedural purposes circumvented an inconvenient common law rule, it did not alter the derivative nature of accessorial liability. Although the modern law no longer requires proof of conviction or punishment, the liability of the accessory is derivative in the sense that the prosecution must still prove that the offence aided or abetted was committed or, at least attempted, by the perpetrator. This feature of complicity remains a cause of continuing conceptual confusion. The doctrines of innocent agency and acting in concert have evolved, in part, to bypass the derivative nature of complicity.

The historical linking of accessorial liability to the perpetrator's offence has had conceptual as well as procedural consequences. Rather than being viewed as an extension of criminal responsibility like the inchoate offences of incitement or conspiracy, accessorial liability is a *mode of participation* in the perpetrator's offence. The ramifications of linking the culpability of the accessory to the perpetrator continue to plague the modern law. This connection between perpetrator and accessory has fuelled controversy over the fault required for complicity, in particular whether an accessory must possess the identical, or at least broadly equivalent, fault element as the perpetrator: see below, 2.6 'The Fault Element', pp 409-411. As KJM Smith noted in his book, *A Modern Treatise on the Law of Criminal Complicity* (Oxford: Clarendon Press, 1991), p 64, this link has forced the courts to return frequently to basic principles:

> Perhaps more than any other form of criminality, complicitous activity raises, in large measure and in complex combinations, questions relating to practically every stage of the imposition of criminal liability, most particularly: the moral basis of responsibility, with in-built issues concerning freedom of choice of action; the acceptability and operation of chance and risk; the meaning of "cause"; the nature and function of harm or wrongdoing; the relevance and relationship of such issues to the justifying aims of punishment.

The historical development of complicity has been particularly sensitive to public concern over collective criminal activity. Like conspiracy, the imperative of devising "catch-all" forms of criminal liability to deal with groups of individuals who jointly agree to commit offences (but who do not necessarily perpetrate them) underlies the historical evolution of the doctrines of "common purpose" and "acting in concert". The doctrine of "common purpose" evolved to impose collateral liability for any offence committed pursuant to an agreement to commit another crime. The development of this doctrine is deeply implicated with the felony-murder rule: Ch 10, 4.2 'Constructive Murder', pp 497ff.

Consequently, the common law imposed harsh and draconian forms of constructive liability, recognising liability for consequences that were neither foreseen nor intended by the parties. Although constructive liability has been banished from the modern law of complicity,[5] a survey of the authorities reveals continuing controversy over the nature and scope of the fault required of individuals who commit offences that were foreseen but not necessarily intended pursuant to a common purpose or joint criminal enterprise.

1.2 THE HIGH COURT ON COMMON PURPOSE AND ACTING IN CONCERT

The High Court has recently reviewed the conceptual foundations and fault elements of the doctrines of "common purpose" and "acting in concert". In relation to "acting in concert", the High Court in *Osland v The Queen* (1998) 159 ALR 170 held that individuals who jointly agree to the commission of an offence and are present during its commission, are liable as principal offenders, *not* as accessories. As we shall explore later in this chapter, the conceptual basis for attributing the criminal acts of one person to another, raises significant questions concerning fault, causation and most fundamentally, the derivative nature of complicity.

In this chapter we will examine the principal statutory and common law modes of complicity:

▬ **aiding, abetting, counselling or procuring;**

▬ **acting in concert; and**

▬ **common purpose.**

These modes are not exhaustive of the forms of complicity. Indeed, the modern trend is to graft ancillary forms of liability onto the offence definition rather than rely on the general principles of complicity outlined below. Statutory forms of complicity, such as "being knowingly concerned" in the importation of prohibited drugs, require separate interpretation and analysis: see Ch 15, pp 843ff. Nevertheless, the principles developed and applied in the context of accessorial liability have relevance to the interpretation of these statutory forms of complicity.

2. ACCESSORIAL LIABILITY

In the previous section we outlined how the common law evolved distinctions between modes of complicity based on the *nature* of the offence assisted or encouraged. The older terminology of principal in the first and second degree and accessories before and after the fact have now evolved into counsellors, procurers, aiders and abettors. The following Table summarises the main differences in terminology across Australian jurisdictions.

---

5   KJM Smith notes that the authorities from the 16th to the 19th centuries suggest "movement from constructive liability for collateral offences through the qualifying guilt of complicity in the primary offence to the application of an objective probable consequences test and later, some form of subjective requirement": *A Modern Treatise on the Law of Criminal Complicity* (Oxford: Clarendon Press, 1991), p 211.

TABLE 1:

Terminology across Jurisdictions

JURISDICTION AND RELEVANT LAW	THOSE WHO PROMOTE A CRIME BEFORE IT OCCURS	THOSE WHO PROMOTE OR ASSIST A CRIME AND ARE PRESENT WHEN IT OCCURS	THOSE WHO CARRY OUT THE CRIME	THOSE WHO ASSIST ANOTHER TO ESCAPE PUNISHMENT AFTER THE EVENT
CTH *Crimes Act* 1914	person who counsels or procures s 5(1)	person who aids or abets s 5(1)	—	accessory after the fact s 6
ACT *Crimes Act* 1900	person who counsels or procures s 345	person who aids or abets s 345	—	accessory after the fact s 346
NSW *Crimes Act* 1900	person who counsels, procures, solicits or incites (s 249F(1)) (corrupt commissions) accessory before the fact (s 346)	person who aids or abets s 249F(1) (corrupt commissions)	principal felon s 346	accessory after the fact ss 347-350
NT *Criminal Code*	person who counsels or procures s 12(1)(c)	person who enables or aids another s 12(1)(a), (b)	—	accessory after the fact s 13
QLD *Criminal Code*	person who counsels or procures s 7(c)	person who enables or aids another s 7(b)	principal offender s 7(a)	accessory after the fact s 10
SA *Criminal Law Consolidation Act* 1935	person who counsels or procures s 267	person who aids or abets s 267	principal offender s 267	accessory s 241
TAS *Criminal Code*	person who instigates s 3(1)(d)	person who aids or enables (s 3(1)(b)) person who abets (s 3(1)(c))	principal offender s 3(1)(a)	accessory after the fact ss 6, 161, 300
VIC *Crimes Act* 1958	person who counsels or procures ss 323, 324	person who aids or abets ss 323, 324	principal offender ss 323, 324	accessory s 325

Table 1 continued

JURISDICTION AND RELEVANT LAW	THOSE WHO PROMOTE A CRIME BEFORE IT OCCURS	THOSE WHO PROMOTE OR ASSIST A CRIME AND ARE PRESENT WHEN IT OCCURS	THOSE WHO CARRY OUT THE CRIME	THOSE WHO ASSIST ANOTHER TO ESCAPE PUNISHMENT AFTER THE EVENT
WA *Criminal Code*	person who counsels or procures s 7(c)	person who enables or aids another s 7(b)	principal offender s 7(a)	accessory after the fact s 10

In this section, we will concentrate on what is meant by aiders, abettors, counsellors and procurers. In the following sections, we will examine the concept of principal offenders and accessories after the fact.

2.1 AIDS, ABETS, COUNSELS OR PROCURES

Traditionally, aiders and abettors refer to those present when the offence is committed while counsellors and procurers are those who are absent.[6] In *Attorney-General's Reference (No 1 of 1975)* [1975] QB 773 it was suggested (at 779) that these words which were set out in s 8 of the *Accessories and Abettors Act* 1961 (UK) should be given their "ordinary meaning". Lord Widgery CJ for the court held that each term has a different shade of meaning and therefore describes a distinct form of accessorial liability. An "aider" is one who helps, supports or assists the principal offender: *Thambiah v The Queen* [1966] AC 37. An "abettor" has been held to be a person who incites or encourages the principal to commit the offence: *Wilcox v Jeffery* [1951] 1 All ER 464. In *R v Giorgi* (1983) 31 SASR 299 Zelling J stated (at 311) that "abet" requires encouragement whereas "aid" does not.

A "counsellor" is one who advises or encourages the principal offender prior to the offence: *R v Calhaem* [1985] QB 808. A "procurer" is one who causes the offence to be committed: *R v Beck* [1985] 1 All ER 571. Lord Widgery held in *Attorney-General's Reference (No 1 of 1975)* [1975] QB 773 (at 779) that "procure" means to "produce by endeavour. You procure a thing by setting out to see that it happens and [by] taking the appropriate steps to produce that happening". By contrast to the word "procure", the term "aids" does not imply a causal connection between the assistance given and the commission of the crime. In other words, a person may aid the commission of the crime, without the perpetrator being aware of the assistance offered. The word "abets" connotes encouragement, implying that the words or conduct must influence the perpetrator's decision to commit a crime, and therefore there must be a causal connection between the acts of encouragement and the crime.[7]

---

6   *Thambiah v The Queen* [1966] AC 37; *Ferguson v Weaving* [1951] 1 KB 814 at 818-819; *Bowker v Premier Drug Co Ltd* [1928] 1 KB 217; KJM Smith, *A Modern Treatise on the Law of Criminal Complicity* (Oxford: Clarendon Press, 1991), p 32.

7   The spectator liability decisions, discussed below in 2.3 'Accessorial Liability by Inactivity', support this view. However Brent Fisse, in *Howard's Criminal Law* (5th ed, Sydney: Law Book Company Ltd, 1990), p 329 argues that such a causal link is not required.

This "ordinary meaning" approach to the phrase "aids, abets, counsels or procures" ignores the haphazard nature of 19th century drafting and the wide range of terms and synonyms used to describe the various conduct giving rise to accessorial liability. Although in "ordinary language" each word may have a different shade of meaning, the preferable view is that the phrase "aids, abets, counsels or procures" is merely descriptive of a general concept.

Cussen ACJ stated in *R v Russell* [1933] VLR 59 (at 66-67):

> All the words ... are ... instances of one general idea, that the person charged as a principal is in some way linked in purpose with the person actually committing the crime, and is by his [or her] words or conduct doing something to bring about, or rendering more likely, such commission.

Similarly, Mason J stated in *Giorgianni v The Queen* (1985) 156 CLR 473 (at 493):

> While it may be that in the circumstances of a particular case one term will be more closely descriptive of the conduct of a secondary party than another, it is important that this not be allowed to obscure the substantial overlap of the terms at common law and the general concept which they embody.

The terminology used to describe accessorial liability is outmoded. Sanford Kadish suggests that accessorial liability should draw a distinction between two forms of conduct — assistance or encouragement.[8] This "plain language" approach is preferable to the arcane terminology of Victorian statutes, and would greatly assist juries in understanding the types of conduct giving rise to accessorial liability.

2.2 THE PHYSICAL ELEMENT OF ACCESSORIAL LIABILITY

An accessory's influence on the commission of an offence may range from the minor role of encouraging by words or supplying materials or information for use in committing an offence,[9] to a major active role such as driving the principal offender to the scene of the crime, keeping watch, or holding the victim so that the principal offender can commit the offence.[10] The main limitation to the liability of an accessory via the doctrine of complicity is that the prosecution must prove that the accessory manifested his or her assent to the principal offender's actions in a manner that promoted their performance.

---

8   See S Kadish, "Complicity, Cause and Blame: A Study in the Interpretation of Doctrine" (1985) 73 *California Law Review* 324; *Blame and Punishment* (New York: MacMillan, 1987). JC Smith speculates that it may be necessary to recognise a third category of conduct, *causing* another person to commit an offence: "Criminal Liability of Accessories: Law and Law Reform" (1997) 113 *Law Quarterly Review* 453 at 453, fn 3.

9   *National Coal Board v Gamble* [1959] 1 QB 11.

10 *R v Clarkson* [1971] 1 WLR 1402; *Betts and Ridley* (1930) 22 Cr App R 148.

The accessory's promotion of or assistance in the crime must be given before, or at the time it is committed. Promotion or assistance given after the principal offender has committed the offence does not attract criminal responsibility as an aider, abettor, counsellor or procurer: *R v Stally* [1959] 3 All ER 814; *R v Maybery* [1973] Qd R 211. Liability may, however be made out in such a situation as an accessory after the fact: see below, 5 'Accessories After the Fact', pp 426ff.

There does not have to be a causal connection between the accessory's assistance and the commission of the crime.[11] For example, if two persons are involved in a fight and a passer-by cheers them on, the passer-by cannot be said to have caused the fight, but may be criminally responsible in the sense that he or she has encouraged the fight: *R v Coney* (1882) 8 QBD 534; *Wilcox v Jeffrey* [1951] 1 All ER 464.

In *Howell v Doyle* [1952] VLR 128 the accused were charged with interfering with the transport of goods with other countries contrary to *Crimes Act* 1914 (Cth), s 30K. They had moved resolutions calling on trade unionists, who were the principal offenders, to boycott certain ships. The principal offenders had been refusing to work on one of the ships before the accuseds' actions and the accused argued that they had not caused the boycott of the ship. The magistrate dismissed the charge. The prosecution successfully appealed. Herring CJ stated (at 134) that there was evidence that the accessories had counselled, aided or abetted the boycott and that no causal link need be shown between the counselling and the offence.

In relation to procuring, however, a causal link may be required: *Attorney-General's Reference (No 1 of 1975)* [1975] QB 773. The act of procuring need not be the sole or dominant cause of the commission of the offence.[12]

2.3 ACCESSORIAL LIABILITY BY INACTIVITY

The courts have grappled with the question as to whether or not a person can be liable as an accessory by simply doing nothing. The individual who is present during the commission of a crime, but who does not intervene, poses a dilemma for the criminal law. The main factual circumstances that give rise to this dilemma concern accessorial liability for "mere presence" and omitting to act.

MERE PRESENCE

The principles governing accessorial liability by "mere presence" have been developed in a series of spectator-liability cases. In these cases, the courts have held that accessorial liability depends on whether the conduct amounts to encouragement. The courts have stressed the "non-accidental" nature of the presence that encouraged the illegal conduct of the perpetrator, and the spectator's intention to encourage that conduct.

---

11 *O'Sullivan v Truth and Sportsman Ltd* (1957) 96 CLR 220; *R v Calhaem* [1985] QB 808. See also KJM Smith, "Complicity and Causation" [1986] *Criminal Law Review* 663; H Benyon, "Causation, Omissions and Complicity" [1987] *Criminal Law Review* 539.

12 *R v Solomon* [1959] Qd R 123 at 129 per Philp J; *Murray v The Queen* [1962] Tas SR 170 at 199 per Crawford J; *Attorney-General v Able* [1984] QB 795.

In general, mere presence at the scene of the crime will not be sufficient for criminal responsibility.[13] For example, in *R v Coney* (1882) 8 QBD 534 Hawkins J stated (at 557-558):

> It is no criminal offence to stand by, a mere passive spectator of a crime, even of a murder.
>
> Non-interference to prevent a crime is not itself a crime.

However, if a person is *deliberately* present at the scene of a crime, this may be taken as evidence that he or she intended to promote or assist the commission of the crime.[14] In *Coney's* case, the accused was among a crowd of spectators who watched two men participate in an illegal prize-fight. The prosecution was unable to prove that the accused took part in the management, or said, or did anything during the prize-fight. The accused was tried for common assault as an accessory.

At trial, the judge held that, as a matter of law, spectators at a prize-fight were guilty of assault. The majority of the Court for Crown Cases Reserved rejected the notion that voluntary presence was, as a matter of law, enough to be guilty as an accessory. Hawkins J held (at 557) that the previous authorities established that "some active steps must be taken by word or action, with intent to instigate the principal, or principals". However, the Court held that mere presence may in certain circumstances amount to proof of participation. Cave J distinguished (at 540) between accidental presence at the scene of a crime and deliberate presence that might amount to evidence of aiding and abetting. He observed (at 540) that "[w]here presence is prima facie not accidental it is evidence, but no more than evidence, for the jury [of abetting the assault]".

In *Wilcox v Jeffery* [1951] 1 All ER 464 the accused attended a concert in which the principal offender, a celebrated saxophone player, gave a performance which was in breach of the *Aliens Order Act* 1920 (UK). The accused, who owned a jazz magazine, knew that the principal offender was only permitted entry into the United Kingdom on condition that he would not take employment and the accused made no protest against the principal offender's actions. The court held that the accused's presence was evidence of aiding and abetting the illegal performance. Here, presence was seen as more than accidental because the accused paid to go to the concert and he went there wanting to report it.

In *R v Clarkson* [1971] 1 WLR 1402 the English Courts-Martial Appeal Court considered whether or not presence during the commission of a rape could give rise to liability as an accessory. A young woman went to a party at an army barracks. At about midnight, she went to the room of a soldier whom she knew well. He was not there. The other soldiers in the room attacked her and subjected her to a gang rape. The two accused, Clarkson and Carroll, did not participate in the rapes. At first, they simply stood outside the room, listening to what was happening. Later they entered the room and remained there while the girl was raped. There was no evidence that the accused had done or said anything to assist or encourage the perpetrators. The Courts Martial Appeal Court, affirming *Coney*, held that being voluntarily and purposely present witnessing the commission of a crime and offering no opposition or dissent, provides cogent evidence that the accused willfully encouraged the crime or activity and so aided and abetted. The Courts Martial Appeal Court stressed that it is important that the presence *in fact* encouraged the principal offenders and that this is a question of fact for the jury.

---

13   *R v Russell* [1933] VLR 59; *Jones and Mirrless* (1977) 65 Cr App R 250; *R v Clarkson* [1971] 1 WLR 1402.

14   *R v Coney* (1882) 8 QBD 534; *R v Russell* [1933] VLR 59; *R v Clarkson* [1971] 1 WLR 1402; *R v Bland* [1988] Crim LR 41; *R v Allan* [1965] 1 QB 130.

The limits of complicity by mere presence were considered again in the English Court of Appeal decision of *R v Bland* [1988] Crim LR 41. The accused cohabited with a drug dealer and was charged with possession of heroin. The prosecution case was that the accused lived with a man who was dealing drugs, and that there was sufficient evidence to prove that she knew of the drug dealing occurring in their flat. On this basis, the prosecution argued that she could be an accessory to the possession of heroin by her "passive assistance". She was convicted and appealed. The Court of Appeal, quashing her conviction, held that presence during the commission of a crime is not *prima facie* evidence of aiding and abetting. In this case, although she knew of the commission of the crime, the court held there was no evidence of assistance, active or passive. To be liable as an accessory there must be evidence of encouragement or some element of control.

AN OMISSION TO ACT

In general, an accessory must assist or encourage the principal offender through a positive act: *R v Coney* (1882) 8 QBD 534; *R v Russell* [1933] VLR 59. However, an omission to act may give rise to criminal responsibility if the person concerned is under a duty to prevent the crime committed by the principal offender or if the person concerned has the power of control over the principal offender but deliberately refrains from preventing the principal offender committing the offence.

In *R v Russell* [1933] VLR 59, the accused had committed bigamy. He told his wife of the bigamous relationship. The wife and two children were found drowned in a public pool. The accused claimed that his wife had drowned the children and then committed suicide by drowning herself. The accused claimed that he tried unsuccessfully to save them and failed to report the drowning because he was frightened. The accused was charged with murder and convicted of manslaughter.

The trial judge directed the jury on two possible scenarios. First, if the accused were merely a silent observer, who stood by and did nothing, then he would be guilty on the basis of manslaughter. His omission could give rise to liability because as a parent he was under a duty to care for his children and hence must prevent his wife murdering his children. Alternatively, if the accused actively encouraged or persuaded his wife to kill the children, he was guilty of murder in that he would be taking part in the crime of murder committed by her. The jury returned a verdict of manslaughter on all three charges.

The first scenario based the accused's liability on his own conduct (in this case an omission). This approach meant that he was directly liable as a principal offender. The second scenario based his liability on his secondary participation in the killings committed by his wife. Cussen ACJ considered the liability on the basis of secondary participation, and so did not focus on the question of parental duty. He reviewed the authorities governing complicity by mere presence, and the earlier decision of *Coney*. Cussen ACJ, stated (at 67) that if a person was present at the scene of a crime, assent to the crime could sometimes be made out by the "absence of dissent, or the absence of what may be called effective dissent". Mann J agreed with Cussen ACJ, but went even further to say (at 75) that the accused's liability arose from a father's duty to save his children. McArthur J, however, stated that mere non-interference was insufficient for liability as an aider and abettor.

Clearly, the requirement of assent (or acquiescence) is an aspect of the fault element for complicity. The requirement of "manifest assent" in cases where the person is present but does nothing to prevent the commission of a crime, may be criticised for blurring the physical and fault elements. However, the role of assent demonstrates the judicial reluctance to impose accessorial liability for inactivity unless there is evidence that individuals knew or intended that their conduct would assist or encourage the principal offender.

The duty to prevent a crime may go beyond the bounds of blood ties. In *Ex parte Parker: Re Brotherson* (1957) 57 SR(NSW) 326 the accused was an employee who allowed the principal offender to steal property from the accused's employer. There was some evidence of positive encouragement, but Walsh J stated (at 330) that in some circumstances a failure to carry out a duty to protect his employer's property arising from a contract could amount to encouragement of the commission of a crime.

In addition, in certain circumstances, a person may be convicted if he or she fails to exercise control over the principal offender. For example, the owner of a car may have the power to control the driver of his or her vehicle and if there is a failure to exercise that power, the owner may be liable.[15] The control principle was confirmed in *Dennis v Plight* (1968) 11 FLR 458, although the accused was not convicted on the facts. The accused allowed the principal offender to drive his car. She drove it in a dangerous manner while the accused was a passenger. The accused was held not guilty because he did not have time to prevent the act of dangerous driving.

In *R v Harris* [1964] Crim LR 54, the accused was supervising a learner driver. He failed to prevent the learner driver's dangerous driving and the learner driver killed a pedestrian. The English Court of Appeal held that the accused was under a legal duty to supervise the learner, and that his failure to control the learner's driving would make him liable as an accessory to causing death by dangerous driving.[16]

A person who owns or possesses land may also have a duty to control those on his or her premises and failure to exercise that duty may lead to criminal liability. In *Tuck v Robson* [1970] All ER 1171 the accused let the principal offender drink alcohol on the accused's licensed premises after closing time. The accused was convicted on the basis that he had a duty to control the principal offender and was present when the offence was committed.

The control principle may extend to property other than vehicles and land. In *Dennis v Pight* (1969) 11 FLR 458 (SC ACT) Smithers J stated (at 460) the principle in these general terms:

> [K]nowledge of an actual or threatened criminal use of one's chattel raises a natural
> obligation to take reasonable steps to prevent such use and ... failure to take such steps is
> evidence of an intention to aid and abet the commission of that criminal offence.

This statement has not as yet been tested in relation to a specific fact situation.

The imposition of accessory liability on the basis of the mere "power to control" the acts of another is a cause for some concern. David Lanham has suggested that there are convincing policy

---

15 *Du Cros v Lambourne* [1907] 1 KB 40. See also *Rubie v Faulkner* [1940] 1 KB 571.

16 See also *R v JJ Alford Transport Ltd* [1997] Crim LR 745 where a similar duty was applied to a company rendering it liable for offences committed by its employees. The English Court of Appeal held that the company and its managers could be guilty of aiding and abetting company drivers who illegally falsified tachograph readings. If they knew that this practice was occurring and took no steps to prevent this misconduct, it would be open to the jury to infer positive encouragement.

reasons for retaining a modified control principle, but only where the right to control property derives from ownership.[17]

However, the Law Commission of England and Wales has proposed that accessorial liability should be further circumscribed. In an early report, it recommended the abolition of accessory liability on the basis of the power to control property: *General Principles, Parties, Complicity and Liability for the Acts of Another*, Working Party No 43, p 35. More recently it suggested that accessorial liability by assistance should be limited to positive acts. Encouragement, by contrast, could be offered by mere presence during the commission of the crime, provided that the presence is intended and does, in fact, encourage the crime: The Law Commission, *Assisting and Encouraging Crime*, Consultation Paper No 131 (London: HMSO, 1993), p 134.

It has been suggested that this radical step of abolishing or restricting accessorial liability by omission is not required in Australia since the fault requirements are more stringent than in England: S Bronitt, "Defending Giorgianni — Part Two: New Solutions for Old Problems in Complicity" (1993) 17 Crim LJ 305 at 311. The requirement in *Russell* that the accessory's presence or inactivity must amount to "assent" to the commission of the offence is underscored in *Giorgianni v The Queen* (1985) 152 CLR 473, the leading High Court decision reviewing the fault elements for accessorial liability: see p 391. The High Court stressed that an accessory must possess an intention to assist or encourage the principal offender's conduct based on "knowledge of the essential matters". Mere recklessness or wilful blindness will not suffice.

This stringent fault element of intention based on knowledge narrows the scope of omission liability considerably. For example, a landlord who knows that a tenant is illegally cultivating illegal drugs would not be an accessory, *unless* the landlord's failure to exercise his or her power to control the property is also intended to assist or encourage the commission of that offence. From the perspective of moral culpability there are few objections to convicting as an accessory, any person who, by failing to exercise a power within his or her control, intends thereby to facilitate the commission of an offence by another.

Nevertheless, imposing liability for complicity on the basis of omissions remains controversial. It places a heavy burden on individuals to control the criminal conduct of individuals under their control, constituting "in one sense a policy of conscripting 'controllers' into the ranks of crime prevention authorities": KJM Smith, *A Modern Treatise on the Law of Criminal Complicity* (Oxford: Clarendon Press, 1991), p 46. From a public policy perspective, these incremental extensions to complicity offer benefits in terms of flexibility, for example, by developing new forms of "server liability" for individuals who supply alcohol but do not take steps to prevent intoxicated persons under their control from driving: HR Weinert, "Social Hosts and Drunken Drivers: A Duty to Intervene?" (1985) 133 *University of Pennsylvania Law Review* 867. While such innovations pursue legitimate policy objectives in relation to the control of supply of intoxicating or dangerous drugs, they significantly extend the reach of the criminal law. Arguably such reforms are better left to the legislature rather than the courts.

---

17   D Lanham, "Drivers, Control and Accomplices" [1982] Crim LR 419.

2.4 SUPPLYING THE "TOOLS OF THE TRADE"

A related question to that of accessorial liability by inactivity is whether or not a person may be guilty as an accessory for supplying goods or advice which subsequently facilitates the principal offender's offence. The cases which have preoccupied academics concern a shopkeeper or assistant who supplies the "tools of the trade" whilst not actually intending to assist or encourage the commission of a crime. The shopkeeper or assistant is simply indifferent to the customer's subsequent use of the goods or advice supplied.

Commentators have long expressed concern that a fault standard for complicity based on recklessness rather than actual knowledge would have the tendency to interfere with legitimate supply and to make crimes out of normal commercial activities, placing an onerous duty on suppliers, requiring them to act as their "customers' keeper". Glanville Williams for example, has argued that "the seller of an ordinary marketable commodity is not his [or her] buyer's keeper in criminal law unless he [or she] is specifically made so by statute. Any other rule would be too wide an extension of criminal responsibility": *Criminal Law: The General Part* (2nd ed, London: Stevens & Sons, 1961), p 373. As previously noted, in the Australian context these fears have been largely allayed. Following *Giorgianni v The Queen* (1985) 156 CLR 473, suppliers will only be liable as an accessory where they have an intention to assist or encourage the crime based on knowledge of the essential matters: S Bronitt, "Defending Giorgianni — Part Two: New Solutions for Old Problems in Complicity" (1993) 17 Crim LJ 305 at 306-311. On the fault element for complicity, see below, 2.6 'The Fault Element', pp 390ff. Suppliers who know that a customer intends to use their goods or services in the commission of a crime must decline to serve that customer to avoid liability as an accessory. This is further complicated when such a course of action would involve breach of a legal obligation to deliver or supply goods. This is a situation that the civil law is extremely reluctant to condone on the basis of mere apprehension that the goods may be used for illegal purposes.[18] Suppliers who do provide goods or services in these circumstances would be liable unless they take steps to frustrate the perpetrator's criminal venture.[19]

THE ENGLISH APPROACH

The English courts have considered the extent of these obligations in cases where the supplier of the goods is under a legal duty to return them, but is aware that the owner intends to use it to commit a crime: see generally, G Williams, "Obedience to Law as a Crime" (1990) 53 *Modern Law Review* 445. To mitigate the obvious injustice that might follow, the English courts developed a special defence. The defence first appears to have been applied in the English decision in *R v Lomas* (1913) 9 Cr App R 220. The accused returned a jemmy at the owner's request, knowing that the owner intended to use the jemmy to commit a burglary. The accused, who was indicted as an accessory before the fact, was convicted of housebreaking. The Court of Criminal Appeal quashed his conviction.

---

18 See *Gollan v Nugent* (1988) 166 CLR 18 where the majority of the High Court held (at 45) that the right to deprive a person of his or her possessory rights existed only in extreme cases, for example, where there is an immediate threat of a physical kind, or where the restoration of property would necessarily involve the person returning that property as a participant in an offence. By contrast, "[m]ere intention to engage in criminal conduct is not sufficient of itself to deny to the plaintiffs their right to possession".

19 In these circumstances, it would it difficult, if not impossible, for the supplier to communicate an effective countermand to the principal: see 2.5 'Withdrawal by an Accessory', p 387.

The reasoning employed by the court is not explicit in the judgment. However, subsequent courts have extrapolated from the decision the principle that a person cannot aid or abet an offence merely by returning property belonging to the perpetrator. The person returning the property, having no lawful right to withhold that property, could not be an accessory, even though he or she knew that the perpetrator intended to use the property in the commission of an offence.

The existence of the *Lomas* defence was affirmed in *National Coal Board v Gamble* [1959] 1 QB 11. In *Gamble*, a weighbridge clerk employed by the National Coal Board had issued a lorry driver with a ticket that permitted the lorry to leave the depot, even though the clerk knew that the vehicle was overloaded with coal. The National Coal Board was charged with aiding and abetting a breach of the Motor Vehicles (Construction and Use) Regulations 1955 (UK) committed by the lorry driver. The National Coal Board argued that the property in the coal had passed, and that, on the basis of *Lomas*, the Board had no lawful right to withhold the coal. Devlin J held that the *Lomas* defence was not available to the National Coal Board "on the facts" since the ownership of the coal did not pass to the driver until after the lorry had been weighed and the clerk had issued the weighbridge ticket. Consequently, the clerk would have been within his legal rights to withhold the transfer, and prevent the overloaded lorry from leaving the depot.[20] Accordingly, the Board's conviction was affirmed.

PROBLEMS WITH THE *LOMAS* DEFENCE

This willingness on the part of the courts to recognise the *Lomas* defence stems from a fundamental commitment to the primacy of possessory rights. However, the scope and status of the *Lomas* defence is unclear. On a strict interpretation, the individual restoring the property (the transferor) can only raise the *Lomas* defence where the person receiving that property (the transferee) has an enforceable remedy for restitution. The availability of the defence depends, not upon the conduct of the transferor, but rather upon the strict legal entitlement of the transferee. However, there is some authority in *Gamble* for a less strict interpretation of *Lomas*, extending the defence to those situations where the accessory *believes* (even erroneously) that he or she is acting according to a legal obligation. Devlin J in *Gamble* suggested that a mistaken view as to the precise nature of a civil obligation would be sufficient to negate an intent to aid: "There is no *mens rea* if the defendant is shown to have a genuine belief in the existence of circumstances which, if true, would negative an intention to aid": [1959] 1 QB 11 at 25. In his view, had the Board raised the argument that the clerk might have acted in a belief that he had no lawful right to withhold the ticket, the Board may well have escaped liability. Unfortunately, the clerk had not been called to give evidence as to his state of mind, and therefore this argument was not fully considered by the court. Devlin J's reasoning is another example where the strict rule that mistake of law affords no defence, has been relaxed: K Amirthalingam, "Mistake of Law: A Criminal Offence or a Reasonable Defence?" (1994) 18 Crim LJ 271 at 278. See Ch 7: pp 364ff.

---

20 In addition to the owner's right to demand the property back, Devlin J identified a further reason preventing the accused in *Lomas* from being an accessory. Lomas could not be an accessory because he had not done a positive act of assistance or encouragement. Devlin J took the view that Lomas had merely refrained from detinue, that is, from using force to keep the property. Only if the accused's failure to act fell within a recognised exception would the courts recognise accessorial liability.

The Law Commission of England and Wales favours this approach as the basis for explaining exculpation in these cases, and proposes the enactment of the following provision:

[A] person is not guilty of an offence as an accessory by reason of anything he [or she] does ... because he [or she] believes that he [or she] is under an obligation to do it and [acts] without the purpose of furthering the commission of the offence.[21]

Fundamental objections may be raised to either interpretation of the defence in *Lomas*. The stricter interpretation of the defence makes its availability turn on fine and subtle distinctions relating to duties under the civil law. On the other hand, a broader interpretation, as favoured by some commentators and the Law Commission, places too much emphasis on an individual's *belief* as to his or her rights under the civil law. Arguably, this would result in "rules of the criminal law introducing pointless complexities or leading to understandable perjuries": G Williams, "Obedience to Law as a Crime" (1990) 53 *Modern Law Review* 445 at 450. Further, it is questionable whether juries in criminal trials should be required to determine such difficult issues of civil liability.

The precise status of this defence in Australia is unclear. It is rarely litigated and has tended to arise in England where the courts are prepared to incriminate accessories on the basis of recklessness rather than intention. It has been suggested that the *Lomas* defence is redundant in Australia following *Giorgianni*: S Bronitt, "Defending Giorgianni — Part Two: New Solutions For Old Problems in Complicity" (1993) 17 Crim LJ 305 at 311-314. That is, individuals who supply goods that facilitate the commission of a crime will only be liable where they act with the intention of assisting or encouraging the perpetrator. Conduct, even that which is strictly required by the civil law, is deservedly criminal when provided with an *intention* to assist or encourage the commission of a crime by another.

2.5 WITHDRAWAL BY AN ACCESSORY

There is a general principle at law that once an offence is committed, nothing the offender does afterwards will affect his or her criminal responsibility. Repentance or attempts to minimise the harm caused will only be relevant to sentencing. With complicity, however, there may be a period of time between the assisting or encouraging of the crime and its actual commission. Considerations of social policy have led to the acceptance of the proposition that if an accessory counters his or her assistance or encouragement with equally obstructive methods, he or she should be acquitted.

The different approach to withdrawal in relation to accessorial liability is justified by reference to its derivative nature: KJM Smith, *A Modern Treatise on the Law of Criminal Complicity* (Oxford: Clarendon Press, 1991), Ch 10. Liability as an accessory does not crystallise until a crime is in fact committed or attempted by the principal offender. Hence, as a matter of logic, if a person withdraws from assisting or encouraging the crime *before* its commission, then there is no accessorial liability.

---

21 Clause 27(6) of the Draft Criminal Code: The Law Commission, *Criminal Law: A Criminal Code for England and Wales*, Report No 177 (London: HMSO, 1989). Williams, favouring a stricter interpretation of *Lomas*, argues that the defence should be restricted to individuals who are acting under a legal duty to transfer or surrender property: "a person will not be an accessory merely because he [or she] returns a thing to its owner, or the apparent owner, provided that he [or she] does not act with the purpose of furthering the commission of the offence": "Obedience to Law as a Crime" (1990) 53 *Modern Law Review* 445 at 445.

There are two possible rationales for exculpation on the basis of withdrawal: KJM Smith, *A Modern Treatise on the Law of Criminal Complicity* (Oxford: Clarendon Press, 1991), pp 251-254. The first approach is that evidence of withdrawal negates key ingredients of accessorial liability. As such, withdrawal is not a defence in itself, rather it is merely evidence that the physical and fault elements of accessorial liability are not fulfilled. Effectively neutralising the assistance or encouragement offered to the perpetrator before the commission of the offence means that the accessory's conduct had no causative influence on the subsequent criminal conduct of the principal offender. This evidence may also support the inference that the accessory lacked the intention to assist or encourage the principal offender.

The alternative "excusing" rationale is based on crime-prevention and can be viewed as a true defence. Withdrawal provides a basis for exculpation because of the "reasonable steps" taken to frustrate the commission of crime. The courts, while recognising that withdrawal may be exculpatory in certain circumstances, rarely articulate its justifying rationale. This conceptual uncertainty explains the conflicting approaches to withdrawal adopted by the courts and why the contours of the defence remain open to challenge.

Withdrawal generally requires some positive act that gives unequivocal notice of a complete withdrawal to the principal offender. A mere change of mind or secret repentance will not be enough.[22] Repentance without a positive act is insufficient because, although the accessory may not possess the requisite fault element at the time of the commission of the crime, he or she will have possessed it at the time of assisting or encouraging the principal offender.

In *White v Ridley* (1978) 140 CLR 342 the accused employed an airline carrier unwittingly to import cannabis from Singapore into Australia. Before the plane took off, the accused was questioned by Customs Officers and he tried to get the airline to cancel delivery of the box containing the drug. The case concerned the doctrine of innocent agency rather than complicity,[23] but the accused claimed that he had withdrawn from the enterprise and therefore was not criminally liable. This argument was rejected by a majority of the High Court.[24] Four of the judges, however, differed as to the nature of withdrawal as an exculpatory factor.

Stephen (at 354) and Aickin JJ (at 363) were of the opinion that withdrawal could not exculpate an accused from criminal responsibility unless it broke the chain of causation. Gibbs J, on the other hand, held (at 350-351) that withdrawal is a defence in its own right, requiring a timely countermand and such action as is reasonably possible to counteract the effect of the previous conduct. Murphy J (at 363) adopted a broader, more flexible test for determining liability, based on whether the accused had done all he reasonably could do to *prevent* the commission of the offence. This test recognises that in some circumstances timely countermand may be impractical (indeed life-threatening) and that informing the police may provide the basis for a good defence of withdrawal.

The New South Wales Court of Criminal Appeal has followed the approach of Gibbs J in treating withdrawal as a defence in its own right: *Tietie* (1988) 34 A Crim R 438. This approach requires both a timely countermand and action to counteract the effect of previous conduct.

---

22 *R v Jensen and Ward* [1980] VR 194 at 201 per the Court; *White v Ridley* (1978) 140 CLR 342; *Becerra* (1975) 62 Cr App R 212; *R v Menniti* [1985] 1 Qd R 520; *R v Saylor* [1963] QWN 14; *R v Solomon* [1959] Qd R 123; *R v Croft* [1944] KB 295.

23 For a discussion of innocent agency, see below, 3.1 'Innocent Agency', pp 402ff.

24 *White v Ridley* (1978) 140 CLR 342, Gibbs, Stephen and Aickin JJ; Jacobs and Murphy JJ dissenting.

An example of such action is informing the police of the proposed crime: *R v Jensen and Ward* [1980] VR 194 at 201.

On Gibbs J's view in *White v Ridley*, the accessory's withdrawal must be communicated to the principal offender. In *R v Whitehouse* (1941) 1 WWR 112 Sloan JA stated (at 115-116):

> Where practicable and reasonable there must be a timely communication of the intention to abandon the common purpose from those who wish to dissociate themselves from the contemplated crime to those who desire to continue it. What is a "timely communication" must be determined by the facts of each case but where practicable and reasonable it ought to be by communication, verbal or otherwise, that will serve unequivocal notice upon the other party to the common unlawful cause that if he [or she] proceeds upon it he [or she] does so without the further aid and assistance of those who withdraw.

In *R v Rook* [1993] 2 All ER 955 the accused agreed with two other men to kill the wife of the instigator of the crime in return for £20,000. The accused did not turn up on the day the killing occurred. He was convicted of murder and on appeal, argued that he had withdrawn from the agreement. The English Court of Appeal dismissed his appeal on the basis that he had failed to communicate his withdrawal to the other men. The Court relied on Dunn LJ's statement in *Whitefield* (1983) 79 Cr App R 36 (at 39-40) that where a secondary party advises or encourages another, he or she must communicate his or her change of mind to the other or others involved, and such communication must provide unequivocal notice that if the others proceed, they do so without the aid and assistance of the party who initially advised and encouraged them.

In *Whitefield's* case itself, the accused had helped plan a burglary with the principal offender, but subsequently informed him that he no longer wished to participate. The accused did not take any physical steps to prevent the principal offender from committing the crime. Nevertheless, the Court of Appeal held that the communication itself amounted to timely and unequivocal notice of withdrawal to the principal offender.

A problem occurs, however, when the desistence is very close to the commission of the crime. For example, in *Becerra* (1976) 62 Cr App R 212 the accused and two other men broke into a house with intent to steal. The accused gave one of the men a knife to use if they were interrupted by anyone. The accused heard the victim coming down the stairs and told the men to leave. The accused jumped out of the window and the other man stabbed the victim and killed him. The accused was convicted of murder. An appeal against conviction was dismissed by the Court of Appeal on the basis that the accused's countermand was ineffective and did not amount to withdrawal. The Court (at 218) followed Sloan JA's approach in *Whitehouse* requiring "timely communication".

Sloan JA's formulation places a fairly heavy onus on the accessory. It would seem that in such a situation nothing short of a physical act on the part of the accused would have stopped the murder occurring.

Further, it is unclear whether an accessory's timely communication to the police or potential victim may amount to an effective act of withdrawal.[25]

---

25   Due to the restrictive nature of the defence, it will be difficult, if not impossible, for suppliers of goods or advice to perpetrators to communicate effective withdrawal: S Bronitt, "Defending Giorgianni — Part Two: New Solutions for Old Problems in Complicity" (1993) 17 Crim LJ 305 at 306-307. See generally, D Lanham, "Accomplices and Withdrawal" [1981] 97 *Law Quarterly Review* 575.

It appears that the degree and type of assistance rendered by the accessory, together with the proximity in time to the commission of the offence will have a bearing on what will constitute an effective withdrawal. It will, for example, be somewhat easier to show withdrawal after counselling or procuring the commission of an offence than aiding or abetting it. If the accessory has only encouraged or advised the principal offender then it may be enough for him or her to tell the principal offender to desist in unequivocal terms.[26]

For example, in *R v Grundy* [1977] Crim LR 543 the accused supplied information to the principal offender in relation to a burglary, but substantial attempts to stop the principal offender breaking in during the two weeks leading up to the offence were held to be sufficient evidence of a valid withdrawal for the jury to consider: see also *Whitefield* (1983) 79 Cr App R 36. Far more will be required if the secondary party supplies the means for committing the crime as the situation in *Becerra* attests.

It is unclear as to whether or not the accused's withdrawal must be voluntary. There is very limited case law in support of this proposition[27] and it has been criticised on the basis that it involves the investigation of motives.[28]

2.6 THE FAULT ELEMENT

This section examines the fault element for accessorial liability. In relation to fault, it is conceptually useful to distinguish between two aspects — those fault elements that concern attitude, and those that concern *cognition*: S Bronitt, "Defending Giorgianni — Part One: The Fault Required for Complicity" (1993) 17 Crim LJ 242 at 244.

The accessory's attitude refers to the mental state that accompanies an accessory's acts that assist or encourage the principal offender to commit the offence. The controversial question in this regard is whether criminal liability for complicity should be restricted to that which is *intended* to assist, or encourage the commission of the principal offender's crime.

The cognition element is that mental state which relates to the accessory's knowledge of the "essential matters". In this context, the question arises whether complicity requires *actual* knowledge or whether some lesser cognitive state, such as recklessness or wilful blindness, will suffice. The authorities however lack this conceptual sophistication, as Glanville Williams in "Complicity, Purpose and the Draft Code — 1" [1990] Crim LR 4 has observed (at 4):

> The authorities do not state a consistent fault principle for accessories. Sometimes they
> require a purpose to bring about the crime; sometimes knowledge; sometimes an intention
> in a wide sense; sometimes they are satisfied with an intention to play some part in
> bringing it about; sometimes they use a formula that embraces recklessness. As so often
> happens, the courts are chiefly concerned to achieve a result that seems right in the
> particular case, leaving commentators to make what they can of what comes out.

---

26   *R v Saunders and Archer* (1576) 2 Plowd 473; 75 ER 706; *R v Croft* [1944] 1 KB 295; *R v Fletcher* [1962] Crim LR 551.

27   *Wilton* (1993) 64 A Crim R 359 at 364 per Zeeman J; *R v Malcolm* [1951] NZLR 470 (CA); *Commonwealth v Doris*, 135 A 313 (1926) (SC Penn).

28   B Fisse, *Howard's Criminal Law* (5th ed, Sydney: Law Book Company Ltd, 1990), p 351; JC Smith and B Hogan, *Criminal Law* (7th ed, London: Butt, 1992), p 155; KJM Smith, "Withdrawal from Criminal Liability for Complicity and Inchoate Offences" (1983) 12 *Anglo-American Law Review* 200 at 213-214.

Is Knowledge of the Essential Matters Sufficient?

The main debate in England concerning the fault element has been focused around an exchange of articles by Ian Dennis and GR Sullivan. Dennis argues that the fault element for complicity, in addition to knowledge, requires some element of purpose. Sullivan, on the other hand, regards knowledge as the exclusive basis for culpability.[29]

HIGH COURT'S APPROACH TO THE FAULT ELEMENT

The principles governing fault in Australia are in a much better state of repair following the High Court decision of *Giorgianni v The Queen* (1985) 156 CLR 473. In that case, Giorgianni leased and operated a prime-mover and trailer. He employed a driver, Renshaw, who lost control of the prime-mover which suffered a brake failure while heavily laden with coal. The prime-mover crashed into two cars, killing five people and seriously injuring another. Giorgianni was charged with five counts of culpable driving causing death and one count of culpable driving causing grievous bodily harm contrary to s 52A of the *Crimes Act* 1900 (NSW). Section 52A is an offence of strict liability: see Chapter 3 'Strict Liability Offences'. The prosecution argued that Giorgianni had procured the act of culpable driving and that he was aware of the prime-mover's brake problems following maintenance work that he had recently undertaken.

The trial judge directed the jury that in order for Giorgianni to have procured the act of culpable driving, he must or *ought to have known* that the brakes were defective. The trial judge went on to direct that that it would equally suffice if Giorgianni had acted recklessly, not caring whether or not the brakes were defective. Giorgianni was convicted and he eventually appealed to the High Court on the basis of the trial judge's directions to the jury.

The High Court overturned Giorgianni's convictions and the majority set out the test for the fault element of complicity. The particular facts of the case required specific consideration of the fault required of an accessory when assisting or encouraging an offence of strict liability. However, the High Court took the opportunity to clarify, in general terms, the fault required for *all* accessories, irrespective of the type of offence assisted or encouraged.

We will first analyse the High Court's decision relating to the fault element concerning *attitude* and in particular whether criminal liability for complicity should be restricted to that which is *intended* to assist or encourage the commission of the perpetrator's crime. We will then turn to the element of *cognition*.

FAULT ELEMENTS CONCERNING ATTITUDE: INTENTIONAL ASSISTANCE OR ENCOURAGEMENT

All of the members of the High Court apart from Mason J, stated that an accessory must intentionally assist or encourage the principal offender: *Giorgianni v The Queen* (1985) 156 CLR 473 at 482 per Gibbs CJ, at 500 per Wilson, Deane and Dawson JJ. Wilson, Dawson and Deane JJ stated (at 505):

---

29 See IH Dennis, "The Mental Element for Accessories" in P Smith (ed), *Criminal Law: Essays in Honour of JC Smith* (London: Butt, 1987), p 40; GR Sullivan, "Intent, Purpose and Complicity" [1988] Crim LR 641; IH Dennis, "Intention and Complicity: A Reply" [1988] Crim LR 649.

> Aiding, abetting, counselling or procuring the commission of an offence requires the intentional assistance or encouragement of the doing of those things which go to make up the offence.

This attitudinal aspect of fault for accessorial liability is extremely controversial. It is not entirely clear what is necessary to constitute intention in this regard. On the one hand it may mean a "specific intent" in the sense of entertaining a conscious purpose to promote the commission of the offence.[30] On the other hand, however, an "oblique intent" may be sufficient in that the secondary party knows the certainty or likelihood that his or her conduct will encourage or assist the principal offender to commit the offence.[31] These different forms of intent have been explored in Chapter 3, pp 177ff.

A careful analysis of the judgment in *Giorgianni* reveals that intention is employed in its narrower sense, requiring the accessory's assistance or encouragement to be accompanied by a specific intent that the principal offender will commit the offence. The majority in *Giorgianni* was cognisant that "intent" had a variable meaning in the criminal law. They stated (at 506):

> For the purposes of many offences it may be true to say that if an act is done with foresight
> of its probable consequences there is sufficient intent in law even if such intent may more
> properly be described as a form of recklessness. There are, however, offences in which it is
> not possible to speak of recklessness as constituting sufficient intent. Attempt is one and
> conspiracy is another. And we think the offences of aiding and abetting and counselling
> and procuring are others. Those offences require intentional participation in a crime by
> lending assistance or encouragement.

The majority (at 506) clearly favoured a requirement of specific intent — requiring that the accessory's acts of assistance or encouragement "be intentionally aimed at the commission of the acts which constitute [the principal offender's offence]".[32] Gibbs CJ held that the natural meaning of the words "aiding, abetting, counselling or procuring" and of their synonyms (for example, help, encourage, advise, persuade, induce or bring about by effort) suggest a more restrictive fault standard based on intent.

---

30 *R v Russell* [1933] VR 59 at 66 per Cussen CJ; *Dennis v Pight* (1968) 11 FLR 458; *Macpherson v Beath* (1975) 12 SASR 174 at 178; *R v Giorgi* (1983) 31 SASR 299 at 310 per Zelling J; *Scott v Killian* (1984) 36 SASR 438; *Mills* (1985) 17 A Crim R 411 at 450 per Roden J; *Gollan v Nugent* (1987) 8 NSWLR 166; *Salford Health Authority; Ex parte Jamaway* [1988] 2 WLR 442; *Attorney-General v Able* [1984] 1 QB 795; *R v Clarkson* [1971] 1 WLR 1402; *National Coal Board v Gamble* [1959] 1 QB 11 at 25-28 per Slade J; *R v Samuels* [1985] 1 NZLR 350.

31 *DPP (Northern Ireland) v Lynch* [1975] AC 653; *DPP (Northern Ireland) v Maxwell* [1978] 1 WLR 1350; *Attorney-General's Reference (No 1 of 1975)* [1975] QB 773; *R v Millar* [1970] 2 QB 54; *National Coal Board v Gamble* [1959] 1 QB 11 at 19 per Lord Goddard CJ, at 22-24 per Devlin J; *R v Miller* (1980) 25 SASR 170 at 200-201 per King CJ; *McLean* (1981) 5 A Crim R 36 at 40-41 per Roden J; *Annakin* (1988) 37 A Crim R 131; *R v Giorgi* (1983) 31 SASR 299 at 302 per King CJ; *Scott v Killian* (1985) 40 SASR 37 at 47 per Matheson J; *Nirta v The Queen* (1983) 51 ALR 53 at 70 per Jenkinson J.

32 The majority also observed that if an alternative, less stringent fault element is permitted, "a person might be guilty of aiding, abetting, counselling or procuring the commission of an offence which formed no part of his [or her] design": *Giorgianni v The Queen* (1985) 156 CLR 473 at 507.

FAULT ELEMENTS CONCERNING COGNITION: KNOWLEDGE OF THE ESSENTIAL FACTS OF THE OFFENCE

The question for the High Court in *Giorgianni* was whether or not an accessory to the offence of culpable driving under s 52A had to possess actual knowledge of the "essential matters" (in this case, knowledge of the defective state of the vehicle), or whether some lesser mental state would suffice.

Prior to *Giorgianni*, the degree of awareness required of an accessory concerning the factual ingredients of the principal offender's crime was unclear. The earlier authorities referred only to actual knowledge as being the fault required for complicity. In *Johnson v Youden* [1959] 1 KB 544, Goddard LCJ described the fault element for complicity in the following terms (at 546):

> Before a person can be convicted of aiding and abetting the commission of an offence he [or she] must at least know the essential matters which constitute that offence. He [or she] need not actually know that an offence has been committed, because he [or she] may not know that the facts constitute an offence and ignorance of the law is not a defence.

Later decisions took a broader approach, supplementing actual knowledge with recklessness or wilful blindness. In *Glennan* (1970) 91 WN (NSW) 609, the New South Wales Court of Criminal Appeal held (at 614) that:

> [I]t must be shown that [the accessory] either knew or suspected the existence of facts which would constitute the commission of the offence or, perhaps, that he [or she] acted recklessly, not caring whether the facts existed or not.

The Court of Criminal Appeal further explained (at 614) that knowledge embraces wilful blindness, that is, "a failure to make an inquiry which is of such a kind as to suggest that the defendant has deliberately abstained from acquiring knowledge because he [or she] suspected the existence of a fact which would have been ascertained on inquiry".

The High Court in *Giorgianni* considered the suggestion in *Glennan* that, as an alternative to actual knowledge, recklessness or wilful blindness would suffice. The majority (Wilson, Deane and Dawson JJ at 506-507) emphatically rejected the notion that recklessness as to the existence of the factual ingredients which constitute the principal offender's offence would suffice:

> It is not sufficient if [the accessory's] knowledge or belief extends only to the possibility or even probability that the acts which he [or she] is assisting or encouraging are such, whether he [or she] realizes it or not, as to constitute the factual ingredients of a crime.

Gibbs CJ (at 487) and Mason J (at 495) agreed with the majority that actual knowledge was required, and that recklessness could never be enough to constitute a person as an accessory. They were prepared (at 482 and 495 respectively), however, to equate wilful blindness with knowledge. This approach has been rejected in subsequent decisions on the role and meaning of wilful blindness, see Chapter 3, p 180.

Applied to the facts, the accused would only be an accessory to the strict liability offence of culpable driving committed by Renshaw, if he had *actual* knowledge of the defective state of the vehicle. Since recklessness did not suffice, a belief that the brakes were possibly (or even probably) defective would be insufficient for liability as an accessory. Therefore, the trial judge's direction to the jury in terms of recklessness amounted to a misdirection, and on that basis the majority of the High Court allowed the appeal.

FAULT AND THE PROBLEM OF DIVERGENCE

There is still some question as to what will constitute knowledge of the essential facts of an offence. Is it knowledge of the factual elements of the crime? Will it be enough for an accessory to know that the principal offender will commit a type of crime rather than a specific crime? Or will knowledge of the principal offender's *intention* to commit a crime suffice? What is the effect if the principal offender's offence diverges from the crime within the accessory's contemplation?

This problem of divergence was considered in *Stokes and Difford* (1990) 51 A Crim R 25. Stokes and Difford were inmates of the Malabar Prison Complex. They were jointly charged with maliciously inflicting grievous bodily harm on another inmate, with intent to inflict grievous bodily harm. At the conclusion of the Crown case the trial judge ruled that there was no case to go to the jury against Difford upon the joint charge, but allowed the jury to consider the alternative charge of maliciously inflicting grievous bodily harm (without the specific intent). Stokes was convicted as a principal offender of maliciously inflicting grievous bodily harm with intent to inflict grievous bodily harm. Difford was convicted as an accessory of maliciously inflicting grievous bodily harm. On appeal, the New South Wales Court of Criminal Appeal quashed Difford's conviction. Hunt J, in delivering the judgment of the Court stated (at 38):

> In relation to [accessories] ... it seems to me, it is usually more appropriate to speak of the accessory's knowledge (or awareness) of the principal offender's *intention* to do an act with a particular state of mind at the time when the accessory aids, abets, counsels or procures the principal offender to commit the crime in question than it is to speak of the accessory's knowledge of the act *done* by the principal offender with that state of mind (emphasis in original).

On the facts, it was held that the prosecution had failed to establish that Difford knew of the intention of Stokes to hit the victim and that Stokes intended to inflict some physical injury or realised the possibility that some such injury might result but nevertheless intended to go ahead and hit the victim.

The case of *Stokes and Difford* therefore stands for the proposition that the knowledge of the principal offender's intention will be enough to satisfy this limb of the fault element: see also *McCarthy and Ryan* (1993) 71 A Crim R 395 (CCA NSW).

Alternatively, the prosecution will have to prove that the accessory had knowledge of the physical elements of the crime. It appears that it will be sufficient if the secondary party had knowledge of the *type of crime* to be committed. In *R v Bainbridge* [1960] 1 QB 129 the accused supplied oxygen-cutting equipment to others who used the equipment to break into a bank and steal cash. The English Court of Appeal held that the accused was liable as he knew, when supplying the equipment, that it would be used for a breaking and entry offence. The Court of Appeal held that a secondary party only needed to know the general type of crime to be committed rather than the specific crime for criminal responsibility as an accessory to be made out.

Similarly, in *DPP (Northern Ireland) v Maxwell* [1978] 3 All ER 1140 the House of Lords held that it was sufficient for liability where the secondary party knew that the crime to be committed was one from a limited range of offences.

In *Ancuta* (1990) 49 A Crim R 307 (CCA Qld) the accused appealed against a conviction for various offences concerning organised car stealing, including three counts of unlawful possession of motor vehicles. The accused had supplied the principal offender with number plates, which several weeks later were attached to a stolen white Commodore. The accused argued that there was insufficient evidence to support the prosecution's argument that he had enabled the principal offender to gain unlawful possession of the white Commodore. The Queensland Court of Criminal Appeal dismissed the accused's appeal on the basis that it was sufficient for the prosecution to establish that the accused had aided or abetted the *type* or *kind* of crime committed by the principal offender. The prosecution did not have to prove that the accused aided and abetted the principal offender's possession of the Commodore that was the subject of the charge.

This process of broadening the knowledge requirement poses the risk of over-criminalisation. The effect of *Bainbridge* is that an accessory who assists or encourages a person to commit a particular crime is theoretically liable for all crimes subsequently committed by the principal offender, no matter how long after the accessory's assistance or encouragement they occur, provided those subsequent crimes are of the same *type* as the crime which the accessory originally contemplated.[33] The risk of over-criminalisation, however, may be exaggerated. John Smith in "Criminal Liability of Accessories: Law and Law Reform" (1997) 113 LQR 453 (at 465) stated:

> What of the *Bainbridge* problem? Ever since the decision in 1959 academic lawyers and students have been having sleepless nights worrying about the seller of a rather durable jemmy being convicted of endless burglaries, of which he [or she] knew nothing, years after the sale. But the issue of multiple convictions did not arise in *Bainbridge* nor, so far as I know, has it arisen in any reported case in 38 years which have elapsed since we were alerted to the existence of the problem. We do not know, of course, that it has not caused concern to prosecutors but it can hardly be seen as a pressing practical problem.

This problem may be theoretical, but it does reveal the conceptual difficulties that arise from linking accessorial liability to the commission of the principal offender's offence. The Law Reform Commission of Canada has suggested a simple and neat solution to the problem of divergence. It proposes that there should be no criminal liability as an accessory where there is a difference between the crime the accessory intends to promote and the crime actually committed by the perpetrator, *except* where that difference relates to the "identity of the victim or to the degree of harm".[34]

---

33   This problem was recognised by the Law Commission of England and Wales in an early Working Paper on secondary liability: The Law Commission, *General Principles, Parties, Complicity and Liability for the Acts of Another*, Working Paper No 43 (London: HMSO, 1972), pp 73-77.

34   Law Reform Commission of Canada, *Secondary Liability: Participation in Crime and Inchoate Offences*, Working Paper No 45 (1985), p 36. This principle is contained in cl 4(6) of the revised *Criminal Code* proposed by the Commission in the *Report on Recodifying Criminal Law* (1987), p 47.

The precise relationship between these earlier English decisions and *Giorgianni* is difficult to determine. The problem lies in reconciling *Bainbridge* and *Maxwell* with the requirement established in *Giorgianni* that an accessory must assist or encourage with an intention that the perpetrator will commit the offence: S Bronitt, "Defending Giorgianni — Part One: The Fault Required for Complicity" (1993) 17 Crim LJ 242 at 256-257.

One interpretation of *Giorgianni* is that an accessory's intention must relate to the *actual* offence that is subsequently committed by the principal offender. It remains unresolved whether a broad qualification, similar to that used in *Bainbridge*, applies to intention as well as to knowledge. Put another way, will it suffice that the accessory intended to assist or encourage the commission of a crime *of the same type* as that which is actually committed by the perpetrator? The obvious way to resolve this uncertainty, and to reconcile these earlier cases with *Giorgianni*, is to extend the qualifications in *Bainbridge* and *Maxwell* to cover intention. This would mean that an accessory need intend only to assist or encourage an offence of the *type* committed in due course by the principal offender. Indeed, this solution to the problem of divergence has been adopted in the *Criminal Code Act* 1995 (Cth). Section 11.2(3)(a) states that for a person to be guilty, he or she must have intended that "his or her conduct would aid, abet, counsel or procure the commission of the offence (including its fault elements) of the type the other person committed".

2.7 PRINCIPAL AND JOINT PRINCIPAL OFFENDERS

The term "principal offender" refers to the person who directly performs the physical elements of the criminal offence. In most cases there is little dispute over who is the principal offender.

However, on occasion, there may be more that one perpetrator of a crime. Two or more persons can be joint principals if they are closely connected to the occurrence of the physical element of the offence: *R v Bingley* (1821) Russ & Ry 446. For example, if a number of individuals attack another intending to kill their victim and the combined effect of their blows is to cause death, each may be said to be a joint principal: *Macklin and Murphy's case* (1838) 2 Lew CC 225.

In *R v Macdonald* [1904] QSR 151 the victim, a young girl, died of starvation and lack of medical care after the two accused brutally mistreated and neglected her. The accused were both convicted of wilful murder on the basis that they were jointly responsible for the victim's death.

Two or more persons may be joint principal offenders where each has the requisite fault element and together perform all the physical elements of the crime.[35] For example, the Law Commission of England and Wales gave as an example the situation where, during a robbery, one party holds a gun or holds down the victim while the other grabs the victim's property: The Law Commission, *Parties, Complicity and Liability for the Act of Another,* Working Paper 43 (London: HMSO, 1972), illustration b at 33. The use of force and stealing are two separate physical elements of the offence of robbery and both have been made out in this situation.

---

35 *R v Clarke and Wilton* [1959] VR 645; *R v Wyles; Ex parte Attorney-General (Qld)* [1977] Qd R 169; *R v Webb; Ex parte Attorney-General* [1990] 2 Qd R 275; *Russell and Russell* (1987) 85 Cr App R 388.

PERSPECTIVES

Domestic Violence and Victim Complicity

The doctrine of complicity has sometimes been used against individuals who assist or encourage their own victimisation. For example, victims of domestic violence have been prosecuted for "aiding and abetting" breaches of restraining orders. Police and prosecutors, frustrated by victims who "invite" perpetrators back to resume cohabitation in breach of their restraining orders, have resorted to this strategy to reinforce to victims and the community the legal significance and inviolability of such orders. In most jurisdictions, the process of criminalisation has occurred surreptitiously, without legislative intervention, through changes to prosecution policies and common law development.

Domestic violence legislation does not *expressly* criminalise victims who aid and abet breaches of restraining orders. In the Australian Capital Territory, however, a person protected by the restraining order must be warned of the possibility of liability for aiding and abetting a breach.[36] The criminalisation of victim-precipitation in the context of domestic violence raises controversial issues of legal principle and policy.

Victim Complicity: An Exceptional Principle or A Matter of Interpretation?

Complicity has the potential to expand significantly the ambit of the criminal law. In relation to victims who "aid and abet" a crime against themselves, the question asked by the court is whether the nature of the offence and/or the purpose behind the relevant legislation excludes accessorial liability. The leading authority on this topic is the English decision of *R v Tyrrell* [1894] 1 QB 710. Section 5(1) of the *Criminal Law Amendment Act* 1885 (UK) created the offence of unlawful carnal knowledge of a female under 16 years of age, an offence which required neither proof of force or lack of consent. The accused, a young girl, was convicted of aiding and abetting the unlawful carnal knowledge of herself. The Court of Crown Cases Reserved held that her conviction should be quashed. Lord Coleridge CJ, with whom the other judges agreed, observed (at 712) that the *Criminal Law Amendment Act* 1885 (UK) was passed for "the purpose of protecting women and girls against themselves". In a judgment of only 15 lines, his Lordship concluded (at 712) that "it is impossible to say that the Act, which is absolutely silent about aiding or abetting, or soliciting or inciting, can have intended that the girls for whose protection it was passed should be punishable under it for the offences committed upon themselves". Mathew J agreed, pointing out (at 712-713) that a contrary decision would result in "nearly every section which deals with offences in respect of women and girls" creating an "offence in the woman or girl. Such a result [could not] have been intended by the legislature. There is no trace in the statute of any intention to treat the woman or girl as criminal".

The rule in *Tyrrell* has been applied to exclude accessorial liability for a prostitute who abetted her husband in living off her immoral earnings: *Congdon* (1990) 140 NLJ 1221. It has also been applied in *R v Whitehouse* [1977] QB 868 to exclude a charge against a father for inciting his daughter to aid and abet him to commit incest with her, no act of sexual intercourse having

---

36 *Domestic Violence Act* 1986 (ACT), s 15(2)(d); *Magistrate's Court Act* 1930 (ACT), s 206E(2)(d). See further, N Seddon, *Domestic Violence in Australia: The Legal Response* (2nd ed, Sydney: Federation Press, 1993), p 97, noting that there has been at least one such conviction in the Australian Capital Territory.

actually occurred. The English Court of Appeal, quashing the father's conviction of incitement, held that the daughter could not be regarded as an accessory to incest for two reasons. First, as the girl was aged 15 she belonged to a class that is protected, but not punished, by the *Sexual Offences Act* 1956. Secondly, the girl was alleged to be the victim of this notional crime. Lord Scarman, for the Court, concluded (at 875):

> In our judgment it is impossible, as a matter of principle, to distinguish *Reg v Tyrrell* from the present case. Clearly the relevant provisions of the *Sexual Offences Act* 1956 are intended to protect women and girls. Most certainly, section 11 is intended to protect girls under the age of 16 from criminal liability, and the Act as a whole exists, in so far as it deals with women and girls exposed to sexual threat, to protect them. The very fact that girls under the age of 16 are protected from criminal liability for what would otherwise be incest demonstrates that this girl who is said to have been the subject of incitement was being incited to do something which, if she did it, could not be a crime by her.

As *Tyrrell* concerned charges of a sexual nature, it is often mischaracterised as establishing a special rule that exempts victims of sexual offences from complicity. For example, recommendation 3.8(g) in the South Australian Penal Methods and Law Reform Commission's Report on *The Substantive Criminal Law* (1977) states (at 309):

> [T]he victim of a sex offence against a person under the age of consent [should] be not liable to conviction as an accomplice, but we do not extend this recommendation to any other situation of the victim of an offence being a willing party to its commission.

The preferable view is that *Tyrrell* is not a special rule, but rather is simply an application of the ordinary principles of statutory interpretation. As the Law Commission of England and Wales observed in *Assisting and Encouraging Crime*, Consultation Paper No 131 (1993), p 48 (footnotes omitted):

> That a rule exists which protects at least the victims of crimes from liability for abetting them is asserted in all the authorities. These, however, also stress the sparse authority for such a rule, and the complete uncertainty as to how far it extends. The principle in reality appears to be one of statutory interpretation that has only been clearly applied in one case, *Tyrrell*, in 1894. It involves identifying a Parliamentary intention that certain parties be exempt from liability, despite their *de facto* aiding, abetting, counselling or procuring of an offence under the statutory provision in question ...
>
> The Court in *Tyrrell* ... exempted the defendant from liability on the basis of an implied statutory intention, rather than by reference to a rule peculiar to victims of sexual offences: indeed, the term "victim" is never used in the judgments. However, the case has since been taken as authority for a supposed principle that the victim of a *sexual* offence, even if he or she encourages its commission, is not liable as an accomplice to that offence if he or she is a member of the class of persons for whose protection the statute was passed".

For a further discussion of the scope of *Tyrrell*, see G Williams, "Victims and Other Exempt Parties in Crime" (1990) 10 *Legal Studies* 245.

Criminalising Victims of Domestic Violence

The legal propriety of victim-criminalisation strategies in the context of domestic violence has rarely been challenged outside courts of summary jurisdiction. An exception is the case of *Michelle Fay Keane* (1997) 95 A Crim R 593. Keane had taken out a restraining order against Smith under s 4 of the *Domestic Violence Act* 1994 (SA). The agreed facts in the Magistrates' Court were that Keane admitted Smith into her home knowing that he was breaching the restraining order. Keane was then charged with aiding or abetting, counselling or procuring, the offence of breaching a restraining order by Smith. Her subsequent conviction provided the Supreme Court of South Australia with an opportunity to review the relevant authorities and principles governing the liability of individuals who aid and abet offences committed on themselves.

King AJ held (at 594) that the action of the appellant in admitting Smith to her home knowing that he was thereby in breach of the restraining order fell within the common law concept of aiding and abetting which is embodied in s 267 of the *Criminal Law Consolidation Act* 1936 (SA). Accordingly, the appellant was guilty unless she could be relieved from criminal liability for her action by some express or implied provision of the law. King AJ considered the relevant authorities on this issue, concluding (at 596) that: "[t]he principle to be derived from [*Tyrrell*], in my opinion, is that accessorial liability is excluded where the Act creating the offence exists for the protection of persons against their own willing participation in the offending conduct". In this case, King AJ concluded (at 596) that the principle had no application to the *Domestic Violence Act* since: "[t]he Act is not aimed at protecting people from themselves but at protecting them from unwanted conduct causing apprehension or fear". Both the nature of the offence and policy behind the Act supported this interpretation. King AJ (at 596) was unable to discern,

> any provision or consideration of policy in the *Domestic Violence Act* giving rise to an implication excluding ordinary accessorial liability ... Where an order is made for a person's benefit, it would seem to be unjust that that person should be able to encourage or facilitate a breach of the order thereby causing another to commit an offence, but escape any liability. Moreover on policy grounds, it is important that curial and police resources should not be wasted in obtaining and enforcing restraining orders, the breach of which the persons for whose benefit they are made, are willing to condone.

From a doctrinal perspective, the decision in *Keane* may be criticised on a number of grounds. The suggestion that *Tyrrell* applies only to crimes which are intended to protect victims *from themselves* is an unduly restrictive reading of the decision. It has the effect of limiting the exclusion of complicity to a narrow range of crimes, such as incest or sex with minors, which apply irrespective of the victim's consent. Such a restriction is inconsistent with dicta in *Giorgianni* (1985) 156 CLR 473 where Mason J (at 491) described the principle in much broader terms:

> In *Mallan v Lee* [(1949) 80 CLR 198, Dixon J at 216] observed that "the application of sections dealing with aiding and abetting may be excluded by the nature of the substantive offence or the general tenor or policy of the provisions by which it is created". A similar approach must be taken to apply to the exclusion of the doctrine of secondary participation at common law. It may, therefore, be inapplicable to a person of a class whom the substantive offence is designed to protect.

Conceived as a principle of interpretation, applicable to statutes and common law offences, complicity cannot be attached to individuals who fall within "a class whom the substantive offence is designed to protect". Arguably, domestic violence victims who are the intended beneficiaries of restraining orders *should* be regarded as falling within this category.

Keane may be further criticised as representing a concealed shift in the approach to "legislative intent". In *Tyrrell,* the court adopted a presumption that victim complicity should not be criminalised unless there is a contrary legislative intent; whereas in *Keane* the court adopted a presumption that victim complicity should be criminalised unless there is a contrary legislative intent. Viewed as a principle of interpretation, rather than as a special exception to complicity, the burden of establishing that the legislature intended not to exclude victim complicity ought to rest with the prosecution. A court must also be satisfied that such an interpretation would not, in the circumstances, constitute a retrospective application of the criminal law. Without fair and reasonable warning of the possibility of accessorial liability, the use of complicity against victims of domestic violence may offend against the principles *nullem crimen sine lege* and *nulla poena sine lege*: see Ch 1, p 8. These principles hold that the State should not deem an act a crime or render it punishable when it was not considered to be a criminal offence under that law at the time of its commission. Clearly this objection is not sustainable in the Australian Capital Territory where the legislation requires victims to be warned of the possibility of liability as an accessory.[37]

From the viewpoint of culpability, criminalising victims who assist or encourage perpetrators of domestic violence to breach a restraining order is problematic. As victims may have suffered repeated violence at the hands of the perpetrator, there may be legitimate doubts about the "voluntariness" of their conduct due to threats, force, feelings of helplessness or economic pressure. These constraints upon the victim's agency do not automatically excuse liability, although they may be raised as relevant to sentence mitigation. To be legally exculpatory, these facts must be successfully translated into legal defences such as automatism, duress, marital coercion or necessity: see Chs 4 and 6. This is an extremely difficult task invariably requiring expert evidence. The prospect of success is remote bearing in mind the lack of legal representation and legal aid available for defending minor criminal matters. Moreover, the fault element for complicity is broad, satisfied by intent to assist or encourage with "knowledge of the essential matters". The victim need not possess knowledge that the perpetrator's conduct (for example, resuming cohabitation) would violate the restraining order. Thus, the victim's ignorance of the law, including her potential liability as an accessory, affords no defence.

Although the law in this area remains uncertain and contentious, the issue of victim complicity has received little attention from law reformers. It was overlooked completely in a recent report examining national domestic violence laws: see Legislation Working Group, *Model Domestic Violence Laws,* Report (April 1999). The matter was raised only tangentially in the section of the Report dealing with breach offences. In determining whether breach of a restraining order should be excused if the protected person had "consented", the Report recognised (p 215) the limited range of choices available to victims of violence:

---

37 For further discussion of *Keane* see M Goode, "Case and Comment: *Keane v Police*" (1998) 22 Crim LJ 237.

> Comments were sought on whether the WA provision [*Restraining Orders Act* 1997
> (WA), s 62], that it is a defence to the breach offence if an aggrieved protected person
> (other than a child or incapable person) consents to the breach represents a desirable
> development. Submissions were largely opposed to this defence being incorporated
> into the Model Laws because of concerns that the "consent" may often have been a
> response to fear or a threat. Further, it was stated in submissions that the defence
> failed to acknowledge that a domestic violence order is an order of a court, and not an
> agreement between two individuals which is capable of being varied at will. The
> Working Group concurred with this reasoning and the defence has been omitted from
> the Model (footnotes omitted).

The construction of "domestic violence", and the responsibility which women are assumed to
play in perpetuating violence against themselves, are politically and legally unstable. The image
of domestic violence victims as lacking agency and capacity to consent may be contrasted with
their alternate construction as culpable accessories to their own victimisation, willing and
competent to instigate breaches of restraining orders. However, these contradictions in legal
discourse seem to be invisible to both law reformers and policy makers. The boundaries of
domestic violence are constantly being reshaped, contingent not only on the "law in the books"
but also on formal and informal interactions between police, prosecutors, judges and
legislatures. Prosecutors and judges seem increasingly prepared to invoke the ordinary
principles of complicity against victims of domestic violence in order to safeguard the rule of law
and judicial authority. The extent to which such strategies will enhance the level of protection
offered against domestic violence is debatable. From a regulatory perspective, criminalising
victims of domestic abuse, while *purporting* to achieve higher levels of protection, may be
counterproductive — victims may be discouraged from seeking restraining orders for fear that
they themselves may be held responsible for breaches which may subsequently occur. Re-
victimisation by gender insensitive laws and procedures is inconsistent with non-binding
international standards laid down in Art 4(f) of the United Nations *Declaration on the Elimination
of Violence Against Women* (DEVAW), which provides that States should:

> Develop, in a comprehensive way, preventive approaches and all those measures of a
> legal, political, administrative and cultural nature that promote the protection of
> women against any form of violence, and ensure that the re-victimization of women
> does not occur because of laws insensitive to gender considerations, enforcement
> practices or other interventions.[38]

Without an unambiguous legislative intent to the contrary, prosecutors and judges should be
cautious in criminalising as accessories, victims who are seeking their protection and a lawful
means of breaking the cycle of violence. Clearly, further research into the domestic violence and
the potential negative effects of victim–complicity is needed before such legal strategies should
be endorsed.

---

38   GA Res 48/104 of 20 December 1993 (85th plen mtg), UN Doc A/RES/48/104.

3. INNOCENT AGENCY AND ACTING IN CONCERT

Because of the derivative nature of counselling, procuring, aiding and abetting, it seems logical that a person cannot be guilty of participating in an offence unless that offence is actually committed.[39] Most of the Australian statutory formulations reflect this by referring to when an offence (or crime) is committed[40] or the commission of an offence.[41]

However, the law has developed avenues by which participants may be held liable even where the principal offender's conduct is not in itself criminal or subject to criminal proceedings. The first main way in which derivative liability may be by-passed is through the doctrine of innocent agency which converts an apparent "aider and abettor" into a principal offender.

The law has also developed in such a way as to enable the conviction of an aider or abettor even where the principal offender is unknown or has been acquitted. There is some controversy concerning this particular area of the law and the recent High Court majority decision in *Osland v The Queen* (1998) 197 CLR 316 has gone some way toward clarifying the law in this area insofar as it relates to those acting in concert.

These two methods of bypassing the concept of derivative liability will be discussed in turn.

3.1 INNOCENT AGENCY

Innocent agency or "perpetration-by-means"[42] is a doctrine that attributes criminal responsibility to a person who has not personally performed the physical elements of a crime. That is, if a person uses an "innocent agent" to commit a crime, it is that person and not the innocent agent who is the principal offender, regardless of whether he or she was present at the scene of the crime.[43]

An innocent agent is one who is not considered criminally responsible by reason of infancy, mental impairment, lack of knowledge of the true facts or belief that the act is not unlawful. The requirement of "innocence" refers to the agent's lack of criminal responsibility rather than lack of moral fault: *Hewitt* (1996) 84 A Crim R 440 at 450 per Winneke P.

---

39 *Morris v Tolman* [1923] 1 KB 166; *Thornton v Mitchell* [1940] 1 All ER 339; *Cain v Doyle* (1946) 72 CLR 409; *R v Williams* (1932) 32 SR(NSW) 504; *Walsh v Sainsbury* (1925) 36 CLR 464; *R v See Lun* (1932) 32 SR(NSW) 363; *R v Demirian* [1989] VR 97; *Osland v The Queen* (1998) 159 ALR 170 at 174 per Gaudron and Gummow JJ, at 189 per McHugh J.

40 *Criminal Code* (NT), ss 8, 9, 12; *Criminal Code* (Qld), ss 7-9; *Criminal Code* (Tas), ss 3-5; *Criminal Code* (WA), ss 7-9.

41 *Crimes Act* (Vic), ss 323, 324; *Criminal Law Consolidation Act* 1935 (SA), s 269.

42 G Fletcher, *Rethinking Criminal Law* (Boston, Mass: Little, Brown and Co, 1978), p 639.

43 *White v Ridley* (1978) 140 CLR 342; *Matusevich v The Queen* (1977) 137 CLR 633; *R v Demirian* [1989] VR 97; *R v Michael* (1840) 9 Car & P 356. See also GF Orchard, "Criminal Responsibility for the Acts of Innocent Agents" (1990) 2 *Criminal Law Forum* 45; G Williams, "Innocent Agency and Causation" (1992) 3 *Criminal Law Forum* 289.

An extensive range of offences have been listed as having been committed by an innocent agent, including murder,[44] administering poison,[45] forgery,[46] theft,[47] offences involving fraud,[48] libel[49] and rape.[50]

In *White v Ridley* (1978) 140 CLR 342 the accused employed an airline carrier to unwittingly import cannabis into Australia. On appeal against conviction, a majority of the High Court held that the accused could be found liable for the importation of drugs via an innocent agent. The majority found (at 354 per Stephen J; at 363 per Aickin J) that a person can be properly convicted of an offence when an innocent agent is used to perform the physical elements of the crime, providing the requisite intent is present and no other cause has intervened to displace the accused's actions as a continuing legal cause of the crime's physical elements.

The doctrine of innocent agency may apply even where the accused is personally unable to commit the crime as a principal offender. For example, in *R v Cogan and Leak* [1976] QB 217 the accused, Leak, persuaded Cogan, his "drunken friend" to have sexual intercourse with Leak's wife. The latter submitted to sex with Cogan out of fear of her husband. She did not struggle with Cogan, but sobbed throughout the ordeal and tried to turn away from him. Cogan was convicted of rape and Leak was convicted of aiding and abetting the rape.

On appeal, Cogan argued that he honestly believed the victim had been consenting. His appeal was allowed and his conviction quashed. Leak then appealed on the ground that he could not be convicted of aiding and abetting Cogan because the latter had been acquitted of the crime of rape. When the case of *Cogan and Leak* was heard, a husband could not be found guilty of raping his wife. Nevertheless, the Court of Appeal upheld Leak's conviction on the basis that he had possessed the necessary fault element for raping his wife and had used Cogan as an "instrument" for the necessary physical act.

The English Court of Appeal clearly viewed Leak as a principal offender rather than an aider and abettor. The Court stated (at 223):

> The modern law allowed Leak to be tried and punished as a principal offender. In our judgment he could have been indicted as a principal offender. It would have been no defence for him to submit that if Cogan was an "innocent" agent, he was necessarily in the old terminology of the law a principal in the first degree, which was a legal impossibility as a man cannot rape his own wife during cohabitation. The law no longer concerns itself with niceties of degrees in participation in crime; but even if it did Leak would still be guilty.

---

44 *Coombes* (1785) 1 Leach 388; *Tyler and Price* (1838)1 Mood CC 428; *Michael* (1840) 9 C & P 356.

45 *Harley* (1830) 4 C & P 369.

46 *Palmer* (1804) 2 Leach 978; *Giles* (1827) 1 Mood CC 166; *Mazeau* (1840) 9 C & P 676; *Clifford* (1845) 2 Car & K 202; *Bull* (1845) 1 Cox 281; *Valler* (1844) 1 Cox 84; *Bannen* (1844) 1 Car & K 295.

47 *Pitman* (1826) 2 C & P 423; *Manley* (1844) 1 Cox 104; *Welham* (1845) 1 Cox 192; *Bleasdale* (1848) 2 Car & K 765; *Flatman* (1880) 14 Cox 396; *Adams* (1812) R & R 225; *Kay* (1857) Dears & B 231; *Paterson* [1976] NZLR 394.

48 *DPP v Stonehouse* [1978] 168 ER 773; *Mutton* (1793) 1 Esp 62; *Brisac and Scott* (1803) East, *PC* iv 164, 102 ER 792; *Butcher* (1858) Bell 6; *Dowey* (1868) 11 Cox 115; *Butt* (1884) 15 Cox 564; *Oliphant* (1905) 2 KB 73.

49 *Johnson* (1805) 29 St Tr 81; *Cooper* (1846) 8 QB 533.

50 *R v Cogan and Leak* [1976] 1 QB 217; *Hewitt* (1996) 84 A Crim R 440. See G Hubble, "Rape by Innocent Agent" (1997) 21 Crim LJ 104.

> The reason a man cannot by his own physical act rape his wife during cohabitation is because the law presumes consent from the marriage ceremony ... There is no such presumption when a man procures a drunken friend to do the physical act for him.

This decision has been criticised on the ground that the "bodily connotations" of rape are so strong that it is incongruous to hold that the offence can be perpetrated by another's act.[51] The Victorian Court of Appeal has stressed, however, that the physical element of rape can be satisfied by an accused sexually penetrating a person who is not consenting or by *causing* such a person to be sexually penetrated.[52]

3.2 ACTING IN CONCERT

Occasionally, it will be difficult to distinguish between whether parties should be termed joint principals, or principal offender and aider or abettor, because of the evidential difficulty in identifying the precise role of each participant. The law has developed another way of holding parties liable through the doctrine of common purpose. This will be explored in the next section: p 411. However, it is important to distinguish between joint principal offenders and complicity in a crime because of the different nature of the fault element involved and because liability as an aider and abettor is derivative and is therefore usually dependent upon the conviction of the principal offender.

In general, there are three ways in which a person may participate by being present at a crime. They are:

═══ primary;

═══ derivative; and

═══ acting in concert.

Consider the following scenarios. First, Jack and Jill attack Mary intending to kill her and the combined effect of their blows causes death. Here, each is said to be a joint principal offender. Their liability is said to be "primary".

Secondly, Jill watches out for passersby whilst Jack hits Mary on the head with an iron bar causing her death. Here, Jack may be said to be the principal offender and Jill the aider and abettor. Jill's liability is said to be "derivative" in that it is dependent on the offence being committed. Jill may be tried and punished *as if* she were the principal offender.

Thirdly, Jack and Jill decide to kill Mary. According to a pre-conceived plan, Jill holds Mary down whilst Jack hits Mary over the head with a brick causing her death. Here, both Jack and Jill are said to be "acting in concert" and each is responsible for the acts of the other in carrying out the crime. On this scenario, Jack and Jill's liability is now considered in Australia to be "primary" and it

---

51 G Williams, *Textbook of Criminal Law* (2nd ed, London: Stevens and Sons, 1983), p 371; see also JC Smith and B Hogan, *Criminal Law* (7th ed, London: Butt, 1992), p 153; D Brown, D Farrier and D Weisbrot, *Criminal Laws: Materials and Commentary on Criminal Law and Process in New South Wales* (2nd ed, Sydney: Federation Press, 1996), pp 1293-1299.

52 *Hewitt* (1996) 84 A Crim R 440. See further G Hubble, "Rape by Innocent Agent" (1997) 21 Crim LJ 204.

will be enough for the prosecution to prove that the acts were performed in the presence of both Jack and Jill and pursuant to a pre-conceived plan.

In relation to this third scenario, in *Lowery v King (No 2)* [1972] VR 560 Smith J stated (at 560):

> The law says that if two or more persons reach an understanding or arrangement that together they will commit a crime and then, while that understanding or arrangement is still on foot and has not been called off, they are both present at the scene of the crime and one or other of them does, or they do between them, in accordance with their under-standing or arrangement, all the things that are necessary to constitute the crime, they are all equally guilty of that crime regardless of what part each played in its commission.

Sometimes, however, it may be difficult to draw a distinction between the second and third scenarios. The general rule appears to be that if it is unclear which party is the principal and which is the aider and abettor, both may nevertheless be convicted of the offence.[53] For example, in *Mohan v The Queen* [1967] 2 AC 187 both accused simultaneously attacked the victim with cutlasses and inflicted two severe injuries. The victim subsequently died. It was possible that only one of the injuries was fatal and it was not proved which of the accused inflicted the one fatal injury. On appeal against conviction, the accused argued that because they did not have a pre-conceived plan, they could not be said to be acting in concert. Further, because it could not be proved who inflicted the fatal wound, their conviction should be quashed. The Privy Council held it irrelevant that it was unknown who struck the fatal blow; since the two accused attacked the victim at the same time with the same intention they were assisting each other and thus were equally guilty: see also *R v Sperotto* (1970) 71 SR (NSW) 344.

A similar view was expressed in *R v Demirian* [1989] VR 97 by McGarvie and O'Bryan JJ who took the view that the theoretical distinction between primary liability for those acting in concert and derivative liability as an aider and abettor is of little practical significance. They stated (at 123):

> When the evidence is that the accused were present acting in concert when the crime was committed it is seldom necessary for a jury to find, or to be concerned, whether individually they were principal offenders or accessories at the crime. They will all fall within one or other of those categories. They may all be convicted of the crime.

However, the conceptual basis for the doctrine of acting in concert has been problematic. In England, the weight of academic opinion favours the view that common purpose or joint enterprise liability is a type of accessorial or derivative liability.[54] A clear conceptual distinction is drawn between the principal offender who actually commits the offence, and the accessories who jointly agree, expressly or impliedly, to its commission. The idea that a person who jointly agrees to the commission of an offence but does not actually commit the physical elements may be deemed to "participate" as a principal offender is viewed as illogical. JC Smith is strongly critical of the trend to view joint enterprise as a means of participating in another person's offence as opposed to simply

---

53   *R v Clough* (1992) 28 NSWLR 396 at 398-399; *R v Swindall and Osborne* (1846) 2 Car & Kir 230.

54   See CMV Clarkson, "Complicity, Powell and Manslaughter" [1998] Crim LR 556; JC Smith, "Criminal Liability of Accessories" [1997] 113 *Law Quarterly Review* 453 at 462. Some judges however have viewed the "doctrine of joint enterprise" as being governed by principles distinct from accessorial liability: *Stewart and Schofield* [1995] 1 Cr App R 441, per Hobhouse LJ.

being an application of ordinary principles of accessorial liability. In his article "Criminal Liability of Accessories: Law and Law Reform" (1997) 113 *Law Quarterly Review* 453 he observed (at 462):

> If D and P set out together to rape (or to murder), how does D "participate" in P's act of sexual intercourse with V (or P's pulling of the trigger and shooting V) except by assisting him [or her] or encouraging him [or her] ... It is submitted that there is no other way.

In *R v Demirian* [1989] VR 97, McGarvie and O'Bryan JJ referred to the cases relating to accused persons acting in concert and stated (at 124):

> In none of the other cases did the court decide that all persons present at the crime and acting in concert were to be treated as principals in the first degree. What was decided was that all were liable to be convicted of the crime.

They therefore appear to be agreeing with the English approach. However, this statement was expressly disapproved of by Callinan J in *Osland v The Queen* (1998) 197 CLR 316 (at 402) on the basis that those who act in concert are to be treated as being "causatively jointly responsible for the commission of the crime". Their responsibility is thus primary, rather than derivative. McHugh J also stated in *Osland* (at 349) that McGarvie and O'Bryan JJ's statement in *Demirian* was inconsistent with previous authority.

Australian academic opinion equally emphatically supports the view that acting in concert is a form of primary rather than derivative liability. For example, in their review of the authorities, Louis Waller and Bob Williams assert in *Brett, Waller and Williams: Criminal Law — Text and Cases* (8th ed, Sydney: Butt, 1997), p 465 that *Lowry v King* established the following principle:

> [E]ven if only one participant performed the acts constituting the crime, each will be guilty as principals in the first degree if the acts were performed in the presence of all and pursuant to a preconceived plan. In this case, the parties are said to be acting in concert.[55]

Conceptually then, the first and third scenarios set out above are examples of primary liability. Each participant is jointly responsible for the commission of the crime. The second scenario, however, provides an example of derivative liability. It is dependent upon the existence of criminal behaviour upon which the aider and abettor's liability may be based.

As stated before, because of the derivative nature of counselling, procuring, aiding and abetting, the principal offence must have been committed before a person falling into one of those categories may be found criminally responsible.[56] However, the concept of "acting in concert" has been used to hold such a person liable even where the perpetrator is not.[57] That is, a person who has assisted or encouraged a crime pursuant to a pre-conceived plan may be convicted even where the

---

55 This statement was approved by McHugh J in *Osland v The Queen* (1998) 197 CLR 316 at 343; see also D Lanham, "Primary and Derivative Criminal Liability: An Australian Perspective" [2000] Crim LR 707 at 714.

56 *Morris v Tolman* [1923] 1 KB 166; *Thornton v Mitchell* [1940] 1 All ER 339; *Cain v Doyle* (1946) 72 CLR 409; *R v Williams* (1932) 32 SR(NSW) 504; *Walsh v Sainsbury* (1925) 36 CLR 464; *R v See Lun* (1932) 32 SR(NSW) 363; *R v Demirian* [1989] VR 97; *Osland v The Queen* (1998) 159 ALR 170 at 174 per Gaudron and Gummow JJ, at 189 per McHugh J.

57 *King v The Queen* (1986) 161 CLR 423; *R v Humphreys and Turner* [1965] 3 All ER 689; *Sweetman v Industries and Commerce Department* [1970] NZLR 139 at 148 per Richmond J; *Andrews Weatherfoil Ltd, Sporle and Day* (1971) 56 Cr App R 31 at 40.

perpetrator has died, is unknown, has not been arrested or has been acquitted.[58] A person acting in concert can still be held liable if the perpetrator is exempt from prosecution[59] or where a defence is available to the perpetrator.[60]

For example in *King v The Queen* (1986) 161 CLR 423 the accused King was jointly charged, together with a man named Matthews, as principal offenders in the murder of King's wife. The prosecution claimed at the trial that Matthews had actually killed the victim. He was acquitted, presumably on the basis that there was a possibility that some other person had killed the victim. King, however was convicted of murder. On appeal, the majority of the High Court stated that there was no inconsistency between the conviction of King and the acquittal of Matthews. On the facts, the accused had encouraged someone to kill the victim and the offence had been carried out. Dawson J stated (at 433-434):

> [W]here two persons are tried jointly upon the one charge as participants in the same degree, it does not inevitably follow that both must be convicted or both must be acquitted ... The evidence may be sufficient to prove the case against one accused beyond reasonable doubt, but be insufficient to prove the case against the other.

In *Matusevich v The Queen* (1977) 137 CLR 633 the accused who had been jointly charged with murder was found guilty despite the principal offender being found not guilty of murder on the ground of insanity. The members of the High Court, however, differed in their reasons for this conclusion. The majority appeared to have supported the principle that it is the acting in concert that extends liability. The accused could be found liable provided that the principal offender knew the nature and quality of the act but did not know that it was wrong. Aickin J specifically referred to acting in concert in this regard (at 633-664) and Mason and Murphy JJ agreed with this (at 645 and 648 respectively). Gibbs and Stephen JJ appear to have gone further in extending liability to a situation where the principal offender did not know the nature and quality of the act. Gibbs J, however, went on to say (at 638) that this fact situation could also be analysed via the doctrine of innocent agency. Gibbs J pointed out (at 638) that the law on this issue was unsettled.

The recent High Court decision in *Osland v The Queen* (1998) 197 CLR 316 also deals with liability for complicity where the principal offender is not convicted. Heather Osland and her son, David Albion were charged with the murder of Frank Osland, Heather Osland's husband and David Albion's stepfather. Frank Osland had a history of violence toward his wife and stepson. Both Osland and Albion dug a grave for the deceased during the day on 30 July 1991. Osland then gave the deceased sedatives in his dinner and was present when Albion struck the fatal blow. They then buried the body and acted as though Frank Osland had simply disappeared, including reporting the deceased as a missing person.

At their trial for the murder of Frank Osland, both Osland and Albion relied on the defences of self-defence and provocation. A clinical and forensic psychologist, Dr Ken Byrne gave evidence concerning battered woman syndrome. This was used in order to bolster the defences of self-defence

---

58 *King v The Queen* (1986) 161 CLR 423; *R v Darby* (1982) 148 CLR 668; *Murray v The Queen* [1962] Tas SR 170; *R v Lopuszynski* [1971] QWN 33; *R v Daniels* [1972] Qd R 323; *O' Sullivan v Thurmer* [1955] SASR 76.

59 *R v Austin* [1981] All ER 374.

60 *Bourne* (1952) 36 Cr App R 125; *Matusevich v The Queen* (1977) 137 CLR 633.

and provocation in relation to Osland. On 2 October 1996, Osland was convicted, but the jury could not reach a verdict in relation to Albion. He was later re-tried and was acquitted on 12 December 1996.

An application for leave to appeal to the Victorian Court of Appeal was dismissed: *Osland* (unrep, 1/8/1997, Winneke P, Hayne and Charles JJA, 279 of 1996). Osland then appealed to the High Court. Just before the special leave application in the High Court, the High Court directed counsel for Osland that it wished to hear argument on the point as to the possible inconsistency of the verdicts. This had not been raised previously.

Accordingly, counsel for Osland argued first, that Osland's conviction was inconsistent with the jury's failure to convict her son and secondly, that it was inconsistent with Albion's subsequent acquittal. All the members of the High Court dismissed the second point, following the reasoning in *King v The Queen* (1986) 161 CLR 423, that different evidence may lead to different outcomes. However, the members of the High Court split 3 to 2 as to the first ground concerning the alleged inconsistency between Osland's conviction and the jury's failure to convict her son at their joint trial.

The prosecution argued at the trial that Osland and Albion were acting pursuant to an understanding or arrangement and they were both liable as principal offenders. No issue was taken to this approach by the defence at trial. The defence accepted the prosecution case that Osland was equally responsible for the acts of Albion and never raised the argument that Osland's conviction was dependent upon the conviction of Albion.

McHugh, Kirby and Callinan JJ held that there was no inconsistency between the verdicts at trial. Where two or more people act in concert, the verdict in relation to each offender may differ. McHugh J said (at 360) that because this was a case of presence at the scene and acting in concert, the jury were entitled to convict Osland and fail to reach a verdict on Albion because the issue of their criminal responsibility was independent. The evidence supporting the defences differed in the case of each accused and was capable of giving rise to different verdicts.

Kirby J expressly agreed with McHugh J on this point in relation to those acting in concert and stated (at 383) that there had not been the slightest suggestion raised at trial that Osland did not actively contribute to Frank Osland's death.

Similarly, Callinan J said (at 402) that where two or more people act in concert they are causatively jointly responsible for the commission of the crime. On the facts, Osland had made a significant contribution to the killing by preparing the grave, drugging Frank Osland, being present at the killing, holding him down on the bed during his death throes and planning the burial and concealment of the grave.

Gaudron and Gummow JJ in the minority agreed (at 325) that there is no necessary inconsistency between the conviction of a person who substantially contributed to the death of another and the acquittal of a person whose act is the immediate cause of death. However Gaudron and Gummow JJ went on to say (at 325-326) that on the facts, the only act done by Osland which might be thought to have contributed to the death of her husband was the mixing of sedatives into his dinner. This was not a substantial contribution given that the judge directed the jury that it could only be the blow that was the operative and substantial cause of death.

Gaudron and Gummow JJ then separated the causation issue from the question of whether or not Osland and Albion acted in concert. They stated (at 327) that the only way in which Osland could be convicted was if Albion had acted pursuant to an understanding or arrangement that they would kill Frank Osland. They were of the view that there could not have been any understanding or arrangement unless the prosecution had negatived self-defence and provocation in relation to Albion. Because these defences had not been negatived, there could not have been an agreement.

This reasoning is very difficult to follow. As McHugh J points out (at 360), there is no inconsistency in finding that Albion was acting in self-defence or under provocation and at the same time acting pursuant to an understanding or arrangement to kill Frank Osland. Nor does it seem logical to divorce the causation issue from that of acting in concert. It seems that Callinan J's view, that where two or more people act in concert they are causatively jointly responsible for the commission of the crime, is to be preferred here.

In all, the significant principles to be derived from *Osland's* case are that the doctrine of acting in concert is a form of primary, rather than derivative liability, and where two or more people act in concert, the verdict in relation to each offender may differ.

PERSPECTIVES

The Future of Derivative Liability

Accessorial liability is derivative in nature, requiring the prosecution to prove that the person who was assisted, or encouraged, committed, or at least attempted to commit, the offence. Consequently, accessorial liability is often described as a form of "secondary liability". The fault required for this mode of complicity is complex because it has "two points of reference rather than one — the wrongful act of the accessory as well as the wrongful act of the principal": I Dennis, "The Mental Element for Accessories" in P Smith (ed), *Criminal Law: Essays in Honour of JC Smith* (London: Butt, 1987), p 58.

The derivative nature of accessorial liability, which links the liability of the accessory to the *guilt* of the principal offender, has been a major source of academic dissatisfaction and has produced many conceptual strains. For example, John Spencer has pointed out that the broad qualification to the knowledge rule in *Bainbridge* (see above pp 349-396) is an unfortunate consequence of tying the liability of the accessory to the commission of the perpetrator's offence. He also suggests that the lack of a non-derivative facilitation offence has caused distortion, in the law of incitement and conspiracy: "Trying to Help Another Person Commit a Crime" in P Smith (ed), *Criminal Law: Essays in Honour of JC Smith* (London: Butt, 1987), p 148. The derivative nature of complicity has two main consequences.

First, there is no liability as an accessory where the perpetrator does not commit the offence or at least get as far as an attempt. Secondly, there is no liability as an accessory where the principal offender is not guilty of an offence because of the existence of a personal defence. These consequences represent serious shortcomings in the present law. In the text (see above, pp 402ff), we have explored how the courts have prevented a person who assists or encourages a perpetrator who has a valid defence from escaping liability by resorting to the doctrine of "innocent agency". Innocent agency is a useful legal fiction although it does strain the notion of human agency and causation in the criminal law almost to breaking point.

The doctrine of acting in concert (see pp 409ff) has similarly been used to bypass the derivate nature of accessorial liability. In *Osland v The Queen* (1998) 197 CLR 316, the High Court held that persons acting in concert would be liable for the acts committed by each other. Under this doctrine the physical acts of one person may be attributed to another person which in turn may give rise to liability as a principal offender: see above, pp 407ff. This is subject to the requirement that the party has agreed jointly to commit the acts constituting the offence and is present during the commission of the acts. Significantly, this form of liability was viewed by the High Court as a form of principal liability rather than accessorial liability, and therefore the availability of personal defences to the person who commits the physical elements are irrelevant to liability.

Another, equally fictive yet pragmatic approach to this problem was suggested in *Bourne* (1952) 36 Cr App R 125 where the English Court of Appeal held that the defence of duress which was relied upon by the principal offender, did not relieve the accessory's guilt. This notion that there are defences that do not relieve an accessory's guilt has been criticised as introducing conceptual distortion into the law.[61]

From the perspective of moral culpability, it has been strongly argued that it should be irrelevant to the liability of the accessory that the person assisted or encouraged did not commit the offence. By parity of reasoning it is also irrelevant in assessing the moral culpability of those who assist or encourage another to commit the offence that the actual perpetrator has a personal defence. The disadvantages that flow from the derivative framework for complicity have prompted calls, from both academics and law reformers, for the creation of a non-derivative criminal facilitation offence.[62]

Such an offence would not only resolve the conceptual strains clearly apparent in the present framework of complicity, it would also plug a "theoretical gap" which exists in the present law. Spencer has drawn attention to the imperfect symmetry between the inchoate offences and complicity. Although the present law contains an inchoate version of complicity by encouragement (namely incitement), there is no inchoate equivalent of complicity by aiding.[63] This is not simply a theoretical problem. The absence of an inchoate offence dealing with assisting another to commit a crime provides a powerful disincentive for the police to intervene to apprehend the person assisting until the principal offender has committed, or at least attempted the crime.

While both academics and law reformers alike have canvassed the creation of a non-derivative form of accessorial liability, the courts have not, until recently, considered it. There are signs that the judiciary, perhaps responding to the weight of academic criticism and legislative inertia, would be amenable to such a challenge.

---

61 It has argued that the conceptual strains apparent in *Bourne* and placed upon the doctrine of innocent agency in *Cogan & Leak* may be seen as a direct consequence of the derivative nature of complicity: SH Kadish, "Complicity, Cause and Blame: A Study in the Interpretation of Doctrine" (1985) 73 *California Law Review* 324 at 378.

62 R Buxton, "Complicity in the Criminal Code" (1969) 85 *Law Quarterly Review* 252 at 268-269; JR Spencer, "Trying to Help Another Person Commit a Crime" in P Smith (ed), *Criminal Law: Essays in Honour of JC Smith* (London: Butt, 1987), p 159. The Law Commission of England and Wales has proposed the creation of non-derivative crime of encouraging and assisting crime: The Law Commission, *Assisting and Encouraging Crime*, Consultation Paper No 131 (London: HMSO, 1993). JC Smith opposes the replacement of accessorial liability with inchoate offences of assisting and encouraging crime, noting that linking the accessory's conduct to the actual harm caused underscores the idea that an accessory is *responsible* (in a moral sense) for the harm caused: "Criminal Liability of Accessories: Law and Law Reform" (1997) 113 *Law Quarterly Review* 568 at 459-461.

63 JR Spencer, "Trying to help another person commit a crime" in PF Smith (ed), *Criminal Law: Essays in Honour of JC Smith* (London: Butt, 1987), p 149. For a discussion of inchoate offences see Chapter 9.

Callinan J in *Osland's* case, reviewed the history of accessorial liability. He concluded that the purpose of the statutory provisions dealing with accessorial liability adopted in England and Australian jurisdictions, "seems to have been to do away with derivative liability": *Osland v The Queen* (1998) 197 CLR 316 at 402-403. The broad interpretation of the effect of these sections has significant import for the derivative nature of accessorial liability:

> If it were necessary to decide the point I would be inclined to hold that the practical effect of the section [*Crimes Act* 1958 (Vic), s 323] is to make it irrelevant to decide whether the accused actually struck the blow or did a final act to complete a crime. The section appears to eliminate the need for a trial of a person formerly thought to be an accessory only, to await and depend upon the attainment or conviction of the principal. The one exception would be punishment which will always look to the particular role of an offender in carrying out a crime.
>
> No matter whether the section is to be taken as procedural or substantive, (a matter which it is not necessary to decide), there is no modern need for any difference in the test to determine the liability of a participant (as a principal in the first degree if that nomenclature still be appropriate) from that provided by Brennan J and McHugh J in *Royall v The Queen* [(1991) 172 CLR 378 at 398, 441]. Their Honours adopted a test of sufficient significant contribution.

Callinan J envisages that these statutory provisions have substantive as well as procedural effects — an interpretation that could break the current derivative link between principal and accessorial liability. He further ventures that the true basis of liability for assisting and encouraging crime is causative: namely, whether assistance or encouragement *caused* another person to commit the offence.

Perhaps this judgment paves the way for a statutory offence of criminal facilitation that does not require the commission of a principal offence.

4. EXTENDING ACCESSORIAL LIABILITY: THE DOCTRINE OF COMMON PURPOSE

The doctrine of common purpose, which is also known as joint enterprise liability, has been regarded as a special form of accessorial liability. See generally, KJM Smith, *A Modern Treatise on the Law of Criminal Complicity* (Oxford: Clarendon Press, 1991), Ch 8. Although conceptually distinct, common purpose is regarded as simply another way of participating in crime as an accessory.[64] It is a mode of

---

64 JC Smith argues that it is not a special form of accessorial liability, but merely an application of the ordinary principles of "aiding, abetting, counselling or procuring" to a particular group based scenario: see "Criminal Liability of Accessories: Law and Law Reform" (1997) 113 *Law Quarterly Review* 453 at 462-463. This modern rationalisation however takes no notice of the historical development of the doctrine or the enactment of distinct common purpose provisions in the 19th century Codes adopted in Australia and Canada.

secondary participation that renders individuals who embark on a joint criminal enterprise or plan to commit an offence (the foundational crime) liable for any further crime (the incidental crime) committed by other group members in the course of that joint criminal enterprise or plan. Common purpose liability at common law is a distinct form of extended secondary liability, imposing accessorial liability in relation to commission of crimes that are not within the scope of that original criminal agreement *but are foreseen as a possible consequence.*

Section 8(1) of the *Criminal Code* (NT) follows the common law approach. The common purpose provisions in the other Code jurisdictions, however, depart from the common law slightly in holding an accessory liable on the basis that the crime committed by the principal offender was a probable consequence of the prosecution of the unlawful purpose: *Criminal Code* (Qld), s 8; *Criminal Code* (Tas), s 4; *Criminal Code* (WA), s 8.

In the Australian context, where ordinary liability for "aiding, abetting, counselling or procuring" requires the accessory to assist or encourage with intention based on knowledge of the essential matters, the doctrine of common purpose considerably widens the net of complicity.

As already noted, the notion of group-based accessorial liability has a controversial history, being tied to constructive forms of liability. Originally, the participants could be held liable for crimes that were neither intended nor foreseen. It was a form of constructive guilt, an ancillary off-spring of the felony–murder rule, which based culpability on the individual's voluntary participation in the original criminal enterprise. It was in effect a form of "guilt by criminal association": S Bronitt, "Defending Giorgianni — Part One: The Fault Required for Complicity" (1993) 17 Crim LJ 242 at 263. To reflect its grafted nature, JC Smith describes this extended form of liability as "parasitic accessory liability": "Criminal Liability of Accessories: Law and Law Reform" (1997) 113 *Law Quarterly Review* 453 at 455. The modern rationale for preserving this extended form of accessorial liability relates to the risk of joint criminal enterprises escalating into the commission of more serious offences and the need to provide effective protection to the public caused by criminals operating in gangs: *R v Powell* [1997] 3 WLR 959 at 966, per Lord Steyn; at 976E per Lord Hutton.

Under this doctrine, the liability of parties turns on whether the crime is "within the scope" of the original common purpose. Initially, this question was determined objectively — whether the offence was a *probable* consequence of the original common purpose.[65] This objective approach is still followed in Queensland, Tasmania and Western Australia. However, with the increasing emphasis on subjective fault elements in the 20th century — that is, intention, knowledge or recklessness — the principle of common purpose was reformulated at common law in terms of subjective agreement, authorisation, contemplation or foresight. The trend of authority has moved slowly toward a "subjectivised" fault element for common purpose. As the High Court in *McAuliffe v The Queen* (1995) 183 CLR 108, observed (at 114):

> Initially the test of what fell within the scope of the common purpose was determined objectively so that liability was imposed for other crimes committed as a consequence of the commission of the crime which was the primary object of the criminal venture, whether or not those other crimes were contemplated by the parties to that venture. However, in

---

65 JC Smith, "Criminal Liability of Accessories: Law and Law Reform" (1997) 113 *Law Quarterly Review* 453 at 456, discussing 18th and 19th century authorities.

accordance with the emphasis which the law now places upon the actual state of mind of an accused person, the test has become a subjective one and the scope of the common purpose is to be determined by what was contemplated by the parties sharing that purpose.[66]

"Acting in concert" must be distinguished from the doctrine of "common purpose". The former doctrine states that it will be enough to establish liability as a principal if the acts were performed in the presence of all and pursuant to a preconceived plan.[67] In this way, the derivative nature of accessorial liability may be by-passed. The doctrine of common purpose on the other hand imposes secondary liability for foreseen, but unintended offences committed by other members who are also participating in original criminal agreement.

There is clearly potential for these two doctrines to overlap on the same facts and juries will require careful direction on which basis of liability — primary or accessorial — the prosecution is relying upon. This is discussed later in 'Procedural Perspectives: Tactical Dilemmas in Charging Complicity': pp 424ff. Problems of divergence — where the crime committed by the principal offender differs in some material respect from the crime contemplated by the other parties — afflict both doctrines. The courts have resolved this problem by attributing or "deeming" the acts of the person committing the crime to other participants in the joint criminal venture. However, the effect of this fiction differs for each doctrine. Acting in concert liability has reconceptualised group-based liability into a non-derivative form. In *Osland v The Queen* (1998) 197 CLR 316, the High Court regarded these cases as an extended form of primary liability rather than accessorial liability. In relation to common purpose however, the courts have not yet abandoned the accessorial principle. Rather they have stretched the derivative link in order to accommodate differential verdicts in a narrow range of cases. For example, in *Barlow v The Queen* (1997) 188 CLR 1, the majority of the High Court held that an accessory may be guilty of manslaughter, even though the perpetrator is guilty of murder, or vice versa.

It is clear that a participant will be liable for all offences committed within the scope of the common purpose.[68] The doctrine of common purpose at common law, however, may also be used to extend criminal liability to situations where the participant contemplated or foresaw the possibility of an offence occurring in furtherance of the common purpose. All cases discussed stress that crimes fall *within* the common purpose — though this has been defined as including crimes foreseen as a possible consequence.

It is this second limb of the doctrine which has attracted much criticism and which is difficult to justify in light of the restrictive fault elements set out in *Giorgianni v The Queen* (1985) 156 CLR 473. These two limbs will be discussed after an exploration of what "the common purpose" means.

---

66 JC Smith, "Criminal Liability of Accessories: Law and Law Reform" (1997) 113 *Law Quarterly Review* 453 at 456, suggests that the shift from objective foreseeability to subjective foresight is recent, emerging first as a submission on what the law *ought* to be in *Russell on Crime* (12th ed, 1964). This formulation was subsequently "incorporated" without acknowledgment into the common law in *R v Smith* [1963] 1 WLR 1200 and *R v Anderson and Morris* [1966] 2 QB 110.

67 *R v Clough* (1992) 28 NSWLR 396; *R v Sperotto* (1970) 71 SR (NSW) 334; *R v Lowery [No 2]* [1972] VR 560; *R v Demirian* [1989] VR 97; *Warren v The Queen* [1987] WAR 314; *Mohan v The Queen* [1967] 2 AC 187.

68 *McAuliffe and McAuliffe v The Queen* (1995) 183 CLR 108; *Betts and Ridley* (1930) 22 Cr App R 148; *R v Adams* [1932] VLR 222; *R v Anderson and Morris* [1966] 2 All ER 644; *Varley v The Queen* (1976) 12 ALR 347; *Johns v The Queen* (1980) 143 CLR 108; *Miller v The Queen* (1980) 32 ALR 321.

4.1 DEFINITION OF THE COMMON PURPOSE

At common law, liability for incidental offences committed pursuant to a common purpose is determined by reference to the subjective state of mind of the parties. Early decisions, such as *R v Anderson and Morris* [1966] 2 QB 110, focussed on the agreement made between the parties. The English Court of Appeal held that individuals were liable for all offences committed in the course of a common purpose or joint enterprise, *except* where the crime committed went beyond that which was tacitly agreed to by the parties.

In *Anderson and Morris*, the two accused set out to find the victim. Anderson was armed with a knife, though Morris denied knowledge of this fact. There was evidence that Anderson was seen punching the victim while Morris stood behind him not taking part in the fight. Morris was convicted of manslaughter. The Court of Appeal accepted (at 118-119 per Lord Parker CJ) the following statement by counsel as a correct summary of the relevant principles:

> where two persons embark on a joint enterprise, each is liable for the acts done in pursuance of that joint enterprise, that that includes liability for unusual consequences if they arise from the execution of the agreed joint enterprise but (and this is the crux of the matter) that, if one of the adventurers goes beyond what has been tacitly agreed as part of the common enterprise, his [or her] co-adventurer is not liable for the consequences of that unauthorised act. ... [I]t is for the jury in every case to decide whether what was done was part of the joint enterprise, or went beyond it and was in fact an act unauthorised by that joint enterprise.

This summary of the law was subsequently affirmed by the High Court in *Varley v The Queen* [1976] 12 ALR 347 at 353.

According to this formulation, the scope of the common purpose is determined by reference to the agreement, express or implied, between the parties. But is agreement exhaustive of the bases of liability in cases of common purpose? The question has arisen whether contemplation, rather than agreement or authorisation, may provide a wider basis for responsibility in cases of common purpose.

In *Johns v The Queen* (1980) 143 CLR 108 the accused participated in a robbery. He waited in the car, while two others entered the premises to commit the robbery. The accused knew that the others were armed with guns and expected the guns to be loaded. He also knew that one of the other two was quick-tempered and violent. In the course of the robbery, there was a struggle with the victim and the victim was shot. The accused was charged as an accessory before the fact to murder and the trial judge, in directing the jury, referred to the doctrine of common purpose. On appeal against conviction, the High Court reviewed the principles of common purpose and concluded that the question for the jury in cases of common purpose was whether the crime committed in furtherance of the criminal plan was contemplated by the parties as a possibility. The majority (Mason, Murphy and Wilson JJ) adopted the following summary of the law (at 130-131):

> [A secondary party] bears ... a criminal liability for an act which was *within the contemplation of both himself [or herself] and the principal* as an act which might be done in the course of carrying out the primary criminal intention — an act contemplated as a possible incident of the originally planned particular venture (emphasis added).

This statement suggests that the common purpose is a consensus between the parties as to the commission of the crime. This consensus may be expressly stated or it may be implied through the conduct of the parties. In *Hui Chi-ming v The Queen* [1991] 3 WLR 495 Lord Lowry stated (at 502):

> It is not necessary that the understanding or arrangement be express. It can be tacit. It can be arrived at by means of actions or words.[69]

In the quotation from *Johns* above the High Court seems to imply that the parties must *jointly* contemplate the offence or one incidental to it. This joint contemplation may not be required in all cases. In *Hui Chi-ming*, Lord Lowry accepted that it many cases there will be joint contemplation, but this does not necessarily follow in every case. He stated (at 509) that the fault for common purpose may be satisfied by examining the contemplation of the secondary party alone:

> [T]he accessory, in order to be guilty, must have foreseen the relevant offence which the principal may commit *as a possible incident of the common unlawful enterprise* and must, with such foresight, still have participated in the enterprise (emphasis in original).

If the principle that there must be a joint or shared contemplation of the offence or one incidental to it, the scope of the common purpose would be restricted. That is, liability would be restricted to situations where there was a consensus between the parties. Some commentators have argued in favour of this restrictive interpretation of common purpose.[70]

The benefit of this restrictive approach is that it would be consistent with the rejection of recklessness for accessorial liability in *Giorgianni v The Queen* (1985) 156 CLR 473[71] where the High Court held that the accessory must assist or encourage with intention based on actual knowledge of the essential matters. Moreover, imposing a requirement of assent or authorisation may counterbalance the breadth of common purpose and its tendency, as noted above, to impose "guilt by criminal association".[72] Regrettably, while common purpose is regarded as a form of accessorial liability, there has been limited consideration by Australian courts of the lack of symmetry between the fault required for accessorial liability by "aiding, abetting, counselling or procuring" and common purpose.[73]

---

69 See also *McAuliffe and McAuliffe v The Queen* (1995) 183 CLR 108 at 114.

70 S Bronitt, "Defending Giorgianni — Part Two: New Solutions for Old Problems in Complicity" (1993) 17 Crim LJ 305 at 317-318; see also S Odgers, Comment on *McAuliffe* in "Criminal Cases in the High Court of Australia" (1996) 20 Crim LJ 43.

71 For a discussion of the fault elment, see above at pp 390ff.

72 In the analogous case where mere presence during the commission of the offence is the basis of accessorial liability, the courts have required an intention, rather than recklessness, on the part of the accessory: see above at p 391.

73 In England, by contrast, the House of Lords have held that foresight, not intention, underlies the basis of accessorial liability both in cases of "aiding and abetting" and joint enterprise: *Powell* [1997] 3 WLR 959 at 964 per Lord Steyn. In Australia, there is no such symmetry since *Giorgianni* held that "aiding and abetting" requires intention based on knowledge of the essential matters.

4.2 THE FOUNDATIONAL CRIME AND COMMON PURPOSE

In recent times, the courts have attempted to limit the scope of liability by imposing a requirement that the original agreement to commit an offence must be operating when the incidental offence is committed. The rationale for this lies in the idea that this form of accessorial liability is "parasitic" upon the original criminal purpose of the parties.

In *Heaney* (1992) 65 A Crim R 428 the Victorian Court of Criminal Appeal held that crimes committed *after* the original plan had been executed or where the party has effectively withdrawn from the original plan are not within the scope of the common purpose. In *Heaney's* case, the three Randall sisters were involved in a plot to kill the deceased, who had been ill-treating one of them. The deceased was lured to Heaney's home and the plan was to mix up amphetamine with battery acid and give it to the deceased who was a drug user. However the injection did not work. Another person present subsequently clubbed the deceased to death. The Randall sisters had left the house before the violence was either discussed or inflicted. The Court of Criminal Appeal allowed the appeals on the ground that the jury had not been directed that the common purpose or design between the parties must be continuing during the commission of the crime.

There is some controversy over whether or not the foundational agreement has to reveal an intention to commit a criminal offence. Would a joint intention to engage merely in dangerous or other antisocial conduct supply the requisite fault element? There is no authority directly on this issue, though the facts of *Miller v The Queen* (1980) 32 ALR 321 reveal the difficulties. The accused was close friends with Worrel and agreed to drive Worrel around looking for women he could "pick up". The typical *modus operandi* was that the accused drove Worrel and a woman to some deserted place so that Worrel could have sex. This occurred many times without incident, but on one occasion Worrel killed his sexual partner. Notwithstanding the killing, the accused continued to drive for Worrel and on six further occasions Worrel murdered the woman they had picked up. The trial judge directed in terms of common purpose — that if it was within the contemplation of the accused that that particular woman might be murdered, he was guilty of murder. The High Court refused special leave to appeal, taking the view that after the first killing, the common purpose between the parties had altered and this would suffice for liability. Brent Fisse in *Howard's Criminal Law* views *Miller* as a departure from the traditional view that there must be a common purpose to commit a criminal offence. Fisse suggest that in *Miller* the common purpose had not been to commit a particular crime, rather it was for "the object of satisfying the perpetrator's sexual appetite in a situation of potential danger to the consenting sexual partner": B Fisse, *Howards Criminal Law* (5th ed, Sydney: Law Book Company Ltd, 1990), p 324. As leave to appeal was refused, little weight may be attached to the discussion of principles in the decision.

The preferable view is that common purpose requires the parties to agree jointly to the commission of a criminal offence. Originally there was no requirement that the incidental crime had to be specifically intended or contemplated by the parties to the common purpose. The only avenue for escape was denial of a common purpose — that there was no common criminal plan between the parties operating.

4.3 COMMON PURPOSE IN QUEENSLAND, TASMANIA AND WESTERN AUSTRALIA

The provisions dealing with common purpose in the *Criminal Codes* of Queensland, Tasmania and Western Australia[74] follow the old common law approach of adopting an objective test of probability in assessing whether the crime committed by the principal offender was a probable consequence of carrying out the common purpose.[75] The word "probable" has been held to mean a "real" or "substantial" possibility: *Hind and Harwood* (1995) 80 A Crim R 105 at 117, 142 and 143. This is the main area in relation to common purpose where these Code jurisdictions and the common law diverge. The test to establish the existence and scope of the common purpose is the same as is the requirement that the original agreement to commit an offence must be operating when the incidental offence is committed: see *R v Phillips and Lawrence* [1967] Qd R 237.

In *Stuart v The Queen* (1974) 134 CLR 426 Gibbs J set out (at 442-443) the objective test in relation to s 8 of the *Criminal Code* (Qld):

> Under s 8 it is necessary for the jury to consider fully and in detail what was the unlawful purpose and what its prosecution was intended to entail and what was the nature of the actual crime committed, and then to decide whether the crime was of such a nature that its omission was a probable consequence of the prosecution of that purpose.

In its *Review of Commonwealth Law, Interim Report: Principles of Criminal Responsibility and Other Matters* (Canberra: AGPS, 1990), the Gibbs Committee regard this objective test as outmoded and recommended the adoption of the current common law approach: pp 205-206. The Model Criminal Code Officers Committee has also recommended following a subjective rather than objective approach: *General Principles of Criminal Responsibility*, Final Report (1992), p 89.

4.4 FORESEEING OFFENCES COMMITTED IN FURTHERANCE OF THE COMMON PURPOSE

The fault element in relation to the doctrine of common purpose has been broadened at common law to include two situations where the accused:

=== foresaw the possibility of an offence committed in furtherance of the original common purpose; or

=== foresaw the possibility of an offence occurring beyond the scope of the original common purpose.

---

74 *Criminal Code* (Qld), s 8; *Criminal Code* (Tas), s 4; *Criminal Code* (WA), s 8.

75 *Stuart v The Queen* (1974) 134 CLR 426; *Brennan v The King* (1936) 55 CLR 253; *Johns v The Queen* (1980) 143 CLR 108 at 126-128, 131 per Mason, Murphy and Wilson J; *R v Solomon* [1959] Qd R 123; *Murray v The Queen* [1962] Tas SR 170; *Borg v The Queen* [1972] WAR 194; *R v Tonkin* [1975] Qd R 1; *Saunders v The Queen* [1980] WAR 183; *Warren v The Queen* [1987] WAR 314; *R v Beck* [1990] 1 Qd R 30.

In looking at the first situation, an accused may be held criminally liable if he or she foresaw the possibility of the occurrence of an offence in the furtherance of the common purpose.[76] For example, if a principal offender takes a gun for the purposes of scaring a victim in order to carry out a robbery and the accessory contemplates that the gun may be used to kill, the latter may be liable for murder if the principal offender kills the victim: *Hui Chi-ming v The Queen* [1991] 3 WLR 495.

It is sufficient that the secondary party contemplate that the principal offender *might* commit the crime in the furtherance of the common purpose: *Hui Chi-ming v The Queen* [1991] 3 WLR 495. That is the secondary offender need only contemplate the possibility rather than the probability of an incidental crime occurring. Mason, Murphy and Wilson JJ in *Johns v The Queen* (1980) 143 CLR 108 (at 131) set out the rationale for the acceptance of a lower threshold test of contemplation as follows:

> The narrow test of criminal liability proposed by the applicant [that of contemplation of the probability of an incidental offence occurring] is plainly unacceptable for the reason that it stakes everything on the probability or improbability of an act, admittedly contemplated, occurring. Suppose a plan made by A, the principal offender, and B, the accessory before the fact, to rob premises, according to which A is to carry out the robbery. It is agreed that A will carry a loaded revolver and use it to overcome resistance in the unlikely event that the premises are attended, previous surveillance having established that the premises are invariably unattended at the time when the robbery is to be carried out. As it happens, a security officer is in attendance when A enters the premises and is shot by A. It would make nonsense to say that B is not guilty merely because it was an unlikely or improbable contingency that the premises would be attended at the time of the robbery, when we know that B assented to the shooting in the event that occurred.

The word "possibility" means a substantial risk, rather than a remote or a negligible possibility.[77]

4.5 FORESEEING OFFENCES OCCURRING BEYOND THE SCOPE OF THE ORIGINAL COMMON PURPOSE

A "wider principle" in relation to the fault element of the common purpose emerged in two Privy Council decisions. In *Chan Wing-Siu v The Queen* [1985] AC 168, the Privy Council reviewed earlier authorities, and relying on Australian authorities including *Johns v The Queen* (1980) 143 CLR 108, Sir Robin Cooke (at 175) concluded that liability for the common purpose is not limited to crimes tacitly agreed, but extends to crimes which the parties *foresee* as a possible incident or consequence of their original enterprise:

---

76 *Johns v The Queen* (1980) 143 CLR 108; *McAuliffe and McAuliffe v The Queen* (1995) 183 CLR 108; *Chan Wing-Siu v The Queen* [1985] AC 168; *R v Hyde, Sussex and Collins* [1990] 3 All ER 892.

77 *Johns v The Queen* (1980) 143 CLR 108 at 164 per Stephen J; *McAuliffe and McAuliffe v The Queen* (1995) 183 CLR 108 at 117; 130 ALR 26; *Chan Wing-Siu v The Queen* [1985] AC 168 at 175.

The case must depend on the wider principle whereby a secondary party is criminally liable for acts by the primary offender of a type which the former foresees but does not necessarily intend. That there is such a principle is not in doubt. It turns on contemplation or, putting the same idea in other words, authorisation, which may be express or is more usually implied. It meets the case of a crime foreseen as a possible incident of the common unlawful enterprise. The criminal culpability lies in participating in the venture with that foresight.

The use of the term "authorisation" caused some confusion as this term is clearly not synonymous with "contemplation" which is a much wider concept. This conflation of two distinct, albeit overlapping states of mind by the Privy Council in *Chan Wing-Siu* was subsequently clarified in *Hui Chi-ming v The Queen* [1991] 3 WLR 495. The Privy Council held that the fault element for common purpose is not confined to authorisation but includes foresight that the crime may be committed as a *possible* incident. In this case, the Privy Council specifically rejected a submission based on *Johns* that joint contemplation between the accessory and perpetrator was required. Although the direction in *Johns* was framed in these terms reflecting the facts of that case, Lord Lowry concluded (at 909-910) that it did not follow that in every case joint contemplation was required. A similar approach was taken in *Sharah v The Queen* (1992) 30 NSWLR 292 at 301 where Carruthers J (for the New South Wales Court of Criminal Appeal) reconciled the apparent conflict between *Johns* and subsequent Privy Council decisions by recognising "two classes of common purpose murder":

▬ **first where there is a shared understanding between the parties as to the commission of the principal offence; and**

▬ **secondly where the accessory foresees the commission of the principal offence.**

As we shall explore in the next section, in *McAuliffe and McAuliffe v The Queen* (1995) 183 CLR 108 the High Court followed the Privy Council's approach of extending the doctrine of common purpose to situations where the parties foresaw the possibility of the offence as a consequence of the original common purpose. The Court stated (at 114):

[E]ach of the parties to the arrangement or understanding is guilty of any other crime falling within the scope of the common purpose which is committed in carrying out that purpose ... [T]he scope of the common purpose is to be determined by what was contemplated by the parties sharing that purpose.

McAuliffe's case therefore holds that where the principal offender goes beyond what was agreed, the secondary party will be liable if he or she foresaw that it was possible that the principal offender would commit that further crime.

CASE STUDIES

When the Common Purpose is Not So Common

In *McAuliffe's* case, two teenage brothers, Sean and David McAuliffe and their friend, Matthew Davis decided to "roll", "rob" or "bash" someone near Bondi Beach. Sean McAuliffe armed himself with a hammer and Davis armed himself with a baton or stick. There was no direct evidence that David McAuliffe knew of this fact before they arrived at a park near the beach which was near cliffs and lookout areas. The three set upon two men, one of whom, Rattanajaturathaporn, was of Thai origin. David McAuliffe and Davis attacked Rattanajaturathaporn, McAuliffe punching and kicking him and Davis beating him with a stick. Davis chased the victim on to an elevated footpath which ran along the top of the cliff. Sean McAuliffe then kicked the victim in the chest and this caused the victim to fall from the footpath into a puddle in the rocks a short distance below.

The victim's body was subsequently found in the sea at the bottom of the cliff, the direct cause of death being the fall from the cliff and drowning. All three youths were convicted of murder and this was upheld by the Supreme Court of New South Wales.

On appeal to the High Court, the McAuliffe brothers argued that they may have intended to cause harm, but they did not intend to inflict grievous bodily harm and therefore could not be found guilty of murder. The prosecution had argued at trial that each of the youths contemplated the intentional infliction of grievous bodily harm as a possible incident in carrying out a common purpose to assault someone.

The High Court, in a joint judgment (Brennan CJ, Deane, Dawson, Toohey, and Gummow JJ, found favour with the prosecution argument and dismissed the McAuliffes' appeals.

It affirmed (at 117-118) that there were two types of common purpose. After discussing the narrower formulation in *Johns*, the Court endorsed the wider principle of liability for common purpose developed by the Privy Council:

> There was no occasion for the Court [in *Johns*] to turn its attention to the situation where one party foresees, but does not agree to, a crime other than that which is planned, and continues to participate in the venture. However, the secondary offender in that situation is as much a party to the crime which is an incident of the agreed venture as he is when the incidental crime falls within the common purpose. Of course, in that situation the prosecution must prove that the individual concerned foresaw that the incidental crime might be committed and cannot rely upon the existence of the common purpose as establishing that state of mind. But there is no other relevant distinction. As Sir Robin Cooke observed [in *Chan Wing-Siu v The Queen*, see above], the criminal culpability lies in the participation in the

---

78   *Sharah v The Queen* (1992) 30 NSWLR 292; *Duong* (1992) 61 A Crim R 140; *R v Anderson and Morris* [1966] 2 QB 110; *R v Smith* [1963] 3 All ER 597; *Reid* (1975) 62 Cr App R 109; *Varley v The Queen* (1976) 12 ALR 347; *Markby v The Queen* (1978) 140 CLR 108.

> joint criminal enterprise with the necessary foresight and that is so whether the
> foresight is that of an individual party or is shared by all parties. That is in
> accordance with the general principle of the criminal law that a person who
> intentionally assists in the commission of a crime or encourages its commission
> may be convicted as a party to it.

If the principal offender deliberately acts outside the scope of the common purpose and commits an act that was not foreseen as a possibility, then no liability will attach to the secondary party.[78] For example, a secondary party will not be liable where he or she has counselled the principal offender to kill a particular person and the latter deliberately kills a different person.[79]

> For a critical review of this "wider principle" governing fault in common purpose see S Bronitt, "Defending Giorgianni — Part One: The Fault Required for Complicity" (1993) 17 Crim LJ 242 at 261-263; S Odgers, Comment on *McAuliffe* in "Criminal Cases in the High Court of Australia" (1996) 20 Crim LJ 43.

4.6 THE FAULT ELEMENTS FOR COMMON PURPOSE AND COMPLICITY

The traditional approach has been to have the same fault element for common purpose as for aiding, abetting, counselling or procuring: B Fisse, *Howard's Criminal Law* (5th ed, Sydney: Law Book Company Ltd, 1990), pp 340-343. The concept of equivalent states of culpability for complicity has been described as the "principle of parallelism" or the "link principle".[80] However, the common law fault standard that is satisfied by foresight of the possibility of a offence occurring in furtherance of the common purpose is much more extensive than the standard of the fault element set out in *Giorgianni v The Queen* (1985) 156 CLR 473. As explored above, *Giorgianni* requires that the secondary party must intentionally assist or encourage the principal offender and must know of the essential matters which constitute the physical elements of the offence.

This area was recently explored in *R v Powell; R v English* [1997] 3 WLR 959. In that case, the House of Lords considered the following question: must an accused participating in a joint enterprise (common purpose) share the perpetrator's *specific intent* for murder (that is, to kill or cause serious bodily injury) or does mere foresight of the possibility of death or serious injury suffice? This appeal raised important issue of principle and policy since the English courts have emphatically rejected recklessness for murder and Parliament maintains mandatory life imprisonment for murder.

---

79 *R v Saunders* (1576) 2 Plowd 473; 75 ER 706.

80 See P Gillies, *Criminal Law* (4th ed, Sydney: LBC, 1997), pp 168-169. Brent Fisse, referring to the "link principle", suggested that "the mental element of complicity in any offence, including a regulatory offence, is always similar to that of the principal offence": B Fisse, "Complicity in Regulatory Offences" (1968) 6 *Melbourne University Law Review* 278 at 278.

In the first appeal concerning Powell, three men went to buy drugs in the course of which one of them shot and killed the drug dealer. The Crown could not prove who was the perpetrator but it was contended that each could be liable for murder on the basis of joint enterprise if they realised that the perpetrator might kill in the course of buying the drugs. On appeal against Powell's conviction for murder, the question was raised whether mere "realisation" is enough or whether the accused must share the intent of the perpetrator.

The House of Lords held that the answer to this question lay simply in the ordinary application of the principles of accessorial liability. The relevant authorities establish that the accessory who is party to a common purpose must foresee or contemplate the possibility that the perpetrator may commit the physical element of the incidental crime with the relevant fault element. Lord Steyn approved JC Smith's summary of the principles governing accessorial liability for murder (at 964-965):

> The accessory to murder, however, must be proved to have been reckless, not merely whether death might be caused, but whether murder might be committed: *he [or she] must have been aware not merely that death or grievous bodily harm might be caused, but that it might be caused intentionally, by a person whom he [or she] was assisting or encouraging to commit a crime* (emphasis added).

While the perpetrator of murder under English law must possess intention, an accessory may be convicted of murder on the basis of a lesser mental state. Similar asymmetry follows in Australian law: to be a liable as a perpetrator of murder, foresight of the probability (not possibility) of death or serious injury is required. However, an accessory participating in a common purpose may be liable for murder on the basis of a lower degree of foresight than the actual principal offender — while the principal offender must intend or foresee the *probability* of death or serious injury, the accessory need only foresee the *possibility* that the perpetrator may kill with either of the relevant mental states required for murder.

Lord Steyn held (at 965-966) that requiring parties to a common purpose to possess the "specific intention" for murder would be impractical in that it would undermine the utility of the accessorial principle and the public interest in deterring group-based criminal activity. In his view, the logical elegance of requiring "strict equivalence" of culpability between the accessory and the perpetrator gave way to the practical needs of the criminal justice system. He acknowledged the potential unfairness of imposing a *mandatory* life sentence for accessories to murder who merely foresee the possibility of serious injury being inflicted by the perpetrator; but was not prepared to distort the ordinary principles of accessorial liability to ameliorate this unfairness.

4.7 THE LINK BETWEEN ACCESSORIAL AND PRIMARY CULPABILITY

Under the doctrine of acting in concert, a person may be held liable even where the principal offender is not and thus differing verdicts are possible: see above, pp 404ff. This is because acting in concert is seen as a form of primary rather than derivative liability.

The doctrine of common purpose, however, is an extension of accessorial liability. Can different verdicts for the principal offender and the accessory be possible? The English and Australian courts have taken different approaches to this question.

In *R v Powell; R v English* [1997] 3 WLR 959, the House of Lords refused to permit differential verdicts, affirming a principle of exact equivalence for accessorial and principal offender culpability. At the same time in Australia, in *R v Barlow* (1997) 188 CLR 1, the High Court considered this question but came to the opposite conclusion.

The High Court in *Barlow's* case reviewed authority from various Commonwealth jurisdictions and concluded that an accessory participating in a common purpose may be liable for manslaughter even where the perpetrator is guilty of murder. Although the case concerned the interpretation of the statutory provisions dealing with the liability of secondary parties who share a "common intention to prosecute an unlawful purpose" contrary to s 8 of the *Criminal Code* (Qld), the majority (Brennan CJ, Dawson and Toohey JJ) held that s 8 operates in the same way as the common law.

The majority posed the question raised by the appeal thus: "Does Barlow avoid liability for manslaughter because the striker of the fatal and unjustified and unexcused blow had an intention that made him liable to punishment for murder?" Such an interpretation, in the opinion of the majority, would be "perverse".

The majority considered that the effect of s 8 is to "deem" the secondary party to have committed the acts of the principal offender. This approach to liability resonates with the approach taken in "acting in concert" cases, although liability under s 8 was viewed as a form of secondary participation rather than primary liability. In such cases, the culpability of the secondary parties is determined by two reference points: first, the parties' original "common intention to prosecute an unlawful purpose" and secondly, the precise mental state of the secondary party at the relevant time. In relation to the latter, the mental state of the accessory could extend to either lesser or greater offences committed by the perpetrator, thus leaving open the possibility of differential verdicts. The majority stated (at 14):

> If, at the time that the act was done or the omission was made, the secondary party had a state of mind which, in combination with an act or omission of the nature which s 8 deems him [or her] to have done or made, renders him [or her] guilty of a more serious offence than the offence of which the principal offender is guilty, the secondary party is liable to conviction of the more serious offence. Thus, the mastermind who, having greater knowledge of the circumstances or the likely result of a minor criminal offence which he [or she] and a comparatively innocent principal offender agree to commit, or who has an evil intent not shared by the principal offender, will be liable according to his [or her] (the secondary party's) state of mind, although the common plan was merely to commit the minor offence.

Kirby J agreed with the majority, pointing out the wide array of legal authority, both statutory as well as common law, supported differential verdicts. In addition to legal authority, Kirby J pointed to reasons of both "principle and policy" supporting differential verdicts (at 346-347) including that they:

allow the trier of fact (usually the jury) "to distinguish between the culpability of the accused and to avoid artificial consequences which may offend the sense of justice";

▬ avoid practical problems in cases where secondary parties and perpetrators are tried separately — in these cases, the trial judge of "the common purpose offender could not finally know the conviction entered against the principal. Yet, on this theory, it is needed in order to define the offence of the co-offender"; and

▬ permit fine-tuning and calibration of culpability — although the law renders an offender liable for the acts of another, each party may have a different state of culpability: "As this is the reality of criminal conduct, even where offences are performed with some degree of common intention, a rational approach to criminal responsibility will permit a reflection of the different specific states of mind of the respective participants".

McHugh J dissented, basing his judgment narrowly on the interpretation of the Code provision. He held that the common law had no bearing on the matter as the legislation, properly construed, required the party of an unlawful common purpose to be acquitted or convicted of the *same offence* as that for which the principal offender was convicted.

Underscoring the legitimacy of differential verdicts is the emerging view that accessorial liability provisions "deem" the acts of the perpetrator to be committed by the accessory. This is reflected in the model provision of s 11.2 of the *Criminal Code Act* 1995 (Cth) that refers to a person who aids, abets, counsels or procures the commission of an offence as being "taken to have committed the offence". By rejecting the idea of strict equivalence of culpability between the accessory and perpetrator, the majority of the High Court in *Barlow* appear to have hammered yet another nail in the coffin of complicity's derivative foundations.

PROCEDURAL PERSPECTIVES

Tactical Dilemmas in Charging Complicity

Although liability for "aiding and abetting" and "acting in concert" are conceptually distinct modes of complicity, they may nevertheless arise on the same facts. As an accused in either case may be charged and indicted as a principal offender, the precise mode of complicity being alleged by the prosecution may not be apparent to the defence. This can cause considerable confusion and unfairness. One solution to this difficulty is for the prosecution to specify the precise mode of complicity relied upon in the indictment. Indeed, in *DPP (Northern Ireland) v Maxwell* [1978] 1 WLR 1350, the House of Lords stressed the desirability of the prosecution specifying in the indictment the mode of complicity alleged, that is whether it was based on aiding and abetting or some broader principle of joint enterprise or common purpose.

In practice, however, this strategy may be difficult to follow in cases where the precise nature of the participation alleged is unclear or contested by the defence. Indeed, the practical difficulty of complying with these requirements has led to the direction in *Maxwell* being universally ignored: see C Clarkson, "Complicity, Powell and Manslaughter" [1998] Crim LR 556 at 561.

An alternative approach is to require the prosecution to outline the conceptual basis of the accused's liability at the commencement of the trial. As Hunt CJ recognised in *Tangye* (1997) 92 A Crim R 545 (at 556), this need to avoid conceptual confusion during the trial places a heavy responsibility on the prosecution, defence and trial judge:

The obligation of the Crown Prosecutor in opening the Crown case is not merely to outline the facts which the Crown proposes to establish in evidence. It is also to indicate, in conceptual terms, the nature of the Crown case. This is to assist both the trial judge and counsel for the accused, more so than the jury. It is essential that any doubt about the nature of the Crown case, conceptually, be removed at that early stage. If it is not done at that stage, or if there had been some change in its nature since the case was opened, it is vital that it be identified with some precision, in the absence the accused, before counsel commence their final addresses. It becomes very difficult for the judge sensibly to make alterations to directions already given once it is learnt that the issues are different to those which had been assumed to exist.

The tactical dilemmas created by the potential doctrinal overlap between aiding and abetting, common purpose and acting in concert were revealed in *Osland v The Queen* (1998) 197 CLR 316. As outlined in the text above, both the defence and prosecution had proceeded at the trial on the basis that this was a case of "acting in concert" rather than accessorial liability: see pp 406ff. McHugh J did point out (at 188) that at the trial and in arguments put before the High Court, there was often a failure by counsel for Osland to distinguish between the situation of a principal offender and aider and abettor and those acting in concert.

The conceptual basis chosen by the prosecution and defence in *Osland* had drastic consequences for the appeal. As Osland had been convicted as a principal offender on the basis of "acting in concert", the acquittal of her son did not render the verdicts inconsistent nor her conviction unsafe. By contrast, had the case been argued on the basis of "aiding and abetting" murder or manslaughter, the jury's failure to reach a verdict on his liability and his subsequent acquittal ought to have precluded liability as an accessory: *R v Cogan and Leak* [1976] 1 QB 217. McHugh J did point out (at 188), however, that it would have been difficult to portray Osland as only an aider and abettor rather than a principal offender given the evidence of her involvement in the crime.

Appeal courts in England have resorted to the doctrine of innocent agency to affirm convictions.[81] They have also suggested that the perpetrator's conduct, though technically not criminal due to the existence of a defence, remained in some sense wrongful: *Bourne* (1952) 36 Cr App R 125. How the prosecution frames its charge of complicity is therefore a crucial issue. As *Osland* illustrates, the mode of complicity relied upon at trial not only affects the ingredients of liability, but it may also establish a conceptual framework for the case that may not be easily challenged on appeal. Indeed, the High Court's licensing of "acting in concert" to combat criminal enterprises may prove to be attractive for prosecutors since it provides yet another means of circumventing the derivative nature and effects of accessorial liability.

Nevertheless, as a matter of fairness, in cases where the prosecution can frame complicity as liability as a principal offender through acting in concert or as an accessory, it is vital that the prosecution should disclose to the accused, before or at the commencement of trial, *precisely* the basis upon which the charge is to proceed.

---

81   The appropriateness of this doctrine, and the conceptual confusion introduced into the law, has been strongly criticised: see G Williams, "Causing Non Crimes: The Procedural Questions" (1990) 140 *New Law Journal* 921.

The conceptual differences between the various modes of complicity — aiding and abetting, acting in concert and the extended concept of common purpose — require careful elaboration to the jury. This is especially important in cases where the facts are contested and support alternative case theories. There is, however, a tendency for trial judges to play safe by offering a "universal complicity direction" which summarises to the jury all conceivable modes of participation, *irrespective* of whether they are applicable to the facts relied upon by the prosecution or the defence. The conceptual confusion caused by jury directions unsupported by the facts may cause unfairness to the accused. Notwithstanding periodic correction on appeal, the practice of trial judges offering unnecessary directions persists. In *Tangye* (1997) 92 A Crim R 545, Hunt CJ strongly criticised this practice, offering the following rebuke (at 556):

> It will be seen from the passages quoted that the judge has referred — apparently interchangeably — to a joint criminal enterprise and to the so-called doctrine of common purpose which extends the concept of a joint enterprise. Where — as here — no such extended concept was relied upon, it was both unnecessary and confusing to refer to it.
>
> The Crown needs to rely upon a straightforward joint criminal enterprise only where — as in the present case — it cannot establish beyond reasonable doubt that the accused was the person who physically committed the offence charged. It needs to rely upon the extended concept of joint criminal enterprise, based on common purpose, only where the offence charged is not the same as the enterprise agreed. *This Court has been making that point for years, and it is a pity that in many trials no heed is taken of what has been said*"[82] (emphasis added).

5. ACCESSORIES AFTER THE FACT

Those who assist offenders after a crime has been committed are generally referred to as accessories after the fact. The crime that the accessory commits is quite separate from the offence committed by the principal offender and any doctrine relating to participation in a crime. Each jurisdiction in Australia, apart from New South Wales, has statutory provisions dealing with accessories after the fact[83] and there are certain provisions in New South Wales which deal with matters of penalty and procedure: for example, *Crimes Act* 1900 (NSW), ss 347 and 371.

Liability as an accessory after the fact only arises if the principal offence has been committed: *Dawson v The Queen* (1961) 106 CLR 1. If the principal offender is acquitted, the accessory after the fact can only be convicted if there is sufficient evidence that the principal offence took place.[84] If the principal offender has been convicted, the accessory may still argue that the principal offence has

---

82 Hunt CJ refers to similar criticisms offered in *Stokes* (1990) 51 A Crim R 25 at 33-37; *Clough* (1992) 64 A Crim R 451 at 455.

83 *Crimes Act* 1914 (Cth), s 6; *Crimes Act* 1900 (ACT), s 346; *Criminal Code* (NT), s 13; *Criminal Code* (Qld), s 10; *Criminal Law Consolidation Act* 1935 (SA), s 241; *Criminal Code* (Tas), ss 6, 161, 300; *Crimes Act* 1958 (Vic), s 325; *Criminal Code* (WA), s 10.

84 *R v Carter* [1990] 2 Qd R 371; *R v Williams* (1932) 32 SR (NSW) 504; *Mahadeo v The King* [1936] All ER 813; *R v Dawson* [1961] VR 773 (revised on other grounds: *Dawson v The Queen* (1961) 106 CLR 1).

not been proved as against him or herself: *Mahadeo v The King* [1936] 2 All ER 813 (PC). Obviously proof of the conviction of the principal offender is admissible and constitutes prima facie evidence that the accessory committed the offence.[85]

The prosecution must prove all the elements of the offence that may be divided into:

▬ **the physical element; and**

▬ **the fault element.**

5.1 THE PHYSICAL ELEMENT

The accessory must perform an act that assists or has the potential to assist the principal offender escape from the administration of justice.[86] Examples of such acts include:

▬ **driving the principal offender away from the scene of the crime;**[87]

▬ **impersonal assistance such as altering the engine number and repainting a stolen car;**[88]

▬ **helping dispose of stolen property;**[89]

▬ **the removal of incriminating evidence after the principal offender has been arrested;**[90] **and**

▬ **buying a car and clothes for the principal offender.**[91]

Indirect assistance may also be sufficient to found liability: *R v McKenna* [1960] 1 QB 411 (CCA). For example, a person who employs another to aid the principal offender may be convicted as an accessory[92] and liability may attach where there is no personal assistance given to the principal offender, but the accessory performs an act such as altering the engine number of a stolen car.[93]

The accessory must perform a positive act. In *R v Ready* [1942] VLR 85 the accused passed a message from an abortionist to the woman operated upon, returning the money paid for the operation in return for the latter's silence. The Victorian Supreme Court held that passing on a message was not sufficiently active assistance to constitute the accused as an accessory. Similarly, merely enjoying the proceeds of the crime will not be sufficient[94] nor will visiting a place where stolen property has been brought with a view to a possible purchase.[95] The special offences and powers dealing with money laundering and proceeds of crime are explored in Chapter 15, pp 863ff.

---

85 *R v Dawson* [1961] VR 773; *Carter and Savage; Ex parte Attorney-General* (1990) 47 A Crim R 55.

86 *R v Tevendale* [1955] VLR 95; *R v McKenna* [1960] 1 QB 411.

87 *R v Holey* [1963] 1 All ER 106.

88 *R v Tevendale* [1955] VLR 95.

89 *R v Butterfield* (1843) 1 Cox CC 39; *R v Williams* (1932) 32 SR (NSW) 504.

90 *R v Levy* [1912] 1 KB 158.

91 *R v Hurley* [1967] VR 526.

92 *R v Jarvis* (1837) 2 Mood and R 40.

93 *R v Tevendale* [1955] VLR 95; *R v Chapple* (1840) 9 Car and P 355.

94 *R v Barlow* (1962) 79 WN (NSW) 756.

95 *R v Rose* [1962] 3 All ER 298.

5.2 THE FAULT ELEMENT

In general, the prosecution must prove beyond reasonable doubt that the accessory:

▬ **knew or believed the principal offender was guilty of the principal offence; and**

▬ **intended to assist the principal offender to escape from the administration of justice.**

KNOWLEDGE OR BELIEF OF THE PRINCIPAL OFFENCE

In the past, it appears that the common law required the accessory to have knowledge of the precise principal offence that had been committed before he or she could be found criminally responsible.[96] Most of the statutory provisions reflect this requirement.[97] However, the South Australian and Victorian provisions have extended the fault element such that it is not necessary for the prosecution to prove that the accessory knew the precise offence or even the particular kind of offence: *Criminal Law Consolidation Act* 1935 (SA), s 241(1); *Crimes Act* 1958 (Vic), s 325(1). In Victoria, it is sufficient if the accessory simply believes that the principal has committed a serious indictable offence. The South Australian provision also extends to a belief that some other offence was committed in the same, or partly in the same, circumstances.

INTENTION TO ASSIST THE PRINCIPAL OFFENDER

The prosecution must further prove that the accessory intended to assist the principal offender to evade justice in some way. This may be to impede the investigation of the offence[98] or to escape apprehension,[99] prosecution,[100] conviction[101] or punishment,[102] or to dispose of the proceeds of the offence.[103] If the accused does an act solely for his or her own benefit, he or she will not be held liable as an accessory.[104] If, however, the accused acts partly for his or her own benefit *and* partly in order to assist the principal offender, as may occur in the situation of receiving stolen goods, he or she will be liable as an accessory.[105] An accessory whose act fails to assist the principal offender may be convicted of an attempt: *R v Maloney* (1901) 18 WN (NSW) 96.

---

96 *R v Tevendale* [1955] VLR 95; *R v Stone* [1981] VR 737 at 741 per Crockett J. For a criticism of this approach see B Fisse, *Howard's Criminal Law* (5th ed, Sydney: Law Book Company Ltd, 1990), p 355.

97 *Crimes Act* 1914 (Cth), s 6; *Crimes Act* 1900 (ACT), s 346; *Criminal Code* (NT), s 13; *Criminal Code* (Qld), s 10; *Criminal Code* (Tas), s 6; *Criminal Code* (WA), s 10.

98 *Criminal Law Consolidation Act* 1935 (SA), s 241(1).

99 *Criminal Law Consolidation Act* 1935 (SA), s 241(1); *Crimes Act* 1958 (Vic), s 325(1).

100 *Criminal Code* (NT), s 13(1); *Criminal Law Consolidation Act* 1935 (SA), s 241(1); *Crimes Act* 1958 (Vic), s 325(1).

101 *Crimes Act* 1958 (Vic), s 325(1).

102 *Crimes Act* 1914 (Cth), s 6; *Crimes Act* 1900 (ACT), s 346; *Criminal Code* (Qld), s 10; *Criminal Code* (Tas), s 6; *Crimes Act* 1958 (Vic), s 325(1); *Criminal Code* (WA), s 10.

103 *Crimes Act* 1914 (Cth), s 6; *Crimes Act* 1900 (ACT), s 346; *Criminal Law Consolidation Act* 1935 (SA), s 241(1).

104 *R v Jones* [1949] 1 KB 194; *R v Barlow* (1962) 79 WN (NSW) 756; *Middap* (1992) 63 A Crim R 434 (CCA Vic).

105 *R v Reeves* (1892) 13 LR(NSW) 220. See also *Leaman v The Queen* [1986] Tas R 223 at 231 per Cox J.

THE DEFENCE OF WITH LAWFUL AUTHORITY OR REASONABLE EXCUSE

In South Australia and Victoria, it is a defence that the accessory's act was done with lawful authority or reasonable excuse: *Criminal Law Consolidation Act* 1935 (SA), s 241(2); *Crimes Act* 1958 (Vic), s 325(1). The term "lawful authority" was stated in the Gibbs Committee's *Review of Commonwealth Criminal Law, Interim Report: Principles of Criminal Responsibility and Other Matters* (Canberra: AGPS, 1990), p 223, as intending to cover executive decision against a prosecution, and "reasonable excuse" related to acts done in pursuance of a legitimate agreement to refrain from prosecuting in consideration of making good the loss caused by the offence. These explanations for the terms appear to be relevant to the South Australian and Victorian provisions. However, the defence of lawful authority does not need statutory expression and an act done under lawful authority cannot be illegal: see *Crafter v Kelly* [1941] SASR 237 at 243 per Napier J.

6. CONCLUSION

The previous sections have identified a number of problems associated with the present state of the law of complicity. There are specific difficulties with details of the law such as whether an omission to act should give rise to accessorial liability and what constitutes knowledge of the essential facts of an offence. There are also broader conceptual difficulties that exist in relation to the derivative nature of accessorial liability and the notion of acting in concert as being a form of primary liability.

In the perspectives sections, we have pointed to a number of issues that need to be considered as this area of law develops. In particular, the question needs to be posed as to whether the current derivative link in accessorial liability should be broken so as to allow for a statutory offence of criminal facilitation in the absence of the commission of a criminal offence. There are signs that the derivative nature of accessorial liability that links the liability of an accessory to the *guilt* of the principal offender is being questioned. Section 11.2(5) of the *Criminal Code Act* 1995 (Cth) states:

> A person may be found guilty of aiding, abetting, counselling or procuring the commission
> of an offence even if the principal offender has not been prosecuted or has not been found
> guilty.

The High Court in *Barlow's* case in supporting differential verdicts in relation to the doctrine of common purpose has certainly challenged the derivative nature of accessorial liability by viewing s 8 of the *Criminal Code* (Qld) as "deeming" the secondary party to have committed the acts of the principal offender.

The law of complicity has thus far developed in a rather haphazard fashion without regard to the conceptual complexities underlying the doctrine of acting in concert, innocent agency and common purpose. Perhaps it is time to heed the Law Commission's call for a new code of statutory offences relating to complicity in order to clarify this increasingly complex area: The Law Commission, Consultation Paper No 131, *Assisting and Encouraging Crime* (London: HMSO, 1993).

9

Inchoate Offences

> **The attempt and not the deed,
> Confounds us**

William Shakespeare,
Macbeth (1606)
Act 2, sc 2, l. 12

1. INTRODUCTION

The term "inchoate" is not one in general use. It stems from the Latin "inchoare" which means to start work on and it therefore can be defined as only partly formed or just begun. There are three "inchoate" offences, namely: attempts, conspiracy and incitement. In general, the common thread amongst these crimes is that they are committed even though the substantive offence that was intended is not completed and no harm is caused. We will explore a little later the various rationales that have been proffered as to why inchoate offences, and in particular, that of conspiracy exist. It is worthwhile noting here, however, that they share a crime prevention rationale. That is, inchoate offences exist to assist the police and law enforcement officials to intervene before the commission of the offence. This is particularly important in the context of drug offences and this will be taken up further in Chapter 15.

The Australian jurisdictions treat inchoate offences as substantive crimes in themselves, separate from the completed offences at which they are aimed. As a result, they are defined broadly in abstract terms and have required a high degree of judicial interpretation. The doctrine of attempts is designed to punish those who intend to commit a crime and who do some acts that are more than merely preparatory to the crime, but are unsuccessful in carrying it out. Conspiracy serves to criminalise an agreement between two or more persons to commit an unlawful act where there is an intention to commit that unlawful act. Incitement is somewhat similar to conspiracy in its time-frame for criminalisation, but covers circumstances where one person tries to persuade another to commit a crime that the inciter wants and intends to have committed.

The origins of attempts, conspiracy and incitement can be traced back to the authority of common law courts to create offences, but the treatment of them as substantive crimes in themselves is of comparatively recent origin.[1] Ira Robbins points out that "despite the independent origins and developments of the three offences, conspiracy and [incitement] can be viewed as early stages of an attempt to commit a completed offense": "Double Inchoate Crimes" (1989) 26(1) *Harvard Journal on Legislation* 1 at 9. Thus, the time-frame of these offences can be visualised as follows:

| No Liability | Conspiracy Incitement | Attempts | Completed Offence |

The traditional division of crimes into "physical" and "fault" elements (see Chapter 3, p 148) does not sit well with the notion of inchoate crimes. In attempts, for example, there is a set fault element, but a loosely defined physical element and in conspiracy, the requirement that an agreement to commit an offence must be identified, may overlap with proving an intention to commit the substantive offence.

As we explore these offences, it is worthwhile keeping in mind the difficulty in dividing conduct into no liability, inchoate liability and liability for the full offence.

Prosecutions for Conspiracy

Although the courts have struggled with defining the element of all three offences, conspiracy, which appears to be charged more often than incitement,[2] is perhaps the vaguest and most problematic. This crime, unlike an attempt, does not require conduct that is proximate to the completion of the substantive offence. This enables criminal responsibility to be proved on the basis of a preliminary plan or consensus between the parties. This obviously has certain advantages to the prosecution, but there is a danger that the crime of conspiracy may be abused if there are unclear limitations on its scope. Gallop J observed in *Nirta v The Queen* (1983) 10 A Crim R 370 at 377 that "[a]n indictment alleging conspiracy has become an increasingly important weapon in the prosecutor's armoury".

Robbins points out that a conceptual approach to inchoate crimes has been overtaken by a functional policy-oriented approach. He argues in "Double Inchoate Crimes" (1989) 26(1) *Harvard Journal on Legislation* 1 at 115 that the courts:

> look first to whether the policy of the criminal law indicates that an individual's acts are sufficiently dangerous to society to warrant judicial intervention and punishment. Only then do they address the issue that the conceptual approach takes up first — whether the particular jurisdiction's definition of attempt, conspiracy, or [incitement] allows a court to punish those acts.

---

1   I Robbins, "Double Inchoate Crimes" (1989) 26(1) *Harvard Journal on Legislation* 1 at 9-10, 25-26, 30-32; F Sayre, "Criminal Attempts" (1928) 4 *Harvard Law Review* 821.

2   The Criminal Law Officers Committee (now the Model Criminal Code Officers Committee) noted that incitement was rarely charged: Criminal Law Officers Committee of the Standing Committee of Attorneys-General, *Chapter 2: General Principles of Criminal Responsibility*, Final Report (December 1992) (Canberra: AGPS, 1993), p 93.

Certainly, a conceptual approach to inchoate crimes has not afforded great clarity or consistency. The following sections show that the way in which the three inchoate offences have developed has been very much on a case-by-case basis, causing difficulties with identifying underlying or consistent principles.

2. ATTEMPTS

General statutory provisions in all Australian jurisdictions establish that attempts to commit certain offences are themselves offences. In this chapter, we will be concentrating on the general doctrine of attempt. There are, however, specific offences relating to attempted crimes such as attempted murder.[3]

The law relating to attempt stems from the early common law. Generally the English courts only punished conduct that resulted in harm, but there are some, albeit rare, 14th century cases where individuals were convicted of heinous felonies even though they had unsuccessfully attempted them. These convictions were based on the principle of *voluntas reputabitur pro facto* (the intention is to be taken for the deed). However, a mere intention was not enough. Some evidence was needed of an act toward the commission of the felony.[4] Attempt as a distinct substantive offence has its origins relatively more recently in the case of *R v Scofield* (1784) Cald Mag Rep 397. In that case, the court indicted the accused on a charge of placing combustible material together with a lighted candle near another's house with intent to burn it down. The court established that it was unnecessary for the house to have caught fire and burnt down for a crime to have occurred. The facts of this case would today give rise to a conviction for attempted arson.

The offence of attempt differs from substantive offences in that it combines the fault element of intention with a loosely defined physical element. Generally, no harm or damage will have occurred in relation to an attempt. Peter Glazebrook has argued that the primary objection to having an attempt as an offence in itself is that any "definition" is inescapably vague and uncertain: "Should We Have a Law of Attempted Crime?" (1969) 85 *Law Quarterly Review* 28. He writes (at 35):

> No one has ever supposed that some single formula might, given a clever enough lawyer, be devised which would embrace the *actus reus* of, for instance, the offences of murder, obtaining property by deception, and the commission of acts of gross indecency between males. Why, then, should it be supposed that a single formula might, when combined with the definitions of those very different crimes, serve to identify the *actus reus* of such disparate offences as attempting to murder, attempting to obtain property by deception, and attempting to commit an act of gross indecency?

---

3   *Crimes Act* 1900 (NSW), ss 27-30; *Criminal Code* (NT), s 165; *Criminal Code* (Qld), s 306; *Criminal Code* (WA), s 283.

4   IP Robbins, "Double Inchoate Crimes" (1989) 26(1) *Harvard Journal on Legislation* 1 at 9, fn 21 and references therein; FB Sayre, "Criminal Attempts" (1928) 41 *Harvard Law Review* 821 at 822-827.

Glazebrook proposes that instead of a general offence of attempt, the legislature should criminalise conduct that is intended to facilitate the future commission of an offence. An example of this approach is the preparatory offence relating to burglary, "going equipped with the instruments of housebreaking" enacted in most jurisdictions: see Ch 13, p 728. Another example is provided by assaults with intent to commit another crime: see Ch 11, p 540.

Turning to justifications for a general law of attempt, we outlined in Chapter 2 how liberal notions of harm have been used to justify what should or should not be criminal conduct. If no harm occurs in an attempt, why is punishment justified?

Generally, there are three answers to this question. First, the "harm" of attempts and the other inchoate offences could be viewed broadly as the *potential* to cause harm. In Chapter 2, we set out, from a philosophical perspective, the "elasticity" of the concept of harm and its ability to accommodate indirect or remote harms. Inchoate crimes can thus be seen in terms of risk management rather than the prevention of harm.

Secondly, Francis Bowes Sayre points out "[t]hat those should not be allowed to go free who attempt to commit some crime but fail, is a feeling deep rooted and universal": "Criminal Attempts" (1928) 41 *Harvard Law Review* 821 at 821. Take, for example, the following scenario from Frederick Forsyth's fictional thriller, *The Day of the Jackal* (London: Hutchinson & Co Ltd, 1971), pp 354-355:

> Six floors up and a hundred and thirty metres away the Jackal held the rifle steady and squinted down the telescopic sight. He could see the features quite clearly, the brow shaded by the peak of the képi, the peering eyes, the prow-like nose. He saw the raised saluting hand come down from the peak of the cap, the crossed wires of the sight were spot on the exposed temple. Softly, gently, he squeezed the trigger ...
>
> A split second later he was staring down into the station forecourt as if he could not believe his eyes. Before the bullet had passed out of the end of the barrel, the President of France had snapped his head forward without warning. As the assassin watched in disbelief, he solemnly planted a kiss on the cheek of the man in front of him ... It was later established the bullet had passed a fraction of an inch behind the moving head.

In terms of moral blameworthiness, one could say that the assassin, the "Jackal" who tried to murder the President of France but failed, is not very different from a person who tried and succeeded. This example suggests that the criminal law should not concentrate on outcomes, but rather focus on culpability instead: see HLA Hart, "The House of Lords on Attempting the Impossible" in C Tapper (ed), *Crime, Proof and Punishment — Essays in Memory of Sir Rupert Cross* (London: Butt, 1981).

The third and final justification for criminalising and punishing attempts is the importance of crime prevention, as mentioned earlier. This is a criminal process argument that the police should be able to step in to *prevent* harm rather than have to wait until after harm has been done. The criminal law should thus punish those who are trying to commit harm as well as those who succeed in so doing.

The source of the definition of an attempt, its application and the penalty imposed varies between Australian jurisdictions. This can be seen from the following Table.

TABLE 1:
Attempts across Jurisdictions

JURISDICTION AND RELEVANT LAW	DEFINITION OF ATTEMPT	APPLICATION TO OFFENCES	PENALTY
CTH *Crimes Act* 1914	**Statutory definition:** s 7	offences against any law of the Commonwealth	same penalty as if offence completed s 7
ACT *Crimes Act* 1900 **Scope:** common law	**Offence:** s 327	offences under a law of the Territory	no specific provision
NSW *Crimes Act* 1900 **Scope:** common law	**Offence:** s 344A	offences under the *Crimes Act* 1900	same penalty as if offence completed s 344A
NT *Criminal Code*	**Statutory definition:** ss 4, 277	any offence	7 years where completed offence is 14 years or upwards; otherwise ½ of greatest punishment for completed offence ss 278, 279
QLD *Criminal Code*	**Statutory definition:** ss 4, 535	indictable offences	7 years where completed offence is 14 years or upwards; otherwise ½ of greatest punishment for completed offence ss 536-538
SA *Criminal Law Consolidation Act* 1935 **Scope:** common law	**Offence:** s 270A	any offence	maximum is ⅔ completed offence s 270A(3)
TAS *Criminal Code*	**Statutory definition:** ss 2, 299	any offence	no specific provision
VIC *Crimes Act* 1958	**Statutory definition:** ss 321M, 321N	indictable offences	penalty is 60% completed offence s 321P
WA *Criminal Code*	**Statutory definition:** ss 4, 552, 555A(1)	any offence	same penalty as if simple offence completed; ½ that of completed indictable offence ss 554, 555A

Despite these variations, the actual substance of the statutory definitions and the common law definition are similar. An attempt involves both physical and fault elements, but as pointed out above, there is great emphasis placed on the fault element. Indeed, without the requisite fault element, the conduct alone may appear inoffensive. Accordingly, the fault element for an attempt generally differs from that of the completed offence in that generally a higher standard must be satisfied.

A definition of an attempt at common law was set out by Murphy J in *Britten v Alpogut* [1987] VR 929 at 938:

> [A] criminal attempt is committed if it is proven that the accused had at all material times the guilty intent to commit a recognised crime and it is proven that at the same time he [or she] did an act or acts (which in appropriate circumstances would include omissions) which are seen to be sufficiently proximate to the commission of the said crime and not seen to be merely preparatory to it.

The same requirements of an intention to commit the completed offence and conduct that is more than merely preparatory are common to all the various statutory definitions of attempt. We will set out the requirements for the physical and fault elements of attempts in turn.

Punishment of Attempts

Table 1 shows that the punishment for an attempt varies across the jurisdictions. David Lewis has argued that it is difficult to find a rationale for leniency in punishing attempts compared to the completed crime. Take the case of the assassin who fires a gun at a public figure and misses and one who fires a gun at a public figure and hits and kills her. They both have the same intention to kill and their conduct is equally dangerous. Why should "failure" or "luck" mean a more lenient punishment? Antony Duff argues that lesser punishment for such an attempt marks the fact that the assassin who missed the target failed to produce the intended effect in the real world. If the potential assassin had a gun in a public place and was caught prior to getting near the target, an argument can perhaps more strongly be made out for a lesser punishment. Andrew Ashworth writes in *Principles of Criminal Law* (3rd ed, Oxford: Oxford University Press, 1999), p 483, that in such a case a more lenient punishment may be justified "because of the possibility of voluntary abandonment of the attempt, because it takes greater nerve to consummate an offence, and because it may be prudent to leave some incentive (that is, reduced punishment) to the incomplete attempter to give up rather than to carry out the full offence". What the punishment should be for attempt is explored in D Lewis, "The Punishment That Leaves Something to Chance" (1989) 18(1) *Philosophy and Public Affairs* 53; RA Duff, *Criminal Attempts* (Oxford: Oxford University Press, 1996), Ch 4 and pp 351-354.

2.1 PHYSICAL ELEMENT

A distinction has generally been drawn between *preparing* to commit a crime and *attempting* to commit it. Only the latter is considered punishable. In *Britten v Alpogut* [1987] VR 929 at 938, Murphy J spoke of conduct being "sufficiently proximate" and not "merely preparatory". The latter term is taken up in s 7(2) of the *Crimes Act* 1914 (Cth), s 321(N)(1) of the *Crimes Act* 1958 (Vic) and s 4 of the *Criminal Code* (WA). The Victorian provision adds a requirement that the conduct be "immediately and not remotely connected" to the commission of the offence. In the Northern Territory and Queensland, the phrase used is "by means adapted to [the crime's] fulfilment": *Criminal Code* (NT), s 4; *Criminal Code* (Qld), s 4. What this means precisely is unclear, but the courts have applied common law decisions on proximity to the Queensland section.[5] Section 2 of the *Criminal Code* (Tas) states that the conduct must not be too remote and part of a series of events that, if not interrupted, would constitute the actual commission of the crime.

All of the statutory provisions and the common law are thus concerned with the notion of proximity. Whether conduct is considered sufficiently proximate to the actual offence is generally a matter for the jury to determine.[6] In Tasmania, however, the question of whether or not conduct was too remote to constitute an attempt is a matter of law for the trial judge to determine: *Criminal Code* (Tas), s 2. Once the trial judge decides that the conduct was not too remote, then it is up to the jury to decide whether the accused would have committed the completed offence if not interrupted.

The difficulty in all jurisdictions lies in determining when conduct is sufficiently proximate to qualify as an attempt. Visually, one has to determine where the accused's act falls on the following continuum:

Mere Preparation ◄----------------------------► **Completed Offence**

In determining where the accused's conduct lies, the courts have developed a number of tests, none of which have proved entirely satisfactory. Salmond J described the problematic process in *R v Barker* [1924] NZLR 865 at 874:

> [T]o constitute a criminal attempt, the first step along the way of criminal intent is not necessarily sufficient and the final step is not necessarily required. The dividing line between preparation and attempt is to be found somewhere between these two extremes; but as to the method by which it is to be determined the authorities give no clear guidance.

In trying to work out whether conduct amounts to an attempt, the courts have referred to whether the conduct is "too remote", "more than merely preparatory", "sufficiently proximate", "the last act", "a substantial step", "on the job" or "unequivocal". We will look at three approaches in the following sections.

---

5   *R v Williams* [1965] Qd R 86 at 102 per Stable J; *R v Chellingworth* [1954] QWN 35 (Circuit Court); *R v Edwards* [1956] QWN 16.

6   *DPP v Stonehouse* [1978] AC 55; *R v Gullefer* [1990] 3 All ER 882 at 884 per Lord Lane CJ.

THE LAST ACT TEST

In the 19th century, the courts took a fairly conservative approach to proximity, requiring a "last act" to have been taken towards the commission of the offence. In *R v Eagleton* (1855) 6 Cox CC 559, the accused made a contract with a local Poor Law authority to supply bread for an agreed weight to the poor. He was to be paid a certain amount per loaf by the authority. The accused supplied underweight loaves, but his conduct was discovered before he was paid. He was charged with attempting to obtain money by false pretences. The case went to the Court for Crown Cases Reserved on the question of law as to whether the accused's activity constituted an attempt. The court held that there had been an attempt. Parke B in delivering the judgment of the Court stated (at 571):

> Acts remotely leading towards the commission of the offence are not to be considered as
> attempts to commit it; but acts immediately connected with it are ... [O]n the statement in
> this case, no other act on the part of the defendant would have been required. It was the
> last act depending on himself towards the payment of the money, and therefore it ought to
> be considered as an attempt.

Parke B here appears to be requiring that the accused do the very last act possible toward the completed offence. This test was taken up in *R v Robinson* [1915] 2 KB 342. In that case, the accused was a jeweller who insured his goods against theft. He faked a robbery by tying himself up and calling for help. He told the police that he had been knocked down and jewellery taken from the safe. The police later found the jewellery in the shop and the accused admitted he intended to put in a false claim to the insurers. The accused's conviction for attempting to obtain money by false pretences was quashed by the Court of Criminal Appeal on the basis that his acts were too remote in that he had not taken the last step of communicating with the insurers and making a false claim.

Glanville Williams described the decision in *Robinson* as being "as favourable to the accused as any that could be found in English law; it seems to be too favourable": *Criminal Law: The General Part* (2nd ed, London: Stevens & Sons, 1961), p 627. Another example of a very favourable result is that of *R v Chellingworth* [1954] QWN 35. In this case, the accused was found in a house at 5.30 in the morning with a half-empty can of petrol. The walls and the floor of the house had been splashed with petrol. Other tins of petrol and bags soaked with petrol were also found. He was charged with attempted arson. The trial judge indicated that on the facts the accused had not shown his intention to carry out the offence of arson within the meaning of the *Criminal Code* (Qld). The prosecution then entered a *nolle prosequi*. The "last act" here would presumably be lighting a match. Here, the "last act" test seems to be unduly restricting the scope of attempts.

The last act test subsequently fell into disfavour by the courts on the basis that some offences may be committed in stages over a period of time: *DPP v Stonehouse* [1978] AC 55 at 86 per Lord Edmund-Davies; *Jones* (1990) 91 Cr App R 351. For example, a person may attempt to kill another by using increasing doses of poison as was the case in *R v White* [1910] 2 KB 124. The last act test is also not useful in situations dealing with guns. If a person buys a rifle, loads it, aims it at the victim and is seized before firing it, this would seem to be sufficient conduct for attempted murder: L Waller and CR Williams, *Brett, Waller and Williams: Criminal Law — Text and Cases* (8th ed, Sydney: Butt, 1997), p 444. According to the last act test, the accused would have to pull the trigger as well, before an attempt could be made out.

The *Criminal Codes* of the Northern Territory, Queensland and Western Australia expressly state that whether or not the accused has done all that is necessary on his or her part for completing the intended offence is immaterial: *Criminal Code* (NT), s 4; *Criminal Code* (Qld), s 4; *Criminal Code* (WA), s 4. The last act test therefore was developed to deal with those situations where a person other than the accused has to do or omit to do something before the offence can be completed. The reasoning in this case has been criticised: see M Goode, "Case and Comment: *O' Connor v Killian*" (1985) 9 Crim LJ 367. In cases where the accused is not dependent on another person, the test seems overly restrictive.

THE UNEQUIVOCALITY TEST

This test is similar to the substantial progress test and requires there to be conduct that unequivocally indicates that the accused intended to commit the offence. Lord Salmond set out this test in *R v Barker* [1924] NZLR 865 at 874:

> [An] act done with intent to commit a crime is not a criminal attempt unless it is of such a nature as to be itself sufficient evidence of the criminal intent with which it is done. A criminal attempt is an act which shows criminal intent on the face of it. The case must be one in which *res ipsa loquitur* [the thing speaks for itself] applies ... That [an accused's] unfulfilled criminal purposes should be punishable, they must be manifested not by his [or her] words merely, or by acts which are themselves of innocent or ambiguous significance, but by overt acts which are sufficient in themselves to declare and proclaim the guilty purpose with which they are done.

This test enables an acquittal if the accused's conduct can be associated with an innocent motive as well as an intention to commit an offence. It has received only limited support in Australia: *R v Williams* [1965] Qd R 86 at 100 per Stable J. For example, in *O' Connor v Killian* (1984) 38 SASR 327, the accused tried to cash bank cheques payable to another. When told they would have to be deposited into a bank account, she opened an account in the other person's name. She was then told to return to the bank with appropriate identification. This she failed to do. She was later charged with attempting to obtain money by false pretences. Her appeal against conviction was unsuccessful. Prior J emphasised the accused's admitted intention to obtain money fraudulently and this was treated as effectively lowering the threshold for conduct constituting an attempt.

The unequivocality test was expressly rejected as a definitive test by the Tasmanian Court of Appeal in *Nicholson* (1994) 76 A Crim R 187 at 190-192 per Underwood J and at 199 per Wright J. However, an admitted intention or an act that unequivocally indicates an intention will be highly persuasive in establishing an attempt.

THE SUBSTANTIAL STEP TEST

This test requires substantial steps to have been made towards the commission of the crime. It looks at how much progress has been made and how much remains to be done. The main case exemplifying this approach is that of *DPP v Stonehouse* [1978] AC 55. The accused, a well-known English politician and Privy Councillor, suffered severe financial difficulties. He decided to fake his own death by drowning and to start life afresh in Australia under a new identity. He took out life insurance with five different companies, naming his wife, who was unaware of the plan, as the beneficiary. The policies totalled £125,000 payable to Barbara Stonehouse upon the death of her husband within five years. The accused went to Florida and staged his apparent death in a drowning incident. He was later caught in Australia.[7] The accused was convicted of a number of dishonesty offences and, in relation to the life insurance, attempting to obtain property by deception. (Section 15(2) of the *Theft Act* 1968 included "enabling another to obtain" as falling within the word "obtain".)

On appeal to the House of Lords, the accused argued that his acts were too remote from the commission of the offence of obtaining property by deception to constitute an attempt. That is, the mere disappearance did not enable Barbara Stonehouse to obtain the property. She would have had to decide to make a claim and communicate that claim before the full offence could be carried out. Lord Diplock (at 68) thought the remoteness point unarguable:

> [T]he accused by November 20, 1974 [when Stonehouse faked his death in Florida], had done all the physical acts lying in his power that were needed to enable Mrs Stonehouse to obtain the policy moneys if all had gone as intended. There was nothing left for him to do thereafter except to avoid detection of his real identity. That was the day on which he crossed his Rubicon and burnt his boats.

As Lord Edmund-Davies pointed out (at 87) not only did Stonehouse's faking of his death go a substantial distance towards the attainment of the complete offence, it was also the final act that *he* could perform.

The substantial step test can be used to focus on what has been done as well as what remains to be done. For example, in *Jones* (1990) 91 Cr App R 351, the victim was in a relationship with the accused's ex-girlfriend. The accused got into the victim's car with a loaded sawn-off shot gun. The victim managed to disarm the accused and the latter was charged with attempted murder. Lord Justice Taylor (at 356), in delivering the judgment of the Court of Appeal, focused on the conduct that had already been committed:

> Clearly his actions in obtaining the gun, in shortening it, in loading it, in putting on his disguise, and in going to the school could only be regarded as preparatory acts. But, in our judgement, once he had got into the car, taken out the loaded gun and pointed it at the victim with the intention of killing him, there was sufficient evidence for the consideration of the jury on the charge of attempted murder.

In comparison, the Court of Appeal in *R v Campbell* [1991] Crim L R 268, focused on the steps that needed to be taken before substantial progress had been made. In that case, the police arrested the accused when he was close to a post office, carrying an imitation firearm and a threatening note. His appeal against conviction for attempted robbery was successful on the basis that he had not entered the post office. This decision seems to imply that the police have to wait until a person is inside a bank or post office and has shown a weapon before an arrest can be made. An alternative approach,

---

7   An entertaining account of the circumstances of this case can be found in G Robertson, *The Justice Game* (London: Chatto and Windus, 1998), pp 62-73. Geoffrey Robertson was junior counsel for Stonehouse in the House of Lords Appeal.

discussed by P Glazebrook, which would avoid this difficulty for the police, is to prosecute the accused for "going equipped with instruments for robbery or burglary": "Should We Have a Law of Attempted Crime?" [1969] 85 *Law Quarterly Review* 28; see Ch 13, p 728.

The substantial progress step test is necessarily vague, being adapted to the facts of each case and providing considerable leeway in determining criminal responsibility.

Legislative Reformulations of the Tests of Proximity

In 1980 the Law Commission of England and Wales produced a report (No 102) reviewing the law of criminal attempts. The Commission concluded that the last act test fixed the point of intervention for criminal liability too late. The Law Commission in an earlier Working Paper (No 50) had provisionally favoured the adoption of a test based on a "substantial step" towards the commission of the offence. In its 1980 Report and in the subsequent enacting legislation, s 1(1) of the *Criminal Attempts Act* 1981 (UK), a formulation based on "acts more than merely preparatory to the commission of the offence" was adopted. The Law Commission rejected the use of the word "proximate" because of the danger that it would suggest that only the last act could be an attempt. Using the words "more than merely preparatory" avoids notions of unequivocality or substantial steps, but JC Smith and Brian Hogan point out that no substantial change in the law set out in *Stonehouse* was intended: *Criminal Law* (6th ed, London: Butt, 1988), p 292. As with the other common law tests, this formulation has been criticised as being too imprecise: I Dennis "The Criminal Attempts Act 1981" [1982] Crim LR 5. Ian Dennis has also suggested that the statutory test could have included a further partial definition of "more than preparation" with suitable illustrations: "The Law Commission Report on Attempt and Impossibility in Relation to Attempt, Conspiracy and Incitement: (1) The Elements of Attempt" [1980] Crim LR 758. Nonetheless the "more than merely preparatory" formulation has been adopted in the s 7(2) of the *Crimes Act* 1914 (Cth), s 321N(1) of the *Crimes Act* 1958 (Vic) and s 4 of the *Criminal Code* (WA). Section 11.1(2) of the *Criminal Code Act* 1995 (Cth) has similarly adopted this more than merely preparatory formula. Whatever words are used in legislation, a completely clear formulation for pinpointing the physical element of an attempt appears to lie in the realm of fantasy.

DESISTANCE

When an accused "desists" or decides not to go ahead with an offence, he or she may still be found criminally liable for an attempt if the conduct performed is considered sufficiently proximate to the completed offence.[8] For example, in *R v Page* [1933] VLR 351, the accused kept watch while another man, Partridge, put a lever under a window in order to break into a shop. Before opening the window, Partridge had a change of heart and decided that he would not "continue with the job". He dropped the lever and descended and the two men were arrested. The Full Court of the Supreme Court of

---

8   *R v Page* [1933] VLR 351 (FC); *R v Collingridge* (1976) 16 SASR 117 (FC); *Criminal Code* (NT), s 4(2); *Criminal Code* (Qld), s 4(2); *Criminal Code* (Tas), s 2(2); *Criminal Code* (WA), s 4. There is no mention of desistance in the Victorian provisions and it would seem that the common law still applies.

Victoria held that what was done by Partridge amounted to an attempt and the fact that he had "desisted of his own volition" made no difference.

In the Northern Territory and Queensland, desistance may be taken into account in reducing the penalty for an attempt: *Criminal Code* (NT), s 279(1); *Criminal Code* (Qld), s 538.

The policy for allowing desistance to exculpate an accused obviously makes more sense the further back the conduct is from the substantive offence. If one takes the view that the fault element is the essential part of an attempt, then it follows that desistance shows that the original intent was not sufficiently firm. A change of mind may be seen as "undoing" the original blameworthy state of mind. Allowing desistance to be taken into account may also show the deterrent effect of criminalising an attempt. In practice, desistance is rarely raised presumably because of the difficulty in arguing that a change of mind was truly voluntary.

IMPOSSIBILITY

An accused may attempt to commit a crime that is in fact impossible to commit due to circumstances unknown to the accused. In a sense, the accused is making a mistake in believing that he or she will be able to accomplish or has accomplished the substantive offence. For this reason, we discussed the law relating to impossibility and inchoate offences in Chapter 7, which dealt with mistake.

2.2 FAULT ELEMENT

In all jurisdictions, the requisite fault element for an attempt is an *intention* to commit the requisite offence.[9] We pointed out in Chapter 3 that the narrow interpretation of intention known as direct intention "connotes a decision to bring about a situation so far as it is possible to do so — to bring about an act of a particular kind or a particular result": *He Kaw Teh v The Queen* (1985) 157 CLR 523 at 569 per Brennan J. This is the form of intention that is generally referred to in the context of attempts. Oblique intention or recklessness is not considered sufficient for attempts to commit offences where the physical element refers to the results or consequences of conduct.

In *Giorgianni v The Queen* (1985) 156 CLR 473, the majority of the High Court (Wilson, Deane and Dawson JJ) stated (at 506), in obiter:

> For the purposes of many offences it may be true to say that if an act is done with foresight of its probable consequences there is sufficient intent in law even if such intent may more properly be described as a form of recklessness. There are, however, offences in which it is not possible to speak of recklessness as constituting a sufficient intent. Attempt is one and conspiracy is another ... Intent is required and it is an intent which must be based upon knowledge or belief of the necessary facts.

This approach that only a direct intention will suffice for an attempted result crime has been followed in subsequent cases. In *Knight v The Queen* (1992) 175 CLR 495, the High Court held that in relation

---

9   *Britten v Alpogut* [1987] VR 929; *Knight v The Queen* (1992) 175 CLR 495 at 501 per Mason CJ and Dawson and Toohey JJ; *Criminal Code* (NT), s 4; *Criminal Code* (Qld), s 4; *Criminal Code* (Tas), s 2(1); *Crimes Act* (Vic), s 321N(2); *Criminal Code* (WA), s 4.

to attempted murder, only an intention to kill would suffice. Mason CJ, Dawson and Toohey JJ stated (at 501):

> [A]n accused is not guilty of attempted murder unless he [or she] intends to kill ... An intention to cause grievous bodily harm may constitute the malice aforethought required for murder where death ensues, but for there to be attempted murder there must be an intention to cause the death which is an essential element of the completed crime of murder.

Brennan J also reinforced this approach in *McGhee v The Queen* (1995) 183 CLR 82 at 85-86:

> [T]he crime of attempted murder at common law has uniformly been held to require an intent to kill ... In principle, that must be so. Not because an intent to kill is a mental element in the crime of murder but because the causing of death is a physical element in the crime of murder and an attempt to commit that crime must have, as its mental element, an intention that death be caused.

This high standard for the fault element in relation to result offences also carries over to strict and absolute liability offences.[10] Following Brennan J's approach, the emphasis is on an intention to commit the physical element of the offence. The fault element, or lack thereof, for the completed offence is irrelevant.

While the fault element therefore appears straightforward in relation to attempted result crimes, the position is less clear regarding attempted crimes where the physical element requires conduct to be performed in certain specified circumstances. In Chapter 12 we explore how, in general, the crime of rape is defined by intentional sexual penetration (conduct) which occurs without the other person's consent (the specified circumstance). For attempted rape, does the fault element have to be an intention to sexually penetrate another *knowing* that the other person is not consenting? Or is it sufficient that the accused intend to sexually penetrate another being *reckless* as to whether the other person is consenting or not?

Section 321N(2)(b) of the *Crimes Act* 1958 (Vic) requires that the accused "intend or believe that any fact or circumstance the existence of which is an element of the offence will exist at the time the offence is to take place". When this test is applied to the crime of rape, for example, the prosecution must show that the accused intended to sexually penetrate another, believing that the other person is not consenting. The fault element is therefore aligned with that of attempted result crimes.

However, there are some cases that support a lower fault standard for attempted rape. In *R v Bell* [1972] Tas SR 127, Neasey J stated (at 131-132) that awareness of the possibility of non-consent would be sufficient for the purpose of attempted rape under the *Criminal Code* (Tas).

In *R v Evans* (1987) 48 SASR 35, the South Australian Court of Criminal Appeal held that attempted rape may be committed when the accused intended to sexually penetrate another, being recklessly indifferent as to the absence of consent. King CJ (at 41) pointed out that the difference between result crimes and crimes involving circumstances led to a difference in fault elements:

---

10   *Trade Practices Commission v Tubemakers of Australia Ltd* (1983) 47 ALR 719 at 737 per Toohey J. For an explanation of strict and absolute liability offences, see Chapter 3: p 191.

The state of facts, the existence of which renders the act of sexual penetration criminal, is the non-consent of the person penetrated. The mental state of the accused in relation to that state of facts, required by the definition of the crime ... includes reckless indifference to its existence. There cannot be an attempt to commit a crime involving particular consequences where those consequences are not intended, because the notion of unintended consequences is inconsistent with the notion of attempt to bring about those consequences. That reasoning does not apply, however, to an accused's state of mind as to the existence of circumstances which render an act criminal.

Special leave to appeal against *Evan's* case was refused by the High Court and it was followed by the English Court of Appeal in *R v Khan* [1990] 2 All ER 783. However, Russell LJ noted (at 819) that the reasoning that explained the inclusion of recklessness in the fault element for attempted rape did not apply equally to all offences. Whether the lower fault element applies to other crimes that include circumstances is unclear.

The Fault Standard for Attempted Rape

Jonathan Clough and Carmel Mulhern are of the opinion that a lower fault standard for attempted rape is difficult to reconcile with the clear requirement that the fault element of an attempt is an intention to commit an offence: *Butterworths Tutorial Series: Criminal Law* (Sydney: Butt, 1999), p 209. They are not convinced that the distinction between result crimes and crimes of circumstance set out in *Evan's* case justifies a lower fault standard. Brent Fisse also points out that because there are no definitive tests for the physical element in attempts, relaxing the fault element may be "dangerous": *Howard's Criminal Law* (5th ed, Sydney: Law Book Company Ltd, 1990), pp 388-389. On the other hand, Ashworth points out in *Principles of Criminal Law* (3rd ed, Oxford: Oxford University Press, 1999), pp 464-465, that if "two men set out to have sexual intercourse with two women, not caring whether they consent or not, it would be absurd if the one who achieved penetration was convicted of rape, whilst the other, who failed to achieve penetration despite trying, was not even liable for attempted rape". It would seem that this "absurdity" may well provide a policy exception to the general principle that only intention should suffice: see G Williams, "The Problem of Reckless Attempts" [1983] *Criminal Law Review* 365; R Buxton, "Circumstances, Consequences and Attempted Rape" [1984] *Criminal Law Review* 25.

3. CONSPIRACY

We have explored how the physical element for attempts is loosely defined. Conspiracy as an offence is even more uncertain in its ambit.

The first statutory reference in England to the crime of conspiracy dates back to the 13th century during the reign of Edward I. James Wallace Bryan in his book on the development of the law of conspiracy refers to the first Ordinance of Conspirators, anno 21 Edward 1, as providing a remedy against "conspirators, inventors and maintainers of false quarrels and their abettors and supporters ... and brokers of debates".[11] Its non-statutory origins may, however, be much older and while the modern law simply requires an agreement to commit an offence, historically, there had to be some act that followed the agreement: JW Bryan, *The Development of the English Law of Conspiracy* (New York: Da Capo Press, 1970), p 14. By the early 17th century, the law altered to the more modern conception of simply requiring an agreement to be established. In the *Poulterers' Case* (1611) 77 ER 813, the Court of Star Chamber held that mere agreement was enough to constitute the offence. Sayre writes that after the abolition of the Star Chamber, the Court of Kings Bench "began to extend the offense so as to cover combinations to commit all crimes of whatsoever nature, misdemeanours as well as felonies": "Criminal Conspiracy" (1922) 35 *Harvard Law Review* 393 at 400.

Conspiracy was thus broadened to include a number of heads such as conspiracy to commit a crime, conspiracy to defraud, conspiracy to pervert the course of justice and conspiracy to corrupt public morals. Until the decision in *DPP v Withers* [1975] AC 842 which restricted the development of conspiracy, it seemed that this offence had the potential for continuous expansion. The House of Lords in *Withers* made it clear that only Parliament and not the courts can add new heads to the offence of conspiracy.

The following section analyses the rationales for the crime of conspiracy, but it is interesting to note here that social factors have at times led to it being viewed as a substantive criminal offence in itself rather than an inchoate offence. This was particularly apparent in England in the 19th century when conspiracy was used to criminalise agreements to engage in unlawful tortious, though not criminal, acts. This was linked to the suppression of trade unionism. Ashworth writes in *Principles of Criminal Law* (3rd ed, Oxford: Oxford University Press, 1999), p 472:

> In the nineteenth century it was accepted that a conviction for criminal conspiracy could be based on an agreement to do any unlawful act, even though that act was not criminal but only a civil wrong, such as a tort or breach of contract. This gave the criminal law a long reach, particularly with regard to the activities of the early trade unions. And the courts upheld conspiracy convictions for what were, in effect, agreements to strike ... In social terms, the criminal law lent its authority to those who wished to suppress organized industrial action.[12]

All Australian jurisdictions criminalise conspiracy to commit certain crimes. However, only Victorian and Commonwealth legislation attempt to define the scope of conspiracy. The common law is still relevant in the other jurisdictions, including the Code jurisdictions, in determining what constitutes conspiracy. In an attempt to limit charges for conspiracy, certain jurisdictions have statutory provisions preventing the commencement of proceedings without the consent of the Director of

---

11 JW Bryan, *The Development of the English Law of Conspiracy* (New York: Da Capo Press, 1970), p 9. See also PH Winfield, *The History of Conspiracy and Abuse of Legal Procedure* (Cambridge: Cambridge University Press, 1921). See also P Gillies, *The Law of Criminal Conspiracy* (2nd ed, Sydney: Federation Press, 1990) for an historical overview of the offence.

12 See also, JV Orth, *Combination and Conspiracy: A Legal History of Trade Unionism, 1721-1906* (Oxford: Clarendon Press, 1991).

Public Prosecutions or Attorney-General.[13] In practice, conspiracy to defraud, conspiracy to commit crimes and conspiracy to pervert the course of justice are the usual forms of conspiracy charged in Australia. Section 321(1) of the *Crimes Act* 1958 (Vic) confirms this limitation.

It is worthwhile noting here that there are certain evidential rules that are specific to conspiracy. For example, the statements of one co-conspirator are admissible in evidence against another where there is other reasonable evidence of the participation of the latter: *Ahern v The Queen* (1988) 165 CLR 87; *R v Masters* (1992) 26 NSWLR 450. This is an exception to the general rule that admissions of one accused cannot be admitted in evidence against another and has been the subject of considerable debate: see B Hocking, "Commentary on *Dellapatrona and Duffield*" (1995) 19 Crim LJ 169 and references therein.

The common law definition of conspiracy was provided by Willes J in *Mulcahy v The Queen* (1868) LR 3 HL 306 at 317:

> A conspiracy consists not merely in the intention of two or more, but in the agreement of two or more to do an unlawful act, or to do a lawful act by unlawful means.

TABLE 2:

Types of Offences to which Conspiracy may Attach

JURISDICTION AND RELEVANT LAW	CONSPIRACY TO ...	PENALTY
CTH *Crimes Act* 1914	commit an offence against a law of the Commonwealth	same penalty as if offence completed or imprisonment of up to 20 years if offence against s 29D of Act (defrauding the Commonwealth)
	s 86	s 86
ACT *Crimes Act* 1900	commit an offence under a law of the Territory prevent or defeat the execution or enforcement of a law effect unlawful purpose effect a lawful purpose by unlawful means	imprisonment for 3 years or, if serious offence, same punishment as for substantive offence
	s 349	s 349
NSW common law	—	no specific provision

13   *Crimes Act* 1914 (Cth), s 86(9); *Criminal Code* (Qld), ss 541(2), 542(2), 543(2); *Crimes Act* 1958 (Vic), s 321(4).

Table 2 continued

JURISDICTION AND RELEVANT LAW	CONSPIRACY TO ...	PENALTY
NT *Criminal Code*	commit any crime or do any act, make any omission or any event that is an offence (s 282) commit a simple offence or do any act, make any omission or any event that is a simple offence (s 283) deceive or defraud (s 284) lay false charge (s 285) pervert the course of justice (s 286) murder (s 287) carry out seditious enterprise (s 288) prevention of execution of statute law etc (s 289)	imprisonment for 7 years or less for serious crime or one year for conspiracy to commit simple offence imprisonment for 14 years for conspiracy to murder imprisonment for 3 years for conspiracy to carry out seditious enterprise or prevention of execution of statute law etc ss 282-289
QLD *Criminal Code*	commit any crime (s 541) any offence which is not a crime (ie, misdemeanour) (s 542) prevention of execution of statute law; cause any injury to person or reputation of person; depreciate the value of any property; prevent the disposition of property; prevent the free and lawful exercise of a person's trade, profession or occupation; effect any unlawful purpose; effect any lawful purpose by any unlawful means (s 543)	imprisonment for 7 years for serious crime or lesser punishment if substantive offence merits less than seven years imprisonment for 3 years for offences that are not crimes or conspiracies under s 543
SA common law	—	no specific provision
TAS *Criminal Code*	kill; obstruct the due course of justice or administration of the law; commit any crime; cheat or defraud the public or person(s); extort any property; inflict any injury or harm upon the public or person(s); facilitate the seduction of a woman; do any act involving public mischief; do any act with intent to injure s 297	no specific provision

Table 2 continued

JURISDICTION AND RELEVANT LAW	CONSPIRACY TO ...	PENALTY
VIC *Crimes Act* 1958	commit an offence (s 321) common law reserved for conspiracies to defraud (s 321F(2))	penalty not exceeding penalty for the relevant offence s 321C
WA *Criminal Code*	commit any indictable offence (s 558) commit any simple offence (s 560)	imprisonment for 14 years where indictable offence is punishable by 14 years or more (s 558) otherwise, punishment equal to the greatest punishment afforded to the relevant offence (ss 558, 560)

The first part of this definition subsumes the second. An agreement to use unlawful means is in itself an agreement to do an unlawful act. This definition therefore appears to be setting out two ways of saying the same thing. It has been endorsed in Australia by Blair CJ in *R v Campbell* [1933] St R Qd 123 at 133 and by Brennan and Toohey JJ in *R v Rogerson* (1992) 174 CLR 268 at 281.

At common law, then, there are in general four matters that must be established by the prosecution:

▬ **an agreement;**

▬ **between two or more persons;**

▬ **to commit an unlawful act;**

▬ **with an intention to commit that unlawful act.**

The Victorian and Commonwealth provisions are stated in similar terms. We will deal with these elements in turn. First, however, it is worthwhile considering the rationales for criminalising agreements to commit offences.

PERSPECTIVES

Rationales for Criminalising Conspiracy

The first main rationale that has been given for criminalising conspiracy is the same as for criminalising inchoate crimes in general: it is appropriate for the police to be able to step in to prevent the commission of a crime. It is also viewed as useful in supplementing the law of attempt. For example, Lord Tucker stated in *Board of Trade v Owen* [1957] AC 602 at 626:

> [I]t seems to me that the whole object of making such agreements punishable is to prevent the commission of the substantive offence before it has even reached the stage of an attempt, and that is all part and parcel of the preservation of the Queen's peace within that realm.

Ian Dennis rightly points out that this rationale in itself is not sufficient. He writes that "[b]y itself, it does not explain what it is about an *agreement* that permits the law to step in to prevent crime where it could not do so without such agreement": "The Rationale of Criminal Conspiracy" (1977) 93 *Law Quarterly Review* 39 at 41.

Sometimes it is claimed that it is necessary to intervene to prevent a crime occurring at such an early stage because members of a group will be more likely to go ahead with a crime than an individual given time to consider the implications: see "Developments in the Law — Criminal Conspiracy" (1959) 72 *Harvard Law Review* 920 at 924. There is some research into social psychology that suggests that people in groups will conform to normative pressure: GM Vaughan and MA Hogg, *Introduction to Social Psychology* (2nd ed, Sydney: Prentice Hall Australia Pty Ltd, 1998), pp 142ff. Whether this translates to two or more people carrying out a crime pursuant to an agreement is debatable. It could be argued that the larger the amount of people involved, the more likely the agreement will be leaked and dissension likely to grow: R Hazell, *Conspiracy and Civil Liberties* (London: Bell, 1974), p 94.

A related rationale for criminalising conspiracy is the notion that a group enterprise is more worthy of punishment than an individual decision to commit a crime. An individual who states an intention to commit a crime will not be punished, but two or more people who agree to do the same thing may be. This ties in with the notion that conspiracy "is said to be a vital legal weapon in the prosecution of 'organized crime', however defined": PE Johnson, "The Unnecessary Crime of Conspiracy" (1973) 61(5) *California Law Review* 1137. Lord Bramwell stated in *Mogul Steamship Company v McGregor, Gow & Co* [1892] AC 25 at 45:

> It has been objected by capable persons, that it is strange that that should be unlawful
> if done by several which is not if done by one ... I think there is an obvious answer,
> indeed two; one is, that a man may encounter the acts of a single person, yet not be
> fairly matched against several. The other is, that the act when done by an individual is
> wrong though not punishable, because the law avoids the multiplicity of crimes ...
> while if done by several it is sufficiently important to be treated as a crime.

This emphasis on the number of people involved has been criticised on the basis that it is the act or agreement that should be central to conspiracy rather than the number involved in the group enterprise: FB Sayre, "Criminal Conspiracy" (1923) 35 *Harvard Law Review* 393 at 411. However, this criticism is based on the notion of individual harm or wrongdoing rather than group harm or wrongdoing upon which the offences of conspiracy and complicity are based.

In practice, conspiracy functions differently from its rationale as an inchoate offence. Usually some overt acts following the agreement have generally taken place before conspiracy is charged. This is because it may be difficult for the prosecution to prove what occurred in a private meeting between conspirators. Further, the prosecution can charge conspiracy where the substantive offence is impossible to commit or where it has in fact been committed. Ashworth in *Principles of Criminal Law* (Oxford: Clarendon Press, 1991), p 410 writes:

> The crime of conspiracy ... remains more than an inchoate offence. While it can be used
> against agreements to commit crimes which have not yet been consummated, and
> agreements which are carried out and yet fail to produce the intended crime, it can also
> be charged where the elements of the substantive offence have been completed. The

justification for this is that the offence of conspiracy gives a more rounded impression of the nature of the criminal enterprise, in terms of planning and concerted action and the different roles of the various participants.

Phillip Johnson agrees that conspiracy is more than an inchoate offence because it invokes several procedural and evidential doctrines. Because of this, he argues that conspiracy only adds confusion to the law: "The Unnecessary Crime of Conspiracy" (1973) 61(5) *California Law Review* 1137 at 1139. In a provocative article he reassesses the rationales for criminalising conspiracy and addresses his reasons for abolishing the crime "to the law reformers of the future": at 1188.

3.1 PHYSICAL ELEMENTS

THE AGREEMENT

As with the law relating to attempts, the traditional division of a crime into physical and fault elements does not fit well with the notion of a conspiracy. The requirement for an agreement between two or more persons may be difficult to separate out from the requirement that there be an intention to commit an unlawful act. Matthew Goode in *Criminal Conspiracy in Canada* (Toronto: Carswell, 1975), p 16 states:

> [T]he concept of *actus reus* is an elusive one, particularly in the area of criminal conspiracy; so much so, in fact, that it may well be possible to say that the crime has no distinguishing mental and physical elements.

Cussen J stated in *R v Orton* [1922] VLR 469 at 473 that an agreement for the purposes of conspiracy is satisfied where there is a "conscious understanding of a common design". There is no liability where two or more individuals are merely talking about the possibility of committing an unlawful act, unless they have reached the stage of agreeing to do that that act. The courts distinguish between cases where the parties have *agreed to do something* and where the parties are *merely negotiating*.

Lord Parker CJ in *Mills* (1963) 47 Cr App R 49 held that determining whether the parties are merely negotiating or whether they have reached an agreement to do something may involve subtle distinctions. He stated (at 54-55):

> [I]t may be that those cases will be decided largely on the form of the reservation. If the reservation is no more than if a policeman is not there, it would be impossible to say that there had not been an agreement. On the other hand, if the matters left outstanding and reserved are of a sufficiently substantial nature, it may well be that the case will fall on the other side of the fence, and it will be said that the matter is merely a matter of negotiation.

If there is an agreement, the crime of conspiracy has been committed: *R v Gunn* (1930) 30 SR (NSW) 336 at 338. While an agreement is required, there need not be evidence of any formal agreement. It is sufficient if there is evidence from which it may be inferred that two or more persons are pursuing the same unlawful purpose and doing so in combination (as opposed to acting in complete independence of each other).

Section 86(3)(c) of the *Crimes Act* 1914 (Cth) now requires that one party must have committed an overt act pursuant to the agreement. In practice, evidence of overt acts will certainly aid the prosecution's case in establishing that an agreement has been reached. For example, in *O' Brien* (1974) 59 Cr App R 222, the accused was charged with conspiring to release two of the "Luton Three" from Bedford Prison and the other member from Winson Green Prison. The members of the "Luton Three", Campbell, Mealey and Sheridan had been gaoled for robbery. It was alleged that they had robbed a bank to gain proceeds for their support of Irish nationalism.

The evidence upon which the prosecution proceeded was that the accused was found taking photographs outside the Winson Green Prison. A search of his house in Luton found literature of a kind that might be associated with those supporting the cause of Irish nationalism. There were annotated maps of Bedford and the prison, and a drawing that may have been some crude attempt to prepare a plan of the interior of Bedford Prison. The English Court of Appeal held (at 226) that there was insufficient evidence to entitle the jury to draw the inference that the accused had agreed *with others* to break into prison. The evidence at the most showed that he had been formulating a plan himself.

WITHDRAWAL

Except at the federal level, once the agreement has been made, a subsequent change of mind or withdrawal from the agreement does not make a difference: *R v Aspinall* (1876) 2 QBD 48.

Section 86(6) of the *Crimes Act* 1914 (Cth) states:

A person cannot be found guilty of conspiracy to commit an offence if, before the commission of an overt act pursuant to the agreement, the person:

(a) withdrew from the agreement; and

(b) took all reasonable steps to prevent the commission of the offence.

As stated above, s 86(3)(c) of the *Crimes Act* 1914 (Cth) requires evidence of the commission of an overt act. This explains why the defence of withdrawal may be allowed. The Criminal Law Officers Committee of the Standing Committee of Attorneys-General, *Chapter 2: General Principles of Criminal Responsibility*, Final Report (1992), p 101 recommended that the *Model Criminal Code* have a similar provision:

The Committee agreed that, if there was a requirement of an overt act, it was impossible to resist the conclusion that there should be a defence of withdrawal or disassociation, for there would be time between the agreement and the commission of the overt act for that to take place.

THE COMMON DESIGN

It is not necessary that all the parties to the agreement should have been in communication with each other, provided they entertained a common design communicated at least to one other party, expressly or tacitly, in relation to the object of the conspiracy.[14]

---

14   *Gerakiteys v The Queen* (1984) 153 CLR 317; *Lee* (1994) 76 A Crim R 271; *R v Griffiths* [1966] 1 QB 589 at 597 per Paull J for the Court; *R v Chrastny (No 1)* [1991] 1 WLR 1381.

Sometimes, however, establishing a conspiracy of the alleged design, rather than a series of connected but separate conspiracies may be problematic. In *Meyrick and Ribuffi* (1929) 21 Cr App R 94, the accused were nightclub owners operating unlicensed nightclubs in London's West End. They bribed a police officer to turn a blind eye to the operation of their respective nightclubs. The accused, together with the police officer, were convicted of conspiracy to contravene the provisions of the *Licensing Acts* and to effect a public mischief by obstructing and corrupting police officers. (The House of Lords subsequently held that there was no common law offence of conspiracy to effect a public mischief: *DPP v Withers* [1975] AC 842.) There was no evidence that the two accused knew each other, or had met each other, or had consulted together.

The Court of Criminal Appeal held that the accused had been rightfully convicted. The Court held that the essential ingredient of conspiracy was the existence of a common design; the prosecution need not establish that the individuals were in direct communication with each other, or directly consulting together, but that they entered into an agreement with a common design. On the facts, the "common design" was to evade the licensing laws. Hewart CJ stated at (101-102):

> [I]t was necessary that the prosecution should establish, not indeed that the individuals were in direct communication with each other, or directly consulting together, but that they entered into an agreement with a common design. Such agreements may be made in various ways. There may be one person ... round whom the rest revolve. The metaphor is the metaphor of the centre of the circle and the circumference. There may be a conspiracy of another kind, where the metaphor would be rather that of a chain; A communicates with B, B with C, C with D, and so on to the end of the conspirators. What has to be ascertained is always the same matter: is it true to say ... that the acts of the accused were done in pursuance of a criminal purpose held in common between them.

It could be said that the police officer on the facts of the case was the person at the centre of the circle around who the rest revolved and that without his coordination, there would have been no common design and hence no conspiracy. The facts suggest separate conspiracies between the police officer and each nightclub owner rather than one general conspiracy that everyone knew about. For example, this can be pictured as follows:

DIAGRAM 1:   Awareness of General Conspiracy

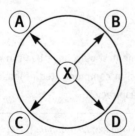

Central figure "X" controlling conspiracy.

"A", "B", "C" and "D" are aware of the general conspiracy.

DIAGRAM 2: **Awareness of Individual Conspiracy**

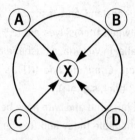

Central figure "X"
controlling conspiracy.

"A", "B", "C" and "D" are only
aware of their own individual
conspiracy with central figure.

The decision in *Meyrick's* case may be questioned in the light of subsequent cases. For example, in *R v Griffiths* [1966] 1 QB 589, the two accused were convicted of conspiring to defraud a government department by claiming false agricultural subsidies on behalf of farmers. The accused brought each farmer into the conspiracy, but none of the farmers knew one another. The prosecution charged one general conspiracy against the accused and the farmers. The Court of Criminal Appeal held that the evidence disclosed not one general conspiracy, but a number of them as portrayed by Diagram 2. That is, there was one general conspiracy between the two accused and several smaller conspiracies involving the accused and each farmer. The accuseds' appeals against conviction were therefore allowed on the basis that there was no evidence of a conspiracy between all those convicted as opposed to a number of separate conspiracies.

The importance of charging specific conspiracies rather than one general one was apparent in the High Court decision of *Gerakiteys v The Queen* (1984) 153 CLR 317. In this case the first accused, a doctor, was charged with conspiring with the second accused, an insurance agent and nine others (the claimants) to defraud a number of insurance companies. The prosecution case was that the first and second accused had arranged the conspiracy. The different claimants had agreed with the first and second accused to defraud a particular insurance company with whom each claimant was insured. Gibbs J stated (at 320):

> The jury in this case could not have found that the applicant and [the insurance agent] and any one or more of the nine claimants were guilty of the conspiracy alleged, because the evidence did not show that the claimant had a common purpose with the applicant and [the insurance agent] to defraud divers insurance companies. Each claimant had only the purpose of defrauding his own insurer. The case resembles *R v Griffiths* [1966] 1 QB 589 ... [A]ssuming the correctness of the Crown evidence, the claimants were parties to a number of different conspiracies, not to one common conspiracy.

The first accused's conviction was therefore quashed. It is therefore essential for the prosecution to consider whether a general conspiracy has taken place rather than a series of connected but separate conspiracies. In cases where there is a lack of consensus between the parties, it has been suggested that prosecutors should resort to charges of aiding and abetting a conspiracy: D Fitzpatrick, "Variations on Conspiracy" (1993) 143 *New Law Journal* 1180.

PARTIES TO CONSPIRACY

The agreement must be between two or more parties.[15] While this rule appears straightforward, there are a number of interesting situations that result from its application.

First, at common law and under statute in Queensland and Tasmania, a husband and wife cannot be criminally responsible for a conspiracy between themselves alone.[16] This rule has been abolished in the Northern Territory and Western Australia. In Victoria, a husband and wife can now be convicted for conspiracy to commit murder or treason: *Criminal Code* (NT), s 291; *Criminal Code Amendment Act (No 2)* 1987 (WA), s 6; *Crimes Act* 1958 (Vic), s 339(1).

The rationale for this rule is that historically, a husband and wife have been viewed in law as forming one personality. This is of course highly questionable today and this remains an anomaly in those jurisdictions where the rule has not been abolished. A husband and wife can nevertheless be liable for a conspiracy involving other persons. There may also be liability where one spouse enters an agreement with the other knowing that he or she is conspiring with a third party: *R v Chrastny (No 1)* [1991] 1 WLR 1381.

Secondly, it has been held that a corporation cannot be liable for conspiracy with a person who is acting as its "directing mind and will": *R v McDonnell* [1966] 1 QB 233. This rule has been abolished at the federal level: *Crimes Act* 1914 (Cth), s 86(4)(b). If a company director conspires with other persons in the course of company business, then criminal liability will exist: *R v ICR Haulage Ltd* [1944] KB 551.

The notion that there must be two or more parties to a conspiracy also raises a number of questions:

▬ **What if one party is exempt from liability?**

▬ **What if the other(s) are acquitted?**

▬ **What if one party is an undercover agent?**

We will deal with these questions in turn.

An Exempt Party

The general rule is that one party may be liable for conspiracy where the other party is exempt from liability for the substantive offence. In *R v Duguid* (1906) 94 LT 887, the accused agreed with a child's mother, to take the child from the possession of her lawful guardian. The child's mother could not herself be convicted of child stealing as the *Offences Against the Person Act* 1861 (UK) exempted parents who took their own children. It was held that the mother's exemption from liability was no bar to the accused being convicted for conspiracy. This common law rule has been enacted in the Northern Territory for cases of conspiracy where the other person lacks the capacity to commit the substantive offence: *Criminal Code* (NT), s 292(e).

15　*Gerakiteys v The Queen* (1984) 153 CLR 317 at 334 per Deane J; *R v Alley; Ex parte Mundell* (1886) 12 VLR 13; *Phillips* (1987) 86 Cr App R 18.

16　*DPP v Blady* [1912] 2 KB 89; *R v McKechie* [1926] NZLR 1; *Kowbel v The Queen* [1954] 4 DLR 337; *Mawji v The Queen* [1957] AC 126; *Criminal Code* (Qld), s 33; *Criminal Code* (Tas), s 297(2).

This rule is analogous to the Australian law relating to the doctrine of acting in concert. In Chapter 8, we explored how a person who has assisted or encouraged a crime pursuant to a pre-conceived plan can still be held liable if the perpetrator is exempt from prosecution or where a defence is available to the perpetrator: see pp 404ff.

There is also authority for the proposition that a person who may personally be exempt from liability can nevertheless be guilty of a conspiracy. In *Burns* (1984) 79 Cr App R 173, a father agreed with others to steal his child from the mother. Again, the father was exempt from the substantive offence of child stealing. The father was convicted of conspiracy and this was upheld on appeal to the English Court of Appeal. Watkins J stated:

> We find [no authority] that leads us to say that it is in any way wrong or unjust for a person who is exempt, in the sense that [the father] was, from prosecution for the substantive offence to be proceeded against for the crime of conspiracy.
>
> The dangers of permitting a father of children to collect a posse of men and suddenly launch a siege of the home of his erstwhile wife, to break in and then snatch away sleeping children are surely evident. The criminal law does not in our view permit that sort of conduct. When a father who is exempt [from prosecution for the substantive offence of child stealing] behaves in that way, it is, in our judgment, not only lawful but right and just that the prosecution should be free to bring a charge of conspiracy against him.

Obviously policy reasons were persuasive in determining the Court of Appeal's decision in *Burns'* case. However, it does not deal with this question: if general principles operate to exempt certain people from liability, why should that legal incapacity be overridden solely in the case of conspiracy? For example, if a person has a serious mental illness such as schizophrenia, why should he or she be considered not criminally responsible for substantive offences and yet, following the *Burns* approach, liable for conspiracy? This decision is highly questionable if conspiracy is viewed as being premised on the need to prohibit agreements between two or more *responsible* persons to commit a crime.

Acquittals

In *Gerakiteys v The Queen* (1984) 153 CLR 317, Deane J stated at 334:

> [A]s a matter of common law principle, an accused may be convicted of conspiring "with a person or persons unknown" to commit an unlawful act.

In *R v Sayers* [1943] SASR 146 it was held that one person could be convicted of conspiracy even where the other person was within the jurisdiction and was not charged. This ruling also covers those situations where one party has been given immunity from prosecution in exchange for giving evidence against the other: see also *Criminal Code* (NT), s 292.

But what if the other person has in fact been acquitted of conspiracy? In England, a distinction was drawn at common law according to the number of persons involved in the alleged conspiracy. In *O'Brien* (1974) 59 Cr App R 222, the trial judge failed to direct the jury as to the effect of one party's acquittal upon the accused's liability for conspiracy *between themselves and persons unknown*. The English Court of Appeal held that the jury should have been directed that if it acquitted one party it had to consider whether there was sufficient evidence that the accused had conspired with persons unknown.

However, where two persons were presented for trial on a single count of conspiracy *between themselves and no other*, the Privy Council in *Dharmasena v The King* [1951] AC 1 held that the acquittal of one necessitates the acquittal of the other. The Privy Council held that where two accused were solely charged with conspiracy, the acquittal of one was inconsistent with sustaining the conviction of the other. Their Lordships stated (at 6):

> It is well-established law that if two persons are accused of conspiracy and one is acquitted the other must also escape condemnation. Two at least are required to commit the crime of conspiracy; one alone cannot do so.

The High Court in *R v Darby* (1982) 148 CLR 668 departed from the common law position set out in *Dharmasena's* case. In that case, the accused and Thomas were tried together on a charge of conspiring to rob. Both were found guilty, but Thomas successfully appealed to the Supreme Court of Victoria which quashed his conviction and ordered that a verdict and judgment of acquittal be entered. The accused (Darby) subsequently argued before the High Court for the continued existence of the rule in *Dharmasena*. This was based on the essence of conspiracy being an agreement of minds and therefore the effect of an acquittal of one party is to deny the very existence of the conspiracy itself.

This argument was rejected by a majority of the High Court. Gibbs CJ, Aickin, Wilson and Brennan JJ referred to Lord Salmon's observations in *DPP v Shannon* [1975] AC 717 at 772. They quoted Lord Salmon's statement (at 677):

> A verdict of not guilty may mean that the jury is certain that the accused is innocent, or it may mean that, although the evidence arouses considerable suspicion, it is insufficient to convince the jury of the accused's guilt beyond reasonable doubt ... The only effect of an acquittal, in law, is that the accused can never again be brought before a criminal court and tried for the same offence.

The majority of the High Court explained that the phenomenon of inconsistent verdicts in joint trials for conspiracy resulted from the jury's obligation to consider separately the guilt of the two accused on the basis of the evidence admissible against each. Gibbs CJ, Aickin, Wilson and Brennan JJ declared the common law of Australia as follows (at 678):

> [T]he conviction of a conspirator whether tried together with or separately from an alleged co-conspirator may stand notwithstanding that the latter is or may be acquitted unless in all circumstances of the case his [or her] conviction is inconsistent with acquittal of the other person. In our opinion such a determination will focus upon the justice of the case rather than upon the technical obscurities that now confound this subject.

This rule is now found in statutory form in s 86(5)(a) of the *Crimes Act* 1914 (Cth) and s 321B of the *Crimes Act* 1958 (Vic). Section 292(d) of the *Criminal Code* (NT) simply states that it is not a defence that the person with whom the accused is alleged to have conspired has been acquitted.

The majority of the High Court were influenced by s 5(8) of the *Criminal Law Act* 1977 (UK). This provides that the acquittal of all the other parties is not a ground for quashing the conviction of the person accused of conspiring with them "unless under all the circumstances of the case his conviction is inconsistent with the acquittal of the other person or persons". Gibbs CJ, Aickin, Wilson and Brennan JJ (at 678) encouraged the practice of separate trials where the evidence against one party was significantly different from the evidence against the other.

There was a very strong dissent from Murphy J, affirming the old law in *Dharmasena*, who argued (at 683) that the members of the majority were degrading the effect of an acquittal:

> In Australia there are no degrees of acquittal. As between the State and the accused, either every judgment of acquittal is conclusive of evidence or none is. The doctrine that acquittal does not mean innocence is unacceptable in a free society.
>
> It is irrelevant that persons may hold private reservations about the acquitted person's innocence. It is irrelevant that remedies may be available in tort or other branches of private law arising out of the conduct of the acquitted person. The relationship between the State and the accused is not to be assimilated to private law relations.

The High Court's ruling in *Darby's* case has been subsequently followed in *R v Brown* [1990] VR 820, *Catalano* (1992) 61 A Crim R 323 and *R v Rogerson* (1991-1992) 174 CLR 269. Nevertheless, Peter Sallmann and John Willis argue that the majority decision in *Darby's* case is "indubitably wrong": "Editorial: Criminal Conspiracy: Takes One to Tango?" (1982) 15 *Australia and New Zealand Journal of Criminology* 129 at 130. Like Murphy J, they emphasise that the essence of conspiracy is an agreement and that to try one accused for conspiracy when the other accused has been acquitted makes a mockery of the acquittal process.

For both exempt parties and acquittals, then, the courts seem prepared to deviate from the group-based rationale for conspiracy.

Undercover Agent

In *Yip Chiu-Cheung v The Queen* [1995] 1 AC 111, the Privy Council held that an accused may be convicted of conspiracy even where the other person was an undercover drug enforcement agent. In that case, the accused was convicted in Hong Kong of conspiracy to traffic in heroin. He had agreed with another man, Needham, to take five kilograms of heroin from Hong Kong to Australia. Needham was in fact an American undercover drug enforcement agent. The plan was that Needham would fly to Hong Kong, pick up the heroin and fly to Australia. Needham had kept the authorities in Hong Kong and Australia informed of the plans and they agreed that he would not be prevented from carrying the heroin to Australia with the aim of identifying both the suppliers and distributors of the drug. In fact, Needham's original flight to Hong Kong was delayed and he missed the rescheduled flight. The accused was arrested at Hong Kong airport and admitted that he was there to meet Needham.

The accused argued on appeal to the Privy Council that he should not have been convicted of conspiracy as Needham was not a co-conspirator because he lacked the fault element for the crime. Lord Griffiths in delivering the judgment of the court held that Needham had in fact the intention to commit the criminal offence of trafficking and therefore could be regarded as a co-conspirator. Lord Griffiths stated (at 118):

> Naturally, Needham never expected to be prosecuted if he carried out the plan as intended. But the fact that in such circumstances the authorities would not prosecute the undercover agent does not mean that he did not commit the crime albeit as part of a wider scheme to combat drug dealing.

Lord Griffiths distinguished (at 117-118) the facts from the situation where the undercover agent has no intention to commit the offence but pretends to join a conspiracy in order to gain information that would frustrate it: *R v Anderson* [1986] AC 27]. The law relating to entrapment and police illegality is discussed in Chapter 15: pp 870ff.

UNLAWFUL ACT

Historically at common law, the definition of an "unlawful act" has been broadly interpreted to include not only crimes,[17] but also agreements to defraud,[18] to commit a tort with intent to cause injury,[19] to corrupt public morals[20] to commit a public mischief[21] and pervert the course of justice.[22] In 1976, the Law Commission of England and Wales recommended that conspiracy be restricted to agreements to commit criminal offences: Law Commission, *Criminal Law: Report on Conspiracy and Criminal Law Reform*, Report No 76 (London: HMSO, 1976). As a consequence, the *Criminal Law Act 1977* (UK) was enacted. Part I of the Act created a statutory offence of conspiracy limited to committing one or more criminal offences. However, conspiracy to defraud and conspiracy to corrupt public morals remained offences at common law in England. The broadening of the scope of conspiracy that occurred in the 1960s and early 1970s was also judicially criticised as not being within the proper domain of the courts.[23]

As mentioned earlier, in practice, conspiracy to defraud, conspiracy to commit crimes and conspiracy to pervert the course of justice are the usual forms of conspiracy charged in Australia. Section 321(1) of the *Crimes Act* 1958 (Vic) confirms this limitation. While most of the legislative provisions set out in Table 2 deal with conspiracies to commit offences in general, specific statutory crimes such as conspiracy to commit murder also exist.[24] The law relating to conspiracy to defraud and conspiracy to pervert the course of justice is often seen as differing from the general law relating to conspiracy and these will be dealt with in the following sections. First, however, it is interesting to take a look at the controversy in England surrounding the development of conspiracy to corrupt public morals.

---

17 *R v Jones* (1832) 4 B & As 345; *Mulcahy v The Queen* (1868) LR 3 HL 306; *R v Kempley* (1944) 44 SR (NSW) 416; *R v Orton* [1922] VLR 469.

18 *Scott v Metropolitan Police Commissioner* [1975] AC 819; *Wai Tsu-tsang v The Queen* [1992] 1 AC 269; *R v Horsington* [1983] 2 NSWLR 72; *R v Walsh* [1984] VR 474.

19 *Kamara v DPP* [1974] AC 104.

20 *Shaw v DPP* [1962] AC 220; *Knuller (Publishing, Printing & Promotions) Ltd v DPP* [1973] AC 435. These cases have not been followed in Australia: *R v Cahill* [1978] 2 NSWLR 453.

21 *R v Boston* (1923) 33 CLR 386; *R v Howes* (1971) 2 SASR 293. In *DPP v Withers* [1975] AC 842, the House of Lords held that there was not a separate and distinct class of conspiracy called conspiracy to effect a public mischief.

22 *R v Grimes* [1968] 3 All ER 179; *R v Baba* [1977] 2 NSWLR 502; *R v Murphy* (1985) 158 CLR 596; *R v Rogerson* (1992) 174 CLR 268.

23 *DPP v Withers* [1975] AC 842; *R v Cahill* [1978] 2 NSWLR 453.

24 *Criminal Code* (NT), s 287; *Criminal Code* (Qld), s 309.

Judicial Law Making: Conspiracy to Corrupt Public Morals

The case of *Shaw v DPP* [1962] AC 220 caused much debate in England concerning the breadth of conspiracy and the power of the courts to create new criminal laws. In that case, the accused published "The Ladies' Directory" which advertised the names and addresses of prostitutes and the sexual acts they were willing to practise. He was convicted of conspiracy to corrupt public morals.

On appeal to the House of Lords, the accused argued that he should only be convicted of conspiracy to commit a crime, and that corrupting public morals was not an established crime. The House of Lords upheld the accused's conviction on the basis that conspiracy to corrupt public morals was an independent offence in itself. The court did not decide as to whether there was a substantive offence of corrupting public morals.

Viscount Simonds, one of the majority judges, relied (at 267) on a residual power in the courts to conserve the "moral welfare of the State" in holding that there was an offence of conspiracy to corrupt public morals. Lord Tucker relied on several decisions that he viewed as implying an offence of conspiracy to corrupt pubic morals.

Lord Reid in dissent saw the majority as inventing an offence. He stated (at 275):

> [T]here are wide differences of opinion today as to how far the law ought to punish immoral acts which are not done in the face of the public. Some think that the law already goes too far, some that it does not go far enough. Parliament is the proper place ... to settle that. When there is sufficient support from public opinion, Parliament does not hesitate to intervene. Where Parliament fears to tread it is not for the courts to rush in.

The decision in *Shaw's* case was affirmed by majority in the House of Lords case *Knuller (Publishing & Printing Promotions) Ltd v DPP* [1973] AC 435. In that case, the accused had agreed to publish advertisements to facilitate homosexual acts. At the time, homosexual acts conducted in private between adult men were no longer considered criminal. Nevertheless, the House of Lords upheld the accused's conviction for conspiracy to "outrage public decency".

The decision in *Shaw's* case was widely criticised on a number of grounds. First, it was argued that if courts could declare new crimes without prior warning, how could individuals avoid being punished for such crimes? Lord Reid in his dissenting judgment stated (at 281) that the criminal law "should be certain: that a [person] should be able to know what conduct is and what is not criminal, particularly when heavy penalties are involved". Similarly HLA Hart in *Law, Liberty and Morality* (Oxford: Oxford University Press, 1963), argued (p 12):

> The particular value which [their Lordships] sacrificed is the principle of legality which requires criminal offences to be as precisely defined as possible, so that it can be known with reasonable certainty beforehand what acts are criminal and what are not. As a result of *Shaw's* case, virtually any cooperative conduct is criminal if a jury consider it *ex post facto* to have been immoral.

Secondly, the court was criticised for usurping the role of the legislature: ATH Smith, "Judicial Lawmaking in the Criminal Law" (1984) 100 LQR 46. This was particularly salient since Parliament had introduced the *Street Offences Act* 1959 a few years prior to the case being heard. This Act had made some limited reforms in the area of prostitution but had not criminalised the corruption of public morals. The importance of the principle of legality is discussed further in Chapter 1 (pp 7ff), and the controversy concerning whether or not the criminal law should be used to enforce moral or community standards is discussed in Chapter 1: pp 51ff.

Any further extension of conspiracy into the realms of immoral or antisocial behaviour was put an end to by the House of Lords in *DPP v Withers* [1975] AC 842. In that case, the court quashed convictions of conspiracy "to effect a public mischief" on the basis that no such general offence was known at law. The House of Lords was of the view that criminal conspiracy should not be extended any further than what was already established. This decision foreshadowed the recommendations of the Law Commission's Report No 76 on *Conspiracy and Criminal Law Reform*: see above, p 458. The subsequent *Criminal Law Act* 1977 (UK) created a statutory offence of conspiracy, but did not completely abolish the existing common law heads. Thus *Shaw's* case and *Knuller's* case still remain authorities in England for conspiracy to corrupt public morals and outrage public decency.

Interestingly, these two cases have never been followed in Australia. In *R v Cahill* [1978] 2 NSWLR 453, an argument was run that the agreements of three Chinese men and three Australian women to marry in order to increase the chances of permanent residency for the men were offensive to public morality. Street CJ made in clear that only Parliament should create new offences involving matters of public morality. He stated (at 455):

> [R]eligious precepts do not in this country affect the application of the ordinary criminal law unless and until such precepts find expression through a validly made law of the Commonwealth or State.

Section 321F(1) of the *Crimes Act* 1958 (Vic) also makes it clear that conspiracy to corrupt public morals or to outrage public decency are not offences in that state. In relation to the ability of the courts to make new offences, McHugh J stated categorically in *R v Rogerson* (1992) 174 CLR 268 at 305 that they "are no longer able to create criminal offences".

Conspiracy to Defraud

The common law offence of conspiracy to defraud is well established.[25] Section 321F(2) of the *Crimes Act* 1958 (Vic) retains this head of the common law and there are statutory provisions in the Northern Territory, Queensland and Tasmania setting out this offence: *Criminal Code* (NT), s 284; *Criminal Code* (Qld), s 430; *Criminal Code* (Tas), s 297(1)(d). The common feature of these provisions and the offence at common law is that liability is extended to fraudulent acts that do not involve theft or any other crime.

In comparison, the Commonwealth and Western Australian provisions deal with conspiracy to defraud in relation to existing statutory crimes.

---

25 *Scott v Metropolitan Police Commissioner* [1975] AC 819; *R v Hersington* [1983] 2 NSWLR 72; *R v Walsh and Harney* [1984] VR 474; *Wai Yu-tsang v The Queen* [1992] 1 AC 269; *Peters v The Queen* (1998) 192 CLR 493.

Section 29D of the *Crimes Act* 1914 (Cth) provides:

A person who defrauds the Commonwealth or a public authority under the Commonwealth
is guilty of an indictable offence.

Penalty: 1000 penalty units or imprisonment for 10 years, or both.

This has been rejected to by the Model Criminal Code Officers Committee (MCCOC) which referred to it
as "conspiracy to defraud without the need for conspiracy": *Theft, Fraud, Bribery and Related
Offences,* Final Report (1995), pp 155-157. It is further explored in Ch 13, p 732. There is also no need
for an agreement as it punishes "a person" rather than two or more. Section 86(2) of the *Crimes Act*
1914 (Cth) retains the conspiracy element as an aggravating factor by setting out that "if a person
conspires with another person to commit an offence against s 29D ... the conspiracy is punishable by a
fine not exceeding 2,000 penalty units, or imprisonment for a period not exceeding 20 years, or both".

Section 409 of the *Criminal Code* (WA) makes it an offence for a person with intent to defraud,
by deceit or any fraudulent means to gain property or any benefit pecuniary or otherwise. Again,
there need be no agreement as one person may be punished under this provision. Section 558 then
presumably applies to a conspiracy to commit the offence under s 409.

The word "defraud" raises the question as to whether or not the prosecution has to prove a
deception. In *Scott v Metropolitan Commissioner of Police* [1975] AC 819, the accused paid
employees of a cinema to lend him films without the knowledge of the cinema owners. He made
copies and then distributed them commercially. He was convicted of conspiracy to defraud the
owners of the copyright in the films. He argued on appeal that there could be no conspiracy to
defraud without deception. This argument was rejected by the House of Lords. It held that "defraud"
was equivalent to "dishonest" and stated (at 839 per Viscount Dilhorne):

[I]t is clearly the law that an agreement by two or more by dishonesty to deprive a person
of something which is his [or hers] or to which he [or she] is or would or might be entitled
and an agreement by two or more to injure some proprietary right of his [or hers], suffices
to constitute the offence of conspiracy to defraud.

The majority of members of the High Court in *Peters v The Queen* (1998) 192 CLR 493 have held that
dishonesty is not a separate element of conspiracy to defraud, but is descriptive of the means used
in order to achieve the design of the conspiracy. This is explored further in the following section on
the fault element for conspiracy to defraud, p 465.

Conspiracy to defraud is not confined to causing economic loss. In *Allsop* (1976) 64 Cr App R
29, the accused was a sub-broker for the victim, a hire-purchase finance company. The accused
agreed with others to enter false particulars on the hire-purchase application forms so that the
company would enter agreements with purchasers whom they would otherwise have rejected. The
accused expected that the company would suffer no economic loss because the creditors would
maintain payments. The Court of Appeal upheld the accused's conviction for conspiracy to defraud on
the basis that the hire-purchase company was being induced into taking a financial or economic risk
that it would not have taken but for the false particulars. It was no excuse that the accused believed
the company would suffer no loss.[26] This may be compared to the position in relation to dishonesty
for theft which is discussed in Chapter 13, pp 675ff.

---

26 See also *R v McGrath and Simonidis* [1983] 2 Qd R 54; (1983) 8 A Crim R 316; *Wau Yu-tsang v The Queen* [1992] 1 AC 269.

The MCCOC considered whether conspiracy to defraud should form part of the *Model Criminal Code: Chapter 3: Conspiracy to Defraud,* Report, May (Canberra: AGPS, 1997). The arguments in favour of its abolition concerned the breadth of the law allowing conduct to be rendered criminal after the event and the fact that the uncertainty surrounding the issue of dishonesty rendered "the criminal law applicable to a number of relationships previously thought to be in the realm of civil remedies": p 25. All the submissions received by the MCCOC, however, were in favour of retaining the offence. The MCCOC stated (at 27):

> [I]t may not be that conspiracy to defraud is justified on the basis of gaps in the existing law (all of which could be addressed through specific legislation) but on the basis that human ingenuity is such that there is a need to have an offence which can be used in relation to newly-devised gaps. Addressing them with specific legislation after the event may be too late.

Conspiracy to Pervert the Course of Justice

Conspiracy to pervert the course of justice is an offence at common law[27] and it also exists in statutory form at the federal level (*Crimes Act* 1914 (Cth), s 42) and in the Code jurisdictions.[28] Interestingly, s 321F(1) of the *Crimes Act* 1958 (Vic) appears to abolish this head of conspiracy. In New South Wales the common law offence has been abolished.[29] In its place, s 319 creates an offence of doing an act with the intention of perverting the course of justice and s 342 confirms that a person may be charged with conspiracy to commit this offence. The MCCOC has noted that there is also a substantive offence of perverting the course of justice independent of conspiracy and has recommended that this be codified: MCCOC, *Chapter 7: Administration of Justice Offences,* Report, July (Canberra: AGPS, 1998), pp 111-119.

The rationale for retaining conspiracy to pervert the course of justice lies in the policy that "the purity and integrity of the course of justice" needs to be maintained: *R v Baba* [1977] 2 NSWLR 502 at 504 per Street J. Accordingly, the courts have taken a broad approach to applying this head of conspiracy. It has been held to cover:

- interference with witnesses;[30]
- fabricating evidence;[31]
- bribing the police to hinder the prosecution;[32] and
- making false statements to the police.[33]

---

27 *R v Grimes* [1968] 3 All ER 179n; *R v Baba* [1977] 2 NSWLR 502; *R v Murphy* (1985) 158 CLR 596; *R v Rogerson* (1992) 174 CLR 268. See also Model Criminal Code Officers Committee, *Chapter 7: Administration of Justice Offences,* Discussion Paper (1997), p 89 and Model Criminal Code Officers Committee, *Chapter 7: Administration of Justice Offences,* Report (1998), p 111.

28 *Criminal Code* (NT), s 286; *Criminal Code* (Qld), s 132; *Criminal Code* (Tas), s 297(1)(2); *Criminal Code* (WA), s 135.

29 *Crimes Act* 1900 (NSW), s 341 as amended by the *Crimes (Public Justice) Amendment Act* 1990.

30 *R v Panayiotou* [1973] 2 All ER 112; *R v Kellett* [1976] QB 372.

31 *R v Vreones* [1891] 1 QB 360.

32 *R v Matthews* [1972] VR 3.

33 *R v Andrew* [1973] 1 QB 422; *Field* (1964) 48 Cr App R 335.

There may also be liability for a conspiracy to pervert the course of justice in relation to the conduct of committal proceedings.[34] In *R v Rogerson* (1992) 174 CLR 268, Mason CJ stated at 278:

> I agree with Brennan and Toohey JJ that an act which has a tendency to deflect the police from prosecuting a criminal offence or instituting disciplinary proceedings before a judicial tribunal, or from adducing evidence of the true facts, is an act which tends to pervert the course of justice

In *R v Rogerson* (1992) 174 CLR 268, the High Court held that there could even be a conspiracy to pervert the course of justice where no relevant police investigation had commenced or judicial proceedings contemplated. There is also some authority that conspiracy to pervert the course of justice may apply to decisions after a sentence has been passed. In *R v Machirus* [1996] 6 NZLR 404, the New Zealand Court of Appeal held that conspiracy to pervert the course of justice encompassed an agreement to try to affect by deceit the decision of the Parole Board. Jeremy Finn writes that this case significantly extends the scope of the offence in New Zealand, "not merely by extending the 'course of justice' to include events occurring after sentence has been imposed, but in determining that the offending conduct need not be concerned with proceedings that are judicial in character": "Case and Comment: *Machirus*" [1997] 21 Crim LJ 51 at 52.

3.2 FAULT ELEMENT

In *Churchill v Walton* [1967] 2 AC 224, the House of Lords held that for conspiracy to be made out, there must be an *intention* to be a party to an agreement to do an unlawful act. This raises the question as to whether there simply has to be an intention to be a party to the agreement (intentional participation in the conspiracy) or must there also be an intention to bring about the unlawful object. Many of the earlier decisions were not explicit as to whether an intention to achieve the unlawful object was required. It now appears clear that an intention to achieve the unlawful object must also be proved. Fisse in *Howard's Criminal Law* (5th ed, Sydney: Law Book Company Ltd, 1990), p 369 writes:

> [I]f the orthodox meaning of the term agreement is accepted, there can be no conspiratorial agreement to commit an unlawful object unless there is a common intention or purpose to achieve that object.

The High Court in *Gerakiteys v The Queen* (1984) 153 CLR 317 insisted upon proof of an intention, shared by all the parties, to commit the unlawful object alleged. As outlined above, in this case, the first accused, a doctor, was charged with conspiring with the second accused, an insurance agent and nine others (the claimants) to defraud a number of insurance companies. Gibbs CJ (at 320), Wilson J (at 323) and Brennan J (at 330) referred to there being a "common purpose" to commit the offence occurring by implication where two or more persons have agreed to commit an offence.

---

34 *R v Murphy* (1985) 158 CLR 596. This case concerned primarily matters of law arising out of the conviction of the High Court justice, the Honourable Lionel Keith Murphy for attempting to pervert the course of justice. For background to this case, see AR Blackshield, "The Murphy Affair" in JA Scutt (ed), *Lionel Murphy: A Radical Judge* (Carlton: McCulloch Publishing, 1987), pp 231-257.

On the facts, the accused's conviction was quashed as the evidence failed to disclose that there was a common purpose to defraud because the claimants had only the purpose of defrauding their own insurance company.

In *Giorgianni v The Queen* (1985) 156 CLR 473, Wilson, Deane and Dawson JJ similarly stated (at 473):

> There are ... offences in which it is not possible to speak of recklessness as constituting a sufficient intent. Attempt is one and conspiracy is another.

Thus, conspiracy will not be made out where an objective is seen as a probable or possible outcome of carrying out an agreement to achieve some other objective. This contrasts with the position in England. The House of Lords in *R v Anderson* [1986] AC 27 held that a person is guilty of conspiracy under s 1 of the *Criminal Law Act* 1977 (UK) irrespective of whether he or she intended that the offence (the subject of the agreement) will be committed. It is sufficient that the parties agree to embark on a course of conduct, being reckless as to whether or not the offence may occur.

The Criminal Law Officers Committee (CLOC) recommended that intention must be established and recklessness should not suffice for the offence of conspiracy: *Chapter 2: General Principles of Criminal Responsibility*, Final Report (December 1992) (Canberra: AGPS, 1993), p 99. At present, s 86(3)(b) of the *Crimes Act* 1914 (Cth) requires that the accused and at least one other party to the agreement must have intended that an offence would be committed pursuant to the agreement. Similarly, s 321(2) of the *Crimes Act* 1958 (Vic) requires that there is an intention that the offence be committed and an intention or belief that any fact or circumstance the existence of which is an element of the offence will exist. Section 11.5(2)(b) of the *Criminal Code Act* 1995 (Cth) also requires an intention that an offence would be committed pursuant to the agreement. The CLOC stated (at 99) that the "concept of recklessness is foreign to an offence based wholly on agreement".

As mentioned above, the fault element in conspiracy overlaps with the physical element of an agreement. Viscount Dilhorne remarked in *Churchill v Walton* [1967] 2 AC 224 at 237:

> In cases of this kind, it is desirable to avoid the use of the phrase *"mens rea"*, which is capable of different meanings, and to concentrate on the terms or effect of the agreement made by the alleged conspirators. The question is, "What did they agree to do?"

In addition, the fault element does not sit easily with subjective notions of intention because liability does not depend solely on the accused's state of mind, but also on that of the other parties to the conspiracy.

As with attempts, the stringent fault standard for conspiracy means that an accused must act with an intention to commit the offence even where it is one of strict liability, negligence or recklessness.[35]

---

35 *Giorgianni v The Queen* (1985) 156 CLR 473; *Kamara v DPP* [1974] AC 104.

THE FAULT ELEMENT IN CONSPIRACY TO PERVERT THE COURSE OF JUSTICE

As with conspiracy in general, the fault element for conspiracy to pervert the course of justice requires an intention to achieve the unlawful object. The leading High Court decision dealing with the fault element in conspiracy to pervert the course of justice is that of *R v Rogerson* (1992) 174 CLR 269. Roger Rogerson, a police officer, Morris Nowytarger and Nicholas Paltros had been convicted of conspiracy to pervert the course of justice. The charge arose out of an alleged agreement to fabricate evidence in order to hinder a police investigation into the possible commission of a crime. The New South Wales Court of Criminal Appeal set aside the convictions: *Rogerson* (1990) 51 A Crim R 359. The prosecution then applied to the High Court for special leave to appeal. Special leave to appeal was granted. The appeal was dismissed in relation to Nowytarger, but allowed for Rogerson and Paltros with orders that the matter be remitted to the Court of Criminal Appeal.

Brennan and Toohey JJ stated (at 281):

> The prosecution [has] to prove that the conspirators intended that, if the relevant act was done pursuant to the conspiracy and in the circumstances contemplated by the conspirators, it would have the effect of perverting the course of justice.

Mason CJ agreed (at 278) that an intention to achieve the result of perverting the course of justice was necessary. McHugh J went somewhat further (at 311) in stating that the offence requires "not merely an intention to pervert the course of justice but an agreement to do something which has the tendency to pervert it". These judgments imply that recklessness will not be sufficient as a fault element.

In the subsequent High Court decision of *Meissner v The Queen* (1995) 184 CLR 132, Brennan and Toohey JJ (at 144) pointed out that an intention to do acts that have the effect of perverting the course of justice may be established even if the conspirator has never heard the expression "perverting the course of justice".

THE FAULT ELEMENT IN CONSPIRACY TO DEFRAUD

The Model Criminal Code Officers Committee (MCCOC) stated in its *Chapter 3: Conspiracy to Defraud* Report (1997) (at 33):

> The fault element of common law conspiracy to defraud is an intent to defraud. As has been seen, this phrase has been interpreted to include within it the concept of dishonesty and an intent to cause a loss, imperil a person's economic interests, or to influence the exercise of a public duty.

Accordingly, the MCCOC recommended that the *Model Criminal Code* provision should include a fault element of dishonesty based on the test set out in *R v Feely* [1973] QB 530 at 537-538 per Lawton LJ and by Lord Lane CJ in *R v Ghosh* [1982] QB 1053 at 1064.

In *Peters v The Queen* (1998) 192 CLR 493, Toohey and Gaudron JJ were highly critical of this approach to the fault element for conspiracy to defraud. In that case, the accused was a solicitor who has been retained by his client, a drug trafficker, to launder money through a series of sham mortgage transactions. He was convicted of conspiracy to defraud the Commonwealth Commissioner of Taxation, but was acquitted of a charge of conspiracy to pervert the course of justice on the basis that he did not know his client's source of income and was simply acting as his solicitor.

All the members of the High Court dismissed the accused's appeal against conviction, but on different grounds. Toohey and Gaudron JJ (at 506-507) criticised the MCCOC's approach and instead took the view that it was superfluous to have a separate direction to the jury as to the meaning of dishonesty. Toohey and Gaudron JJ stated (at 509):

> [T]he offence of conspiracy to defraud involves dishonesty at two levels. First, it involves an agreement to use dishonest means ... And quite apart from the use of dishonest means, the offence involves an agreement to bring about a situation prejudicing or imperilling existing legal rights or interests of others. That too, is dishonest by ordinary standards.

They went on to state (at 510):

> [I]t will ordinarily be sufficient to instruct the jury as to the facts they must find if the agreed means are to be characterised as dishonest. Alternatively, it will be sufficient to instruct them that, if satisfied as to those facts, they will be satisfied that the agreed means were dishonest. Only in the borderline case will it be necessary for the question whether the means are to be so characterised to be left to the jury.

In those borderline cases, Toohey and Gaudron JJ were of the view that "dishonesty" is a question of fact to be determined by the jury, applying the current standards of ordinary decent people. This was the test set out in *R v Feely* [1973] QB 530 at 537-538 per Lawton LJ and by Lord Lane CJ in *R v Ghosh* [1982] QB 1053 at 1064.

McHugh and Gummow JJ went further in holding that dishonesty was not a separate element of conspiracy to defraud and no direction as to dishonesty need be given even in borderline cases. McHugh J, with whom Gummow J agreed, held that dishonesty does not constitute a distinct or separate element of the offence but is simply descriptive of the means used to accomplish the fraud. The term "dishonesty" characterises the conduct and would be evidenced by an intention to prejudice another person's right or interest or performance of public duty by (a) making or taking advantage of representations or promises which they knew were false or would not be carried out; (b) concealing facts which they had a duty to disclose; or (c) engaging in conduct in which they had no right to engage. Dishonesty could be inferred from an intention to engage in any of these forms of wrongful conduct. McHugh J stated (at 527):

> The authors of *Archbold* [*Criminal Pleading, Evidence and Practice*, (1996), Vol 2, para 17-102] seem to have been voices in the wilderness in robustly maintaining the view that it is "superfluous" to direct a jury as to dishonesty. In my opinion, however, the authors of *Archbold* are right. A successful prosecution for conspiracy to defraud does not require proof that the accused knew that he or she was acting dishonestly either in a *Ghosh* sense or a wholly subjective sense.

Kirby J regarded dishonesty as a separate fault element, but in order to provide "clear instruction to those who have responsibility for conducting criminal trials" (at 556) he withdrew his own opinion and concurred with the views expressed by Toohey and Gaudron JJ that conspiracy involves dishonesty at two levels. In Kirby J's opinion (at 555):

Dishonesty of its essential nature connotes conscious wrongdoing. It is not dishonesty by the standards of other persons but by the appreciation and understanding of the accused personally.

It would seem then as a result of *Peters'* case there must be an intention to use dishonest means to prejudice another person's right, interest or performance of public duty. There is no requirement for dishonesty to be a separate element above and beyond these concepts. See also R Evans, *"Peters"* (1998) 22 Crim LJ 230 and Chapter 13 on the meaning of dishonesty: pp 675ff.

The intention to prejudice another person's right or interest was interpreted in *Scott v Metropolitan Commissioner of Police* [1975] AC 819 by Lord Diplock as meaning an intention to cause *economic loss* by depriving the other person of some property or right to which he or she was or might be entitled. This interpretation limits the fault element quite substantially as often those involved in fraud want to make a profit for themselves rather than cause an economic loss to others. Toohey and Gaudron JJ pointed out in *Peters* case (at 506-507) that there are difficulties associated with Lord Diplock's approach and stated that the offence of conspiracy to defraud is not limited to an agreement involving an intention to cause economic loss. It is therefore doubtful that Lord Diplock's approach holds sway in Australia.

The fault element for conspiracy to defraud also extends to an intention to prejudice another person's performance of public duty. This is broader than an intention to prejudice another person's right or interest in that no economic loss need be intended.[36]

4. INCITEMENT

Except in the Northern Territory and Queensland, it is an offence to incite another person to commit an offence, even if that offence is not carried out and even if the incitement has no effect on the other person.[37] The existence of the offence can be dated back to the case of *R v Higgins* (1801) 2 East 5, where a conviction for inciting a person to steal another person's property was upheld. At common law, incitement to commit any offence is a misdemeanour and this has been retained in New South Wales and South Australia. Statutory provisions now exist in the Australian Capital Territory, Tasmania, Victoria, Western Australia and at the Commonwealth level. An overview of these provisions is set out in the following Table.

While incitement is not an offence in the Northern Territory and Queensland, those jurisdictions in addition to Western Australia, have the analogous offence of attempting to procure the commission of an offence.[38]

---

36 *Welham v DPP* [1961] AC 103; *R v Howes* (1971) 2 SASR 293; *Scott v Metropolitan Police Commissioner* [1975] AC 819; *R v Horsington* [1983] 2 NSWLR 72; *R v Simonidis* [1983] 2 Qd R 54.

37 *R v Higgins* (1801) 2 East 5; *Crimes Act* 1914 (Cth), s 7A(a); *Crimes Act* 1900 (ACT), s 348; *Criminal Code* (Tas), s 298; *Crimes Act* 1958 (Vic), ss 321G-321I; *Criminal Code* (WA), ss 553, 555A. In this case New South Wales and South Australia are both governed by the common law.

38 *Criminal Code* (NT), s 280; *Criminal Code* (Qld), s 539; *Criminal Code* (WA), s 556.

TABLE 3:

Incitement across Jurisdictions

JURISDICTION AND RELEVANT LAW	DEFINITION OF INCITEMENT	APPLICATION TO OFFENCES	PENALTY
CTH *Crimes Act* 1914	**Statutory definition:** s 7A(a)	offences against any law of the Commonwealth	imprisonment for 12 months s 7A
ACT *Crimes Act* 1900 **Scope**: common law	**Offence:** s 348	offences under a law of the Territory	incitement to commit murder: punishment for life incitement for any other offence: 12 months imprisonment/$2000 fine or both s 348
NSW **Scope**: common law	**Offence:** common law	any offence	misdemeanour: discretionary penalty
SA **Scope**: common law	**Offence:** common law	any offence	misdemeanour: discretionary penalty
TAS *Criminal Code*	**Statutory definition:** ss 2, 298	any offence	discretionary penalty
VIC *Crimes Act* 1958	**Statutory definition:** ss 321G-321I	any offence including those outside Victoria where the inciter is in Victoria s 321H	incitement is in itself an indictable offence: penalty is generally the same as for substantive offence s 321I
WA *Criminal Code*	**Statutory definition:** ss 1, 553, 555A	incitement of indictable offence (s 553) incitement of simple offence (s 555A)	incitement to commit an indictable offence where punishable for imprisonment for life: imprisonment for 14 years in any other case: punishment equal to one half the greatest punishment for the indictable offence (s 554) punishment for simple offence: punishment as for substantive offence (s 555A)

The above Table shows that liability for incitement exists in relation to all offences, whether indictable or summary. Section 321G(1) of the *Crimes Act* 1958 (Vic) states that the offence is an indictable one, and this remains the case even where the offence intended is only a summary one. It seems anomalous that an incitement should be treated more seriously than the offence intended and the Western Australian approach of having different penalties for incitement to commit indictable as opposed to simple offences seems preferable.

Incitement can be seen as analogous to aiding and abetting in complicity in the sense that both forms of liability depend upon the doing of an act in furtherance of a crime. However, incitement is viewed as a form of primary liability since the accused will be held liable for what he or she does, whereas aiding and abetting is a form of derivative liability because it depends partly on what another person has done. This leads to the peculiar situation that a person will be criminally responsible if he or she *incites* another who fails to commit the crime, but will not be criminally responsible for *aiding* another who fails to commit the crime. This asymmetry in the law is conceptually indefensible: see further Ch 8, pp 404ff.

It is unclear whether a person can be held responsible for inciting another inchoate offence. JC Smith and Brian Hogan point out that it may be technically possible to incite an attempt to commit an offence: *Criminal Law* (7th ed, London: Butt, 1992), p 267. They refer to the example of an accused giving another person a substance that the accused knows to be harmless. The accused says that it is poison and urges the other person to give it to the "victim". Smith and Hogan state that the accused cannot be convicted of attempted murder, but may be guilty of inciting an attempt to murder. The complete dearth of case law on this point implies that there is a consensus that there is no such offence as inciting an attempt and belief that "double inchoate" offences extend the boundaries of the criminal law too far.

Inciting a conspiracy, on the other hand, is perhaps more readily understandable. Section 321F(3) of the *Crimes Act* 1958 (Vic) specifically abolishes this offence, but it may remain an offence at common law. The Criminal Law Officers Committee has recommended that it should not be possible to incite a conspiracy or an attempt because "[t]here has to be some limit on preliminary offences".[39]

For incitement to be made out, there must be conduct amounting to incitement and an intention that the offence be committed. We will examine these elements in turn.

4.1 PHYSICAL ELEMENT

Incitement involves seeking to encourage or persuade another person to commit an offence: *Invicta Plastics v Clare* [1976] Crim LR 131. Section 1 of the *Criminal Code* (WA) refers to the word "incite" as encompassing "solicits and endeavours to persuade" and s 2A(1) of the *Crimes Act* 1958 (Vic) refers to "incite" as including "command, request, propose, advise, encourage or authorize". The Commonwealth and Australian Capital Territory provisions also refer to a person who "prints or

---

39 Criminal Law Officers Committee of the Standing Committee of Attorneys-General, *Chapter 2: General Principles of Criminal Responsibility*, Final Report (December 1992) (Canberra: AGPS, 1993), p 95; see further IP Robbins, "Double Inchoate Crimes" (1989) 26(1) *Harvard Journal on Legislation* 1.

publishes any writing which incites to, urges, aids or encourages" the commission of an offence as an offence: *Crimes Act* 1914 (Cth), s 7A(b); *Crimes Act* 1900 (ACT), s 348(b). The Criminal Law Officers Committee (CLOC) has suggested that the word "urges" should be used in preference to "incites": *Chapter 2: General Principles of Criminal Responsibility*, Final Report (December 1992) (Canberra: AGPS, 1993), p 93. In CLOC's opinion, the word "incites" could be interpreted as only requiring the accused to have *caused* rather than *advocating* the offence.

Whatever word is used, it is clear that there must be proof of persuasion or encouragement; a mere intent to commit an offence is insufficient.[40] As well as positive encouragement, incitement encompasses negative threats or pressure: *Race Relations Board v Applin* [1973] QB 815. The encouragement or persuasion must be communicated to the other person: *R v Krause* (1902) 66 JP 1902. If it fails to be communicated, there may still be liability for attempted incitement: *R v Ransford* (1874) 13 Cox CC 9. The encouragement may be directed towards the world at large rather than a specified person. For example, in *R v Most* (1881) 7 QBD 244, the accused published an article in a London newspaper encouraging readers to kill their Heads of State. The accused was convicted of incitement to murder and this was upheld by the Court for Crown Cases Reserved.

Except in Victoria, the person incited need not act on the incitement for the physical element to be made out: *Dimozantos* (1991) 56 A Crim R 345. Providing the accused incited the other person it is irrelevant that the latter is not influenced or unwilling to commit the offence: *R v Higgins* (1801) 2 East 5; *R v Krause* (1902) 66 JP 1902. However, s 321G(1) of the *Crimes Act* 1958 (Vic) makes it clear that an element of the offence is that "the inciting is acted on in accordance with the inciter's intention". This substantially narrows the scope of the offence. CLOC pointed out that while incitement is rarely charged, "circumstances may arise that are so serious that an appropriate offence is required": *Chapter 2: General Principles of Criminal Responsibility*, Final Report (December 1992) (1993), p 93. The Committee therefore rejected the Victorian approach.

There is some lack of clarity as to the law concerning inciting a person, such as a child, who is exempt from criminal responsibility for the substantive offence. Section 321G(1) of the *Crimes Act* 1958 (Vic) states that incitement in these circumstances will still attract criminal responsibility. However, at common law, there is some suggestion that the accused will not be criminally responsible in such circumstances.

For example, in *R v Whitehouse* [1977] QB 868, the accused incited his 15-year-old daughter to commit incest with him. Under s 1(1) of the *Sexual Offences Act* 1956, a girl under the age of 16 could not be convicted of an offence by permitting a man to commit incest with her. This decision contrasts with the position taken in the law relating to conspiracy. In *Burns* (1984) 79 Cr App R 173, it was held that there can be liability for conspiracy with a party excused from criminal responsibility. In addition, we explored in Chapter 8 at pp 404ff how a person who has assisted or encouraged a crime pursuant to a pre-conceived plan may be convicted even where the perpetrator has died, is unknown, has not been arrested or has been acquitted. A person acting in concert can still be held liable if the perpetrator is exempt from prosecution or where a defence is available to the perpetrator.

It therefore seems that the Victorian approach reflects that taken in the law relating to conspiracy and acting in concert. The decision in *Whitehouse's* case may not therefore be good law in Australia.

---

40   *R v Chrichton* [1915] SALR 1; *Invicta Plastics Ltd v Clare* [1976] Crim LR 131.

4.2 FAULT ELEMENT

The case law is silent as to the fault element for incitement. In *Giorgianni v The Queen* (1985) 156 CLR 473, Wilson, Deane and Dawson JJ (at 506) rejected recklessness in relation to complicity and the inchoate offences of attempt and conspiracy on the ground that:

> [t]hose offences require intentional participation in a crime by lending assistance or encouragement.

While strictly obiter, it may be inferred that the fault element for incitement will also be an intention to commit the substantive offence. Section 321G(2) of the *Crimes Act* 1958 (Vic) clearly sets out a strict fault element for incitement that is in line with the fault element for attempts:

> For a person to be guilty ... of incitement the person
>
> **(a)** must intend that the offence the subject of the incitement be committed; and
>
> **(b)** must intend or believe that any fact or circumstance the existence of which is an element of the offence in question will exist at the time when the conduct constituting the offence is to take place.

CLOC has pointed out that having a lesser fault element of recklessness would mean too great a threat to free speech: *Chapter 2: General Principles of Criminal Responsibility*, Final Report (December 1992) (Canberra: AGPS, 1993), p 95. Accordingly, s 11.5(2) of the *Criminal Code Act* 1995 (Cth) requires an intention that the offence incited be committed.

PROCEDURAL PERSPECTIVES

The Link Between Inchoate and Substantive Offences

A conviction for an attempt as well as for the substantive offence is procedurally impermissible: *Wesley-Smith v Balzary* (1977) 14 ALR 681 (SC NT) at 685 per Forster J; *R v Lee* (1990) 1 WAR 411 at 426 per Malcolm J, at 434 per Kennedy J; s 342(3) *Criminal Code* (Tas). A conviction for both an attempt and the substantive attempt is said to be contrary to the rule against double jeopardy (that is, punishing a person twice for what is substantially the same offence). However, currently, there is no legal barrier to enabling a conviction both for conspiracy to commit a crime and actually committing the offence. The situation is unclear with respect to incitement, probably because it is rarely charged.

In *R v Hoar* (1981) 148 CLR 32, Gibbs CJ, Mason, Aickin and Brennan JJ stated (at 38) that it was "undesirable" for conspiracy to be charged when a substantive offence had been committed. Nevertheless the ability to charge both conspiracy and the crime intended may be attractive to the prosecution because it enables it to allege a wide-ranging scheme of criminal activity without having to pinpoint the accused's precise role. It provides a "fall back" charge for the jury of the substantive elements if the full offence cannot be proven. That is if both conspiracy and the substantive crime can be charged, the evidence at trial may establish the accused's involvement in the conspiracy but not the commission of the substantive offence or vice versa.

The Law Commission of England and Wales in its Report No 76, *Codification of the Criminal Law: General Principles, Inchoate Offences. Conspiracy, Attempt and Incitement* (London: HMSO, 1976) set out the traditional practical criticisms to allowing conspiracy and the substantive offence to be charged as follows (at 27-28):

(i) inclusion of a conspiracy count adds to the length and complexity of trials and, in particular, complicates the task of summing up to a jury;

(ii) a conspiracy count tends to obscure questions of fact vital to a decision on the substantive charges;

(iii) joinder of a conspiracy and substantive offences tends to produce inconsistent verdicts;

(iv) evidence relevant to the conspiracy count may have, despite any warning against relying upon it, a prejudicial effect on an accused in relation to one or more of the substantive counts [references to cases omitted].

In addition, there is a broader conceptual difficulty with this approach. There is a real danger that allowing conspiracy and the substantive offence to be charged amounts to double jeopardy. That is convicting a person of both conspiracy and the substantive crime is akin to punishing a person twice for what is substantially the same offence.

The argument that, unlike attempt, conspiracy involves additional harms to those of the substantive offence is not persuasive in this context. The principle should simply be that the inchoate crime and the substantive crime cannot be charged together. For a further discussion of the concept of fairness in the context of a criminal trial, see Chapter 2.

5. CONCLUSION: THE FUTURE OF INCHOATE OFFENCES

In its Final Report on *General Principles of Criminal Responsibility* CLOC only considered the possibility of abolishing conspiracy. They noted (at 93) that incitement was rarely charged, but did not consider abolishing it, presumably on the basis that "circumstances may arise that are so serious that an appropriate offence is required".

There is, however, a need to rethink the conceptual basis of primary and derivative liability as it relates to incitement and aiding and abetting. It was previously pointed out (at p 469) that a person will be criminally responsible if he or she *incites* another who fails to commit the crime, but will not be criminally responsible for *aiding* another who fails to commit the crime. A move to remodelling aiding and abetting as a non-derivative crime might very well make incitement redundant.

CLOC did consider (at 85) limiting attempts to those relating to indictable offences, but ultimately dismissed this suggestion because of the "seriousness of offences which are classified as summary". It did not discuss abolishing attempts.

Similarly, the Gibbs Committee in its *Review of Commonwealth Criminal Law* (1990) did not consider the abolition of attempts, but stated (at 361) in relation to conspiracy:

Conspiracy is a crime which is regarded by many criminal lawyers with suspicion and distaste, not only because of the wide and imprecise scope of the offence itself, but also because the evidentiary rules peculiarly applicable to the offence may cause unfairness in particular cases. However, all the submissions received by the Review Committee express the opinion that the offence of conspiracy is one that must be retained, although one submission, that of the New South Wales Bar Association, reached this conclusion with reluctance. The Review Committee has no doubt that conspiracy should be retained in the law of the Commonwealth as an offence.

The three inchoate offences thus remain firmly in place in Australian jurisdictions. We have outlined how the three offences do not "fit" neatly with the division of crimes into physical and fault elements. They are also exceptional in imposing criminal responsibility in circumstances that depart from, or simply ignore, fundamental principles. This deviation is undoubtedly related to the importance attached to crime prevention and the suppression of organised crime.

Because the law in this area has often been developed on an ad hoc basis, there is perhaps a need for a more restrictive approach to be followed in the future as to the ambit of inchoate offences. Confining the fault element to an intention to commit the substantive offence has been one step in the right direction, although we recognise the policy reasons for enabling recklessness to be the fault element for attempted rape. Another way of restricting inchoate offences is to confine them to preparatory conduct for serious crimes rather than for serious *and* summary offences.

PART IV

Specific Crimes

10

Unlawful Killing

John Webster, (1580-1625)
The Duchess of Malfi,
IV:2 Line 260 (London:
Penguin Books Ltd, 1972), p 260

> **Other sins only speak;
> murder shrieks out**

1. INTRODUCTION

"Homicide" is a general term that has been used to refer to the unlawful killing of a human being. It encompasses offences such as murder, manslaughter, infanticide, and culpable driving causing death. Other closely related offences include assisting and encouraging suicide, child destruction, abortion and concealment of birth. All these offences will be discussed in this chapter with the exception of infanticide which has already been analysed in Chapter 4.

Interestingly, only ss 157, 159, 160 of the *Criminal Code* (Tas) specifically use the term "homicide". In the other Codes, the term "unlawful homicide" is used as a heading. All jurisdictions apart from Tasmania refer specifically to either "murder" or "manslaughter" or "unlawful killing". We will follow the general pattern in this chapter by referring to "unlawful killing" as a generic term and "murder" "manslaughter" and "culpable driving" as sub-categories of unlawful killing.

All Australian jurisdictions distinguish between the various forms of unlawful killing with the primary distinction being that between murder and manslaughter. The physical elements of murder and manslaughter are the same, namely causing the death of a human being. Murder involves in addition some form of specific fault element, whilst manslaughter is a residual category that contains a collection of disparate types of killing such as causing death by negligence or intentional killing that involves mitigating circumstances.

We will explore in this chapter not only the difficulty associated with the types of unlawful killing that manslaughter should cover, but also the controversy concerning whether culpable driving causing death should exist as a sub-category of unlawful killing or be abolished. We will also spend some time looking at the political, social and legal debate concerning the criminalisation of abortion. Practice in this area does not fully accord with what the law prohibits, as criminal prosecutions for abortion and child destruction are rare.

The various forms of unlawful killing are often referred to as "result crimes" in that the physical element refers to the results or consequences of conduct rather than the conduct itself: see Ch 3, pp 161ff. For example, what is prohibited in the crime of murder and manslaughter is the death of the victim rather than the conduct that caused the death. It is irrelevant what conduct was undertaken which caused the death; providing the conduct of the accused *results* in the death of the victim, the physical element will be established.

> According to the Australian Institute of Criminology, there were 333 victims of murder and manslaughter recorded by the police in Australia in 1998, with 1.8 victims per 100,000 population: Australian Institute of Criminology, *Australian Crime, Facts and Figures* (Canberra: AIC, 1999), p 14. In all age categories, except the 65 and over group, the probability of being a victim of murder or manslaughter was far greater for males than for females: p 15. In relation to homicide of women, there is a significantly increased risk of victimization by intimate partners: see J Mouzos, *Femicide: The Killing of Women in Australia 1989-1998* (Canberra: AIC, 1999).

There is a need to be wary of what statistics tell us. In the context of unlawful killing, there are a number of factors that may play a role in distorting the true rate in Australia. Many deaths are not constructed as unlawful killings, such as industrial or sporting "accidents". Criminological research on occupational fatalities in Victoria has suggested that the criminal law is not routinely invoked to deal with industrial deaths. This is the case even where there is a potential accused (either corporate or individual) whose conduct was sufficiently blameworthy to merit punishment through manslaughter by criminal negligence: S Perrone, "Workplace Fatalities and the Adequacy of Prosecution" (1995) 13(1) *Law in Context* 81, discussed in R White and S Perrone, *Crime and Social Control* (Oxford: Oxford University Press, 1997), pp 102-105: see above, Ch 1, p 13; Ch 3, p 154. Further, in those cases of "extreme" employer negligence that prompt criminal prosecution, the charge most likely to be pursued is an offence under the Occupational Health and Safety legislation rather than manslaughter.

Andrew Ashworth writes that for practical purposes, "the culpable causing of another person's death may fairly be regarded as the most serious offence in the criminal calendar": *Principles of Criminal Law* (3rd ed, Oxford: Oxford University Press, 1999), p 263. However, the context in which the killing occurs, such as whether it is caused by culpable driving or in the context of employment, has traditionally affected just how seriously it is taken by police and prosecutors.

The first sections of this chapter will concentrate on murder and manslaughter, then we will examine other specific offences closely related to unlawful killing.

2. CAUSING THE DEATH OF A HUMAN BEING

The following Table shows that the crimes of murder and manslaughter only differ in Australian jurisdictions as to the fault element required to establish the offence. The physical element for both is the same. That is, the accused must cause the death of a human being.

The Table sets out an overview of the physical and fault elements required for murder and manslaughter in Australian jurisdictions. In this section we will concentrate on the physical element, then, after exploring the relationship between euthanasia and unlawful killing, we will provide an overview of the fault elements of murder and manslaughter.

TABLE 1:
Physical and Fault Elements of Murder

JURISDICTION AND RELEVANT LAW	PHYSICAL ELEMENT	FAULT ELEMENT
ACT *Crimes Act* 1900	causes the death of another person s 12(1)	intending to cause death reckless indifference to the probability of causing death s 12(1)(a), (b)
NSW *Crimes Act* 1900	act or omission causing death (s 18(1)) constructive murder (s 18(1))	intent to kill or inflict grievous bodily harm reckless indifference to human life s 18(1)
NT *Criminal Code*	unlawfully kills another (s 161) constructive murder (s 162)	intends to cause death or grievous harm s 161
QLD *Criminal Code*	causes the death of another (ss 291, 293, 300) constructive murder (s 302)	intends to cause death or grievous bodily harm s 302(1)
SA common law *Criminal Law Consolidation Act* 1935	unlawfully kills "any reasonable creature in being" constructive murder (s 12A)	intention to cause death or grievous bodily harm foreseeability of death as a probable consequence of action

Table 1 continued

JURISDICTION AND RELEVANT LAW	PHYSICAL ELEMENT	FAULT ELEMENT
TAS *Criminal Code*	culpable homicide (ss 156(2), 157, 158) constructive murder (s 157(1)(d))	intention to cause death intention to cause bodily harm which the offender knew to be likely to cause death unlawful act or omission which the offender knew or ought to have known to be likely to cause death ss 156, 157
VIC common law *Crimes Act* 1958	unlawfully kills "any reasonable creature in being" constructive murder (s 3A)	intention to cause death or grievous bodily harm foreseeability of death as a *probable* consequence of action
WA *Criminal Code*	unlawfully kills another (ss 268, 279) constructive murder (s 279)	wilful murder: intends to cause death (s 278) intends to do grievous bodily harm (ss 268, 279)

Two questions therefore arise here: first, who is considered to be a human being and secondly, what tests need to be applied in establishing causation? The latter question has been dealt with in detail in Chapter 3, pp 164ff, and only a summary will be provided here.

2.1 A HUMAN BEING

The concept of a human being encompasses questions concerning birth and death. Is a foetus a human being for the purposes of the law? What about a person in a "persistent vegetative state"? Is he or she a human being capable of being killed? The rise of new medical technology that takes over the functions of breathing and circulation has meant that lives may be prolonged for substantial periods of time. The following provides a brief overview of the current law dealing with questions relating to the beginning and end of life while the next section raises some of the ethical and legal questions relating to euthanasia.

THE BEGINNING OF LIFE

The legal status of the human foetus has in recent years become the focus of debate in bioethical and legal literature: see in general J Seymour, *Childbirth and the Law* (Oxford: Oxford University Press, 2000). This is partly because of the discovery by medical researchers that human foetal tissue from aborted foetuses can be transplanted in order to treat a range of debilitating conditions and illnesses.[1]

Just how to categorise the human foetus for the purposes of the law has proven to be very difficult. There is a division between those who argue that the foetus is akin to a body part of its mother,[2] those who argue it is some form of separate entity[3] and those who have advocated a third model which sees the foetus and its mother as indivisibly linked: J Seymour, *Fetal Welfare and the Law: A Report of an Inquiry Commissioned by the Australian Medical Association* (1995), p 55. In *Attorney-General (Qld) (Ex rel Kerr) v T* (1983) 57 ALJR 285 at 286, Gibbs CJ (sitting alone) stated that "a foetus has no rights of its own until it is born and has a separate existence from its mother". Similarly, in the English decisions of *Paton v British Pregnancy Advisory Service Trustees* [1979] QB 276 and *C v S* [1988] QB 135 it was held that the foetus acquires no legal rights prior to having a separate existence of its own. However, Les Haberfield has argued that there has been some minimal recognition of the foetus as having some legal rights in both property law and torts.[4]

In relation to the criminal law, the killing of a child in the womb or in the process of being born is not considered murder or manslaughter, but may give rise to other criminal offences such as abortion and child destruction: see below, pp 518ff, 523ff. In *R v Hutty* [1953] VR 338, Barry J held at 339 that murder could only be committed on a person who is "in being" and "legally a person is not in being until he or she is fully born in a living state".

This begs the question as to when a child can be considered "fully born". Barry J (at 339) then set out the test at common law as follows:

> A baby is fully and completely born when it is completely delivered from the body of its mother and it has a separate and independent existence in the sense that it does not derive its power of living from its mother. It is not material that the child may still be attached to its mother by the umbilical cord; that does not prevent it from having a separate existence. But it is required, before the child can be the victim of murder or of manslaughter or of infanticide, that the child should have an existence separate from and independent of its mother, and that occurs when the child is fully extruded from the mother's body and is living by virtue of the functioning of its own organs.

This test is followed in the common law states of South Australia and Victoria and the *Criminal Codes* are very similar in setting out the requirement that the child be "completely extruded" from the body of its mother and in a "living" state.[5] There is no requirement that the child should have breathed,

---

1   On this issue, see L Haberfield, "The Transplantation of Human Fetal Tissue in Australia: Abortion, Consent and Other Legal Issues" (1996) 4(2) *Journal of Law and Medicine* 144 at 153. See also A Stuhmcke, "The Legal Regulation of Fetal Tissue Transplantation" (1996) 4(2) *Journal of Law and Medicine* 131.

2   See, for example, E Deutsch, "The Use of Human Tissue, Particularly Foetal Tissue, in Neurosurgery" (1990) 9 *Medicine and Law* 671 at 673. See also RS Magnusson, "The Recognition of Proprietary Rights in Human Tissue in Common Law Jurisdictions" (1992) 18 *Melbourne University Law Review* 601 at 628.

3   For a discussion of this argument, see J Seymour, *Fetal Welfare and the Law: A Report of an Inquiry Commissioned by the Australian Medical Association* (1995), p 50.

4   L Haberfield, "The Transplantation of Human Fetal Tissue in Australia: Abortion, Consent and Other Legal Issues" (1996) 4(2) *Journal of Law and Medicine* 144 at 153. See also B Bennett, "The Human Embryo as Property? Cyropreservation and the Challenges for the Law" (2000) 7(4) *Journal of Law and Medicine* 434.

5   *Criminal Code* (NT), s 16; *Criminal Code* (Qld), s 292; *Criminal Code* (Tas), s 153(4); *Criminal Code* (WA), s 269.

perhaps because a child may be born alive, but not breathe for some time after birth: *R v Brain* (1834) 6 C & P 349 at 350 per Park J.

The tests in the Australian Capital Territory and New South Wales are a little different in specifically requiring that the child has breathed. Section 20 of the *Crimes Act* (NSW) 1900 states:

> On the trial of a person for the murder of a child, such child shall be held to have been born alive if it has breathed, and has been wholly born into the world whether it has an independent circulation or not.

This suggests that when a child is completely removed from the body of its mother, it is fully born even though it is still attached via the umbilicus. This test of breathing and being wholly born applies in the Australian Capital Territory not only to a charge of murder, but also manslaughter and other offences against the person: *Crimes Act* 1900 (ACT), s 10. The reference to independent circulation is unnecessary given that a foetus has independent circulation for some months before birth: see in general K Moore and TVN Persaud, *The Developing Human — Clinically Oriented Embryology* (6th ed, Philadelphia: WB Saunders Company, 1998), pp 350ff.

The line between murder and manslaughter and other crimes is therefore very much a matter of timing. In jurisdictions other than New South Wales and South Australia, the crime of child destruction has been created to overcome the difficulty that may arise where a child is killed in the process of being born.[6] This offence will be dealt with more fully later in this chapter, but it is worthwhile noting here that one of the elements of the offence is that the child must be "capable of being born alive". Section 10(2) of the *Crimes Act* 1958 (Vic) sets out a statutory presumption that a foetus is capable of being born alive after a gestation period of 28 weeks. There is considerable difficulty, however, in establishing whether a foetus of less than 28 weeks is capable of being born alive. In *Rance v Mid-Downs Health Authority* [1991] 1 QB 587, Brooke J held at 621 that a 27-week-old foetus was "capable of being born alive" if it was capable of "breathing and living by reason of its breathing through its own lungs alone".

As discussed in Chapter 3 at p 178 until 1997, it was generally accepted that an accused who inflicts injuries to the foetus who is later born alive but subsequently dies from those injuries, may be guilty of murder or manslaughter depending on what fault element existed at the time of the action.[7] However, in *Attorney-General's Reference (No 3 of 1994)* [1997] 3 WLR 421 in discussing the law relating to transferred intention, the House of Lords unanimously held that only manslaughter and not murder may be committed in these circumstances. In *Martin* (1995) 85 A Crim R 587 Owen J held that a conviction for "unlawful killing" under the *Criminal Code* (WA) could arise out of similar circumstances to those in *Attorney-General's Reference (No 3 of 1994)*. An appeal against this finding was dismissed by the Full Court of the Supreme Court of Western Australia: *Martin (No 2)* (1996) 86 A Crim R 133. Because the law of homicide in Australia has developed in a different way to that of England, it would seem that the approach in *Martin's* case will probably hold sway.

---

6   *Crimes Act* 1900 (ACT), s 40; *Criminal Code* (NT), s 170; *Criminal Code* (Qld), s 313; *Criminal Code* (Tas), s 165; *Crimes Act* 1958 (Vic), s 10; *Criminal Code* (WA), s 290.

7   *R v West* (1848) 2 Cox CC 500; *Kwok Ming v The Queen (No 1)* [1963] HKLR 349; *Martin* (1995) 85 A Crim R 587 .

THE END OF LIFE

Death was traditionally defined as the absence of breathing and circulation of the blood. However, the advancement of medical technology that enables breathing and circulatory support means that this definition is no longer appropriate. Most jurisdictions now have legislation deeming a person dead where there has occurred either irreversible cessation of all functions of the brain or irreversible cessation of the circulation of blood.[8]

The requirement for the irreversible cessation of *all* functions of the brain is significant. The brain stem regulates reflex activities such as heart rate and respiration whereas the forebrain mediates the complex functions of voluntary movement, sensory input and cognitive processes. A patient may have severe damage to the forebrain causing a lack of awareness, but if the brain stem is still functioning, then the patient is still legally alive. The term "persistent vegetative state" (PVS) is generally used to refer to this clinical condition. In 1994, the Multi-Society Task Force on PVS set out a list of criteria for the diagnosis of the condition: "Medical Aspects of the Persistent Vegetative State Part One" (1994) 330(21) *New England Journal of Medicine* 1499 and "Part Two" (1994) 330(22) *New England Journal of Medicine* 1572. The criteria include no evidence of awareness of self or environment and inability to interact with others; no evidence of sustained, reproducible, purposeful, or voluntary behavioural responses to visual, auditory tactile or noxious stimuli; and no evidence of language comprehension or expression. In a PVS, the patient's eyes remain open, but there are no detectable responses to visual, auditory or tactile stimuli. However, autonomic reflexes that are controlled by the brain stem such as breathing, coughing and even swallowing may be retained.

There are some conditions that are similar to the PVS such as coma, the locked-in syndrome and akinetic mutism: see "The Persistent Vegetative State and Brainstem Death" in I Kerridge, M Lowe and J McPhee, *Ethics and Law for the Health Professions* (Katoomba, NSW: Social Science Press, 1998), pp 420 at 421. In 1996, Keith Andrews and colleagues published a controversial study in the *British Medical Journal* which found that of 40 patients admitted over three years to a single unit specialising in the rehabilitation of patients with profound brain damage, 17 of the patients or 43% were misdiagnosed as being in a PVS: K Andrews, L Murphy, R Munday and C Littlewood, "Misdiagnosis of the Vegetative State: Retrospective Study in a Rehabilitation Unit" (1996) 313 *British Medical Journal* 13. The 17 misdiagnosed patients were able to communicate consistently using eye pointing or a touch sensitive buzzer.

Because those in a PVS have some function in the brain stem, they are not considered dead for the purposes of organ transplantation. However, it may not be necessary to keep such patients alive through artificial nutrition and hydration. This is explored more fully below in 3 'Euthanasia and Unlawful Killing': p 485.

---

8   *Transplantation and Anatomy Act 1978* (ACT), s 45; *Human Tissue Act 1983* (NSW), s 33; *Human Tissue Transplantation Act 1979* (NT), s 23; *Death (Definition) Act 1983* (SA), s 2; *Human Transplantation and Anatomy Act 1979* (Qld), s 45 (applying only to the act and not generally). There is no statutory definition of death in Western Australia, but s 24(2) of the *Human Tissue and Transplant Act 1979* (NT) states that tissue shall not be removed unless two medical practitioners have declared that "irreversible cessation of all function of the brain of the person has occurred".

The ability of modern medical technology to maintain respiration and circulation of the blood in the presence of brain death raises the importance of adequate tests to determine the difference between the cessation of all functioning of the brain, comas and PVS. It also raises important ethical questions about the nature of "personhood". Those considered brain dead do not easily fit within our concept of a dead person in that they are "pink and warm, their hearts beat and they continue to breathe with the aid of a ventilator": "The Persistent Vegetative State and Brainstem Death" in I Kerridge, M Lowe and J McPhee, *Ethics and Law for the Health Professions* (Katoomba, NSW: Social Science Press, 1998), p 420 at 425. Some have argued that the pressing need for organs for transplantation should lead to the concept of death being redefined to the cessation of functioning of the forebrain or "higher brain" which would enable those in a PVS to be considered legally dead.[9] Shann points out, however, that "paradoxically some of the strongest opposition to change, or even discussion of the issues involved, comes from the transplant lobby — who fear that any suggestion of change will be misinterpreted as an attempt to snatch organs, and so undermine public confidence in the public system": "A Personal Comment: Whole Brain Death Versus Cortical Death" (1995) 23(1) *Anaesthesia Intensive Care* 14.

The Model Criminal Code Officers Committee has recommended that there be no change to the legal definition of death because the ramifications of such a change would "extend beyond the criminal law": *Fatal Offences Against the Person*, Discussion Paper (1998).

2.2 CAUSATION

As well as proving that the accused unlawfully killed a human being, the other physical element for both murder and manslaughter is that the accused *caused* the victim's death. In Chapter 3, we explored this requirement in some detail: pp 164ff. It will be recalled that the courts have developed a number of different tests to establish causation such as the:

- **reasonable foreseeability test;**

- **substantial cause test; and**

- **natural consequence test.**

The more modern cases appear to favour the substantial cause test, but sometimes these tests are used interchangeably. *Royall v The Queen* (1991) 172 CLR 378 shows how seven judges applied three different tests to the facts, with the majority (Mason CJ, Deane and Dawson JJ) favouring the natural consequence test. Whilst much academic debate has surrounded the concept of causation, it should be kept in mind that the issue rarely arises in practice.

---

9   A Asai, "Should a Patient in a Persistent Vegetative State Live?" (1999) 18(2) *Monash Bioethics Review* 25.

3. EUTHANASIA AND UNLAWFUL KILLING

At common law, a competent adult patient has the right to refuse medical treatment, although this generally does not extend to palliative care.[10] The right to refuse treatment has now been recognised in some Australian jurisdictions.[11] But what of taking active steps to hasten death?

Euthanasia has been the subject of intense debate in Australia and elsewhere in recent years. Some confusion surrounds the use of the term and it is important to note that euthanasia may be divided into the categories of voluntary, non-voluntary and involuntary. Euthanasia is said to be voluntary where there is an intentional taking of life to relieve suffering in response to the sufferer's request. It is non-voluntary when the intentional taking of life occurs where the patient is incapable of communicating or forming an opinion as to euthanasia. The most common situation where the question of non-voluntary euthanasia may arise is where a patient is in a persistent vegetative state. Involuntary euthanasia occurs where intentional killing is carried out against the known wishes of the patient. Closely connected to these forms of euthanasia is physician-assisted suicide where a medical practitioner assists a patient to kill him or herself by providing the means to allow the patient to take his or her own life, but does not actually administer any fatal treatment.

Voluntary and involuntary euthanasia[12] and physician assisted suicide[13] are illegal in Australia though prosecutions of medical practitioners are rare. Prosecution of spouses or relatives is more common, though there is still evidence of leniency in relation to charging and sentencing practices: M Otlowski, "Mercy killing cases in the Australian Criminal Justice System" (1993) 17 Crim LJ 10. Non-voluntary euthanasia may be permitted in narrow circumstances through the withdrawal of hydration and nutrition from patients in a PVS: *Airedale NHS Trust v Bland* [1993] 2 WLR 316. See below (p 490) for a discussion of this case and its implications for Australia. The ethical issues arising from voluntary and non-voluntary euthanasia are discussed below.

3.1 VOLUNTARY EUTHANASIA — THE NORTHERN TERRITORY EXPERIMENT

The debate concerning voluntary euthanasia and assisted suicide became prominent in Australia with the passage of the *Rights of the Terminally Ill Act* 1995 (NT). That Act enabled an individual over the age of 18 and suffering from a "terminal illness" to request a physician to assist him or her to die.

---

10 *Re T (Adult: Refusal of Medical Treatment)* [1992] 4 All ER 649; *Re C (Adult: Refusal of Medical Treatment)* [1994] 4 All ER 819; *Malette v Shulman* (1990) 67 DLR (4th) 321.

11 *Medical Treatment Act* 1994 (ACT); *Natural Death Act* 1988 (NT); *Consent to Medical Treatment and Palliative Care Act* 1995 (SA); *Medical Treatment Act* 1988 (Vic).

12 H Palmer, "Dr Adams' Trial for Murder" [1957] Crim LR 365 at 375; *R v Cox* (1992) 12 BMLR 38; *Airedale NHS Trust v Bland* [1993] 2 WLR 316. For a review of these cases and recent prosecutions in England, see A Arlidge, "The Trial of Dr David Moor" [2000] Crim LR 31; JC Smith, "A Comment on Moor's Case" [2000] Crim LR 41.

13 *Crimes Act* 1900 (ACT), s 17; *Crimes Act* 1900 (NSW), s 31C; *Criminal Code* (NT), s 168; *Criminal Code* (Qld), s 311; *Criminal Code Consolidation Act* 1935 (SA), s 13A(5), (7); *Criminal Code* (Tas), s 163; *Crimes Act* 1958 (Vic), s 6B(2); *Criminal Code* (WA), s 288.

"Terminal illness" was defined in s 3 of the *Rights of the Terminally Ill Act* 1995 (NT) as "an illness which, in reasonable medical judgment will, in the normal course, without the application of extraordinary measures or of treatment unacceptable to the patient, result in the death of the patient". A number of safeguards were built into the Act, including being assessed by a specialist in the illness and a psychiatrist: s 7(1)(c). The latter had to be satisfied that the individual was not suffering from a "treatable clinical depression in respect of the illness": s 7(1)(c)(iv). A physician who acted in accordance with the Act could not be held guilty of any crime or professional misconduct, nor could he or she be liable in a civil action to any claim for damages: s 20(1).

The *Rights of the Terminally Ill Act* 1995 (NT) was repealed by the *Euthanasia Laws Act* 1997 (Cth). This denied the Northern Territory, the Australian Capital Territory and Norfolk Island the power to make laws "which permit or have the effect of permitting (whether subject to conditions or not) the form of intentional killing of another called euthanasia (which includes mercy killing) or the assisting of a person to terminate his or her life": Sch 1.

> In the short time that the *Rights of the Terminally Ill Act* 1995 (NT) was in force, Dr Phillip Nitschke used a computerised system that allowed patients to give them- selves a lethal dose of medication to end their life. This was therefore a form of assisted suicide rather than active voluntary euthanasia. At the time of its repeal, four people were reported to have received assistance to die in accordance with the terms of the Act: Senate Legal and Constitutional Legislation Committee, *Consideration of Legislation Referred to the Committee: Euthanasia Laws Bill 1996* (1997), pp 10-11. Bob Dent became the first person to die pursuant to the Northern Territory legislation on 22 September 1996. He was followed by South Australian cancer sufferer Janet Mills on 2 January 1997; a 69-year-old unnamed Darwin man on 20 January 1997; and a 72-year-old unnamed Sydney woman on 1 March 1997: G Alcorn, "Euthanasia Law Assists New Death" *The Age*, 5 March 1997, A7.

In the debate surrounding the enactment and subsequent repeal of the *Rights of the Terminally Ill Act* 1995 (NT), a number of ethical arguments surfaced in favour of and against voluntary euthanasia and assisted suicide. The following is a brief outline of the main arguments.

3.2 ARGUMENTS IN FAVOUR OF VOLUNTARY EUTHANASIA

RIGHTS-BASED ARGUMENTS

In 1914, Cardozo J stated that "every human being of adult years and sound mind has a right to determine what shall be done with his [or her] own body": *Schloendorff v Society of New York Hospital*, 105 NE 92 at 93 (SCNY 1914). This stemmed from John Stuart Mill's oft-quoted harm principle that "the only purpose for which power can be rightfully exercised over any member of a civilized community, against his will, is to prevent harm to others": *On Liberty* (Harmondsworth, Middlesex: Penguin Books Ltd, 1987) (first published 1859), p 68; see Ch 1, 3.1 'The Prevention of Harm', p 49.

Proponents of voluntary euthanasia argue from this starting point that if an individual chooses to end his or her own life, the State has no business interfering with that choice or invoking criminal penalties to stop the individual acting on it. Further, "if the person who has made the decision needs the assistance of another to help him or her carry it out, and that other person is also an adult of sound mind, who after careful reflection is willing to assist the first person in carrying the decision out, the state also ought not to invoke criminal penalties against the person who assists": H Kuhse and P Singer, "Active Voluntary Euthanasia, Morality and the Law" (1995) 3(2) *Journal of Law and Medicine* 129 at 130.

Some have also argued for the existence of a right to die. In his dissenting judgment in *Rodriguez v Attorney-General (British Columbia)* [1993] 3 SCR 519 Cory J saw the right to die as an extension of a right to life which finds expression in s 7 of the Canadian *Charter of Rights and Freedoms* (at 630):

> If, as I believe, dying is an integral part of living, then as a part of life it is entitled to the constitutional protection provided by s 7. It follows that the right to die with dignity should be as well protected as is any other aspect of the right to life. State prohibitions that would force a dreadful, painful death on a rational, but incapacitated terminally ill patient are an affront to human dignity.

The eminent philosophers Max Charlesworth and Ronald Dworkin have written about voluntary euthanasia in the context of an expression of autonomy, integrity and dignity: M Charlesworth, *Bioethics in a Liberal Society* (Cambridge: Cambridge University Press, 1993); R Dworkin, *Life's Dominion: An Argument About Abortion and Euthanasia* (London: Harper Collins, 1993).

BENEFICENCE

Voluntary euthanasia has also been advocated where it is in "the best interests" of the individual concerned. This stems from the ethical principle of beneficence that holds that there is a moral obligation to promote the welfare of individuals: TL Beauchamp and JF Childress, *Principles of Biomedical Ethics* (4th ed, Oxford: Oxford University Press, 1994), p 249.

In this sense, it has been argued that if there is a choice between a long, drawn out and painful death or a quick death by lethal injection, a person acts with beneficence by giving the appropriate injection. It is this argument that gives rise to voluntary euthanasia sometimes being referred to as "mercy killing": A Flew, "The Principle of Euthanasia" in AB Downing and B Smoker (eds), *Voluntary Euthanasia: Experts Debate the Right to Die* (London: Peter Owen, 1986), p 43. The notion of beneficence is also implicit in comparisons between the death of animals and humans, expressed in statements such as "we should have been punished by the State if we kept an animal alive in a similar

---

14   H Kuhse and P Singer, "Voluntary Euthanasia and the Nurse: An Australian Study" (1993) 4 *International Journal of Nursing Studies* 311; H Kuhse, P Singer, P Baume, M Clarke and M Rickard, "End-of-Life Decisions in Australian Medical Practice" (1997) 166(4) *Medical Journal of Australia* 191; P Baume and E O'Malley, "Euthanasia: Attitudes and Practices of Medical Practitioners" (1994) 161(2) *Medical Journal of Australia* 137; BJ Ward and PA Tate, "Attitudes Among NHS Doctors to Requests for Euthanasia" (1994) 308 *British Medical Journal* 1332; ME Suarez-Almazor, M Belzile and E Bruera, "Euthanasia and Physician-Assisted Suicide: A Comparative Survey of Physicians, Terminally-Ill Cancer Patients and the General Population" (1997) 15(2) *Journal of Clinical Oncology* 413.

physical condition": AB Downing, "Euthanasia: The Human Context" in AB Downing and B Smoker (eds), *Voluntary Euthanasia: Experts Debate the Right to Die* (London: Peter Owen, 1986), p 18.

PUBLIC SUPPORT

International and Australian studies suggest there is strong support for the idea of voluntary euthanasia.[14] However, there are often methodological problems associated with opinion surveys, not the least of which is the phrasing of the questions posed. It is also problematic relying on polls and questionnaires to determine what should be legally permissible: see further Ch 1, 3.3 'The Public Interest', p 56. As Ian Kerridge, Michael Lowe and John McPhee point out, there are plenty of instances in recent history "where both popular approval and the law approved major violations of human rights": I Kerridge, M Lowe and J McPhee, *Ethics and Law for the Health Professions* (Katoomba, NSW: Social Science Press, 1998), p 468.

3.3 ARGUMENTS OPPOSING VOLUNTARY EUTHANASIA

SANCTITY OF LIFE

Those opposed to voluntary euthanasia often refer to the idea that human life has an inherent value such that it is always ethically impermissible to intentionally end human life. Often, but not always, this argument is based on religious or moral principles: see further Ch 1, 3.2 'Morality', p 51.

In *Airedale NHS Trust v Bland* [1993] AC 789 at 893, Lord Mustill explained that in circumstances where active steps are taken to end life, even with humanitarian motives, "the interest of the state in preserving life overrides the otherwise all-powerful interest of patient autonomy". The Supreme Court of the United States took a similar position in deciding that statutes prohibiting physician-assisted suicide are constitutionally valid.[15]

SLIPPERY SLOPE

The "slippery slope" argument is that the legalisation of voluntary euthanasia will lead to active non-voluntary and involuntary euthanasia in that it will open the way for killing individuals who are not competent to make end of life decisions. For an exploration of this argument, see J Rachels, *The End of Life* (Oxford: Oxford University Press, 1986), pp 170ff.

Linked to this is the argument that legalising voluntary euthanasia will open the way for interpersonal, professional and institutional abuse: M Battin, *The Least Worst Death* (New York: Oxford University Press, 1994), p 173. It is of course difficult to prove or disprove consequentialist arguments such as these in the absence of legalised voluntary euthanasia. However, some authors point to the Remmelink Report that was carried out in 1990 for a government-appointed committee of inquiry into the Dutch experience of voluntary euthanasia as supporting the "slippery slope"

---

15 *Vacco, Attorney-General of New York v Quill*, 521 S 793 (1997); *Washington v Glucksberg*, 521 US 702 (1997). For the Canadian position, see *Rodriguez v Attorney-General (British Columbia)* [1993] 3 SCR 519.

argument.[16] This Report showed that 1000 deaths occurred with the explicit purpose of ending life, but *without* an explicit request from the patient. These figures have been questioned, and Helga Kuhse and Peter Singer have argued that in Australia where voluntary euthanasia is illegal, the rate of ending a patient's life without the patient's explicit request was five times higher than in Holland: H Kuhse, P Singer, P Baume, M Clark and R Maurice, "End-of-Life Decisions in Australian Medical Practice" (1997) 166(4) *Medical Journal of Australia* 191.

THE INTEGRITY OF THE MEDICAL PROFESSION AND PALLIATIVE CARE

The Australian Medical Association has stated that medical practitioners have an "ethical obligation to preserve health": *Position Statement on Care of Severely and Terminally Ill Patients* (1996), p 1. Some doctors have argued that if they are allowed to end their patients' lives, then "the profession ... will never again be worthy of trust and respect as healer and comforter and protector of life in all its frailty".[17]

There was evidence placed before the Senate Legal and Constitutional Legislation Committee that after the enactment of the *Rights of the Terminally Ill Act* 1995 (NT) members of Aboriginal communities became reluctant to attend clinics or to go to hospital: Senate Legal and Constitutional Committee, *Consideration of Legislation Referred to the Committee: Euthanasia Laws Bill 1996* (Canberra: 1997), p 50, quoting Mr Mackinolty.

Health practitioners working in palliative care have also expressed concern about voluntary euthanasia. For example, Michael Ashby in "Hard Cases, Causation and Care of the Dying" (1995) 3(2) *Journal of Law and Medicine* 152 writes (at 152):

> Palliative care practitioners believe that intentional ending of life is not a part of currently accepted palliative care practice. They are not persuaded by what well people say in opinion polls, nor by arguments which appear to intellectually undermine the doctrine of double effect or the sanctity of life. For many doctors, and particularly those who care for dying people, there is a profound moral intuitive objection to intentionally and actively causing the death of a patient.

The Model Criminal Code Officers Committee in its Discussion Paper on *Fatal Offences Against the Person* (1998) has stated (p 187) that the *Model Criminal Code* should not permit voluntary euthanasia or assisted suicide:

> Any such change would be radical, controversial and beyond the Committee's brief to propose a uniform code which reflects a consensus on matters of legal principle.

---

16   These findings were reported in P van der Maas, J van Delden, L Pijnendorg, C Looman, "Euthanasia and Other Medical Decisions Concerning the End of Life" (1991) 338 *The Lancet* 669, September 14th. See also, P van der Maas, G van der Wal, I Haverkate, C de Graaff, J Kester, B Onwuteaka-Philipsen, A van der Heide, J Bosma and D Willems, "Euthanasia, Physician-Assisted Suicide and Other Medical Practices Involving the End of Life in the Netherlands, 1990-1995" (1996) 335 *New England Journal of Medicine* 1699.

17   W Gaylin, LR Kass, ED Pellegrino and M Siegler, "Doctors Must Not Kill" in RM Baird and SE Rosenbaum, *Euthanasia: The Moral Issues* (New York: Prometheus Books, 1989), p 25 at 27. See also, P Mullen, "Euthanasia: An Impoverished Construction of Life and Death" (1995) 3 *Journal of Law and Medicine* 121 at 124; K Healey (ed), *Euthanasia* (Sydney: The Spinney Press, 1997), p 13.

3.4 NON-VOLUNTARY EUTHANASIA — *BLAND* AND *CURZAN*

Anthony Bland was a victim of the 1989 Hillsborough Football Ground disaster in England. At that time he was aged 17½ and he suffered a severe crushed chest injury that gave rise to hypoxic brain damage. His condition deteriorated such that he was considered to be in a persistent vegetative state with no hope whatsoever of improvement. His doctors supported by his parents formed the view that there was no useful purpose in prolonging his medical care and that it was appropriate to stop artificial feeding and other measures keeping him alive. Because of doubts about the legality of such conduct, the responsible hospital authority sought declarations from the High Court that the doctors could lawfully discontinue all life-sustaining treatment and medical supportive measures including artificial hydration and nutrition. This was granted by the President of the Family Division and, later on appeal, by the Court of Appeal and ultimately the House of Lords: *Airedale NHS Trust v Bland* [1993] AC 789.

In assessing whether the withdrawal of nutrition and hydration could amount to a criminal offence, the House of Lords considered the extent of the duty owed by the hospital and the doctors to their patient. Where a legal duty exists to do a certain act that an accused failed to do, that *omission* may amount to the physical element for unlawful killing. The House of Lords considered there was *no* duty of care to provide Anthony Bland with medical care and food for an indefinite period.

Bland relied upon a previous House of Lords decision *In Re F* [1990] 2 AC 1. That case laid down the principle that, based on concepts of necessity, a doctor can lawfully treat a patient who cannot consent to treatment if it is determined to be "in the best interests" of the patient to receive such treatment: see Ch 6, p 332. Following on from that principle, the House of Lords held in *Bland's* case that the right to administer invasive medical care is wholly dependent upon such care being in the best interests of the patient. The critical issue therefore became whether or not it was in the best interests of the patient to continue the invasive medical care involved in artificial feeding. The medical evidence was such that continuance of medical treatment would confer no benefit on Anthony Bland and accordingly, the House of Lords held that existence in a PVS was not in the best interests of the patient. Thus, there was no duty to provide Anthony Bland with medical care and food for an indefinite period of time and the withdrawal of artificial nutrition and hydration would not amount to an unlawful killing.

The United States Supreme Court has taken a different approach to a similar fact situation. In 1983, Nancy Beth Cruzan was involved in a car accident that left her in a PVS. A gastronomy tube was implanted to allow for artificial feeding. After five years, the Cruzan family requested removal of the feeding tube. The doctors involved refused to honour the request without a court order. The Missouri trial court held that Nancy Cruzan had a right to have "death-prolonging" procedures removed. The Supreme Court of Missouri reversed this decision, stating that it would only give permission for the discontinuance of artificial feeding if there was convincing evidence that Cruzan would have wanted to be allowed to die. No such evidence had been presented to the court.

On appeal, the United States Supreme Court in a five to four decision, upheld the approach of the Supreme Court of Missouri: 497 S 261; 110 S Ct 2841 (1990). The majority held that medical treatment and artificial nutrition and hydration must be continued *unless* there is clear evidence indicating that the patient would not have wished to be kept alive in the circumstances. The focus of this case, therefore, was not on the best interests of the patient, but on evidence of any advance directives as to withdrawal of treatment. Six months after the Supreme Court decision, three new witnesses testified as to Nancy's prior wishes that medical treatment should cease if she were in such circumstances and the Missouri court then allowed Nancy Cruzan to die.

The significance of the *Bland* case for Australian jurisdictions is unclear. Ian Freckelton points out that Australian health professionals have not followed the English approach of applying to courts for declaratory orders in decision-making on cessation or withdrawal of treatment, but adds that "in circumstances that are unusual it may very well be that the English-style approach would be prudent for the treating doctor or responsible hospital": I Freckelton, "Withdrawal of Life Support: The 'Persistent Vegetative State Conundrum'" (1993) 1(1) *Journal of Law and Medicine* 35 at 46.

In South Australia, the American approach has to some extent found its way into legislation. Section 7(1)(a) of the *Consent to Medical Treatment and Palliative Care Act* 1995 (SA) allows a person to give an advance direction refusing treatment in the event that he or she is at some future time in the terminal phase of a terminal illness or in a persistent vegetative state.

Many commentators have queried the distinction in *Bland's* case between an *omission* to treat and active forms of non-voluntary euthanasia.[18] Lord Goff was careful to point out (at 865) that an omission is not the same as the taking of some positive step to bring life to an end, because "the law does not feel able to authorise [active] euthanasia, even in circumstances such as these; for once euthanasia is recognised as lawful in these circumstances, it is difficult to see any logical basis for excluding it in others".

Lord Browne-Wilkinson (at 879) posed the ethical question arising from *Bland's* case as follows:

> [S]hould society draw a distinction (which some would see as artificial) between adopting a course of action designed to produce certain death, on the one hand through the lack of food, and on the other from a fatal injection, the former being permissible and the latter (euthanasia) prohibited?

The answer to this question will no doubt continue to be vigorously debated.

The Philosophical Debate about Act and Omissions

In 1975, James Rachels, a bioethicist, set out two hypothetical cases to argue that there was no moral difference between passive and active euthanasia. In the first case, Smith stands to gain a large inheritance if his six-year-old cousin dies. One evening, as the six-year-old is taking his bath, Smith slips into the bathroom and drowns his cousin, making it look like an accident. In the second case, Jones also stands to

---

18   For example, M Bagaric, "Active and Passive Euthanasia: Is There a Moral Distinction and Should There Be a Legal Difference?" (1997) 5(2) *Journal of Law and Medicine* 143; C Favour, "Puzzling Cases about Killing and Letting Die" (1996) 1 *Res Publica: A Journal of Legal and Social Philosophy* 18; J Finnis, "Bland: Crossing the Rubicon?" (1993) 109 LQR 329; G Gillett, "Euthanasia, Letting Die and the Pause" (1988) 14 *Journal of Medical Ethics* 61; J Rachels, "Active and Passive Euthanasia" (1975) *New England Journal of Medicine* 78.

benefit if his six-year-old cousin dies. Like Smith, Jones slips into the bathroom intending to drown his cousin. However, as he enters he sees the child slip, hit his head and fall face down in the bath. Jones watches and does nothing as the child drowns. According to Rachels, Jones' conduct is no less reprehensible than Smith's. From these cases, Rachels argues that there is no moral difference between killing and letting die. Tom Beauchamp, however, argues that Rachels' cases are not analogous to killing and letting die as they relate to euthanasia: J Rachels, "Active and Passive Euthanasia" in T Beauchamp and L Walters (eds), *Contemporary Issues in Bioethics* (4th ed, Belmont, California: Wadsworth Publishing Company, 1994), pp 439-442. TL Beauchamp, "A Reply to Rachels on Active and Passive Euthanasia" in TL Beauchamp and L Walters (eds), *Contemporary Issues in Bioethics* (4th ed, Belmont, California: Wadsworth Publishing Company, 1994), pp 442-449. For an earlier article which adopts a similar philosophical position, see T Campbell, "Euthanasia and the Law" (1979) 17(2) *Alberta Law Review* 188.

4. THE FAULT ELEMENTS OF MURDER AND MANSLAUGHTER

We have previously explored the physical elements of unlawful killing which are the same for both murder and manslaughter. In relation to fault elements, murder involves some form of specific fault element, whilst manslaughter is a residual category that contains a collection of disparate types of killing such as causing death by negligence or intentional killing that involves mitigating circumstances.

4.1 MURDER

According to the traditional common law, the requisite fault element for murder was "malice aforethought": E Coke, *Institutes of the Laws of England — Part 3* (London: Lee & Pakeman, 1644) 3 Inst 47. This is no longer relevant as murder may be established where the accused has not acted "maliciously" and where there is no pre-meditation. Whilst s 18(2)(a) of the *Crimes Act* 1900 (NSW) provides that no act or omission is murder unless it is "malicious" this appears to be redundant: *Royall v The Queen* (1990) 172 CLR 378 at 416 per Deane and Dawson JJ, at 428-429 per Toohey and Gaudron JJ. A motive for murder need not be proved, although evidence of motive is admissible to show the accused possessed the requisite fault element: *Plomp v The Queen* (1963) 110 CLR 234.

Australian jurisdictions vary in the fault elements required for murder. While all jurisdictions include an intention to kill within the fault elements, seven include an intention to cause some form of serious bodily harm, five include recklessness as to causing death and only two jurisdictions include recklessness as to causing grievous bodily harm: see Table 1.

All jurisdictions apart from the Australian Capital Territory also include a category of murder known as "constructive murder" whereby a fault element is "constructed" out of a set of circumstances. We shall outline how this particular category of murder has been very difficult to justify in terms of a presumption of a subjective fault element for serious crimes.

INTENTION TO KILL

An intention to kill satisfies the fault element for murder in all jurisdictions. This element is set out in legislation in all jurisdictions[19] apart from South Australia and Victoria where the common law holds sway to the same effect: *R v Crabbe* (1985) 156 CLR 464.

In Chapter 3, we set out that intention in relation to the results or consequences of conduct requires the prosecution to prove that the accused's *purpose* was to bring about the consequences. In relation to murder, this requires proof that the accused intended death to ensue from the conduct.[20] This is sometimes referred to as specific intent: *He Kaw Teh v The Queen* (1985) 157 CLR 523 at 569-570 per Brennan J. However, the prosecution need not prove the accused intended the exact mode of death: *R v Demirian* [1989] VR 97; *R v Willmot (No 2)* [1985] 2 Qd R 413 at 415 per Campbell J. We also explored the problematic distinction between "direct" and "oblique" intention. Brennan J in *He Kaw Teh v The Queen* (1985) 157 CLR 523 referred to (at 569) intention in its narrow sense as a decision to bring about a particular result. However, the English courts have developed a broader approach to intention — oblique intent — to encompass a person's awareness or belief that particular consequences are virtually certain to occur. This approach overlaps with the concept of recklessness and may be explained by the fact that the fault element for murder in England remains an intention to kill or to cause grievous bodily harm and does not include a separate category for recklessness: JC Smith and B Hogan, *Criminal Law* (7th ed, London: Butt, 1992), pp 346-347. The High Court has yet to comprehensively define the meaning of intention. In *Royall v The Queen* (1991) 172 CLR 378 it was unsuccessfully argued that intention in s 18(1)(a) of the *Crimes Act* 1900 (NSW) included knowledge of likelihood and it may well be the case that the narrow interpretation of intention holds sway in Australia.

The doctrine of transferred intention applies to the situation where an accused intends to kill a certain person and commits the required physical elements for murder, but kills another. In such a situation, the accused is still liable for the death of the person killed: see Ch 3, pp 177ff.[21]

INTENTION TO INFLICT SERIOUS BODILY HARM

In all jurisdictions except for the Australian Capital Territory, the fault element for murder includes an intention to inflict some form of serious bodily harm.[22] In New South Wales, Queensland, Western Australia and at common law, the term "grievous bodily harm" is used. In the Northern Territory, the term used is "grievous harm" and in Tasmania, an intention to cause "bodily harm" is sufficient where the accused knows that death is likely to be caused.

---

19 *Crimes Act* 1900 (ACT), s 12(1)(a); *Crimes Act* 1900 (NSW), s 18(1)(a); *Criminal Code* (NT), s 162(1)(a); *Criminal Code* (Qld), s 302(1); *Criminal Code* (Tas), s 157; *Criminal Code* (WA), s 279(1).

20 *La Fontaine v The Queen* (1976) 136 CLR 62; *R v Crabbe* (1985) 156 CLR 464; *Boughey v The Queen* (1986) 161 CLR 10; *R v Demirian* [1989] VR 97.

21 *Crimes Act* 1900 (ACT), s 12(1)(b); *Crimes Act* 1900 (NSW), s 18(1)(a); *Criminal Code* (NT), s 162(3); *Criminal Code* (Qld), s 301(1)(a); *Criminal Code* (Tas), ss 13(3), 157(1)(a); *Criminal Code* (WA), ss 278, 279(1); *R v Michael* (1840) 169 ER 48; *R v Saunders and Archer* (1573) 2 Plowd 473; *Attorney-General's Reference (No 3 of 1994)* [1997] 3 WLR 421.

22 *Crimes Act* 1900 (NSW), s 18(1)(a); *Criminal Code* (NT), s 162(1)(a); *Criminal Code* (Qld), s 302(1)(a); *Criminal Code* (Tas), s 157(1)(b); *Criminal Code* (WA), s 279(1)(a); *Pemble v The Queen* (1971) 124 CLR 107.

What is meant by "grievous bodily harm" varies amongst the jurisdictions. At common law, it has been interpreted as meaning "really serious bodily injury": *DPP v Smith* [1961] AC 290 at 334 per Viscount Kilmuir LC; *Pemble v The Queen* (1971) 124 CLR 107. Section 4(1) of the *Crimes Act* 1900 (NSW) has an inclusive definition of the term in that it is defined as including "any permanent or serious disfiguring of the person". In the Northern Territory, "grievous harm" is defined as "any physical or mental injury of such a nature as to endanger or be likely to endanger or to cause or be likely to cause permanent injury to health": *Criminal Code* (NT), s 1; *Charlie v The Queen* (1998) 119 NTR 1. In Queensland and Western Australia, "grievous bodily harm" is defined as "any bodily injury of such a nature that, if left untreated, would endanger or be likely to endanger life, or to cause or be likely to cause permanent injury to health".[23] Section 1(4) of the *Criminal Code* (WA) extends this definition to include a "serious disease". The Tasmanian definition of "bodily harm" is the same as in the Queensland and Western Australian Codes except that the term "serious injury" is used in place of "permanent injury". It is up to the jury to interpret whether the harm intended amounted to grievous bodily harm: *R v Watson* [1987] 1 Qd R 440 at 458 per Dowsett J; *R v Miller* [1951] VLR 346.

In 1991, the Victorian Law Reform Commission called for the abolition of the category of murder based on intent to do grievous bodily harm: *Homicide*, Report No 40 (1991), pp 53-56. This was on the basis that there is a significant difference between the moral blameworthiness of someone who intends to kill and someone who intends to do serious injury, but does not intend or foresee death. The Commission also pointed out (at 54) that the outcome of cases based on grievous bodily harm might be arbitrary, given that it is up to the jury to decide whether the harm intended amounted to grievous bodily harm:

> One jury might conclude, for example, that the intention of putting a pillow over someone's mouth in order to render the victim unconscious amounts to an intent to do grievous bodily harm. Another jury might conclude on exactly the same facts, that it does not.

The Victorian Law Reform Commission proposed that such circumstances should be seen as manslaughter rather than murder. The inclusion of this fault element for murder also troubled Lord Edmund-Davies in *R v Cunningham* [1982] AC 566 when he stated (at 582-583):

> I find it passing strange that a person can be convicted or murder if death results from, say, his [or her] intentional breaking of another's arm, an action which, while undoubtedly involving the infliction of "really serious harm" and, as such, calling for severe punishment, would in most cases be unlikely to kill.

The definition of "grievous bodily harm" in the Code jurisdictions does go some way in alleviating Lord Edmund-Davies' concern because they include the requirement for the likelihood of the injury endangering life. A broken arm would not appear to fall within this particular definition, though such an injury may be seriously life threatening if the victim is elderly or very frail. In this sense, what constitutes "serious injury" is context-dependent: S Bronitt, "Spreading Disease and the Criminal Law" [1994] Crim LR 21 at 28, giving the example that a common cold may amount to "serious injury" where the person infected is suffering from AIDS and has a dysfunctional immune system.

---

23 *Criminal Code* (Qld), s 1; *Criminal Code* (WA), s 1; *R v Lobston* [1983] 2 Qd R 720 at 721 per Douglas J.

The Model Criminal Code Officers Committee (MCCOC) has recommended that this form of the fault element for murder be abolished: *Fatal Offences Against the Person*, Discussion Paper (June 1988), p 53. It states:

> The serious harm category of murder diminishes [the] intent-based approach by allowing
> something less than an intention to kill to constitute murder. The Committee's view is that
> murder should in some way be linked to death as the contemplated harm rather than
> merely serious harm.

The MCCOC suggests that killing in such circumstances should be viewed as manslaughter rather than murder. Several other law reform bodies have also suggested the abolition of an intention to cause grievous bodily harm as a separate fault element for murder.[24]

RECKLESSNESS AS TO CAUSING DEATH

The Australian Capital Territory, New South Wales, South Australia, Tasmania and Victoria include recklessness as to causing death within the fault elements for murder.[25] The test is whether the accused knew that death was a *probable* (as opposed to possible) consequence of his or her conduct: *R v Crabbe* (1985) 156 CLR 464. This test is subjective in that it must be proved that the accused rather than an "ordinary" or "reasonable" person knew of the likelihood of causing death. This is despite the fact that the *Criminal Code* (Tas) uses the words "ought to have known".[26] In Chapter 3, we explored how this subjective test for recklessness differs from the English approach taken in *Commissioner of Police of the Metropolis v Caldwell* [1982] AC 341: see p 184.

There are no statutory provisions in the Queensland, Western Australian and Northern Territory *Criminal Codes* dealing with recklessness as a fault element for murder. If intention is defined broadly in the "oblique" sense to include awareness of likelihood, then these jurisdictions may have a fault element that overlaps somewhat with the notion of recklessness. In *Vallance v The Queen* (1961) 108 CLR 56 a minority of the High Court took this broader approach to the term "intentional" in s 13 of the *Criminal Code* (Tas). However, as previously stated, the High Court has yet to provide a definition for "intention" and it would seem that at present, recklessness is not sufficient in Queensland, the Northern Territory and Western Australia. See further IG Campbell, "Recklessness in Intentional Murder Under the Australian Codes" (1986) 10 Crim LJ 3.

In the Australian Capital Territory and New South Wales the statutory references to reckless murder refer respectively to "reckless indifference to human life" and "reckless indifference to the probability of causing death": *Crimes Act* 1900 (ACT), s 12(1)(b); *Crimes Act* 1900 (NSW), s 18(1)(a). In Chapter 3, we outlined how the High Court in *R v Crabbe* (1985) 156 CLR 464 (at 470) was of the

---

24 Mitchell Committee, *Criminal Law and Penal Methods Reform Committee of South Australia* (Adelaide: Government Printer, 1977); Law Reform Commissioner of Victoria, *Criminal Procedure: Miscellaneous Reforms* (Melbourne: Law Reform Commission, 1974); House of Lords Select Committee, *Report of the Select Committee on Murder and Life Imprisonment* (London: HMSO, 1989) Law Reform Commission of Canada, *Homicide,* Working Paper No 33 (1984), pp 85-86.

25 *Crimes Act* 1900 (ACT), s 12(1)(b); *Crimes Act* 1900 (NSW), s 18(1)(a); *Criminal Code* (Tas), s 157(1)(b); *R v Crabbe* (1985) 156 CLR 464.

26 *Boughey v The Queen* (1986) 161 CLR 10 at 28-29 per Mason, Wilson and Deane JJ; *Simpson v The Queen* [1989] ALR 571.

opinion that it was unnecessary that the accused's knowledge of the probable consequences of his or her actions be accompanied by indifference. The Federal Court has held that in relation to the Australian Capital Territory position, the common law should apply and therefore it is immaterial whether or not the accused was indifferent to the risk: *R v Brown* (1987) 78 ALR 368. It is unclear, however, whether the common law applies to the New South Wales provision given that Mason CJ pointed out in *Royall v The Queen* (1990) 172 CLR 378 at 395 that s 18 departs from the common law in not having a category of awareness of the probability of grievous bodily harm. Leader-Elliott has argued that the common law should apply to the New South Wales provision, although this "flies in the face of conventional definitions of murder": "Recklessness in Murder" (1981) 5 Crim LJ 84 at 84.

The exact meaning of knowledge that death was a probable consequence is unclear. The risk of death must be more than a mere possibility (*R v Crabbe* (1985) 156 CLR 464 at 469), but the courts have been loath to apply any form of statistical analysis to the notion of probability. In *Boughey v The Queen* (1986) 161 CLR 10 it was argued that the words "likely to cause death" in s 157(1)(c) of the *Criminal Code* (Tas) meant that the likelihood of death was more likely than not. The High Court rejected this analysis and instead stated that the risk had to be "substantial" or "real and not remote". The Court then went on to say that "likely" and "a good chance" were synonyms for "probable". It could be argued that the words "likely" or "a good chance" lower the standard of the test somewhat. This case is further explored in Chapter 12, 'Case Studies: Death by Sexual Misadventure': p 586.

In the case of *R v Leslie Peter Faure* [1999] 2 VR 537, Brooking JA, with whom Winneke P and Ormiston JA agreed, stated that probability should not be approached in terms of "an odds on chance". *Faure's* case concerned a game of Russian roulette where the accused claimed that his girlfriend had agreed that they would fire no more than two shots at each other from a six-shot revolver. The cylinder was spun each time before the trigger was pulled. The victim pulled the trigger first, then the accused, followed by the victim again. The fourth time, when the accused fired, the revolver discharged and the victim was killed. Brooking JA stated (at 547) that the actual probability of the gun discharging was 671/1296. However, he took the view that the jury should be directed not in terms of percentages but that "probable" meant a substantial or real and not remote chance, whether or not it was more than 50%: at 551. In ordering a retrial, Brooking JA commented (at 552) that he would not expect a jury, if they believed the game took place, to have any difficulty in concluding that the accused's act was dangerous in the sense necessary for reckless murder.

As explored in Chapter 3, the High Court in *Crabbe's* case has relegated wilful blindness to an evidential role and it falls short of the fault element required for reckless murder: *R v Crabbe* (1985) 156 CLR 464 at 470-471; see p 183.

RECKLESSNESS AS TO INFLICTING GRIEVOUS BODILY HARM

Under the common law which applies in South Australia and Victoria, it is murder if the accused killed another, knowing that his or her conduct would probably cause grievous bodily harm: *R v Crabbe* (1985) 156 CLR 464. Reckless murder was justified in *Crabbe's* case on the basis that the "conduct of a person who does an act, knowing that death or grievous bodily harm is a probable consequence ... [is] just as blameworthy as the conduct of one who does an act intended to kill or do grievous bodily harm": at 469. However, one can argue that knowing that grievous bodily harm will probably result from conduct is not in the same category of blameworthiness as intending to kill. The MCCOC has recommended this particular fault element be abolished and that a person who kills in such circumstances be convicted of manslaughter: *Chapter 5 — Fatal Offences Against the Person*, Discussion Paper (1988), p 59.

4.2 CONSTRUCTIVE MURDER

All Australian jurisdictions apart from the Australian Capital Territory recognise a category of "constructive" murder — this is also known as the felony murder rule. This applies where a subjective fault element of intention or recklessness to kill or cause GBH is not present, but the circumstances are such that a fault element is "constructed" or that is, imputed to the accused. In general, this category of murder applies where the accused kills the victim during the course of a serious crime or violence, or, in South Australia and Victoria, whilst resisting lawful arrest: *R v Ryan and Walker* [1966] VR 553. The following Table sets out the differing requirements for this rule.

TABLE 2:
Constructive Murder

JURISDICTION AND RELEVANT LAW	COMMISSION OF CERTAIN OFFENCES
NSW *Crimes Act* 1900	in the course or furtherance of a crime punishable by penal servitude for life or for 25 years s 18(1)(a)
NT *Criminal Code*	prescribed offence provided it is of such a nature as to be likely to endanger life (s 161(1)(b)) administering any stupefying or overpowering thing/wilfully stopping the breath of any person for the purpose of assisting the commission of, or the flight of someone who has committed or attempted a prescribe offence (s 162(1)(c), (d)) prescribed offence is any crime punishable by 14 years imprisonment or longer, any crime of which an assault or an intention to do or cause any injury or damage is an element and which is punishable by imprisonment for seven years or more and offences relating to escape from custody (s 161(2))
QLD *Criminal Code*	act done in the prosecution of an unlawful purpose, where the act is of such a nature as to be likely to endanger human life (s 302(1)(b)) administering any stupefying or overpowering thing/wilfully stopping the breath of any person for the purpose of facilitating either the commission of a crime which is subject to arrest without warrant or the flight of an offender who has committed, or attempted to commit any such crime (s 302(1)(c))

Table 2 continued

JURISDICTION AND RELEVANT LAW	COMMISSION OF CERTAIN OFFENCES
SA common law *R v Van Beelen* (1973) 4 SASR 353	felony murder rule (common law) act involving violence or danger to another (*R v Van Beelen* (1973) 4 SASR 353)
TAS *Criminal Code*	any unlawful act or omission which the accused knew or ought to have know to be likely to cause death in the circumstances (s 157(1)(c)) administering any stupefying or overpowering thing/wilfully stopping the breath of any person for the purpose of assisting the commission of, or the flight of someone who has committed or attempted piracy, murder, escape or rescue from prison or lawful custody, resisting lawful apprehension, rape, forcible abduction, robbery, burglary and arson (ss 157(1)(e), (f), 157(2))
VIC *Crimes Act* 1958	act of violence done in the course or furtherance of a crime the necessary elements of which include violence and which is punishable by imprisonment for life or for 10 years or more s 3A
WA *Criminal Code*	act done in the prosecution of an unlawful purpose, where the act is of such a nature as to be likely to endanger human life (s 279(2)) administering any stupefying or overpowering thing/wilfully stopping the breath of any person for the purpose of facilitating either the commission of a crime which is subject to arrest without warrant or the flight of an offender who has committed, or attempted to commit any such crime (s 279(4), (5))

The physical elements for constructive murder are similar to that for murder and manslaughter in that the accused must have caused the death of the victim. However, there are further requirements in that the victim's death must be connected in some way to the commission of a specified offence.

In relation to the connection between the victim's death and the commission of an offence, the law in South Australia and Victoria requires that the death be caused "in the course or furtherance of" a specified offence: *Criminal Law Consolidation Act* 1935 (SA), s 12A; *Crimes Act* 1958 (Vic), s 3A. The New South Wales provision appears to be broader requiring that the act causing death be done "in an attempt to commit, or during or immediately after the commission by the accused, or an accomplice, of a crime punishable by penal servitude for life or for 25 years": *Crimes Act* 1900 (NSW), s 18(1)(a). However, in *Mraz v The Queen* (1955) 93 CLR 493 Williams, Webb and Taylor JJ required (at 505) that there be more than just a temporal connection in that the act causing death should be "associated with or done in the furtherance of the commission of" the felony.

Section 162(1)(b) of the *Criminal Code* (NT) refers to "committing or attempting to commit" the specified offence. A temporal connection would therefore seem to be sufficient. However, the Queensland and Western Australian provisions use the expression "in the prosecution of" an unlawful purpose, and require that the act causing death facilitate the relevant unlawful activity.[27] In Tasmania, the act causing death must have been committed "for the purpose of facilitating the commission of" the specified offence: *Criminal Code* (Tas), s 157(1)(d).

The specified offences vary between jurisdictions as set out in the above table. In South Australia, the conduct causing death must be violent or dangerous: *R v Van Beelen* (1973) 4 SASR 353; *Ryan v The Queen* (1967) 121 CLR 205. The words used in s 3A of the *Crimes Act* 1958 (Vic) are an offence "the necessary elements of which *include* violence". The meaning of this expression was considered by the Full Court of the Supreme Court of Victoria in *R v Butcher* [1986] VR 43. In that case, the accused had waved a knife at the victim whilst demanding money. The accused claimed the victim was stabbed when he ran at the accused. The victim died and the prosecution argued that this was a case of constructive murder in that the death occurred in the course of an armed robbery that was a crime, the necessary elements of which include violence. The accused argued that there was no act of violence as he had only intended to scare the victim and secondly, because robbery could be made out by a threat of force, it could not be said that violence was an essential element.

The Court held that armed robbery *was* a crime, the necessary elements of which include violence for the purpose of s 3A. It reasoned that at common law "violence" had not been restricted to physical force, but included threats of force and therefore robbery, in having as its element, a threat *or* use of force, must be a crime of violence. There is no equivalent requirement that the offence be violent in other jurisdictions. Section 18(1)(a) of the *Crimes Act* 1900 (NSW) states that the offence must be a crime punishable by life imprisonment or a maximum of 25 years in prison. Thus in Victoria, only a small number of crimes will be relevant to constructive murder.

In Queensland and Western Australia, the act performed in the prosecution of an unlawful purpose must be of a nature likely to endanger human life: *Criminal Code* (Qld), s 302(1)(b); *Criminal Code* (WA), s 279(2). Similarly, in the Northern Territory, the act done when committing an offence that carries a maximum penalty of 14 years imprisonment or seven years where assault, intention to cause injury or damage to property is an element, must be of such a nature as to be likely to endanger life: *Criminal Code* (NT), s 162(1)(b). Section 157(1)(d), (2) of the *Criminal Code* (Tas) states that the accused must have intended to inflict grievous bodily harm for the purpose of facilitating crimes such as murder, rape and robbery. In South Australia and Victoria, the common law rule that it is murder to cause death by a violent act whilst resisting arrest still remains: *R v Ryan and Walker* [1966] VR 553. The Victorian Supreme Court set out the rule (at 564) as follows:

> [T]he killing of a person by the intentional use of force, knowingly to prevent such person from making an arrest which he [or she] is authorised by common law to make, is murder even if the person using the force did not intend to kill or do grievous bodily harm, and even if he [or she] did not foresee that he [or she] was likely to do so.

---

27 *Criminal Code* (Qld), s 302(1)(b); *Criminal Code* (WA), s 279(2).

The justification for dispensing with the subjective fault element for murder in the circumstances outlined, is said to be that the blameworthiness accompanying the killing is supplied by the foundational offence as illustrated in *Mraz v The Queen* (1955) 93 CLR 493 at 505 per Williams, Webb and Taylor JJ:

> If upon the evidence the jury was prepared to conclude that the crime of rape had been committed and that the acts of the appellant associated with or done in the furtherance of his purpose had caused the death, it was unnecessary that they should embark upon an independent inquiry to ascertain whether those acts were malicious. The very fact that they were so associated or so done established beyond question that they were done "of malice". On the other hand unless the jury was satisfied that rape had taken place the appellant, as the learned trial judge pointed out, should have been acquitted for, in those circumstances, there was no evidence of any act of the accused amounting either to murder or manslaughter.

There has been a vast amount of criticism of constructive murder.[28] Constructive murder in the guise of the common law felony murder rule was repealed in England by s 1(2) of the *Homicide Act* 1957 (UK) following a recommendation by the *Royal Commission on Capital Punishment: Report* (London: HMSO, 1953), para 111. Constructive murder provisions in the Canadian *Criminal Code* have also been struck down by the Supreme Court of Canada as unconstitutional.[29] In *Vaillancourt v The Queen* [1987] 2 SCR 636 (at 653) Lamer J writing for himself and three other judges, noted that murder is a serious crime with a corresponding "special stigma". He further stated (at 654):

> I am presently of the view that it is a principle of fundamental justice that a conviction for murder cannot rest on anything less than proof beyond a reasonable doubt of subjective foresight.

This notion that constructive murder offends against the fundamental principle of justice that serious crimes require a subjective fault element, forms the basis for much criticism of the doctrine. The Model Criminal Code Officers Committee (MCCOC) has echoed other Law Reform Committees' calls for its abolition.[30] The MCCOC has stated in *Chapter 5: Fatal Offences Against the Person*, Discussion Paper (1998), p 63:

> The lack of intention or other culpable state of mind for murder on behalf of the person committing the felony or seeking to escape underlies the inappropriateness of this doctrine. To equate accidental killings with murder is contrary to the Committee's fault-based approach to determining culpability. In as far as the law of fatal offences is concerned, persons who kill while committing a felony or attempting to escape should be

---

28 For example, D Lanham "Felony Murder — Ancient and Modern" (1983) 7 Crim LJ 90; J Willis, "Felony Murder at Common Law in Australia" (1977) 1 Crim LJ 231.

29 *Vaillancourt v The Queen* [1987] 2 SCR 636; *R v Martineau* (1990) 58 CCC (3d) 353. See also I Grant, "The Impact of *Vaillancourt v The Queen* on Canadian Criminal Law" (1990) 28 (2) *Alberta Law Review* 443.

30 Model Criminal Code Officers Committee, *Chapter 5: Fatal Offences Against the Person*, Discussion Paper (1998), p 65; Victorian Law Reform Commission, *Homicide*, Report 40 (1991); The Criminal Law and Penal Methods Reform Committee of South Australia, *The Substantive Criminal Law*, Fourth Report (the Mitchell Committee), 1977.

treated in the same way as any other person. If they intended to kill or are reckless as to death they will be convicted of murder pursuant to the existing rules regarding intentional and reckless killing. In the absence of these circumstances — where the death is truly accidental — murder should not be an issue. In these cases, manslaughter by gross negligence may be an appropriate charge but in any event the defendant can be prosecuted for the offence he or she intended to commit.

4.3 MANSLAUGHTER

Where an unlawful killing does not amount to murder, it may nevertheless constitute manslaughter.[31] Traditionally, the two main categories of manslaughter have been divided into "voluntary" and "involuntary" manslaughter where "voluntary" manslaughter refers to the situation where an accused commits murder, but is convicted of manslaughter due to mitigating circumstances such as provocation, diminished responsibility or in pursuance of a suicide pact. "Involuntary" manslaughter refers to unlawful killing where the accused caused the death of the victim but did not possess the relevant fault element for murder.

The terms "voluntary" and "involuntary" are highly misleading in regard to manslaughter. As outlined in Chapter 3, p 163, the term "involuntary" generally refers to conduct that is accidental or a reflex action because it is "unwilled". This is not the case with involuntary manslaughter.

We have already outlined those defences to murder that may lead to a finding of manslaughter: see Ch 5. This section deals with two main categories of manslaughter, that of unlawful and dangerous act manslaughter and negligent manslaughter. A third category, battery manslaughter was abolished by the High Court in *Wilson v The Queen* (1992) 174 CLR 313. Manslaughter at common law is broadly the same as under the *Criminal Codes* which define manslaughter as unlawful killing not amounting to murder.[32] The Northern Territory, however, does not have a category of unlawful and dangerous act manslaughter.

The two categories of unlawful and dangerous act manslaughter and negligent manslaughter may overlap. The accused may be charged with the one generic offence of manslaughter and then it is for the prosecution to produce evidence to show liability falling into one or both categories.

UNLAWFUL AND DANGEROUS ACT MANSLAUGHTER

At common law, an unlawful and dangerous act causing death will render an accused liable for manslaughter: *R v Larkin* [1943] 1 All ER 217 at 219 per Humphreys J; *Bedkinov* (1997) 95 A Crim R 200. In practice, it is generally an assault leading to death that gives rise to liability under this head.[33]

The early common law provided that for a conviction of manslaughter all that was required was that the accused caused the death of another by an unlawful act. In that respect it was similar to

---

31 *Crimes Act* 1900 (ACT), s 15(1); *Crimes Act* 1900 (NSW), s 18(1)(b); *Criminal Code* (NT), s 163; *Criminal Code* (Qld), s 303; *Criminal Code* (Tas), s 159; *Criminal Code* (WA), s 280. The common law exists in South Australia and Victoria.

32 *Criminal Code* (NT), s 163; *Criminal Code* (Qld), s 300; *Criminal Code* (Tas), s 159; *Criminal Code* (WA), s 277.

33 For example, *R v Wills* [1983] 2 VR 201; *R v Holzer* [1968] VR 481; *R v Simpson* (1959) 76 WN (NSW) 589; *R v Larkin* [1943] KB 174; *R v Jarmain* [1945] 2 All ER 613: *Kwaku Mensah v The Queen* [1946] AC 83.

the felony murder rule, except that the unlawful act did not have to be a felony. The unlawful act doctrine may well have originated as a constructive form of liability: *Wilson v The Queen* (1992) 174 CLR 313 at 319-323 per Mason CJ, Toohey, Gaudron and McHugh JJ. However, in the 19th century the English courts restricted its operation to unlawful acts causing death which were also *dangerous* in the sense of "likely to injure another person": *R v Larkin* [1943] KB 174; *R v Church* [1966] 1 QB 59. The existence of this category of manslaughter by an unlawful and dangerous act was affirmed in England by the House of Lords in *DPP v Newbury & Jones* [1977] AC 500.

There is no separate category of unlawful and dangerous act manslaughter set out in the *Criminal Codes*. However, the provisions relating to unlawful killing in Queensland, Tasmania and Western Australia have been interpreted as including a class of manslaughter consistent with unlawful and dangerous act manslaughter at common law.[34] In Queensland and Western Australia, it is the intentional infliction of harm less than grievous bodily harm that gives rise to manslaughter: *Criminal Code* (Qld), s 291; *Criminal Code* (WA), s 268. Section 156(2)(c) of the *Criminal Code* (Tas) states that it is culpable homicide to kill "by any unlawful act". This has been interpreted along with s 159(1) as meaning that manslaughter arises where death is caused by an unlawful and dangerous act.[35] The common law tests for unlawfulness and dangerousness are relevant in this regard.[36] Section 31 of the *Criminal Code* (NT) excludes this category of manslaughter. Manslaughter is instead confined to situations where the death was intended or foreseen by the accused as possible and, where the death was foreseen as possible but not intended, a reasonable person in similar circumstances would not have proceeded with the conduct.

As with all unlawful killings, the prosecution must prove beyond reasonable doubt that the accused's act *caused* the victim's death: see above, p 479. This question generally precedes the exploration of whether or not the accused's act was unlawful and dangerous.

Unlawful Act

The act must be unlawful in the sense that it is a criminal act rather than merely a civil wrong.[37] As stated above, generally this has been an assault, but other offences which have been treated as unlawful for the purpose of this head of manslaughter include attempted assault,[38] unlawful wounding,[39] attempted robbery,[40] burglary,[41] arson,[42] abortion,[43] and discharging a firearm in a public place.[44]

---

34 *Pemble v The Queen* (1971) 124 CLR 107 at 122 per Barwick CJ; *Boughey v The Queen* (1986) 161 CLR 10 at 40 per Brennan J; *R v Van Den Bend* (1994) 170 CLR 137.

35 *R v Phillips* (1971) 45 ALJR 467; *R v Rau* [1972] Tas SR 59; *R v Davis* [1955] Tas SR 52 at 55 per Crisp J; *R v McCallum* [1969] Tas SR 73.

36 *Boughey v The Queen* (1986) 161 CLR 10 at 34, 40 per Brennan J; *R v Rau* [1972] Tas SR 59; *R v McCallum* [1969] Tas SR 73; *Murray v The Queen* [1962] Tas SR 170.

37 *Pemble v The Queen* (1971) 124 CLR 107 at 122 per Barwick CJ; *R v Haywood* [1971] VR 755; *R v Bush* [1970] 3 NSWR 500 at 504; *R v Davis* [1955] Tas SR 52; *R v Lamb* [1967] 2 QB 981.

38 *Pemble v The Queen* (1971) 124 CLR 107 at 123 per Barwick CJ, at 137 per Windeyer J.

39 *R v McCallum* [1969] Tas SR 73.

40 *R v Dawson* (1985) 81 Cr App R 150.

41 *R v Watson* [1989] 1 WLR 684.

42 *R v Goodfellow* (1986) 83 Cr App R 23.

43 *R v Creamer* [1966] 1 QB 72; *R v Buck* (1960) 44 Cr App R 213.

44 *Pemble v The Queen* (1971) 124 CLR 107 at 127 per McTiernan J; *R v Haywood* [1971] VR 755 at 758 per Crockett J.

Offences of negligence or carelessness such as dangerous driving have however been excluded from the category of unlawful act. In *Andrews v DPP* [1937] AC 576, Lord Atkins stated (at 585):

> There is an obvious difference in the law of manslaughter between doing an unlawful act
> and doing a lawful act with a degree of carelessness which the Legislature makes criminal.
> If it were otherwise a man [or woman] who killed another while driving without due care
> and attention would ex necessitate commit manslaughter.

If a death occurs in such circumstances, it is generally charged as culpable driving or negligent manslaughter.

It is important that the prosecution prove each element of the unlawful act, including the requisite fault element, if required by the offence. In *R v Lamb* [1967] 2 QB 981 the accused shot and killed his best friend whilst fooling around with a revolver. It was conceded that the accused was acting in jest, with no intention to harm the victim. Neither the accused nor the victim understood the operation of the revolver, that a shot may be fired even though the firing chamber may be empty: the chamber rotates as the trigger is pulled. The trial judge was of the opinion that the pulling of the trigger amounted to an unlawful act even though there was no intent to alarm or intent to injure. On appeal, the English Court of Appeal held that there was no evidence of an assault of any kind because there was no intention to commit an assault.

The courts have sometimes taken a broad approach to what may be considered unlawful. In *R v Cato* [1976] 1 WLR 110 the English Court of Appeal appeared to find an act unlawful simply because it was dangerous. In that case, the accused and his friend injected each other a number of times with heroin. Both became very ill and the friend died. The accused was convicted of manslaughter. On appeal, it was argued that there was no unlawful act because the administration of a drug to another with consent did not of itself amount to an offence. The Court of Appeal upheld the accused's conviction for manslaughter stating (at 118, per Lord Widgery) that "the unlawful act would be described as injecting the deceased ... with a mixture of heroin and water which at the time of the injection and for the purposes of the injection the accused had unlawfully taken into his possession". This reasoning is difficult to follow given that the possession of the heroin did not cause the death and the actual administration of heroin was not a crime. It was perhaps the fact that the act was dangerous that influenced the Court's finding, though this approach is difficult to reconcile with the requirement that "unlawful" and "dangerous" are distinct requirements.

Another case which shows disparate approaches to the "unlawfulness" element is *Pemble v The Queen* (1971) 124 CLR 107. In that case, the accused had approached his ex-lover from behind carrying a sawn-off rifle. The rifle discharged and the victim died of a wound to her head. The accused argued that he had only wanted to frighten the victim and that the rifle had accidentally discharged. The accused was convicted of murder. On appeal to the High Court, the Court held that the trial judge's direction to the jury had been defective and a majority of three to two judges substituted a verdict of manslaughter.

However, those three judges took different views as to what constituted the unlawful act. Barwick CJ categorised the unlawful act as an *attempted* assault (there was evidence that the victim had not been aware of the gun being pointed at her and so had not been assaulted): *Pemble v The*

Queen (1971) 124 CLR 107 at 122. Windeyer J agreed with the judgment of Barwick CJ that there should be a verdict of manslaughter, but saw it as manslaughter by gross negligence: at 137-139. McTiernan J stated (at 127) that the accused had committed the unlawful act of discharging a firearm in a public place. The dissenting judges, Menzies and Owen JJ, held that a new trial should be ordered and were of the opinion that there has been no unlawful act committed given that the accused had not committed an assault.

Given the diversity of opinion in *Pemble*, it is questionable whether the requirement of unlawfulness is workable. The Victorian Law Reform Commission in *Homicide*, Report No 40 (1991) has stated (p 113):

> The requirement of unlawfulness has nothing relevant to add. Dangerousness is the key
> element here, and it is assessed by an objective test. This head of manslaughter is
> therefore already based on negligence.

The Commission accordingly suggested merging the two categories of manslaughter into one category of "dangerous act or omission manslaughter": p 116. This proposal is considered later in the perspectives section on the future of manslaughter.

Dangerous Act

The act must not only be unlawful but also dangerous to ground a conviction for manslaughter under this head. The High Court in *Wilson v The Queen* (1992) 174 CLR 313 laid down (per Mason CJ, Toohey, Gaudron and McHugh JJ) the common law test of dangerousness as follows at 335:

> In the end the jury [has] to determine whether the [accused's act in relation to] the
> deceased was, from the standpoint of a reasonable person, an act carrying with it an
> appreciable risk of serious injury to the deceased.

This test departs slightly from the test set out by Smith J in the Victorian case of *R v Holzer* [1968] VR 481 at 482 in that "an appreciable risk of *really* serious injury" has been changed to the lesser standard of "an appreciable risk of serious injury". This lesser standard meant that the pre-existing category of "battery manslaughter" whereby an accused could be convicted of manslaughter based on an intention to cause some physical injury not merely of a trivial or negligible nature was no longer necessary: *Wilson v The Queen* (1992) 174 CLR 313 at 342.

The test for assessing dangerousness is an objective one. The prosecution therefore need not prove that the accused knew that the act was dangerous.[45] In *R v Wills* [1983] 2 VR 201 at 214 Fullagar J stated that it is inappropriate to attach to the reasonable person "anything personal" to the accused.

"Serious injury" means more than trivial or negligible injury.[46] There is a suggestion that psychiatric harm will not be sufficient: *R v Dawson* (1985) 81 Cr App R 150 (CA). The meaning of an "appreciable risk" of serious injury was not defined in *Wilson's* case. What appears to be required is a risk that is significant rather than remote.

---

45 *Coomer* (1989) 40 A Crim R 417; *Zikovic* (1985) 17 A Crim R 396; *R v Wills* [1983] VR 201; *R v McCallum* [1969]
    Tas SR 73.

46 *Wilson v The Queen* (1992) 174 CLR 313 at 333-334 per Mason CJ, Toohey, Gaudron and McHugh JJ.

NEGLIGENT MANSLAUGHTER

A killing that occurs through gross negligence amounts to manslaughter in all jurisdictions.[47] The wording differs slightly across jurisdictions, but the general gist of the crime is the same. At common law, the test is whether there was "a great falling short of the standard of care" that a reasonable person would have exercised, involving "such a high risk that death or grievous bodily harm would follow that the doing of the act merited criminal punishment": *Nydam v The Queen* [1977] VR 430 at 445 per Young CJ, McInerney J and Crockett J (the Full Court).

In the Northern Territory, Queensland and Western Australia, a killing that occurs in breach of a statutory duty to avoid danger or preserve human life will constitute manslaughter if the breach is criminally negligent. The requirement of criminal negligence is not expressly stated in the Codes but has been implied: *R v Scarth* [1945] St R Qd 38; *Callaghan v The Queen* (1952) 87 CLR 115. Section 156(2)(b) of the *Criminal Code* (Tas) makes it culpable homicide where there is an omission amounting to "culpable negligence" to perform a duty to preserve human life.

In general, negligent manslaughter requires the prosecution to prove that there was:

▬▬ **a duty of care owed by the accused to the victim; and**

▬▬ **a breach of the high standard of care required.**

Duty of Care

Where the death of a victim is caused by an act, the prosecution must prove that the accused was under a general duty to act in such a way as not to cause harm to others. A general duty not to cause harm exists at common law.[48] In Queensland, Tasmania and Western Australia, the accused must have breached the duty to avoid danger or to preserve life.[49]

Where an accused *omits* to act in a manner that causes the victim's death, criminal liability will only be imposed where the accused was under a duty to act. As stated in Chapter 3 (see p 162), a duty to act may arise at common law as a result of a family relationship between the parties[50] or as a result of a person undertaking to care for another who is unable to care for him or herself.[51] In *R v Miller* [1983] 2 AC 161 Lord Diplock also referred (at 176) to there being "no rational ground for excluding from conduct capable of giving rise to criminal liability conduct which consists of failing to take measures that lie within one's power to counter act a danger that one has oneself created". Statutory examples of the imposition of a duty to act include a duty to provide necessities.[52]

---

47 *Criminal Code* (NT), s 163; *Criminal Code* (Qld), s 303; *Criminal Code* (Tas), s 156(2)(b); *Criminal Code* (WA), s 280; *Nydam v The Queen* [1977] VR 430.

48 *R v Doherty* (1887) 16 Cox CC 206 at 309 per Stephen J; implicit in *Nydam v The Queen* [1977] VR 430 at 445 per the Court.

49 *Criminal Code* (NT), ss 149-155; *Criminal Code* (Qld), s 289; *Criminal Code* (Tas), s 150; *Criminal Code* (WA), s 266. The Northern Territory provision lacks such a mandatory emphasis.

50 *R v Russell* [1933] VLR 59; *R v Clarke and Wilton* [1959] VR 645.

51 *R v Instan* [1893] 1 QB 450; (1893) 17 Cox CC 602; *Lee v The Queen* (1917) 13 Cr App R 39 at 41 per Darling J; *Gibbins v The Queen* (1918) 13 Cr App R 134; *R v Stone and Dobinson* [1977] QB 354; (1976) 64 Cr App R 186; *Taktak* (1988) 34 A Crim R 334.

52 *Crimes Act* 1900 (NSW), s 44; *Criminal Code* (NT), s 183; *Criminal Code* (Qld), s 285; *Criminal Law Consolidation Act* 1935 (SA), s 30; *Criminal Code* (Tas), s 144; *Criminal Code* (WA), s 262.

The issues involved in imposing liability for omissions are taken up later in the text: see p 512.

Standard of Care

The standard of care for negligent manslaughter is an objective standard in that it is based on the concept of a "reasonable" person in the same situation as the accused.[53] At common law, this is linked to the risk of causing death or grievous bodily harm,[54] whilst in the Northern Territory, Queensland, Tasmania and Western Australia, it is linked to the failure to perform a relevant statutory duty.[55]

There has been some confusion in the case law as to the emphasis that should be placed on whether or not the accused foresaw the likelihood or possibility of causing grievous bodily harm, thus importing a subjective element into the standard of care. Several cases seem to suggest that the state of mind of the accused is a relevant factor to be taken into account. In *Andrews v DPP* [1937] AC 573 Lord Atkin stated (at 583) that "a very high degree of negligence is required to be proved before the felony is established. Probably of all the epithets that can be applied 'reckless' most nearly covers the case".

This reference to recklessness was picked up in several subsequent cases. In *R v Lamb* [1967] 2 QB 981 Sachs LJ stated (at 990):

> When the gravamen of a charge is criminal negligence — often referred to as recklessness — of the accused, the jury have to consider among other matters the state of his [or her] mind, and that includes the question of whether or not he [or she] thought that that which he [or she] was doing was safe.

This may be regarded as importing a subjective element into manslaughter by criminal negligence. However, this view was rejected in England in *DPP v Newbury and Jones* [1976] 2 WLR 918. In that case, Lord Salmon stated that *Lamb's* case should not be taken as supporting the idea that the correct test is anything but objective. He stated (at 992) that "the test is not did the accused recognise that it was too dangerous but would all sober and reasonable people recognise its danger".

The confusion over the precise meaning of negligence persisted in *R v Stone & Dobinson* [1977] 1 QB 354. The Court of Appeal (at 363 per Lane LJ) referred to *Andrews'* case and concluded that the accused's failure to act must have been reckless:

> that is to say a reckless disregard of danger to the health and welfare of the infirm person. Mere inadvertence is not enough. The defendant must be proved to have been indifferent to an obvious risk of injury to health or actually have foreseen the risk but to have determined nevertheless to run it.

---

53   *Nydam v The Queen* [1977] VR 430 at 439-446 rejecting a subjective standard referred to by Smith J in *R v Holzer* [1968] VR 481.

54   *Nydam v The Queen* [1977] VR 430.

55   *Criminal Code* (NT), ss 150, 151; *Criminal Code* (Qld), s 289; *Criminal Code* (WA), s 266; *Criminal Code* (Tas), s 150.

Stone and Dobinson's case was cited in *R v Taktak* (1988) 14 NSWLR 226. In that case, Yeldham J (at 247-248) appeared to endorse the above passage in *Stone and Dobinson* that suggested that the test was subjective and that the defendant must have "a reckless disregard to the health and welfare of the infirm person": Loveday J concurring. However, this is of limited weight given that *Nydam v The Queen* [1977] VR 430 was not discussed.

In the Northern Territory, the approach in *Stone and Dobinson* holds sway in that the accused must have foreseen death as a possible consequence of the breach of the duty of care.[56] However, this approach imposing the necessity of proving foreseeability is *not* good law in the other Australian jurisdictions for two reasons. First, the comments in *Stone and Dobinson's* case suggest that the standard of care is partially subjective and this approach was expressly rejected in *Taylor* (1983) 9 A Crim R 358. Secondly, *Stone and Dobinson's* case suggests that the risk associated with the defendant's conduct (whether determined objectively or subjectively) need only be of "injury to health or welfare", rather than "death or grievous bodily harm".

Recklessness should not be treated as a synonym for criminal negligence. In Australia, the better view is that adopted by the Victorian Court of Appeal in *Taylor's* case, namely that the accused's state of mind is irrelevant to the determination of criminal negligence. In that case, the accused had administered a lethal dosage of a sedative to her hyperactive six-year-old child. The normal dose had been 5 ml but her doctor had told the accused that it was safe to use a "higher dosage" or "a little bit more than 5 ml". The accused was convicted and appealed. The issue on appeal was as follows: what *circumstances* are relevant to the determination that the accused's conduct, which caused the death, was criminally negligent?

The Court held that the view expressed in *Lamb's* case that the accused's actual state of mind is relevant to criminal negligence is *not* good law in either England or Victoria. Whether the acts of the accused were criminally negligent is to be objectively determined, without reference to the particular belief of the accused. However the Court of Appeal held that the trial judge's direction had not been deficient. The essential issue was whether a reasonable hypothetical person, placed in the same circumstances as the accused (particularly having regard to the advice given by the doctor), would have appreciated the probability of death or serious bodily harm as a result of their actions. The jury was entitled to consider whether a reasonable person, in the accused's position, might have entertained the mistaken belief held by the accused.

The irrelevance of the accused's state of mind to "gross negligence" was recently confirmed by the House of Lords in the context of manslaughter in *R v Adomako* [1995] 1 AC 171. This leads on to the next question concerning the extent to which the particular characteristics and circumstances of the accused are to be attributed to the reasonable person. In Chapter 3, we discussed how in *R v Stone and Dobinson* [1977] 1 QB 354 the objective standard posed severe problems for the accused who were unable to reach the standards of the reasonable person because of inherent physical and intellectual disabilities: see p 186. In Tasmania, the age of the accused has been taken into account (*R v Holness* [1970] Tas SR 74 (SC)), but it appears that other physical characteristics of the accused will be ignored. On the other hand, if the accused has specialist knowledge of some type, the test will become that of a "reasonable person with that knowledge": *R v Wills* [1983] 2 VR 201.

---

56 *Criminal Code* (NT), s 31. This is the case except where ss 154-155 apply. The High Court examined the relationship between s 31 and murder proscribed in s 162(1)(a) in *Charlie v The Queen* (1999) 162 ALR 463.

This area again shows the difficulties with applying a reasonable or ordinary person standard. The Victorian Law Reform Commission in *Homicide*, Report No 40 (1991) has recommended (at 116) that any person charged with manslaughter by criminal negligence should be afforded a defence if by reason of some physical or intellectual disability he or she could not reach the standard expected from non-disabled persons. The Model Criminal Code Officers Committee (MCCOC) has also suggested that the objective standard for negligence "require the reasonable person to step into the shoes of the [accused] at the relevant time": *Chapter 5 — Fatal Offences Against the Person*, Discussion Paper (1998), p 153.

Breach of Duty of Care

The degree of negligence required to establish criminal liability is higher than that for the civil law.[57] Lord Atkin in *Andrews v DPP (UK)* [1937] AC 576 reviewed the 19th century cases that had defined this category of manslaughter using epithets such as "criminal misconduct" and "criminal inattention". Lord Atkin (at 582) conceded that the use of the "word 'criminal' in any attempt to define a crime is perhaps not the most helpful". However, these early definitions had intended to convey that only a very high degree of negligence would suffice:

> Simple lack of care such as will constitute civil liability is not enough: for the purposes of
> the criminal law there are degrees of negligence: and a very high degree of negligence is
> required to be proved before the felony is established.[58]

In *Nydam v The Queen* [1977] VR 430 at 445, the Full Court of the Victorian Supreme Court referred to "a great falling short of the standard of care" involving a high risk of death or serious harm. Just what will amount to "a great falling short" is unclear and is perhaps incapable of judicial definition.

The principles of criminal or gross negligence have been examined by the House of Lords in *R v Adomako* [1995] 1 AC 171. Lord Mackay LC held (at 187) that the "ordinary principles of the law of negligence" apply to ascertain whether or not the accused had been in breach of a duty of care and whether that breach caused the victim's death. The jury must consider whether that breach constituted "gross negligence". Lord Mackay LC observed (at 187) that the question for the jury is whether the departure from the proper standards involved "a risk of death ... such that it should be judged criminal". This formulation seems to be more restrictive than *Nydam*, excluding negligence in cases involving a risk of serious bodily injury only.

PERSPECTIVES

Merging the Divisions in Manslaughter

In relation to manslaughter the courts are primarily concerned with conduct that, objectively speaking, involves a *high risk of death or serious harm*. There is accordingly a high degree of overlap between the categories of unlawful and dangerous act manslaughter and negligent manslaughter. Waller and Williams suggest that "it would not require a very bold judicial step to treat unlawful and dangerous act manslaughter as merging into negligent manslaughter.

---

57 *Callaghan v The Queen* (1952) 87 CLR 115; *R v White* (1951) 51 SR (NSW) 188; *Re Lamperd* (1983) 63 FLR 470; *Evgeniou v The Queen* [1965] ALR 209; *Mamote-Kulang of Tamagot v The Queen* (1964) 111 CLR 62.

58 *Andrews v DPP* [1937] AC 576 at 583.

Certainly such a development would be desirable": *Brett, Waller and Williams: Criminal Law — Cases and Materials* (8th ed, Sydney: Butt, 1997), at 6.18, p 267.

In *R v Wills* [1983] 2 VR 201 Lush J concluded (at 212):

> The unlawfulness of the [unlawful and dangerous] act stands parallel with criminal negligence of negligent manslaughter, and equally the risk factor relevant to manslaughter by unlawful and dangerous act stands as an objective consideration parallel with the objective danger assessment of negligent manslaughter.

This overlap led to the Victorian Law Reform Commission's recommendation that there should be one category of "dangerous act or omission manslaughter": *Homicide*, Report No 40 (1991) Recommendation 33, p 132. The Commission proposed that the test should be whether or not the accused performed an act in gross breach of duty (or omitted to do an act where there was a duty to act) which a reasonable person would have realised exposed another to a substantial and unjustifiable risk of life-endangering injury: Recommendation 34, p 132.

Although the High Court in *Wilson v The Queen* (1992) 174 CLR 313 acknowledged that there have been calls to replace the two remaining categories with one, the majority rejected this because the test for dangerousness between the categories of manslaughter differs in two ways. First, for manslaughter by criminal negligence, the test is a *high* risk that death or grievous bodily harm would follow: *Nydam v DPP* [1977] VR 430 at 445. In contrast, unlawful and dangerous act manslaughter requires an appreciable risk of serious injury. However, if the unamended test in *R v Holzer* [1968] VR 481 is applied ("*really* serious harm") the difference becomes insignificant. Secondly, for manslaughter by criminal negligence, the accused's act need not be unlawful: *Andrews v DPP* [1937] AC 576; see also *R v Larkin* [1942] 1 All ER 217. However, this distinction is illusory as there is no requirement (or restriction) that the accused's behaviour must *not* be criminal.

The MCCOC, like the Victorian Law Reform Commission, has suggested abolishing unlawful and dangerous act manslaughter and replacing negligent manslaughter with the offence of "dangerous conduct causing death": *Chapter 5 — Fatal Offences Against the Person*, Discussion Paper (1998), pp 145-160. An intention to cause or recklessness about causing serious harm would form the basis of a separate general category of manslaughter: pp 160-161. The MCCOC has stated (at 153):

> There are a number of coincidental reasons which make it attractive to retain some form of unlawful homicide by gross negligence as an offence. It signals to society acceptable standards of behaviour and, at the same time, importantly acts to re-enforce the value of human life. It also significantly overlaps with manslaughter by dangerous and unlawful act, thus discouraging people from dangerous unlawful conduct. Therefore abolition of the offence of manslaughter by dangerous and unlawful act is made less consequential in the result if unlawful homicide by gross negligence continues to be an offence.

This recommendation is logical and sensible. Perhaps the real problem lies in setting out the standard to be applied in an offence of "dangerous conduct causing death". We have already outlined the problems with having a "reasonable person" standard that takes no account of the characteristics of the accused that bear on his or her ability to comply with that objective standard. The MCCOC has suggested that the objective standards for negligence "require the reasonable person to step into the shoes of the [accused] at the relevant time": p 153. This would place a more onerous standard on those with professional skills and also take into account the characteristics of those with mental and/or physical disabilities. This suggestion may go some way in reforming the problematic concept of the "reasonable person".

5. CULPABLE DRIVING

All Australian jurisdictions, with the exception of the Northern Territory, have created specific offences dealing with driving causing death: see Table 3. Instances of dangerous driving may sometimes be prosecuted under s 154 of the *Criminal Code* (NT) which deals with "dangerous acts or omissions".

Technically, where a driver causes a victim's death in circumstances that amount to manslaughter at common law or under the Codes, he or she should be convicted of manslaughter: *R v Pullman* (1991) 25 NSWLR 89. However, the statutory culpable driving offences have been created because juries have traditionally been viewed as reluctant to convict drivers of negligent manslaughter: MCCOC, *Chapter 5 — Fatal Offences Against the Person,* Discussion Paper (1998), p 161 and references therein.

The following Table sets out the elements of culpable driving causing death or grievous bodily harm.

TABLE 3:

Culpable Driving Causing Death

JURISDICTION AND RELEVANT LAW	OFFENCE
ACT *Crimes Act* 1900	offence where motor vehicle is driven negligently or while under the influence of alcohol, or a drug, to such an extent as to be incapable of having proper control of the vehicle s 29
NSW *Crimes Act* 1900	offence where motor vehicle driven by the accused causes death or grievous bodily harm and at the time of the impact, the accused is driving under the influence of alcohol or a drug, or at a dangerous speed or in a dangerous manner (s 52A) offence of predatory driving (s 51A)
NT *Criminal Code*	general offence where act or omission causes serious danger to the life, health or safety of any person s 154

Table 3 continued

JURISDICTION AND RELEVANT LAW	OFFENCE
QLD *Criminal Code*	a person who operates a vehicle dangerously in any place commits a misdemeanour s 328A
SA *Criminal Law Consolidation Act* 1935	offence where a person drives a motor vehicle in a culpably negligent manner, recklessly, or at a speed or in a manner dangerous to the public s 19A(1)
TAS *Criminal Code*	offence where any person causes the death of another by the driving of a motor vehicle at a speed or in a manner which is dangerous to the public s 167A
VIC *Crimes Act* 1958	offence where any person causes the death of another by driving a motor vehicle recklessly, negligently or whilst under the influence of alcohol or a drug to such an extent as to be incapable of having proper control of the vehicle s 318
WA *Road Traffic Act* 1974	offence where a person causes the death of another by driving a motor vehicle in a manner that is dangerous to the public or to any person s 59

The main question concerning culpable driving causing death as a sub-category of unlawful killing is whether or not it should exist at all. Section 318 of the *Crimes Act* 1958 (Vic) for example, provides four circumstances of culpability in relation to a victim's death, that of driving recklessly, negligently or while under the influence of alcohol or a drug so as to be incapable of having proper control of the car. In 1991, the Law Reform Commission of Victoria noted in *Death Caused by Dangerous Driving*, Discussion Paper 21 (July 1991), p 15:

> The main difficulty with retaining a separate offence of causing death by culpable driving is
> that it appears to give entirely the wrong message to the community — that killing while
> using a motor vehicle is not as serious as killing while using something else.

The Commission proposed (at 21) that this separate offence be abolished and situations of causing death by culpable driving be charged as reckless murder or manslaughter. It also proposed a range of lesser alternative offences to cover cases where the accused's liability was less than these offences.

Alldridge in "Manslaughter and Causing Death by Driving Recklessly" (1980) 144 *Justice of the Peace* 569 (at 571) echoed the Law Reform Commission of Victoria in stating:

> [I]t is not a principle of English jurisprudence that offences ought to be named palliatively
> so as to increase the conviction rate, nor is it just that one who kills with a car should be
> exposed to a lower maximum penalty than one who, no more culpably, kills otherwise.

The New South Wales provision, on the other hand, goes further than simply making a "palliative" name change for negligent manslaughter. The offence of dangerous driving causing death is one of strict liability: *Crimes Act* 1900 (NSW), s 52A; *Jiminez v The Queen* (1992) 173 CLR 572. That is, an accused will be guilty unless the defence of reasonable mistake of fact is made out. Departure from a reasonable person standard does not have to be proved as is the case for negligent manslaughter.

The MCCOC in assessing current law, has suggested that the introduction of a general offence of "dangerous conduct causing death" would do away with the necessity for a separate offence of culpable driving: *Chapter 5 — Fatal Offences Against the Person,* Discussion Paper (June 1998), p 165. It considered a special offence imposing strict liability as in New South Wales, but concluded that in "principle, a special offence that dispenses with any need for proof of fault and imposes a severe penalty is difficult to justify": p 171.

As mentioned in 'Perspectives: Merging the Divisions in Manslaughter', the MCCOC recommendation for an offence of "dangerous conduct causing death" would go a long way toward providing a logical rationale for manslaughter as a category of unlawful killing. It would also do away with any need for a special offence of culpable driving causing death and go some way toward combating "a pervasive and unwarranted social tolerance for careless or dangerous driving practices": p 165.

PERSPECTIVES

Omissions and Unlawful Killing

In most instances of unlawful killing, some form of conduct will have caused the victim's death. However, murder, manslaughter or culpable driving may occur where an accused has breached a legal duty to act.

The Northern Territory is the only jurisdiction that establishes a general duty to act so as to avoid death or danger to another: *Criminal Code* (NT), s 154(1). The other jurisdictions set out more specific duties. There has been a traditional reluctance to use the criminal law to punish those who omit to act in the absence of a legal duty. It has been thought that the criminal law should not be used to compel or encourage the doing of good and that it is too harsh a method of punishing the ignorant or neglectful.[59] Furthermore, a general duty to intervene means that a large number of people who fail to act in certain circumstances would be held responsible. If a beggar dies of starvation or neglect, how many people could be held criminally responsible?[60]

The main legal duties to act arise from a special relationship between the accused and the victim,[61] as a result of a person voluntarily undertaking the care of another,[62] to act in order to

---

59 See JP McCutcheon, "Omissions and Criminal Liability" (1993-1995) 28-30 *The Irish Jurist (New Series)* 56 at 57ff; G Williams, "Criminal Omissions — the Conventional View" (1991) 107 *Law Quarterly Review* 86.

60 Indian Law Commission, *A Penal Code Prepared by the Indian Law Commissioners* (Birmingham, Alabama: Legal Classics Library, 1987, first published 1837), pp 53, 56.

61 *R v Russell* [1933] VLR 59; *Criminal Code* (Qld), s 286; *Criminal Code* (Tas), s 145; *Criminal Code* (WA), s 263.

62 *R v Instan* [1893] 1 QB 450; (1893) 17 Cox CC 602; *R v Stone and Dobinson* [1977] QB 354; *R v Taktak* (1988) 14 NSWLR 226; *Criminal Code* (Qld), s 287; *Criminal Code* (NT), s 149; *Criminal Code* (Tas), s 147; *Criminal Code* (WA), s 264. Under the Codes, there is also a duty to provide the necessaries of life: *Criminal Code* (NT), s 155; *Criminal Code* (Qld), s 285; *Criminal Code* (Tas), s 144; *Criminal Code* (WA), s 262.

avoid certain dangers[63] and where an accused has created a situation of danger: *R v Miller* [1982] 2 All ER 386.

Certain professionals such as doctors may also be under legal duties to act. In 3.4 'Non-Voluntary Euthanasia — Bland and Curzan', we outlined the facts in *Airedale NHS Trust v Bland* [1993] AC 789. The House of Lords held that an omission to provide the invasive medical care involved in artificial feeding did not breach the duty owed by the hospital and the doctors to act in the best interests of the patient.

An omission to act arises most commonly in the context of manslaughter by negligence. In relation to unlawful and dangerous act manslaughter, the unlawful act must be an act, not an omission: *R v Lowe* [1973] 1 QB 702. However, negligent manslaughter encompasses a sub-category of negligence by omission. As with negligent act manslaughter, there must be a legal duty of care owed by the accused to the victim and a breach of the high standard of care required.

In *R v Russell* [1933] VLR 59 the accused's children and wife drowned. The prosecution case was that the accused had deliberately drowned them. On his version of the facts, his wife drowned the children and he stood by helplessly as she drowned. His convictions for manslaughter of his two children were upheld on appeal on the basis that a parent has a legal duty to come to the assistance of a young child. McArthur J (at 83) stated that no similar duty extended to safeguard the accused's wife as there was no duty to protect "adults who are not helpless, but are quite capable mentally and physically of looking after themselves": see also *R v Gorman* (unrep, 15/5/1997, CCA NSW Gleeson CJ, Hunt and Sperling JJ, 60373/95).

If the adult is "helpless" and the accused has voluntarily assumed responsibility for him or her, then the courts are prepared to establish a legal duty of care. For example, a woman was found guilty of manslaughter for failing to seek medical treatment for her aunt who had asked the accused to live with her at the aunt's expense in return for her niece looking after her: *R v Instan* [1893] 1 QB 450. Even a person with no blood ties to the victim may be held responsible for negligence by omission. In *R v Taktak* (1988) 14 NSWLR 226, the accused was an associate of a proprietor of a "dog shop" and a drug dealer who asked the accused to procure him two prostitutes. The drug dealer rang the accused later that night asking him to collect one of the girls who had taken too much heroin. The accused took her to his flat, tried to awaken her by washing and slapping her face, pumped her chest and gave her mouth-to-mouth resuscitation. He said he did not call a doctor because he believed that the girl would recover. She subsequently died and at the accused's trial for manslaughter, there was conflicting medical opinion as to the exact time of death. The accused was convicted and on appeal the court examined whether the accused, by his actions, had assumed a duty of care.

Yeldham J held (at 246) "with some hesitation" there was evidence to support the jury's conclusion that the accused had assumed a legal duty to seek medical aid for the victim. He focused on the fact that the accused had made an effort to care. Carruthers J (at 250) had no difficulties recognising a duty to care for the victim which "flowed from his [the accused's] taking her [the victim's] unconscious body into his exclusive custody and control and thereby removing

---

63 For example, the duty to carry out dangerous acts with care: *Criminal Code* (NT), ss 150-151, 154; *Criminal Code* (Qld), ss 288-289; *Criminal Code* (Tas), ss 149-150; *Criminal Code* (WA), ss 265-266.

her from the potentiality of appropriate aid from others". Both Yeldham and Carruthers JJ agreed that the conviction should be quashed since the inconsistent medical evidence made it impossible to determine whether the accused's conduct had amounted to *criminal* negligence and whether this conduct *caused* the death of the victim.

These cases raise the question as to the extent to which the law should impose upon individuals a *legal duty* to come to the aid of others, particularly where the person concerned is actively refusing assistance. In the medical context, it is clear that health care practitioners are under a legal duty to treat their patients, and to use reasonable care and skill in the discharge of that duty. However, the law does not require medical treatment to be administered to competent patients who refuse treatment. Similarly the law does not require prison authorities to force-feed prisoners who have decided to go on hunger strike: see the decision of Thorpe J in *Secretary of State for the Home Department v Robb* [1995] 1 Fam LR 127.

Hazel Biggs has highlighted the differing approach of the law in these contexts in "Euthanasia and Death with Dignity: Still Poised on the Fulcrum of Homicide" [1996] Crim LR 878. She compares *Stone and Dobinson* [1977] QB 354 where the two mentally and physically disabled accused were convicted of the manslaughter of Stone's sister Fanny despite their ineffectual attempts to gain assistance with the later decision of *Airedale NHS Trust v Bland* [1993] AC 789. She states (at 883):

> The duty of care ... appears to adopt a different criminal significance depending on whether the potential defendant is a member of the public or a medical profession ... Why is it that a professionally imposed duty extended only as far as determining the best interests of a patient who could not consent, while the scope of the voluntarily assumed duty in *Stone and Dobinson* included the obligation to overrule the autonomous wishes of the "patient" [Stone's sister, Fanny]? *Smith* [1979] Crim LR 251 suggests that a person who is capable of *rational* decision-making could relieve a relative of a common law duty of care, but this fails to reconcile conflicting dicta. Bland was incapable of making any decisions and his carers were absolved of responsibility, while Stone's sister purposefully declined the provision of food and medical aid by her carers and they were culpable.

6. OFFENCES RELATED TO SUICIDE

It is difficult in modern times to understand why suicide at common law was considered a felony and attempted suicide a misdemeanour.[64] How can a person who commits suicide be punished?

The Church viewed suicide as a mortal sin and the person who committed suicide was punished by a denial of Christian burial: WE Mickell, "Is Suicide Murder?" (1903) 3 *Columbia Law Review* 379 at 383. The criminal law became involved in punishing those who committed suicide through a process of forfeiture. One of the early criminal sanctions was that of "attainder", the forfeiture of property and land when judgment of death was recorded against a person convicted of treason or felony: see Ch 2, pp 97-98. As early as 967, attainder attached to suicide: J Barry, "Suicide and the Law" (1965) 5 *Melbourne University Law Review* 1 at 2. Because of this penalty, suicide became known as a felony. As Barry states (at 2-3):

> There is good reason to believe that suicide became a felony by arguing backwards, thus: suicide attracts a forfeiture, forfeiture is a consequence of felony, therefore suicide is a felony.

Barry points out (at 5) that attempted suicide became an offence only in the middle of the 19th century:

> The reasoning was simple: an attempt to commit a felony is a misdemeanour; suicide is a felony; an attempt to commit it is, therefore, a misdemeanour, and in 1854 the law was so declared.

6.1 ASSISTING OR ENCOURAGING SUICIDE

While suicide is no longer an offence in Australia,[65] and attempted suicide is not unlawful, assisting or encouraging another to attempt to commit suicide is an offence in all jurisdictions.[66] Further, in five jurisdictions, assisting or encouraging another *to attempt* to commit suicide is also an offence.[67]

"Assisting" or "encouraging" is described in various ways as set out in the following Table and the meaning of these terms is the same as for the law set out in Chapter 8 'Complicity'.

---

64 W Hawkins, *A Treatise of the Pleas of the Crown*, Vol 1 (London: J Curwood, 1824), p 77. See also J Barry, "Suicide and the Law" (1965) 5 *Melbourne University Law Review* 1; GV Williams, *The Sanctity of Life and the Criminal Law* (London: Faber, 1958), Ch 7.

65 The common law offences of suicide and attempted suicide have been abrogated by *Crimes Act* 1900 (ACT), s 16; *Crimes Act* 1900 (NSW), s 31A; *Criminal Law Consolidation Act* 1935 (SA), s 13A(1); *Crimes Act* 1958 (Vic), s 6A. In the Code jurisdictions, unlawful killing requires the killing of another person: *Criminal Code* (NT), s 161; *Criminal Code* (Qld), s 300; *Criminal Code* (Tas), s 153; *Criminal Code* (WA), s 277.

66 *Crimes Act* 1900 (ACT), s 17; *Crimes Act* 1900 (NSW), s 31C; *Criminal Code* (NT), s 168; *Criminal Code* (Qld), s 311; *Criminal Law Consolidation Act* 1935 (SA), s 13A(5)(7); *Criminal Code* (Tas), s 163; *Crimes Act* 1958 (Vic), s 6B(2); *Criminal Code* (WA), s 288.

67 *Crimes Act* 1900 (ACT), s 17; *Crimes Act* 1900 (NSW), s 31C; *Criminal Code* (NT), s 168; *Criminal Law Consolidation Act* 1935 (SA), s 13A(5); *Crimes Act* 1958 (Vic), s 6B(2).

TABLE 4:

Terms used for Assisting or Encouraging Suicide

JURISDICTION AND RELEVANT LAW	TERM
ACT *Crimes Act* 1900	aiding or abetting/inciting or counselling s 17
NSW *Crimes Act* 1900	aiding or abetting/inciting or counselling s 31C
NT *Criminal Code*	procures/counsels/aids s 168
QLD *Criminal Code*	procures/counsels/aids s 311
SA *Criminal Law Consolidation Act* 1935	aid/abet or counsel s 13A(5)
TAS *Criminal Code*	instigate or aid (s 163) instigate means "counsel, procure or command" (s 1)
VIC *Crimes Act* 1958	inciting/aiding or abetting s 6B(2)
WA *Criminal Code*	procures/counsels/aids s 288

In general, there must be a causal connection between the assisting and encouraging and the actual suicide.[68] The prosecution must also prove that the accused intended to assist or encourage another to commit or attempt to commit suicide. In *Attorney-General v Able* [1984] QB 785 Woolf J held that the publication of material on euthanasia could only amount to an offence if the distributor had an intention to assist or encourage the reader to take or attempt to take his or her own life and that the material actually did assist or encourage such an act. On the facts of that case, it was held that a booklet entitled "A Guide to Self-Deliverance" published by the Voluntary Euthanasia Society did not satisfy the elements of the offences of assisting or encouraging suicide or attempted suicide. The MCCOC has recommended that assisting or encouraging suicide should remain unlawful, with assisting suicide attracting a higher penalty than encouraging: *Chapter 5 — Fatal Offences Against the Person*, Discussion Paper (1998), p 181.

Even though suicide is no longer unlawful, there still exist some statutory provisions that enable the use of reasonable force to prevent suicide.[69]

---

68 *Crimes Act* 1900 (ACT), s 17; *Crimes Act* 1900 (NSW), s 31C; *Criminal Code* (NT), s 168; *Criminal Code* (Qld), s 311; *Crimes Act* 1958 (Vic), s 6B(2)(a); *Criminal Code* (WA), s 288. No causal connection is required in Tasmania. No causal connection is required in South Australia for aiding, abetting or counselling, but s 13A(7) of the *Criminal Law Consolidation Act* 1935 (SA) requires a causal connection for murder or attempted murder to be proved where an accused procures a suicide or attempted suicide by means of "fraud, duress or undue influence".

69 *Crimes Act* 1900 (ACT), s 18; *Crimes Act* 1900 (NSW), s 574B; *Criminal Code* (NT), s 27(pa); *Criminal Law Consolidation Act* 1935 (SA), s 13A(2); *Crimes Act* 1958 (Vic), s 463B.

6.2 SUICIDE PACT

A "suicide pact" is an agreement between two or more persons where the purpose is the death of all of them.[70] In New South Wales, South Australia and Victoria, if an accused kills another pursuant to a suicide pact, he or she may be partly excused. In South Australia and Victoria, the offence will be reduced from murder to manslaughter,[71] whereas in New South Wales, the survivor of a suicide pact will not be guilty of murder or manslaughter,[72] but of the lesser offence of assisting or encouraging suicide.[73] Section 13A(11) of the *Criminal Law Consolidation Act* 1935 (SA) states that an accused will be unable to rely upon a suicide pact where he or she induced another to enter the pact by way of fraud, duress or undue influence. The accused's conduct must have been performed with the intention to die pursuant to the pact.[74]

The MCCOC has recommended that participation in a suicide pact should not serve as a partial excuse: *Chapter 5 — Fatal Offences Against the Person*, Discussion Paper (1998), p 184. It stated (p 183) in relation to a pact where all agree to commit suicide:

> The aspect of the [accused's] conduct which attracts criminal sanction, and which is sought to be deterred, relates to being involved in *another's* self-killing.

Further, the MCCOC is of the opinion that it should still be murder where a survivor has killed another pursuant to a "consensual murder pact". The circumstances of the killing may be taken into account in sentencing: p 183. This approach is consistent with motive not being taken into account in establishing criminal liability for unlawful killing.

7. ABORTION, CHILD DESTRUCTION AND CONCEALMENT OF BIRTH

The criminal law in relation to abortion continues to attract political, social and legal debate. It is perhaps the one area of law where practice does not fully accord with what the law prohibits, as criminal prosecutions for abortion and child destruction are rare. For a historical review of these "reproduction" offences see S Davies, "Captives of their Bodies — Women, Law and Punishment, 1880–1980s" in D Kirkby (ed), *Sex, Power and Justice* (Melbourne: Oxford University Press, 1995), pp 105-110.

South Australia and the Northern Territory have statutory regimes that permit a slightly more liberal approach to abortion than in other jurisdictions. However, from the legal point of view, abortion is not available "on demand", but must be justified in terms of necessity gauged by examining the risks to the health of the pregnant woman.

---

70 *Crimes Act* 1900 (NSW), s 31B(2); *Criminal Law Consolidation Act* 1935 (SA), s 13A(10)(a); *Crimes Act* 1958 (Vic), s 6B(4).

71 *Criminal Law Consolidation Act* 1935 (SA), s 13A(2); *Crimes Act* 1958 (Vic), s 6B(1).

72 *Crimes Act* 1900 (NSW), s 31B(1).

73 *Crimes Act* 1900 (NSW), s 31C.

74 *Crimes Act* 1900 (NSW), s 31B(2); *Criminal Law Consolidation Act* 1935 (SA), s 13A(10)(a); *Crimes Act* 1958 (Vic), s 6B(4).

The offence of child destruction exists in all jurisdictions apart from New South Wales and South Australia. This offence covers the gap between abortion and murder where a person unlawfully kills a child "capable of being born alive". If there is insufficient evidence for a conviction for murder, manslaughter or infanticide, an accused may be charged with the offence of concealment of birth. These three offences will be discussed in turn.

7.1 ABORTION

Much of the philosophical literature on abortion deals with competing "rights". For example, according to the *Declaration on Procured Abortion* by the Catholic Church,[75] the rights of the unborn child justify State involvement in prohibiting abortion:

> It is true that it is not the task of the law to choose between points of view or to impose one rather than another. But the life of the child takes precedence over all opinions. One cannot invoke freedom of thought to destroy this life ... It is at all times the task of the State to preserve each person's rights and to protect the weakest.[76]

Liberals, on the other hand, argue that a woman's right to personal liberty in regard to reproductive decisions is the most important consideration. As Mary Anne Warren states in "Abortion" in P Singer (ed), *A Companion to Ethics* (Oxford: Blackwell, 1991), p 306, "there is no other case in which the law requires individuals (who have been convicted of no crime) to sacrifice liberty, self-determination and bodily integrity in order to preserve the lives of others".

In recent times, philosophical debate has turned to the controls the State may place on women's access to abortions. For example, the Australian Capital Territory and Western Australian governments enacted legislation concerning counselling of women who seek abortions.[77] These steps followed the decision of the United States Supreme Court in *Planned Parenthood v Casey*, 505 US 833 (1992). In that case, the Court held (at 872) that state governments can legitimately take steps to "enact rules and regulations designed to encourage [pregnant women] to know that there are philosophical and social arguments of great weight that can be brought to bear in favour of continuing the pregnancy to full term". The Court held that the *Pennsylvania Abortion Control Act* was not unconstitutional and did not impose an "undue burden" on a woman seeking an abortion. The Act required women seeking abortions to be provided with information about the nature and risks of abortion and stipulated that an abortion could only be performed at least 24 hours after the woman had received the information. Some authors have argued that "forced contemplation" is unnecessary given that the decision to have an abortion is usually seriously and carefully considered.[78]

---

75 Sacred Congregation for the Doctrine of Faith, *Declaration on Procured Abortion* (November 18, 1974); found at http://www.catholic.org/newadvent/docs/df75ab.htm.

76 Sacred Congregation for the Doctrine of Faith, *Declaration on Procured Abortion* (November 18, 1974); found at http://www.catholic.org/newadvent/docs/df75ab.htm, paras 20, 21.

77 *Health Regulation (Maternal Health Information) Act* 1998 (ACT); *Health Act* 1911 (WA) as amended by *Acts Amendment (Abortion) Act* 1998 (WA).

78 L Cannold, *The Abortion Myth* (Sydney: Allen and Unwin, 1998); R Graycar and J Morgan, *The Hidden Gender of Law* (Sydney: Federation Press, 1990), Ch 9; K Luker, *Abortion and the Politics of Motherhood* (Berkeley: University of California Press, 1984).

The MCCOC has suggested that the Model Criminal Code should reflect the current law in the Northern Territory and South Australia: *Chapter 5 — Non-Fatal Offences Against the Person,* Discussion Paper (1996), p 85. It points out (p 81) that "[w]ith the exception of South Australia and the Northern Territory, the political process in Australia has been unable to deal with the issue for a century, and that position is unlikely to change".

At present, there are three indictable offences connected with abortion:

=== **procuring one's own miscarriage;**[79]

=== **procuring another's miscarriage;**[80] **and**

=== **the supply of means for a miscarriage with knowledge that those means are intended to be used for that purpose.**[81]

The MCCOC has pointed out in *Chapter 5 — Non-Fatal Offences Against the Person,* Discussion Paper (1996) (p 80) that the latter offence is redundant given the breadth of the existing law of complicity. Accordingly, it will not be discussed in this chapter.

PHYSICAL AND FAULT ELEMENTS

Except in Queensland, the current abortion provisions are cast in terms of the pregnant woman[82] or other person unlawfully administering or causing to be taken any poison, drug or noxious thing or using any instrument, force of any kind or other means with an intention to cause a miscarriage.

The terms "administer" and "causes to be taken" have been interpreted very broadly. For example, to constitute an administering, it is not necessary that there should be a "delivery by hand": *R v Harley* (1830) 172 ER 744 at 745 per Park J. See also *R v Dale* (1852) 6 Cox CC 14 at 17. The term "causing to be taken" can extend to instances where a woman consumes a substance when the accused is not present: *R v Wilson* (1856) 169 ER 945; *R v Farrow* (1857) 169 ER 961. Failing to warn the victim of the need to take a safe dose has been taken to amount to "causing" the substance to be taken: *R v Turner* (1910) 4 Cr App R 203, 206.

The substance used to procure an abortion must be a poison, drug, or noxious thing depending upon the jurisdiction. A poison has been held to be any substance calculated to destroy life: *R v Haydon* (1845) 1 Cox CC 184. A noxious thing is a substance that has a deleterious as

---

79 *Crimes Act* 1900 (ACT), s 42; *Crimes Act* 1900 (NSW), s 82; *Criminal Code* (Qld), s 225; *Criminal Law Consolidation Act* 1935 (SA), s 81(1); *Criminal Code* (Tas), s 134(1); *Crimes Act* 1958 (Vic), s 65. This offence does not appear to exist in the Northern Territory and Western Australia as s 172 of the *Criminal Code* (NT) and s 199 of the *Criminal Code* (WA) only prohibit "any person" and "a person" respectively from procuring the abortion of another. Section 174 of the *Criminal Code* (NT) and s 82A of the *Criminal Law Consolidation Act* 1935 (SA) deal with the medical termination of pregnancy.

80 *Crimes Act* 1900 (ACT), s 43; *Crimes Act* 1900 (NSW), s 83; *Criminal Code* (NT), s 173; *Criminal Code* (Qld), s 224; *Criminal Law Consolidation Act* 1935 (SA), s 81(2); *Criminal Code* (Tas), s 134(2); *Crimes Act* 1958 (Vic), s 65; *Criminal Code* (WA), s 199 (perform an abortion).

81 *Crimes Act* 1900 (ACT), s 44; *Crimes Act* 1900 (NSW), s 84; *Criminal Code* (NT), s 173; *Criminal Code* (Qld), s 226; *Criminal Law Consolidation Act* 1935 (SA), s 81(2); *Criminal Code* (Tas), s 135; *Crimes Act* 1958 (Vic), s 66. A similar provision was repealed in Western Australia by the *Act Amendment (Abortion) Act* 1998 (WA).

82 In Queensland, this prohibition applies whether or not the woman is pregnant: *Criminal Code* (Qld), s 225. This offence does not appear to apply in the Northern Territory or Western Australia.

opposed to a minor effect on the body.[83] A drug does not necessarily mean a noxious thing,[84] but it is likely that its meaning will be linked to the terms poison and noxious thing and some early cases have used these terms interchangeably.[85] O'Bryan J stated in *McAvoy v Gray* [1946] ALR 459 (at 460):

> A common meaning of "drug" is any organic or inorganic substance which, used as a medicine or as an ingredient in medicines especially, is a narcotic or poison.

Where a substance which is harmless in small doses but is administered in excessive doses making it harmful, it will be considered to be a noxious thing.[86] The substance in question need not be an abortifacient: *R v Marlow* (1964) 49 Cr App R 49 at 55 per Brabin J.

The word "instrument" is used in its ordinary sense and it is immaterial whether or not the instrument was capable of causing a miscarriage.[87] The term "means" connotes the doing of something that is capable of producing a miscarriage.[88]

The term "miscarriage" in law is generally taken to refer to the premature ending of a pregnancy that is presumed to begin when the ovum is fertilised.[89] The use of modern techniques such as the intra-uterine device, prostaglandin, the morning-after pill and the drug RU-486 which do not prevent conception but which operate after the fertilisation of the ovum by the sperm has taken place, have raised doubts about the viability of this definition of miscarriage. It has been argued that the use of such techniques amounts to procuring a miscarriage: V Tunkel, "Modern Anti-Pregnancy Techniques and the Criminal Law" [1974] Crim LR 461 at 462. However, there is some, albeit slight support for the view that any technique used before implantation of the fertilised egg into the womb is not an abortifacient because conception actually occurs upon nidation[90] or implantation.[91]

---

83   *R v Perry* (1847) 2 Cox CC 223. The substance must be either a noxious thing in itself (*R v Isaacs* (1862) 169 ER 1371 at 1373 per Pollock CB) (cf *R v Coe* (1834) 6 Car & P 1295) or it must have been administered in sufficient quantity to be noxious (*R v Hennah* (1877) 13 Cox CC 547 (cantharides); *R v Cramp* (1880) 5 QBD 307 (juniper oil); *R v Turner* (1910) 4 Cr App R 203 (bitter apple); *R v Barton* (1931) 25 QJPR 81 (Beecham's pills, quinine and gin)).

84   *R v Duffy* (1901) 1 SR (NSW) 20.

85   *R v Farrow* (1857) 169 ER 961; *R v Isaacs* (1862) 169 ER 1371; *R v Turner* (1910) 4 Cr App R 203. Heroin has been held to be a noxious thing in itself: *R v Cato* [1976] 1 All ER 260. Amphetamines have also been held to be noxious: *R v Hill* (1986) Cr App R 386 (HL).

86   *R v Cramp* [1880] 5 QBD 307 at 309 per Coleridge CJ; *R v Bickley* (1909) 2 Cr App R 53; *R v Turner* (1910) 4 Cr App R 203; *R v Barton* (1931) 25 QJPR 81.

87   *R v Doucette* (1949) 93 CCC 202. In that case, a piece of tubing which was inserted into a woman's vagina and which was used to pump a chemical solution was held to be an instrument for the purposes of the *Criminal Code* (Can).

88   *R v Lindner* [1938] SASR 412 at 415. In that case, innocuous pills were held not to fall within the terms "other means whatsoever".

89   N Cica, "The Inadequacies of Australian Abortion Law" (1991) 5 *Australian Journal of Family Law* 37 at 50. See further K Martyn, "Technological Advances and *Roe v Wade*: The Need to Rethink Abortion Law" (1982) 29 *University of California Los Angeles Law Review* 1194; N Rhoden, "Trimesters and Technology: Revamping *Roe v Wade*" (1986) 95 Yale LJ 639; J Rubenfeld, "On the Legal Status of the Proposition that 'Life Begins at Conception'" (1991) 43 *Stanford Law Review* 599.

90   The embedding of the early embryo into the uterine mucosa. See *Oxford English Dictionary* (2nd ed, Oxford: Clarendon Press, 1988), Vol X, p 397.

91   In *R v Price* [1969] 1 QB 541, the Court implied that the use of an intra-uterine device would not amount to an abortion merely because it operates after the ovum is fertilised by acting to prevent nidation or implantation. See further G Williams, *Textbook of Criminal Law* (2nd ed, London: Stevens & Sons, 1983), pp 294-295; R Cook, "Legal Abortion: Limits and Contributions to Human Life" in R Porter and M O'Connor (eds), *Ciba Foundation Symposium 115 - Abortion: Medical Progress and Social Implications* (London: Pitman Publishing, 1985), p 212.

In relation to the fault element, the offences of procuring one's own miscarriage and procuring another's miscarriage both require an intention to procure such miscarriage. The intention must be genuine and not merely feigned: *R v A* (1944) 83 CCC 94.

The law relating to abortion was amended in Western Australia by the *Acts Amendment (Abortion) Act* 1998 (WA). Section 199 of the *Criminal Code* (WA) avoids the expression "procuring a miscarriage" and simply states that it is unlawful to perform an abortion unless it is "performed by a medical practitioner in good faith and with reasonable care and skill" and conforms with the provisions of the *Health Act* 1911 (WA). Section 334 of the latter Act requires the medical practitioner to offer the woman referral to "appropriate and adequate counselling" and to explain the risks and matters associated with the termination of pregnancy. Similar requirements are set out in s 8 of the *Health Regulation (Maternal Health Information) Act* 1998 (ACT).

UNLAWFUL ABORTIONS

In all jurisdictions, the prosecution must prove that the abortion was "unlawful". In practice, this has meant looking at the extent to which medical terminations of pregnancy can be considered "lawful". The main rationale for considering an abortion lawful depends upon the concept of necessity: see Ch 6, pp 325ff. South Australia, the Northern Territory and Western Australia have special provisions for the medical termination of pregnancy, but a broad concept of necessity forms an essential part of these provisions.

In the Australian Capital Territory, New South Wales and Victoria the defence of necessity is available at common law to abortion related offences. In *R v Davidson* [1969] VR 667 (at 671), Menhennit J defined the element of necessity in terms of an honest and reasonable belief that the steps taken are required to preserve the woman from some serious danger and are proportionate to the need to preserve the woman from serious danger.[92] The requirement of proportionality may have been included to emphasise that the later the abortion takes place, the greater the danger for the health of the woman: I Elliott, "Australian Letter" [1969] *Criminal Law Review* 511 at 524-525. This part of the test, however, seems largely redundant as if the test of necessity is satisfied because the termination was needed to preserve the woman from serious danger to life or health, then it would seem that the termination was proportionate as well.

The danger may be existing or potential and means serious danger to physical or mental health and not merely a normal danger associated with pregnancy and child birth.[93] Economic and social factors may be taken into account in assessing the question of serious danger, but they are not in themselves sufficient grounds for rendering a termination lawful: *R v Wald* (1971) 3 DCR (NSW) 25 at 29 per Levine J. As McGuire J noted in *R v Bayliss* (1986) 9 QL 8 (at 45) this test does not allow abortion on demand.

---

92   *R v Wald* (1971) 3 NSWDCR 25 at 29; *K v Minister for Youth and Community Services* [1982] 1 NSWLR 311 at 318; *CES v Superclinics Australia Pty Ltd* (1995) 38 NSWLR 47.

93   *R v Davidson* [1969] VR 667 at 672 per Menhennit J; *CES v Superclinics Australia Pty Ltd* (1995) 38 NSWLR 47 at 59-60 per Kirby P.

CASE STUDIES

The High Court and Abortion

On 15 April 1996, an application for special leave to appeal against the New South Wales Court of Appeal decision in *CES v Superclinics* (1995) 38 NSWLR 47 was heard by the High Court. Dawson, Toohey and Gummow JJ granted leave to appeal. The case concerned a civil action for "wrongful birth". A 21-year-old woman went to a 24-hour medical clinic on a number of occasions believing she might be pregnant and wanting a termination if that was the case. Her pregnancy was not diagnosed until 19.5 weeks at which time she was told the pregnancy could not be terminated safely. Newman J in the New South Wales Supreme Court case, *CES v Superclinics* (unrep, 18/4/1994, 14479 of 1998) found the defendant doctors and the clinic had breached their duty of care but denied the woman's claim for damages on the ground that she had merely lost the opportunity to perform a hypothetically illegal abortion. On appeal to the New South Wales Court of Appeal, Kirby ACJ and Priestley JA, with Meagher JA dissenting, reversed the decision. However, the majority could not agree on how the damages should be assessed. By granting leave to appeal, it was thought that the High Court could authoritatively rule on what constituted an "unlawful" abortion. However, after applications were made for leave to intervene by the Australian Health Care Association, the Australian Episcopal Conference and the Abortion Providers Federation of Australasia in September 1996, the matter was settled out of court. See L Crowley-Smith, "Therapeutic Abortions and the Emergence of Wrongful Birth Actions in Australia: A Serious Danger to Mental Health?" (1996) 3 *Journal of Law and Medicine* 359; R Graycar and J Morgan, "'Unnatural Rejection of Womanhood and Motherhood': Pregnancy, Damages and the Law" (1996) 18 *Sydney Law Review* 323; K Petersen, "Wrongful Conception and Birth" (1996) 18 *Sydney Law Review* 501; W Neville, "Abortion before the High Court — What Next? Caveat Interventus: A Note on *Superclinics Australia Pty Ltd v CES*" (1998) 20 *Adelaide Law Review* 183.

In the Code jurisdictions, apart from the Northern Territory, an abortion will be lawful where the pregnancy is terminated by a registered medical practitioner in good faith and with reasonable skill. The performance of the operation must be reasonable and for the patient's benefit, having regard to the patient's state at the time and all the circumstances of the case.[94] In addition, in Queensland, Tasmania and Western Australia, a person is not criminally responsible for performing a surgical operation upon an unborn child for the preservation of the mother's life. Again, the performance of the operation must be reasonable, having regard to the patient's state at the time and to the

---

94 *Criminal Code* (Qld), s 282; *Criminal Code* (Tas), s 51; *Criminal Code* (WA), s 259. These sections are not limited to the case where the accused believes the abortion necessary to preserve the woman's life, but merely lays down the general requirement of reasonableness in all the circumstances. The common law defence of necessity is also preserved in Tasmania by reason of s 8 of the *Criminal Code*. These provisions in the *Criminal Codes* of Queensland, Tasmania and Western Australia have been taken to incorporate the test set out in *R v Davidson* [1969] VR 667 at 671: *R v Bayliss* (1986) 9 QL 8, per McGuire J at 45; *Re Bayliss* (unrep, 24/5/1985, SC QLD McPherson J, 376 of 1985); *K v T* [1983] 1 Qd R 396, Williams J at 398.

circumstances of the case.[95] In Western Australia, s 334 of the *Health Act* 1911 (WA) sets out that an abortion will be lawful if serious danger to the physical or mental health of the woman concerned will result if the abortion is not performed or the pregnancy of the woman concerned is causing serious danger to her physical or mental health. This section also seems to go further than the common law in stating that an abortion is justified if the woman has given informed consent or she will suffer serious personal, family or social consequences if the abortion is not performed.

A statutory defence of necessity also applies in South Australia and the Northern Territory. Section 82(1)(b) of the *Criminal Law Consolidation Act* 1935 (SA) requires that the termination be performed in good faith where immediately necessary to save the life, or to prevent grave injury to the physical or mental health, of the pregnant woman. Under s 174(1)(b) of the *Criminal Code* (NT) a defence is available where the woman has been pregnant for not more than 23 weeks and the medical practitioner is of the opinion, formed in good faith that the termination of the pregnancy is immediately necessary to prevent grave injury to the woman's physical or mental health. In the Northern Territory, there is also a statutory defence of necessity which applies to medical practitioners who terminate a pregnancy in good faith for the purpose only of preserving the woman's life: s 174(1)(c).

An abortion will also be lawful in the Northern Territory and South Australia where the termination of the pregnancy is carried out in a hospital and certain conditions are met. In the opinion of two medical practitioners, the termination is necessary either because the continuance of the pregnancy would cause a greater risk to the life or mental health of the woman or because there is a substantial risk that if the pregnancy were not terminated, the child would suffer from such physical or mental abnormalities as to be seriously handicapped: *Criminal Code Act* 1983 (NT), s 174(1)(a); *Criminal Law Consolidation Act* 1935 (SA), s 82a(1)(a). In the Northern Territory, the woman must have been pregnant for not more than 14 weeks for this section to apply. In South Australia, in determining whether the continuance of a pregnancy would involve a risk of injury to the physical or mental health of a pregnant woman, account may be taken of the woman's actual or reasonably forseeable environment: *Criminal Law Consolidation Act* 1935 (SA), s 82a(3).

7.2 CHILD DESTRUCTION

The offence of child destruction involves the killing, prior to birth, of a child capable of being born alive. It exists in all jurisdictions other than New South Wales and South Australia.[96] There is, however, a related offence in s 21 of the *Crimes Act* 1900 (NSW) whereby a woman who is acquitted of the murder of a child she has delivered may be found guilty of an offence if she has wilfully contributed to the death of the child during delivery or at or after its birth. In Queensland, an assault on a pregnant woman that seriously injures or kills her unborn child, may also give rise to the offence of "killing an unborn child": *Criminal Code* (Qld), s 313 amended by s 47(2) of the *Criminal Law Amendment Act* 1996 (Qld).

---

95 *Criminal Code* (Qld), s 282; *Criminal Code* (Tas), s 165(2); *Criminal Code* (WA), s 259.

96 *Crimes Act* 1900 (ACT), s 40; *Criminal Code* (NT), s 170; *Criminal Code* (Qld), s 313; *Criminal Code* (Tas), s 165; *Crimes Act* 1958 (Vic), s 10; *Criminal Code* (WA), s 290.

The offence deals with cases of a child being born dead because of acts that would have amounted to murder or manslaughter if the child died after birth. It differs from abortion in that it is linked to the killing of a viable foetus, or one that is "capable of being born alive". Nevertheless, it is closely linked to abortion and technically, those who commit late term abortions may be liable for child destruction. The physical and fault elements differ between jurisdictions, but, in general, the prosecution must prove:

- the foetus was capable of being born alive;

- the act or omission must be linked to a certain time-frame;

- the killing must be unlawful; and

- the requisite fault element such as intention or recklessness must be present.

PHYSICAL ELEMENTS

The victim must be a child capable of being born alive.[97] Section 10(2) of the *Crimes Act* 1958 (Vic) sets out a statutory presumption that a foetus is capable of being born alive after a gestation period of 28 weeks. There is no corresponding presumption in other jurisdictions.

Where the child is less than 28 weeks old, it may be regarded as capable of being born alive if it could breathe independently without deriving any of its living or power of living by or through any connection with its mother. In *Rance v Mid-Downs Health Authority* [1991] 1 QB 587 (at 621) Brook J held that foetus less than 28-weeks-old was "capable of being born alive" if it was capable of "breathing and living by reason of its breathing through its own lungs alone". This opens the way (at least theoretically) for medical practitioners who perform late term abortions to be prosecuted for child destruction. If the foetus is born alive in the course of an abortion, Gerard Wright argues that this may constitute murder should the foetus die: "The Legality of Abortion by Prostaglandin" [1984] Crim LR 347. The question of the legal status of a foetus born alive in the course of an abortion is further explored by Michael Eburn in "The Legal Status of a Living Abortus" (1997) 4(4) *Journal of Law and Medicine* 373. In practice, however, prosecutions for child destruction are rare.[98]

The timing of the act or omission causing death is expressed differently from one jurisdiction to another. Under s 40 of the *Crimes Act* (ACT) the act or omission must have occurred "in relation to a childbirth". In the Northern Territory, Queensland and Western Australia, the fatal conduct must have occurred "when a woman is about to be delivered of a child": *Criminal Code* (NT), s 170;

---

97 This is expressly provided for in s 10(1) of the *Crimes Act* 1958 (Vic). It is implied in the other jurisdictions where the provisions impose criminal liability for an act or omission that prevents a child being born alive: *Crimes Act* 1900 (ACT), s 40; *Criminal Code* (NT), s 170; *Criminal Code* (Qld), s 313; *Criminal Code* (Tas), s 165; *Criminal Code* (WA), s 290.

98 See further L Waller, "Tracy Maund Memorial Lecture: Any Reasonable Creature in Being" (1987) 13 *Monash Law Review* 37; IJ Keown, "The Scope of the Offence of Child Destruction" (1988) 104 *Law Quarterly Review* 120; V Tunkel, "Late Abortions and the Crime of Child Destruction: (1) A Reply" [1985] Crim LR 133; G Wright, "Late Abortions and the Crime of Child Destruction: (2) A Rejoinder" [1985] Crim LR 140; K Norrie, "Abortions in Great Britain: One Act, Two Laws" [1985] Crim LR 475; DPT Price, "How Viable is the Present Scope of the Offence of Child Destruction?" (1987) 16 *Anglo-Am LR* 220; G Wright, "Capable of Being Born Alive?" (1981) 131 *New Law Journal* 188; DPT Price, "Selective Reduction and Feticide: The Parameters of Abortion" [1988] Crim LR 199.

Criminal Code (Qld), s 313; *Criminal Code* (WA), s 290. The offence is therefore linked to the process of birth of a viable foetus. In Tasmania and Victoria, the time frame is much broader in that the relevant time is governed by the capacity of the child to be born alive: *Criminal Code* (Tas), s 165(1); *Crimes Act* 1958 (Vic), s 10(1). In these jurisdictions, the offence extends to any act or omission during pregnancy that causes the death of a viable foetus.

Another physical element of the offence is that the killing must have been unlawful. This is specifically required under s 10(1) of the *Crimes Act* 1958 (Vic). In Queensland, Tasmania and Western Australia the requirement appears in the form of provisions exempting from liability an accused who has acted in good faith for the preservation of the mother's life: *Criminal Code* (Qld), s 313; *Criminal Code* (Tas), s 165(2); *Criminal Code* (WA), s 290. In the Australian Capital Territory and Victoria, the common law defence of necessity in the context of abortion appears to apply equally to child destruction. Under s 33 of the *Criminal Code* (NT) the applicable defence is one of sudden and extraordinary emergency.

FAULT ELEMENT

The fault element for the offence varies widely from one jurisdiction to the other, but, in general, intention or recklessness is required. Section 40 of the *Crimes Act* 1900 (ACT) stipulates an intentional or reckless prevention of live birth or contribution to death of the child. In the Northern Territory, Queensland and Western Australia the mental element is required to be the same as that for "an unlawful killing" which means that any mental state sufficient for murder or manslaughter will suffice: *Criminal Code* (NT), s 170; *Criminal Code* (Qld), s 313(1); *Criminal Code* (WA), s 290. Section 10(1) of the *Crimes Act* 1958 (Vic) requires an intention to destroy the life of the child. In Tasmania, the accused must have caused the death "in such a manner that he would have been guilty of murder" had the child been born alive: *Criminal Code* (Tas), s 165(1). Hence, intentional killings are sufficient as are those which would have constituted reckless or constructive murder.

7.3 CONCEALMENT OF BIRTH

Concealment of birth is an offence that exists in all jurisdictions to cover cases where there is insufficient evidence of the murder or manslaughter of a child. Most of the cases dealing with the offence date from the 19th century and it has fallen into disuse in recent times. Whilst not an example of "unlawful killing" it is closely tied to such offences and is best dealt with in this chapter.

In relation to the physical elements of the offence, there must be a "secret disposition" of a child's body for the offence to be made out.[99] The word "secret" implies some form of concealment. There was held to be no secret disposition where the child's body was left in a toilet where the mother had been confined,[100] nor where the child's body was covered with a petticoat on the bed where the mother lay: *R v Rosenberg* (1906) 70 JP 264. However, a secret disposition was held to

---

99   *Crimes Act* 1900 (ACT), s 45(1); *Crimes Act* 1900 (NSW), s 85(1); *Criminal Code* (NT), s 171; *Criminal Code* (Qld), s 314; *Criminal Law Consolidation Act* 1935 (SA), s 83(1); *Criminal Code* (Tas), s 166(1); *Crimes Act* 1958 (Vic), s 67; *Criminal Code* (WA), s 291.

100   *R v Derham* (1843) 1 Cox CC 56; cf *R v Hughes* (1850) 4 Cox CC 447.

have occurred where the accused put the body under a bolster upon which she put her head: *R v Perry* (1855) Dears CC 471; see also *R v Veaty* (1910) 74 JP Jo 352.

In *R v Brown* (1870) 11 Cox CC 517, Bovil CJ (at 247) stated that leaving the child's body fully exposed, but in a secluded place such as "on top of a mountain" would amount to a secret disposition. Leaving the dead body in a street, however, would not be sufficient.[101] The concealment does not mean from a particular individual, but from the world at large.[102]

The disposition must be that of a dead body,[103] although it is irrelevant, whether or not the child was born dead: *R v Donoghue* [1914] VLR 195. The offence does not cover those cases of concealment of the body of a child born or aborted in the early stages of pregnancy. The child must have had "a fair chance of life when born".[104] In the Australian Capital Territory and New South Wales, it is a defence if the child had issued from the body of the mother before the expiration of the 28th week of pregnancy: *Crimes Act* (ACT), s 45(2); *Crimes Act* 1900 (NSW), s 85(2). Under s 166(2) of the *Criminal Code* (Tas) the offence does not apply to the situation where the child has not reached such a stage of maturity as would in the ordinary course of nature render it probable that such child would live.

In relation to the fault element, the offence requires an intention to conceal the birth of a child from the world at large. This requirement is clearly set out in the Australian Capital Territory and New South Wales legislation,[105] and is implicit in the term "endeavours" in the appropriate sections of the other jurisdictions.[106] The offence is not made out where the accused simply intended to conceal the fact of birth from an individual or individuals: *R v Jacobs* [1932] SASR 456 at 458 per Parsons J.

The lack of use of this offence in recent times has led to calls for its abolition. Peter English in "Homicide other than Murder" [1977] Crim LR 79 writes (at 89):

> The offence seems to be of only minor importance and it is submitted that it could be safely repealed, leaving the conduct presently covered by it to be dealt with by the general law on improper disposal of dead bodies.

The MCCOC has also recommended in its Discussion Paper on *Fatal Offences Against the Person* (1998) (p 197) that this offence be abolished and given the lack of prosecutions under this head, we support this recommendation.

---

101 *R v Clark* (1883) 15 Cox CC 171. See also *R v Sleep* (1864) 9 Cox CC 559; *R v Cook* (1870) 11 Cox CC 542; *R v Rosenberg* (1906) 70 JP 264; *R v George* (1868) 11 Cox CC 41; *R v Waterage* (1846) 1 Cox CC 338; *R v Mappin* (1904) 6 WALR 161; *R v Narden* (1873) 12 SCR(NSW) 160.

102 *R v Morris* (1848) 2 Cox CC 489; *R v Higley* (1830) 4 C & P 366; *R v Jacob* [1932] SASR 456.

103 *R v Turner* (1846) 173 ER 704.

104 *R v Hewitt and Smith* (1866) 4 F & F 1101; *R v Berriman* (1854) 6 Cox CC 388. Cf *R v Colmer* (1864) 9 Cox CC 506 where Martin B held that a foetus not bigger than a finger, but having the shape of a child could be considered to be a child for the purposes of the appropriate legislation.

105 *Crimes Act* 1900 (ACT), s 45(1); *Crimes Act* 1900 (NSW), s 85(1).

106 *Criminal Code* (NT), s 171; *Criminal Code* (Qld), s 314; *Criminal Law Consolidation Act* 1935 (SA), s 83(1); *Criminal Code* (Tas), s 166(1); *Crimes Act* 1958 (Vic), s 67; *Criminal Code* (WA), s 291.

8. CONCLUSION

In this overview of unlawful killing and associated offences, we have identified a number of problematic issues. The continued advances in medical technology confront our conceptions of "personhood" in relation to unlawful killing and crimes such as abortion and child destruction. If we consider criminal culpability, the following questions need to be considered:

▬ **Should there be a category of murder based on intent to do grievous bodily harm?**

▬ **Should there be a category of reckless murder?**

▬ **Should there be a category of constructive murder?**

▬ **Should there be a single category of dangerous act or omission manslaughter?**

▬ **Should there be a separate offence of causing death through culpable driving?**

▬ **Should participation in a suicide pact serve as an excuse?**

▬ **What should the role of the criminal law play in relation to abortion?**

As outlined in the introduction, many deaths are not constructed as unlawful killings, such as industrial or sporting "accidents". Perhaps the underlying central question is whether or not the criminal law should spread a wider net in relation to unlawful killing so as to encourage, for example, safer working conditions or whether current practice is satisfactory.

11

Offences Against the Person

> **Man's inhumanity to man**
> **Makes countless thousands mourn**

Robert Burns, (1759-1796) *Man was Made to*
Mourn in R Burns, *Poems 1786 and 1787*
(Menston: The Scholar Press Ltd, 1971), p 160

1. INTRODUCTION

The criminal law relating to offences against the person is primarily statutory and encompasses a wide range of offences such as assault, unlawful wounding, kidnapping and the relevant newcomers, stalking and female genital mutilation. In most Australian jurisdictions, offences against the person are based on modifications of the *Offences Against the Person Act* 1861 (UK) 24 & 25 Vict c 100. This Act largely consolidated the common law together with a variety of statutory provisions.

The structure of the offences in the *Offences Against the Person Act* leaves much to be desired. Sir James Stephen wrote in this regard:

> Their arrangement is so obscure, their language so lengthy and cumbrous, and they are
> based upon and assume the existence of so many singular common law principles that no-
> one who was not already well acquainted with the law would derive any information from
> reading them.[1]

---

1   From a Letter to Sir John Holker 20 January 1877, cited by R Cross, "The Reports of the Criminal Law Commissioners
     (1833–1849) and the Abortive Bills of 1853" in P Glazebrook (ed), *Reshaping the Criminal Law* (London: Stevens &
     Sons, 1978), p 10.

In 1985, the Victorian Parliament enacted a scheme of offences that departed quite dramatically from the 1861 statutory provisions. This scheme was based on a proposal originally put forward by the English Criminal Law Revision Committee in 1980: *Offences Against the Person*, Fourteenth Report (Cmnd 7844, 1980). The proposal was again recommended in a modified form by the English Law Commission in *Criminal Law: A Criminal Code for England and Wales* (Law Comm 177, 1989) and again in *Legislating the Criminal Code: Offences Against the Person and General Principles* (Law Comm No 218, 1993). The Victorian scheme sets out offences based on causing injury, thereby focussing on the degree of harm caused. The Model Criminal Code Officers Committee (MCCOC) has suggested that a similar scheme based on degrees of fault and seriousness of injury should provide the basis for the *Model Criminal Code: Chapter 5 — Non-Fatal Offences Against the Person*, Discussion Paper (1996); *Chapter 5 — Non-Fatal Offences Against the Person*, Report (1998).

At present, there is much overlap between offences and accordingly a great deal of discretion has been given to the police, prosecuting authorities, magistrates and judges in the trial process. Social attitudes toward particular types of violence can be highly persuasive in defining what constitutes offences against the person. Historically, for example, there has been a reluctance to prosecute assaults that occur in the context of the home: A Cretney and G Davis, "Prosecuting 'Domestic' Assault" [1996] Crim LR 162 at 163. Nicholas Seddon writes in his book *Domestic Violence in Australia* (2nd ed, Sydney: The Federation Press, 1993), p iv that this may partly be because of the shame felt by victims of domestic violence:

> Though violence against a family member is undoubtedly criminal conduct, deep-seated
> beliefs about the privacy of the family and shame about exposing a failure in the family
> relationship to the outside world act as powerful deterrents. Resort to law is, therefore,
> often a sign of desperation.

It has been exceptionally difficult to deal with violence that occurs in the domestic arena because of complex social attitudes toward the private realm. However, in the past two decades, there has been a growing awareness of the personal and social costs caused by domestic violence. This has elicited a range of legislative and policy responses.

In September 1996, the Federal Government convened the National Domestic Violence Forum in Canberra. This resulted in a Discussion Paper released in November 1997[2] and a Report published in April 1999.[3] Both papers focus on protection orders and the need for a uniform approach across Australian jurisdictions. Rosemary Hunter and Julie Stubbs have criticised the Discussion Paper as being too technical and concentrating on discrete sectors in the absence of any guiding principles: R Hunter and J Stubbs, "Model Laws or Missed Opportunity" (1999) 24(1) *Alternative Law Journal* 12. They also point out that it fails to consider issues of criminal and family law relevant to domestic violence. We will concentrate on the public order problems associated with prosecuting offences that occur in the domestic context in Chapter 14: pp 756ff. We have also considered the notion of domestic violence and victim complicity in Chapter 8, pp 397-401.

---

2   Domestic Violence Legislation Working Group, *Model Domestic Violence Laws*, Discussion Paper (1997).
3   Domestic Violence Legislation Working Group, *Model Domestic Violence Laws,* Report (1999).

In 1996, the Australian Bureau of Statistics conducted a National Women's Safety Study that involved interviewing 6300 women. In that sample, 23% of women who had ever been married or in a de facto relationship had experienced violence. "Violence" was defined as any incident involving the occurrence or attempt or threat of either physical or sexual assault: Australian Bureau of Statistics, *Women's Safety, Australia* (Canberra: AGPS, 1996). See further S Parker, P Parkinson and J Behrens, *Australian Family Law in Context — Commentary and Materials* (2nd ed, Sydney: LBC Information Services, 1999), pp 357-366.

In 1996, the British Crime Survey conducted by the Home Office used a computer-assisted self-interviewing questionnaire on domestic violence. Analysis of the data found that 23% of women and 15% of men aged 16-59 said they had been physically assaulted by a current or former partner at some time. Twenty-eight per cent of women aged 20-24 said they had been assaulted by a partner at some time and 34% had been threatened or assaulted. Women were more likely to be injured (47%) than men (31%). The majority of female victims said they had been very frightened, compared to a minority of men. Although the questions asked about incidents that would legally be considered assaults, only 17% of incidents counted by the survey were considered to be crimes by their victims: C Mirrlees-Black, Home Office Research Study 191, *Domestic Violence: Findings from a New British Crime Survey Self-Completion Questionnaire* (London: Home Office, 1999).

In this chapter, we will outline the current law relating to the offences of assault, aggravated assault and the related offences of threats, offences endangering life or personal safety and false imprisonment, child abduction and kidnapping. We will also outline the different categories of lawful assault, paying particular attention to the issue of consent as well as having separate sections on female genital mutilation, stalking and consent relating to sadomasochism. The final concluding section will deal with the proposals for reform put forward by the MCCOC.

2. ASSAULT

The term assault is now generally used to encompass two types of unlawful interference with the person of another. In the first instance, an assault is any act committed intentionally or recklessly which puts another person in fear of immediate and unlawful personal violence. In addition, the term assault may be used to encompass the situation where a person causes force to be applied to the body or clothing of another. This type of assault was formerly referred to at common law as "battery", but this distinction no longer applies as both statute and case law use the term "assault" to cover both putting another in fear and the use of force: *R v Lynsey* [1995] 3 All ER 654. In this chapter, the first type of assault will be referred to as "assault by the threat of force" and the second "assault using force".

The various statutory provisions also draw a distinction between "common" assault and a number of more serious offences, generally termed aggravated assaults, which are built upon the proof of the commission of an assault. "Common" assault exists in statutory form in all jurisdictions apart from Victoria.[4] Despite the new statutory scheme in Victoria, common assault at common law was not abolished and it continues to carry a penalty at the judge's discretion.[5]

> In 1998, there were 132,297 assaults in Australia recorded by the police. There were more male victims of assault than females in all age categories and both males and females were most at risk of being a victim of assault while aged between 15-24. A large majority of male victims (72%) were assaulted in non-residential locations, whereas a majority (58%) of female victims were assaulted in residential premises: Australian Institute of Criminology, *Australian Crime, Facts and Figures* (Canberra: AIC, 1999).

The structure of the more serious assaults divides them into common assaults aggravated either by the nature of the intent of the accused, the status of the victim or by the harm thereby done. Because these offences share the fact that they are built upon the occurrence of a common assault, an alternative verdict of common assault is generally available where the circumstances of aggravation or its accompanying mental state are not proven. For example, in the Australian Capital Territory, the Northern Territory, Queensland, Tasmania and Western Australia, common assault is an alternative verdict to wounding.[6]

2.1 COMMON ASSAULT — PHYSICAL ELEMENTS

Common assault may occur either by the threat of force or through the use of force. The common law definition of assault applies in the Australian Capital Territory, New South Wales, South Australia and Victoria. The leading case setting out this definition is *Fagan v Commissioner of Metropolitan Police* [1969] 1 QB 439. James LJ stated in that case (at 444):

> An assault is any act which intentionally — or possibly/recklessly — causes another person to apprehend immediate and unlawful personal violence ... and the actual intended use of unlawful force to another person without his [or her] consent.

The Code jurisdictions offer statutory definitions of assault that are of similar effect.[7]

---

4   *Crimes Act* 1900 (ACT), s 26; *Crimes Act* 1900 (NSW), s 61; *Criminal Code* (NT), s 188; *Criminal Code* (Qld), s 335; *Criminal Law Consolidation Act* 1935 (SA), s 39; *Criminal Code* (Tas), s 184; *Criminal Code* (WA), s 313.

5   *R v Patton* [1998] 1 VR 7. Section 31 of the *Crimes Acts* 1958 (Vic) is entitled "assault", but is limited to assaults with intent to commit an indictable offence, assaults on police or those aiding police and assaults permitted in order to resist or prevent lawful detention.

6   *Crimes Act* 1900 (ACT), s 47; *Criminal Code* (NT), s 315; *Criminal Code* (Qld), s 575; *Criminal Code* (Tas), s 334A; *Criminal Code* (WA), s 594.

7   *Criminal Code* (NT), s 187; *Criminal Code* (Qld), s 245(1); *Criminal Code* (Tas), s 182; *Criminal Code* (WA), s 222.

THE THREAT OF FORCE

An assault by the threat of force is any act committed intentionally or recklessly which puts another person in fear of immediate and unlawful personal violence or, in the Code jurisdictions, indicates an actual or apparent present ability to apply force.[8]

There are divergent views between jurisdictions as to the answers to the following four questions:

▬ **What sort of conduct is sufficient to amount to a threat of force?**

▬ **Must the victim know of the accused's act?**

▬ **What constitutes the requirement of immediacy or actual or apparent present ability to commit force?**

▬ **Will a conditional threat suffice?**

Conduct Constituting a Threat of Force

In relation to the first area of concern, *Fagan v Commissioner of Metropolitan Police* [1969] 1 QB 439 at 444 per James LJ, set out a general principle that an omission to act cannot constitute an assault. Some form of positive act is necessary such as a threatening gesture.[9] In Tasmania, and, by implication, Queensland and Western Australia,[10] the use of words alone cannot constitute an assault. In contrast, in the Northern Territory,[11] and at common law,[12] an assault by the threat of force may be evidenced either by bodily movement or threatening words by themselves.

Threatening words made over the telephone may amount to an assault at common law.[13] But what of silence? In the case of *R v Ireland; R v Burstow* [1998] AC 147 the House of Lords took a broad approach to the definition of a positive act in holding that the making of a series of silent telephone calls that caused fear of immediate and unlawful bodily harm amounted to assault. Lord Steyn stated (at 162):

> [T]he critical question [is] whether a silent caller may be guilty of an assault. The answer to this question seems to me to be "Yes, depending on the facts." ... Take now the case of the silent caller. He intends by his silence to cause fear and he is so understood ... As a matter

---

8   *Criminal Code* (NT), s 187(b); *Criminal Code* (Qld), s 245; *Criminal Code* (Tas), s 182(1); *Criminal Code* (WA), s 222; *Fagan v Commissioner of Metropolitan Police* [1969] 1 QB 439; *R v Venna* [1975] 3 All ER 788; *Rozsa v Samuels* [1969] SASR 205; *Knight* (1988) 35 A Crim R 314,

9   *Beal v Kelley* [1951] 2 All ER 763; *Fairclough v Whipp* [1951] 2 All ER 834; *DPP v Rogers* [1953] 2 All ER 644; *Rolfe* (1952) 36 Cr App Rep 4 at 6 (CCA); *R v Dale* [1969] QWN 30; *Hall v Foneca* [1983] WAR 309.

10 *Criminal Code* (Tas), s 182(2). Section 245 of the *Criminal Code* (Qld) and s 222 of the *Criminal Code* (WA) use wording appropriate only to physical gestures.

11 *Criminal Code* (NT), s 187(b); *R v Secretary* (1996) 5 NTLR 96 per Mildren J.

12 *R v Wilson* [1955] 1 All ER 744; *R v Tout* (1987) 11 NSWLR 251 at 256-257 per Lee J; *Barton v Armstrong* [1969] 2 NSWR 451 at 455 per Taylor J; *Knight* (1988) 35 A Crim R 314 at 318 per Lee J; *R v Ireland; R v Burstow* [1998] AC 147 at 162 per Lord Steyn.

13 *Barton v Armstrong* [1969] 2 NSWR 451 at 455 per Taylor J; *R v Knight* [1998] 35 A Crim R 31; *R v Ireland; R v Burstow* [1997] 3 WLR 534 at 546 per Lord Steyn.

of law the caller may be guilty of an assault: whether he is or not will depend on the circumstance and in particular on the impact of the caller's potentially menacing call or calls on the victim.

The Victim's Mental State

The second divergent area concerns the victim's mental state. At common law, the act constituting assault must be such as to raise in the mind of the person threatened an apprehension of immediate bodily harm: *R v McNamara* [1954] VLR 137 at 138; *Brady v Schatzel* [1911] QSR 206. This is generally assessed by reference to whether or not a reasonable person would have been put in fear: *Barton v Armstrong* [1969] 2 NSWR 451 at 455 per Taylor J. At common law, assault by the threat of force requires the victim's knowledge[14] and an apprehension of personal violence may exist even where the accused is not in a position to carry out the threat.

For example, if a victim reasonably believes that a firearm may be loaded and that he or she is within range, the accused's actions may amount to an assault whether the gun is actually loaded or not.[15] In *R v Everingham* (1949) 66 WN (NSW) 122 the accused pointed a toy gun at a taxi driver who thought that it was real. The New South Wales Court of Appeal held (at 122) that these facts established "as clear a case of assault" as could be imagined.

At the opposite end of the scale, there may be no assault where the victim believes in facts that remove the apprehension. The facts of the following case illustrate this point. In *R v Lamb* [1967] 2 QB 981, the accused and the victim were playing "Russian Roulette" with a loaded revolver. In this case apprehension normally experienced by a person at which a loaded gun is pointed was absent. This was due to a mistaken belief, shared by the accused and the victim that neither of the two bullets in the chamber would be discharged because they were not opposite the firing pin.

In the Code jurisdictions, however, it appears possible for an assault to occur where a person has an actual ability to apply force to another regardless of whether or not the victim has knowledge of that ability.[16] Emphasis in these jurisdictions is placed on an *actual* present ability to apply force or an *apparent* present ability. Where there is an *actual* ability, it is irrelevant whether or not the victim has knowledge of that ability.[17] Where, however, there is an *apparent* present ability, the emphasis on the victim's apprehension is similar as for the common law. The victim must believe that the accused has an ability to apply force. This belief, in Tasmania, must be based upon reasonable grounds: *Criminal Code* (Tas), s 182(1).

The inquiry into the victim's apprehension of the accused's ability to apply force involves a subjective test. It does not depend upon what a reasonable person would have apprehended, but what the victim him or herself apprehended. In *Barton v Armstrong* [1969] 2 NSWLR 451 in the context of determining the civil liability for assault, the Supreme Court of New South Wales set out an objective test, but this has not been followed: see, for example, *MacPherson v Beath* (1975) 12 SASR 174 at 177 per Bray CJ.

---

14   *State v Barry* (1912) 45 Mont 598; *Pemble v The Queen* (1971) 124 CLR 107 at 134 per Menzies J and at 141 per Owens J; *R v Lamb* [1967] 2 QB 981. Pointing a gun at the back of a person's head or holding a knife over a sleeping person would therefore not constitute an assault at common law.

15   *R v St George* (1840) 9 Car & P 483; *R v Everingham* (1949) 66 WN (NSW) 122; *Logdon v DPP* [1976] Crim LR 121.

16   *Criminal Code* (NT), s 187(b); *Criminal Code* (Qld), s 245; *Criminal Code* (Tas), s 182(1); *Criminal Code* (WA), s 222.

17   *Criminal Code* (NT), s 187(b); *Criminal Code* (Qld), s 245; *Criminal Code* (Tas), s 182(1); *Criminal Code* (WA), s 222.

Perhaps because the inquiry into the victim's apprehension is subjective, there is some confusion in the case law as to whether or not the prosecution must show that the accused was *in fact* put in fear. In *Brady v Schatzel; Ex parte Brady* [1911] St R Qd 206 the victim gave evidence that when the accused pointed a gun at him, he did not believe the accused would fire it. It was argued that because the victim was not afraid, there was no assault. This argument was rejected and it was held that there could be an assault even where the victim was not put in fear. Chubb J of the Queensland Supreme Court stated (at 208):

> [I]t is not material that the person assaulted should be put in fear ... If that were so, it would make an assault not dependent upon the intention of the assailant, but upon the question whether the party assaulted was a courageous or a timid person.

All that is needed on this view, is the anticipation of the application of unlawful personal violence. In *Ryan v Kuhl; Wilson Kuhl* [1979] VR 315 the victim was in a cubicle in a public toilet at a railway station. The accused pushed a knife through a hole in the partition between the cubicles in order, he claimed, to stop the victim from annoying him. McGarvie J of the Supreme Court of Victoria held (at 327) that there was no assault in these circumstances because the victim had not been put in fear:

> [O]n the evidence it could not be inferred that the defendant's conduct created in Matthews [the "victim"] a fear of violence. Matthews said that he realized at the time that the person in the next cubicle could not harm him with the knife while he remained in his cubicle. He also said that the sight of the knife had not scared him and said that he had not gone to the station master because he was frightened. On the other hand he also gave evidence that the sight of the knife had shocked him, that he said out aloud, "Are you mad or something?", then opened the door and walked quickly out of the toilet.

These differing viewpoints may partly be caused by the common law placing more emphasis on the accused's state of mind than in the Code jurisdictions. That of course begs the question *should* the victim's state of mind be the focus here at all? Isn't the doing of an act with the intention of causing fear enough to attract criminal liability? The latter certainly complies with the general principle of taking one's victim as one finds him or her. This principle has certainly been at the forefront of the law relating to unlawful killing.[18] However, if the Model Criminal Code Officers Committee (MCCOC) approach is to be followed, the focus will be on the degree of harm caused and therefore the *effect* of the threat of force on the victim will be of central concern: *Chapter 5 — Non-Fatal Offences Against the Person,* Report (1998).

The Notion of Immediacy

There is a further lack of clarity as to what is meant by the requirement of immediacy or actual or apparent present ability to commit force. At common law, there must be an apprehension of *immediate* bodily harm.[19] Instances of where bodily harm has been considered to be immediate include:

---

18   See, for example, *Mamote-Kulang of Tamagot v The Queen* (1964) 111 CLR 62; *R v Blaue* [1975] 1 WLR 1411; *Hubert* (1993) 67 A Crim R 181.

19   *Wilson v Pringle* [1986] 2 All ER 440; *Logdon v DPP* [1976] Crim LR 121; *Knight* (1988) 35 A Crim R 314.

▬ where the accused was in another room;[20]

▬ where the accused was on the other side of a locked door apparently about to break it down;[21]

▬ where the accused opened a drawer and showed the victim a gun declaring that he would hold her hostage;[22] and

▬ where the accused peered in through a bedroom window at the victim who was wearing her night clothes.[23]

The general rule is that where a threat is made, even in the most menacing fashion, of future violence, an assault will not be made out. For example, in *Knight* (1988) 35 A Crim R 314 the accused had made a series of threatening phone calls. The New South Wales Court of Appeal held (at 317) that since the calls were made from an appreciable distance away and the recipients of the calls were not in any danger of immediate violence there was no conduct that could constitute an assault: "They were mere threats which may have been executed at anytime if at all", per Lee J.

However, the requirement of immediacy has been criticised as being too restrictive. In *Barton v Armstrong* [1969] 2 NSWLR 451 which concerned a tort action for assault, Taylor J commented (at 455):

> Being able to immediately carry out the threat or being thus perceived by [the victim] is but one way of creating the fear of apprehension, but not the only way. There are other ways, more subtle and perhaps more effective ... If the threat produces the fear or apprehension of physical violence then I am of [the] opinion that the law is breached, although the victim does not know when that physical violence may be effected.

In that case, a telephone threat of serious violence by a person in authority whom the victim feared was held to constitute an assault.

There is no requirement of immediacy in the Code jurisdictions. Rather, the emphasis is on the "present ability" of the accused to carry out the threat.[24] This term is said to bear its ordinary meaning,[25] but just what time period is appropriate for a "present" ability is unclear.

There is some reason to believe that at common law, the requirement for immediacy may be relaxed in some circumstances. For example, in *Zanker v Vartzokas* (1988) 34 A Crim R 11, the victim accepted a lift from the accused. Once in the car, the accused offered the victim money for sex. The victim refused and demanded that she be let out of the car. The accused kept accelerating the car and stated: "I am going to take you to my mate's house. He will really fix you up". The victim then jumped out of the car. The Supreme Court of South Australia held (at 14 per White J) that:

---

20 *R v Lewis* [1970] Crim LR 647 (CA).

21 *Beech* (1912) 7 Cr App R 197.

22 *Logdon v DPP* [1976] Crim LR 121.

23 *Smith v Chief Superintendent Woking Police Station* (1983) 76 Cr App R 234.

24 *Criminal Code* (NT), s 187; *Criminal Code* (Qld), s 245; *Criminal Code* (Tas), s 182; *Criminal Code* (WA), s 222.

25 *R v Secretary* (1996) 5 NTLR 96 at 104-105.

A present fear of relatively immediate imminent violence was instilled in her mind from the moment the words were uttered and that fear was kept alive in her mind, in the continuing present, by continuing progress with her as prisoner, towards the house where the feared sexual violence was to occur.

The House of Lords in *R v Ireland; R v Burstow* [1998] AC 147 held that, depending on the circumstances, there may be an apprehension of immediate violence present when a silent telephone call is made. Lord Steyn stated (at 162):

[The silent caller] intends by his silence to cause fear and he is so understood. The victim is assailed by uncertainty about his intentions. Fear may dominate her emotions, and it may be the fear that the caller's arrival at her door may be imminent. She may fear the *possibility* of immediate personal violence.

Lord Steyn went on to criticise the need for the concept of an assault to involve an element of immediate personal violence because it was a complicating factor in prosecutions for stalking and silent telephone callers. He supported the creation of proposals for the abolition of this requirement and (at 162) a statutory offence of intentionally or recklessly causing injury.

Conditional Threats

Finally, there is some lack of clarity as to whether a conditional threat will suffice for assault. This matter was raised in *Rozsa v Samuels* [1969] SASR 205. The accused was a taxi driver who was convicted of assaulting another taxi driver who had objected to his queue jumping. The victim had remonstrated with the accused and said he would punch the accused in the head. The accused produced a knife and said "I will cut you to bits if you try it". The question on appeal to the Supreme Court of South Australia was whether or not the threat to use force, accompanied by words which indicate the threat was conditional, constituted an assault. The Court held that the mere fact that the threat was conditional did not prevent it constituting one of the elements necessary to establish assault.

The Supreme Court accepted that the common law draws a distinction between

- **a conditional threat which is unlawful (one that the party has no right to impose) which constitutes an assault; and**

- **a conditional threat which is lawful (one that the party has the right to impose) which is not an assault. An example of this would be where the threat is made to apply force unless the person threatened desists from some unlawful course of action.**

On the facts, the accused's conditional threat was considered unlawful because it went beyond what was reasonable in self-defence and his appeal was therefore dismissed. It is unclear whether this interpretation carries over into the Code jurisdictions. It could be argued that it does given there is no requirement for immediacy. In *Secretary* (1996) 86 A Crim R 119 the Northern Territory Court of Criminal Appeal held that a threat can be of future violence and the issue of "present ability" is to be determined with reference to the circumstances at the time when the threat would supposedly be carried out. On this basis, a conditional threat can be assessed in relation to when it would be carried out.

THE USE OF FORCE

An assault by the use of force occurs where a person, intentionally or recklessly, causes force to be applied to the body or clothing of another.[26] An assault may occur not only where force is applied to the body of the victim, but also where clothing is slashed or rubbed: *R v Day* (1845) 1 Cox 207; *Thomas* (1985) 81 Cr App R 331. The force used need not be violent, but can be as slight as a mere touch: *Collins v Wilcock* [1984] 3 All ER 374. Thus, kissing or touching another who does not consent to such conduct may constitute an assault. If an injury results from the application of force and it is more than minor, then the accused may be charged with an aggravated assault.

Usually an assault is committed by delivering a blow with a limb or using a weapon of some kind. However, the Queensland and Western Australian provisions specifically define the use of force so as to include the application of heat, light, electrical force, gas or odour so as to cause injury or personal discomfort: *Criminal Code* (Qld), s 245; *Criminal Code* (WA), s 222.

At common law, it appears that the application of force must be direct in that it must be aimed at the victim or an object on which the victim is supported.[27] In comparison, in the Code jurisdictions, indirect application of force is sufficient provided that there is adequate evidence of causation.[28]

2.2 COMMON ASSAULT — THE FAULT ELEMENT

In all jurisdictions, a common assault may be committed intentionally or recklessly.[29] Although the Queensland and Western Australian *Criminal Codes* do not specify the fault requirement for an assault, in *Hall v Fonceca* [1983] WAR 309 it was accepted at 314 that the fault element was the same as for common law. Assault has been referred to as a crime of basic intent[30] in that it is a crime involving a specified form of conduct and intention therefore refers to the accused meaning to perform the conduct. Thus for assault by the threat of force, the accused must mean to commit the act creating an apprehension of immediate and unlawful personal violence. Similarly, for assault using force, the accused must mean to use force on the victim.

If the MCCOC's recommendation is followed in setting out a series of statutory crimes based on causing harm,[31] these crimes could be viewed as result rather than conduct crimes. In relation to

---

26 *Beal v Kelley* [1951] 2 All ER 763; *Fairclough v Whipp* [1951] 2 All ER 834; *DPP v Rogers* [1953] 2 All ER 644; *Rolfe* (1952) 36 Cr App R 4; *R v McCormack* [1969] 2 QB 442; *Fagan v Metropolitan Police Commissioner* [1969] 1 QB 439; *R v Venna* [1976] QB 421; *R v Spratt* [1990] 1 WLR 1073; *R v Parmenter* [1991] 3 WLR 914; *Criminal Code* (NT), s 187(a); *Criminal Code* (Qld), s 245; *Criminal Code* (Tas), s 182(1); *Criminal Code* (WA), s 222.

27 *R v Salisbury* [1976] VR 452; *Commissioner of Police v Wilson* [1984] AC 242; *R v Sheriff* [1969] Crim LR 260.

28 *Criminal Code* (NT), s 187(a); *Criminal Code* (Qld), s 245; *Criminal Code* (Tas), s 182(1); *Criminal Code* (WA), s 222.

29 *R v Spratt* [1991] 2 All ER 210; *Vallance v The Queen* (1961) 108 CLR 56; *Leonard v Morris* (1975) 10 SASR 528; *MacPherson v Brown* (1975) 12 SASR 184; *R v Bacash* [1981] VR 923; *Criminal Code* (NT), s 31; *Criminal Code* (Qld), s 23; *Criminal Code* (Tas), s 182; *Criminal Code* (WA), s 23.

30 *R v O' Connor* (1980) 146 CLR 64; *DPP v Majewski* [1977] AC 443; *Duffy v The Queen* [1981] WAR 72.

31 Model Criminal Code Officers Committee, *Chapter 5: Non Fatal Offences Against the Person*, Discussion Paper (1996), p 26; Model Criminal Code Officers Committee, *Chapter 5: Non Fatal Offences Against the Person*, Report (1998), p 13.

the physical element as the results or consequences of conduct, the prosecution must prove that the accused's *purpose* was to bring about the results or consequences of the conduct.[32] In relation to a statutory crime of intentionally causing harm, the accused must be shown to have intended to cause that harm and not just the *act* that may have resulted in harm. However, the existing law in relation to assaults occasioning actual bodily harm views intention as relating to the use of force rather than the resulting bodily harm: see below, p 549. This offence is therefore viewed as a conduct rather than a result crime and the MCCOC has made it clear that this should carry over to the MCCOC's scheme: *Chapter 5 — Non Fatal Offences Against the Person*, Discussion Paper (1996), p 29.

In keeping common assault as a conduct crime, a narrow, direct form of intention appears appropriate. Brennan J stated in this regard in *He Kaw Teh v The Queen* (1985) 157 CLR 523 at 569 that intention "connotes a decision to bring about a situation so far as it is possible to do so — to bring about an act of a particular kind or a particular result".

The concept of recklessness in relation to common assault is somewhat unclear. An assault will be made out if the accused foresaw unlawful force or the act causing an apprehension of immediate and unlawful personal violence: *Fagan v Commissioner of Metropolitan Police* [1969] 1 QB 439 at 444 per James LJ. However, the *degree* of foresight required is uncertain. Some authorities simply refer to the need for recklessness to be proven without further explanation.[33] However, in *MacPherson v Brown* (1975) 12 SASR 184 Bray CJ stated (at 187) that it will be enough that the accused foresaw the *possibility* that force might be inflicted.[34] The alternative is that the accused must have foreseen that force would *probably* be inflicted. In *R v Campbell* [1997] 2 VR 585 Hayne J and Crockett AJA spoke with approval of the High Court test of recklessness in relation to murder as set out in *R v Crabbe* (1985) 156 CLR 464. Hayne J and Crockett AJA concluded (at 592-593) in relation to the offence of recklessly causing serious injury:

> We have no doubt that the appropriate test to apply is that it is possession of foresight that injury *probably* will result that must be proved (original emphasis).[35]

Phillips CJ agreed with this point at 586.

Campbell's case, however, applies to the statutory offence of recklessly causing injury and not to common assault. The weight of common law authority does seem to be in favour of foresight in terms of possibility rather than probability. This requirement is also clearly set out in the Northern Territory. Section 31 of the *Criminal Code* (NT) specifies that an assault is committed whether the harm is "intended or foreseen ... as a possible consequence of [the accused's] conduct".

---

32 *La Fontaine v The Queen* (1976) 136 CLR 62; *R v Crabbe* (1985) 156 CLR 464; *Boughey v The Queen* (1986) 161 CLR 10; *R v Demirian* [1989] VR 97.

33 *Fagan v Commissioner of Metropolitan Police* [1969] 1 QB 439 at 444; *Logdon v DPP* [1976] Crim LR 121 at 122; *R v Venna* [1976] QB 421.

34 See also *Williams* (1990) 50 A Crim R 213; *R v Coleman* (1990) 19 NSWLR 467 at 475-478 per Hunt J; *R v Lovett* [1975] VR 488 at 493-494 per Harris J: *R v Savage* [1992] 1 AC 699 at 752 per Lord Ackner.

35 Also see *R v Crabbe* (1985) 156 CLR 464 at 592-593 per Phillips CJ.

2.3 AGGRAVATED ASSAULTS

A wide variety of statutory offences generally termed "aggravated assaults" authorise the imposition of greater penalties than for common assault. These statutory offences can be divided into three classes:

=== assaults accompanied by an intention of a particular kind;

=== assaults committed on particular classes of people; and

=== assaults resulting in harm of a particular kind.

ASSAULTS ACCOMPANIED BY AN INTENTION OF A PARTICULAR KIND

The most serious form of aggravated assault involving a particular intention is assault with intent to commit murder.[36] The accused must intend to kill as opposed to intending to inflict grievous bodily harm even though that would be sufficient to render the accused guilty of murder if death resulted.[37] It is not sufficient that the accused acted with recklessness as to the possibility of death: *R v Belfon* [1976] 3 All ER 46.

There are also statutory provisions dealing with assaults with intent to commit another crime.[38] In all jurisdictions, it is an offence to commit an assault with intent to resist or prevent the lawful apprehension of the accused or of any other person for any offence.[39] The arrest that the accused was seeking to resist or prevent must have been in exercise of a legal right. The question is not whether the accused believed that the arrest was lawful, but whether such arrest was in fact lawful: *R v Heavey* (1965) 84 WN (Pt 1) NSW 248; *Williams v The Queen* (1986) 161 CLR 278.

ASSAULTS COMMITTED ON PARTICULAR CLASSES OF PEOPLE

Assaults on particular classes of people are viewed as aggravated because of the special status of the people concerned. For example, it is an offence to assault a police officer in the execution of his or her duty.[40] Except in Victoria, it is not necessary for the prosecution to prove that the accused

---

36 *Crimes Act* 1900 (NSW), s 27; *Criminal Code* (NT), s 165; *Criminal Code* (Qld), s 306; *Criminal Code* (WA), s 283. In the other jurisdictions, the crime of attempted murder falls under the general law of attempt: see Ch 9, p 435.

37 *Whybrow* (1951) 35 Cr App Rep 141; *R v Grimwood* [1962] 2 QB 621; *R v Bozikis* [1981] VR 587 at 591.

38 *Crimes Act* 1900 (ACT), s 22; *Crimes Act* 1900 (NSW), s 58; *Criminal Code* (NT), s 193; *Criminal Code* (Qld), s 340(a); *Criminal Law Consolidation Act* 1935 (SA), s 270B; *Criminal Code* (Tas), s 183(a); *Crimes Act* 1958 (Vic), s 31(1)(a); *Criminal Code* (WA), s 317A.

39 *Crimes Act* 1900 (ACT), ss 27(4)(b), 32(1)(b); *Crimes Act* 1900 (NSW), ss 58, 61k; *Criminal Code* (NT), ss 188(2)(h), 189A; *Criminal Code* (Qld), s 340(a)-(e); *Criminal Law Consolidation Act* 1935 (SA), s 43(c); *Criminal Code* (Tas), s 183(a); *Crimes Act* 1958 (Vic), s 31(1)(c); *Criminal Code* (WA), s 317A(c).

40 *Crimes Act* 1900 (ACT), ss 27(4)(c), 32(1)(b); *Crimes Act* 1900 (NSW), s 58; *Criminal Code* (NT), s 188(2)(h); *Criminal Code* (Qld), s 340(b), (e); *Criminal Law Consolidation Act* 1935 (SA), s 43(b); *Police Offences Act* 1935 (Tas), s 34B(1); *Crimes Act* 1958 (Vic), s 31(1)(b); *Criminal Code* (WA), s 318(1)(d)-(f).

knew that the person assaulted was a police officer.[41] In comparison, s 31(b) of the *Crimes Act* 1958 (Vic) requires the prosecution to prove that the accused *knew* that the person was a police officer. The offence is committed only if the officer is acting in the execution of his or her duty.[42] This has been defined very broadly. The Federal Court stated in *R v K* (1993) 118 ALR 596 (at 601):

> [A] police officer acts in the execution of his [or her] duty from the moment he [or she] embarks upon a lawful task connected with his [or her] functions as a police officer, and continues to act in the execution of that duty for as long as he [or she] is engaged in pursuing the task and until it is completed, provided that he [or she] does not in the course of the task do anything outside the ambit of his [or her] duty so as to cease to be acting therein.

The scope of police duties is not confined to the apprehension of crime, but extends to taking reasonable steps to prevent crime and disorder: see Ch 14, 2.3 'Policing Public Order', pp 761ff. Other classes of person receive special protection in certain jurisdictions. These include:

▬ **women;[43]**

▬ **those under a certain age;[44]**

▬ **those unable to defend themselves by reason of infirmity, age, physique, situation or other disability;[45]**

▬ **members of Parliament where the assault is committed because of such membership;[46]**

▬ **members of the public service or the judiciary;[47]**

▬ **those serving court documents[48] or executing any process against lands or goods;[49]**

▬ **those protecting wrecked vessels;[50]**

---

41 *R v Forbes & Webb* (1865) 10 Cox CC 362; *R v Reynhoudt* (1962) 107 CLR 381; *McBride v Turnock* [1964] Crim LR 456; *McArdle v Wallace* [1964] Crim LR 467.

42 *R v Cumpton* (1880) 5 QBD 341; *Davis v Lisle* [1936] 2 KB 434; *Duncan v Jones* [1936] 1 KB 218; *R v Waterfield* [1964] 1 QB 164; *McArdle v Wallace* [1964] Crim LR 467; *Kenlin v Gardiner* [1967] 2 QB 510; *Donnelly v Jackman* [1970] 1 All ER 987; *Gardner* (1979) 71 Cr App Rep 13; *Coffin v Smith* (1980) 71 Cr App Rep 221; *Lindley v Rutter* (1980) 72 Cr App Rep 1; *Pedro v Diss* [1981] 2 All ER 59; *Collins v Wilcock* [1984] 1 WLR 1172; *Weight v Long* [1986] Crim LR 746; *Noordhof v Bartlett* (1986) 69 ALR 323.

43 *Criminal Code* (NT), s 188(2)(b). Section 35(2) of the *Police Offences Act* 1935 (Tas) enables the imposition of a heavier penalty if the assault is on a female or a child and is of an aggravated nature.

44 *Crimes Act* 1900 (NSW), s 43; *Criminal Code* (NT), s 188(2)(c); *Criminal Code* (Qld), s 340(g); *Police Offences Act* (SA), 1935.

45 *Crimes Act* 1900 (NSW), s 44; *Criminal Code* (NT), s 188(2)(d).

46 *Criminal Code* (NT), s 188(2)(e); *Criminal Code* (WA), s 318(1)(d)-(f).

47 *Crimes Act* (NSW), ss 58, 326; *Criminal Code* (NT), ss 188(2)(f), 190; *District Courts Act* 1967 (Qld), s 129; *Criminal Code Consolidation Act* 1935 (SA), s 42; *Criminal Code* (WA), s 318A.

48 *Criminal Code* (NT), s 188(2)(h).

49 *Criminal Code* (Tas), s 183(b).

50 *Crimes Act* 1900 (NSW), s 57; *Criminal Code* (Qld), s 338; *Criminal Law Consolidation Act* 1935 (SA), s 42.

▬ members of a crew on board an aircraft;[51]

▬ members of the clergy;[52] and

▬ seamen.[53]

These classes reflect a degree of outmoded paternalism toward those perceived to need extra protection such as women and children, and the law's general abhorrence toward those who commit assaults on public officials. The Model Criminal Code Officers Committee (MCCOC) has suggested that there be increased penalties for assaults where factors of aggravation exist: *Chapter 5 — Non-Fatal Offences Against the Person*, Discussion Paper (August 1996), pp 92ff; *Chapter 5 — Non-Fatal Offences Against the Person,* Report (September 1998), pp 111ff. A modified version of these classes of person has been outlined. The MCCOC suggests the following categories:

▬ **public officials defined as including members of parliament, a Minister of the Crown, a judicial officer, a police officer, a person appointed by or employed by the Government of a Government agency;**

▬ **a person who was involved in any capacity in judicial proceedings;**

▬ **a child under the age of 10 years; and**

▬ **those to whom the accused is in a position of trust.**

The MCCOC approach is to place circumstances of aggravation into the sentencing stage of procedure, rather than have separate statutory crimes of causing harm to certain classes of person.

ASSAULTS RESULTING IN HARM OF A PARTICULAR KIND

We have already pointed out that the MCCOC has suggested that a scheme of non fatal offences against the person based on degrees of fault and seriousness of injury should provide the basis for the *Model Criminal Code: Chapter 5 — Non-Fatal Offences Against the Person*, Report (September 1998). In all jurisdictions, except Tasmania, there already exists a division between assaults causing actual bodily harm or injury, and grievous bodily harm or serious injury. There is also a related offence that exists in all jurisdictions apart from Victoria and the Northern Territory of unlawful wounding. Section 183 of the *Criminal Code* (Tas) creates a separate crime of aggravated assault and describes it as assault with intent to commit a crime or to resist lawful apprehension and the assault of a person in the lawful execution of process against land and goods. However, s 172 provides that any person who "causes grievous bodily harm to any person by any means whatever is guilty of a crime".

---

51 *Civil Aviation Act* 1988 (Cth), s 24; *Crimes (Aviation) Act* 1991 (Cth), s 21; *Crimes Act* 1900 (NSW), s 206; *Criminal Code* (NT), s 191; *Criminal Code* (Qld), s 338A; *Criminal Code* (WA), s 318A.

52 *Crimes Act* (NSW), s 56; *Criminal Law Consolidation Act* 1935 (SA), s 41.

53 *Criminal Law Consolidation Act* 1935 (SA), s 44.

Definitions of Types of Harm

The problem with the term "bodily harm" is that it appears to ignore the psychological harm that may result from an assault. Thus, at common law, an assault that causes shock or an hysterical reaction may amount to an assault occasioning actual bodily harm.[55] In *R v Chan-Fook* [1994] 2 ER 552 the Court held (at 559) that actual bodily harm includes "psychiatric injury", but it does not include mere emotions such as fear or distress or panic nor does it include states of mind that are not evidence of some "identifiable clinical condition".

The House of Lords in *R v Ireland; R v Burstow* [1997] 3 WLR 534, confirmed that bodily harm was no longer confined to physical harm and could include mental harm provided that it amounted to a "recognisable psychiatric illness".[54] In coming to this conclusion in *R v Ireland; R v Burstow* [1998] AC 147, Lord Steyn (at 159) was influenced by the position in the law of negligence in relation to nervous shock cases where the common law, supported by advances in modern psychiatry, no longer drew a rigid distinction between the mind and body. He concluded (at 159) that the term "bodily harm" used in the *Offences Against the Person Act* 1861 (UK) should be interpreted in light of these legal and scientific developments: "the statute must be interpreted in the light of the best current scientific appreciation of the link between the body and psychiatric injury". This decision has serious implications for the scope of many offences against the person in Australia which employ identical definitions of bodily harm, modelled on the *Offences Against the Person Act* 1861 (UK). The judicial expansion of bodily injury to include psychic injury is arguably unnecessary in light of the statutory offences of stalking recently enacted in all Australian jurisdictions: see below p 568.

The MCCOC has recommended that "harm" and "serious harm" are more appropriate terms: *Chapter 5 — Non-Fatal Offences Against the Person,* Report (1998), pp 21ff.

The main difference between these forms of aggravated assaults and unlawful wounding lies in the definition of the relevant types of harm. In relation to the offence of unlawful wounding,[56] a wound at common law consists of an injury involving a breaking through both the inner and outer skin.[57] The term is not defined in the *Criminal Codes*, but the common law definition has been applied by the Queensland Court of Criminal Appeal in *Jervis* (1991) 56 A Crim R 374. The word "unlawfully" in relation to this offence appears to be largely redundant in that it does no more than express the principle that certain uses of force may be lawful or justifiable if used in self-defence and arrest situations. The fault elements for this offence are the same as for assaults resulting in grievous bodily harm which will be discussed later: p 549.

---

54 For a critical review of these recent developments see L Dunford and V Pickford, "Is There a Qualitative Difference Between Physical and Psychiatric Harm in English Law?" (1999) 7 *Journal of Law and Medicine* 36 at 42ff; J Horder, "Reconsidering Psychic Assault" [1998] Crim LR 392.

55 *R v Miller* [1954] 2 QB 282; *R v Chan-Fook* [1994] 2 All ER 552; *R v Ireland; R v Burstow* [1997] 3 WLR 534 at 546-547 per Lord Steyn.

56 *Crimes Act* 1900 (ACT), s 21; *Crimes Act* 1900 (NSW), ss 33, 35; *Criminal Code* (Qld), s 323(1); *Criminal Law Consolidation Act* 1935 (SA), ss 21, 23; *Criminal Code* (Tas), s 172; *Criminal Code* (WA), s 301.

57 *R v Wood and McMahon* (1830) 1 Mood CC 278; *Moriarty v Brooks* (1834) 6 C & P 684; *R v Beckett* (1836) 1 Mood & R 526; *Vallance v The Queen* (1961) 108 CLR 56 at 77; *R v Berwick* [1979] Tas R 101.

In the Australian Capital Territory, New South Wales and South Australia, the relevant provisions refer to "actual bodily harm"[58] whereas the Code jurisdictions, apart from Tasmania, use "bodily harm".[59] In Victoria, the word used is "injury": *Crimes Act* 1958 (Vic), s 18. At common law, it has been held that the words "actual bodily harm" should be given their ordinary and natural meaning: *R v Metharam* [1961] 3 All ER 200. In Victoria, injury is defined in s 15 of the *Crimes Act* 1958 as including "unconsciousness, hysteria, pain and any substantial impairment of bodily function".

"Actual bodily harm" need not be permanent, but must be more than merely transient or trifling: *R v Donovan* [1934] 2 KB 498 at 509. The Code jurisdictions' definitions of "bodily harm" are similar. In the Northern Territory, "bodily injury" includes any hurt or injury that interferes with health[60] and in Queensland[61] and Western Australia,[62] this is extended to an interference with health or comfort. In *Wayne v Boldiston* (1992) 85 NTR 8, Mildren J stated that an assessment of bodily harm required focussing on the injury and its immediate consequences. In that case, the victim had received two cuts to the face that, after medical treatment, resulted in a slight cosmetic disfigurement. In upholding a conviction of assault causing bodily harm, Mildren J stated (at 13-14) that the fact the victim was left with only cosmetic injuries was irrelevant if the *immediate* result of the injury temporarily interfered with health. However, in *R v Tranby* [1992] 1 Qd R 432 De Jersey J held that "health" meant freedom from disease or ailment and an injury to body parts that have no function and do not cause disease or physical ailment would be insufficient.

In all jurisdictions, there exists an offence of assault resulting in some form of serious harm. The term "grievous bodily harm" is used in most jurisdictions,[63] with "grievous harm" used in the Northern Territory[64] and "serious injury" in Victoria.[65] "Grievous bodily harm" has been interpreted at common law as meaning bodily harm of a serious character.[66] It is a matter for the jury as to whether the injury complained of amounts to grievous bodily harm.[67] In the Australian Capital Territory and New South Wales, grievous bodily harm is defined as including "any permanent or serious disfiguring of the person".[68] "Serious injury" is defined in s 15 of the *Crimes Act* 1958 (Vic) as including "a combination of injuries".

The Code jurisdictions provide statutory definitions of the relevant terms. "Grievous bodily harm" is defined under s 1 of the *Criminal Code* (Qld) as the loss of a distinct part or an organ of the body, serious disfigurement or "any bodily injury of such a nature that, if left untreated, would

---

58   *Crimes Act* 1900 (ACT), s 24; *Crimes Act* 1900 (NSW), s 59; *Criminal Law Consolidation Act* 1935 (SA), s 40.

59   *Criminal Code* (NT), s 186; *Criminal Code* (Qld), s 328; *Criminal Code* (WA), s 306.

60   *Criminal Code* (NT), s 1.

61   *Criminal Code* (Qld), s 1.

62   *Criminal Code* (WA), s 1.

63   *Crimes Act* 1900 (ACT), ss 19, 20, 25; *Crimes Act* 1900 (NSW), ss 35, 54; *Criminal Code* (Qld), ss 317, 320; *Criminal Law Consolidation Act* 1935 (SA), ss 21, 23; *Criminal Code* (Tas), ss 170, 172; *Criminal Code* (WA), ss 294, 297.

64   *Criminal Code* (NT), ss 177, 181.

65   *Crimes Act* 1958 (Vic), ss 16, 17, 24.

66   *DPP v Smith* [1961] AC 290 at 334 per Viscount Kilmuir LC; *R v Metharam* [1961] 3 All ER 200; *R v Cunningham* [1982] AC 566; *R v Saunders* [1985] Crim LR 230 (CA).

67   *R v Miller* [1951] VLR 346 at 356-357; *R v Van Beelen* (1973) 4 SASR 353 at 404; *R v Perks* (1986) 41 SASR 335; *R v Blevins* (1988) 48 SASR 65 at 68; *DPP v Smith* [1961] AC 290 at 335; *Hyam v DPP* [1975] AC 55 at 68, 84, 94.

68   *Crimes Act* 1900 (ACT), s 4; *Crimes Act* 1900 (NSW), s 4(1).

endanger or be likely to endanger life, or to cause or be likely to cause permanent injury to health". The Western Australian definition is the same as this latter quoted part. However, s 1(4) of the *Criminal Code* extends it to include a "serious disease". The Tasmanian definition is also the same as the quoted part of the Queensland definition, but the words "serious injury" are used instead of "permanent injury".

Under s 1 of the *Criminal Code* (NT) "grievous harm" is similarly defined as "any physical or mental injury of such a nature as to endanger or be likely to endanger or to cause or be likely to cause permanent injury to health".

Working Definitions of Bodily Harm and Grievous Bodily Harm

Whether an injury reaches the threshold of "actual" or "grievous" bodily harm or is merely "transient or trifling" is a factual matter for the jury. The victim's own physiology and availability of medical treatment will play a determining role in how serious an injury will be for the victim. As Lord Mustill noted in *R v Brown* [1993] 2 WLR 556 at 600, some of the sado-masochistic activities of the accused involved a risk of genito-urinary infection and septicaemia, which though grave in former times, had been greatly reduced by modern medical science. From a practical perspective, the question of the seriousness of the injury (and thus the offence charged) will be determined when the charges are laid. In this regard, the police and prosecution play a significant role in determining the scope and content of concepts such as actual and grievous bodily harm. The discretion over the choice of charge will be influenced by substantive legal definitions as well as "working definitions" that operate through internal guidelines or policy documents. A study of hospital admissions in England identified a wide-range of factors that influence whether or not an assault will be criminalised. However, the researchers concluded that there was no relationship between offence seriousness (measured in terms of culpability and harm) and the likelihood of reporting, investigation, prosecution and punishment: C Clarkson, A Cretney, G Davies and J Shepherd, "Assaults: The Relationship between Seriousness, Criminalisation and Punishment" [1994] Crim LR 4.

PERSPECTIVES ON PUBLIC HEALTH

Grievous Bodily Harm and HIV/AIDS

There is some question as to whether grievous bodily harm encompasses serious diseases, particularly sexually transmitted diseases. In *R v Clarence* (1888) 22 QBD 23, the communication of a venereal disease was held not to amount to an infliction of grievous bodily harm. The consequences of this decision have recently been reconsidered in the light of incidents involving conduct that may result in the transmission of HIV/AIDS.

In the early 1990s, some jurisdictions decided to criminalise the spreading of a serious disease by enacting specific statutory provisions. For example, s 36 of the *Crimes Act* 1900 (NSW) was introduced by the *Crimes (Injuries) Amendment Act* 1990 (NSW). This criminalises causing or attempting to cause a "grievous bodily disease". Section 317 of the *Criminal Code* (Qld) has been extended to cover the intentional transmission of a serious disease. A serious disease is defined in s 1 as "a disease that would, if left untreated, be of such a nature as to —

(a) cause or be likely to cause any loss of a distinct part or organ of the body; or

(b) cause or be likely to cause serious disfigurement; or

(c) endanger or be likely to endanger life or to cause or be likely to cause permanent injury to health;

whether or not treatment is or could have been available.

Section 294(8) of the *Criminal Code* (WA) was introduced by the *Criminal Law Amendment Act (No 2)* 1992 (WA). This makes it an offence to do any act that is likely to result in a person contracting a serious disease with intent to do that person grievous bodily harm. As stated above, s 1(4) of the *Criminal Code* (WA) now extends the meaning of "grievous bodily harm" to include a "serious disease". This is further defined in s 1(1) as a disease that is of such a nature as to endanger, or be likely to endanger, life or to cause or be likely to cause permanent injury to health. Finally, s 19A of the *Crimes Act* 1958 (Vic) was introduced by the *Crimes (HIV) Act* 1993 (Vic). This makes it an offence to cause another person to be infected with a very serious disease which is defined to mean HIV. Cases where the person has not contracted HIV have been prosecuted under s 22 of the *Crimes Act* 1958 (Vic) which concerns recklessly engaging in conduct that places or may place another person in danger of death: see below, p 570.

These provisions raise the question as to whether the criminal law is the appropriate avenue for controlling such conduct. In 1992, the Final Report of the Legal Working Party on the Intergovernmental Committee on AIDS recommended:

A public health offence should exist where a person knows that he or she is HIV-infected and significantly exposes or infects another person without his or her consent ... Special as opposed to existing general criminal law sanctions should be carefully considered by State and Territory governments because of the danger of stigmatising already alienated groups.[69]

As well as the stigma involved, criminalising conduct that transmits HIV raises concerns about excessive government intervention into the private realm, the potential for selective prosecutions (why HIV and not other diseases?) and difficulties in proving the fault element of such an offence. There are also extensive civil powers of detention relating to the spread of infectious diseases already in operation: see B McSherry, "'Dangerousness' and Public Health" (1998) 23(6) *Alternative law Journal* 276. For an essay examining the legal regulation of life-threatening disease, drawing on republican theory and strategies of regulation see S Bronitt, "The Transmission of Life-Threatening Injections: A New Regulatory Strategy" in R Smith (ed), *Health Care, Crime and Regulatory Control* (Sydney: Hawkins Press, 1998), Ch 13: see Ch 1, pp 59-63.

---

69 Legal Working Party of the Intergovernmental Committee on AIDS, *Legislative Approaches to Public Health Control of HIV Infection* (1992), pp 21-22. See further S Bronitt, "Criminal Liability for the Transmission of HIV/AIDS" (1992) 16 Crim LJ 85; S Bronitt, "Spreading Disease and the Criminal Law" [1994] Crim LR 21: D Ormerod and M Gunn, "Criminal Liability for the Transmission of HIV" (1996) 1 *Web Journal of Current Legal Issues* (http://webcli.ncl.ac.uk/1996/issue1/ormerod1.html); J Godwin, J Hamblin, D Patterson and D Buchanan, *Australian HIV/AIDS Legal Guide* (2nd ed, Sydney: Federation Press, 1993).

On the other hand, conduct resulting in harm to others is already criminalised and the transmission of HIV with its potentially lethal consequences should be seen as a criminal act. Alan Turner in his article "Criminal Liability and AIDS" (1995) *Auckland University Review* 875 at 887 summarises the arguments for criminalising the transmission of HIV as follows (at 887):

> The criminal law would be a valuable tool for assisting and reinforcing education in this area. The criminal law clearly defines the standards of behaviour which society deems to be unacceptable, and imposes sanctions on those persons whose conduct falls within these bounds. Knowingly transmitting HIV is a cruel, anti-social act that is deserving of stigmatisation by the criminal law. Criminalisation can also be justified on the basis that individuals, and society as a whole, are entitled to be protected from harmful behaviour.

The Model Criminal Code Officers Committee (MCCOC) is of the opinion that the transmission of HIV should be criminalised: *Chapter 5 — Non Fatal Offences Against the Person*, Report (September 1998), p 85. It recommends, however, that a specific offence need not be enacted, but a general endangerment offence will suffice: p 87. For a critical review of these proposals see S Bronitt, "HIV/AIDS and the *Model Criminal Code:* Endangering Public Health?" (1997) 8(4) *HIV/AIDS Legal Link* 14. See also below as to offences of endangerment: p 570.

Causing or Inflicting Harm

The jurisdictions differ as to the verb used in relation to actual or grievous bodily harm. It may be "causing", "inflicting", "occasioning" or "doing".

The verbs "causing" and arguably, "occasioning" can be viewed as broader than "inflicting" or "doing". The MCCOC points to the case of *R v Nicholson* [1916] VR 130 as exemplifying this distinction: *Chapter 5 — Non-Fatal Offences Against the Person,* Report (September 1998), p 17. The accused entered a house with the purpose of removing two gas meters. He failed to properly plug the gas pipe in one meter. When the occupants of the house subsequently lit a lamp, the gas exploded and injured them. The accused was convicted of negligently "causing" injury. It was held that the accused indirectly "caused" the injury and an argument that "causing" was limited to "direct" injury was dismissed.

"Inflicting" grievous bodily harm, in comparison, has been said to involve the direct or indirect *application of force* to the victim. For example where a person does an act calculated to cause a panic in a public assembly, he or she may be guilty of the offence of inflicting grievous bodily harm if injury results.[70]

However, in practice, little rides on the difference between these verbs because the word "inflict" has been interpreted broadly in recent years to include causing psychiatric illness: *R v Ireland; R v Burstow* [1998] AC 147. The MCCOC recommends casting offences resulting in harm in terms of "causing" the prohibited consequences: *Chapter 5 — Non-Fatal Offences Against the Person,* Report (1998), p 17.

---

70 *R v Martin* (1881) 8 QBD 54; *R v Clarence* (1888) 22 QBD 23 at 36 per Wills J; *R v Chapin* (1909) 74 JP 71;
R v Salisbury [1976] VR 452.

TABLE 1:

Terms Used in Relation to Actual or Grievous Bodily Harm

JURISDICTION AND RELEVANT LAW	CAUSING	INFLICTING	OCCASIONING	DOING
ACT *Crimes Act* 1900	causing grievous bodily harm s 25	inflicting actual bodily harm (s 23) inflicting grievous bodily harm (ss 19, 20)	assault occasioning actual bodily harm s 24	—
NSW *Crimes Act* 1900	causing grievous bodily harm s 54	inflicting grievous bodily harm s 35	assault occasioning actual bodily harm s 59	—
NT *Criminal Code*	unlawfully causes bodily harm (s 186) causing grievous harm (ss 177, 181)	—	—	—
QLD *Criminal Code*	unlawfully causes bodily harm (s 328) causing grievous bodily harm (s 317)	—	occasioning bodily harm s 339	doing grievous bodily harm s 320
SA *Criminal Law Consolidation Act* 1935	causing grievous bodily harm s 21	inflicting grievous bodily harm s 23	assault occasioning actual bodily harm s 40	—
TAS *Criminal Code*	causing grievous bodily harm s 172	—	—	doing grievous bodily harm s 170
VIC *Crimes Act* 1958	causes injury (s 18) causing serious injury (ss 16, 17, 24)	—	—	—
WA *Criminal Code*	unlawfully causes bodily harm (s 306) causing grievous bodily harm (s 294)	—	occasioning bodily harm s 317	doing grievous bodily harm s 297

The Fault Element

The fault element required for assaults resulting in actual bodily harm is the same as for common assault in that intention or recklessness will suffice. The intention or recklessness relates to the use (or threatened use) of force, rather than the actual bodily harm, rendering this a conduct rather than a result crime.[71]

The fault element in relation to assaults resulting in grievous bodily harm varies between jurisdictions. Intention[72] and recklessness[73] are mentioned in most jurisdictions. However, the relevant Queensland, Northern Territory and Western Australian provisions contain no mention of intention or recklessness.[74] These fault elements will nevertheless be relevant to show that the act did not occur involuntarily or by accident.[75]

It would seem that the intention required is the same as for the offences of assault and assault resulting in bodily harm. In *Bennett* (1989) 45 A Crim R 45, the Tasmanian provision was viewed as a crime of basic rather than specific intent.

The test for recklessness varies between jurisdictions. In *R v Campbell* [1997] 2 VR 585 Hayne and Crockett JJ stated that the test for recklessly causing serious injury was foresight of the *probability* that injury will result. At common law, however, Diplock LJ stated in *R v Mowatt* [1968] 1 QB 421 (at 426) that the offence of inflicting grievous bodily harm required the accused to "foresee that some physical harm to some person, albeit of a minor character, might result". (This view was relied on by the House of Lords in *R v Savage and Parmenter* [1992] 1 AC 699 at 716.) This seems to imply a lesser standard of foresight.

The New South Wales provisions refer to maliciously inflicting grievous bodily harm with intent to do grievous bodily harm[76] and maliciously inflicting grievous bodily harm.[77] Section 5 of the *Crimes Act* 1900 (NSW) defines "malice" as acting with indifference to human life or suffering, or with intent to injure some person or persons, and in any such case without lawful cause or excuse, or acting recklessly or wantonly. If the offence is sought to be established by proof of recklessness, it is sufficient that the accused foresaw the possibility as opposed to probability of some harm resulting from the accused's act: *R v Coleman* (1990) 19 NSWLR 467 at 475; *Stokes* (1990) 51 A Crim R 25 at 40.

Some jurisdictions also have statutory provisions relating to causing grievous bodily harm through a negligent act or omission.[78] In *R v Shields* [1981] VR 717, the Full Court of the Supreme Court of Victoria held that the standard of negligence required was the same as for negligent manslaughter. The latter test is set out at common law in *Nydam v The Queen* [1977] VR 430 at 455 and is discussed in Chapter 10: pp 505ff.

---

71   *R v Venna* [1975] 3 WLR 737 at 742 per James LJ; *R v Percali* (1986) 42 SASR 46; *Coulter v The Queen* (1988) 164 CLR 350; *Savage v DPP* [1991] 3 WLR 914 at 930; *Williams* (1990) 50 A Crim R 213.

72   *Crimes Act* 1900 (ACT), s 19; *Criminal Code* (NT), s 177; *Criminal Law Consolidation Act* 1935 (SA), s 21(b); *Criminal Code* (Tas), s 170; *Crimes Act* 1958 (Vic), s 16.

73   *Crimes Act* 1900 (ACT), s 20; *Criminal Code* (NT), s 181; *Criminal Law Consolidation Act* 1935 (SA), s 29(2)(b); *Crimes Act* 1958 (Vic), s 17.

74   *Criminal Code* (Qld), s 320; *Criminal Code* (NT), s 181; *Criminal Code* (WA), s 297.

75   *Criminal Code* (Qld), s 23; *Criminal Code* (WA), s 23; *R v Fitzgerald* (1999) 106 A Crim R 215.

76   *Crimes Act* 1900 (NSW), s 33.

77   *Crimes Act* 1900 (NSW), s 35.

78   *Crimes Act* 1900 (ACT), s 25; *Crimes Act* 1900 (NSW), s 54; *Criminal Code* (Qld), s 328; *Crimes Act* 1958 (Vic), s 24.

The MCCOC has recommended that an offence of negligently causing serious harm should form part of the *Model Criminal Code* partly because it "is necessary in order to criminalise those instances of gross negligence that cause serious harm, such as the removal of safety equipment in the workplace": *Chapter 5: Non Fatal Offences Against the Person*, Discussion Paper (August 1996), p 33.

CULTURAL PERSPECTIVES

Female Genital Mutilation

Female genital mutilation ("FGM") is a term used to describe a variety of ritual practices ranging from scraping or cutting the clitoris to the excision of the clitoris, labia minora and parts of the labia majora: see Queensland Law Reform Commission, *Female Genital Mutilation*, Report No 47 (September 1994), pp 7-8. FGM was first described as "female circumcision" reflecting its religious significance in some cultures. In recent years, however, the language of human rights abuse has displaced the "traditional" language: see, for example, Australian Medical Association, *Female Genital Mutilation*, Position Statement, (1994). FGM is portrayed as a form of torture, or as cruel, inhuman or degrading treatment. Its redefinition as "mutilation" denotes more clearly the physical, sexual and aesthetic boundary violations involved in these practices: M Douglas, *Purity and Danger* (London: Routledge & Kegan Paul, 1992).

Although much has been written on the origins of the practice, primarily to dispute the authenticity of its basis in the *Koran* or religious law,[79] little attention has been paid to its therapeutic and experimental use by the medical profession in the United Kingdom throughout the 19th century. As Susan Edwards in her book *Female Sexuality and the Law* (Oxford: Martin Robertson, 1981) notes (p 87):

> Contrary to popular belief, this ancient and primitive custom [clitoridectomy] is not just a "survival" from the past that persists in peasant and pastoral societies; it was an advanced cure for a wide variety of female disorders in nineteenth-century gynaecological practice.

In the United Kingdom, the performance of FGM has now been criminalised. The *Prohibition of Female Circumcision Act* 1985 (UK) made it an offence to "excise, infibulate or otherwise mutilate the labia", but makes it a defence if it is performed by a doctor and is intended to benefit the person in a therapeutic context: *Prohibition of Female Circumcision Act* 1985 (UK), s 1. The offence, punishable by a maximum of five years imprisonment, extends to individuals who aid, abet, counsel or procure the performance of the procedure. Similar legislation exists in some Australian jurisdictions.[80] Other jurisdictions have not enacted special legislation, content to rely on the ordinary law of assault.[81]

---

79 See Family Law Council, *Female Genital Mutilation*, Discussion Paper (January 1994); Family Law Council, *Female Genital Mutilation*, Report (June 1994). For a commentary on the Report, see B Hughes, "Female Genital Mutilation: The Complementary Roles of Education and Legislation in Combating the Practice in Australia" (1995) 3 *Journal of Law and Medicine* 202.

80 *Crimes Act* 1900 (ACT), Pt 111B; *Crimes Act* 1900 (NSW), s 45; *Criminal Code* (NT), Pt VI Divn 4A; *Criminal Code* (Tas), ss 178A-178C.

81 The Australian Law Reform Commission rejected calls for special FGM offences, favouring the view that the practice constitutes an offence under the general law: Australian Law Reform Commission, *Multiculturalism: Criminal Law*, Discussion Paper No 48 (1991), p 23. For a critical review of its recommendations see S Bronitt and K Amirthalingam, "Cultural Blindness and the Criminal Law" (1996) 21(2) *Alternative Law Journal* 58.

FGM has been represented as a both a human rights and a health issue. When FGM is considered as a human rights issue, women's rights have tended to trump the cultural and religious rights of minority groups. The *Declaration on Violence Against Women* (1993) adopted by the United Nations defined "violence" as including "female genital mutilation and other traditional practices to women". Anticipating the clash between cultural and feminist claims to equality, the Declaration stated that "custom, tradition or religion cannot be invoked by States to avoid their obligations with respect to the elimination of violence against women". The Declaration draws on the rights contained in the *Universal Declaration of Human Rights* 1948 (UDHR) and the *International Covenant on Civil and Political Rights* 1966 (ICCPR). The UDHR and ICCPR contain the right not to be subject to torture, or to cruel, inhuman or degrading treatment or punishment and the right to liberty and security of person. The ICCPR specifically protects ethnic and cultural rights under the guarantee of freedom of religion and the right of ethnic, religious or linguistic minorities to enjoy their own culture, religion or language: Arts 18 and 27.

The problem that occurs here is that imposing western human rights standards on individuals of other cultures may lead to FGM being driven "underground". The Family Law Council in its Report, *Female Genital Mutilation* (1994), points out (para 5.10, p 31):

> Many people who practise female genital mutilation see western societies as sexually promiscuous, decadent and in the process of disintegration. They cite female genital mutilation as a defence against such corrupting influences. They see the attack on female genital mutilation as an attempt to disintegrate their social order and thereby speed up their Europeanisation.

The health objections levelled at FGM raise the possibilities of a range of short-term and long-term complications: Queensland Law Reform Commission, *Female Genital Mutilation*, Report No 47 (September 1994), pp 22-24. While these objections are indeed significant, they overlook the broader cultural justifications that underlie some forms of surgical procedure. The law has never cast doubt on the legality of ritual circumcision performed on newly-born male infants for religious or cultural reasons. Within Jewish and Islamic communities, these operations are often performed in non-sterile environments without anaesthesia by individuals who lack formal medical training. Post-operative complications do occur, although prosecution is rarely instituted even in cases where the infant suffers severe infection or permanent physical impairment. The changing social and medical attitudes to male circumcision for non-medical purposes have raised the question whether the assumed legality of the religious circumcision could be challenged before the courts: see D Richards, "Male Circumcision: Medical or Ritual" (1996) 3(4) *Journal of Law and Medicine* 371; G Boyle, J Svoboda, C Price and J Turner, "Circumcision of Healthy Boys: Criminal Assault?" (2000) 7(3) *Journal of Law and Medicine* 301. FGM and male circumcision can be viewed as qualitatively different procedures, the latter having no or only limited impact on sexual or reproductive functioning. While this may be true, the point revealed by this comparison is that the legal legitimacy of surgical interference does not rest *exclusively* on its medical utility. Indeed, it is important to recognise that justifications based on medical utility often blur with those derived from the patient's religious, cultural and aesthetic beliefs. Further, compliance with deeply-held beliefs is often claimed by the medical profession to yield therapeutic or psychological benefits for the patient.

The present legal approach toward FGM fails to take seriously the rights relating to both individual and cultural autonomy. Clearly arguments based on autonomy have less weight with respect to FGM performed on children. Indeed, FGM should *never* be performed on a child. As Art 24(3) of the *Convention on the Rights of the Child* (1989) states, parties must "take all effective and appropriate measures with a view to abolishing traditional practices prejudicial to the health of children". However, dismissing the consent of adult women who wish to undergo FGM may compound their lack of autonomy and sense of alienation: S Pritchard, "The Jurisprudence of Human Rights: Some Critical Thought and Developments in Practice" (1995) 2(1) *Australian Journal of Human Rights* at 23, fn 87.

A different approach to FGM, one that is rarely discussed, is regulation rather than prohibition. As with other controversial procedures, such as abortion, the law could impose restrictions relating to consent such as requiring mandatory counselling before obtaining an "informed consent", coupled with limits on the *type* of the procedure permitted. This together with education programmes such as those run by the Ecumenical Migration Centre in Victoria, may provide a better alternative than criminalisation of the practice.[82] As experience in drug law demonstrates, strict enforcement of prohibition can be counterproductive, resulting in less rather than more control. Realistically, the present strategy of global prohibition of FGM is unlikely to stamp out the practice. A policy of strict enforcement is much more likely to produce unintended consequences by driving the practice underground. For example, this may severely compromise the strategies in place to control the transmission of HIV and other blood-borne infections: see generally, P Grabosky, "Counterproductive Regulation" (1995) 23 *International Journal of the Sociology of Law* 347. Policy in this area should pursue the "least worst solution".

The "unprincipled" but practical approach mooted here may seem abhorrent. However, resolving clashes between cultural, moral and political imperatives requires imaginative policy-making. By advocating effective regulation that is based on education and harm-minimisation, medico-legal discourse could exert greater influence on these traditional practices, and perhaps, over time, transform these initiation rituals into symbolic covenants rather than surgical ones.

3. LAWFUL ASSAULT

As the law of assault and related offences has developed, a number of ways of avoiding criminal responsibility have also arisen. The use of force may be considered lawful if:

=== it forms part of ordinary social activity;

=== it forms the basis for an arrest or steps taken to prevent a breach of the peace;

=== it is used in self-defence;

=== in some jurisdictions, it is used as a result of provocation; or

=== it is used reasonably and moderately to chastise children.

---

82   For an argument in favour of education over legislation, see M Ierodiaconou, "'Listen to Us!' Female Genital Mutilation, Feminism and the Law in Australia" (1995) 20 *Melbourne University Law Review* 562.

Consent to a common assault renders the act lawful, but there is considerable debate about the role of consent in relation to aggravated assault. We will examine all these areas in turn.

3.1 ORDINARY SOCIAL ACTIVITY

An act that is part of ordinary social activity is not an assault.[83] Physical conduct that is generally acceptable in the ordinary course of everyday life includes the jostling that may occur on public transport or in a busy street or handshaking at a party: *Collins v Wilcock* [1984] 3 All ER 374 at 378. Similarly, it is not an assault to give a slight touch in friendship or to seek the attention of another by tapping on that person's shoulder.[84]

3.2 ARREST

A person exercising a lawful power of arrest is entitled to use reasonable force where it is necessary in order to effect that arrest.[85] The old common law drew a distinction between the use of force in relation to resisting arrest and in relation to fleeing from arrest. The provisions in the Queensland and Western Australian *Criminal Codes* still retain this distinction with more limitations being placed on the force used in relation to fleeing from arrest.

What amounts to reasonable force is a question of fact that depends upon the circumstances of the particular case including the nature of the resistance put up by the accused: *R v Turner* [1962] VR 30 (SC). There is also a corresponding right to use reasonable force to resist unlawful arrest[86] and again what amounts to reasonable force is a question of fact. The use of force to prevent a breach of the peace is explored in Chapter 14: pp 764-767.

3.3 SELF-DEFENCE

The defence of self-defence is available to crimes involving the use of or threat of force to the person such as assault and it results in a complete acquittal. As explored in Chapter 6, the test for self-defence varies across jurisdictions.

In the Australian Capital Territory, New South Wales and Victoria, the common law holds sway. Wilson, Dawson and Toohey JJ set out the requirements for the defence in *Zecevic v DPP* (1987) 162 CLR 645 (at 661) as follows:

---

83 *Collins v Wilcock* [1984] 1 WLR 1172; *R v Boughey* (1986) 161 CLR 10; *Criminal Code* (NT), s 187(e); *Criminal Code* (Tas), s 182(3).

84 *Coward v Baddeley* (1859) 4 H&N 478; *Donnolly v Jackman* [1970] 1 All ER 987; *R v Phillips* (1971) ALR 740 at 746; *Boughey v The Queen* (1986) 161 CLR 10 at 24 per Mason, Wilson and Deane JJ.

85 *R v Turner* [1962] VR 30; *Crimes Act* 1914 (Cth), s 3ZC(2)(a); *Crimes Act* 1900 (ACT), s 349ZE; *Criminal Code* (NT), ss 27, 28; *Criminal Law Consolidation Act* 1935 (SA), s 15(1)(b); *Criminal Code* (Qld), ss 256-257; *Criminal Code* (Tas), ss 30-31, 26-27; *Police Offences Act* 1935 (Tas), s 55; *Criminal Code* (WA), s 237.

86 *R v Ryan* (1890) 11 LR(NSW) 171; *McLiney v Minister* [1911] VLR 347; *R v Marshall* (1987) 49 SASR 133; *R v Fry* (1992) 58 SASR 424; *Criminal Code* (NT), ss 27(g), 28(f); *Criminal Code* (Qld), s 271; *Criminal Code* (WA), s 248. See also Self-Defence in Chapter 6.

The question to be asked in the end is quite simple. It is whether the accused believed upon reasonable grounds that it was necessary in self-defence to do what he [or she] did. If he [or she] had that belief and there were reasonable grounds for it, or if the jury is left in reasonable doubt about the matter, then he [or she] is entitled to an acquittal. Stated in this form, the question is one of general application and is not limited to cases of homicide.[87]

Section 46 of the *Criminal Code* (Tas) states that:

A person is justified in using, in defence of himself or another person, such force as, in the circumstances as he [or she] believes them to be, it is reasonable to use.

This test is partly subjective and partly objective. It requires two questions to be answered. First, what were the circumstances as the accused believed them to be? Secondly, was the use of force reasonable in those circumstances?

Similarly, s 15(1) of the *Criminal Law Consolidation Act* 1935 (SA) allows an accused to use force if that person believes that the force is necessary and reasonable for self-defence and conduct was reasonably proportionate to the threat that the accused genuinely believed to exist.

The provisions in the Queensland, Northern Territory and Western Australian *Criminal Codes* are more complex and supplement the core element of "reasonable necessity" with additional rules that limit the use of permissible force. Section 283 of the *Criminal Code* (Qld) and s 260 of the *Criminal Code* (WA) distinguish between self-defence as it relates to provoked and unprovoked attacks. In relation to an unprovoked attack:

[I]t is lawful for [the accused] to use such force to the assailant as is reasonably necessary to make effectual defence against the assault, provided that the force used is not intended and is not such as is likely, to cause death or grievous bodily harm.

Here, the test is objective in determining whether or not the force used by the accused was reasonably necessary.

3.4 PROVOCATION

Provocation in some jurisdictions is not only a defence to murder, but may also apply as a defence to assault. In the Northern Territory, Queensland and Western Australia, provocation is also a complete defence to offences that have assault as a defined element: *Criminal Code* (NT), s 34; *Criminal Code* (Qld), s 269; *Criminal Code* (WA), s 246. It is, however, not applicable to offences such as doing bodily harm, grievous bodily harm or wounding where assault is not a defined element: *Kaporonovski v The Queen* (1973) 133 CLR 209.

In the Australian Capital Territory, New South Wales and Victoria, provocation is a qualified defence to an assault which is defined to include the word "murder" such as wounding with intent to

---

87 *Zecevic v DPP* (1987) 162 CLR 645 (approved of at 654 per Mason CJ and at 666 per Brennan J). It also seems that the dissenting judges approved of this statement of the law: at 681 per Deane J and at 685 per Gaudron J.

murder: *R v Newman* [1948] VLR 61; *Helmhout v The Queen* (1980) 49 FLR 1. In South Australia, provocation does not appear to apply as there are no offences of assault defined to include the word "murder". Provocation is, however, a defence to an attempted murder in South Australia,[88] but not, it appears, in Victoria.[89]

There is no specific provision relating to provocation in relation to assaults in Tasmania. However s 8 of the *Criminal Code* (Tas) states:

> All rules and principles of the common law which render any circumstances a justification
> or excuse for any act or omission, or a defence to a charge upon indictment, shall remain in
> force and apply to any defence to a charge upon indictment, except insofar as they are
> altered by, or are inconsistent with, the Code.

This implies that in theory, the common law definition of provocation can apply to Code offences defining assault as including the word "murder". However, in practice, it appears that because there are no Code offences in these terms, provocation only applies to murder.

In the Australian Capital Territory, New South Wales and Victoria, the test for provocation is that for murder: see Ch 5, pp 256ff. It appears that in relation to assaults with an intention to murder, provocation acts as a complete rather than a partial defence: *R v Duvivier* (1982) 29 SASR 217.

In Queensland and Western Australia, the definition of provocation as it applies to assault differs from that of the common law: *Criminal Code* (Qld), s 268; *Criminal Code* (WA), s 245. For example, s 268 of the *Criminal Code* (Qld) provides:

> The term "provocation", used with reference to an offence of which an assault is an
> element means and includes ... any wrongful act or insult of such a nature as to be likely,
> when done to an ordinary person, or in the presence of an ordinary person to another who
> is under his [or her] immediate care, or to whom he [or she] stands in a conjugal, parental,
> filial, or fraternal relation, or in the relation of master or servant, to deprive him [or her] of
> the power of self-control, and to induce him [or her] to assault the person by whom the act
> or insult is done or offered

The MCCOC in its Report, *Chapter 5: Non Fatal Offences Against the Person* (1998), has recommended that provocation should not be a defence to assault.: It states (p 141):

> [O]ne of the many conceptual problems with the doctrine of provocation is that it artificially
> forces attention to what is likely to be but one of the factors that precipitated the violence,
> and is to that extent misleading. In cases where there is no mandatory sentence, (as with
> all offences under consideration here) the circumstances of provocation can be taken into
> account together with the other factors precipitating the offence in sentence.

The criticisms of provocation discussed in Chapter 5 are equally applicable here: see p 285.

---

88   *R v Duvivier* (1982) 29 SASR 217, overruling *R v Wells* (1981) 28 SASR 63.

89   *R v Farrar* [1992] 1 VR 207 at 208-209 per Hampel J.

3.5 LAWFUL CORRECTION OF CHILDREN

The common law enabled the lawful correction of certain classes or persons such as children, servants, the crew of ships, apprentices and, though subject to debate, wives. The lawful chastisement of wives was ruled out in *R v Jackson* [1891] 1 QB 671.

It appears that currently, parents are entitled to use reasonable and moderate force to chastise their children.[90] There is also some authority to the effect that teachers or those "in *loco parentis*" to the child may use some degree of force to correct a child as "lawful correction": *Cleary v Booth* [1893] 1 QB 465; *Mansell v Griffin* [1908] 1 KB 160. This is reflected in legislation in some jurisdictions. For example, s 257 of the *Criminal Code* (WA) states:

> It is lawful for a parent or a person in the place of a parent, or for a school master or master,
> to use, by way of correction, towards a child, pupil, or apprentice, under his [or her] care,
> such force as is reasonable under the circumstances.[91]

In Victoria, corporal punishment in State schools was prohibited by reg XVI of the *Education Act* 1958 (Vic). Section 14 of the *Education and Public Instruction Act* 1987 (NSW) enabled Discipline Codes to be formulated for State schools after consultation with parents. In 1990, the National Committee on Violence recommended in *Violence: Directions for Australia* (Canberra: Australian Institute of Criminology, 1990) that corporal punishment in all schools be illegal. See also Australian Law Reform Commission, *Seen and Heard: Priority for Children in the Legal Process*, Report No 84 (1997), Recommendation 50, p 217.

There is scant authority defining the scope and degree of force implied by the words "reasonable correction" as it relates to parents or teachers. In *R v Terry* [1955] VLR 114, Sholl J stated (at 116):

> [T]here are exceedingly strict limits to that right [to use reasonable force on a child]. In the
> first place, the punishment must be moderate and reasonable. In the second place, it must
> have a proper relation to the age, physique and mentality of the child, and in the third
> place, it must be carried out with a reasonable means or instrument.[92]

In a Discussion Paper commissioned by the Commonwealth Department of Human Services and Health, Judy Cashmore and Nicola de Haas undertook an extensive examination of the existing law. They concluded that the law currently does not provide a clear and consistent guide as to what behaviour is and is not acceptable and does not provide children with the protection available to other members of society: *Legal and Social Aspects of the Physical Punishment of Children* (ACT: Commonwealth of Australia, 1995).

Recently, it has been argued that the use of force against children should fall within the context of assault. Rochelle Urlich, for example, has argued that physical discipline is ineffective, is linked to child abuse, teaches children that violence is a legitimate means of problem solving and erodes children's rights: "Physical Discipline in the Home" [1994] 7(3) *Auckland University Law Review* 851.

---

90 *Criminal Code* (NT), s 11 (delegation of power); *Criminal Code* (Qld), s 280; *Criminal Code* (Tas), s 50; *Criminal Code* (WA), s 257; *R v Hopley* 2 F & F 202; *Smith v Byrne* (1894) QCR 252 at 253; *R v Terry* [1955] VLR 114 at 116-117 (SC).

91 See also *Criminal Code* (Qld), s 280.

92 See also *R v Atkinson* [1994] 9 WWR 485.

The common law governing lawful correction was recently challenged before the European Court of Human Rights as violating Art 3 of the *European Convention on Human Rights* (ECHR). This states that "[n]o one shall be subjected to torture or to inhuman or degrading treatment or punishment".

The European Court in *A v The United Kingdom* (Eur Court HR, 23 September 1998, *Reports of Judgments and Decisions* 1998–VI) held (at para 22, p 2699) that Art 3 imposes on the State an obligation "to take measures designed to ensure that individuals within their jurisdiction are not subjected to torture or inhuman or degrading treatment or punishment, including such ill-treatment administered by private individuals". In that case, a nine-year-old boy was beaten repeatedly with a garden cane by his step-father with "considerable force" resulting in severe bruising. The step-father was charged and acquitted of assault and the child sought a ruling from the ECHR that the common law defence of reasonable chastisement violated Art 3. The Court held, and the United Kingdom Government conceded, that the notion of reasonable correction embodied in the common law exception to assault did not offer adequate protection against inhuman or degrading treatment or punishment contrary to Art 3.

Article 19(1) of the *Convention on the Rights of the Child*[93] is similar to Art 3 in that it states:

> [P]arties shall take all appropriate legislative, administrative, social and educational measures to protect the child from all forms of physical or mental violence, injury or abuse, neglect or negligent treatment, maltreatment or exploitation, including sexual abuse, while in the care of parent(s), legal guardian(s) or any other person who has the care of the child.

As the MCCOC noted, the Australian Government has taken one view that this article does not require the prohibition of reasonable correction: *Chapter 5 — Non-Fatal Offences Against the Person,* Report (1998), p 137. Nevertheless the MCCOC has recommended the introduction of the following qualifications on "reasonable correction". First, that reasonable correction be lawful when conducted by a parent or another person who takes care of the child where the parent has so consented. Secondly, in relation to what constitutes reasonable correction, the MCCOC proposed that:

> Conduct can amount to reasonable correction of a child only if it is reasonable in the circumstances for the purposes of the discipline, management or control of the child. The following conduct does not amount to reasonable correction of a child:
>
> **(a)** causing or threatening to cause harm to a child that lasts for more than a short period; or
>
> **(b)** causing harm to a child by use of a stick, belt or other object (other than an open hand).

This proposal, defining and limiting the scope of "reasonable correction", addresses the concerns raised about the defence in *A v The United Kingdom*. If adopted, it would be difficult to sustain an argument that the criminal law authorised or excused inhuman or degrading treatment or punishment contrary to international human rights law.

---

93 *Convention on the Rights of the Child*, opened for signature 20 November 1989, ATS 1991 No 4 (entered into force in Australia 19 January 1991).

3.6 CONSENT

Consent to a common assault renders the act lawful.[94] In *Schloss v Maguire* (1897) 8 QLJ 21 the Supreme Court of Queensland commented (at 22):

> [T]he term assault of itself involves the notion of want of consent. An assault with consent is not an assault at all.

Consent may be express or implied.[95] The rule that an act that is part of ordinary social activity is not an assault is sometimes justified on the basis of implied consent: *Boughey v The Queen* (1986) 161 CLR 10 at 24 per Mason, Wilson and Deane JJ. Consent must be freely given and not induced by fraud, force or threats: *Criminal Code* (Tas), s 2A; *Wooley v Fitzgerald* [1969] Tas SR 65.

The situation in relation to aggravated assaults differs quite markedly from consent as it relates to common assault. There are a number of English cases setting out the general rule that a victim cannot consent to an act that has the purpose of causing, or will probably cause, him or her actual bodily harm.[96] There are no decisions in Australian common law jurisdictions that directly address this point. In *Lergesner v Carroll* (1989) 49 A Crim R 51 the Queensland Court of Criminal Appeal held that consent may in some cases be a "defence" to an assault occasioning actual bodily harm. However, consent does not appear to be relevant where the force applied amounts to grievous bodily harm or wounding.

The rationale for the English rule that consent is irrelevant where actual bodily harm occurs, lies in the notion that it is not in the public interest that a person should cause bodily harm to another for no good reason: *Attorney-General's Reference (No 6 of 1980)* [1981] QB 715 at 719.

What constitutes a "good reason" for causing consensual bodily harm includes:

▄▄ **for personal adornment such as tattooing, body piercing and branding;**

▄▄ **surgery; and**

▄▄ **rough "horseplay" and violent sports.**

Consensual sadomasochistic sexual activities have been viewed as not providing a "good reason" for the infliction of bodily harm: *R v Brown* [1993] 2 WLR 556. This point is taken up later (p 562) and also in Chapter 12, 1.1 'Constructing Sexual Crimes: Sexual Violence or Violent Sex': p 581.

PERSONAL ADORNMENT

Various cultures have sanctioned the infliction of harm upon the body in the form of such conduct as tattooing, piercing, footbinding, headmoulding or genital rearrangement: see in general A Favazza,

---

94 *R v Donovan* [1934] 2 KB 498; *Attorney-General's Reference (No 6 of 1980)* [1981] QB 715; *R v Brown* [1993] 2 WLR 556; *Criminal Code* (NT), s 187; *Criminal Code* (Qld), s 245; *Criminal Code* (Tas), s 182; *Criminal Code* (WA), s 222.

95 *Beer v McCann* [1993] 1 Qd R 25 at 28-29 per Derrington J; *Collins v Wilcock* [1984] 1 WLR 1172 at 1177-1178 per Goff LJ; *Carroll v Lergesner* [1991] 1 Qd R 206.

96 *R v Coney* (1882) 8 QBD 534 (prize fighting); *Rex v Donovan* [1934] 2 KB 498 (caning a 17-year-old girl for sexual gratification); *Attorney General's Reference (No 6 of 1980)* [1981] QB 715; *R v Brown* [1993] 2 WLR 556.

Bodies Under Seige (Baltimore: John Hopkins University Press, 1992). In Western society, body piercing has increased in popularity in recent years: see I Freckelton, "Masochism, Self-mutilation and the Limits of Consent" (1994) 2(1) *Journal of Law and Medicine* 48 at 50. While tattooing and body piercing may seem to result from the quest for personal adornment, there is an argument that self-injurious behaviour may be sexual in nature. As stated by Ian Freckelton (at 51) the relationship between sadomasochistic behaviour and injurious behaviour is "difficult to define and as yet the subject of little analysis". Freckelton goes on to say (at 55):

> Because of the emphasis that Western society places on health, idealised appearance and our abhorrence of suffering, the voluntary assumption of pain has a taboo or subversive aspect for most. It should not be surprising, therefore, that this status alone should provoke a sub-culture of limited and stylised self-harm, shared among the initiated and either revealed only to one another or brandished to the uninitiate as a statement of identity and "otherness".

The leading case dealing with bodily harm for "personal adornment" is that of *R v Wilson* [1996] 3 WLR 125. In that case, the accused branded his initials on his wife's buttocks with a hot knife. He was charged and convicted of assault occasioning actual bodily harm. He argued that the act was consensual. On appeal, the Court of Appeal quashed the conviction on the basis that what the accused did was on a par with tattooing which did not involve an offence. Russell LJ in delivering the judgment of the Court, stated (at 128):

> For our part, we cannot detect any logical difference between what the appellant did and what he might have done in the way of tattooing. The latter activity apparently requires no state authorisation, and the appellant was as free to engage in it as anyone else. We do not think that we are entitled to assume that the method adopted by the appellant and his wife was any more dangerous or painful than tattooing.

Just where the line is to be drawn between allowing consent to personal adornment by way of tattooing, body piercing and branding and criminalising other conduct that causes bodily harm is very difficult. See generally, L Bibbings and P Alldridge, "Sexual Expression, Body Alteration and the Defence of Consent" (1993) 20(3) *Journal of Law and Society* 356; A Watkins, "Score and Pierce: Crimes of Fashion? Body Alteration and Consent to Assault" (1998) 28(2) *Victoria University of Wellington Law Review* 371. This issue is taken up further in the ensuing section on consent and sadomasochism: p 562.

SURGERY

Surgery is viewed as lawful when performed with the patient's consent despite it involving serious bodily harm.[97] Consent may be oral, written or implied: *Re T (Adult: Refusal of Treatment)* [1993] Fam 95 at 102 per Lord Donaldson MR. Valid consent requires that the patient has the capacity to consent

---

97 *Department of Health and Community Services (NT) v JWB (Marion's case)* (1992) 175 CLR 218 at 232; *Criminal Code* (Tas), s 51(1).

and is capable of understanding the treatment: *Department of Health and Community Services (NT) v JWB (Marion's Case)* (1992) 175 CLR 218. Consent must also be voluntary[98] and pertain to the act performed.[99]

If a patient is unable to give consent, another person may be authorised to give consent on that person's behalf.[100] In Tasmania, surgical operations performed in good faith and with reasonable care and skill upon a person incapable of giving consent are lawful: *Criminal Code* (Tas), s 51(3). In the Northern Territory, Queensland and South Australia, doctors have statutory powers to give treatment without consent in an emergency[101] and it appears that there is a common law doctrine of emergency that is applicable in other Australian jurisdictions: L Skene, *Law and Medical Practice: Rights, Duties, Claims and Defences* (Sydney: Butt, 1998), pp 82-83. An emergency situation is one where the treatment is essential to preserve the patient's life or to prevent serious permanent injury.[102] It does not extend to treatment that is convenient. For example, in *Murray v McMurchy* [1949] 2 DLR 442 the patient was undergoing a Caesarean delivery when the doctor discovered fibroids in the patient's uterus. The doctor performed a sterilisation on the basis that the patient should not undergo another pregnancy and it was more convenient to carry out the procedure at that time. The doctor was found liable for damages (at 445) as there was "no evidence that these tumours were presently at the time of the operation dangerous to her life or health".

Treatment may also be justified in the absence of consent on the basis of a common law doctrine of necessity. This was explored in Chapter 6: p 332.

ROUGH HORSEPLAY AND VIOLENT SPORTS

The courts have permitted consent to operate as a defence to bodily harm in the course of certain activities such as "rough horseplay" and violent sports. In *R v Aitken* [1992] 1 WLR 1006 the three accused and the "victim" were members of the Royal Air Force in the United Kingdom. They went to a party at the completion of their formal flying training and they consumed a "considerable quantity" of alcohol. Later that night when two officers who were wearing fire resistant flying suits fell asleep, some of the men set fire to their suits. The suits burned enough to wake the officers and they both treated this as a joke. After the party broke up, the three men followed Flying Officer Gibson, caught him, poured spirit over his suit and set fire to it. This time, the flames engulfed Gibson and he suffered extremely severe burning. The three accused were convicted at a general court-martial of inflicting grievous bodily harm. They appealed to the Courts-Martial Appeal Court which quashed the convictions.

Cazalet J who delivered the judgment of the Court stated (at 1020) that the judge advocate had failed to give any direction in relation to Gibson's consent to "rough and undisciplined horseplay". Cazalet J went on to set out (at 1021) the direction that should have been given:

---

98 *Re T (Adult: Refusal of Treatment)* [1992] 3 WLR 782.

99 *Walker v Bradley* (unrep, 15/12/1993, NSW Dist Ct Kirkham J, 1919 of 1989); *Murray v McMurchy* [1949] 2 DLR 442.

100 See B Bennett, *Law and Medicine* (Sydney: LBC Information Services, 1997), pp 21-29; L Skene, *Law and Medical Practice: Rights, Duties, Claims and Defences* (Sydney: Butt, 1998), Chs 4, 5.

101 *Emergency Operations Act* 1973 (NT), s 3(1); *Voluntary Aid in Emergency Act* 1973 (Qld), s 3; *Consent to Medical Treatment and Palliative Care Act* 1995 (SA), s 13(1).

102 *Walker v Bradley* (unrep, 15/12/1993, Dist Ct NSW Kirkham J, 1919 of 1989); *Murray v McMurchy* [1949] 2 DLR 442.

It is common ground that there was no intention to cause any injury to Gibson. In those circumstances, if Gibson consented to take part in rough and undisciplined mess games involving the use of force towards those involved, no assault is proved in respect of any defendant whose participation extended only to taking part in such an activity.

It is uncertain what status this case has in Australia given the decision in *Lergesner v Carroll* (1989) 49 A Crim R 51 that implies consent will be irrelevant to a situation where grievous bodily harm is caused. The injuries suffered by Gibson would seem to fall within this category.

There is slightly more authority on the role of consent in relation to sports violence. Sports such as boxing, wrestling, football and hockey involve body contact that may lead to serious harm. The general rule is by engaging in sport, the participant accepts the inherent risks involved in that sport: *Billinghurst* [1978] Crim LR 553. For the purpose of civil law the status of professional boxing matches was considered in *Pallante v Stadiums Pty Ltd (No 1)* [1976] VR 331. McInerney J stated (at 343):

> [B]oxing is not an unlawful and criminal activity so long as, whether for reward or not, it is engaged in by a contestant as a boxing sport or contest, not from motive of personal animosity, or at all events not predominantly from that motive, but predominantly as an exercise of boxing skill and physical condition in accordance with rules and in conditions the object of which is to ensure that the infliction of bodily injury is kept within reasonable bounds, so as to preclude or reduce, so far as is practicable, the risk of either contestant incurring serious bodily injury, and to ensure that victory shall be achieved in accordance with the rules by the person demonstrating the greater skill as a boxer.

In some sports such as Australian Rules Football, however, it is recognised that the rules will be breached on a regular basis and participants accept this within reasonable limits. Legoe J pointed out in *McAvaney v Quigley* (1992) 58 A Crim R 457 at 459-460 that "opposing players will not always abide by the rules and it cannot be said that every infringement of the rules resulting in physical contact that directly results in injury can amount to a criminal act".

Similarly, in *R v Carr* (unrep, 17/10/1990, CCA NSW), the New South Wales Court of Criminal Appeal upheld the accused's conviction for assault occasioning actual bodily harm. In a particularly violent rugby league match, the accused had executed a head high swinging arm tackle that broke the victim's jaw. The Court upheld the conviction on the basis that the tackle was in breach of the rules of the game and players did not consent to major breaches of the rules that led to injuries of the type sustained on the facts.[103]

There has, however, been a marked reluctance in Australia to invoke the law of assault in relation to sports violence. Most disciplinary action is brought by way of the relevant governing bodies of the sports concerned. In Canada, by contrast, where ice hockey involves a great deal of bodily contact, more than 100 criminal convictions were made for offences involving violence

---

103 See also *Watherston v Woolven* (1988) 139 LSJS 366; *R v Stanley* (unrep, 7/4/1995, CCA NSW, No 60554 of 1994); D Garnsey, "Rugby League Player Jailed for On-Field Assault" (1995) 5(2) *ANZSLA Newsletter* 7; *Abbott v The Queen* (unrep, 25/7/1995, CCA WA, No 98 of 1995); H Opie, "Aussie Rules Player Jailed for Behind-Play Assault" (1996) 6(2) *ANZSLA Newsletter* 3.

between players in the 1970-1985 period: D White, "Sports Violence as Criminal Assault: Development of the Doctrine by Canadian Courts" (1986) 6 *Duke Law Journal* 1030 at 1034. In Australia, however, there have only been a handful of prosecutions and of those cases reported, Paul Farrugia writes that the courts "have apparently not been concerned with applying, or formulating any form of workable test for the scope of consent on the sports field": "The Consent Defence: Sports Violence, Sadomasochism, and the Criminal Law" (1997) 8(2) *Auckland University Review* 472 at 485.

All that can be drawn from the limited case law on sports violence is that the courts will focus on "the rules of the game, the degree to which the victim actually or could have consented to the behaviour and importantly its outcome, and the varying degrees of express or implied intention in the mind of the perpetrator at the time of the incident in question".[104]

PERSPECTIVES

Consent and Sadomasochism

In the course of an investigation into child pornography in England, the police discovered a number of videotapes that were originally thought to be "snuff" movies: S Edwards, "No Defence for a Sado-Masochistic Libido" (1993) 143 *New Law Journal* 406 at 406. The videotapes in fact showed a group of homosexual men engaging in sadomasochistic sex with one another. Some of the acts that were portrayed involved whipping, branding and the infliction of wounds to the genitals, including the insertion of safety pins and fish hooks into the penis, the dripping of hot wax into the urethra and the nailing of a penis into a bench.[105]

These activities had taken place over a period of 10 years at a number of different locations, including rooms equipped as torture chambers. The activities were videotaped and the tapes then copied and distributed amongst members of the group.

The men involved were charged with a number of offences including charges of assault occasioning actual bodily harm. The men argued that they had committed no crimes as all the activities were consensual. They said there was no permanent injury, and that there was no infection of the wounds, and they used a code word to halt the infliction of pain if necessary.

After a ruling by the trial judge that they could not rely on consent as an answer to the prosecution case, the men changed their pleas of not guilty to guilty. On 19 December 1990, the men were sentenced. Some of the men were given terms of imprisonment, one receiving a prison sentence of four and a half years. Six of the men appealed to the Court of Appeal. That Court reduced the sentences but upheld the convictions: *R v Brown* [1992] 2 WLR 441.

In a joint judgment delivered by Lord Lane CJ, the judges followed *Attorney-General's Reference (No 6 of 1980)* [1981] QB 715 in which the Court stated (at 719):

> [I]t is not in the public interest that people should try to cause, or should cause, each other actual bodily harm for no good reason.

---

104 I Warren, "Violence, Sport and the Law: A Critical Discussion" in D Hemphill (ed), *All Part of the Game: Violence and Australian Sport* (Melbourne: Walla Walla Press, 1998), p 87 at p 99.

105 Details of the activities are set out in the Court of Appeal judgment in *R v Brown* [1992] 2 WLR 441.

The Court of Appeal stated in *Brown's* case (at 449) that:

> [W]e agree with the trial judge that the satisfying of sadomasochistic libido does not come within the category of good reason nor can the injuries be described as merely transient or trifling.

Five of the men then appealed to the House of Lords. A majority of three judges to two dismissed their appeal: *R v Brown* [1993] 2 WLR 556. The judges in the majority stressed that consent could not be a defence to a charge of assault occasioning actual bodily harm unless the circumstances fell within pre-existing categories of exceptions such as sporting contests or reasonable surgery. The words used by the majority judges display a degree of moral censure. For example, Lord Templeman stated (at 566):

> Society is entitled and bound to protect itself against a cult of violence. Pleasure derived from the infliction of pain is an evil thing. Cruelty is uncivilised.

Similarly, Lord Lowry (at 583) referred to the men suffering injury in order to:

> satisfy a perverted and depraved sexual desire. Sadomasochistic homosexual activity cannot be regarded as conducive to the enhancement or enjoyment of family life or conducive to the welfare of society.

These views echo the position of the distinguished English judge, Lord Patrick Devlin who in the 1960s argued that certain kinds of conduct ought to be prohibited and punished by the law simply because they are immoral according to the norms of a given society: P Devlin, *The Enforcement of Morals* (London: Oxford University Press, 1965). See further, Ch 1, 3.2 'Morality' at p 51. He argued that certain types of consensual conduct such as homosexual acts should be criminalised in order to preserve society, its essential institutions and what he termed its "positive morality" from disintegration.

The opposing view was taken up by Herbert Hart,[106] who, following the tradition of John Stuart Mill,[107] argued that conduct should only be criminalised if it caused harm to others. What people did with consent in private was their business and not that of the criminal law.

This view was followed by the dissenting judges in *Brown's* case. Lord Mustill, in particular, stated (at 599) that questions dealing with morally acceptable behaviour "are questions of private morality: the standards upon which they fall to be judged are not those of the criminal law".

Three of the accused in *Brown* then took the matter to the European Court of Human Rights, arguing that the British justice system had violated their human rights, in particular, their right to privacy: *Laskey, Jaggard and Brown v The United Kingdom* (Eur Court HR, 19 February 1997), *Reports of Judgments and Decisions* 1997-I, 120. A unanimous nine-judge decision of the European Court held that it found no basis for allegations that the British courts were biased against homosexual men and that it had been necessary to delve into the men's private lives "for the protection of health".

---

106 HLA Hart, *Law, Liberty and Morality* (London: Oxford University Press, 1963). See further, Ch 1, 3.1 'Prevention of Harm', p 49.

107 JS Mill, *On Liberty* (London: Harmondsworth, Penguin 1974; first published 1859).

Should the acts done by the men in *Brown's* case be punishable by the criminal law? A positive answer could be justified by recourse to Lord Devlin's moralistic approach. A negative answer could be based on Professor's Hart's liberal approach. Interestingly, the European Court of Human Right's approach seems to fall somewhere in between, in that it could be argued that such conduct should be criminalised because, even though consensual, it is likely to cause harm to health.

Brown's case was widely reported in the media and has been subject to a great deal of academic debate.[108] From a doctrinal perspective, the decision was criticised as representing a concealed shift in the approach to consent in the criminal law. For example, Nicola Padfield suggested that *Brown* represented a fundamental shift in philosophy:

> In the past, consent had been seen as a defence in all but a few cases where the judiciary specifically ruled that it could not apply. Now the courts seem to be saying that consent can only be used in those few circumstances defined by the judiciary. [109]

Brown's case also provided a focus for renewed discussion in England and Australia on the limits of consent in the criminal law, producing analyses of sadomasochism from various perspectives including liberalism, feminism, critical theory and human rights.[110]

A similar approach to the majority view in *Brown's* case was expressed by the Ontario Court of Appeal in *R v Welch* (1996) 101 CCC (3d) 216. In the course of consensual sado-masochistic activity, the "victim" suffered "obvious and extensive bruising" and (possible) injury

---

108 See for example, PJ Farrugia, "The Consent Defence: Sports Violence, Sadomasochism and the Criminal Law" (1997) 8(2) *Auckland University Law Review* 472; P Roberts, "Consent to Injury: How Far Can You Go?" (1997) 113 *Law Quarterly Review* 27; S Bronitt, "The Right to Sexual Privacy, Sadomasochism and the *Human Rights (Sexual Conduct) Act* 1994 (Cth)" (1995) 21(2) *Australian Journal of Human Rights* 59; Law Commission Consultation Paper No 139, *Consent in the Criminal Law* (December 1995); I Freckelton, "Masochism, Self-mutilation and the Limits of Consent" (1994) 2(1) *Journal of Law and Medicine* 48; M Giles, "*R v Brown*: Consensual Harm and the Public Interest" (1994) 57 *Modern Law Review* 101; N Bamforth, "Sado-masochism and Consent" [1994] Crim LR 661; D Kell, "Social Disutility and the Law of Consent" (1994) 14 *Oxford Journal of Legal Studies* 121; D Kell, "Bodily Harm in the Court of Appeal" (1993) 109 *Law Quarterly Review* 199.

109 N Padfield, "Consent and the Public Interest" [1992] *New Law Journal* 430 at 430. For a similar argument made in the context of the *Criminal Code* (Qld), see D Kell, "Consent to Harmful Assaults Under the Queensland *Criminal Code*: Time for a Reappraisal?" (1994) 68 ALJ 363.

110 For an analysis drawing on medico-legal perspectives and liberal theory, see I Freckelton, "Sado-masochism, Repeated Self-mutilation and Consent" (1994) 2 *Journal of Law and Medicine* 48. For a feminist analysis, see S Edwards, *Sex and Gender in the Legal Process* (London: Blackstone Press, 1996), pp 77-89; S Jeffreys, "Consent and the Politics of Sexuality" (1993) 5(2) *Current Issues in Criminal Justice* 173 and C Smart, *Law, Crime and Sexuality* (London: Sage, 1995), pp 110-123. For a discourse analysis drawing on critical theory, see C Stychin, "Unmanly Diversions: The Construction of the Homosexual Body (Politic) in English Law" (1994) 32 *Osgoode Hall Law Journal* 503 and S Chandra-Shekeran, "Theorising the Limits of the 'Sado-masochistic homosexual' identity in *R v Brown*" [1997] 21 *Melbourne University Law Review* 584. For a human rights analysis, see S Bronitt, "The Right to Sexual Privacy, Sado-masochism and the *Human Rights (Sexual Conduct) Act* 1994 (Cth)" (1995) 2(1) *Australian Journal of Human Rights* 59. Other discussions of the case can be found in P Farrugia, "The Consent Defence: Sports Violence, Sadomasochism and the Criminal Law" (1997) 8(2) *Auckland University Law Review* 472; P Roberts, "Consent to Injury: How Far Can You Go?" (1997) 113 *Law Quarterly Review* 27; Law Commission *Consent in the Criminal Law*, Consultation Paper No 139 (December 1995); M Giles, "*R v Brown*: Consensual Harm and the Public Interest" (1994) 57 *Modern Law Review* 101; N Bamforth, "Sado-masochism and Consent" [1994] *Criminal Law Review* 661; D Kell, "Social Disutility and the Law of Consent" (1994) 14 *Oxford Journal of Legal Studies* 121; D Kell, "Bodily Harm in the Court of Appeal" (1993) 109 *Law Quarterly Review* 199.

to the rectum. The Court affirmed (at 239) that the trial judge had been correct in withdrawing the issue of consent from the jury on the following basis:

> Although the law must recognise individual freedom and autonomy, when the activity in question involves pursuing sexual gratification by deliberately inflicting pain upon another that gives rise to bodily harm, then the personal interest of the individuals involved must yield to the more compelling societal interests which are challenged by such behaviour.

A subsequent decision of the English Court of Appeal, *R v Emmett* (unrep, 18/6/1999, CA Rose LJ, Wright and Kay JJ, No 9901191/Z2) has confirmed the principle arising from *Brown's* case and refused to draw a distinction between sadomasochistic activity on a heterosexual basis and that which is conducted in a homosexual context. In *Emmett's* case, the accused was living with the "victim" at the time of the alleged assaults and they afterwards married. The evidence of injuries came from a doctor whom the victim had consulted. The victim herself did not give evidence at the trial. The accused was charged with five offences of assault occasioning actual bodily harm, but this was dropped to two at the trial. Emmett was convicted of assault occasioning actual bodily harm on one count and in the light of the judge's direction, the accused pleaded guilty to a further count of assault occasioning actual bodily harm. He was sentenced to nine months' imprisonment on each count consecutive, the sentence being suspended for two years.

The first incident that gave rise to the conviction concerned a process of partial asphyxiation through a plastic bag being tightly tied around the victim's neck during the course of the accused engaging in oral sex with her. The victim lost consciousness due to loss of oxygen. The following day her eyes became progressively bloodshot and when she went to her doctor, he found subconjunctival haemorrhages in both eyes due to the lack of oxygen and bruising around the neck due to the tight ligature holding the plastic bag in place. No treatment was given and after about a week, the bloodshot eyes returned to normal.

The second incident occurred a few weeks later when during sexual activity, the accused poured lighter fuel on the victim's breasts and set light to it. The accused said the victim had panicked and would not keep still, so he could not extinguish the flames immediately. She suffered a 6 cm x 4 cm third degree burn that became infected. The doctor initially thought it might need a skin graft but the burn eventually healed over without scarring.

The accused appealed against conviction upon a certificate granted by the trial judge setting out the following question for the court's determination:

> Where two adult persons consent to participate in sexual activity in private not intended to cause any physical injury but which does in fact cause or risk actual bodily harm, the potential for such harm being foreseen by both parties, does consent to such activity constitute a defence to an allegation of assault occasioning actual bodily harm contrary to s 47 of the *Offences Against the Person Act* 1861.

The Court of Appeal held that consent could not amount to a defence in such circumstances. The accused relied upon *R v Wilson* [1996] 3 WLR 125 in which Russell LJ observed that consensual activity between husband and wife, in the privacy of the matrimonial home, is not a proper matter for criminal investigation or prosecution. However, the Court of Appeal in *R v Emmet* drew a distinction (at 4) between the type of harm in *Wilson* (branding for personal adornment) and the actual or potential damage suffered by the victim during the course of sexual activity on the facts:

> The lady suffered a serious, and what must have been, an excruciating painful burn which became infected, and the appellant himself recognised that it required medical attention. As to the process of partial asphyxiation, to which she was subjected on the earlier occasion, while it may ... now be fairly known that the restriction of oxygen to the brain is capable of heightening sexual sensation, it is also, or should be, equally well-known that such a practice contains within itself a grave danger of brain damage or even death.

The Court of Appeal found that the facts of *Emmett* were similar to that in *Brown*, observing (at 3) that there was "no reason in principle ... to draw any distinction between sadomasochistic activity on a heterosexual basis and that which is conducted in a homosexual context". The Court concluded by agreeing with the trial judge's comments (at 4):

> In this case, the degree of actual and potential harm was such and also the degree of unpredictability as to injury was such as to make it a proper cause for the criminal law to intervene. This was not tattooing, it was not something which absented pain or dangerousness and the agreed medical evidence is in each case, certainly on the first occasion, there was a very considerable degree of danger to life; on the second, there was a degree of injury to the body.

It is unclear whether these English decisions will be followed in Australia, although there is some slight indication that they may be. In *R v McIntosh* (unrep, 3/9/1999, SC Vic Sentence by Vincent J, No 1412 of 1999; [1999] VSC 358) the accused pleaded guilty to manslaughter. His sexual partner died during bondage sex after the accused deliberately pulled on the rope around the deceased's neck on the theory that near asphyxia can heighten sexual pleasure. There was no evidence that the deceased had not consented to the rope being placed around his neck and there was evidence that the accused and the deceased had periodically engaged in bondage type sex. In the course of sentencing the accused to five years imprisonment, Vincent J remarked (at 4-5) in relation to whether the activity was unlawful for the purpose of unlawful and dangerous act manslaughter:

> [I]t is not, of itself, and I repeat that expression, of itself, in the case of consenting adult persons, contrary to the law of this jurisdiction to engage in activities that could be described as bondage or sexual sadomasochism ... In my opinion, if the sado-masochistic activity or bondage activity to which a victim consents involves the infliction of any such injury or the reckless acceptance of the risk that it will occur, then the consent of the victim will not be recognized.

Here, Vincent J appears, like the Court of Appeal in *Emmett's* case, to be focussing on the degree of harm involved in order to provide a threshold for consent to sadomasochistic activities.

The regulation of sadomasochistic activities is particularly difficult because such activities combine sex with violence and therefore raise issues for the law relating to sexual offences as well as assault. Susan Edwards in "No Defence for Sado-masochistic Libido" (1994) *New Law Journal* 406, for example, has stated:

> In our desire to preserve privacy, individual liberty, and freedom from state intervention we are in danger of missing what lies at the heart of sado-masochism — its potential for violence. Why is it that for some the prefix "sex" functions as a protective shield? We need to recognise, as we move increasingly into a world of sexual violence, the dangers of placing this so-called "sex" beyond the rule of law.

The physical expression of sexuality takes many different forms, and this may include sado-masochistic violence.[111] The malleability of the distinction between "sex" and "violence", and its scope for legal inversion, is explored in Chapter 12: pp 581ff.

The present law may offer some degree of protection by setting limits on the *degree of harm* to which a person can validly consent. An alternative framework for developing safeguards for those engaging in sadomasochistic activities may lie in the concept of consent rather than the degree of harm. The law relating to consent for common assault at present offers little (if any) protection to those individuals who are especially vulnerable because of youth, inexperience or dependency. The general position is that provided the person is sufficiently mature to understand the nature of the relevant act or risk, consent operates as a complete defence. By contrast, recent reforms to the law governing consent to sexual intercourse offers greater protection to vulnerable parties. In Chapter 12, we explore how free agreement to sexual intercourse may be negated by, for example, intoxication, the abuse of authority, threats or mental incapacity. In the context of offences against the person, similar rules should be developed to ensure that the consent of the parties is given freely, without constraint. This could involve the adoption of a positive consent standard for sadomasochistic activities that involve the risk of bodily harm to the participants: S Bronitt, "The Right to Sexual Privacy, Sado-Masochism and the *Human Rights (Sexual Conduct) Act* 1994 (Cth)" (1995) 2(1) *Australian Journal of Human Rights* 59 at 72.

4. THREATS

We have outlined how assault by the threat of force involves any act committed intentionally or recklessly which puts another person in fear of immediate and unlawful personal violence. Threats independently of assault may also give rise to a criminal offence.

The most serious of the threat offences that exist in all jurisdictions are threats to kill and threats to cause harm or injury. In New South Wales, Queensland and Tasmania, a threat to kill must be put in writing.[112] In the other jurisdictions, the threat can be by words or conduct.[113] For example,

---

111 For a discussion of activities concerning the causing of pain to enhance sexual pleasure, see The Law Commission, *Consent in the Criminal Law*, Consultation Paper No 139 (London: HMSO, 1995), pp 133ff.

112 *Crimes Act* 1900 (NSW), s 31; *Criminal Code* (Qld), s 308; *Criminal Code* (Tas), s 162.

113 *Crimes Act* 1900 (ACT), s 30; *Criminal Code* (NT), s 166; *Criminal Law Consolidation Act* 1935 (SA), s 19; *Crimes Act* 1958 (Vic), s 20; *Criminal Code* (WA), s 338B.

s 19(3) of the *Criminal Law Consolidation Act* 1935 (SA) states that a threat may be "directly or indirectly communicated by words (written or spoken) or by conduct, or partially by words and partially by conduct".

All jurisdictions apart from Queensland require an intention to cause the victim's fear that the threat will be carried out. In Queensland, it is enough that there is proof that the accused knew of the contents of any writing threatening to kill another. Some jurisdictions also contain recklessness as a fault element.[114]

The Australian Capital Territory and the Northern Territory also impose an additional reasonable person test. Section 30 of the *Crimes Act* 1900 (ACT) states that the circumstances must be such that a reasonable person would fear that the threat would be carried out. Similarly, under s 166 of the *Criminal Code* (NT), the threat must be of such a nature as to cause fear to any person of reasonable firmness and courage. It is a defence in that Territory that the making of the threat was reasonable by the standards of an ordinary person in similar circumstances to the accused: s 166.

It is also an offence in all jurisdictions to threaten harm or injury to another.[115] How that harm or injury is constituted varies between jurisdictions. In the Australian Capital Territory, the term is "grievous bodily harm" and in New South Wales, "bodily harm". In the Northern Territory and Queensland, it is "any injury" or "any detriment" and in Victoria, "serious injury". In Western Australia, the offence covers threats to "injure, endanger or harm". In Tasmania, it covers threats to "apply force" to another.

The MCCOC has recommended in its Report, *Chapter 5: Non-Fatal Offences Against the Person* (1998), p 48, that threats to kill and to cause serious harm remain offences. The Committee was not certain as to whether to criminalise threats to cause non-serious harm as "threats to cause minor harms are part of everyday life": p 49. It concluded that such an offence, if it is to be enacted, should be triable summarily: p 51.

PERSPECTIVES FROM PSYCHIATRY

Stalking

Stalking is now an offence in all jurisdictions.[116] From the legal viewpoint stalking refers to a pattern of behaviour that results in some form of psychological harm. Matthew Goode in his article "Stalking: Crime of the Nineties?" (1995) 19 Crim LJ 21 writes (at 21):

> The essence of this behaviour is intentionally harassing, threatening, and/or intimidating a person by following them about, sending them articles, telephoning them, waiting outside their house and the like.

---

114 *Crimes Act* 1900 (ACT), s 30; *Criminal Law Consolidation Act* 1935 (SA), s 19; *Crimes Act* 1958 (Vic), s 20.

115 *Crimes Act* 1900 (ACT), s 31; *Crimes Act* 1900 (NSW), s 31; *Criminal Code* (NT), s 200; *Criminal Code* (Qld), s 359; *Criminal Law Consolidation Act* 1935 (SA), s 19; *Criminal Code* (Tas), s 182; *Crimes Act* 1958 (Vic), s 21; *Criminal Code* (WA), ss 338, 338B.

116 *Crimes Act* 1900 (ACT), s 34A; *Crimes Act* 1900 (NSW), s 562AB; *Criminal Code* (NT), s 189; *Criminal Code* (Qld), s 359A; *Criminal Law Consolidation Act* 1935 (SA), s 19AA; *Criminal Code* (Tas), s 192; *Crimes Act* 1958 (Vic), s 21A; *Criminal Code* (WA), s 338D.

Paul Mullen and Michelle Pathé are two psychiatrists who have carried out substantial research into stalking behaviour. In 1997, they defined stalking as "a constellation of behaviours in which one individual inflicts on another repeated unwanted intrusions and communications": "The Impact of Stalkers on their Victims" (1997) 170 *British Journal of Psychiatry* 12 at 12.[117] In a recent book written with Rosemary Purcell (P Mullen, M Pathé and R Purcell, *Stalkers and Their Victims* (Cambridge: Cambridge University Press, 2000)) they suggest that there are five primary types of stalkers:

— **Intimacy Seekers** who respond to loneliness by attempting to establish a close relationship. They tend to be prolific letter writers and gift senders and are often impervious to legal sanctions, believing such sanctions to be the price of true love.
— **The Resentful** who respond to a perceived insult or injury by conduct aimed not just at revenge but at vindication. They are the most likely to threaten, but the least likely to proceed to an actual assault. They are usually self-righteous and are difficult to engage in treatment, but will often withdraw from stalking when faced with legal sanctions.
— **The Rejected** who respond to an unwelcome end to a close relationship. They seek reconciliation or reparation or both. They use the widest range of stalking behaviours and are the most responsive to threats or the reality of legal sanctions.
— **The Predatory** who pursue sexual gratification and control both in and through their stalking. They concentrate almost exclusively on furtively following and maintaining surveillance of their victims and their stalking behaviour is intended as preparatory to an assault, usually sexual, upon the victim. They form a small subset of stalkers and treatment may be difficult because of the existence of sexually aberrant behaviours.
— **The Incompetents** who are would be suitors. They seek a relationship by methods that are at best counterproductive and at worst terrifying. They can usually be persuaded to abandon their stalking of a particular victim, but the challenge is preventing them latching on to a new victim.

While Mullen, Pathé and Purcell point out that these different types of stalkers and stalking behaviour have existed for centuries, it was only in the late 20th century that the word "stalking" became one of general parlance in Western cultures. It was during the 1980s and 1990s that the media began to focus on the stalking of high profile celebrities by their "fans" and the violence that occurred in the pursuit of ex-intimate partners. Novels such as Ian McEwan's *Enduring Love* (1997) and films such as Adrian Lyne's *Fatal Attraction* (1987) and Martin Scorcese's remake of *Cape Fear* (1991) also served to bring stalking behaviours into the popular imagination.

This increased focus on stalking behaviours highlighted the deficiencies in the law. For example, in New South Wales, there was an outcry concerning the murder of Andrea Patrick by an ex-lover after severe harassment that occurred in violation of a protection order. This was one of

---

117 See also P Mullen and M Pathé, "The Pathological Extensions of Love" (1994) 165 *British Journal of Psychiatry* 614; P Mullen and M Pathé, "Stalking and the Pathologies of Love" (1994) 28 *Australian and New Zealand Journal of Psychiatry* 469; P Mullen, M Pathé, R Purcell and GW Stuart, "A Study of Stalkers" (1999) 156 *American Journal of Psychiatry* 1244.

the catalysts for the enactment of stalking legislation in New South Wales: *Crimes (Domestic Violence) Amendment Act* 1993 (NSW). While certain stalking behaviour could possibly have been prosecuted under existing law such as assault through the threat of force or general threat provisions, certain acts when considered individually such as sending flowers or letters could seem innocuous to the uninvolved observer. Accordingly, stalking provisions were designed to cover a course of conduct that causes fear. Amanda Pearce and Patricia Easteal have written about the high incidence of "domestic" stalking and police reactions to it in the Australian Capital Territory: A Pearce and P Easteal, "The 'Domestic' in Stalking" (1999) 24(4) *Alternative Law Journal* 165.

Celia Wells writes that the introduction of specific stalking provisions arose from "two of the anxieties of the late 20th century — how to determine the boundaries of acceptable sexual behaviour and whether to admit psychiatric damage to the front row of significant personal harms": "Stalking: The Criminal Law Response" [1997] Crim LR 463 at 463. The types of stalker set out above do suggest a sexual connection to the harassing behaviour. In Chapter 12, we explore how the legal classification of conduct as sexual or non-sexual, violent or non-violent, criminal or non-criminal depends on various factors including the age, consent, gender and/or sexuality of the parties. Further, the willingness of the courts to consider "bodily harm" as including pure psychiatric illness as in the House of Lords decision in *R v Ireland; R v Burstow* [1998] AC 147, has allowed the criminalisation of some forms of stalking as an assault occasioning actual bodily harm.

Mullen, Pathé and Purcell would view "the rejected" as the mainstayers of domestic stalking. However, their types of stalker show that there are added layers to stalking behaviour. Because of the differences in motives, psychiatric status and response to treatment amongst stalkers, it is very difficult to establish workable definitions and sanctions. Mullen, Pathé and Purcell in *Stalkers and Their Victims* (Cambridge: Cambridge University Press, 2000), pp 277-278 sound the following warning:

> The constellation of behaviours associated with stalking frequently involves legitimate and otherwise innocuous activities, such as telephone calls, letters, sending "gifts", or approaches to the public. Requiring as few as *two* prohibited actions to constitute the offence will assist the proscription of behaviour prior to an escalation of violence. However, in the absence of sufficient safeguards, these laws increase the likelihood that inadvertent and legitimate behaviours will be regarded, and prosecuted, as "stalking" ... [T]here are natural limits to what the law can do to help to protect victims and prevent unwanted forms of conduct. It remains to be seen whether anti-stalking laws in their current form will prove an effective remedy to the problem of stalking, and, in many jurisdictions, in what form these contentious laws will eventually survive.

5. OFFENCES ENDANGERING LIFE OR PERSONAL SAFETY

There are numerous miscellaneous statutory offences dealing with the concept of endangering life or personal safety. There are, for example, provisions against administering drugs or poisons with intent to commit an offence,[118] setting traps[119] and offences relating to explosives.[120] There are also more general offences such as conduct endangering life or personal safety and engaging in dangerous conduct. We will deal with these latter offences in this section.

In the Northern Territory, South Australia and Victoria, there are provisions dealing with endangerment of life or personal safety. These provisions vary in their elements. Under s 154 of the *Criminal Code* (NT) any person who causes serious danger to the lives, health or safety of the public is guilty of an offence. This is assessed on the basis of whether an ordinary person would have foreseen the danger and not done the act or omission: s 154. In *Hoessinger v The Queen* (1992) 107 FLR 99 Gallop J held that the accused need not have clearly foreseen the danger, it is enough if an ordinary person "similarly circumstanced" would have foreseen the danger.

The South Australian provision, in contrast, contains a subjective element. It is an offence in South Australia where a person does an act or makes an omission knowing that it is likely to endanger the life of another or intending to endanger the life of another or being recklessly indifferent as to whether the life of another is endangered.[121]

Section 22 of the *Crimes Act* 1958 (Vic) sets out the offence of recklessly engaging in conduct that places, or may place, another person in danger of death. Section 23 is similar, but deals with serious injury rather than death. The victim need not have suffered harm. It is enough that he or she was placed in danger of death or serious injury.

In *R v Nuri* [1990] VR 641 the Supreme Court of Victoria held that s 22 involves proof of both subjective *and* objective elements. The prosecution must prove that a reasonable person in the accused's position, engaging in the conduct of the accused, would have realised that his or her conduct had placed, or might place, another person in danger of death. The subjective element requires proof that the accused intended to engage in the relevant conduct, realising that the probable consequence of that conduct would be to place another in danger of death.

This objective and subjective test has proved problematic in relation to prosecuting HIV positive accused who have engaged in unprotected intercourse. In *B* (unrep, 3/7/1995, SC Vic), Teague J held that the probability requirement in s 22 required proof of a "level of dangerousness" in the sense of an appreciable rather than a merely remote risk. In that case, there was uncontradicted

---

118 *Crimes (Internationally Protected Persons) Act* 1976 (Cth), ss 8(2), 8(7)(c); *Crimes Act* 1900 (ACT), ss 27(3)(b), 27(4)(a); *Crimes Act* 1900 (NSW), ss 38, 39; *Criminal Code* (NT), s 176; *Criminal Code* (Qld), ss 316, 322; *Criminal Law Consolidation Act* 1935 (SA), ss 25(c), 26; *Criminal Code* (Tas), ss 169, 175; *Crimes Act* 1958 (Vic), s 19 (there is no requirement that there be an intent to commit an indictable offence); *Criminal Code* (WA), ss 293, 300.

119 *Crimes Act* 1900 (ACT), ss 27(3)(f), 28(2)(c); *Crimes Act* 1900 (NSW), s 49(1); *Criminal Code* (NT), s 185; *Criminal Code* (Qld), s 327 *Criminal Code* (Tas), s 179; *Crimes Act* 1958 (Vic), ss 25, 26; *Criminal Code* (WA), s 305.

120 *Crimes Act* 1900 (ACT), ss 27(3)(e), 28(2)(b); *Crimes Act* 1900 (NSW), ss 46, 47, 48, 55; *Criminal Code* (NT), ss 177, 182; *Criminal Code* (Qld), ss 317, 321, 540; *Criminal Law Consolidation Act* 1935 (SA), ss 25(c), 26; *Criminal Code* (Tas), ss 170, 181; *Crimes Act* 1958 (Vic), s 317; *Criminal Code* (WA), ss 294, 298, 299, 557.

121 *Criminal Law Consolidation Act* 1935 (SA), s 29; *Bedi v The Queen* (1993) 61 SASR 269; *R v Teremoana* (1990) 54 SASR 30.

expert evidence led to the effect that the risk of transmission of HIV arising from unprotected intercourse was around one in 200. The jury was accordingly directed to return a verdict of not guilty: see also *D* (1997) 21 Crim LJ 40.

In *Mutemeri v Cheesman* (1999) 100 A Crim R 397 the accused who was HIV positive, had been convicted by a magistrate of recklessly engaging in conduct that may place another in danger of death after he had unprotected intercourse on several occasions with the same woman. No evidence was led as to the statistical risk of HIV transmission. On appeal, Mandie J set aside the convictions, sentences and orders of the Magistrates' Court. Mandie J was of the opinion that s 22 was concerned with foresight of the probability of the other person's exposure to risk of death. Following *Nuri's* case, he held (at 401) that the test has both subjective and objective elements, namely that:

(1) the accused intended to do an act having realised the probable consequence of that act would be to place another in danger of death; and

(2) a reasonable person in the accused's position would realise that act had placed or may place another in danger of death.

Mandie J held (at 406) that it was not open for the magistrate to find that the accused's conduct placed his partner in danger of death without expert evidence directed to the risk associated with the particular conduct in issue. Matthew Groves in "Commentary" (1998) 22 Crim LJ 357 writes (at 359):

> [T]he essential issue for the magistrate concerned the level of risk of [the victim] contracting HIV by her contact with Mutemeri, *and then* dying as a result. It followed that the expert should have provided evidence on the chances of the survival of [the victim] if she had contracted HIV from Mutemeri, including the possible length of survival, during which a cure or further life prolonging treatments might be developed, and also her chance of outright survival.

This subjective/objective test and the need for expert evidence seems unduly complicated and it may be that having either a subjective or an objective test would provide greater clarity: see further D Lanham, "Danger Down Under" [1999] Crim LR 960.

Some of the other jurisdictions impose duties on those engaging in conduct that may be dangerous to health such as surgical or medical treatment.[122] In all jurisdictions apart from the Australian Capital Territory and Victoria, it is a criminal offence to fail to provide the necessaries of life where there is a duty to do so.[123] There is also a range of offences in jurisdictions other than South Australia and Victoria dealing with endangering the life of a child by abandonment or exposure.[124]

The MCCOC has recommended the enactment of a general endangerment provision divided into recklessness as to the danger of death and recklessness as to the danger of serious harm: *Chapter 5 — Non-Fatal Offences Against the Person*, Report (1998), p 64. The wording is similar to the Victorian provisions, but the MCCOC did not discuss the objective/subjective test and dismissed the criticism that a comprehensible test for recklessness is difficult to establish: p 71. Instead, it

---

122 *Criminal Code* (NT), s 150; *Criminal Code* (Qld), s 288; *Criminal Code* (WA), s 265.

123 *Crimes Act* 1900 (NSW), s 44; *Criminal Code* (NT), s 183; *Criminal Code* (Qld), s 285; *Criminal Law Consolidation Act* 1935 (SA), s 30; *Criminal Code* (Tas), s 144; *Criminal Code* (WA), s 262.

124 *Crimes Act* 1900 (ACT), s 39; *Crimes Act* 1900 (NSW), s 43; *Criminal Code* (NT), s 184; *Criminal Code* (Qld), ss 326, 364; *Criminal Code* (Tas), s 178; *Criminal Code* (WA), ss 304, 344.

quoted with approval Hampel J's way of explaining the idea to the jury. In *D* (1997) 21 Crim LJ 40, Hampel J considered the test of recklessness in relation to the transmission of HIV (at 43):

> [T]he question of whether the risk of danger involved is an appreciable risk is one for the jury. The jury is entitled to go beyond the population figure and consider the nature of the infection ... the manner in which it is transmitted, and the various epidemiological studies ... in order to determine, without relying on statistical or arithmetical calculations of probabilities, whether the risk of infection in respect of each act charged was an appreciable risk of danger or a mere remote possibility.

This seems to relate to an objective measurement. The MCCOC, however, did not make any mention of a reasonable person test in this regard.

6. FALSE IMPRISONMENT, KIDNAPPING AND ABDUCTION

The offences of false imprisonment and kidnapping exist in certain jurisdictions. There is some overlap between these offences, but false imprisonment refers to the deprivation of liberty of another, whereas kidnapping refers to the forcible taking away of another. Abduction generally refers to the taking or detaining of a person for a sexual purpose.

At common law, every unlawful restraint of the liberty of one person under the custody of another, either in a prison, house or in the street, constitutes the tort of false imprisonment which is also a misdemenour.[125] The corresponding offence of "unlawful deprivation of liberty" exists in the Code jurisdictions[126] and in the Australian Capital Territory, it is an offence to unlawfully confine or imprison another person: *Crimes Act* 1900 (ACT), s 34.

The offence of false imprisonment is made out if a person is detained in consequence of threats whether or not those threats relate to the person detained or to another: *R v Garrett* (1988) 30 SASR 392. There is no imprisonment, however, if a person blocks the path of another so that he or she cannot go in a particular direction: *Bird v Jones* (1845) 7 QB 742.

An imprisonment may occur even where the detained person is not aware that he or she is being detained.[127] The restraint of a child's freedom of movement by a parent may amount to an unlawful imprisonment where the restraint extends to detention that is outside the realms of reasonable parental discipline: *Rahman* (1985) 81 Cr App Rep 349 (CA).

It is an offence at common law to unlawfully take and carry away a person or hold a person in secret against his or her will: *R v D* [1984] AC 778 (HL). All that must be proved is a deprivation of liberty and a taking away of the victim from the place he or she wishes to be. It is unnecessary to prove that the kidnapper took the victim to the place he or she intended: *Wellard* (1978) 67 Cr App R 364 (CA).

---

125 *Emmett v Lyne* (1805) 1 Bos & PNR 255; *R v Lesley* (1860) Bell CC 220; *Hunter v Johnson* (1884) 13 QBD 225; *Mee v Cruickshank* (1902) 20 Cox CC 210; *Macpherson v Brown* (1975) SASR 184; *Rahman* (1985) 81 Cr App R 349.

126 *Criminal Code* (NT), s 196; *Criminal Code* (Qld), s 355; *Criminal Code* (Tas), ss 186, 191; *Criminal Code* (WA), s 333.

127 *Meering v Grahame-White Aviation Co Ltd* (1919) 122 LT 44 (CA); cf *Herring v Boyle* (1834) 1 Cr M & R 377.

A statutory offence of kidnapping a person for ransom or for any other advantage exists in all jurisdictions.[128] The Western Australian provision is the most extensive in that it covers the detention of a person where the accused intends to gain a benefit, pecuniary or otherwise, for any person or cause a detriment, pecuniary or otherwise to any person as well as the intention to prevent the doing of an act or to compel the doing of an act. A parent may be convicted of kidnapping his or her own child: *R v D* [1984] AC 778.

In the Northern Territory and Queensland it is also a statutory offence for a person to take, entice away or detain another person with intent to compel that other person to work for him or her: *Criminal Code* (NT), s 195; *Criminal Code* (Qld), s 354.

The offence of "abduction" exists in all jurisdictions apart from the Northern Territory and Western Australia.[129] The offence was originally designed to protect the fortunes of heiresses. A statute was passed in the reign of Henry VII making it a felony to "taketh any woman against her will unlawfully" if she had land or goods or was heir to the same and the taking was for "motives of lucre": 3 Hen 7.2 (UK); Hawkins PC 109. The New South Wales and Queensland provisions still retain vestiges of the old law, in that only a woman can be abducted and the accused must have a "motive of lucre" and the woman have an "interest in property, or who is a presumptive heiress or ... next of kin to any person who has such an interest".[130] The other current provisions do not refer to such motives, but rather to the taking or detaining of a person against his or her will with the intent to have sexual intercourse or to marry.

Some States have specific provisions dealing with the abduction of children under the age of 16[131] and child stealing.[132] Section 65Y of the *Family Law Act* 1975 (Cth) also allows for imprisonment for up to three years if an accused takes a child outside Australia in breach of a residence, contact or care order of the court. A similar penalty can be imposed where the removal occurs when such proceedings are pending: *Family Law Act* 1975 (Cth), s 65Z. If a child is taken to another country, whether or not the child can be returned will depend upon whether the countries involved are contracting parties to the Hague *Convention on the Civil Aspects of International Child Abduction*.[133] If both countries are contracting parties, a child under the age of 16 may be the subject of an order to return to the country of origin.

The *Family Law Act* provisions are of limited power in that the majority of child abductions occur when there are no family law proceedings pending. They also do not apply where a child has been taken overseas with consent, but one parent decides to keep the child there.

---

128 *Crimes (Internationally Protected Persons) Act* 1976 (Cth), s 8; *Crimes Act* 1900 (ACT), s 37; *Crimes Act* 1900 (NSW), s 90A; *Criminal Code* (NT), s 194; *Criminal Code* (Qld), s 354A; *Kidnapping Act* 1960 (SA), s 4; *Criminal Code* (Tas), s 191A; *Crimes Act* 1958 (Vic), s 63A; *Criminal Code* (WA), s 332.

129 *Crimes Act* 1900 (ACT), s 92M; *Crimes Act* 1900 (NSW), ss 86, 89; *Criminal Code* (Qld), s 351(1); *Criminal Law Consolidation Act* 1935 (SA), s 59; *Criminal Code* (Tas), s 186; *Crimes Act* 1958 (Vic), s 55.

130 *Crimes Act* 1900 (NSW), s 86; *Criminal Code* (Qld), s 351. Section 89 of the *Crimes Act* 1900 (NSW) refers to forcible abduction which does not require "motives of lucre".

131 *Crimes Act* 1900 (NSW), s 90; *Criminal Code* (Qld), s 219(1); *Criminal Code* (Tas), s 189; *Criminal Code* (NT), s 202; *Criminal Law Consolidation Act* 1935 (SA), s 80; *Crimes Act* (Vic), s 56.

132 *Crimes Act* 1900 (NSW), s 91; *Criminal Code* (Qld), s 363; *Criminal Code* (WA), s 343; *Crimes Act* 1958 (Vic), s 63.

133 The Hague 25 October 1980 [1987] ATS 2 19 ILM 1501. This is implemented in Australia by the Family Law (Child Abduction Convention) Regulations (Cth). See further D Chaikin, "International Extradition and Parental Child Abduction" (1993) 5 *Bond Law Review* 129.

The MCCOC has recommended an offence of child abduction be enacted, but has specifically excluded parental child abduction from that offence: *Chapter 5 — Non-Fatal Offences Against the Person,* Report (September 1998), pp 88-91. In 1998, the Family Law Council considered whether or not child abduction by a parent should be criminalised and recommended that it should not: *Parental Child Abduction,* A Report to the Attorney-General (January 1998), p 32. The Report set out a number of grounds for this conclusion, including that criminalisation would have negative effects on parent-child and parent-parent relationships; it might operate to the disadvantage of women fleeing domestic violence and it could operate to the disadvantage of economically and socially weaker members of the community: p 33.

7. CONCLUSION

This exploration of the law of assault and related offences shows that there is much left to be desired in terms of the existing structure because of the considerable overlap between offences. Obviously, there is an urgent need for the rationalisation and reform of the hierarchy of offences against the person. Andrew Ashworth in his book *Principles of Criminal Law* (3rd ed, Oxford: Oxford University Press, 1999) writes in this regard (p 345):

> How might the non-fatal offences be reformed? It is important to start by affirming the principle of maximum certainty, the principle of correspondence and the principle of fair labelling, and in particular to ensure that the new scheme of offences is not so dominated by concerns about efficient administration (usually, prosecutorial convenience) as to produce wide, catch-all offences of the kind found in public order legislation.

The MCCOC was drawn to the scheme of offences against the person proposed by the English Criminal Law Reform Committee in its Fourteenth Report, *Offences Against the Person* (London: HMSO, Cmnd 7844, 1980) upon which the Victorian provisions are based.[134] This scheme replaces assault provisions with those focusing on different types of injury accompanied by different fault elements. Similarly, the Home Office in England circulated a draft Bill for comment in 1998: *Violence: Reforming the Offences Against the Person Act 1861* (1998). This Bill again proposed a scheme based on the seriousness of the harm caused and the degree of the fault element involved.

The MCCOC scheme is to have four divisions based on causing harm, threats and stalking, endangerment and finally, kidnapping, child abduction and unlawful detention. The use of the term "causing harm" goes further than the Victorian provisions that refer to "inflicting injury". As explored above, the notion of causation here is broader than infliction and "harm" is used rather than "injury" in order to include "psychiatric harm" within the purview of the term. The MCCOC approach also differs from the Victorian in defining more fully the scope of physical harm and harm to a person's mental health. Section 5.4 of the *Criminal Code Act 1995* (Cth) already defines the fault element of recklessness and this may go some way in avoiding the uncertainty that has surrounded the interpretation of the Victorian provisions using this term.

---

134 Model Criminal Code Officers Committee, *Chapter 5: Non-Fatal Offences Against the Person*, Discussion Paper (1996); Model Criminal Code Officers Committee, *Chapter 5: Non Fatal Offences Against the Person*, Report (1998).

The MCCOC scheme has much to recommend it. However, any reform to the law of offences against the person needs to be accompanied by reform to the public order offences, such as offensive conduct, affray and violent disorder, which are explored in Chapter 14. The traditional legal separation between "public" offences against the person and "private" domestic violence offences also needs continued review in order to ensure that violence against women and children is reported and charged because of the harm caused, rather than where they occur.

12

Sexual Offences

> A little still she strove,
> and much repented,
> And whispering
> "I will ne'er consent" — consented

Lord Byron, *Don Juan* (1819-1824)
canto 1, st 92

1. SEX, VIOLENCE AND THE CRIMINAL LAW

This chapter explores the relationship between sex, violence and the criminal law through an examination of selected sexual offences, namely, rape, sexual assault and indecency offences. The term "sexual violence", while widely used by criminologists and sociologists, has no stable or consistent meaning from a legal perspective. The legal classification of conduct as sexual or non-sexual, violent or non-violent, criminal or non-criminal depends on various factors including the age, consent, gender and/or sexuality of the parties. There is considerable conceptual difficulty in identifying unifying characteristics, raising uncertainty whether pornography, prostitution, stalking and sexual harassment constitute sexual violence. This difficulty stems from the fact that "sexual violence" is more than a descriptive label. It performs a normative function that allows the police, prosecutors, judges and law-makers to distinguish legitimate from illegitimate sexual behaviour.

From a technical perspective, efforts to categorise crimes as "sexual offences" pose similar difficulties. Kate Warner in her Subtitle on sexual offences in *The Laws of Australia* (Sydney: LBC, 1996–) offers the following definition: "Sexual offences encompass a variety of sexual conduct which is either prohibited because it is non-consensual, offensive or exploitative": 10.3 'Sexual Offences', para 1. Accordingly, her Subtitle includes sexual assault, indecency as well as other "sexual offences against public morality" such as prostitution. Interestingly, the transmission of a serious disease (such as HIV) by sexual intercourse is viewed as sexual offence, rather than as a specie of assault. The difficulty with such a wide embracing definition is that it obscures the highly differentiated nature of offences with a sexual dimension. Crimes of rape, sexual or indecent assault prohibit unwelcome or unwanted sexual conduct: the presence or absence of the victim's consent distinguishes between legitimate and illegitimate behaviour. Other types of sexual activity, such as prostitution, pornography and homosexual sadomasochism, may be unlawful notwithstanding their apparently consensual and "victimless" nature. In some situations, the conduct may be constructed by police, prosecutors, judges or law-makers in terms that conceal its sexual dimension altogether. In cases of stalking, for example, the sexual dimension of the accused's conduct may be concealed behind charges of common assault or public order offences, or may be viewed as a "non-criminal" matter leaving victims to invoke civil remedies, such as restraining orders. See further, Ch 14, pp 756ff.

The law governing sexual offences does not merely regulate conduct. It also plays an important role in constituting sexual identities. This function of the criminal law is often overlooked since, according to traditional liberal accounts, the law is (or ought to be) concerned with regulating conduct, not criminal types. This point was explored in Chapter 1, 2.1 'Crime and the Rule of Law'. Ostensibly the law governing sexual offences fits this mould, prohibiting specific sexual conduct such as buggery or gross indecency rather than different types of sexuality such as homosexuality. Notwithstanding these powerful ideological claims of neutrality, the criminal law plays a role, together with other disciplinary discourses such as medical science and politics, in creating and sustaining categories of sexual deviance.

Sexual Pathology and Sexual Politics

In medical science, there is considerable controversy surrounding the role of psychiatry in constituting, diagnosing and treating homosexuality as a "sexual disorder": E Shorter, *A History of Psychiatry* (London: Sage, 1995). Edward Shorter traces the political controversy surrounding the inclusion of homosexuality in the illness list as a "sexual deviation". A sub-committee of the American Psychiatric Association (APA) reviewed the scientific data on homosexuals. Unable to agree on the issue, the matter was put to referendum of members and in 1974 the APA removed homosexuality from the *Diagnostic and Statistical Manual of Mental Disorders* (DSM). As Shorter noted, "At a stroke, what had been considered for a century or more a grave psychiatric disorder ceased to exist": p 304. Political discourse has also played a significant role in creating and sustaining homosexuality as a subversive sexual and identity. The ambivalence toward homosexual reform in political texts, such as parliamentary debates and legislative preambles, is explored in E Henderson, "Of Signifiers and Sodomy: Privacy, Public Morality and Sex in the Decriminalisation Debates" (1996) 20 *Melbourne University Law Review* 1023. See generally, J Weeks, *Coming Out: Homosexual Politics in Britain from the 19th Century to the Present* (London: Quartet Books, 1977); M Kirby, "Psychiatry, Psychology and Law: Uncomfortable Bedfellows" (2000) 7(2) *Psychiatry, Psychology and Law* 139.

Carl Stychin in *Law's Desire: Sexuality and the Limits of Justice* (London: Routledge, 1995) points out that "legal discourse is an important site for the constitution, consolidation and regulation of sexuality and, in particular, the hetero-homo sexual division": p 7. Transgressive sexuality clearly plays an important role in constituting and re-affirming the boundaries of "normal" (hetero)sexuality:

> In order for heterosexuality to remain intact, it requires an intelligible conception of its
> boundaries and that which lies beyond its limits. Thus, homosexuality, as the counter-
> structure of heterosexuality, emerges as a desire that must be produced in order to be
> repressed. Far from being outside of discourse, the continuous exclusion of homosexuality
> is integral to the formulation of a dominant heterosexual identity.[1]

The production of sexual identities under the criminal law involves affirming or repressing sexuality. But some types of sexuality are considered so marginal or incomprehensible that their status as deviant is not legally recognised. While male homosexuality has been the historical site of repressive religious and legal controls against buggery and gross indecency, lesbianism has stood largely outside the sphere of legal regulation. Neither legitimate nor illegitimate, this aspect of female sexuality has been regarded simply as legally "unimaginable". As Ruth Ford concludes in her examination of the legal treatment of lesbians in Australia in the mid-20th century:

> The exclusion of lesbian sexual practices from the statutes provided most lesbian women
> with areas of silence and immunity, free from persecution and prosecution. That lesbian
> acts were not criminalised meant that there was less public discussion and little awareness
> of lesbianism. This created a space for women to have relationships unsuspected and often
> without intervention. Lesbian women did not experience the ongoing and direct
> persecution by the legal system that gay men did.[2]

Sexual offences have provided the focus for much philosophical discussion of the nature and functions of the criminal law. Liberalism and feminism have debated the purpose and scope of sexual offences, influencing both legislative reform and common law development. As discussed in Chapter 1, 3.1-3.2 the liberal values of autonomy and privacy have played a significant role in reconstituting the boundaries between licit and illicit forms of sexuality, particularly in relation to laws governing prostitution and homosexuality: *Report of the Committee on Homosexual Offences and Prostitution* (London: HMSO, Cmnd 247, 1957).

The failure of the common law or statute to provide adequate protection to a right to sexual privacy may result in a challenge under Art 17 of the *International Covenant on Civil and Political Rights* (ICCPR) 1966. The scope and legitimate restrictions on privacy under the ICCPR have been discussed in Chapter 2, 3.5 'The Principle of Privacy'. Following the adoption of the Optional Protocol,

---

1   S Chandra-Shekeran, "Theorising the Limits of the 'Sadomasochistic Homosexual' identity in *R v Brown*" (1997) 21 *Melbourne University Law Review* 584 at 592. See also L Moran, *The Homosexual(ity) of Law* (London: Routledge, 1996).

2   R Ford, "'Lady-friends' and 'sexual deviationists': Lesbians and law in Australia, 1920s-1950s" in D Kirkby (ed), *Sex, Power and Justice* (Melbourne: Oxford University Press, 1995), pp 47-48. Although sexual conduct between women never constituted an offence under the common law or statute, Ford notes that police surveillance and harassment of "known" lesbians was not uncommon.

Tasmanian gross indecency laws prohibiting sexual conduct between consenting adult males in private have been held to violate the right to privacy guaranteed under Art 17 of the ICCPR: *Toonen v Australia* (1994) 1 PLPR 50 (Communication No 488/1992, UN Doc CCPR/C/50/D/488/1992, 4 April 1994). The *Toonen* ruling was given domestic effect by the *Human Rights (Sexual Conduct) Act* 1994 (Cth). Section 4 of the Act renders inoperative to the extent of inconsistency any Commonwealth, State or Territory law that constitutes an arbitrary interference with sexual conduct between consenting adults in private. The Act creates a legally protected zone of sexual privacy with potential implications for the laws governing the age of consent (which varies between heterosexual and homosexual conduct) and the blanket criminalisation of otherwise "consensual" sexual acts between adults such as prostitution and homosexual sadomasochism.[3]

In the next section, the role of the criminal law in constituting and delineating "sex" from "violence" is explored through two case studies: sadomasochism (S&M) and death by sexual misadventure. Since S&M involves the mutual infliction of pain to obtain sexual pleasure, it straddles the binary classification of conduct as either "sex" or "violence". The inclusion of sadomasochism in our chapters dealing with sexual offences *and* offences against the person recognises the instability of the categorisation "sex" and "violence". Traversing the conventional doctrinal lines drawn around S&M reveals the complex contradictory and contingent nature of legal categorisation. The other case study on death by sexual misadventure examines the role and significance of "consent" in regulating potentially harmful sexual activity. A careful examination of the cases reveals that the legality of dangerous sexual conduct is not determined solely by the level of harm or risk involved. Rather, legality is contingent on a range of factors including the gender and sexuality of the participants.

The law inscribes, and in some cases saturates, legal subjects with sex. Legal discourse produces and subordinates sexual subjects in contradictory ways. Sadomasochistic homosexuals participate in legally incomprehensible acts of "violence" rather than consensual sex, while heterosexual males engage in legitimate acts of "rough sex" with women who it is alleged gain sexual pleasure from the intentional infliction of pain. To achieve this legal contradiction, fundamental tenets of liberalism, such as autonomy and privacy, must be invoked selectively. The decision to restrict or respect autonomy in an individual case is represented as a matter of weighing these liberal values against competing considerations of policy and public interest: *R v Brown* [1994] 1 AC 212 at 234. The controversy surrounding the limits of autonomy and privacy in the context of sado-masochism shadows the theoretical struggle between the principles of liberalism, morality and welfare as the appropriate markers for criminalisation. The influence of these principles have been explored in Chapter 1, 3.1-3.4. The criminal law's margin of sexual tolerance, though often couched in the language of liberalism, is highly contingent on prevailing social and cultural understandings of sexuality and sexual deviance. These understandings, which are neither fixed nor immutable, play a significant role in constituting and policing the borders between legitimate and transgressive forms of sexuality.

---

3   See further S Bronitt, "The Right to Sexual Privacy, Sado-masochism and the *Human Rights (Sexual Conduct) Act* 1994 (Cth)" (1995) 2(1) *Australian Journal of Human Rights* 59.

1.1 CONSTRUCTING SEXUAL CRIMES: SEXUAL VIOLENCE OR VIOLENT SEX

R v Brown [1993] 2 WLR 556 was not merely a judgment about the legality of sadomasochism for the purpose of the law of assault: Ch 11, pp 562ff. The criminalisation of sadomasochism in that case appeared to be tied to the construction and suppression of a distinct legal subject — the "sadomasochistic homosexual": S Chandra-Shekeran, "Theorising the Limits of the 'Sado-masochistic homosexual' identity in *R v Brown*" [1997] 21 *Melbourne University Law Review* 584, p 586. Pathologised as both sexually deviant and a carrier of deadly disease, in this case HIV/AIDS, the sadomasochistic homosexual was viewed simultaneously as a victim and perpetrator of violence.[4] The sexual dimensions of sadomasochism were concealed behind the judicial depiction of the conduct as involving cruel violence, not merely sex: at 235. As Lord Templeman concluded (at 566) in *Brown*:

> The violence of sadists and the degradation of their victims have sexual motivations but sex is no excuse for violence ... Society is entitled and bound to protect itself against a cult of violence. Pleasure derived from the infliction of pain is an evil thing. Cruelty is uncivilised.

The European Court of Human Rights has similarly constructed sadomasochism as violence. The accused argued that English law, as applied in *Brown*, discriminated on the grounds of sexuality and therefore violated the *European Convention on Human Rights*. The Court rejected this reading of the judgments in *Brown*, observing that "it is clear from the judgment of the House of Lords that the opinions of the majority were based on the extreme nature of the practices involved and not the sexual proclivities of the applicants": *Laskey, Jaggard and Brown v the United Kingdom* (Eur Court HR, 19 February 1997) *Reports of Judgments and Decisions* 1997-I at para 47. From both a domestic and international perspective, sadomasochism is legally incomprehensible as *sexual* activity.

The common law framework for consent adopted by the House of Lords in *Brown* required the accused to establish that sadomasochism fell within a recognised public interest exception. Cast in this way, the task of justifying sadomasochism becomes legally impossible. Making little effort to understand the varied meanings and complexities of the rituals involved, the majority held that the accused had not established that inflicting pain for sexual gratification could be beneficial. The majority discounted precautions taken to respect the autonomy and welfare of the participants, such as code-words, because in the words of Lord Templeman "no one can feel the pain of another": at 565. They also took judicial notice that homosexual men were carriers of the deadly virus HIV, and that S&M posed an obvious *risk* of serious personal injury and blood infection, although there was no evidence that any of these practices had caused the infection: at 565. As David Fraser concludes, the House of Lords could hardly validate a "contract for death": "Father Knows Best: Transgressive

---

4   The police cautioned 26 "victims" on the basis that their willing participation amounted to aiding and abetting offences against themselves: L Bibbings and P Allridge, "Sexual Expression, Body Alteration and the Defence of Consent" (1993) 20(3) *Journal of Law and Society* 356. On the use of complicity against individuals who incite their own victimisation, see Chapter 8: pp 397ff.

Sexualities (?) and the Rule of Law" (1995) 7(1) *Current Issues in Criminal Justice* 82 at 84. The majority did not consider that S&M might involve less serious injury, or that S&M practices were not restricted to groups of homosexual men.[5]

Through this language of addiction, seduction and contagion, the majority constructed gay male sexuality exclusively in negative terms: C Stychin, "Unmanly Diversions: The Construction of the Homosexual Body (Politic) in English Law" (1994) 32 *Osgoode Hall Law Journal* 503. The majority did not consider whether the public interest would similarly override consent in other cases, such as unprotected heterosexual intercourse or body-contact sports, which similarly involve the risk of HIV infection. The Law Commission of England and Wales developed a more complex account of sado-masochism, drawing on public submissions from S&M enthusiasts and comparative research: *Consent in the Criminal Law,* Consultation Paper No 139 (London: HMSO, 1995), Pt X.

The instability of the categorisation of sadomasochism as "violence" rather than "sex" is apparent in the opening line of the dissenting speech of Lord Mustill: "My Lords, this is a case about the criminal law of violence. In my opinion, it should be a case about the criminal law of private sexual relations, if about anything at all": at 584. Indeed, the charges initially contemplated were sexual offences, gross indecency between males, though these were statutorily time-barred. The activities, which had occurred many years previously, only came to police attention through a video tape made at the time. This tape provided the basis for charges against some of the accused involved, who pleaded guilty to the publication and possession of obscene or indecent articles, an offence that carried a longer sentence than assault. Others pleaded guilty to "keeping a disorderly house", a charge usually reserved for brothel keepers. In practical as well as conceptual terms, the sexual and violent dimensions of conduct may be accentuated or concealed by the type of offence charged.

CASE STUDIES

The Legitimacy of "Rough Sex" in Rape and Indecent Assault Cases

R v Brown [1993] 2 WLR 556 demonstrates that the criminal law, to borrow Lord Mustill's words, does not possess a "general theory of consent and violence": at 591. While the consent of sadomasochistic homosexuals in the context of assault and related offences is legally disregarded as "worthless" for reasons of public policy, for the purposes of the law of rape, consent remains contestable even where the victim is subjected to very serious injury during sex. However serious the injury inflicted during sexual intercourse, consent is a live issue that the prosecution must disprove in every case.[6]

---

5   C Smart, *Law, Crime and Sexuality* (London: Sage, 1995), p 119. The legality of body piercing and performance art involving these practices was thrown into doubt following the decision in *Brown*. In England, performers were instructed by lawyers that while self-mutilation was not unlawful, individuals who assisted by inserting the needles would be guilty of aiding and abetting an assault: see C Armistead, "Piercing Thoughts", *Guardian Weekly*, 17 July 1994. See further Ch 11, pp 558ff.

6   This lack of symmetry between the ordinary law of assault and rape is explored further in S Bronitt, "Rape and Lack of Consent" (1992) 16 Crim LJ 289 at 303-305.

Combined with the exculpatory effect of a mistaken belief in consent, the law offers limited protection to women. Under the common law, a mistaken belief in consent, even if unreasonable, may negate the accused's intent or recklessness: *DPP v Morgan* [1976] AC 182. The effect of mistake of fact on culpability was explored in Chapter 7, pp 338ff. This "defence" of unreasonable mistake operates to legitimate men who understand sexual relations in terms of dangerous rape myths such as "No means Yes". The asymmetry in the law is highly revealing. Carol Smart in *Law, Crime and Sexuality* (London: Sage, 1995) summarises the law's divergent approach as follows (pp 120-121):

> The *Brown* decision has left Britain with a law of sexuality which states — symbolically at least — that when women say No to rape they mean Yes, but when men say Yes to homosexual sex they mean No.
>
> In rape even the bruises and physical injuries sustained are typically subordinated to an understanding of the event as one of sexual passion, notwithstanding that neither aspects were consensual. In S/M the sexual gratification is subordinated to the physical harm, notwithstanding that the latter was consensual. It is hard to avoid concluding that the court's response to such cases embodies a tolerance of non-consensual heterosex and a continuing desire to sanction consensual homosexual sex.

The law of consent for indecent assault, like rape, reveals a similar margin of tolerance towards heterosexual "rough sex". The common law is well established that a person cannot ordinarily consent to bodily injury unless it falls within a recognised exception. We have previously explored in Chapter 11 (pp 558-559) how the law of assault may stretch these "recognised exceptions" to permit consent to operate as a defence to some rough sexual activity. For example, in one recent English case, buttock branding with a hot knife was distinguished from sadomasochism by likening it to tattooing: *Wilson* [1996] 2 Cr App R 241.

The definition of bodily injury also provides some margin for tolerance for rough sex. In *Donovan* (1934) 25 Cr App R 1, the accused raised consent as a defence to a charge of indecent assault upon a young woman arising from an act of flagellation perpetrated for his own sexual gratification. The English Court of Criminal Appeal held that the trial judge had failed to adequately distinguish between those activities to which consent could be raised as a defence, and those where consent was deemed to be immaterial. In its view, consent would be immaterial where the conduct is intended or is likely to cause actual bodily harm unless the conduct falls within a recognised exception. "Bodily harm" was defined to include (at 13) any hurt or injury calculated to interfere with the health or comfort of the victim, but excluded injuries that were "merely transient or trifling".

Flagellation for sexual gratification did not fall within any of these exceptions.[7] However, the Court of Criminal Appeal in *Donovan* did accept (at 13-14) that, in relation to

---

7   There is authority that flagellation for the purpose of religious mortification is justified in the public interest: *William Fraser* [1847] Ark 280, 302 discussed in Law Commission, *Consent in the Criminal Law*, Consultation Paper No 139 (London: HMSO, 1995), pp 130-133.

assault and indecent assault, consent may operate as a defence to sexual conduct involving "transient or trifling injuries". Significantly, the Court did not find that the beating inflicted by the accused exceeded this threshold of "transient and trifling" injury — this was an issue of fact that had to be left to the jury to decide. This aspect of the decision in *Donovan* is often misunderstood. As Lord Mustill in *Brown* points out (at 596), the decision did *not* establish that flagellation for sexual gratification is a special category of beating which, for reasons of public policy, is automatically criminal.

The extent that "rough sex" between heterosexuals may be legally tolerable is apparent in the English Court of Appeal decision of *R v Boyea* (1992) Crim LR 574. In this case, the accused was convicted of indecent assault arising from a violent attack in which he inserted his hand into the victim's vagina and twisted it round inside causing internal and external injuries. The accused raised consent as a defence but the trial judge directed the jury, in accordance with *Donovan*, that an accused cannot raise consent where the conduct is intended or is likely to cause bodily injury unless the injuries are "transient or trifling" concluding:

> Two people in the course of sexual activity may agree to rough behaviour in the same way that people in sport may agree to behaviour which but for their agreement would constitute an assault.

Lord Glidewell approved this direction, offering the following qualification to assist the jury in its determination of what would constitute "transient and trifling":

> The court must take into account that social attitudes have changed over the years, particularly in the field of sexual relations between adults. As a generality, the level of vigour in sexual congress which is generally acceptable, and therefore the voluntarily accepted risk of incurring some injury, is probably higher now than it was in 1934. It follows, in our view, that the phrase "transient or trifling" must be understood in the light of conditions in 1992 rather than those nearly 60 years ago.

The decision was briefly reviewed in *Brown*, although Lord Jauncey distinguished the availability of consent as a defence in cases such as *Donovan* and *Boyea* on the ground that the injuries inflicted "could not have been described as in any way serious": at 244.

Through this complex doctrinal web, the criminal law constitutes sexuality as either legitimate or deviant. Transgressive sexual encounters between sadomasochistic homosexuals are criminalised as unlawful acts of violence, while injuries deliberately inflicted during heterosexual encounters may be construed as trifling incidents of "rough sex", consent to which negates liability for both rape and indecent assault. As a result, the criminal law entrenches dangerous stereotypes about gender and sexuality such as women are masochistic and enjoy "rough sex" and that men may legitimately use force through "rough handling" as a means of sexual foreplay.

Judicial directions to juries will reflect these legal understandings of sexuality. When viewed against the background of the above authorities, the highly publicised directions of Bollen J in *R v Johns* (unrep, 26/8/1992, SC SA, No SCCRM/91/452, transcript pp 12-13) on the meaning of consent in a rape trial in South Australia seem legally warrantable (if no less morally objectionable):

> "Consent" means free voluntary agreement to engage in an act of sexual inter-course at the relevant time. Submission is not consent. Of course, you may run into considering in this case the question of, shall I say, persuasion. There is, of course, nothing wrong with a husband, faced with his wife's initial refusal to engage in intercourse, in attempting, in an acceptable way, to persuade her to change her mind, and that may involve a measure of rougher than usual handling. It may be, in the end, that handling and persuasion will persuade the wife to agree. Sometimes it is a fine line between not agreeing, then changing of the mind, and consenting.

The subsequent appeal by the Director of Public Prosecutions on a point of law provided an opportunity for the South Australian Court of Criminal Appeal to review the correctness of the direction. The majority pointed out that Bollen J's remarks were a misdirection since they wrongly suggested that men could use some degree of force against resistant women in order to persuade them to have sex. The dissenting judge, King CJ, considered that Bollen's remarks may have been misleading, but they were not strictly an error of law: "if sexual intercourse follows persuasion, whatever form the persuasion takes, the issue as to consent is whether the wife freely and voluntarily consented to such intercourse and did not merely submit to force or threats": *Question of Law Reserved on Acquittal Pursuant to Section 351(1A), Criminal Law Consolidation Act (No 1 of 1993)* (1993) 59 SASR 214. From a legal analytical perspective, the approach by the Chief Justice, a distinguished criminal lawyer, is unobjectionable. The difficulty with such direction is that they embody a paradigmatic experience of sex which permits force to play *some* legitimate role in procuring consent, leaving the jury the complex task of determining whether the force induced consent freely or conversely vitiated consent. For policy reasons, it has been argued that the use of violence, threats or coercion is incompatible with notions of free agreement and that in such cases, the prosecution should be relieved of the burden of proving lack of consent: S Bronitt, "Rape and Lack of Consent" (1992) 16 Crim LJ 289 at 308-310.

The notorious "rougher than usual handling" direction emerges against a legal land-scape that condones some degree of "roughness" as a prelude for normal (hetero)sexual encounters. The direction may be viewed not as a deviation from the law, but rather as recognition that the rules governing consent licence the use of *some* force (as in *Donovan* and *Boyea*) as a legitimate part of sexual relations. As we shall explore below, this toleration of roughness as part of "normal sex" must be understood in the context of the prevailing model of sexual relations between men and women that is both penetrative/coercive and non-communicative.

The Role of Risk and HIV/AIDS in Lethal Sexualities

The spectre of HIV and AIDS looms large in *Brown's* case as a potentially lethal risk of homosexual sadomasochistic activity. The prostitute has been similarly constructed as an "emissary of death": R Davenport-Hines, *Sex, Death and Punishment* (London: Collins, 1990), p 169. Contagious diseases legislation was enacted in England and Australia in the 19th century to protect men (not women) from deadly sexual disease. To do this, Indigenous and working class women were subject to discriminatory and coercive medico-legal surveillance and control: K Saunders, "Controlling (hetero)sexuality: The implementation and operation of contagious diseases legislation in Australia, 1868-1945" in D Kirkby (ed), *Sex, Power and Justice: Historical Perspectives on Law in Australia* (Melbourne: Oxford University Press, 1995). The approach is discriminatory because, in objective terms, the "occupational risk" of sex workers contracting and transmitting disease is the same as the "recreational risk" of clients contracting and transmitting the disease. Even today, modern public health laws perpetuate discrimination by imposing a different regime of surveillance and controls on sex workers and their clients: N Greenberg, "The Rhetoric of Risk" (1997) 22(1) *Alternative Law Journal* 11; B McSherry, "Dangerousness and Public Health" (1998) 23(6) *Alternative Law Journal* 276. See further Chapter 11, pp 571ff on the use of endangerment offences in this context.

CASE STUDIES

Death by Sexual Misadventure

The judicial tolerance of rough sex can be seen in those cases involving "death by sexual misadventure". These cases are not typically prosecuted as murder on the basis of recklessness. Rather this type of homicide is more likely to result, often through plea-bargaining, in a guilty plea of manslaughter. The legal boundaries of consensual "rough sex" are more likely to be considered incidentally during sentencing, usually raised as factor relevant to mitigation, as in *R v McIntosh* [1999] VSC 358, which is reviewed in Chapter 11: pp 566ff. In that case, as part of bondage sex, the accused tied a rope around the victim's neck for the purpose of heightening sexual pleasure. The victim died as a result of strangulation. The accused entered a guilty plea of manslaughter. In sentencing the accused, Vincent J doubted whether the principle in *Brown* (that a person could never consent to bondage or sexual sadomasochism) was good law in Victoria: para 11. A person may consent to the risk of some injury, though not amounting to significant physical injury. This case involved extremely dangerous activities to which consent would not operate as a defence. The judge stressed that the significant sentence imposed was a reflection of the inherent danger involved in the bondage and the accused's lack of care for his partner and was not based on any moralistic response to their sexual predilections. As discussed in Chapter 11, it is difficult to reconcile such dicta with *Brown*. It is possible that Australian courts, when they eventually consider the legality of "homosexual sadomasochism", may demonstrate greater respect for individual autonomy and the principle of non-discrimination on the ground of sexual orientation than the English courts.

Dangerous, apparently consensual, sexual conduct leading to death has on occasion resulted in murder charges. This occurred in *Boughey v The Queen* (1986) 161 CLR 10. The accused, a doctor, engaged in a range of unconventional sexual activities with a Fijian woman who came to live with him in Hobart. It was not disputed that her death had been caused by manual strangulation involving applying pressure to the carotid arteries on the neck during sexual intercourse. The accused claimed that this had been done with no intention to cause injury but to induce light-headedness to increase his partner's sexual excitement. At trial, the judge directed that murder under s 157 of the *Criminal Code* (Tas) may be committed by an "unlawful act or omission which the accused knew or ought to have known to be likely to cause death". He further directed that an assault would be "unlawful" only if it were perpetrated without the victim's consent. The accused had claimed that these practices did not constitute an assault because his partner had consented. He was convicted of murder and the appeal to the High Court ranged across various aspects of the trial judge's direction including the meaning of the phrase "likely to cause death" and the effect of the absence of hostility on intent. The decision however is curiously silent about the judge's directions on the consent issue. Only Brennan J (at 37) identifies the trial judge's misdirection, noting that the *Criminal Code*, like the common law, precludes consent as a defence to the infliction of injury likely to cause death: s 53(b). However, since the matter was not raised by the parties on the appeal and the direction clearly benefited the accused, there was no further consideration of this issue.

Boughey's case is remarkable in two respects. First, notwithstanding the formal irrelevance of consent, both the trial judge, the prosecution and the High Court (with the exception of Brennan J) assumed that consent could be raised as a defence to the type of injuries inflicted by the accused. Secondly, the sexual deviation of Dr Boughey, though considered bizarre, escaped the kind of moral condemnation and fear of death that coloured the majority's judgments in *Brown*. His activity was constructed as sexual conduct "gone wrong", rather than as a senseless act of violence for sadomasochistic pleasure. Although the High Court ultimately upheld his conviction for murder, the judgment's curious moral silence about the accused's conduct signifies both the sanctity of the heterosexual bedroom and the margin of tolerance toward dangerous but consensual heterosexual activity.

Similar assumptions about the legitimacy of roughness during heterosexual encounters are also evident in another recent manslaughter case in England. In *Slingsby* [1995] Crim LR 570, the accused was charged with manslaughter arising from unintentional injuries inflicted upon his sexual partner during rough sex. The victim had suffered cuts to her anus and vagina caused by his signet ring during consensual sexual activity. These cuts became infected and she died of septicaemia. Judge J ruled (at 571) that the charge of unlawful act manslaughter could not be sustained. In his view, this was not an area of sexual activity in which the law dispensed with the defence of consent. He distinguished *Donovan*, *Brown* and *Boyea* on the ground that the bodily injury caused was neither intended nor could have been foreseen. As a consequences of his ruling, the Crown offered no evidence and the judge entered a verdict of acquittal. This approach to "sexual accidents" arguably misreads the authorities on consent, in particular the public interest qualification in *Brown*. Under the common law, consent is unavailable as a defence not only where the party intends or foresees bodily injury, but also where the activity *causes* or is likely to cause bodily injury: see JC Smith, "Commentary" [1995] Crim LR 571-572. The accused's conduct in this case *caused* death and therefore consent should have been withdrawn. The fact that the injury was unforeseeable is relevant only to issue of causation or fault. The judicial reluctance to withdraw consent in cases of "death by sexual misadventure" is yet another illustration of the law's tolerance of rough sex.

1.2 PRIVACY AND THE LEGITIMATION OF SEXUAL VIOLENCE

For feminists, "rough sex" including S&M raises controversial questions relating to the nature of autonomy, subordination and privacy. Liberal defences of S&M practices, which were considered in Chapter 11, are based on traditional notions of privacy and autonomy. These justifications have raised objections from feminists, such as Susan Edwards in "No Shield for a Sado-masochistic Libido" (1993) 143 *New Law Journal* 406 (at 407):

> In our desire to preserve privacy, individual liberty and freedom from state intervention we
> are in danger of missing what lies at the heart of sado-masochism — its potential for
> violence. Why is it that for some the prefix "sex" functions as a protective shield? We need
> to recognise, as we move increasingly into a world of sexual violence, the dangers of
> placing this so-called "sex" beyond the rule of law.[8]

From this perspective, the right to privacy conceals sexual violence from public view, while rights to autonomy only legitimate and normalise violence in sexual relations: S Jeffreys, "Consent and the Politics of Sexuality" (1993) 5(2) *Current Issues in Criminal Justice* 173. These feminist concerns, though couched in the language of abuse of power rather than moral danger, resonate with some of the majority views in *Brown*. As Smart observed in *Law, Crime and Sexuality* (London: Sage, 1995), p 118, Lord Templeman's comment that sadomasochism was concerned not only with sex but with violence could equally have been penned by a feminist:

> It was almost as if a feminist were speaking about rape — although no judge has, to my
> knowledge, uttered these sentiments in cases of non-consensual sexual abuse of women.

Whether motivated by moral or feminist concerns, such perspectives overlook the malleability, contingency and normative dimensions of "sex" and "violence" in the criminal law.

---

8   See also S Edwards, *Sex and Gender in the Legal Process* (London: Blackstone Press, 1996), pp 77-89. The Law
     Commission similarly argued that right to privacy would not protect *violence* simply because it is sexual in nature
     and occurs in private: Law Commission, *Criminal Law: Consent and Offences against the Person*, Consultation Paper
     No 134 (London: HMSO, 1994), para 33.2.

Traditional liberal notions of privacy, conceived as an individual's right to be left alone, have potentially repressive qualities in the sexual sphere. As previously explored in Chapter 2, feminist scholarship has revealed how the division between the public and the private spheres has played and continues to play a significant role in concealing and legitimating the subordination of women in their sexual and other relations with men. Privacy also subordinates and discriminates against gays, lesbians and other marginalised sexual identities. As Wayne Morgan observed in "Identifying Evil for What it is: Tasmania, Sexual Perversity and the United Nations" (1994) 19(3) *Melbourne University Law Review* 740 (at 756):

> As long as contested sexual identities are kept closeted, secret, private; as long as gay men
> and lesbians appear as straight, no damage is done to the unitary, hegemonic construction
> of heterosexuality dominant in popular and institutional discourse.

The protection and limits of this legal "closet" of privacy are apparent in those rights recognised under international human rights law. We have previously explored in Chapter 2 how the right to privacy under the *International Covenant on Civil and Political Rights* (ICCPR) has been used to challenge homosexual offences in Tasmania that criminalised consenting sexual conduct between adult males in private. The protective shield of privacy recognised by the *Human Rights (Sexual Conduct) Act* 1995 (Cth) is not absolute, but is subject to reasonable restrictions. In this respect, the limits on privacy, like consent under the common law, are defined by the public interest.

The relative ease with which the right to privacy is qualified and curtailed in cases of "sexual perversion" is readily apparent. In *R v Brown* [1993] 2 WLR 556, the majority quickly dismissed arguments based on the right to privacy, which were guaranteed by Art 8 of the *European Convention on Human Rights* (ECHR). Adopting a narrow literal reading of the right to privacy under Art 8, Lord Templeman doubted whether the accused were exercising rights in respect of "private and family life" and that even if they were, the ECHR did not invalidate a law which forbids violence which is *intentionally* harmful to body and mind: at 566.[9] Even the minority judgments expressed some scepticism at the value of privacy in this context. Lord Mustill doubted whether the language of the ECHR could offer any guidance, refusing to pronounce in favour of "libertarian doctrine specifically related to sexual matters": at 599. Lord Slynn similarly found that the answer to the appeal lay in the settled doctrine, and the law should not deny consent as a defence as a matter of policy unless there were compelling public interest arguments: at 608.

Having exhausted domestic remedies, several of the accused in *Brown* appealed to the European Court of Human Rights (ECHR) alleging a violation of their right to privacy: *Laskey, Jaggard and Brown v United Kingdom* (Eur Court HR, 19 February 1997, *Reports of Judgments and Decisions* 1997-I). The Court held that the prosecution of the accused in this case did interfere with their private lives. However, Art 8 envisages (at para 43) that the State may impose restrictions on privacy that are "necessary in a democratic society":

---

9   Lord Lowry (at 256) offered different reasons for rejecting Art 8: the ECHR was not part of domestic law; as the
     domestic statute was not ambiguous, it was unnecessary to construe it so as to conform with Art 8; and finally, no
     "public authority" had interfered with the exercise of the right to privacy.

> One of the roles which the State is unquestionably entitled to undertake is to seek to regulate, through the operation of the criminal law, activities which involve the infliction of physical harm. This is so whether the activities in question occur in the course of sexual conduct or otherwise.

The interference with privacy must be proportionate to the objective of protecting the participants' health, though in this respect, the Court held that the national authorities have a "margin of appreciation" in how they respond.

The European Court's decision to uphold the public interest limitations to consent in *Brown* will undoubtedly influence the interpretation of the right to privacy created by the *Human Rights (Sexual Conduct) Act* 1995 (Cth). As discussed in Chapter 2 (pp 142ff), s 4 of the Act renders inoperative any law (statute or common law) in Australia that arbitrarily interferes with the sexual conduct of adults in private. In light of this ruling, it is doubtful whether the Federal sexual privacy shield would render inoperative the common law rule that consent is no defence in cases involving the infliction of significant injury for the purpose of sexual gratification.[10]

The view that privacy is simply a cloak for legitimating sexual violence (including sadomasochism) is not shared by all feminists. In *Law, Crime and Sexuality* (London: Sage, 1995) Smart draws upon the ideas of ethical feminism to create a legal space for the legitimate expression of diverse sexualities including sadomasochism. She reviews research that challenges the dominant conceptualisation of sadomasochism as a form of sexual oppression of the weak by the powerful: pp 114-116. Such research suggests that fantasy and theatre are essential to the understanding of these practices, and that masochists are not disempowered victims but rather possess power, through cues and signals, to control the behaviour of the sadist: p 114. In her view, feminists who simply dismiss agency and consent in these cases are assuming that "women are cultural dupes just waiting to be saved or to see the light": p 117. The banishment of individual agency and consent simply replaces liberal concepts with the "public interest", an amorphous legal category that empowers the judiciary, on a case by case basis, to determine whether dangerous activity should be lawful. Smart concludes that the criminal law is capable of greater sexual tolerance in cases where the harm involved is not significant. As she notes, the injuries in *Brown* were not permanent and certainly no greater than the violence generated in football matches or boxing contests.[11] The ordinary law of assault through its recognised public interest exceptions provides considerable scope for the legitimation of traditional forms of "homosocial" violence involved in sports, dangerous exhibitions and rough horse-play. The issue of sports violence has been explored in Chapter 11: pp 560ff. Although accepting that privacy traditionally has offered few benefits for women, Smart concludes that it does provide a "private space which, if not absolutely inviolate, does prevent the criminal law exercising its remit overzealously": p 117.[12]

---

10 For a contrary argument, see S Bronitt, "The Right to Sexual Privacy, Sado-masochism and the *Human Rights (Sexual Conduct) Act* 1994 (Cth)" (1995) 2(1) *Australian Journal of Human Rights* 59 at 68-72.

11 For an excellent review of the public interest arguments against boxing in its present form see M Gunn and D Ormerod, "The Legality of Boxing" (1995) 15(2) *Legal Studies* 181.

12 "Although boundaries are being drawn in new and imaginative ways, and denied under circumstances of abuse or hurt in the erstwhile private sphere, nevertheless some protection of the private life against totalitarianism is acknowledged": K O'Donovan, "Book Review: Public and Private Feminist Legal Debates" (1996) 18(1) *Adelaide Law Review* 113.

We believe that the problem of negotiating and redressing power imbalances that potentially arise in sexual encounters is better addressed through redefining rather than eliminating consent from sexual offences. Rather than banish consent in situations of perceived inequality under the rubric of public interest, an alternate approach is to refurbish consent in terms of a positive obligation to communicate before and during sexual activity. A more communicative model of autonomy is emerging in the criminal law. For example, in the Australian Capital Territory, for the purposes of sexual assault (though not ordinary assault) consent is deemed not to be "freely given" where it is obtained through abuse of power or a position of trust or authority: *Crimes Act* 1900 (ACT), s 92P(1). Such reforms have the potential to challenge dangerous stereotypes about sexuality.

The reform of sexual offences should involve rethinking the values and interests protected by the law, particularly the meaning and scope of autonomy in the sexual context. The emergence of a positive consent standard challenges the passive consent standard recognised in present legal doctrines such as "implied" consent. Indeed, international law may provide the basis for reforming laws that condone discriminatory stereotypes about female sexuality. This occurred recently in Canada, where the Supreme Court, drawing inspiration from the *Convention on the Elimination of All Form of Discrimination Against Women* (CEDAW), held that the doctrine of implied consent had no application to sexual assault: *R v Ewanchuk* [1999] 1 SCR 330, see above, pp 130ff. The role of international law in reshaping the criminal law, particularly the use of human rights treaties to develop the common law and interpret statutes, has been discussed in Chapter 2: pp 111ff.

2. RAPE AND SEXUAL ASSAULT

2.1 PHYSICAL ELEMENTS: SEXUAL INTERCOURSE WITHOUT CONSENT

Modern statutory formulations of rape or sexual assault define the prohibited conduct as sexual intercourse without consent. Table 1 sets out the elements of this offence in Australian jurisdictions.

TABLE 1:

Physical and Fault Elements for Rape and Sexual Assault

JURISDICTION AND RELEVANT LAW	OFFENCE	PHYSICAL ELEMENT	FAULT ELEMENT
ACT *Crimes Act* 1900 s 92D	sexual assault without consent	sexual intercourse without consent	intent to engage in sexual intercourse knows or is reckless to consent
NSW *Crimes Act* 1900 s 61I	sexual assault	sexual intercourse without consent	knowledge of no consent

Table 1 continued

JURISDICTION AND RELEVANT LAW	OFFENCE	PHYSICAL ELEMENT	FAULT ELEMENT
NT *Criminal Code* s 192(3)	sexual intercourse without consent	sexual intercourse without consent	(strict liability)
QLD *Criminal Code* s 47	rape	carnal knowledge without consent	(strict liability)
SA *Criminal Law Consolidation Act* 1935 s 48	rape	sexual intercourse	knowing no consent or recklessly indifferent as to consent
TAS *Criminal Code Act* 1924 s 185	rape	sexual intercourse without consent	(strict liability)
VIC *Crimes Act* 1958 s 38(a)(b)	rape	(a) sexually penetrates or (b) does not withdraw	intentionally sexually penetrates or does not withdraw and aware that person is not consenting or might not be consenting
WA *Criminal Code Act Compilation Act* 1913 s 325	sexual penetration without consent	sexual penetration without consent	(strict liability)

THE MEANING OF SEXUAL INTERCOURSE

Under the common law, the boundaries of rape were fixed by the narrow and the restrictive definition of sexual intercourse or penetration of the vagina by the penis. The common law definition was gender-specific and excluded non-penetrative or non-penile forms of sexual activity: L Tyler, "Towards a Redefinition of Rape" (1994) *New Law Journal* 860. In Australia, these definitional limitations have been largely remedied by statute.[13] In some jurisdictions, the definition is both gender and sexuality neutral, encompassing a wide variety of conduct. For example, s 61H of the *Crimes* Act 1900 (NSW) defines "sexual intercourse" as vaginal or anal sexual penetration, fellatio and cunnilingus. The proposed *Model Criminal Code* defines sexual penetration in the following terms:

---

13 South Australia was the first jurisdiction to extend the definition "sexual intercourse" to include penetration of the mouth or anus as well as the vagina, although "penetration" still had to involve a penis: s 5 of the *Criminal Law Consolidation Act* 1935 (SA), as amended by s 3 of the *Criminal Law Consolidation Act Amendment Act* 1976 (SA).

5.2.1 Sexual penetration

(1) In this Part, *sexually penetrates* means:

(a) penetrate (to any extent) the genitalia or anus of a person by any part of the body of a person or by any object manipulated by a person; or

(b) penetrate (to any extent) the mouth of a person by the penis of a person; or

(c) continue to sexually penetrate as defined in paragraph (a) or (b).

(2) For the purpose of this Part, the genitalia or other parts of the body of a person include surgically constructed genitalia or other part of the body of the person.

As the Model Criminal Code Officers Committee (MCCOC) concluded, the use of gender and sexuality neutral definitions for these purpose avoids the need for specific homosexual offences: *Chapter 5 — Sexual Offences Against the Person*, Report (1999), pp 15-19. The MCCOC favoured the adoption of a core offence called "unlawful sexual penetration", reflecting the fact that the offence may be committed by a wider range of violations than the present law: p 65.

The danger with gender neutrality or compendious definitions such as "unlawful sexual penetration" is that they conceal the fact that *most* sexual harm is gender-based, perpetrated by males against females. This argument does not deny the reality of "male rape" or child sexual abuse against boys. Indeed, it is clear that male sexual abuse within institutional settings such as prisons requires greater political and legal attention: G Mezey and M King, *Male Victims of Sexual Assault* (Oxford: Oxford University Press, 1991). However, on a symbolic and political level, definitional neutrality can have a negative impact on women, as well as other victimised groups, by rendering invisible the distinctive nature and causes of their sexual abuse.

Sex with Virgins and Transsexuals

The law of rape and sexual assault exhibits a phallocentric focus notwithstanding extensive redefinition of the physical element. Sexual intercourse requires the sexual *penetration* of a vagina, whether by penis, other body part, or an object. It has been pointed out that a woman may be subject to sexual interference (by penis or finger) that does not in fact penetrate her vagina because of the elasticity of the hymen. The lack of proof of vaginal penetration would exclude rape as a matter of law: N Puren, "Defining the Hymen in the *Model Criminal Code*" (1997) 9 *Australian Feminist Law Journal* 96, discussing *Holland v The Queen* (1993) 67 ALJR 946. Notwithstanding Nina Puren's submission, the narrow definition of penetration was not discussed in either the Discussion Paper or Final Report: see *Model Criminal Code: Chapter 5 — Sexual Offences Against the Person*, Report (1999). In some jurisdictions, the definition of vagina includes a "surgically constructed vagina": *Crimes Act* 1900 (NSW), s 61H; *Crimes Act* 1958 (Vic), s 35; *Criminal Code* (NT), s 1; *Criminal Code* (WA), Sch 5. While offering some protection for post-operative transsexuals, this extended definition does not extend to pre-operative transsexuals who may be excluded from the protection offered by rape and sexual assault laws. For a review of the difficulties in invoking the criminal law to deal with the sexual abuse of transsexuals see A Sharpe, "The Precarious Position of the Transsexual Rape Victim" (1994) 6 (2) *Current Issues in Criminal Justice* 303; A Sharpe, "Attempting the 'Impossible': The Case of Transsexual Rape" (1997) 21 Crim LJ 23.

THE FUNDAMENTAL ELEMENT: LACK OF CONSENT

Within the present law of rape and sexual assault, consent occupies a central place. In every rape trial the prosecution must prove, as an ingredient of the offence, that intercourse occurred without the victim's consent. Consequently, the victim's state of mind before and during intercourse with the accused will always be relevant, not only in those cases where the issue of consent has been raised by the defence: *R v Olugboja* [1982] QB 320 at 332.

The shift in the legal definition of rape from sexual intercourse "against her will" to "without consent" in the mid-19th century did not alter the presumption that unless a woman resisted or struggled in some way, the act of penetration was not rape. As late as 1965, the English Court of Criminal Appeal in *R v Howard* [1966] 1 WLR 13 concluded (at 13) that:

> [T]he prosecution, in order to prove rape, must prove either that [the complainant] physically resisted, or if she did not, that her understanding and knowledge was such that she was not in a position to decide whether to consent or resist.[14]

Although the substantive law no longer requires evidence of resistance, an outward manifestation of lack of consent,[15] there is empirical research that suggests that conviction is harder without evidence that injuries had been sustained that required medical treatment: Victorian Law Reform Commission, *Rape: Reform of Law and Procedures*, Appendix to Interim Report No 42 (1991), pp 95-95.

Carol Smart in "Law's Truth/Women's Experience" in R Graycar (ed), *Dissenting Opinions — Feminist Explorations in Law and Society* (Sydney: Allen and Unwin, 1990) has concluded (p 14) that it is the victim's experience rather than the accused's behaviour that lies at the heart of the rape trial:

> The central concerns of the rape trial are consent and pleasure. Although the law is framed around *mens rea* and consent, the issue of *mens rea* only becomes relevant if consent/pleasure cannot be established. The man's intentions are therefore not a priority, the whole focus is on the woman, her intentions and her pleasure.

This focus on consent is supported by empirical research that in the majority of rape trials the accused will not dispute that some form of sexual activity took place but will claim that it occurred with consent: Law Reform Commission of Victoria, *Rape: Reform of Law and Procedure*, Appendixes to Interim Report No 42 (1991), App 3, p 86; New South Wales Department for Women, *Heroines of Fortitude: The Experiences of Women in Court as Victims of Sexual Assault* (1996), p 52.

Lack of consent plays a dual role in rape, defining the physical element and the fault element. As Nicola Lacey has pointed out in *Unspeakable Subjects* (Oxford: Hart Publishing, 1998), p 112:

> In definitions of offences such as rape, however, a "mental" element is part of not only the *mens rea* but also the *actus reus*: whilst the defendant's lack of belief in the victim's consent is part of the *mens rea* requirement, the victim's lack of consent itself is part of the *actus reus*.

---

14   See also *Chadderton* (1908) 1 Cr App R 229; *Harling* (1938) 26 Cr App R 127; *Lang* (1975) 62 Cr App R 50 and more recently, *Singh* (unrep, 18/12/1990, CCA Vic, No 226 of 1990), at 7-8.

15   This is confirmed by legislation in some jurisdictions: *Crimes Act* 1900 (ACT), s 92P(3); *Criminal Code* (NT), s 192A; *Crimes Act* 1900 (NSW), s 61R(2)(d); *Criminal Law Consolidation Act* 1935 (SA), s 48; *Crimes Act* 1958 (Vic), s 61R(2)(d); *Criminal Code* (WA), s 319(2)(d).

In the context of rape, the strict dualism between physical and fault elements, which runs through the criminal law, seems to break-down. In many cases, defence claims of consent and belief in consent are inextricably meshed. An accused who says that the other party "consented" is invariably claiming simultaneously that sexual activity was consensual and was *believed* to be consensual.

The MCCOC has proposed that sexual offences should retain the dualist structure and that lack of consent on the part of the victim should ordinarily constitute the physical element: *Model Criminal Code: Chapter 5 — Sexual Offences Against the Person*, Report (1999), p 31. It rejected academic proposals that offences of rape or sexual assault should be defined without reference to lack of consent. However, the claims of the centrality of consent to rape and sexual assault laws warrant further scrutiny. Under the present law, the prosecution must prove that the victim did not consent even where there was evidence of serious injuries being inflicted during sex. The Supreme Court of Canada, however, has adopted a different approach to consent under the statutory offence of sexual assault, limiting its availability as a defence in those cases where bodily harm was intended or likely to occur: *R v Welch* (1995) 101 CCC (3d) 216. The idea that consent is deemed irrelevant where the accused engages in sexual conduct involving bodily harm to another is consistent with the approach taken in the law of assault. The public interest limitations on consent for offences against the person were previously considered in Chapter 11, 3 'Lawful Assault', pp 552ff.

COMPARATIVE PERSPECTIVES

Redefining Rape as Sexual Assault

Pioneering reforms of rape law in Michigan in the United States in the 1970s dispensed with the requirement that the prosecution had to prove lack of consent in cases where sexual penetration was accomplished by "force or coercion". These reforms are discussed in S Bronitt, "Rape and Lack of Consent" (1992) 16 Crim LJ 289 at 307-310. However, the Michigan legislation defined force or coercion narrowly as including circumstances where the accused uses actual physical force or violence, threatens to use force or violence, retaliation (including threats of physical punishment, kidnapping and extortion), engages in unethical and unacceptable medical treat-ment, or acts through concealment or surprise: *Criminal Conduct Act* 1974 (Mich), s 520b(1)(f)(i)-(iv). The legislative exclusion of consent was further undermined by judicial interpretation. While the prosecution no longer need prove lack of consent, the accused could always raise consent as a "defence" to an allegation of force: *People v Hearn* (1981) Mich App 300 NW 2d 396.

In the 1980s, New South Wales and the Australian Capital Territory remodelled selected sexual offences following the Michigan model. In New South Wales, the common law offence of rape was abolished and replaced with the statutory offence of sexual assault to reflect the violent rather than the sexual nature of the offence. Sexual assault was graded into four degrees mirroring the level of violence used by the perpetrator. On a theoretical level, sexual assault laws were modelled around rape as violence, rather than sex. This approach drew on the work of feminists such as Susan Brownmiller, *Against Our Will: Men, Women and Rape* (New York: Simon & Schuster, 1974). However, some feminists, notably Catharine MacKinnon have disputed this interpretation of rape as violence. In *Toward A Feminist Theory of the State* (Cambridge, MA: Harvard University Press, 1989), MacKinnon highlights (p 175) the sexual rather than violent dimension of rape and the difficulty of distinguishing sex from rape in a situation where women are subordinated by male power:

> The law of rape presents consent as free exercise of sexual choice under conditions of equality of power without exposing the underlying structure of constraint and disparity.

In many respects, the reforms in New South Wales proved to be counterproductive. For an evaluation of the impact of these changes see D Brown, D Farrier and D Weisbrot, *Criminal Laws* (2nd ed, Sydney: Federation Press, 1996), pp 857-859. The added requirement of proving violence (actual or threatened) for sexual assault had the effect of prolonging rape trials and downgrading the perceived seriousness of non-violent rapes. Indeed, as a result of these unintended effects, the New South Wales law was amended in 1989. Lack of consent was reinstated as the central element of the principal offences of sexual assault and aggravated sexual assault: *Crimes Act* 1900 (NSW), ss 61I, 61J. Supplementary sexual offences did however retain some features of the Michigan reforms: see "assault with intent to have sexual intercourse" and "sexual intercourse by means of a non-violent threat": ss 61K and 65A(2) respectively. Section 61K modified rather than abrogated the requirement of lack of consent. That is, proof of non-consent was required only in relation to the basic element of inflicting actual bodily harm, not the intended sexual act. More drastically, s 65A(2) dispensed with lack of consent completely:

> A person who has intercourse with another person shall, if the other person submits to the sexual intercourse as a result of a non violent threat and could not in the circumstances be reasonably expected to resist the threat, be liable to penal servitude for 6 years.

Non-violent threat was defined as "intimidatory or coercive conduct or other threat which does not involve a threat of physical force": s 65A(1). To be guilty, the accused must have known that the person concerned submitted to intercourse as a result of the non-violent threat: s 65A(3). While avoiding the specificity of the Michigan model, the offence leaves the question of intimidation, coercion or non-violent threat as a question of fact for the jury. There are considerable uncertainties surrounding the scope of non-violent threat. For example, would the offence criminalise economic sexual coercion, such as a threat of loss of employment or promotion prospects? Within this framework, the issue of causation, namely whether the threat was "operative", may continue to focus attention on the state of mind of the victim thereby "providing a backdoor mechanism for reintroducing consent": S Bronitt, "Rape and Lack of Consent" (1992) 16 Crim LJ 289 at 309. The task facing the judge and jury in resolving this definitional uncertainty is similar to the problems of resolving consent under the existing law, in particular, the difficulty in identifying the precise circumstances where consent may be vitiated.

As we shall explore below, many of the core definitional questions in sexual offences are elusive because of the profound moral disagreement over whether particular behaviour is sufficient to warrant criminalisation. Juries may be considered well-qualified to resolve moral disagreements. However, the lack of certainty in such core definitions (whether under statute or common law) provides considerable scope for discriminatory myths and stereotypes about female sexuality to operate unchallenged.

After reviewing the Michigan reforms, the Victorian Law Reform Commission concluded that shifting from the language of consent to coercion would be a "semantic change" in the law of rape. In its view, the circumstances of coercion or exploitation would operate "in reality no more than indicators of lack of consent": *Rape: Reform of Law and Procedure*, Report No 43 (1991), p 6. This criticism of the Michigan reforms is heavily coloured by the particular structural weakness of the legislation and the subsequent judicial interpretation of sections that retained an implied "defence" of consent in every case.

Consent remains central to social understandings of sexual wrongfulness. An empirical study of attitudes toward sexual violence confirmed the centrality of consent as a defining concept for young people, government agencies and community services in Australia: L Daws, J Brannock, R Brooker, W Patton, G Smeal, S Warren (eds), *Young People's Perceptions of and Attitudes to Sexual Violence* (Hobart: National Clearinghouse of Youth Studies, 1995). Nevertheless, a new rape offence could be envisaged that dispenses with consent. Rather than require proof of lack of consent or allow consent as a defence, rape or sexual assault could be defined as sexual conduct in circumstances of coercion or exploitation.

Excising lack of consent from rape law has the advantage of shifting the focus of the trial away from the complainant, but invariably leads to the accusation that sexual autonomy for women would be denied. This accusation however ignores the improverished and restrictive notion of consent in the present law and that notions of autonomy for many women are highly constrained: C MacKinnon, *Toward A Feminist Theory of the State* (Cambridge, Mass: Harvard University Press, 1989), Ch 9. More recently, some feminists have sought to retrieve and reconstruct the concept of autonomy. Nicola Lacey in Chapter 4 of *Unspeakable Subjects* (Oxford: Hart Publishing, 1998), has pointed out that sexual autonomy as protected by the present law is understood narrowly in terms of property or ownership over one's own body. As we shall explore in the next two sections, it is possible to reconstruct the concept of sexual autonomy (and thus consent) in terms that protect a wider range of interests.

THE PRINCIPLE OF SEXUAL AUTONOMY: FROM AGAINST HER WILL TO WITHOUT HER CONSENT

Law reform in Australia has proceeded on the basis that lack of consent must remain the key element of the sexual offences, except those dealing with children or persons with mental impairment. The MCCOC's recommendation to retain consent for the core sexual offences undoubtedly relates to the importance attached to the right to autonomy. The idea that violating sexual autonomy is the rationale for criminalisation is apparent from the novel title to the chapter on sexual offences in the *Model Criminal Code*, namely "Sexual Offences *against* the Person".

As Lacey has observed, rather than being a universal and timeless feature of sexual offences, the "discourse of sexual autonomy is, of course, a recent one": *Unspeakable Subjects* (Oxford: Hart Publishing, 1998), p 104. The notion of "consent" as a mediating concept for differentiating lawful from unlawful sexual activity emerged only in the mid-19th century. In medieval times, rape was concerned with the ravishment or abduction of unmarried women without paternal consent. By the 18th century, the English courts, drawing from various statutory sex crimes, had identified the felony of rape at common law. The capital felony of rape was narrowly defined as "carnal knowledge" (sexual penetration) of a woman "forcibly and against her will": W Blackstone, *Commentaries on the Laws of England* (Oxford: Clarendon Press, first published 1769) Vol IV, p 210; Hale, *The History of the Pleas of the Crown* (1736) Vol 1, pp 628-629. With the relaxation of the death penalty in the mid-19th century, the English courts gradually reformulated the definition of rape in broader terms of "sexual intercourse without consent". This occurred in order to criminalise cases where no force or fraud had been used against the victim because she was insensible through drink or asleep: *Camplin* (1845) 1 Cox CC 220; *Young* (1878) 12 Cox CC 114.

The definitional shift to "without consent" in the 19th century was not merely a semantic change. It reflected the modernising influence of liberal values on the criminal law and the tendency of enlightenment philosophy to view social relations between individuals in contractual or quasi-contractual terms: C Pateman, *The Sexual Contract* (Cambridge: Polity, 1988). While contractual concepts, like implied consent, have exerted some influence over legal development in this area, sexual offences have never been a perfect expression of liberalism. In some areas, such as homosexual and prostitution offences, the legal commitment to the liberal values of autonomy and privacy can be quite weak. The impact of the right to privacy on the criminal law has been considered in Chapter 2: pp 141ff. It would seem that sexual autonomy and privacy may be qualified by competing policy considerations. "Statutory rape" provisions criminalising sex with minors or other vulnerable individuals provide examples where the principle of autonomy is legally subordinated to overriding concerns about moral and physical welfare of those individuals, as well as doubts about their legal capacity to give "true" consent.

The common law does not recognise for the purpose of sexual offences a general age of majority that determines the capacity to consent. In the absence of any statutory provision on this issue, the validity of consent is determined solely by reference to the person's understanding of the nature and character of the act. As we shall explore below, the rules governing consent laid down by statute for different offences are not consistent. The "age of consent" is contingent on diverse factors such as the sex and sexual orientation of the parties, the type of conduct involved and whether it occurred in public or in private.

Andrew Ashworth has characterised individual autonomy as a general principle that has "factual and normative elements": *Principles of Criminal Law* (3rd ed, Oxford: Oxford University Press, 1999), pp 27-29. The principle of autonomy, as explored in Chapter 3, underlies the significance attached to free-will and voluntariness in attributing criminal responsibility. It also underwrites the role of consent as a "defence" in relation to offences such as assault and theft. However, the principle of autonomy is not absolute. Many liberal theorists, including Ashworth, are prepared to concede that there are limits to the principle of individual autonomy, and that while utmost respect should be accorded to the principle, it may be qualified by the principle of welfare and the interests of the community: see Ch 1, 3.4 'Preservation of Welfare', pp 57ff.

Within the sexual sphere, the principle of autonomy is typically conceived in terms of bodily ownership or control. As Lacey points out: "sexual autonomy simply *is* proprietary autonomy: the choice to exclude another from access to bodily 'property'": pp 112-113. Sex, as a "thing" to be owned and controlled, must be protected from wrongful interference by others. Proprietary conceptions of sex and sexuality promote a contractual or quasi-contractual view of sexual relations.

The commodification of sex as property that may be bargained and exchanged underscores the traditional immunity for rape within marriage. Until abolished by statute and the High Court in *R v L* (1991) 174 CLR 379, this immunity applied irrespective of the lack of consent of the woman or intent of the husband on the basis that the parties had *by their contract of marriage* offered an irrevocable consent to have sex with each other. Although the immunity has now gone, the commodity theory of sex continues to influence how legal academics, lawyers and judges conceptualise consent and thus distinguish between rape and non-rape. In Chapter 1, we explored how "Law and Economics" has used the commodity theory to critique and propose reform of rape law.

Under the current law, juries are often directed that consent (rather like acceptance of an offer in contract law) need not be express through words, but may also be "implied" from conduct: J Glissan and S Tilmouth, *Australian Criminal Trial Directions* (Sydney: Butt, 1996), Ch 5, 5-1100-25. Such directions are premised on presumptions of (female) sexual access and that parties bear the risk of unwanted sex in cases where their conduct has been misunderstood as indicating consent by the other person. The Supreme Court of Canada has recently held in *R v Ewanchuk* [1999] 1 SCR 330 that the doctrine of "implied consent" has no place in the modern law of sexual assault. The concept of implied consent suggests that the mind of the victim was severable from her conduct, a prospect that would operate to entrench and legitimate dangerous myths about female sexuality, in particular that consent may be implied from appearance or prior sexual conduct and the like.

By focussing on proprietary control over the person, the concept of sexual autonomy overlooks other values associated with sex, such as mutual respect, trust, love and pleasure. These values, which Lacey describes as "affective" and "relational" values, play a significant role in the wider social discourse of sexuality. Within the law of rape, however, the protection of these values have played a marginal role. At present, they are relevant only as sentencing factors to gauge the "seriousness" of harm caused to the victim. In Lacey's view, there is little scope within the current legal framework structured around autonomy for victims to express the full range of interests harmed by the accused's conduct: p 116. More positively, Kathy Laster and Pat O'Malley have observed a general reassertion of emotionality in legal discourse with the effect of displacing or qualifying traditional rationalist and positivist values. The authors cite developments in the law of rape and domestic violence as evidence of greater legal sensitivity to emotions and other intangible interests: "Sensitive New-Age Laws: The Reassertion of Emotionality in Law" (1996) 24(1) *International Journal of the Sociology of Law* 21.

RAPE WITHIN MARRIAGE: AN IMPLIED AND CONTINUING CONSENT

Consent is represented as an essential or fundamental concept for distinguishing between lawful and unlawful sexuality. Until recently, however, consent was deemed an irrelevant consideration in relation to marital sex. The origins of the "marital rape immunity" is invariably traced to the views of English judge and jurist, Matthew Hale, in the 18th century. The passage, most widely cited, stated that a husband could not be guilty of committing rape upon his wife because by "mutual matrimonial consent the wife hath given up herself in this kind unto her husband which she cannot retract": *The History of the Pleas of the Crown* (1736), Vol 1, p 629.

Although Hale cited no authority for the proposition, the immunity was clearly not his own invention. The idea that a husband could not be guilty of rape at that time was firmly supported by ecclesiastical law: J Barton, "The Story of Marital Rape" (1992) 108 *Law Quarterly Review* 260. Hale is often accused of misogyny, though the idea of viewing sexual relations within marriage as being governing by "implied" terms of the marriage contract demonstrated a relatively liberal and modern outlook compared to the traditional ecclesiastical view that a husband had a "conjugal right" to extract a sexual debt from his wife. While recognising the immunity for rape, Hale doubted whether the husband could lawfully use force against a reluctant wife. As David Lanham concluded in "Hale, Misogyny and Rape" (1983) 7 Crim LJ 148 at 156:

> What is clear is that in selecting the marital contract theory, Hale turned his back on some
> of the more preposterous bases which have been suggested by others, like the fictional
> unity of the husband and wife, the theory that a wife is the property of the husband, or that
> the wife is under a duty to obey her husband.

By the late 20th century, the immunity had become increasingly untenable. Judges placed limits on the immunity, deciding that it had no application where the husband and wife had revoked their consent by an act of separation pursuant to a court order. Yet, even in the 1980s there were still legal scholars who were prepared to defend the immunity. Lanham concluded his excellent historical review of the immunity, which debunked many of the myths about Hale's misogyny, with the following caution about the dangers of criminalising marital rape (at 166):

> It is submitted that the law of rape is too blunt an instrument for dealing with the relation-
> ship between husband and wife and that marital immunity should be retained at least where
> the parties are living together. Where the marriage as a whole has become intolerable
> because of an act of unwanted intercourse the appropriate remedy is divorce or separation.
> Where force is used there is the possibility of criminal proceedings for crimes from assault
> to causing grievous bodily harm. In other cases the criminal law should keep out of it.

This submission fell on deaf ears as the marital rape immunity became the focus of increasing feminist activism. By the late 1980s, the immunity had been abolished by legislation in every Australian State and Territory.

The status of the immunity was further undermined by judicial decisions. *R v R* [1992] 1 AC 599 provided the House of Lords with its first opportunity to review the marital rape immunity. The accused did not dispute the fact that he had violently had sex with his wife who at the time was living separately from him though not pursuant to a court order. Rather than infer a revocation of consent by *de facto* separation, the trial judge in this case simply refused to recognise that the immunity existed in the modern law. The accused appealed against his conviction. The House of Lords, affirming the conviction, agreed with the Court of Appeal, that the immunity was a "common law fiction which has become anachronistic and offensive": at 623. The decision to abolish the marital rape immunity was widely welcomed, although some concern was expressed over the *process* by which the immunity was abolished. The decision to abolish the immunity may be viewed as the creation of a crime of marital rape that previously did not exist, therefore raising concerns about retrospectivity: M Giles, "Judicial Law Making in the Criminal Courts: The Case of Marital Rape" (1991) Crim LR 407. This question was considered by the European Court of Human Rights in *SW v the*

United Kingdom; CR v the United Kingdom (Eur Court HR, 22 November 1999) *Reports of Judgments and Decisions*, Series A no 335; (1996) 21 EHRR 363. The Court noted that the common law doctrine of precedent legitimately facilitated legal development. Offences may be broadened and defences narrowed by common law development. This would not violate the principle against retrospectivity provided that the development is consistent with the essence of the offence and could have been reasonably foreseen: para 36, p 42; para 34, p 69.

While the fate of marital immunity was being decided in England, the High Court was considering the same issue in Australia. Although the immunity had been abolished by statute in every Australian jurisdiction, its precise status as part of the common law of Australia was reviewed in *R v L* (1991) 174 CLR 379. The accused was charged and convicted with raping his wife. In South Australia the immunity had been abolished by statute, and the accused argued on appeal that the South Australia provision conflicted with a provision of the *Family Law Act* 1975 (Cth). The Commonwealth provision allowed the Family Court to make an order relieving a party to a marriage from rendering conjugal rights. When the *Family Law Act* was enacted, conjugal rights included the right, under the criminal law, to have marital intercourse without consent. The accused submitted that there was an inconsistency between State and Commonwealth provisions. Section 109 of the Constitution states that in the event of a conflict between State and Commonwealth law, the Commonwealth law prevails. The High Court rejected the appeal on a number of grounds, including that there was no inconsistency between the provisions. Nevertheless the High Court took the opportunity to clarify the status of the immunity. The majority of the High Court (at 390) doubted whether the immunity had been part of the common law, and concluded that they "would be justified in refusing to accept a notion that is so out of keeping with the view society now takes of the relationship between the parties to a marriage".

PROCEDURAL PERSPECTIVES

Marital Rape

Although the immunity has been formally abolished, there is evidence that rape within marriage is viewed as a less serious form of rape by police, prosecutors and sentencing judges. While marital rape has been an offence for 20 years in some Australian jurisdictions, few prosecutions are initiated against husbands who commit rape on their wives. This dearth of prosecution of marital rape may be contrasted with the scale of the crime reported through victimisation studies. Patricia Easteal notes that available victim surveys suggest that husbands or ex-partners are named as the perpetrator by between 13-15% of respondents: "Rape in Marriage: Has the Licence Lapsed?" in P Easteal (ed), *Balancing the Scales — Rape, Law Reform and Australian Culture* (Sydney: Federation Press, 1998), p 113. See also, P Easteal, *Voices of the Survivors* (Melbourne: Spinifex Press, 1994), p 56; New South Wales Sexual Assault Committee, *Sexual Assault Phone-In Report* (Sydney: Ministry for the Status and Advancement of Women, 1993). Victims however are reluctant to disclose or report the matter to the police. When matters do proceed to court, they are most likely to be cases involving extreme violence.

Marital rape is grossly under-reported. Even where the complaint does result in a guilty plea or conviction, the "domestic nature" of the rape has been taken into account by courts as a matter in mitigation of sentence. For a recent example, see *Spencer* (unrep, CCA Qld, No 80 of

1991) discussed in S Kift, "That All Rape is Rape Even if Not by a Stranger" (1995) 4 *Griffith Law Review* 60 at 99. The working judicial assumption is that marital rape is less serious than rape by a stranger. In the United Kingdom, Sue Lees' empirical study of rape trials revealed that estranged husbands' punishments were "frequently lower than in other rape cases": *Ruling Passions: Sexual Violence, Reputation and the Law* (Buckingham: Open University Press, 1997), p 123. Easteal cites similar attitudes being expressed by sentencing courts cases in Australia: pp 118-119. More positively, there have been recent cases where the opposite view has been taken that rape within marriage is an aggravating factor because it involves a "breach of trust": *R v S* [1991] Tas R 273. Warner has suggested that there is a growing trend against leniency on the ground that the rape or sexual assault was committed within or against the background of a sexual relationship with the victim: "Sentencing for Rape" in P Easteal (ed), *Balancing the Scales* (Sydney: Federation Press, 1998). The relative invisibility of these decisions, most of which are unreported, has meant that sentencing principles in rape cases are undeveloped, although Warner's survey of the authorities reveals growing consensus on a range of issues such as the irrelevance of the victim's sexual history, "provocative" dress and conduct, or the type of penetration involved (whether by penis or object). Clearly there is scope for further guidelines on how judges should evaluate the seriousness of rape and sexual assaults to prevent the downgrading of "domestic rape".

The Problem of Domestic Rape: When Rape is (not) Rape

The reasons for treating marital rape as less serious than stranger rape is reflected in a series of articles by Glanville Williams. In "The Problem of Domestic Rape" (1991) 141 *New Law Journal* 205 Williams proposed that while marital rape should be criminalised, it should be downgraded in seriousness to an offence in the nature of an assault punishable by fine or binding-over. *R v R* [1992] 1 AC 599 provided the opportunity to revisit the topic in a rather misleadingly titled article, "Rape is Rape" (1992) 142 *New Law Journal* 11. In this piece he identified "four powerful reasons" for treating marital rape differently from stranger rape: (i) the harm is less serious because of past sexual contact; (ii) strangers cause more fear in society than non-strangers; (iii) failure to provide sex on demand is a form of "unfaithfulness" that provokes men to lose control and is therefore less culpable; (iv) victims are often willing to forgive their partners. These arguments have been subject to extensive criticism: see H Fenwick, "Marital Rights or Partial Immunity" (1992) 142 *New Law Journal* 831; S Kift, "That All Rape is Rape Even if Not by a Stranger" (1995) 4 *Griffith Law Review* 60. Although Williams' proposal has been dismissed by law reformers, his "commonsense" continues to be evidenced in the attitudes of some police, prosecutors and sentencing courts.

DEFINING LACK OF CONSENT: THE ORDINARY MEANING APPROACH

In *R v Olugboja* [1982] QB 320, the English Court of Appeal held that consent is a question of fact for the jury and that in the majority of cases the jury need only be directed to adopt an "ordinary meaning" of consent for the purpose of determining rape (at 332):

[The jury] should be directed to concentrate on the state of mind of the victim immediately before the act of sexual intercourse, having regard to all the relevant circumstances; and in particular, the events leading up to the act and her reaction to them showing their impact on her mind.

By requiring juries to apply their commonsense, further judicial elaboration on the meaning of consent is limited only to unusual cases, for example, where guidance is needed on the distinction between consent and submission due to the effect of force or threats. This "ordinary meaning" approach mirrors the preferred direction for several fundamental concepts of criminal responsibility, such as intention, causation, dishonesty, offensiveness and indecency. Attributing the "ordinary meaning" to fundamental concepts has the moral appeal that community standards are explicitly incorporated into the criminal law. The neutrality of these objective standards, and the role of morality and community in sustaining them, is critically reviewed in Chapter 1, 3.3 'The Public Interest'.

In rape cases, the ordinary meaning approach permits the jury to scrutinise the quality of consent in each individual case taking into account the subjective perceptual capacities of the complainant. This is particularly important where it is alleged that the accused obtained consent by pressure, fraud or abuse of power. The difficulty with this approach is that consent, like many fundamental concepts in the criminal law, does not possess a settled or shared meaning within the community.[16] In aligning the legal and moral understanding of consent, juries will be left to "legislate" the precise boundaries of rape in particular cases. Juries would be required to act "as a kind of sovereign legislature", determining what constitutes the offence of rape on the facts of each case.[17] However, the advantage of *Olugboja* is that consent is comprehended in terms that demonstrate greater respect to the complainant's perception of the situation, albeit "arguably at the expense of values such as determinacy and the wish to treat like cases alike": S Gardiner, "Appreciating *Olugboja*" (1996) 16(3) *Legal Studies* 275 at 275-276.

The decision in *Olugboja* set the law of consent on a new path. However, leaving the jury such a wide latitude to determine whether there is or is not consent raises concerns beyond consistency and predictability. There is a danger that discriminatory assumptions and myths about consent are simply removed from substantive definitions, only to resurface and reinstate themselves as the "ordinary meaning" of consent. Understood in its "ordinary" sense, consent will be determined by prevailing cultural stereotypes and myths about appropriate standards of female sexuality. An Australia-wide study on attitudes to rape, summarised by Easteal (ed) in *Balancing the Scales — Rape, Law Reform and Australian Culture* (Sydney: Federation Press, 1998), reveals (p 10) the prevalence and enduring quality of myths and stereotypes:

▬▬▬ **one third of the males were either undecided or agreed that "women who hitchhike have only themselves to blame if they are raped";**

---

16 A similar point has been made in relation to intention in the context of murder in N Lacey, "A Clear Concept of Intention: Elusive or Illusory" (1993) 56 *Modern Law Review* 621.

17 G Williams, *Textbook of Criminal Law* (2nd ed, London: Stevens & Sons, 1983), p 554. The Criminal Law Revision Committee rejected the suggestion in *Olugboja* that consent should simply be left as a question for the jury: *Fifteenth Report, Sexual Offences* (London: HMSO Cmnd 9213, 1984), p 10.

- about 16 of every 100 male respondents either believed that "no" means "yes" or they were undecided;

- almost four out of every 10 males either disagreed or were undecided about the statement that "there is no behaviour on the part of a woman that should be considered justification for rape";

- almost three out of every 10 males agreed or were undecided with the statement that "most charges of rape are unfounded"; and

- more than one quarter of males agreed that a rape victim's past sexual history should be relevant evidence in the courtroom.

When consent is left to commonsense, juries must determine where the line between consent and non-consent must be drawn in each case. Questions would arise whether lack of resistance or dissent was indicative of consent; whether "rough handling" by the accused was persuasion that induced consent; or whether "no" meant "yes" or perhaps "maybe". Without firmer definitions, contradictory meanings of consent can operate simultaneously in the law, leaving considerable scope for discriminatory myths about female sexuality to operate unchallenged. Indeed, Bollen J's infamous direction that there was nothing wrong in a husband using "rougher than usual handling" to overcome a wife's initial resistance was preceded by a direction that "Consent means free voluntary agreement to engage in an act of sexual intercourse at the relevant time": *R v Johns* (unrep, 26/8/1992, SC SA, No SCCRM/91/452), transcript p 12.

Conscious of these dangers, some jurisdictions have adopted an explicit definition of consent, supported by a range of mandatory directions designed to neutralise the effect of some of these enduring myths.

Sentencing and Myths Surrounding the Harm of Rape

Like the rape of a wife or co-habitee, some judges have held that the rape of a prostitute is less serious than the rape of a chaste woman: *R v Hakopian* (unrep, 8/8/1991, County Ct Vic). The judicial assumption that the likely psychological traumatisation of rape would likely be reduced where the victim is a prostitute has been strongly criticised by feminists: D Cass, *"R v Hakopian"* (1993) 1 *Feminist Legal Studies* 203. For an article defending Hakopian by reference to previous authority and basic sentencing principles see M Sharpley, "Heroes as Villain: A Defence of the Judicial Approach to Hakopian" (1993) 67(11) *Law Institute Journal* 1064.

MANDATORY JURY DIRECTIONS ON CONSENT

Rape myths develop against the background of community beliefs about what is considered normal and abnormal heterosexual behaviour. Normality in the context of sexuality is structured in the law around a "penetrative/coercive" model of sexuality. This model is based on two main assumptions about heterosexuality. The first is that sexuality is somehow centred upon the act of penetration and the second is that women enjoy being "coerced" or persuaded to engage in sexual intercourse: B McSherry, "Constructing Lack of Consent" in P Easteal (ed), *Balancing the Scales* (Sydney:

Federation Press, 1998), Ch 3. In relation to the latter assumption, there is a general belief that the art of "seduction" allows for any reservations on the part of the woman to be rightfully overcome by the persistence of the man. In this model of sexuality, women are viewed as submissive, as acquiescing to sexual intercourse *unless* they resist in some way. This is reflected in judicial comments that physical inaction on the part of the woman may signal consent: *Maes* [1975] VR 541. The penetrative/coercive model also underlies much legal scholarship, surfacing in many authoritative academic analyses of the law: B McSherry, "Constructing Lack of Consent" in P Easteal (ed), *Balancing the Scales* (Sydney: Federation Press, 1998), p 28.

The model presupposes that violence and resistance is indicative of "real rape" and this is reflected in the types of cases selected for prosecution. It has been noted that the vast majority of rape charges involve allegations of physical coercion: Victorian Law Reform Commission, *Rape: Reform of Law and Procedure* (1991), Appendixes to Interim Report No 43, p 41. Of course, the prevalence of coercion in rape prosecution figures is misleading. It ignores the filtering process at work that exclude from prosecution rapes, such as marital or acquaintance rapes, that do not involve violence or result in the infliction of injury, as well as the high levels of under-reporting of sexual violence where the accused is a current partner: C Coumarelos and J Allen, "Predicting Women's Responses to Violence: The 1996 Women's Safety Survey" (1999) *Crime and Justice Bulletin*, No 47 (New South Wales Bureau of Crime Statistics and Research).

The evidential presumption of consent that operates in rape law (in effect, a presumption of female sexual accessibility) may be contrasted with the approach taken in the civil law. In relation to potentially invasive medical procedures, the tort of trespass and negligence has moved strongly to a more positive "informed" standard of consent and disclosure of risk: B McSherry, "Constructing Lack of Consent" in P Easteal (ed), *Balancing the Scales* (Sydney: Federation Press, 1998), p 29. The positive consent standard attaches importance to mutuality and sexual pleasure during sexual encounters. As Lois Pineau points out in "Date Rape: A Feminist Analysis" (1989) 9 *Law and Philosophy* 217 at 234:

> if a man wants to be sure that he is not forcing himself on a woman, he has an obligation
> either to ensure that the encounter really is mutually enjoyable, or to know the reasons
> why she would want to continue the encounter in spite of her lack of enjoyment.

Pineau writes that under the positive communicative model of sexuality, these burdens are of an ongoing and continuing nature: at 240. They may be contrasted with the traditional contractual concept of consent as an agreement negotiated beforehand, a process where both the "offer" and the "acceptance" may be implied rather than express.

The rules governing consent have been modified by statute. Legislation in the Australian Capital Territory, New South Wales, the Northern Territory, South Australia, Victoria and Western Australia expressly provides that failure to manifest physical resistance to a sexual assault does not *of itself* indicate consent.[18] As a matter of *substantive* law, resistance is not required. However, from an evidential perspective the prosecution's burden of proving "lack of consent" on the criminal standard of beyond reasonable doubt will be made easier in cases where there are signs of active

---

18 *Crimes Act* (ACT), s 92P(2); *Crimes Act* (NSW), s 61R(2)(d); *Criminal Code Act* (NT), s 192(A); *Criminal Law Consolidation Act* 1935 (SA), s 48; *Crimes Act* 1958 (Vic), s 37(6)(i); *Criminal Code* (WA), s 319(2)(b).

dissent or physical resistance. This tactical reality has been explained by Fisse, in *Howard's Criminal Law* (5th ed, Sydney: Law Book Company Ltd, 1990) as follows (p 179):

> [A]lthough in theory D [the defendant] is not entitled to make any presumption of consent, the fact that P [the prosecution] must prove non-consent as part of his case means in practice that if V [the victim] consciously submits with passive acquiescence, subject only to a mental reservation, D should be acquitted unless V's acquiescence is explicable in the context as arising from fear of the consequences of resistance. V must make it clear to D, up to the moment of intercourse, that she does not consent, but in so doing she is not required to incur the risk of brutality.

Victoria has attempted to address this "covert" resistance standard through the adoption of mandatory jury directions. These laws are unique in Australia with the potential to replace the traditional penetrative/coercive model of sexuality with a more positive communicative model.

The changes to the law followed an extensive review of the law by the Law Reform Commission of Victoria: *Rape — Reform of Law and Procedure*, Report No 43 (1991). As a consequence of that review, the Parliament enacted the *Crimes (Rape) Act* 1991, amending the *Crimes Act* 1958 (Vic). Section 36 of the *Crimes Act* provides that "consent means free agreement". Similar formulations of consent or agreement freely or voluntarily given have been adopted in other jurisdictions: *Criminal Code* (NT), s 192(1); *Criminal Code* (Tas), s 2A; *Criminal Code* (WA), s 319(2)(a). Section 36 then enumerates the non-exhaustive list of situations where free agreement is *not* present (the rules governing vitiation of consent are considered in the next section). This "two-pronged" approach to consent has been endorsed by the MCCOC: *Chapter 5 — Sexual Offences Against the Person*, Report (1999), p 41. The Committee (p 43) also favoured the use of the term "agreement" because it emphasises that consent should be seen as a positive state of mind.

By far the most significant and progressive reform in Victoria relates to the introduction of mandatory jury directions on consent. Section 37 of the *Crimes Act* 1958 (Vic) (which covers jury directions on consent) states that in a relevant case the judge must direct the jury that:

(a) the fact that a person did not say or do anything to indicate free agreement to a sexual act is normally enough to show that the act took place without that person's free agreement

(b) a person is not to be regarded as having freely agreed to a sexual act just because —

    (i) she or he did not protest or physically resist; or

    (ii) she or he did not sustain physical injury; or

    (iii) on that or an earlier occasion she or he freely agreed to engage in another sexual act (whether or not of the same type) with that person, or a sexual act with another person;

(c) in considering the accused's alleged belief that the complainant was consenting to the sexual act, it must take into account whether that belief was reasonable in all the relevant circumstances.

Physical inactivity or passive acquiescence now means non-consent rather than the opposite. The objectives behind the jury directions, namely to confront the discriminatory assumptions around consent and to educate the community generally, has been approved by the MCCOC: *Chapter 5 — Sexual Offences Against the Person,* Report (1999), p 263. However, the Committee felt that s 37(a) went too far. The use of the word "normally" in para (a) implies that the burden is on the defence to raise evidence displacing this presumption. The Committee proposed that the provision should be redrafted so that the judge must direct the jury that "a person is not to be regarded as having consented to a sexual act just because: (a) the person did not say or do anything to indicate that she or he did not consent": s 5.2.43.

The evidential effect of s 37 was recently considered by the Supreme Court of Victoria in *R v Laz* [1998] 1 VR 453. The Court held that it was a misdirection to say that the victim's failure to do or say anything was evidence or "prima facie proof" that free agreement was absent. The reforms were not intended to alter the burden on the prosecution to prove lack of free agreement. The Supreme Court held (at 460) that the expression used in s 37(a) "does no more than require a trial judge to draw to the jury's attention the necessity, when considering the issue of consent, to have regard to the common human experience that, in general, people do not engage voluntarily in sexual activities without indicating by word or action in some way their preparedness to do so".

These mandatory jury directions aim to counteract the informal presumptions of consent. They challenge the traditional model of sexuality which views women as passively acquiescing to penetration. The jury directions promote a "communication standard" in sexual relationships that confronts and undermines the penetrative/coercive model of sexuality. While some lawyers have argued that these laws do not reflect contemporary ideas about sexual relations, it has been pointed out that the criminal law has a role to play in setting sexual standards, not merely reflecting them: R Weiner, "Shifting the Communication Burden: A Meaningful Consent Standard in Rape" (1983) 6 *Harvard Women's Law Journal* 143 at 160-161.

The positive consent standard created by these mandatory jury directions would be further reinforced by the reforms adopted in Canada that limit defence claims of mistaken belief in consent to cases where the accused has taken "reasonable steps" to ascertain consent: S Bronitt, "The Direction of Rape Law in Australia: Toward a Positive Consent Standard" (1994) 18 Crim LJ 249. This proposal is discussed below: pp 622ff. The communicative model of sexuality is not confined to heterosexual activity, but may be usefully employed in promoting more effective communication and ensuring mutual sexual pleasure in other contexts such as sadomasochism.

From No means Yes, To *Only* Yes means Yes

A model of sexuality constructed around mutuality and communication rather than consent has been sketched by a number of feminist writers: R Wiener, "Shifting the Communication Burden: A Meaningful Consent Standard in Rape" (1983) 6 *Harvard Women's Law Journal* 143; M Chamallas, "Consent, Equality and the Legal Control of Sexual Conduct" (1988) 61 *Southern California Law Review* 777; L Pineau, "Date Rape: A Feminist Analysis" (1989) 9 *Law and Philosophy* 217; L Remick, "Read Her Lips: An Argument For a Verbal Consent Standard in Rape" (1993) 141 *University of Pennsylvania Law Review* 1103; B McSherry, "Constructing Lack of Consent" in P Easteal (ed), *Balancing the Scales* (Sydney: Federation Press, 1998), Ch 3; N Lacey, *Unspeakable Subjects* (Oxford: Hart Publishing, 1998), Ch 4, pp 121-122.

Experimenting with Mandatory Jury Directions

The reforms in Victoria have been subjected to close empirical scrutiny: Department of Justice, *Rape Law Reform Evaluation Project — The Crimes (Rape) Act* 1991 (1997). The researchers, Melanie Heenan and Helen McKelvie, reviewed 27 jury directions offered in rape trials in Victoria. The research revealed that most judges gave the mandatory directions on consent where "relevant", although a small number of judges failed to direct the jury in cases where the researchers believed that the directions were appropriate: p 298. The finding implies that "relevance" may mean different things to different judges. Even where the judge accepts the "relevance" of the warning, its effect may be subverted by the way in which the jury direction is given.

Feeling resentment at being compelled to offer guidance that does not accord with common-sense or personal experience, some judges have sought to subvert the mandatory directions. For example, the trial judge in *Defina* (1994) 18 Crim LJ 293 (at 296), prefaced the mandatory warning with the following cautionary statement: "I am required by the Parliament to tell you the following, which is contained in our Act, and I will read it to you". On appeal, the Court of Criminal Appeal concluded this direction was inadequate as it failed to convey that "the sections contained *the law*" and the judge further failed to relate the directions to the facts. By implying that directions were simply fashionable political symbolism, the jury may be encouraged to give them little weight or disregard them completely.

Approximately 50% of the judges and legal practitioners interviewed expressed reservations about the mandatory reforms. Why is the legal community resistant to these reforms? The main criticism was that the mandatory jury direction did not accord with the way in which people relate to one another. As one barrister said (p 317):

> I just don't think that accords with human nature and ... normal interrelationship ... I
> shouldn't assume other people's experience, but I hazard a guess that in a vast number
> of sexual encounters there is nothing said one way or another about agreement or no
> agreement. It's all done by way of the normal messages that people give each other.

This comment may well be a reasonable assessment of many "normal" heterosexual negotiations. The question arises whether assumptions about implied agreement (which may be true for *some* men and women, *some* of the time) should become the "norm" around which the law of consent for rape or sexual assault is constructed. For those who believe the penetrative/coercive model of sexuality is "normal" because it has existed for centuries and arises from some innate biological differences between men and women that causes men to be dominant and women to be submissive, then no harm can be seen as emanating from such practices. On the other hand, for those who believe that a penetrative/coercive model of sexuality leads to a denial of women as agents of their own sexual pleasure as well as to the idea of aggressive male domination of women as a natural right, the law can be seen as a vehicle for preventing harm to women by defining what is and what is not consensual intercourse.

Admittedly, in many sexual encounters the burden of positive verbal communication may seem heavy or awkward. However, mutual discomfort may be tolerable if harmful myths about female sexuality are challenged rather than being condoned by the law. Having a standard that consent needs to be communicated benefits both men and women. The presumption that a woman's silence or inactivity is consistent with her sexual fulfilment implies that her partner intuitively knows how to discern her sexual needs correctly. This is also unfair on men since "[t]he 'silent is sexy' view of sexual relationships ... unrealistically presupposes male sexual omniscience": L Remick, "Read Her Lips: An Argument For a Verbal Consent Standard in Rape" (1993) 141 *University of Pennsylvania Law Review* 1103 at 1150. In the ultimate analysis, we believe that the Victorian reforms, by tackling discriminatory and dangerous myths about consent and female sexuality, are a step in the right direction.

THE STATUTORY RULES NEGATING CONSENT: A QUESTION OF LAW OR FACT?

Both the courts and legislatures have been reluctant to permit the jury a completely free hand in determining whether the sexual conduct occurred "without consent". Complex legal rules have been developed to identify those circumstances where the victim's "apparent" or purported consent to intercourse is negated. The approach of the common law and supplementary legislation has been to identify the problem cases where the victim is not regarded as having consented. As noted above, even the "ordinary meaning" approach to consent recognises that some cases may require further direction on consent, as for example, where the person's sexual submission was procured by threats.

Early legislation simply disposed of problematic consent cases by "deeming" sexual inter-course in particular circumstances to be rape. For example, s 4 of the *Criminal Law Amendment Act* 1885 (UK) deemed cases of spousal impersonation to be rape. Modern statutes have defined the circumstances not as rape or sexual assault, but rather as "circumstances" where consent is "deemed to be negated"; or where the person "does not freely agree" or is "not to be taken to consent": *Crimes Act* 1900 (ACT), s 92P; *Crimes Act* 1900 (NSW), s 62R(2); *Crimes Act* 1958 (Vic), s 37. In South Australia, legislation provided that no person under the age of 18 years shall be "deemed capable of consenting to any indecent assault committed by any person who is his or her guardian, teacher, schoolmaster or schoolmistress": *Criminal Law Consolidation Act* 1935 (SA), s 57.

In some jurisdictions, these common law rules governing vitiation of consent have been clarified and expanded by statute. The Victorian provision on consent, adopted in 1991, defines consent for the purposes of rape and other prescribed sexual offences as "free agreement" and provides a non-exhaustive list of the circumstances where a person does not consent to intercourse: *Crimes Act* 1958 (Vic), s 36. The list includes the following: where the person submits through force, fear, unlawful detention; where the person is unconscious, incapable of understanding the sexual nature of the act, mistaken about the sexual nature of the act or identity of the other person, or mistaken about the medical or hygienic purpose. In the Code States of Queensland and Western Australia, consent must be "freely and voluntarily given": *Criminal Code* (Qld), s 347; *Criminal Code* (WA), 319(2).

Drawing on these various statutory models of consent, particularly the Victorian reforms, the Model Criminal Code Officers Committee (MCCOC) recommended in *Chapter 5: Sexual Offences Against the Person*, Report (1999), (p 38) the following definition of consent:

5.2.3 Consent

(1) In this Part, consent means free and voluntary agreement.

(2) Examples of circumstances in which a person does not consent to an act include the following:

(a) the person submits to the act because of force or the fear of force to the person or to someone else;

(b) the person submits to the act because the person is unlawfully detained;

(c) the person is asleep or unconscious, or is so affected by alcohol or another drug as to be incapable of consenting;

(d) the person is incapable of understanding the essential nature of the act;

(e) the person is mistaken about the essential nature of the act (for example, the person mistakenly believes that the act is for medical or hygienic purposes).

The proposed list of circumstances negating consent is an amalgam of common law and statutory rules. However, the list is not exhaustive. Outside the defined circumstances, consent is defined as "free and voluntary agreement". As the MCCOC noted: "The only effect of the list is that, once the listed circumstances are established, then lack of consent is automatically established. It has no effect on unlisted circumstances": p 41. In cases where the jury finds certain facts to exist, consent is "irrebuttably" defined to be absent: p 51.

Rather than adopt this strict division between fact and law, the statutory framework governing vitiation of consent could adopt the middle ground of viewing consent in every case as a "mixed question of law and fact": S Bronitt, "Rape and Lack of Consent" (1992) 16 Crim LJ 289 at 291-292. On this view, the judge should direct the jury as to the factors that are *capable* of vitiating consent, but it is for the jury to determine whether those factors did, in fact, vitiate consent. This "mixed" fact and law approach to consent represents the position in the present common law.

NEGATING CONSENT BY VIOLENCE, THREATS AND FEAR

The English Court of Appeal in *Olugboja* [1982] QB 320 drew a critical distinction (at 332) between submission by force or fraud, and consent; "every consent involves submission, but it by no means follows that a mere submission involves consent", citing Coleridge J in *R v Day* (1841) 9 C & P 722 at 724. Without further elaboration from the judge, the distinction between submission and consent would be difficult for the jury to comprehend. The English Criminal Law Revision Committee concluded that the jury required guidance on the line between submission and consent, and recommended that the types of threats or frauds vitiating consent should be identified by statute: Fifteenth Report, *Sexual Offences* (London: HMSO, 1984), pp 10-11.

Using violence or threats of violence to procure sexual submission cannot result in a consent freely or voluntarily given. The difficulty with coercion, and therefore consent, is that it lies on a continuum. The principles have been summarised by King CJ in *Case Stated by DPP (No 1)* (1993) 66 A Crim R 259 at 265:

The law on the topic of consent is not in doubt. Consent must be a free and voluntary consent. It is not necessary for the victim to struggle or scream. Mere submission in consequence of force or threats is not consent. The relevant time for consent is the time when sexual intercourse occurs. Consent, previously given, may be withdrawn, thereby rendering the act non-consensual. A previous refusal may be reversed thereby rendering the act consensual. That may occur as a consequence of persuasion, but, if it does, the consequent consent must, of course, be free and voluntary and not mere submission to improper persuasion by means of force or threats.

It follows that the use of pressure, not amounting to coercion, will not vitiate consent. It has been said that consent may be "hesitant, reluctant, grudging or tearful, but if she consciously permits it (provided her permission is not obtained by force, threat, fear or fraud) it is not rape": *Holman v The Queen* [1970] WAR 2 at 6 per Jackson CJ. Thus, the use of harassment or emotional pressure to procure consent falls outside the scope of rape or sexual assault. The difficulty in differentiating submission from consent is that some force by the male and reluctance by the female is viewed as a normal and legitimate part of seduction or foreplay: see above, pp 585ff. To deal with this problem, a separate offence of using non-violent threats to procure sexual intercourse has been created in New South Wales: *Crimes Act* 1900 (NSW), s 65A. "Non-violent threat" is defined as "intimidatory or coercive conduct or other threat which does not involve a threat of physical force". The background and scope of this offence is considered below.

There is some uncertainty over the scope of the common law rules governing negation of consent by force, threats and fear, in particular whether vitiation of consent is confined to the application (or threatened application) of *immediate* force; and whether the force or threats may be directed at someone other than the victim.[19] The common law and statutory provisions were reviewed in the Report, *Model Criminal Code: Chapter 5 — Sexual Offences Against the Person* (1999). The MCCOC concluded that the deeming provisions negating consent should be limited to force or threats of force, whether express or implicit: p 47. The MCCOC felt that the comprehensive list of circumstances negating consent adopted in the Australian Capital Territory was inappropriate. Section 92P(1) of the *Crimes Act* 1900 (ACT) provides that the consent of the victim is deemed to be negated if caused by:

- **the infliction (or threatened infliction) of violence or force;**

- **a threat to use extortion, threats of public humiliation or disgrace or physical or mental harassment;**

- **or the abuse of authority over, or professional or other trust in relation to the victim.**

Section 92P(1)(a)-(b) expressly states that the violence or force may be directed at the accused or a third person who is present or nearby. Section 36(b) of the *Crimes Act* 1958 (Vic) similarly states that there is not free agreement where a person submits because of the "fear of harm of *any type* to that

---

19   J Scutt, "Consent Versus Submission: Threats and the Element of Fear in Rape" [1977] 13 *University of Western Australia Law Review* 52; G Syrota, "Rape: When does Fraud Vitiate Consent?" (1995) 25 *Western Australian Law Review* 334.

person or someone else" (emphasis added). Potentially, these provisions could mean that the threat of economic harm, such as the loss of a job or blackmail, could negate free agreement. The MCCOC felt that these non-coercive circumstances should not *automatically* negate consent. However, since the definition of consent was non-exhaustive, it acknowledged (p 51) that fear of economic harm could support a finding that there was no free and voluntary agreement.

Commercial Intrusions into Consent: Unconscionability

Some feminists have argued that the law should recognise a wider range of conduct and situations where consent may be negated. The concepts of fraud, duress and unconscionability used in contract and commercial law have been suggested as models for the law of consent. Jocelynne Scutt in "Consent Versus Submission: Threats and the Element of Fear in Rape" [1977] 13 *University of Western Australia Law Review* 52 developed the argument (at 63-64) that the standard of duress in contract should be applied in determining whether a person's consent to sexual intercourse had been vitiated. More recently, Vicki Waye in "Rape and the Unconscionable Bargain" (1991) 16 Crim LJ 94 proposed that the common law could draw on the equitable doctrine of unconscionability in contract law to provide a new basis for determining whether consent was freely given. Waye envisaged that unconscionability vitiating consent might arise through fraud, emotional abuse or economic blackmail. For criticism of this approach and the danger of overcriminalisation, see S Bronitt, "Rape and Lack of Consent" 16 Crim LJ 289 at 298-300.

There is some doubt as to whether the victim's response to the accused's threats or intimidation must be "reasonable": B Fisse, *Howard's Criminal Law* (5th ed, Sydney: Law Book Company Ltd, 1990), p 183. Arguing that consent should be treated as *exclusively* a question of fact for the jury, Scutt has argued (at 66) strongly against the notion of "reasonable" fear:

> it would seem irrelevant that another person would not have been terrified or her reason overcome, by a threat of a similar nature. What might validly interfere with one person's ability to consent may be of no moment to another. The definition of rape is *not* that it is "sexual intercourse without consent of the reasonable man".

This subjective approach to fear is consistent with the policy of "taking your victims as you find them". Under this approach, the jury must consider as a factual matter whether the nature of the threat and the degree of fear engendered by the accused was sufficient to destroy the person's consent: S Bronitt, "Rape and Lack of Consent" 16 Crim LJ 289 at 292-293.

NEGATING CONSENT BY FRAUD OR MISTAKE

There is similar uncertainty over the effect of fraud and mistakes on consent. The early common law was reluctant to recognise that fraud would vitiate consent. James Fitzjames Stephen, a distinguished English judge and jurist, took the view in his *Digest of the Criminal Law* (3rd ed, London: Macmillan, 1883) that "where consent is obtained by fraud the act does not amount to rape": p 185. The English authorities in the 19th century had been ambivalent as to whether it would be rape to have sexual intercourse by impersonating a married woman's husband. As noted above, the uncertainty was eventually resolved by legislation that stated that intercourse in such circumstances would be "deemed" to be rape.[20]

In cases other than spousal impersonation, the effect of fraud on consent remained unclear until the issue was considered in *R v Clarence* (1888) 22 QBD 23. The case actually concerned consent in the context of offences against the person (assault occasioning actual bodily harm), though the principles have been held to have general application. The accused knowingly infected his wife with gonorrhoea, a fatal disease in the 19th century. He was convicted of inflicting grievous bodily harm and assault occasioning actual bodily harm. The majority of the Court of Crown Cases Reserved quashed the conviction on the ground that the statutory offences of inflicting grievous bodily harm and assault occasioning actual bodily harm did not cover the accused's behaviour; that is, infection of another with a disease through sexual intercourse. Since lack of consent was an essential ingredient for both offences, the court also considered whether the wife's consent had been vitiated by the accused's failure to disclose the infection. In light of his earlier reservations about fraud, Stephen J rejected the simple idea that fraud would vitiate consent in criminal matters (at 43):

> [I]f fraud vitiates consent, every case in which a man infects a woman or commits bigamy ...
> [without informing the woman of his infection or the existence of the first marriage,
> respectively] ... is also a case of rape. Many seductions would be rapes, and so might acts
> of prostitution procured by fraud, as for instance by promises not intended to be fulfilled.

Based on his review of earlier authorities, Stephen J concluded (at 44) that consent would only be vitiated where the fraud related to "the nature of the act itself, or as to the identity of the person who does the act". In this case, the husband could not be guilty of assault, and by implication rape, since the wife's consent was "as full and conscious as consent could be. It was not obtained by any fraud either as to the nature of the act or the identity of the agent": at 44.

Although *Clarence* dealt with vitiation of consent in the context of offences against the person, it is clear that the principles apply equally to rape and sexual assault: *Papadimitropoulos v The Queen* (1957) 98 CLR 249; *R v Mobilio* [1991] 1 VR 339. In *Papadimitropoulos*, the accused fraudulently procured sexual intercourse from a young Greek woman recently arrived in Australia by tricking her into believing that she had gone through a marriage ceremony with him. In fact, the accused had simply given notice of his intention to marry at the Melbourne Registry Office. With this belief she consented to sexual intercourse on their "honeymoon". There was some evidence that the young woman never intended to consent to intercourse outside marriage. The accused deserted her shortly after the honeymoon. The matter was reported to the police, and he was charged and convicted of rape.

The High Court in *Papadimitropoulos* traced the development of the principles governing vitiation of consent. The High Court held (at 261) that consent to sexual penetration requires:

> a perception as to what is about to take place, as to the identity of the man and the
> character of what he is doing. But once the consent is comprehending and actual the
> inducing causes cannot destroy its reality and leave the man guilty of rape.

---

20 *Criminal Law Amendment Act* 1885 (UK), s 4; now see *Sexual Offences Act* 1956 (UK), s 1.

The High Court affirmed the formulation in *Clarence* that the mistake induced by the fraud must relate to the "nature and character of the act". The High Court was not prepared to extend vitiation of consent beyond a mistake relating to "the identity of the physical act and the immediate conditions affecting its nature" (at 261). This qualification provides a control mechanism for the courts. On the facts of *Papadimitropoulos* the mistake made by the young woman was insufficient to destroy consent since it related to an "antecedent inducing cause — the existence of a valid marriage" (at 261). As she had understood the physical act (the act of sexual intercourse), the accused could not be guilty of rape. The High Court recognised that the accused's fraudulent conduct inducing consent, although not amounting to rape, could be punished as another less serious criminal offence, namely, procuring sexual intercourse by fraud or false pretences.[21] It should be noted that the effect of *Papadimitropoulos* has been reversed by statute in New South Wales, which provides that a person who consents to intercourse "under a mistaken belief that the other person is married to the person" is to be taken not to consent to intercourse: *Crimes Act* 1900 (NSW), s 61R(2)(a)(ii).

The members of the High Court in *Papadimitropoulos* emphasised that it was a victim's *mistake* as to the nature and character of the act or identity of the accused rather than the accused's *fraud* that vitiated consent. In their view, the focus on fraud in the earlier cases distracted attention from the essential inquiry, namely "whether the consent is no consent because it is not directed to the nature and character of the act" (at 260).

This subtle shift in emphasis from fraud to mistake is significant. By giving greater weight to the victim's perception of events, it widens the scope of the offence considerably. It means that any error or failure in appreciating the nature and character of the act or identity of the other party may negate consent irrespective of whether the accused's conduct had induced that mistake. This approach has been criticised for focusing the investigation and the trial upon the victim and her state of mind, rather than on the accused's dishonesty in inducing that state of mind. As Jennifer Morgan has observed in "Rape in Medical Treatment: the Patient as Victim" (1991) 18 *Melbourne University Law Review* 403 (at 413), this may have consequences for how the offence of rape is perceived within the community:

> By emphasizing the mistake (made by the woman) rather than the fraud (perpetrated by the man) we have surely lowered the perceived seriousness of the offence. A mistake is a human error, something minor; fraud is a deliberate decision. There are specific statutory offences of inducing sexual intercourse by fraud or false pretences; these are not rape but some lesser offence.

Similar criticism may be levelled at the statutory formulations of consent in New South Wales and Victoria that identify particular mistakes by the victim rather than the accused's fraud as the circumstance where consent is negated (see above). In related common law jurisdictions, such as Canada, the courts have continued to emphasise that the accused's dishonesty and deception are the basis for negating consent to sexual intercourse: *R v Cuerrier* [1998] 2 SCR 371, discussed below, p 618.

---

21 *Crimes Act* 1900 (NSW), s 66; *Criminal Code* (Qld), s 218; *Criminal Law Consolidation Act* (SA), s 64(b); *Criminal Code* (Tas), s 129(b); *Crimes Act* 1958 (Vic), s 129(b); *Criminal Code* (WA), s 192. Rather than enact a separate offence in the Australian Capital Territory, consent is deemed to be negated where it was obtained by "a fraudulent misrepresentation of any fact made by the other person, or by a third person to the knowledge of the other person": *Crimes Act* 1900 (ACT), s 92P(1)(g).

The MCCOC expressed concern about broadening the types of mistake that automatically negate consent: see *Chapter 5 — Sexual Offences Against the Person*, Report (1999). The MCCOC concluded that misunderstandings should be limited to cases where "the person is incapable of understanding the essential nature of the act", or "the person is mistaken about the essential nature of the act": p 38. It rejected that the facts of *Papadimitropoulos automatically* amount to the basic offence of sexual assault, though the jury would be at liberty to consider whether there had been "free and voluntary agreement" on these facts: p 49.

The judicial and legislative reforms of the law of consent have been piecemeal, tackling the symptoms rather than the cause of the problem. The cause of "consent problems" in the present law is that the victim is not required to possess an understanding or appreciation of the *significance* of those acts. To address these shortcomings, some academics have argued that consent to sexual intercourse requires an understanding of the purpose behind the accused's act: G Roberts, "Dr Bolduc's Speculum and the Victorian Rape Provisions" (1984) 8 Crim LJ 296 at 300. In her examination of the decision in *Mobilio*, Morgan has stressed the importance of understanding the *context* of the act: "Rape in Medical Treatment: the Patient as Victim" (1991) 18 *Melbourne University Law Review* 403 at 427.

No matter how the rule for consent is formulated (whether it is said to require an understanding of the significance, purpose or context of the act) the fundamental difficulty is the extent to which the "nature and character of the act" should take into account the wider *moral* dimension of the intercourse. Scutt has forcefully argued that the nature and character of the act has a moral dimension: "Fraud and Consent in Rape: Comprehension of the Nature and Character of the Act and its Moral Implications" (1976) 18 *Criminal Law Quarterly* 312. Drawing inspiration from Canadian authorities, she argued (p 319) that the jury should be invited to consider the moral dimension of the intercourse because

> the moral aspect of sexual activity being as fundamentally important as it is, in terms of our current social and moral values, consent in the moral sense is equally important in any sexual transaction as is consent in the physical sense.

Scutt suggested that the trial judge should direct the jury that it is simply a question of fact whether the mistake as to the moral significance of that act was sufficient to vitiate the victim's consent. This approach raises concerns over the lack of certainty and predictability in fixing the boundaries of rape. It raises the spectre of many forms of sexual dishonesty, such as bigamy and adultery, giving rise to liability for rape. This approach could leave the accused in *Papadimitropoulos* guilty of rape since there was some evidence that the woman would not have consented to intercourse if she had known the truth. The question for the jury would be whether mistake in this case related to the moral significance of the intercourse. There was little evidence directly on this issue. Certainly a person with strong religious beliefs might regard intercourse outside marriage as having a different moral significance from intercourse within marriage. This approach would certainly require extensive examination and cross-examination in the trial as to the significance of the moral beliefs of the victim.

In *Chapter 5: Sexual Offences Against the Person*, Report (1999), the MCCOC did not elaborate further on the types of mistakes that automatically vitiate consent. The list is deliberately narrow. Because the list is non-exhaustive, the jury remains at liberty to decide whether the mistake in the particular case prevented the agreement being "free and voluntary": p 51. There are however a number of problems with this approach. The mistakes included in the list that are deemed to negate consent must relate to the "essential nature of the act": *Model Criminal Code*, cl 5.2.3(2)(d) and (e). Does mistake as to the "essential nature of the act" differ from the common law version of mistake as to the "nature or character" of the act? Undoubtedly, in interpreting this phrase the courts would be required to consider as yet unresolved questions about the legal effect of mistakes as to the moral, social and cultural significance of the sexual act on consent. In relation to mistakes that fall outside the list, do the common law principles governing the effect of mistake in *Papadimitropoulos* apply? Moreover, how will the jury know that they have this residual power to determine the effect of such mistakes without direction from the judge? The MCCOC skirts this issue, leaving "consent problems" to be determined on the facts of the particular case: p 51.

An alternative approach is to require further specification of the types of mistake that *may* vitiate consent and/or to create new offences of sexual dishonesty: S Bronitt, "Rape and Lack of Consent" (1992) 16 Crim LJ 289 at 303. Under both the present law and proposals for reform, the malleability of key legal definitions conceal the moral and political disagreement over the meaning and scope of consent. The jury will be left to resolve the question of rape or sexual assault by reference to the concepts of "free and voluntary agreement" and whether the mistakes related to the "essential nature" of the act. Within these boundaries the offence of rape and sexual autonomy are legally constructed. Without further legislative guidance, there is a danger that judges and juries will draw heavily on discriminatory myths about female sexuality and their own notions of what constitutes "real rape".

CASE STUDIES

Consent: Medical Fraud and Spreading Disease

The concept of "nature and character of the act" has a narrow definition in the common law. This is most apparent from the decision of the Supreme Court of Victoria (Court of Criminal Appeal) in *R v Mobilio* [1991] 1 VR 339. The accused, a radiographer, conducted a series of internal vaginal examinations upon several female patients using ultrasound transducers. These internal scans had no medical value and were done solely for the accused's sexual gratification. He was charged with rape under the extended definition of sexual intercourse in Victoria and convicted.[22] The Court of Criminal Appeal considered whether the victims had consented to intercourse, focusing particularly on directions given on the vitiation of consent. Affirming *Papadimitropoulos v The Queen* (1957) 98 CLR 249, the Court held that to vitiate consent, a person's mistake must relate to the nature and character of the act or identity. Thus, a mere mistake as to the man's purpose would not be sufficient: "it is established in Australia by the High Court that if the woman consented to an act knowing it to be an act of sexual intercourse, no mistake as to the man's purpose deprives her consent

---

22 "Rape" in s 2A of the *Crimes Act* 1958 (Vic) as amended by the *Crimes (Sexual Offences Act)* 1980 includes inter alia the introduction of "(b) an object (not being part of the body) manipulated by a person (whether male of female) into the vagina or anus of another person (whether male or female)" in circumstances where the introduction of the penis would have amounted to rape.

of reality": at 344. Applied to the facts of *Mobilio*, as each patient had understood the nature of the physical act perpetrated upon them (the insertion of the ultrasound transducer into their vagina) their consent had not been vitiated.

The cause of the problem in the present law is the critical distinction between understanding what is being done and why it is being done: B Fisse, *Howard's Criminal Law* (5th ed, Sydney: Law Book Company Ltd, 1990), p 181. The effect of this restrictive interpretation of the nature and character of the act is that the concept of consent in the criminal law is limited to a person's appreciation of what is physically being done to them.[23] In *Mobilio*, the victims were not mistaken about what was physically happening to them. The physical act (the insertion of the ultrasound transducer) would be the same whether the act was done for a medical purpose or for sexual gratification. But clearly the victims were not consenting to interference with their vaginas for the accused's sexual pleasure. The common law has decided that a mistake as to the *significance* of the act is not sufficient to vitiate consent. *Mobilio* is subjected to a detailed discussion and analysis in J Morgan, "Rape in Medical Treatment: the Patient as Victim" (1991) 18 *Melbourne University Law Review* 403.

The effect of *Mobilio* has since been reversed by statute in Victoria in 1991. Section 36(g) of the *Crimes Act* 1958 (Vic) provides that a person does not freely agree to an act in circumstances where that person "mistakenly believes that the act is for medical or hygienic purposes".[24] As a result of concerns about *Mobilio*, the MCCOC has proposed a provision in cl 5.2.3 (see above, p 610) clarifying that a mistaken belief that the act is for a medical or hygienic purpose is an "example" of a mistake about the "essential nature" of the act.

Another controversial consent question concerns the effect of a failure to disclose a sexual disease prior to intercourse. Does a failure to disclose a serious infection (such as HIV) amount to a fraud or mistake vitiating consent, leaving the infected person open to a charge of assault, sexual assault and/or rape? The 19th century decision in *R v Clarence* (1888) 22 QBD 23 appeared to preclude prosecution even where the accused knowingly and dishonestly failed to disclose the infection to his or her sexual partner: S Bronitt, "Spreading Disease and the Criminal Law" (1994) Crim LR 21; see above, p 613. From a regulatory and policy perspective, the criminalisation of disease transmission in the context of otherwise lawful activity raises complex questions about the relationship between public health law and criminal law: S Bronitt, "The Transmission of Life-Threatening Infections: A New Regulatory Strategy" in R Smith (ed), *Health Care, Crime and Regulatory Control* (Sydney: Hawkins Press, 1998).

---

23 It is difficult to reconcile the old consent cases with this distinction. In *R v Flattery* (1877) 2 QBD 410 and *R v Williams* [1923] 1 KB 340 consent was held not to exist because the woman mistakenly believed that penetration was a medical treatment. Although the correctness of these decisions has not been doubted, they can only be reconciled with the distinction made in the present law if we accept that the victims' complete naivety about sex prevented them from comprehending what was physically being done to them.

24 The original amendment to s 36 introduced by the *Crimes (Sexual Offences) Act* 1991 (Vic), provided that consent had no effect "if it was obtained by a false representation that the conduct was for medical or hygienic purposes". The present section follows the approach in *Papadimitropoulos* (focusing on mistakes rather than fraud) and implements the recommendations of the Law Reform Commission of Victoria in *Rape: Reform of Law and Procedure*, Report No 42 (1991).

Concern that culpable instances of transmission of a lethal disease like HIV may not fall within the scope of the ordinary criminal law have led to criticisms of *Clarence* and suggestions that the courts should, through common law development, re-fashion the rules governing fraud and consent: H Power, "Consensual Sex, Disease and the Criminal Law" (1996) 60(4) *Journal of Criminal Law* 412. Clearly, it would be possible for the courts to depart from *Clarence* and to develop the common law in a way which better reflects modern understandings of consent, in particular the importance of disclosure of risks and obtaining an "informed consent". Indeed, this strategy has been recently adopted by the Supreme Court of Canada in *R v Cuerrier* [1998] 2 SCR 371. In this case the accused had unprotected sexual intercourse with two women without informing them that he was HIV-positive. Both complainants consented to unprotected sexual intercourse. However the complainants testified at trial that they would not have consented had they known the accused was HIV-positive. The accused was charged with aggravated assault. The majority concluded (at 127) that consent to sexual intercourse in these cases could amount to a fraud relating to the "nature and character" of the act:

> Without disclosure of HIV status there cannot be a true consent. The consent cannot simply be to have sexual intercourse. Rather it must be consent to have intercourse with a partner who is HIV-positive.

The majority stressed that the accused's failure to disclose his HIV-positive status must: (a) be fraudulent in the sense of dishonesty; and (b) have resulted in deprivation by putting the complainant at a significant risk of suffering serious bodily harm: at 128. Although dealing with the interpretation of the *Criminal Code* (Can), the Supreme Court's discussion and rejection of *Clarence* clearly has implications for the common law rules governing consent.

2.2 FAULT ELEMENTS FOR RAPE AND SEXUAL ASSAULT

The principle of contemporaneity or correspondence suggests that physical and fault elements must be correlated. As "sexual conduct without consent" constitutes the relevant physical conduct for the purpose of rape or sexual assault, the fault element (intention, knowledge or recklessness) must relate to the sexual conduct and the lack of consent. In the majority of cases, there is no controversy over whether the accused intended to have sexual intercourse. As the MCCOC noted, the more controversial issue is whether the accused had the necessary fault with respect to lack of consent: *Model Criminal Code: Chapter 5 — Sexual Offences Against the Person,* Report (1999), p 67.

BELIEF IN CONSENT: THE SUBJECTIVE VERSUS OBJECTIVE APPROACH

The fault element for the common law offence of rape is satisfied by an "intention to have sexual intercourse without consent": *DPP v Morgan* [1976] AC 182. The House of Lords has clarified that this intent will be satisfied by either knowledge that the victim is not consenting or recklessness as to consent. The statutory formulations of rape adopted in the Australian Capital Territory, New South Wales, South Australia and Victoria have followed the common law: *Crimes Act* 1900 (ACT), s 92D; *Crimes Act* 1900 (NSW), s 61R(1); *Criminal Law Consolidation Act* 1935 (SA), s 48(1); *Crimes Act* 1958 (Vic), s 38. By contrast, the Code States of the Northern Territory, Queensland, Tasmania and Western Australia, have been less faithful to the principle of correspondence and "subjective" mental states: *Criminal Code* (NT), s 192(3); *Criminal Code* (Qld), s 347; *Criminal Code* (Tas), s 185; *Criminal Code* (WA), s 324D. In interpreting rape under their respective Codes, the courts have held that the mental state for rape is satisfied by a mere intention to have sexual intercourse and the prosecution is not required to prove knowledge of the victim's lack of consent to intercourse or recklessness as to whether or not the victim was consenting. Rather, the accused may raise mistaken belief in consent as a "defence". As a defence the "belief in consent" must be both honest and reasonable: *R v Daniels* (1989) 1 WAR 435. This defence was explored in Chapter 7: p 341.

The different approaches to the fault element for sexual offences in the Code and common law jurisdictions may be understood in terms of the traditional controversy between "subjective" and "objective" liability. The common law approach demonstrates a high degree of fidelity to the principle of correspondence and the primacy of subjective mental states. In *DPP v Morgan* [1976] AC 182, the House of Lords considered the legal effect of a mistaken belief by an accused that the victim was consenting. Morgan, a senior member of the RAF, invited three junior colleagues home to have sexual intercourse with his wife. On her evidence, she was woken and frog-marched into another room where she was restrained and forced to have sexual intercourse with each of the men. The three younger men were charged with rape and Morgan was charged with aiding and abetting these rapes. The three younger men claimed at trial that Morgan had urged them to ignore any protests or resistance saying his wife was "kinky" and that these protests were merely simulations designed to increase sexual pleasure. The trial judge directed the jury that the accused would not be guilty if they honestly believed that the woman was consenting and that the belief was reasonably held. The majority of the House of Lords held this to be a misdirection. Nevertheless, the House of Lords dismissed the appeal on the ground that had the jury been properly directed, it was unlikely that there would have been a different verdict. The majority affirmed that the jury should have been directed that a man is not guilty of rape where he had sexual intercourse in the mistaken belief, however unreasonable, that the woman was consenting. For further analysis of this decision see Chapter 7, pp 338ff.

The reasoning applied by the majority has been widely criticised. It was heralded by the English press as a "Rapist's Charter", precipitating a major review into the laws governing sexual offences: Jennifer Temkin, *Rape and the Legal Process* (London: Sweet and Maxwell, 1987), pp 79-82. The split decision in *Morgan* (5:3) revealed that there was serious uncertainty about the scope of the existing law and its future direction. Before *Morgan*, it was well established that mistake could be raised as a defence, but only where the mistake was reasonable: "an honest and reasonable belief in the existence of circumstances, which if true, would make the act of the prisoner an innocent act, has always been held to be a good defence": *R v Tolson* (1889) 23 QBD 168 at 181, per Cave J. Indeed, this position at common law had been reflected in the Australian Codes enacted in the 19th century. The majority in *Morgan* held that the *Tolson* defence had no application to these facts. Mistake was not a "defence" for rape, strictly speaking. Rather mistake simply provided an evidential foundation for raising doubt over whether the accused possessed the requisite mental state. In cases of rape, the prosecution had to prove beyond reasonable doubt that the accused believed the other person was not consenting or be reckless as to consent. Since rape required the accused to either know or be reckless as to whether the woman was consenting, as a matter of "inexorable logic", a mistaken belief in consent however unreasonable must negate liability for rape: at 214.

The principle identified in *Morgan* had previously been applied to the offence of rape in South Australia and Victoria without the media and political controversy that ensued in England: *R v Brown* [1975] 10 SASR 139; *R v Flannery* [1969] VR 31; *R v Maes* [1975] VR 541. *Morgan* was subsequently affirmed as a correct statement of the common law in New South Wales in *R v McEwan* [1979] 2 NSWLR 926. Moreover, *Morgan* has been approved by the High Court as a correct statement of law in relation to the effect of mistake for crimes requiring proof of a subjective mental state: *He Kaw Teh v The Queen* (1985) 157 CLR 523 at 592 per Dawson J. By contrast, the equivalent offences of rape and sexual assault in the Code jurisdictions of the Northern Territory, Queensland, Tasmania and Western Australia do *not* require proof of knowledge or recklessness as to the victim's lack of consent. Consequently, the principle in *Morgan* has been held to have no application. In the Code jurisdictions, where the accused's belief in consent is raised as a defence, the *Tolson* principle applies and the mistake must be both honest and reasonable.

The MCCOC in *Model Criminal Code: Chapter 5 — Sexual Offences Against the Person,* Report (1999) (p 73) has summarised the "two positions" in Australia as follows:

▬ *Common law jurisdictions:* **"Did the accused believe that the other person was consenting?"**

▬ *Code jurisdictions:* **"Did the accused believe the other person was consenting. If so, was that belief reasonable?"**

The reasonableness test has been formulated in some Code jurisdictions as a "reasonable person" test. In *Daniels v The Queen* (1989) 1 WAR 435, the Supreme Court of Western Australia (Criminal Court of Appeal) held (at 445) that "whether it was a reasonable mistake depended on whether an ordinary and reasonable man [or woman] would have made it in the circumstances which the jury found to have existed". The reasonable person is presumed to be sober and if the accused has "that belief [in consent] by reason of his [or her] state of intoxication at the time, it does not avail him [or her] if a reasonable man [or woman] would not have been mistaken": at 445.

The principle of correspondence and subjectivism leads to the disconcerting logic that could justify acquittals on the facts of *Morgan*. Some feminists have argued that the principle of subjectivism, while perhaps fundamental, must give way on policy grounds. Adopting this pragmatic approach, Jennifer Temkin in *Rape and the Legal Process* (London: Sweet and Maxwell, 1987) casts the issues surrounding the fault element as follows (p 84):

> The ultimate question which arises in this area of law is whether a commitment to subjectivism should override all other considerations regardless of circumstances or social cost. It is suggested that where a woman demonstrates her lack of consent, it is no hardship for a man to enquire whether her consent is present and that as a matter of policy the law should demand that he do so.

From a more principled standpoint, Celia Wells attacked the common law's fetish for subjectivity in her article "Swatting the Subjectivist Bug" [1982] Crim LR 209. Rather than subjectivism as the default standard for fault, Wells proposed a framework of culpability for rape which encompasses both subjective *and* objective standards.

From a law reform perspective, proposals to reverse *Morgan* have been rejected on the basis that a serious crime, such as rape, should not be made an offence of strict liability or negligence. Such reform would be an exception to the general principle of the criminal law that serious offences require proof of intention or recklessness: see Heilbron Committee, *Report of the Advisory Group on the Law of Rape* (1975); Criminal Law Revision Committee, *Fifteenth Report, Sexual Offences* (1984); Law Reform Commission of Victoria, *Rape: Reform of Law and Procedure*, Report No 43 (1991). Of course, these objections are persuasive only if the idea of "true fault" in the criminal law is conceived in purely "subjective" terms. Both as an explanatory and normative principle, subjective fault in the criminal law has never been the *only* basis for criminal responsibility: see Ch 3. As we shall explore below, there are signs that some judges and law reformers are prepared to adopt an objective fault standard based on culpable inadvertence, where the accused has failed to advert to the question of consent completely.

Merely moving to an objective standard for judging the accused's mistaken belief in consent may not resolve the problems of *Morgan*. Not all feminists have embraced the "reasonable person" as the solution to the appropriate fault standard for rape. Scutt doubts whether the introduction of a reasonableness test would advance the situation for women at all, for the simple reason that "what a *woman* actually believes is reasonable, and what the law has traditionally regarded as reasonable are quite different".[25]

Drawing parallels with the difficulties of an objective standard for the defence of provocation, doubts have been expressed whether the reasonable person could play any significant role in shaping male attitudes toward female sexual autonomy and protecting a woman's right to refuse to engage in sexual activity: S Bronitt, "Rape and Lack of Consent" (1992) 16 Crim LJ 289 at 306. In applying a reasonableness test, the jury must consider whether a "reasonable person" in the position of the accused would have believed the victim was consenting. In those jurisdictions that apply a reasonableness test, juries have been directed to give this hypothetical person the gender of the accused: *Daniels v The Queen* (1989) 1 WAR 435 at 445. The further question arises whether the legal fiction of the reasonable man should be given familiar male stereotypes about female sexuality, for example, that women are masochistic by nature and enjoy being hurt in sexual encounters and that "No means Yes"? If the reasonable person is given the ethnic and cultural background of the accused, misogynous attitudes which are traditional and culturally acceptable could be taken into account.

A reasonableness test that introduced an objective principle of fault for rape may be a retrograde step. The question of the "reasonableness" of the accused's mistaken belief in consent will be inevitably tied in the minds of the jury to the "reasonableness" of the victim's conduct.

---

25 J Scutt, *Women and The Law* (Sydney: Law Book Company Ltd, 1990), p 479. Catharine MacKinnon has doubted whether using subjective or objective perspectives for determining fault makes any significant difference: "Measuring consent from the socially reasonable, meaning objective man's, point of view reproduces the same problem [as measuring consent from the assailant's point of view] under a more elevated label": *Toward A Feminist Theory of the State* (Cambridge Mass: Harvard University Press, 1989), p 181.

This provides considerable scope for the jury to apply its own standards of morality to evaluate the "contributory" behaviour of the victim, including the discriminatory rape myths considered above: pp 603ff. An objective standard would further maintain the legal focus during the trial on the victim's conduct rather than the accused's blameworthy conduct. Basing that standard on the reasonable person used in the civil law of negligence may also downgrade the perceived seriousness of the crime of rape. Indeed, concern that objective standards of fault would weaken perceptions of rape as a serious crime led to its rejection by the MCCOC in *Chapter 5: Sexual Offences Against the Person*, Report (1999), p 75.

RESTRICTING THE MISTAKEN BELIEF IN CONSENT DEFENCE

An alternative compromise approach, that cuts across the "subjective versus objective" debate, is to retain the subjective fault standard but impose some restrictions as to when mistaken belief in consent may be raised by the accused. To some extent, this middle ground is achieved in the present law. The standard *Morgan* direction does this already by encouraging the jury to take a "hard look" at the evidence before accepting a claim of mistaken belief in consent. The first part of the direction instructs the jury of the central importance of a subjective mental state for criminal liability and that, *as a matter of law*, a belief in consent, however unreasonable, must lead to an acquittal. But this direction is then qualified by the further instruction that, *as a matter of evidence*, the less reasonable the mistake is, the less likely it is that the accused actually held that belief. Even Lord Hailsham in *Morgan* recognised that the presence or absence of reasonable grounds for the accused's belief in consent would be relevant evidence in determining the likelihood that the accused honestly believed the woman was consenting: at 214. Several jurisdictions now require judges to give a direction in these terms,[26] and the MCCOC has recommended that in a relevant case a mandatory jury direction in these terms should be given: *Model Criminal Code: Chapter 5 — Sexual Offences against the Person*, Report (1999), s 5.2.43, p 263.

A further judicial qualification often incorporated into the standard direction is the requirement that the accused's mistake must be "honest" or "genuine". This qualification is logically redundant. Lord Edmund-Davies in *Morgan* described "honest" as a "superfluous, but convenient adjective": at 227. A person is either mistaken or is not. A "dishonest mistake" in relation to consent is not a mistake — it is a lie. While simultaneously paying lip-service to individual justice and the central importance of subjective mental states, the judicial stress on honesty and genuine belief in this direction may be viewed as an encouragement for the jury to apply a sceptical eye to claims of mistaken belief in consent. It is an example of raising the judicial eyebrow, or as Alan Norrie might say, an instance of the law "having its subjectivist cake and eating it": *Crime Reason and History* (London: Weidenfeld and Nicolson, 1993), p 52.

A more overt restriction on the accused's mistaken belief in consent was adopted in Canada in 1992. Bill C-49 enacted a statutory definition of consent listing the circumstances where a person is

---

26   See *Criminal Code* (NT), s 194A; *Crimes Act* 1958 (Vic), s 37(c); *Criminal Code* (Can), s 265(4); *Sexual Offences (Amendment) Act* 1976 (UK), s 2(1).

taken not to consent: *Criminal Code* (Can), s 273.1(1). The most significant reform was the modification of the fault element for sexual assault. Although the reforms do not dispense with the subjective fault element, the *Criminal Code* provides that the mistake defence is not available where "the accused did not take reasonable steps in the circumstances known to the accused at the time, to ascertain that the complainant was consenting": s 273.2. The Code also excludes the defence where the accused's mistake arises from self-induced intoxication, recklessness or wilful blindness. This is a dramatic departure from the common law, as expounded in *Morgan*, which had previously been endorsed by the Supreme Court of Canada in *Pappajohn v The Queen* (1980) 52 CCC (2d) 481. It is perhaps premature to make an assessment of the significance and impact of these changes. Orthodox subjectivists will criticise this reform as a violation of their fundamental article of faith which requires proof of a subjective mental state for all serious crimes. Since the Supreme Court of Canada has held that the *Charter of Rights and Freedoms* requires subjective foresight for some serious offences, like murder and theft, this issue has constitutional significance — a Charter challenge to these reforms on this basis may be inevitable: D Stuart, "Sexual Assault: Substantive Issues Before and After Bill C-49" [1993] 35 *Criminal Law Quarterly* 241 at 259. The question remains how the requirement of "reasonable steps" will be interpreted. Clearly, in conjunction with the positive consent standard sketched above based on free agreement, the accused will be placed under a duty to ascertain whether the other person has freely agreed to intercourse. This formulation provides a basis for tackling discriminatory stereotypes about female sexuality, rather than simply condoning them as in *Morgan*.

MULTIPLE MEANINGS OF RECKLESSNESS IN RAPE AND SEXUAL ASSAULT

As a matter of common law, the courts have established that the fault element for rape may be satisfied by either intention or recklessness. This dual approach, exhibiting a preference for subjective mental states, has been incorporated into statutory definitions of rape or sexual assault adopted in the common law jurisdictions.[27] The provisions dealing with rape or carnal knowledge in the Codes, by contrast, make no reference to either knowledge or recklessness. In the Code jurisdictions, liability is strict requiring merely an intention to have sexual intercourse. As a leading textbook on the Code jurisdictions noted, "the question becomes simply: Did the victim consent?": RG Kenny, *An Introduction to Criminal Law in Queensland and Western Australia* (5th ed, Sydney: Butt, 2000), p 248.

But what does recklessness in the context of rape or sexual assault *actually* mean? Significantly, the term recklessness was not employed by Lord Hailsham LC in his summary of the requisite fault for the offence of rape in *DPP v Morgan* [1976] AC 182 (at 215):

> I am content to rest my view of the instant case on the crime of rape by saying that is my
> opinion that the prohibited act is and always has been intercourse without consent of the

---

27 *Crimes Act* 1900 (ACT), s 92P(3); *Crimes Act* 1900 (NSW), s 61R(1); *Criminal Law Consolidation Act* 1935 (SA), s 48; *Crimes Act* 1958 (Vic), s 38.

victim and the mental element is and always has been the intention to commit that act, or the equivalent intention of having intercourse willy-nilly not caring whether the victim consents or no. A failure to prove this involves an acquittal because the intent, an essential ingredient, is lacking. It matters not why it is lacking if only it is not there, and in particular it matters not that the intention is lacking only because of a belief not based on reasonable grounds.

"Not caring whether the victim consents" suggests carelessness or inadvertence as to the possibility that the other person is not consenting suffices for rape. Subsequent English decisions have explained this passage as meaning that to be convicted, the accused must appreciate the risk that the victim is not consenting; it will not suffice that the risk is obvious to the ordinary person: *Satnam and Kewal* (1983) 78 Cr App Rep 149. See Chapter 3 for further discussion of the notion of objective or *Caldwell* recklessness: p 184. This form of subjective recklessness based on the foresight of the possibility that the other person is not consenting has been placed on a statutory footing in some jurisdictions. In Victoria, subjective recklessness for rape has been formulated in plain English, as either awareness that the person is not consenting or that they might not be consenting: *Crimes Act 1957* (Vic), s 36.

In New South Wales, the concept of recklessness has been extended beyond subjective foresight to embrace a state of culpable inadvertence, that is, "not caring" whether the other person consents. The offence of sexual assault defines the fault element in terms of knowledge, but this is defined in another section as including recklessness: a person who is "reckless" as to whether the other person consents to intercourse "is taken to know that the other person does not consent to the sexual intercourse": *Crimes Act* 1900 (NSW), s 61R(1). Since the term recklessness is not further defined in the *Crimes Act*, its meaning and scope for the purpose of sexual offences has needed interpretation by the courts. In *Hemsley* (1988) 36 A Crim R 334 the New South Wales Court of Criminal Appeal considered that the degree of foresight involved in recklessness was based on the possibility rather than probability of non-consent. In *R v Kitchener* (1993) 29 NSWLR 696 the Court of Criminal Appeal held that recklessness, in addition to foresight of the possibility that the other person is not consenting, may include a culpable state of inadvertence.

The latter concept has been further explored and developed in *R v Tolmie* (1995) 37 NSWLR 660. In this case, the accused challenged the correctness of the trial judge's direction on the definition of recklessness on the grounds that the direction had embraced a state of inadvertence. Kirby P reviewed the law of recklessness in the context of sexual offences. Both the majority and minority speeches in *Morgan v DPP* [1976] AC 182 had viewed the fault element for rape being satisfied by:

- "at least indifference to the woman's consent" (at 203, per Lord Cross); or

- by acting "recklessly, without caring whether or not she was a consenting party" (at 225, per Lord Edmund-Davis); or

- by "having intercourse willy-nilly, not caring whether the victim consents or no" (at 215, per Lord Hailsham).

Kirby P concluded that these dicta supported an objective aspect to recklessness based on inadvertence. He was careful to reconcile this concept with the decision in *Morgan,* noting that this concept of recklessness did not prevent an accused relying on a *positive* mistaken (albeit unreasonable) belief in consent: "In this sense if amounting to an inadvertent test, recklessness is limited to cases in which the accused did not consider the question of consent *at all*" (at 668, emphasis added). In other words, the objective aspect of recklessness was not a standard of negligence based on the reasonable person standard, but rather a *negative* state of mind based on a complete failure to consider the autonomy interests of the other person. As Kirby P acknowledges, such cases would be rare. He could only point to examples given by Carruthers J in *Kitchener,* where the inadvertence had been caused through intoxication or lack of intellect: at 669. However, he accepted that "at least theoretically" such inadvertence could found recklessness in law.

The accused's inadvertence to the other person's autonomy could in these circumstances provide the moral basis for legal culpability (at 671):

> In the context of sexual activity the difference between someone who is put on conscious notice or who is forced by circumstances to actually consider the issue of consent of a sexual partner, is likely to be where that person is more sensitive to the other's autonomy, dignity and value. The criminal law, at least in respect of conduct as seriously invasive as sexual intercourse, should not fall more heavily on those who exhibit some attention to the rights of others while exculping those who are so insensitive to the rights of others that they do not consider their wishes in respect of sexual intercourse although they are necessarily relevant and important in the process of initiation and continuation of sexual intercourse.

Kirby P later concluded (at 672):

> To allow accused persons to escape conviction merely because they do not realise the significance of what they have done, where they have completely ignored the requirement of consent as a prerequisite for sexual interaction, is completely antithetical to the attainment of the goals which the criminal law properly sets for itself in this area.

The definition applied here has been applied to recklessness for the purpose of indecent assault: *Fitzgerald v Kennard* (1995) 38 NSWLR 184.

While transcending the sterility of the subjective versus objective debate, the test of inadvertent recklessness is not without difficulties. First, the test requires proof that the accused failed *completely* to advert to the issue of consent. This excludes the situation where the accused has sexual intercourse believing in dangerous rape myths such as "no means yes" or that some "rough handling" is a legitimate means of persuasion or overcoming resistance. These states of mind demonstrate little or no respect for the other person's sexual autonomy, though it would not be possible to say that these are cases of total inadvertence to the other person's consent. Such individuals merely live their sexual lives according to a set of dangerous mythologies about female sexuality and the types of behaviour that signify consent.

Another difficulty with this extended definition of recklessness is that inadvertence to the issue of consent must also be shared by the reasonable or ordinary person. Kirby P traced the emergence of objective notions of recklessness in *R v Caldwell* [1982] AC 341, where the English courts, resorting to the "ordinary meaning" of the concept, embraced as a specie of reckless inadvertence to risks that would be "obvious" to the reasonable or ordinary person. The concept of inadvertent recklessness in *Tolmie* attempts to avoid the worst aspects of the objective standards. The ordinary person is presumed to have the accused's mental capacity. For the purpose of sexual assault, recklessness was defined in the following terms (at 672):

> where the accused has not considered the question of consent and a risk that the complainant was not consenting to sexual intercourse would have been obvious to someone with the accused's mental capacity if they had had turned their mind to it.

The MCCOC has recommended that the fault element for sexual assault and indecency offences should include a definition of recklessness that includes "not giving any thought to whether or not the other person is consenting": *Chapter 5 — Sexual Offences against the Person,* Report (1999), s 5.2.6(3) (p 88). Like *Tolmie*, the provision preserves the positive mistaken belief in consent, and therefore is susceptible to the objections outlined above. Sharing the sentiments expressed by Kirby P above, the Committee concluded that it would be "absurd" not to criminalise the person "who is absolutely uncaring" about the other person's sexual wishes and desires.

In many respects, the interminable controversy over subjective *versus* objective guilt has hijacked debates over rape law reform. It has consumed a disproportionate amount of both academic and political attention. This focus on fault and mistake may be unjustified since there is empirical research suggesting that the dangers of acquittals from applying *Morgan* logic are over-estimated. The Victorian Law Reform Commission conducted a comprehensive study of rape trials in 1989 (the "DPP Study") that considered the impact of *Morgan: Rape: Reform of Law and Procedure*, Interim Report No 42; Report No 43 (1991), App 3. The study showed that in most rape cases the battle between the prosecution and defence centred on the issue of consent rather than the effect of mistake on the fault element: D Brereton, "Real Rape, Law Reform and the Role of Research: The Evolution of the *Victorian Crimes (Rape) Act* 1991" (1994) 27 *Australian and New Zealand Journal of Criminology* 74. It also suggested that mistaken belief in consent was not an attractive strategy for those accused of rape (it was raised in only 23% of cases), and that compared with other lines of defence is least likely to result in an acquittal.

The reason that the *Morgan* principle is not a "Rapists' Charter" may be related to the effect of ambivalent jury directions on the effect of an mistaken belief in consent: see above, p 622. The DPP study convinced the Victorian Law Reform Commission to reject calls for the statutory repeal of *Morgan*. The Law Reform Commission data has been supported by a recent study published by the Department of Justice, *Evaluation of the Crimes (Rape) Act 1991* (1997). The researchers, Melanie Heenan and Helen McKelvie, reviewed 27 jury directions offered in rape trials. Most of the directions involved cases where the primary issue in the trial was consent (37%), the accused's belief in consent (7.4%), or a combination of consent and belief in consent (25.9%): p 296.

PERSPECTIVES

Empirical Data on Consent:
An Illuminating or Misleading Use of Facts?

Jeremy Gans in "Rape Trial Studies: Handle with Care" (1997) 30 *Australian and New Zealand Journal of Criminology* 27 raises some objections to the academic and political uses of the data produced by the Victorian Law Reform Commission's DPP study. He points out that the research did not reveal how the subjective test had an impact on pre-trial decision-making or how the directions on belief in consent (which were often given where there was no real issue of mistake raised on the facts) had an impact on the jury. He also raises concern about the researcher's categorisation of directions, in particular the conceptual difficulty in separating defence claims of "consent" from "belief in consent": pp 31-33. In many cases, such claims will amount to the same thing. Immediately after this article, David Brereton, one of the principal researchers involved, replied to Gans' critique of the Director of Public Prosecutions' study. Accepting the limitations of the empirical research undertaken, he welcomed the "Rolls Royce" research project that involved interviewing police, prosecutors and jurors. While this approach *might* have yielded further insight on the practical effect of the law, it did not detract from the methodological soundness and reliability of the research undertaken. Brereton concludes that Gans' paper is "long on criticism and short on either data or practical suggestions about how researchers might go about gathering that data": p 39.

Empirical research has a valuable role to play in highlighting *real* as opposed to perceived problems with rape law. Law reform must broaden its methodological horizons beyond merely doctrinal and philosophical perspectives. Indeed, the rape trial studies in Victoria and New South Wales have demonstrated the limitations of law reform that is addressed solely to the structure and content of legal rules. The failure of substantive and evidential reforms to challenge judicial practices, especially the informal working definitions of consent and complainant credibility, has led to the adoption of mandatory jury directions.

A different, more communicative model of sexuality will not be promoted through merely changing the substantive definition of "consent" to "free and voluntary agreement". The reform of sexual offences must aim to educate judges, juries and the community about the range of interests and values relevant to sexual integrity. Lacey's idea of sexual integrity extends beyond the traditional legal idea of "*individual* autonomy as bodily property" to a "relational and embodied autonomy" based on values such as communication, trust, mutual respect, care, pleasure and so on: *Unspeakable Subjects* (Oxford: Hart Publishing, 1998), p 121. While the English law remains trapped in the traditional penetrative/coercive model of sexuality, in Australia and Canada the courts and legislature have begun this task of normative reconstruction, taking their tentative first steps toward a new vision of sexual integrity in the criminal law.

2.3 RAPE LAW REFORM: ACCOMPLISHMENT AND COMPROMISE

Gail Mason has suggested that the history of rape law reform in Australia may be characterised in terms of accomplishment and compromise: "Reforming the Law of Rape: Incursion into the Masculinist Sanctum" in D Kirkby (ed), *Sex, Power and Justice: Historical Perspectives on Law in Australia* (Melbourne: Oxford University Press, 1995), p 50. The reform process began only 30 years ago, with the legislative move to replace rape under the common law with "sexual assault" in New South Wales. This legislative innovation, reflecting feminist scholarship of that time, sought to reconceptualise rape as an act of violence rather than as sex: S Brownmiller, *Against Our Will: Men, Women and Rape* (Harmondsworth: Penguin Books, 1975). As previously noted, these early statutory reforms replaced the single common law offence of rape with a graded scheme of sexual assault and aggravated sexual assault crimes.

Feminist legal scholarship has played a significant role in highlighting the inadequacies and discriminatory nature of substantive laws and procedures dealing with sexual offences. See, for example, the influential monograph by Temkin, *Rape and the Legal Process* (London: Sweet & Maxwell, 1987). The treatment of rape victims during cross-examination by the defence acquired considerable notoriety as a form of re-victimisation by the legal process. This led to the enactment of protective "rape shield laws" in many jurisdictions. The legal process, rather than directing attention towards the accused's conduct, focused disproportionately on the conduct and character of the complainant. The substantive law reinforced this victimisation in a number of ways. As the prosecution bears the burden of proving lack of consent, the complainant's state of mind before and during sexual intercourse is a central concern of the trial. Moreover, the rules governing consent and the fault element operate to entrench and legitimate dangerous stereotypes about female sexuality, such as "no means yes" and that women are sexually masochistic. These discriminatory aspects of the law have only begun to be addressed by reformers, for example, through the adoption of mandatory directions on consent enacted in Victoria: see above, pp 604ff.

Feminist reformers have achieved some success in removing the most glaring examples of gender discrimination such as marital rape immunity: see above, pp 599ff. The common law immunity from prosecution for husbands who raped their wives has been removed by legislation in all Australian jurisdictions. However, it remained part of the common law until formally abolished by the House of Lords and High Court: *R v R* [1992] 1 AC 599 and *R v L* (1992) 174 CLR 379 respectively.

Numerous official reports and studies examining the offences of rape and sexual assault have identified the need for the reform of substantive and procedural laws dealing with rape.[28] Although many changes to the law have occurred over the past 20 years, recent empirical studies of rape trials conducted in New South Wales and Victoria reveal that these reforms have not been completely

---

28 Victorian Law Reform Commission, *Rape: Reform of Law and Procedure,* Report No 43 (1991); J Bargen and E Fishwick, *Sexual Assault Law Reform: A National Perspective* (Sydney: Office of the Status of Women, 1995); Model Criminal Code Officers Committee, *Model Criminal Code: Chapter 5 — Sexual Offences Against the Person,* Report (1999).

effective: Department of Women (NSW), *Heroines of Fortitude* (1996); Department of Justice (Vic*)*, *Rape Law Reform Evaluation Project — The Crimes (Rape) Act 1991* (1997), Ch 1, 2.2.

The reason for the failure of rape law reform is complex and multi-layered: P Easteal (ed), *Balancing the Scales: Rape, Law Reform and Australian Culture* (Sydney: Federation Press, 1998), p 1. Evidential and procedural reforms can be subverted by a legal culture where judges and lawyers continue to discredit women who allege sexual abuse. The rationale and attempted reforms of the "special" rules governing sexual offences trials are considered in the next section. At the broader level, legislative reforms have been qualified by the courts which have jealously upheld competing values in the criminal justice system, such as the right to a fair trial. When feminist reforms are considered to undermine the right of the accused to a fair trial, the former necessarily gives way to the latter. In Chapter 2 (pp 104ff), we explored how feminists have challenged traditional (masculinist) notions of "fairness" that have excluded the interests of women as "victims" and members of the community demanding the protection of the criminal law.

According to Gail Mason the difficulty is that most rape law reform, while inspired by feminism, is "grounded in liberalism": "Reforming the Law of Rape: Incursion into the Masculinist Sanctum" in D Kirkby (ed), *Sex, Power and Justice: Historical Perspectives on Law in Australia* (Melbourne: Oxford University Press, 1995), p 52. Feminists who remain optimistic about the value of using legal strategies for promoting social change must divide their attention between a macro-analysis of general principles, such as fairness, equality and privacy, and a micro-analysis of the specific legal rules, such as the rules of evidence and procedure and the substantive definitions of consent and fault. Reform of sexual offences should not be limited to merely restructuring legal definitions. Although such changes may be symbolically important, there is a danger that substantive restructuring merely frees the trial judge to apply discriminatory myths and misconceptions about female sexuality to the remodelled definitions of consent, relevance and credibility. Behind such "ordinary" meanings, myths and misconceptions can be reinforced by the trial judge and accepted by the jury without challenge: S Bronitt, "The Rules of Recent Complaint" in P Easteal (ed), *Balancing the Scales* (Sydney: Federation Press, 1998), pp 42-43.

There is increasing awareness that an integrated or holistic approach to reform is required. Substantive definitions of sexual offences must be understood within their wider procedural and evidential context. In *Chapter 5: Sexual Offences against the Person*, Report (1999) the MCCOC took the view that evidential provisions with regard to sexual offences were "inextricably bound up with the reform of the substantive law": p 215. Indeed, the common law rules governing mistaken belief in consent (which allow the defence to rely on dangerous myths about female sexuality) have a direct impact on the notion of legal relevance. Within this definitional framework, it would be unfair to deny the admissibility of evidence of the complainant's sexual past with the accused or other men if this may legitimately be relevant to a "defence" based on an honest, albeit unreasonable, mistaken belief in consent: *DPP v Morgan* [1976] AC 182. The recent empirical studies of rape laws in Australia, as discussed above, highlight the importance of legal culture in the reform process, and suggest that greater attention must be paid to non-legal strategies such as legal education and gender awareness training for judges and lawyers.

PERSPECTIVES

Special Procedural and Evidential Rules for Sexual Offences

In many respects, the procedural and evidential rules governing sexual offence trials are "exceptional". Special rules, both common law and statutory, have been developed to regulate criminal trials involving sexual allegations: Model Criminal Code Officers Committee, *Chapter 5: Sexual Offences Against the Person,* Report (1999), pp 215-288. Most of these rules share a central concern about the credibility (truthfulness) of complainants in sexual offences trials.

The importance of the complainant's reputation in evaluating an allegation of rape was apparent in the early substantive law. The law of rape did not aim to protect female sexual autonomy, but rather provided a remedy for the fathers and husbands of respectable women who had been devalued in social and economic terms: J Carter, *Rape in Medieval England: An Historical and Sociological Study* (Lanham: University Press of America, Lanham, 1985), Ch 6. Blackstone could proudly proclaim in 1769 that even "common prostitutes" were protected under the laws of England, though he knew that reputation and prior sexual experience of the complainant were crucial factors in a successful prosecution: *Commentaries on the Laws of England* (Oxford: Clarendon Press, 1769), Vol IV, p 213. Rape trials were transformed into pornographic morality plays in which the sexual experience and morals of the complainant were intricately scrutinised by the lawyers and judges for the benefit of the jury and the prurient interest of the public: A Clarke, *Women's Silence, Men's Violence: Sexual Assault in England 1770-1845* (London: Pandora, 1987), p 54. In the context of rape trials in 19th century Australia, Jill Bavin-Mizzi suggests that the declining conviction rate over that century was not due to the reluctance of juries to condemn men to death for mere sexual transgression, but rather to the increasing legal attention being paid to the issue of "bad character" of the complainant: "Understandings of Justice: Australian Rape and Carnal Knowledge Cases 1876-1924" in D Kirkby (ed), *Sex, Power and Justice: Historical Perspectives on Law in Australia* (Melbourne: Oxford University Press, 1995), Ch 2, p 21.

Sexual offences trials, then as now, fixate to an unusual degree on the moral character of the complainant. Respectable women who had physically resisted their attackers and promptly complained of their abuse may seek the protection of the criminal law. This standard of behaviour continues to shape assumptions in the modern law governing the admissibility of "recent complaint" and the warnings that should be given where the complaint is delayed: S Bronitt, "The Rules of Recent Complaint: Rape Myths and the Legal Construction of the 'Reasonable' Rape Victim" in P Easteal (ed), *Balancing the Scales* (Sydney: Federation Press, 1998), Ch 4. Evidence of the complainant's sexual reputation, although strictly hearsay, was admitted as relevant to the issues of consent and/or credibility. Concerns about female fabrication and fantasy in sexual matters were reflected in the customary warnings to juries about the dangers of relying on the complainant's testimony in the absence of corroboration. Although often traced to 17th and 18th century Institutional writers, such as Hale and Blackstone, corroboration warnings only became formalised as a mandatory warning in sexual trials toward the end of 19th century and the early 20th century: see generally Law Commission of England and Wales, *Criminal Law: Corroboration of Evidence in Criminal Trials,* Report No 202 (London: HMSO, 1991). The judicial "experience" from which these corroboration warnings grew was bolstered by psycho-analysis, in particular, Sigmund Freud's famous recantation made in 1897 that female claims of "seduction" in childhood were not actual instances of sexual abuse, but rather were inventions of hysterical women: J Astbury, *Crazy For You: The Making of Women's Madness* (Oxford: Oxford University Press, 1996).

Since the 1970s, rape law reform in Australia has targeted these discriminatory rules of evidence and procedure. The mandatory duty to offer a corroboration warning in sexual offences cases has been abolished in Australian jurisdictions. However, these reforms do not prevent the judge from commenting on the reliability of particular testimony. As the High Court noted in *Longman v The Queen* (1989) 168 CLR 79, a corroboration warning tailored to the facts of the case may be needed to avoid a miscarriage of justice. In this case, a warning was required because of the significant delays in bringing the complaints, the risk of sexual fantasy and the possibility of hatred as a motive to lie. The MCCOC regarded that any further restriction on the judge's right to comment on the reliability of a particular complainant would be an unacceptable restriction on judicial discretion: *Model Criminal Code: Chapter 5 — Sexual Offences Against the Person,* Report (1999), p 251. See also Law Commission, *Criminal Law: Corroboration of Evidence in Criminal Trials*, Report No 202 (1991), pp 15-16. It seems that the solution lies not with increasingly prescriptive legal rules, but rather with judicial education to dispel the myths and stereotypes surrounding the nature of the offence and the "reasonable" behaviour of rape victims.

"Rape shields" were enacted to restrict the admission of evidence of the complainant's sexual reputation and sexual history in an effort to protect complainants from further victimisation by the legal process. In most jurisdictions, the shield is a structured discretion to exclude evidence in certain circumstances. The strongest shield contains no discretion, simply prohibiting admission of reputation and sexual history unless certain exceptions apply: eg *Crimes Act* 1900 (NSW), s 409B. However, empirical research in New South Wales, Tasmania and Victoria suggests that the rape shields have not significantly improved the treatment of women during cross-examination: T Henning and S Bronitt, "Rape Victims on Trial: Regulating the Use and Abuse of Sexual History Evidence" in P Easteal (ed), *Balancing the Scales* (Sydney: Federation Press, 1998), Ch 6. In some instances, trial judges admitted evidence of sexual reputation and previous sexual history with scant regard to the statutory restriction or the "relevance" of the evidence to the issues in dispute in the case. In other cases, the trial judge, mindful of the overriding duty to ensure a "fair trial", has given the provision a more restrictive interpretation than the drafters intended: see for example *Bull v The Queen* [2000] HCA 24 (11 May 2000). As Therese Henning and Simon Bronitt conclude, the failure of the rape shield laws is a combination of deficient legislation and non-compliance and resistance within the legal profession: p 93. Judges often strive for a "balanced" position between the feminist objectives of the reform and the overriding right of the accused to a fair trial. As noted in Chapter 2, from a feminist perspective, this traditional balance may be structurally flawed when the concept of fairness is constructed in a manner that denies or minimises the legitimate interests of women as victims, witnesses and members of the community.

3. SEXUAL OFFENCES INVOLVING CHILDREN AND PERSONS WITH MENTAL IMPAIRMENT

Gayle Rubin, "Thinking Sex: Notes for a Radical Theory of the Politics of Sexuality" in C Vance (ed), *Pleasure and Danger* (London: Pandora, 1989), p 270

> For over a century, no tactic for stirring up erotic hysteria has been as reliable as the appeal to protect children. The current wave of erotic terror has reached deepest into those areas bordered in some way, if only symbolically, by the sexuality of the young.

3.1 SEXUAL OFFENCES INVOLVING CHILDREN

For the purpose of determining consent, the criminal law does not contain an "age of consent" as such. Rather, specific offences impose restrictions on certain types of sexual conduct depending on the age of the parties. Where the victim is below a certain age, proof of consent is no longer a defence. However, the criminal law is not consistent in its approach to sexual maturity. As Rubin points out, the laws governing sexual conduct have been shaped in response to successive moral panics about white sex slavery in the 1880s, the anti-homosexual campaigns of the 1950s and child pornography in the 1970s: p 296. At the turn of this century, Australian sex laws are being further reshaped by moral panics about the spread of HIV/AIDS, organised (homosexual) paedophile rings, pornography on the internet and sexual trafficking.

The criminalisation of sex with children first became a "law and order" issue in the 19th century. Statutory offences of carnal knowledge were enacted in all Australian jurisdictions to protect young girls from sexual exploitation. These laws dispensed with the need to prove lack of consent. The effect of these crimes of "statutory rape" was that the age for consensual sexual activity was set differently in different Australian colonies at different times: J Bavin-Mizzi, "Understandings of Justice: Australian Rape and Carnal Knowledge Cases, 1876-1924" in D Kirkby (ed), *Sex, Power and Justice* (Melbourne: Oxford University Press, 1995), Ch 2. The political impetus for these new laws was "agitation by women's groups and political liberals": p 20. Further offences of maintaining sexual relationships with minors were later added in some jurisdictions.

Interestingly, incest has never been an offence at common law, though the ecclesiastical courts exercised some jurisdiction over sex between family members because of the religious prohibition on consanguinity in relation to marriage and procreation. The criminalisation of incest by statute in the 19th century occurred as a result of the efforts of Victorian moral reformers. Reform of incest laws is discussed below at p 637. Table 2 sets out the current law relating to incest in the Australian jurisdictions.

TABLE 2:
Incest Offences in Australia

JURISDICTION AND RELEVANT LAW	OFFENCE	FAULT ELEMENTS	PENALTY
Crimes Act 1900 (ACT)	incest s 92L(3)	knowledge that related 16 years or older	10 years
	s 92L(2)	under 16 years	15 years
	s 92L(1)	under 10 years	20 years
Crimes Act 1900 (NSW)	incest s 78A	male has carnal knowledge of female relative over age of 16 years	7 years
	attempted incest s 78B	attempt by male to commit incest	2 years
Criminal Code (NT)	incest s 134	knowledge that related by male with female	12 years
	incest s 135	knowledge that related by adult female with male	7 years
Criminal Code (Qld)	incest s 222	knowledge that related	10 years
Criminal Law Consolidation Act 1935 (SA)	incest s 72	not specified	7 years
Criminal Code (Tas)	incest s 133(1)	knowledge that related	7 years
	permitting incest s 133(2)	16 years or older permits sexual inter- course with a relation knowledge that related	7 years
Crimes Act 1958 (Vic)	incest s 44	knowledge that related (presumption in section)	25 years
	s 44(1), (2)	under 18 years	
	s 44(3), (4)	if 18 years or older	5 years

Table 2 continued

JURISDICTION AND RELEVANT LAW	OFFENCE	FAULT ELEMENTS	PENALTY
Criminal Code (WA)	incest s 329	knowledge that related (statutory presumption)	
		18 years or older	3 years
		sexual penetration or procuring sexual behaviour with child:	
		if under 16 years	20 years
		if over 16 years	10 years
		indecent dealing or procuring indecent dealing with child:	
		if under 16 years	10 years
		if over 16 years	5 years

Homosexual or "unnatural offences" similarly dispensed with the requirement of lack of consent. Although "unnatural" intercourse was policed under the capital offence of buggery, the "male homosexual", as a distinct criminal identity, became one target of special laws in the late 19th century. Victorian concerns about homosexuality, in particular fears about the corruption of youth, led to the introduction of statutory offences of indecency between males: see below, pp 640ff. These distinct "homosexual" offences were aggravated where the victim was a minor, or where the accused exercised authority over the child as a teacher, father or stepfather: eg *Crimes Act* 1900 (NSW), s 78N.

Over the past 20 years, many jurisdictions have abolished or reformed these homosexual offences in order to decriminalise homosexual conduct between adults in private. In many jurisdictions, these reforms created different "ages of consent" for homosexual and heterosexual conduct. The MCCOC in *Chapter 5: Sexual Offences against the Person,* Report (1999), has summarised the state of the law on age of consent as follows (p 119):

> Australian jurisdictions currently have widely divergent ages of consent. Often, there are different ages of consent within a jurisdiction as well, based upon gender or sexuality or some other factor.

The MCCOC had some difficulty reconciling the divergent positions, noting that public consultation revealed that many respondents "had very little idea about what the age of consent was in their own State or Territory, let alone anywhere else": p 123.

Rubin noted that the "amount of law devoted to protecting young people from premature exposure to sexuality is breathtaking": "Thinking Sex: Notes for a Radical Theory of the Politics of Sexuality" in C Vance (ed), *Pleasure and Danger* (London: Pandora, 1989), p 290. The list below summarises the laws governing the ages below which it is unlawful to engage in sexual conduct in Australia. Sexual conduct in this context is defined narrowly and excludes the laws governing the age for accessing restricted classified material (pornography) or restricted premises (sex shops) or participating in the sex industry lawfully (prostitution).

▬ *AUSTRALIAN CAPITAL TERRITORY:* sexual intercourse or the maintenance of a sexual relationship with a person under the age of 16 years is illegal, but the provisions do not distinguish between heterosexual or homosexual activity: *Crimes Act* 1900 (ACT), ss 2E(2), 92EA(2).

▬ *NEW SOUTH WALES:* homosexual intercourse, including anal penetration and fellatio, with a male under the age of 18 years is an offence: *Crimes Act* 1900 (NSW), s 78K. It is an offence to engage in an act of gross indecency committed with a male person under the age of 18 years: s 78Q. However, heterosexual intercourse and acts of indecency are only unlawful if committed with a child under the age of 16: ss 66C(1) and 61N respectively.

▬ *NORTHERN TERRITORY:* it is an offence for a male to have carnal knowledge of a male under 18 years, or to commit an act of gross indecency with a male who is not an adult: *Criminal Code* (NT), s 128(1) (a), (b). However, carnal knowledge or gross indecency involving a female is only an offence if she is under 16 years old: s 133.

▬ *QUEENSLAND:* carnal knowledge by anal intercourse of any person not an adult is unlawful: *Criminal Code* (WA), s 208(1). "Adult" is defined as a person of or above 18 years of age: s 1. In contrast, carnal knowledge of a girl is only unlawful where she is under 16 years of age: s 215(1).

▬ *SOUTH AUSTRALIA:* the age of legality for sexual activity is the same for both homosexual and heterosexual sex. Sexual intercourse is only an offence with a person under the age of 17 years: *Criminal Law Consolidation Act* 1935 (SA), s 49(3). Sexual intercourse is defined to include both heterosexual and homosexual activity: s 5.

▬ *TASMANIA:* heterosexual sexual intercourse is only unlawful with a person under the age of 17 years: *Criminal Code* (Tas), s 124. "Sexual intercourse" is defined as including anal penetration: s 1. Note that sexual intercourse "against the order of nature" contrary to s 122 of the *Criminal Code* (Tas) was only recently repealed by s 4 of the *Criminal Code Amendment Act* 1997 [No 12 of 1997].

▬ *VICTORIA:* uniform age of consent for both anal and vaginal sexual penetration, set at 16 years, and the provision does not distinguish between heterosexual and homosexual activity: *Crimes Act* 1958 (Vic), s 46(1).

▬ *WESTERN AUSTRALIA:* sexual penetration of a child under the age of 16 is an offence: *Criminal Code* (WA), s 321. A male adult who penetrates a juvenile male (between the age of 16 and 21 years) or who allows a juvenile male to penetrate him is guilty of a crime: s 322A. It is in Western Australia that the distinction between the age of consent for heterosexual and homosexual activity is the greatest.

Not surprisingly, the MCCOC strongly favoured a uniform approach to the age of consent. But what age should this be? The MCCOC noted that the Australian Capital Territory, South Australia and Victoria had adopted a consistent age below which both homosexual and heterosexual intercourse is an offence. This was 17-years-old in South Australia and 16-years-old in Victoria and the Australian Capital Territory.[29] By contrast, New South Wales, the Northern Territory, Queensland and Western

---

29   See *Criminal Law Consolidation Act* 1935 (SA), s 49(3); *Crimes Act* 1958 (Vic), s 46(1); *Crimes Act* 1900 (ACT), s 92E(2).

Australia had all adopted different ages of consent for homosexual and heterosexual conduct. New South Wales, the Northern Territory and Queensland limited lawful homosexual sex to adult males,[30] while sexual intercourse with a girl was only an offence if she was under the age of 16.[31] In Western Australia, anal penetration of a male under the age of 21 remains an offence under s 322A, while sexual penetration of a child is only unlawful if the child is under the age of 16: *Criminal Code Act 1913* (WA), s 321.

The legislative power to enact laws interfering with sexual conduct in private is circumscribed by the *Human Rights (Sexual Conduct) Act* 1994 (Cth). The Federal legislation renders inoperative any State or Territory law that constitutes an arbitrary interference with sexual conduct between adults in private: s 4. The legislation was considered necessary following a decision of the Human Rights Committee that Tasmanian offences criminalising intercourse "against the order of nature" and gross indecency between males violated the right to privacy under the *International Covenant on Civil and Political Rights* 1966. The litigation led to the Commonwealth intervention, and the creation of a right to privacy in relation to sexual conduct between adults in private. "Adult" is specifically defined as a person over the age of 18 years. As the law renders inoperative any inconsistent law, there is some doubt whether the Western Australian laws that limit lawful homosexual conduct to males under the age of 21 years would survive a challenge before the High Court: *Criminal Code Act* 1913 (WA), s 322A. The background and scope of the federal sexual privacy law has been explored in Chapter 2: pp 141ff.

The MCCOC found this area of law highly unsatisfactory. Its proposal for a "uniform" age of consent throughout Australia diverged from an earlier recommendation against the creation of separate homosexual offences: *Chapter 5 — Sexual Offences Against the Person,* Report (1999), p 19. It followed therefore that the age of consent should apply to male and females regardless of the nature of the sexual contact, whether it be "straight, male homosexual or lesbian": p 123. As for the precise age of consent the MCCOC made no firm recommendations, no doubt mindful of the political implications of lowering the homosexual act of consent. The tenor of the Report suggests that it favoured, without actually recommending, that the uniform age of consent should be either 16 or 17 years of age. It should be noted that the MCCOC proposed that the age of consent should be higher (by two years) in cases where the sexual penetration, indecent touching or indecent act involving a young person has been perpetrated by a person in a position of authority, that is, a teacher, parent, step-parent, foster parent, guardian, custodian, religious instructor, counsellor, health profession or a police or prison officer: *Model Criminal Code*, s 5.2.21. In these cases, consent would not be a defence: *Model Criminal Code*, s 5.2.25.

The trend in the modern criminal law, reflected in these proposals for reform, is to adopt a "neutral" stance between homosexual and heterosexual sex offenders. Indeed, the MCCOC has proposed that no special homosexual offences should be included in the Code: p 19.

By contrast, in relation to incest, a substantive distinction is drawn between sexual abuse within and outside the family. Although incest was an ecclesiastical crime in England, it was not recognised as a felony or misdemeanour under the common law. Following the lead from England,

---

30 See *Crimes Act* 1900 (NSW), s 78K; *Criminal Code* 1983 (NT), s 128; *Criminal Code* 1899 (Qld), s 208(1).

31 See *Crimes Act* 1900 (NSW), s 66C(1); *Criminal Code* 1983 (NT), s 129; *Criminal Code* 1899 (Qld), s 215(1).

incest was criminalised by statute in all Australian States between 1876 and 1924: J Bavin-Mizzi, "Understandings of Justice: Australian Rape and Carnal Knowledge Cases 1876-1924" in D Kirkby (ed), *Sex, Power and Justice: Historical Perspectives on Law in Australia* (Melbourne: Oxford University Press, 1995), p 19. The concerns underlying the offence have changed over time. The offence of incest was created to reinforce the moral and religious taboo against consanguinity, though in recent years the focus has been more associated with protecting children from sexual abuse within the family: MCCOC, *Chapter 5: Sexual Offences Against the Person,* Report (1999), p 189.

The legal distinction drawn between familial and non-familial sexual abuse has been criticised as anomalous. In relation to child sexual abuse, the offending conduct may be dealt with under existing laws. In relation to adult incest, there are concerns about the criminal law unduly interfering with sexual activity of consenting adults in the absence of significant harm to others: p 189. The countervailing argument is that there are harms associated with adult incest, such as an increased risk of genetic defects from inbreeding and the violation of basic moral and religious taboos: p 189. A separate offence of incest signifies the different "family context" of the abuse and a serious breach of trust involved. The arguments for and against its retention are finely balanced, and the MCCOC tentatively recommended in its Discussion Paper that incest should be abolished. This recommendation produced a strong adverse reaction within the community. Although the MCCOC was only recommending the decriminalisation of *adult* incest, most responses proceeded on the misunderstanding that it was proposing the legalisation of sexual abuse within the family. The adverse reaction was sufficient enough for the MCCOC to resile from its earlier tentative recommendation to abolish incest. In the final Report, the MCCOC recommended that the *Model Criminal Code* should contain an offence of incest: p 197.

Although the law of sexual offences may adopt a formal stance of neutrality between different types of offenders and victims for the purpose of criminalisation, such distinctions continue to have practical significance within the criminal justice system. The offender's sexual orientation and whether the abuse occurred within or outside the family continue to play a significant role in determining the perceived seriousness of offence, the level of available resources and methods of investigation used by law enforcement agencies. The practical significance of these distinctions is apparent in the findings and recommendation of a recent inquiry into paedophilia in New South Wales headed by Justice Wood: *Paedophile Inquiry Report, The Royal Commission into the New South Wales Police Service* (1997). In defining the scope of the inquiry, the Wood Royal Commission considered the range of classifications used by psychiatrists specialising in child sex offenders. The Commission concluded that a distinction could be drawn between familial and extra-familial child sexual abuse on the ground that the latter type of offender could be regarded as more fixated and dangerous. This classification led the Commission to focus its paedophilia inquiry on the "homosexual, extra-familial offender". However, as Annie Cossins points out, the classification is not consistent with either psychological literature or data about sex abuse gathered by victim report studies: "A Reply to the NSW Royal Commission Inquiry into Paedophilia: Victim Report Studies and Child Sex Offender Profiles — A Bad Match?" (1999) 32(1) *Australian and New Zealand Journal of Criminology* 42 at 46-54. She summarises her concerns with the Commission's approach to research as follows (p 54):

In summary, a distinction based on the abuse of children inside and outside the home is problematic since it ignores the possibility that offenders may choose their victims merely because of access and opportunity and perpetuates the unsupported assumption that intrafamilial abuse of girls is less serious or less damaging than extrafamilial abuse of boys. Such a distinction also obscures the substantial body of empirical data that shows that a significant proportion of so-called regressed offenders do not confine themselves to the sexual abuse of children within the family and that some also abuse male children.

The distinction drawn by the Royal Commission, while empirically dubious and strictly legally irrelevant, remains significant in both practical and political terms. The recommendations for new police powers and laws were directed primarily to child sexual abuse that occurred *outside* the family. As a result, specialised police units, such as the Child Protection Enforcement Agency in New South Wales, have been established to investigate paedophiles, distinguishing themselves from "normal child abuse investigations" on the ground that (homosexual) paedophilia was more organised and that the threats were international as well as domestic. It was made clear that these investigative units would not ordinarily be concerned with child sexual abuse by family members: p 55.

As Cossins concludes, the moral panic about paedophilia and allegations about police involvement in protecting "known" paedophiles has resulted in law enforcement resources being channelled into investigating the "extra-familial homosexual offender". This in turn has diverted resources and public attention from the most common form of child sexual abuse, namely child sexual abuse against females. Such abuse remains protected within the private sphere of the family, left in the hands of the family and to be resolved by welfare services and social workers, rather than police and prosecutors: p 56. Although the criminal law may remove the substantive distinctions between types of child sexual abuse based on either the sexual orientation of the offender or the familial relationship with the victim, Cossin's research demonstrates that such distinctions remain crucial in practice for determining the availability of investigative resources and the likelihood of prosecution.

3.2 SEXUAL OFFENCES INVOLVING PERSONS WITH MENTAL IMPAIRMENT

The present law of rape and sexual assault provides only limited protection for adults who engage in sexual intercourse while suffering from some form of mental impairment. Individuals with intellectual disability are especially vulnerable to sexual exploitation. Numerous studies have revealed that individuals with intellectual disabilities are prone to much higher rates of victimisation through sexual assault as well as other crimes generally.[32] The standard offences of rape, sexual assault and

---

32   See M Carmody, *Sexual Assault of People With an Intellectual Disability* (Sydney: NSW Women's Coordination Unit, 1990); B McSherry, "A Review of the New South Wales Law Reform Commission's Report, People with an Intellectual Disability and the Criminal Justice System" (1999) 25(1) *Monash University Law Review* 166 at 166-167 and references therein.

indecent assault are difficult to apply because of problems with proving lack of consent. In many cases, the victim, lacking sexual experience, may simply acquiesce to the accused's requests unaware of the moral and social significance of the act: *R v Beattie* (1981) 26 SASR 481. As we have explored above, under the common law consent requires an understanding of the "nature and character of the act": pp 614ff. Fraudulent conduct by the accused or mistakes by the victim that relate to the nature and character of the act may negate consent. However, as previously noted, the law governing vitiation of consent does not require the person to understand the moral or social significance of the act. All that is required is comprehension of the *physical* nature and character of the act. This narrow legal standard of consent may be contrasted with the broader medical and ethical standard of *informed* consent that requires not only an understanding of the nature and quality of the act, but also an appreciation of the risks, harms and benefits of both allowing or refusing the act.[33] As noted above, this notion of consent under the common law has been replaced in some jurisdictions by a statutory positive consent standard based on free or voluntary agreement. In Victoria, this reform of the rules governing consent included an express provision that there is no free agreement where "the person is incapable of understanding the sexual nature of the act": *Crimes Act* 1958 (Vic), s 37(e). In similar terms, consent is negated in the Australian Capital Territory where it is caused "by the person's physical helplessness or mental incapacity to understand the nature of the act in relation to which the consent is given": *Crimes Act* 1900 (ACT), s 92P(i). Although such statutory provisions are an improvement, in each case the prosecution must prove that the victim *completely* lacked capacity in relation to consent.

The alternative approach to relying on ordinary sexual offences such as rape or sexual assault is to enact special offences prohibiting sexual activity with a person with mental impairment irrespective of consent. These offences have the advantage of by-passing lack of consent and may relieve from the victim the burden and distress of testifying. Under these offences the person with the mental impairment is variously described as mentally ill or handicapped, intellectually impaired or disabled, insane or as a defective female.[34] Some of these laws are gender-specific, directed to the protection of females only. These laws have a strongly paternalistic tone. They were enacted at a time when women with mental difficulties were routinely sterilised for their own protection and where the rules governing the institutionalisation of the mentally ill prohibited any form of sexual activity. As these offences do not require proof of lack of consent, an accused may also be charged with the more serious crime of rape, providing the jury with a "fall back" offence. The difficulty is that special offences that dispense with consent as a defence deny the rights to sexual autonomy and privacy of persons with mental disabilities, a right that is recognised under numerous international treaties. Laws must demonstrate maximum respect for these rights and interference with these rights will only be justified where there is proven harm or dangers of exploitation.

---

33 B McSherry, "Sexual Assault Against Individuals with Mental Impairment: Are Criminal Laws Adequate?" (1998) 5(1) *Psychiatry, Psychology and Law* 107 at 109. See also B McSherry, "A Review of the New South Wales Law Reform Commission's Report, *People with an Intellectual Disability and the Criminal Justice System*" (1999) 25(1) *Monash University Law Review* 166.

34 See *Crimes Act* 1900 (NSW), s 66F(3); *Criminal Code* (NT), s 130; *Criminal Code* (Qld), s 216; *Criminal Law Consolidation Act* 1935 (SA), s 49(6); *Criminal Code* (Tas), s 126; *Criminal Code* (WA), s 330.

In *Chapter 5: Sexual Offences against the Person,* Report (1999), the MCCOC recommended the creation of three sexual offences against persons with mental impairment: sexual penetration, indecent touching and indecent act. Concerns about overcriminalisation were addressed by limiting the offences to individuals who are responsible for the care of a person with mental impairment: *Model Criminal Code,* ss 5.2.29-5.2.31. While lack of consent is not an element of these offences, it is a defence if the person with the mental impairment consents *and* the giving of the consent was not unduly influenced by the fact that the person was responsible for the care of the person with the mental impairment: p 180. This approach aims to balance the needs of protecting vulnerable individuals from exploitation, while demonstrating respect for their sexual autonomy and privacy.

4. INDECENCY OFFENCES

4.1 REGULATING SEXUAL DECENCY

Although autonomy is much vaunted in legal rhetoric, the vast majority of sexual offences, regardless of whether they require proof of lack of consent, function as public order offences.[35] This is particularly true of indecency offences. These offences range from "indecent assaults" involving non-consensual physical interference in indecent circumstances, through to "acts of indecency" or "gross indecency" involving no such interference, such as indecent exposure involving flashing or sexual activity in public and even nudism.[36]

Indecency offences are statutory in origin, modelled on English reforms enacted in the 19th century. These laws were primarily enacted to protect females against sexual predation that did not constitute the full offence of rape or an attempt. With the adoption of the extended definitions of "sexual intercourse" to include non-penile sexual interference in the modern law of rape and sexual assault, there is now a substantial overlap with indecency offences.

As noted above, indecency offences come in many forms. The issue of consent is not dealt with uniformly. While consent cannot be raised as a defence to acts of indecency with minors or where the indecent conduct occurred in public, the prosecution must prove lack of consent for indecent assault. In relation to indecent assault, the elements of common assault must be proved. In most cases, the common assault element will be satisfied by a non-consensual touching of another person or the infliction of actual bodily harm: see *R v Kimber* [1983] 1 WLR 1118 and *Donovan* (1934) 25 Cr App R 1 respectively. As Lord Ackner noted in *R v Court* [1989] 1 AC 28, the authorities also established that an indecent assault "need not involve any physical contact but may consist

---

35 N Lacey, *Unspeakable Subjects* (Oxford: Hart Publishing, 1998), p 104. Reflecting this reality, textbooks may discuss indecency offences in the chapter dealing with public order rather than sexual offences: D Brown, D Farrier and D Weisbrot, *Criminal Laws* (2nd ed, Sydney: Federation Press, 1996), p 945.

36 Indecency is an element of a wide range of offences: see *Crimes Act* 1900 (ACT), ss 46, 92F-K, 92NA, 546A, 546B; *Crimes Act* 1900 (NSW), ss 61L, 61M, 61N, 61O, 78Q, 81C, 578C; *Criminal Code* (NT), ss 125B, 125C, 127, 128, 129, 130, 131, 132, 133, 140, 188(2), 192, 201; *Criminal Code* (Qld), ss 210, 216, 227, 228 236, 337; *Criminal Law Consolidation Act* 1935 (SA), ss 56, 58, 58A; *Criminal Code* (Tas), ss 127, 127A, 137, 138, 139(b); *Crimes Act* 1957 (Vic), ss 39, 47, 49, 51, 52, 60; *Criminal Code* (WA), ss 184, 203, 204, 214, 320, 321, 322, 322A, 323, 324.

merely of conduct which causes the victim to apprehend immediate and unlawful personal violence":
at 42. In relation to common assault, consent ordinarily vitiates liability. This rule is subject to the
public policy proviso that consent is no defence to conduct that is intended or likely to cause bodily
harm unless it falls within a recognised exception such as lawful sports or games, medical treatment
and so on: *R v Brown* [1993] 2 WLR 556. This public interest limitation would presumably be applied
to indecent assault, and exclude consent as a defence for most forms of heterosexual or homosexual
sadomasochism. The use of any physical force by an accused in this context may also raise the
possibility that the consent to otherwise indecent conduct has been vitiated under the common law
rules. These rules have been considered above in the context of sexual offences, and in Chapter 11 in
the context of assault.

The key element of all offences of indecency, that places them within the framework of sexual
offences rather than offences against the person, is the requirement that the accused's conduct was
objectively "indecent" as determined by community standards, and was accompanied by an indecent
intent.

TESTS OF SEXUAL INDECENCY

Two questions arise in regard to offences dealing with indecency. First, what constitutes an act of
indecency? Secondly, must the accused know that the act committed is indecent? In other words,
must the accused act with indecent motives? In *R v Court* [1989] AC 28 the House of Lords
considered the definition of indecency for the purpose of indecent assault. The accused had
spanked a 12-year-old girl 12 times across her bottom. When asked by the police why he did it, he
replied "I don't know, buttock fetish". He was convicted of indecent assault and the questions on
the appeal related to the meaning of indecency and whether the accused had to have an indecent
purpose or intention. Lord Ackner, with whom the majority agreed, made the following points:
at 45-46. On a charge of indecent assault the prosecution must prove that:

(1) the accused intentionally assaulted the victim;

(2) the assault, or the assault and the circumstances accompanying it, are capable of being
considered by right-minded persons as indecent; and

(3) the accused intended to commit such an assault as is referred to in (2).

Lord Ackner noted (at 42) that the trial judge defined indecent as meaning "overtly sexual", applying
a definition offered by Williams in *Textbook of Criminal Law* (2nd ed, London: Stevens & Sons, 1983),
p 231. While a convenient shorthand, this definition did not encompass those cases where the
conduct "may have only sexual undertones". Consequently, Lord Ackner offered the following
alternate definition of indecency (at 42):

> A simpler way of putting the matter to the jury is to ask them to decide whether "right-
> minded persons would consider the conduct indecent or not." It is for the jury to decide
> whether what occurred was so offensive to contemporary standards of modesty and
> privacy as to be indecent.

This objective test of indecency departs from the earlier view that a common assault combined with an indecent motive or intent constituted an indecent assault. Lord Ackner stressed that the conduct must also be indecent according to community standards, and that if the conduct was incapable of being so regarded, it could not be converted into an offence by the mere existence of an undisclosed or secret indecent intent: at 42. This two stage test for indecency is similar in its structure and function to the test of dishonesty applied to property offences, as discussed in Chapter 13: pp 677ff.

The majority in *R v Court* held, dismissing the appeal, that on these facts the assault was capable of being indecent since the accused's "explanation" demonstrated that his conduct was intended to be indecent. Lord Ackner drew a distinction (at 43) between two situations:

▪ **the first related to conduct which was "inherently indecent", where the facts of the case "*devoid of any explanation*, would give rise to an irresistible inference that the defendant intended to assault his victim in a manner which a right-minded person would clearly think was indecent";**

▪ **the second related to conduct which was equivocal, where the facts of the case are consistent with an innocent as well as an indecent interpretation.**

In the latter situation, in determining whether such conduct would be regarded as indecent, the jury may consider a range of factors, including (at 43):

> the relationship of the defendant to his victim — were they relatives, friends or virtually complete strangers? How had the defendant come to embark on this conduct and *why* was he behaving in this way? Aided by such material, a jury would be helped to determine the quality of the act, the true nature of the assault and to answer the vital question — were they sure that the defendant not only intended to commit an assault upon the girl, but an assault which was indecent — was such an inference irresistible? (emphasis in original)

An indecent intention was crucial in equivocal cases such as buttock spanking of a child which may be consistent with innocent conduct, namely reasonable chastisement. Lord Ackner firmly rejected the view (which had been held by the Court of Appeal) that mere awareness or recklessness as to indecent circumstances could suffice: at 44-45. Accordingly, the accused's statement about his fetish was admissible as revealing his sexual motives for spanking the girl, from which an indecent intention could be inferred: at 35 per Lord Griffiths.

While the majority emphasised the importance of a subjective intent and sexual motives, Lord Goff, dissenting, held that an intention to obtain sexual gratification should not be an element of the offence and that proof of indecent intent is not required. He pointed out that under the majority's view, a man who forcibly undresses a woman in public just because he is a misogynist, or because he wants to embarrass her, or because he is mischievous, is not guilty of indecent assault: at 49.

The "ordinary meaning" approach to indecency applied by the House of Lords has been followed by the New South Wales Court of Criminal Appeal in *Harkin* (1989) 38 A Crim R 296. The accused was a "family friend" of two young girls who often came to stay with him during the school holidays. The accused took the girls, who were both 11, for a drive in his car to a nearby bush track. Each girl then had a turn at steering the car whilst sitting on his lap. While one of the girls was steering, the accused fondled her breasts and vagina. He fondled the breasts of the second girl in a similar fashion. The trial judge directed that indecency is to be determined by the "ordinary standards of morality of respectable people within the community". The accused was convicted. On appeal to the New South Wales Court of Criminal Appeal, the defence claimed that it was a misdirection to use "morality" as the standard to determine indecency. Lee J approved the definition of indecency applied by Lord Ackner in *R v Court*. Defining indecency in terms of the "ordinary standards of morality of respectable people within the community" was not a misdirection, and indeed served to remind jurors of their task in maintaining the standards of decency in the community to which they belonged: at 300.

The second ground for appeal was that the trial judge had not directed that the accused's acts were intended by him for his sexual gratification. The Court held that for indecent assault the assault must have a sexual connotation. This may be objectively determined by the "area of the body" of either the victim or the accused: "[t]he genitals and anus of both male and female and the breast of the female are the relevant areas": at 301. Thus, intentionally touching the breast of a girl would be sufficient to give the assault the necessary sexual connotation and to render it capable of being indecent. For these cases, the purpose or motive of the accused is irrelevant and the intentional doing of the act is sufficient to put the matter to the jury. This formulation expands the test in *R v Court*: it omits Lord Ackner's qualification that inherently indecent conduct gives rise to an irresistible inference of indecency only in cases "devoid of any explanation" and thus would preclude the accused raising an innocent explanation to negate the inference of indecency. In other cases where the sexual connotation of the alleged conduct was objectively "equivocal", Lee J affirmed (at 301) the approach in *R v Court* noting that the assault must be accompanied by "some intention to obtain sexual gratification".

The case law in this area draws a clear distinction between acts of indecency that are (1) unequivocal, in which case an inference of indecency arises; or (2) equivocal, in which case the conduct may become indecent if the accused has a sexual purpose or motive. The tests of indecency in the existing law confer a wide discretion to juries in determining indecency. Lord Ackner in *R v Court* suggested (at 42) that indecency was determined principally by whether "right-minded persons would consider the conduct indecent or not" and it was for the jury to decide whether what occurred was "so offensive to contemporary standards of modesty or privacy as to be indecent". *Harkin* attempted to further limit this discretion by stipulating that deliberate interference involving "defined areas" of the body are presumed to have a sexual connotation. While the MCCOC endorsed the community standards approach to indecency in *R v Court*, it rejected the idea in *Harkin* of listing body parts or acts as "inappropriately inflexible": *Model Criminal Code: Chapter 5 — Sexual Offences Against the Person,* Report (1999), p 107.

The fictional "right-minded person" that lies at the heart of the legal definition of indecency fixes the boundaries of sexual propriety and decency. Like the reasonable person standard applied elsewhere in the criminal law, the right-minded person provides the external objective assessment of the community standards. As we shall see below, while these standards purport to be neutral, they may be defined and applied in ways that perpetuate discrimination against sexual minorities.

PERSPECTIVES

Policing Homosexual and Heterosexual Decency

The trend in the modern criminal law, as reflected in the MCCOC's recommendations in Chapter 5: *Sexual Offences Against the Person*, Report (1999), is firmly against the enactment of distinct "homosexual offences".[37] Nevertheless, some jurisdictions continue to maintain indecency offences specifically aimed at sexual conduct between males, which often carry aggravated penalties.[38] Some of these indecency laws, such as the offence of gross indecency, involve policing the public/private boundary. Sexual conduct between consenting adults may be criminalised in cases where it has transgressed this boundary and would be regarded by "right-thinking" persons as indecent. Indecency offences tend to operate as public order laws, overlapping with the offensive conduct or behaviour crimes. These public order offences are discussed in Chapter 14, 3.1 'Offensive Conduct and Language Crimes', pp 786ff.

A fundamental right to privacy in relation to sexual conduct between adults has been created by the *Human Rights (Sexual Conduct) Act* 1994 (Cth). As explored in Chapter 2, the Federal Act renders inoperative any State or Territory law that arbitrarily interferes with sexual conduct between consenting adults "in private": s 4. The limiting phrase "in private" is a significant restriction on the Act's ability to protect important facets of human sexuality: S Bronitt, "The Right to Sexual Privacy, Sado-masochism and the *Human Rights (Sexual Conduct) Act* 1994 (Cth)" (1995) 2(1) *Australian Journal of Human Rights* 59 at 64-65. Framed in this way, the Act will not restrict the operation of indecency offences proscribing sexual conduct that occurs in public. These limitations, as well as restrictions on sexual acts with minors, would fall within the legitimate restrictions on the right to privacy recognised under international human rights jurisprudence. Engaging in explicit sexual activity (either homosexual or heterosexual) in a public place may cause serious affront and distress to others, and could therefore be regarded as a form of harm that would justify restriction.[39] Milder forms of sexual expression in public may not cause sufficient "offense to others" to justify criminalisation. Clearly, the tribunal of fact, in applying the community standards of decency, will be left to grapple with these boundaries with no guidance on the limits of sexual tolerance that should be demonstrated towards sexual minorities. Similar questions have arisen over racist insults and whether these are sufficiently harmful to warrant criminalisation, see further Chapter 14: pp 769ff.

---

37 The offence of gross indecency between males criminalises sexual conduct in public or with minors: *Crimes Act* 1900 (NSW), s 78Q; *Criminal Code* (NT), ss 127, 128; *Criminal Code* (WA), s 184. An extensive array of offences have been enacted in New South Wales, proscribing "homosexual intercourse" with males under 10 years; under 18 years and where the accused is a person in authority such as teacher schoolmaster or other teacher, or a father: *Crimes Act* 1900 (NSW), ss 78H, 78I, 78K, 78L, 78N, 78O. These offences include attempts and have adopted an extended definition of homosexual intercourse as including other non-penetrative acts such oral sex: s 78G.

38 For example, s 127 of the *Criminal Code* (NT) provides a penalty of seven years imprisonment for an act of gross indecency in public between males, while the equivalent general offence of gross indecency only attracts a penalty of two years. See also s 184 of the *Criminal Code* (WA).

39 In all jurisdictions in Australia it is an offence to engage in an act of indecency in public. In the Northern Territory and Western Australia there are aggravated offences dealing with acts of gross indecency in public between males which carry significantly higher penalties: *Criminal Code Act* 1983 (NT), s 127; *Criminal Code Act* 1913 (WA), s 184. Whether an act is indecent is determined according to ordinary standards of morality and decency within the community: see *Harkin* (1989) 38 A Crim R 296 (CCA NSW).

The boundaries between the public and private spheres, as well as the concept of harm itself, are both contingent and highly elastic. As we explored in Chapter 2, the definitions of privacy in the criminal law have tended to reflect liberal and negative notions of privacy as the right to protection from arbitrary State interference with property or person, rather than the positive concept of privacy as the right to establish, develop and fulfil one's own emotional needs: pp 143ff. Indeed, a notion of indecency could be developed in the future that embraces an inclusive standard of sexual decency that recognises the value of sexual expression and diversity as an aspect of the fundamental human right to privacy.

Although the modern approach to sexual offences, including indecency, does not distinguish between different types of sexuality for the purpose of offence description or punishment, clearly there is considerable scope for the repression of sexual minorities whose conduct would be considered "indecent" by "right-minded persons". The legal standards of indecency are constructed by reference to a *norm of sexual decency* that is implicitly heterosexual, and thus discriminates against sexual minorities. As Lord Ackner indicated in *R v Court*, the jury must evaluate the question of indecency by reference to the community standards of sexual propriety. In this regard, he noted that factors such as "modesty" and "privacy" will be relevant.

A wide definition of indecency leaves homosexuals susceptible to arrest and prosecution for any sexual conduct that occurs in public. While a young girl and boy passionately kissing or engaged in "heavy petting" in public would not be considered indecent, a male couple kissing in a public street may be considered indecent conduct, possibly even insulting conduct likely to provoke public disorder.[40] Of course, there are times within certain communities where these standards of sexual decency may be relaxed, as witnessed during the annual Sydney Gay and Lesbian Mardi Gras. Nevertheless, public expression of homosexual and other transgressive sexualities is usually tolerated only within the narrowly defined sphere of privacy. Stepping outside that metaphorical closet and strictly enforced zone of privacy will invite criminalisation through either indecency offences or public order crimes such as offensive conduct or behaviour.

The implicitly heterosexed nature of decency not only affects the legal evaluation of conduct alleged to be indecent, it also influences law enforcement decision-making particularly the exercise of police and prosecution discretion. Sexual conduct between homosexual males, in both public and private spaces, provokes hostile responses from the community (in some cases leading to violence and gay-hate murder), as well as discriminatory policing and law enforcement: G Mason and S Tomsen (eds), *Homophobic Violence* (Sydney: Hawkins Press, 1997). Notwithstanding the removal of criminal prohibitions on homosexual conduct between adult males in private, the police continue to conduct widespread covert and proactive investigations against homosexual activity: L Moran, *The Homosexual(ity) of Law* (New York: Routledge, 1996), Chs 6 and 7. Undercover policing, including surveillance and entrapment, is often used against homosexual men who engage in sexual acts in public or semi-public spaces.

---

40 *Masterson and Cooper v Holden* [1986] Crim LR 688 (HC Eng) held that overt homosexual conduct could be insulting behaviour likely to cause a breach of the peace. This was a question for the decider of fact. In this case, two males kissed and fondled each other to the annoyance of passers-by. The conduct occurred at a bus stop in the early hours in Oxford Street, and the couple was unaware that anyone was watching them. The court held that this type of conduct could be insulting, even though it is not deliberately aimed at someone.

To address concerns about discriminatory and unfair policing practices around public toilets (known as "beats"), guidelines have been developed by the police in New South Wales and South Australia to restrict the use of undercover operations. For an evaluation of these police initiatives and reforms to eradicate discriminatory policing of homosexual males, see G Mason and S Tomsen (eds), *Homophobic Violence* (Sydney: Hawkins Press, 1997), Chs 9 and 10.

4.2 OBSCENE AND INDECENT PUBLICATIONS: THE LEGAL REGULATION OF PORNOGRAPHY

> I shall not today attempt further to define the kinds of material I understand to be embraced within that shorthand description [hardcore pornography]; and perhaps I could never succeed in intelligibly doing so. But I know it when I see it ...

Jacobellis v Ohio, 387 US 184 (1964), at 197 per Stewart J

THE LEGAL DEFINITION OF OBSCENITY

An important subset of indecency laws regulates the production, supply and possession of pornography. Legal concepts such as obscenity, indecency and offensiveness play a key role in delineating between lawful and unlawful sexual material. Because obscenity laws raise concerns about freedom of expression and sexual privacy, they are generally examined in courses dealing with human rights rather than the criminal law.[41] This is unfortunate. From a criminal perspective, indecency offences provide further material upon which we may critically examine the function and values behind objective standards (in this case decency standards) and the role of legal theory, particularly liberalism and feminism, in shaping legal policy.

Under the common law, the crime of "obscene libel" prohibited any publication that had the tendency to deprave or corrupt those minds who are open to immoral influences: *R v Hicklin* (1868) LR 3 QB 360; *Bremner v Walker* (1885) 6 LR (NSW) 276. As we shall see below, this common law definition formed the basis of further statutory offences dealing with obscene and/or indecent publication or articles. Although the offence originated in the ecclesiastical jurisdiction, in the modern era it performs a secular function suppressing publications perceived by the State to be politically, socially and morally subversive.

---

41   E Campbell and H Whitmore, *Freedom in Australia* (Revised ed, Sydney: Sydney University Press, 1973), Ch 13; G Flick, *Civil Liberties in Australia* (Sydney: Law Book Company Ltd, 1981), Ch 8; N O'Neill and R Handley, *Retreat From Injustice* (Sydney: Federation Press, 1995), Ch 14; B Gaze and M Jones, *Law, Liberty and Australian Democracy* (Sydney: Law Book Company Ltd, 1990), Ch 10.

In Australia, the history of these laws is bound up with State efforts to curb press freedom and impose censorship on political and literary radicals: M Pollak, *Sense and Censorship — Commentaries on Censorship Violence in Australia* (Sydney: Reed, 1990). There has been a significant shift in the use of obscenity laws in the 20th century. As political censorship of the theatre and novels became increasingly untenable, the focus of obscenity laws have shifted to the regulation of sexually explicit material.

> **Blasphemy or blasphemous libel is also an offence under the common law and statute, though there has only been one recorded prosecution in New South Wales: New South Wales Law Reform Commission, *Blasphemy: A Discussion Paper* (1992), p 17. The offence is constituted by published words or matters which are "scoffing" or "reviling" of the basic tenets of Christianity as defined by the Church of England: p 18. The offence, though rarely used, discriminates against other religions and threatens freedom of speech. It is difficult to reconcile the offence with the secular nature of government in multicultural Australia.**

Pornography, as distinct from "the erotic", emerges at a particular historical moment. During the revolutionary period in Europe, especially in France, pornography played a significant cultural role in constructing myths about women's bodies and feminine sexuality, male domination and female submission.[42] With the advent of photography in the late 19th century, the objects of obscenity could be packaged and commodified, further distanced from the "erotic" literature and art of previous eras.

Obscenity laws played a crucial role, through concepts of decency based on community standards, in regulating this emerging market in sexually explicit material. The legal definition of obscenity is notoriously elusive. Justice Stewart's famous dictum on pornography — "I know it when I see it" — typifies the definitional difficulty confronting judges.[43] This fundamental indeterminacy not only affects the common law. Key statutory concepts in statutory offences are left to judges and juries with limited guidance. Like Justice Stewart, Barwick CJ in *Crowe v Graham* (1968) 121 CLR 375 doubted the wisdom of defining terms like "indecent" or "indecency", concluding (at 379) simply that material that offended "the modesty of the average man or woman in sexual matters" would be an indecent article for the purpose of the *Obscene and Indecent Publications Act* 1901-1955 (NSW). Until this landmark High Court decision, there was considerable confusion over the precise relationship between indecency and obscenity, with some courts suggesting that indecency was concerned with protecting the general public from offensive content, whereas obscenity was concerned with protecting individuals from immorality. Windeyer J (at 389) emphatically rejected that indecency was distinct from obscenity, even if the terms appeared disjunctively in a particular section.

The High Court's judgment in *Crowe* signalled a fundamental shift from the approach taken to obscene libel in *R v Hicklin* (1868) LR 3 QB 360, which focused on the tendency of material to

---

42 A Orford, "Liberty, Equality, Pornography: The Bodies of Women and Human Rights Discourse" (1994) 3 *Australian Feminist Law Journal* 72 at 81-87.

43 *Jacobellis v Ohio*, 378 US 184 (1964), at 197. For a review of the law of obscenity and pornography see S Rozanski, "Obscenity: Common Law and the Abuse of Women" (1991) 13 *Adelaide Law Review* 163. See also C MacKinnon, *Only Words* (Cambridge, MA: Harvard University Press, 1993).

"deprave and corrupt", to a forensic inquiry into whether the impugned material is acceptable by current community standards: A Blackshield, "Censorship and the Law" in G Dutton and M Harris (eds), *Australia's Censorship Crisis* (Melbourne: Sun Books, 1970), p 23. This modernisation of the law governing obscenity, however, offered limited guidance for those individuals entrusted with upholding these legal standards, namely the censors (since replaced with classification boards), law enforcement officials and the courts. In the United States, obscenity laws were constrained by constitutional rights relating to freedom of speech and privacy. This jurisprudence on obscenity has had no impact on the development of the Australian common law. As Windeyer J in *Crowe v Graham* (1968) 121 CLR 375 held (at 398-399), considerations of liberty, such as freedom of speech, were not relevant to the task of determining the community standard of decency:

> their Honours [in the court below] were wrong in invoking considerations of "private liberty
> as a basic right and need of modern man" as an aid for the interpretation of a statute of the
> Parliament of New South Wales dealing with obscenity and indecency. And I think too that
> their references in this connexion to judgments delivered in courts of the United States
> were only remotely relevant.

Judges and juries are left to determine the standards of indecency by reference to their under-standing of prevailing sexual mores, in particular the level of sexual tolerance that would be acceptable to the community. The inherently conservative values of judges (which can exert considerable influence on the jury)[44] may operate to discriminate against individuals or groups that hold unconventional views on sexual matters.

In light of the significant statutory reforms in this area, the offence of obscene libel would rarely be prosecuted nowadays. It does not follow that the crime of obscenity is obsolete. Indeed, the potential breadth and indeterminacy of common law and statutory offences dealing with obscene and indecent material are fundamental to the effective operation of the national system of cooperative regulation and classification scheme, discussed below. The uncertainty surrounding the scope of Commonwealth, State and Territory offences encourages publishers and suppliers of potentially obscene or indecent material to submit to a "voluntary" *National Code of Classification*, compliance with which confers immunity from prosecution. These nebulous definitions of obscenity and indecency also empower informal censorship by law enforcement officials such as the police and customs officials, and encourage a high degree of self-censorship by publishers and suppliers.

The common law is supplemented by a wide range of statutory crimes prohibiting the publication, possession and supply of indecent articles and books, magazines, films and computer games. In addition to these State and Territory offences, the Commonwealth has powers over the sale and supply of obscene publications through its constitutional power to regulate postal services, broadcasting and the import/export of goods: N O'Neill and R Handley, *Retreat From Injustice* (Sydney: Federation Press, 1995), pp 270-282. These offences are supplemented by extensive law enforcement powers of search, seizure and confiscation.

---

44 Geoffrey Robertson in *The Justice Game* (London: Vintage, 1999), Ch 3, recounts how the trial judge in a famous obscenity trial swayed the jury by comments and body language that disparaged the accused and their defence expert witnesses. His blatant bias led to the reversal of the convictions on appeal: *R v Anderson, Neville, Dennis and Oz Publications Ink Ltd* (1972) 1 QB 304.

> Obscenity prosecutions are rare. They are often selective prosecutions targeting members of subversive or anti-establishment groups. One of the most infamous obscenity prosecutions in England in the 1970s targeted three editors of a satirical magazine called *Oz*. The prosecution focused on a special "Schoolkids' Edition" which contained allegedly obscene cartoons featuring the infamous "Rupert Bear Strip". Geoffrey Robertson QC appeared as junior counsel for the defence and has provided an insightful account of the trial and subsequent appeal in *The Justice Game* (London: Vintage, 1999), Ch 3.

The laws governing obscenity, particularly obscene publications, constitute a complex web of Federal, State and Territory regulation. The censorship of publications (which include films, video tapes and computer games) is governed by a cooperative arrangement established by the *Classification (Publications, Films and Computer Games) Act* 1995 (Cth). Under this Act, the Classification Board (which is located within the Office of Film and Literature Classification) is empowered to make classification decisions for publications, films and computer games. Section 3 of the Act provides:

> The purpose of this Act is to provide for the classification of publications, films and computer games for the Australian Capital Territory. This Act is intended to form part of a Commonwealth/State/Territory scheme for the classification of publications, films and computer games and for the enforcement of those classifications.
>
> Note: Provisions dealing with the consequences of not having material classified and the enforcement of classification decisions are to be found in complementary laws of the States and Territories.

The Board also makes classification decisions on behalf of participating States and Territories using a National Classification Code (NCC) that ensures the development of uniform and consistent standards. Different classifications apply to publications, films and computer games. With respect to films there are seven classification categories: *Classification (Publications, Films and Computer Games) Act* 1995 (Cth), s 7 described in the Schedule to the Act. These are set out in Table 3.

TABLE 3:

Commonwealth Classification Standards for Films

ADVISORY CLASSIFICATIONS

G (General) [45]

All other computer games.
All other films.

PG (Parental Guidance)

Films (except RC films, R films, X films, MA films and M films) that cannot be recommended for viewing by persons who are under 15 without the guidance of their parents or guardians.

M (Mature)

Films (except RC films, R films, X films, MA films and M films) that cannot be recommended for viewing by persons who are under 15 without the guidance of their parents or guardians.

Computer games (except RC, MA (15+) and M (15+) computer games) that cannot be recommended for viewing or playing by persons who are under 8.

LEGALLY RESTRICTED CLASSIFICATIONS

MA (Mature Accompanied)

Films (except RC films, X films and R films) that depict, express or otherwise deal with sex, violence or coarse language in such a manner as to be unsuitable for viewing by persons under 15.

Computer games (except RC computer games) that depict, express or otherwise deal with sex, violence or coarse language in such a manner as to be unsuitable for viewing or playing by persons under 15.

R (Restricted)

Films (except RC films and X films) that are unsuitable for a minor to see.

Category 2 restricted: Publications (except RC publications) that:
(a) explicitly depict sexual or sexually related activity between consenting adults in a way that is likely to cause offence to a reasonable adult; or
(b) depict, describe or express revolting or abhorrent phenomena in a way that is likely to cause offence to a reasonable adult and are unsuitable for a minor to see or read.

Category 1 restricted: Publications (except RC publications and Category 2 restricted publications) that:
(a) explicitly depict nudity, or describe or impliedly depict sexual or sexually related activity between consenting adults, in a way that is likely to cause offence to a reasonable adult; or
(b) describe or express in detail violence or sexual activity between consenting adults in a way that is likely to cause offence to a reasonable adult; or
(c) are unsuitable for a minor to see or read.

X (Restricted)

Films (except RC films) that:
(a) explicitly depict sexual activity between adults, where there is no sexual violence, coercion or non-consent of any kind, in a way that is likely to cause offence to a reasonable adult; and
(b) are unsuitable for a minor to see.

RC (Refused Classification)

Publications, films, computer games[46] that:
(a) describe, depict, express or otherwise deal with matters of sex, drug misuse or addiction, crime, cruelty, violence or revolting or abhorrent phenomena in such a way that they offend against the standards of morality, decency and propriety generally accepted by reasonable adults to the extent that they should not be classified; or
(b) describe or depict in a way that is likely to cause offence to a reasonable adult, a minor who is, or who appears to be, under 16 (whether the minor is engaged in sexual activity or not); or
(c) promote, incite or instruct in matters of crime or violence.

---

45 The category "unrestricted" is used to signify all publications which are not classified R or RC.

46 There is a special fourth option for RC computer games: "Computer games that ... (d) are unsuitable for a minor to see or play": *Classification (Publications, Films and Computer Games) Act* 1995 (Cth), Schedule.

Individual States and Territories have adopted their own classification schemes that mirror, to a greater or lesser extent, the Commonwealth scheme, as discussed below.

Classification provides protection from prosecution under Commonwealth, State or Territory laws, though the scope of this immunity is not uniform. Queensland has the most limited immunity. Only publications classified as "unrestricted" are exempt from prosecution as indecent or obscene publications. Moreover, not all classifications are recognised in every jurisdiction. In New South Wales, a film classified as X rated is deemed to have been refused classification with the effect of forfeiting immunity from prosecution.[47] In Victoria, possession of RC or X films for the purpose of supply or exhibition is an offence. Section 23(1) of the *Classification (Publications, Films And Computer Games) (Enforcement) Act* 1995 (Vic) provides that:

A person who possesses —

(a) a film classified RC or X; or

(b) an unclassified film which would, if classified, be classified RC, X, R or MA —

with the intention of selling or exhibiting the film is guilty of an offence.

Some jurisdictions, such as the Northern Territory and Victoria, have enacted specific provisions relating to "on-line" computer services.[48] In Victoria, for example:

A person must not use an on-line information service to publish or transmit, or make available for transmission, objectionable material.[49]

The *Broadcasting Services Amendment (Online Services) Act* 1999 (Cth) goes further and requires, if there has been a complaint to the Australian Broadcasting Authority, internet service providers and content hosts[50] to prevent access to materials hosted in Australia and classified RC.

Section 11 of the *Classification (Publications, Films and Computer Games) Act* 1995 (Cth) identifies the following matters to be taken into account in classification decisions:

(a) the standards of morality, decency and propriety generally accepted by reasonable adults; and

(b) the literary, artistic or educational merit (if any) of the publication, film or computer game; and

---

47 Section 9A of the *Film and Computer Game Classification Act* 1984 (NSW), as amended by the *Film and Video Tape Classification (Amendment) Act* 1993 (NSW). The *National Classification Code* defines X rated material as follows: "This classification is a special and legally restricted category which only contains sexually explicit material. That is material which contains depictions of actual sexual intercourse and other sexual activity, including mild fetishes such as rubber and leather wear. It does not contain any depictions of sexual violence, sexualised violence or coercion, or grossly exploitative depictions".

48 *Classification of Publications, Films And Computer Games Act* (NT), ss 50X, 50Z; *Classification (Publications, Films And Computer Games) (Enforcement) Act* 1995 (Vic), ss 56, 57, 58.

49 *Classification (Publications, Films And Computer Games) (Enforcement) Act* 1995 (Vic), s 57(1). "Objectionable material" is defined in s 56 of the Act to include material which is or would be classified RC; see s 3 of the Act for definitions of "objectionable publication" and "objectionable film".

50 "Internet content hosts" are broadly defined in Sch 1 of the *Broadcasting Services Amendment (Online Services) Act* 1999 (Cth). See B Scott, "The Dawn of a New Dark Age: Censorship and Amendments to the *Broadcasting Services Act*" (1999) 38 *Computers & Law* 39, and K Koomen, "Illegal and Harmful Content on the Internet: Some Issues and Options" (1998) 35 *Computers & Law* 1.

(c) the general character of the publication, film or computer game, including whether it is of a medical, legal or scientific character; and

(d) the persons or class of persons to or amongst whom it is published or is intended or likely to be published.

The *National Classification Code*, contained in the Schedule to the Act, provides that classification decisions are to give effect, as far as possible, to the following principles:

(a) adults should be able to read, hear and see what they want;

(b) minors should be protected from material likely to harm or disturb them;

(c) everyone should be protected from exposure to unsolicited material that they find offensive;

(d) the need to take account of community concerns about:

(i) depictions that condone or incite violence, particularly sexual violence; and

(ii) the portrayal of persons in a demeaning manner.

As reviewed in Chapter 2, interference with privacy in order to protect morals in the absence of any harm to others is controversial. Liberalism rejects the idea that the criminal law should be used to enforce a particular conception of private morality, and legal philosophers, such as Ronald Dworkin, have argued that there is a right to pornography as an exercise of the freedom of moral responsibility: R Dworkin, "Is There a Right to Pornography" (1981) 1 *Oxford Journal of Legal Studies* 177. While the first principle contained in the *National Classification Code* demonstrates some commitment to *individual* freedom, classification (and hence legal availability) is also determined by reference to the *community* standards of morality, decency and propriety.

Under the existing legal framework, moral standards are applied in a number of ways — the decision makers must reflect community standards in applying standards of morality, decency and propriety of "reasonable adults": s 11. The Act requires that members of the Classification Board be "broadly representative of the Australian community": s 48(2). The Act and *National Classification Code* offer no guidance on how these conflicting communal and individual interests should be reconciled. Presumably, the tribunal determining the matter must engage in a some form of balancing exercise. In Chapter 2 we explored how the process of balancing rights tends to prioritise communal/majority interests over individual/minority interests. Anne Orford has noted that a review of international and comparative jurisprudence in this area reveals that the liberal principles of free speech and privacy are held not to be infringed by obscenity laws based on "community standards".[51]

The European Court of Human Rights (ECHR) has held that the freedom of expression may be justifiably restricted in order to protect "public morals". In *Handyside v the United Kingdom* (1976) Series A, No 24, 1 EHRR 737, the applicant, an English publisher, was charged and convicted under the *Obscene Publications Acts* 1959 and 1964 (UK) for having obscene books in his possession for publication or gain. Copies of the books were seized, forfeited and destroyed, and the applicant was

---

51   A Orford, "Liberty, Equality, Pornography: The Bodies of Women and Human Rights Discourse" (1994) 3 *Australian Feminist Law Journal* 72 at 79, discussing case law in the United States, Europe, New Zealand and Canada.

fined and ordered to pay costs. The applicant argued that this action constituted a breach of Art 10 of the *European Convention on Human Rights*, which protects freedom of expression from "interference". The ECHR held that the interference with an individual's rights under Art 10 was "necessary in a democratic society ... for the protection of morals". Accordingly, there had been no breach of Art 10: at 746, para 59. This decision is significant since the freedom of expression is similarly protected under Art 19 of the *International Covenant on Civil and Political Rights* (ICCPR) and may be subject to restrictions in accordance with the law and where necessary: (1) for respect of the rights or reputation of others; and (2) for the protection of national security or of public order or of public health or morals: Art 19(3).

In Australia, the legal standards of decency are based on "the reasonable person" or "the community". As in other areas of the criminal law, this raises questions about how tribunals construct objective standards, particularly those based on morality and decency, within a secular, multicultural and pluralistic society. As pointed out in Chapter 2, the stability of objective and neutral concepts has been challenged from both feminist and critical perspectives. While liberals object to the breadth and arbitrariness of legal definitions of obscenity, feminists and critical legal scholars raise concern that the legal standards of indecency operate in discriminatory ways against women and sexual minorities such as gays and lesbians.

MacKinnon has noted that obscenity laws in the United States have rarely operated to prohibit the publication, sale and supply of sexually explicit material. She concludes that persistent judicial refusal in the case law to define obscenity is systematic and determinate. It is part of an epistemological process by which the legal standard of obscenity "is built on what the male standpoint sees": *Towards A Feminist Theory of State* (Cambridge: Harvard University Press, 1989), p 197. As well as being a gendered construct, the legal concept of decency is historically contingent. A comparison of "unrestricted" magazines freely available in Australia today with publications deemed to be "obscene" 50 years ago would reveal radical changes to the standards of decency, particularly in relation to acceptable levels of female nudity in "lifestyle" magazines and "mainstream" advertising.

Jurisdictional inconsistencies undermine the Commonwealth's vision of a national scheme of classification applying consistent standards across Australia. Such variations are difficult to reconcile with the fact that the standards of decency applied to State and Territory indecency offences are constructed by reference to prevailing *Australian* community standards rather than those of individual States or Territories. For a review of the statutory provisions and offences in all Australian jurisdictions, see N O'Neill and R Handley, *Retreat From Injustice* (Sydney: Federation Press, 1995), Ch 14.

REDEFINING PORNOGRAPHY LAWS: A RIGHT TO EQUALITY?

As feminist scholars have pointed out, the debate about the regulation of pornography is deeply implicated in questions about gender, in particular the role of the public/private dichotomy: N Lacey, *Unspeakable Subjects* (Oxford: Hart Publishing, 1998), Ch 3. Feminist anti-pornography arguments are confronted with the assertion of both public and private rights. As Lacey has observed (p 88):

The liberal analysis which constructs pornography as a matter of private sexual preference in one breath constructs it as a matter of public right to free expression in the next. In what might be called a "no-lose situation" for the producers and consumers of pornography, the production of pornography is seen as a matter of public right, and hence protected, whilst its consumption is constructed as a matter of private interest, and hence also protected.

Debates over the legal regulation of pornography produce a strange coalition between religious moralism and radical feminism.[52] While both seek to impose restrictions on the availability of sexually explicit material, the justifications for so doing are fundamentally different. Rather than focus on the perceived sinful or immoral nature of pornography, the feminist critique conceives it as a harmful social practice that both expresses and causes the subordination of women. Pornography is defined *as* sex discrimination. Viewing pornography as a matter of discrimination deftly avoids the intractable controversy over whether pornography causes or contributes to violence against women.

The feminist critique does not necessarily compel the adoption of criminal prohibition as the regulatory solution. By focusing on discrimination and inequality, only certain forms of sexually explicit materials would be censured. Indeed, in the United States, Indianapolis enacted an anti-pornography ordinance based on a model law drafted by leading feminist legal academics, Andrea Dworkin and Catharine MacKinnon. This model conceptualised pornography as sex discrimination, creating a wide range of civil causes of action to individuals harmed by pornography. Ultimately, the law was held to be constitutionally invalid for unduly interfering with freedom of speech protected by the First Amendment.[53]

Unlike the MacKinnon–Dworkin anti-pornography ordinance, the laws regulating pornography in Australia lack a clear, coherent and consistent philosophical basis. As noted above, decisions about classification (and hence legal availability) incorporate a wide range of interests, many of which potentially conflict with each other. The *Classification (Publications, Films and Computer Games) Act* 1995 (Cth) and the *National Classification Code* identify as relevant considerations various and competing rights, values and interests (in no particular hierarchy). Communal interests relating to morality and offensiveness must be balanced against individual interests relating to privacy and freedom of moral choice. Sexual equality and in particular the interests of women play no visible role. It is only made relevant obliquely in the National Classification Code through "community concerns" about depictions that condone or incite violence, particularly sexual violence and the portrayal of persons in a demeaning manner.

As Orford points out in "Liberty, Equality, Pornography: The Bodies of Women and Human Rights Discourse" (1994) 3 *Australian Feminist Law Journal* 72 (at 97-99), the process of building "community" in legal discourse continues to exclude women's interests:

> The silencing of the voices of women enables the construction of "community consensus" in liberal theory, of a false universal which assimilates all difference in the public sphere.

---

52 For a review of the conflicting perspectives — moral, feminist and liberal — on pornography, see H Potter, *Pornography* (Sydney: Federation Press, 1996).

53 *American Booksellers v William Hudnutt III, Mayor, City of Indianapolis*, 771 F 2d 323 (7th Cir 1985). The background to the ordinance and the constitutional challenge are reviewed in R Graycar and J Morgan, *The Hidden Gender of Law* (Sydney: Federation Press, 1990), pp 375-390.

The idea of moral consensus has been used by liberal theorists and judges, both to uphold or propose regimes for criminalising or regulating "obscenity", and to argue that anti-pornography ordinances based on feminist perspectives are an infringement of individual freedom.

The present law seems ill-equipped to deal with the problematic aspects of pornography. The existing regulatory strategy strives for uniformity and consistency in decision-making on the question of indecency without any coherent philosophical or political principles guiding the content and scope of these standards. As with prostitution and the sex industry generally, law-makers have pragmatically adopted a policy of "harm minimisation". This strategy aims to minimise the harms that would otherwise flow from strict prohibition. It has been influential in the reform of some drug laws, such as the possession of cannabis, discussed in Chapter 15: pp 817ff. By creating a lawful market for obscene and indecent material, the State minimises the involvement of organised crime, corruption and threats to public health. It also profits through the imposition of substantial taxes on pornography.

Rather than employ a "balancing" discretion for classification, a regulatory framework could be reconstructed around a different set of values. The liberal conceptions of equality, the idea of equality as mere sameness, has failed to address the structural disadvantage of historically marginalised and disempowered groups. A more contextual approach to equality is emerging in some jurisdictions. In Canada, for example, depictions of degrading and dehumanising stereotyping of women have been held to constitute an interference with the right to equality and therefore may be justifiably restricted by obscenity laws.[54] We must be cautious about the liberal promise of equality. As explored in Chapter 2, the principle of equality can have counterproductive effects and often works against legislative reforms designed to alleviate disadvantage. Indeed, for this reason, Lacey has expressed doubts about the value of reforms of pornography laws based on equality. This is because of the individuated nature of the anti-discrimination laws and its limited ability to redress group based harms: *Unspeakable Subjects* (Oxford: Hart Publishing, 1998), pp 92-97.

Debates about legislative strategy, including much feminist critique, seem trapped within a liberal dichotomy drawn between private and public interests. Rather than accept this dichotomy, Lacey argues that the dichotomy needs to be reconceptualised. While feminists have sought to relocate sexual harms against women from the private/unregulated sphere to the public/regulated sphere, they have largely overlooked the potential of privacy to maximise human autonomy through positive regulation. In Chapter 2, we explored how privacy may be constructed as a positive right to personal and emotional development, rather than a negative right to be protected from interference, in other words, the right to be left alone. Lacey's perspective provides the platform from which feminists may challenge serious autonomy-reducing sexual practices ranging from rape to violent pornography: p 96. She doubts the value of pursuing the legislative strategies of the sort adopted in the United States, placing greater emphasis on the power of feminist critique to transcend the public/private dichotomy and to raise consciousness: p 97. Smart, while recognising the importance

---

54 This equality-based approach was taken to impose restrictions on obscene materials in Canada: *R v Butler* [1992]
    1 SCR 452 (Supreme Court of Canada). See A Orford, "Liberty, Equality, Pornography: The Bodies of Women and
    Human Rights Discourse" (1994) 3 *Australian Feminist Law Journal* 72 at 97.

of such feminist strategies, argues that "consciousness raising is a starting point not the finishing post": "Law's Truth/Women's experience" in R Graycar (ed), *Dissenting Opinions* (Sydney: Allen and Unwin, 1990), p 13. Law's truths about women and female sexuality must be confronted within the legal as well as political and social arena.

A republican analysis of pornography would be more optimistic about the instrumental and symbolic value of using law to challenge sexual oppression and inequality. As explored in Chapter 2, republican theorists would examine the extent to which a particular activity interferes with freedom. While some regulation of pornography would be justifiable to protect the rights of those individuals involved in the industry and those members of the general public who did not wish to view such material, the prohibition of sexual material on the ground that it causes offense to the moral standards of a hypothetical "reasonable person" would not be justifiable: J Braithwaite and P Pettit, *Not Just Deserts* (Oxford: Clarendon Press, 1990), p 96. However, material that sexualises domination, such as pornography that involves or depicts sexual violence against women and children, could be arguably limited on the ground that it condones sexual coercion and perpetuates inequality. This would be distinguished from pornography that promotes positive and empowering images of female sexuality. Admittedly, such a vision of pornography seems remote, bearing in mind the prevailing genre that sexualises dominance. Feminists have argued that pornography is a site of struggle against male colonisation of female sexuality. Strategies for confronting these truths about women and sexuality are not restricted to legal regulation. Some feminists have argued that the violence of pornography will only be eliminated by increasing women's power as producers and consumers of sexual imagery.[55] The republican approach to regulation would counsel restraint in the use of criminal sanctions in favour of civil actions along the lines proposed by MacKinnon and Dworkin. To maximise freedom, including rights of sexual expression and privacy, republicanism would require clear articulation of the key definitions for distinguishing between lawful and unlawful material.

With an increasingly regulated and therefore legitimated sex industry in Australia, pornography is no longer a serious cause for community concern. Public attention has shifted to problematic forms of pornography. Indeed, there is widespread moral panic about pornography and children. Principally, this concern is directed toward two distinct problems:

=== **the unrestricted availability and access of sexually explicit material by children, particularly through the internet; and**

=== **child pornography.**

PERSPECTIVES ON INDECENCY

Children, Pornography and the Internet

Australia and the wider international community are gripped by a moral panic about children and pornography. In the hierarchy of sexual deviance, sex involving children seems to generate the majority of this concern. Community panic is fuelled by sensational media stories about the

---

55 These views are discussed in A Orford, "Liberty, Equality, Pornography: The Bodies of Women and Human Rights Discourse" (1994) 3 *Australian Feminist Law Journal* 72 at 91.

existence of national and transnational paedophile networks that use sophisticated technologies, such email and the internet, to solicit victims and to disseminate child pornography.[56] Research has revealed that child pornography is currently available in Australia on internet newsgroups and to a lesser extent on the world wide web: P Forde and A Patterson, "Paedophile Internet Activity" (1998) 97 *Trends and Issues in Crime and Criminal Justice* 1 at 3.

As discussed above, the criminal law has experienced difficulty defining the age of sexual maturity. In relation to *actual participation* in sexual acts, the "age of consent" varies according to type of sexual conduct, the sexual orientation and/or gender of the parties: see above, p 635. Similar uncertainties bedevil the definitions used for obscenity laws proscribing the description or depiction of sexual acts involving minors.

The sexual maturity of young persons is made relevant to our obscenity laws in a number of ways. In fixing the community standards, the *National Classification Code* states that minors should be protected from material likely to harm or disturb them (see above). While this principle is central to determining the standards of decency within the community, the term "minor" is not defined. In relation to the classification "RC" (Refused Classification), the Code is more prescriptive. It states that classification should be refused to any publications that "describe or depict in a way that is likely to cause offence to a reasonable adult, a minor who is, or who appears to be, under 16 (whether the minor is engaged in sexual activity or not)": *Classifications (Publications, Films and Computer Games) Act* 1995 (Cth), Schedule. As previously noted, the effect of classification is crucial to the operation of various State and Territory offences relating to possession, or possession for sale or exhibition, copying, sale, or production or publishing of films, books or computer games.

Child pornography has been addressed at the international level by the *Convention on the Rights of the Child*.[57] Art 34 provides:

> Parties shall in particular take all appropriate national, bilateral and multilateral measures to prevent: —
>
> **(c)** The exploitative use of children in pornographic performances and materials.

As Australia is a party to the Convention, this provision could provide the constitutional basis for Federal offences under the "external affairs" power, s 51(xxix) of the Constitution. The *National Classification Code* provides some evidence of compliance with Art 34 of the Convention, however, it arguably diverges from the Convention by fixing the age of majority at 16 rather than 18 years.[58]

---

56 See UN General Assembly Resolution No 48/156, *Need to Adopt Efficient International Measures for the Prevention of the Sale of Children, Child Prostitution and Child Pornography* [20 December 1993].

57 Adopted and opened for signature, ratification and accession by General Assembly resolution 44/25 of 20 November 1989, entry into force 2 September 1990, in accordance with Art 49. In general see P Alston, S Parker, J Seymour, *Children, Rights and the Law* (Oxford: Clarendon Press, 1992). In Australia see the Parliament of the Commonwealth of Australia: Joint Standing Committee on Treaties, *United Nations Convention on the Rights of the Child*, 17th Report (Canberra, ACT: CanPrint Communications, 1998).

58 Art 1 of the *Convention on the Rights of the Child* provides that: "For the purposes of the present Convention, a child means every human being below the age of eighteen years unless under the law applicable to the child, majority is attained earlier."

Child pornography may be dealt with under existing indecency offences. However, legislatures around Australia, responding to international and domestic pressures, have enacted new offences against child pornography carrying severe penalties. These offences criminalise most dealing with material that indecently "describes or depicts persons under the age of 16". Structured in this way, these offences relieve the prosecution of the burden of proving the actual age of those involved. Neither do these offences, with the exception of Queensland and Victoria, require express proof of fault on the part of the accused.[59] Where strict liability is imposed the accused may rely on the defence of reasonable mistaken belief that the person depicted was over the age of 16. In addition, specific defences to child pornography offences have been included. For example, possession in the line of duty for law officers or classifiers has also been exempted in some jurisdictions.[60] In other jurisdictions, it is a defence that the material possessed had "artistic merit"[61] or served some scientific, medical or educational purposes.[62] For example, the offence provision (s 58) of the *Censorship Act* 1996 (WA) states that:

> It is a defence ... to prove that the article concerned is —
>
> **(a)** an article of recognized literary, artistic or scientific merit; ... and that publishing
> the article is justified as being for the public good.

These defences provide some measure of protection to those involved in law enforcement activities, as well as protecting freedom of expression and facilitating legitimate research. The extent of this protection rests on the interpretation and values of the tribunal of fact, and there is a danger that the inclusion of this type of "defence" simply legitimates the sexualisation of children provided that it is packaged with certain aesthetic conventions or scientific criteria in mind.

---

59 In Queensland, the offence requires that the accused "knowingly" possessed the prohibited material: *Classification of Computer Games and Images Act* 1995 (Qld), s 26(3); *Classification of Films Act* 1991 (Qld), s 41(3); *Classification of Publications Act* 1991 (Qld), s 14. See the similar position in Victoria under s 70(1) of the *Crimes Act* 1958 (Vic).

60 *Classification (Publications, Films and Computer Games) (Enforcement) Act* 1995 (ACT), ss 24, 32, 43; *Crimes Act* 1900 (NSW), s 578B(3); *Crimes Act* 1958 (Vic), s 70(4).

61 These jurisdictions are the Northern Territory, South Australia, Victoria and Western Australia. But in Victoria the defence of "artistic merit" does not apply if the person depicted is actually under 16: *Crimes Act* 1958 (Vic), s 70(3). In Western Australia there is an added "public good" requirement: *Censorship Act* 1996 (WA), s 58. In South Australia there should not be "undue emphasis on — indecent or offensive aspects": *Summary Offences Act* 1953 (SA), s 33(5). In the Northern Territory, with respect to computer services, the material must be of "recognised" literary or artistic merit: *Classification of Publications, Films and Computer Games Act* (NT), s 50Z(2).

62 It is a defence "if the defendant did not know, or could not reasonably be expected to have known, that the film, publication or computer game concerned is classified RC or would be classified RC": *Crimes Act* 1900 (NSW), s 578B(5)(a), or if the person depicted actually was 16 or over: s 578(5)(b). In Victoria, it is a defence if the material "possesses artistic merit or is for a genuine medical, legal, scientific or educational purpose" or "the defendant believed on reasonable grounds that the minor was aged 16 years or older or that he or she was married to the minor": see s 70(2) of the *Crimes Act* 1958 (Vic) for these and other defences. See s 58 of the *Censorship Act* 1996 (WA): "It is a defence to a charge of an offence in this Division to prove that the article concerned is (a) an article of recognized literary, artistic or scientific merit; or (b) a bona fide medical article, and that publishing the article is justified as being for the public good". See also *Summary Offences Act* 1953 (SA), s 33(5); *Classification (Publications, Films and Computer Games) Enforcement Act* 1995 (Tas), s 81(1); *Criminal Code* (NT), s 125B(5)(b); *Classification of Publications, Films and Computer Games Act* (NT), s 50Z(2). A prior written exemption is possible in Queensland: *Classification of Publications Act* 1991 (Qld), s 37; *Classification of Computer Games and Images Act* 1995 (Qld), s 59(1); *Classification of Films Act* 1991(Qld), s 58.

Technology has posed new challenges for obscenity laws: P Grabosky and R Smith, *Crime In the Digital Age* (Sydney: Federation Press, 1998), Ch 6. With the growth of cyber-porn, a problem arises in relation to the physical aspect of "possession" of indecent material where it is stored in an electronic form. A "computer generated image" has been included within the scope of "publication" for the purpose of the *Classifications (Publications, Films and Computer Games) Act* 1995 (Cth) and similar broadened definitions apply under various State and Territory offences. However, it is unclear whether "possession" for the purpose of the offences extend to unsolicited images sent as an email attachment that have not yet been deleted from the hard drive of a computer (or have been "deleted", though remain stored in the computer's recycling bin). This problem is resolved in some jurisdictions by enacting offences that do not require possession, but rather specifically criminalise the use of computer services, or phone lines, to transmit objectionable material or child pornography.[63] The question would remain, however, whether as a matter of policy the legislature intended to penalise those visiting child pornography sites unwittingly, or those visiting on purpose or those sending such material. Also, practical problems may exist with the efficacy of any 'blocking' regime set up under the *Broadcasting Services Amendment (Online Services) Act* 1999 (Cth).[64] For a review of the various regulatory approach to cyper-porn generally, including possible counterproductive effects of prohibition and criminalisation, see P Grabosky and R Smith, *Crime In the Digital Age* (Sydney: Federation Press, 1998), Ch 6. Computer offences are further explored in Chapter 13: p 697.

5. CONCLUSION

This chapter has examined how the criminal law responds to sexual wrongdoing. The process of criminalising sexual behaviour contingent on a range of factors. Age, gender and sexual orientation of both perpetrators and victims, as well as the nature of the conduct itself, are relevant to criminalisation. An important function of sexual offences, often neglected in traditional legal analysis, is the role of the criminal law in the construction of sexual identities as either "deviant" or "normal". Both female and male sexuality is constructed through legal discourse.

Feminist scholarship has rightly pointed out how the criminal law has privileged male interests and perspectives. In *Feminism and Criminology* (Sydney: Allen & Unwin, 1997), Ngaire Naffine explored how rape law constructs and legitimates a coercive form of masculine sexuality with disastrous consequences for women (p 110):

---

63 *Classification of Publications, Films and Computer Games Act* (NT), s 50Z; *Classification (Publications, Films and Computer Games) (Enforcement) Act* 1995 (Vic), ss 57, 58. See also *Crimes Act* 1914 (Cth), ss 85ZE(1)(b), 85ZE(2), 85ZE(3).

64 Parliament of the Commonwealth of Australia, Senate Select Committee on Information Technologies, *Report on the Broadcasting Services Amendment (Online Services) Bill 1999*, at 18, quoting Mr Cheah, General Manager, Regulatory Framework and Bandwidth: National Office for the Information Economy, Department of Communications, Information Technology and the Arts: "The Government accepts that no blocking technology is going to be 100 per cent effective". See also P Grabosky and R Smith, *Crime in the Digital Age* (Sydney: Federation Press, 1998), pp 133-134.

The modern law of rape generally rewards the strong male seducer for his absorption in his own sexuality. In law the man who can see only what he desires and needs, and who interprets a woman's reactions as invariably congruent with his own, whatever she does, has sex with the law's sanction.

As we have explored, recent reforms of the substantive law, procedure and evidence have confronted this model of sexuality, with mixed results, by redefining key concepts such as consent, fault and relevance.

Applying the label of "sexual violence" to rape and other sexual wrongdoing performs an important symbolic function, challenging the traditional downgrading of the seriousness of sexual abuse against women and children. While politically necessary, conjoining "sex" with "violence" has problematic legal consequences. The case studies in this chapter reveal the instability of the category "sexual violence", in particular the law's difficulties in distinguishing between sexual coercion and sexual pleasure. Such demarcation is an evaluative and normative process in which the sexuality of parties, not merely their sex and the level of harm involved, plays a crucial role. As Smart has observed in *Law, Crime and Sexuality* (London: Sage, 1995) (p 121):

> In rape even the bruises and physical injuries are typically subordinated to an understanding of the event as one of sexual passion, notwithstanding that neither aspects were consensual. In S/M [sadomasochism] the sexual gratification is subordinated to the physical harm, notwithstanding that the latter was consensual. It is hard to avoid concluding that the court's responses to such cases embodies a tolerance of non-consensual heterosex and a continuing desire to sanction consensual homosexual sex.

Critical legal analysis reveals that the criminal law embodies multiple, often conflicting, discourses on sexuality. Liberalism has exerted considerable influence on the modern law of sexual offences, with individual rights of autonomy and privacy playing important roles in reshaping laws proscribing homosexual conduct and prostitution. Paradigm sexual offences, such as rape and sexual assault, are structured around the principle of individual autonomy. Consent plays a central role in distinguishing between lawful and unlawful sexual conduct. It is important to note that liberal discourse has not always exerted such sway over rape law. Until this century, rape was not considered a sexual offence *against* the person. Under the common law, male privilege rather than (female) autonomy provided the basis for criminalisation, as reflected in the traditional immunity for rape within marriage. In the modern law, the concept of consent is entrenched and seems unassailable. Yet autonomy for the purpose of sexual offences is conceived narrowly as possession and control over one's own body. Contractual understandings of consent are evident in the case law, reflected in notions of "implied consent" and the rules governing vitiation of consent on the grounds of "fundamental mistake". This impoverished concept of consent, which reinforces a coercive/non-communicative model of sexual relations, has been rightly criticised by feminist legal scholars.

Responding to these concerns, some jurisdictions, such as New South Wales, have removed lack of consent as an ingredient for certain sexual offences, focusing on the accused's harmful conduct rather than the victim's state of mind. Other jurisdictions have adopted a positive communication standard for sexual offences, redefining consent as a "free and voluntary agreement". Though these reforms are significant, the law must address the underlying cultural and social assumptions that legitimate some degree of sexual coercion in "normal" sexual relations. Outside the criminal law the idea of sexual integrity rests upon a wide range of values beyond simple respect for personal autonomy. Values such as trust, honesty, care, respect, love, communication and pleasure are considered vital. Yet under existing sexual offences, such relational values play a limited role in shaping our understanding of the requisite physical and fault elements.

There are signs that courts, as well as legislatures, are prepared to promote a model of sexuality based on communication, trust and respect. Kirby P in *R v Tolmie* (1995) 37 NSWLR held that the complete failure to consider the consent of the other person was a blameworthy state of mind and as such constituted "recklessness" for the purpose of sexual assault. Although the decision concerned the interpretation of legislation, a similar approach to fault could be adopted in the common law. A broadened notion of recklessness will undoubtedly raise the objection that serious sexual offences must not be converted into crimes of negligence or strict liability. However, such criticism is misdirected. In *Tolmie*, Kirby P firmly reiterated that penalising "culpable inadvertence" did not alter the general principle in *Morgan* that a mistaken belief (however unreasonable) in consent negated the requisite fault element. He also stressed that the fault element based on inadvertence was not founded on a hypothetical reasonable person standard, but rather on the accused's complete failure to consider the issue of consent in circumstances where the risk of non-consent would have been obvious to someone with the accused's mental capacity. Commendably, the approach to fault in *Tolmie* traversed the traditional binary opposition of subjectivism versus objectivism. While demonstrating fidelity to fundamental principles of individual justice in the process of fault attribution, the decision recognised that the criminal law, consistent with the objectives of rape law reform, must impose an ethic of care and responsibility on individuals who engage in acts of sexual intimacy.

The law of sexual offences is also concerned with upholding and policing sexual decency. There is a tension within legal discourse between the principles of liberalism and welfare. This tension, which is evident in many compartments of the criminal law, has been explored in Chapter 1. Individual rights of autonomy and privacy compete with community interests. For some offences, maintaining community standards of sexual decency are dominant considerations, subordinating individual rights of autonomy and privacy. Sexual offences such as gross indecency and obscenity demonstrate little (if any) concern for individual rights or freedoms, functioning primarily as public order offences. Conceived as "offences against public morality", these crimes protect the community from conduct or material considered offensive. In the modern context, the limits of sexual decency are fixed objectively by reference to "community standards" of decency. The notion of "community" plays an important symbolic and ideological function in drawing the boundaries between legitimate and deviant sexuality. However, a standard of decency based on the "right-minded" or "reasonable" person has potentially repressive consequences. This standard implicitly fixes male heterosexuality as the norm of comparison, significantly restricting the scope for sexual diversity and toleration.

Community interests may trample upon individual autonomy and privacy, leading to accusations of moral and legal paternalism. In some cases, this paternalism is justified because the victim is vulnerable to sexual exploitation. Legislation has identified categories of vulnerable "victims" who are to be protected from sexual activity regardless of consent. For offences involving children or mentally impaired persons, concern about impaired capacity to consent mingle with moral objections to the nature of the sexual attraction. For example, in the area of child sexual exploitation, the patterns of law enforcement and level of punishment are contingent both on the nature of the relationship between the offender and the victim (intra-familial/extra-familial) and the sexual orientation of the offender. Society is presently gripped in a moral panic about homosexual pedophilia, which is viewed with greater moral repugnance than other forms of child sexual abuse. This differential response to homosexual/heterosexual child sexual exploitation reveals the political influences involved in the construction of sexual deviance, and how the private sphere continues to be implicated in concealing and downgrading sexual abuse that occurs within the family.

The law governing sexual offences is not a coherent or unified body of law. The level of diversification is a reflection of the fact that sexual offences perform a wide variety of functions in modern society. In symbolic terms, sexual offences have become an arena in which the claims of liberalism, morality and feminism are contested. This conflict, which is often suppressed in legal discourse, reflects the pluralism of values and interests that legitimately impinge on the criminalisation of sexual behaviour. Sexuality is essential to human flourishing and a criminal law that acknowledges the value of sexual pluralism, rather than simply perpetuating sexual repression, would, in our opinion, provide a better blueprint for future legal development.

13

Property Offences

> A lawyer with his briefcase can steal more than a thousand men with guns

Mario Puzo,
The Godfather (1969)

1. INTRODUCTION

This chapter examines a wide range of offences against property. In this area, the law is principally concerned with the protection of private property.[1] It achieves this protection through offences such as larceny, theft and fraud.[2] Across these areas, the criminal law has experienced acute difficulties in adapting existing offences to new situations. The industrial revolution in the 19th century heralded increasingly complex commercial dealings that relied upon cheques, credit and other negotiable instruments. Yet the common law of larceny, geared toward the physical taking and carrying away of portable chattels, found it difficult to accommodate novel forms of fraud involving intangible property. A plethora of statutory offences was enacted to plug the gaps in larceny. The common law also responded to the growth in commercial fraud by fashioning a "catch-all" offence from the law of conspiracy. The inchoate offence of conspiracy to defraud has been examined in Chapter 9: pp 46off.

---

1   This was not always the case. Reflecting the approach of Roman law, the early common law of larceny in the 15th century was more concerned with keeping the peace than protecting private property. At that time, obtaining property by deception, fraud or breach of trust was not considered a public wrong: D Brown, D Farrier and D Weisbrot, *Criminal Laws* (2nd ed, Sydney: Federation Press, 1996), p 1104.

2   The protection of property also relies on offences against criminal damage. While these offences overlap with the modern law of theft, they are beyond the scope this chapter. Due to the conceptual differences between theft and criminal damage, there is a proposal that criminal damage should be included in a separate chapter of the *Model Criminal Code*: Model Criminal Code Officers Committee, *Chapter 4: Damage and Computer Offences*, Discussion Paper (2000).

At the end of the 20th century, the "Information Technology Revolution" heralded yet another dramatic change in the nature of commercial activity, creating new opportunities for the fraudulent appropriation of property and challenges for the criminal law. Uncertainty over the nature of information *as property* and whether particular forms of dishonesty are covered by existing laws have led to new crimes against computer fraud. Similar questions have arisen over criminal damage and whether interference with intangible property in the form of computer data should be criminalised as a distinct offence.

In addition to these substantive questions, the complexity of modern commercial transactions raises concern that the procedures for dealing with "serious commercial fraud" are inadequate. It has been argued that non-expert jurors may be less capable of evaluating financial impropriety, thereby increasing the costs and delays in prosecution, as well as the risk of unwarranted acquittals. As we shall explore below at p 685, the definition of dishonesty depends on establishing and applying community standards, which can present difficulties for jurors (and judges) in the context of complex commercial transactions. Although these procedural and evidential questions are clearly related to the substantive law, they have usually been addressed as separate law reform projects.[3]

In terms of law reform, this area of the criminal law has been subject to extensive refurbishment. In the 1960s, the Criminal Law Revision Committee (CLRC) in the United Kingdom recommended the abolition of the common law of larceny. Rather than continue an ad hoc and piecemeal approach to modernisation through statutory supplementation, the CLRC recommended that larceny and related offences should be replaced with a comprehensive code dealing with property offences. This model was enacted by the *Theft Act* 1968 (UK). The United Kingdom Act has formed the basis of the property offences enacted by the *Crimes (Theft) Act* 1973 (Vic), and the *Crimes (Amendment) Act (No 4)* 1985 (ACT). It has also influenced the approach adopted to the offence of "stealing" enacted in s 209 of the *Criminal Code* (NT).

More than a decade ago, Brent Fisse in *Howard's Criminal Law* (5th ed, Sydney: Law Book Company Ltd, 1990), doubted at pp 283-315, 198 whether the United Kingdom *Theft Act* model would bring the simplifications hoped for. His chapter examined the reforms enacted in the Australian Capital Territory and Victoria as a postscript to the examination of larceny. This chapter proceeds with greater optimism about the *Theft Act* model and the prospects for modernisation and codification in this area. Since Fisse's somewhat pessimistic assessment, the Model Criminal Code Officers Committee (MCCOC) has recommended that the *Theft Act* model, with minor modifications, should be adopted in all jurisdictions: *Chapter 3 — Theft, Fraud, Bribery and Related Offences*, Final Report (1995), p 6. While the process of codification has been slower than expected, a Bill is currently before the Commonwealth Parliament that will enact the *Theft Act* model for federal property offences. Indeed, the movement towards uniformity in relation to property offences appears to be stronger than in other areas. There is a widespread perception that larceny and its complex array of

---

3   In the United Kingdom, the obstacles to the investigation and prosecution of serious commercial fraud were examined by the Roskill Committee: *Fraud Trials Committee Report* (London: HMSO, 1986). Such reviews have led to the establishment of specialised multidisciplinary investigative bodies of accountants, police and lawyers empowered to investigate commercial fraud. For a review of these new investigators in Australia see M Findlay, S Odgers and S Yeo, *Australian Criminal Justice* (2nd ed, Melbourne: Oxford University Press, 1999), Ch 3.

supplementary offences is unable to cope with sophisticated fraud. Within a federal criminal system, there is considerable anxiety that jurisdictional differences means that sophisticated crime and criminals will be drawn to those jurisdictions with the weakest criminal laws and powers of enforcement. As the MCCOC noted (p vi):

> Whether a person gets convicted of theft, forgery or bribery or a related offence should not depend on those offences having different elements on one side of the River Tweed from the other. Justice and efficiency demand consistent if not uniform offence provisions.

Later the MCCOC stated (p vi-vii):

> More than most offences, fraud knows no jurisdictional boundaries and, in view of what has come to be termed "the excesses of the 80s", the need for a uniform and principled approach to the problems of fraud and these related offences has never been greater.

The Committee noted that there was overwhelming support from respondents for the *Theft Act* model and the goal of uniformity.

Uniformity also offers administrative benefits in terms of simplification and streamlining. As the MCCOC noted, the 150 offences dealing with theft, fraud and related offences in New South Wales would be replaced by a code of about 20 offences contained in Chapter 3 of the *Model Criminal Code*: p 1. The administration of uniform laws offer practical advantages in terms of legal training, production of reference material, development of precedent and consistency of sentencing across jurisdictions.

> **Property crime is very common, accounting for 86% of the major crimes reported to the police. Unlawful entry (burglary) and motor vehicle theft accounted for 33% and 10% of recorded offences respectively, while other types of theft (for example, stealing, pickpocketing) accounted for 43% of the total: Australian Institute of Criminology, *Australian Crime — Facts and Figures* (1999), pp 10-11.**

The *Theft Act* model offers the prospect of greater certainty, consistency and predictability in the criminal law. The liberal promise of codification has been critically evaluated in Chapter 2: pp 70ff. Simplification was an important aim of the original drafters. It was hoped that fundamental legal concepts, such as dishonesty, could be applied by the jury according to their "ordinary meaning" without complex technical directions from the trial judge. The statutory offence of theft tried to avoid the complexities of civil law governing the transfer of ownership that had bedevilled larceny, especially in cases of mistake. This objective of simplification has remained illusive, as the MCCOC has noted (p 5):

> There is an irreducible level of complexity that comes with complex financial transactions and apparently straightforward transactions like writing a cheque can raise complex issues of civil law and the nature of intangible property and who owns it.

While the common law of larceny centres on the physical element of taking property, the *Theft Act* model focuses to a greater degree on the fault element. The concept of dishonesty is crucial in distinguishing between a legitimate and illegitimate interference with another person's property:

MCCOC, *Chapter 3: Theft, Fraud, Bribery and Related Offences*, Final Report (1995), p 11. While dishonesty plays a fundamental role in controlling the scope of theft, there remains uncertainty over its meaning, in particular whether it is determined by reference to the accused's belief (subjective) and/or community standards (objective). As we shall see, the definition of dishonesty remains controversial despite the recent decision of the High Court in *Peters v The Queen* (1998) 192 CLR 493.

Notwithstanding the ambitions of the drafters to minimise reliance on case law to determine the meaning of key elements of theft, the *Theft Acts* have generated a steady stream of appeals in England and Australia. Like its predecessor larceny, the modern law of theft is continually challenged by technological and commercial innovation. Property offences have particularly been tested by the criminal ingenuity involved in "white collar crime". As the mafia in *The Godfather* could attest, professional groups such as lawyers, accountants and other advisers can be employed to create complex "paper trails" concealing the tainted origins of property or profits obtained from illegal activities. Indeed, it is no coincidence that the recent High Court decision of *Peters v The Queen* (1998) 192 CLR 493 reviewing the definition of dishonesty arose from the conviction of a solicitor for fraud who had helped a client to launder money through a series of sham mortgage transactions. The elements of conspiracy to defraud are discussed in Chapter 9, pp 460ff. In addition to fraud offences, these activities may now be caught by money-laundering offences and the wide-ranging powers to confiscate the proceeds of crime enacted in most jurisdictions: see, for example, *Proceeds of Crime Act* 1987 (Cth). Money laundering, which may be regarded as the "new property" crime, is further examined in Chapter 15: pp 863ff.

2. THE COMMON LAW OF LARCENY

The common law of larceny applies in New South Wales and South Australia, though it has been supplemented by statutory provisions. The basic offence of larceny is also complemented by an array of aggravated and related offences. Larceny provided the basis, with minor amendment, for the statutory offences enacted in the Code jurisdictions of Queensland, Tasmania and Western Australia. It also formed the basis the property offences enacted to protect Commonwealth property inserted into the *Crimes Act* 1914 (Cth).[4]

Larceny is one of the most complex common law offences, "more distinguished perhaps than any other offence by its anomalies and irrationalities": B Fisse, *Howard's Criminal Law* (5th ed, Sydney: Law Book Company Ltd, 1990), p 198. The technical complexity of larceny may be explained by the array of overlapping statutory offences enacted to plug gaps that appeared in the basic offence.[5]

---

4   The principal property offences in the *Crimes Act* 1914 (Cth) are s 71 (stealing Commonwealth property); s 29 (destroying or damaging Commonwealth property); s 29A (false pretences); s 29D (defrauding the Commonwealth); s 29B (false representation).

5   For an excellent socio-historical account of larceny see J Hall, *Theft, Law and Society* (2nd ed, Bloomington, IN: Bobbs-Merrill, 1952). See also CR Williams, *Property Offences* (3rd ed, Sydney: LBC, 1999), pp 2-7; D Brown, D Farrier and D Weisbrot, *Criminal Laws* (2nd ed, Sydney: Federation Press, 1996), pp 1110-1115.

As Chapter 1 highlighted, it is also important to appreciate how changes in criminal procedure can have an impact on the development of substantive law: p 15. In England, "simple larceny" was distinguished from the more serious offence of "grand larceny", which applied where the stolen property was worth more than one shilling.[6] With the effects of inflation over time, the scope of the offence grew wider and wider. To limit the scope of this capital offence, the courts drew elaborate and technical distinctions between different types of misappropriation. Parliament was often compelled to intervene enacting a wide range of supplementary offences. Although larceny is no longer a capital offence, its irrational elements are considered too well-established to be abolished except by way of legislation.[7]

Larceny and theft share some common elements. This section contains an overview of the distinctive physical and fault elements of larceny. Since many of the provisions introduced by the *Theft Act* model address perceived deficiencies in the common law, the discussion of some aspects of the common law (such as the effect of mistake on transfer of property) will be deferred until the next section. The following Table sets out the elements of larceny and theft offences across Australian jurisdictions.

TABLE 1:

Basic Larceny and Theft Offences

JURISDICTION	OFFENCE	FAULT ELEMENTS		PHYSICAL ELEMENTS	
ACT *Crimes Act* 1900	theft s 99	dishonest s 94	intention permanently to deprive s 94	appropriation s 94	property belonging to another person s 94
NSW common law	larceny *Crimes Act* 1900 (NSW), s 117	fraudulent	intention permanently to deprive	taking and carrying away without con- sent of owner or person in possession or control	property belonging to another
NT *Criminal Code*	stealing s 210	—	intention of depriving s 209(1)	unlawful appropriation s 209	property of another s 209

---

6   The distinctions between simple and grand larceny have not been retained in Australia: see for example *Crimes Act* 1900 (NSW), s 116.

7   In *Croton v The Queen* (1967) 117 CLR 326 the High Court held that the common law of larceny did not extend to stealing intangible property such as debts. Such an extension, which was clearly needed, had to be effected by legislation rather than common law development.

Table 1 continued

JURISDICTION	OFFENCE	FAULT ELEMENTS		PHYSICAL ELEMENTS	
QLD *Criminal Code*	stealing	fraudulent	fraudulent requires intention permanently to deprive	taking or converting	anything that is the property of any person which is moveable or capable of being made moveable
	s 398(1)	s 391(1), (2)	s 391(2)	s 391(1)	s 390
SA common law	larceny *Criminal Law Consolidation Act* 1935 (SA), s 131	fraudulent	intention permanently to deprive	taking and carrying away without consent of owner or person in possession or control	property belonging to another
TAS *Criminal Code*	stealing	dishonestly	intention permanently to deprive	taking or converting without consent of owner, possessor or controller	every movable thing which is the property of any person, or a thing which is attached to or forms part of any real property as soon as it is completely severed therefrom
	s 234	s 226(1)	s 226(1)	s 226(1) and (2)	s 227
VIC *Crimes Act* 1958	theft	dishonest s 72(1)	intention of permanently depriving	appropriation	property belonging to another
	s 74	s 73	s 72(1)	s 72(1)	s 72(1)
WA *Criminal Code*	stealing	fraudulent	fraudulent requires intention permanently to deprive	taking or converting	every inanimate thing which is the property of any person, and which is movable, or capable of being made moveable
	s 371(1)	s 371(1) and (2)	s 371(2)	s 371(1)	s 370

Table 1 continued

JURISDICTION	OFFENCE	FAULT ELEMENTS		PHYSICAL ELEMENTS	
Model Criminal Code	theft s 15.1	dishonesty	intention to deprive permanently	appropriation	property belonging to another

2.1 THE PHYSICAL ELEMENT: TAKING AND CARRYING AWAY

The key element of larceny is "asportation", that is, the physical taking and carrying away of property. The courts took a generous view of this requirement holding that the slightest movement of any part of the property could suffice.[8] The removal of the property had to occur against the owner's will, which in the modern law is now understood as without the owner's consent: *Kennison v Daire* (1985) 38 SASR 404 at 412, per Jacobs J. The common law also required that the initial taking of the property and the fraudulent intent must coincide. This requirement exposed major deficiencies in the law which, as we shall explore below, were remedied by postponing the moment of taking through the use of legal fictions such as the doctrine of "continuing possession" and "breaking bulk".

The general requirement of concurrence between the physical and fault elements precluded a conviction for larceny in cases where the accused innocently acquired property without committing a trespass. For example, a person who obtained possession by mistake could not be guilty of larceny. A subsequent fraudulent intention to retain or deal with the property did not convert the original innocent asportation into larceny. However, the 19th century courts in Australia were understandably reluctant to allow acquittals in these circumstances. There was a strong line of authority establishing that innocent acquisition of another person's sheep or cattle would not preclude larceny in cases where the person continued in the unlawful possession (constituting a tort of trespass) in the knowledge that he or she was not entitled to that property: *R v Finlayson* (1864) 3 SCR (NSW) 301. There remained some uncertainty over the precise rationale and scope of this rule, including doubts as to whether it could be applied to inanimate as well as animate objects: B Fisse, *Howard's Criminal Law* (5th ed, Sydney: Law Book Company Ltd, 1990), pp 202-205. The 19th century judges resorted to the legal fiction of "continuing possession" to overcome the narrowness of the doctrines of asportation and concurrence. As Fisse notes, "The only purpose served by the idea of continuing trespass is the preservation of the old rule that there is no larceny unless the intention to steal coincides in time with the wrongful taking": p 204.

The conceptual strains placed on larceny to accommodate cases of "fraudulent conversion" led to further modifications in the 19th century. Under the codes enacted in Queensland and Western Australia, the statutory offence of stealing was extended to include the fraudulent taking or conversion of property: *Criminal Code* (Qld), s 391; *Criminal Code* (WA), s 371. Any subsequent

---

8   *R v Lapier* (1784) 168 ER 263; *R v Walsh* (1824) 168 ER 1166; *R v Taylor* [1911] 1 KB 674; *Wallis v Lane* [1964] VR 293. The principles developed in these cases is explored in B Fisse, *Howard's Criminal Law* (5th ed, Sydney: Law Book Company Ltd, 1990), p 201.

dealing with the property inconsistent with the rights of the owner could constitute fraudulent conversion: *Ilich v The Queen* (1987) 162 CLR 100 at 116, per Gibbs CJ. The statutory distinction between taking and conversion in the Code jurisdictions now assumes less significance following the gradual acceptance of the notion that taking may be a "continuing act".[9] As we shall explore below at p 689, the *Theft Act* model has applied a similarly elastic approach to the physical element of dishonest appropriation, which extends to cases where a person innocently comes by property without stealing it, and then subsequently decides to keep it or deal with the property as the owner: *Crimes Act* 1900 (ACT), s 96(2); *Criminal Code* (NT), s 209(1); *Crimes Act* 1958 (Vic), s 73(4).

Similar problems of conversion have arisen in relation to "larceny by bailee". A bailment arises where the owner grants possession of property to another with specific instructions for its use or safekeeping. Since the initial possession was not a trespass against the will of the owner, there was uncertainty as to whether the employees who appropriated property entrusted to them by their employers could be guilty of larceny. Even before the doctrine of continuing possession emerged, the common law had held that a servant who received possession of a consignment of goods, and subsequently appropriated them, could be guilty of larceny: *Carriers Case* (1473) YB 13 Edw. The rationale for the decision came to be based on the fact that the servant only acquired possession when he or she "broke bulk" and took the contents of the consignment.

To keep the scope of larceny by bailee within proper bounds, the courts carefully scrutinised the nature, scope and obligations imposed on the bailee. A number of uncertainties arose over whether larceny could be applied to the misappropriation of *the proceeds* of the property bailed or was limited to the property itself. Parliament also intervened in the 18th century enacting special offences that targeted theft within the employment context. The statutory offence of embezzlement dispensed with the requirement of initial trespass to property and criminalised misappropriation of property (including money and other valuable securities) and proceeds already in the possession of the servant. These offences were determined by reference to the occupational status of the accused, and tended to be restricted to individuals with special fiduciary obligations such as agents, clerks and servants, tenants and lodgers, company officers, trustees, public servants, partners and joint owners and persons exercising a power of attorney.[10] As we shall explore in the next section, the *Theft Act* model has not recognised a separate specie of "theft by bailee", but contains general provisions dealing with individuals who receive property initially without stealing it, and are under a legal obligation to account for property or its proceeds in particular ways.

In relation to larceny, another critical distinction emerged between taking property *without consent*, and obtaining property *with consent* through trickery or deception. A number of legal questions arose in relation to "larceny by trick". Originally obtaining property by fraud was not considered to be larceny, but rather the less serious misdemeanour of public cheating. The offence

---

9 RG Kenny, *An Introduction to Criminal Law in Queensland and Western Australia* (5th ed, Sydney: Butt, 2000), p 267, citing *R v Johnston* [1973] Qd R 303; *R v Hennessey* [1976] Tas SR (NC) 4, 154; *Coyne v Dreyer* (1991) 13 MVR 540; *R v McDonald* [1992] 2 Qd R 634.

10 See *Crimes Act* 1900 (NSW), ss 155-178A; *Criminal Law Consolidation Act* 1935 (SA), ss 176-192; *Criminal Code* (Qld), ss 398(5)-(8); *Criminal Code* (WA), ss 378(6)-(9). B Fisse, *Howard's Criminal Law* (Sydney: Law Book Company Ltd, 1990), pp 209-210. The historical development of these laws is explored in D Brown, D Farrier and D Weisbrot, *Criminal Laws* (2nd ed, Sydney: Federation Press, 1996), pp 1110-1115.

distinguished between conduct that aimed to defraud "the public" and "private cheats" which only gave rise to civil liability. The misdemeanour of cheating has largely fallen into disuse in Australia. Indeed, the statutory offences of cheating included in the 19th century Griffiths code have recently been abolished in Queensland and Western Australia.[11]

Tax Cheats

In the United Kingdom, the common law offence of public cheating has recently been revived to deal with tax evasion schemes not caught by existing theft and revenue offences: D Ormerod, "Cheating the Revenue" [1998] *Criminal Law Review* 627.

At the end of the 18th century, there was considerable uncertainty as to whether larceny could be used against obtaining property by fraud or deception. The courts eventually resolved the uncertainty by recognising "larceny by trick" but only in cases where the accused had used deception to obtain the initial possession: *R v Pear* (1779) 168 ER 208; see further G Ferris, "The Origins of 'Larceny by Trick' and 'Constructive Possession'" [1998] Crim LR 175. The legislature also intervened to create a general offence of obtaining property by false pretences. Although there is an obvious overlap between the common law and statutory offences, the courts drew complex distinctions in an effort to preserve the conceptual unity of larceny and to avoid duplication of charges. Larceny by trick involved fraudulent conduct that had induced the victim to transfer *possession* of his or her property, whereas the statutory offence of obtaining property by false pretences involved conduct that induced the victim to transfer *ownership* as well: *R v Ward* (1938) 38 SR (NSW) 308 at 313. This distinction preserved the idea that larceny under the common law was a crime against possession — since fraud was used to obtain possession, the victim's consent to the taking by the accused was negated, leaving the accused guilty of larceny. This distinction between these two offences has been criticised as being artificial since in both cases the accused acts with the same fraudulent intent and causes the same harm to the interests of the property owner.[12] A review of the available authorities reveals that the distinction was not always applied in a consistent or principled manner by the courts.[13]

Since it was firmly established that an accused could not be guilty of both charges on the same facts, the uncertain relationship between larceny and the statutory offence of obtaining by false pretences has provided scope for appeals on technicalities often leading to unmeritorious

---

11   The statutory offences of cheating were enacted in s 429 of the *Criminal Code* (Qld), and s 411 of the *Criminal Code* (WA) (though these offences were abolished in 1997 and 1990 respectively). Cheating remains an offence under s 252 of the *Criminal Code* (Tas): "Any person who, with intent to defraud, by means of any trick or device, obtains from any person, or induces any person to deliver to any person, anything capable of being stolen, is guilty of a crime."

12   CR Williams, *Property Offences* (3rd ed, Sydney: LBC, 1999), p 144 discussing the views of J Hall, *Theft, Law and Society* (2nd ed, Bloomington, IN: Bobbs-Merrill, 1952), p 45.

13   The artificiality of the distinction is apparent in the cases involving "ringing the changes", a common trick where in the course of a transaction, the accused asks for change, and then confusing the teller by producing further money and altering the request. Although the parties intend the ownership in the money to pass, the courts have always treated this case as larceny by trick. On the malleability of this distinction, see B Fisse, *Howard's Criminal Law* (5th ed, Sydney: Law Book Company Ltd, 1990), p 222; CR Williams and M Weinberg, *Property Offences* (2nd ed, Sydney: Law Book Company Ltd, 1986), pp 123-124.

acquittals: *R v Mark* (1902) 28 VLR 610. In jurisdictions that draw this distinction, the prosecutor's dilemma over which offence to charge has been addressed by special statutory rules allowing for alternate verdicts.[14]

Another complicating factor in deceit cases is that the property obtained is typically money. Money is both intangible and fungible property. Money is intangible in the sense that the true value of each note or coin is that it represents a debt (*chose in action*). Fungible property, being substitutable by nature, presents difficulties in cases where a person obtaining the money has an intention to repay it *in specie*, that is, using notes of equivalent value. Does the inability to repay the *exact* notes originally obtained leave that person open to charges of larceny or obtaining by false pretences? As we shall explore below at p 723, the Australian Capital Territory has addressed this problem through deeming provisions. The confusing position under the common law is discussed in B Fisse, *Howard's Criminal Law* (5th ed, Sydney: Law Book Company Ltd, 1990), pp 217-219.

Cheating on Tax and Welfare: Same Fraud, Different Outcome

David Brown and Russell Hogg in *Rethinking Law and Order* (Sydney: Pluto Press, 1998) note (pp 95-98) that the majority of tax and Medicare fraud is dealt with by civil and administrative measures to recover losses, rather than by criminal prosecution. Welfare fraud, by contrast, seems much more likely to be prosecuted. The authors conclude that the distinction in levels of enforcement activity could be explained as a product of class bias, or that there exist sound organisational and economic reasons for not enforcing criminal sanctions in cases of tax and Medicare fraud. In relation to the latter, the lower level of enforcement may reflect the resources and powers available to investigators, as well as the capabilities of those accused of fraud to defend themselves. Whatever the reason, it is clear that the criminal law operates in a non-egalitarian manner. More significantly, this research reveals that "a private form of administrating justice" has grown up to replace the criminal law: the departments involved (such as the Australian Tax Office) give priority to administrative "penalties" and debt recovery through civil courts. These processes can achieve the same educative and punitive outcome as the criminal law without incurring the cost of criminal litigation. Operating in the shadow of the criminal law, these processes are largely disinterested in moral evaluations of the offender's conduct. This process of pervasive demoralisation, with its emphasis on cost-effectiveness and efficiency, is consistent with the "technocratic" model of criminal justice, discussed in Chapter 1: pp 40ff.

---

14 *Crimes Act* 1900 (NSW), ss 120, 183; *Criminal Code* (Qld), s 581; *Criminal Code* (Tas), s 338; *Criminal Code* (WA), s 599.

2.2 THE FAULT ELEMENT: FRAUDULENT INTENT

The concept of fraudulent intent under the common law (and its statutory variant) plays an important role in distinguishing between theft and other forms of taking that are not considered sufficiently morally objectionable to warrant criminalisation. The courts are vigilant not to apply the stigma of larceny or theft to conduct that lacks "moral obloquy". As Lawton LJ noted in *R v Feely* [1973] QB 530 at 541, it is the fault element "whether it is labelled 'fraudulently' or 'dishonestly', which distinguishes a taking without consent from stealing".

The common law requirement of fraudulent intent developed case-by-case with the courts attempting to identify situations where the taking of property warranted criminal condemnation. In terms of fault, the early common law emphasised simply that the taking of property must be "without a claim of right", that is, without a lawful right to the property. In the early 19th century the word "fraudulently" was used interchangeably with "without a claim of right": *R v Holloway* (1849) 3 Cox 241 at 244. By the middle of the 20th century, some court emphasised that the fault element for larceny required proof of a positive, subjective mental state on the part of the accused. The requirement that the taking of property must be without claim of right was gradually refashioned into a mental state based on the *belief* that the taking is without a claim of right. In *R v Williams* [1953] 1 QB 660, the English Court of Criminal Appeal considered the fault required for the statutory offence of larceny in the *Larceny Act* 1916 (UK). Lord Goddard CJ emphasised (at 668) that the requirement that the property was taken "without claim of right" and "fraudulently" meant that individuals "knew that they had no right to take the money which they knew was not their money".[15]

Formulated as a subjective test, the courts have held that it does not matter whether that belief in the legal claim to the property is unfounded either in fact or law provided the belief is honest.[16] As we shall explore in the next section, the *Theft Act* model has retained a claim of right by incorporating the concept into the definition of dishonesty — an appropriation of property under a belief in a claim of right is deemed not to be dishonest.

In addition to the development of a claim of right, the common law has identified a number of situations where there is a strong inference of fraud. The following statutory definition, which is generally considered an accurate summary of the existing common law, was adopted in s 391(2) of the *Criminal Code* (Qld) and s 371(2) of the *Criminal Code* (WA). Section 391(2) states that:

> A person who takes or converts anything capable of being stolen is deemed to do so fraudulently if the person does so with any of the following intents, that is to say —

---

15 This decision was considered in *R v Cockburn* [1968] 1 All ER 466. In that case, the Court of Appeal emphasised that lack of moral obloquy was not a necessary element of larceny, though it may constitute substantial mitigation of sentence. The Court stressed that larceny is the taking of property against the will of the owner without any claim of right, and with intent of taking it permanently to deprive the owner of it: at 468, per Winn LJ. The decision left the law in a state of uncertainty since it suggested that the term fraudulently did not require proof of a subjective requirement beyond an intent to permanently deprive.

16 *R v Bernhard* [1938] 2 KB 264 at 270; *R v Powell* [1962] QWN 123 at 129, per Gibbs J; *R v Hancock* [1963] Crim LR 572.

(a) an intent to permanently deprive the owner of the thing of it;

(b) an intent to permanently deprive any person who has any special property in the thing of such property;

(c) an intent to use the thing as a pledge or security;

(d) an intent to part with it on a condition as to its return which the person taking or converting it may be unable to perform;

(e) an intent to deal with it in such a manner that it cannot be returned in the condition in which it was at the time of the taking or conversion;

(f) in the case of money — an intent to use it at the will of the person who takes or converts it, although the person may intend to afterwards repay the amount to the owner.

As we shall see below, these definitions of fraudulent intent form the basis of the statutory definition of dishonesty, though the fault elements are not identical. In those jurisdictions that continue to apply larceny, the courts are increasingly willing to consult appellate authorities on the *Theft Act* model for guidance on the meaning and scope of fraudulent intent. In *R v Glenister* [1980] 2 NSWLR 597, for example, the New South Wales Court of Criminal Appeal held that the meaning of "fraudulently appropriates" under an offence dealing with company directors had the same meaning as "dishonestly appropriates" under the *Theft Act* model. The Court applied the leading English authorities, directing the jury that the question of dishonesty should be determined by reference to the "current standards of ordinary decent people". As in other areas of the criminal law where there is some degree of legislative variation, such as provocation, the courts are striving to develop uniformity in the interpretation of fundamental concepts in the criminal law: see Ch 2, pp 72-73.

3. THEFT OFFENCES

The first Australian jurisdiction to adopt the *Theft Act* model based on the *Theft Act* 1968 (UK) was Victoria in 1974. Victoria abolished the crime of larceny and replaced it with a statutory offence of theft. It also abolished related offences that had been enacted to plug gaps in the common law, such as embezzlement. Other offences such as obtaining by false pretences and receiving stolen property were replaced by new offences of obtaining property by deception and handling stolen property: *Crimes Act* 1958 (Vic), ss 71-96. In 1985, the Australian Capital Territory abolished larceny and related common law offences and adopted the *Theft Act* model: *Crimes Act* 1900 (ACT), ss 93-126. This reform followed the same general pattern of reforms in the United Kingdom and Victoria, though in one respect diverged from the *Theft Act* model by including obtaining property by deception within the basic offence of theft. There are further minor divergences where the Australian Capital Territory legislature sought to address complications that had emerged in the operation of the existing theft offences enacted in the United Kingdom and Victoria. The Northern Territory also remodelled its offence of stealing: *Criminal Code* (NT), s 209. Although the offence is structured differently, the definitions used are substantially similar to those contained in the *Theft Act* model.

The key elements of the theft offences in the various jurisdictions are the same, and for the purpose of the following discussion we will discuss the law in general terms, identifying jurisdictional differences as appropriate. We will then examine the provisions of the *Model Criminal Code* and the extent to which they diverge from existing approaches.

The basic offence of theft under the *Theft Act* model is committed where a person dishonestly appropriates property belonging to another with an intention to permanently deprive the other of it: *Crimes Act* 1900 (ACT), s 94; *Crimes Act* 1958 (Vic), s 72. These sections designate this conduct as "stealing", which is then stated as constituting the offence of theft. The Model Criminal Code Officers Committee (MCCOC) suggested that the reference to "stealing" in these definition sections is unnecessary, and proposed its deletion from the Code: *Chapter 3 — Theft, Fraud, Bribery and Related Offences*, Final Report (1995), p 31. The MCCOC concluded (p 31) that the core offence of theft had six elements:

(1) dishonesty;

(2) appropriation;

(3) property;

(4) belonging to another;

(5) intention to deprive permanently; and

(6) the requirement that all the elements exist at the same time.

The inclusion of the last element, namely the requirement of concurrence, followed the classification of the offence in Fisse, *Howard's Criminal Law* (5th ed, Sydney: Law Book Company Ltd, 1990), p 285. It should be noted that concurrence is a general requirement in the criminal law, not a specific element of theft. The principle of concurrence or contemporaneity is considered more generally in Chapter 3, p 192. In this chapter, we do not propose to devote a separate section to this requirement, but will examine the concurrence issues as they arise in the context of the specific elements, such as dishonesty, appropriation and property belonging to another.

The brevity and apparent simplicity of the basic formulation of theft is misleading. Each element is supplemented by an extensive definition section clarifying its meaning and scope, as well as case law examining its application in particular contexts.

3.1 DISHONESTY

Reflecting its fundamental importance to the operation of the modern law of theft and related offences, dishonesty is the first concept defined in the *Model Criminal Code: Chapter 3 — Theft, Fraud, Bribery and Related Offences*, Final Report (1995), p 10. As the "core fault element" for the offences contained in this Chapter of the *Model Criminal Code*, dishonesty replaced the common law requirement of fraudulent intent for larceny.

The *Theft Act* 1968 (UK) did not define dishonesty, leaving the matter for the jury to decide as a question of fact: Criminal Law Revision Committee, *Theft and Related Offences*, Eighth Report (London: HMSO Cmnd 2977, 1966), para 20. However, the legislation offered a partial (negative) definition identifying those circumstances that are *not* to be regarded as dishonest. The definition sections, which have also been enacted in Australia, state that a person shall not be regarded as dishonest if he or she appropriates property:

(a) in the belief that he or she has a lawful right to deprive the other person of the property on behalf of himself or herself or a third person;

(b) he or she appropriates the property in the belief that the other person would consent to the appropriation if the other person knew of it and of the circumstances in which it was done; or

(c) in the case of property other than property held by the person as trustee or personal representative — he or she appropriates the property in the belief that the person to whom the property belongs cannot be discovered by taking reasonable steps.[17]

The *Theft Act* model also includes a partial (positive) definition of dishonesty relating to an accused's intention to pay for the property appropriated: *Theft Act* 1968 (UK), s 2(2). Similar provisions have been adopted in the Australian Capital Territory, the Northern Territory and Victoria, which state that a person who appropriates property belonging to another person may be dishonest notwithstanding that he or she is willing to pay for the property.[18]

These statutory definitions of dishonesty are not exhaustive. There is some doubt as to whether further guidance on the concept should be offered beyond the express definitions included in the legislation. Appellate courts in England and Australia have grappled with the *general* meaning of dishonesty. The controversy over this fault element has centred on two issues, namely:

▬ whether dishonesty is a question of fact or law; and

▬ whether dishonesty is a subjective, objective or hybrid concept.

As we shall explore below, the English courts have adopted an "ordinary meaning" approach to dishonesty. Under this approach, the tribunal of fact (the jury or magistrate) evaluates the accused's dishonesty by reference to the standards of ordinary decent people: *R v Feely* [1973] QB 530; *R v Ghosh* [1982] 3 WLR 110. In the Australian Capital Territory and Victoria, the courts have refused to follow the English approach, viewing dishonesty as a legal rather than a moral question upon which the courts should give guidance to the jury or magistrate. Although the Australian tests of dishonesty have considerable merit, the High Court in *Peters v The Queen* (1998) 192 CLR 493 has recently endorsed the English tests of dishonesty in the context of conspiracy to defraud. The decision has clearly exposed the tensions between these two competing conceptions of dishonesty, leaving unresolved questions about the meaning of dishonesty for property offences generally. Does the majority judgment of the High Court in *Peters* represent the state of the common law of Australia generally on the meaning of dishonesty? In order to answer this question, it is first necessary to examine critically the English authorities on dishonesty and why they received such a hostile reception in the Australian jurisdictions that substantially adopted the *Theft Act* 1968 (UK).

17 *Theft Act* 1968 (UK), s 2(1); *Crimes Act* 1900 (ACT), s 96(4); *Criminal Code* (NT), s 209(1); *Crimes Act* 1958 (Vic), s 73(2).

18 *Crimes Act* 1900 (ACT), s 96(3); *Criminal Code* (NT), s 209(1); *Crimes Act* 1958 (Vic), s 73(3).

THE ORDINARY MEANING APPROACH TO DISHONESTY

The first English case examining the general meaning of dishonesty under the *Theft Act* 1968 (UK) was *R v Feely* [1973] QB 530. The accused was the manager of a bookmakers. His employers issued a circular that the practice of employees borrowing money from the till was to stop. The accused took money, £30, from the till. When the deficiency was discovered, he provided an "IOU" and said that he intended to repay the money and that, in any event, the employer owed him £70 in wages and commissions. The trial judge directed that it was no defence that the accused intended to repay the money or that his employer owed more than the sum taken. The accused appealed against his conviction. At trial, the following statements were made by the trial judge:

> the accused had intended to permanently deprive the owner of the specific notes taken and the fact that the accused knew his employer (the owner of the money) did not permit that taking meant the accused was dishonest.

These directions followed the earlier approach taken to larceny, confining the fault element to situations where the accused believed he or she had no legal right to appropriate the property.

The Court of Appeal held that trial judges should not define the meaning of "dishonesty" for the purpose of s 1(1) of the *Theft Act* 1968 (UK). The issue of whether taking money from the till was dishonest was an issue for the jury. Lawton LJ, delivering the judgment of the Court, held (at 537-538):

> We do not agree that judges should define what "dishonestly" means. The word is in common use ... Jurors, when deciding whether an appropriation was dishonest can be reasonably expected to, and should, apply the current standards of ordinary decent people. In their own lives they have to decide what is and what is not dishonest. We can see no reason why, when in a jury box, they should require the help of a judge to tell them what amounts to dishonesty.

The decision had two effects. It freed the mental element of theft from the exclusive focus on "claim of right" as had previously been the case for "fraudulently" under the law of larceny. It also restricted the judicial role in determining whether the accused was dishonest. An "ordinary meaning" approach had similarly been adopted in *Brutus v Cozens* (1972) 56 Cr App R 799 where the House of Lords held that the question whether conduct was "insulting" under s 5 of the *Public Order Act* 1936 (UK) was a question of fact, not law, for the jury. In Chapter 14 at pp 790-791, we explore how the apparent objectivity and neutrality of the legal standard of "offensiveness" can operate in a highly discretionary and discriminatory fashion.

The ordinary meaning approach to dishonesty has received strong criticism from legal academics.[19] The "ordinary meaning" approach leaves the question of dishonesty entirely to the

---

19 JC Smith, "Commentary on *R v Feely*" [1973] Crim LR 192; DW Elliot, "Dishonesty in Theft: A Dispensable Concept" [1982] Crim LR 395; E Griew, "Dishonesty: The Objections to *Feely* and *Ghosh*" [1985] Crim LR 341; A Halpin, "The Test for Dishonesty" [1996] Crim LR 283.

unstructured discretion of a jury. As DW Elliot concluded in "Law and Fact in *Theft Act* Cases" [1976] Crim LR 707 at 711:

> No perverse verdict on the issue of honesty is possible. The jury have complete control of the question. The word does not mean what it ordinarily means. It means what a jury decides it means, which is not the same thing.

The Law Commission of England and Wales has criticised this approach to dishonesty on the ground that the jury is not merely applying a standard set by the law, but constructing it: *Legislating the Criminal Code: Fraud and Deception*, Consultation Paper No 155 (London: HMSO, 1999), para 5.13. Moral views will diverge on the questions of honesty in specific contexts (consider for example community attitudes towards pilfering stationery from work and fiddling tax), and different juries will come to different conclusions. The Law Commission concluded that this "endemic inconsistency" undermined the idea that "like cases should be treated alike"; an idea that is vital to principle of fairness and the rule of law: para 5.15. This type of objection to the "ordinary meaning approach" stems from the overriding importance attached to the legal values of certainty, consistency and uniformity, as well as the importance of fundamental principles such as fairness and equality. We have explored the centrality of these liberal values to the criminal law in Chapter 2.

For these reasons, the Supreme Court of Victoria in *R v Salvo* [1980] VR 401 refused to follow *Feely*. The majority rejected the ordinary meaning approach to dishonesty developed by the English Court of Appeal. Fullagar J defined dishonesty as meaning obtaining property "without any belief that [the accused] has any legal right to deprive the other of it": at 432. Murphy J also rejected the *Feely* approach.[20] He stated that regarding the question of dishonesty as a factual and moral matter was fraught with danger. Murphy J considered (at 430-431) that determining guilt by reference to notions of abstract justice or current standards of honesty or morality would weaken confidence in both the courts and juries. Allowing dishonesty to be determined on purely moral grounds would inevitably lead to different outcomes. Murphy J noted that if moral consensus on dishonesty could not be achieved among judges and academics, then it would be difficult to see how a jury would have any greater capacity for uniformity: at 431.

This liberal perspective however ignores the normative function of dishonesty in the modern law of theft, particularly its role in evaluating the moral wrongfulness of the accused's conduct. Those who argue in support of *Feely* point out that the jury arguably is well placed to perform this normative evaluation. The jury is not constructing and applying its own standards, but rather standards accepted within the community. This type of inquiry is applied in relation to sexual offences (indecency and obscenity) and public order crimes (offensive and insulting conduct): see Chs 12 and 14, pp 640ff and pp 786ff respectively. Although there is always some room for difference of view on the meaning of dishonesty, in the majority of cases the jury will have no difficulty in

---

20 It is arguable that Murphy J did not go as far as Fullagar J in holding that dishonesty means without claim of legal right for the purpose of obtaining property by deception: CR Williams, *Property Offences* (3rd ed, Sydney: LBC, 1999), p 135. However, Young CJ, Crockett and Tadgell JJ in the subsequent case of *R v Brow* [1981] VR 783 interpreted Murphy J's judgment as agreeing fully with that of Fullagar J. In *R v Bonollo* [1981] VR 633, McInerney and McGarvie JJ reluctantly joined with Young CJ in holding that dishonesty means without claim of legal right. CR Williams argues that this trilogy of cases has been significantly undermined by the High Court decision in *Peters v The Queen* (1998) 192 CLR 493: "The Shifting Meaning of Dishonesty" (1999) 23(5) Crim LJ 275.

deciding whether the act was done honestly or dishonestly. As McInerney J observed in his dissenting judgment in *R v Salvo* [1980] VR 401 (at 408-409):

> If or in so far as this requires the fact-finding tribunal to undertake the task of ascertaining and applying the standard of honesty, accepted in the community, it is complying with the will of Parliament which has imposed on it that very task. Nor is there any great novelty in judges or fact-finding tribunals assuming to act as judges of moral standards: such a task is commonly committed to them by legislation, as, in my opinion, by the provisions of the *Theft Act*.

The use of "fact-finder" rather than jury in this passage recognises that dishonesty may be determined by magistrates or judges sitting without a jury. As we shall explore below, much of the discussion concerning the advantages and disadvantages of the "ordinary meaning approach" to dishonesty proceeds on the mistaken assumption that the construction of independent, objective standards is undertaken by a jury. The concerns about the legitimacy of judicial involvement in determining and applying moral standards of "the community" is critically examined below: pp 684-685.

The question of dishonesty was again reviewed in *R v Ghosh* [1982] 3 WLR 110. In this case, the English Court of Appeal offered further guidance on the meaning of dishonesty. The Court of Appeal, mindful of the academic criticism levelled at the "ordinary meaning" and "objective standard" of dishonesty, redirected the inquiry onto the dishonest *mental state* of the accused. The accused was a surgeon who worked as a locum in a hospital. He claimed payments for certain procedures that were not carried out by himself or which were covered by the National Health Service provisions. He was charged with obtaining money by deception. Obtaining by deception has the same requirement of dishonesty as the basic offence of theft. In accordance with *Feely*, the jury was directed by the trial judge that dishonesty was a matter for it to decide applying contemporary standards of honesty and dishonesty. Jurors were told that dishonesty may include "getting something for nothing, sharp practice, manipulating systems and many other matters that may come to your mind". The accused was convicted and appealed. One of the grounds of appeal was that the jury direction incorrectly adopted an objective rather than a subjective test of dishonesty.

The Court of Appeal in *Ghosh* reviewed the authorities on dishonesty. It noted that a distinction had emerged between an objective approach to dishonesty for theft and a subjective approach for conspiracy to defraud; in relation to the latter proof of dishonesty in the mind of the accused was required: *Scott v Commissioner of Police for the Metropolis* [1975] AC 819. The court concluded (at 116) that this difference in approach was unprincipled and that reconciling the two conflicting lines of authority (as in *R v McIvor* [1982] 1 WLR 409) was "an attempt to reconcile the irreconcilable".

Having established the need for a uniform approach to dishonesty, the Court of Appeal in *Ghosh* returned to its earlier decision in *Feely*. While *Feely* was often treated as having laid down an objective test, Lord Lane CJ took the view that this decision had simply established the following propositions (at 695):

▬ **it is for the jury to determine whether the accused acted "dishonestly" and not for the judge;**

▬ **the word "dishonestly" can only relate to the accused's own state of mind; and**

▬ **it is unnecessary and undesirable for judges to define what is meant by "dishonestly".**

Feely did not establish a *purely* objective test for dishonesty. A requirement that dishonesty should be determined by reference to the community standards did *not* mean that dishonesty could be found independently of the knowledge or belief of the actual accused. It was not an independent inquiry into what the accused *ought* to have known, or whether the ordinary reasonable person would have known that the conduct was dishonest. Lord Lane CJ gave the following example to illustrate the pre-eminent importance of a subjective mental state:

> Take for example a man who comes from a country where public transport is free. On his first day here he travels on a bus. He gets off without paying. He never had any intention of paying. His mind is clearly honest; but his conduct, judged objectively by what he has done, is dishonest. It seems to us that, in using the word "dishonestly" in the 1968 Act, Parliament cannot have intended to catch dishonest conduct in that sense, that is to say conduct to which no moral obloquy could possibly attach. ...
>
> If we are right that dishonesty is something in the mind of the accused (what Professor Glanville Williams calls "a special mental state"), then if the mind of the accused is honest it cannot be deemed dishonest merely because members of the jury would have regarded it as dishonest to embark on that course of conduct.

Lord Lane CJ distilled the proper approach to dishonesty into a two-pronged test: at 696.

▬ First, the jury must decide whether the accused's conduct was dishonest according to the "ordinary standards of reasonable and decent people". If the accused's conduct is not dishonest by that objective standard, then that is the end of the matter.

▬ Secondly, if it is dishonest, then the jury must consider whether the accused realised that his or her conduct was, by those standards, dishonest.

In coming to its conclusion, the Court of Appeal rejected concerns that a subjective approach abandoned fault to the idiosyncratic standards of honesty of the accused. The subjective approach to dishonesty did not lead to a "Robin Hood" defence, as Lord Lane CJ concluded (at 696):

> Robin Hood or those ardent anti-vivisectionists who remove animals from vivisection laboratories are acting dishonestly, even though they consider themselves to be morally justified in doing what they do, because they know that ordinary people would consider these actions to be dishonest.

Legal academics have criticised the test as unduly complicated and as placing an onerous burden on the prosecution to prove that the accused believed that ordinary people in the community considered his or her conduct to be dishonest.[21]

> Until the decision in *R v Ghosh* [1982] 3 WLR 110, the precise scope of *R v Feely* [1973] QB 530 was unclear. Some judges directed that the test of dishonesty should be exclusively determined by objective standards, while others persisted in definitions that stressed the importance of a dishonest *mental state* on the part of the accused.

---

21   D Elliott, "Dishonesty in Theft" [1982] Crim LR 395; G Williams, "The Standard of Honesty" (1983) 133 *New Law Journal* 636; E Griew, "Dishonesty: Objections to *Feely* and *Ghosh*" [1985] Crim LR 341.

> Martin Wasik in *"Mens Rea*, Motive and the Problem of 'Dishonesty' in the Law of Theft" [1979] *Criminal Law Review* 543 reviewed these inconsistent approaches and proposed a third way to determine dishonesty, namely, "by reference to two standards: those of the accused and those of society at large". Wasik's perceptive analysis was not mentioned in *Ghosh*, though it bears an uncanny similarity to the two-stage test for dishonesty adopted by the English Court of Appeal. There is a strong tradition at the English bar and bench of not citing academic opinion until the learned author is dead!

The Model Criminal Code Officers Committee (MCCOC) in *Chapter 3: Theft, Fraud, Bribery and Related Offences*, Final Report (1995) examined the arguments for and against the *Feely/Ghosh* test: pp 17-29. The principal arguments against the test were that it was an abdication of legislative and judicial responsibility leading to a departure from the standards of precision and certainty that should characterise the criminal law. This approach would also lead to inconsistent verdicts. Although it was commonly claimed that the *Feely/Ghosh* test "casts the law forth into a sea of moral confusion and uncertainty", the MCCOC found that "the cases where dishonesty is a genuine issue are few": p 19. The MCCOC rejected the approach to dishonesty applied in Victoria, which had limited the issue of dishonesty to the provisions expressly contained in the legislation. It finally recommended the adoption of the *Feely/Ghosh* test on the ground (p 25) that:

> it is necessary for the offence of theft to retain a broad concept of dishonesty in order to reflect the essential character of the offences in this chapter as involving moral wrongdoing.

The MCCOC noted (p 27) that leaving the residual notion of dishonesty for the jury or magistrate to determine by reference to community standards was consistent with the approach taken to negligence. Indeed, the prediction of inconsistent verdicts, and therefore loss of respect in the criminal law and its administration, has not been borne out by a large number of cases decided over the last 30 years in England and Australia. The MCCOC noted that, as a practical matter, dishonesty only arises as *the* issue infrequently in the very difficult cases: p 27.

The MCCOC was particularly influenced by the widespread support for the *Feely/Ghosh* test among judges and prosecutors. Indeed, it was noted that the *Feely/Ghosh* test had been used to determine the meaning of "fraudulently" in larceny offences in New South Wales and South Australia, as well as the meaning of "intent to defraud" and "dishonesty" within the Code juris-dictions: p 29. As we shall further explore below, the MCCOC could now enlist the support of the High Court in *Peters v The Queen* (1998) 192 CLR 493, which has endorsed the *Feely/Ghosh* test of dishonesty in relation to conspiracy to defraud.

To entrench the *Feely/Ghosh* test, the MCCOC recommended the inclusion of the following definition section:

Dishonesty

14.2

(1) In this Chapter, **"dishonest"** means dishonest according to the standards of ordinary people and known by the defendant to be dishonest according to the standards of ordinary people.

(2) In a prosecution for an offence, **dishonesty** is a matter for the trier of fact.

Further provisions bearing on the issue of dishonesty also apply such as:

▬▬ **belief in a claim of right (s 9.5);**

▬▬ **a belief that the owner cannot be found by taking reasonable steps (s 15.2.1); or**

▬▬ **the person is willing to pay (s 15.2.2).**

These sections have been considered above. On the claim of right defence, see Chapter 7: p 366.

DISSENTING JURISPRUDENCE ON DISHONESTY

The MCCOC identified widespread support for the *Feely/Ghosh* test among judges and prosecutors: *Chapter 3 — Theft, Fraud, Bribery and Related Offences*, Final Report (1995). The MCCOC acknowledged the strong dissent on this question in Victoria, but concluded that the "majority consensus across the jurisdictions" favoured the *Feely/Ghosh* test: p 29. The MCCOC's claim of widespread support for the English test for dishonesty in Australia overlooked some significant dissent in the Australian Capital Territory.

The *Crimes Act* 1900 (ACT) explicitly incorporated aspects of the dissenting Victorian jurisprudence into its statutory definition of dishonesty. Section 96(4)(b) of the Act states that a person shall not be regarded as dishonest where:

> he or she appropriates the property in the belief that the appropriation will not cause any
> significant practical detriment to the interests of the person to whom the property belongs
> in relation to that property;

The provision can be traced directly to the general definition of dishonesty offered by McGarvie J in *R v Bonollo* [1981] VR 633. In that case, McGarvie J defined dishonesty (at 668) as consciously producing a consequence affecting the interests of the person deprived of the property; and the consequence is one that would be detrimental to those interests in a "significant practical way". In the ultimate analysis he rejected his preferred view of dishonesty because he considered he was bound to follow previous authority in Victoria that confined dishonesty to meaning "without belief in a claim of right": see *R v Salvo* [1980] VR 401; *R v Brow* [1981] VR 783; CR Williams, "The Shifting Meaning of Dishonesty" (1999) 23(5) Crim LJ 275.

The precise effect of the partial definition of dishonesty in s 96(4)(b) of the *Crimes Act* 1900 (ACT) remains uncertain. The use of unfamiliar terms raises concern that the section could operate as a "Robin Hood" defence — legitimating appropriation from individuals or corporations who are believed not to be disadvantaged by the loss of their property. It may be argued that the belief that there is no significant practical detriment must relate to the *particular* property appropriated, not to the general capacity of the owner of the property to withstand its loss. McGarvie J himself was conscious of the need to avoid a "Robin Hood" defence and so proposed dishonesty as a two-stage inquiry:

▬▬ **first, the jury had to be satisfied that the accused believed that obtaining the property would produce a particular consequence affecting the interests of the person deprived of it; and**

▬▬ **then that the particular consequence was one which would be detrimental to those interests in a "significant practical way": at 657.**

Framed in this way, the test of dishonesty was not determined *exclusively* by reference to the accused's internal values. The accused must know that he or she is adversely affecting the interests of the victim. However, the jury must determine whether or not the detriment is "practically significant" in any particular case. In the latter inquiry, the accused's beliefs are tested against "the standard of whether an ordinary person would regard that consequence as one which would be detrimental in a significant practical way to the interests of the other person": at 657. McGarvie J compared (at 657) the two-stage test proposed to the bifurcated test applied to determine the standard of self-control for the defence of provocation: see Ch 5, p 265.

The statutory reformulation of this test has not been litigated in the Australian Capital Territory. Although the test has attracted academic support,[22] the MCCOC rejected McGarvie J's approach to dishonesty as vague and unduly restrictive because of its narrow focus on activity believed to be detrimental or adverse to the rights of the owner.[23]

The rejection of the *Feely/Ghosh* test in the Australian Capital Territory was firmly stated in *Mattingley v Tuckwood* (1989) 88 ACTR 1. In this case, the Supreme Court, examining the meaning of "dishonesty" in the *Crimes Act* 1900 (ACT), refused to apply the English test of dishonesty. Kelly J held (at 13) that the meaning of dishonesty is not simply one of fact for the jury or the magistrate:

> I think the word "dishonestly" used in Pt IV of the Act is to be taken as a conscious departure from a community standard consciously understood. It was for the magistrate to decide as a matter of law whether on the facts found by him there could be such a departure from such a standard. This test seems to accord with the intention of the legislature ... and to be preferable to those laid down in *R v Feely* [1973] 1 QB 530 and *R v Ghosh* [1982] 1 QB 1053.

Due to the brevity of the judgment, the reasoning underlying this departure from the English cases is not apparent. However, Kelly J's judgment clearly stresses the subjective aspects of dishonesty. Moreover, it is clear that dishonesty should not be treated as a moral question for the fact-finder, but its meaning is a legal one upon which judges, both at trial and appellate level, have a legitimate role to play.

The MCCOC's unqualified support for the *Feely/Ghosh* test may be weakened by the criticism levelled at the test by the Law Commission of England and Wales in Consultation Paper No 155, *Legislating the Criminal Code: Fraud and Deception* (London: HMSO, 1999). These criticisms are thoughtfully reviewed by Alex Steel in "The Appropriate Test for Dishonesty" (2000) 24 Crim LJ 46. Steel concluded that the *Model Criminal Code* should reject the English tests of dishonesty, and the MCCOC should adopt instead the subjective test proposed by McGarvie J in *Bonollo* [1981] VR 633 at 653.

---

22 Cf DW Eilliot, "Dishonesty in Theft: A Dispensable Concept" [1982] Crim LR 395, who considered McGarvie J's approach as preferable to the test laid down in *Feely*: at 408. The author proposed that the term "dishonesty" could be removed entirely from the Act and could simply identify the beliefs which were inconsistent with theft. He remodelled McGarvie's test of "insignificance" into the definition of appropriation: "No appropriation of property belonging to another which is not detrimental to the interests of the other in a significant practical way shall amount to theft of property": at 410.

23 See Model Criminal Code Officers Committee, *Chapter 3: Theft, Fraud, Bribery and Related Offences*, Final Report (1995), p 25, endorsing the views of the Gibbs Committee, *Review of Commonwealth Criminal Law*, Interim Report (Canberra: AGPS, November 1991), pp 132-133.

Dishonesty and Summary Justice

The tests of dishonesty in *Feely/Ghosh* above largely proceed on the assumption that community standards will be determined by a jury. That is, the relevant standard will be constructed by reference to the values and experiences of jurors as representatives of the wider community. These assumptions fail to recognise that the task of judging conduct as dishonest is more likely to be performed by a magistrate or a judge sitting without a jury.

Penny Darbyshire in "An Essay on the Importance and Neglect of the Magistracy" [1997] Crim LR 627 has pointed out that much legal discussion of dishonesty is "unreal" being modelled on the assumption that this element of the offence will be determined by a jury. In reality, as Darbyshire notes (at 636), the majority of theft cases are decided by magistrates, not juries:

> The overwhelming bulk of trials for offences of dishonesty are summary but because the precedents *Feely* and *Ghosh* lay down tests designed for jury trial, all academic discussion follows suit.

As explored in Chapter 2 at pp 37-38, this observation supports Doreen McBarnet's thesis that there are two tiers of criminal justice and that an "ideology of triviality" surrounds the lower tier of summary justice: *Conviction: Law, The State and the Construction of Justice* (London: MacMillan Press, 1981), Ch 7.

While Darbyshire's article highlights the invisibility of magistrates within legal discourse, the particular implications for dishonesty were not further explored. Would simply including references to summary jurisdiction in academic commentary and judicial decisions dealing with dishonesty address the "neglect of the magistracy"? Clearly, what needs to be examined is how (if at all) the task of determining dishonesty differs for a magistrate or judge sitting without a jury. An obvious difference is the discomfort at the prospect of judges exchanging their legal mantle for a moral one, and the increased scope for public criticism of individual cases based on the moral values of the judges involved.

R v Salvo [1980] VR 401 is one of the cases in which it has been noted that the moral evaluation of the accused's behaviour, as required by *Feely,* is more likely to be undertaken by magistrates. The drafters of the *Theft Acts* in England and Victoria had adopted an ordinary meaning approach to dishonesty, presuming that this factual determination would be undertaken by the jury. But as Fullagar J noted (at 430-431):

> it is simply not true to say that the statute in either country leaves it only to juries. Magistrates have to deal with prosecutions before them under the section and have to decide these questions of morals, and a very large number of cases come before them for decision. The reported cases in England, since 1970 show the almost insoluble problems with which this legislation, as interpreted in England, has forced them to wrestle. In my opinion this is calculated to bring the courts into contempt by reason of different decisions being given on similar facts, because this is a field where quite demonstrably "all do not have the same intuitions".

The Law Commission of England and Wales raised similar concerns in Consultation Paper No 155, *Legislating the Criminal Code: Fraud and Deception* (London: HMSO, 1999), para 5.17. The Commission doubted whether there existed a unified conception of honesty based on the ordinary standards of reasonable and honest people. Modern society is heterodox and pluralistic, and there may be difficulties in identifying a consensus on whether the conduct is dishonest. As Steel has pointed out, this consensus will be absent in cases of white-collar commercial fraud, because of the complexity and lack of experience of the transactions involved.[24]

Magistrates and judges sitting with a jury may seek to down-play the significance of their personal values in determining dishonesty in particular cases. The facts of the case may be "squeezed" into the existing statutory definitions dealing with dishonesty. In the exceptional "hard case", where the legislation does not assist, magistrates and judges may develop their own informal guidelines for decision-making in the "shadow of the law". We have explored in Chapter 1 how "bench books" and other professional manuals constitute a significant, though largely neglected, legal source that can promote uniformity in the administration of the law.

The *Feely/Ghosh* test entrusts the jury or magistrate with the role of policing community standards of honesty. As noted above, the explicit intrusion of moral values in this role exposes the decision-maker to criticism on moral, rather than strictly legal grounds. The constitution of the jury as randomly selected (if not representative) members of the community seems to provide some protective shield for this moralising function. Unlike magistrates, the jury is not required to reveal the reasoning supporting its verdict. However, it is important not to over-emphasise the moral autonomy of the jury. As we explored in Chapter 2, the trial judge can exert considerable influence on how the jury evaluates the evidence, determines the facts, and applies the law to those facts. In relation to dishonesty, there is plenty of scope for the personal moral values and attitudes of the trial judge to influence the jury's assessment of the facts. While the *Feely/Ghosh* test grants the jury a wide latitude in determining dishonesty, it may be counteracted by judicial efforts to guide the jury to the "right conclusion" through careful direction on the facts and summing up. This shepherding may in fact explain why the *Feely/Ghosh* test has not led to wildly inconsistent verdicts in practice. Although much of the criticism of the *Feely/Ghosh* test is based on a concern over jury usurpation of legislative and judicial functions, available research reviewed in Chapter 2 at pp 123ff, suggests that the autonomy of jury deliberation (even in relation to fact-finding) is always exercised within the parameters fixed by the trial judge.

> The penalties provisions for minor theft involving property below a prescribed value have been lower in some jurisdictions to allow the matter to be tried summarily before a magistrate: for example, *Crimes Act* 1900 (ACT), s 99A. In other jurisdictions, theft has been classified as an offence "triable either way" and so the accused may elect to be tried by a superior court judge sitting without a jury. The summary/indictable/ hybrid distinction has been examined in Chapter 2: p 99. There are considerable pressures on police and prosecutors to "downgrade" theft to facilitate summary jurisdiction. A single event may be broken into several counts of minor theft to avoid the cost and delays of trial by jury.

---

24 A Steel, "The Appropriate Test for Dishonesty" (2000) 24 *Criminal Law Journal* 46, discussing the views of E Griew, "Dishonesty: Objections to *Feely* and *Ghosh*" [1985] *Criminal Law Review* 341.

TOWARDS UNIFORM STANDARDS OF DISHONESTY IN PROPERTY OFFENCES

The entrenchment of the *Feely/Ghosh* test of dishonesty for property offences may have been further consolidated by the decision of the High Court in *Peters v The Queen* (1998) 192 CLR 493. The decision concerned the role of dishonesty in the statutory offence of conspiracy to defraud the Commonwealth. The implications of this decision for conspiracy to defraud, and the MCCOC's proposals for reform of this offence, have been examined in Chapter 9, pp 465-467. The accused was a solicitor who had helped a client to launder money through a series of sham mortgage transactions. At trial, directions were given in line with the decision of the English Court of Appeal in *Ghosh*. The jury was instructed that it had to be satisfied that what the accused agreed to do was dishonest by the current standards of ordinary and reasonable people and, if it was, that the accused must have realised it was dishonest by those standards. The question was whether those instructions were correct. The accused argued that the trial judge misdirected the jury as to the test of dishonesty. In this regard, he argued that the jury should have been instructed to apply a subjective test in accordance with the Victorian decision of *R v Salvo* and not the test adopted in *R v Ghosh*. Specifically, the accused argued that the jury should have been instructed that the prosecution had to prove that the accused had "an absence of belief that he had a legal right to do what he did".

All the members of the High Court dismissed the appeal, but did so on different grounds. McHugh J, with whom Gummow J agreed, held that dishonesty was not relevant to the charge of conspiracy to defraud. His reasoning was examined in Chapter 9, p 466. Toohey and Gaudron JJ adopted a different view, concluding that dishonesty was relevant to conspiracy to defraud "at two levels". First, the agreement must be to use dishonest means; and secondly, it must be to bring about a situation prejudicing or imperilling existing legal rights or interests of others. The means will be dishonest if the accused asserts as true something which is false and which is known to be false or not believed to be true or if means are used that the conspirators know they have no right to use or do not believe that they have any right to use. If addressed in this way, a further direction that the accused must have acted dishonestly is "superfluous". In cases where "dishonestly" was prescribed by statute, as in this case, the term may bear in its ordinary meaning (as understood in *Feely/Ghosh*) or be used in a "special sense". In relation to the ordinary meaning, the trial judge should follow the formulation applied in the *Feely/Ghosh* test, instructing the jury that "the question whether they are to be characterised as dishonest is to be determined by application of the standards of ordinary reasonable people": at 508. In most cases, questions as to whether the accused was dishonest are usually not in issue. In an exceptional case where dishonesty was an issue, the judge should direct the jury on the importance of the proof of intent, knowledge or belief relied upon by the prosecution, and the question of whether that mental state is dishonest should be left to the jury.

Kirby J agreed with Toohey and Gaudron JJ. Kirby J came to this conclusion by way of a dissenting opinion that had strongly favoured (at 552) a subjective standard based on the actual intent of the accused rather than "a fiction based on objective standards". But since the other judges had intended to dismiss the appeal, he decided to endorse the judgment of Toohey and Gaudron JJ so as to constitute a technical majority view on the proper test of dishonesty.

While *Peters v The Queen* (1998) 192 CLR 493 brings some degree of certainty to the meaning of dishonesty for the purpose of conspiracy, its impact on the law of theft remains unclear. On a strict reading, the endorsement of *Ghosh* applies only to conspiracy to defraud. It has been suggested that the decision has wider ramifications. It has been heralded by some academics as further evidence of the legal consensus on the appropriate directions on dishonesty. Indeed, the rejection of the *Feely/Ghosh* test in both the Australian Capital Territory and Victoria is now open to challenge on the basis of *Peters v The Queen* (1998) 192 CLR 493.

CR Williams has recently suggested in "The Shifting Meaning of Dishonesty" (1999) 5 Crim LJ 275 that the High Court has substantially undermined the Victorian approach to dishonesty, which treated dishonesty as a question of law and confined the concept to the partial definitions contained in s 73(2) of the *Crimes Act* 1958 (Vic). While the decision represents a firm step towards uniformity and the development of an Australian common law on dishonesty, the decision leaves some questions unresolved. As Williams pointed out (at 284), the majority required directions on dishonesty in "borderline" or "exceptional" cases, "leaving open the question of the criteria to be applied by the judge ... so as to require a *Feely/Ghosh* direction". He notes that the English authorities are not so restricted, requiring this direction where dishonesty is a real issue in the case.

Not all academics have welcomed the decision. Steel in "The Appropriate Test for Dishonesty" (2000) 24 Crim LJ 46 argues that *Peters* is not beyond challenge. As well as identifying the criticisms levelled at the *Feely/Ghosh* test discussed above, he notes (at 57) that the High Court decision does not constitute an endorsement of the "full *Ghosh* test". The Toohey/Gaudron test requires a distinction between offences that refer to dishonesty in its "general sense" and those that refer to it in its "special sense". The present test does not assist in distinguishing between these "senses" of dishonesty. Steel suggests that the idea of two concepts of dishonesty reflects the different functions it performs for different offences. Drawing on ideas developed by the Law Commission of England and Wales in Consultation Paper No 155, *Legislating the Criminal Code: Fraud and Deception* (London: HMSO, 1999), he draws a distinction between negative and positive dishonesty: para 3.15. The negative definition corresponds to dishonesty in its "general sense" and the positive definition corresponds to dishonesty in its "special sense":

Negative Dishonesty
For offences involving conduct that is inherently objectionable, such as obtaining property by deception or without consent, dishonesty plays a less significant role. The deception or trespass to the property provides the wrongfulness necessary for criminal liability. In these cases, dishonesty is not a special requirement. It is a negative form of dishonesty since the accused is left to raise an honest belief or intention.

Positive Dishonesty
For offences involving conduct that is inherently unobjectionable, such as conspiracy to defraud, dishonesty will be crucial. In relation to conspiracy to defraud, an agreement to prejudice the rights and interests of others was not intrinsically wrongful. As Steel noted: "It is the stuff of competition and commerce. In such a crime dishonesty is a positive element and 'does all the work'": at 58. Since culpability cannot be *inferred* from the wrongfulness of the conduct, further direction on the dishonesty of the accused's subjective mental state is required.

While highly refined, Steel's analysis provides practical guidance on the application of the Toohey/Gaudron test in *Peters*. The model of dishonesty proposed by Steel addresses the definitional defects identified by Williams above. It also transcends the traditional dichotomy between subjective versus objective fault in the criminal law. The "special test" is reserved for those cases where a subjective inquiry into fault is most needed, namely, those cases where the conduct of the accused is not objectively wrongful. In cases that involve some additional element of wrongfulness, a "general test" based on the standards of ordinary decent people will suffice with the additional safeguard that an accused may raise a positive honest belief as a basis for exculpation. The combined effect of these tests will ensure the criminal law does not impose punishment on morally blameless conduct. For further discussion of the fundamental importance of this principle, see Chapter 3: p 187.

PERSPECTIVES

Dishonesty and the Relevance of Motive

Martin Wasik in "Mens Rea, Motive, and the Problem of 'Dishonesty' in the Law of Theft" [1979] Crim LR 543 at 549 concluded that, notwithstanding the repeated articulation of the principle that motive is irrelevant in the criminal law, "motive really *is* admitted as relevant to responsibility in a significant, and increasing, number of cases". Wasik used theft as a case study to demonstrate how the concept of dishonesty allowed the accused to explain *why* the alleged offence occurred, not just *how* it occurred: at 550. He concluded that the difficulties in relation to dishonesty reflected the dilemma which is introduced by allowing an accused to call upon motive in support of a claim that he or she should be excused. Dishonesty provided the opportunity for the accused to offer explanations (and therefore excuses) for conduct that are "inherently disrespectful to the underlying assumptions of the criminal law" — in particular respect for private property and ownership rights. In most cases, the jury will have no difficulties balancing the beliefs of the accused concerning the honesty of his or her standards, and the independent standards of the community. In extreme cases, however, Wasik suggested that the judge, as a matter of law, should have the power to declare whether certain explanations for conduct phrased in terms of "honest" motives are capable of founding a defence in law: at 557.

As explored in Chapter 3 at p 176, the general rule of the criminal law is that motive is irrelevant to questions of fault, though may legitimately be considered relevant to sentencing. Critical scholars have observed that the exclusionary approach to motive in the criminal law seeks to suppress the socio-political context of the offending, but is rarely completely successful. While philosophers of the criminal law struggle to maintain this strict conceptual division between fault and motive, the law in relation to defences such as duress and provocation does recognise that motive (the *reasons* for behaviour) is relevant to legal as well as moral blame: A Norrie, *Crime, Reason and History* (London: Weidenfeld & Nicolson, 1993), Ch 3. Such insights suggest that a re-evaluation of the exclusionary approach to motive is required. Others theorists have sought to reconcile this apparent contradiction, arguing that the true principle is that motive while *ordinarily irrelevant* to fault determination, may be morally and legally significant in some cases: A Duff, "Principle and Contradiction in the Criminal Law: Motives and Criminal Liability" in A Duff (ed), *Philosophy and the Criminal Law: Principle and Critique* (Cambridge: Cambridge University Press, 1998), pp 170-173.

3.2 APPROPRIATION

Appropriation replaced the common law concept of asportation used in larceny, namely, the taking and carrying away of property without the consent of the owner. The *Theft Act* model adopted in the United Kingdom and Victoria defines "appropriation" as "any assumption by a person of the rights of an owner": *Theft Act* 1968 (UK), s 3(1); *Crimes Act* 1958 (Vic), s 73(4). As we shall explore below, the Australian Capital Territory has adopted a different formulation, reflecting the subsequent case law that elaborated on the meaning and scope of "appropriation". Section 209(1) of the *Criminal Code* (NT), basically adopting the *Theft Act* model, defines "appropriates" as meaning "assumes the rights of the owner of the property".

The difficulties experienced in larceny in cases where the initial possession occurred with consent or without fraudulent intent are expressly addressed in these sections, which define "appropriation" as including cases where the accused "has come by the property (innocently or not) without stealing it, any later assumption of a right to it by keeping or dealing with it as owner": see *Crimes Act* 1900 (ACT), s 96(2); *Crimes Act* 1958 (Vic), s 73(4). While this extended definition of appropriation overcomes the concurrence problems of larceny caused by the delayed formation of an intent to steal, Fisse in *Howard's Criminal Law* (5th ed, Sydney: Law Book Company Ltd, 1990) has raised the concern that the provision carries the danger of "over-criminalisation": p 205. As we shall see below, the legislature has imposed limits on the concept by creating exemptions in favour of bona fide purchasers for value. Also, some courts have sought to define the concept of appropriation in a more restrictive way, so that it applies only to conduct which is inherently and unambiguously wrongful.

APPROPRIATION: ASSUMPTION OF THE RIGHTS OF AN OWNER

The concept of appropriation is much broader than the requirement of "taking and carrying away" in larceny. It extends to the assumption of rights in relation to the property that could be exercised by its owner. In addition to the "ordinary" case of theft based on *taking* property belonging to another, many other forms of property interference could fall within this definition of appropriation, including the:

- use of property;

- destruction or damage of property;

- selling or pledge of property;

- lending or borrowing property;

- retention of property or refusing to return property.[25]

---

25 L Waller and CR Williams, *Brett, Waller and Williams: Criminal Law — Text and Cases* (8th ed, Sydney: Butt, 1997), p 355.

The question has arisen in the United Kingdom and Victoria as to whether an appropriation involves the assumption of *any* of the rights of an owner. As noted above, the legislation simply states that "any assumption by a person of the rights of an owner amounts to an appropriation". As a preliminary matter, it should be noted that this provision does not require interference with rights that are currently exercised by the owner. Rather, the rights that are interfered with must be rights *exercisable by an owner*. This formulation reflects the fact that the concept of appropriation relates to "property *belonging* to another person". Thus, a person may appropriate their own property or even appropriate property from a thief who lacks legal title to that property. Interference with "owner-like" rights, rather than the owner's rights, is the essence of appropriation.

The potential breadth of appropriation is apparent in *Stein v Henshall* [1976] VR 612. The accused was found by police officers near a stolen car in a street in Kensington, Victoria. He was charged with the theft of the car. The defence argued that he had not stolen the car and that someone else had stolen the car. The accused, knowing that the car was stolen, had used the car on at least two occasions. The defence stated that the accused had only used the car on a few occasions and therefore had not interfered with all the rights of the owner. It was argued that the original thief had not given up all of his possessor rights in the car. Lush J held (at 615) that whether the original thief had given up his possessory rights was irrelevant: "The question is — and is only — whether the defendant acted in relation to the car in a manner in which the owner would have the right to act". On these facts, this was clearly satisfied since the accused had used the car for his own purposes and "use" was one of the rights of the owner of the car. As we shall explore below, the House of Lords took a similar approach to appropriation in *R v Morris* [1984] AC 320.

In *Wilson v Woodrow* (1987) 26 A Crim R 387, the Supreme Court of Victoria held that sitting on the back-seat of a stolen car could be an appropriation. The court referred with approval to *Stein v Henshall* and held that being a passenger in a motor vehicle was one of the rights of ownership. Whether or not there was an intention to permanently deprive in both the above cases is a more difficult question. To overcome the difficulty of proving this intention in the case of "joyriding", the legislature in Victoria has enacted a special deeming provision. Section 73(14) of the *Crimes Act* 1958 (Vic) states that in any proceedings for stealing (or attempted stealing) of a motor car or an aircraft, proof that the person charged took or in any manner used the motor car or aircraft without the consent of the owner or person in lawful possession is conclusive evidence that the person charged intended to permanently deprive the owner of it. In other jurisdictions, specific "joyriding" offences have been enacted to deal with the unlawful use of vehicles or other conveyances to catch those individuals who do not intend permanently to deprive the owner of the property: *Crimes Act* 1900 (ACT), s 120; *Crimes Act* 1900 (NSW), s 154A; *Criminal Code* (NT), s 218; *Criminal Code* (Qld), s 408A; *Criminal Code* (WA), s 371A.[26]

> The Model Criminal Code Officers Committee (MCCOC) has noted that pointing to another person's car and offering it for sale, or simply sitting on a car bonnet, would amount to appropriation because these are some of the rights of an owner: *Chapter 3 — Theft, Fraud, Bribery and Related Offences*, Final Report (1995), pp 35, 43.

26   In most jurisdictions, unlawful use of a motor vehicle is a summary offence carrying a lesser penalty than larceny or theft. In New South Wales, stealing a motor vehicle is an aggravated offence carrying a maximum penalty of 10 years imprisonment, twice the penalty for simple larceny. There is empirical evidence that the majority of car theft is committed by "joyriders": D Brown, D Farrier and D Weisbrot, *Criminal Laws* (2nd ed, Sydney: Federation Press, 1996), pp 1128-1130.

The Law Commission of England and Wales has similarly noted that a person who selects a newspaper to buy at a newsagent's has committed all the elements of theft except for dishonesty: *Legislating the Criminal Code — Fraud and Deception*, Consultation Paper No 155 (London: HMSO, 1999), para 3.17.

APPROPRIATION: ADVERSE INTERFERENCE WITH THE RIGHTS OF OWNERS

Does appropriation require the assumption of rights of an owner to occur "without consent"? The MCCOC in *Chapter 3: Theft, Fraud, Bribery and Related Offences*, Final Report (1995) reviewed this issue, concluding that the concept of "without consent" was vital for distinguishing between theft and fraud. This requirement of "adverse interference" is consistent with the requirement of the law of larceny that the taking and carrying away of property must be without the consent of the owner.

Until the House of Lords decision in *R v Gomez* [1993] AC 442 there was considerable uncertainty as to relevance of lack of consent to appropriation. The uncertainty stemmed from an irreconcilable conflict between dicta in two House of Lords decisions, *Lawrence v Metropolitan Police Commissioner* [1972] AC 626 and *R v Morris* [1984] AC 320.

In *Lawrence* the accused was a taxi driver. Occhi was an Italian student who spoke very little English and was on his first visit to England. At Victoria Station Occhi went to a taxi driver (Lawrence) and showed him an address indicating he wanted to go that address. Lawrence said that the place was very far and would be very expensive. Occhi offered Lawrence £1, but Lawrence said that was not sufficient. He took the £1 and a further £1 and £5 note from Occhi's open wallet which Occhi held out to Lawrence. The lawful fare was 10/6d. Lawrence was charged with theft of the £6. On appeal to the House of Lords it was argued that there was no appropriation of the money since Occhi had consented to the money being taken. Dismissing the appeal, Viscount Lord Dilhorne, delivering the judgment of the House of Lords, held (at 631-632) that the *Theft Act* should be construed as a new code, and that "without consent" should not be implied into the definition of the offence.

The question of "consent" in relation to appropriation was revisited in *R v Morris* [1984] AC 320. The case involved two appeals heard together. In the first case the accused, Burnside, had been charged with theft of a joint of pork. He had switched the price labels and placed a lower price on a larger joint. He was caught at the checkout before he paid for it. In the second case, Morris had taken some goods from the shelves of a supermarket and replaced the price labels with lower prices. He paid the lower prices at the checkout and was charged with both theft and obtaining property by deception. Both were convicted and appealed. Counsel for the accused argued that there could not have been an appropriation until they had passed the checkout. On this view, Burnside had not committed theft, and Morris could only be guilty of obtaining property by deception. Counsel further argued that if the swapping labels and removing of the goods from the shelves was an appropriation, then Morris would effectively be obtaining by deception goods that he had already stolen.

Lord Roskill, giving the judgment of the House of Lords, defined appropriation as an adverse interference with or usurpation of *any* of the rights of an owner. The House of Lords affirmed that an appropriation did not require an assumption of *all* the rights of an owner — any interference with *any* rights of the owner was sufficient. This point has been further explored above. On these facts, the swapping of price labels was clearly an interference with the right of an owner to sell goods at the correct price. The House of Lords also affirmed that the assumption of rights had to be *adverse* to the rights of an owner. As Lord Roskill concluded (at 332), "the concept of appropriation in my view involves not an act expressly or impliedly authorised by the owner but an act by way of adverse interference with or usurpation of those rights". He rejected the Crown's submission that the *Theft Act* 1968 (UK) intended to treat as an appropriation the act of an honest shopper who removes goods from the shelf and places them in a trolley with the implied authority of the supermarket.

In the instant case, the House of Lords was of the view that the actions of both accused constituted an appropriation. The combination of removing the items from the shelf and switching the prices was evidence of appropriation. Mere removal from the shelves would not be an appropriation, as this is something that the owner impliedly authorised. Lord Roskill also suggested (at 332) that it would not be an appropriation to merely switch price labels, for example as part of a practical joke, but not remove the items from the shelves.

It is difficult to draw a principled distinction between unauthorised touching and unauthorised label switching. Fisse has suggested in *Howard's Criminal Law* (5th ed, Sydney: Law Book Company Ltd, 1990), p 288 that label switching alone, as a form of unauthorised touching, does amount to an adverse interference, concluding that the concept of appropriation in *Morris* seemed "erratically elastic". The better view is that the prankster has technically "appropriated" the property, though may not be guilty of theft because of doubts about her or his dishonesty or intention to permanently deprive the owner of that property. We will examine the overlap of appropriation with obtaining property by deception below: p 694.

Although *Lawrence* was not technically overruled, the decision in *Morris* was considered the correct approach to appropriation in England until the matter was again revisited by the House of Lords in *R v Gomez* [1993] AC 442. By contrast, the Victorian courts adopted a middle course. Rather than simply ignoring *Lawrence*, the Supreme Court of Victoria in *R v Roffel* [1985] VR 511 attempted to reconcile the two decisions. Both Young CJ and Crockett J doubted whether the decisions were in conflict: at 513 and 521, respectively. The starting point of the analysis of appropriation for both judges was the definition applied in *Morris*. Crockett J pointed out that absence of consent will often be relevant to a determination of whether there had been an adverse interference with or usurpation of some right of the owner. However, in some cases, this right does not appear to be usurped because the appropriation is "seemingly consensual, due to deception": at 521. In these cases of fraud or deception, the apparent consent of the victim from whom the property is obtained is vitiated: see, for example, *R v Baruday* [1984] VR 685. *Lawrence* may be treated as a "special case" where fraud vitiates consent, leaving undisturbed the requirement in *Morris* that an appropriation is *ordinarily* an adverse (non-consensual) interference with or usurpation of the rights of an owner.

The conflict between these authorities was since been authoritatively resolved by the House of Lords in *R v Gomez* [1993] AC 442. The accused was an assistant manager at an electrical goods store. A friend of his asked him to supply some goods which would be paid for with stolen building society cheques. The accused agreed and prepared the goods for supply and sought the manager's authorisation. The manager asked whether the cheques were good and the accused assured him they were. Authorisation was given and the transaction made. The cheques were later found to be stolen, and the accused and his friend were charged with theft and convicted. On appeal, the accused argued that there had not been any appropriation because the manager had authorised the transactions. The Court of Appeal agreed and quashed the conviction, but allowed the Crown to appeal the following point of law to the House of Lords: When theft is alleged and that which is alleged to be stolen passes to the accused with the consent of the owner, but that has been obtained by a false representation:

(1) has an appropriation within the meaning of s1 of the *Theft Act* taken place; or

(2) must such a passing of property necessarily involve an element of adverse interference with or usurpation of some right of the owner?

R v Gomez provided an opportunity to decide whether *Lawrence* or *Morris* was the correct approach to appropriation. Unlike the Supreme Court of Victoria in *R v Roffel* (1985) VR 511, the House of Lords held that *Lawrence* and *Morris* were irreconcilable, although the outcomes in each case were correct on the facts. The *Lawrence* position was that consent to the taking was not relevant to appropriation and was only relevant to dishonesty. The *Morris* position was that consent was relevant to appropriation, as well as dishonesty. Lord Keith of Kinkel, delivering the judgment of the court, held that *Lawrence* was the better approach, and that *Morris* was wrong and should no longer be followed. He referred to Lord Roskill's example of the prankster who switched labels without removing the items and said that that was sufficient to be an appropriation because it was an assumption of the owner's rights. As already noted, there would be no theft because there would neither be the element of dishonesty nor the intent to permanently deprive.

R v Gomez [1993] AC 442 may be criticised on the ground that it extends appropriation to cover *any* dealing (not merely unwanted interference) with property belonging to another. According to *Morris*, theft always required a *trespass to property*. This requirement differentiated theft from cases of obtaining property by deception in which the property was obtained with consent. Although formally separate offences in the United Kingdom and Victoria, *Gomez* blurs the conceptual and practical distinction between theft and obtaining property by deception. Although this is a substantial criticism of the decision, CR Williams concluded in *Property Offences* (3rd ed, Sydney: LBC, 1999), p 338, that the approach to appropriation in *Gomez* is correct and should be followed in Australia:

> There is no good reason why an accused who has dishonestly obtained the property of
> another by deception should not be regarded as having appropriated that property. Any
> consent implicit in such a transaction is vitiated by fraud and is not true consent.

Rationalising the decision in *Gomez* in terms of vitiation of consent begs further questions about the nature of the fraud that vitiates consent. As we explored in Chapters 11 and 12, the type of frauds vitiating consent for the purpose of assault and sexual offences has continued to preoccupy judges, legislatures and academics.

Whether *Gomez* will be followed by the High Court remains open. While some overlap in property offences will be inevitable and tolerable, *Gomez* actually obliterates the distinction between theft and other forms of fraud. As Williams himself conceded, all cases of obtaining property by deception, with the exception of land, may now be prosecuted as theft: p 188. The extended definition of appropriation in *Gomez* leaves open the possibility of multiple charges arising out of a single transaction. The discretion of the police and prosecutor will be critical to prevent the over-use of charges in such cases.

One advantage of *R v Gomez* [1993] AC 442 is that it overcomes the obstacle to convictions for theft in cases where a company director has authorised the company to give him or her company assets. Under the *Morris* approach, there is no appropriation where the company, as a separate legal entity, has authorised the (dishonest) transfer of property to the director: *R v Roffel* [1985] VR 511 at 515, per Young CJ. Under the *Gomez* approach, the consent of the owner is irrelevant, and the only issue would be whether the assumption of the rights of an owner was dishonest. This had been the approach of the dissenting judge, Brooking J, who preferred *Lawrence* over *Morris*, and would have dismissed the appeal against conviction.[27]

While the decision in *R v Gomez* [1993] AC 442 raises questions about the scope of appropriation in Victoria, the definition in the Australian Capital Territory expressly incorporated the *Morris* formulation, that is, appropriation is defined as "an adverse interference with or usurpation of any of the rights of the owner". This more restrictive definition of appropriation has no practical effect on the scope of theft since the Act adopts the following expanded definition of appropriation that includes obtaining property by deception:

96. Appropriation and dishonest appropriation — interpretation

(1) For the purposes of this Part, a person shall be taken to have appropriated property if:

(a) he or she obtains by deception the ownership, possession or control of the property for himself or herself or for any other person; or

(b) he or she adversely interferes with or usurps any of the rights of an owner of the property.

This definition section achieves the same result as *Gomez*, collapsing the distinction between theft and obtaining property by deception. The advantage of a single offence covering both theft and obtaining property by deception is that the prosecution is relieved of the burden of choosing between the charges at a time when the factual circumstances surrounding the alleged offence may not be revealed. Another way of overcoming this charging dilemma is the enactment of a provision allowing for an alternate verdict of obtaining property by deception in cases of theft.[28] Provisions governing an alternative verdict have been included in the *Model Criminal Code*: see s 17.2(6), Model Criminal Code Officers Committee (MCCOC) in *Chapter 3: Theft, Fraud, Bribery and Related Offences*, Final Report (1995), p 39. The expanded approach to appropriation also obviates the need for the development of complex rules governing vitiation of consent, as noted above.

The effect of this expanded definition of appropriation is to place greater emphasis on dishonesty as a means of distinguishing between wrongful and non-wrongful dealing in property. As the MCCOC noted, "if virtually any dealing with goods counts as an appropriation, the more work dishonesty has to do to distinguish theft from innocent transactions": *Chapter 3 — Theft, Fraud, Bribery and Related Offences*, Final Report (1995) p 37. While dishonesty performs an important

---

27 Careful attention must be paid to the corporate structure and its legal authority to transfer property to directors. *Roffel* was distinguished in *Clarkson and Lyon* (1986) 24 A Crim R 54 on the basis that a building society was prohibited by legislation from entering into the particular transaction with the accused (the Chairman of the building society) and therefore his assumption of rights had been without consent.

28 A similar provision exists in relation to larceny and fraud in s 183 of the *Crimes Act* 1900 (NSW).

control function, the MCCOC expressed preference for the development of "clear-cut criteria" for this purpose. In this regard the MCCOC was highly critical of the approach taken to appropriation in the English cases of *Lawrence* and *Gomez*.

The MCCOC has sought to limit the concept of appropriation in two ways. First, the MCCOC imposed a requirement that the assumption of rights of an owner had to be "without consent".[29] Secondly, the MCCOC recommended that the rights of an owner had to relate to "ownership, possession or control of property": s 15.3(1). The MCCOC had noted that English courts had recently sought to place limits on the concept of appropriation by excluding trivial interference such as picking up property in a supermarket and reshelving it: *Gallasso* [1993] Crim LR 459. The parameters and principles underlying this *de minimis* rule are not clear. However, the MCCOC recommended that a similar effect may be achieved legislatively by limiting the assumption of rights to those relating to "ownership, possession or control": s 15.3(1). It is unclear how this formulation in fact excludes trivial interference with property. Control is a broad term that extends to any physical dealing with property (apart from accidental touching) however brief. The breadth of appropriation under the present law potentially renders redundant many other property and damage offences, and confers upon the police and prosecution a wide and unstructured discretion in framing charges.

PERSPECTIVES

ATM Fraud and Computer Misuse

In *Kennison v Daire* (1986) 160 CLR 129 the High Court considered an appeal from a conviction of larceny contrary to s 131 of the *Criminal Law Consolidation Act* 1935 (SA). The accused closed his bank account, though continued to use his card to withdraw funds from an automated teller machine (ATM). He was still able to withdraw funds when the ATM was "off-line" because the computer was programmed to allow the withdrawal of up to $200 by any person who placed a card in the teller and gave the correct personal identification number (PIN). The defence argued that as the bank had consented to the taking, the accused was not guilty of larceny. The defence argued that the ATM was like a bank teller who had intended the property in the money to pass to the accused. The High Court unanimously dismissed the appeal. In a remarkably brief judgment, the High Court held (at 132) that merely because the bank programmed the ATM in a way that facilitated the fraud by the customer does not mean that the bank consented to the withdrawal. A machine cannot give consent, and it is not appropriate to treat a machine as though it were a person in authority. The bank did not give consent to withdrawing money beyond the balance in the account or (as in this case) where there was no account. The scope of consent would be inferred from the conditions of use supplied by the bank with the ATM card. The High Court (at 132) specifically left open the question of whether the person who withdrew funds in excess of their balance or approved overdraft limit would be guilty of larceny.

---

29 The MCCOC was persuaded to drop the formulation "adverse interference or usurpation" applied in *Morris* and the *Crimes Act* 1900 (ACT) in favour of "any assumption of the rights of an owner without consent". In reaching this conclusion, the MCCOC was persuaded by a submission received from Ian Leader-Elliott who had argued that the key concept consent (or lack thereof) was "a robust concept which provides a base for vigorous and intelligible argument: p 39.

Later cases, applying *Kennison v Daire*, established that a bank does not consent to money obtained from an ATM where the customer has overdrawn in excess of their credit limit or withdrawn funds against a cheque that has not cleared: *Evenett* (1987) 24 A Crim R 330; *Munjunen* (1993) 67 A Crim R 350. It would also follow that a person who obtained funds from an ATM using another person's card is also acting without the consent of the bank. Although obtained by consent of the cardholder, the notes are obtained without consent of the bank which imposes a strict condition that the ATM card and PIN are not used by persons other than those authorised by the bank. (In these situations, it is the bank, not the cardholder, who owns and possesses the notes in the machine). However, an appropriation of funds in this situation may not be dishonest if the person believes that the owner had consented to the taking.

Remarkably, the High Court in *Kennison v Daire* did not consider whether the property in the money belonged to the bank or whether it had passed to the accused at the moment of taking. At this time, whether or not property had passed in mistake cases had not been authoritatively resolved by the court. The law remained in an uncertain and controversial state particularly in relation to the overpayment of money. The High Court in *Kennison v Daire* deftly avoided the issue of computerised mistakes, leaving the principles governing fundamental mistakes negating passing of property to be developed in a more typical case of overpayment involving human rather than computer error: see *Ilich v The Queen* (1987) 162 CLR 110, discussed below.

Many forms of ATM fraud may be prosecuted as obtaining property by deception — the deception is that the customer has the authority to use the card and is operating the account in accordance with the terms and condition of use (which include that the cardholder has a sufficient balance in the account to cover the amount requested). Using another person's ATM card and PIN would similarly constitute a deception. This raises the question as to whether a deception may be practised on a machine or is limited to human beings.

There is dicta in *Kennison v Daire* (1985) 16 A Crim R 338 suggesting that a machine cannot be deceived — this was strictly *obiter* since the accused was charged with theft not obtaining property by deception. O'Loughlin J in the Supreme Court of South Australia observed (at 348):

> There is no question of deception to be considered; deception, as a concept, can only arise when a human being is the subject of the deceit ... Simply expressed, one would not equate an automatic [teller] machine, and its computerised functions, with the conduct of a human being who is capable of being deceived - who is capable of being the victim of a false pretence or a fraud.

Responding to this potential gap in the law, legislatures have broadened the offence of obtaining property or services by deception to include deceptions aimed at: (1) a computer system; or (2) a machine that is designed to operate by means of payment or identification: *Crimes Act* 1900 (NSW), s 178BA; *Crimes Act* 1958 (Vic), s 81(4). The issue is further explored below at p 735.

Rather than attempt to stretch existing property offences to cover ATM misuse, the Australian Capital Territory has enacted a special offence relating to the dishonest use of computers. Section 135L of the *Crimes Act* 1900 (ACT) provides:

Dishonest use of computers

(1) A person who, by any means, dishonestly uses, or causes to be used, a computer or other machine, or part of a computer or other machine, with intent to obtain by that use a gain for himself or herself or another person, or to cause by that use a loss to another person, is guilty of an offence punishable, on conviction, by imprisonment for 10 years.

(2) In this section, "machine" means a machine designed to be operated by means of a coin, bank-note, token, disc, tape or any identifying card or article.

The question of ATM fraud was briefly examined by the MCCOC in *Chapter 3: Theft, Fraud, Bribery and Related Offences*, Final Report (1995), pp 137-139. The MCCOC recommended the adoption of the Victorian extended definition of deception in preference to the enactment of a general offence against computer fraud. In addition to obtaining property by deception, ATM fraud may involve the commission of other offences relating to forgery and computer trespass: *Director of Public Prosecutions v Murdoch* [1993] 1 VR 406. The issues of trespass and fraud in relation to ATMs are further explored in I Leader-Elliott and M Goode, "Criminal Law" (1993) *An Annual Survey of Australian Law* 181 at 221-226. See also C Sullivan, "The Response of the Criminal Law in Australia to Electronic Funds Transfer Abuse" in G Hughes (ed), *Essays on Computer Law* (Melbourne: Longman Professional: 1990), Ch 14. On the legal policy and regulatory issues surrounding ATM misuse, see P Grabosky and R Smith, *Crime in the Digital Age* (Sydney: Transaction Publishers/Federation Press, 1998), Ch 8, especially pp 161-169

Plugging Gaps: Computer Crime and the New Property Offences

To deal with the perceived gaps in property offences, legislatures have enacted a range of computer offences. Australia's response to computer misuse has been marked by disharmony and illogicality: see G Hughes, *Data Protection in Australia* (Sydney: Law Book Company Ltd, 1991), Ch 8. The *Review of Commonwealth Criminal Law: Interim Report on Computer Crime* (1988) (the "Gibbs Committee") recommended the creation of specific computer offences dealing with unlawful access to computers and damage to data. These recommendations were enacted for the Commonwealth and also provided the basis for reform in New South Wales: *Crimes Act* 1914 (Cth), ss 76A-F; *Crimes Act* 1900 (NSW), ss 308-310. Other jurisdictions have developed their own approach to computer crime. As noted above, s 135L of the *Crimes Act* 1900 (ACT) was an early response to a perceived gap in the law. As this offence of dishonest use of computers did not cover hacking, additional offences were enacted against unlawful access and damage to computer data: *Crimes Act* 1900 (ACT), ss 135H-135K. Broadly drafted hacking offences have been enacted in most jurisdictions.[30] For a review of this inconsistent patchwork of offences see O Akindemowo, *Information Technology Law in Australia* (Sydney: LBC, 1999), Ch 5. The MCCOC has recently released a discussion paper on this topic: *Chapter 4 — Damage and Computer Offences* (2000).

---

30 See *Criminal Code* (Qld), s 408D (hacking and computer misuse); *Summary Offences Act* 1953 (SA), s 44 (unauthorised use); *Criminal Code* (Tas), ss 257A-F; *Summary Offences Act* 1966 (Vic), s 9A (computer trespass); *Criminal Code* (WA), s 440A(2) (unlawful operation).

APPROPRIATION: BONA FIDE PURCHASERS FOR VALUE

The rights of purchasers who acquire interests in property in good faith for value are given considerable protection by the law of property, equity and contracts.[31] A similar concession has been incorporated into the *Theft Act* model exempting from the law of theft the person who purchases property in good faith and for value. Mirroring the provisions in the *Theft Act* 1968 (UK), s 73(5) of the *Crimes Act* 1958 (Vic) provides:

> Where property or a right or interest in property is or purports to be transferred for value to a person acting in good faith, no later assumption by him [or her] of rights which he [or she] believed himself [or herself] to be acquiring shall, by reason of any defect in the transferor's title, amount to theft of the property.

A similar exemption occurs in s 96(5) of the *Crimes Act* 1900 (ACT).

These provisions counterbalance the extended definition of appropriation which, as noted above, includes cases where the person who initially comes by property innocently and subsequently keeps or deals with it as an owner: *Crimes Act* 1900 (ACT), s 96(2); *Crimes Act* 1958 (Vic), s 73(4). Under the common law, such cases did not amount to larceny because of the requirement that the initial taking of possession had to coincide with a fraudulent intent. While innocent purchasers of stolen goods who, on discovering the truth, decide to keep or sell the stolen property would not be guilty of larceny under the common law, they may now be liable for theft under the extended statutory definition of appropriation: *Wheeler* (1990) 92 Cr App R 279.

Questions have arisen as to whether this exemption confers too much protection for bona fide purchasers of stolen property. As CR Williams has pointed out in *Property Offences* (3rd ed, Sydney: LBC, 1999), the scope of the protection is quite limited because of the operation of the separate offence of obtaining property by deception: p 124. The exemption provides protection from liability for theft in relation to purchasers for value who retain or transfer property upon which there is a defect in the title. However, where the purchaser sells the property to a third party, that transaction is not protected. In that situation, the purchase money has been obtained by an untrue representation (express or implied) that the vendor has good title to the property offered for sale and thus gives rise to potential liability for the offence of obtaining property by deception. Moreover, if the second purchaser is aware of the true facts then that person will also be guilty of theft, and the first purchaser will be guilty as a party to that crime on the ordinary principles of accessorial liability. For a discussion of the principles governing complicity, see Chapter 8. The MCCOC in *Chapter 3: Theft, Fraud, Bribery and Related Offences*, Final Report (1995) reviewed the scope of this exemption and concluded that the protection should not be limited to transfers for value. The MCCOC recommended

---

31   See generally, E Sykes, *The Law of Securities* (5th ed, Sydney: Law Book Company Ltd, 1993), pp 527-529. As R Meagher, W Gummow and J Lehane, *Equity: Doctrines and Remedies* (3rd ed, Sydney: Butt, 1992) observe (p 256), "The doctrine of 'bona fide purchaser for value without notice of the legal estate' applies as much to personalty as to realty". Denning LJ in *Bishopgate Motor Finance Corp v Transport Brakes Ltd* [1949] 1 KB 332 held (at 336-337): "In the development of our law, two principles have striven for mastery. The first is for the protection of property; no one can give a better title than [that person] possesses. The second is for the protection of commercial transactions; the person who takes in good faith and for value without notice should get a better title. The first principle has held sway for a long time, but it has been modified by the common law itself and by statute to meet the needs of our time". For further discussion see K Sutton, *Sales and Consumer Law* (4th ed, Sydney: Law Book Company Ltd, 1995), pp 430-431.

that the defence should provide protection to all persons who receive property in good faith, not just bona fide purchasers, because "in both these cases the defendant initially believed he or she had become the owner of the goods": p 43.

> ### Misappropriation — A Dangerous Queensland Supplement
>
> The term appropriation has a different meaning in jurisdictions that retain larceny as the basis for property offences. These jurisdictions have supplemented the basic crime of larceny with statutory offences of "misappropriation of property": *Crimes Act* 1900 (NSW), s 178A; *Criminal Code*, s 408C(1) (Qld); *Criminal Law Consolidation Act* 1935 (SA), s 184; *Criminal Code* (Tas), s 261. These offences are limited to individuals who are entrusted with money or valuable security. The Queensland offence applies to any person who dishonestly "applies to his [or her] own use or to the use of any person (a) property belonging to another; or (b) property belonging to him [or her], which is in the possession or control, (either solely or conjointly with any other person) subject to a trust, direction, condition or on account of any other person". This offence punishes dishonest (not necessarily unauthorised) use of property (including property owned by the accused but controlled by another). It applies to temporary use of property and there is no requirement of obtaining gain or inflicting loss. The offence has been considered broad enough to catch computer hacking, obviating the need for special computer offences in Queensland: see G Hughes, *Data Protection in Australia* (Sydney: Law Book Company Ltd, 1991), p 286.

3.3 PROPERTY

The common law of larceny was originally limited to tangible property capable of being taken and carried away. It followed that the common law excluded larceny of land and intangible property. For these reasons, larceny is usually described as a crime against possession, and is contrasted with modern statutory offences that establish crimes against the rights of an owner: *Parsons v The Queen* (1999) 195 CLR 619 at 625. Not surprisingly, legislation has made a number of significant changes to the definition of property to overcome the limitations of the common law.

STATUTORY DEFINITIONS OF "PROPERTY"

Although significantly extended by legislation, the precise definition and scope of "property" varies from one jurisdiction to another. For example, the definition of property expressly includes "real property" in s 93 of the *Crimes Act* 1900 (ACT). By contrast, s 71 of the *Crimes Act* 1958 (Vic) defines property as including "real property" subject to the following qualifications in s 73(6):

> A person cannot steal land, or things forming part of land and severed from it by him [or her] or by his [or her] directions, except in the following cases, that is to say —
>
> **(a)** when he [or she] is a trustee or personal representative, or is authorized by power of attorney, or as liquidator of a company, or otherwise, to sell or dispose of land belonging to another, and he [or she] appropriates the land or anything forming part of it by dealing with it in breach of the confidence reposed in him [or her]; or

(b) when he [or she] is not in possession of the land and appropriates any thing forming part of the land by severing it or causing it to be severed, or after it has been severed; or

(c) when, being in possession of the land under a tenancy, he [or she] appropriates the whole or part of any fixture or structure let to be used with the land.

This narrower formulation of property has been recommended for adoption in the *Model Criminal Code*: see s 14.4, which is discussed in *Chapter 3: Theft, Fraud, Bribery and Related Offences*, Final Report (1995), pp 47-49. The MCCOC noted that these restrictions were based on the concept of theft as involving property that can be taken and carried away, and that appropriation of land should be dealt with under a separate fraud offence. It also noted that trespass to land was adequately protected by the law of property and that it would be anomalous if a person who lawfully acquired property by the doctrine of adverse possession (say by uninterrupted possession for 15 years) could be charged with theft. Although not addressed in the Report, the general exclusion of land would also preclude Indigenous communities claiming that the wrongful dispossession of their property constituted theft.

Intangible property has also raised vexed problems for the law of larceny and theft. Funds held in bank accounts have posed particular difficulties for the law of larceny since, from a strict legal perspective, "money in the bank" is intangible property, namely, a debt owed by the bank to the account holder. In *Croton v The Queen* (1967) 117 CLR 326, the High Court affirmed that, apart from special statutory provisions, larceny can only be committed in relation to property that is capable of physical possession and removal. While paper money or coin was properly the subject-matter of a charge of larceny, appropriating funds from a joint bank account was not. A majority of the High Court held that a conviction for larceny was not open in these circumstances since a *chose in action* (in this case, a debt owed by the bank to the account holder, as represented by the bank balance) was not property capable of being stolen.

Legislation has cured the defect in *Croton v The Queen* (1967) 117 CLR 326 in all jurisdictions and the definition of property has been broadened to include *choses in action* or "things in action", as well as intangible property more generally. Indeed, the MCCOC in *Chapter 3: Theft, Fraud, Bribery and Related Offences*, Final Report (1995) recommended (p 46) the following non-exhaustive definition of property in s 14.4:

"property" includes all real or person property, including:

(a) money; and

(b) things in action or other intangible property; and

(c) electricity; and

(d) a wild creature that is tamed or ordinarily kept in captivity or that is reduced (or in the course of being reduced) into the possession of a person.[32]

---

32 *Crimes Act* 1900 (ACT), s 93; *Criminal Code* (NT), s 1; *Criminal Code* (Qld), s 1; *Criminal Law Consolidation Act* 1935 (SA), s 142; *Criminal Code* (Tas), s 237; *Crimes Act* 1958 (Vic), s 73(7); *Criminal Code* (WA), s 370. In New South Wales, the extended definition applies only to offences of criminal destruction and damage, not larceny: *Crimes Act* 1900 (NSW), s 194(1). The offences relating to larceny of animals is limited to domesticated animals such as cattle and dogs: *Crimes Act* 1900 (NSW), ss 126-133.

There is legitimate concern about the role and limits of the criminal law in the protection of commercial secrets and intellectual property rights. The courts have been grappling with the changing nature of "property", in particular whether appropriation of intangible property, such as confidential information or computer data, may constitute theft. As we shall explore below, at pp 704ff, there is little legislative consensus on whether "on-line fraud" should be brought within the framework of existing property offences or should be dealt with by special computer crimes.

THE MEANING OF "INTANGIBLE PROPERTY"

While most statutory definitions extend to "intangible" property or things, the boundaries of this concept remain hazy. It is particularly difficult in the digital age to determine whether intangible property has been appropriated or is simply an identical copy or reproduction. As Jacqueline Lipton has pointed out in "Property Offences in the Electronic Age" (1998) 72 *Law Institute Journal* 54 at 54:

> The problem with these offences based on "property belonging to another" is that, with many forms of intangible property, it is difficult to establish that the property in the hands of the wrongdoer is actually the same as that which was lost by the victim. In other words, it is difficult to prove that what the defendant actually received was "property belonging to another" as opposed to some other forms of financial gain which happens to correspond with that loss.

As a consequence, fraud involving electronic funds transfers has posed considerable difficulties for the law of theft. The status of "electronic money" has been considered in the English decision of *R v Preddy* [1996] AC 815. In this case, the accused obtained mortgage advances on properties from a number of lending institutions by providing false information. The accused claimed that obtaining property by deception had not been committed because they intended to repay the money when the properties were resold. The accused were convicted. The convictions were quashed on appeal. The House of Lords held that since the deception involved the debiting of one person's bank account and the corresponding crediting of another's account, there was no obtaining of property belonging to another. The property belonging to the lenders was a debt owed by the bank to them. The property ultimately received by the accused was a new *chose in action*, a debt owed by their own bank to them. Although the two debts corresponded in value, they were distinct and separate items of property. The House of Lords also noted that the cheques that had been obtained by the accused were not property belonging to another since, from the moment they were drawn in their favour as the payee, they could not be regarded as property belonging to another. Lord Goff, whose reasons were adopted by the other judges, held (at 835):

> I start with the time when the cheque form is simply a piece of paper in the possession of the drawer. He [or she] makes out a cheque in favour of the payee, and delivers it to him [or her]. The cheque then constitutes a chose in action of the payee, which he [or she] can enforce against the drawer. At that time, therefore, the cheque constitutes "property" of the payee within section 4(1) [of the *Theft Act* 1968].

Lord Goff held (at 835) that at the crucial time that the cheque was obtained by deception, the property in the cheque (that is, the debt or *chose in action*) belonged to the payee with the consequence that "there was no chose in action belonging to the drawer which could be the subject of a charge of obtaining by deception". He also noted (at 836-837) that while the tangible piece of paper on which the cheque drawn still belongs the drawer, a charge of theft of the "cheque form" would also fail because "there can have been no intention on the part of the payee permanently to deprive the drawer of the cheque form, which would on presentation of the cheque for payment be returned to the drawer via his [or her] bank".

As Lipton observed (at 55) *Preddy* leads to an apparent inconsistency between payments in cash and those made by electronic transfers or cheques. The decision creates a legal distinction based on the mode of transfer with the result that fraud involving electronically-registered shares (as distinct from actual share certificates) may be immune from charges of theft or obtaining property by deception. This anomaly has been rectified in the United Kingdom by the enactment of a statutory offence of obtaining a money transfer by deception: see *Theft Act* 1968 (UK), s 15A.

The decision in *Preddy* has been trenchantly criticised by academics. JC Smith in "Obtaining Cheques by Deception or Theft" [1997] Crim LR 396 argued that *Preddy* was wrong and ignored the practical realities of the situation. He argued (at 400) that a cheque may be regarded as "(i) a piece of paper which (ii) creates a thing in action but it is also ... (iii) a valuable security". As such, a cheque may be regarded as a special form of property belonging to both the drawer and the payee simultaneously.

The implications of *Preddy* have been considered by the Victorian Court of Appeal and, more recently, by the High Court. In *R v Parsons* [1998] 2 VR 478, the Victorian Court of Appeal considered an argument, based on *Preddy*, that cheques drawn in favour of the accused (as a result of a deception) could not be regarded as property belonging to another. Winneke ACJ, delivering the judgment of the Court, rejected Lord Goff's reasoning in *Preddy* on a number of grounds. First, he noted that prior to *Preddy*, obtaining cheques by deception (even those drawn in favour of the fraudster) had been successfully prosecuted as obtaining property belonging to another in Victoria and other jurisdictions. Winneke ACJ also noted that Lord Goff's comments on the nature of cheques were strictly *obiter* since the facts of *Preddy* concerned electronic funds transfer, not cheque fraud. Winneke ACJ found persuasive the arguments in JC Smith's article, concluding (at 487-488):

> If a person, by deception, induces another to make out a cheque and deliver it to him [or her], the fraudster has obtained an instrument of value at the expense of the victim ... These sentiments seem to me to accord with practical reality. In my view the courts of this State have regarded cheques as instruments of inherent value which are capable of being stolen or obtained, and not simply as intangible property or choses in action.

The decision of the Court of Appeal was reviewed by the High Court in *Parsons v The Queen* (1999) 195 CLR 619. The High Court, unanimously upholding the conviction, substantially endorsed the reasoning of Winneke ACJ. The High Court (at 632-633) relied on the law governing negotiable instruments, including provisions of the *Cheques Act* 1986 (Cth), to find that cheques possessed:

> various legal characteristics giving them then a value beyond what otherwise was their quality as mere pieces of paper. The cheques, being complete in form, contained a mandate by the respective drawer to its bank to reduce the credit of its account by payment in favour of a person answering the statutory description of a holder ... It follows that both

the bank cheques and the cheques, at the time they were, by a deception, dishonestly obtained by the appellant, were property within the meaning of the definition in s 71(1) of the *Crimes Act*.

Lipton has further explored the problems posed by electronic fraud in "Property Offences into the 21st century" (1999) (1) *The Journal of Information Law and Technology* (http://www.law.warwick.ac.uk/jilt/99-1/lipton.html).

The High Court's decision in *Parsons* could be summarised as follows: a cheque is a special kind of *tangible* property which embodies valuable intangible characteristics, and is capable of being "owned", "controlled" or "possessed" by both the drawer and the payee for the purposes of the relevant property offences. Although the High Court resolved the legal status of cheques for property offences, the facts of that case did not require an examination of whether the narrower *ratio* in *Preddy* relating to electronic funds transfer should also be followed. As Lipton pointed out, the uncertainties over the requirement of "property belonging to another" in relation to fraudulent electronic funds transfers may be avoided in Victoria by relying on alternate offences such as obtaining a financial advantage by deception (*Crimes Act* 1958 (Vic), s 82) or procuring the execution of a valuable security by deception (*Crimes Act* 1958 (Vic), s 86(2)).

Jurisdictions may be tempted to address these uncertainties by redrafting traditional property offences in more general terms, substituting offences based on dishonest appropriation or obtaining of property from one person to another with general offences of dishonestly procuring gain for oneself or causing loss to others. While this approach may be considered necessary to keep pace with crime in the digital age, it presents clear dangers of over-criminalisation. Indeed, precisely for this reason the Model Criminal Code Officers Committee (MCCOC) in *Chapter 3: Theft, Fraud, Bribery and Related Offences*, Final Report (1995) rejected proposals for a general dishonesty offence: p 171. As explored above, the MCCOC considered that the inherent wrongfulness of the *conduct* was as important as its dishonesty. Within capitalist economies, where so much commercial activity is directed toward inflicting loss or obtaining gain from competitors, dishonesty should not be the sole concept for distinguishing innocent from criminal conduct.

The digital age has exposed a number of gaps in the law governing property offences particularly in relation to the concepts of "property" and "belonging to another". Legislatures and the courts should be cautious in expanding the frontiers of the criminal law without considering any potential counterproductive effects. While information is considered a valuable and tradeable commodity in the digital age, particularly in the form of computer data, traditional property offences may not be an appropriate legal route for vindicating these proprietary interests. In this regard, the civil law clearly has an important regulatory role to play. As Lipton has noted: "It may be that the most effective forms of protection for such assets will develop in the civil law context as remedies for misuse of intellectual property or associated rights, rather than as a matter of criminal law": "Property Offences into the 21st Century" (1999) (1) *The Journal of Information Law and Technology* (http://www.law.warwick.ac.uk/jilt/99-1/lipton.html). For a further examination of criminal justice and regulatory issues surrounding "electronic funds transfer crime", see P Grabosky and R Smith, *Crime in the Digital Age* (Sydney: Transaction Publishers/Federation Press, 1998), Ch 8.

"Fiddling the Books": The Doctrine of General Deficiency

The law of larceny required misappropriation or conversion of *specific* property. To overcome the difficulties of proof in relation to minor alterations of financial accounts, the courts developed a doctrine that the prosecution need only prove a general deficiency of accounts, rather than larceny of specific sums. The case law is reviewed in Fisse, *Howard's Criminal Law* (5th ed, Sydney: Law Book Company Ltd, 1990), p 213. This rule has been enacted into legislation in most jurisdictions: *Crimes Act* 1900 (ACT), s 124; *Crimes Act* 1900 (NSW), s 161; *Criminal Code* (Qld), s 568(1); *Criminal Law Consolidation Act* 1935 (SA), s 179; *Criminal Code* (WA), s 568(1). The MCCOC recommended the retention of this doctrine in the form of an evidential provision applicable to "money or other property": *Chapter 3 — Theft, Fraud, Bribery and Related Offences*, Final Report (1995), p 77. It should also be noted that Rule 6 of the 6th Schedule to the *Crimes Act* 1958 (Vic) has effected a more general alteration of the common law requirement that *specific* property must be identified as appropriated or obtained by deception: "The description of property ... shall be in ordinary language and such as to indicate with reasonable clearness the property referred to". There is no corresponding provision in the *Crimes Act* 1900 (ACT) or proposed for the *Model Criminal Code*.

Theft of Intangible Property

Technology seems destined to outstrip the capacity of the criminal law to keep pace. The criminal law has struggled with the meaning of "property", especially intangible things that cannot be taken or carried away. Earlier this century, the uncertainties surrounding whether electricity was property capable of being stolen led to the enactment of statutory offences dealing with the illegal abstraction of electricity in many jurisdictions.[33] In the late 20th century, there are similar uncertainties surrounding the application of the concept of "property" to "information". For a review of these issues see G Hughes, "Computers, Crime and the Concept of 'Property'" (1990) 1 *Intellectual Property Journal* 154.

Although statutory definitions of property expressly include "intangible things", the question remains whether information (which is clearly intangible) should be regarded as "property" or a "thing" capable of being stolen. In *Oxford v Moss* (1978) 68 Cr App R 183 the Divisional Court in England held that copying information contained in an examination paper could not be regarded as property capable of being stolen in the *Theft Act* 1968 (UK), notwithstanding that the statutory definition in s 4(1) applied to "other intangible property". The case suggested that "information", even confidential and valuable information, should not be regarded as property capable of being stolen. It should be noted that the decision to quash the conviction

---

33 See, for example, *Crimes Act* 1900 (ACT), s 114; *Criminal Code* (Qld), s 408; *Criminal Code* (NT), s 221; *Criminal Law Consolidation Act* 1935 (SA) s 154; *Criminal Code* (Tas), s 233; *Criminal Code* (WA), s 390. In other jurisdictions, as noted above, the definition of property expressly includes electricity.

in this case was justified on the alternate ground that the accused had merely "borrowed" the exam paper and therefore lacked the intention to deprive the owner of it permanently.

The courts in Canada have similarly grappled with the question as to whether confidential information could be regarded as property for the purpose of theft. In *R v Stewart* (1983) 149 DLR (3d) 583, the accused, a consultant, approached a security guard of a hotel with a view to obtaining the names, addresses and other relevant information about the staff of the hotel. The union, frustrated by a hostile management, had enlisted the services of the accused to obtain information about the hotel staff. The information was contained on the hotel's personnel files and payroll print-out, which was regarded as confidential and protected under the hotel's security arrangements. The security guard reported the approach to the police, and the accused was charged with the statutory offence of counselling theft (an inchoate offence equivalent to incitement). He was acquitted of the offence and the Crown appealed. The majority of the Court of Appeal of Ontario upheld the appeal and substituted a conviction for counselling theft. They specifically rejected the approach in *Oxford v Moss,* holding that confidential information could fall within the scope of theft. Section 283 of the *Criminal Code* (Can) did not use the term "property" and extended to any fraudulent taking or conversion of "anything whether animate or inanimate". The majority noted that not all forms of information were property, but that confidential information gathered through the expenditure of time, effort and money by a commercial enterprise for the purpose of its business should be protected by the criminal law. For a critique of this decision see G Hammond, "Theft of Information" (1984) 100 *Law Quarterly Review* 252. Significantly, the Alberta Court of Appeal refused to follow *Stewart,* favouring the approach taken in *Oxford v Moss* (1978) 68 Cr App R 183: see *R v Offley* (1986) 51 CR (3d) 378.

The uncertainty whether information could be property capable of being stolen was finally resolved by the Supreme Court of Canada: *Stewart v The Queen* (1988) 41 CCC (3d) 481. Lamer J, giving the judgment of the Court, allowed the appeal against conviction for counselling theft on a number of grounds. First, the criminal law should not recognise information as property because the civil law had not yet recognised that proprietary rights existed in information. The protection of information in the present law derived from intellectual property law or from the equitable nature of the relationship (a relationship of good faith or confidence) rather than from the idea of a proprietary right in information. Secondly, the physical elements of theft required the property to be "taken or converted". If information is property, it is intangible property. As such, intangible property cannot be "taken". It is only possible to take an intangible thing if it is embodied in a tangible form such as a document. Conversion may be satisfied (interference with the rights of the owner) but there must be deprivation of the the the use and possession of the property. In this case, there was no deprivation of the use or possession of the information. Copying did not deprive the hotel of the information itself. The Ontario Court of Appeal had held the hotel would have been deprived of the "confidentiality" of the information. But as the Lamer J pointed out (at 494) in the Supreme Court, there can be no property in confidentiality: "One cannot be deprived of confidentiality, because one cannot own confidentiality. One enjoys it".

On the basis of the decision in *Stewart,* Gordon Hughes has suggested that the unauthorised extraction of data from a computer may not constitute theft, stealing or larceny in Australia: "Computers, Crime and the Concept of 'Property'" (1990) 1 *Intellectual Property Journal*

154 at 158. Where information has been stored as data on a computer, special computer offences relating to unauthorised access and damage may apply. The scope of these offences have been briefly considered above at p 697. The Northern Territory contains an offence of "unlawfully abstracting confidential information from any register, document or computer, or other repository of information": *Criminal Code* (NT), s 222; see *Snell v Pryce* (1990) FLR 213.

3.4 BELONGING TO ANOTHER

The *Theft Act* model aimed to avoid the complexity of the civil law relating to ownership and possession by resorting to the concept of "belonging to another". While the legislature and the courts have promoted the ordinary meaning approach to key definitions for theft, it is impossible to free the law entirely from the complexity of the civil law. In many cases, particularly those involving complex commercial transactions, the courts will be under a duty to explain and apply complex civil law concepts that affect the possession of and control over property. Although the definition of "belonging" avoids the use of the term "ownership", it still resorts to traditional proprietary concepts. Section 71(2) of the *Crimes Act* 1958 (Vic) provides:

> In this Division property shall be regarded as belonging to any person having possession or
> control of it, or having in it any proprietary right or interest (not being an equitable interest
> arising only from an agreement to transfer or grant an interest).

In this respect, see also s 95(1) of the *Crimes Act* 1900 (ACT). Indeed, the rights of ownership clearly fall within the broad umbrella of "any proprietary interest".

THE SCOPE OF POSSESSION, CONTROL AND OTHER PROPRIETARY RIGHTS OR INTERESTS

Since property is regarded as belonging to any person having "possession or control of it, or having in it any proprietary right or interest", a single item of property may belong to more than one person for the purposes of theft. While theft of joint property is not controversial, the definition is more problematic in cases where the legal owner is alleged to have appropriated his or her own property by adversely interfering or usurping the rights of others who have (for the time being) the right to possess or control that property. In practical terms, cases of owners "stealing their own property" are unlikely to succeed because of the requirement of dishonesty, and the inevitable reliance upon a defence of claim of right. As discussed above, in the absence of clarifying legislation, there is uncertainty whether an appropriation must be "without consent of the owner". Should judges insist that lack of consent is an essential requirement, this would further preclude the conviction of owners who appropriate their own property.

The potential breadth of "belonging to another" was revealed in *R v Turner (No 2)* [1971] 2 All ER 441. The accused took his car to a garage for repairs, and following a dispute with the garage, removed his car without paying for the repairs. At the trial, the trial judge considered that the nature and scope of the repairer's proprietary interests in the accused's car to be irrelevant, specifically whether or not the repairer had a lien (security) over the property. (Under the civil law, a creditor may have the right to hold property as a security until a debt is discharged.) The sole question was whether the owner of the garage had "possession or control" of the car. The accused was convicted of theft of his car and appealed to the Court of Appeal. At the appeal, the defence argued that, in the absence of proof of a lien over the car, the repairer had no right to retain the property as against the owner. The Court of Appeal examined the relevant section dealing with property belonging to another. The Court held (at 443) that the words "possession and control" required no qualification in this case. Accordingly, it is sufficient if the person from whom the property was taken had, at the time of the appropriation, "possession" or "control" of the property.

Conceivably, an owner who removed his or her property from the possession or control of a thief may be appropriating property belonging to another. While the judicial desire to avoid introducing complex questions of civil law is understandable, a preferable approach is to impose a requirement that the possession, control or proprietary interest in the property must be *lawful* in the circumstances. This may require the courts to address incident questions of civil law and to determine the priority of interests in the property in cases of conflict. The need to determine the legal nature of the interests in property will occur only rarely, as in the case of *Turner (No 2)*. This requirement is consistent with the idea that the conduct of the accused must be wrongful, and that the fault element of dishonesty, while important, should not perform "all the work" in relation to distinguishing between innocent and criminal dealings in property. Regrettably, this question was not addressed by the *Model Criminal Code*, which largely accepted the existing statutory definition.

The definition of "belonging to another" recommended by the MCCOC contained one significant change from the *Theft Act* model. The MCCOC recommended that the exemption in relation to equitable interests should be extended expressly to cover interests in or arising from a constructive trust: *Model Criminal Code*, s 14.5, discussed in *Chapter 3: Theft, Fraud, Bribery and Related Offences*, Final Report (1995), pp 50-51. The MCCOC considered that this equitable exemption (which included constructive trusts) was justified because of the existence of a wide range of civil law remedies for unjust enrichment and unconscionable dealing. The MCCOC considered that any extension of the law of theft to deal with the appropriation of equitable interests would "stray too far from the common conception of theft and the much more culpable sort of dishonesty involved in theft": p 53.[34]

> One route to solving the problem of property passing under a mistake is to take an expansive approach to the definition of proprietary interest. Thus, an owner who passes property to another by mistake may retain some equitable proprietary (beneficial) interest in that property once the recipient is aware of the mistake. This approach was adopted in the English Court of Appeal in *Shadrokh-Cigari* [1988] Crim LR 465. As noted above, the MCCOC recommended against stretching the definition of "proprietary interest" to encompass interests arising under equitable remedies, such as constructive trusts or tracing, on the grounds of complexity and the availability of civil remedies. It should be noted that such an extension is also unnecessary since these many cases will trigger the statutory provisions that deem the property passed by mistake to belong to the person entitled by law to restoration.

---

34 This position reflected the approach taken in *Attorney-General Reference (No 1 of 1985)* [1986] 1 QB 491 at 503, where the English Court of Appeal refused to extend the law of theft in aid of constructive trusts. See further ATH Smith, "Constructive Trusts in the Law of Theft" [1977] Crim LR 395.

THE DEEMING PROVISIONS: PROPERTY WITH SPECIAL OBLIGATIONS

The common law has had difficulties with the person who, receiving property subject to a legal obligation to deal with it in a particular manner, fraudulently appropriated or converted it for his or her own benefit. The *Theft Act* model addressed this problem of "larceny by bailee" in a number of ways. As explored above, the concept of appropriation was extended to cases where the accused initially received the property innocently, but later kept or dealt with it as an owner. The other problem arising in these cases was that the legal ownership, possession or control of the property had passed to another person. The *Theft Act* model addressed this obstacle by "deeming" that the property belonged to another for the purposes of theft. Following the provisions in the *Theft Act* 1968 (UK), s 73 of the *Crimes Act* 1958 (Vic) provides:

> **(8)** Where property is subject to a trust, the persons to whom it belongs shall be regarded as including any person having a right to enforce the trust, and an intention to defeat the trust shall be regarded accordingly as an intention to deprive of the property any person having that right.

> **(9)** Where a person receives property from or on account of another, and is under an obligation to the other to retain and deal with that property or its proceeds in a particular way, the property or proceeds shall be regarded (as against him [or her]) as belonging to the other.

See also s 95(2) and (3) of the *Crimes Act* 1900 (ACT).

Property subject to a trust

Section 73(8) above deals with the trustee who appropriates property held in trust. The legal ownership vests in the trustee, who has an obligation to hold the property in trust for the benefit of other persons. As the beneficiaries have equitable rights in the property subject to the trust, their interests may fall with the broad definition of "property" as discussed above. It may also be deemed to be property belonging to the beneficiaries by virtue of the obligation imposed on the trustee to deal and retain the property in a particular way, as discussed below. In reality, this section deals with residual cases where property is held on trust, but there is no ascertained beneficiary as in the case of "purpose trusts". In these cases, special provisions deem that the trust property belongs to any person who has a right to enforce the trust.

Property received on account of another

A person may receive money or other property in circumstances in which he or she falls under an obligation either to the person from whom it is received or to some other person, to deal with that property in a particular way. The Criminal Law Revision Committee which drafted the *Theft Act* 1968 (UK) gave the example of the treasurer of a holiday fund, who is the legal owner of the fund, but is under an obligation to retain the money received as agreed: *Theft and Related Offences* (London: HMSO Cmnd 2977, 1966), p 127. The *Theft Act* 1968 (UK) simply provided that the recipient of the property had to be under an "obligation" to deal with the property or its proceeds in a particular manner. It is not clear from this formulation whether the issue should be treated as one of law or fact; or whether the obligations imposed on the accused are confined to those recognised and enforceable under the civil law. There is also uncertainty over the nature and scope of the obligations arising in relation to money and other fungibles.

The obligation to retain and deal with money received for particular purposes was considered by the English Court of Appeal in *R v Hall* [1972] 2 All ER 1009. The accused was a partner in a firm of travel agents in Manchester. He received money from clients for trips to America and deposited this money into the firm's general trading account. The flights did not materialise. The accused was charged with theft of the money received and convicted. The question on appeal was whether, at the time of the appropriation, the property belonged to another person. The problem with this case was that, at the time of the appropriation, the accused had possession of the money, raising the question whether the deeming provisions in s 5(3) of the *Theft Act* 1968 (UK) applied. (This section is identical to s 73(9) of the *Crimes Act* 1958 (Vic).)

The Court of Appeal considered whether the accused was under an obligation to account for money provided by the clients. The accused had argued that he was not under any obligation to his clients to retain or deal with the money in a particular way. Edmund-Davies LJ, delivering the judgment of the Court, held (at 1101) that the obligation was determined by examining the expectation of the party handing over the money. The manner in which the accused subsequently dealt with the property (paying it into a general trading account rather than holding it separately) would not be determinative of the issue. In this type of case, the expectation of the clients after making payment was that they would receive, in due course, air tickets and other documents necessary for their holiday. The travel firm was under an obligation to fulfil this expectation, but there was no expectation on the part of the client that the accused would "retain and deal with that money in a particular way". Therefore the situation did not attract the operation of s 5(3). Edmund-Davies LJ made it clear that "each case turns on its own facts", and that there may be "special arrangements" where the client could impose an obligation to retain the money in a particular way, but this would require proof preferably evidenced by documents. In this case, the prosecution had not established that the clients expected the accused to deal with the property (the money) in a particular way, nor had the prosecution shown that the accused had assumed such an obligation. Although the accused's conduct was scandalous, it could not be regarded as theft.

By focusing the inquiry on the particular expectations of the clients when depositing the property, *R v Hall* skirted over whether the obligation to account should be confined to those arising under the civil law. Edmund-Davies LJ did allude to this issue indirectly. He noted that in the present case, the issue as to whether the property was entrusted for and on account of another could be regarded as a question of fact for the jury.[35] In more complex cases, he suggested that the question of whether an obligation to account existed would be a "mixed question of law and fact": at 1012.

The legal basis for the obligation to account was further explored in *R v Meech* [1973] 3 All ER 939. McCord, a second-hand car dealer owed the accused £40. McCord had obtained from a hire-purchase company a cheque for £1450 by means of a forged document. McCord asked the accused, Meech, to cash the cheque, retain his £40 and return £1410 to McCord. Before drawing against the

---

35 In support of this approach, Edmund-Davies cited *R v Sheaf* (1927) 134 LT 127, a case decided under the *Larceny Act* 1916 (UK).

sum, Meech became aware that the cheque was obtained by fraud. Meech then decided to double-cross McCord. He withdrew £1410 and then with the assistance of two accomplices, Parslow and Jolliffe, staged a fake robbery with a view to keeping the balance of the money. Meech reported the fake robbery to the police who got suspicious and investigated. The trio was charged and convicted of theft of £1410.

The Crown had argued, applying s 5(3), that at all material times there was an obligation on Meech to McCord to deal with the cheque in a particular way. The defence argued that the section did not apply — since the cheque had been obtained by a forged instrument, that illegality meant that there was no *legal* obligation on the accused enforceable at civil law to retain or deal with that property in a particular way. The defence pointed to the authorities and academic commentary that supported the contention that the "obligation" means "legal obligation". While accepting this premise, the Court of Appeal nevertheless held that the submission was unsound in principle: at 942. Roskill LJ, delivering the judgment of the Court, held that the question must be viewed from the accused's point of view and not the victim's point of view. From Meech's point of view, at the time he took the cheque he clearly considered that he was under an obligation to McCord to deal with the cheque in a specific way. The fact that under the civil law the obligation to account would be unenforceable due to public policy or illegality was irrelevant. The existence of the obligation was determined at the time of the creation or acceptance of that obligation, and not at a subsequent stage where there may be legal obstacles to its performance. The accused raised a second argument: if he accepted that initially he was under an obligation to account for the proceeds to McCord, once he became aware that the cheque was obtained by a forged instrument, he was no longer under an obligation to account for the property or proceeds. The Court rejected this argument too. The time at which to determine the obligation was the time of the assumption of the obligation not the time of the performance of the obligation.

In most cases, the question as to whether there is an obligation to account is a straight-forward matter determined by examining the intention of the person transferring the property. For example in *Wakeman v Farrar* [1974] Crim LR 136 the accused made a claim for a benefit from the Department of Health and Social Security. He was sent a cheque that never arrived. The accused informed the Department which asked him to sign a declaration that if the cheque subsequently arrived he would return it to them. The money was then given to the accused over the counter. Later the cheque arrived and the accused cashed it. He was charged with theft. The magistrates dismissed the charge on the ground that the property did not belong to the Department at the time it was cashed. The prosecution appealed and the Queen's Bench Divisional Court reinstated the charges on the ground that the deeming provisions in s 5(3) of the *Theft Act* 1968 (UK) applied on these facts. By virtue of the signed declaration, the accused had been placed under a legal (not merely moral obligation) to deal with the cheque in a certain way. The Divisional Court also noted that the Department retained a proprietary interest in the cheque, even though it had been drawn in favour of the accused — this aspect of the ruling diverges from dicta in the House of Lords relating to the ownership of cheques in *R v Preddy* [1996] 3 WLR 255, though is consistent with the High Court approach in *Parsons v The Queen* (1999) 195 CLR 619, discussed above: pp 701ff.

Subsequent cases have established that the deeming section is confined to "legal obligations", the precise scope of which is properly a matter for the courts: *R v Mainwaring* (1981) 74

Cr App R 99 at 107, per Lawton LJ. It has also been firmly established that these legal obligations to retain and deal with property imposed on the accused are not necessarily *identical* to those arising under the civil law: see Lord Widgery CJ in *R v Hayes* (1976) 64 Cr App R 82 at 85. By treating this question of legal obligation as *sui generis* (in a category all of its own), the courts have attempted to prevent the complexities of the civil law unnecessarily intruding into the law of theft. The courts have remained mindful of the dangers of judges usurping the fact-finder's function, stressing that the question of whether the "obligation" (as judicially interpreted) has arisen on the particular facts is for the jury or magistrate.[36] However, in complex cases, as suggested by Edmund-Davis LJ in *R v Hall*, this issue should be regarded as a mixed question of law and fact.

> Section 95(3) of the *Crimes Act* 1900 (ACT) expressly states that the recipient of the property must be under a "legal obligation" to that person to retain and deal with the property in a particular way. The Model Criminal Code Officers Committee (MCCOC) has similarly adopted this formulation, though the Report provides no further explanation or clarification of the meaning of "legal obligation", or in particular, the relevance of the civil law to this question.

Property received by mistake

One of the most perplexing areas of the law of theft relates to property obtained by mistake and the effect of mistake on whether the property "belongs to another". As in cases of receiving property on account of another, the question whether or not property has passed to the accused before the act of appropriation involves some examination of civil law concepts and obligations.

The common law of larceny lacked a clear consensus on whether property transferred by mistake vitiated the consent of the owner to that transaction. If it was held that legal ownership of the property had *already* passed to the accused, then there could be no larceny by any subsequent taking or conversion. To avoid this unsatisfactory outcome, the common law developed complex rules governing the effect of "fundamental mistakes" on consent and the intent to pass property. The English law on mistake, following *R v Middleton* (1873) LR 2 CCR 38 and *R v Ashwell* (1885) 16 QBD 190, remained in a highly confused state. It seemed that both consent and intent in relation to transfers of property could be negated where the accused was aware of the mistake before or during the transaction, as well as in cases where the accused having received the property by mistake, subsequently became aware of the error. The difficulties in extrapolating a workable principle from the available authorities are apparent in *R v Potisk* (1973) 6 SASR 389, where the Supreme Court of South Australia simply declined to apply the English decisions.

The uncertainty over the effect of mistake for larceny under the common law was not resolved until the High Court decision in *Ilich v The Queen* (1987) 162 CLR 110, which is discussed in the case study below. In relation to the statutory offence of theft, the definition of appropriation extends the offence to cases where the accused "has come by the property (innocently or not) without stealing it, any later assumption of a right to it by keeping or dealing with it as owner": *Crimes Act* 1900 (ACT),

---

36   For an attempt to reconcile the seemingly contradictory dicta in this area see *R v Dubar* [1994] 1 WLR 1484 at 1492, per McKinnon J.

s 96(2); *Crimes Act* 1958 (Vic), s 73(4). However, in these cases, the question still arises as to whether the property passed by mistake "belongs to another" at the critical moment of appropriation. As the MCCOC noted in *Chapter 3: Theft, Fraud, Bribery and Related Offences*, Final Report (1995), "there are a number of routes to the conclusion that it does" (p 61).

CASE STUDIES

Fundamental Mistakes and the Negation of Consent

The principal route under the common law for resolving "mistake problems" in relation to property offences was identified in *Ilich v The Queen* (1987) 162 CLR 110. Though this case concerned the offence of stealing under the *Criminal Code* (WA), in the absence of legislative guidance on the effect of mistake, the High Court applied the common law — as such, the principles identified by the High Court have application to larceny, offences under the Codes and even offences based on the *Theft Act* model in situations where the statutory deeming provisions in relation to mistake have no application. As we shall see below, the principles in *Ilich* have also been influential in developing new mistake provisions for the *Model Criminal Code*.

In this case, the High Court approached the issue by examining the effect of the mistake on the transfer of possession and ownership of property. The accused was a locum vet who worked for another vet, Brighton, while he was away. On his return, Brighton was upset with the way the accused had run the practice and sacked him. The accused said that Brighton gave him a packet of money and was told to sign for it without counting it. He did so and went home and found there was extra money in the packet. The accused claimed that he kept the extra money separately in his car. The police were called to investigate and the accused denied having any extra money. The excess money was found in his car. The accused claimed that he did not intend to take it but was waiting for Brighton to call him so that he could have the upper hand.

The High Court considered the effect of mistake in terms of its impact on the intention of the person passing the property. The accused had argued that the owner of the money, Brighton, notwithstanding his mistake, had intended the property in the envelope to pass to him. The accused argued that since the property had passed on receipt of his envelope, the money did not "belong to another" and therefore could not be stealing. (It should be noted that "lack of consent" to the taking or conversion was not a requirement of the statutory offence under the Code.) The sole issue in this case was whether, at the latter stage of fraudulent conversion, the property in the money had already passed to the accused.

According to the majority of the High Court (Wilson and Dawson JJ with whom Deane J agreed), there are only three kinds of mistake of a "sufficiently fundamental kind" that would negate the apparent consent and prevent property passing (at 126):

— a mistake as to the identity of the transferee; or

— a mistake as to the identity of the thing delivered; or

— a mistake as to the quantity of the thing delivered, though there is an exception relating to money where property passes with the change of possession.

In cases where the error cannot be classified as "fundamental", consent is not vitiated and thus possession and ownership passes in accordance with the apparent intention of the owner. In *Ilich v The Queen* the overpayment involved a mistake that was of a non-fundamental kind — it related to the quantity of money passed. As the property in the money passed with possession, there was neither a fraudulent taking nor subsequent conversion when the accused realised Brighton's mistake.

The approach based on vitiation of consent in *Ilich v The Queen* is not the only legal route whereby a mistake may be held to prevent the passing of possession and ownership of property. As noted above, the *Theft Act* model enacted in the United Kingdom, the Australian Capital Territory and Victoria contain provisions that deem property *not* to belong to another where it is received by mistake.

The precise relationship between the statutory provisions and the common law remains unclear. The statutory provisions are clearly broader than the common law since they are not confined to mistakes of a "fundamental character" as defined by the High Court in *Ilich*. In cases of non-fundamental mistakes, although the possession and ownership of property has passed, the statutory provisions can apply and deem the property to belong to another. As we shall see below, the breadth of the statutory provisions obviate reliance on the principles in *Ilich*, though the common law may continue to have relevance to the interpretation of these statutory provisions and provide guidance in cases where the mistake does not fall squarely within the terms of statute. As we shall explore below, the MCCOC in *Chapter 3: Theft, Fraud, Bribery and Related Offences*, Final Report (1995), recommended (p 65) that the *Theft Act* provisions should be remodelled (subject to minor qualifications) to incorporate the concept of "fundamental mistake" established by the High Court in *Ilich*.

Mirroring the *Theft Act* 1968 (UK), s 73(10) of the *Crimes Act* 1958 (Vic) deals with the effect of property received by mistake in the following way:

> Where a person gets property by another's mistake, and is under an obligation to make restoration (in whole or in part) of the property or its proceeds or of the value thereof, then to the extent of that obligation the property or proceeds shall be regarded (as against him [or her]) as belonging to the person entitled to restoration, and an intention not to make restoration shall be regarded accordingly as an intention to deprive that person of the property or proceeds.

See also s 95(4) of the *Crimes Act* 1900 (ACT). Unlike the common law approach in *Ilich*, the mistake does not vitiate or negate possession or ownership. However, it achieves the equivalent effect by deeming the property in the possession of the person who received it by mistake as belonging to the person entitled to restoration. The section also provides that an intention not to make restoration amounts to an intention to permanently deprive the owner of it.

It has been established that the obligation to make restoration must be a *legal* obligation, not merely a moral or social one. In *R v Gilks* [1972] 1 WLR 1341, the accused placed a number of bets with a bookmaker. When the accused collected his winnings, he was overpaid £106 by the bookmaker.

The accused kept the money, although he was aware at the time that the bookmaker had made a mistake. The accused was convicted of theft of this sum. The question on appeal was whether, at the time of the appropriation, the property belonged to another. The accused argued that s 5(4) of the *Theft Act* 1968 (UK) dealing with mistake did not apply. This provision is equivalent to s 95(4) of the *Crimes Act* 1900 (ACT) and s 73(10) of the *Crimes Act* 1958 (Vic). The accused relied on a civil case which held that debts arising through gambling were not legally enforceable. Under the common law, gaming contracts are not legally enforceable — winnings are regarded simply as gifts of money. Although the money had passed under a mistake, the accused was not under a legal obligation to make restitution, and therefore the property could not be deemed to belong to the bookmaker.

The English Court of Appeal held (at 1345) that s 5(4) only applied to cases where there was a legal obligation to make restoration. The court rejected the view taken by the magistrate that the subsection includes obligations to restore property that are moral or social, as distinct from legal. The principle in *Gilks* that the obligation to make restoration must be "legal" has been incorporated into s 95(4) of the *Crimes Act* 1900 (ACT) and the equivalent section (s 15.5(3)) proposed for the *Model Criminal Code*: see *Chapter 3: Theft, Fraud, Bribery and Related Offences*, Final Report (1995), p 61. Notwithstanding this restrictive interpretation of the phrase "an obligation to make restoration", the Court of Appeal in *Gilks* nevertheless affirmed the conviction for theft. The accused was guilty of theft because the property had never passed to the accused. The Court of Appeal affirmed the rule in the earlier case of *Middleton*, discussed above, that property does not pass from the owner where the accused receives an overpayment of money if he or she is aware of the mistake at the time of its receipt.

On this view, the *Theft Act* provisions on mistake *only* apply to cases of mutual mistakes, that is, where the recipient of the property is unaware of the mistake made by the transferee. This aspect of the law of mistake was not specifically addressed in *Ilich* and there remains some uncertainty over this question. It may be argued that the distinction between mutual and unilateral mistakes should have no legal bearing on whether property passes. This is consistent with dicta in *Ilich* that the *characterisation* of the mistake as "fundamental" determined whether or not property passed, not the knowledge or intention of the transferee.

The Model Criminal Code Officers Committee (MCCOC) reviewed the complex rules governing mistake and concluded that the law should not distinguish between unilateral and mutual mistakes *except* in "special cases" of overpayment by cash, cheque or direct credit. In this situation, a distinction should be drawn between individuals who are aware of the overpayment at the time of the receipt of the property, and individuals who became aware of the overpayment at a later stage. In the former case, the MCCOC noted (p 67) that "the absence of the inertia factor" made the situation case sufficiently like the "finding cases" to warrant criminalisation as theft. In the latter case, the imposition of liability for theft would place an onerous duty on the person innocently receiving the property to rectify the mistake on pain of committing theft. In such circumstances, it was more appropriate that victims seek recovery of the overpayment through the civil law. Earlier in the report, the MCCOC had noted (p 63) that the criminal law should not be used to relieve businesses of their responsibility to establish and maintain reliable payment systems and that, in any event, the culpability was much reduced in cases where the accused "has had temptation thrust upon him or her".

While it is clear that the obligation to make restoration is a "legal obligation", there are doubts whether the duty to make restoration is identical and restricted to those imposed under the civil law. Another case where s 5(4) of the *Theft Act* 1968 (UK) was held to apply was *Attorney-General's Reference (No 1 of 1983)* [1984] 3 WLR 686. The accused was a police officer and her salary was paid into her bank account by a direct debit system. She was wrongly credited £74.74 for her wages and overtime for a day on which she did not work. There was evidence that she became aware of the overpayment, but decided to do nothing about it and simply left the money in the account. She was charged with theft of £74.74. The trial judge directed an acquittal and the Attorney-General made the following reference to the Court of Appeal. The Attorney-General asked the Court of Appeal whether a person who was overpaid, who becomes aware of that mistake and then fails to repay that debt, is guilty of theft.

The first question addressed by the Court was what property the accused had appropriated. Lord Lane CJ, delivering the judgment of the Court, rejected the prosecution view that the accused had appropriated £74.74. He held (at 690) that it was not money, but rather the debt due to the accused from her own bank (a *chose in action*) that was the property subject of the charge. As a logical consequence, the accused had appropriated a debt which in fact belonged to herself. The Court further examined whether the deeming provision dealing with mistake could be applied to the facts in this case. The Court considered (at 691) that the obligation of "making restoration" of property or proceeds under s 5(4) of the *Theft Act* was the same as "making restitution". The law of restitution provided a wide range of rights and remedies under civil law to prevent unjust enrichment. In cases of over-payment, the Court turned to the following general principles of restitution (at 691):

> Generally speaking the respondent [the accused], in these circumstances, is obliged to pay for a benefit received when the benefit has been given under a mistake on the part of the giver as to a material fact. The mistake must be as to a fundamental or essential fact and the payment must have been due to that fundamental or essential fact. The mistake here was that this police officer had been working on a day when she had been at home and not working at all.

As a result of s 5(4), the property, which was obtained by a mistake, was deemed to belong to the person entitled to restoration, in this case the Metropolitan Police. Under the section, the accused's intention not to make restoration is regarded as an intention to permanently deprive. The preparedness of the Court of Appeal in mistake cases to use the principles of restitution may be contrasted with its reticence in using the civil law to resolve the nature of the obligations in cases where property has been received from or on account of another: see above, p 711.

The MCCOC expressed general concern over leaving the effect of mistake "at large" for judges to determine using civil law principles. The MCCOC concluded (p 65) that "civil law distinctions — while appropriate to the context of determining civil recovery — are too obscure on the whole to define the boundaries of an offence as serious as theft". The MCCOC decided (p 50) to define and limit the principles governing mistake to the existing law as stated by the High Court in *Ilich v The Queen*, subject to the following qualifications and clarifications:

Belonging to another — interpretation

15.5

(3) If a person gets property by another's fundamental mistake, and is under a legal obligation to make restoration (in whole or in part) of the property or its proceeds, then to the extent of that obligation the property or proceeds belongs (as against the person) to the person entitled to restoration. Accordingly, an intention not to make restoration is an intention to deprive the person so entitled of the property or proceeds, and an appropriation of the property or proceeds without the consent of the person entitled to the restoration.

(4) For the purpose of subsection (3), a fundamental mistake is:

(a) a mistake about the identity of the person getting the property or a mistake as to the essential nature of the property; or

(b) a mistake about the amount of any money, direct credit into an account, cheque or other negotiable instrument if the person getting the property is aware of the mistake at the time of getting the property.

These principles are purportedly exhaustive, and while avoiding reliance on civil law concepts, will undoubtedly require judicial interpretation. The rule governing mistake as to the "essential nature of the property" is conceptually similar to the rules governing vitiation of consent in offences against the person and sexual offences. Chapter 12 at pp 612ff has explored the complexity and continuing controversy surrounding the meaning and scope of mistakes as to the "nature and character of the act". Like autonomy, the concept of property belonging to another is amenable to competing and contestable interpretations.

PERSPECTIVES

Evasion of Liability and Self-Service Operations

The requirement that the property must belong to another at the moment of the dishonest appropriation presents difficulties in cases where the owner intends the customer to take possession of the goods prior to purchase. In supermarkets, for example, the property taken by the customer from the shelves still "belongs to another" at the moment of the appropriation since the supermarket maintains both control and a proprietary interest in those goods. Different considerations apply in cases of fungible property, where possession and indeed all the proprietary interests in that property, are intended to pass to the customer. Indeed, the only legal interest of the person who has passed the property is the contractual right to obtain payment from the customer. Common examples of this situation include property or services obtained in self-service petrol stations, restaurants, taxis and hotels.

The obstacles to obtaining a conviction in cases where the customer has received possession of the property innocently and then dishonestly evades payment were revealed in the English case of *R v Greenberg* [1972] Crim LR 331. The accused filled up his car with petrol intending to pay, but later decided not to pay and drove off. He was convicted of theft and appealed. The Court of Appeal held that this was not theft; the accused's act of filling his car with petrol was not an appropriation since the rights in the petrol were assumed with the owner's consent. Nor was the accused acting dishonestly at the time that he took possession of the petrol. The *Theft Act* 1968 (UK) defined "appropriation" as including the person who innocently comes by property without stealing it, and then later decides to keep it or deal with the property as the owner: see *Crimes Act* 1900 (ACT), s 96(2); *Crimes Act* 1958 (Vic), s 73(4). While the subsequent act of keeping the petrol and driving off could constitute a dishonest appropriation, the Crown had to establish that the property belonged to another at that time. The obstacle to conviction when the accused drove away was that the petrol had already been transferred to his possession. The service station owner retained no identifiable *proprietary* interest in the petrol transferred, which had now mingled with the accused's petrol in his tank. Moreover, none of the deeming provisions discussed above applied; the property had not been received on account of another or under a mistake. Since the petrol "belonged to the accused", he could not be guilty of theft. It should also be noted that he could be guilty of obtaining property by deception only if, *at the outset*, he had intention to make off without payment. In such a case, the act of entering into a self-service station and filling up with petrol would constitute the operative deception — a false implied representation that he was customer willing to pay for the petrol received. If a person formed the intention to keep the property *after* receiving the petrol, as in *R v Greenberg*, he or she could not be guilty of obtaining property belonging to another by deception. The property was not initially obtained by a deception and, moreover, at the critical moment, the property did not belong to another.

To plug these obvious gaps in the law, the *Theft Act* 1968 (UK) was amended in 1973, and an offence of making off without payment was created: *Theft Act* 1973 (UK), s 3. A similar offence has been enacted by s 107 of the *Crimes Act* 1900 (ACT) which provides:

Making off without payment

(1) A person who, knowing that immediate payment for any goods supplied or services provided or expected from him or her, dishonestly makes off without having paid and with intent to avoid payment of the amount due, is guilty of an offence punishable, on conviction, by imprisonment for 2 years.

(2) Sub-section (1) does not apply to or in relation to —

   (a) the supply of goods or the provision of a service where that supply or provision is contrary to law; or

   (b) payment for the provision of a service where that payment is not legally enforceable.

(3) In this section, a reference to immediate payment shall be read as including a reference to payment at the time of collecting goods in respect of which a service has been provided.

There is no equivalent provision in Victoria. The MCCOC has recommended the inclusion of a similar provision in the *Model Criminal Code*: s 16.6, discussed in *Chapter 3: Theft, Fraud, Bribery and Related Offences*, Final Report (1995), pp 99-101. The fault element of the "making off without payment" offence is knowledge that immediate payment is due, and dishonesty. Dishonesty bears the same meaning (and therefore uncertainties) as for the basic offence of theft and the case law, discussed above, will be relevant to the determination of this element of the offence.

There has been one appellate decision examining the meaning of the term "intent to avoid the amount due". In *R v Allen* [1985] 1 AC 1029 the accused stayed at a hotel for 10 days and left without paying the bill of £1286. He telephoned two days later and said that he was having financial difficulties, but promised to return within two days to collect his belongings and to leave his Australian passport as security. Upon his return, he was arrested. The accused was convicted of making off without payment under the above section. The appeal to the House of Lords considered whether "intent to avoid payment" is satisfied by an intent to avoid payment at the place when payment was expected. The accused argued that the prosecution had to prove an intent *permanently* to avoid payment, and not just an intent to avoid payment when it was expected. The House of Lords agreed with the accused's analysis and allowed his appeal. Their Lordships referred to the Criminal Law Revision Committee report that had led to the section and noted that the Committee took the view that the "making off" offence should only cover individuals who leave without paying never intending to pay. "Making off without payment" therefore requires proof that the accused had formed an intention to avoid payment altogether and excludes the customer who intends merely to delay or defer payment. As the MCCOC observed (p 101): "The need to prove intent to avoid payment altogether parallels the requirement of intent to permanently deprive in theft".

3.5 INTENTION TO PERMANENTLY DEPRIVE

The *Theft Act* model, in addition to dishonesty, requires an intention to permanently deprive the other person of the property. Drawn directly from the common law, this requirement draws a distinction between theft and other forms of dishonest dealing in property such as unauthorised borrowing. As noted above, at p 690, this requirement has presented obstacles to conviction for larceny and theft in relation to the taking of motor vehicles. Removing a vehicle without the consent of the owner could not be larceny or theft because the "joyrider" lacked an intention to deprive permanently the owner of the vehicle. To deal with this type of "dishonest borrowing", special statutory offences prohibiting unauthorised use of a motor vehicle have been enacted in most jurisdictions. In Victoria and Western Australia, rather than enact a special offence, the basic offence of theft has dispensed with the requirement of an intention to permanently deprive in cases involving vehicles: *Crimes Act* 1958 (Vic), s 73(14); *Criminal Code* (WA), s 371A.

The *Theft Act* model has addressed the problem by expanding the definition of intention to permanently deprive to include an intention to borrow or lend property, but only in circumstances where it is equivalent to an outright taking or disposal. The MCCOC examined (p 73) whether this fault element was redundant in light of the role played by dishonesty. In favour of abolition, it could be argued that the intention to permanently deprive had grown less significant: the requirement had been abolished in specific situations (as in the case of vehicle theft) and the deeming provisions in the *Theft Act* had stretched the concept to encompass many forms of dishonest borrowing. In favour of retention, it could be argued that the offence of theft should be restricted to permanent deprivations — a person who intends to return the property should not be regarded as a thief.

Also, that the deeming provisions relating to intention to permanently deprive in the *Theft Act* were simply "fair extensions of the concept". While the dishonest borrowing of another's property could clearly interfere with the enjoyment of rights of ownership and possession, the civil remedies available in tort provided more than adequate remedies for such temporary deprivations of property. Reflecting the majority of submissions, the MCCOC recommended the retention of the concept. The reforms recommended by the MCCOC are considered below.

INTENTION TO DISPOSE OF PROPERTY REGARDLESS OF THE RIGHTS OF THE OTHER PERSON

Mirroring the approach in the *Theft Act* 1968 (UK), s 73 of the *Crimes Act* 1958 (Vic) provides:

> **(12)** A person appropriating property belonging to another without meaning the other permanently to lose the thing itself is nevertheless to be regarded as having the intention of permanently depriving the other of it if his [or her] intention is to treat the thing as his [or her] own to dispose of regardless of the other's rights; and a borrowing or lending of it may amount to so treating it if, but only if, the borrowing or lending is for a period and in circumstances making it equivalent to an outright taking or disposal.

> **(13)** Without prejudice to the generality of sub-section (12) where a person, having possession or control (lawfully or not) of property belonging to another, parts with the property under a condition as to its return which he [or she] may not be able to perform, this (if done for purposes of his [or her] own and without the other's authority) amounts to treating the property as his [or her] own to dispose of regardless of the other's rights.

With minor changes, this provision has been enacted in s 97(1), (2), (3) of the *Crimes Act* 1900 (ACT). It also substantially mirrors the proposed definition section (s 15.6 (1) and (2)) of the *Model Criminal Code: Chapter 3 — Theft, Fraud, Bribery and Related Offences*, Final Report (1995), pp 70-75.

The above definition requires proof of an *actual* intention on the part of the accused to permanently deprive the other person of the property. This fault element is based on the subjective state of mind of the accused, and arguably is restricted to intention in the narrower sense of purpose. The uncertain and variable meaning of intention in the criminal law, including the controversy over "oblique intent", has been examined in Chapter 3: p 176. There is no need to rely on the common law to extend the scope of intention since the legislation expressly expands the concept to include an intention to treat the property as one's own to dispose of regardless of the rights of the other person. Although an accused may lack an intention to permanently deprive, the subsection deems that intention to exist where he or she has an intention to treat the property as his or her own to dispose of regardless of the rights of the other person. Thus, destroying the property, if it meets this standard, may satisfy this fault element.

It has been argued that this expanded definition of intention to permanently deprive imports the notion of negligence or inadvertence into the law of theft. As the MCCOC observed, an intention to dispose of property "regardless" of the rights of the other person should not be understood as an objective standard of fault based on negligence. Rather it involves a sort of recklessness about permanent deprivations and is consistent with the general principles of criminal responsibility in Chapter 2 of the *Model Criminal Code* which makes recklessness the basic fault element. Regrettably, the type of recklessness implicit within this expanded definition of intention is not specified either in the existing legislation or the provisions proposed for the *Model Criminal Code*.

Since the concept of recklessness, like intention, bears different meanings for different offences, there is clearly a need to clarify whether this specie of recklessness is restricted to actual foresight of the probability of deprivation, or extends, more broadly, to culpable states of inadvertence. This question has caused considerable controversy in New South Wales in relation to the scope of recklessness in relation to the offence of sexual assault: see further Ch 12, pp 623ff.

It has also been suggested that subsections relating to borrowing and lending, and parting with property on conditions as to its return that the accused may not be able to perform, add little to the concept of permanent deprivation. The deeming provisions are not exhaustive and simply extend or clarify the meaning of intention to permanently deprive. As the MCCOC noted (p 75), these provisions are simply "examples" of disposing of property regardless of the other person's rights. The subsections do not limit or otherwise restrict the general definition contained in that section. This point has been made by Edmund-Davies LJ in *R v Warner* (1970) 55 Cr App R 93 at 96-97.

The scope of the definition and the effect of the subsections above were considered by the English Court of Appeal in *R v Lloyd* [1985] QB 829. The accused, a cinema projectionist, and a number of others were charged and convicted of conspiracy to steal. The charge related to the projectionist's removal of feature films and lending them to two other men for the purpose of making master copies from which "pirate" video tapes were produced. The films were removed for a few hours on each occasion, and then returned before their absence was noticed. The principal question on appeal was whether the accused had an intention to permanently deprive the other person of the feature films. Lord Lane CJ, delivering the judgment of the court, characterised (at 834) the above section dealing with borrowing or lending as "abstruse". In his view, the section must mean:

> if nothing else, that there are circumstances in which a defendant may be deemed to have the intention permanently to deprive, even though he [or she] may intend the owner eventually to get back the object which has been taken.

Lord Lane CJ held (at 835) that the deeming provisions should only be invoked in "exceptional cases" where the accused did not have an intention to permanently deprive. In the majority of cases, the question of intent could be resolved without resort to these sections. In *Lloyd*, the sections were relevant since the accused had only an intention to deprive the owners of the films temporarily. The court considered whether the deeming provision applied, specifically whether the borrowing in this case was for "a period or in such circumstances as to make it equivalent to an outright taking or disposal". Lord Lane CJ noted (at 836) that an intention to borrow is never enough for theft unless the intention is to return the property in such a changed state that it can truly be said that all its goodness or virtue has gone. He gave the example of *R v Beecham* (1851) 5 Cox CC 181, where the accused had appropriated a railway ticket intending that it should be returned to the railway company at the end of the journey. In this case, the accused was rightly convicted of larceny.

Applied to the facts in *Lloyd*, it was clear that the feature films did not fall into this category as "the goodness, the virtue, the practical value of the films to the owners has not gone out of the articles": at 837. The films could still be shown to audiences and were not diminished in value. Although the copyright swindle clearly caused damage to the owner's commercial interests, the borrowing was not for a period that made it equivalent to an outright taking. There was, in the words of Lord Lane CJ, "still virtue in the film": at 837. The remedies in this case were limited to those available in intellectual property law for infringement of copyright, rather than the law of theft.

PERSPECTIVES

Piracy and Theft of Copyright

In *R v Lloyd* [1985] QB 829, considered above, the defence submitted that the charges against the accused related to the appropriation of the "value" or "virtue" of the feature film. The defence argued that this "value" could not properly be regarded as "property" for the purpose of the *Theft Act* 1968 (UK). Since the appeal was allowed on other grounds, the Court of Appeal did not address this submission. The defence had specifically relied on *Rank Film Distributors Ltd v Video Information Centre* [1981] 2 All ER 76 where several members of the House of Lords had expressed the view that copyright could not be regarded as "property" for the purpose of theft. These comments were made in the context of an appeal reviewing an order obtained by Rank Films to search for and seize any infringing "pirate" copies of films and any related documents in the possession of the respondent. The Court of Appeal had quashed the orders on the grounds that it would violate the respondent's privilege against self-incrimination. The House of Lords, agreeing with the Court of Appeal, dismissed the appeal on the ground that a charge of conspiracy to defraud was a real possibility in this case. In the course of the judgment, the Court considered, strictly *obiter*, whether the respondent might also be guilty of theft of copyright. Lord Wilberforce took the view that the risk of prosecution was remote (at 81) since "[i]Infringement of copyright is not theft", and Lord Fraser of Tullybelton noted (at 83) that under the *Theft Act* 1968 (UK) property is "defined in a way that does not appear to include copyright".

The issue of theft of copyright has also been considered by the Supreme Court of Canada in *Stewart v The Queen* (1988) 41 CCC (3d) 481: see above at p 705. This case considered whether the act of copying confidential information could be theft. Although copying information may be an infringement of the rights of the copyright owner, it was not theft because the owner would never suffer any deprivation of the copyright: "whether or not copyright is property, it cannot be the object of theft": at 495 per Lamer J for the court.

In Australia, appropriation does not require actual deprivation of property — copying material may be properly regarded as usurping or interfering with one of the rights of the owner. Even if video or software "pirating" was held to constitute a dishonest appropriation, there remains doubt as to whether the person pirating films or software has an intention to permanently deprive the owner of that copyright. As the MCCOC concluded in *Chapter 3: Theft, Fraud, Bribery and Related Offences*, Final Report (1995), p 47:

> Mere breach of a copyright or use of a trade secret might involve breach of the
> copyright or the trade secret but would not be theft (assuming a trade secret amounts

to intangible property) because there is no intent to permanently deprive the owner ...
MCCOC has decided not to deal with this issue in the context of theft.

The uncertainty over the application of theft to copyright may be avoided by resorting to the offences contained in s 132(1)-(9) of the *Copyright Act* 1968 (Cth). These offences, which carry a lesser penalty than theft, prohibit a wide range of dealing in articles (including manufacture, sale, hire, exhibit, commercial importing, distribution and so on) where the "person knows, or ought reasonably to know that the article is an infringing copy of the work". It is also an offence to possess a device that is used for making infringing copies of the work: s 132(3). These offences are directed to those who profit from pirating, rather than consumers who purchase infringing copies. While the possession of an infringing copy is not a criminal offence, to overcome difficulties of proof, criminal liability has been extended to include possession for the purpose of sale, hire or distribution, and so on: s 132(2A). Transmitting a computer program so as to result in the creation of an infringing copy shall be deemed to be a distribution by the person of that infringing copy: s 132(5A).

Although copyright offences carrying significant penalties (including a maximum of five years imprisonment), these offences are summary in nature. The fault element of these offences is also downgraded to an objective standard based on what the accused "ought reasonably to have known". The difficulties of penetrating illicit markets and obtaining evidence against those individuals who profit from the illegal trade have justified these draconian measures. These derogations from general principles of criminal responsibility follow the pattern of criminalisation for illicit drugs: see further, Ch 15.

DEEMED INTENTION: PAWNING, PLEDGING AND BORROWING ANOTHER'S PROPERTY

Under the *Theft Act* model a person who, having possession or control of property whether innocently or not, parts with it under a condition as to its return which he or she may not be able to perform, is deemed to have disposed of that property regardless of the rights of the other person: *Crimes Act* 1958 (Vic), s 76(13). This provision was included to resolve the uncertainty over whether the accused who dishonestly pledged or pawned property belonging to another would possess the intent to permanently deprive at the relevant time. An example would be the person who took jewellery from the victim (whether innocently or not) and pawned it in exchange for cash with an intention to redeem and return the jewellery to the owner. In this case, there is no intention to permanently deprive the owner of the property, strictly speaking. However, the subsection provides that the parting with the property under a condition that may not be performed (that is, the future redemption of the pawned property) is deemed to be a disposal regardless of the rights of the other. By virtue of this provision, an intention to part with the property may be equated with an intention to permanently deprive.

The requirement of intention to permanently deprive has also presented difficulties in cases involving the appropriation of fungible property (namely goods which are interchangeable such as money, petrol or milk). The person appropriating this type of property may intend to replace the goods taken with equivalent, though non-identical, property. Although this conduct is popularly regarded as "borrowing", in legal terms it amounts to an appropriation (taking or conversion) with an intention to permanently deprive the owner of those *particular* goods. This feature of appropriation of fungibles is apparent in *R v Cockburn* [1968] 1 All ER 466 where the accused took £50 from his employer's till with an intention to replace it with equivalent notes or a cheque. The English Court of Appeal, upholding the conviction for larceny, held that the accused had an intention permanently to deprive the owner of those notes taken, notwithstanding his intention to replace it with equivalent sums. The Court held that the accused's intention to repay the money, while constituting good mitigation of sentence, did not preclude a conviction of larceny.

The potential unfairness of this decision, which effectively deletes the requirement of intention to permanently deprive in relation to persons who appropriate fungibles, has been partially addressed in s 97(4) of the *Crimes Act* 1900 (ACT):

> Notwithstanding anything in this section, a person who appropriates a sum of money belonging to another person shall not be taken to have intended to deprive the other person of the money permanently by reason only of the fact that he or she did not, at the time of the appropriation, intend to return the money in specie.

No equivalent provision has been enacted in the United Kingdom or Victoria. The main criticism of this subsection is that the exception is limited to money, and does not apply to other types of fungibles such as milk or petrol. The MCCOC in *Chapter 3: Theft, Fraud, Bribery and Related Offences*, Final Report (1995) considered whether this provision should be included in the *Model Criminal Code* and whether it should be expanded to fungibles generally. The MCCOC recommended (p 75) that the provision was unnecessary since the proverbial "borrower" of fungible property could not be regarded as dishonest.

A CONDITIONAL INTENTION TO DEPRIVE

The term "conditional intent" is used to describe the state of mind of a person who intends to deprive the victim of property *only* in certain circumstances. The problems presented for the law of theft in such cases were revealed in *R v Easom* [1971] 2 QB 315. In this case, the accused rifled through a woman's handbag in a darkened cinema. The woman was in fact an undercover police constable. The bag was placed at her feet and attached to her wrist by a piece of string. The accused examined the contents of the bag, and finding nothing of value to take, replaced it. The accused was arrested, charged and eventually convicted of theft of the handbag and its contents. In this case the English Court of Appeal held that this could not constitute theft since the appropriation was not accompanied by an intention to permanently deprive. Edmund-Davies LJ, delivering the judgment of the Court, held (at 319) as follows:

> In every case of theft the appropriation must be accompanied by the intention of permanently depriving the owner of his [or her] property. What may be loosely described as a "conditional" appropriation will not do. If the appropriator has it in mind merely to deprive the owner of such of his [or her] property as, on examination, proves worth taking and then, finding that the booty is valueless to the appropriator, leaves it ready to hand to be repossessed by the owner, the appropriator has not stolen.

If the accused was guilty of a crime, the appropriate charge was attempted theft of unspecified items. Yet attempting to steal property that does not in fact exist raises the problem of impossibility. The common law relating to impossible attempts and statutory modifications have been considered in Chapter 7, pp 355ff. In jurisdictions where physical or factual impossibility is no longer a bar to a conviction, the accused in *Easom* could be convicted of attempted theft.

In this case, the police had set a trap for the accused. Entrapment is not a defence in England or Australia. Consequently, police methods of investigation have no bearing on the question of guilt or innocence of the accused. While not a substantive defence, illegal or improper conduct by the police may provide a basis for excluding evidence and/or granting a stay of proceedings. As we shall explore in relation to drug investigation in Chapter 15, some forms of undercover policing and proactive investigation pose a serious threat to the rule of law and the right to a fair trial. A distinction is emerging, fostered by international human rights jurisprudence, between on the one hand, actively inciting an offence, which infringes the right to a fair trial, and on the other hand, passively creating an opportunity to commit that offence, which does not. The strict approach to intention to permanently deprive adopted by the court in *Easom* may have been in part a reaction to the covert methods of policing. As entrapment was not raised at trial, there is uncertainty as to whether the accused was a suspected thief specifically targeted by the police or an ordinary citizen being subject to "random virtue testing" by the police.

> *Easom* did not escape academic criticism. Glanville Williams regarded the decision as a "rogues' charter", providing a defence to thieves who intend to return goods to the owner if they are insufficiently valuable. He suggested that the rule would apply even in cases where the person drove off with property and subsequently finding that they were valueless, dumped them at the police station: "Three Rogues' Charters" [1980] Crim LR 263 at 264. See also L Koffman, "Conditional Intention to Steal" [1980] Crim LR 463; G Williams, "Temporary Appropriation Should be Theft" [1981] Crim LR 129.

Perhaps mindful of the criticisms of *Easom* as a "Rogues' Charter", a more restrictive approach to the scope of intention to permanently deprive was adopted by the Supreme Court of Victoria in *Sharp v McCormick* [1986] VR 869. The accused took a starter coil from his employer which he intended to fit to his car. He claimed that if the coil did not fit he intended to return it. The magistrate held, applying *Easom*, that there was no case to answer because the accused only had a "conditional intention". The prosecution sought an order to reinstate the charge. Murray J held (at 871) that in the present case it was unnecessary to decide whether *Easom* was correctly decided since it was "plainly distinguishable in a critical respect". He pointed out that in *Easom* the accused never intended to steal the handbag and it was this fact that made it difficult for the Court of Appeal to sustain a conviction for theft of the handbag. In this case, by contrast, the accused took the starter coil and was caught in the process of taking it home to see if it fitted his car when he was apprehended. The intent is determined by looking at the state of mind of the accused at the time of the appropriation of the property. Murray J held that the accused had the necessary intent for theft if, at the time of appropriation, he intended to keep the coil unless he *later* decided to return it. If the mental state is posed the other way as an intention to return the coil unless he later decided to keep it, this could fall within the expanded definition contained in s 73(12) — "[h]is reservation of the probability or possibility of keeping it would amount to an intention to treat the coil as his own to dispose of regardless of the owner's rights": p 872. On these facts, at the moment of the appropriation, the accused did not intend to return the property unless it was not suitable. His subsequent intent to return the property was simply a matter of choice on his part, and there was clearly evidence on these facts that he intended to dispose of the property regardless of the rights of the owner.

3.6 RELATED OFFENCES: ROBBERY, BURGLARY AND RECEIVING

There are a wide range of related offences, many of which carry harsher penalties than the basic offence of theft or larceny. As discussed above, those jurisdictions that base their laws on the common law of larceny have enacted special offences with increased penalties depending on factors such as the type of property stolen or the relationship of the accused to the victim: at p 670. The *Theft Act* model largely avoids this complexity, though these factors may be taken into account in sentencing. In this section, we examine the related offences of robbery, burglary and receiving.

ROBBERY

At common law, robbery is defined as taking property by force or threat of force.[37] As a form of aggravated larceny, the offence is punishable more severely than simple larceny. The offence of robbery under the *Theft Act* model does not significantly alter the structure of the common law offence. Section 75(1) of the *Crimes Act* 1958 (Vic) provides:

> **(1)** A person is guilty of robbery if he [or she] steals, and immediately before or at the time of doing so, and in order to do so, he [or she] uses force on any person or puts or seeks to put any person in fear that he [or she] or another person will be then and there subjected to force.
>
> **(2)** A person guilty of robbery, or of an assault with intent to rob, is guilty of an indictable offence and liable to level 4 imprisonment (15 years maximum).

Although not clear from its structure, the section creates two offences of robbery and assault with intent to rob. This is made explicit in ss 100 and 101 of the *Crimes Act* 1900 (ACT). There are further aggravated offences of armed robbery, which apply where the person committing the robbery also has possession of a firearm, imitation firearm, offensive weapon, explosive or imitation explosive: *Crimes Act* 1900 (ACT), s 101; *Crimes Act* 1958 (Vic), s 75A.

---

37 *Crimes Act* 1900 (NSW), s 94(1); *Criminal Code* (NT), s 211(1); *Criminal Code* (Qld), s 409; *Consolidation Act* 1935 (SA), s 155; *Criminal Code* (Tas), s 240; *Criminal Code* (WA), s 391. The elements of the offence at common law are explored in CR Williams, *Property Offences* (3rd ed, Sydney: LBC, 1999), pp 192-202 and Code jurisdictions: pp 204-207. There are other offences related to robbery. Offences have been enacted prohibiting stealing from the person and assault with intent to rob, which deal with "pick-pocketing" and with inchoate forms of the offence. There are also aggravated forms of robbery involving violence and weapons: pp 202-207.

For the purpose of these offences, and the related offences of armed robbery, stealing is defined by reference to the offence of theft, the elements of which have been discussed above. The requirements of taking and carrying away in larceny have been replaced by appropriation — this avoids the difficulties faced when the accused interfered with property but did not actually physically remove it.

The key element of the offence of robbery is the application of force or threatened or apprehended application. The force must be used to steal, but it is not necessary that it is directed at the victim of the theft. A threat to hurt another person unless property was handed over would suffice. The ingredients of assault, which are clearly relevant to the definition of robbery and assault with intent to rob, were explored in Chapter 11.

BURGLARY AND RELATED OFFENCES

The *Theft Act* model avoided the complex body of law that had developed around the common law felony of burglary that was defined in terms of "break and enter". At common law, the offence did not apply to "break-ins" committed during the daytime, which were punishable by the lesser misdemeanour of house-breaking. These offences are now defined by statute in all jurisdictions.[38] The offences of burglary enacted in the Australian Capital Territory and Victoria mirror the reforms to burglary enacted by the *Theft Act* 1968 (UK). Section 76 of the *Crimes Act* 1958 (Vic) defines the offence of burglary as follows:

(1) A person is guilty of burglary if he [or she] enters any building or part of a building as a trespasser with intent —

(a) to steal anything in the building or part in question; or

(b) to commit an offence —

(i) involving an assault to a person in the building or part in question; or

(ii) involving any damage to the building or to property in the building or part in question —

which is punishable with imprisonment for a term of five years or more.

(2) References in sub-section (1) to a building shall apply also to an inhabited vehicle or vessel, and shall apply to any such vehicle or vessel at times when the person having a habitation in it is not there as well as at times when he is.

(3) A person guilty of burglary is guilty of an indictable offence and liable to level 5 imprisonment (10 years maximum).

The offence of burglary recommended by the MCCOC in *Chapter 3: Theft, Fraud, Bribery and Related Offences*, Final Report (1995) is similarly based on trespass rather than breaking and entering.

---

38 See *Crimes Act* 1900 (ACT), ss 102; *Crimes Act* 1900 (NSW), s 109(1); *Criminal Code* (NT), s 213; *Criminal Code* (Qld), s 419; *Criminal Law Consolidation Act* 1935 (SA), s 168; *Criminal Code* (Tas), ss 244; *Crimes Act* 1958 (Vic), s 76; *Criminal Code* (WA), s 401. The common law is explained in *Property Offences* (3rd ed, Sydney: LBC, 1999), pp 217-221.

Although burglary is popularly understood as a specie of aggravated theft, the offence does not require proof of theft or even an attempt. At common law, the offence of breaking and entering merely required proof of an intent to commit any felony. The offence of burglary in the Australian Capital Territory and Victoria, following the *Theft Act* 1968 (UK), is limited to trespass with an intent to commit an unlawful assault or criminal damage. The MCCOC proposed that the offence of burglary should be limited to trespassers who enter or remain in any building with the intent to commit: (1) theft; or (2) an offence punishable by five years imprisonment and that involves harm to person or damage to property: *Model Criminal Code*, s 16.3. The basic offence is punishable by 12 years imprisonment. Following the structure of existing burglary offences, the MCCOC also recommended the inclusion of an offence of aggravated burglary, which would apply where burglary is committed in the company of others or with an offensive weapon, punishable by 15 years imprisonment.

The key element of the modern offence of burglary is a trespass to property, a concept which is determined by the civil law. Whether or not a person's presence constitutes a trespass will be determined by examining the scope of the licence granted by the owner to enter and remain on the premises. Although this element is straightforward in most cases, the High Court decision of *Barker v The Queen* (1983) 153 CLR 338 reveals the potential complexities surrounding trespass in the context of burglary offences. The accused had been convicted of burglary contrary to s 76 of the *Crimes Act* 1958 (Vic). The accused had been given the key of a neighbour's house for the purpose of caring for the property while they were away on holiday. The accused used the key to enter the house and steal property while the owners were away. The accused was charged with and convicted of burglary. The question on appeal turned on the scope of the accused's licence or authority to enter the premises. The majority held that the accused entered the property beyond the purpose of the licence granted to him by the owners, and therefore committed a trespass and therefore burglary. Brennan and Deane JJ distinguished the case where the owners had placed no restrictions on entry, either expressly or by necessary implication. In such cases, it would not be appropriate to limit the licence or authority on the grounds that the owner would have objected to entry if they had known that it was for an illegal purpose. They concluded (at 364-365):

> The answer to the question [of who is a trespasser] is not complicated by artificial notions that permission must be qualified by reference to authorised purpose or by artificial doctrines of relation back … If the permission was not subject to any express or implied limitation which excluded the entry from its scope, the entry was not as a trespasser. If permission was subject to an actual express or implied limitation which excluded the actual entry, the entry was as a trespasser.

This refinement avoids the possibility that shoplifters who enter shop premises for the purpose of stealing would be rendered trespassers, and therefore guilty of burglary rather than merely theft. By contrast to the majority, Murphy J expressed concern that this approach to trespass was too complicated and could convert pilfering cleaners, employees and shoplifters from thieves into burglars depending on the terms (express or implied) of the licence to enter the premises. This dissenting view has found favour with the Model Criminal Code Officers Committee (MCCOC) in *Chapter 3: Theft, Fraud, Bribery and Related Offences*, Final Report (1995). In a case like *Barker*, the MCCOC reasoned that the rights to restrict entry had not been violated since the owner had agreed to the accused being on the premises, though not for the purpose of theft. Although not guilty of burglary, the accused may be liable for other offences such as theft or criminal damage or assault. To avoid the complexities of *Barker*, the MCCOC proposed the inclusion of the following provision in s 16.3(2) of the *Model Criminal Code*:

> A person is not a trespasser merely because the person is permitted to enter or remain in the building for a purpose that is not the person's intended purpose, or as a result of fraud, misrepresentation or another's mistake.

The MCCOC also recommended that the offence of burglary should be extended to "break outs" — that is, where the accused obtains entry to premises with consent, but remains on premises after the initial consent has been revoked. An offence modelled along these lines has been enacted in South Australia, though it is limited to cases where the initial entry was with an intent to commit an offence: *Criminal Law Consolidation Act* 1935 (SA), s 168. To address the perceived gap in the law, the MCCOC recommended that the offence of burglary should be extended to a person who "enters or remains in any building as a trespasser with intent": *Model Criminal Code*, s 16.4.

Most jurisdictions contain preparatory offences related to burglary that criminalise the possession of implements or equipment used for housebreaking. These offences were needed because of the narrow test of proximity developed in the law of criminal attempts. As we have discussed in Chapter 9 at p 433, under the early common law, individuals would only be liable for attempts where they had committed an act immediately and not remotely connected to the substantive offence.

The legislature has enacted a wide range of offences punishing the possession of implements and other equipment capable of use in the commission of burglary or related offences.[39] These offences criminalise preparatory acts not constituting the offence of criminal attempt. The offence has been held to apply to cases where the accused has not yet formed an intention in relation to a *specific* offence; it suffices that the accused had a general intention to use the implements for *some* burglary, theft or cheat: *R v Ellames* [1974] 1 WLR 1391 at 1397.

In New South Wales, the offence includes a qualification that the possession of implements must be "without lawful excuse". The legislation generally casts the burden in relation to proving the excuse onto the accused: *Crimes Act* 1900 (NSW), s 417. In the context of a similar offence, the English Court of Appeal has held that where the accused is found in possession of implements capable of use in housebreaking, the burden is cast on the defence to prove on the balance of probabilities that there was a lawful excuse for the possession of the implements: *R v Patterson* [1962] 2 QB 429. Bearing in mind the breadth of the physical element (which applies to the possession of articles that have other legitimate uses), the state of mind of the accused is crucial in terms of culpability. In this context, shifting the legal burden to the accused in relation to such a fundamental element of the offence (albeit on a lower civil standard of proof) is unfair and oppressive. The *Theft Act* model did not

---

39   *Crimes Act* 1900 (ACT), s 116; *Crimes Act* 1900 (NSW), s 114(1)(b); *Criminal Code* (NT), s 57(1)(e); *Criminal Code* (Qld), s 425; *Criminal Code* (Tas), s 248; *Criminal Code* (WA), s 407. The equivalent offence in the *Criminal Law Consolidation Act* 1935 (SA) was remodelled in 1994; s 171(2) provides: "A person who is in possession, at night, of housebreaking equipment, without lawful excuse, is guilty of an offence". See further CR Williams, *Property Offences* (3rd ed, Sydney: LBC, 1999), pp 221-226 and pp 224-243.

modify the burden of proof in this way, although it contained a subsection stating that being found in possession of an instrument "adapted" for housebreaking constitutes evidence of intent to use that article for burglary, theft or cheat: *Crimes Act* 1900 (ACT), s 116(3); *Crimes Act* 1958 (Vic), s 91(3).

The MCCOC in *Chapter 3: Theft, Fraud, Bribery and Related Offences*, Final Report (1995) recommended (p 103) that no special evidential provision should be retained for this offence. The MCCOC pointed out that such provisions constituted an averment of a fault element, which is expressly prohibited under s 13.6 of the *Model Criminal Code*. Inferences from the possession of adapted implements may be drawn in the ordinary way without the need to resort to any special provisions. The MCCOC also recommended that the offence should be extended to the possession of equipment for use in robbery and taking a motor vehicle without authority: p 103.

"Home Invasion" Defences: A Potent Symbol or Redundant Law?

Responding to uncertainty within the community about the legality of householders using force to defend their property from "home invasion" by intruders, the New South Wales legislature enacted the *Home Invasion (Occupants Protection) Act* 1998 (NSW). This Act clarifies that the common law of self defence in *Zecevic v DPP* (1987) 162 CLR 645 applies to protection of a dwelling house: ss 6-8. As the Act reflected the common law as it had been developed by the courts in New South Wales, the aim of the Act was primarily educative and symbolic: *Conlon* (1993) 69 A Crim R 92. See further Ch 6, pp 297.

RECEIVING AND HANDLING STOLEN PROPERTY

Offences exist in every jurisdiction prohibiting individuals from dealing in stolen property. Statutory offences against receiving stolen goods were enacted in the 19th century. These laws overcame the difficulties of applying accessorial liability to this type of activity, and aimed to remove the financial incentives for theft by punishing individuals who profited from, and thus sustained, the illicit market in stolen goods.[40]

The *Theft Act* model reconceived the offence as one of handling rather than receiving. The term "handling" was intended to denote the wider scope of the offence. Section 88 of the *Crimes Act* 1958 (Vic) defines the offence of handling stolen goods as follows:

(1) A person handles stolen goods if (otherwise than in the course of the stealing) knowing or believing them to be stolen goods he [or she] dishonestly receives the goods or brings them into Victoria, or dishonestly undertakes or assists in bringing them into Victoria or in their retention, removal, disposal or realization by or for the benefit of another person, or if he [or she] arranges to do so.

(2) A person guilty of handling stolen goods is guilty of an indictable offence and liable to level 4 imprisonment (15 years maximum).

---

40 For a review of the historical development of the receiving offences see J Hall, *Theft, Law and Society* (2nd ed, Bloomington, IN: Bobbs-Merrill, 1952), pp 164-189.

There are four elements of the offence (1) dishonesty; (2) handling; (3) stolen property and (4) knowledge or belief that the property is stolen.

Handling grafts a variety of modes of complicity onto the basic offence. As CR Williams has pointed out, there at least 23 ways in which this offence may be committed: *Property Offences* (3rd ed, Sydney: LBC, 1999), p 293. Notwithstanding the differentiated structure of the offence, the physical element of handling may be performed in one of two ways — receiving stolen goods or dealing in stolen goods independently of the initial receiving. In the Australian Capital Territory, the offence of handling is slightly broader than the Victorian offence, applying to a person who "has stolen property in his or her possession": *Crimes Act* 1900 (ACT), s 113. The MCCOC recommended in *Chapter 3: Theft, Fraud, Bribery and Related Offences*, Final Report (1995) that the offence definition should not be further expanded or complicated by the inclusion of these ancillary forms of receiving. In its view, these forms of receiving are better dealt with by applying the ordinary principles of complicity: p 109. The MCCOC proposed the following streamlined definition of the offence:

> A person who dishonestly receives stolen property knowing or believing the property to be stolen, is guilty of the offence of receiving.

The MCCOC recommended that the offence should be described as receiving rather than handling, since the former is the more common terminology in Australia: p 109.

The breadth of receiving and handling offences also raises concern about the potential overlap with theft. It should be noted that many instances of receiving and handling stolen property could amount to an appropriation under the extended definition discussed above at p 690. Indeed, the retention of separate offences of receiving or handling could be viewed as redundant. Although acknowledging the overlap, the MCCOC concluded that a separate offence of receiving should be retained since this conduct was commonly understood within the community as denoting a form of criminality distinct from theft: p 107.

The offence of handling in s 88 of the *Crimes Act* 1958 (Vic), modelled on the *Theft Act* 1968 (UK), aimed to minimise this potential overlap by limiting the offence to cases of handling "otherwise than in the course of stealing": see also *Crimes Act* 1900 (ACT), s 113(2). Thus, proof that the accused had stolen the goods would constitute a defence to handling: CR Williams, *Property Offences* (3rd ed, Sydney: LBC, 1999), p 301. In cases where the accused is found in possession of stolen goods, but it is unclear whether theft or handling has been committed, the prosecution may charge both offences.[41]

---

41 The High Court in *Gilson v The Queen* (1991) 172 CLR 353 held that in cases where the jury is satisfied beyond reasonable doubt that the accused committed either theft or handling, but is unsure which one, then the jury should return the less serious offence. The MCCOC recommended that the Code should make provision for alternate verdicts in prosecutions of theft and handling, and that in cases of uncertainty as in *Gilson* where both offences have been charged, the trier of fact should convict of the offence which is more probable, rather than the offence which is less serious: *Chapter 3 — Theft, Fraud, Bribery and Related Offences*, Final Report (1995), pp 111-113.

PERSPECTIVES

The Regulation of Illicit Markets in Stolen Goods

There is empirical evidence that the bulk of household theft is carried out in order to sell the goods either to consumers directly or through an intermediary "fence" who trades professionally in stolen goods: R Jochelson, "Household Break-ins and the Market for Stolen Goods" in *Crime and Justice Bulletin*, No 24 (Sydney: NSW Bureau of Crime Statistics and Research, 1995). Russell Hogg and David Brown in *Rethinking Law and Order* (Annandale: Pluto Press, 1998) explore (pp 82-85) the complex relationship between illegal and legal markets, pointing out that patterns of property crime are highly responsive to market demand. The authors note that while national victim survey data suggest that burglary is perceived to be a major crime threat, the market in stolen goods is sustained by a widespread community tolerance towards goods that have euphemistically "fallen off the back of a lorry". The authors speculate that the doubling in the rates of reported burglary and motor vehicle theft in Australia over the last 20 years is due not only to higher levels of ownership of consumer items, but also to the increasingly depersonalised nature of property and economic activity in modern capitalist societies: p 83. Insurance explains the increased levels of reporting of burglary and motor vehicle theft, as well as the moral indifference toward the market in the consumer goods of dubious provenance.

Hogg and Brown also observe that the market in stolen goods is often connected with organised crime leading the police to participate in elaborate "sting" operations that target weak links such as "fences". One such example is the Queensland case of *D'Arrigo* (1991) 58 A Crim R 71. In this case the police conducted an undercover operation against a group of individuals suspected of involvement in a scheme where motor vehicles would be stolen and then disguised or dismantled for the purpose of resale. An informer, guided by the police and granted complete immunity, participated in the theft of 68 motor vehicles from innocent citizens. On the basis of the informer's evidence, the group was charged with a wide range of property offences. The Queensland Court of Criminal Appeal held that the informer's evidence should have been excluded on the basis of public policy. In addition to illegality, the strategies in *D'Arrigo* raise questions about the limits of entrapment and the prejudice to the principle of fairness in the criminal process. The evidential and procedural remedies for entrapment are further discussed in relation to covert drug investigation in Chapter 15, at pp 870ff.

The police use of a decoy in undercover operations targeting receiving may mean that the accused is found in possession of goods that are no longer technically stolen. Under common law, the doctrine of impossibility would seem to preclude a conviction: *Haughton v Smith* [1975] AC 476. In jurisdictions where this doctrine is no longer a bar to conviction, individuals may be convicted of an attempt for receiving or handling goods that they mistakenly believed are stolen. The practical implications for law enforcement and the recent reforms to the law governing impossible attempts are further considered in Chapter 7, pp 355-360.

4. FRAUD AND DECEPTION OFFENCES

As the above section reveals, the legislature has plugged many of the gaps that have emerged in the law of larceny and theft. We have explored how specific loopholes arising in cases of dishonest use of computers, cheques, motor vehicles and making off without payment have been remedied by specific provisions or the creation of new offences. The process of gap-filling has not been entirely legislative. The courts have also fashioned a common law offence of conspiracy to defraud to deal with a wide range of fraudulent conduct not caught by larceny or theft. The concerns about the breadth of conspiracy to defraud have been explored in Chapter 9: pp 460-462. In this section we examine the principal fraud offences relating to obtaining by deception.

Other fraud offences relating to blackmail, forgery, bribery, extortion and secret commissions have also been enacted. The MCCOC grouped these offences together with theft and fraud in *Chapter 3: Theft, Fraud, Bribery and Related Offences*, Final Report (1995), pp 195-314. In many respects, these disparate offences bear few conceptual or analytical similarities to theft and fraud beyond the common concern to punish conduct displaying some form of "moral obloquy". As Peter Alldridge provocatively argued in *Relocating Criminal Law* (Aldershot: Ashgate, 2000), Chapter 6, it is more useful to conceive offences of forgery, bribery and corruption as a "criminal law of markets" rather than as offences of dishonesty. The essence of the harm common to all these activities is that they "prevent the market functioning in accordance with its professed objectives": p 167. As we shall explore below, the MCCOC has generally resisted moves to reshape property offences into "offences of dishonesty" — a nebulous and potentially over-reaching category.

In Alldridge's analysis, the criminal law of market may be divided into the following categories:

- crimes to guarantee the unit of exchange;

- crimes to prevent manipulation and exploitation of markets;

- crimes to establish borders to markets; and

- crimes to prevent commodification of specific areas of human activity.

This framework provides conceptual coherence and a clear set of goals and policies (beyond simply punishing blameworthy conduct) for these disparate offences. Within these categories fall many important though "anomalous" offences such as money laundering, insider dealing and sexual trafficking offences. For these conceptual reasons, as well as the practical limitations of space, the offences of blackmail, forgery, bribery, extortion and secret commissions lie beyond the scope of this chapter.

The principal fraud offence is obtaining property by deception. In some jurisdictions, this conduct is subsumed within a general "omnibus" fraud offence that does not require proof of deception. For example, s 29D of the *Crimes Act* 1914 (Cth) provides:

> A person who defrauds the Commonwealth or a public authority under the Commonwealth is guilty of an indictable offence.
>
> **Penalty:** 1,000 penalty units or imprisonment for 10 years, or both.

See also s 409 of the *Criminal Code* (WA), which punishes a wide range of conduct and is not limited to dishonest dealings in property.[42] Combined with new crimes against "organised fraud",[43] the scope of the criminal fraud has been significantly expanded, rendering many of the property offences examined above superfluous. Indeed, these new offences are even broader than the offence of conspiracy to defraud. Conspiracy to defraud, while considered by many commentators to be draconian, at least requires proof that the accused entered into an *agreement* with others to defraud. No such restriction applies to these general offences against fraud.

The MCCOC in *Chapter 3: Theft, Fraud, Bribery and Related Offences*, Final Report (1995) has recommended against the adoption of general offences of dishonesty on the ground that, while flexible and adaptable, they would offend the principle that criminal offences should be certain and knowable in advance. The MCCOC concluded (p 169):

> The *Theft Act* offences are already expressed in a more general or abstract way than the preceding law. To take the further step of dispensing with the need to prove an appropriation without consent or that there was a deception is to go too far. Problems in specific areas like tax and social security can and have been dealt with under specific legislative provisions.

For similar reasons the MCCOC recommended (p 183) that the *Model Criminal Code* should not include an organised fraud offence.

4.1 OBTAINING BY DECEPTION

The offence of obtaining property by deception overlaps with theft. As these two offences share common elements, the statutory definitions and authorities discussed above are relevant. In the United Kingdom and Victoria, the offences of obtaining property by deception are distinct from theft. The common law relating to "larceny by trick" and the offences of obtaining property by false pretences have been examined above, at p 671. The Code jurisdictions similarly maintain a distinction between the basic offence of stealing/larceny and fraud/deception.[44] Uniquely, the Australian Capital Territory has collapsed theft and fraud into a single offence that defines appropriation as including adverse interference/usurpation and obtaining property by deception: *Crimes Act* 1900 (ACT), s 96(1)(a) and (b), discussed above, p 694.

The MCCOC considered that the "fundamental question" in this area was whether the two offences should be amalgamated following the Australian Capital Territory model. Although amalgamation had the support of legal academics and an earlier Commonwealth

---

42 See generally G Syrota, "Criminal Fraud in Western Australia: A Vague, Sweeping and Arbitrary Offence" (1994) 24 *Western Australian Law Review* 261.

43 *Proceeds of Crime Act* 1987 (Cth), s 83; *Proceeds of Crime Act* 1991 (ACT), s 76.

44 The fraud offences in the Code jurisdictions cover a wide range of conduct including *inter alia* obtaining by deception, procuring financial advantage/detriment, and making off without payment: *Criminal Code* (Qld), 408C; *Criminal Code* (WA), s 409. See discussion in RG Kenny, *An Introduction to Criminal Law in Queensland and Western Australia* (5th ed, Sydney: Butt, 2000), pp 280-281.

review,[45] the MCCOC resolved the question in favour of retention of a separate fraud offence. In its view, the essence of theft was appropriating property *without consent*, which could be distinguished from obtaining property *with consent* by deceptive conduct. The distinction mirrored the community's understanding of different types of dishonesty. Although the distinction has been blurred by the House of Lords in *R v Gomez* [1993] AC 442 and abolished by the legislature in the Australian Capital Territory, fraud should not be labelled as theft. The MCCOC concluded (p 131) that the distinction was necessary as a matter of "fair labelling":

> The law should employ terms which communicate the nature of the proscribed conduct
> unless there are strong reasons to the contrary. Artificially collapsing categories is as bad
> as artificial distinctions. It undermines public acceptance of the law and confuses juries by
> lumping disparate forms of behaviour together.

An amalgamated offence covering theft and obtaining property by deception also poses dangers of unfairness. This is because the prosecution is not obliged to disclose before trial which form of "appropriation" is being alleged against the accused. This would clearly hamper the preparation of the defence, and could only be remedied by the adoption of procedural rules requiring the prosecution to provide further particulars where the appropriation being relied upon was a deception. The MCCOC concluded (p 133) that the charging dilemmas experienced by the prosecution caused by the overlap between theft and obtaining property by deception were better addressed by provisions allowing for alternate verdicts. The existing rules governing alternate verdicts, and the MCCOC's recommendations for reform, have been discussed above at p 694.

In this section, we focus on the *Theft Act* model offence of obtaining by deception, which has the following elements:

- **dishonestly**
- **obtaining by deception**
- **property**
- **belonging to another**
- **intent to permanently deprive.**

The offence of obtaining property by deception shares its elements and definitions with the basic offence of theft. Many of the cases discussed above examining the meaning of dishonesty and other elements have also involved charges of obtaining property by deception. We have examined the definition of dishonesty developed in Victoria in a succession of cases involving obtaining property by deception, discussed above at pp 682ff. For a comprehensive discussion of the elements of obtaining property by deception, see CR Williams, *Property Offences* (3rd ed, Sydney: LBC, 1999), pp 171-191. In the following section, we will focus on the elements that are *specific* to this offence — obtaining by deception.

---

45 Gibbs Committee, *Review of Commonwealth Criminal Law*, Interim Report (Canberra: AGPS, November 1991), pp 128-131 and CR Williams and M Weinberg, *Property Offences* (2nd ed, Sydney: Law Book Company Ltd, 1986), p 413. Williams has since recanted on this earlier view on the ground that the "two crimes are principally aimed at different activity": *Property Offences* (3rd ed, Sydney: LBC, 1999), p 339.

THE MEANING OF "OBTAINING BY DECEPTION"

The Victorian offence of obtaining property by deception mirrors the offence contained in *Theft Act* 1968 (UK):

81. Obtaining property by deception

    (1) A person who by any deception dishonestly obtains property belonging to another, with the intention of permanently depriving the other of it, is guilty of an indictable offence and liable to level 5 imprisonment (10 years maximum).

    (2) For purposes of this section a person is to be treated as obtaining property if he obtains ownership, possession or control of it, and "obtain" includes obtaining for another or enabling another to obtain or to retain.

    (3) Sub-sections (12) and (13) of section 73 shall apply for purposes of this section, with the necessary adaptation of the reference to appropriating, as it applies for purposes of section 72.

A similar offence has been enacted in s 227 of the *Criminal Code* (NT).

Obtaining property by deception replaced the earlier concept of obtaining by false pretences. The reformulation was intended to refocus the inquiry on the *effect* on the mind of the victim rather than simply on the accused's conduct: Criminal Law Revision Committee, *Theft and Related Offences* (London: HMSO Cmnd 2977, 1966), para 87. The element of obtaining is wider than the predecessor offence of false pretences which only applied to obtaining *ownership* by deception. Like theft, the offence of obtaining property by deception is extended to obtaining ownership, possession or control of property. Furthermore, it extends to obtaining for the benefit of another or enabling another to obtain, or to retain the property.

The *Theft Act* model, which formed the template for the above offences, included an extended definition of deception. This definition is contained in s 81(4) of the *Crimes Act* 1958 (Vic):

    For the purposes of this section, "deception" —

    (a) means any deception (whether deliberate or reckless) by words or conduct as to fact or as to law, including a deception as to the present intentions of the person using the deception or any other person; and

    (b) includes an act or thing done or omitted to be done with the intention of causing —

        (i) a computer system; or

        (ii) a machine that is designed to operate by means of payment or identification —

    to make a response that the person doing or omitting to do the act or thing is not authorised to cause the computer system or machine to make.

See also s 93 of the *Crimes Act* 1900 (ACT). Uncertainties over deception aimed at computers led to this extended definition in Victoria and the adoption of a special offence of dishonest use of computers contained in s 135L of the *Crimes Act* 1900 (ACT). The legal issues surrounding ATM misuse have been considered above, at pp 695-697.

Recklessness for the purpose of this section has been defined in subjective terms. It has been defined as including knowledge or awareness of a "substantial risk" that the words or conduct were untrue: *R v Smith* (1982) A Crim R 437; *Mattingley v Tuckwood* (1988) 88 ACTR 1. The formulation of foresight of "substantial risk" is suggestive of a high degree of foresight based on probability rather than possibility. This would be inconsistent with the approach taken to the meaning of recklessness in other areas, where (apart from murder) recklessness is satisfied by foresight of possibility.[46] The variable meaning of recklessness in the criminal law has been explored in Chapter 3, at pp 181-184. The deception may relate to matters of law, as well as fact.[47]

OBTAINING PROPERTY, SERVICES AND FINANCIAL ADVANTAGE

The above offence is limited to obtaining "property" by deception, which bears the same meaning as property for the purpose of theft. We have also considered above, at p 701, the difficulties of applying obtaining property by deception to individuals who have dishonestly used false representations to obtain cheques, negotiable instruments and electronic funds transfers. Some jurisdictions have enacted separate fraud offences relating to obtaining services; a pecuniary or financial advantage; and evading a liability.[48]

Obtaining a pecuniary or financial advantage by deception is broader than the other obtaining offences since it does not require an intention to permanently deprive. As the MCCOC noted (p 149) the offence is broad enough to encompass virtually all cases of obtaining property by deception. As we shall explore below, some cases where the accused obtained property by deception have been charged as obtaining a financial advantage. In some situations, this offence offers certain tactical advantages to the prosecution. As the MCCOC noted (p 149), the breadth of the offence is often controlled by prosecution guidelines, as in Victoria, where the offence is limited to cases *not* involving property, that is, where the accused has obtained credit or other financial services by deception.

For the offence of obtaining a pecuniary or financial advantage, there is no requirement that the person deceived must suffer any loss arising from the deception. All that is required is that there is a causal relationship between the deception and the pecuniary advantage. This feature of the offence is important in cases of cheque fraud where the deception is often directed at the supplier of goods, but the financial advantage is obtained from the bank or credit provider: *R v Kovacs* [1974] 1 WLR 370.

A pecuniary or financial advantage to the accused must be proved, not assumed — this element plays a significant role in controlling the scope of an offence that may be applied to cases

---

46 CR Williams has argued that "substantial risk" should be interpreted as imposing a less stringent standard than that applied in "reckless murder", suggesting that "foresight of 'substantial risk' is lower on the scale of probabilities than probable or more likely than not": *Property Offences* (3rd ed, Sydney: LBC, 1999), pp 172-173.

47 The High Court has held that a statement of claim in a civil action which contained a false assertion would not constitute a making of a false representation for the purposes of obtaining by deception: *Jamieson and Brugmans v The Queen* (1993) 177 CLR 574.

48 *Crimes Act* 1900 (ACT), ss 104-106; *Crimes Act* 1958 (Vic), s 82. See also obtaining credit by false pretences: *Crimes Act* 1900 (NSW), s 178C;

where the financial advantage obtained by deception is only temporary. The importance of this element was firmly reiterated by the Supreme Court of the Australian Capital Territory in *Fisher v Bennett* (1987) 85 FLR 469. The accused required some money to enter into a business transaction. He asked a friend to make out a cheque in his favour for $10,000. The friend obtained an overdraft on his own account in order to make out the cheque. The agreement was that the accused would pay the amount borrowed, plus interest and bank charges. The accused did not repay for a while. He then paid some interest but delayed on the capital repayments. The friend demanded the money and the accused made out a cheque for $10,000 which was dishonoured by the bank because of insufficient funds. He was charged and convicted of obtaining a financial advantage by deception contrary to s 178C of the *Crimes Act* 1900 (NSW), in its application to the Australian Capital Territory — this offence has since has been enacted as s 104 of the *Crimes Act* 1900 (ACT). The section provided:

> A person who, by any deception, dishonestly obtains for himself [or herself] or any other
> person any money or valuable thing or any financial advantage is guilty of an offence
> punishable, on conviction, by imprisonment for a term not exceeding 5 years.

The question on appeal was whether the accused had obtained a financial advantage. Miles CJ approved dicta in *Mathews v Fountain* [1982] VR 1045, where Gray J of the Supreme Court of Victoria had held that there could be cases, admittedly rare, where despite the proffering of a valueless cheque, there was no financial advantage. Miles CJ held (at 472) that "financial advantage" bears the following meaning: "When one speaks of obtaining a financial advantage by deception there is imported in my view the notion of improving a financial situation by means of that deception".

The accused in this case had not improved his financial situation by means of the deception; he had obtained no forbearance to sue from the cheated creditor and there was no reducing or forgiving the debt. Interest continued to accrue on the amount borrowed. The accused was no better off than when he started. He had merely retained a continuing benefit, not obtained a new financial advantage. This decision clearly demonstratesd the difference between obtaining a financial advantage and unilateral evasion of a financial liability.

DECEPTION BY CONDUCT: IMPLIED REPRESENTATIONS

The Criminal Law Revision Committee favoured deception because, unlike false pretences, the concept seemed "more apt in relation to deception by conduct": *Theft and Related Offences* (London: HMSO Cmnd 2977, 1966), para 87. As noted above, the property, service or financial advantage must be obtained *as a result* of the deception — there must be a causal nexus between the accused's deception and the thing obtained. Therefore, there must be evidence that the deception affected the mind of the victim. In many cases, the deception is a false representation by the accused that induces another person to provide property or services. Difficulties have commonly arisen in cases involving representations by conduct and whether such implied representations actually operated on the minds of the victims inducing them to provide property, service or a financial advantage to the accused.

The boundaries of implied representation have been expanded by the decisions recognising that an implied representation may be "continuing" in nature. The limits of implied representations by conduct were explored by the House of Lords in *DPP v Ray* [1974] AC 370. The accused had dinner at a restaurant with some friends. At the time of ordering the food the accused intended to pay for it. After the meal, he decided not to pay and ran off. The accused was not charged with obtaining property or services by deception presumably because the prosecution accepted that, at the moment the meal was obtained, there was no deception being practised by the accused. The accused was charged with dishonestly obtaining a pecuniary advantage by deception contrary to s 16(1) of the *Theft Act* 1968 (UK). The Divisional Court held that there was no deception in this case and quashed the conviction. The prosecution appealed. The questions certified the appeal to the House of Lords were first, whether the accused had practised a deception, and secondly, if he had, was his evasion of the debt obtained by that deception.

The majority upheld the appeal and restored the conviction. In this case, the deception was that the accused had impliedly represented by his conduct in ordering the meal that he was an ordinary customer intending to pay for it. By continuing in that same role, he continued with his original representation. This constituted a deception on the waiter because the accused's intention had in fact changed. As Lord Morris noted (at 386) the representation could be regarded as a continuing one that "remained alive and operative and had already resulted in the accused being taken on trust and treated as ordinary, honest customers". According to Lord MacDermott (at 382) the representation covered "the whole transaction up to and including payment and must therefore be considered ... as continuing and still active at the time of the change of mind". Lords Reid and Hodson dissented on the basis that there was no deception practised in this case. The accused's continuing act of sitting in the restaurant after he had changed his mind had not exercised any influence on the mind of the waiter.

The concept of continuing representations by conduct was applied in *R v Benli* [1998] 2 VR 149. The accused, a driving instructor, had had his license to drive and therefore to instruct suspended. He continued to conduct lessons and obtain fees. He was charged with obtaining property by deception. Evidence was given at trial that the students had believed he was a licensed instructor and that they would not have used his services if they had known that he was not licensed. The Victorian Court of Appeal, dismissing the appeal against conviction, held that although there was no express representation that he was licensed instructor, this was implied by his conduct.

Both decisions raise doubts as to whether there was sufficient evidence that the victims had been misled by the accused. Strictly speaking, the prosecution must prove that the false representation acted on the mind of the victim. In early cases, the courts suggested that this element had to be proved by direct evidence, though recent decisions have relaxed this requirement emphasising that the operative nature of the inducement may be inferred from the totality of evidence.[49] This inferential approach is particularly necessary in cases where the fraud is directed toward a government department, statutory authority or company rather than a specific individual: see *Low v The Queen* (1978) 23 ALR 616. Indeed, in cases like *DPP v Ray* and *R v Benli,* it is only by resorting to hindsight and putative beliefs that it is possible to say that the implied representation

---

49   See *R v Laverty* [1970] 3 All ER 432; cf *Collis-Smith* [1971] Crim LR 716.

operated on the minds of the victims causing them to part with their property or services. Rather than rely on the somewhat nebulous concept of implied continuing representations, the facts of the case may suggest that the statutory offence of making off without payment is the more appropriate charge, discussed above: p 717.

There has been some uncertainty as to whether a deception is operative on the mind of the victim in cases where the property, services or financial advantage have been dishonestly obtained using cheques, credit cards or charge cards. We have explored the problems of ATM misuse and the special provisions enacted to deal with deception of computers, at p 735. In cases of credit card fraud, there may be difficulty in establishing an operative deception in relation to an actual employee. In many cases, there may be no reliance by the employee conducting the transaction on any express or implied representation of the customer. This is because the employee knows that the bank operating the particular payment system (for example, credit card or cheque guarantee card) will honour the debt, even in cases where the card is stolen.

This question of operative deception was explored by the House of Lords in *R v Lambie* [1982] AC 449. The accused had a bank credit card, a Barclaycard, with a limit of £200. She exceeded that limit and was asked by the bank to return the card. She did not, and continued to incur expenditure on the card amounting to £1005. The last use was at a shop where she made a purchase of around £10. She was then charged with and convicted of obtaining a pecuniary advantage by deception. The prosecution decided not to charge her with obtaining property by deception, a decision which was criticised by the House of Lords. On appeal, the House of Lords considered whether or not the store manager had been induced or parted with the property *because of* the deception. In other words, had the deception been operative? The problem in relation to payment systems such as credit cards, is that the merchant has an arrangement with the bank that it would transact with any customer who presents a Barclaycard — indeed, the manager's deposition clearly stated that before and during the transaction she had made no assumptions about the customer's credit standing with the bank. The Court of Appeal accepted the defence submission that consequently the accused's deception had not induced the manager to part with the property. The manager had simply relied on the agreement with the bank and not on any representation made by the accused.

The House of Lords disagreed with this approach. Lord Roskill, delivering the judgment of their Lordships, held that the Court of Appeal below had attached too much emphasis to the evidence of the manager. Lord Roskill held that presenting a credit card is *not* an implied representation as to the customer's credit standing, but rather a representation of actual authority to make a contract with the store on the bank's behalf, which the bank will honour when the transaction voucher is presented. Since this is the implied representation, the only question remaining was whether it induced the manager to proceed with the transaction and allow the accused to remove the goods. Undoubtedly, had the manager known that the accused lacked the authority to use that card, then she would not have allowed the transaction to proceed. As the MCCOC noted in *Chapter 3: Theft, Fraud, Bribery and Related Offences*, Final Report (1995), any sales assistant who admitted that they knew that the card was not authorised would probably be guilty of conspiracy with the customer to defraud the merchant: p 141.

The law requires evidence that the deception *caused* the other person to part with the goods or services. As Lord Roskill conceded (at 460), in most cases it will be difficult or impossible for an employee to remember individual transactions and whether the actions of a particular customer had induced them to part with the goods or services. However, the absence of direct evidence will not be fatal to a prosecution. The question of proof should be simply left to the jury (or magistrate) to resolve in light of the totality of evidence, drawing inferences as appropriate.

The difficulties in establishing an operative deception in cases involving credit cards may be overcome by the application of "common-sense" and careful directions to the jury. In reality, many victims of credit card fraud pay no attention or are simply ignorant of the implied legal representations underlying these commercial transactions. In such cases, the question of whether a deception was operative on the mind of the victim can only be resolved evidentially by resorting to the fiction of what that person would have done, *or rather be assumed to have done,* had the truth been known about the customer's lack of authority to use the card. Hindsight is being equated for the state of mind of the victim at the time of the deception. By this evidential sleight of hand, the law is reconstructing the deception, imputing (objectively) rather than inferring (subjectively) the victim's reliance upon the implied representation that the customer has authority to use the card.

While this judicial creativity avoids unmeritorious acquittals, there are significant theoretical objections to the strains being placed on the causal requirement that lies at the heart of criminal deception. ATH Smith in "The Idea of Criminal Deception" [1982] Crim LR 721 suggested (at 726) that the courts in *Ray* and *Lambie* are developing a law of "constructive deception" rather than confining the concept to what actually passes through the mind of the victim. He concluded (at 731) that the law governing deception "is beginning to drift off course, and that it is for the courts to re-assert the basic principle that deception exists not just in the acts of the cheats, but also in the minds of his [or her] victim".

5. CONCLUSION

There are a number of themes explored in this chapter. The first theme is the complex array of social, political and economic forces shaping the development of larceny and theft. From a simple crime against possession, the offences dealing with stealing have been significantly remodelled to capture new forms of fraudulent and dishonest dealings in property. The modern law of theft protects a wide range of proprietary interests beyond simple possession. This evolution has required the courts and legislatures to adapt the law to reflect the changing nature of property and ways of doing business: from protecting coins and tangible chattels, to credit cards and intangible interests, the law governing property offences has been subject to a constant cycle of legislative reform and judicial development.

Another theme is the emerging consensus that dishonesty is the hallmark of culpability for *all* property offences. Much of the academic discussion in this area of the criminal law is devoted to resolving authoritatively the meaning and scope of dishonesty. Notwithstanding the recent decision of the High Court in *Peters v The Queen* (1998) 192 CLR 493, there is still controversy over whether the concept should be defined objectively or subjectively. The preoccupation — perhaps even obsession — with the fault element for property offences distracts attention from examining the wrongfulness of the conduct element. As dishonesty becomes the principal criterion for wrongfulness, the physical elements (such as the trespass to property or the deception) appear increasingly redundant. This is reflected in the broad, all-encompassing definition of appropriation for theft which punishes *any* dishonest dealing in property without proof of a trespass, and the enactment of general fraud offences which dispense with the requirement of an operative deception.

Another theme running through this chapter is the impact of technology on theft and fraud. In the 1980s and 1990s the difficulties in using existing property offences against computer fraud led to the enactment of remedial provisions and/or specialised computer offences analogous to unlawful trespass and criminal damage.[50] From being an adjunct to property offences, computer crime is now considered a discrete field of the criminal law raising its own legal and policy issues. Indeed, this is reflected in its separate treatment in the *Model Criminal Code: Chapter 4 — Damage and Computer Offences,* Discussion Paper (2000). The Model Criminal Code Officers Committee (MCCOC) has recommended that computer offences should be confined to damage to computer systems, while "computer fraud" should be dealt with under general offences of theft and related offences, amended where necessary to cover computers. This template for reform provides conceptual coherence to the legal response to computer misuse, and overcomes the erratic and piecemeal approach to reform that has hitherto characterised this area of the criminal law. Like property offences generally, these proposed reforms follow the model adopted in the United Kingdom by the *Computer Misuse Act* 1990 (UK).

Technology also exposes the limitations of territoriality in the criminal law. The MCCOC report on computer offences contained significant proposals to reform the general rules governing jurisdiction. These provisions have already been considered in Chapter 2, p 89. The MCCOC's reminder that in the digital age "fraud knows no boundaries", creates further challenges for law enforcement as well as raising legitimate concerns over the proper reach of the criminal law. With increasing concern about the global nature of organised crime, in particular "white collar crime", there will be concerted pressure at the international level to create new laws, supported by specialised investigative agencies, to combat transnational property crime in the 21st century.

---

50   The *Review of Commonwealth Criminal Law: Interim Report on Computer Crime* (1988) (the Gibbs Committee) recommended the creation of specific computer offences dealing with unlawful access and damage to data. These reforms were enacted in ss 76A-F of the *Crimes Act* 1914 (Cth)and ss 308-310 of the *Crimes Act* 1900 (NSW). Different approaches have been adopted in other jurisdictions: *Crimes Act* 1900 (ACT), ss 135H-135L (unlawful access; damaging data and dishonest use); *Summary Offences Act* 1966 (Vic), s 9A (computer trespass); *Summary Offences Act* 1953 (SA), s 44 (unauthorised use); *Criminal Code* (Qld), s 408D (hacking and computer misuse); *Criminal Code* (WA), s 440A(2) (unlawful operation). See generally, O Akindemowo, *Information Technology Law in Australia* (Sydney: LBC, 1999), Ch 5.

14

Public Order

> **Good order is the foundation of all good things**

Edmund Burke,
Reflections on the Revolution in France
(Hammondsworth: Penguin, 1970), p 372

1. INTRODUCTION

The scope of "public order" law is broad and overlaps with many other areas of the criminal law. For example, stalking spans both offences against the person and public order. Although stalking is now a distinct offence (as explored in Chapter 11, p 568), it may also trigger the exercise of a wide range of public order powers. In New South Wales, for example, stalking is one of the grounds for granting an apprehended violence order: *Crimes Act* 1900 (NSW), ss 562AB, 562B. Moreover, offences against "public morals" such as gross indecency and prostitution function more like public order offences than sexual offences: see further Ch 12, pp 640ff.

Public order law is also highly diversified. Crimes range from relatively minor offences such as drunkeness and offensive language, to some of the most serious crimes against the State such as unlawful assembly and riot. Minor public order offences, which form the bulk of prosecutions, are routinely dealt with by way of summons or even an infringement notice. For an explanation of infringement notices and expiation schemes, see Chapter 1, p 42.

1.1 THE POLITICS OF PUBLIC ORDER

Crime and safety surveys in Australia have revealed that concerns about crime and public nuisances within the local neighbourhood are divided between, on the one hand, offences such as burglary, drugs and car theft, and nuisances such as dangerous/noisy driving, louts/young gangs and vandalism/graffitti: S Mukherjee, C Carcach and K Higgins, *A Statistical Profile of Crime in Australia* (Canberra: AIC, 1997), p 62.

TABLE 1:

Australia, State/Territory Crime and Safety Surveys, 1995
Victims and Non-Victims of Personal Crime
Perceptions of Crime or Public Nuisance Problems in the Neighbourhood

CRIME OR PUBLIC NUISANCE PROBLEM	NSW	QLD	WA	SA	ACT
None	48.6	48.1	42.6	50.8	46.3
Burglary	18.1	44.3	32.0	21.6	23.2
Dangerous/noisy driving	10.7	20.1	6.5	7.0	10.3
Louts/young gangs	6.8	10.9	3.9	2.8	3.1
Vandalism/graffiti	3.9	6.7	4.6	8.1	7.8
Illegal drugs	3.7	4.1	3.0	1.2	2.4
Car theft	2.6	2.1	3.1	1.4	1.0

As Table 1 illustrates, the maintenance of public order is a major community preoccupation. Moral panics about hooliganism and juvenile delinquency produces demands for new offences and wider police powers to deal with disorderly elements.[1] As a consequence, the debate about public order reform is highly susceptible to an uncivil politics of "law and order": R Hogg and D Brown, *Rethinking Law and Order* (Sydney: Pluto Press, 1998).

Potentially, any conduct that causes public alarm or community disquiet may justify a legislative response. Law and order campaigns tend to generate hastily drafted criminal laws that pay only scant attention to the adequacy or potential overlap of existing police powers and offences. While the criminalisation of stalking throughout Australia directly responds to community fears, these new offences are open to the accusation of redundancy on the ground that existing public order laws and offences against the person are more than adequate for the task. As Celia Wells noted in "Stalking: The Criminal Law Response" [1997] Crim LR 463, public order legislation responding to public fears tends to follow the same pattern of "addressing a narrowly conceived social harm with a widely drawn provision, often supplementing and overlapping with existing offences": p 464.

The emergence of a new threat to public order — "contamination of goods" — illustrates the historical and political contingency of criminalisation. The issue of "product tampering" and

---

1   The term "moral panic" was coined by Stanley Cohen in a famous book, *Folk Devils and Moral Panics: The Creation of the Mods and Rockers* (St Albans, Herts: Paladin, 1973).

"consumer terrorism" seized the imagination of the media, the general public and law-makers as a result of a series of cases in the 1990s. Following a highly publicised threat of contamination targetting Arnotts biscuits in February 1997, the company recalled all of its products in Australian supermarkets with devastating financial consequences for shareholders and employees. As a direct result of this case, the Commonwealth Attorney-General referred the issue to the Model Criminal Code Officers Committee (MCCOC) for consideration. In its Discussion Paper and Final Report, the MCCOC concluded that existing criminal laws were inadequate and inappropriate, and proposed that special offences dealing with contamination of goods should be enacted: *Chapter 8: Public Order Offences — Contamination of Goods*, Report (1998). The Report concluded that new offences were needed because of the special nature of the harm and the need to adopt tougher penalties and rules for extra-territorial jurisdiction: p 5. Concerns about the inadequacy of existing penalties and territorial jurisdiction raise general questions *distinct from criminalisation*. These perceived inadequacies could have been addressed without creating new offences. The Report gave no consideration to the designation of the proposed offences as public order offences, and only briefly examined their relationship to existing criminal laws. The political imperative to adopt a legislative response to community and corporate panic about contamination of goods overcame the objection that this conduct could be adequately addressed through existing offences such as offences against the person, endangerment, administering poisons/noxious substances, public nuisance, extortion, blackmail and conspiracy to defraud and so on: p 3.

The political dimension of "consumer terrorism", both at a domestic and international level, played a significant role in the process of criminalisation. The proposed offences were modelled directly on contamination of goods legislation enacted in the United States and the United Kingdom: *Public Order Act* 1986 (UK), s 38. Even before the Report had been released, offences had been enacted in New South Wales, Queensland and Victoria. South Australia and Tasmania have since followed suit.[2] The political consensus and speed of reform stand in stark contrast to the usual difficulties of achieving uniformity for the criminal law within our federal system.

Offences against public order must be understood in the context of their enforcement. Part I of this chapter examines the extensive powers under common law and statute to prevent and suppress disorder. The policing of public order situations does not always result in formal intervention such as arrest or prosecution. This emphasis on order-maintenance and prevention of crime and disorder explains its relative invisibility in official statistics and reported decisions. Indeed, public order offences tend to operate primarily as a resource that police may draw upon to negotiate situations with a *potential* for disorder. As Denis Galligan noted in "Preserving Public Protest: the Legal Approach" in L Gostin (ed), *Civil Liberties in Conflict* (London and New York: Routledge, 1988), p 49:

> The law may have little impact, being more in the nature of a resource to be used as a last resort in ensuring compliance with the police's conceptions of good order.

---

2   See *Crimes Act* 1900 (NSW), s 93ID; *Criminal Law Consolidation Act* 1935 (SA), s 251; *Criminal Code Amendment (Contamination of Goods) Act* 1999 (Tas), Ch XXXIIB ss 287D, E, F; *Crimes Act* 1958 (Vic), s 251. In Tasmania and Victoria the legislation makes no distinction between contamination which does or does not cause harm. In New South Wales and South Australia, the legislation additionally includes aggravated offences for contamination which causes harm or threatens public health.

The threat of formal intervention such as arrest is merely one resource that police may draw upon. There are also wide ranging "quasi-criminal" powers, falling short of arrest, available to citizens, police and magistrates to prevent crime and disorder. As we shall explore in the next section, the exercise of these powers may have serious implications for the exercise of fundamental human rights, including the right to privacy, as well as civil and political rights such as freedom of expression, assembly and association.

The paramount duty of the police is to prevent crime and disorder. This responsibility formed part of the original mandate of modern policing in the 19th century, and is now incorporated into police service codes of conduct and statements of values. It has been recognised by the courts and is now entrenched by legislation in some jurisdictions. The law has imposed few formal constraints on operational police decision-making, especially in public order situations. The police often claim (in their interactions with citizens) that they have minimal discretion. The myth of full enforcement identifies the police with the rule of law, giving their authority both moral and political legitimacy. However, it has been empirically demonstrated that in the execution of their duties, police possess a wide discretion. Moreover, from a normative legal perspective, the ideal of full enforcement has been rejected in favour of a discretionary approach to policing. Both the courts and legislatures have imposed only minimal fetters on the exercise of police discretion.

The wide discretion recognised by the courts in relation to public order should not be viewed as a deviation from legality, but rather is condoned by the courts both as a necessary and legitimate feature of modern policing. The standards of legality and fairness that should constrain police decision-making (through the substantive law and judicial review) are, in reality, far from the minds of those police confronted with the practical task of maintaining order. As we shall explore below, it is police culture rather than legal standards that determine how situations with potential for disorder, such as "political protests" or "domestic disputes", will be managed.[3]

Police have considerable leeway in how to respond to threats to public order. This discretion is supported by broad and nebulous definitions that lie at the core of many powers and offences, such as "breach of the peace" or "offensive conduct". The summary nature of these offences has meant that there has only been limited appellate clarification of key concepts. As Lawrence Lustgarten observed in "The Police and the Substantive Criminal Law" [1987] *British Journal of Criminology* 24 at 29:

> a key characteristic of all preventative public order offences, is that the police are a
> complainant, judge, and, in all but a few cases, jury as well. This is because the vast bulk of
> prosecutions are conducted using summary trial, in which the accused is denied the
> protection of a jury verdict and in which magistrates are notorious for accepting police
> officers' versions of key facts.

As in other areas of the criminal law, the summary nature of most public order offences reinforces an "ideology of triviality": D McBarnet, *Conviction* (London: Macmillan Press, 1981), discussed above in Chapter 2: p 96.

---

3   For an excellent analysis of police discretion and a survey of criminological research on police culture in the
    Australian context, see S James and I Warren, "Police Culture" in J Bessant, K Carrington and S Cook (eds),
    Cultures of Crime and Violence (Bundoora: La Trobe University Press, 1995), p 3.

As Nicola Lacey and Celia Wells have pointed out, the traditional triviality and invisibility of public order law must be resisted by legal scholars and criminal lawyers: *Reconstructing Criminal Law* (2nd ed, London: Butt, 1998), p 92. Not only does this much neglected part of the criminal law loom large in the daily lives of the citizens, the police, criminal lawyers and magistrates, it also reveals important perspectives on the process of criminalisation, the nature and structure of criminal liability, and the political, social and cultural context of law enforcement.

2. PUBLIC ORDER POWERS

William Blackstone,
Commentaries on the Laws of England (9th ed,
London: Garland, 1978),
(first published 1765),
Book IV, p 251

> **[P]reventive Justice is upon every principle, of reason, of humanity, and of sound policy, preferable in all respects to *punishing* justice**

2.1 PREVENTIVE JUSTICE AND BINDING OVER

The common law dealing with breach of the peace has an ancient pedigree dating back to 10th century Norman England: D Feldman, "The King's Peace, The Royal Prerogative and Public Order: The Roots and Early Development of Binding Over Powers" [1988] 47(1) *Cambridge Law Journal* 101. From the 14th century onwards, English statutes granted Justices of the Peace (the forerunner of the modern magistrate) wide powers to prevent, and later to punish, threats to the "king's peace". Justices of the Peace were empowered to require a person to enter into a recognisance (a written undertaking), with or without sureties (a pledge of money) to "keep the peace and/or be of good behaviour". The practice of binding over to ensure "good behaviour", as distinct from keeping the peace, derives from the *Justices of the Peace Act* 1361 (34 Edw 3 c 1) and the nature of the oath-taking by Justices of the Peace: *Forbutt v Blake* [1981] 51 FLR 465 at 473. The High Court has confirmed that the common law and 14th century English statutes broadening these powers were received into the common law of Australia and are exercisable by Justices of the Peace or any court that has inherited its jurisdiction: *Devine v The Queen* (1967) 119 CLR 506 at 514, per Windeyer J; see also *Forbutt v Blake* [1981] 51 FLR 465 at 474. For a detailed discussion of the history and evolution of the magistracy in Australia see J Lowndes, "The Australian Magistracy: From Justices of the Peace to Judges and Beyond — Part I" (2000) 74 *Australian Law Journal* 509; "Part II" (2000) 74 *Australian Law Journal* 592.

Blackstone venerated binding over as an example of "preventive justice" (as exemplified in the above quotation). From an 18th century perspective, preventive justice was clearly preferable to punishing justice. In the absence of a professional, disciplined police force, responsibility for law enforcement was shared between local constables and lay Justices of the Peace. Though administered by amateurs, the criminal justice system was not benign. Felonies were routinely punishable by death. Against this backdrop, binding over became an indispensable aspect of local summary justice. As a crime control measure administered by local Justices, it was a more merciful alternative to prosecution and conviction before the itinerant judges of the Royal Courts. From a 21st century perspective, these feudal powers to bind over, to obtain a promise from individuals to keep the peace and/or be of good behaviour seem anomalous and quaint.

Binding over straddles the border between the criminal and civil law. Although binding over carries the risk of imprisonment, if a person refuses to enter into or breaches the recognisance, it is not in the nature of punishment. Rather, binding over is "a precautionary measure to prevent a future crime, and is not by way of punishment for something past": *Ex parte Davis* (1871) 24 LT 547. See P Power, "'An Honour and Almost a Singular One': A Review of the Justices' Preventive Jurisdiction" (1982) 8 *Monash University Law Review* 69. Binding over may be applied to any conduct likely to cause a breach of the peace.[4] In *Forbutt v Blake* [1981] 51 FLR 465, Connor ACJ held (at 475) that "a binding over order may be available against a person who has not committed any offence in circumstances where the consequence of his [or her] lawful conduct is likely to produce a breach of the peace by other persons". Binding over may also be used to restrain peaceful and perfectly lawful conduct.[5] Magistrates may bind over individuals engaged in peaceful and otherwise lawful conduct on the ground that it provoked or was likely to provoke *others* to violence. Binding over orders have been used in a wide variety of situations including cases where the person to be bound over had:

- obstructed the highway;

- obstructed the police in the execution of their duty;

- used threatening, abusive or insulting words; or

- engaged in conduct which caused, or was likely to cause, a breach of the peace.[6]

The potential for these laws to operate as a "prior restraint" on individuals engaged in peaceful political protest is explored below, pp 771ff.

A binding over order may be imposed on the court's own initiative, or where legislation provides, following the laying of a complaint, information or summons. Before requiring the defendant to enter into a recognisance, the magistrate must be satisfied that the alleged apprehension of a breach of the peace was "reasonable": see *Crimes Act* 1900 (ACT), s 547(1); *Crimes Act* 1900 (NSW), s 547(1). Since a binding over order is not the equivalent of a criminal conviction, the standard of proof in making the order and determining whether an alleged breach has been established is the civil standard of balance of probabilities, although it has been suggested that in evaluating the strength of the evidence to establish the basis of an order, the court must take into

---

4   Binding over is not confined to conduct causing an actual or threatened breach of the peace, but may be used in any case where the person commits or threatens to commit *any* criminal offence: *R v Wright; Ex parte Klar* (1971) 1 SASR 103 at 106-107.

5   *R v Pinney* (1832) 5 Car & P, 254, 271-273; *Wise v Dunning* [1902] 1 KB 167; *Carr v Werry* [1979] 1 NSWLR 144.

6   *Wise v Dunning* [1962] 1 KB 167; *Lansbury v Riley* [1914] 3 KB 229; *R v Sandbach; Ex parte Williams* [1935] 2 KB 192; *Everett v Ribbands* [1932] 2 QB 198; *R v Aubrey-Fletcher; Ex parte Thompson* [1969] 2 All ER 846. For a review of English decisions on binding over orders see DGT Williams, "Protest and Public Order'" (1970) *Cambridge Law Journal* 96 at 104.

account the seriousness of the allegation against the person against whom the complaint is made: see further, Ch 2, p 122.[7] As well as forfeiture of the surety, the breach of the recognisance may result in fines or imprisonment: see *Crimes Act* 1900 (NSW), s 547(1), (2).[8] Although the obligation to keep the peace and be of good behaviour is imprecise, the High Court has established "that most conduct which justifies the making of a binding over order can also serve as the basis for forfeiture": *Devine v The Queen* (1967) 119 CLR 506 at 516, per Windeyer J.

In all jurisdictions, except Victoria, the common law has been codified and/or supplemented by legislation.[9] Such legislation has preserved the key features of the common law, including its anomalies. For example, s 19B of the *Crimes Act* 1914 (Cth) allows a court of summary jurisdiction to release an offender on a binding over order without having to proceed to a conviction. As we shall examine below, the historic lineage of these preventive powers obscures the significant role that the modern courts and parliaments have played in developing and expanding the common law to meet the needs of public order policing in the late 20th century. Binding over has also provided the template for specialised statutory protection orders to restrain domestic violence, as well as other forms of apprehended violence such as stalking, intimidation and molestation.

Binding over offers many advantages for defendants, police, prosecutors and judges. The avoidance of prosecution and conviction for a criminal offence may be attractive to defendants. From the "official" perspective, the power to bind over "provides a flexible way to deal with cases arising out of disputes between neighbours and minor public order problems without the need for a full hearing. It saves time and money": D Feldman, "The King's Peace, The Royal Prerogative and Public Order: The Roots and Early Development of Binding Over Powers" [1988] 47(1) *Cambridge Law Journal* 101 at 101.

HUMAN RIGHTS PERSPECTIVES

Binding Over and Quasi-Criminal Laws

Summary preventive powers, while not entailing conviction or punishment, are neither benign nor lacking in punitive force. The European Court of Human Rights has recently considered whether the power to arrest and bind over individuals who are likely to commit a breach of the peace violates the right to liberty and security of the person, contrary to Art 5 of the *European Convention on Human Rights* (ECHR): *Steel and Others v United Kingdom* (67/1997/851/1058, 28 September 1998) (1999); 28 EHRR 603. Article 5 contains exceptions where the deprivation of liberty will be justified, and these include:

— detention after conviction;

---

7   *Hulett v Laidlaw* (1996) 89 A Crim R 240, Fitzgerald P at 243 (CA Qld), following *Briginshaw v Briginshaw* (1938) 60 CLR 517. By contrast the English courts have applied the criminal standard of proof, requiring the facts upon which the order is granted to be proved beyond reasonable doubt: *R v London Quarter Sessions; Ex parte Metropolitan Police Commissioner* [1940] KB 670.

8   Cf ss 19B and 20 of the *Crimes Act* 1914 (Cth) which provide that imprisonment is not available for default of the recognisance.

9   *Crimes Act* 1914 (Cth), s 19B; *Magistrates Court Act* 1930 (ACT), ss 80-79 and 196-197, 205; *Crimes Act* 1900 (NSW), s 547(1) and (2); *Peace and Good Behaviour Act* 1982 (Qld), s 6(3)(b); *Justices Act* 1980 (NT), ss 99-100; *Summary Procedure Act* 1921 (SA), ss 99-99K; *Justices Act* 1959 (Tas), ss 93-105; *Justices Act* 1902 (WA), s 172 — repealed by *Restraining Orders Act* 1997 (WA).

— lawful arrest or detention for the non-compliance of a lawful order of a court (eg contempt); or

— lawful arrest or detention for the purpose of bringing a person, reasonably suspected of having committed an offence to court or to prevent a person committing an offence or fleeing. The European Court held that breach of the peace, whatever its domestic characterisation, must be regarded as an "offence" for the purpose of Art 5 of the ECHR: para 49. As such, any deprivation of liberty and detention must comply with domestic law and procedures and must not be arbitrary: para 54. Although the scope of the "breach of the peace" concept had been unclear, the Court observed that recent decisions over the past two decades had resolved much uncertainty. It concluded that the powers and procedures governing the breach of the peace were sufficiently clear to comply with the requirements of the ECHR. Since the *International Covenant on Civil and Political Rights*, to which Australia is a signatory, also contains a right to liberty and security of person and immunity from arbitrary arrest and detention (Art 9), this decision is similarly relevant to the common law and statutory powers of arrest and binding over to prevent a breach of the peace in Australia.

The finding that binding over orders were sufficiently clear to satisfy the ECHR is surprising, in light of the earlier criticism offered by the Law Commission of England and Wales. After reviewing the authorities on binding over, the Commission recommended in its Report 222, *Binding Over* (London: HMSO, 1994) its abolition on the following grounds (para 6.27):

> These objections are, in summary, that the conduct which can be the ground for a binding over order is too vaguely defined; that binding over orders when made are in terms which are too vague and are therefore potentially oppressive; that the power to imprison someone if he or she refuses to consent to be bound over is anomalous; that orders which restrain a subject's freedom can be made without the discharge of the criminal, or indeed any clearly defined, burden of proof; and that witnesses, complainants or even acquitted defendants can be bound over without adequate prior information of any charge or complaint against them.

As well as raising concerns about the rule of law and due process, binding over orders raise concerns about imposing unjustified restrictions on the right to peaceful assembly. The decision in *Steel and Others v United Kingdom* (1999) 28 EHRR 603 explored this question, specifically, whether the power to arrest and bind over individuals engaged in political protest interferes with freedom of speech, assembly and association protected by the ECHR: see below, p 775.

2.2 DEFINING PUBLIC ORDER: POLICING ACROSS PUBLIC AND PRIVATE SPHERES

The law governing public order traverses both the public and private spheres. The common law powers and offences dealing with public order are not confined to public places, but may be applied to disorder that occurs on private property. In an effort to limit the intrusive exercise of police powers, statutory powers and offences are sometimes restricted to "public places", such as the police power to request individuals to "move-on", and public indecency/offensive conduct crimes. The statutory definition of "public place" is broad, expressly covering places to which members of the public ordinarily have access: see for example, *Summary Offences Act* 1988 (NSW), s 3. The scope of "public place" is determined by habitual use by members of the public, rather than by strict legal rights. By adopting this extended definition, public order powers and offences are extended to "semi-private" places such as public lavatories and clubs, as well as commercial spaces such as shopping malls. Indeed, a police "lock-up" has been claimed as a public place in a prosecution for using offensive language in the presence of a police officer. The discriminatory effect of these laws against young people and minority groups is considered below: see pp 792-793.

Not all statutory public order offences and powers are limited to public spaces. In New South Wales, the statutory offences of riot, affray and violent disorder "may be committed in private as well as in public places": *Crimes Act* 1900 (NSW), ss 93B(5), 93C(5); *Summary Offences* Act 1988 (NSW), s 11A, respectively. It may be argued that the public interest in preventing and suppressing serious disorder trumps rights of ownership and private property. The strength of such an argument is weakened by the fact that the offence of violent disorder, as reflected in its summary nature and penalties, was enacted to deal with minor cases of disorder not resulting in *actual* injury or property damage.

PUBLIC ORDER AND THE RIGHT TO PROPERTY AND PRIVACY

Public order law constitutes a significant threat to "private" interests relating to privacy and property. The question whether police action to prevent disorder is a *justifiable* interference with privacy, a right which is protected by international human rights treaties, has recently been considered by the European Court of Human Rights in *McLeod v the United Kingdom* (1999) 27 EHRR 493.

CASE STUDIES

Policing Domestics: Public Order versus Private Interest

McLeod v the United Kingdom (1999) 27 EHRR 493 explored whether common law powers to prevent a breach of the peace exercised in dealing with a domestic dispute violated the right to privacy. Following a bitter and acrimonious divorce and property settlement, the applicant, Mrs McLeod, was ordered by the court to return specified property to her former husband by a certain date. Mr McLeod was under the belief that the applicant had agreed that he could collect the property on a certain date, saving her the trouble of delivering it to him. Because of previous difficulties in obtaining cooperation from the applicant, Mr McLeod's solicitors had arranged for police officers to be present because of the potential for a breach of the peace. The applicant was not at home when Mr McLeod and the police entered the premises. The police remained on the premises (mainly outside in the driveway) during the removal of the property. The applicant arrived at the scene later and strongly objected to the removal of the property. The police intervened and insisted that Mr McLeod be allowed to remove the property on the ground that if she obstructed him further, there was likely to be a breach of the peace.

The applicant instituted a criminal prosecution against the police, but was unsuccessful. A civil action for trespass to her property also failed. The English Court of Appeal dismissed her appeal, affirming the existence of the power under common law to enter and remain on private property in order to prevent a breach of the peace: *McLeod v Commissioner of Police of the Metropolis* [1994] All ER 553. Her claim of trespass to her chattels also failed since the police had not participated in the removal of the goods. Having exhausted her domestic remedies, and leave to appeal to the House of Lords having been refused, she appealed to the European Court of Human Rights alleging an interference with her right to respect for private life and home, contrary to Art 8 of the *European Convention on Human Rights* (ECHR).

The European Court of Human Rights ruled there was no doubt that the entry onto the applicant's premises violated Art 8 of the ECHR. The critical issue in this case was whether the interference was justifiable under Art 8(2) which provides:

> There shall be no interference by a public authority with the exercise of this right except such as in accordance with the law and is necessary in a democratic society in the interests of national security, public safety or the economic well-being of the country, for the prevention of disorder or crime, for the protection of health or morals, or for the protection of the rights and freedoms of others.

The Court held that the interference with the applicant's privacy was "in accordance with law". Although there had been some uncertainty over the scope of breach of the peace, it had been clarified over the past two decades: para 42. The common law defined with sufficient precision the powers of a person to enter private property without warrant in order to prevent a breach of the peace: para 45. This power also served a legitimate aim of preventing disorder or crime: para 48.

As well as corresponding to a pressing social need, the interference must also be proportionate to the legitimate aim pursued. The European Court viewed its task as striking "a fair balance between the relevant interests, namely the applicant's right to respect for her private life and home, on the one hand, and the prevention of disorder and crime, on the other": para 53. The Court concluded that the means employed by the police in this case were disproportionate to the legitimate aim. The Court noted that police did not take any steps to verify whether Mr McLeod was entitled to enter the property and remove property and should not have assumed that the verbal agreement had superseded the court order. In light of these facts, it was stated (at para 57) that the police should have not intervened at that stage:

> The Court considers further that, upon being informed that the applicant was not present, the police officers should not have entered her house, as it should have been clear to them that there was little or no risk of disorder or crime occurring.

In light of the ruling in *McLeod*, the common law would seem to be deficient in relation to the exercise of public order powers that interfere with the right to respect for one's private life and home.

The principles articulated in *McLeod* suggest that some reordering of both the common law and legislation may be required in order to meet Australia's international obligations under the *International Covenant on Civil and Political Rights* (ICCPR), New York, 19 December 1966, 999 UNTS, [1980] ATS 23. Like Art 8 of the *European Convention on Human Rights*, Art 17 of the ICCPR prohibits any arbitrary interference with privacy, family, home or correspondence. The fundamental importance and limits of privacy as a general principle are discussed in Chapter 2. Article 17 reiterates the fundamental importance of privacy, and demands that interference with privacy through the exercise of public order powers or offences must be justified as necessary and reasonable in the circumstances.

The potential negative impact of public order powers on rights to privacy was foreshadowed by the Australian Law Reform Commission (ALRC) in *Domestic Violence*, Report No 30 (Canberra: AGPS, 1986). After reviewing the common law and statutory powers of entry onto private property in order to deal with domestic violence, the ALRC cautioned that any "liberalisation" of the power must conform with the ICCPR: para 37. Without the benefit of the subsequent privacy jurisprudence under the ECHR and ICCPR, particularly the development of the tests of reasonableness and proportionality, it was not surprising that the ALRC was unable to venture any further opinion on how compliance with Art 17 might be achieved.

The decision of the European Court in *McLeod* stresses the fundamental primacy attached to private interests, particularly the right to property. Interference with privacy will be prohibited unless it is established to be necessary and reasonable in the circumstances. Under Art 17, interference with privacy is only prohibited where it is "arbitrary". The scope and meaning of arbitrary interference has been recently reviewed in relation to the challenge to homosexual offences in Tasmania on the ground that it interfered with privacy rights: *Toonen v Australia* (1994) 3 Int Hum Rts Reports 97. The Human Rights Committee in this case recalled (at para 8.3) that:

> [t]he introduction of the concept of arbitrariness is intended to guarantee that even interference provided for by the law should be in accordance with the provisions, aims and objectives of the Covenant and should be, in any event, reasonable in the circumstances.

Compliance with Art 17 in the context of preventive powers may be addressed in a number of ways. Under the existing common law, the powers to prevent a breach of the peace may only be exercised where the apprehended breach is "imminent" or "proximate". However, as we shall explore below, these concepts are highly elastic and provide considerable latitude in determining when the police may intervene in public order situations. To satisfy the conditions of necessity and proportionality, a more stringent common law test based on immediacy rather than imminence could be developed in situations involving trespass to private property: see below, p 767. Although the ruling in *McLeod* was concerned with trespass to property, public order powers that involved either trespass to the person or a person's chattels would pose the risk of interference with privacy and similarly would have to satisfy these more stringent tests.

Significantly the ruling in *McLeod* was not unanimous. The two dissenting judges took the view that the police were "fully entitled on the evidence to fear a breach of the peace": para 2. They expressed concern that the majority's ruling may significantly weaken the position of the police in dealing with cases of domestic violence. They stated (at para 4) that there were clear dangers of escalation in this situation:

> as a matter of common knowledge, the intensity and bitterness of domestic disputes tend all too often to escalate into disorder or violence, particularly where the division of property is involved; and it is by no means unusual for the British police to be called on to intervene to prevent such escalation.

In light of this tendency, the dissenting judges concluded that the interference in this case was not disproportionate. They stressed that throughout the incident the police remained on the premises, acting discreetly and with restraint, until there was no longer any threat of a breach of the peace.

In an attempt to clarify the common law, in several Australian jurisdictions the powers of the police to enter and remain on private premises in order to prevent a breach of the peace have been placed on a statutory footing. For example, ss 349A, 349C of the *Crimes Act* 1900 (ACT) provide:

Division 1A — Preventative action

349A. Police powers of entry

A police officer may enter premises, and may take such action as is necessary and reasonable to prevent the commission or repetition of an offence or of a breach of the peace or to protect life or property:

(a) when invited onto the premises by a person who is or is reasonably believed to be a resident of the premises for the purpose of giving assistance to a person on the premises who has suffered, or is in imminent danger of suffering, physical injury at the hands of some other person;

(b) in pursuance of a warrant issued under section 349B; or

(c) in circumstances of seriousness and urgency, in accordance with section 349C ...

349C. Entry in emergencies

A police officer may enter premises where the officer believes on reasonable grounds that:

(a) an offence or a breach of the peace is being or is likely to be committed, or a person has suffered physical injury or there is imminent danger of injury to a person or damage to property; and

(b) it is necessary to enter the premises immediately for the purpose of preventing the commission or repetition of an offence or a breach of the peace or to protect life or property.

These provisions are similar to those enacted in New South Wales, though the powers there are restricted to cases involving "domestic violence" offences: *Crimes Act* 1900 (NSW), s 357F(2)-(3). Similar proposals are contained in the *Model Domestic Violence Laws*, Report (1999), though these powers are not intended to limit or replace those available under the common law: p 180. Unlike the earlier ALRC Report, the Intergovernmental Working Group did not consider the privacy or broader human rights implications of such powers.

Like the common law, these statutory powers of entry rely on flexible concepts, such as "imminence", "circumstances of seriousness and urgency", and "breach of the peace". While such powers may pursue a legitimate aim of preventing crime and disorder, as in *McLeod* they are open to challenge on the ground of reasonableness and/or proportionality. Clearly, it is impossible and impractical to define with any absolute precision the circumstances in which a threat of disorder justifies trespass onto private premises. Police discretion is unavoidable in this context, and it would be retrograde to deny entry onto private property unless violence had *actually* occurred. To give effect to the ruling in *McLeod*, however, it may be necessary to give greater priority to privacy interests under the common law. This could be achieved by structuring police decision-making under the legislation. To give greater respect to privacy, the police could be required to consider whether the intervention proposed would be justified under Art 17, and whether alternative steps were available to prevent disorder that did not violate, or at least minimised, interference with property and privacy rights.

RECONSTRUCTING PRIVACY: PROTECTING FAMILY LIFE AND PERSONHOOD

The legal boundaries between the public/private sphere are malleable and contingent. At the domestic level, the courts and legislatures have imposed restrictions on the intrusion of public order laws into the private sphere, though not always consistently. The notion of protected "private spaces" where public order laws are inapplicable, contrasts starkly with other areas of the criminal law, such as drug offences: see Ch 15. At the international level, the European Court recently recognised that any interference with privacy through the exercise of public order powers must be justified as necessary, reasonable and proportionate: see above, pp 751ff. As the right to privacy is not absolute, the domestic law will be required to strike a "balance" between respect for privacy and the legitimate interests in preventing disorder and crime. In the present law, the balance struck between privacy and public order is not consistent across the common law and statute. To the extent that the right to privacy is recognised at all, it is strongest in relation to tangible interests such as property.

Feminists have pointed out that the public/private dichotomy is both functional and ideological. Women have been largely excluded from the rights enjoyable in the public sphere, and conversely denied legal protection within the (unregulated) private sphere. For a critical review of privacy from a feminist perspective, see Chapter 2, 'Feminist Perspectives: The Fair Trial Principle: A Flawed Balance?': pp 104ff. The liberal conception of privacy is a *negative* right (freedom from State interference, in effect, the individuals right to be left alone). However, this concept of private life is not immutable and there are indications that privacy may be remodelled into a *positive* right to establish, develop and fulfil one's own emotional needs. Viewed in relational terms, the concept of privacy could provide a basis for empowering rather than disempowering victims of domestic violence. Article 17 of the *International Covenant on Civil and Political Rights* (ICCPR) could provide a warrant for legal intervention to secure for women a positive right to enjoy a secure home and family life without fear of physical and emotional abuse. In this respect, different aspects of privacy collide (the right to property *versus* the right to family life). Sometimes resort to balancing metaphors cannot resolve this clash of moral imperatives, and the legislature and the courts simply must choose between these competing interests. This broader normative vision however does not undermine the powerful feminist critique that privacy *as presently conceived* creates and sustains an unregulated "private sphere" that renders invisible and condones violence against women and children. In the next section, we examine how family privacy has traditionally impeded the use of the criminal law as a remedy for violence against women and children within the home.

It is important to appreciate that the privacy zone that conceals and legitimates domestic violence is not *solely* a matter of legal rules. While police possess wide powers under public order law and the criminal law to deal with family violence, law enforcement policy and culture may strongly discourage legal intervention into "domestic disputes". The policies and culture of the police play a crucial role in sustaining the legal invisibility of domestic violence. As the dissenting judges in *McLeod* observed, the wide powers to combat domestic violence, though invasive of privacy, may be reasonable and proportionate in order to overcome the reluctance of law enforcement officials to intervene in "private disputes".

POLICING VIOLENCE AGAINST WOMEN AND CHILDREN: "JUST ANOTHER DOMESTIC?"

The reluctance of the police to intervene in "domestic disputes" has a long history: M Finnane, *Police and Government* (Melbourne: Oxford University Press, 1994), pp 104-110. Non-intervention by the State in such disputes has left generations of women and children vulnerable to serious physical and emotional abuse. The reasons for non-intervention by law enforcement officials are many and complex. See generally J Stubbs (ed), *Women, Male Violence and the Law* (Sydney: The Institute of Criminology, 1994) and S Cook and J Bessant (eds), *Women's Encounters with Violence — Australian Experiences* (Thousand Oaks, CA: Sage Publications Inc, 1997).

> In 1996, a National Women's Safety Study of 6300 women revealed that almost one quarter (23%) of women surveyed who had been married or in a de facto relationship had experienced violence (physical, sexual, threats or attempts): Australian Bureau of Statistics, *Women's Safety Australia* (Canberra: AGPS, 1996). See further S Parker, P Parkinson and J Behrens, *Australian Family Law in Context* (2nd ed, Sydney: LBC, 1999), Ch 10.

The foremost reason for non-intervention is the concern about unduly interfering with private family business. From the inception of modern policing in the mid-19th century, police standing orders prohibited unnecessary interference in family quarrels between a husband and his wife unless required to prevent disorder or serious violence. As Mark Finnane has pointed out, such instructions and policies formally persisted in some Australian states until the 1980s, and continue, informally, to reflect the attitudes of many police officers called to attend "domestics": p 104. Even where the police are willing to intervene in domestic situations, their mandate is conflicted between the duty to respect private property on the one hand, and the duty to prevent disorder and crime on the other. The duties of the police are discussed in the next section.

Migrant and Aboriginal women, because of social isolation and cultural reasons, may have greater difficulties in reporting abuse: P Easteal, *Shattered Dreams: Marital Violence Among Overseas-born in Australia* (Canberra: AGPS, 1996) and M Lucashenko, "Violence Against Indigenous Women: Public and Private Dimensions" in S Cook and J Bessant (eds), *Women's Encounters with Violence — Australian Experiences* (Thousand Oaks, CA: Sage Publications Inc, 1997), Ch 9.

The legal treatment of domestic violence has also played a role in sustaining its invisibility. The common law historically authorised the use of violence against wives under the rubric of "reasonable chastisement". The limits of "reasonableness" in the context of patriarchal discipline have been unclear and eventually the defence was ruled out in *R v Jackson* [1891] 1 QB 671. As pointed out in Chapter 11 the modern law still authorises reasonable chastisement of children, though there is considerable uncertainty surrounding the limits of parental discipline. Indeed, the defence of reasonable chastisement under the common law has been successfully challenged under Art 3 of the *European Convention on Human Rights* as a violation of the right not to be subjected to torture or inhuman or degrading treatment or punishment: see Ch 11, p 557. Even in cases resulting in prosecution and conviction, domestic violence has also been regarded as less serious from a sentencing perspective. The domestic context has often justified a more lenient penalty or the imposition of binding over orders instead of conviction.

From the law enforcement perspective, police have traditionally claimed that their hands were tied in domestic violence cases. Police often claimed that they lacked sufficient authority to intervene unless an actual offence had been committed, and the victim or another witness was unwilling to testify against the abuser. As Nicholas Seddon has pointed out, prior to the introduction of domestic violence protection orders, police complained that they had to rely on a mixture of bluff, subterfuge and ignorance of the offender's rights in order to gain entry to private premises: *Domestic Violence in Australia — The Legal Response* (2nd ed, Sydney: Federation Press, 1993), p 34.

The true legal position, as distinct from the police *mis*-perception about their powers to deal with domestic disputes, is somewhat different. In the next section we examine the wide powers under the common law to take necessary and reasonable steps to prevent crime and disorder, including powers of arrest without warrant and the power to enter and remain on private property. Moreover, the ordinary law of assault, supplemented by the doctrine of attempt and the new statutory offence of stalking, provides a broad basis for police intervention *before* actual harm has been inflicted: see Ch 11. This suggests that police claims of insufficient or ineffective powers are unfounded or, at least, overstated. Clearly police prefer to rely on specific statutory powers and offences, rather than on the common law, which is more difficult to access and often misunderstood by the police: D Dixon, *Law in Policing: Legal Regulation and Police Practices* (Oxford: Oxford University Press, 1997), p 205. Upon closer inspection, the traditional reluctance to intervene in violence within families is largely the product of police culture and entrenched attitudes that legitimate domestic violence or at least regard it as less serious than other types of violence.

The Use of Protection Orders

Although "domestic violence" involves breaches of the ordinary criminal law (such as assault, sexual assault, stalking, criminal damage and so on), legislation has been enacted in all jurisdictions, including the Commonwealth, to provide alternative remedies for domestic violence. These laws were enacted to address perceived inadequacies of existing powers and offences, and have performed an important educative function in relation to community and police attitudes toward domestic violence: Australian Law Reform Commission (ALRC), *Domestic Violence*, Report No 30 (Canberra: AGPS, 1986), para 110.

Protection orders granted under State and Territory laws are overlaid by a national system created by the *Family Law Act* 1975 (Cth). Under this legislation, the Family Court may issue an injunction aimed at preventing spousal violence or harassment (s 114(1)) or similar conduct direct to a child (s 70C(1)). From an enforcement perspective, the Family Law jurisdiction is not as effective as the equivalent regimes established under State and Territory laws. While there is a power of arrest under the *Family Law Act* for breach of an injunction, persons protected by the injunction must institute contempt proceedings on their own initiative. This rarely happens in practice. Nicholas Seddon in *Domestic Violence in Australia — The Legal Response* (2nd ed, Sydney: Federation Press, 1993) (p 73), has summed up the weakness of the injunction under the *Family Law Act* as follows:

> Enforcement is therefore not a police or State matter. The burden of enforcement invariably falls on the applicant. This is to be contrasted with breaches of protection orders under State or Territory legislation which are criminal offences prosecuted by the State. This is the main fault of the Family Court injunction. It is expensive and slow.

More commonly, victims of domestic violence will obtain a protection order under State or Territory legislation. The nomenclature, criteria and scope of these protection orders significantly differ between jurisdictions. These orders are variously described as "protection orders", "restraining orders", "domestic protection orders", "restraint orders" and "intervention orders". There is considerable diversity in these laws particularly in relation to who may seek an order. In most jurisdictions, the persons protected by an order are restricted to spouses, de facto spouses and other family members. However, in New South Wales, Tasmania and Western Australia, the orders are not restricted to domestic violence situations. For a comprehensive review of these jurisdictional differences see N Seddon, *Domestic Violence in Australia — The Legal Response* (2nd ed, Sydney: Federation Press, 1993), Ch 5.

The Australian Law Reform Commission (ALRC) in *Domestic Violence*, Report No 30 (Canberra: AGPS, 1986) viewed these laws as a supplement to rather than as a substitute for, the criminal law. In the ALRC's view, protection orders should not be regarded as a "soft option": para 90. Protection orders are designed to restrain conduct that falls outside the scope of the traditional criminal law, such as intimidation. Intimidation includes harassment, molestation and causing the apprehension of injury or property damage: for example, *Crimes Act* 1900 (NSW), s 562A(1). To grant an order, the relevant facts must be proved on the balance of probabilities.

The ALRC considered that the higher criminal standard of beyond reasonable doubt operated as a significant hurdle in the way of victims of domestic violence invoking the ordinary criminal law and caused a "lower strike rate": para 80. The protection order offers greater flexibility than binding over since the court may impose prohibitions or restrictions on behaviour as appear necessary and desirable to the court: for example, *Crimes Act* 1900 (NSW), s 562B(4). Protection orders may be tailored to the specific facts of the case; orders commonly restrain defendants from contacting specified persons; entering or remaining in specified places. They may also require positive action, such as the return of specific property, and so can perform a restitutionary as well as protective function. An interim order may be granted, and in some instances this may be done by telephone, providing police and victims with "on the spot" remedies: s 562H. Breach of an order is an arrestable offence and, without further proof of actual or apprehended violence, is punishable by fine or imprisonment: s 562I. As breach is an offence, it must be proved to the criminal standard of beyond reasonable doubt.

As part of the Commonwealth's Partnerships Against Domestic Violence, an Intergovernmental Working Group was recently established to examine the operation of protection orders in Australia with a view to developing a uniform domestic violence law: *Model Domestic Violence Laws*, Report (1999). The Group favoured a scheme of protection orders that was restricted to domestic violence situations and rejected proposals to extend the laws "to situations of a casual or purely temporary nature, such as dating relationships": p 27. The Report contains model legislation for protection orders with detailed rules governing the scope and conditions upon which these protection orders may be granted, as well as provisions governing the mutual recognition of orders across all Australian jurisdictions and New Zealand. Cross jurisdictional enforcement will be aided by the establishment of a national database of protection orders called "CrimTrac".

Protection orders in cases of domestic violence were enacted to deal with perceived deficiencies with existing criminal laws and the *Family Law Act* injunction: N Seddon, *Domestic Violence in Australia — The Legal Response* (2nd ed, Sydney: Federation Press, 1993), p 76. In the view of the ALRC, existing remedies such as binding over were inflexible, cumbersome, and lacked effective enforcement procedures: ALRC, para 85. Claims by the ALRC that breach proceedings could not be easily invoked were arguably overstated. Under the existing common law, *apprehended* as well as actual violence or property damage may justify entry, arrest without warrant and detention under the general powers to prevent a breach of the peace: see below, p 765. Existing public order powers provide a wide range of "on-the-spot" remedies, as well as legal authority to arrest a person who is causing or likely to cause a breach of the peace, and convey him or her to a magistrate for the purpose of binding over, or to be punished if any existing recognisance has been breached.

As noted previously, binding over is neither benign nor lacking in punitive force: refusal to consent to binding over, as well as breach, may result in fines or imprisonment. Outside the domestic violence context, the police regard binding over orders as an effective means of preventing and restraining threatening or harassing conduct not amounting to a criminal offence. In these cases, binding over offers the police, prosecutors and magistrates a powerful diversionary tool that restrains future violence while avoiding the stigma of conviction. As Seddon has pointed out, ordinary public order powers such as binding over can still be used as "gap-fillers" to deal with cases that do not fall within the terms of domestic violence legislation: p 77.

From a legal perspective, protective orders offer some improvement on binding over and the reliance on the ordinary criminal law. The principal advantages of protective orders relate to their clarity (and hence educative function) and "streamlined" enforcement procedure. By comparison to binding over, protective orders can be tailored to particular circumstances, imposing specific rather than vague prohibitions on the defendant. The real difficulty faced by women victimised by domestic violence is not the absence of adequate laws, but rather the unwillingness of the police to take action. Even in relation to protective orders designed to deal with domestic violence, police attitudes are a key factor in their effectiveness. As Ngaire Naffine observed in her evaluation of protection orders in South Australia ("Domestic Violence and the Law: a Study of s 99 of the *Justices Act* (SA)" (Adelaide: Women's Adviser's Office, Dept of the Premier and Cabinet, 1985), p 94):

> [A] common theme ... is that whenever the police are committed, enthusiastic and conscientious, victims of domestic violence receive justice.

Naffine's research is discussed in ALRC, *Domestic Violence*, Report No 30 (Canberra: AGPS, 1986), p 48. Research from other jurisdictions, such as Queensland, reach the similar conclusion that the provision of express powers to deal with domestic violence have significantly changed police attitudes to intervening in these cases. This research is reviewed in Mark Finnane, *Police and Government* (Melbourne: Oxford University Press, 1994), p 109.

Some jurisdictions have directly addressed the common law's reluctance to interfere with the exercise of police discretion in domestic violence cases. Legislation mandating investigation of such cases has been introduced in some jurisdictions. Mandatory policing is a radical deviation from the doctrine of police independence which is reflected in the judicial reluctance to interfere in the ordinary exercise of the police discretion not to intervene in a particular case. In New South Wales and Queensland, for example, the legislature has enacted a statutory duty to investigate whether an act of domestic violence has been committed in cases where the police officer believes or suspects that domestic violence has been, is being or is likely to be committed: *Crimes Act* 1900 (NSW), s 562H; *Domestic Violence (Family Protection) Act* 1989 (Qld), s 67. The Intergovernmental Working Party has recommended the adoption of a similar statutory duty to investigate in cases of domestic violence: *Model Domestic Violence Laws*, Report (1999), pp 38-41. This statutory duty may be contrasted with the wide discretion granted to police in relation operational decision-making for other offences. The centrality of discretion to public order policing generally is reviewed below at pp 780ff.

The Role of Victims: Aiding and Abetting Domestic Violence

The restricted choices open to women in abusive relationships often results in the resumption of cohabitation in breach of the order. Frustrated by this seemingly unending cycle of violence and reconciliation, police and prosecutors have begun to institute charges of aiding and abetting against women who have "invited" the defendant into their homes in violation of the protection order. The issues of legal principle and policy surrounding this use of complicity are discussed in Chapter 8: pp 397ff.

Rather than view the question of the appropriate legal response in terms of either criminal or civil law, it is possible to develop an integrated regulatory strategy based on the "enforcement pyramid": see Ch 1, p 62. John Braithwaite has conceptualised the enforcement pyramid for domestic violence as follows:

DIAGRAM 1:   **Example of a Domestic Violence Enforcement Pyramid**

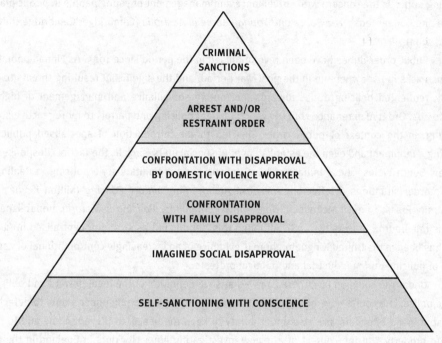

J Braithwaite, "Inequality and Republican Criminology", J Hagan and R Peterson (eds), *Crime and Inequality* (Stanford, CA: Stanford University Press, 1995), p 301.

Consistent with his republican principles (see Chapter 1, p 61), criminal sanctions would be used as a "last resort", and greater attention would be given to strengthen community based crime prevention programs.

2.3 POLICING PUBLIC DISORDER

More than any other area of the criminal law, public order law delimits the function of the police in modern society. Public order laws reinforce the mission of the police as one of "order maintenance" rather than "law enforcement". As reflected in the founding Commissioners' Instructions for police forces established in 19th century England and Australia, the paramount duty of the police was the prevention of disorder and crime rather than law enforcement. As Finnane points out, policing in the 19th century was an exercise in the governance of drunks, prostitutes, vagrants and other disorderly elements for the benefit of the respectable classes: *Police and Government* (Melbourne: Oxford University Press, 1994), Ch 1. Keeping the peace demarcated the "respectable" from the "rough" classes, and thus played a crucial role in "reproducing inequalities in society or even in enhancing them": p 103.

In modern policing the primary task assigned to police remains "moral street-sweeping": R Reiner, "Policing and the Police" in M Maguire, R Morgan and R Reiner (eds), *The Oxford Handbook of Criminology* (Oxford: Oxford University Press, 1994), p 742. Indeed, the primacy of peace-keeping has been further reinforced in the 20th century by hiving off crime detection as a "specialised" function of non-uniformed detectives working within the Criminal Investigation Department or Bureau (CID or CIB). As we shall see below (p 784), in the Australian context, a large part of general policing duties is the concern with surveillance and management of young people in public places: R White and C Alder (eds), *The Police and Young People in Australia* (Cambridge: Cambridge University Press, 1994).

Public order duties have been revolutionised in the period since 1945. As Finnane points out, the increases in car ownership in the post-war period, and the significant resulting threats to public safety, reoriented policing duties towards the routine surveillance and management of highways: pp 100-104. Order maintenance shifted away from beat policing and patrols to more reactive styles of policing. In the context of public order, this led to the introduction of specialised public order training, equipment and even the establishment of special units, such as the Tactical Response Group in New South Wales. These initiatives have encouraged paramilitary-style policing in dealing with public order situations: T Jefferson, *The Case Against Paramilitary Policing* (Milton Keynes: Open University Press, 1990); J McCulloch, *Blue Army: Paramilitary Policing in Victoria*, unpublished PhD Thesis (Melbourne University, 1998). Although this trend is not as strong or centralised in Australia as it has been in the United Kingdom, there is evidence of an increasingly confrontational or assertive style of policing during industrial and political protests.

Under the common law, there is no exhaustive definition of the legal powers and obligations of the police. The courts have observed that the police, as well as being under a duty to detect crime and apprehend offenders, are also under a duty to keep the peace, to prevent crime and to protect private property.[10] In the context of a review investigating inner city riots in England in the 1980s, Lord Scarman argued that the primary duty of the police was the maintenance of the Queen's Peace, a duty that is more fundamental than upholding the law: *The Brixton Disorders 10-12 April 1981* (London: HMSO, Cmnd 8427), pp 62-63.

A similar view has been expressed by judges in Australia. As Wright J observed in *North Broken Hill; Ex parte Commissioner of Police (Tas)* (1992) 61 A Crim R 390 the "peacekeeping powers of the police are of supreme importance": at 396. The importance of public order to modern policing is reflected in the *National Code of Ethics for the Police in Australia* (1981), which identifies the following objectives for the police:

(i) the preservation of the peace;

(ii) the protection of life and property; and

(iii) the prevention and detection of crime.

---

10 *R v Waterfield* [1964] 1 QB 164 at 170; *R v Metropolitan Police Commissioner; Ex parte Blackburn* [1968] 2 QB 118; *R v Metropolitan Police Commissioner; Ex parte Blackburn (No 3)* [1973] QB 241; *R v Chief Constable of Sussex; Ex parte International Trader's Ferry Ltd* [1999] 2 AC 418.

These duties have been enacted into legislation by s 8 of the *Australian Federal Police Act* 1979 (Cth); s 6 of the *Police Service Act* 1990 (NSW); s 2(3), (4) of the *Police Service Administration Act* 1990 (Qld); Pt V of the *Police Act* 1892 (WA). See further D Bradley, "Policing" in K Hazlehurst (ed), *Crime and Justice* (Sydney: LBC, 1996), pp 353-354.

In most jurisdictions, the common law powers to prevent and suppress public disorder are supplemented and extended by a wide range of statutory powers reserved exclusively for the police. These statutory powers cover a vast terrain, empowering the police to "move on" individuals in public places; to stop, question and search suspected persons; to enter and remain on property to prevent disorder; to summons or arrest individuals involved in disorderly conduct not involving actual or threatened violence. Moreover, special "non-criminal" powers have been granted to the police to deal with particular threats to public order, such as "domestic violence", individuals whose state of intoxication or mental illness makes them a threat to themselves or others. It is important, when reviewing public order law, to recognise that these specific statutory police powers and offences supplement the extensive powers to prevent crime and disorder under the common law.

Breach of the Peace: A Common Law Renaissance

Academic discussion of public order law in the 1970s and 1980s focused on public order offences such as riot, rout, unlawful assembly and obstruction offences: A Hiller, *Public Order and the Law* (Sydney: Law Book Company Ltd, 1983), pp 149ff. Because of the uncertainty around the concept, breach of the peace was considered largely of historical interest: E Campbell and H Whitmore, *Freedom in Australia* (Revised ed, Sydney: Sydney University Press, 1973), pp 139-144; G Flick, *Civil Liberties in Australia* (Sydney: Law Book Company Ltd, 1981), pp 15-18 and Ch 4. Following the clarification of the concept of breach of the peace in *R v Howell* [1982] QB 416, the police became more confident in the exercise of their common law powers. For a review of the cases where the common law governing breach of the peace was invoked to deal with public protests and industrial picketing see B Gaze and M Jones, *Law, Liberty and Australian Democracy* (Sydney: Law Book Company Ltd, 1990), pp 134-152.

2.4 BREACH OF THE PEACE

The common law concept of "breach of the peace" remains central to public order law in Australia. Breach of the peace provides the basis for exercising the common law powers to prevent disorder. It is not an offence of itself, though engaging in conduct that causes or is likely to cause a breach of the peace may involve the commission of other offences, such as assault, affray, or criminal damage. Breach of the peace is also an ingredient of other offences such as unlawful assembly and riot. As noted in the preceding section (see p 754), the concept of breach of the peace has been incorporated into the statutory powers available to the police to enter onto private premises in situations of emergency: *Crimes Act* 1900 (ACT), ss 349A-C. Although the police often prefer to rely on statutory powers, the common law remains a residual source of powers when the former do not cover the particular situation confronting the police.

MEANING AND SCOPE OF "BREACH OF THE PEACE"

The leading authority on breach of the peace is the English Court of Appeal decision in *R v Howell* [1982] QB 416. In this case, Watkins LJ (at 427) held that the concept should be defined as follows:

> there is a breach of the peace whenever harm is actually done or is likely to be done to a person or in his [or her] presence to his [or her] property or a person is in fear of being so harmed through an assault, an affray, a riot, unlawful assembly or other disturbance.

The definition of "breach of the peace" in *Howell* included apprehended as well as actual harm to persons or property. The inclusion of harm to property constituted a significant extension of the common law. Prior to this "clarification", a review of the available precedent on breach of the peace revealed a lack of authoritative definition, though the courts seemed to suggest that breach of the peace must involve "some danger to the person": G Williams, "Arrest for Breach of the Peace" [1954] Crim LR 578 at 579. Significantly, in providing an authoritative definition of breach of the peace, the Court of Appeal (at 426) in *Howell* attached little weight to these older authorities:

> The older cases are of considerable interest but they are not a sure guide to what the term is understood to mean today, since keeping the peace in this country in the latter half of the 20th century presents formidable problems which bear upon the evolving process of the development of this [branch] of the common law.

The social forces at work in shaping public order law in England in the mid-1980s were high levels of unemployment coupled with poor community-policing relations that had sparked large-scale inner-city riots across the country. These riots produced major changes to the traditional reactive style of policing public disorder, as subsequently witnessed in the coordinated and pro-active policing of disorder during the protracted Miners' Strike: B Fine and R Millar (eds), *Policing the Miners' Strike* (London: Lawrence and Wishart, 1985); S McCabe and P Wallington, *The Police, Public Order and Civil Liberties: Legacies of the Miners' Strike* (London: Routledge, 1988).

Although the public order problems in Australian society have been less serious, the broad definition of "breach of the peace" in *Howell* has been accepted as a correct statement of the common law in Australia: *Innes v Weate* [1984] Tas SR 14 at 22, per Cosgrove J; *Panos v Hayes* (1987) 44 SASR 148 at 151, Legoe J.

POWERS TO PREVENT A BREACH OF THE PEACE: NECESSARY AND REASONABLE STEPS

Under the common law, any citizen is empowered to take any necessary steps to prevent or suppress a breach of the peace. In the 20th century, the courts have imposed the further condition that these steps must be reasonable in the circumstances. In *Albert v Lavin* [1982] AC 546, Lord Diplock (at 565) held that:

> [E]very citizen in whose presence a breach of the peace is being, or reasonably appears to be about to be, committed has the right to take reasonable steps to make the person who is breaking or threatening to break the peace refrain from doing so; and those reasonable steps in appropriate cases will include detaining him [or her] against his [or her] will.

At common law this is not only the right of every citizen, it is also his [or her] duty, although, except in the case of a citizen who is a constable, it is a duty of imperfect obligation.

The common law has conferred both criminal and civil immunity for individuals who take necessary and reasonable steps to prevent or suppress a breach of the peace. These steps have included trespass, assault, dispersal, detention, confiscation of property, erecting roadblocks and even controlling the numbers of individuals on a picket line.[11] As a measure of last resort, the common law confers on individuals, including police, the power to arrest without warrant any person whose conduct is causing or is likely to cause a breach of the peace.[12] This power may be contrasted with the general power of arrest without warrant which only permits apprehension and detention where the person has committed, or is in the act of committing, an offence for the purpose of bringing that person before a court to answer charges: *Williams v the Queen* (1986) 161 CLR 278. In relation to breach of the peace, a power of arrest without warrant has been granted for the purpose of *preventing* crime and disorder rather than as a forensic tool for commencing proceedings against persons suspected of a criminal offence.

In Queensland, the common law power to deal with a breach of the peace has been clarified and supplemented by the *Police Powers And Responsibilities Act* 1997 (Qld). Section 89 of this legislation contains examples to guide the police in the practical application of these powers:

Dealing with breach of the peace

(1) This section applies if a police officer reasonably suspects —

    (a) a breach of the peace is happening or has happened; or

    (b) there is an imminent likelihood of a breach of the peace; or

    (c) there is a threatened breach of the peace.

(2) It is lawful for a police officer to take the steps the police officer considers reasonably necessary to prevent the breach of the peace happening or continuing, or the conduct constituting the breach of the peace again happening, even though the conduct prevented might otherwise be lawful.

Examples —

1. The police officer may detain a person until the need for the detention no longer exists.

2. A person who pushes in to the front of a queue may be directed to go to the end of the queue.

3. Property that may be used in or for breaching the peace may be seized to prevent the danger.

---

11 *Humphries v Connor* (1864) 171 CLR 1 (assault); *O' Kelly v Harvey* (1883) 15 Cox CC 435 (assault); *Thomas v Sawkin* [1935] 2 KB 249 (trespass to property); *Albert v Lavin* [1981] 3 WLR 955 (detention); *Piddington v Bates* [1961] 1 WLR 162 (power to limit the number of picketers); *Moss v McLachlan* [1984] IRLR 76 (power to use road blocks by the police to prevent secondary picketing); *Minot v McKay (Police)* [1987] BCL 722 (power to confiscate a protestor's megaphone); *Commissioner of Police (Tas); Ex parte North Broken Hill Ltd* (1992) 61 A Crim R 390 (power to disperse picketers). See W Birtles, "The Common Law Power of Police to Control Public Meetings" (1973) 34 MLR 587 at 590.

12 *R v Howell* [1982] QB 416 at 427; *Innes v Weate* [1984] Tas R 14 at 22; *Nicolson v Avon* [1991] 1 VR 212 at 223; *Commissioner of Police (Tas); Ex parte North Broken Hill Ltd* (1992) 61 A Crim R 390 at 396.

Preventing a Breach of the Peace: A Citizen's Right or Duty

In *Albert v Lavin* [1982] AC 546, Lord Diplock suggested (strictly obiter) that it was the duty of every citizen to assist preventing breaches of the peace: at 565. Is this duty placed on citizens to assist police to suppress disorder a moral or legal one? In earlier times, the obligation to assist suppressing a breach of the peace could be viewed as a legal duty since failure to do so was a misdemeanour. In *Brown* (1841) Car & M 314 the accused refused to help quell a riot arising from an illegal prize fight and was convicted of refusing to assist a person who was taking action to prevent a breach of the peace. This offence has been codified in Tasmania, where it is an offence to neglect to aid the police in suppressing a riot or arresting an offender or in preserving the peace: *Criminal Code* 1924 (Tas), ss 116-117. In South Australia and Western Australia, the Commissioner of Police has power to issue directions for regulating traffic, preventing obstructions and maintaining order. It is an offence not to comply with request of police officers to observe directions if acquainted with directions: *Summary Offences Act* 1953 (SA), s 59; *Police Act* 1892 (WA), s 52. In common law jurisdictions, the offence of refusing to assist the police in preserving the public peace, though technically extant, has fallen into disuse. See further D Nicolson, "The Citizen's Duty to Assist the Police" [1992] Crim LR 611.

The formula of "necessary and reasonable steps" to prevent a breach of the peace is highly permissive, providing a wide range of police powers to prevent disorder. As Simon Bronitt and George Williams have concluded in "Political Freedom as an Outlaw: Republican Theory and Political Protest" (1996) 18(2) *Adelaide Law Review* 289 (at 322):

> The list of measures available to prevent a breach of the peace is not closed ... Within this broad and open-ended framework, the only limit upon the further development of preventive measures is the ingenuity and imagination of the police and the judicial acceptance that the steps taken are "reasonable" in the circumstances.

Because of their potential breadth, the courts have counselled restraint in the exercise of these preventive measures. The use of arrest is discouraged except as a "measure of last resort": *Commissioner of Police (Tas); Ex parte North Broken Hill Ltd* (1992) 61 A Crim R 390 at 396. In this case Wright J held (at 397) that police on duty at the picket line had at their disposal a wide range of "transitory preventive measures" falling short of arrest to prevent a violent confrontation:

> [I]f police do intervene at this point, they do not have to arrest. They may be able to persuade the picketer to move away or they may be able to physically remove him [or her] before an actual offence has been committed. They have the power to do this and do not commit an unlawful assault themselves in doing so.

In *Forbutt v Blake* (1981) 51 FLR 465 Connor ACJ held that preventive powers, such as dispersal and arrest, may be exercised only where there is a reasonable apprehension or belief that a breach of the peace is imminent: at 469-470. Adopting the test applied in the English decision of *Piddington v Bates* [1961] 1 WLR 162, Connor ACJ (at 469) stressed that the belief in the imminence of disorder must be reasonable:

a mere statement by a police constable that he [or she] anticipated a breach of the peace is not enough to justify his [or her] taking action to prevent it; the facts must be such that he [or she] could reasonably anticipate not a remote, but a real, possibility of a breach of the peace.

The requirement that a breach of the peace be reasonably anticipated as a real possibility reinforces the conditional authority of the power of arrest. But how is imminence of disorder to be determined under this formula? Imminence may be measured both in temporal terms, as well as physical proximity. However, as Connor ACJ acknowledged, the test could not be defined with precision. He concluded that imminence must be a "relative concept": at 471. On these facts, he accepted that the risk of disorder occurring within five to ten minutes could be an imminent breach of the peace.

Notions of imminence have tended to be excessively deferential to the police assessment of the likelihood of disorder: see, for example, *Moss v McLachlan* [1985] IRLR 76. In *Forbutt v Blake*, considerable evidential weight was attached to the assessment and experience of the police in determining imminence. Not only were police able to rely on their own observation at the scene to determine the imminence of disorder, Connor ACJ accepted (at 470) that the police could legitimately consider media reports, including reports of the protestors' *own* fears that their conduct may provoke a hostile response. Concerned about the flexibility of these tests, some academics have argued that prior restraint of peaceful and otherwise lawful exercise of civil and political rights requires *substantial* evidence of the nature and likelihood of the threat to public order: SA de Smith, *Constitutional and Administrative Law* (7th ed, Harmondsworth: Penguin, 1996), pp 495-496.

The elasticity of "reasonable anticipation" and "imminence" in English and Australian law may be contrasted with the more stringent approach taken in the United States. Mindful that prior restraint of conduct may unduly interfere with freedom of speech and peaceful assembly constitutionally protected by the Bill of Rights, the Supreme Court has held that there must be a "clear and present danger" of violence before these rights may be justifiably restricted: *Whitney v California*, 274 US 357 (1927). It has been suggested that the implied freedom of political discussion under the Commonwealth Constitution "might be applied, in a case involving a restriction upon political discussion, to achieve a common law concept of imminence much closer to that developed in the United States": S Bronitt and G Williams, "Political Freedom as an Outlaw: Republican Theory and Political Protest" (1996) 18(2) *Adelaide Law Review* 289 at 324.

PROVOKING A BREACH OF THE PEACE: A SUBJECTIVE OR OBJECTIVE TEST

Preventive powers of arrest, detention and dispersal may be exercised against peaceful and otherwise lawful conduct on the ground that it causes or is likely to cause *others* to commit a breach of the peace. Questions have arisen whether the test for determining whether such conduct is likely to cause a breach of the peace should be judged subjectively or objectively. If an entirely subjective approach is taken, breach of the peace can operate as a "Hecklers' Charter".

A subjective approach to this question was adopted in *Jordan v Burgoyne* [1963] 2 WLR 1045. In this case, the accused, a speaker for a political party called The National Front, attempted to address a rally in Trafalgar Square in London. In the course of his speech, he directed racially inflammatory remarks, such as "Hitler was right", at a small group of hecklers within the audience who were attempting to disrupt his speech. The group was described in the head-note as comprising "many Jews, CND [Campaign For Nuclear Disarmament] supporters and communists". The Divisional Court had to determine whether the speaker's conduct constituted offensive conduct likely to provoke a breach of the peace contrary to s 5 of the *Public Order Act* 1936 (UK).

Delivering the judgment of the court, Lord Parker CJ held (at 1047-1048) that the test of whether conduct is likely to provoke a breach of the peace is a subjective one:

> [T]here is no room here for any test as to whether any member of the audience is a reasonable man [or woman] or ordinary citizen ... [the accused] must take his [or her] audience as he [or she] finds them, and if those words to that audience or that part of the audience are likely to provoke a breach of the peace, then the speaker is guilty of an offence.

Lord Parker CJ attached no significant weight to the importance of freedom of speech or assembly. The decision affirmed that peaceful and otherwise lawful conduct may be criminalised simply because of its offensive impact on members of the audience and its tendency to provoke them to violence.

Lord Parker CJ adopted a *subjective* or natural consequence approach to causation, adapting the principle of causation used in tort and criminal law that "defendants must take their victims as they find them": see Ch 3, pp 167ff. This approach has serious ramifications for those individuals who wish to express unpopular political ideas to a potentially hostile audience.

The alternative approach would apply an *objective* standard based on the likely reaction of the reasonable or ordinary person, and whether she (or he) would be provoked to violence. There is some support for an objective test at first instance, though the matter has not yet been fully argued before an appellate court.[13] An objective approach would also be consistent with the test for offensive conduct, where offensiveness is determined by reference to the reasonable person who is presumed to be broad-minded and politically tolerant in her (or his) opinions: see below 3.1 'Offensive Conduct and Language Crimes': p 789.

The freedom to protest is regarded by police and judges as a question of balancing the legitimate aims of protecting civil and political liberties on the one hand, with the importance of preventing and suppressing crime and disorder on the other: *Commissioner of Police v Allen* (1984) 14 A Crim R 244, discussed below, 3.2 'Unlawful Assembly', p 797. The weakness of the "balancing approach" is that the exercise of civil and political rights is not accorded any fundamental status under the common law. As Bronitt and Williams have observed in "Political Freedom as an Outlaw: Republican Theory and Political Protest" (1996) 18(2) *Adelaide Law Review* 289 (at 294):

> Both the police and the courts are required to make decisions about the importance of competing interests within a legal framework which does not attach a relative weighting or significance to each of the interests in competition.

The scope for balancing is limited within a regulatory framework that does not recognise an express right to protest, and where the residue of political freedom is constantly under siege from an

---

13 *Commissioner of Police (Tas); Ex parte Nth Broken Hill Ltd* (1992) 61 A Crim R 390. Wright J held (at 396) that the issue was whether actions of the protesters "should give rise to a reasonable apprehension of a breach of the peace on the part of reasonable men and women".

expanding range of police powers and public order offences. For a critique of this utilitarian approach to balancing rights and interests in the context of public order powers, see B Gaze and M Jones, *Law, Liberty and Australian Democracy* (Sydney: Law Book Company Ltd, 1990), p 168.

The presumption in favour of preventive rather than remedial intervention, raises concern about the prior restraint of peaceful and otherwise lawful processions, assemblies and demonstrations on the ground that they are likely to provoke a violent or hostile response from opposing groups. As Denis Galligan has observed in "Preserving Public Protest: the Legal Approach" in L Gostin (ed), *Civil Liberties in Conflict* (London and New York: Routledge, 1988), pp 54-55:

> The trouble with this approach is that it gives insufficient importance to the freedom of protest; if it is vulnerable to the disruptive tactics of opposing groups, that freedom is of slight weight. It means that any protest, no matter how peaceful and orderly itself, may be the subject of intervention by the police merely because those hostile to its aims are able to create disruption amounting to a threat to the peace.

PERSPECTIVES ON HATE CRIMES

Free Speech or Psychic Injury

The legal protection accorded to peaceful yet provocative speech cases like *Jordan v Burgoyne* [1963] 2 WLR 1045 may depend on the nature of the accused's motivations. Under international human rights law, the prohibition of racist speech is considered a justifiable restriction on the freedoms of expression and assembly. Article 20(2) of the *International Covenant on Civil and Political Rights* (ICCPR) provides that "Any advocacy of national, racial or religious hatred that constitutes incitement to discrimination, hostility or violence shall be prohibited by law". Indeed, the *Convention on the Elimination of All Forms of Racial Discrimination* (CERD) New York, 7 March 1966, 660 UNTS 195, ATS 1975 No 40, goes further, and requires Member States to declare as an offence punishable by law all dissemination of ideas based on racial superiority or hatred: Art 4(a). At the time of ratification, the Australian Government noted that such conduct was not presently treated as an offence, though it was the intention to enact such legislation "at the first suitable moment". On 6 November 1984 Australia withdrew reservations and declarations to the ICCPR with the exception of reservations including a reservation to Art 20 (ATS 1984 No 1, p 12). The reservation states that "Australia interprets the rights provided for by Article 19, 21 and 22 as consistent with Article 20; accordingly, the Commonwealth and States having legislated with respect to the subject matter of the Article in matters of practical concern in the interests of public, the right is reserved not to introduce any further legislative provision on these matters."

Racial vilification was not made an offence under the *Racial Discrimination Act* 1975 (Cth). Rather, this Commonwealth Act, which was enacted to implement the obligations in CERD, made it "unlawful" to engage, otherwise than in private, in offensive conduct because of race, colour or national or ethnic origin: s 18C. Racial vilification provides a ground for making a complaint to the Human Rights and Equal Opportunity Commission (HREOC) for conciliation or adjudication: ss 22, 24. The legislation does not exclude the operation of State and Territory anti-discrimination provisions (including offences) prohibiting racial vilification: s 18.

In many jurisdictions, the racial insults hurled in *Jordan* could now be prosecuted under special offences prohibiting incitement to racial hatred: s 5A of the *Public Order Act* 1936 (UK), amended by s 70 of the *Race Relations Act* 1976 (UK). The various legislative models for vilification offences enacted in Canada, Europe, New Zealand, New South Wales, United States and the United Kingdom are reviewed in HREOC, *Racist Violence* (Canberra: AGPS, 1991), Ch 11. In New South Wales, the offence of "serious racial vilification" is contained in s 20D of the *Anti-Discrimination Act* 1977 (NSW). The vilification must manifest itself by a "public act" (s 20B) and occur by means which include threats of physical harm towards persons or groups of persons or property or inciting others to perpetrate such threats (s 20D). Clearly such threats and incitement could be prosecuted under the general criminal law, though the racial motivation behind such conduct should be deemed legally irrelevant by the court: HREOC, *Racist Violence* (Canberra: AGPS, 1991), p 276. Some empirical evidence suggests that racial motivation may lead to more lenient treatment by police and prosecutors, operating as a mitigating rather than aggravating factor: p 277. Unlike the general criminal law which tends to suppress the political motivation for conduct, racial vilification offences direct legal attention towards the motives of the accused.

HREOC recommended that Australia should implement the CERD without reservation. It proposed that specific offences under the *Crimes Act* 1914 (Cth) should be enacted proscribing (i) racist violence and intimidation; and (ii) incitement to racial violence: *Racist Violence* (Canberra: AGPS, 1991), pp 296-302. Unfortunately, these proposals have not been implemented. This reticence may be due to the concern that laws against racial vilification may violate the implied freedom of political discussion under the Commonwealth Constitution recognised by the High Court in *Australian Capital Television Pty Ltd v Commonwealth* (1992) 177 CLR 106. However, it has been suggested that these constitutional concerns are overstated since "there is no basis for concluding that racial vilification is 'political speech' in terms relevant to the implied constitutional freedom recognised by the High Court": L McNamara and T Solomon, "The Commonwealth Racial Hatred Act 1995: Achievement or Disappointment?" (1996) 18(2) *Adelaide Law Review* 259 at 281.

From a philosophical perspective, the outlawing of racial vilification may be viewed as a justifiable restriction on freedom of speech, assembly and association because of the "harm" that it causes to others. Wojciech Sadurski identified three harms associated with racist hate speech in "Racial Vilification, Psychic Harm and Affirmative Action", T Campbell and W Sadurski (eds), *Freedom of Communication* (Aldershot: Dartmouth, 1994):

1. harm results from violent reactions by the victims; (as in *Jordan*)

2. others are incited to commit violence;

3. victims suffer psychic injury.

In Sadurski's view, (1) and (2) pose little difficulty for liberal theory and may be accommodated fairly easily within the present law. In the absence of violence, however, interference with racist speech poses greater difficulties in terms of justification. Rather than seeking to justify prohibition on the grounds of affirmative action, Sadurski argues that offensive speech may be prohibited where it constitutes a form of "psychic injury". The implications of this approach are further explored below in 3.1 'Offensive Conduct and Language Crimes'.

Racial vilification offences perform an important symbolic role in outlawing racist violence. However, there is a contrary argument that it would be far better, symbolically and practically, to promote the rigorous enforcement of the existing offences (of which there are no shortage) and forthright punishment of such conduct: P Gordon, "Racist Harassment and Violence" in E Stanko (ed), *Perspectives on Violence* (London: Quartet Books, 1994), p 51.

A range of similar issues has arisen in relation to the criminalisation of hate speech targeting gays and lesbians, and whether such vilification may be legitimately prohibited by the criminal law. For a review of hate crime generally, see C Cunneen, D Fraser and S Tomsen (eds), *Faces of Hate — Hate Crime in Australia* (Sydney: Hawkins Press, 1997).

PROVOKING A BREACH OF THE PEACE: PRIOR RESTRAINT OF PEACEFUL PROTEST

Some judges have sought to impose restrictions on public order laws that have the potential to operate as a prior restraint on political protest. In *Forbutt v Blake* [1981] 51 FLR 465 the police took action to prevent members of an organisation called "Women Against Rape" from participating in the annual ANZAC parade in Canberra. Dressed in black and carrying placards stating "Soldiers are Phallic Murderers", "Patriots Kill" and "Heroes Rape", the group of women assembled to march about 500 metres (five or six minutes' walk) from the Australian War Memorial. The police stopped them marching on the ground that their behaviour was likely to provoke a breach of the peace. When the group refused to disperse, the women were arrested, charged and convicted with obstructing a police member in the execution of his duty contrary to s 64 of the *Australian Federal Police Act* 1979 (Cth).

The use of the offence of "obstructing police" provided the Supreme Court of the Australian Capital Territory with an opportunity to examine the common law powers to prevent a breach of the peace. Connor ACJ (at 469) noted that the sole basis for the police intervention in this case "was that some members of the public might be provoked into committing acts against the group which would constitute a breach or breaches of the peace". The issue raised at the appeal was whether the police had the power to stop lawful and peaceful conduct merely because it was likely to provoke violence by others.

Connor ACJ declined to follow an earlier English decision *Duncan v Jones* [1936] 1 KB 218 that had supported a conviction for obstruction on similar facts. By drawing a distinction between those powers that derived from the common law preventive jurisdiction (breach of the peace) and those that are conferred by statute (obstructing police), he concluded (at 475) that the police "in executing their duty to keep the peace, were restricted to the means recognised in that jurisdiction". He acknowledged that any concerns about conceptual purity were subsidiary to the dangers of adopting any alternative construction of the offence. In the opinion of Connor ACJ, the alternative (broader) construction of obstruction could lead to "quite extraordinary results", including that Members of Parliament could be forbidden to address hostile audiences during election campaigns. Having regard to the seriousness of the offence of obstruction, Connor ACJ concluded (at 475):

> I am quite unable to attribute an intention to the legislature to expose a person to such a penalty for disobeying a police order to cease a lawful activity in circumstances where the only relevant police duty is to prevent a breach of the peace by other citizens against him [or her].

The imaginative interpretive strategy employed by Connor ACJ in *Forbutt* offers some protection against prior restraint of peaceful and otherwise lawful forms of protest. In these cases, policing should not be directed against those who are being threatened, but rather at those who are threatening violence. Connor ACJ endorsed (at 475) earlier judicial dicta in *R v Londonderry Justices* (1891) 28 LR Ir 440 at 450 per O'Brien J:

> If danger arises from the exercise of lawful rights resulting in a breach of the peace, the remedy is the presence of sufficient force to prevent the result, not the legal condemnation of those who exercise those rights.

The rejection of *Duncan v Jones* and the attempt to impose limits on the offence of obstruction in *Forbutt* have been commended by English commentators: DGT Williams, "Criminal Law and Administrative Law: Problems of Procedure and Reasonableness" in P Smith (ed), *Criminal Law: Essays in Honour of JC Smith* (London: Butt, 1987), p 179.

Notwithstanding this resounding caution against prior restraint in *Forbutt,* the decision hardly provides a secure legal foothold for freedom of expression, assembly and association. Although disobedience of the police in such situations cannot constitute the offence of obstruction, Connor ACJ affirmed (at 476) that a demonstrator who is engaged in peaceful and other lawful protest may still be liable to other types of intervention, including arrest, to prevent a breach of the peace. Also, the limitation on obstruction applies only where the police are exercising *common law* powers. Thus, a charge of obstruction is presumably available against persons involved in peaceful conduct that interferes with statutory powers, such as the power to enter and remain on premises to prevent the commission of an offence, to prevent a breach of the peace, or to protect life or property under ss 349A-C of the *Crimes Act* 1900 (ACT). The scope of *Forbutt* has been further restricted by legislation in many jurisdictions that imposes on police statutory duties to keep the peace, prevent crime and disorder: see above, p 763. A person who obstructs or hinders police while exercising these statutory duties would be guilty of obstruction.

The judicial concern about prior restraint in *Forbutt* resonates with the approach taken in *Beatty v Gillbanks* (1882) 9 QBD 308. In this case, members of the Salvation Army were bound over to keep the peace for participating in a parade on the ground that their conduct was likely to provoke a tumultuous assembly by an opposing group, the Skeleton Army. An appeal against the binding over was allowed on the grounds that an assembly of Salvationists pursuing a lawful and peaceful activity could not constitute an unlawful assembly merely because of the presence of others who caused or threatened to cause a breach of the peace. The judges affirmed that the assembly of the Salvationists was lawful, that it had not intended to provoke violence and that the violence threatened stemmed entirely from the hostile members of the opposing group. In upholding the appeal, Field J concluded (at 314) that the justices had wrongly based their decision on the idea "that a man [or woman] may be convicted for doing a lawful act if he [or she] knows that his [or her] doing it may cause another to do an unlawful act. There is no authority for such a proposition ...".

Beatty v Gillbanks provided a glimmer of hope that the courts, without the assistance of an entrenched Bill of Rights or statutory right of peaceful assembly, can resist the prior restraint of peaceful political protest. Unfortunately, the decision has been confined to its facts and distinguished in subsequent cases. In *Duncan v Jones* [1936] 1 KB 218, Lord Hewitt CJ described the case as "unsatisfactory" and affirmed that a person who refused to comply with a police request to desist in peaceful and otherwise lawful conduct may quite properly be guilty of the statutory offence of obstructing the police: T Daintith, "Disobeying a Policeman. A Fresh Look at *Duncan v Jones*" [1966] *Public Law* 248 at 249-251. Although *Duncan v Jones* has not been followed in Australia (see *Forbutt v Blake* [1981] 51 FLR 465, discussed above, p 771), the residual legal space for engaging in peaceful protest is limited, and under constant threat from further statutory incursion. As DGT Williams has pointed out, the protective scope of *Beatty* is limited "as those who seek to protest in public can very easily run foul of the battery of laws and powers available to the police and prosecutors": "The Principle of *Beatty v Gillbanks*: A Reappraisal" in A Doob and E Greenspan (eds), *Perspectives in Criminal Law: Essays in Honour of John Edwards* (Ontario: Canada Law Book Inc, 1985), p 117. Notwithstanding this limitation, Williams argues that *Beatty v Gillbanks* may still have a role to play as a direction to judges (rather than to the police) cautioning against any peremptory exercise of public order powers or offences against peaceful and otherwise lawful conduct. In Williams' view, a distinction should be drawn between "prior control" and "instant response". In relation to the latter, restriction of peaceful and otherwise lawful conduct may be justifiable in situations where the police "on the spot" reasonably anticipate that a breach of the peace is imminent: p 116. In cases involving hostile audiences, the appropriate response is the presence of sufficient numbers of police to ensure that the individuals threatening violence can be contained. Although this is a desirable outcome, in operational terms such an approach may place intolerable financial and human resource burdens on the police. This was apparent in the APPM case at Burnie (considered below, p 781): see also *R v Chief Constable of Sussex; Ex parte International Traders Ferry Ltd* [1999] 2 AC 418. In that case police intervention against the hostile elements obstructing individuals who wished to return to work required one of the largest police operations ever mounted in Tasmania and resulted in a serious escalation in the tension and violence on the picket line.

Galligan states that the authorities on hostile audiences reflect "two different and conflicting approaches, one more protective of public protest than the others, but neither developed adequately": "Preserving Public Protest: the Legal Approach" in L Gostin (ed), *Civil Liberties in Conflict* (London and New York: Routledge, 1988), p 55. The principle in *Beatty v Gillbanks*, though more protective of political freedom at one level, offers no guidance to the police or the courts in situations where *both* groups of protestors legitimately claim to be exercising lawful rights. The principle proves difficult, if not impossible, to apply where the opposing groups are comprised of *both* peaceful and hostile elements. The lack of guidance on how the police and judges should prioritise the exercise of conflicting lawful rights is apparent in the judgment of Wright J in *Commissioner of Police (Tas); Ex parte North Broken Hill Ltd* (1992) 61 A Crim R 390. In reviewing the legality of police action at a picket line in Burnie, Wright J directed the police to break through the picket line on the ground that workers, who were exercising their lawful right to work, were being obstructed by picketers. In support of his decision, Wright J approved (at 398) the dicta in *R v Londonderry Justices* also cited in *Forbutt's Case*: p 772. In his view, it made no difference that the picketers were acting in a peaceful and lawful manner: an obstruction involving face to face confrontation is conduct likely to provoke violence on the part of the workers who were exercising their lawful right to work. No special weight was attached to the fact that the picketers were exercising their right to freedom of expression, assembly and association protected under the *International Covenant on Civil and*

Political Rights. Wright J dismissed an argument that the protestors on the picket line had lawful rights, concluding that "persons picketing in furtherance of an industrial dispute have no special rights in the eyes of the law": at 395. The judicial attention to the fundamental human rights in conflict is inadequate. As Bronitt and Williams conclude in "Political Freedom as an Outlaw: Republican Theory and Political Protest" (1996) 18(2) *Adelaide Law Review* 289 (at 320):

> What is remarkable is that three fundamental human rights, namely the freedoms of expression, assembly and association, can be "lost" within the interstices of the common law. To ensure that this does not occur, the law ought to provide explicit guidance (both to the police and the courts) as to how the exercise of *competing* lawful rights should be accommodated and how those rights should be prioritised.

The law in this area has tended to suppress political and human rights questions, resolving the legitimacy of peaceful conduct provoking disorder through legal technicalities such as subjective or objective tests. As in other areas of the criminal law, the courts have reiterated the formal irrelevance of the (political) motives of participants. Though these powers to prevent disorder are represented as value-neutral, it is impossible to avoid the highly politicised context within which they are often exercised. The suppression of politics in public order law can only be partial. Indeed, the political, social and moral context of the disorder is often simply displaced to the less visible arena of police discretion and operational policies on arrest and prosecution. As Lacey and Wells in *Reconstructing Criminal Law* (2nd ed, London: Butt, 1998), p 153 state:

> Legal categories encapsulate the authoritative view of what constitutes illegitimate disorder, and more over, do so in a way which is not overtly political. The traditional doctrinal story about clear and general rules which are promulgated and applied as announced allows the political sting to be taken out of the suppression of disorder. Political power is exercised with a low profile by means of a wide discretionary power at all stages of the criminal process, leaving the law clean of political taint.

HUMAN RIGHTS PERSPECTIVES

Public Order and the Right to Protest

Under the common law the freedom to engage in political protest is not a positive legal or constitutional right, but rather is a residual and negative liberty. Freedom of speech, assembly and association is nothing more than the liberty of individuals, alone or in combination with others, to engage in conduct that is not prohibited by law: AV Dicey, *Introduction to the Study of the Law of the Constitution* (10th ed, London: Macmillan, 1959). As the Community Law Reform Committee of the Australian Capital Territory recently concluded, the right to assembly under the common law is nothing more than "the residue of freedom remaining when the restrictions imposed by law are taken into account": *Public Assemblies and Street Offences: Issues Paper No 10* (Canberra: ACT Government, 1994), p 6. The freedom to protest, rather than being protected by positive rights in legislation or a constitutional Bill of Rights, rests on interpretive presumptions or implications in favour of individual liberty: *Re Bolton; Ex parte Beane* (1987) 162 CLR 514 at 523 per Brennan J.

This model of civil liberties requires judicial vigilance since the "residue" of personal liberty is under constant threat from legislative incursion. As Connor Gearty and Keith Ewing have observed, "Freedom retreats in the face of laws that are constantly emerging, evolving and accumulating — but very rarely disappearing. They originate not only in Parliament but also in the courts. The residual nature of liberty means that it can never fight back": *Freedom Under Thatcher: Civil Liberties in Modern Britain* (Oxford: Clarendon Press, 1990), p 11.

The legislative expansion of public order powers and offences in the late 20th century has dramatically reduced the residual sphere of freedom within which fundamental freedoms may be exercised. In many cases the presumption of liberty is overlooked by the courts, or, where it is considered relevant, it is outweighed by the legitimate interest in preventing crime and disorder. In the absence of an express legal right to engage in peaceful protest, political freedom in Australia depends upon policing restraint, in particular the benevolent exercise of discretion *not* to use public order powers and offences.

Unlike the common law, peaceful assembly and the related rights of free expression and association are expressly protected under Arts 19 and 20 of the *Universal Declaration of Human Rights* (UDHR) and Arts 19, 21 and 22 of the *International Covenant of Civil and Political Rights* (ICCPR). However, these rights are not unqualified. Restrictions may be imposed on the right of peaceful assembly in accordance with the law and where necessary in a democratic society in the interests of national security or public safety, public order, protection of public health or morals or the protection of the rights and freedoms of others: Art 21. The common law powers to prevent a breach of the peace were recently challenged have been challenged on the ground that they violate the right to freedom of expression (Art 10), and assembly and association (Art 11) protected under the *European Convention on Human Rights* (ECHR). In *Steel and Others v the United Kingdom* (1999) 28 EHRR 603, the European Court of Human Rights held that laws governing breach of the peace, while impinging on the exercise of the freedom of expression, may be justified for the legitimate aim of preventing disorder and protecting the rights of others: para 96. In this case, the applicants had engaged in various acts of protest ranging from physical disruption of a grouse shoot and construction of a motorway, to the peaceful distribution of leaflets protesting arms sales outside a conference venue. The Court held that the arrests and detention of the applicants for interference or obstruction of lawful activities on the ground that it may provoke a breach of the peace had to satisfy the proportionality principle. That is, the interference with freedom of expression had to be proportionate to the legitimate aim pursued, due regard being had to the importance of freedom of expression: para 101. The Court held that the arrest and detention of the applicants who were interfering with the grouse shoot and motorway construction could be justified on the ground that it was "dangerous conduct". The further imprisonment of one applicant for refusing to accept the binding over order was upheld by the European Court on the ground that it was likely that she would have continued with the protest and that it was necessary for the maintenance of the rule of law and the authority of the judiciary: para 107. By contrast, the arrest and detention of the applicants who were peacefully distributing leaflets was not in accordance with law and was disproportionate: para 110.

Public order laws in Australia similarly impinge on freedoms of expression, association and assembly protected under the ICCPR. Queensland is the only jurisdiction that has reformed its public order laws to ensure that the right to peaceful assembly under the ICCPR is protected. This reform occurred as a reaction to the repressive public order laws and policies adopted in the 1970s: F Brennan, *Too Much Order With Too Little Law* (St Lucia, Qld: University of Queensland Press, 1983). As a consequence, Queensland is the only jurisdiction in Australia to have enacted a statutory right of peaceful public assembly: *Peaceful Assembly Act* 1992 (Qld), s 5(1). This Act draws expressly on the right to peaceful assembly and the grounds for restriction contained in Art 21 of the ICCPR. To protect the statutory right of peaceful assembly, the legislation provides immunity from liability for various laws that would otherwise prohibit or restrict the exercise of that right, such as laws governing the movement of traffic and pedestrians, as well as loitering and obstruction offences: s 6. The immunity is available only where the assembly has been subject to prior police approval, though participation in an assembly which is not approved does not of itself constitute an offence. Organisers and protesters participating without approval simply forfeit their immunity from prosecution under prescribed offences: ss 3, 6(1). This framework regulating public assemblies in Queensland conforms with the ICCPR since the grounds for restricting assemblies precisely mirrors the restrictions applied in Art 21. The Act aims to balance the rights of those participating in the assembly against the legitimate interests in maintaining public order, decency and amenity. The legislative objectives contained in s 2(1)(c) provides that the existence of the right to participate in public assemblies is subject only to such restrictions as are necessary and reasonable in a democratic society in the interests of:

(i) public safety;

(ii) public order; or

(iii) protection of rights and freedoms of other persons.

The right of peaceful assembly contained in the ICCPR could provide a template for domestic legislation, as in Queensland. It also may be considered relevant to the interpretation of existing legislation and operate as a legitimate influence on the development of the common law: *Mabo v Queensland (No 2)* (1992) 175 CLR 1; *Dietrich v The Queen* (1992) 177 CLR 292, and see generally Ch 2, p 11. Following *Minister for Immigration and Ethnic Affairs v Teoh* (1995) 183 CLR 273, it has been suggested that Australia's ratification of the ICCPR may also give rise to a "legitimate expectation" on the part of protestors that police decisions to curtail freedom of expression, assembly and association will consider the relevant rights contained in the ICCPR: S Bronitt and G Williams, "Political Freedom as an Outlaw: Republican Theory and Political Protest" (1996) 18(2) *Adelaide Law Review* 289 at 326-327. Such a transformation would require significant shifts in police and judicial attitudes. As yet, administrative law has not played any significant role in clarifying or confining the scope of police discretion.

While stronger legislative or judicial recognition of the rights under the ICCPR would be a positive step, it is important to recognise the importance of cultural attitudes of tolerance toward political protest. As Denis Galligan concludes in "Preserving Public Protest: the Legal Approach" in L Gostin (ed), *Civil Liberties in Conflict* (London and New York: Routledge, 1988) p 62:

The proclamation of a right to protest might go some way towards establishing a more secure legal footing, but it is surely folly to think that that in itself is the final solution. The real problem lies in the attitudes of officials — legislators, judges, police and others; those attitudes have produced the present position, and it is only if they change that the value of public tumults will be secured.

Public order laws also potentially raise questions of constitutional validity where they interfere with the implied freedom of political communication under the Commonwealth Constitution. See S Bronitt and S Ford, 10.10 "Public Order" in Title 10 CRIMINAL OFFENCES, *The Laws of Australia* (Sydney: LBC, 1996—), paras 4-11. See also S Bronitt and G Williams, "Political Freedom as an Outlaw: Republican Theory and Political Protest" (1996) 18(2) *Adelaide Law Review* 289. The latter article examines freedom of protest from a constitutional and public order perspective, developing a regulatory model for political protest drawing on the principles and presumptions of republican theory of criminal justice in J Braithwaite and P Pettit, *Not Just Deserts* (Oxford: Clarendon Press, 1990). For a discussion of republicanism and its implications for the criminal law generally, see Chapter 1.

2.5 SELECTED STATUTORY PUBLIC ORDER POWERS

The powers to prevent crime and disorder under the common law have been supplemented by a wide range of statutory powers. In this section, we examine two powers commonly used by the police to deal with minor threats to public order:

- the power to remove individuals who are causing disturbances in public places; and

- the power to deal with individuals who are drunk in a public place.

We have previously examined the extensive statutory powers available for preventing domestic violence, for example, authorising entry onto private premises and obtaining a protection order.

STATUTORY MOVE-ON POWERS

Statutory move-on powers are triggered by a wide range of disorderly conduct including violence (actual or threatened), property damage, harassment or intimidation. These powers supplement and extend the existing powers to disperse individuals to prevent a breach of the peace under the common law, and the rarely exercised statutory powers of dispersal to prevent a riot, which are considered below: see p 810. In relation to move-on powers, it is only an offence where the person directed to leave an area by the police refuses to comply. For example, in the Australian Capital Territory, police have the power to direct a person to leave the vicinity of a public place "where a police officer has reasonable grounds for believing that a person in a public place has engaged, or is likely to engage, in violent conduct in that place": *Crime Prevention Powers Act* 1998 (ACT), s 4. "Violent conduct" is defined in the Act as violence to, or intimidation of, a person, or damage to property: s 35(4). Similar move-on powers exist in New South Wales and Queensland: *Summary Offences Act* 1988 (NSW), s 28F; *Police Powers And Responsibilities Act* 1997 (Qld), s 88(1).

To provide guidance on how move-on powers should be exercised in Queensland, the legislation includes the following examples:

Examples for subsection (1)

1. If a person sitting in the entrance to a shop is stopping people entering or leaving the shop when it is open for business and the occupier complains, a police officer may give to the person a direction to move away from the entrance.

2. If a group of people have been fighting in a night club car park, a police officer may give the people involved in the fight a direction to leave the premises in opposite directions to separate the aggressors.

3. If a person has approached a primary school child in circumstances that would cause anxiety to a reasonable parent, a police officer may give the person a direction to leave the area near the school.

Making disobedience of a police officer an offence serves to reinforce police authority on the streets, as much as to prevent crime or disorder. These powers promote a "Do As I Say" style of policing and contradict the traditional ideal that policing should rest on the consent of the community. The courts have often pointed out that citizens, while under a moral or social duty to help police, are not under a legal duty to do so. In the absence of statutory compulsion, a failure to assist the police does not constitute the offence of obstruction of a police officer in the execution of his or her duties: *Rice v Connolly* [1966] 2 QB 414.

Such common law idealism that citizens are not legally obliged to assist the police with their inquiries would severely limit the traditional role of the police as moral street-sweepers. Not surprisingly, the common law has been extensively modified by statute. Thus, a failure to provide identification details or produce a drivers' licence to the police when asked is an offence in many jurisdictions: S Bronitt and S Ford, 10.10 "Public Order" in Title 10 CRIMINAL OFFENCES, *The Laws of Australia* (Sydney: LBC, 1996–), para 23. Criminalising such disobedience through statutory provisions may be viewed as a further derogation from that policing model where officers are viewed as "citizens in uniform" exercising powers to prevent crime and disorder available to any person.

Although statutory move-on powers are widely drawn, in many respects they are less flexible and more restricted than the common law powers to prevent a breach of the peace. Move-on powers are limited to persons engaging in or threatening disorderly conduct in public places, and the power of arrest is only available where the person has previously refused to comply with police directions. By contrast, there is no requirement to give directions and warnings before exercising the common law powers of dispersal or arrest in order to prevent or stop a breach of the peace. Moreover, the common law is not restricted to disorderly conduct that occurs in public places, and may be applied to peaceful and otherwise lawful conduct that provokes or is likely to provoke others to cause a breach of the peace. Most significantly, move-on powers may not be available in cases where individuals are exercising rights of peaceful protest. For example, s 35(3) of the *Crime Prevention Powers Act* 1998 (ACT) provides that the move-on powers and the associated offence do not apply to individuals involved in picketing a place of employment, demonstrating or protesting about a particular matter or speaking, bearing or otherwise identifying with a banner, placard, or sign or otherwise behaving in a way that is apparently intended to publicise the person's views about a particular matter. Under s 88(2) of the *Police Powers And Responsibilities Act* 1997 (Qld) a police officer must not give a direction that interferes with a person's right of peaceful assembly unless it is reasonably necessary in the interests of:

(1) public safety;

(2) public order; or

(3) the protection of the rights and freedoms of other persons.

These limitations are consistent with the permissible restrictions on the right to peaceful protest under the ICCPR considered above, p 776.

DRUNK AND DISORDERLY: CRIMINALISATION VERSUS WELFARE MODELS

From early colonial times, managing public drunkenness has been a major concern and preoccupation of law enforcement officials in Australia: P Grabosky, *Sydney in Ferment* (Canberra: ANU Press, 1977), p 8. The policing role in relation to drunk and disorderly individuals has continued, and even intensified, through the course of the 20th century. As Peter Grabosky has noted, between 1943 and 1970, arrests for drunkenness steadily increased from 32% to 54% of all arrests, excluding traffic violations: p 135. As Chris Cunneen points out, even in relation to serious disorder at public events, such as the Bathurst race riots in the 1980s, the police most commonly used offences against drunkenness and traffic violations rather than more serious public order offences, such as riot or unlawful assembly: "The Policing of Public Order: Some Thoughts on Culture, Space and Political Economy" in M Findlay and R Hogg (eds), *Understanding Crime and Criminal Justice* (Sydney: Law Book Company Ltd, 1988), p 196. Public drunkenness was the most commonly prosecuted public order offence in the 20th century: D Brown, D Farrier and D Weisbrot, *Criminal Laws* (2nd ed, Sydney: Federation Press, 1996), p 922.

Community attitudes to intoxicated persons have changed over time and offences of public drunkenness have been repealed in most Australian jurisdictions. Brown, Farrier and Weisbrot (above) reviewed the history of drunkenness laws and the reforms introduced in the 1970s in New South Wales. In 1979, drunkenness in a public place was decriminalised. Rather than using a criminal model, the new laws governing public intoxication were geared towards a social welfare or medical model. Although arrest and prosecution for public drunkenness were no longer available, intoxicated persons could be detained for their own protection for up to eight hours: *Intoxicated Persons Act* 1979 (NSW).

Though non-criminal, these civil powers can have coercive and punitive qualities. These powers are determined and exercised by the police and the welfare of the intoxicated person is typically protected by detention in a "lock up" or other designated place: p 923. Although drunkenness has been "decriminalised", the police continue to rely on these civil powers as well as other public order offences to control intoxicated individuals. These reforms have not affected the multitude of offences enacted under local council by-laws that proscribe the consumption of alcohol in the vicinity of certain proclaimed places, such as taxi ranks. Moreover, it seems that other "street offences" prohibiting offensive/indecent behaviour continue to be applied against individuals who have been drinking in public places. Available empirical data, discussed below, pp 792-793, reveals that these crimes of offensive conduct are enforced in a discriminatory manner, having a harsh impact on minorities and those who resist police authority.

On the general exculpatory effect of intoxication on the voluntariness of conduct and criminal fault, see Chapter 4.

2.6 PUBLIC ORDER AND THE CENTRALITY OF POLICE DISCRETION

As David Williams pointed out, discretion lies at the heart of public order powers: *Keeping the Peace* (London: Hutchinson, 1967), pp 15-17. The law has imposed minimal restrictions on how the police and magistrates should exercise their powers to prevent disorder. In relation to these powers, the courts have been reluctant to apply even basic standards of "reasonableness" required by administrative law: DGT Williams, "Criminal Law and Administrative Law: Problems of Procedure and Reasonableness" in P Smith (ed), *Criminal Law: Essays in Honour of JC Smith* (London: Butt, 1987). Administrative law and judicial review remains, as yet, an untapped resource for controlling pre-trial decision-making: DJ Galligan, "Regulating Pre-Trial Decisions" in N Lacey (ed), *A Reader on Criminal Justice* (Oxford: Oxford University Press, 1994). The discretionary approach to peace-keeping may be contrasted with the strict approach taken by the courts to the powers of arrest, detention, search and seizure, where the courts have demonstrated considerable vigilance in safe-guarding the interests of personal liberty and private property: *Williams v The Queen* (1986) 161 CLR 278 (arrest and detention for the purpose of investigation); *Coco v The Queen* (1994) 179 CLR 427 (trespass for the purpose of installing listening devices).

Citizens are rarely in a position to challenge action taken by the police to prevent disorder. The legal basis for police action is very difficult to review in cases where the police or prosecution decline to institute further proceedings, which is often the case where the individual has acted in a peaceful and otherwise lawful manner. Even where the person is prosecuted for a public order offence, the arbitrary or unreasonable exercise of police discretion cannot be raised as a defence to liability. As Kerr J noted in *Wright v McQualter* (1970) 17 FLR 305 (at 320):

> [S]o far as the courts are concerned, when offences are alleged to have been committed and the police make arrests and prosecutions follow, the role of the courts is simply to decide the question of guilt or innocence and the penalty to be imposed in the event of a finding of guilt. It is for other parts of the structure of democratic institutions in society to deal with the problems, if any, of selective law-enforcement.

Individuals adversely affected by the exercise of these powers are left to contest the legality of police conduct through judicial review, private prosecution or civil actions for trespass, assault and/or unlawful imprisonment. To remedy the problem of selective enforcement in cases of domestic violence, some jurisdictions have imposed a statutory duty on police to investigate. These reforms have been discussed above, at p 760.

Collateral challenges to the legality of police conduct are difficult and rare. The lack of an effective framework of judicial review is apparent in those few cases where individuals have sought court orders to compel or restrain police conduct. Invoking the notion of constabulary independence, the courts have affirmed that police officers possess a wide discretion in exercising their duties that is *ordinarily* not reviewable: *R v Metropolitan Police Commissioner; Ex parte Blackburn* [1968] 2 QB 118. Operational decisions and law enforcement policies are difficult to challenge in cases where the grounds for police action (or inaction) have not been publicised or remain invisible to those affected by the decision. Because of the coercive effect of many preventive powers, there is risk that the process *itself* becomes the punishment: M Feeley, *The Process is the Punishment* (New York: Russell Sage Foundation, 1979).

In some cases, the grounds for non-prosecution are promulgated as a formal policy. In the mid-1980s, the Commonwealth Director of Public Prosecutions issued Prosecution Guidelines that expressly stated that the arrest of a person engaged in civil disobedience may provide a sufficient penalty for the conduct in question because of the deprivation of liberty caused by the arrest. Such a policy, which probably operated informally before the guidelines, encouraged the arrest, detention and release without charge of any peaceful protestors who had engaged in disruptive conduct. The Federal Human Rights Commission examined this policy and concluded that the use of arrest as an "extra-judicial punishment" was incompatible with the guarantee against arbitrary arrest and detention contained in the ICCPR: *Civil Disobedience and the Use of Arrest as Punishment: Some Human Rights Issues* (Canberra: AGPS, 1986). The Prosecution Guidelines were subsequently amended and the offending paragraphs were deleted. Notwithstanding these formal changes, at the street level, political and moral judgments continue to influence whether and when the police will intervene, arrest, prosecute or caution individuals engaged in non-violent protest that is potentially disruptive. It is also important to remember that while the use of arrest *as a form of punishment* is clearly prohibited under international human rights law, arrest for the purpose of *preventing* public disorder is not: *Steel and Others v United Kingdom* (1999) 28 EHRR 603: see discussion above, p 775.

There is some authority in Australia that the police discretion not to intervene is restricted where a breach of the peace or any other crime occurs (or is likely to occur) in the presence of the police: *Commissioner of Police (Tas); Ex parte North Broken Hill Ltd* (1992) 61 A Crim R 390 at 398. The human rights implications of this decision have been reviewed above at p 773. In determining whether or not the police should intervene to disperse a picket line, Wright J held that neither the industrial genesis of the dispute nor the lack of police resources were legitimate reasons for not intervening: at 398. Police had discretion in how — *not whether* — to proceed in cases where the obstruction of workers wishing to return to work was likely to provoke a breach of the peace. Although the police were under a duty to intervene, Wright J declined to grant an order of mandamus since the police officers at the scene had exercised their powers under a misapprehension of the law, and their inaction was not a deliberate decision to flout the law. This ruling led to immediate police action, provoking violent confrontations and arrests on the picket line. Margaret Otlowski has described the ensuing police operation in "The Legal Fallout from the APPM Dispute" (1992) 5 *Australian Journal of Labour Law* 287 (at 292):

> In response to the court's ruling, the following day police numbers at the Burnie mill were dramatically increased in one of the state's biggest police operations. During the course of the day, there were violent clashes as police helped employees wanting to return to work to break the picket line. Forty one picketers were arrested and charges were laid for obstruction and assault. A picketer and a policeman had to be taken to hospital as a result of the injuries sustained in the confrontation.

The decision clarifies police duties in relation to picket lines.[14] From the perspective of industrial law, the decision, though first instance, has had far-reaching implications. As Otlowski concluded, "a new precedent has been established with regard to the duties of police in relation to picketing which virtually eliminates police discretion not to intervene in such cases": at 294. The lack of a legal basis for picketing under domestic civil and criminal laws raises concerns about compliance with the ICCPR, see R Hale, "Peaceful Picketing in Australia: The Failure to Guarantee a Basic Human Right" in *The Right of Peaceful Protest Seminar, Human Rights Commission Occasional Paper No 14* (Canberra: AGPS, 1986).

3. PUBLIC ORDER OFFENCES

DGT Williams, "Freedom of Assembly and Free Speech: Changes and Reforms in England" (1975) 1(2) *University of New South Wales Law Journal* 97 at 100-101

> The law of public order in no way resembles a code of public order. It is an amalgam of particular offences which have been devised to meet particular problems at particular times. It fluctuates wildly in its emphasis and usage. Some offences disappear through statutory repeal, others fade away through what is effectively a process of desuetude, while a few rest in a state of suspended animation awaiting resusitation at the behest of an ingenious prosecutor

Offences against public order are highly diversified. Some offences such as riot are concerned with serious threats to State security and social and political order, while others such as offensive conduct are concerned with minor nuisances that interfere with the peace and amenity of the neighbourhood. What is common to these offences is the *process of criminalisation*. Public order law is particularly susceptible to moral panics within the community about crime and disorder. The process of identification and criminalisation of "new" public order threats is sensitive to local as well as international "law and order" politics. This process is not merely legislative. As Williams observed in the above quotation, the contours of public order law are also shaped through prosecutorial discretion and judicial development of the common law.

MAKING PUBLIC ORDER CRIMES: PROSECUTORIAL, JUDICIAL AND LEGISLATIVE DEVELOPMENT

In policing and prosecuting disorder, a number of offences such as public nuisance and offensive conduct operate as "backstops" and "gapfillers". Public nuisance, which is both a crime and a tort under the common law, is sufficiently broad to criminalise any conduct that poses danger to the community at large. While much dangerous and antisocial conduct could be prosecuted as a public nuisance, the offence has been limited to conduct that is indiscriminate in nature rather than targeted at specific individuals: *Attorney-General v PYA Quarries Ltd* [1957] 2 QB 169 at 184, per

---

14   On this topic see generally, R Handley, "Preventive Powers and NUM Pickets" (1986) 10 Crim LJ 93.

Romer LJ. Public nuisance is highly adaptable. In the public order context, it has been used to prosecute individuals who perpetrated a bomb hoax and, more recently, property owners who rented land for the purpose of holding "raves".[15]

Recent authorities on public nuisance have established that the conduct must present a "real risk" (not a remote risk) of danger to the public. The breadth of the conduct constituting a public nuisance is matched by its fault element. The English Court of Appeal in *R v Shorrock* [1993] 3 WLR 698 has affirmed the fault element for the crime of public nuisance is the same as for the tort of private and public nuisance. The offence is attractive to prosecutors because the fault element is satisfied by mere negligence. Public nuisance requires that the accused knew or *ought to have known* (in the sense that the means of knowledge were available to him or her) that there was a real risk that his or her conduct would endanger the public: at 706.

In this area of the law, there has been a close correlation between prosecutorial and judicial development of the common law and legislative intervention. Soon after *Shorrock*, the *Criminal Justice and Public Order Act* 1994 (UK) was enacted conferring on police special powers to deal with "raves". This required the creation of a new legal category of disorder called "raves", which s 63 of the Act defined as follows:

> a gathering on land in the open air of 100 or more persons (whether or not trespassers) at
> which amplified music is played during the night (with or without intermission) and is such
> as, by reason of its loudness and duration and the time at which it is played, is likely to
> cause serious distress to the inhabitants of the locality.

The Act empowers the police to disperse individuals, to enter and seize vehicles and sound equipment, as well as to stop and divert persons travelling to raves: ss 64-65. The police prefer to rely on specific powers and offences rather than on broad and nebulous laws governing breach of the peace and public nuisance. There are dangers that these "tailored" public order laws are discriminatory against minority groups, and have the effect of criminalising alternative lifestyles. For a discussion of the criminalisation of aggravated trespass to deal with nomadic "travellers" see S Campbell, "Gypsies: The Criminalisation of a Way of Life?" [1995] Crim LR 28.

A similar pattern of criminalisation of disorder emerges in Australia. Moral panics about beachside drag car racing in New South Wales led to new offences of deliberate tyre spinning on ordinary and oil-slicked roads ("wheelies" and "doughnuts") and menacing driving: ss 4BA, 4BB, 4BC of the *Traffic Act* 1909 (NSW), discussed in (1997) 21 Crim LJ 152. These provisions have been repealed and replaced by ss 40-43 of the *Road Transport (Safety and Traffic Management) Act* 1999 (NSW). These new offences were supplemented by extensive powers of vehicle seizure and confiscation. These laws against "hooning" overlap existing motor traffic offences such as driving in "intimidatory manner" contrary to s 11H of the *Summary Offences Act* 1988 (NSW).

---

15   *R v Madden* [1975] 1 WLR 1379; *R v Shorrock* [1993] 3 WLR 698 respectively. The usefulness of public nuisance is not limited to public order situations. In Canada and England the offence has been used to deal with individuals who expose others to the risk of HIV infection: S Bronitt, "Donating HIV-infected Blood: A Public Nuisance?" (1994) 1 *Journal of Law and Medicine* 245; S Bronitt, "Fracturing the Criminal Law: Disease Control and the Limits of Law-making" (1996) 4(1) *Health Care Analysis* 59.

Intimidatory use of vehicles and vessels

(1) A person must not operate a motorised vehicle or motorised vessel in a public place:

    (a) in such a manner as to harass or intimidate another person, or

    (b) in such a manner as would be likely to cause a person of reasonable firmness to fear for his or her personal safety.

Maximum penalty: 6 penalty units.

(2) No person of reasonable firmness need actually be, or be likely to be, present at the scene.

Although legally redundant, these new "public order" crimes are politically and symbolically important — they represent a firm legislative response to a new public order threat, increasing the range of penalties and providing the police with new powers of seizure and confiscation of motor vehicles.

Public Order: Policing the Streets and Juvenile Delinquency

For a collection of essays examining the treatment of juveniles by the criminal justice system see R White and C Alder (eds), *The Police and Young People in Australia* (Cambridge: Cambridge University Press, 1994). Public order looms large in several of these essays. While public order offences do not formally target juvenile delinquency, they are disproportionately enforced against young people in Australia. Finnane examined how the need to control disorderly youth historically shaped the role of policing in Australia: "Larrikins, Delinquents and Cops: Police and Young People in Australian History", Ch 1. The inevitable collision on the streets between young people and police asserting authority over public space has resulted in strained community relations, harassment and police violence: R White, "Street Life: Police Practices and Youth Behaviour", Ch 5. In many jurisdictions, public order powers and policies have been shaped by perceived "law and order" concerns, resulting in harsh and discriminatory policing methods against Indigenous youth: C Cunneen, "Enforcing Genocide? Aboriginal Young People and the Police", Ch 6. In "Policing Youth in 'Ethnic' Communities", Ch 8, Janet Chan reviewed the role of ethnicity and racism in policing young people. While racial prejudice and stereotyping is evident in policing, she concluded that "the more problematic area is the police's perception of their work, particularly in relation to juveniles": p 196. Chan concluded that juvenile justice reform requires more than the adoption of a friendly and tolerant style of "community policing". Fundamental shifts in police attitudes to young people and their rights are required, in particular that "the police, as professional law enforcement workers, *have genuine regard for due process of the law*" (original emphasis): p 192.

THE TERRITORY OF PUBLIC ORDER OFFENCES: GENERAL ACTS AND LOCAL BY-LAWS

As well as being diversified, public order offences can be highly localised. It is important to appreciate that many public order powers and offences are not solely found in Federal, State and

Territory legislation of general application. Local by-laws and council regulations play a significant role in the abatement of a wide range of nuisances.[16] Because these offences are not contained in public general Acts, they have less legal visibility. Nevertheless, these local laws impose a wide range of restrictions on the use of highways, public spaces and semi-private places such as malls and shopping precincts.

By-laws may have dire implications for individuals engaged in political protest. In *Foley v Padley* (1984) 154 CLR 349, the High Court considered the validity of a by-law that made it an offence to distribute anything in the Rundle Street Mall without the permission of the Adelaide Council. The by-law was made under s 11(1)(a) of the *Rundle Street Mall Act* 1975 (SA) that permitted the Council to regulate, control or prohibit any activity in the Mall likely to affect its use or enjoyment. Similar provisions exist governing the use of commercial public spaces in cities and towns throughout Australia. The majority upheld the validity of the by-law. Murphy and Brennan JJ, dissenting, held that the by-law was not a valid exercise of the Council's powers to make by-laws. Murphy J held that the by-law granted the Council the unfettered discretionary power to negative the prohibition by granting permission. By this route the Council avoided statutory safeguards, and was improperly exercising a form of legislative power. Murphy J concluded (at 362) that:

> If freedom of expression is to be maintained by-laws which may be used to restrict expression must be clearly authorized by enabling legislation and procedural safeguards must be strictly observed.

Brennan J (at 373) focused on the technical rather than human rights aspects of the case, concluding that the blanket prohibition interfered with conduct that did *not* affect the use and enjoyment of the Mall, and therefore was ultra vires. See also *Melbourne Corporation v Barry* (1922) 31 CLR 174.

Public order offences may also be tied to "protected" locations or persons. Special diplomatic offences dealing with aggravated trespass and disorder have been enacted by the Commonwealth under the *Public Order (Protection of Persons and Property) Act* 1971 (Cth).[17] Legislatures around Australia have enacted especially draconian laws for dispersing and criminalising public assemblies in the vicinity of parliamentary buildings. A recent inquiry into the right to protest or demonstrate in the vicinity of Federal Parliament identified more than 20 offences under Commonwealth and Australian Capital Territory statutes that potentially have an impact upon the right to protest: The Parliament of the Commonwealth of Australia, *A Right To Protest* (Canberra: AGPS, 1997). The inquiry identified several obscure and largely dormant offences with the capacity to interfere with most forms of peaceful political protest in Canberra, including draconian offences such as "unlawful assembly" and "interference with political liberty": *Crimes Act* 1914 (Cth), s 28; *Unlawful Assemblies Ordinance* 1937 (ACT), s 3(2). Enacted in the early years of Federation, these political offences reflected concerns about political instability in Australia at the outbreak of World War I and the rising tides of fascism and communism. Although rarely prosecuted, such dragnet offences provided a legal backstop for the police in their negotiation over the manner, form and duration of political protests. It has been suggested that these offences are clearly incompatible with the political rights and

---

16   See, for example, *Burswood Park By-laws* 1988 (WA), s 19 (offensive or indecent behaviour).
17   See further S Bronitt and S Ford, 10.10 'Public Order' in Title 10 CRIMINAL OFFENCES, *The Laws of Australia* (Sydney: LBC, 1996—), paras 29-30.

freedoms implied within the Constitution and protected by Art 19, 21 and 22 of the *International Covenant on Civil and Political Rights* (ICCPR): S Bronitt and G Williams, "Political Freedom as an Outlaw: Republican Theory and Political Protest" (1996) 18(2) *Adelaide Law Review* 289. The offence of unlawful assembly is considered below: see p 797.

3.1 OFFENSIVE CONDUCT AND LANGUAGE CRIMES

In Australia, the criminal laws prohibiting offensive conduct and language are not tied to causing harm to others or to property, and consequently can be deployed in a broad range of situations.[18] Offensive and/or indecent conduct may be an aggravating element of other offences.[19]

Criminalising offensive language or conduct has the potential to interfere with the freedom of expression, assembly and association protected by Arts 19, 21 and 22 of the ICCPR. As previously noted, restrictions on these freedoms may be imposed where necessary to protect the rights or reputation of others (Art 19); and the interests of national security or public safety, public order, protection of public health or morals or the protection of the rights and freedoms of others (Arts 19, 21 and 22). From a theoretical perspective, restricting fundamental rights for "protection of morals" without any need to establish harm to others is considered a serious weakness in international human rights law: D Feldman, *Civil Liberties and Human Rights in England and Wales* (Oxford: Clarendon Press, 1993), p 523. According to the harm principle, the State would only be justified in restricting individual freedom in order to prevent harm to others. The "harm principle" and its theoretical rivals (namely "moral protection" and "welfare") were explored in Chapter 1: pp 49ff. Not surprisingly, liberal scholars concerned with maximising liberty have argued against the criminalisation of offensive speech: J Braithwaite and P Pettit, *Not Just Deserts — A Republican Theory of Criminal Justice* (Oxford: Clarendon Press, 1990), p 95. Others have argued that "causing offense" to deeply held moral beliefs may be treated as a form of personal harm that may be justifiably and therefore legally restricted: J Feinberg, *The Moral Limits of the Criminal Law: Offense to Others* (New York: Oxford University Press, 1985).

The expansion of harm to include "causing offense to others" applies "symmetrically". It allows racists/sexists to claim offense at hearing the views of minorities/feminists, and vice-versa. Notwithstanding its seemingly neutral stance, offensive conduct crimes have tended to entrench rather than redress discrimination against minorities. Although offensive conduct and language crimes in Australia *could* be used to criminalise acts of racial vilification, empirical evidence has revealed that these laws tend to be enforced *against* minorities. As Wojciech Sadurski points out, this pattern of law enforcement "over-emphasises the seriousness of insults against majority (in particular, against enforcement agents themselves) and undervalues insults against disadvantaged

---

18 *Crimes Act* 1900 (ACT), s 546A; *Summary Offences Act* 1988 (NSW), ss 4, 4A; *Summary Offences Act* 1988 (NT), s 47; *Summary Offences Act* 1953 (SA), s 7; *Police Offences Act* 1935 (Tas), ss 12 and 13; *Summary Offences Act* 1966 (Vic), s 17; *Police Act* 1892 (WA), ss 54, 59. In Queensland, indecent or offensive behaviour provides a basis for exercising move on powers contained in the *Police Powers and Responsibilities Act* 1997(Qld), s 83.

19 Offensive conduct may be an element of other crimes, such as aggravated trespass on Territory, Commonwealth or diplomatic premises: *Public Order (Protection of Persons and Property) Act* 1971 (Cth), ss 11(2)(b), 12(2)(b), 20(2)(b).

minorities": "Racial Vilification, Psychic Harm and Affirmative Action", T Campbell and W Sadurski (eds), *Freedom of Communication* (Aldershot: Dartmouth, 1994), p 90. As we shall examine below (see p 792), there is empirical data in New South Wales revealing that offensive conduct crimes have a disproportionate impact on Indigenous communities, being used primarily to deal with young people who swear at the police or otherwise demonstrate disrespect to authority.

Rather than resort to the principle of equality and affirmative action for drawing distinctions between cases, Sadurski justifies the prohibition of offensive speech on the ground that it constitutes a type of "psychic injury".

To warrant criminalisation, offensive epithets must:

- **constitute personally abusive insults;**
- **be addressed in a face-to-face manner;**
- **target a specific individual and be descriptive of that individual; and**
- **be addressed to an individual unable to avoid the assaultive message (p 88).**

There are some signs that the courts are imposing tougher thresholds for the criminalisation of offensive conduct, particularly in cases where there was no intention to cause hurt to another person and/or the conduct has an obvious political dimension. Perhaps mindful of the potentially discriminatory and repressive uses of offensive conduct laws, some judges have sought to restrict the scope of these crimes by requiring the offending conduct to be placed in its broader political and social context: see below, pp 793-795.

As with other public order crimes, police discretion is crucial in fixing the limits of offensive conduct within public places. Offensiveness is largely determined by police conceptions of public decency and "good order". While offensiveness is "objectively" determined, the response of the police in attendance, as an evidential matter, will be crucial in identifying the likely emotional response of the reasonable, hypothetical person: see below, p 791.

> The centrality of police attitudes to the behaviour alleged to be offensive is supported by empirical research. A study of prosecutions for offensive language in the 1980s in New South Wales revealed that the police were the "victims" in two thirds of the cases. That is, the insulting language was directed to the police or towards the police and another person present: S Egger and M Findlay, "The Politics of Police Discretion" in M Findlay and R Hogg (eds), *Understanding Crime and Criminal Justice* (Sydney: Law Book Company Ltd, 1988), p 218.

FAULT ELEMENT: DELIBERATE OR ACCIDENTAL OFFENSE

An important safeguard imposing limits on the scope of offensive conduct or language crimes is the requirement of an intention to arouse feelings of anger, resentment, disgust or outrage in others. Historically, the courts have not required proof of fault for minor public order crimes such as offensive conduct. Although the commitment to subjectivism remains weak for most public offences, some courts have emphasised the importance of intention in cases where the crime carries a penalty of imprisonment: *Jeffs v Graham* (1987) 8 NSWLR 292.

The requirement that the prosecution must prove that offensive behaviour was "intended" was affirmed in *Daire v Stone* (1991) 56 SASR 90. In this case, the accused was charged with behaving in a "disorderly manner" in a public place contrary to s 7 of the *Summary Offences Act* 1953 (SA), which expressly included behaving in an "offensive manner". The allegation was that the accused had "eyed off" females in a store. The charge was dismissed and the prosecution appealed. The Supreme Court of South Australia (at 93, per Legoe J) dismissed the appeal by the prosecution on the ground that the offence of disorderly behaviour requires proof beyond reasonable doubt that:

> there is a conscious and deliberate course of conduct by the accused person which
> constitutes this interference with the comfort of other people such as to leave the tribunal
> of fact with no reasonable doubt that the conduct of the accused person was intentionally
> done to bring about such interference.

On these facts, there was no evidence of the purpose or intention of the accused so to establish that the conduct was directed at the victims.

Since obscene language is often used unconsciously as a means of linguistic emphasis or general expletives, requiring a proof of subjective fault is an important limitation on the scope of this offence.

Intentional conduct may be distinguished from conduct that is intended to cause offense. In relation to the latter, the strength of the judicial commitment to subjectivism may be doubted following *Police v Pfeifer* (1997) 68 SASR 285. In this case, the accused wore a t-shirt in public emblazoned with the words "Too Drunk to Fuck". He was convicted of behaving in an offensive manner contrary to s 7 of the *Summary Offences Act* 1953 (SA). The Supreme Court of South Australia, dismissing the appeal, held that s 7 did *not* require the prosecution to prove intention or knowledge. The Court reviewed recent authorities that had favoured a subjective fault requirement for offensive conduct crimes.[20] Applying the principles laid down by the High Court in *He Kaw Teh v The Queen* (1985) 157 CLR 523, the Supreme Court held that the presumption that intent or knowledge is an essential element of s 7 had been rebutted. The principles in *He Kaw Teh v The Queen* (1985) 157 CLR 523 are discussed in Chapter 3 at pp 190ff. Doyle CJ, with whom Debelle and Lander JJ agreed, attached particular relevance was the language of the section (noting that other crimes of offensiveness in the Act expressly required intention) and the subject matter of the provision (at 292):

> It appears to me to be a provision intended to protect members of society from disturbance
> and annoyance through offensive behaviour, intended to prevent the sort of disputes and
> disturbances that might arise if such behaviour is not prevented by law with the conse-
> quence that members of society react to it or resist it in other ways. To convict only those
> who intentionally or knowingly offend will achieve a good deal, but does not go that extra
> step of requiring members of society to take care to ensure that they do not breach
> generally accepted standards of behaviour.

While the prosecution need not prove intention or knowledge, the defence may raise an honest and reasonable belief that the behaviour would not be offensive according to community standards of decency.

---

20 Early decisions on offensive behaviour did not require proof of subjective intent: see *Densley v Merton* [1943] SASR 144; *Normandale v Brassey* [1970] SASR 177; *Ellis v Fingleton* (1972) 3 SASR 437. Later decisions, applying *He Kaw Teh*, required proof that the conduct which caused offense had been intentional: *Daire v Stone* (1991) 56 SASR 90; *Stone v Ford* (1993) 59 SASR 444.

MEASURING OFFENSIVENESS: THE REASONABLE PERSON TEST

Attempts by the police to suppress conduct they deem offensive have not always been successful. The courts have imposed some limits on the scope of offensiveness in cases where the conduct is obviously "political". The meaning of offensiveness in the context of a political demonstration was considered in *Ball v McIntyre* (1966) 9 FLR 237. In this case, the police attempted to prevent an anti-Vietnam protest outside Parliament House in Canberra. Desmond Ball, a university student, had climbed on a statue of George V and hung a placard that read "I will not fight in Vietnam". The accused refused to remove the placard or climb down, as requested by the police. When he eventually came down he was arrested and prosecuted for behaving in an offensive manner in a public place contrary to s 17(d) of the *Police Offences Ordinance* 1930-1961 (ACT): now see s 546A of the *Crimes Act* 1900 (ACT).

Reflecting the sensitivity and division within the community over Australia's military involvement in Vietnam, the relevant behaviour deemed offensive was carefully constructed by the arresting police officers. At the trial the police emphasised that neither the political nature of the demonstration nor the student's refusal to obey their instructions had caused them offense. Rather the police testified that it was the accused's act of climbing on a public monument and hanging a placard (in effect, using the statue for a non-designated purpose) that had caused offense. As empirical studies have verified, the case was a typical application of offensive conduct crimes, where the only "victims" offended by the accused's conduct were the police officers themselves: see above, p 787.

The critical issue in this case was whether the student's behaviour was "offensive". Although the term was not defined in the Act, Kerr J held (at 243) that to be offensive, the behaviour must be "calculated to wound the feelings, arouse anger or resentment or disgust or outrage in the mind of a reasonable person". By applying an objective test, the political context of the accused's behaviour could be introduced as a relevant factor. As Kerr J acknowledged (at 244),

> The average man [or woman], the reasonable man [or woman], being present on such an occasion, would readily see that the defendant was engaged in a political demonstration. He [or she] would doubtless think that climbing on the pedestal and placing the placard on the statue was rather foolish and a misguided method of political protest, that it offended against the canons of good taste, that it was in that sense improper conduct, but I do not believe that the reasonable man [or woman] seeing such conduct to be truly political conduct, would have his [or her] feelings wounded or anger, resentment, disgust or outrage roused.

And later (at 245),

> I recognize that different minds may well come to different conclusions as to the reaction of the reasonable man [or woman] in situations involving attitudes and beliefs and values in the community, but for my part I believe that a so-called reasonable man [or woman] is reasonably tolerant and understanding, and reasonably contemporary in his [or her] reactions.

An objective standard of "offensive conduct" which explicitly provides room for dissent appears to be more protective of political protest. It avoids the problems associated with breach of the peace, where the right to engage in peaceful and otherwise lawful conduct is held hostage to the subjective responses (however unreasonable) of a hostile audience. Under Kerr J's definition, the political motives behind the accused's words and conduct are relevant to determining offensiveness. In this sense, it may be viewed as an exception to the general rule that motive is irrelevant to the criminal law: see Ch 3, p 176.

In many respects *Ball v McIntyre* (1966) 9 FLR 237 is an exceptional case. It stands in stark contrast to the approach taken by the English courts where the question of offense is regarded exclusively as a matter of fact for the tribunal. In *Brutus v Cozens* (1972) 56 Cr App R 799, the accused disrupted a tennis match at Wimbledon throwing leaflets protesting against apartheid around the court (one of the players was South African). The incident lasted two to three minutes before he left the court voluntarily. He was charged with using "threatening, abusive or insulting" words or behaviour likely to cause a breach of the peace contrary to s 5 of the *Public Order Act* 1936 (UK). The magistrate dismissed the charge on the ground that the accused's conduct was not "insulting". The prosecution appealed to the Divisional Court, which held that the conduct could be insulting as a matter of law and remitted the matter to the magistrate.

The accused appealed to the House of Lords. The case provided their Lordships with an opportunity to consider the meaning of the phrase "insulting words or conduct". The court held unanimously that the determination of whether words or conduct was "insulting" is a question of fact for the tribunal. This does not mean that judges have no role to play in interpreting statutes. As Lord Reid pointed out (at 804), in every case, the proper construction of a statute is a question of law for the courts. For this offence, Parliament intended that the words used should be given their ordinary meaning:

> It is for the tribunal which decides the case to consider, not as law but as fact, whether in
> the whole circumstances the words of the statute do or do not as a matter of ordinary
> usage of English language cover or apply to the facts which have been proved.

Lord Reid rejected the definition of offensiveness proposed by the Divisional Court, namely, that the conduct must affront other people, demonstrate a disrespect or contempt for their rights and constitute behaviour that reasonable persons would foresee is likely to cause resentment or protest. This test was not dissimilar to the definition of offensive conduct offered by Kerr J in *Ball v McIntyre* above. Lord Reid pointed out (at 805) that the qualifying adjectives, "threatening, abusive or insulting", had been employed by Parliament to define the limits of free speech. Conduct would not be caught by the section provided that a person's words or behaviour did not transgress these limits, even though it posed some threat of disorder. In light of this purpose, the terms required no further elaboration. In relation to insulting words or behaviour, Lord Reid rejected the dictionary definition approach favoured by the Divisional Court: "There can be no definition. But an ordinary sensible man knows an insult when he [or she] sees or hears it". He later stated (at 806): "Insulting means insulting and nothing else".[21] The ordinary meaning test for offensive conduct leaves the police,

---

21 On the meaning of "insulting", see further *DPP v Orum* [1983] 3 All ER 449; *R v Ball* (1990) 90 Cr App R 378; *DPP v Clarke and Others* (1992) 94 Cr App R 359. Cases following this approach: *Jeffrey Stephen Vigon v DPP* [1997] EWHC 854 (30 October 1997) *Manning*; *R v Cally* [1997] EWCA 3657 (22 October 1997).

prosecutors, judges and juries with a broad discretion for defining the relevant legal standards, and mirrors the definitional approach taken to offences relating to sexual indecency, obscenity and dishonesty: see Chs 12 and 13.

It is important not to overstate the differences between these two approaches. Whether the courts adopt an objective test based on the "reasonable person" or an "ordinary usage" approach to offensive conduct, the standards being applied are determined by reference to the wider community rather than the "victims" (including the police in attendance) or the tribunal determining the matter. But who is "the community" in this context? Do we comprise the community of a broad cross-section of society, both young and old? Or is it drawn more selectively and respectably from law-abiding and "right-thinking" persons whose conduct would not ordinarily come to the attention of the police? Although legal definitions based on the hypothetical reasonable or ordinary person are represented as external and neutral standards, they are in fact highly discretionary. As Lacey and Wells point out in *Reconstructing Criminal Law* (2nd ed, London: Butt, 1998), p 44:

> Where "reasonableness" tests are in play, doctrine fails to ask whose standard is the objective standard: who, in other words, is the "reasonable person"? The operation of "objective" tests in fact results in highly discretionary regulation. The tribunal here is effectively constructing the standard against which the defendant is being judged: the legal process goes on to legitimise that standard as "objective" and neutral.

In determining the ordinary or reasonable response to behaviour alleged to be offensive, the tribunal of fact will invariably defer to the judgment of the police. In determining the likely reactions of the "reasonable person", the tribunal may regard the evidence of police as the best guide of what reasonable and respectable persons would find offensive. In many cases the assessment of the reasonable person and the police officers in attendance converge. For example, in *Ball v McIntyre,* the police claimed that neither the political nature of the student's conduct nor the disrespect directed to a deceased monarch was offensive. In this respect, Kerr J concluded (at 240) that "the sergeant's approach is that of a reasonable man".

Even within liberal democracies that tolerate some measure of political dissent, there is a danger that crimes of offensiveness operate unfairly against unpopular and/or disempowered groups in society. Whether a person's conduct is constructed as legitimate protest or disorderly conduct will depend on factors such as age, gender, ethnicity, class and so on. The identification of conduct as "political protest" by police, lawyers and judges can confer some measure of protection to otherwise offensive conduct.

And Well May God Save Mr Ball and the Governor-General!

Unlike many threatened with arrest for offensive conduct, the accused in *Ball v McIntyre* (1966) 9 FLR 237 fended off his arrest for some time with reasoned legal debate. In his negotiations with police, Ball had the advantage of advice about his legal rights from law students attending the demonstration. After his brush with the law, Ball resumed his studies, predictably pursuing research on the United States' foreign policy. He is now a Professor of Strategic and Defence Studies at the Australian National University in Canberra. The judge in the case, Kerr J, proceeded to eternal political infamy as the Governor-General who sacked Gough Whitlam.

Most individuals whose conduct comes to the attention of the police are not ordinarily in a position to contest the official assessment of offensiveness by police and magistrates. Aboriginal youths will hardly be in a position to argue that their conduct deemed offensive by police has a deeper political meaning and value. Indeed, individuals who attempt to assert their legal rights in their interactions with police are more likely to become the subject of further investigation since "knowledge of rights" is regarded as evidence of previous contact with police: J Chan "Policing Youth in 'Ethnic' Communities", R White and C Alder (eds), *The Police and Young People in Australia* (Cambridge: Cambridge University Press, 1994), p 191.

Policing strategies within Aboriginal communities must be understood within the broader historical and contemporary demand of colonial order. The police have performed an array of welfare functions in Indigenous communities, culminating in their complicity in the forcible removal of children in the 1950s. High levels of resistance to policing in Indigenous communities produces saturation policing, "law and order" campaigns against "Aboriginal" juveniles and the extension of police powers: C Cunneen, "Enforcing Genocide? Aboriginal Young People and the Police", R White and C Alder (eds), *The Police and Young People in Australia* (Cambridge: Cambridge University Press, 1994), Ch 6. In charting these patterns of colonial governance, Chris Cunneen concludes (at 154) that police intervention in the lives of Aboriginal young people has "shifted from one of government-authorised removal policies to increasing criminalisation".

EMPIRICAL PERSPECTIVES

Offensive Conduct and Indigenous Policing

There has been increasing awareness that the use of minor public order offences, such as offensive conduct and language, significantly contribute to the high rates of arrest and prosecution of Indigenous persons. Although the arrest rate for offensive conduct and language has been declining overall, an empirical study in New South Wales has established that minor public order offences continue to have a disproportionate impact on individuals from Indigenous backgrounds: R Jochelson, "Aborigines and Public Order Legislation in New South Wales" (1997) *Crime and Justice Bulletin* No 34. The study revealed that Aboriginal persons continue to be grossly over-represented among arrests for offensive language and conduct offences, and that there was a positive and statistically significant correlation between areas with higher proportions of Aboriginal residents and areas with higher court appearance rates for offensive conduct and language. A qualitative analysis of police narratives describing these incidents, randomly selected, showed (at 15) that the majority involved excessive alcohol consumption and/or interpersonal conflict:

> In the high Aboriginal country area this conflict often involves seemingly ritual confrontations between police and Aboriginal people over swearing in public places or at police themselves. Sometimes the person reported for offensive behaviour and/or offensive language seems to have taken the initiative in provoking the confrontation. Sometimes the confrontation occurs when police question or attempt to detain an Aboriginal person in relation to matters unrelated to offensive behaviour or, alternatively, when police attend an altercation or dispute among Aboriginal people or between non-Aboriginal and Aboriginal people.

Robert Jochelson concluded (at 15) that "arrests for offensive language or behaviour only seem to exacerbate or perpetuate problems of public order rather than reduce them". This seems especially true in country towns where Aboriginal-police relations are strained due to over-policing and the imposition of curfews without legal authority: N O'Neill and R Handley, *Retreat From Injustice* (Sydney: Federation Press, 1995), pp 410-412.

The structure and linguistic forms of Aboriginal English may also contribute to the high rates of arrest for offensive language: B Walsh, "Offensive Language" in D Eades (ed), *Language in Evidence* (Sydney: University of New South Wales Press, 1995).

TABLE 2:

Charges in Local Court Appearances Finalised (NSW)

TYPE OF OFFENCE CHARGED	1993-94	1994-95	1995-96	1996-97	1997-98
offensive behaviour	8418	8290	7753	7197	6923
other offences against good order	3024	3045	3285	3828	3832

Source: *NSW Bureau of Crime Statistics and Research*, http://www.lawlink.nsw.gov.au (as at 25/05/00).

MEASURING OFFENSIVENESS: SOCIAL AND CULTURAL CONTEXT OF LANGUAGE

Mindful of the potential abuse of offensive conduct charges by the police, some courts have held that the use of obscene language is not always criminal — the behaviour alleged to be offensive must be understood in its context. In *Hortin v Rowbottom* (1993) 68 A Crim R 381, the police were called to a domestic dispute in which the accused continually used the word "fuck" during a heated argument with his de-facto spouse outside their home. When the accused refused to calm down and desist from using bad language, he was arrested, charged and ultimately convicted of using indecent language in a public place contrary to s 22 of the *Summary Offences Act* 1953 (SA). Allowing the appeal, the Supreme Court of South Australia held that the magistrate had wrongly concluded (at 384) that the word "fuck" is necessarily indecent regardless of the context or circumstances in which it is used. Mullighan J (at 385-386) reviewed the authorities dealing with indecency in other contexts and highlighted the difficulties in determining a "community standard of decency". These cases revealed that the context and potential audience were critical considerations in determining offensiveness. In this case, the accused did not use the words in their primary sense. Rather the accused had used them as "intensives" or "expletives" in order to give emphasis to the message he was seeking to convey. In this case, the accused had directed the language to persons well-known to him in the context of a family argument and when in a highly emotional state: at 389. Although such language was coarse, and would be offensive to some sections of the community, such language was now commonly used in ordinary conversation by both men and women in many sections of the community, sometimes in its primary sense but more often in its secondary sense, without offending contemporary standards of decency. A similar approach was adopted in Western Australia when the Supreme Court quashed the conviction of Keft (also known as "Rodney Rude") for using the word "fuck" in a public performance: *Keft v Fraser* (unrep, 21/4/1986, 6251).

The courts have held that police officers are persons *capable* of being offended by the accused's conduct. This is a significant concession since the police may be the only individuals present during the alleged offensive behaviour. To hold otherwise, would provide individuals with a license to abuse, harass or intimidate the police. This approach to offensive conduct was taken in the English decision of *DPP v Orum* [1988] Crim LR 848, though with some cautions and caveats. The accused was arrested by police who attended an argument between the accused and his girlfriend late at night in a residential street. The police advised the accused that he was causing a breach of the peace. The accused refused to be quiet, saying "You fuck off. This is a domestic and you can't do nothing. You can't fucking arrest me. I know my rights. If you don't go away, I am going to hit you." He was charged with the offence of using threatening, abusive or insulting words or behaviour within the hearing or sight of a person likely to be caused harassment, alarm or distress: *Public Order Act* 1986 (UK), s 5. The magistrate dismissed the charges on the ground that there were no other persons present — except the police — who were likely to have been harassed, alarmed or distressed. The Divisional Court upheld the Crown's appeal, noting that the attending police were persons capable of being harassed, alarmed or distressed by the accused's conduct. The question of whether harassment, alarm or distress was caused was simply one of fact for the tribunal of fact to determine, though the court pointed out that in most cases, the words and behaviour would be wearily familiar to police and have little emotional impact save that of boredom!

The importance of context was again emphasised in *Saunders v Herold* (1991) 105 FLR 1. The accused, an Aborginal man, and his friends were asked to leave the Canberra Workers Club, which they did. Outside, the accused was approached by police, and was alleged to have said "Why don't you cunts just fuck off and leave us alone?" His conviction for offensive conduct was quashed by Higgins J (at 5):

> What constitutes behaving in an offensive manner depends very much on the circumstances. Conduct and language engaged in at a football match or on a tennis or squash court may be acceptable, or, at least, unremarkable, but offensive if engaged in during a church service or a formal social event.

In this case, the words were vulgar and crude, but understood in the context of a verbal disagreement with the police at 3 am in a deserted street, the conduct could not be regarded by the reasonable bystander as offensive: at 6-8.

A similar approach to offensive language was adopted by White J in *E (A Child) v The Queen* (1994) 76 A Crim R 343. In this case, the accused was convicted of disorderly conduct, which includes using obscene language, by virtue of ss 54 and 59 of the *Police Act* 1892 (WA). The youth had been picked up on the street late at night and taken to the police station to wait there until a responsible adult came to pick him up. The youth, frustrated and distressed, challenged the authority of the police to hold him. In the course of that conversation with a female officer he said "I'm leaving. You have no right to hold me here. I want to fucking go". His swearing led to a warning that he would be arrested for obscene language, which prompted the reply "You can get fucked" and "Fuck you". The magistrate found the language to be obscene and he was convicted.

On appeal, White J held that the question of whether language is obscene must be determined according to community standards, not the standards of a particular witness. He then reviewed the available case law, including many of the decisions discussed above. White J stated that the question of whether language was obscene must be understood in its context. The use of the word "fuck" as an expletive, where there were no sexual overtones or implications, was not obscene language. The conviction also failed on the ground that a lock up was not a "public place" for the purpose of the Act. In this case, the obscenity of language was measured in "neutral" linguistic terms: using the word "fuck" merely as a general expletive did not violate community standards. However, this approach does not reveal the true political context of the words. In this case, the accused was an Aboriginal youth who was resisting police authority to impose a curfew and to detain him without proper legal authority (this significant issue was neither explored at trial nor raised on appeal). In the absence of formal powers to detain him, offensive language provided the police with a "holding charge" and a legal basis for exercising authority over the youth. The judgment of Wright J did not fully expose the legal or political context surrounding the use of offensive words. Nevertheless, the decision does constitute a judicial attempt to place limits on the offence and prevent its overuse against young people and minorities.

> In *Burns v Seagrave & Anor* [2000] NSWSC 77 (23 February 2000), the accused went to Kings Cross police station to complain about drug dealing in the neighbourhood. He was very upset and challenged the police refusal to take action. He refused to give his name when asked and told the sergeant "I don't have to give you anything, you fat spiv. You're nothing but a useless fat spiv. I don't have to talk you, you giraffe." In another exchange, the accused said to the sergeant: "I'm not speaking to you, you're not my type." He was charged with using offensive language and the evidence tendered claimed that the sergeant was extremely offended by the homosexual connotation. The magistrate dismissed the charge. The DPP successfully appealed against the dismissal of the charge, with the Supreme Court of New South Wales agreeing that there was sufficient evidence to allow the case to proceed.

The legal concepts of offensiveness and indecency lie at the heart of many public order offences. Decisions such as *Ball v McIntyre* and *Saunders v Herold* are important particularly as guides to magistrates charged with the duty of determining whether particular conduct is offensive — as one judge recently noted, "some of these cases are so familiar as to be old friends".[22] Although the law determines offensiveness by reference to an "objective test" based on community standards, it is not a value-neutral concept. The conceptions of good order and decency created and applied by both police officers and magistrates have the potential to operate unfairly against minorities who are perceived to be a threat to social order and/or police authority. For a review of the wide range of conduct that has been caught by these laws, see D Brown, D Farrier and D Weisbrot, *Criminal Laws* (2nd ed, Sydney: Federation Press, 1996), pp 957-959.

---

22 *Burns v Seagrave* [2000] NSWSC 77 at para 12, Simpson J.

CASE STUDIES

Socio-Economic and Political Factors in Sentencing Indigenous Persons

While the broader context of "offensive" conduct is often suppressed during the trial process, it may assert itself post-conviction as a factor relevant to sentencing. The relevance of socio-economic and political factors in sentencing Indigenous persons was raised in the High Court decision in *Neal v The Queen* (1982) 149 CLR 305. In this case, the accused, an Aboriginal community leader living on a reserve in Queensland, was convicted of an assault for swearing and spitting at Mr Collins, the manager of the local store and reserve superintendent. The incident arose after an argument over whether the white people on the reserve should leave. In passing sentence, the magistrate took into account that persons of Mr Neal's "type" had been responsible for growing hatred of black against white, and by his agitation was disturbing the "happy life" of Aboriginal people living on the reserve. The Court of Criminal Appeal (Supreme Court of Queensland), on an appeal against sentence, exercised its power to *increase* the term of imprisonment. It did so without hearing argument from Mr Neal why the sentence should not be increased! The High Court reversed that decision and reinstated the original sentence of the magistrate.[23]

The judgment contains a valuable discussion of the relevance of ethnicity to sentencing by Brennan and Murphy JJ. Brennan J offered some important guidance on the relevance of racial factors and the principle of equality before the law to sentencing. This has been explored in Ch 2, p 135. Brennan J approached the issue of race primarily in personal terms, focusing on the stress of an Aboriginal living on a reserve.[24]

By contrast, Murphy J (at 316) viewed the matter as a "race relations" case. As a consequence, his judgment addressed the wider political context of the accused's conduct. While accepting that Mr Neal's conduct constituted an unlawful assault, Murphy J held (at 312) that the assault had to be kept in perspective. In his view, the conditions and race relations on the reserve were relevant mitigating factors. Indeed, he noted (at 316) that the magistrate who passed the original sentence had wrongly concluded that political agitation by Mr Neal and his attempt to change conditions on the reserve were factors aggravating the penalty. Murphy J, citing Oscar Wilde (at 317) regarding the importance of agitators to the advancement of civilisation, concluded that "Mr Neal is entitled to be an agitator". The evidence before the Court revealed that Aborigines on this particular reserve had a deep sense of grievance at their paternalistic treatment by white authorities "in charge" including Mr Collins. Murphy J referred to wide range of historical, political and criminological literature to explain the powerlessness of Aborigines communities in the face of white colonisation.

---

23 Gibbs CJ and Wilson J held that the Court of Criminal Appeal should not have granted leave to appeal in these circumstances and so declined to examine the factors that should properly influence sentencing in this type of case.

24 The judgments of Brennan and Murphy JJ are compared in J Clarke, "Lionel Murphy and Indigenous Australians" in M Coper and G Williams (eds), *Justice Lionel Murphy Influential or Merely Prescient?* (Sydney: Federation Press, 1997), pp 139-144.

Drawing on psychological research, he explained (at 319) how spitting was a typical response of children and others without power who were attempting to degrade and humiliate those who are seen as oppressors. Unlike other members of the court, Murphy J did not reinstate the magistrate's original sentence, but exercised the discretion himself, imposing a fine of one week's sentence. Murphy J's judgment is a rare example of how the meaning of conduct alleged to be offensive and degrading to others can only be truly understood when placed in its wider political and socio-economic context.

Jennifer Clarke has offered the following assessment of the impact of Murphy J's judgment in *Neal*:

> Has Justice Murphy's approach had any impact? The High Court continues to leave sentences largely to the State appeal courts, but there are indications that "Aboriginality", including "the conditions in which the offender lives", is considered to be a relevant factor in sentencing. There is some evidence that Aborigines or Torres Strait Islanders are receiving lighter sentences than other offenders, perhaps because judges are "bending over backwards" to avoid making racially discriminatory decisions. If this is the case, the increasing over-representation of Indigenous people in the criminal justice system must be attributed to other factors, including the continued availability to police of broad discretion to lock up drunks and others who for cultural reasons offend standards of "public order", a more serious problem of increased violence in Aboriginal communities and the complex and related problems of alcohol and substance abuse (footnotes omitted).[25]

3.2 UNLAWFUL ASSEMBLY

The common law misdemeanour of unlawful assembly has been defined as an assembly of three or more persons with intent to commit a crime by open force, or with such an intent to carry out any common purpose, either lawful or unlawful, in such a manner as to endanger the public peace, or to give firm and courageous persons in the neighbourhood of the assembly reasonable grounds to apprehend a breach of the peace as a consequence of it: J Stephen, *A History of the Criminal Law of England* (London: Macmillan, 1883), Vol 2, pp 385-386. Like affray, unlawful assembly requires proof of fear or terror caused to innocent parties present nearby. It is distinguished from affray by the requirement of a common purpose and actual violence is unnecessary provided that the public peace is endangered: *Kamara v DPP* [1974] AC 104 at 116, per Lord Hailsham.

The common law offence, and its statutory variants, have been used against disorderly meetings and gatherings. Indeed, the history of the statutory offence of unlawful assembly in New South Wales is linked to the law and order campaign by the conservative Bavin Government in the 1920s to prevent mass picketing by the Timber Workers Union: D Brown, D Farrier and D Weisbrot,

---

25 J Clarke, "Lionel Murphy and Indigenous Australians" in M Coper and G Williams (eds), *Justice Lionel Murphy Influential or Merely Prescient?* (Sydney: Federation Press, 1997), pp 142-143.

Criminal Laws (2nd ed, Sydney: Federation Press, 1996), p 979. The language of the offences of unlawful and riotous assembly (see below) seem anomalous in the modern age and may explain why conviction rates are relatively low.

At common law, the basic element of the offence of unlawful assembly is causing other persons who are not participating in the assembly, but are present or nearby, to fear on reasonable grounds a breach of the peace: *Kamara v DPP* [1974] AC 104 at 115-116, per Lord Hailsham. The offence is not restricted to assemblies in "public places" and may be committed on private premises provided that the other elements of the offence are satisfied: at 115. In determining whether an assembly is unlawful the court may consider a range of factors including the purpose of the assembly in question, the duration of the use, the place and the hour and whether any obstruction was trivial, casual or temporary, and without wrongful intent: *Lowdens v Keaveny* [1903] 2 IR 82 at 90-91, per Gibson J. This definition has been applied to statutory offences of unlawful assembly enacted in Code and common law jurisdictions in Australia.[26]

The common law offence of unlawful assembly now requires proof of fault. This has been defined as assembling with the necessary intent to use violence or to engage knowingly in conduct that causes or is likely to cause a breach of the peace: *R v Hunt and Others* (1820) 1 State Tr NS 435; *R v Stephens* (1839) 3 State Tr NS 1189 at 1234 per Patterson J. It has been suggested that the fault element will turn on the particular facts of case: *Wise v Dunning* [1902] 1 KB 167 at 178, per Darling J. A leading English textbook has suggested that "it must be proved that [the accused] intended to use or abet the use of violence; or do or abet acts which he [or she] knows to be likely to cause a breach of the peace": JC Smith and B Hogan, *Criminal Law* (5th ed, London: Sweet & Maxwell, 1983), p 732. It is clear that there is no further requirement that participants have knowledge of the unlawfulness of the purpose of the assembly: *R v Fursey* (1833) 6 C & P 80. Mere assembly with the necessary intent constitutes the offence, notwithstanding that the participants subsequently changed their minds and dispersed without any further action: *R v Birt* (1831) 5 C & P 154.

The offence of unlawful assembly is related to other public order offences. Causing another person to be harmed or fear harm through an assault, affray, unlawful assembly or riot is a breach of the peace: see above, p 764. An unlawful assembly may be converted into a riot when a breach of the peace actually occurs: see below, p 809. An assembly of individuals becomes riotous when alarming force or violence begins to be used. The offences of unlawful assembly and riot are closely related, and as Sach LJ noted in *R v Caird* (1970) 54 Cr App Rep 499 (at 504-505) the precise relation between riot and unlawful assembly had not been fully resolved. Sach LJ pointed out (at 505) that the offence is sufficiently broad to criminalise the facilitation of unlawful assemblies, so any person who actively encouraged or promoted an unlawful assembly or riot, whether by words, signs or actions or who participated in it, is guilty of the offence.

---

26 See *Crimes Act* 1900 (NSW), s 545C; *Criminal Code* 1899 (Qld), s 61; *Criminal Code* 1913 (WA), s 62; *Criminal Code* 1924 (Tas), s 73. See generally A Hiller, *Public Order and the Law* (Sydney: Law Book Company Ltd, 1983), p 75. There are also specific offences making it unlawful to assemble at or in the vicinity of certain designated places, such as Parliament House: see *Unlawful Assemblies Ordinance* 1937 (ACT); *Unlawful Assemblies and Processions Act* 1958 (Vic). For further discussion of these political offences, see S Bronitt and S Ford, 10.10 "Public Order" in Title 10 CRIMINAL OFFENCES, *The Laws of Australia* (Sydney: LBC, 1996—), para 34.

In New South Wales, the summary offence of unlawful assembly does not appear to abrogate the common law, though it has been held that the common law has largely fallen into disuse: *Black v Corkery* (1988) 33 A Crim R 134 at 138, per Young J. The statutory offence provides that a person who knowingly joins an unlawful assembly or continues in it shall be taken to be a member of that assembly: *Crimes Act* 1900 (NSW), s 545C (1), see further *R v O' Sullivan* (1948) 54 WN (NSW) 155 at 156, per Jordan CJ. Unlawful assembly is defined in s 545C(3):

> Any assembly of five or more persons whose common object is by means of intimidation or
> injury to compel any person to do what the person is not legally bound to do or to abstain
> from doing what the person is legally entitled to do, shall be deemed to be an unlawful
> assembly.

This offence carries a maximum penalty of six months imprisonment, which is increased to 12 months where weapons are carried: *Crimes Act* 1900 (NSW), s 545C(1), (2). There was uncertainty whether participating in an assembly following the issuing of the proclamation under the Act deems a person to be guilty of the offence. The procedure for issuing a proclamation to disperse an unlawful or riotous assembly is discussed below. However, as Young J noted in *Black v Corkery* (1988) 33 A Crim R 134 (at 140), there was no magic in the reading of a proclamation. A proclamation merely marks the point after which the unlawful assembly must be shown to have continued for the accused to have been found guilty of the offence:

> The mere presence of the person at the spot where an unlawful assembly is taking place is
> some evidence that he [or she] is a member of it but it is not conclusive evidence and the
> tribunal of fact must weigh all the circumstances.

OBSTRUCTION OF THE HIGHWAY

An assembly, meeting or procession on public land, including highways, does not necessarily constitute a trespass unless prior permission is required under relevant statutes or by-laws. This is because the primary purpose of a highway is passage, and accordingly members of the public have a legal right to use a highway for "passing and repassing": *Hubbard v Pitt* [1976] QB 142. Activities incidental to the right of passage have been held to fall within the concept of reasonable and ordinary use of the highway and these include the distribution of leaflets, market research, carol singing, Morris dancing, carnival parades and flag selling: *Nagy v Weston* [1965] 1 All ER 78.

While the common law recognises that an individual or a group of individuals are free to make incidental use of the highway for protest activity, this freedom is severely curtailed by the statutory offences of obstruction that exists in all jurisdictions.[27] The High Court has held that any assembly or meeting on a public street may constitute an obstruction of the highway contrary to statute or local by-laws: *Haywood v Mumford* (1908) 7 CLR 133. In this case, two members of the

---

27 See *Public Order (Protection of Persons and Property) Act* 1971 (Cth), s 9; *Traffic Act* 1937 (ACT), s 21; *Summary Offences Act* 1988 (NSW), s 6; *Police Offences Act* 1953 (SA), s 58; *Police Offences Act* 1935 (Tas), s 15(1)(a); *Summary Offences Act* 1958 (Vic), ss 4 and 5; *Traffic Regulations* 1962 (Qld), regs 44(1), 144 (1); *Traffic (Miscellaneous) Regulations* 1968 (Tas), regs 97, 101, 102.

Salvation Army were convicted of obstructing the highway after they refused to stop singing and playing musical instruments in a street. Their conduct had caused a crowd of about 80 persons to gather in the street, although the magistrate conceded that the conduct had not caused any actual interference with traffic and was not an unreasonable use of the street. The members of the High Court attached no significance to the fundamental importance of peaceful assembly or the danger of prior restraint. Adopting a highly formalistic approach, O'Connor J defined obstruction expansively (at 140) as "any obstruction which interferes to an appreciable practical extent with the right which every member of the public has to use the highway, and to use it at all times and under all circumstances". The effect of obstruction is that the law draws a distinction between processions that constitute a "reasonable exercise" of the right to use the highway for passage, and stationary assemblies, meetings and pickets that cause an obstruction and therefore do not constitute a reasonable use of the highway.[28]

Obstruction of the highway does not require proof of fault on the part of the accused, except in the Australian Capital Territory and New South Wales: *Traffic Act* 1937 (ACT), s 21 (wilful or negligent obstruction); *Summary Offences Act* 1988 (NSW), s 6 (wilful obstruction). In *Fitzgerald v Montoya* (1989) 16 NSWLR 164, Kirby P held (at 166) that the term "wilful" used in the offence of obstruction should be construed narrowly, as a broader construction could become "a means of oppressing those whose presence in a public place is a source of irritation to the overly sensitive". Accordingly, the term "wilful" means intention or knowledge that the conduct would have the effect of preventing the free passage of someone else without any lawful excuse for doing so. Other legislation requires proof that the conduct of the accused amounted to an "unreasonable" or "undue" obstruction, though these concepts are not defined.[29]

LICENSING PUBLIC ASSEMBLIES: IMMUNITIES AND PRIOR RESTRAINT

Like many other public order laws, unlawful assembly poses the danger of prior restraint of peaceful and otherwise lawful protest. It may be argued, applying the common law principle in *Beatty v Gillbanks* (1882) 9 QBD 308, that a peaceful and lawful assembly should not be rendered unlawful by the mere presence of hostile opponents who cause or threaten to cause a breach of the peace: see above, pp 771. However, the common law caution against imposing prior restraint on peaceful assemblies has been significantly diluted by the legislative licensing schemes for public assemblies or processions. In the Australian Capital Territory, the Northern Territory, Tasmania and Western Australia it is an offence to organise an assembly without a permit or licence. In the other jurisdictions, obtaining a licence or permit is not mandatory, though it furnishes essential immunity from liability for "street offences" such as causing obstruction of the highway and unlawful

---

28 A Goodhart, "Public Meetings and Processions" (1936) 6 *Cambridge Law Journal* 161 at 169; E Ivamy "The Right of Public Meeting" (1949) 2 *Current Legal Problems* 183 at 192; H Wade, "The Law of Public Meeting" (1938) 2 *Modern Law Review* 177.

29 *Public Order (Protection of Persons and Places) Act* 1988 (Cth), s 9; *Summary Offences Act* 1958 (Vic), s 5. These offences are further discussed in S Bronitt and S Ford, 10.10 "Public Order" in Title 10 CRIMINAL OFFENCES, *The Laws of Australia* (Sydney: LBC, 1996–), paras 43-44.

assembly.[30] These licensing laws have a broadly similar effect, though in Queensland, the legislation creates a statutory right of peaceful assembly that may only be curtailed in accordance with the restriction contained in the *International Covenant on Civil and Political Rights*: see above, p 774.

Under these licensing laws, law enforcement officials and judges possess wide powers to impose restrictions and prohibitions upon assemblies or processions. In most jurisdictions, the relevant legislation provides little guidance to the police or the courts on whether an assembly or procession should be prohibited or allowed to proceed under certain conditions. Restrictions and prohibitions that are imposed are reviewable before the courts. One of the few reported cases reviewing the power to impose restrictions on public assemblies is *Commissioner of Police v Allen* (1984) 14 A Crim R 244, where the New South Wales Police Commissioner sought an order to prohibit Women Against Rape participating in the annual Anzac parade in Sydney. Hunt J noted that the *Public Assemblies Act* 1979 (NSW) was completely silent on the criteria to be applied by the Commissioner or the court. In his view, assembly or procession would be commonly prohibited or otherwise restricted where it is likely to provoke others to cause a breach of the peace or other offences: at 250. However, potential disorder was not the only basis for prohibiting assemblies or processions. The legislature identified that the time, the place, the number of people involved and the purpose of the proposed assembly or procession were also relevant. Hunt J held (at 251) that the order of prohibition had to be determined by balancing competing interests:

> What both the Commissioner and the court must do, it seems to me, is to balance the democratic right of every person in this community to exercise his or her freedom of speech and freedom of assembly with the democratic rights of others to be spared unnecessary offence [sic] or affront by the exercise of those freedoms of speech and assembly.

Causing serious offense and affront could provide the basis for restricting the march. Hunt J warned that this did not mean that courts should prohibit an assembly or procession solely on the ground that the views expressed are unpopular or may provoke a strong reaction in those who disagree with them. As Hunt J noted (at 251), Australian society and the police are made of "sufficiently stern stuff as to be able to cope with disputes of that type". Nevertheless, it was the emotional reaction that the proposed march would create, not the physical competition between the two marches, that constituted the basis for prohibiting the proposed assembly: at 253. The proposed assembly and procession were considered likely to cause grave offense, and were likely to constitute a massive affront to those who were about to participate in or view the Anzac Day march.

Since "causing serious offense and affront" provides a ground for prohibiting public assemblies or processions, there is a serious danger that the law will operate as a "heckler's charter" unduly restricting freedom of speech, assembly and association. In Hunt J's view, it did not matter whether the offense was intended or not, merely that it will occur: at 252. The threat of prior restraint and the difficulties faced by police and judges required to balance the exercise of competing lawful rights have been discussed above: see pp 772-773. See further R Handley, "'Serious Affront' and the

---

30 Public Parks Regulations 1930 (ACT), reg 21; Traffic Regulations 1949 (NT), reg 134; Traffic (Miscellaneous) Regulations 1968 (Tas), regs 99(3), (4), 110(2); *Police Act* 1892 (WA), ss 52(3), 54(B). For a discussion of the various powers to licence, control and prohibit public assemblies or processions, see S Bronitt and S Ford, 10.10 "Public Order" in Title 10 Criminal Offences, *The Laws of Australia* (Sydney: LBC, 1996–).

NSW Public Assemblies Legislation" (1986) 10 Crim LJ 287; C Ronalds, "Anzac Day and the Aftermath" (1983) 8 *Legal Services Bulletin* 133.

   The prohibition order issued by Hunt J did not make it an offence for the women to assemble or march, though it did mean that the organisers and participants forfeited their immunity from prosecution for various street offences. As a consequence, 168 women protestors who marched on Anzac Day were arrested, prosecuted and convicted of the summary offence of causing serious alarm or affront and their convictions were upheld on appeal: *Connolly v Willis* [1984] 1 NSWLR 373.[31] (The offence has since been repealed and replaced by the crime of offensive conduct.)

3.3 AFFRAY AND FIGHTING IN PUBLIC PLACES

The common law misdemeanour of affray is committed by a person who engages in a display of force that causes terror to others, or participates in actual violence that induces others to fear personal violence: *Taylor v DPP* [1973] AC 964 at 989 per Lord Reid.[32] Affray is commonly used to deal with brawling and fighting. The common law offence of affray applies in South Australia and Victoria and has also been preserved by s 72 of the *Criminal Code* (Qld), s 80 of the *Criminal Code* (Tas) and s 71 of the Criminal Code (WA). In the Australian Capital Territory, the common law offence of affray has been abolished by s 25 of the *Public Order (Protection of Persons and Property) Act* 1971 (Cth) and replaced by a statutory offence of fighting in any public place: *Crimes Act* 1900 (ACT), s 545A. In New South Wales, the common law offence of affray has not been abolished, though a statutory offence of affray has recently been enacted modelled on the *Public Order Act* 1986 (UK): *Crimes Act* 1900 (NSW), s 93C. In the Northern Territory it is an offence to go armed in public and to issue a challenge to fight a duel: *Criminal Code* (NT), ss 69, 70.

   The common law misdemeanour of affray had largely fallen into disuse by the end of the 19th century in England and Australia. As Lord Reid noted in *Taylor v DPP* [1973] AC 964 (at 988):

> For some reason which I have not discovered there were few prosecutions for this offence
> for a very long period before the middle of this century. But then the practical advantages
> to the prosecution of using this offence must have occurred to somebody.

Affray was revived by prosecutors in England in the 1950s and 1960s: I Brownlie, "The Renovation of Affray" [1965] Crim LR 479. The offence became useful to prosecutors to deal with the outbreak of "hooliganism" and fights between gangs disrupting the relative stability of the postwar period.[33] The use of affray, along with the common law offences such as riot and rout, was the result of the efforts of prosecutors as well as the courts willing to adapt and refine (where necessary) these common law

---

31   For a discussion of the political background to the various Anzac Day parades involving Women Against Rape during the 1980s, see B Gaze and M Jones, *Law, Liberty and Australian Democracy* (Sydney: Law Book Company Ltd, 1990), pp 161-167.

32   *R v Sharp and Johnson* [1957] 1 All ER 577. See *R v Button and Swain* [1966] 3 AC 591 at 623-627, per Lord Gardiner LC, for a discussion of the historical background to the offence of affray.

33   For a discussion of these developments in the Australian context, see R White (ed), *Youth Subcultures: Theory, History and the Australian Experience* (Hobart: National Clearinghouse for Youth Studies, 1993).

offences to modern conditions: DGT Williams, "Freedom of Assembly and Free Speech: Changes and Reforms in England" (1975) 1(2) *University of New South Wales Law Journal* 97 at 101.

A similar pattern is evident in Australian jurisdictions. In New South Wales, the revival of the use of affray to deal with public order situations has been facilitated by legislation. The following provisions were inserted into the *Crimes Act* 1900 (NSW):

93C Affray

(1) A person who uses or threatens unlawful violence toward another and whose conduct is such as would cause a person of reasonable firmness present at the scene to fear for his or her personal safety is guilty of affray and liable to penal servitude for 5 years.

(2) If 2 or more persons use or threaten the unlawful violence, it is the conduct of them taken together that must be considered for the purpose of subsection (1).

(3) The common purpose may be inferred from conduct.

(4) No person of reasonable firmness need actually be, or be likely to be present at the scene.

(5) Affray may be committed in private as well as in public places.

The definition section defines "violence" as follows:

93A Definition. In this Part —

"violence" means any violent conduct, so that —

(a) it includes violent conduct towards property as well as violent conduct towards persons, and

(b) it is not restricted to conduct causing or intended to cause injury or damage but includes any other violent conduct (for example, throwing at or towards a person a missile of a kind capable of causing injury which does not hit or falls short).

The offence is identical to the statutory offence of affray enacted by the *Public Order Act* 1986 (UK). The "law and order" campaign in New South Wales that led to the modernisation of riot and affray is discussed below: see Resuscitating Riot and Affray in New South Wales, p 805.

The common law and statutory offences of affray overlap with other crimes of violence, such as assault and reckless endangerment. As a consequence, the offence is often viewed as an offence against the person rather than a public order offence.[34] This view is not shared by the Model Criminal Code Officers Committee, and affray was not included in the chapter dealing with offences against the person: *Chapter 5 — Non Fatal Offences Against the Person,* Report (Canberra: AGPS, 1998). More likely, the offence of affray will be included in the forthcoming chapter of the *Model Criminal Code* dealing with Offences Against Public Order.

The boundaries of affray are hazy, overlapping with offences such as assault and grievous bodily harm. Within the hierarchy of public order offences, affray is regarded as an intermediate offence — less serious than riot but more serious than disorderly conduct — for dealing with small

---

34 Affray has been categorised as an offence against the person in P Fairall 10.2 "Assault and Related Offences" in Title 10 CRIMINAL OFFENCES, *The Laws of Australia* (Sydney: LBC, 1996–), Part J.

scale public order threats. As Nicola Lacey and Celia Wells conclude: "Affray is a common choice of charge after Saturday night pub brawls": *Reconstructing Criminal Law* (2nd ed, London: Butt, 1998), p 116. The advantage of affray from the law enforcement perspective is that it is not necessary for the prosecution to prove that individual blows were inflicted without consent. Rather the focus of the charge is whether the conduct is capable, objectively speaking, of causing alarm and fear to the public. This may have practical advantages in cases where the participants and potential victims are unwilling to cooperate with the prosecution or where it is difficult to identify who inflicted which blow and caused which injury.

The common law of affray has been progressively broadened by judicial development: *R v Sharp* [1957] 1 QB 552. In relation to the number of persons necessary to constitute the offence, it has been held that "it may well be that if two people fight and one is acting in self-defence that man cannot be said to be guilty of an affray, but it would appear to this court that there is no reason why his attacker, whether acting alone or jointly with another attacker, should not be guilty of the affray": *Scarrow* (1968) 52 Cr App R 591 at 596; see also *Summers* (1972) 56 Cr App R 604. Thus, the courts have upheld the conviction of a single aggressor who so ferociously attacked his victim as to terrify a member of the public who witnessed the attack: *R v Button and Swain* [1966] AC 591. Although the nature of the offence typically involves conduct by more than one person, a person brandishing a rifle in a manner calculated to terrify a bystander has been held to be an affray: *Taylor v DPP* [1973] AC 964 at 991, per Lord Morris.

The public order dimension of affray is a requirement of public alarm, namely that the display of force or participation in violence must be such as to put bystanders in terror or fear of personal violence: *R v Button and Swain* [1966] AC 591; *Taylor v DPP* [1973] AC 964; *Attorney-General's Reference (No 3 of 1983)* [1985] QB 242. The original common law requirement that the affray cause actual terror or occur in a public place is no longer necessary: *R v Button and Swain* [1966] AC 591; *R v Summers* (1972) 56 Cr App R 604. In *Taylor v DPP* [1973] AC 964 the House of Lords held (at 987) that in cases where an affray is committed in a public place, it is no longer necessary to prove that members of the public were present and were terrified. It is sufficient to show that the violence used was of such a kind as to render the place unusable by persons of a reasonably firm disposition. In cases where an affray occurs in a private place, it is necessary to prove the presence of persons who were not engaged in the fighting: at 988. The statutory definitions of affray reflect this widened definition. For example, the statutory offence of affray in New South Wales provides that an affray may be committed in private as well as public places: *Crimes Act* 1900 (NSW), s 93C(5). Even in those jurisdictions that followed the old common law and limited the offence of affray to public places, the legislation usually adopts an extended definition of public place to include any place to which members of the public ordinarily have access.[35] The New South Wales offence also dispenses with the common law requirement of proving that a person actually experienced terror as a result of the accused's conduct. It is sufficient if the conduct would be likely to cause a hypothetical person of "reasonable firmness" present at the scene to fear for his or her personal safety: s 93C(4).

---

35 See for example, the *Crimes Act* 1900 (ACT), s 8, which deems the following to be a "public place": "a vessel or vehicle only, or a room, or field, or place, ordinarily private, was at the time used for a public purpose, or as a place of common resort, or was open to the public on the payment of money or otherwise".

Resuscitating Riot and Affray in New South Wales

In August 1986, following a week of escalating tension with the police, a group of Aboriginal youths in Bourke went on a rampage. Police called to investigate a broken shop window were pelted with rocks and bottles. The local police responded by clearing the street and calling for back up from riot squads. Eleven of the 16 people arrested were juveniles. Ten were charged with common law riot, an offence carrying life imprisonment. Similar clashes between Aboriginal youths and paramilitary riot police units (euphemistically called the "Tactical Response Group") in Redfern in 1988 led to an immediate Government pledge of legislative intervention. A package of reforms creating new offences of riot, affray and violent disorder were copied *verbatim* from the *Public Order Act* 1986 (UK). This historical background, and the role of politics in generating a "law and order" campaign against Aboriginal youth is discussed in C Cunneen, "Enforcing Genocide? Aboriginal Young People and the Police" in R White and C Alder (eds), *The Police and Young People in Australia* (Cambridge: Cambridge University Press, 1994), pp 146-148. See also, C Cunneen, "The Policing of Public Order: Some Thoughts on Culture, Space and Political Economy" in M Findlay and R Hogg (eds), *Understanding Crime and Criminal Justice* (Sydney: Law Book Company Ltd, 1988).

3.4 ROUT AND VIOLENT DISORDER

The offence of affray is closely related to the common law misdemeanour of rout. This offence has been defined as a disturbance of the peace by three or more persons who have assembled together with the intention to do a thing which, if executed, would make them rioters, and have actually taken steps to execute their purpose: A Hiller, *Public Order and the Law* (Sydney: Law Book Company Ltd, 1983), pp 69-70; M Supperstone, *Brownlie's Law of Public Order and National Security* (2nd ed, London: Butt, 1981), p 130. Unlike riot, rout may be complete without the execution of the intended common purpose.

The offence is obscure and has largely fallen into disuse. The common law offences of riot, rout and affray have been abolished in New South Wales: *Crimes Act* 1900 (NSW), s 93E. These have been replaced by the statutory offences of riot and affray: ss 93B, 93C. There is no equivalent intermediate offence of rout in the Northern Territory, Queensland, Tasmania and Western Australia.

In New South Wales, the statutory offences of riot and affray are supplemented by an "intermediate" offence of violent disorder. Section 11A (formerly s 28) of the *Summary Offences Act* 1988 (NSW) provides:

11A Violent disorder

(1) If 3 or more persons who are present together use or threaten unlawful violence and the conduct of them (taken together) is such as would cause a person of reasonable firmness present at the scene to fear for his or her personal safety, each of the persons using or threatening unlawful violence is guilty of an offence.

Maximum penalty: 10 penalty units or imprisonment for 6 months.

(2) It is immaterial whether or not the 3 or more persons use or threaten unlawful violence simultaneously.

(3) No person of reasonable firmness need actually be, or be likely to be, present at the scene.

(4) An offence under subsection (1) may be committed in private as well as in public places.

(5) A person is guilty of an offence under subsection (1) only if he or she intends to use or threaten violence or is aware that his or her conduct may be violent or threaten violence.

(6) Subsection (5) does not affect the determination for the purposes of subsection (1) of the number of persons who use or threaten violence.

(7) In this section:

violence means any violent conduct, so that:

(a) it includes violent conduct towards property as well as violent conduct towards persons, and

(b) it is not restricted to conduct causing or intended to cause injury or damage but includes any other violent conduct (for example, throwing at or towards a person a missile of a kind capable of causing injury which does not hit or falls short).

Like the statutory offences of affray and riot, the offence of violent disorder is borrowed from the *Public Order Act* 1986 (UK). The elements of violent disorder have been discussed in the following cases: *Mahroof* [1989] Crim LR 72, at 74; *Fleming & Robinson* [1989] Crim LR 658; *McGuigan & Cameron* [1991] Crim LR 719; *Jefferson* [1994] 1 All ER 270.

The purpose of the violent disorder offence was to deal with disorderly conduct that threatened public safety and property. The offence targets disturbances and rowdy conduct of a relatively minor nature. The less serious nature of the offence is reflected in its inclusion in the *Summary Offences Act* 1988 (NSW) rather than the *Crimes Act* 1900 (NSW), and the relatively lenient maximum penalty of six months imprisonment. The offence is defined in similar terms to affray, which is a more serious offence carrying a maximum penalty of five years imprisonment. Indeed, the principal difference between affray and violent disorder is that an affray involves two or more persons, while violent disorder involves three or more persons. In this regard, the hierarchy of seriousness seems counterintuitive. Ordinarily, the presence of other individuals sharing a common purpose aggravates the seriousness of the offence. Yet, in New South Wales, a group of persons engaging in violent disorder may be punished more leniently than two individuals engaged in a fight amounting to an affray. Because of the summary jurisdiction and the more lenient penalty in New South Wales, the offence of violent disorder is more commonly prosecuted than riot or affray.

3.5 SEDITION AND RIOT

In historical terms, sedition and riot were among the most serious public order offences under the common law. In the modern context, these offences have generally declined in significance. Sedition, in particular, was rarely used in the 20th century. The practical demise of sedition is related to its breadth and potential to interfere with peaceful agitation for political and constitutional change. The political implications of sedition make the offence unattractive to prosecutors. Also, the offence cannot be prosecuted without the consent of the Attorney-General or Director of Public Prosecutions and, in any event, carries a lesser penalty than many other public order offences.

SEDITION

Under the common law, the crime of sedition covers any conduct (acts, words, writing or publications) accompanied by a "seditious intent". The definition of seditious intent under s 24A of the *Crimes Act* 1914 (Cth) mirrors the common law, and is typical of the provisions enacted in the Code jurisdictions: *Criminal Code* (NT), ss 44-48; *Criminal Code* (Qld), ss 44-52; *Criminal Code* (Tas), ss 66-67; *Criminal Code* (WA), ss 44-52.

> **SECT 24A — Definition of seditious intention**
>
> An intention to effect any of the following purposes, that is to say:
>
> **(a)** to bring the Sovereign into hatred or contempt;
>
> **(d)** to excite disaffection against the Government or Constitution of the Commonwealth or against either House of the Parliament of the Commonwealth;
>
> **(f)** to excite Her Majesty's subjects to attempt to procure the alteration, otherwise than by lawful means, of any matter in the Commonwealth established by law of the Commonwealth; or
>
> **(g)** to promote feelings of ill-will and hostility between different classes of Her Majesty's subjects so as to endanger the peace, order or good government of the Commonwealth;
>
> is a seditious intention.

The High Court, upholding the constitutional validity of this offence, confirmed a person could be convicted of sedition even where the conduct did not cause or incite violence or public disorder: *R v Sharkey* (1949) 79 CLR 121. While potentially broad, the High Court has emphasised that political criticism directed at public officials, even when it brings them into disrepute, would not constitute sedition: *Burns v Ransley* (1949) 79 CLR 101 at 115. Reflecting this concern, the Code jurisdictions have enacted a broad defence based on "innocent intentions" that offers protection to individuals who in good faith attempt to bring about political and constitutional change by lawful and peaceful means.[36]

> **Except for its brief renaissance to combat Communism in the late 1940s, leading to the prosecution of agitators such as Burns and Sharkey, the offence of sedition seems to be a dead-letter.**

---

36 *Criminal Code* (NT), s 48; *Criminal Code* (Qld), s 45; *Criminal Code* (Tas), s 68; *Criminal Code* (WA), s 24.

Though fallen into disuse, the offence of sedition, like affray, is always capable of resuscitation. While prosecution has been rare in Australia, sedition is not benign and can continue to have a "chilling effect" on publishers, individuals and organisations that criticise organs of government. As Enid Campbell and Harry Whitmore have pointed out, "When the law may have such broad application, it is only the executive discretion as to prosecution which stands in the way of governmental suppression of political views": *Freedom in Australia* (Revised ed, Sydney: Sydney University Press, 1973), p 329. In the authors' view, sedition requires reform and incitement to violence and civil disorder should be made an essential ingredient of the offence: p 329. This re-focusing on disorder would lead to a significant overlap with existing public order offences and would render the offence of sedition legally redundant.

In jurisdictions which have not enacted racial vilification offences, there may be scope for prosecutors to use sedition against individuals who incite racial hatred on the basis that their conduct would "promote feelings of ill-will and hostility between different classes of Her Majesty's subjects".[37]

RIOT

Riot is the most serious public order offence and under the common law carries the maximum penalty of life imprisonment. The offence applies to groups of individuals who perpetrate violence with others in a manner that causes public alarm. Participants must act with a "common purpose" that encompasses not only violence, but also a common intention to use force against any person who opposes them.

The common law governing riot assumed its modern features in the 18th century as prosecutors and judges in England sought to maintain control faced by increasing levels of disorder and political agitation by the urban poor. Bread and food riots were commonplace at this time. The responsibility for restoring order remained with local constables supervised by Justices of the Peace. Increasing concern about the dangers of revolution often resulted in over-reaction with bloody consequences, especially where the magistrates sought assistance from the military to suppress unlawful and riotous assemblies.

Rioting in early colonial Australia stemmed largely from drunken and disorderly mobs: P Grabosky, *Sydney in Ferment* (Canberra: ANU Press, 1977). As a consequence, riots were viewed as the work of larrikin elements rather than the revolutionary mobs that were agitating for political change in Europe. The fear of revolution led to the enactment of draconian statutory powers to disperse crowds, including authorising the use of lethal force where necessary, after the reading of a proclamation in accordance with the *Riot Act* 1715 (UK).

The *Riot Act* 1715 (UK) was received into the Australian colonies and several Australian jurisdictions continue to retain the provisions relating to proclamation (reading the *Riot Act*) and the wide immunities for those who disperse riotous assemblies. The advent of professional policing in England and the Australian colonies in the 19th century led to a decreased reliance on riot offences

---

37   For a discussion of the difficulties in using sedition to criminalise racial vilification, see Human Rights and Equal Opportunity Commission, *Racist Violence* (Canberra: AGPS, 1991), pp 29-31.

and draconian powers of dispersal. In the postwar period, powers and offences dealing with riotous assemblies have been revived to deal with unruly and violent crowds in a variety of situations including public disturbances outside a police station (*R v McCormack* [1981] VR 104); violence at motorcycle races and soccer matches (*Anderson v Attorney-General (NSW)* (1987) 10 NSWLR 198); and outbreaks of disorder following incidents of racial discrimination: Human Rights and Equal Opportunity Commission, *Toomelah Report* (Sydney: HREOC, 1988); *R v Muranyi* (1986) 8 Cr App Rep (S) 176.

The precise scope of riot under the common law was unclear until clarified in the early 20th century. In *Field v Receiver of Metropolitan Police* [1907] 2 KB 853, Phillimore J (at 860) reviewed the available authorities and defined riot as requiring proof of the following elements:

(1) three or more persons;

(2) acting with a common purpose;

(3) which has been executed or incepted;

(4) with the intent to help one another by force if necessary against any person who may oppose them in the execution of their common purpose; and

(5) applying the use of force or violence, not merely used in demolishing, but displayed in such a manner as to alarm at least one person of reasonable firmness and courage.[38]

If there is force or violence present, it is immaterial if the purpose intended to be executed is lawful or unlawful: *R v Soley* (1707) 11 Mod Rep 115; *R v Graham* (1888) 16 Cox CC 420, per Charles J at 427.

In his review of the law of riot, Geoffrey Flick in *Civil Liberties in Australia* (Sydney: Law Book Company Ltd, 1981), p 102, suggests that there would be no riot where the common purpose has been executed in consequence of a lawful authority and no more force is displayed than is reasonably necessary. This is simply an acknowledgment that self-defence, as a general defence, may be raised as a defence to a charge of riot.

The common law offence of riot requires proof of public alarm. In the 19th century, courts held that to satisfy this element of the offence, the prosecution had to adduce evidence of one witness that she or he was terrified: *R v Langford* (1842) 174 ER 653. The renaissance of the riot in the mid-20th century led to reformulation of this element into an objective test. Lord Goddard CJ in *R v Sharp* [1957] 1 QB 552 held (at 560) that it suffices if the natural tendency of the conduct involved would be to cause alarm to members of the public. The statutory offence of riot has adopted a similar objective test requiring fear on the part of the (hypothetical) person of reasonable firmness: see below, p 810. The opposition to lawful authority is also an element of riot. In *R v Hunt* (1845) 1 Cox CC 177 Alderson J held (at 177) that "there must be some sort of resistance to lawful authority to constitute [a riot]".

---

38 This statement of principle was applied in *Ford v Receiver for the Metropolitan Police District* [1921] 2 KB 344 at 349-350; *Pitchers v Surrey County Council* [1923] 2 KB 57 at 60-61; *JW Dwyer Ltd v Receiver for the Metropolitan Police District* [1967] 2 QB 970 at 977-978.

Reading the Riot Act: God Save the Queen!

Statutory powers exist in all jurisdictions except New South Wales governing the dispersal of an unlawful or riotous assembly. These provisions are modelled on the *Riot Act* 1714 (UK) (1 Geo 1 Stat 2 c 5) which requires a proclamation or order to be read to the assembly directing them to disperse within a certain time, with criminal liability attaching to failure to disperse: see Table below, pp 811-812. Section 64(1) of the *Criminal Code* (Qld) contains a typical proclamation:

> Our Sovereign Lady the Queen charges and commands all persons here assembled immediately to disperse themselves and peaceably to depart to their habitations or to their lawful business, or they will be guilty of a crime, and will be liable to be imprisoned for life. God Save the Queen!

Legislation identifies the persons authorised to read the proclamations, such as the Sheriff or Under Sheriff, the Mayor of a municipality or a Justice of the Peace, or police officer. It is an offence to remain assembled after the reading of the proclamation. A person who obstructs, opposes or prevents a person from making or beginning to make such a proclamation or order is also guilty of a crime. These offences are punishable by a maximum of life imprisonment in some jurisdictions. Although these draconian powers and offences have been preserved in Australia, the *Riot Act* 1715 (UK) was abolished in England in 1973. See generally, A Hiller, *Public Order and the Law* (Sydney: Law Book Company Ltd, 1983), pp 77-85.

Statutory offences of riot (or riotous assembly) have been adopted in all jurisdictions, except South Australia: see Table 3. The statutory offence of riot in s 93B of the *Crimes Act* 1900 (NSW), follows the definition in the *Public Order Act* 1986 (UK).

Riot

(1) Where 12 or more persons who are present together use or threaten unlawful violence for a common purpose and the conduct of them (taken together) is such as would cause a person of reasonable firmness present at the scene to fear for his or her personal safety, each of the persons using unlawful violence for the common purpose is guilty of riot and liable to imprisonment for 10 years.

(2) It is immaterial whether or not the 12 or more persons use or threaten unlawful violence simultaneously.

(3) The common purpose may be inferred from conduct.

(4) No person of reasonable firmness need actually be, or be likely to be, present at the scene.

(5) Riot may be committed in private as well as in public places.

Section 5 of the *Unlawful Assemblies and Processions Act* 1958 (Vic) has broadened the common law offence of riot to include riotous assemblies. In Queensland and Western Australia, an unlawful assembly becomes a riot when the assembly begins to act in such a tumultuous manner as to disturb the peace and the persons then assembled are regarded as riotously assembled: *Criminal Code* 1899 (Qld), s 61(4); *Criminal Code* 1913 (WA), s 62. Section 73(3) of the *Criminal Code* 1924 (Tas) defines a "riot" as an unlawful assembly that has begun to put into execution the common purpose. The minimum number of persons required to constitute the offence of riot varies from jurisdiction to jurisdiction: see Table below.

TABLE 3:
Riot and Related Offences

JURISDICTION	TYPE OF OFFENCE	NUMBER OF PARTICIPANTS	STATUTE/ COMMON LAW	MAX. PENALTY
CTH	riot abolished	—	—	—
	refusal to disperse	12	*Public Order (Protection of Persons and Property) Act* 1971, ss 8, 17	6 months
ACT	riot abolished	—	—	—
		20	*Unlawful Assemblies Ordinance* 1937, s 3(2)	6 months or $200 fine
	refusal to disperse	12	*Public Order (Protection of Persons and Property) Act* 1971, ss 8, 17	6 months
NSW	riot	12	*Crimes Act* 1900, s 93B	10 years
NT	riot	3	*Criminal Code*, s 63(4)	14 years
	refusal to disperse	12	*Criminal Code*, s 66(4)	6 months
			Public Order (Protection of Persons and Property) Act 1971, s 8, 17	
QLD	riot	3	*Criminal Code*, s 63	3 years
	refusal to disperse	12	*Criminal Code*, s 66	7 years
SA	riot	3	common law	—

Table 3 continued

JURISDICTION	TYPE OF OFFENCE	NUMBER OF PARTICIPANTS	STATUTE/ COMMON LAW	MAX. PENALTY
TAS	riot	3	*Criminal Code*, ss 73(3), 75	–
	refusal to disperse	12	*Criminal Code*, s 77	–
VIC	riotous assembly	3	*Unlawful Assemblies and Processions Act 1958*, ss 5, 6 and 10	–
	refusal to disperse	–	*Unlawful Assemblies and Processions Act 1958*, s 12	3 months
WA	riot	3	*Criminal Code*, s 64	3 years
	refusal to disperse	12	*Criminal Code*, s 65	14 years

The Code jurisdictions have enacted aggravated riot offences. For example, it is an offence, punishable by life imprisonment, to participate in a riot that demolishes a building: *Criminal Code* (NT), s 67; *Criminal Code* (Qld), s 65; *Criminal Code* (WA), s 65. Participating in a prison riot, unlawful assembly or mutiny is a separate statutory offence under s 92 of the *Corrective Services Act* 1988 (Qld). Under this offence, a prisoner can be convicted of taking part in a prison riot even though fewer than two other prisoners are convicted of taking part in the same riot: *R v Thomas* [1993] 1 Qd R 323. The prisoner must take part in the actions which make the assembly a "riot". If the behaviour consists of a number of elements, the accused must be involved in at least some of that activity. The question of whether a particular prisoner is sufficiently involved is a question of fact for the jury. The words "take part in" must be given their ordinary meaning of active involvement and once riotous behaviour is discerned by part of the unlawfully assembled group, all the members of the group are thereby guilty of riot: *R v Cook* (1994) 74 A Crim R 1.

4. CONCLUSION

> This area has great intrinsic interest and importance,
> but is generally taught in law schools in the context of courses
> on civil liberties, thus diverting its attention away from its
> implications for the general structure of criminal law.
> How can this area of criminal regulation, which impinges
> on some of the most contested areas of social life,
> illuminate our general understanding of criminal law?

Nicola Lacey and Celia Wells,
Reconstructing Criminal Law
(London: Butt, 1998), p 92

Many themes have been identified in this review of public order powers and offences. These include the relative legal invisibility of summary offences and preventive powers; the centrality of police discretion; their discriminatory use against minorities; the malleability of the public/private distinction and their susceptibility of "law and order" politics.

Public order remains a neglected part of the criminal law. To borrow Doreen McBarnet's phrase, an "ideology of triviality" pervades the legal discourse surrounding public order offences: *Conviction: Law, the State and the Construction of Justice* (London: MacMillan, 1981), Ch 7, discussed in Ch 1, p 37. Although practically and numerically significant, public order offences receive only limited attention from legal academics and appellate courts. Confined largely to the summary level, many fundamental definitions (such as "breach of the peace" and "offensive conduct") remain indeterminate and under-analysed. Public order offences further reinforce this marginal status by often dispensing with fundamental principles of the criminal law such as the presumption of a fault element: see above, pp 787-788.

The jurisdiction of public order offences and powers seems constrained to "public" spaces. Yet, as in other areas, the public/private dichotomy is neither stable nor immutable. While some "private" forms of disorder such as domestic violence have been accorded immunity, in recent years legislation has extended the powers and offences to deal with disorder to private as well as public spaces. The boundaries of public order offences are malleable, potentially subsuming any behaviour that violates the criminal law and which can therefore be constructed as a "law and order" problem: N Lacey and C Wells, *Reconstructing Criminal Law* (2nd ed, London: Butt, 1998), pp 115-116. As a consequence, public order law is highly susceptible to what David Brown and Russell Hogg describe as an "uncivil politics of law and order": *Rethinking Law and Order* (Sydney: Pluto Press, 1998). Moral panics about the lawlessness of particular groups have justified the rapid expansion of police powers and the range of public order offences.

The hallmark of public order law is the indeterminacy of its key powers and offences. This confers upon police officers a wide scope of discretion. In many cases, the law operates as a resource for the police to negotiate situations with a potential for disorder. As noted above, since police intervention does not always follow with an arrest or charge, there is a danger that the *process is the punishment*. While providing flexibility for the police, the judicial reluctance to guide police discretion has had adverse implications for those engaged in peaceful protest or women suffering domestic violence. In relation to these issues, we have examined how legislative reform has sought to influence and constrain the exercise of police discretion.

Public order law strives to suppress the political and social context of "disorder". Inevitably, these efforts are only partially successful. The legal controversies that surround key definitions, as well as policies of law enforcement, are inevitably bound up in wider political and societal conflicts. We examined how public order powers and offences may infringe upon fundamental civil and political rights, and how they continue to be implicated in the over-policing and harassment of disadvantaged groups, such as Indigenous youth. Public order law plays an important symbolic as well instrumental role in order maintenance.

As well as providing legal powers to respond to outbreaks of disorder, it establishes and maintains police authority over defined spaces. Within these spaces, the legitimacy of political and social activity rests upon police conceptions of good order and decency. It is this role that symbolically supports the conception of the police (and public order law) as the "thin blue line" between order and anarchy.

15

Drug Offences

Carl Gustav Jung "Erinnerungen, Träume,
Gedanken", recorded and edited by Aniela Jaffé,
translated from German by Richard and
Clara Winston (New York: Pantheon Books,
1973), p 361

> **Every form of addiction is bad,
> no matter whether the narcotic be
> alcohol or morphine or idealism**

1. INTRODUCTION

Since the middle of the 20th century, drug offences have become the driving force propelling the criminal justice system: P Alldridge, *Relocating Criminal Law* (Aldershot: Ashgate, 2000), Ch 7. At a practical level, drug offences have revolutionised criminal justice priorities and policies both domestically and internationally. Yet drug offences continue to be omitted from many standard textbooks and courses in criminal law.[1] Although comprising a sizeable portion of criminal matters both in higher and lower courts, drug offences are considered marginal both to the academic enterprise and legal education which, as noted in Chapter 2 is preoccupied with identifying and elucidating upon general principles. In this regard, drug offences do not provide a fertile field of inquiry since they derogate from many purportedly universal and fundamental principles, such as the burden of proof and the presumption in favour of subjective mental states.

Drugs have been effectively quarantined as a specialist area of the criminal law and practice. The few texts that focus on drug offences concentrate primarily on questions of procedure, evidence

---

1   Drugs are not addressed in B Fisse, *Howard's Criminal Law* (Sydney: Law Book Company Ltd, 1990). An early and notable exception was the first contextual casebook in criminal law by A Bates, T Buddin and D Meure, *The System of Criminal Law* (Sydney: Butt, 1979).

and technical definition, such as the meaning and scope of possession, supply and trafficking.[2] Because of this practical focus, little or no attention is paid to broader policy questions such as: the rationale or justification for criminalisation; the historical evolution of drugs laws; the relationship of criminalisation to other regulatory strategies; and options for law reform.[3] Most strikingly, unlike other areas of the criminal law dealing with "consensual harm", liberal and moral philosophical ideas have not significantly informed legal debate about the purpose, scope and limits of drug offences: D Husak, *Drugs and Rights* (Cambridge: Cambridge University Press, 1992).

In many respects, the criminal law dealing with illicit drugs most closely conforms to Pat O'Malley's "technocratic model of criminal justice". As discussed in Chapter 1, p 42, the increasingly actuarial/bureaucratic emphasis within the criminal justice system results in the displacement of legal strategies based on crime control/due process in favour of risk management. A consequence of this approach is that the content of the criminal law is significantly "de-moralised". This model explains the trend in some jurisdictions to "decriminalise" the possession of small quantities of "soft drugs" like cannabis through the introduction of infringement notice schemes or "on the spot" fines.

The legal discourse surrounding illicit drugs is a striking example of law's disciplinary autonomy. The law has proven adept at resisting external sources of knowledge — whether historical sociological, criminological or public health — about drugs and their users. Drawing upon these perspectives, this chapter hopes to offer an antidote to such legal myopia. This chapter provides an overview of the development and operation of the principal offences and powers of investigation relating to illicit drugs. In relation to reform, it is necessarily selective, focusing on key policy issues such as the desirability of alternative legal strategies based on regulation rather than prohibition.

1.1 THE CRIMINALISATION OF DRUGS: THE LOGIC AND COSTS OF PROHIBITION

The logic of prohibition is rarely subject to wider scrutiny, and fundamental questions about the legitimacy of criminalisation are often deemed "political" and therefore beyond the scope of the reform enterprise. This approach characterises the Model Criminal Code Officers Committee's recent review of drug law in Australia: *Model Criminal Code, Chapter 6: Serious Drug Offences*, Report (1998). The MCCOC viewed its task largely as a technical exercise in legislative clarification. A priori questions relating to criminalisation and legal policy were considered largely beyond the scope of its terms of reference. This approach to law reform contrasts starkly with its approach in other areas, such as *Sexual Offences Against the Person*, where the MCCOC examined alternate models for sexual offences and relevant feminist and critical legal scholarship: see Ch 12.

---

2   See P Zahra, R Arden, M Ierace and B Schurr, *Drug Law in New South Wales* (2nd ed, Sydney: Federation Press, 1998); P Alcorn, P Zahra and R Arden, *Drug Law in the Code States* (Sydney: Federation Press, 1993). See also F Rinaldi and P Gillies, *Narcotic Offences* (Sydney: Law Book Company Ltd, 1991).

3   A notable exception is the discussion contained in C Reynolds, *Public Health Law in Australia* (Sydney: Federation Press, 1995), pp 202-210.

In the last decade, the most significant principle bearing on debates about drug law reform has been "harm minimisation". This principle, which has formed the basis of Australia's *National Strategy on Drugs*, aims to minimise or reduce the harms suffered by users, including the adverse effects of criminalisation itself: MCCOC, *Model Criminal Code, Chapter 6: Serious Drug Offences*, Report (1998), pp 6-11. A central tenet of harm minimisation is that "[p]olicies designed to discourage drug consumption should only be supported if they prevent more harm than they cause": A Wodak and R Owens, *Drug Prohibition: A Call for Change* (Sydney: UNSW Press, 1996), p 42. This is a variant of utilitarianism, where maximising "the happiness of the greatest number is replaced by the promotion of 'the least harm of the greatest number'.[4]

Harm minimisation balances the harms of drugs use against the harms caused by prohibition. But as Stephen Mugford points out, weighing and aggregating different types of harm is an impossible task — how do we measure and compare public health harms directly flowing from drug use against harms indirectly flowing from strict policies of prohibition, such as increased risks of corruption and police illegality?[5] Also how do we balance individual harms against wider harm to the community? Mugford also notes that utilitarian analysis falls into a major trap by not recognising and valuing the pleasures of drug consumption. Moral neutrality on the "benefits" of drug consumption may lend political credence to harm minimisation as a strategy for policy and law reform, but its exclusive focus on measurable *economic* costs is a significant weakness. Mugford's approach to drug control, which is based on regulating rather than prohibiting the market for pleasurable (yet risky) commodities, is further explored below.

Consistent with the principle of harm minimisation, the MCCOC drew a distinction between personal use on the one hand, and dealing in drugs for profit on the other hand: *Model Criminal Code, Chapter 6: Serious Drug Offences*, Report (1998). The Report proposed that the former should be viewed as "health and regulatory" offences, while the latter should be viewed as more serious "trafficking offences". Any potential overlap between these offences would be resolved by prosecutorial discretion. The MCCOC recommended (p 5) that distinct methods of enforcement, fault elements, proof requirements and a range of penalties were necessary for these different types of offences. As our historical examination will demonstrate, knowledge about drugs, including this crucial distinction between use and trafficking, has been influenced by numerous Royal Commissions and inquiries into drugs conducted in the 1970s and 1980s.

In the modern law, attention has been increasingly directed away from users towards those individuals who profit from the trade in illegal drugs. Dealing in drugs within an illicit framework is highly exploitative of users. Indeed, Peter Alldridge has observed that drug dealing possesses analytical and moral similarities to blackmail: "Dealers in addictive drugs obtain money by very unpleasant menaces. They sell protection from withdrawal symptoms. This is blackmail or its moral equivalent": *Relocating Criminal Law* (Aldershot: Ashgate, 2000), p 205. Viewed in this way, the user

---

4   S Mugford, "Harm Reduction: Does it Lead Where its Proponents Imagine?" in N Heather, A Wodax, E Nadelmann and P O'Hare (eds), *Psychoactive Drugs and Harm Reduction: From Faith to Science* (London: Whurr Publishers, 1993), p 29.

5   S Mugford, "Harm Reduction: Does it Lead Where its Proponents Imagine?" in N Heather, A Wodax, E Nadelmann and P O'Hare (eds), *Psychoactive Drugs and Harm Reduction: From Faith to Science* (London: Whurr Publishers, 1993), p 29.

ceases to become the wrongdoer but rather a pitiable "victim" who should be protected. While the MCCOC did not endorse the decriminalisation of possession and use of drugs, the recommendation that this conduct should be dealt under a less serious "health and regulatory" offence reflects a more sympathetic approach to users.

The legal dichotomy drawn here between "addict/use" and "dealer/trafficking" warrants critical attention on a number of levels. Chris Reynolds has suggested in *Public Health Law in Australia* (Sydney: Federation Press, 1995) that the dichotomy is "flawed" since "[m]any users deal in a small way in order to fund their habit or to obtain drugs for friends": p 204. It also ignores the involvement of undercover police in "controlled operations" who may encourage and assist users to participate in the lucrative trade in drugs. While the rhetoric of the present law and legal policy sustains attention on drug traffickers and organised crime, the reality is that drug offences in Australia continue to be enforced primarily against users, with the possession of small quantities of "soft" drugs, such as cannabis, constituting the bulk of arrests and convictions: *Australian Illicit Drug Report 1997-1998* (Canberra: Australian Bureau of Criminal Intelligence, 1999), p 2. Even in relation to "hard" drugs such as heroin, the Report points to empirical research that suggests (p 39) consumers rather than providers constitute the bulk of arrests in Australian jurisdictions. Rather than reflect upon the soundness of basing laws and policies on this distinction, these data are explained simply as further evidence of the elusive nature of drug trafficking and the difficulties, using conventional law enforcement methods, of apprehending the "Mr Bigs" of organised crime.

Another "truth" constructed through legal discourse is that all illicit drugs warrant similar treatment, notwithstanding the existence of scientific evidence suggesting that different drugs pose different dangers. The MCCOC embraced this undifferentiated approach to illegal drugs — all drugs deemed illegal must be treated the same, even if they pose different dangers to the health of the users, because trafficking in any prohibited drug is "associated with the same evils of corruption, violence and the financial derelictions of the black market economy": *Model Criminal Code, Chapter 6: Serious Drug Offences*, Report (1998), p 14. Even though the MCCOC acknowledged that a reduction in penalties for trafficking in some drugs, such as cannabis, might reduce black-market prices and so reduce incentives for organised crime, the case for decriminalisation was considered to involve issues of policy "which are beyond the scope of the Committee's deliberations": p 15. The MCCOC expressed concern that "decriminalisation by degrees" could be taken as a signal of lessening governmental concern over illicit cannabis use and supply and so concluded that "In this area, deployment of the symbolism of prohibition and punishment is a matter for political judgment by government rather than the Committee": p 16.

The logic of prohibition, outlined above, is both perplexing and self-reinforcing. Prohibition of *any* pleasurable commodity or service could result in an illicit market with the consequential risks of endangering the health of consumers, encouraging corruption of public officials and enriching black-market profiteers. Lumping the associated harms of prohibition into the criminalisation calculus means that the target for the criminal law is blurred. It is not the inherent moral, social or public health harms associated with the drug or its use that warrant criminalisation, but rather the collateral or indirect harms arising from the unintended effects of prohibition.

It has been said that law, viewed as an exercise in governance, contains elements of attempt and incompleteness: A Hunt and G Wickham, *Foucault and Law* (London: Pluto Press, 1994), p 79. This hypothesis is clearly evident in the history of drug law which may be represented as a perpetual cycle of attempts at legal repression, which being incomplete, lead to resistance, adaptation and further attempts at repression. It accounts for the almost constant amending and expansion of offences and legal powers dealing with illicit drugs. What is striking about drugs is that this legal cycle persists without critical reflection upon or empirical scrutiny of existing regulatory strategies.

There is a significant disjunction between research and policy development on illicit drugs — to borrow a medical concept, drug law is not "evidence based". Indeed, those responsible for making and enforcing drug laws measure effectiveness by reference to the level of criminal justice *activity* (drug arrests, seizures, convictions and the like) rather than the impact on patterns of drug use, supply, drug-related crime and public health.[6]

Although there is a sizeable academic critique of prohibition, the criminal law remains remarkably resistant to external sources of knowledge — whether scientific, sociological or cultural — about the drugs themselves, and the unintended effects of criminalisation.[7] Criminological research has revealed that the prohibition of illicit drugs has been ineffective, even counterproductive. In the drug context, criminalisation and law enforcement strategies based on prohibition have brought about many unintended and undesirable side effects: G Wardlaw, "Drug Control Policies and Organised Crime" in M Findlay and R Hogg (eds), *Understanding Crime and Criminal Justice* (Sydney: Law Book Company Ltd, 1988), Ch 7. Grant Wardlaw has observed (pp 153-154) that the present policy, which he characterises as one of "overcriminalisation", has produced a myriad of negative consequences, including the following:

- the criminalisation of a particular drug drives up its price, which in turn forces some users into money-producing crime to support their habits;[8]

- the high price of illegal drugs makes trafficking very lucrative, encouraging sophisticated and organised criminals and groups into the market, as well as increasing the amount of violence employed within the circle of drug users and traffickers;

- the illegal context means that much drug use occurs in marginal social settings thus associating drugs with other undesirable features of contemporary life and bringing young people into contact with them;

---

6   S James and A Sutton, "Joining the War Against Drugs? Assessing Law Enforcement Approaches to Illicit Drug Control" in D Chappell and P Wilson (eds), *Australian Policing — Contemporary Issues* (2nd ed, Sydney: Butt, 1996), p 153.

7   W Morrison, "Modernity, Knowledge and the Criminalisation of Drug Usage" in I Loveland (ed), *Frontiers of Criminality* (London: Sweet and Maxwell, 1995), p 215, drawing on Gunther Teubner, *Law as an Autopoietic System* (Oxford: Basil Blackwell, 1993).

8   This is not a universal effect of prohibition. Over the past decade the price of heroin on the streets has decreased as a result of the increased availability, notwithstanding increased law enforcement activity.

==== the covert context of drug use poses health risks (such as the spread of HIV and hepatitis);

==== other medical risks associated with using adulterated drugs (overdose, morbidity and mortality); and

==== criminalisation places significant strains on law enforcement and the criminal justice system, overloading the courts, prisons and probation system, leading to the corruption of officials and engendering changes to our legal system which undermine some of its basic precepts (such as the reversal of the burden of proof and dispensing with proof of fault).

In examining any proposals for legal regulation, policy-makers, legislators and regulatory agencies should consider the possible counterproductive effects of criminalisation: P Grabosky, "Counterproductive Regulation" (1995) 23 *International Journal of the Sociology of Law* 347. Concern about unintended effects of prohibition has been crucial in mustering support for harm minimisation and implementing some significant law reform measures. For example, community fear about the spread of HIV within drug-using communities in the 1980s reconceptualised illicit drugs as a public health issue: E Drucker, "Drug Prohibition and Public Health: It's A Crime" (1995) 28 *Australian and New Zealand Journal of Criminology* 67, special issue on "Crime, Criminology and Public Health". As we shall explore in the next section, the public health concern about HIV and "unsafe" injecting practices has led the introduction of syringe/needle distribution and exchange programs and safe-injecting rooms in many jurisdictions.

The Economic Costs of Prohibition: Creating Crime Tariffs

From an economic perspective, criminalising drugs, or indeed any other commodity for which there is demand, may create a lucrative illicit market. Although drugs laws were not designed to operate as a "tariff", by limiting supply and increasing costs to suppliers and sellers, prohibition has invariably had this effect: H Packer, *The Limits of the Criminal Sanction* (Stanford, CA: Stanford University Press, 1968), pp 277-282. Herbert Packer suggests that removing these tariffs would lead to the price of narcotics plummeting and cause the financial ruin of illegal suppliers: p 280. It is often argued that relaxing prohibition would increase the availability and consumption of drugs, producing social and economic problems following wide-spread addiction. This argument in favour of prohibition (rather than regulation) ignores those users who do not come to the attention of the medical profession or the police and impose little costs on society. For a discussion of these arguments in the context of the heroin market in Australia see R Marks, "Prohibition or Regulation: An Economist's View of Australian Heroin Policy" (1990) 23 *Australian and New Zealand Journal of Criminology* 65.

PERSPECTIVES ON PUBLIC HEALTH

Harm Minimisation: Promoting Safe-Injecting Practices

The *National HIV/AIDS Strategy* (Canberra: AGPS, 1989) proposed that needle and syringe exchange programs (NSE) should be established as a matter of priority to combat the spread of HIV. Concern however was expressed that this strategy would be impeded by laws that criminalised the possession and supply of drug-injecting equipment.[9] Section 31(1)(c) of the *Controlled Substances Act* 1984 (SA) prohibits the possession of "any piece of equipment for use in connection with the smoking, consumption or administration of [a drug] … or the preparation of such a drug or substance for smoking, consumption or administration. Section 83A(1) of the *Poisons Act* 1971 (Tas) prohibits the possession of "any pipe, syringe or other utensil, or any other appliance or thing, for use or designed to be used in connection with the preparation … administration, or taking of [a drug]". Section 12(5), (2) of the *Misuse of Drugs Act* 1990 (NT) criminalises the supply and possession of hypodermic syringes for drug use, however, it is a defence under s 5(3) if the syringes were supplied by a medical practitioner or other authorised body. Similar provisions exist in s 10(3) of the *Drug Misuse Act* 1986 (Qld).

The Legal Working Party of the Intergovernmental Committee on AIDS noted that there had been some changes to the law to facilitate the introduction of NSE programs, such as the removal of possession of needles or exchanges as an offence. However, the Committee concluded that these reforms did not go far enough since supplying a syringe or indeed advice as part of a needle exchange program could still expose health-workers to aiding and abetting charges: *The Final Report of The Legal Working Party of the Intergovernmental Committee on AIDS* (1992), Ch 8. The Committee recommended that legal protection for these programs, which should extend to offering advice on safe injecting techniques, should be conferred by legislation. A statutory framework for the lawful provision of needles and syringes by approved persons is preferable to the position in other jurisdictions, such as in New South Wales, where supply is merely tolerated under non-prosecution policies. That said, whether based in legislation or executive policy, the adoption of public health strategies by law enforcement agencies in Australia may be contrasted to the policies of strict criminalisation that continue to hamper efforts to respond to the HIV pandemic in the United States: E Drucker, "Drug Prohibition and Public Health: It's A Crime" (1995) *Australian and New Zealand Journal of Criminology* 67 at 68-69, special issue on "Crime, Criminology and Public Health".

Legislative reform has occurred in some jurisdictions including the Australian Capital Territory, New South Wales, Queensland and Western Australia.[10] The legislative scheme adopted in the Australian Capital Territory permits, in certain circumstances, the lawful supply of syringes to drug users. Part VII of the *Drugs of Dependence Act* 1989 (ACT) establishes a system of syringe distribution through "approved persons". A medical practitioner, pharmacist, nurse or health

---

9   For an excellent review of the State and Territory criminal laws governing intravenous drug use, see J Godwin, J Hamblin, D Patterson and D Buchanan, *Australian HIV/AIDS Legal Guide* (2nd ed, Sydney: Federation Press, 1993), Ch 7.

10 See *Drugs Dependence Act* 1989 (ACT), Pt VII; *Drug Misuse and Trafficking Act* 1985 (NSW), s 36N(2); *Drug Misuse Act* 1986 (Qld), s 10(3); *Poisons Act* 1964 (WA), s 36A, as amended by *Poisons Amendment Act* 1994 (WA), s 7.

worker may apply to the Australian Capital Territory Medical Officer of Health for an approval to supply syringes: s 86. Section 93(1) addresses the risk of accessorial liability arising from syringe supply:

> An approved person who supplies a syringe to another person shall not, by reason only of that supply, be taken to commit any offence under or by virtue of a provision in Part VIII of the *Crimes Act 1900* if
>
> (a) the supply is in the course of the professional practice or occupational duties of the approved person; and
>
> (b) the approved person has reasonable grounds for believing that —
>
>   (i) the syringe might be used for the purpose of the administration to the other person of a drug of dependence or prohibited substance; and
>
>   (ii) the supply of the syringe might assist in preventing the spread of disease.

In the late 1990s, the establishment of safe-injecting rooms (SIRs) has also been debated. The matter was first placed on the political and legislative agenda by the proposed clinical trials that would have supplied heroin to registered addicts. The "Heroin Trial", which is further discussed below, was vetoed by the Commonwealth in 1997. The introduction of SIRs have continued to be mooted at State and Territory level. Indeed, the introduction of SIRs for heroin users was one of the recommendations of the Royal Commission into the New South Wales Police Service, *Final Report* (1997), Recommendation 2.19.

SIRs have been introduced in Switzerland, Germany and the Netherlands, and now have the broad support of the Australian legal profession: Law Council of Australia, Media Release, 20 April 2000. These schemes cannot assume responsibility for the provision of the illicit drugs to users without Commonwealth cooperation. The possession of illicit drugs would need to comply with the licensing requirements under the *Therapeutic Drugs Act* 1989 (Cth) and other Federal legislation: S Bronitt, *Criminal Liability Issues Associated with a Heroin Trial: Working Paper No 13, Feasibility Research into the Controlled Availability of Opioids Stage 2* (Canberra: NCEPH and AIC, 1995). Nevertheless they are attractive from a harm minimisation/reduction perspective as they provide a safer environment for injecting drugs, with medical resources on hand to deal with emergencies such as overdoses.

> A recent study of drug dealing in Cabramatta suggests that aggressive "street-level" policing based on "zero-tolerance" can be counterproductive, increasing the likelihood of risky injection practices: see D Dixon, M Lynskey and W Hall, *Running the Risks: Heroin, Health and Harm in South West Sydney* (Sydney: National Drug and Alcohol Centre, UNSW, 1998) NDARC Monograph No 38, p 126.

From a regulatory perspective, the decision to outlaw drugs, users and suppliers places a large sphere of social activity *beyond* legal control. Rather than maintain a system of prohibition based largely on outmoded temperance ideals developed in the 19th century, it is often argued that drug control should be placed within a public health framework and based on a policy of minimising the harms to individuals and the community posed by dangerous drugs: C Reynolds, *Public Health Law in*

Australia (Sydney: Federation Press, 1995). As such a model encompasses both individual and community interests, it invokes consideration of competing liberal and welfare theories of criminalisation.

It is often claimed that prohibition, through deterrence, incapacitation and rehabilitation, protects and promotes the welfare of the community. This supports a regulatory model based on philosophies and policies that aim to protect public health. Drugs cause harm to users, their families and impose enormous costs on the public health system. For this reason, modern drug laws may be justified within the welfare model of criminalisation developed by Nicola Lacey, and reviewed in Chapter 1, pp 57-59.

> The *Australian Illicit Drug Report 1997-1998* (Canberra: Australian Bureau of Criminal Intelligence, 1999) notes that the "economic cost associated with the prevention and treatment of drug-related illness, loss of productivity in the workplace, property crime, theft, accidents and law enforcement activity has been estimated to be in excess of $18 billion. Almost 67.3% ($12.7 billion) of this is attributable to tobacco use; 23.8% ($4.49 billion) is attributable to alcohol abuse and 8.9% ($1.68 billion) to illicit drugs": p 1.

Notwithstanding the high cost of drug use to the community, liberalism opposes the criminalisation of conduct unless it causes "harm to others". To maximise individual freedom, particularly the rights of autonomy and privacy, "self-harming" conduct should be immune from the criminal law.[11] While the criminalisation of self administration of drugs may be difficult to justify within a liberal theoretical framework, the prohibition of dealing in drugs is less problematic. Trafficking, it is claimed, falls within the compass of the harm principle; it involves the exploitation of drug users (in Alldridge's terms, the moral analogue of blackmail) and therefore causes "harm to others". However, as noted above, it remains difficult within a framework of prohibition to extrapolate the direct harms of drug use and supply from the indirect harms caused by prohibition, such as corruption and dangers to public health caused by an illicit market. As noted in Chapter 1 at pp 49-51, the elasticity of the harm principle significantly weakens its utility as a either a guide for, or limit upon, criminalisation.

Liberalism falters when it seeks to claim rights of autonomy on behalf of drug users. It is commonly noted that drug users, as a result of the damaging effects of habitual use over time, cease to exercise "free choice" in relation to consumption. Even those sympathetic to liberalism and the decriminalisation of drugs concede this point. In *Not Just Deserts* (Oxford: Clarendon Press, 1990), republican theorists, John Braithwaite and Philip Pettit, generally reject the criminalisation of "consensual" crimes on the grounds that it diminishes liberty: pp 97-99. Using an example of a masochist who requests to be spanked by a prostitute, the authors point out that criminalisation is unjustified because the consensual nature of the "harm" means that the victim's liberty-prospects have not been reduced. The authors however concede that in relation to drug suppliers, this type of argument has less weight since "in the long term, addiction will reduce the dominion of the

---

11   For an extended analysis of the application of the harm principle to drug use see P Alldridge, *Relocating Criminal Law* (Aldershot: Ashgate, 2000), pp 212-213.

consensual victim": p 97. This suggests that some legal regulation may be justifiable. However, in light of the republican commitment to minimal criminalisation (the principle of parsimony), the authors reject prohibition. Rather, they support a legal policy of decriminalisation that would place all potentially dangerous drugs within a doctor–patient–pharmacist framework: p 98. Since republican theory is also concerned with the costs and counterproductive effects of prohibition, they note that decriminalisation would remove the substantial costs to individual freedom at the surveillance, investigation and enforcement stages: p 98. Braithwaite and Pettit nevertheless remain cautious about the strategy of decriminalisation. Rejecting the case for free availability of drugs such as heroin, they recognise that a regulatory legal framework governing supply and consumption would need to be coupled with a community education campaign, as with tobacco and alcohol, on the inherent hazards of using a particular drug.

Drug reform has been delayed by the search for the "perfect" model for drug control. Prohibition remains entrenched, while a perpetual cycle of commissions and inquiries search for the answers to the drug problem. There is no assurance that the ideas of controlled supply sketched above would completely eliminate public health concerns and (notwithstanding economists' predictions) that the illicit market in drugs would been displaced. As Stephen Mugford has observed, policy makers and reformers should give up the illusory quest for perfection, contenting themselves with the "least bad solution to the drugs problem".[12]

The Case for Free Availability of Drugs

Richard Miller's *The Case for Legalizing Drugs* (NY: Prager, 1991) is a critical examination of prohibition and the "War Against Drugs" in the American context. Using historical, scientific and criminological material, Miller concluded that the claims made about the harmfulness of illicit drugs are unverified or routinely exaggerated. Like Desmond Manderson (see below, pp 834ff), he identifies racism (against Chinese, Africans and Mexicans) as a significant factor in criminalisation of drugs. He concludes that levels of use should be achieved by means other than law: "The law does not restrain people from destroying themselves; intelligence does. There is no reason to anticipate an epidemic of stupidity sweeping the land if illicit drugs are legalized": p 143. However experience of other markets in pleasurable commodities such as alcohol, cannabis and gambling suggest that freer increased availability *does* lead to increased and more problematic forms of use: see also D Manderson, "Metamorphoses: Clashing Symbols in the Social Construction of Drugs" (1995) 25 *Journal of Drug Issues* 799.

While the range and level of harm associated with illicit drugs are debatable, in comparative terms it is clear that *lawful* drugs pose a much greater threat to public health. Available data demonstrates that tobacco and alcohol use are responsible for the vast majority of drug-related deaths. A recent report noted that 80% of preventable deaths were attributable to smoking, 16% to alcohol and only 3% to illicit drugs: *Australian Illicit Drug Report 1997-1998* (Canberra: Australian Bureau of Criminal

---

12 S Mugford, "Least Bad Solutions to the 'Drugs Problem'" (1991) 10 *Drug and Alcohol Review* 401. At the heart of this strategy, of course, lies "harm minimisation".

Intelligence, 1996), p 1. Even in relation to the significant increases in mortality rates in relation to illicit drugs, empirical research suggests that the risk of overdose is increased by mixing opioids with other central nervous depressants such as alcohol: p 43. Alcohol abuse, and poly-drug use, rather than potency and impurity of illicit drugs may have a greater causal relationship to mortality rates in users.

> **A national inquiry into substance abuse has recently been instituted. In early 2000, the House of Representatives Family and Commonwealth Affairs Committee of the Commonwealth Parliament began investigating the social and economic costs of both legal and illegal drugs in Australian society.**

While drugs like opium, heroin, cocaine and cannabis are subject to coercive legal controls, other "domesticated" yet potentially more dangerous drugs are subject to minimal legal regulation. Reynolds rightly describes the present regulatory responses to drugs as "topsy turvy".[13] Although tobacco and alcohol have been included within the National Drugs Strategy, the Liberal Government gave priority to its National *Illicit* Drugs Strategy, also known as "Tough on Drugs". Launched in 1997, this program responded to community concerns about illicit drugs, particularly concerns about increased heroin use and overdoses. The strategy has resulted in significant increases in the level of resources available for drug law enforcement. While the Federal Government has not formally repudiated the strategy of "harm minimisation", it has been placed within an "integrated framework" that seeks to reduce the drug supply and control demand through tough legal measures. It will be difficult (if not impossible) to realise the objectives of harm minimisation, discussed above, within a regulatory framework that aims to be "tough on drugs" and favours "zero tolerance".[14] Abstinence is the ultimate goal of strict prohibition, whereas harm minimisation accepts that illicit drug use is inevitable and so favours a public health/medical model based on minimising or alleviating the harmful effects of both drug use *and* policies of strict law enforcement.

Australia's *National Drug Strategy* has been regarded as one of the most progressive in the world, especially in relation to harm minimisation and the development of an integrated approach that encompasses both licit and illicit drugs. By the mid-1990s, it appeared that the "War Against Drugs", so favoured in the United States, had been abandoned in Australia. Researchers identified a malaise within the specialised law enforcement agencies responsible for illicit drugs about their role in fighting drugs within a policy based on harm minimisation.[15] In the intervening period, enthusiasm for criminal law as the principal vehicle for drug control has increased. The growing influence of "zero tolerance" at the national level has legitimised the increased use of the criminal

---

13 C Reynolds, "Can We Make Sense of Drug Laws in Australia? A Case Study of the South Australian Legislation" (1995) 1 *Flinders Journal of Law Reform* 73 at 74.

14 In the United States, the policy of zero tolerance to illicit drugs has prevented the development of public health strategies based on harm minimisation: E Drucker, "Drug Prohibition and Public Health: It's A Crime" (1995) *Australian and New Zealand Journal of Criminology* 67 at 72, special issue on "Crime, Criminology and Public Health".

15 S James and A Sutton, "Joining the War Against Drugs? Assessing Law Enforcement Approaches to Illicit Drug Control" in D Chappell and P Wilson (eds), *Australian Policing — Contemporary Issues* (2nd ed, Sydney: Butt, 1996), p 162.

law against street-level drug use and dealing.[16] It has also led to new forms of procedure and punishment tailored for drug offences. For example, to address the perceived ineffectiveness of traditional punishment options for drug offenders, policy-makers are exploring the benefits of specialised "drug courts", modelled on American initiatives, with broader powers to supervise the treatment of drug addiction with the ultimate goal of achieving abstinence.

PROCEDURAL PERSPECTIVES

Drug Courts: Therapeutic Justice

In 1998, New South Wales enacted legislation to formally constitute the first drug courts in Australia: *Drug Court Act* 1998 (NSW), s 3. A pilot scheme along similar lines has recently been established in Queensland: *Rehabilitation (Court Diversion Act) Act* 1999 (Qld). Arie Freiberg has defined the drug court as "a court specifically designated to administer cases referred for judicially supervised drug treatment and rehabilitation within a jurisdiction": "Australian Drug Courts" (2000) 24 Crim LJ 213 at 214. He suggests (at 222) that there are significant differences between drug courts and traditional courts:

> Whereas traditional courts focus on dispute resolution, drug courts focus on problem solving. Traditional courts seek legal outcomes while drug courts seek therapeutic outcomes. The differences are numerous: adversarial vs collaborative process; case orientation vs people orientation; rights-based vs interest — or needs-based; backward looking vs forward looking; judges as arbiters vs judges as coaches; precedent-based vs planning-based; individualistic vs interdependent; formal vs informal; legalistic vs common-sensical.

Bearing in mind the sizeable number of drug prosecutions, it can be argued that conventional courts already function — in all but name — as drug courts. In many jurisdictions, judges possess the powers to supervise drug offenders pre-trial through bail schemes and post-conviction through the imposition of conditional sentences. As Freiberg points out, the new "drug courts" established in New South Wales deal only with a very small proportion of drug related offending: at 227.

While the instrumental impact of drug courts may be limited at present, they symbolise a significant shift in criminal justice philosophy towards the establishment of a "therapeutic jurisprudence", in which the criminal law and its various institutions operate as agencies for healing offenders. This model has also informed the development of specialised courts to deal with mental health crime and domestic violence in the United States. But as Freiberg observes (at 222), the concept of "therapeutic justice" has overtones of paternalism with the potential to displace important interests such as the autonomy and other basic human rights of the offender.

In Chapter 1 at pp 22-23, we reviewed how an emphasis on rehabilitation can excessively pathologise offending, producing forms of "treatment" which are as degrading and punitive as more conventional (that is, retributivist) forms of punishment. For a general review of issues surrounding drug courts see T Makkai, "Drug Courts: Issues and Prospects" (1998), *Trends and Issues in Crime and Criminal Justice*, No 95 (Canberra: AIC, 1998).

---

16   A recent study of heroin use in Sydney has revealed the effect of "zero tolerance" on street level drug policing strategy, resulting in the displacement of crime to other areas and seriously undermining the effectiveness of public health strategies: L Maher, D Dixon, M Lynskey and W Hall, *Running the Risks: Heroin, Health and Harm in South West Sydney* (Sydney: National Drug and Alcohol Centre, UNSW, 1998), NDARC Monograph No 38.

The growing commitment in drug policy to "zero tolerance" was symbolised by the withdrawal of Commonwealth support for the "Heroin Trial" in 1997. The research trial, which was to be conducted initially in the Australian Capital Territory, would have involved heroin being prescribed and administered to a small group of users under medical supervision with a view to comparing heroin maintenance with other forms of treatment for opioid dependence such as methadone. The trial also would have examined the health and social impact (including involvement in criminal activity) of different types of treatment. Similar programs have been successfully implemented in the United Kingdom and Switzerland with marked improvements in the health of the users, significant reduction in crime rates and the rehabilitation of users back into mainstream society.[17] Although the program of research had been approved by the Ministerial Council on Drug Strategy (comprising Federal, State and Territory ministers responsible for health and law enforcement), the Prime Minister John Howard vetoed the trial. Concern that the Heroin Trial would send the "wrong message" to the community about drugs was undoubtedly politically influential. Reflecting this significant shift in drug policy, the Commonwealth has now abandoned its "integrated" approach to public drug education, which included lawful dangerous drugs such as tobacco and alcohol, in favour of an anti-drug message that focuses exclusively on illicit drugs. To borrow Russell Hogg and David Brown's phrase, drug reform is peculiarly susceptible to an "uncivil politics of law and order": *Rethinking Law and Order* (Annandale: Pluto Press, 1998), Ch 1.

> **Heroin (or diacetylmorphine) belongs to the opiate group of narcotic drugs. It was first synthesised from morphine in 1874 by a British scientist, but it was the German pharmaceutical company, Bayer, which patented and marketed the drug under the brand name "Heroin" as a cough suppressant in 1898.**

EMPIRICAL PERSPECTIVES

The Drug–Crime Nexus

Another widely held view is that drug use is implicated, directly or indirectly, in non-drug related criminal activity. Heroin in particular, is associated with crime. Consider the claim made in the *Australian Illicit Drug Report 1995-1996* (Canberra: Australian Bureau of Criminal Intelligence, 1996) that "The nature of heroin addiction is considered responsible for a large proportion of drug related crime, and contributes to social problems, as well as injuries and deaths related to overdosing": p 3. The Report later concedes that the crime-drug nexus is difficult to establish since the motives for offending are many and varied and that many addicts had criminal histories before commencing heroin use: p 12.

Research has explored the correlation between illicit drug use and other crime. The drug-crime nexus has been extensively explored, but the direction, size and existence of a causal relationship is problematic. Early research suggested that many addicts were involved in crime *before* they turned to drugs. Later research has qualified these findings demonstrating that while drug use does not lead to an increased *involvement* in crime, it may increase the *frequency* of

---

17   This comparative research is reviewed in Joint Select Committee into Safe Injection Rooms, Parliament of New South Wales, *Report on the Establishment or Trial of Safe Injection Rooms* (1998).

offending of addicts who are already involved in crime.[18] As one study concluded "the evidence suggests that heroin dependence exacerbates offending among those already committing crimes, rather than actually causing a law-abiding person to turn to a life of crime": Queensland Criminal Justice Commission, *Residential Burglary in Queensland,* Research Paper Series, Vol 3 (1), (1996).

The preliminary findings of the "Drug Use Monitoring in Australia Project" confirm the link between illicit drugs and other crimes. This national study conducted screening for illicit drugs of arrestees for various offences (violence/property/drug/road traffic) in several jurisdictions. The overwhelming majority of arrestees tested positive for some illicit drug use (cannabis being the most common).

TABLE 1:

Drug Use Among Adult Detainees

POSITIVE TEST BY OFFENCE TYPE	VIOLENCE	PROPERTY	DRUGS	ROAD TRAFFIC
any drug*	70%	86%	89%	73%
any drug (excluding cannabis)	34%	62%	42%	30%

Data from T Makkai, *Drug Use Monitoring in Australia — 1999 Annual Report on Drug Use Among Adult Detainees*, Australian Institute of Criminology, Research and Public Policy Series, No 26 (Canberra: AIC, 2000).

*The illicit drugs tested were amphetamines, benzodiasepines, cannabis, and opiates.

The prevalence of drug use in those apprehended by police may be explained in a number of ways. The wide use of cannabis may be attributed to its tendency to be used by young persons, a group which is disproportionately subject to police attention. The phenomenon of over-policing of young people and minorities is further explored in Chapter 14 in the context of public order offences. The data also have implications for the welfare of potentially intoxicated suspects in custody, as well as the relevance of intoxication to the denial of criminal responsibility. The role of intoxication in relation to criminal fault and defences is explored in Chapter 4.

It is important not to overstate the prevalence of positive drug testing among detainees. The tests indicate recent usage. It does not establish that the level of use caused, or was likely to cause, impairment of mental functioning. Recent empirical research, based on surveys of detainees, legal aid solicitors and community correction officers, suggests that the correlation between drug use and property offences and violent crime is weaker than commonly claimed: T Makkai, "Drugs and Property Crime" in *Australian Illicit Drug Report 1997-1998* (Canberra: Australian Bureau of Criminal Intelligence, 1999), Ch 8. Toni Makkai concludes that the available data based on self-reporting suggest that less than half of drug users commit crime to support

---

18   The research is reviewed in R Homel and M Bull, "Under the Influence: Alcohol, Drugs and Crime" in K Hazlehurst (ed), *Crime and Justice — An Australian Textbook in Criminology* (Sydney: LBC, 1996), p 167.

their habit, though the real figure is probably closer to a quarter or one third: p 112. She concludes that "Drug use may be a major factor for some property offenders, but it is not a factor for others". The correlation is weaker for violent offenders.

More generally, we must be cautious about drawing implications from research that focuses exclusively on prison or "captive" populations. Other empirical studies have focused on users who have not come to the attention of the criminal justice system, revealing a different image of the lifestyle and effects of illicit drug use. "Recreational users" are less crime-prone and have much higher levels of social integration and organisation.[19] Mugford's studies on cocaine demonstrate that the majority of users were able to manage the drug; the serious dangers attached to its use being contained and managed: "Recreational Cocaine Use in Three Australian Cities" (1994) 2 *Addiction Research* 95. The users of cocaine are "young, educated, individualists engaged in a peer orientated pattern of non-work activity in which partying looms large": at 128. Rather than focus on medical, legal or criminological explanations of drug use, this research raises questions about the role of leisure and entertainment in postmodern society. The regulatory implications of re-conceptualising drugs as "pleasurable commodities" are discussed below.

When this research on non-captive populations is taken into account, the drug-crime nexus looks more tenuous. Empirical research, while usefully challenging widely-held myths about drugs, has primarily been concerned to measure "deficits". Researchers have focused on exploring the commonalities between users of drugs, rather than on the diverse settings within which drug use, both licit and illicit, occurs. As Phyll Dance and Stephen Mugford have pointed out, deficit studies can grossly distort our "knowledge" of drugs and their users:

> Such discussions usually centre upon psychological variables (eg poor impulse control), social-psychological contexts (eg lack of family integration) or socio-economic matters (eg lack of jobs, crime as source of revenue). In so doing, the historical and cultural context of drug use, and the meanings that are created and sustained by users, vanishes.[20]

In the next two sections, we offer some sociological, historical and cultural perspectives on drugs, users and the battery of laws that have been enacted to control them.

---

19 S Mugford, "Controlled Drug Use Among Recreational Users: Sociological Perspectives" in N Heather, W Miller and J Greeley (eds), *Self Control and the Addictive Behaviours* (Sydney: Macmillan, 1991), Ch 8. Researchers have identified communities of "drug enthusiasts" who consume drugs heavily and organise their lives around drug use, but do not conform to the pathological or "deficit model" of drug addiction: P Dance and S Mugford, "The St. Oswald's Day Celebrations: 'Carnival' versus 'Sobriety' in an Australian Drug Enthusiast Group" (1992) 22(3) *Journal of Drug Issues* 591.

20 P Dance and S Mugford, "The St. Oswald's Day Celebrations: 'Carnival' versus 'Sobriety' in an Australian Drug Enthusiast Group" (1992) 22(3) *Journal of Drug Issues* 591 at 603.

1.2 SOCIO-HISTORICAL PERSPECTIVES ON DRUG OFFENCES

It is important to recognise that the prohibition of certain drugs did not occur as response to the perceived risk of addiction or dangers to public health. Mugford has observed that the status of a particular drug as licit or illicit has more to do with a range of economic, political and cultural factors than a rational appraisal of its potential harm.[21] Legal discussion of drug offences, including options for reform, often proceeds without appreciation of the historical forces that have shaped Australia's drug laws. Such historical myopia is unfortunate. An historical analysis is vital for revealing the political, economic and social forces, as well as powerful and enduring cultural myths, impinging on the process of criminalisation.

From a historical perspective, the philosophies of welfare and liberalism relating to public health or harm prevention do not provide an adequate explanation for the development of drug laws in Australia, or indeed any other jurisdiction. As Desmond Manderson noted in *From Mr Sin to Mr Big — A History of Australian Drug Laws* (Melbourne: Oxford University Press, 1993), p 12:

> There is no simple or overarching reason for the development of drug laws in Australia. But there is one clear message: no matter what we are told, "drug laws" have *not* been about health or addiction at all. They have been an expression of bigotry, class, and deep-rooted social fears, a function of Australia's international subservience to other powers, and a field in which politicians and bureaucrats have sought power. Drugs have been the subject of our laws, but not their object.

In the late 20th century, it is undeniable that medical discourse has assumed the dominant role in shaping our knowledge of drugs and legal responses to the "drug problem". It is impossible to dismiss the harmful health effects of drugs. However, the concept of drug addiction and dependence may lead policy makers to an excessive focus on clinical intervention and treatment as the appropriate regulatory solution.

Mugford has pointed out that a wider "social historical" perspective on drugs reveals that medical and legal discourses are not the only ways of controlling drugs: "Controlled Drug Use Among Recreational Users: Sociological Perspectives" in N Heather, W Miller and J Greeley (eds), *Self Control and the Addictive Behaviours* (Sydney: Macmillan, 1991). Drug use, when understood as a *social practice*, has had different meanings at different times. Through history and across different cultures the consumption of intoxicating substances, rather than being an aberrant feature, reflects the central values of a society. In modern Western societies, Mugford suggests that drugs may be better understood in terms of the commodification of pleasure and the pleasure of commodities: p 255. The pursuit of pleasure by means of illegal drugs is prohibited because of the perceived threats to decorum and social order. Mugford represents this tension as a conflict between the Protestant work ethic and the hedonist ethic: p 258. In later work, this tension is understood in terms of a struggle over the body, between the classical body (ordered, closed, unambiguous and seemly) and the

---

21   S Mugford, "Policing of Euphoria: The Politics and Pragmatics of Drug Control" in P Moir and H Eijkman (eds), *Policing Australia: Old Issues, New Perspectives* (South Melbourne: MacMillan, 1992), p 183.

grotesque body (open, ambiguous, disorderly and flagrant): "Policing of Euphoria: The Politics and Pragmatics of Drug Control" in P Moir and H Eijkman (eds), *Policing Australia: Old Issues, New Perspectives* (Sydney: Macmillan: 1992), p 200.

Such an approach exposes the historical and cultural specificity of prohibition and how particular drugs are condemned, while others are legitimated. Mugford's research also highlights neglected insights on regulating drugs such as the centrality of pleasure and commodification. This approach may yield practical benefits since it allows policy-makers, law-makers and regulators to reconceptualise the "drug problem" in terms of the regulation of a market for pleasurable commodities. This regulatory approach would be similar to that adopted for other social activities for which there is strong public demand yet simultaneously pose dangers to the community, such as prostitution, pornography and gambling. Clearly, a wider range of regulatory strategies should be considered that do not depend on pathologising drug use and viewing medical treatment as the *only* appropriate regulatory intervention. Within this regulatory framework, the State (though *not* necessarily the criminal law) would play a significant role in the regulation of pleasurable commodities.

Any regulatory framework that proposes to make the use of intoxicating substances lawful raises concern about the visibility of drug use and the potential for public nuisance. Indeed, the delays over the introduction of SIRs are related to concerns over location and public visibility. In an early article calling for the introduction of a comprehensive scheme of opioid maintenance, Ian Leader-Elliot raised the issue of "urban aesthetics": "Prohibitions Against Heroin Use: Can They Be Justified?" (1986) 19 *Australian and New Zealand Journal of Criminology* 225. He concluded (at 244-245) that the lawful supply of intoxicants (including alcohol) raised the prospect of social congregation and attendant risk of public nuisance and disorder:

> More permissive regimes of control may also intensify problems of urban aesthetics. When users are not punished, and attempts to drive them underground are abandoned, the undesirable effects of recreational opiate use may be even more visible than they are now. For many, the spectacle is offensive. One would add, however, that Australians are not unused to viewing the degrading spectacle of public intoxication and appallingly primitive and disorganized methods of purveying liquor.

1.3 CULTURAL PERSPECTIVES ON DRUG LAWS AND THE "WAR ON DRUGS"

When examining drug law and policies it is important to appreciate the power of symbolism and mythology in constructing our knowledge of drugs and their users. The imagery and symbolism around drugs and users are historically contingent: D Manderson, "Metamorphoses: Clashing Symbols in the Social Construction of Drugs" (1995) 25 *Journal of Drug Issues* 799. In the 19th century moral and political campaigns to criminalise drug use were directed specifically to the "Chinese vice" of opium-smoking. In the 20th century, the threats posed by drugs are now personified by the disease-ridden and crime-prone "junkie" and the "Mr Bigs" of organised crime.

Similarly potent imagery has developed around drug law enforcement where the dominant metaphor is that the international and domestic community is engaged in a "War Against Drugs".[22] In times of war, "extraordinary measures" are needed, and the suspension of fundamental rights is justifiable. The metaphorical War Against Drugs has produced draconian offences against trafficking, and money laundering and the reintroduction of forfeiture laws to prevent participants in drug dealing profiting from their crime. From a law enforcement perspective, drugs have empowered new investigative agencies with national and international jurisdiction (such as the National Crime Authority). They have also justified the use of intrusive investigative powers, such as electronic surveillance and police entrapment.

Deviation from normal investigative methods is tolerated by the courts and condoned by the legislature as necessary measures to fight the War Against Drugs. Legislation has provided legal authority for electronic surveillance and "controlled operations" in which police and their informers can participate in the illegal importation and supply of drugs. The trend is firmly in favour of the "normalisation" of these exceptional investigative powers. When the system of regulation of phone-tapping was introduced in 1970s, it was initially restricted to Federal police involved in the investigation of "serious narcotic offences". The range of offences for which interception may be authorised under the *Telecommunications (Interception) Act* 1979 (Cth) has been extended to include serious offences against the person, computer and property offences and even tax evasion. The powers have also been extended to State and Territory police and specialised investigative agencies such as the National Crime Authority. Electronic surveillance, like emergency legislation adopted to combat terrorism, was initially tolerated as an exceptional measure for designated offences not amenable to ordinary investigative techniques. But once adopted, these exceptional powers have become an accepted and, in due course, an indispensable feature of the Australian criminal justice system: S Bronitt, "Electronic Surveillance, Human Rights and Criminal Justice" (1997) Vol 3(2) *Australian Journal of Human Rights* 183 at 189.

> In the United States, as noted above, the advent of drug courts have provided the template for new specialist courts for dealing with domestic violence; driving under the influence (DUI); neighbourhood courts; mental health courts; teen courts; juvenile drug courts and native drug courts: A Freiberg, "Australian Drug Courts" (2000) 24 Crim LJ 213 at 235.

It would seem that drug law, both in relation to investigation as well as procedure, has been an area of unrestrained *legal* experimentation.

Criminal justice scholars often represent the "War Against Drugs" as a struggle between legality and crime control. As Francis Allen, a leading American legal scholar of criminal justice, observed in *The Habits of Legality* (New York: Oxford University Press, 1996), the true casualty of this war is the rule of law (p 39):

---

22 S James and A Sutton, "Joining the War Against Drugs? Assessing Law Enforcement Approaches to Illicit Drug Control" in D Chappell and P Wilson (eds), *Australian Policing — Contemporary Issues* (2nd ed, Sydney: Butt, 1996); W Morrison, "Modernity, Knowledge and the Criminalisation of Drug Usage" in I Loveland (ed), *Frontiers of Criminality* (London: Sweet and Maxwell, 1995); P O'Malley and S Mugford, "The Demand for Intoxicating Commodities: Implications for the 'War on Drugs'" (1991) 18(4) *Social Justice* 49 at 50.

The war on drugs has contributed importantly to the environment in which the rule of law functions today. Any rational appraisal of the war on drugs as it has emerged in the last decade and a half must focus in large measure on the cost of present drug policy. One category of costs largely neglected in modern political discourse is that resulting in debilitation of the legality ideal, and the weakening of the habits of legality.

Illicit drugs represent a threat not only to users or the community, but to the integrity of the criminal justice system. As explored in Chapter 2, the rule of law performs an important symbolic and ideological function within liberal democracies. Within the criminal justice system, legality and fairness limit the power of the State to censure and punish individuals. As such, it is an important source of political legitimacy for the criminal law. Liberal scholars of criminal justice such as Allen conceive criminal justice as a balance between two competing models: crime control versus due process: Ch 1 pp 34-36. Like Herbert Packer's influential two models of criminal justice outlined 30 years earlier in *The Limits of the Criminal Sanction* (Stanford, CA: Stanford University Press, 1968), the crisis of criminal justice is that the system's equilibrium is becoming unbalanced in favour of crime control. Critical scholars, such as Doreen McBarnet, would reject this dichotomised approach to criminal justice implicit within most liberal scholarship. In her view, the concepts of legality and fairness rarely stand in the way of conviction. Rather than restraining crime control, she concludes that "due process *is for* crime control": *Conviction: Law, The State and the Construction of Justice* (London: MacMillan Press, 1981), pp 155-156. It is not that the police, prosecutors and judges collude in deviation from principles of legality and fairness, but rather that the law itself licences this deviation. Drug offences and the specialised investigative methods employed to detect them provide many illustrations where the rhetoric of legality and fairness not only fails to be realised, but in fact serves the interests of the State.

The Significance of Culture: Drug, Mindset and Setting

The effects and dangers of drugs are contingent on the nature of the drug, the expectations or mindset of the user and the setting within which consumption takes place: N Zinberg, *Drug, Set and Setting: The Basis for Controlled Intoxicant Use* (New Haven, CT: Yale University Press, 1984). The setting and mindset may dramatically differ for the same drug. Mugford's research on "crack" and cocaine revealed that although these substances are identical chemical compounds, the setting for use and the mindset of the users are very different: "Despite the common chemical structure, the drugs are understood and used differently with different outcomes": "Studies in the Natural History of Cocaine Use — Theoretical Afterword" (1994) 2(1) *Addiction Research* 127 at 130. Unlike junkies addicted to "crack", recreational users of cocaine conform to a different socio-economic profile — young, single, urban, moderate in education and income, secular and non-traditional: at 131. Mugford's socio-historical approach to drugs cautions against simplistic caricatures of drugs or their user for guiding legal regulation and drug policy, highlighting that a single drug may have many and varied meanings and uses, and that these may change over time: "Controlled Drug Use Among Recreational Users: Sociological Perspectives" in N Heather, W Miller and J Greeley (eds), *Self Control and the Addictive Behaviours* (Sydney: Macmillan, 1991).

1.4 THE HISTORY OF DRUG LAW IN AUSTRALIA

Until recently, the history of drug law in Australia has been largely neglected. Researchers have tended to adopt the subservient view that the history of drugs in Australia was similar to that of the United Kingdom and United States though "necessarily briefer and less complex": J Krivanek, *Heroin — Myths and Reality* (Sydney: Allen and Unwin, 1988), p 32. This historical blind-spot has been largely rectified by Desmond Manderson's book, *From Mr Sin to Mr Big — A History of Australian Drug Laws* (Melbourne: Oxford University Press, 1993). This lively historical account explores the multitude of domestic and international forces shaping drug laws in Australia during the late 19th century and early 20th century. Manderson locates the impetus for criminalisation of drugs in a complex interaction of factors that include racism, the rise of the medical profession, bureaucratic attitudes, the pressure of the international community, the emergence of a drug mythology, and political convenience: p 11.

In the first two chapters, Manderson examines how the first wave of opiate prohibition was the product of racism directed toward the "Chinese vice" of opium-smoking and religious moralism in the form of temperance crusades. At this time, Australia was at the forefront of drug regulation. Some of the early Australian prohibitions on the supply and use of opiates predated laws in Britain and the United States.

The early prohibitions in Australia were directed to local concerns. For example, the first drug laws in Australia prohibited the supply of "any opium to aboriginal natives of Australia or half caste of that race except for medicinal purposes": *Sale and Use of Poisons Act* 1891 (Qld). While formally neutral, this Act was in fact directed against the Chinese customary usage of opium as a means of barter and exchange. The Act was the product of xenophobia, economic protectionism and paternalism toward Aboriginal people. It is important to appreciate that the restrictions on dealing in opiates were directed only to opium suitable for smoking and did not restrict its widespread medicinal use. These early laws distinguished between the vice of opium-smoking and the ingestion of opiates in the form of patent and proprietary medicines. These medicines (few of which actually were patented) were often simply pure alcohol or opiate preparations. As Manderson points out, the consumption of patent medicines was widespread with Australia having the largest per capita levels of consumption in the world at the turn of the century: p 53. The general public only became aware of the opiate content of the "secret ingredients" in patent medicines through a New South Wales Royal Commission into Secret Drugs, Cures and Foods in 1905. The exposé by the Commission, rather than leading to prohibition or tighter control over medicinal opiates, simply led to the introduction of Commonwealth laws requiring accurate labelling of contents for medicines. The patent medicine industry, from which newspapers generated huge profits through advertising revenues, continued to flourish with minimal restrictions.

The prohibition on the supply of opium to Aboriginal natives in Queensland was eventually extended to the general population. Although the prohibition on opiates purported to have general application, enforcement policies continued to focus on the problem of intoxication and drug abuse within Aboriginal communities. Even though opium-smoking by the Chinese community was reviled in the general community, the prohibition was only loosely enforced against them. Rather than implement the prohibition as legislation dictated, police and customs officials operated an administrative regime for licensing and taxing the supply of non-medicinal opium until the end of the century: D Manderson, *From Mr Sin to Mr Big — A History of Australian Drug Laws* (Melbourne: Oxford University Press, 1993), p 34. Such pragmatic strategies resonate with the regulatory policies of decriminalisation that have been adopted for some "recreational drugs" such as cannabis.

Drug law developed its modern character in the latter half of the 20th century. The offences have quickly proliferated beyond possession, use and supply, to a wider range of trafficking and drug related activities, such as money laundering. It was not until the 1970s that the extremely high penalties (such as life imprisonment) for drug offences were adopted, and offence and penalty provisions began to distinguish between personal use and commercial dealing. The explosion in legislative activity in the 1970s, supported by numerous Royal Commissions and official inquiries into illicit drugs,[23] coincides with a moral panic about drugs and the corruption of Australian youth. Chris Reynolds in *Public Health Law in Australia* (Sydney: Federation Press, 1995) summarised (p 204) the social forces promoting legislative activity during the 1970s and 1980s as follows:

> This legislative flurry seemed to be a product of the wider social event of the time, the Vietnam war, fear about the rebelliousness of youth and the "pop" culture all combined with drugs to make a high profile issue of concern. The laws were populist responses, designed to protect Australia's youth from the outside influences of dangerous drugs and ideas.

This historical survey of the formation of drug laws in Australia highlights the danger of over-reliance on formal legal sources, such as legislation, to understand the purpose, operation and effects of the criminal law. Lifeless statutes provide only a partial account of the complex process of criminalisation. Legal history clearly plays a vital role in revealing the social, economic and political forces that have shaped, and continue to shape, the development of drug law in Australia.

The Discovery of Addiction and the Creation of the Disease Model

Harry Levine explores the discovery of addiction, and the changing societal attitudes toward intoxication through drugs in "The Discovery of Addiction: Changing Conceptions of Habitual Drunkenness in America" (1978) 39(1) *Journal of Studies on Alcohol* 143. Levine traces how the concept of drug and alcohol "addiction" as a disease emerged in the late 19th century. The medical profession conceptualised drug use as a progressive disease, the principal symptom of addiction being the loss of control over usage which could only be cured by abstinence. A similar process was applied to the discovery of alcohol addiction, which generated new laws and powers for dealing with *habitual* drunkenness: see Ch 14, p 779.

---

23 The Royal Commissions held in Australia between 1977-1980 symbolised official and community anxiety about the growth of illicit drug use: D Manderson, *From Mr Sin to Mr Big* (Melbourne: Oxford University Press, 1993), p 170. The Commissions played a significant role in reshaping attitudes toward drugs, particularly in solidifying the distinction between users (who required treatment) and traffickers. From 1980, there were a further 13 commissions or inquiries into drugs in Australia: D Brown, D Farrier and D Weisbrot, *Criminal Laws* (2nd ed, Sydney: Federation Press, 1996), pp 1047-1050.

The medicalisation of drug use is consistent with Michel Foucault's identification of the "clinical gaze": *The Birth of the Clinic* (New York: Vintage Press, 1975). Diagnosising social as well as biological diseases empowered medical science and the medical profession as the appropriate disciplinary authority over drug users. Levine concluded that the concept of addiction should be understood not as an independent medical or scientific discovery but rather "as part of a transformation in social thought grounded in fundamental changes in social life — in the structure of society": pp 165-166. The medical model remains highly influential in regulatory strategies based on harm minimisation, supporting treatment in the form of methadone programs and scientific research such as the proposed "Heroin Trial".

COMPARATIVE PERSPECTIVES

Drugs in the United Kingdom, United States and Australia

More than any other area of the criminal law, drug law has been influenced by political pressure from powerful individual nations, such as the United States, and the wider international community. The following comparative history of drug law relies heavily on Jara Krivanek's, *Heroin — Myths and Reality* (Sydney: Allen and Unwin, 1988), Ch 2. As Krivanek points out, the first nation to become concerned about opiate misuse was China, reacting to concerns about the high level of imports from India by the British East India Company. Opium for non-medicinal use was outlawed in China in 1726 primarily for economic reasons. In an attempt to preserve this trading arrangement whereby valuable tea, silk and spice were exchanged for opium, the United Kingdom was ultimately prepared to use force (the so-called "Opium Wars") to protect their interests. The domestic acceptability of opium began to change in the 19th century with the emergence of temperance movements, such as the Society for the Suppression of Opium Trade established by Quakers in 1874.

The prohibition movement was aided by the medical profession which from the 1870s onwards viewed habitual non-medicinal drug use as a disease — "addiction". By pathologising drug use, the medical profession gained control over drug users and entrenched its monopoly over the use of narcotic drugs for medicinal purposes: T Parssinen and K Kerner, "Development of the Disease Model of Drug Addiction in Britain, 1870-1926" (1980) 24 *Medical History* 275. As early as 1895, a Royal Commission on Opium took the view that drug addiction was a disease requiring medical treatment. Indeed, the problematic aspects of drug use were reflected in the belief that addiction caused mental infirmity and sometimes insanity. Moreover, the *Mental Deficiency Act* 1913 (UK) was extended to "intoxicants", who were defined as addicts of sedatives, narcotics and stimulant drugs. This Act allowed for the detention of "moral imbeciles" in asylums or the appointment of guardians.

The United Kingdom ratified the *Hague Convention* in 1912, an international treaty aiming to bring about the gradual suppression of the "abuse of drugs" specifically opium, morphine and cocaine. Significantly, the Convention's definition of drug abuse excluded the medical use of drugs. The medical control over drug use was further entrenched by an official inquiry into drugs conducted by the Rolleston Committee in 1924. This Committee, comprised entirely of medics, concluded that drug addiction should be viewed primarily as a disease rather than as a vice: "the taking of a narcotic drug of addiction for a few doses may be termed as a vice, but if the administration is continued for a month or so a true disease condition becomes established with a definite pathology and symptoms": cited in J Krivanek, *Heroin — Myths and Reality* (Sydney: Allen and Unwin, 1988), p 36.

The so-called "British system" separated out the pathological from the moral and legal aspects of drug use, conferring on the medical profession the principal responsibility for controlling "the addict" through treatment. Such treatment in many cases involved simply controlling opiate addiction through *maintenance*, namely providing a controlled dose with a view to avoid the symptoms of withdrawal, rather than to cure the addiction. The system required no registration of addicts, though the Committee did lay down some guidelines on how addicts should be maintained by doctors. For example, addicts should not be informed of the name of the drug and in no circumstances should inject themselves.

Until the 1950s, there was no significant illicit market in opiates in Britain. A series of medical abuses in prescribing drugs in the 1950s and 1960s, coupled with the emergence of an affluent, rebellious and drug using youth culture led to calls for tighter regulations. The medical profession increasingly sought to distinguish between therapeutic and non-therapeutic addiction. The Home Office adopted this distinction in 1958, and it appears that 80% of cases of drug addiction at this time were characterised as therapeutic, that is, addicted through medical contact. The recreational use of drugs was properly the subject of criminal prosecution. In this sense, the law entrenched a dichotomy between lawful (medically supervised) drug use and unlawful recreational use. As Manderson observes in *Mr Sin to Mr Big* (p 105),

> In stark contrast to the medical and legal authority that jointly demonised the transgressor of drug laws, those who accepted the legal and medical boundaries that had been set in place met with support and reassurance. Even "drug addicts" were able to continue their habit if they did so legally and under medical supervision.

The Brain Committee in the 1960s generally endorsed the medical model adopted in the 1920s, but recommended measures to control over-prescribing drugs including the establishment of special centres and specialist care, notification of addicts to central authority and powers of compulsory detention for the purpose of treatment: Ministry of Health and Scottish Home and Health Department, *Drug Addiction*, The Second Report of the Interdepartmental Committee (London: HMSO, 1965) (the Brain Committee). These clinics reduced the size of doses and used substitutes like methadone to maintain addiction.

The "British system" was largely followed in Australia. Although some States forbade the supply of opiates for the purpose of addiction, as Manderson has pointed out, the essence of the Commonwealth policy remained the "institutionalisation and medicalisation of drug use": p 107. For example, heroin was widely used in the first half of the 20th century in the United Kingdom and Australia by the medical profession. It was used not merely as a treatment for morphine addiction, but was also prescribed for the alleviation of pain experienced as a result of cancer and even childbirth. As Manderson further notes (p 110),

> In 1931 Australia consumed 3.10 kilograms of heroin per one million persons, more in total than the United States, Canada or Germany and, per capita, behind only New Zealand. Australia consumed three times as much heroin per capita as the United Kingdom and twice as much cocaine. Hitherto we had been world leaders in the popping of patent medicines pills; now we had moved on to other drugs.

Due to increasing international pressure and treaties requiring more stringent prohibition, the importation of heroin was banned in Australia in 1953, notwithstanding protests from the medical profession at the time.

The history of the regulation of opiates in the United States differs from the medical and bureaucratic model adopted in the United Kingdom: see generally, J Krivanek, *Heroin — Myths and Reality* (Sydney: Allen and Unwin, 1988), Ch 2. The "British system", while highly influential in Australia, was never adopted in the United States. Opiate addiction first became visible at the end of the American Civil War in the 1860s. The introduction of the intravenous syringe on the battlefield allowed morphine to be used as an effective pain-killer. The consequent addiction to morphine became known as "army disease". Returning soldiers continued to obtain their supplies of opiates lawfully through doctors and pharmacists. Indeed, a wide range of opiates were available by mail order through the Sears-Roebuck catalogues in the 1890s. In 19th century America, opium addiction was not widely associated with vice or crime.

As in Australia, a number of factors were critical in changing public attitudes towards opium in the United States — the rise of the Temperance Movement and the arrival of Chinese workers. In relation to the latter, opium became a symbol of Chinese vice and its criminalisation a means of attacking the social and economic challenges that they presented. As Thomas Szasz noted: "After all Americans could not admit they hated and feared the Chinese because the Chinese worked harder and were willing to work for lower wages than they did": *Ceremonial Chemistry* (London: Routledge and Kegan Paul, 1975), p 76. In 1875 San Francisco enacted laws prohibiting the keeping of opium dens and opium smoking. In 1883 the Chinese were prohibited from importing opium, though no similar restrictions were placed on importation by Americans. For an excellent article examining the historical forces behind opium offences in the United States, see P Morgan, "The Legislation of Drug Law: Economic Crisis and Social Control" (1978) 8(1) *Journal of Drug Issues* 53.

Following the *Hague Convention* in 1912, the *Harrison Act* 1914 was enacted by Congress. The Act had three central provisions:

— to provide information about legal opiate traffic;

— to introduce a tax on those who handled drugs; and

— to prohibit the purchase of opiates except on the prescription of a physician for a "legitimate medical purpose".

The Act severely limited the availability of opiates resulting in the medical profession becoming besieged with addicts. Special clinics were established but quickly became unmanageable and were all closed by 1921. Also, individual States began to prosecute doctors who were prescribing drugs for addicts. An early decision of the Supreme Court in 1919 further limited medical involvement in regulating the supply of opiates. The Supreme Court held that prescription for the purpose of maintaining habitual use, rather than for the purpose of curing addiction was not permitted under the *Harrison Act*.[24] Although this decision was reversed in 1925, the reticence of the medical profession to supply opiates to addicts fostered a black-market for drugs and organised crime.

The regulation of drug use was conceived as a criminal justice issue, an approach promoted by newly created national agencies, such as the Federal Bureau of Narcotics (FBN). The FBN played a significant role in marshalling and shaping public concern about marijuana misuse. Propaganda films like "Reefer Madness" portrayed cannabis as a drug capable of inducing sexual frenzy and homicidal rage. Howard Becker has stressed the critical role played by "moral entrepreneurs", such as Harry Anslinger, the head of the FBN from the 1920s to the 1960s, who once described marijuana as "the assassin of youth": *Outsiders: Studies in the Sociology of Deviance* (London: Collier McMillan, 1963). Other researchers have stressed the role of racism directed toward Mexican migrant workers (the principal consumers of "marijuana") and the bureaucratic needs in explaining prohibition: S Bottomley and S Parker, *Law in Context* (2nd ed, Sydney: Federation Press, 1997), pp 177-179. What is striking is how our understanding of cannabis has changed from one of a dangerous sexual stimulant in the 1930s, to a relaxant associated with the hippy youth culture in the 1960s and 1970s.

While there is clearly an international dimension to the criminalisation of drugs, as reflected in the narcotic treaties adopted in the 20th century, the intensity and nature of legal regulation has varied from jurisdiction to jurisdiction. These variations reflect the different meanings and symbols of drug law in different places at different times. Australia's legal response to opium, like the United States, was affected by the problem of "Chinese vice". As Manderson concludes in "Substances as Symbols: Race Rhetoric and the Tropes of Australian Drug History" (1997) 6 (3) *Social and Legal Studies* 383 (at 384), opium in the 19th century became an important symbolic expression of anti-Chinese sentiment:

> [T]he very first, anti-opium, drug laws arose in many countries — in Australia and New Zealand, South Africa and Canada, as well as in the United States — specifically because of the association of Chinese immigrants with opium use. In each case it was not the dangers of the substance itself but its use by these minority groups which caused public outcry and outlawry.

In the United Kingdom, the medical control of drugs remained dominant. This regulatory approach was not affected by the moral crusades against Chinese vice in the United States and Australia — significantly, the United Kingdom had not experienced Chinese migration to any large extent. Thus, drugs simply symbolised sickness rather than vice. As Krivanek concludes, "where Britain espoused a disease model, the United States took an essentially moral stance on opiate addiction, and that stance remains basically unchanged today": *Heroin — Myths and Reality* (Sydney: Allen and Unwin, 1988), p 59. Australia may be viewed as falling between these two models — a dualist approach based on prohibition tempered by medical pragmatism that continues to influence regulatory strategies today.

---

24 *Webb v US*, 249 US 96 (1919). This decision was followed in *US v Behrman*, 258 US 280 (1922) but subsequently overruled in *Linder v US*, 268 US 5 (1925).

The *National Drug Strategy Household Survey* in 1998 indicated that 2.2% of the population surveyed had tried heroin. By contrast, 39.3% of the population surveyed had consumed cannabis. Whilst comprising a relatively small part of the illicit drug market, heroin users are disproportionately targeted for regulation by law enforcement agencies and the present government's National Illicit Drugs Strategy.

2. SERIOUS DRUG OFFENCES

2.1 THE FEDERAL AND INTERNATIONAL FRAMEWORK FOR DRUG OFFENCES

The early drug laws in the 19th century, particularly those dealing with opium smoking, were local attempts to impose legal controls on suspect populations and their "peculiar" vices. As noted above, even when these laws were extended to the general populace in the late 19th century, they continued to be enforced by law enforcement officials in a discriminatory fashion along racial lines. The next phase of legal regulation for drugs in the 20th century witnessed a new player enter the regulatory arena — the newly established Commonwealth of Australia sought tighter controls, backed by the federal criminal law, over illicit drugs. The period from Federation at the turn of the century to the end of the Second World War witnessed a dramatic expansion in drug laws. At the State level, the early restrictions on opium were extended to heroin, morphine, cocaine and other "dangerous drugs". At the federal level, the Commonwealth enacted the first *national* drug offences. The result was that the responsibility for drug offences and enforcement is now shared between the Commonwealth, States and Territories. The next section examines the scope of federal jurisdiction over drugs and the principal offences. The key federal drug offences are contained in two statutes:

▬ *Customs Act* 1901 (Cth), as amended by the *Customs Act* 1967 (Cth);

▬ *Crimes (Traffic in Narcotic Drugs and Psychotropic Substances) Act* 1990 (Cth).

In the next section, we focus on the leading High Court and other appellate decisions relating to the physical and fault elements of drug offences. The dominance of federal offences reflects the growing international character of drug law, which implement various international conventions on illicit drugs. The next section briefly examines the evidential and procedural issues relating to "controlled operations", in particular the legal and policy concerns relating to the use of police entrapment. It also contains a case study on heroin law reform. The plethora of drug offences under State and Territory laws are beyond the scope of an introductory chapter. These offences, however, are comprehensively reviewed in specialist texts dealing with the Code and common law jurisdictions respectively.[25]

---

25 See P Zahra, R Arden, M Ierace and B Schurr, *Drug Law in New South Wales* (2nd ed, Sydney: Federation Press, 1998); P Alcorn, P Zahra and R Arden, *Drug Law in the Code States* (Sydney: Federation Press, 1993).

2.2 THE SCOPE OF FEDERAL JURISDICTION

The Commonwealth's competence to enact laws in this area is based on two heads of power in the Constitution: the "trade and commerce" power and the "external affairs" power under ss 51(i) and (xxix) respectively. The trade and commerce power permits the Commonwealth to restrict or prohibit the importation and exportation of any goods including drugs. Under the *Customs Act* 1901 (Cth) the Governor General may prohibit, by way of regulation, the importation of goods into Australia.[26] The external affairs power permits the Commonwealth to enact laws implementing the terms of the international treaties and conventions dealing with drugs. It has been suggested that the external affairs power is sufficiently broad to permit the Commonwealth to assume total control over the regulation of drugs: R Brown, "Federal Drug-Control Laws: Present and Future" (1977) 8 *Federal Law Review* 435.

Although transferring the responsibility for drug offences to the Commonwealth would simplify the administration of drug law in Australia, it would be politically unacceptable to the States and Territories which are keen to preserve their competence to legislate and enforce laws against drugs. Following its review of federal criminal law, the Gibbs Committee affirmed the present split between federal and State/Territory legislation on drugs, and proposed that any future recommendations for reform and consolidation should proceed on that assumption: Review of Commonwealth Criminal Law, *Drug Offences*, Discussion Paper No 13 (1988), p 8.

Federal laws prohibiting the importation and exportation of illegal drugs have been held to be a valid exercise of the trade and commerce power in the Constitution: *Milicevic v Campbell* (1975) 132 CLR 307. Because of the constitutional limitations on federal jurisdiction, the courts have viewed the purpose of State and Territory drug laws as legally distinct. As the New South Wales Court of Criminal Appeal observed in *R v Stevens* (1991) 23 NSWLR 75 (at 82):

> The Commonwealth Act, it may be said, erects, in s 233B, a barrier or defence against narcotics coming into Australia, whilst the *Drugs Misuse and Trafficking Act* [NSW] is a measure which enables the State to police the use of and trafficking in narcotics in New South Wales. The two laws will, in given circumstances overlap and apply to the same set of circumstances but the purpose of each remains fundamentally different. As the purpose of the two Acts is entirely different they are not, under s 109 of the Constitution, to be regarded as inconsistent.

The scope for overlap between Federal, State and Territory offences is extensive. As we shall explore below, federal offences relating to "prohibited imports" have been broadly interpreted. State and Territory drug offences are used principally where the criminal activity has no international dimension. Offences against the administration, possession and supply of prohibited drugs exist in

---

26 *Customs Act* 1901 (Cth), s 50(1). It is an offence to import a prohibited import under s 51(1) of the *Customs Act* 1901 (Cth).

every jurisdiction in Australia.[27] It should be noted however, that State and Territory offences of possession and supply may be used as "back-up" charges where crucial evidence relating to proof of importation is absent or has been judicially excluded because of illegal activity of the police: *Ridgeway v The Queen* (1995) 184 CLR 19 at 43. See the discussion of entrapment below: pp 870ff.

> Possession offences are said to be "creatures of statute". The common law historically has been wary of imposing criminal liability on the basis of possession alone. It was held that an indictment charging a person for mere possession of articles that may have criminal uses does not charge "an act" and therefore is bad at common law: G Williams, *Criminal Law: The General Part* (2nd ed, London: Stevens and Sons, 1961), p 8.

2.3 IMPORTATION OFFENCES

The principal drug provision under federal law is s 233B of the *Customs Act* 1901 (Cth). This section is an "omnibus" provision catching a wide range of drug-related activity. It states:

Special provisions with respect to narcotic goods

(1) Any person who:

(a) without any reasonable excuse (proof whereof shall lie upon him) has in his possession, on board any ship or aircraft, any prohibited imports to which this section applies; or

(aa) without reasonable excuse (proof whereof shall lie upon the person) brings, attempts to bring, or causes to be brought, into Australia any prohibited imports to which this section applies;

(b) imports, or attempts to import, into Australia any prohibited imports to which this section applies or exports, or attempts to export, from Australia any prohibited exports to which this section applies; or

(c) without reasonable excuse (proof whereof shall lie upon him) has in his possession, or attempts to obtain possession of, any prohibited imports to which this section applies which have been imported into Australia in contravention of this Act; or

(caa) without reasonable excuse (proof whereof shall lie upon him) conveys, or attempts to convey, any prohibited imports to which this section applies which have been imported into Australia in contravention of this Act; or

---

27 For offences dealing with supply of drugs see *Drugs of Dependence Act* 1989 (ACT), s 164; *Drugs Misuse and Trafficking Act* 1985 (NSW), s 25; *Misuse of Drugs Act* 1990 (NT), s 5; *Drugs Misuse Act* 1986 (Qld), s 6; *Controlled Substances Act* 1984 (SA), s 32; *Poisons Act* 1971 (Tas), s 47; *Misuse of Drugs Act* 1981 (WA), s 6(1)(c). In Victoria, supply of drugs is covered by the "trafficking" offence in *Drugs, Poisons and Controlled Substances Act* 1981 (Vic), s 71, which the courts have interpreted broadly to include supply: *R v Clarke and Johnstone* [1986] VR 643. For offences dealing with possession of drugs see *Drugs of Dependence Act* 1989 (ACT), s 171(1); *Drugs Misuse and Trafficking Act* 1981 (NSW), s 10(1); *Misuses of Drugs Act* 1990 (NT), s 9; *Drugs Misuse Act* 1986 (Qld), s 9; *Controlled Substances Act* 1984 (SA), s 31; *Poisons Act* 1971 (Tas), s 48; *Drugs, Poisons and Controlled Substances Act* 1981 (Vic), s 73; *Poisons Act* 1964 (WA), s 42.

(ca) without reasonable excuse (proof whereof shall lie upon him) has in his possession, or attempts to obtain possession of, any prohibited imports to which this section applies which are reasonably suspected of having been imported into Australia in contravention of this Act; or

(cb) conspires with another person or other persons to import, bring, or cause to be brought, into Australia any prohibited imports to which this section applies or to export from Australia any prohibited exports to which this section applies; or

(d) aids, abets, counsels, or procures, or is in any way knowingly concerned in, the importation, or bringing, into Australia of any prohibited imports to which this section applies, or the exportation from Australia of any prohibited exports to which this section applies; or

(e) fails to disclose to an officer on demand any knowledge in his possession or power concerning the importation or intended importation, or bringing or intended bringing, into Australia of any prohibited imports to which this section applies or the exportation or intended exportation from Australia of any prohibited exports to which this section applies;

shall be guilty of an offence.

Although seemingly a single offence provision, the High Court has construed each of the above paragraphs as a separate offence: *Kingswell v The Queen* (1985) 159 CLR 264. The offences created by the provision encompass both principal and secondary participation, as well as inchoate forms of liability such as conspiracy and attempts.

THE PHYSICAL ELEMENT: THE MEANING OF IMPORTATION

The scope of the prohibition on "importation" in s 233B(1)(a) of the *Customs Act* 1901 (Cth) has been confined to cases where the goods have been imported. In *R v Bull* (1974) 131 CLR 203 the High Court held (at 220, 254) that goods intercepted within Australia's territorial waters, were not to be regarded as imported. Goods in transit therefore would not necessarily be imported. This decision has not unduly hampered law enforcement. Indeed, subsequent decisions have adopted a more flexible approach to importation, construing this element as including activities that took place outside the jurisdiction and used innocent agents, such as airlines, to bring the drugs into Australia. The High Court in *White v Ridley* (1978) 140 CLR 342 established that despatching goods from outside the jurisdiction with the intention that the goods should be landed in Australia fell within the scope of s 233(1)(b): at 359. The scope of importation offences have been further broadened by s 233B(1)(aa) which criminalises any person who "brings or attempts to bring, or causes to be brought, into Australia any prohibited imports".

The scope of importation is further broadened by its conjunction with ancillary offences such as "being knowingly concerned" in the importation of drugs. Recent cases have tended to view importation as a process rather than an event. This approach means that individuals whose involvement commences *after* the physical landing of the drugs into the country may nevertheless participate in that importation. In *Leff* (1996) 86 A Crim R 212, the accused was charged with being knowingly concerned in the importation of cocaine, contrary to s 233B. The accused claimed that her involvement in the criminal enterprise occurred *after* the importation had occurred. The New South Wales Court of Criminal Appeal upheld her conviction. Even on the most favourable view of the evidence, the Court held that her involvement (conversations with the courier after the drugs were landed) could support her conviction. (In fact, the conversations took place while the courier was under arrest and helping the police with their inquiries). James J pointed out that importation was a continuing process that was not extinguished by interception by law enforcement officials: at 223. Gleeson CJ endorsed this approach (at 214), adding that both "importation" and "being concerned" were flexible concepts:

> The concepts of importation, and of being concerned in an importation, are both sufficiently flexible to cover a case such as the present. ... [I]mportation is a process, or a venture, not a physical act which occurs or ceases at the moment of import. Furthermore, concern in an importation can commence at a time when it has apparently broken down, and where efforts are being made to bring it to fruition.

Such an interpretation raises questions about the limits of the concept, in particular when an importation has ceased. Are these limits determined solely by the needs of the law enforcement officials conducting covert operations? Clearly some flexibility in these concepts is considered essential to facilitate the controlled delivery of drugs. There are however dangers that the original importation is only remotely or tangentially related to those individuals who subsequently become "knowingly concerned" in the distribution of those drugs. This often occurs when undercover police and informers incite others to become concerned in the distribution and supply of illegal drugs. The permissible limits of police participation in the drug trade and the use of entrapment are usually considered as separate procedural or evidential issues, though they clearly have implications for the substantive law, such as the meaning and scope of importation.[28]

The structure and form of s 233B(1) reflects the limits of legislative competence under the trade and commerce power in the Constitution. Federal regulation of drugs is seemingly restricted to acts of importation, and any consequent dealings in those imported goods. However, the section is not strictly confined to trafficking illegal drugs across national borders. Section 233B(1)(c) prohibits mere possession, though the prosecution must prove that the drugs were imported in contravention of the Act. Possession has been subsequently expanded to its constitutional limits to include possession of drugs "reasonably suspected" of having been imported in contravention of the Act by s 233b(1)(ca). While this concept stretches the federal jurisdiction considerably, a wider mandate for federal drug law can be located in the external affairs power of the Constitution since Australia has ratified numerous international treaties and conventions on illicit drugs. The impact of international law on drug control, particularly the growing internationalisation of drug law, is explored below: pp 859-861.

---

28 See for example *R v Chow* (1987) 11 NSWLR 561 where the New South Wales Court of Criminal Appeal rejected the argument that since the Australian Federal Police had imported the heroin it could no longer be treated as a prohibited import under the *Customs Act* 1901 (Cth).

The prohibited "imports" and "exports" to which this section applies are "goods that consist of a narcotic substance". This means a substance or thing that is named or described in column 1 of Sch VI or any other substance or thing for the time being declared by the regulations to be a narcotic substance: *Customs Act* 1901 (Cth), s 4(1). Schedule VI includes the commonly-known illicit drugs such as cannabis, cocaine, heroin (diacetylmorphine), LSD, morphine, methadone, as well as many other less familiar drugs. Although the legislation defines the illicit drugs as containing a "narcotic substance", many of the drugs prohibited do not belong to the opioid group and have very different pharmacological structures and effects.

The frontiers of modern drug laws are highly sensitive to drug markets and the emergence of new "recreational" drugs. Rather than enact specific offences to deal with particular substances, omnibus provisions such as s 233B(1) criminalise prohibited *categories* of drug. These categories, such as "prohibited import or narcotic drug", are then defined in schedules appended to the legislation or contained in subordinate regulations. A similar framework applies for State and Territory drug offences. The use of regulations permits drug offences to be amended rapidly without the need to redraft the Principal Act. Indeed, the Model Criminal Code Officers Committee (MCCOC) recommended that drug tables should not be included in legislation but should be located in regulations: *Chapter 6 — Serious Drug Offences,* Report (1998), p 23. Although acknowledging that legislating new offences by regulation was undesirable in terms of criminal law principles (as they are less visible to the public and by-pass direct parliamentary scrutiny), this development was "practically unavoidable" because of the need to amend drug laws quickly in response to emerging threats. The MCCOC stated (p 21) "recent problems with a sudden surge in the supply of GHB or "fantasy" in Queensland and the scramble in all jurisdictions to add the drug to their tables is an example of this".

The ease with which new drugs (which share no common pharmacological characteristics) are prohibited, by-passes the opportunity for informed debate within the community about the danger of such drugs, or the positive and negative effects of prohibition.

Concern about the misuse of drugs in sport in the 1980s resulted in calls for tighter controls over performance enhancing substances, such as anabolic steroids, and led to the establishment of a new regulatory body, the Australian Drugs Sports Agency. At present, steroids are not prohibited under international conventions and trafficking in steroids is not an offence in most jurisdictions. Nevertheless, the MCCOC has recommended that anabolic steroids should be included within the definition of "controlled drug" for the purpose of trafficking and related offences. The MCCOC noted that there had been opposition to this proposal from the Commonwealth Department of Health and Family Services on the ground that steroid users were not dependent on the drug and that the use of drugs in sport fell within the regulatory jurisdiction of the Australian Drugs Sports Agency: p 265. In the MCCOC's view, however, criminalisation of trafficking in steroids was warranted because of the growing international trade in steroids, the potential negative health consequences of non-medical usage and the potential for criminal profit and development of a black market structures.

> Concern about the diversion of animal steroid products used legitimately by veterinarians into the illicit drug market has led to tighter restrictions in some jurisdictions, and calls for further federal offences to stem the influx of these substances from overseas: *Australian Illicit Drug Report 1997-1998* (Canberra: Australian Bureau of Criminal Intelligence, 1999), pp 90-95.

REVERSING THE BURDEN OF PROOF: THE DEFENCE OF "REASONABLE EXCUSE"

Section 233B(1) has many curious features. In addition to the wide range of conduct and numerous overlapping offences dealt within a single provision, the section also modifies the burden of proof in relation to defences. As discussed in Chapter 2 at pp 114ff, the House of Lords in *Woolmington v DPP* [1935] AC 462 established that the prosecution ordinarily bears the burden of proof to establish the elements of the offence and rebut available defences. Although much revered as the "golden thread" of the criminal law, the presumption has been subject to extensive derogation and qualification by statute.

Section 233B(1) of the *Customs Act* 1901 (Cth) is typical of many summary offences in that it places on the accused a legal burden of disproving key elements of the offence or establishing defences such as "reasonable excuse". The difference however is that the reversal in s 233(1) does not apply to a minor "regulatory" offence, but rather to a serious offence punishable by a maximum sentence of life imprisonment. The draconian nature of such sentencing powers is considered in the next section.

The key defence for offences contained in s 233B(1) is "reasonable excuse". The term is not defined in the Act. The statutory excuse operates alongside the general defences available under the common law, such as mistake of fact. There is some clarification of its scope under the Customs (Prohibited Imports) Regulations, which permits importation and exportation where a person has obtained both a licence to import a drug and permission to import a drug has been granted by the federal minister for health: reg 5(1)(a). The conditions governing the issuing of licenses are contained in Regulation 5(7). The specific conditions governing the use of the drug for medical or scientific purposes are contained in Regulation 5(10)(b).

Reasonable excuse may permit issues relating to "necessity" to be raised as a defence. This proposition has not yet been tested in Australian courts, though there have been suggestion that possession or supply could be justified on the basis of medical necessity: D Heilpern with G Rayner, "Drug Law and Necessity" (1997) 22(4) *Alternative Law Journal* 188. As we have explored in Chapter 6, the precise boundaries and elements of the common law doctrine of necessity are vague: pp 325ff. Nevertheless, the common law may provide a justification for illegal conduct on medical grounds of necessity. For example, necessity has provided a defence (and hence a lawful basis) for the medical provision of abortions in Australia. The debate about necessity and drugs has focused on the medicinal use of cannabis: M Kyriagis, "Marijuana — Just What the Doctor Ordered?" (1997) 20(3) *University of New South Wales Law Journal* 594. There is scientific and medical evidence demonstrating that the active properties of cannabis (THC) is an effective drug for the treatment of medical conditions such as glaucoma and for relieving the symptoms of disease such as nausea and vomiting. It is also considered a pain relieving analgesic: National Drug Strategy, *Report of the Task Force on Cannabis* (Canberra: AGPS, 1994). As a prohibited drug, however, further research on the therapeutic effects of cannabis and THC has been largely blocked.

In the United States, since the 1970s, State courts have recognised that the possession of cannabis may be justified on the grounds of medical necessity, and following recent referenda in Arizona and California, doctors in those jurisdictions have been permitted to prescribe cannabis for use in medical treatment. As Michael Kyriagis points out, the difficulty with partial legalisation is that cannabis remains firmly prohibited under US Federal law, and the legal position of those involved in the supply and use of the drug remains ambiguous (pp 616-630). In light of the "Tough on Drugs" policy recently adopted in Australia and the Commonwealth's rejection of the "Heroin Trial", it is unlikely that there will be legislation forthcoming to provide a lawful basis for the medicinal use of cannabis (or even research into its therapeutic effects). The absence of legislation, however, does not preclude further judicial development of the medical necessity defence. As David Heilpern and Georgia Rayner conclude (at 191):

> This is not drug law reform by the back door. It is applying established principles of common law in an innovative way in an effort to remedy injustice.

As the history of abortion in Australia reveals, political and legislative stalemates on matters of moral concern can be overcome by judicial expansion of existing common law doctrines such as necessity: see further Ch 10, pp 521-523.

> **Therapeutic morphine used in medical practice can be imported and exported under license granted by the federal Minister for Health. To obtain permission to import a narcotic, the Commonwealth must be satisfied that the importation does not exceed the annual estimates, as determined by the International Narcotic Control Board, on how much narcotic Australia needs to import to avoid stockpiling. Under the *Single Convention on Narcotic Drugs* (1961), the Board monitors and supervises the international movement of licit narcotics. It should be noted that Tasmania is one of the world's largest growers and producers of licit opiates: *Australian Illicit Drug Report 1997-1998* (Canberra: Australian Bureau of Criminal Intelligence, 1999), pp 41-42.**

"CIRCUMSTANCES OF AGGRAVATION": A PHYSICAL ELEMENT OR SENTENCING PROVISION?

The penalty provisions for the above offences, contained in s 235 of the *Customs Act* 1901 (Cth), are potentially very harsh. In the absence of aggravating factors, the penalty is two years imprisonment or a fine not exceeding $2,000. The presence of aggravating circumstances increases the penalties in graduated steps to the maximum of imprisonment for life. The penalty for an offence against s 233B(1) varies according to a number of circumstances, including whether the quantity of the narcotic goods exceeded either a commercial quantity or a trafficable quantity (as defined by Sch VI) and whether the offender had previously been convicted of an offence of a specified kind involving narcotic goods: s 235(2)(c). The breadth of penalties for these offences — ranging from two years to life imprisonment — is staggering.

The provisions in s 235 have presented some difficulties. There has been uncertainty as to whether the aggravating circumstances are an element of the offence to be determined by the jury as part of the trial, or should be determined by the court as part of sentencing. If the latter approach is adopted, a potential constitutional problem arises — does s 235 conform with s 80 of the Constitution which requires that a trial on indictment of any Commonwealth offence shall be by jury? The High Court has held that the circumstances of aggravation in s 235 were matters relevant to the maximum sentence that could be imposed, and were not ingredients of an offence. As such, these matters were properly left to the determination of the sentencing court, not the jury: *Kingswell v The Queen* (1985) 159 CLR 264 at 276. On the constitutional issue, the majority held that s 235 did not contravene the right to a jury trial secured by s 80 of the Constitution.

For the purpose of fixing the sentence, the judge must form a view of the facts. This was a legitimate function of the court, the only limitation being that the judicial view of the facts must not conflict with the jury's verdict. The majority observed (at 276) that the constitutional right to a jury trial for federal offences was very limited: "Section 80 says nothing as to the manner in which an offence is to be defined". However, as a matter of practice, the majority proposed that these aggravating circumstances should nevertheless be included in the indictment. Although the inclusion of these circumstances in the indictment was desirable, failure to do so would not result in a miscarriage of justice. As Gibbs CJ subsequently pointed out in *R v Meaton* (1986) 160 CLR 359 (at 363-364):

> The inclusion in the indictment of matters of fact, which, although not elements of the offence, render the accused liable to a greater maximum punishment, serves the double purpose of informing the accused of a very important feature of the case made against him and of enabling the jury (in the event of a trial by jury) to decide questions of fact which may very materially affect the maximum punishment to which the accused is exposed.

The practice of including aggravating circumstances in the indictment poses difficulties where a past conviction for narcotic offences is being relied upon to aggravate the penalty. The introduction of these facts, while not requiring proof at trial, would pose a danger of unfairness to the accused through the risk of prejudicing the jury. In some jurisdictions, the indictment in such cases must be framed without reference to any previous conviction, and only upon conviction for the subsequent offence will the jury be asked to determine whether the accused has been previously convicted: *Crimes Act* 1900 (NSW), ss 394 and 414, discussed in *Kingswell v The Queen* (1985) 159 CLR 264 at 284.

The difficulty with s 235 is that it tries to do too much. The High Court has drawn (primarily for constitutional purposes) a strict conceptual distinction between guilt attribution (a matter for the jury) and sentencing (a matter for the court). The difficulty is that the concept of aggravation in the section spans both functions. The rule of practice applied in *Kingswell* overcomes this disjunction recognising that these factors significantly alter the nature of the offence and liability to punishment. The present practice permits the jury to play a role in determining whether these aggravating factors are present. Indeed, the majority in *R v Meaton* (1986) 160 CLR 359 advocated (at 364) that "the preferable course for the prosecution is to lay one charge which includes the circumstances of aggravation; the jury can then be directed that it would be open to them (in appropriate circumstances) to find the accused guilty of the charge without those circumstances of aggravation". This practice, unsupported by statute, would require careful judicial direction on the range of verdict options available to the jury.

Brennan and Deane JJ strongly dissented (at 366) on the appropriateness of these procedural manoeuvres. In their view, it was fundamental that strict congruence between criminal practice and the substantive law should be maintained — simply put, if aggravation is not an element of the offence, then it should not be included in the indictment. Underlying this controversy is the importance of avoiding unfairness to the accused, particularly that the defence should be in a position before trial to know the true nature of the charge and potential liability to punishment. As discussed in Chapter 2, the right to a fair trial is fundamental, and the accused has a right to know the nature of the charge against him or her and be given an opportunity to obtain an acquittal from a jury fully informed of the relevant facts. The right to a fair trial, a right which is fundamental under the common law, must be given utmost protection in trials where the accused is exposed to the risk of life imprisonment.

THE FAULT ELEMENT FOR IMPORTATION OFFENCES

Before the High Court decision of *He Kaw Teh v The Queen* (1985) 157 CLR 523, drug offences were almost universally considered to be offences of strict liability. There was no requirement for the prosecution to prove any fault element, either subjective or objective, on the part of the accused. All that was required was the importation/exportation/possession of a thing listed on the schedule as a prohibited drug. Barwick CJ in *R v Bull* (1974) 131 CLR 203 at 220 held that knowledge of the nature of the thing was not essential to the commission of the importation offence under s 233B(1)(a). However, the High Court held that the section did not exclude the exculpatory principle by which the person charged may prove an honest belief on reasonable grounds in the existence of circumstances which, if true, would make innocent that with which he or she is charged. The Court held that this defence was permitted under the terms of the section which allowed for any reasonable excuse, proof of which is to lie on the accused. The scope of the mistake of fact defence available to crimes of "strict liability" is explored in Chapter 7.

Dispensing with proof of fault for federal narcotic offences stemmed from the placement of these offences within a statutory framework of customs prohibitions on particular imports and exports. Drugs were simply added to an existing Act as a special class of prohibited goods, namely "narcotic goods". The *Customs Act* 1901 (Cth) performs a wide range of functions related to trade and commerce, taxation and public health. While strict liability may be appropriate for regulatory offences prohibiting the importation of otherwise harmless goods into Australia, the question arises whether a similar approach should be adopted for serious drug offences, which carry a maximum penalty of life imprisonment.

Although the offences created under s 233B do not expressly require proof of fault (intention, knowledge or recklessness), the High Court has been generally unwilling to dispense with subjective fault for offences that carry severe penalties.

The High Court on No-Fault Liability for Drug Trafficking

The High Court decision in *He Kaw Teh v The Queen* (1985) 157 CLR 523 contains some of the strongest judicial statements on the fundamental importance of fault for criminal liability. In that case, the accused was convicted of two offences under s 233B(1)(b) and (c) of the *Customs Act* 1901 (Cth), importing and being in possession of a prohibited import (heroin) respectively. The decision provided the opportunity to affirm the importance of fault in attributing criminal liability, a value underlying the presumption of a fault element applicable to both common law and statutory offences. The High Court affirmed that there was a tripartite classification for criminal offences — crimes requiring proof of fault, strict liability or absolute liability. These different forms of liability have implications for the degree of blameworthiness required, particularly whether and on what condition a mistake of fact will be exculpatory. This aspect of the judgment in *He Kaw Teh* has been reviewed in Chapter 3: pp 190-192.

The High Court attempted to provide guidance on how the courts should construe offence provisions that do not expressly identify the fault element. The basic question is whether the presumption of a fault element had been displaced and Parliament intended that the offence should have no mental ingredient. In resolving this question, Gibbs CJ held (at 529) that a number of matters would be relevant:

(a) the words used in the statute;

(b) the subject matter of the statute;

(c) the extent to which strict liability assists in enforcement.

In determining whether Parliament intended that there should be no mental ingredient for the offence of importing/exporting prohibited imports/exports contrary to s 233B(1)(b), Gibbs CJ examined the provision itself and compared it to the surrounding offences. He noted (at 529) that the omission of the "reasonable excuse" defence in s 233B(1)(b) would be productive of injustice in some cases:

> That [the omission of the words "reasonable excuse"] would lead absurdly Draconian result if it meant that a person who unwittingly brought into Australia narcotics which had been planted in his [or her] baggage might be liable to life imprisonment notwithstanding that he [or she] was completely innocent of any connection with the narcotics and that he [or she] was unaware that he [or she] was carrying anything illicit.

Gibbs CJ then examined the second factor, the subject matter of the statute. These provisions of the *Customs Act* 1901 (Cth) dealt with the "grave social evil" of drug trafficking, which Gibbs CJ described in the following terms (at 529-530):

> The importation of and trade in narcotics creates a serious threat to the well-being of the Australian community. It has led to a great increase in crime, to corruption and to the ruin of innocent lives. The fact that the consequences of an offence

> against s 233B(1)(b) may be so serious suggests that the Parliament may have
> intended to make the offence an absolute one ... On the contrary, offences of this
> kind, at least where heroin in commercial quantities is involved, are truly criminal;
> a convicted offender is exposed to obloquy and disgrace and becomes liable to the
> highest penalty that may be imposed under the law. It is unlikely that the
> Parliament intended that the consequences of committing an offence so serious
> should be visited on a person who had no intention to do anything wrong and no
> knowledge that he [or she] was doing so.

The third factor considered relevant was the extent to which strict liability assisted in
enforcement. Gibbs CJ considered whether strict liability would promote the objectives of the
legislation and discussed the earlier Privy Council decision of *Lim Chin Aik v The Queen* [1963]
AC 160. Although strict liability would have the effect of encouraging travellers to take
extreme care to ensure that they were not importing drugs, it would serve no purpose to
penalise a person who had taken reasonable care and yet had unknowingly been an innocent
agent to import the drugs. What possible steps could such an innocent person take, who has
nothing to arouse his or her suspicions, to prevent a stranger secreting narcotics in his or her
luggage? He concluded that these three factors (words in the section, subject matter and
whether strict liability would assist enforcement) suggested that Parliament did not intend to
rebut the presumption of a fault element.

The next question for judicial consideration in *He Kaw Teh* was the nature and scope
of the requisite fault for these drug offences. Gibbs CJ traced the evolution of strict liability
and the three-fold classification of fault into crimes with a fault element, strict liability
offences and absolute liability offences. This analysis drew heavily on the classification
developed by the Supreme Court of Canada in *R v City of Sault St Marie* [1978] 2 SCR 1299.
The Supreme Court had held (at 1325) that strict liability is a "middle position between cases
where full *mens rea* is required and cases of absolute liability" where the accused can raise
the defence of mistake of fact based on honest and reasonable grounds. The Supreme Court
of Canada had held that absolute liability was limited to "public welfare offences" or
"regulatory offence". Gibbs CJ however found the Canadian method of classification unhelpful
and instead focused on legislative intent (at 535):

> it is more likely that the Parliament will have intended that full mens rea, in the
> sense of guilty intention or guilty knowledge, will be an element if an offence is one
> of a serious kind.

As this offence was one of the most serious in the criminal calendar, it seemed improbable
that Parliament would have intended to impose the sentence of life imprisonment for an
offence on the basis of "mere negligence". Neither would punishing negligence assist with
enforcement. Gibbs CJ noted earlier that there was nothing that a person, unaware that drugs
had been secreted into his or her baggage, could do to prevent an importation. It followed
therefore that the presumption of a fault element was not displaced and so the prosecution
must prove that the accused knew that he or she was importing a narcotic substance.

Gibbs CJ then went on to consider the allied offence of possession of a prohibited import under s 233b(1)(c). The ordinary meaning of the words used in the section "has in his [or her] possession" connoted a state of mind, namely awareness of the thing that was in fact in the possessor's physical control. Gibbs CJ left open (at 538) whether the accused must know the *quality* of the thing in the possessor's physical control, in this case whether the parcel contained narcotics. He noted that there was no unanimity on this question and that the present case did not require them to consider the issue. Brennan J took a firmer view (at 589):

> On a count of possession ... the onus is on the prosecution to prove that an accused, at the time when he [or she] had physical custody or control of narcotics goods, knew of the existence and nature, or of the likely existence and likely nature, of the narcotic goods in question.

Dawson J took a different view in relation to the extent of knowledge required under this offence holding (at 602) that a person possesses a prohibited import under this section (in this case narcotics) if the person is aware of possessing something but is not aware that what he or she possesses are in fact narcotics.

As David Brown, David Farrier and David Weisbrot point out in *Criminal Laws* (2nd ed, Sydney: Federation Press, 1996), p 370:

> The High Court decision of *He Kaw Teh* has significance beyond its narrow ratio decidendi. It provides a framework for analysing statutory criminal offences, and indicates a number of alternatives which are available when courts have to address *mens rea* questions about the *actus reus* of a particular offence.

Brennan J's judgment is regarded as an authoritative summary of general principles governing fault in the criminal law. The decision has also been influential for drug offences generally. Although concerned with specific importation and possession offences under Commonwealth legislation, the statements of principle have been applied to State/Territory offences dealing with the possession of drugs: F Rinaldi and P Gillies, *Narcotic Offences* (Sydney: Law Book Company Ltd, 1991), p 38.

As an authority on these specific provisions of the *Customs Act* 1901 (Cth), *He Kaw Teh* has been largely overtaken by subsequent decisions. In *Kural v The Queen* (1987) 162 CLR 502, the High Court clarified that the requisite intent for importation offences is not limited to *actual* knowledge, but may rest on *awareness* that the thing in possession is a narcotic drug. It is not necessary to show that the person in possession had detailed knowledge of the chemical composition of the drug or even that it is a particular type of drug; it is only necessary to prove knowledge that the thing possessed is, or is likely to be, an illicit drug. A similarly flexible approach to knowledge was adopted for the possession offence by the High Court in *Saad v The Queen* (1987) 70 ALR 667. This approach to knowledge has been described as the "genus principle": P Gillies, *Criminal Law* (4th ed, Sydney: Federation Press, 1997), p 801.

A more stringent approach to the fault for serious drug offences has been recommended by the Model Criminal Code Officers Committee (MCCOC) in *Chapter 6: Serious Drug Offences*, Report (1998). In the MCCOC's view, the imposition of absolute liability, or the reversal of the burden of proof, was considered appropriate only for regulatory offences carrying a comparatively light penalty. In relation to trafficking and related drug offences, as a matter of principle and policy, the prosecution should be required to prove intent or recklessness beyond reasonable doubt: pp 63-64. The MCCOC also recommended a partial defence of mistake which would apply to cases where the offender made a mistake as to the nature of the controlled drug. The defence of mistake however would be limited in its application to aggravated drug offences (such as commercial trafficking), simply reducing liability to the lesser offence contemplated by the accused. This partial defence of mistake was considered to be an acceptable compromise between the requirements of effective law enforcement and the principle that absolute liability should not be imposed on offences carrying moral stigma and severe penalties: p 213. As the MCCOC noted, this approach to culpability is consistent with the approach taken to impossible attempts, where the accused is judged liable according to the facts as he or she mistakenly believed them to be. The effect of mistake and impossibility on the law of attempts has have been explored in Chapter 7, 5 'Mistake and Inchoate Offences': pp 352ff.

2.4 TRAFFICKING OFFENCES

In the 19th century, the statutes prohibiting drugs as types of poison focused primarily on restraining their use or administration. In the 20th century, the focus of drug legislation shifted to commercial dealing, in particular to the problem of drug trafficking and organised crime. This is consistent with the emerging policy distinction between use and trafficking, with the latter being the focus of increasingly punitive measures.

Since the 1970s, the emergence of links between organised crime and drugs have produced even tougher laws and penalties for drug trafficking. Separate and higher penalties for the supply or sale of "traffickable quantities" of drugs, were enacted in several jurisdictions.[29] Penalties relating to "commercial quantities" were aggravated to a maximum of 25 years' imprisonment.[30] Commercial manufacture and cultivation of drugs were also brought within the framework of trafficking offences, implementing the obligations contained in the various international treaties against drugs, discussed below.[31]

---

29   Section 21A of the *Poisons Amendment Act* 1970 (NSW) introduced a maximum penalty of up to 10 years' imprisonment. Similar provisions were enacted by the *Dangerous Drugs Amendment Act (No 2)* 1970 (SA), s 5; *Health Act Amendment Act* 1971 (Qld), ss 7, 12; *Poisons (Drugs of Addiction) Act* 1976 (Vic), s 6.

30   *Drugs Misuse and Trafficking Act* 1985 (NSW), s 33 ($500,000 fine or life imprisonment); *Drugs Misuse Act* 1986 (Qld), s 8; *Drugs, Poisons and Controlled Substances (Amendment) Act* 1983 (Vic), s 7.

31   There is no consistent approach to these offences, and in some jurisdictions, manufacture falls within the scope of trafficking offences; see for example *Drugs, Poisons and Controlled Substances Act* 1981 (Vic). The *Model Criminal Code* however recommends the creation of a separate offence of manufacture of a controlled drug: s 6.3. This proposal envisages a series of aggravated offences that increase the punishment in graded steps where the accused has manufactured a commercial quantity or large commercial quantity of controlled drug: Model Criminal Code Officers Committee, *Chapter 6: Serious Drug Offences*, Report (1998), pp 107-109.

At both the international and national level, the focus of concern has shifted away from individual drug users to organised crime networks considered responsible for trafficking. Reflecting the concern about trafficking, the reach of the Commonwealth regulation was significantly extended by the *Crimes (Traffic in Narcotic Drugs and Psychotropic Substances) Act* 1990 (Cth). This Act contains several offences targeting the activities of individuals involved in drug trafficking. The Act received Royal Assent on 29 November 1990, but its commencement was deferred until in 14th February 1993, the day that Australia ratified the United Nations' *Convention Against Illicit Traffic in Narcotic Drugs and Psychotropic Substances* (1988). The principal offence — possession of prohibited drugs, equipment or materials with knowledge that they are being used in or for "dealing in drugs" — is an offence under s 9. The Act also prohibits dealing in drugs on board an Australian aircraft (s 10) and on board an Australian ship (s 11). The "dealing in drugs" must constitute an offence against a law of the Commonwealth, of a State or Territory or of a foreign country: s 9(b). In this sense, these trafficking provisions are *parasitic* upon the commission of other offences. Consistent with the objectives of the Convention, the offence aims to tackle the international dimension of the trade in illicit drugs. Section 6 contains an extensive list of activity that can constitute "dealing in drugs":

(1) For the purposes of this Act, each of the following is a dealing in drugs:

(a) the cultivation of opium poppy, coca bush or cannabis plant for the purpose of producing narcotic drugs;

(b) the separation of opium, coca leaves, cannabis or cannabis resin from the plant from which they are obtained;

(c) the manufacture, extraction or preparation of a narcotic drug or psychotropic substance;

(d) the possession of a narcotic drug or psychotropic substance for the purpose of the manufacture, extraction or preparation of another such drug or substance;

(e) the sale, supply, or possession for the purpose of sale or supply, of a narcotic drug or psychotropic substance;

(f) the importation into Australia, exportation from Australia, or possession for the purpose of such importation or exportation, of a narcotic drug or psychotropic substance;

(fa) the manufacture, transport or distribution of any substance listed in Table I or Table II in the Annex to the Convention or of equipment or materials, with the knowledge that the substance, equipment or materials are to be used for a purpose set out in paragraph (a), (b) or (c);

(fb) organising, managing or financing a dealing in drugs referred to in paragraphs (a), (b), (c), (d), (e), (f) or (fa);

(g) the possession of any substance listed in Table I or Table II in the Annex to the Convention or of any equipment or materials, with the knowledge that the substance, equipment or materials are being used or are to be used for a purpose set out in paragraph (a), (b) or (c).

(2) For the purposes of this Act, each of the following is also a dealing in drugs:

(a) a conspiracy or attempt to engage in conduct that is, under subsection (1), a dealing in drugs;

(b) being a party to any dealing in drugs referred to in subsection (1);

(ba) aiding, abetting, counselling or procuring, or being by act or omission in any way directly or indirectly knowingly concerned in, any conduct that is, under subsection (1), a dealing in drugs;

(c) inciting to, urging or encouraging, any conduct that is, under subsection (1), a dealing in drugs.

There is clearly an overlap with the *Customs Act* 1901 (Cth) provisions. However, the *Crimes (Traffic in Narcotic Drugs and Psychotropic Substances) Act* 1990 (Cth) does not limit the operation of any other law of the Commonwealth, or any law of a State or Territory: s 5(1).

The increasing focus on drug traffickers rather than users was reinforced by the successive governmental inquiries into drugs from the 1970s to the 1990s. The Royal Commission headed by Justice Williams in 1980 affirmed the importance of this distinction, and proposed that offences relating to use and trafficking should be dealt with in separate legislation. In *From Mr Sin to Mr Big* (Melbourne: Oxford University Press, 1993), Manderson summarises the bifurcated legislative model recommended by the Commission as follows (p 181):

> The proposed Drugs of Dependence Act punished minor offences including possession and use. It accepted that users were sick and in need of help; penalties were relatively slight, and the emphasis was placed on treatment and community services. The proposed Drug Trafficking Act was designed to facilitate the detection and punishment of trafficking. It assumed that the drug problem was a question of law enforcement requiring stiff penalties, broad search powers, and complicated provisions for the forfeiture of assets. Illness and vice were treated in isolation as if the problems they addressed were unrelated (footnotes omitted).

The idea of separate legislation was never implemented, though it continues to be the model favoured by law reformers. Indeed, the *Model Criminal Code* proposes only to deal with serious drug offences, leaving minor possession and use as minor regulatory offences to be dealt with by public health legislation: Model Criminal Code Officers Committee, *Chapter 6: Serious Drug Offences*, Report (1998). The offences proposed for the *Model Criminal Code* focused on commercial dealing in drugs, namely "trafficking". The removal of "use" offences from the "criminal" framework is consistent with the policy of harm minimisation that guided the MCCOC's work; namely, that drug laws should aim to minimise or moderate the harms suffered by users.

While no jurisdiction has adopted the model based on separate legislation, a clear distinction between use and trafficking is apparent in all State and Territory legislation. For illustrative purposes, we will examine the Australian Capital Territory legislation, which substantially implemented the recommendations of the Williams Royal Commission in 1981 and was intended to be a model for other jurisdictions.

The regulatory framework in the *Drugs of Dependence Act* 1989 (ACT) draws a distinction between "prohibited substances" and "drugs of dependence". The list of prohibited substances and drugs of dependence is contained in schedules under Drugs of Dependence Regulations — heroin (diacetylmorphine) is a prohibited substance while methadone is a drug of dependence. From a medical perspective, both type of drugs have similar pharmacological properties and the potential to cause addiction and to adversely affect health if misused. The distinction is ultimately based on the legality of the drug, and plays a crucial moral as well as legal role in differentiating between the legitimate treatment involving the medical use of methadone and the illegitimate recreational use of "dangerous" drugs such as heroin. The Act itself does not explain the basis for this two-fold classification, although the rationale provided in the Explanatory Statement accompanying the Act is that while drugs of dependence have medical use, prohibited substances have no medical use and are harmful for recreational purposes.[32] This explanation is hardly convincing when one considers that heroin, which is classified as a dangerous drug, had a wide and legitimate use in medical treatment prior to its complete prohibition in the 1950s.

The following Table contains a comparison of offences dealing with heroin, revealing the diversity of approaches to criminalisation, structure of offences and range of penalties. The Table was included in the Model Criminal Code Officers Committee, *Chapter 6: Serious Drug Offences*, Report, (1998), p 342:

TABLE 2:

Australian Drug Legislation — Comparative Tables (Heroin)

Note: penalties given are in relation to sale/supply/trafficking of quantities of more than the amount shown.

JURISDICTION	PURE OR MIXED	POSSESSION (users)	SMALL QUANTITY	TRAFFICABLE QUANTITY (raises presumption)	COMMERCIAL QUANTITY
MCC	pure or mixed	NE	NE	3 g pure or mixed 10 years	25 g pure 50 g mixed 20 years
CTH	pure	—	2 years +/ $2,000	2 g 25 years +/ $100,000	1.5 kg life
ACT	pure	less than 2 g 2 years +/ $5,000	—	2 g (less than 1.5 kg) 25 years +/ $100,000	1.5 kg life

32 A similar point was made about the non-therapeutic use of recreational drugs by the Model Criminal Code Officers Committee, though it did concede that such categorisation was not immutable in light of recent research suggesting that cannabis can play a role in legitimate medical treatment: *Chapter 6: Serious Drug Offences*, Report (1998), p 4, fn 5.

Table 2 continued

JURISDICTION	PURE OR MIXED	POSSESSION (users)	SMALL QUANTITY	TRAFFICABLE QUANTITY (raises presumption)	COMMERCIAL QUANTITY
NSW	mixed	2 years +/ 20 penalty units	1 g 2 years +/ 1,000 penalty units	3 g 2 years +/ 100 penalty units	250 g 20 years +/ 3,500 penalty units
NT	mixed	less than 2 g 5 years or $10,000 (public place) 2 years or $5,000 elsewhere	—	2 g (less than 40 g) 14 years	40 g 25 years
QLD	mixed	less than 2 g 15 years	—	2 g (less than 200 g) 25 years	200 g
SA	mixed	less than 2 g 2 years +/$2,000	—	2 g (less than 300 g) 25 years +/ $200,000	300 g life +/ $500,000
TAS	mixed	2 years +/50 penalty units	—	0.5 g (any amount) 25 years +/ $100,000	—
VIC	pure or mixed	1 year +/ 30 penalty units	1 g pure or mixed	3 g pure or mixed 15 years +/ 1,000 penalty units	250 g pure 500 g mixed 25 years +/ 2,500 penalty units
WA	mixed	—	2 g (any amount) 25 years +/ $100,000	—	—

SALE, SUPPLY AND POSSESSION WITH INTENT TO TRAFFICK

Trafficking offences are considered notoriously difficult to prove because of the absence of victims willing to complain or testify. As a consequence, some offences extend to the possession of drugs with intent to traffic. Section 164(3) of the *Drugs of Dependence Act* 1989 (ACT) is a typical example where the offence of sale or supply is broadened to include possession for the purpose of sale or supply:

> (3) A person shall not —
>
> **(a)** sell or supply a prohibited substance to any person;
>
> **(b)** participate in the sale or supply of a prohibited substance to any person; or
>
> **(d)** possess a prohibited substance for the purpose of sale or supply to any person.

For the purposes of the *Drugs of Dependence Act* 1989 (ACT) "supply" is defined as including an "offer to supply but does not include administer": s 3(1). In interpreting this offence, the courts have applied the ordinary meaning of the term "supply", which in this context means the transfer of physical control of the property from one person to another.[33]

The penalties are more severe where the conduct involves either "commercial" or "traffickable" quantities of the substance,[34] or involves the sale or supply of a prohibited substance to persons under the age of 18 years.[35] Proof of intent to traffic is further facilitated by the liberal use of presumptions such as s 164(8) which states that

> where a person has more than the traffickable quantity of a drug of dependence or a prohibited substance in his or her possession, it shall be presumed that the possession is for the purpose of sale or supply to another person, but that presumption is rebuttable.[36]

The amount of drugs constituting a "traffickable" or "commercial" quantity varies between different types of drug and jurisdictions: see Table 2 above. The Model Criminal Code Officers Committee (MCCOC) in *Chapter 6: Serious Drug Offences* (1998) recommended the three graded trafficking offences rather than a single offence with defined circumstances of aggravation (p 66):

---

33 *Excell v Dellaca* (1987) 26 A Crim R 410 at 412, per Kelly J (SC ACT). In this case, the accused had agreed with a friend "to mind" a quantity of cannabis for one day. The court held that the since the accused intended to return the cannabis to his friend, he was properly convicted of possession of a controlled substance with an intention to supply. Supply therefore does not depend on legal ownership or lawful possession of the property transferred. The meaning of supply in the context of narcotic offences is explored in F Rinaldi and P Gillies, *Narcotic Offences* (Sydney: Law Book Company Ltd, 1991), pp 90-93.

34 "Commercial" and "traffickable" are used to describe different quantities of drug or substance prescribed under s 160(1) of the *Drugs of Dependence Act* 1989 (ACT).

35 *Drugs of Dependence Act* 1989 (ACT), s 164(3). Note also the separate provisions dealing with the wholesale sale or supply of drugs of dependence or prohibited substances: *Drugs of Dependence Act* 1989 (ACT), s 163.

36 Similar presumptions apply in other jurisdictions: *Drug Misuse and Trafficking Act* 1985 (NSW), s 29; *Misuse of Drugs Act* 1990 (NT), s 40(c); *Controlled Substances Act* 1984 (SA), s 32(3); *Poisons Act* 1971 (Tas), s 47(7); *Misuse of Drugs Act* 1981 (WA), s 11(a); *Drugs, Poisons and Controlled Substances Act* 1981 (Vic), s 73(2).

TABLE 3:

Model Criminal Code Proposals: Aggravated Trafficking Offences

OFFENCE	PENALTY
trafficking in a large commercial quantity of a controlled drug	life imprisonment
trafficking in a commercial quantity of a controlled drug	20 years imprisonment
trafficking in a controlled drug	10 years imprisonment

As the MCCOC noted, the specifications of "large commercial" quantity and "commercial" quantity are based on the (undisclosed) field reports of law enforcement officers.

The severity of trafficking offences may be contrasted with those offences prohibiting the possession and administration of illicit drugs. In the Australian Capital Territory, for example, the possession offence penalises possession for "personal use".[37] Administration of a prohibited substance is also an offence under the Act: "A person shall not administer, or cause or permit to be administered, to himself or herself a prohibited substance": *Drugs of Dependence Act* 1989 (ACT), s 171(2). Both offences are punishable by a $5000 fine or imprisonment for two years. In cases of possession of a quantity of cannabis not exceeding 25 grams a penalty of $100 applies: *Drugs of Dependence Act* 1989 (ACT), s 171(1)(a). This minor penalty is further mitigated by the use of an expiation scheme, as discussed in Chapter 1, p 42.

PERSPECTIVES ON INTERNATIONAL LAW

Conventions on Illicit Drugs

The development of drug law in Australia in the 20th century was different from that which occured in the 19th century. International treaties have played an increasingly significant and determining role. As international law dictated that domestic drug laws must be strengthened and multiplied, the policy of prohibition became self-validating and self-reinforcing. Drug users had become criminals, and with the increasingly severe penalties accompanying narcotic offences drug use became associated in the public mind as an instance of serious criminality. Moreover, the reputation of these drugs for their addictiveness provided another reason for their prohibition and regulation. This coincided with the emergence of specialised law enforcement agencies in the United States, like the Federal Bureau of Narcotics.

After World War II, the international regime of drug control was considerably strengthened by the Paris Protocol of the Geneva Convention, signed in 1948, which placed upon any new narcotic drug the same controls and prohibitions that applied to heroin, morphine and cocaine. Notwithstanding these restrictions, medically-prescribed heroin consumption in Australia remained very high. Fearing that its international reputation would be tarnished, the

---

37 *Drugs of Dependence Act* 1989 (ACT), s 171(1). Possession for the purpose of sale or supply is prohibited in s 164(3).

Commonwealth Government acted to prohibit heroin importation in 1953. The Commonwealth put pressure on the States and Territories to prohibit the use, possession and manufacture of heroin and total prohibition was accomplished by 1955. Despite the absence of a significant domestic "drug problem", the Australian public were led to believe that the total ban of heroin was necessary due to high levels of heroin addiction. These drug laws were rarely invoked until the 1960s when patterns of drug use began to change and illicit "recreational" drug consumption became an issue of public concern.

The restrictions placed on the opioids were extended to other drugs as they were developed and in 1961 these various treaties were codified into the *Single Convention on Narcotic Drugs* the purpose of which was to require State Parties to regulate *by law*, the production, distribution and supply of the controlled substances. Activities that did not fall under the narrow medical or scientific derogations had to be the subject of criminal offences. Under the *Single Convention on Narcotic Drugs* (1961) heroin is classified under Schedule IV as a drug having "particularly dangerous properties". Article 36(1) of the Convention requires the prohibition of the following drug-related activities:

> Subject to its constitutional limitations, each Party shall adopt such measures as will ensure that cultivation, production, manufacture, extraction, preparation, possession, offering, offering for sale, distribution, purchase, sale, delivery on any terms whatsoever, brokerage, dispatch, dispatch in transit, transport, importation and exportation of drugs contrary to the provisions of this Convention, and any other action which in the opinion of such Party may be contrary to the provisions of this Convention, shall be punishable offences, when committed intentionally, and that serious offences shall be liable to adequate punishment particularly by imprisonment or other penalties of deprivation of liberty.

Under this Article, the prohibition on "possession" does not distinguish between possession for personal or recreational use, and possession for the purposes of trafficking. This ambiguity has allowed some jurisdictions to adopt "decriminalisation" strategies for the possession of drugs for personal use. The subsequent clarifications of the scope of prohibition in Art 3(2) of the United Nations *Convention Against Illicit Traffic in Narcotic Drugs and Psychotropic Substances* (1988) suggest that possession for personal consumption should be criminalised:

> Subject to its constitutional principles and the basic concepts of its legal system, each Party shall adopt such measures as may be necessary to establish as a criminal offence under its domestic law, when committed intentionally, *the possession, purchase or cultivation of narcotic drugs or psychotropic substances for personal consumption* contrary to the provisions of the 1961 Convention, the 1961 Convention as amended or the 1971 Convention (emphasis added).

Notwithstanding these uncertainties about the scope of prohibition demanded by international law, the possession and cultivation of small quantities of cannabis have been "decriminalised" by expiation and infringement notice systems (in the Australian Capital Territory, the Northern Territory and South Australia) or by establishing a system of caution notices (Tasmania and

Victoria). The International Narcotics Control Board in 1997 expressed concern over "the discussion of legalisation of cannabis consumption in Australia, where already, in some States, possession of cannabis for personal use is not prosecuted" (discussed in *Australian Illicit Drug Report 1997-1998* (Canberra: Australian Bureau of Criminal Intelligence, 1999), p 23). As the Report notes, the Board's criticism misunderstands the distinction between decriminalisation and legalisation. It is highly unlikely that an expiation/infringement notice scheme which introduces "civil or administrative penalties" while retaining prosecution in the case of non-payment, would be held to violate the obligations under international law. Such "concerns" nevertheless place international pressure on those jurisdictions committed to reform based on the principle of harm minimisation.

It is often claimed that legalising the supply of drugs as part of a Heroin Trial (see above, p 827) would place Australia in violation of its international obligations.[38] However, the *Single Convention* permits the use of drugs for "medical and scientific research". Article 2(5) of the Convention provides:

> **(b)** A Party shall, if in its opinion the prevailing conditions in its country render it the most appropriate means of protecting the public health and welfare, prohibit the production, manufacture, export and import of, trade in, possession or use of any such drug *except for amounts which may be necessary for medical and scientific research only, including clinical trials therewith to be conducted under or subject to the direct supervision of the Party* (emphasis added).

Reflecting this derogation, the *Drugs of Dependence Act* 1989 (ACT) contains "research and education" exemptions for supply and possession. Under s 32, the supply and possession of a drug of dependence or prohibited substance may be authorised under the Act for the purpose of a "program of research or education". Where the Minister of Health has granted such authorisation, the Act exempts those individuals conducting a program of research or education from liability for those offences relating to the possession or supply of a prohibited substance provided that they adhere to the terms and conditions of the authorisation.[39]

3. DRUG LAW ENFORCEMENT

The arena of drug law enforcement has witnessed significant reforms widening investigative powers. Significant innovations in undercover policing in drug investigations. The deployment of surveillance technology and proactive policing methods are common features of many drug operations. As noted above, pp 831-833, these "extraordinary powers" introduced for the "War Against Drugs" are invariably normalised, becoming indispensible tools in law enforcement in other areas.

---

38 These objections and the domestic legal issues arising from the proposed heroin trial were reviewed in S Bronitt, *Criminal Liability Issues Associated with a Heroin Trial* (Canberra: NCEPH and AIC, 1995), Working Paper No 13, *Feasibility Research into the Controlled Availability of Opioids Stage 2.*

39 The conditions of authorisation are outlined in Pt IV, Divn 1 of the *Drugs of Dependence Act* 1989 (ACT). The exemptions in the Act are found in s 164(5) (exemption for supply) and s 171(4)(a) (exemption for possession). Note that researchers are not exempt from the prohibition on the sale or administration of prohibited substances.

The job of drug law enforcement has been diverted from traditional police forces to specialised drug agencies. The national and international dimensions of drug trafficking, money laundering and organised crime have justified the creation of new investigative agencies, such as the National Crime Authority and State Crime Commissions. These agencies have extensive statutory powers to investigate crime and concerns have been expressed regarding the breadth and potential abuse of these powers: M Findlay, S Odgers and S Yeo, *Australian Criminal Justice* (2nd ed, Melbourne: Oxford University Press, 1999, Ch 3).

Questions arise about the effectiveness of these considerable drug law enforcement efforts. Official reports on illicit drugs tend to focus on the levels of drug seizure, arrest, prosecution and conviction as indicia of effectiveness: see, for example, *Australian Illicit Drug Report 1997-1998* (Canberra: Australian Bureau of Criminal Intelligence, 1999). We have already noted above the importance of measuring the impact, as well as effectiveness, of law enforcement.[40] Until recently, there were limited data on the impact of drug laws and their enforcement on drug availability, price, purity, movements, social and health impacts or levels of drug-related crime. A significant exception is the empirical research undertaken on the (unintended) effects of cannabis decriminalisation, discussed in Chapter 1, p 42 and recent research on the link between illicit drug use and property crime discussed above, pp 827-829.

In the next section we examine several important powers used in the investigation of drug offences:

▬ money laundering and confiscation of the proceeds of crime; and

▬ entrapment.

Public versus Private Drug Law Enforcement

Most of the discussion about drug law focuses on public (State-sponsored) enforcement activity against illicit drugs. However, private (corporate-sponsored) enforcement activity has grown significantly in recent years with the introduction of random drug testing (RDT): P O'Malley and S Mugford, "Moral Technology: The Political Agenda of Random Drug Testing" (1991) 18 *Social Justice* 122. RDT has been embraced by large corporations in the United States, though in Australia it has been largely confined to sports and sensitive employment fields, such as defence and law enforcement. Although unable to impose formal punishment, these systems of parallel justice can exert discipline — via civil law and the employment contract — inflicting loss of earnings, licence revocation and adverse publicity on drug users. As O'Malley and Mugford conclude (at 222), RDT is not just about risk management — it is also a deeply moral and moralising activity. However, operating in the shadow of the criminal law, these systems of private discipline develop definitions of wrongdoing and methods of adjudication that, while mimicking the criminal law, lack the necessary safeguards of certainty, transparency and accountability.

---

40 S James and A Sutton, "Joining the War Against Drugs? Assessing Law Enforcement Approaches to Illicit Drug Control" in D Chappell and P Wilson (eds), *Australian Policing — Contemporary Issues* (2nd ed, Sydney: Butt, 1996), p 153.

3.1 MONEY LAUNDERING AND CONFISCATION OF THE PROCEEDS OF CRIME

Money laundering and the confiscation of proceeds relating to drug dealing were placed on the international agenda by the United Nations *Convention Against Illicit Trafficking in Narcotic Drugs and Psychotropic Substances* (1988). The Convention recognised that the international drug trade could only be stemmed through measures designed to undermine the power of organised crime and to remove the profits from trafficking: WC Gilmore, *Dirty Money: The Evolution of Money Laundering Counter-Measures* (The Netherlands: Council of Europe Press, 1995), p 64. The Convention required the criminalisation of certain offences, including the acquisition, possession or use of property, knowing at the time of receipt that it was derived from drug trafficking (Art 3(1)(c)(i)), as well as conspiracy, aiding and abetting, and facilitating the commission of drug trafficking offences, including money laundering (Art 3(1)(c)(ii)).

MONEY LAUNDERING MEASURES

Money laundering encompasses a wide range of practices that facilitate the concealment of the true origins of proceeds of crime in order to avoid detection by law enforcement authorities. The *United Nations International Drug Control Program* (1997) defines money laundering as "the process by which one conceals the existence, illegal source, or illegal application of income and then disguises or converts that income to make it appear legitimate": p 137, cited in *Australian Illicit Drug Report 1997-1998* (Canberra: Australian Bureau of Criminal Intelligence, 1999), p 130. It appears that money laundering occurs in three basic ways:

- illicit cash can be converted into a less suspicious form of currency or some other type of asset, such as real estate or high value goods;

- illicit cash can be converted into an alternate form in a manner that conceals its origin, ownership or other suspicious factors surrounding the cash.

- illicit cash can be converted into an alternate form, concealing the true source or ownership of the funds, and creating a legitimate source for subsequent use of the cash.[41]

There are three stages to money laundering — placement, layering and integration.

Placement: this is the process by which the cash is disposed of physically. This may be done by depositing the cash in a domestic bank or other financial institution, formal or informal, or a foreign financial institution or by the purchase of high value goods for resale. In response to legislation containing reporting requirements for "suspect" transactions involving large sums of cash, placement is done by "smurfs" who deposit sums less than $10,000 to avoid triggering the mandatory reporting thereby minimising the risk of detection by law enforcement agencies. The *Cash Transactions Reports Act* 1988 (Cth) is discussed below: p 865.

---

41 National Crime Authority, *Taken to the Cleaners: Money Laundering in Australia*: Vol 1 (Canberra: AGPS, 1992), p 11.

Layering: the second phase involves complex layers of financial transactions undertaken in order to separate the illicit cash from its source and disguise the audit trail, making it impossible for criminal investigators to reconstruct any criminal activity. This is done in a number of ways, ranging from conversion of cash into monetary instruments like bonds, stocks and shares, resale of high value goods and investment in real estate and legitimate businesses. A favoured method for carrying out this phase is via shelf companies run by lawyers and registered in off-shore havens like the Cayman Islands. This has the effect of hiding the identity of the real beneficiaries of the company by the combination of restrictive bank secrecy laws and lawyer–client privilege.

Integration: the final phase is the integration of the illicit proceeds back into the legitimate market. This is done by companies "lending" money back to the owner of the company, a loan which exists only on paper, and over-invoicing or producing false invoices for goods "sold" across borders, where, again, the sale only takes place on paper, and no goods actually change hands.

For a review of the international and national examples of money-laundering, including case studies, see *Australian Illicit Drug Report 1997-1998* (Canberra: Australian Bureau of Criminal Intelligence, 1999), Ch 10. Money laundering is a major problem world-wide, and continues to grow each year. Recent estimates suggest that nearly $4 billion is laundered through Australia annually: N Mackrell, "Economic Consequences of Money Laundering" in *Money Laundering in the 21st Century: Risks and Countermeasures* (Canberra: Australian Institute of Criminology, 1996), p 29.

The issue of knowledge, intent or purpose in relation to any of the offences listed in the Convention is addressed in Art 3(3), which provides that those factors may be inferred from objective factual circumstances.

The Convention also addresses, and promotes, international cooperation in investigation and extradition. Article 5(4) provides a mandatory framework for cooperation among law enforcement agencies, while retaining a substantial element of flexibility necessary for domestic-based legislation. It contemplates two approaches for cooperation: receiving a request for an order for confiscation, granting the order and giving effect to it, and receiving a completed order for confiscation from the requesting party and giving effect to that order. Therefore, while the ultimate outcome is the same, namely the confiscation of tainted property, the terms of the confiscation order may come either from the requesting or the requested State.

Extradition law generally contains a double criminality requirement, that is, the offence for which extradition is sought must be a criminal offence under the law of both the requesting and the requested State. While narcotics offences are almost universally recognised as an extractable offence, "narcotics related money laundering is a new criminal offence for many states and has not been traditionally recognised as an extradictable offence": W Gilmore, *Dirty Money: The Evolution of Money Laundering Counter-Measures* (The Netherlands: Council of Europe Press, 1995), p 66. By requiring State parties to criminalise narcotics related money laundering, the Convention addresses double criminality and facilitates extradition for those offences. Although Art 5(4) does not eliminate the possibility of invoking two other traditional restrictions on international cooperation, namely refusing to extradite in relation to political or fiscal offences, it limits the possibility of invoking those grounds in the context of narcotics related money laundering: p 67.

The other major aspect of the *Convention Against Illicit Trafficking in Narcotic Drugs and Psychotropic Substances* (1988) is the principle that domestic bank secrecy provisions should not unduly hinder the progress and operation of international criminal investigations. Article 5(3), which provides that a party may not refuse to empower its law enforcement authorities, including its courts, to order that bank, financial or commercial records be made available or seized on the basis of bank secrecy laws, has been flagged by William Gilmore as "one of the most important measures in combating drug money laundering operations": p 69.

Two major international bodies, amongst others, have been set up to monitor and assist in the implementation of anti-money laundering legislation and activities. The United Nations International Drug Control Program (UNDCP) provides assistance to States in devising legislative schemes to combat money laundering activities. Similarly, the Financial Action Task Force (FATF) specialises in and concentrates solely on the fight against money laundering, focusing its efforts primarily at a policy-based level. Set up by G7 governments in 1989, FATF has representatives from 24 OECD countries, and has issued "Forty Recommendations" for appropriate countermeasures that countries can adopt to address money laundering.

Australian law prohibiting money laundering goes one step further than international provisions on this subject matter, in that the crimes covered by Australian domestic law go beyond drug offences. Under s 4 of the *Proceeds of Crime Act* 1987 (Cth), "proceeds of crime" is defined to include any property derived or realised, directly or indirectly, by any person from the commission of an offence against the law of the Commonwealth, or a Territory of Australia, that may be dealt with as an indictable offence. Property constituting the proceeds of crime includes real or personal property, tangible or intangible, of every description, whether located in Australia or elsewhere, and includes an interest in such property. States and Territories within Australia have, for the most part, enacted similar legislation relating to the proceeds of crime derived from the commission of acts which are indictable offences under the relevant State or Territory law.

Section 81(3) of the *Proceeds of Crime Act* 1987 (Cth) provides that persons shall be taken to be engaging in the laundering of money if they engage in a transaction that involves the proceeds of crime, or if they receive, possess, conceal, dispose of or bring into Australia money or other property that are the proceeds of crime. Knowledge, or imputed knowledge whereby a reasonable person in the situation of the person ought to have reasonably known, that the money or other property derives from criminal activity is an element of the offence. Section 81(2) criminalises the act of money laundering and provides for penalties: up to $200,000 or 20 years imprisonment for an individual, and up to $600,000 for a body corporate. Section 85(1)-(4) provides that the knowledge of an employee, servant or agent of a corporation is attributed to a corporation, including the principals of a firm.

The operation of the *Proceeds of Crime Act* 1987 (Cth) is facilitated by the *Cash Transactions Reports Act* 1988 (Cth). The latter Act provides for a system of reporting significant cash transactions (s 7) and suspicious transactions (s 16). The reporting of suspicious transactions or cash transactions over a certain monetary limit greatly assists law enforcement authorities to properly administer the provisions of the *Proceeds of Crime Act* 1987 (Cth).

Legal provisions prohibiting money laundering have a very real impact on corporate financial institutions due to the use of those institutions by organised crime bosses and other persons to cleanse "dirty money". While banks have been the focus of the Convention, FATF's Forty Recommendations have also recognised the role of life insurance companies, non-bank financial institutions and financial regulatory authorities in the fight against money laundering. FATF has recommended that such institutions strengthen their ability to identify customers, keep and maintain accurate records of financial transactions and cooperate with law enforcement authorities by providing them with financial records for the purposes of investigation and prosecution. The recommendations also encourage institutions to adopt good internal policies, procedures and controls, to prevent staff from turning a blind-eye to suspicious transactions. The implication is that financial institutions should no longer keep anonymous accounts, which constitutes a serious obstacle to investigators to following the financial "paper trail" of money laundering operations.

Another issue pertaining to corporate legal entities is "the failure of traditional corporate crime control strategies and the need to re-fashion both the law and enforcement strategies in this area": D Chappell and P Wilson, *The Australian Criminal Justice System: The Mid 1990s* (Sydney: Butt, 1994), p 263. Corporate criminal offences are often not prosecuted. Sanctions may bear no relation to the harm suffered or may not be sufficient to deter would-be offenders, and accountability under corporate criminal law itself may provide a further bar: Ch 3, pp 154-156. It is arguable that, in line with FATF's recommendations, strengthening provisions concerning the duties of corporate entities and money laundering would go a long way to assist in the detection and prevention of money laundering. Money laundering provisions also need to be extended to non-bank financial institutions, and possibly to other institutions such as import/export companies, which facilitate money laundering schemes. Another area for reform arises from the Convention concerning a provision for overriding bank secrecy laws. While this provision is useful, it can be "an illusory benefit in cases where a second layer of secrecy, such as anonymous trusts and shell companies, is available": W Gilmore, *Dirty Money: The Evolution of Money Laundering Counter-measures* (The Netherlands: Council of Europe Press, 1995), p 69. As noted, this also provides particular problems in jurisdictions with no anti-money laundering provisions in place. Some countries, such as Burma, have refused to sign the Convention and implement anti-money laundering laws, claiming their economies would collapse if the influx of laundered money was to cease.

Other areas deserving of attention include electronic money and its effect on money laundering operations, and the extension of international cooperation to serious offences not including narcotics, as has been included in Australian legislation. Finally, legal provisions allowing law enforcement authorities to lift the "corporate veil" to identify the individuals party to suspicious transactions, would be useful in stemming the tide of money laundering operations.

> In 1991, the large multinational, the Bank of Credit and Commercial International (BCCI) collapsed after it was revealed that it had, over many years, been involved in complex money laundering operations in over 70 countries for the benefit of drug dealers, arms dealers, and terrorists. See further, G Stessens, *Money Laundering: A New International Law Enforcement Model* (Cambridge: Cambridge University Press, 2000).

CONFISCATION OF THE PROCEEDS OF CRIME

Article 5 of the *Convention Against Illicit Trafficking in Narcotic Drugs and Psychotropic Substances* (1988) also required the adoption of confiscation measures. By the 1980s, the powers of the Crown to obtain forfeiture consequent upon a felony conviction had fallen into disuse and were finally abolished by statute: see Ch 2, p 98. In the field of drug enforcement, however, confiscation of property has remained a significant weapon in the "War Against Drugs". The basis for property confiscation was originally limited to the *Customs Act* 1901 (Cth), which empowered customs officers to confiscate unlawful imports/exports and property used in that unlawful importation or exportation.[42] These draconian civil powers permit confiscation without proof of conviction or even subjective awareness on the part of the owner that the property was being put to unlawful use: *Forbes v Traders' Finance Corporation Ltd* (1972) 126 CLR 429.

In an effort to combat drug trafficking, all jurisdictions have reinstated forfeiture through property confiscation legislation.[43] While the powers of confiscation and pecuniary order under the *Customs Act* are not conditional upon proof of conviction, confiscation under the *Proceeds of Crime Act* 1987 (Cth) requires proof beyond reasonable doubt that an indictable offence has been committed. This scheme is administered by the Commonwealth Director of Public Prosecutions.

Although implementing the terms of the United Nations Convention, as noted above, the Act is not confined to drug trafficking. The Act make generous use of rebuttable presumptions such as that property in the possession of the accused (at, or immediately after, the commission of the offence) was used in, or in conjunction with, the commission of the offence: s 18(4). The Act reverses the burden of proof, as the accused must prove that the assets currently owned, or transferred to him or her within a specified period, were not derived from unlawful sources: s 27. Where tainted property cannot be identified, there are also wide powers to impose pecuniary penalties equivalent to the value of the benefits derived from the criminal activity: s 26. Once forfeiture or pecuniary proceedings have commenced, there are powers to make restraining orders to prevent the property being moved beyond the jurisdiction: s 43. After conviction for a trafficking offence, property covered by a restraining order will be automatically forfeited unless the accused can prove that the property was lawfully acquired and was not used in any unlawful activity: s 48(4). Proving not merely lawful title, but that the property has not been used in any illegal activity (not restricted to drug trafficking) is often difficult. These provisions have been judicially described as "novel, drastic and Draconian": *DPP (Cth) v Jeffery* (1992) 58 A Crim R 310 at 320 per Hunt CJ.

In some jurisdictions, these powers of forfeiture have been further broadened, dispensing with the requirement of proof of conviction and permitting orders to be made in civil proceedings. Within the civil sphere, the ordinary procedural and evidential safeguards such as the standard of proof based on beyond reasonable doubt, are deemed not to apply. The provisions under proceeds of crime legislation, such as the *Drug Trafficking (Civil Proceedings) Act* 1990 (NSW), derogate from fundamental common law presumption of innocence and the right to enjoyment of property:

---

42 *Customs Act* 1901 (Cth), s 229(1). There are specific powers relating to the forfeiture of proceeds of drug trafficking in ss 229A and 243A. See discussion in P Zahra, R Arden, M Ierace, B Schurr, *Drug Law in New South Wales* (2nd ed, Sydney: Federation Press, 1998), pp 338-342.

43 *Proceeds of Crime Act* 1987 (Cth); *Proceeds of Crime Act* 1991 (ACT); *Criminal Assets Recovery Act* 1990 (NSW); *Confiscation of the Proceeds of Crime Act* 1989 (NSW); *Crimes (Forfeiture of Proceeds) Act* 1988 (NT); *Crimes (Confiscation of Profits) Act* 1989 (Qld); *Crimes (Confiscation of Profits) Act* 1986 (SA); *Crimes (Confiscation of Profits) Act* 1993 (Tas); *Confiscation Act* 1997 (Vic); *Crimes (Confiscation of Profits) Act* 1988 (WA). On these developments see B Fisse, D Fraser and G Coss, *The Money Trail: Confiscation of Proceeds of Crime, Money Laundering and Cash Transaction Reporting* (Sydney: Law Book Company Ltd, 1992). See also D Brown, D Farrier and D Weisbrot, *Criminal Laws* (2nd ed, Sydney: Federation Press, 1996), pp 1088-1095.

NSW Crime Commission v Younan (1993) 31 NSWLR 44 at 48. In reviewing these confiscation powers, the Court of Criminal Appeal highlighted that in exercising the discretion to confiscate assets the judge must ensure that the confiscation order did not deny the accused a fair trial by denying access to funds for his or her legal defence. On the importance of legal representation to the fair trial principle, see Chapter 2, p 103. The New South Wales legislation has been proposed as the model for the provisions related to property derived from drug offences contained inMCCOC, *Chapter 6: Serious Drug Offences*, Report (1998), p 223.

These powers of confiscation are not regarded as punishment — they are considered fundamentally civil measures designed to ensure that the offenders do not profit from their crime: M Bagaric, "The Disunity of Sentencing and Confiscation" (1997) 21 Crim LJ 191. Confiscation has deterrent and incapacitative effects, and, in this sense, there is an overlap with the traditional objectives of punishment. Although Bagaric identifies this overlap in purpose, he concludes (p 192) that it is merely "incidental" and that fusion of these two distinct processes would be undesirable. The categorisation of confiscation as a civil measure conceals the punitive effects of these laws. Indeed, the severance of confiscation powers from proof of conviction, as well as other ordinary safeguards relating to the burden and standard of proof, pose the danger that the process becomes the punishment. The importance of the burden and standard of proof to the fair trial principle was explored in Chapter 2, pp 114ff. These laws have been subject to extensive academic criticism: see for example A Frieberg, "Criminal Confiscation, Profit and Liberty" (1992) 25 *Australian and New Zealand Journal of Criminology* 44.

Significantly, the MCCOC has proposed that strict liability is inappropriate for any serious drug offence, including those offences related to property derived from drug offences: *Chapter 6 — Serious Drug Offences*, Report (1998), p 231. Notwithstanding strong objections from law enforcement agencies, the MCCOC recommended (p 231) that offences which would carry 20 years imprisonment should only be applied to accused persons who knew that the property being dealt with was "tainted". The MCCOC was influenced by the sustained academic criticism of the unfairness of the offences under the *Proceeds of Crime* Act 1987 (Cth).

The extraordinary powers deemed necessary for drug investigation have been gradually extended to other offences. For example, in New South Wales, the confiscation legislation was initially confined to drug related activity and required proof of conviction. In 1997 the *Drug Trafficking (Civil Proceedings) Act* 1990 (NSW) was renamed the *Criminal Assets Recovery Act* 1990 (NSW). The new Act dispensed with the requirement of conviction and extended these powers to any serious crime related activity that included non-drug related offences such as theft, fraud, obtaining financial benefit from the crime of another, money laundering, extortion, violence, bribery, corruption, harbouring criminals, blackmail, obtaining or offering a secret commission, perverting the course of justice, tax or revenue evasion, illegal gambling, forgery and homicide: *Criminal Assets Recovery Act* 1990 (NSW), s 6(2).[44]

---

44 These provisions are discussed in P Zahra, R Arden, M Ierace, B Schurr, *Drug Law in New South Wales* (2nd ed, Sydney: Federation Press, 1998), Ch 10.

In Tasmania, the Port Arthur massacre provided the political impetus for enacting laws authorising the forfeiture of offenders' assets and distribution to the offenders' victims: *Criminal Injuries Compensation Amendment Act* 1996 (Tas), discussed in C Möller, "Legislation Comment: Serious Money, Funny Legislation: Tasmania and the Politics of Criminal Forfeiture" (1998) 22 Crim LJ 99. These forfeiture powers were not limited to the proceeds of crime, but extended to *any* assets owned by perpetrators of serious crimes. This Act effectively re-instituted the old forfeiture rules based on the doctrine of attainder under the common law: see Ch 2, p 98.

At the international level, these laws have been challenged (unsuccessfully) as violating fundamental human rights relating to property and a fair trial. Although conceding these powers do interfere with rights of ownership, the European Court of Human Rights held in *Air Canada v United Kingdom* [1995] 20 EHRR 150 that seizure of private property used for the importation of drugs (in that case a commercial jet) did not violate the rights of property or the right to a fair trial under the *European Convention on Human Rights*. The Court held that the interference with property was justifiable since the temporary detention (until Air Canada paid a specified sum of money to Customs to release the property) was a necessary and proportionate measure for pursuing the general interest in combating international trafficking. The proceeding was held to be a civil rather than a criminal matter, and as such access to the courts through judicial review was sufficient to comply with the right to a fair hearing under Art 6. There was a strong dissent in which two judges took the view that the proceedings were equivalent to a "criminal" charge and it was unfair to impose a sanction on the airline without proof of fault.[45]

Extension of Jurisdiction: The International Reach of Drug Offences

Many of the above offences and powers have extra-territorial effect. Dealing in drugs outside Australia is an offence if the conduct constitutes an offence against the law of a foreign country; and the conduct would constitute an offence against a law in force in a State or Territory if it were engaged in by the person in that State or Territory: *Crimes (Traffic in Narcotic Drugs and Psychotropic Substances) Act* 1989 (Cth), s 12. It is also an offence to deal in drugs outside Australia with a view to the commission of the offence in Australia: s 13. Similarly, a conspiracy outside Australia to commit an offence inside Australia is an offence: s 14. The offences related to money laundering and the confiscation of proceeds of crime have been extended to property derived from drug offences committed in other countries: *Proceeds of Crime Act* 1987 (Cth), s 12. The extension of jurisdiction implements the obligations imposed by Art 4 of the United Nations' *Convention Against Illicit Traffic in Narcotic Drugs and Psychotropic Substances* (1988). The MCCOC envisaged that these specific extra-territoriality provisions will be superseded by the general jurisdictional rules developed for the *Model Criminal Code*. These new principles of jurisdiction have been examined in Chapter 2: p 89.

---

45 In *Welch v United Kingdom* [1995] 20 EHRR 247, the European Court held that legislation empowering confiscation implemented after the commission of the offence though before the trial would violate the principle against retrospectivity.

3.2 ENTRAPMENT

Drug investigations rely heavily on undercover policing, the use of informers, surveillance technology and use of pro-active investigative methods. These features may be viewed as part of a increasing global trend away from coercion toward deception in criminal investigation.[46]

"Entrapment" is not a legal term of art. The definitional boundaries of the concept remain controversial and illusive. The term encompasses a wide-range of pro-active investigative techniques ranging from "manna from heaven" operations where unguarded valuables are placed in public view in order to tempt passers-by, to complex undercover "stings" involving collaboration between international law enforcement agencies for months or even years. It is claimed that entrapment is necessary to overcome the reluctance of victims and witnesses of "consensual" crimes such as drug trafficking. Consequently, law enforcement officials are compelled to conduct "controlled operations" in which they organise the purchase, importation and supply of illegal drugs to suspects, sometimes across several jurisdictions. From a substantive and evidential perspective, the difficulty is that such law enforcement conduct may involve police illegality in the form of complicity, incitement or conspiracy.[47] On the potential liability of law enforcement officials for inchoate offences see Chapter 9: pp 457-458.

> Entrapment is not confined to drug investigations. Geoffrey Robertson QC provides an account of the elaborate efforts of British and American intelligence agencies to incite an Arab business man to supply "nuclear triggers" to Iraq, and the subsequent trial and successful appeal against his conviction: "Ali Daghir and the Forty Nuclear Triggers" in *The Justice Game* (London: Vintage, 1999).

In Australia, the law governing entrapment is an amalgam of evidential discretion and recent federal and State legislation governing the use of controlled operations. Unlike the United States, the common law of England and Australia has refused to recognise a substantive defence of entrapment.[48] As a result, the definitional limits of entrapment remain hazy, particularly in relation to the significance of the suspect's predisposition to commit the offence incited by the police. Legal discussion in Australia has focused not on the subjective or objective "tests" of entrapment, but rather on the nature and scope of available remedies.[49] The question arises as to whether entrapment would trigger the discretion to exclude otherwise relevant and admissible evidence on

---

46 A Ashworth, "Should the Police Be Allowed to Use Deceptive Practices" (1998) 114 LQR 108 at 108. See G Marx, *Undercover — Police Surveillance in America* (Berkeley: University. of California Press, 1988); C Fijnaut and G Marx (eds), *Undercover — Police Surveillance in Comparative Perspective* (The Hague: Kluwer, 1995).

47 *Yip Chiu-cheung v The Queen* [1994] 2 All ER 924 (PC), 928 per Lord Griffiths. There may be no liability for conspiracy in cases where undercover police or agents, having no intention to commit the offence, merely pretend to join a conspiracy in order to gain information that would frustrate it: *R v Anderson* [1985] 2 All ER 961 at 965 per Lord Bridge.

48 The basis of the defence is a statutory presumption that Congress does not intend its criminal statutes to be used to entrap otherwise innocent citizens: *Sorrells v United States*, 287 US 435 (1932); *Sherman v United States*, 356 US 369 (1958); *United States v Russell*, 411 US 423 (1973); *Hampton v United States*, 425 US 484 (1976); *Jacobson v United States*, 503 US 540 (1992).

49 An analysis of case law prior to *Ridgeway v The Queen* (1995) 184 CLR 19 revealed a judicial commitment to both subjective and objective tests: W Harris, "Entrapment" (1994) 18 Crim LJ 197 at 214.

public policy grounds established in *Bunning v Cross* (1978) 141 CLR 54.[50] This discretion involves balancing the competing public interest in promoting crime control against the negative impact of judicial approval of illegally or improper investigative methods: at 74. The public policy considerations underlying the discretion include promoting respect for the "rule of law" among those entrusted with its enforcement, but also protecting citizens from arbitrary intrusions into their privacy: at 75.

> In Canada and England, the trial judge has a discretion to grant a stay of proceedings in cases involving entrapment on the grounds of abuse of process: *R v Mack* (1988) 44 CCC (3d) 513 and *R v Latif* [1996] 1 WLR 104. Rather than extend this rarely used procedural remedy in *Ridgeway v The Queen* (1995) 184 CLR 19, the High Court addressed the issue of entrapment by extending the discretion to exclude evidence on the grounds of illegality.

The application of the public policy discretion to police entrapment was reviewed by the High Court in *Ridgeway v The Queen* (1995) 184 CLR 19. In this case, the accused had contacted a man whom he had met in an Australian prison to propose a heroin smuggling operation. Unbeknown to the accused, his contact had become a police informant, and alerted the authorities. With the cooperation and assistance of the Australian Federal Police and Customs, the informant and a Malaysian Police officer purchased and imported a quantity of heroin and sold the heroin to the accused. He was charged and convicted of the possession of a quantity of illegally imported heroin contrary to s 233B of the *Customs Act* 1901 (Cth). The ingredients of this offence have been discussed above.

On appeal to the High Court, six of seven judges (McHugh J dissenting) quashed the conviction. The majority held that the public policy discretion to exclude evidence obtained by unlawful conduct recognised in *Bunning v Cross* (1978) 141 CLR 54 could be extended "by analogy" to exclude evidence of a person's guilt or elements of an offence, where the actual commission was procured by unlawful conduct on the part of law enforcement officials. Mason CJ, Deane and Dawson JJ (at 41-42) held that considerations of public policy were at the heart of this discretion to exclude evidence:

> The critical question was whether, in all the circumstances of the case, the considerations of public policy favouring exclusion of the evidence of the appellant's offence, namely, the public interest in maintaining the integrity of the courts and of ensuring the observance of the law and minimum standards of propriety by those entrusted with powers of law enforcement, outweighed the obvious public interest in the conviction and punishment of the appellant of and for the crime ...

In determining whether to exclude evidence of an offence procured by entrapment, the relative weight of the public interest in convicting the guilty and maintaining confidence in the administration of criminal justice will vary according to various factors including (at 38):

---

50 In this landmark case, the High Court refused to follow the House of Lords decision in *R v Sang* [1979] 3 WLR 263, which held that there is no discretion to exclude evidence merely on the ground that it was obtained by improper or unfair means such as grounds that it was obtained by improper or unfair means or as the result of the activities of an agent provocateur: at 271, per Lord Diplock.

═══ the nature, the seriousness and the effect of the illegal or improper conduct engaged in by the law enforcement officers; and

═══ whether such conduct is encouraged or tolerated by those in higher authority in the police force or, in the case of illegal conduct, by those responsible for the institution of criminal proceedings.[51]

The rationale of exclusion was public policy, not the fairness of the methods used to obtain evidence of guilt. According to the majority unfairness to the accused arising from the illegal conduct will "ordinarily be of no more than peripheral importance": at 38. Applied to the facts, a majority of the High Court held that had the trial judge exercised this discretion properly, evidence of illegal importation by police should have been excluded.[52] Since the exclusion of this evidence deprived the prosecution of proof of a fundamental element of the offence — namely, that the drugs had been illegally imported — the majority directed that to allow proceedings to continue in these circumstances would have amounted to an abuse of process.

The decision of the High Court may be understood in terms of Herbert Packer's competing models of criminal justice — crime control versus due process: *The Limits of the Criminal Sanction* (Stanford: Stanford University Press, 1969), discussed in Ch 2, at pp 34-40. In Packer's terms, the outcome in *Ridgeway* appears to be a triumph for due process over crime control. Closer scrutiny reveals that this judicial veneration of legality and the rule of law, while constituting powerful rhetoric, rarely stands in the way of convictions. A study of reported and unreported cases reveals that in every case (except one) in which *Ridgeway* was considered, the judicial discretion was exercised in favour of the reception of the evidence obtained by unlawful police entrapment.[53] The limited impact of the exclusionary discretion on entrapment practices is related to the narrow basis of the discretion in *Ridgeway*. The majority held (at 39) that evidence would likely be excluded where the illegal conduct of the police creates an essential ingredient of the charged offence, or is itself the principal offence to which the offence is ancillary. By contrast, unlawful police conduct that did not constitute an essential ingredient of the offence (as in *Ridgeway*) would not usually warrant exclusion. In these cases, the majority noted (at 39) that the public interest in the conviction and punishment of those guilty of crime is likely to prevail over other considerations, and the evidence should generally be admitted. Most cases of entrapment will fall into the latter category rather than the former.

This analysis of entrapment is consistent with Doreen McBarnet's theories about the nature of criminal justice. The importance of McBarnet's sociolegal research on the criminal process has

---

51 These factors have been incorporated into the statutory discretion contained in *Evidence Act* 1995 (Cth), s 138; *Evidence Act* 1995 (ACT), s 138; *Evidence Act* 1995 (NSW), s 138.

52 On these facts, the judge should have granted a stay of proceedings on the grounds of abuse of process since the exclusion of evidence meant that "the proceedings will necessarily fail with the consequence that a continuance of them would be oppressive and vexatious": *Ridgeway v The Queen* (1995) 184 CLR 19 at 41.

53 S Bronitt and D Roche, "Between Rhetoric and Reality: Sociolegal and Republican Perspectives on Entrapment" (2000) 4(2) *International Journal of Evidence And Proof* 77 at 89. The authors' study of trials in which *Ridgeway* was argued by the defence revealed that the decision was routinely distinguished. Indeed, in only one case did the application of the discretion result in evidence of entrapment being excluded: *Dau v Emanuele* (unrep, 4/12/1995, Fed Ct); see "Comment" by M Bartlett (1996) 20 Crim LJ 219.

been explored in Chapter 1, p 36 and Chapter 2, p 95. As David Dixon has observed, McBarnet's thesis usefully explains the contradictions within the law — the tensions are not between crime control and due process as Packer maintained, but rather "between the rhetoric of legality (in which due process and other rights are venerated) on one side, and the reality of legal rules and procedures (which routinely deny them) on the other": *Law in Policing: Legal Regulation and Police Practices* (Oxford: Clarendon Press, 1997), p 29. Judicial rhetoric venerates the principles of legality and fairness in the administration of criminal justice while routinely denying them in the application of specific rules and remedies, such as the discretion to exclude evidence obtained by illegal or improper means. Deviation by the police and trial judges is not a departure from the norms of legality, but rather is something permitted — in effect, *licensed* — by the law. The Australian approach to entrapment confirms McBarnet's assessment, that if "we bring due process down from the dizzy heights of abstraction and subject it to empirical scrutiny, the conclusion must be that *due process is for crime control*": *Conviction: Law, The State and The Construction of Justice* (London: MacMillan Press, 1981), pp 155-156.

The legal commitment to fundamental values, such as the rule of law and public confidence in the administration of criminal justice, has been further eroded by remedial legislation enacted by the Commonwealth, New South Wales and South Australian parliaments: *Crimes Amendment (Controlled Operations) Act* 1996 (Cth); *Law Enforcement (Controlled Operations) Act* 1997 (NSW); *Criminal Law (Undercover Operations) Act* 1995 (SA). These statutes responded to law enforcement concerns that *Ridgeway* would unduly hamper (if not completely prohibit) the use of controlled operations in drug law enforcement. The objective of this legislation was to exempt from criminal liability those law enforcement officials who engage in unlawful conduct to obtain evidence of offences relating to narcotics. This immunity had the effect of removing the threat of prosecution for police involved in undercover work. The legislation did not abolish the discretion in *Ridgeway*.[54] However, it does have the practical effect of limiting the scope of public policy discretion by removing the taint of illegality attached to the investigative methods during authorised operations.

While the legislation authorising controlled operations confers a wide immunity to police, it establishes some safeguards by imposing restrictions on the scope and duration of controlled operations. The *Crimes Amendment (Controlled Operations) Act* 1996 (Cth) permits senior officers in the Australian Federal Police (the Commissioner, or Deputy or Assistant Commissioner) or a member of the National Crime Authority to authorise unlawful conduct by law enforcement officers. Under s 15M, the authorising officer must be satisfied that the person targeted by the operation is likely to commit an offence against s 233B of the *Customs Act* 1901 (Cth) or an associated offence whether or not the operation takes place. Also, the authorising officer must be satisfied that the operation will make it much easier to obtain evidence that may lead to the prosecution of the person for such an offence. The immunity from criminal liability is subject to the following qualification in s 15I(2):

(a) the conduct of the officer involves intentionally inducing the person targeted by the operation to commit an offence against s 233B of the *Customs Act* 1901 or an associated offence; and

---

54 The *Crimes Amendment (Controlled Operations) Act* 1996 (Cth) explicitly acknowledges that it is not intended to limit the judicial discretion to exclude evidence in criminal proceedings or to stay criminal proceedings in the interests of justice: s 15G(2).

(b) the person would not otherwise have had the intent to commit that offence or an offence of that kind. Authorisation does not apply if officers induced commission of the offence, and the person would not otherwise have had intent.

There are a number of weaknesses in this system of regulation. The model of oversight is based on internal police supervision, requiring the approval by senior police officers. From the perspectives of "checks and balances", some degree of external oversight (along the lines developed for warrants for listening devices and telecommunications interception) would be preferable. The breadth of the immunity in New South Wales is also a cause for concern. While the Commonwealth and South Australian legislative schemes regulating controlled operations are restricted to controlled operations for narcotic offences, the New South Wales legislation applies to controlled operations in relation to *any* criminal or corrupt conduct. It may be applied to civilian informers as well as to police, and may be applied retrospectively in cases where there is no time to make an application.[55] Significant criticism, both theoretical and practical, can be directed at the breadth of powers and immunities conferred to police involved in undercover operations.[56]

Compared to the post hoc control of police investigation based on judicial discretion, a statutory framework has many advantages. Individuals who are targeted for investigation and are subsequently prosecuted will be made aware that these methods have been used, a fact which is not always disclosed under present arrangements. Transparency and accountability in relation to controlled operations will be promoted through mandatory requirements to submit reports on controlled operations to the responsible Minister and to Parliament: ss 15R and T. The authorisation framework also imposes time-limits on these operations, avoiding the risk that suspects may be targeted for highly-intrusive, potentially unlimited, undercover investigation.

Entrapment in Australia, Canada and England has raised important questions concerning the role of judges in upholding legality (the rule of law) and maintaining public confidence in the administration of criminal justice. In common law jurisdictions, the issue of fairness, in particular whether entrapment impinges on the right to a fair trial, has not exerted significant influence on legal discussion. A recent judgment of the European Court of Human Rights however suggests that in some circumstances proactive policing methods may violate the right to a fair trial protected by international law.

In *Teixeira de Castro v Portugal* (Eur Court HR, 9 June 1998, *Reports of Judgments and Decisions* 1998-IV) two Portuguese undercover police officers pressured a cannabis user to introduce his supplier to them. Unable to locate his normal supplier, the cannabis user identified the accused as a potential supplier of heroin. The informer arranged a meeting with the accused during which the undercover police indicated that they wished to buy 20 grams of heroin. The accused procured the heroin and was arrested and subsequently convicted of a drug offence. Having exhausted domestic remedies, the accused appealed to the European Court alleging that he had been deprived of a fair trial guaranteed by Art 6 of the *European Convention on Human Rights* (ECHR).

---

55 *Law Enforcement (Controlled Operations) Act* 1997 (NSW), s 14. For an illustration of the extraordinary scope of these provisions see P Zahra, P Arden, M Ierace, B Schurr, *Drug Law in New South Wales* (Sydney: Federation Press, 1998), p 192.

56 For a discussion of Australian and English case law on entrapment using empirical perspectives and republican principles, see S Bronitt and D Roche, "Between Rhetoric and Reality: Sociolegal and Republican Perspectives on Entrapment" (2000) 4(2) *International Journal of Evidence And Proof* 77.

The Court held that the guarantee of fairness under international human rights law is not limited to the trial, but underpins the proceedings as a whole including "the way in which evidence was taken": at para 34. In its view, police incitement posed a clear threat to the right to fair administration of justice (at para 36):

> The use of undercover agents must be restricted and safeguards put in place even in cases concerning the fight against drug trafficking. While the rise in organised crime undoubtedly requires that appropriate measures be taken, the right to a fair administration of justice nevertheless holds such a prominent place ... that it cannot be sacrificed for the sake of expedience. The general requirements of fairness embodied in Art 6 apply to proceedings concerning all types of criminal offence, from the most straightforward to the most complex. The public interest cannot justify the use of evidence obtained as a result of police incitement.

The right to a fair trial under the ECHR is breached where law enforcement officials do not confine themselves to investigating criminal activity in a passive manner, but actively engage in incitement. On these facts, the police had actively instigated the offence and there was no evidence that the accused was predisposed to commit the offence. Indeed, the accused had to obtain the drug from a third party and was found in possession of no more drugs than were being solicited by the police. The investigative techniques caused unfairness in the administration of justice because the police officers had acted on their own initiative without judicial supervision or good reasons to suspect that the accused was a drug trafficker: at para 39.

Since the right to a fair trial in Art 14 of the *International Covenant on Civil and Political Rights* (ICCPR) mirrors Art 6 of the ECHR, the *Teixeira* ruling has implications for Australian law in this area. By extending the right to fairness into the pre-trial phase, the international human rights law imposes new standards for criminal investigation and evidence-gathering. It may be argued that this broader notion of fairness is legitimately relevant to the exercise of the discretion to exclude evidence and to stay legal proceedings on the ground of abuse of process. Indeed, the ruling is directly relevant to the discretion to exclude evidence in jurisdictions applying the *Uniform Evidence Act*, which expressly provides that evidence obtained in probable breach of a right protected by the ICCPR is considered relevant to the exercise of the common law and statutory discretion to exclude improperly obtained evidence.[57]

Although remedies for breach of international human rights are a matter for the domestic legal system, it has been argued that staying the proceedings as an abuse of process, rather than merely excluding the evidence, is the appropriate remedy for unfair police incitement. In determining the unfairness of investigative methods, the fundamental question should be whether the police actively incited the accused (who was not otherwise predisposed) to commit the offence.[58] This would require a significant change to the present common law laid down in *Ridgeway*, where the

---

57 The *Evidence Act* 1995 (Cth), s 138(3) and the *Evidence Act* 1995 (NSW), s 138(3) provide that a trial judge, in exercising the discretion to exclude evidence obtained improperly, *must* consider a range of factors including inter alia "(f) whether the impropriety or contravention was contrary to or inconsistent with a right of a person recognised by the *International Covenant on Civil and Political Rights*".

58 A subjective approach to predisposition was taken by the House of Lords in *R v Latif* [1996] 1 WLR 104 at 113.

tests formulated by the majority focused on police illegality and public policy considerations, rather than on the unfairness of those processes and their subjective effect on the suspect. As foreshadowed above, the subjective test of predisposition has already been imported into the federally controlled operations legislation, acting as a limitation on the immunities granted to the police. A test based on subjective predisposition has been criticised because of its tendency to focus exclusively on the character of the accused and render suspects with known past criminal records "fair game" for such tactics: S Bronitt and D Roche, "Between Rhetoric and Reality: Sociolegal and Republican Perspectives on Entrapment" (2000) 4(2) *International Journal of Evidence and Proof* 77. Attempting to minimise the risk of unfair harassment, Andrew Ashworth suggests that the term "predisposition" should be abandoned because of its connotation with previous convictions, in favour of more contemporaneous terms such as "presently disposed" or "ready and willing": "What is Wrong with Entrapment" [1999] *Singapore Journal of Legal Studies* 293. This would assist the courts in drawing the line between providing an opportunity (acceptable) and encouraging or inducing the suspect to commit an offence (unacceptable).

An alternate model focusing on the conduct of the law enforcement officials rather than the criminal character/disposition of the accused was favoured by the Supreme Court of Canada in *R v Mack* (1988) 44 CCC (3d) 513. Lamer CJ held (at 554) that proceedings should be halted as an abuse of process where the authorities have:

(a) provided the accused with an opportunity to commit an offence without having reasonable suspicion or acting pursuant to a bona fide inquiry; or

(b) gone beyond providing an opportunity and have induced the commission of an offence.

The law of entrapment is in a state of flux. While there has been some legislative reform in Australia, the remedial legislation has focused on the problem of police illegality raised in *Ridgeway*, rather than the potential negative impact of entrapment on the accused's rights to a fair trial and privacy. A discrepancy has emerged between the rights of individuals targeted by proactive investigative methods under international law, and those recognised by Australian law. While international law does not mandate particular definitions or remedies for entrapment, the recent decision by the ECHR examining the effect of police incitement on the right to a fair trial is clearly relevant to future development of this area of the law. The role of human rights in the development of the common law has been considered in Chapter 2, p 111.

The use of undercover policing and entrapment is not new. Prior to the formation of professional policing in the 19th century, *agent provocateurs* would instigate crime and informers would supply evidence (often fabricated) for reward: L Radzinowicz, *A History of English Criminal Law and its Administration from 1750* (London: Stevens & Sons Ltd, 1956), Vol 2, pp 307-346. As a result, law enforcement in the 18th century was highly disreputable. The need to provide a legitimate moral and political basis for modern policing in the early 19th century led away from these potentially corrupt and unreliable investigative methods. This moratorium on proactive policing largely persisted until the "War Against Drugs" was declared in the mid-20th century. The metaphor of "War" has justified the development and gradual expansion of extraordinary measures such as electronic surveillance and entrapment. It falls to the courts, as well as to the legislature, to impose limits on these developments and to ensure that law enforcement officials show respect for fundamental legal rights, especially those protected by the ICCPR. Within the judicial arena, the question is often posed as balancing the interests of crime control against due process. As Kirby J recently observed in *R v Swaffield; Pavic v The Queen* (1998) 192 CLR 159 (at 220-221) (a case examining the admissibility of a confession elicited by an informer acting on police instructions):

> Subterfuge, ruses and tricks may be lawfully employed by police, acting in the public interest. There is nothing improper in these tactics where they are lawfully deployed in the endeavour to investigate crime so as to bring the guilty to justice. Nor is there anything wrong in the use of technology, such as telephonic interception and listening devices although this will commonly require statutory authority. Such facilities must be employed by any modern police service. The critical question is ... whether the trick may be thought to involve such unfairness to the accused or otherwise to be so contrary to public policy that a court should exercise its discretion to exclude the evidence notwithstanding its high probative value (footnotes omitted).

While such rhetoric demonstrates fidelity to fundamental principles of criminal justice, it is situated within a utilitarian framework that balances the rights of persons engaged in drug trafficking against the practical needs of law enforcement. Invariably, the rhetoric of fundamental rights and justice is trumped by the rhetoric of War Against Drugs. For further critique of "balancing" in the criminal justice context, see Chapter 1: pp 39ff.

4. CONCLUSION

Pat O'Malley and Stephen Mugford have identified four discourses relating to drugs: pathology, profit, the State and pleasure.[59] Pathology and profit discourses tend to cluster together. Modern drug laws are primarily directed against "profit" (derived from trafficking and organised crime), while "pathology" (the view of drug users as persons requiring treatment rather than punishment) supports strategies of harm minimisation and decriminalisation. The discourse concerning "the State" centres on legislation, and how legislative power has been deployed in the 19th and 20th centuries to impose controls over the suspect activities of minorities, such as the Chinese. Drug law enforcement has also provided the arena in which the State has committed itself zealously to pursuing a "War Against Drugs", a mission which has led to confrontation with fundamental legal values such as legality, fairness and human rights. What is strikingly absent from the debate about drugs, especially to anyone who has consumed psychotropic substances, is the discourse of "pleasure". Adopting this perspective reveals that law and legal regulation, though not necessarily the criminal law, has a significant role to play in controlling the markets for these pleasurable commodities that involve risks to consumers.

The explanations for drug laws are rarely formulated in terms of moral protection or prevention of harm. The logic of prohibition is autonomous and self-referential. It is highly resistant to external perspectives — whether historical, sociological, criminological or medical — that could

---

59 "The Demand for Intoxicating Commodities: Implications for the 'War on Drugs'" (1991) 18(4) *Social Justice* 49 and "Heroin Policy and Deficit Models — The Limits of Left Realism" (1991) 15 *Crime, Law and Social Change* 19.

inform our understanding of the "drug problem". What is patently clear is that drugs have become the object of a relentless cycle of legal repression — a "War Againt Drugs" — in which the legislature is engaged in a constant process of expanding the range of offences and investigative powers relating to illicit drugs.

The myriad of negative consequences of waging this war has produced a rival discourse of harm-minimisation. This strategy maintains an illusory dichotomy between use/addict and trafficking/dealer, advocating policies of decriminalisation for the former, while permitting the proliferation of crimes and penalties for the latter. Although harm-minimisation has operated as a constraint on criminalisation in some contexts, such as needle and syringe exchange schemes, it does not directly address the normative or moral basis for drug control. Many liberal scholars committed to harm minimisation suggest that drug use should be reconceived as an issue of public health rather than criminal law. It is important to appreciate that State coercion comes in many varied forms, and that the "preventive" powers of civil detention and treatment under public health law also have the potential to be coercive and disrespectful of fundamental human rights. Within this private sphere of civil regulatory power, there is a real danger that the *process is the punishment*.

Drug courts are the latest experiment to have captured the attention of policy-makers, diverting attention away from criminalisation, in particular, the question of prohibition versus regulation. The advent of specialised drug courts in Australia may be viewed as a re-alignment of pathology and State discourses on drugs — through legislation the State has co-opted the courts into the therapeutic enterprise of supervising and rehabilating addicts. While "therapeutic jurisprudence" purports to be more humane and effective than incarceration (especially compared with overcrowded and drug-ridden prisons), it raises fundamental questions about the proper nature and limits of judicial power. Indeed, the drug court legislation may generate a constitutional challenge, based on *Kable v DPP (NSW)* (1996) 189 CLR 51, that the allocation of therapeutic powers to a court is inconsistent with the judicial function. Whether placed within the criminal or civil framework, legal interventions against drug users must respect the basic principles of justice and human rights.

Peter Alldridge in *Relocating Crime* (Aldershot: Ashgate, 2000), describing the position in the United Kingdom, predicts that there are two possible paths for the development of drug laws:

> Extrapolating from the current rates of escalation in drug-related crime, the next 10 years
> will either see measures of decriminalisation put in place, or the preponderance of the
> resources of the criminal justice system devoted to drug offenders.

Within Australia's federal structure of drug control, which divides responsibility for legal control between the Commonwealth, States and Territories, these two contradictory strategies are being pursued concurrently. In symbolic terms, "contradiction" characterises much of Australia's approach to illicit drugs. It is incumbent on the legal community to expose and challenge this substantive irrationality and strive for a more humane and workable approach to all drugs (whether illicit or licit) which pose a risk of harm to users. In a recent address entitled "The Future of Criminal Law" (1999) 23 Crim LJ 263 at 272, Kirby J highlighted the costs, both in economic and human terms, of the present policy toward drugs. In his view, legal change is inevitable, concluding (at 273) that:

Criminal lawyers, who see the human face of those caught up in the law concerning illegal drug use have an obligation to bring what they see to the notice of their fellow citizens who may have more confidence than is warranted in the capacity of criminal law and punishment to deliver results.

Index